WITHDRAWN

CHINESE
STYLE

the art of living

CHINESE STYLE

Bradley Quinn

Foreword by Ou Baholyodhin

Special photography by Jan Baldwin

Styling by Lyndsay Milne

First published in 2002 by

Conran Octopus Limited

a part of Octopus Publishing Group

2–4 Heron Quays, London E14 4JP

www.conran-octopus.co.uk

Publishing director: Lorraine Dickey

Senior editor: Muna Reyal

Editor: Alison Wormleighton

Creative director: Leslie Harrington

Design: Megan Smith and Lucy Gowans

Photographer: Jan Baldwin

Stylist: Lyndsay Milne

Senior picture researcher: Rachel Davies

Calligraphy artist: Su Ling Wang

Senior production controller: Manjit Sihra

British Library Cataloguing-in-Publication Data.

A catalogue record for this book is available from

the British Library.

ISBN 1 84091 275 8

Printed in China

contents

FOREWORD BY OU BAHOLYODHIN 7

INTRODUCTION 8

ARCHITECTURE **16**
THE FORMAL ROOMS 22
THE FAMILY RESIDENCE 28
THE COURTYARD 34
YIN & YANG 36

LIVING **40**
SYMBOLS 44
FESTIVALS 48
EATING 56
TEA 62
FLOWERS & PLANTS 66
WALLPAPER 70
LIGHTING 76
COLOUR 84

FURNITURE **92**
WOOD 102
LACQUER 108
BAMBOO 110
DETAIL 114

TEXTILES **116**
CARPETS 126
HANGING FABRICS 132
EMBROIDERY 134
IMPERIAL DRESS 138

DECORATIVE DETAILS **140**
CRAFTSMANSHIP 148
LACQUERWARE 154
JADE & PRECIOUS STONES 158
FANS 160
DISPLAY 162
CALLIGRAPHY 166

CERAMICS **170**
PATTERN & MOTIF 178
GLAZES 180
FORMS 182

BUYING ANTIQUES 188
CHRONOLOGY 188
INDEX 189
ACKNOWLEDGEMENTS 191

FOREWORD

The principal decorative features of the Chinese interior are contemplated in terms of their natural beauty. The wood-grain of timber provided muted, unassuming textures, while the smooth patterns of stone floor tiles enhanced the rich brown and red tones of the woodwork. This formula has remained unchanged for several hundred years, creating settings as distinctive in the twenty-first century as they were in the fourteenth-century Ming interior. Contemporary designers such as Ou Baholyodhin, who designed this interior and Hong Kong chair, create dramatic visions of modern elegance by drawing upon the simplicity of Chinese style.

My first childhood design-conscious memory is of the dramatic, classical Chinese Dragon column carved out of solid rosewood and set within a sleek modernist interior of my grand parents mid-century home in Bangkok. Such unexpected theatrical juxtaposition of two culturally diverse symbols was my initiation to a strain of accidental post-modernism, and more significantly, an early instance of contemporary east meets west.

I have always been intrigued by Chinese style's staying power – how it has managed to remain so hip throughout the last three centuries and still cast an influence today, perhaps more strongly than ever.

Chinese style has become de rigueur in private residences as well as public spaces. The proof is in the ubiquitous pair of antique Chinese chairs or an antique Chinese lacquer chest of some description in just about every issue of a contemporary interior design magazine.

On a more subtle level, we owe much of the sensibility in the approach to contemporary design to the Chinese tradition of cultural refinement and their understanding of nature. Indeed, the emphasis on the importance of spirituality and well being in the contemporary interior is very much a Chinese concept.

Many of us, myself included, do not really appreciate the profound meanings of yin and yang, the intricacies of *qi*, the complexity of feng shui, but somehow we can recognize the harmony of a simple, but perfectly formed contemporary ceramic vase or the poise and tranquillity of an east-meets-west modern interior. Such intricate studies, although complex in formulation, have roots so sensitively grounded and are so primal that they consequently come to us naturally. The modern use of natural materials and surfaces, the preference for simplicity over contrived is so akin to the philosophy of Ming scholars and artisans.

Chinese style is so accessible to all of us; it brings warmth and exoticism to our homes whilst fulfilling our perpetual longing for travel and adventure.

Ou Baholyodhin

INTRODUCTION

Acelebrated Tang poet of the eighth century wrote, 'Heavy over distant peaks, only sky limits the emperor's earthly reign. Dare we ever dream of a world beyond this one? Here, among men, lies the enchanted middle kingdom.' To the Chinese their land has always been the middle kingdom. Not merely a vast empire stretching between two oceans and the steppes of Asia, but a realm between heaven and earth inhabited by humans of such refinement that they could only describe the cultures existing outside their domain as 'barbaric'. The belief that their land bridges heaven and earth was so deeply etched upon the minds and values of the Chinese people that their society evolved to mirror heavenly aspirations and express incredibly subtle beauty in art, furniture, ceramics and architecture.

For centuries, Chinese style has caught the imagination of the West. A civilization like that of the Chinese has never existed anywhere else: the mixture of philosophy, scholarship, ceremony and fine art that flourished for centuries created one of the most heavily aestheticized societies the world has ever known. To the ancient Chinese, the home was inextricably bound to a reverence for nature and a fundamental, almost superstitious, belief that balance and harmony must be achieved in the interior. Colours, symbolism, form and function were carefully considered to create objects and images that performed aesthetic as well as practical roles. Each dynasty developed a signature style; each applied purity of form to all aspects of design and emphasized exquisite craftsmanship, leaving a legacy of designs, shapes and elegant motifs that still appear timeless today.

Even before the first decorative works made by Oriental cultures were brought to Europe, the exotic East seemed enigmatic, alluring and mysterious. From the thirteenth century, the extraordinary tales of explorers like Marco Polo described an intriguing and romantic fantasy land called Cathay, where fiery dragons moved amidst palaces and pagodas that were inhabited by exquisite concubines and moustachioed mandarins. These legends of splendour and adventure fired the European imagination, creating a fascination for all things Chinese and an insatiable demand for vestiges of life in that mystic land.

Trade between East and West had always been sporadic, and the land of Cathay was largely presumed to be myth rather than reality. When the port city of Canton (Guangzhou) opened to the West in the seventeenth century, merchant adventurers returned with cargos of porcelain, silk, lacquer and tea, bringing with

Hand-painted with delicate, adept brush strokes and subtle applications of colour, this wallpaper depicting courtly gentlemen captures a mood of scholarly debate. Composition details such as the rock and the bamboo tree evoke Taoist sentiments of wisdom and virtue, while fans depicted in portraits often denoted rank.

them promises of even more resplendent goods to come. Though the traders bore proof that Cathay did exist, the romantic speculation and fantastic visions of pleasure and opulence had already taken hold. Merchants embellished their stock with tales so fantastic that Europeans remained spellbound for two centuries.

By the beginning of the eighteenth century, the widespread enthusiasm for Chinese objects had grown to affect almost every decorative art found in the interior. Furniture, wallpaper, silk hangings, lacquerwares and ceramics featured whimsical motifs of men with embroidered robes and diadem hats, willowy ladies in flowing gowns, performing acrobats, latticed temples and pagodas, mythological animals and trailing flowers. At first only a handful of these decorative objects had found their way to Europe, brought by the crews of trading ships from the East India Company, who were sent primarily to purchase tea and raw silk. The growing demand therefore led European craftsmen to attempt their own imitations of Chinese decorative styles, recklessly using virtually any motif culled from the East, whether it was known to be Chinese or not. As more envoys visited Asia, greater authenticity did become possible, but fantasy seemed to be more appealing to the European taste.

The French court became devoted to the Chinese style, dubbing it 'chinoiserie', which led to its popularity in other parts of Europe. During the seventeenth century, Chinese style became assimilated into the prevailing taste for Baroque. While the Baroque incorporated chinoiserie into its general fascination with the exotic, the craftsmen of the Rococo period, the predominant style of the first half of the eighteenth century, found that chinoiserie decoration captured the essence of European Rococo perfectly. Both diverged from Classical concepts of symmetry and restraint – as the Rococo turned its back on Classical features, the naturalistic motifs and asymmetrical patterns of chinoiserie inspired many of its designs. Although chinoiserie is considered characteristic of the Rococo style, it remained popular even after the advent of Neoclassicism in the second half of the eighteenth century.

At Versailles, the Rococo style of Louis XV was especially compatible with chinoiserie. Whole rooms, such as those at Chantilly, were painted with compositions in chinoiserie, and artists like Jean-Antoine Watteau brought consummate craftsmanship to the look. Thomas Chippendale, the chief advocate of Chinese style in England, was heavily influenced by patterns of latticework and decorative motifs expressed in Chinese architecture, absorbing them into his distinctive vocabulary. The craze even reached the American colonies, where Chinese wallpaper was as popular in colonial homes as it was in the grand palaces of Europe. In Philadelphia especially, chinoiserie had a pronounced effect upon colonial interiors.

In Europe, chinoiserie culminated in whole interiors being decorated in the style, most famously at the Petit Trianon in Versailles and the legendary apartments decorated by Madame de Pompadour, who remained faithful to chinoiserie

Early Chinese potters were believed to use magic to transform earth, fire and water into works of beauty and functionality. By the fourteenth century, ceramics were considered to be one of China's highest art forms, and *longquan* vessels like these were found in temples and palaces. A type of celadon, *longquan* was made throughout the Song dynasty, and was widely exported for centuries afterwards.

Although the Chinese had the technology and materials to make glass goblets, custom dictated that liquids were served in porcelain vessels decorated with elaborate, almost ceremonial, motifs. Wine cups like these were made in the palace workshops during the Kangxi reign. They were highly prized by French merchants, who dubbed them *famille rose* because of their tints of delicate pink.

throughout her life. King Adolf Fredrik of Sweden famously built an entire Chinese pavilion at Drottningholm Palace, near Stockholm, which he presented to his German-born wife, Queen Lovisa Ulrika, on her thirty-fourth birthday. The two-storey pavilion consists of an oval reception room, opening into drawing rooms on either side, which in turn open into galleries. Some of the most complete and perfect examples of chinoiserie interiors, the rooms are brilliant in colour and extravagantly mirrored. Wall paintings depict the mythical inhabitants of Cathay, idling away their time as they arrange flowers, play musical instruments and lie in dreamy reverie under parasols. In other parts of the pavilion, walls are panelled with the lacquered sections of Chinese screens, and delicately carved furniture is upholstered in embroidered silk. Walls are covered with Chinese wallpaper and woodwork trim is painted dark red to match, while every niche, shelf and alcove is filled with porcelain treasures. Not to be outdone, the queen's relations built chinoiserie pavilions across Germany with great speed, many of which survive today.

Chinoiserie, despite its Westernized shapes and decorations, remains an important part of China's own cultural history, where it also represents the continuation of a long tradition of manufacturing export goods. Over several millennia, Chinese traders had established workshops across the country to produce goods for exchange along the Silk Route. Long before China began trading with the West, Persian and Arabic merchants had commissioned its workshops and factories to manufacture wares specifically for export to Asia and the Middle East.

In the minds of Europeans, chinoiserie conjured up images of elaborately decorated Chinese homes rich in colours, textures and embroideries. To a large extent, Europeans believed that the exotic interiors they created were accurate replications of authentic Chinese interiors. In fact, the decorative arts made for export by the Chinese bore little resemblance to authentic decoration found in China. Little did the Europeans realize that merchants had encountered Ming styles years earlier, but judging them too austere for European tastes, focused on exporting the staples of tea and silk instead. As Guangzhou (Canton), for many years the sole point of commercial contact with the West, became more industrialized, European merchants commissioned elaborate objects for export just as the Persian and Arabic merchants had done along the Silk Route many centuries before.

Early in the Ming dynasty, the fourteenth-century missionary visitors to China who managed to penetrate the homes of rich merchants and high nobles were struck by their relative simplicity. Few decorative surfaces or soft furnishings were found, while simple but sophisticated paintings and hanging scrolls took the place of the wall murals and tapestries they were familiar with in Europe. Those were described in the sixteenth century, by the Augustinian friar, Juan Gonzalez de Mendoza, who wrote in awe of houses as large as entire European villages, but seemed unimpressed by their white walls, stone floors and wooden ceilings.

Prior to the Ming dynasty, Chinese interiors had been even simpler, resembling those prevalent in Japan today. As most activities took place at floor level, mats were used in place of chairs. Footwear was removed and seating was either directly on the floor or on low platforms covered with matting or textiles. The Japanese adopted the lifestyle of the Chinese during the Tang dynasty and conserved and adapted it for many centuries to follow.

Despite the seemingly austere shapes and undecorated surfaces of the Ming dynasty, architecture, furniture and home decoration reached their zenith during this period. Lines were clean and spare, with much emphasis placed on the lustre and grain of the wood itself. Every conceivable decorative detail was carefully considered, before being incorporated into a system so highly aestheticized that the scale and proportion of architecture determined the design not only of the furniture but also of the tiniest craft details. In a decorative context, Ming style can be loosely compared to the Puritan simplicity of England in the sixteenth and seventeenth centuries, which ended with the Restoration in 1660, when Charles II and his courtiers returned from Europe with a taste for opulence. Echoes of the Ming style can also be found in the Shaker style of nineteenth-century America.

The elegance of Ming style was achieved by a sophistication in materials, construction and design motifs that was expressed in architecture, furniture and ornamentation. Few foreign influences affected the style; from around 1450 Ming rulers pursued a policy of isolationism and forbade foreigners to enter the country, and this was continued for several centuries. Despite China's vast size, the principles of Ming design was practised throughout the country, uniting it in a style that amplified the esoteric principles of house design outlined by the ancients. Ming artisans reinterpreted the Chinese preference for living amidst elements from the natural world, articulating a system of balancing the natural with the artificial that continues today.

Following the collapse of the Ming dynasty in 1644, the understated tastes of the Han Chinese (the native Chinese ethnicity) slowly gave way to the exaggeratedly ornate style of the Manchu conquerors. The Manchu rulers displayed their power in expansive gowns and headdresses designed to reflect the very breadth of their magnificence, and decorated their homes with equal panache. During the Qing dynasty, established by the Manchus, arts and crafts seemed to be a part of the political agenda, driving Manchu tastes and values into the home itself. This was the antithesis of the classical Ming style, which was considered to be the height of Han Chinese sensibilities.

The Manchus introduced deep hues of red and yellow to the home interior, with accents of gold, turquoise, black and light green. Red became emblematic of the power and vibrancy of the Manchu reign, and still has these associations for the Chinese today. The Manchus were strictly Buddhist rather than Taoist or Confucian, and their tastes were influenced by temple decoration, whose bright colours had probably originally come from India centuries before as the teachings of the Buddha spread east. Qing decoration brings warmth to any interior, but with it comes the

The Manchu rulers of the Qing dynasty created some of the most opulent fashions ever worn in China, as seen on this Manchu bride of the late nineteenth century. Her outer robe was made to wear over a gown coloured in deep red and bright gold, probably with stiff cuffs styled in the shape of a horseshoe, and heavily ornamented with embroidery. The headdress, like her gown, would have been made in red and gold. Many of the Manchu elite dressed in this style every day.

struggle to keep the rest of the decor simple. Ironically, the word *qing* means 'clarity' or 'purity', which is at odds with the confusing styles and chaotic tastes that characterized the dynasty.

By the mid- to late nineteenth century, Chinese interiors had become brightly coloured and heavily ornamented, emulating European Baroque and Rococo styles. This is attributed to the relatively relaxed foreign policy of the Qing sovereigns; under their rule the West was able to explore China beyond the trading ports, and the occasional emissary was received in the capital. Many European courts presented gifts of furniture and textiles to the emperor, and these objects influenced the decor of the palace and the interiors of the nobility, trickling down to the homes of mandarins and merchants. Chinese furniture and screens became heavy, dark and carved; ceramics lost their refinement and appeared ornate and heavily embellished; curtains and drapes were made of thick velvet and richly embroidered; and lanterns became laden with medallions and red tassels.

In the mid-eighteenth century, at the height of the Qing period, the Emperor Qianlong decided to construct Yuanmingyuan, a complex of European palaces loosely based on Versailles. Vast Neoclassical pavilions, garden mazes and mechanical fountains, great marble arches, galleries and banquet halls all created in Beijing an image of 'Europeanoiserie' built astride Chinese-style parkland. The palaces themselves were seldom referred to in the West, but the magnificent gardens served as the inspiration for many of the beautiful chinoiserie gardens that were built throughout Europe in the eighteenth and nineteenth centuries.

The fall of the Qing dynasty in 1911 didn't end Qing style or chinoiserie; they spread further west as the Chinese emigrated to Europe and North America, where many Chinese homes and restaurants are decorated in pastiche versions of Qing style today. In China, the Qing treasures were shared with the people by opening palaces to the public and turning grand estates into public parks. To the Chinese, Qing seems a bit old-fashioned. Though the period began and ended in political turmoil, Qing will always seem tied to its Manchu heritage and Western chinoiserie. Ming styles are making a marked comeback, with many classical Ming shapes regarded as contemporary today. Qing and Ming styles came closer together when the Qing aesthetic gave way to Art Deco, creating streamlined shapes that recalled the elegance associated with Ming.

Often modern Chinese choose to return to the reverence for simplicity that characterized the Ming period, pushing excessive ornamentation aside and highlighting only essential elements and subtle colours. The recent resurgence of

The ceramics of the Tang dynasty were characterized by rich colours and bold patterns that today are mirrored in some of the abstract patterns created by contemporary ceramicists. Vibrant motifs like the one on this platter were created by mixing pieces of straw with the wet glaze, or dusting the piece with charcoal and ash before firing.

An indicator of status, dragons were associated with power and protection. This Qing dish is adorned with scrolling rims and wave motifs that recall the blue-and-white ceramics typical of the early Yuan dynasty. A plate of this design would have been used on formal or ritual occasions, given as a gift, or awarded to officials for services to the court.

Ming style shows how well these timelessly classic pieces work with modern trends. This type of minimalism not only involves negation, subtraction and purity, but also reduces the decorative process to the basic concepts of light, volume and mass. By eliminating all superfluous ornamentation, Ming designers were able to make features out of the home's interior proportions by contrasting strict symmetry with irregular shapes. For modern minimalists, the Ming style returns to the starting point of interior design to arrive at the essence of elegant style. But the possibilities for injecting Chinese style into the home are not simply limited to minimalism – the lavish ornamentation of the Qing period creates rich, exotic overtones that either transform an interior into a shrine of Oriental splendour or denote the decadence of an opium den.

In recent years the concept of Chinese design has been restricted to archaeological pieces in museums or those mass-produced, poor-quality wares branded with the ubiquitous 'Made in China' label. As twenty-first century China takes its next great leap forward, Chinese designers and manufacturers have started working from a point where they can adopt ancient principles and at the same time express contemporary, visionary attitudes that will redefine the historic notions of Chinese style. The teapot has, for example, been produced for over a thousand years while the rice bowl and the high-necked vase have been produced continuously for three thousand years. Compared with the West, where an object manufactured continuously for a mere fifty years is celebrated as a design classic, China has a rich sense of design history that is astounding and inspirational.

As the best and most appealing aspects of Chinese style and design are brought vividly to life in this book, the timeless elements of the Ming and Qing periods have been adapted for the contemporary interior along with the more exotic visions of some of the world's leading contemporary designers. Chinese Style is a fascinating journey through the Chinese interior itself, juxtaposing its rich, detailed history with bold new directions for the home. Organized in six practical sections, the book explores the vibrancy and equanimity that this seductive style can bring to the Western interior. Drawing inspiration from furniture, ceramics, textiles and artefacts, Chinese Style is a comprehensive study that examines the design principles behind Chinese architecture and space planning, the beauty of antiques and decorative arts, and the uses of traditional colours and motifs. As a practical guide to introducing elements of Chinese chic into the Western home, Chinese Style offers accessible ways to inject new inspiration into the interior, or completely rethink your living space in line with Chinese sensibilities. Chinese Style will appeal to anyone with an appreciation of pure form, innovative design, understated luxury or exotic decor.

ARCHITECTURE

ARCHITECTURE

In China, architecture has been considered an extension of nature since ancient times. The wood and stone harvested from forests and quarries remained a part of the natural world even after they had been reborn as houses and temples. All buildings were regarded as an integral part of their surroundings, their placement influenced by their proximity to rivers, plains, mountains and the sea. The ancients believed that forces in the natural world held the secret to prosperity, longevity and happiness, and Chinese architecture became an essential part of a system advocating living in harmony with the environment and the earth. Philosophers believed that the presence of *qi, or chi*, meaning 'life energy', in the landscape would indicate the areas most fertile for agriculture and best sheltered from inclement weather. Their regard for these places determined where people would live, cultivate land, build temples and bury their dead. The belief in invisible forces generated a profound respect for all aspects of the physical world, gradually evolving into the concepts of yin and yang, feng shui, Taoism and the *Yijing* (the *I Ching*, or the 'Book of Changes'), which are still observed in modern times.

Feng shui translates as 'wind and water'. According to this philosophy our lives and destinies are closely interwoven by the workings of the universe and of nature. The invisible *qi* can be directed into a harmonious flowing energy that enhances the life force in our bodies, eliminating any element that may cause an imbalance. The aim of feng shui is to add balance to the surrounding environment so that harmonious energy fields prevail throughout. The ideal living space can be perfectly aligned with the cosmos, by bringing it in line with the polarities of north and south, symbolically linking it with heaven as well as earth.

Traditionally, the most auspicious places to dwell are found on flat terrain among hills or mountain ranges. The ancients searched far and wide to find the most powerful sites in the landscape, where houses and tombs could be built in close proximity to hills and rivers. While any house could be constructed to counteract unlucky forces, those built on hill plateaus with an open southerly view over a gentle river or stream were thought to be protected from the effects of negative *qi*. The proximity to flowing water would increase the flow of positive *qi* around the house, while the hills surrounding the site at the rear and sides would prevent it from flowing away too quickly.

Auspicious spots were usually associated with energy lines in the landscape, and whole cities would be erected on so-called 'dragon lines of *qi*'. Individual homes were planned in relation to sources of *qi* in the natural world, and also to those in the man-made landscape. The Chinese character for 'wall' and 'city' is one and the same; the massive walls built to fortify cities also served as a starting point for the symmetrical division of space in the north–south orientation. Homes throughout the land were built on a north–south axis, with the main part of the house positioned to face south, flanked by rooms of lesser importance on the east and west. Houses were typically enclosed by thick walls, resembling complexes of cloistered buildings separated by courtyards.

The formula for domestic architecture and its principal decorative features has changed very little over the last three thousand years. Large family homes often originated as modest dwellings with only a set of rooms surrounding a walled garden,

which grew in size as subsequent generations added more rooms and additional courtyards. The household often included groups of seven or eight families, or large clans sharing several interlocking dwellings. In ancient times tax relief was given to individual households, regardless of their size. The taxation laws were complex, and as they changed from taxing the household to taxing the married couple, clans moved apart, but several generations of the same family remained together – a tradition that continues today.

Despite their unpredicted expansion, homes of this type were well planned, with the space apportioned into four different areas: the formal reception rooms, the family's residence, the garden courtyard and the studio. Although vernacular Chinese architecture differed among its varied landscapes and many far-flung provinces, common to all was a careful balance between the practical needs of the household, the concept of *ya*, or elegance, and the designation of separate living spaces. By creating several very different environments under a single roof, the Chinese achieved varied surroundings in which the household could find beauty and serenity when they closed the doors on the outside world.

The basic structure of a traditional Ming house involved a network of timber columns that were interconnected by horizontal beams, supporting a curved, overhanging roof made of ceramic tiles. The columns rested on round stone plinths and rose in an unbroken line from the floor through to the open rafters. The upturned eaves were designed to direct rainfall away from the house, while also letting more light through to the rooms within. The roof tiles were angled to form gullies that channelled water over the eaves, with triangular drip tiles turning the flow of water into a curtain of raindrops.

Throughout the house, the height of the rooms extended to the eaves, where panels of fretwork buttressed the columns or lined the beams overhead. The soft tones of native hardwoods gradually deepened over the years to a warm brown, and the fragrance of the wood lingered in the interior for years. The rich natural pattern of woodgrain was highly regarded, and wood was treated as a decorative element in itself. Stone was held in the same esteem; marble, jade and amber were inset into the wall or mounted on it to highlight the beauty of the shapes contained in their grain. Floors were laid in terracotta, granite or other light-coloured stone, and sporadically covered with rugs made of cotton or wool. The natural colours created a sense of visual harmony, with the smoothness and cool colouring of the floor tiles enhancing the rich brown and red tones of the wood.

Window openings were spaced unevenly to counter the precise symmetry of the architectural supports, while the fretwork covering them was also designed to contain subtle differences to create variety within uniformity. The contrasts between open window frames and solid walls were seen as a juxtaposition of positive and negative shapes, providing a subtle representation of yin and yang. Windows overlooking a garden were sometimes cut into the shape of lanterns, flowers, moons or fans. Regarded as 'picture windows', they literally framed a carefully composed 'painting' of beautiful plants and flowers.

Page 19 Large Chinese homes almost always included a study or studio to which individuals could withdraw for some peace and quiet. Today Western architects recognize the value of such spaces, designating tranquil areas where the occupants can relax, and escape from the pressures of modern life. Latticework window shutters have always provided privacy, also filtering the sunlight and camouflaging urban scenery.

Above The Chinese often treat the view as part of a picture. Window openings are cut in a variety of shapes and configurations, framing the view of the plants in the garden beyond. They may also be fitted with geometrical fretwork or elaborate carvings, such as this silhouette with its poetic depictions of nature.

The Formal Rooms

Situated along a north–south axis, the house was traditionally built with the formal rooms to the south, so that they overlooked both the gate at the front of the house and the courtyard at the centre; the private rooms for the family were built on the other side of the courtyard, to the north. In the formal rooms, visitors were received, guests entertained and business transacted. The formality and status of these rooms were emphasized by the poetic names they were given. Titles like the 'Hall of Gathering Elegance' and the 'Hall of Ascending to the Clouds' were especially popular.

Depending on the wealth and status of the owners, the formal part of the house could be a large, single room, or several interconnecting rooms separated by screens or double doors. These rooms were usually rectangular in shape, divided by columns into several bays with banks of alcoves on either side. Latticework screens provided intimacy within the large rooms, creating an internal structure and dividing up the space. A screen was typically constructed to span the space between two columns, which supported it on either side. When placed directly in front of a doorway, screens were believed to ward off spirits, since the Chinese ghosts of legend cannot turn sharp corners. Ghosts cannot step over obstructions either, which is why the menkan, a raised wooden threshold, would be placed across each doorway.

Below left Latticework screens can be fitted from floor to ceiling to restructure a room, providing both privacy and a sense of scale without blocking the passage of light. Free-standing screens also make practical room dividers as they can be easily moved to redefine floor space and living areas, or create shadows and diffused lighting.

Opposite Traditional domestic architecture divided the Chinese home into four distinct living spaces: the formal rooms, the family's private residence, the courtyard garden and the studio or study. The private rooms for the family were where the children played and the family worked and slept, prepared food and carried out domestic chores.

Floor space was determined more by the positioning of screens than by the design and layout of the room. Because screens were treated as partition walls and were generally placed at right angles to the existing walls, they divided the floor space into rectangles, with the furniture arranged between them.

Although important pieces like armchairs and couch beds were usually placed in the centre of the room, secondary items such as straight-backed chairs and occasional tables usually lined the walls. This maximized the open spaces in the interior, allowing the eye to travel uninterrupted from wall to wall.

When family gatherings or social events were held, the furniture was pulled into the centre of the room, opening up space along the walls for people to move freely from one side of the room to another.

Opposite The main entrance to a Chinese home is often described as the front gate, which historically was wide enough for a sedan chair or carriage to enter. In China today this gate is usually replaced by a reinforced door, but some homes symbolically recreate it through latticework panels or elaborate door frames. Superstition dictated that *menkan*, raised wooden thresholds, were fitted to ward off spirits, since the Chinese ghosts of legend are not able to pass over obstructions. *Menkan* are a distant memory in modern China.

Above The shape and style of Ming tables often determined their function. Square tables were usually designated for game playing, flanked by matching stools or high-backed chairs. These armless 'official's chairs' are so called because the top of the backrest resembles the shape of the hat worn as part of the bureaucrat's uniform. The small, square pieces pictured here, however, were crafted in a uniquely multipurpose design; they were made to double as stools or occasional tables, or for use as steps to reach high places.

The streamlined elegance of Ming style resurfaced in the early twentieth century to influence Art Deco styles. The contours of this set of modern furniture mirror the graceful shapes of Ming style, while the upholstery recalls the signature crimson of the Qing dynasty. The fusion of gentle shapes and rich colours counters the angular architecture of this minimal twenty-first-century interior.

The balance and harmony achieved in Ming interiors were attributed to the precise symmetry followed in furniture placement. The alignment of the chairs shown here defines the different living areas of the room; they are an effective and unobtrusive means of dividing space.

The Family Residence

The residence was less formal in its arrangement of furniture and perhaps the cosiest part of the house. It contained the rooms where the family worked and slept, located at the rear of the house near the kitchen, or situated on the first floor where they were accessed via enclosed staircases. Long corridors running parallel to the formal rooms led from the entrance directly into the family rooms or the kitchen, allowing members of the household to bypass the main parts of the house as they came and went.

The kitchen stove – usually a mammoth brick or earthenware structure – was constructed by the house builders. Though stoves of this type are no longer built, many still survive and remain in use today. This type of stove had a chimney but bore little resemblance to a European fireplace or ceramic stove. It was stoked with wood or coal from underneath and cooking was done in pots and pans set into its oven-like alcoves.

Whether the home was humble or palatial, no more than one stove would ever be built, as the Chinese believe that the family who eats food prepared in the same stove is symbolically one unit. If two brothers decided to split their families apart and live separately, the ashes of the communal stove would be distributed between them to represent the division.

The stove was also the location of one of the most powerful household deities, the kitchen god, who watches over all family activities and reports annually to the heavenly emperor on their behaviour. His shrine – also shared with his wife and children – is built into the stove as a shelf on the chimney. Families burned incense and presented fragrant offerings in their attempts to placate this revered spirit. The main household shrine was usually situated in the formal rooms. Elaborately decorated with pictures of Buddhist deities and statues of the Buddha, it was also adorned with devotional objects. Flower vases, scented candles and porcelain bowls of fruit offerings fill the air with the fragrances of lemon, sweet basil, citronella, sandalwood and rosewood.

Despite China's temperate climate the winters can be severe, and the risks of using open fireplaces in a wooden house horrified the Chinese. Therefore, in the cooler seasons coals from the stove would be shovelled into metal braziers and placed throughout the house. The family insulated the rooms by hanging heavy, padded textiles over the doorways and window shutters, and around beds and sleeping areas. In the north of China, domestic architecture was characterized by substantial stoves and the large *kang* built in the family rooms, many of which are still in use today. Resembling a raised brick platform with a stove underneath, a *kang* can occupy a third of a room, and provides a place for sleeping, eating and relaxing in the winter months. Homes in the northern regions were often built with flat roofs to keep the warm air circulating in the living space rather than letting it escape to the rafters above.

The studio was a room, or a set of rooms, devoted to the practice of the visual arts. Writing, like painting, was considered an art form, and the calligrapher and painter worked seated at desks and tables rather than standing at easels. Typically located in a quiet part of the house, the studio was a place where members of the household could retreat in solitude. Here the scholar might write poetry, create flower arrangements, study the Confucian classics, or spend evenings gazing upon the moon in quiet contemplation.

Opposite Families surrounded themselves with stylized 'ancestor portraits', which were painted on scrolled parchment or silk and hung in places of honour. They were venerated by the family, who burned candles and incense to appease their spirits and invoke their continued benevolence and protection.

Page 30 Architectural features are sometimes the starting point for transforming a Western interior into a Chinese room. This fire surround recalls the Western trend for chinoiserie elements and creates a focal point around which other Chinese details have been added.

The sense of symmetry characteristic of Chinese interiors illustrates the ancient expression, 'All good things come in pairs'. The pairing of two pieces of furniture is considered auspicious. According to Chinese legend, placing two objects alongside each other creates a cosmic gateway though which invisible blessings can come. The Ming tables, chairs and benches give this contemporary study a tranquil feel.

Opposite and this page Ming style easily lends itself to the most minimal modern living space. Featuring a few period pieces in a contemporary setting injects the flair of another era to create an artistic feel. This approach works best with smooth surfaces and subtle colours that allow antiques to stand out. Though the low table (below) is more than six hundred years old, its streamlined style seems just as contemporary as the modular furniture surrounding it. The dining table and benches (opposite) are also antique, their unadorned shapes adding a rustic element to the room.

The Courtyard

As we l as being designated for the cultivation of plants, flowers and small trees, the courtyard served as an extension of the house. Either it was situated in the middle of the house, surrounded by rooms on all four sides, or it was enclosed by rooms on three sides and the high, white-washed perimeter wall on the fourth side. Every house was defined by its surrounding wall, and to create a garden without enclosing it on all sides was almost unthinkable to the Chinese. The courtyards were paved with bricks or terracotta tiles. The eighteenth-century Emperor Qianlong started a vogue for bluish-grey terracotta tiles when he built his own garden courtyard in the Forbidden City in Beijing.

Water was the garden courtyard's main focus as well as its physical centre. Small ponds were dug in irregular shapes to create narrow coves that could be spanned by stone bridges – either arched or zigzag in shape – creating the illusion that water continued to flow into unseen parts of the landscape. The ponds were filled with lotus pods, lily beds and goldfish with bulging dragon eyes and ribbon-like tail fins. The murmuring sound of tiny waterfalls and winding rivulets of water flowing over pebbles and rocks filled the air, along with birdsong and the chirping of crickets. Children caught crickets in special cages to bring their rhythmic tones indoors for the adults to hear, or captured fireflies to use in lanterns as nightlights.

Water immediately brings to mind the principles of yin and yang so fundamental to Chinese architecture. In contrast to the inherent yang of the hard, dry stone, clay and timber used to construct the house, the water nourishing the core of the home brought yielding yin elements of softness, moisture and coolness. Its vitality nourished foliage around it and represented a continuation of the life force for the plants and the inhabitants. To the Chinese, water also signifies that which is pure and noble, and ultimately true to its nature, following its own path and seeking its own level.

Porches or pavilions were built in styles and proportions appropriate to the house, providing additional spaces for entertaining, relaxing or carrying out household tasks. Larger homes occasionally featured pavilions and pagodas in architectural styles that differentiated them from the main house, so as to create a trompe l'oeil effect that made the rest of the house virtually disappear from view. These areas were especially inviting in the summer months, where they would have been cooled by the water around them and the breezes passing through the lattice-work walls.

Those who did not venture into the garden could enjoy nature in the form of elegant *penjing*, or 'flowerpot landscapes', similar to the *bonsai* known in Japan. Held in the same artistic esteem as painting or poetry, these displays of miniature landscapes created for the interior were painstakingly detailed and true to nature. Proud gardeners might commission a replica of their own garden or a model of an area of outstanding natural beauty nearby. These were generally made specifically for each home, and great sensitivity was practised in choosing the colours, lines and textures of the plant material and the platter. Minute trees appeared to grow at the base of rocks grouped to resemble miniature mountains, transforming pebbles into boulders. Creating these table landscapes is by no means a lost art in China: they remain an area of both popular and scholarly interest and are found in homes, shop windows and botanical gardens.

The garden courtyard was the hub of the traditional Chinese house; it bridged the formal rooms and the private residence. The rooms adjacent to the courtyard were designed with doors and windows that opened onto it, inviting the fragrance of flowers and plants and the gentle sound of running water into the house. Guests were expected to admire the garden, and etiquette dictated that they be seated with a garden view, while the hosts would face in the direction of the front gate.

Yin & Yang

The active energy of yang and the passive energy of yin symbolically reverberates throughout the rest of the structure and into the interior itself. Balance is considered an important element in every aspect of the home, from the shape and location of rooms to the arrangement of furniture. Chinese architecture incorporates polarities of light and dark, soft and hard, rounded and angled. The circle is used to counter the triangle, and dark colours and shade are juxtaposed against sunlight and brightness: constant reminders that life should be lived in balance. This philosophy does not stand independently from other everyday customs of design and decoration, and is integrated into everyday life where it continues to play a role today.

The concepts of yin and yang imply both independence and interaction, their combinations symbolizing infinite change in nature as in life, all leading towards ultimate harmony in the universe. Both of these opposites are half-completed statements, awaiting unification with the other half. To the Chinese, balance is not stasis, but a controlled fluctuation of the extremes. In a spatial sense, this can be achieved by the combination of different elements that remain distinct from each other but ultimately blend into a harmonious whole.

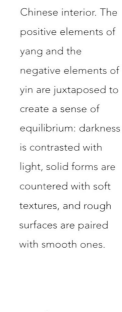

This page and opposite The principles of yin and yang are fundamental to the Chinese interior. The positive elements of yang and the negative elements of yin are juxtaposed to create a sense of equilibrium: darkness is contrasted with light, solid forms are countered with soft textures, and rough surfaces are paired with smooth ones.

The materials used to build a traditional home were also perceived in terms of their characteristics. The strength of timber enabled it to support a heavy roof and tolerate harsh weather, and, with its unassuming beauty, provided an unfinished surface that could be beautifully ornamented. Such characteristics were metaphors for the upright character of the Confucian scholar, who was humble yet dared to uphold principles when challenged, and remained true to his spiritual nature despite worldly temptations, fashioning his character with few superficial influences.

Applied to the Western interior the principles of yin and yang can also be used to create contrasting areas, or to design interiors that can be easily changed between contrasting moods. The relationship of darkness and light can be reversed using curtains, blinds, screens, candles and incense to change the room's mood in an instant. This system, so utterly simple in principle, provides the basis to experiment and vary surroundings into an ever-changing, multi-functional environment. To explore fully the many functions furniture can have, create contrasts and discover unexpected juxtapositions is to allow the interior to work its own magic.

The Ming aesthetic still has an impact on homes today, as modern minimalism and Eastern philosophies converge to shape contemporary interiors. The surfaces of this room reveal the beauty of line and form, and the effect of vibrant colour. The low Ming altar table juxtaposes the old with the new, the light with the dark and the smooth with the patinated.

Great sensitivity was shown in coordinating a room's elements with its architecture; and the furniture and ornaments were designed to occupy specific places in the interior. High-backed chairs were made to be positioned in the centre of the room, facing each other or grouped around square tables. Low-backed chairs were intended to be placed under windows, or against the walls. The chairs shown here bear the shape of the 'official's hat chairs' shown on pages 25 and 27, but are crafted in lighter wood and fitted with armrests.

LIVING

The fabrics, furnishings and decorated objects prized by the West may have created a rich mythology of ancient Cathay, but they provided little insight into the customs, rites and rituals which they represented in the Chinese household. The tradition of the extended family living under the same roof is one of the oldest in China. The eldest male was considered to be the head of the family, while the women of the household, as a rule, were expected to obey their father in youth, their husband in marriage, and their son in old age. When a woman married, she would move to her husband's home and would remain with his family throughout her life, often forbidden to remarry if her husband died before her.

Not only was the family unit bound through kinship, but it was also united materially and ethically. Traditionally, China's entire social system tended to be family-centred, rather than oriented towards religion or the political state. The family was the chief source of economic sustenance, security, education and recreation and was even the primary religious focus through ancestor worship. Most household activities were strictly segregated by sex. Men usually ran the family business or worked as civil bureaucrats, and presided over the household's religious ceremonies, education, books, artwork and gardening, while women supervised domestic activities, the sewing of clothes and the weaving of textiles. Daily life for women was lived in accordance with the maxim, 'A girl's first concern is to be virtuous, her second, industrious'.

居住 LIVING

The most powerful female figure in China was Yehonala (1834–1908), the formidable Qing consort better known by the title of the Dowager Empress Cixi, whose strong control over the nation was unprecedented by any woman before her. Her lifetime spanned the gradual opening up of court life and signalled changes in status for all Chinese women. Criticized for her vanity, for her liberalism and ultimately for causing the collapse of the imperial regime, she circulated photographs of herself that were contrived to remind her subjects that reforms were taking shape at every level of Chinese society. Cixi famously composed her own photographic portraits, sometimes posing for the camera without wearing formal outer robes, in a breathtaking breach of protocol.

Historically, Chinese society was divided into four classes – mandarins (officials), peasants, artisans and merchants – and respected in that order. Though all aspired to serve the government in an official capacity, most of the population were resigned to humbler lifestyles. The Chinese elite were taught to idolize the humbler members of society. Following the example set by the renowned poet, Tao Qian (365–427), who abandoned the city for a home in the countryside, numerous urban scholars romanticized in poetry and literature the rustic lifestyle of provincial villagers.

The ancient Chinese applied the same intensity to building an environment for the afterlife as they did to creating their living spaces. They believed that life continued in the same form after death, so the dead should be as well equipped as the living. Tombs were constructed below ground, sumptuously equipped with all the furniture, utensils and clothing necessary for daily life. Buildings above ground were considered places provided for and protected by the ancestors for their living descendants – as long as they continued to respect and care for the well-being of the dead.

The Qing dynasty was established in 1644 by a coup d'état. Although the Manchus embraced the native Chinese culture of the Han people, they never completely adopted their styles of dress or interior decor. The Dowager Empress Cixi, photographed here in an opulent Qing interior at the turn of the twentieth century, wears traditional court robes and a distinctive Manchu headdress. Fashion and interior design were inextricably linked – both were designed to express the magnificence of the Manchu empire.

Symbols

Throughout their long history, the Chinese have always placed great faith in the power of magic symbols. Every occasion has its symbolic emblems and rituals, from school ceremonies and religious observances to the birth, marriage and death of the ordinary citizen. The references are religious, superstitious or mythological, be they depictions of natural phenomena such as clouds, mist and rolling waves, or a zoology of exotic animals. Birds are bestowed with moral and symbolic qualities: orioles represent the sun, the mandarin duck is associated with fidelity, while the magpie is a traditional symbol of luck. Dragons and other mythological beasts, lotus blossoms and chrysanthemums all remind the Chinese of an invisible world.

Each written Chinese character is pronounced as a single syllable, making the Chinese language rich in homophones, or words that have the same sound but different meanings. For example, fu, the Chinese word for bat, has the same sound as the term for good fortune; hence an image of the bat symbolized the word. As an image it was immediately recognizable by those who couldn't read or write, and such visual puns play an essential role in the choice of symbols for decoration.

Stoves are often decorated with images of fish because yu, the Chinese word for fish, is also a homophone for the word meaning plentiful, and the family hope that their food supply will always be abundant. Many motifs result from the symbolic meanings given to words that have the same pronunciation as certain ambitions or blessings, giving birds and animals an important role in the visual language of decoration.

The twelve animals of the zodiac – rat, ox, tiger, hare, dragon, snake, horse, sheep, monkey, rooster, dog and boar – represent the characters of humans born under their sign and the basis of predictions for the future. In the astrological chart, the animals are paired with twelve 'earthly branches' in a system that combines them with ten 'heavenly stems' to form a cycle of sixty. The system is commonly used today as a way of marking time, identifying compatibility between individuals and divining the future. These signs are best known in the West among those interested in Chinese astrology, divination and the occult aspects of Chinese philosophies.

Symbols have high aesthetic and decorative value as well as symbolic meaning. Although a mantis (above left) sometimes represented cruelty, its presence in a motif also symbolized mystery. Birds (above centre) served as family emblems in ancient China and are often associated with allegorical folk tales. A river crab (above right) is a symbol of fertility. The dragon (opposite) rules over all other mythical creatures, but does not have the fierce reputation of its European counterparts. It is also an indicator of imperial rank.

The ancient Chinese delighted in natural forms preferring motifs featuring flora, fauna (including mythological beasts), the changing seasons and landscape. Images of dragons range in shape and style from heavy, bulbous and rigid to the lithe and serpentine creatures shown here (above left). Sprays of wintersweet (above centre) remain as popular in modern fashion as they were on ancient robes. This bat (above right) flies among scrolling clouds set against a night sky. Scrolling clouds (right) were associated with deities, foretelling their arrival. The ubiquitous longevity symbol (left) was often considered a talisman to confer long life on the wearer. As well as appearing on textiles, it featured on ceramics and cloisonné, and on furniture during the Qing dynasty, when it was widely used.

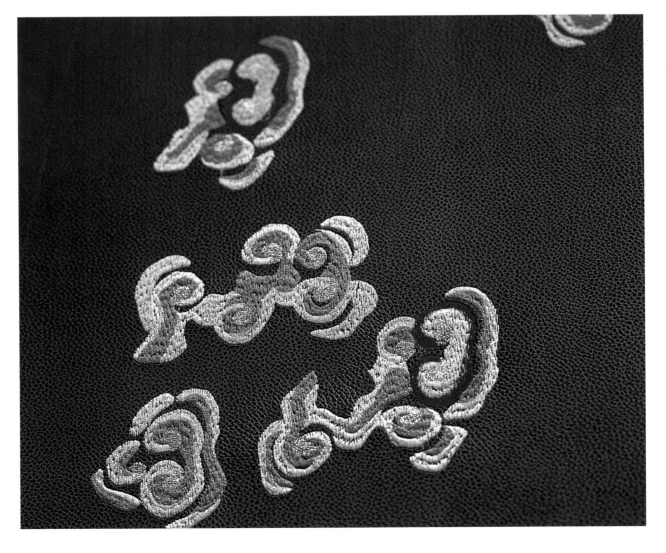

Festivals

The ancient Qing Ming Festival exemplifies the fundamental belief systems of the Chinese people. For thousands of years Chinese society has been organized on lines of respect for elders rather than the recognition of individual rights. Observance of respect to ancestors is an integral part of this system, and is a natural extension of the respect paid to living people who are older than oneself. It is the obligation of the young to show respect to their elders, and equally, the responsibility of the aged to teach these values to the young. Although the festival has a focus on remembering the dead, it is very much about the living family.

Qing Ming, meaning 'Clear and Bright', comes at the start of spring, when flowers are newly blossoming and the days are longer and brighter. In the Chinese lunar calendar, it is observed on the fourteenth day of the second month – in early April. Qing Ming is also associated with decorating graves and paying respect to the dead, which traditionally included preparing food offerings and burning goods in order to convey them to ancestors in heaven. Today, the living family enjoys the food, and the burnt offerings are made out of paper. Packets of paper clothing can be bought in Hong Kong and China to burn for the dead, sending them contemporary fashions to wear in the afterlife. The Chinese burn 'Bank of Hell' notes at the same time to distract any evil spirits attempting to intercept the goods; while the evil spirits are chasing the Bank of Hell money, the valuable goods pass safely to the dead.

Ever since the Xia dynasty, around four thousand years ago, the first day of the first moon in the lunar calendar has been a cause for celebration. New Year carnivals offer lantern and flower displays, lion dances, firecrackers and dragon processions. The celebrations – in early February – sometimes continue for an entire week, with preparations beginning weeks beforehand. The house is cleaned from top to bottom and decorated with fragrant fruits and flowers, and branches of pussy willow, plum or persimmon. The characters for health, wealth, longevity and good fortune are written on red paper in black or gold ink, then stuck to walls throughout the house.

Perhaps the most popular of all Chinese festivals, the New Year is regarded as an important family holiday. On New Year's Eve (the last day of the twelfth moon in the Chinese lunar calendar) the family gathers for a sumptuous meal, where everyone is careful not to drop their chopsticks, which could bring bad luck. The last baths of the year are taken to wash away all old luck, then everyone dresses in a new outfit to greet the year ahead. The entire family embarks on ritual 'New Year Visiting', when friends and relations greet each other and exchange good wishes. Known as the 'eight treasures', boxes of sweets, dried fruits, savoury nuts and seeds are prepared as snacks for visiting guests. It is also traditional to eat melon seeds to bring luck in the year ahead.

New Year's Day can start with children receiving from their parents their first red envelopes containing packets of 'lucky money'. Throughout the coming days friends and relatives give children more red envelopes – all to be immediately saved in a piggybank and increased throughout the year. No scissors or knives can be used on New Year's Day in case they 'cut short' the good luck that the New Year just brought in, so food is prepared the day before. Nothing can be washed all day either, to prevent the new luck from being rinsed away.

The Lantern Festival has been held for thousands of years. Today people still gather at dusk for the festival and fill the streets, carrying glowing lanterns and studying the sky overhead for the first signs of fireworks. Many families hang red lanterns over their doorways as their ancestors did, but chemical glow-sticks and mini-torches replace precarious flames. The lantern shown here is a modern reproduction of a traditional design.

The Lantern Festival falls on the fifteenth day of the first month in the Chinese lunar calendar usually at the end of February. The exact origins of the tradition are unknown, but it may have evolved out of celebrations for the lengthening daylight that followed closely on from the New Year. Legends recall a Han dynasty emperor who ordered displays of light on the fifteenth night of the first lunar month to pay homage to Buddha, and Buddhists carried lanterns on this night to pay their respects. The festival itself takes its name from the Tang dynasty custom of hanging out lanterns on the night of the first full moon o the lunar year and lighting them nightly for several weeks afterwards.

The festival once lasted for forty-five days, but was gradually shortened to one week, then five days, and then three. Today, lanterns continue to be hung outside and throughout the house, and carried through the streets by children. The event is also famous for the moon-shaped rice flour dumplings filled with a variety of sweet fillings, popularly known as *yuanxiao* (literally 'round and little', like their shape), which is another name for the festival. Cities throughout China, Hong Kong and Taiwan hold elaborate festivals and huge lantern displays; coloured lanterns are strung together to form a shimmering lantern 'wall', and traditional dances are performed by dancers wearing costumes that glitter and sparkle in the light.

Few occasions are more joyous to the Chinese than a wedding. It is immediately distinguishable from other festivities, because almost everything relating to it is coloured red. Deep shades of scarlet, rich crimson, maroon and dark pink colour banners, lanterns, table coverings and garments. Traditionally, even the bride wears red, and the couple spend the wedding night sleeping in red linen. The 'double happiness' character (see page 169) – the symbol for marital bliss – originated in the Song dynasty, when a legendary scholar and statesman was a student awaiting his examination results. They arrived on his wedding day, with the news that his high score would almost certainly attract an imperial post. He expressed his delight by writing the character for happiness twice and joining them together as an expression of the double joy he experienced.

From this comes the Chinese saying, 'All good things come in pairs'. It is considered auspicious to put two chairs together or place two matching tables in a room. Portraits and scrolls are hung in pairs, while even lanterns are paired and potted plants placed side by side. A dragon and a phoenix are a mythical pair that represent the coupling of male and female virtues – the heavenly pairing of yin and yang energies. In Chinese eyes placing two objects alongside each other creates a cosmic opening, a symbolic corridor though which invisible blessings can come.

On the wedding day, the groom calls for the bride at her home, and takes her to the wedding. The bride's friends demand 'lucky door money' before they allow the groom to collect her. The groom then counts the money aloud in denominations of nine, because the words *jiu* in Mandarin and *gao* in Cantonese, both meaning nine, are homophones for 'everlasting'. Whether the money adds up to ninety-nine pence or ninety-nine pounds is irrelevant – the ritual lends a witty modern twist to the ancient custom of the groom declaring an everlasting commitment to the bride and her family before the wedding. After the wedding, the food, gifts and decorations at the banquet feature in pairs and the table, utensils and dishes are all coloured in shades of red.

Pages 50 & 51 The first day of the first moon in the lunar calendar was recognized as the official start of the Chinese calendar year, and a cause for celebration. Traditionally, the interior would be decorated with symbols of health, wealth, longevity and good fortune, but modern households may hang only paper lanterns, their glowing orbs mimicking the shimmer of moonlight. *Opposite* Dragon decorations can recall the festive spirit of the Chinese New Year. Origami dragons are easily refolded and stored, and they take seconds to hang up and create a festive mood. Paper dragons and dragon masks originated as an art form, requiring the combined skills of painters and sculptors to create their menacing faces and other-worldly bodies.

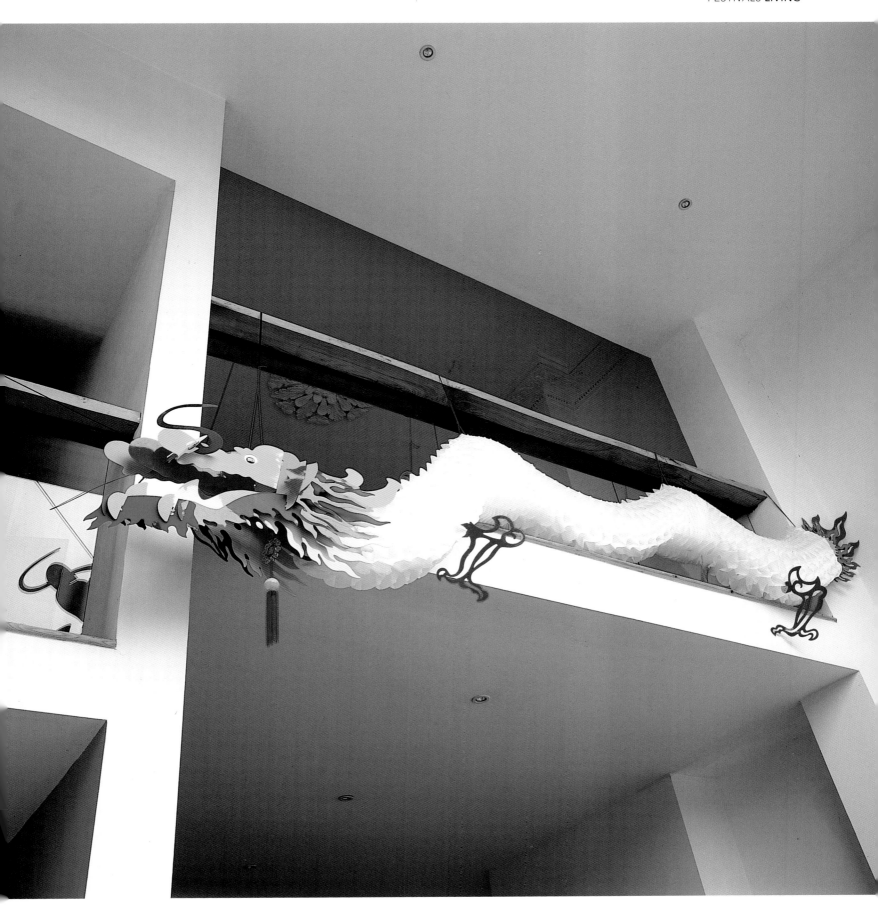

This page Supported
here by a pair of Ming
stands, the hanging
lanterns appear as
festive when placed
on a table as they
do suspended from
the ceiling.
Opposite These
crimson bed clothes
are reminiscent of a
Chinese marital bed.
Tradition dictated
that newlywed
couples spent their
first nights together
in a bed swathed in
red fabrics.

Eating

Living together and often working together, the family would also be united at mealtimes, religious ceremonies and festivals. Dining tables could be built to seat a family of ten or twelve; they were usually round, and of a size that would allow those seated to reach comfortably the dishes placed at the table's centre. Stools were universally used at dining tables, with only the aged seated at chairs. Traditionally, it was not unusual for the overall family unit to number well into the twenties or thirties – large households had to set up several tables at mealtime to accommodate the entire household. This is still the custom today, though families are much smaller now or live apart. Even at formal gatherings or festival dinners, groupings of smaller tables are customary rather than the long banquet tables used at formal dinners in the West.

Though meal presentation is a very important part of Chinese culture, there are fewer rules of etiquette to observe. The table setting has less importance than in the West – the placement of dishes and eating utensils is less formal. The Chinese begin the meal in order of seniority, with each diner beginning only after the older generations have started. Individual place settings include a rice bowl, a saucer, a pair of chopsticks and a flat-bottomed soup spoon, with rests for chopsticks and spoons placed alongside the rice bowl. Typically these are crafted in white porcelain decorated with coloured motifs and symbols conveying luck, long life and good fortune.

Below The Chinese have long preferred chopsticks to knives and forks, which they associate more with weapons and violence than with mealtime. Spoons (below centre) with 'lucky' symbols and spines crafted to mimic the segments of a bamboo tree were made for export in the Qing dynasty.

雲中彩鳳卿五色

Contemporary Chinese tableware combines ceramics, wood and lacquer to create modern displays based on historic designs. Platters crafted from bamboo are popular in the West for their stylish shapes as well as their antibacterial properties. Set on lacquerware flats, they inject a note of rustic elegance into a contemporary table setting, harmonizing with the altar scroll in the background.

Left Large, round tables are traditionally used at family mealtimes. Although rectilinear Western-style tables are becoming popular in the modern Chinese household, stools, rather than chairs, are likely to be used with them. Today's versions are made from metal with padded seats and swivel bases to suit contemporary sectional tables. All of the pieces shown here can be easily dismantled between dinner parties.

Opposite The hardwoods chosen for table tops are characterized by their fine grains and beautiful markings, which are left untreated, but are polished to a high sheen. This table was cut as individual quarters. Two of the quarters were cut on the cross grain and the other two on the lengthwise grain. When the segments are joined together into a circle, their grains create a contrasting pattern.

Chopsticks are thought to reflect the elegance and moderation encouraged in the teachings of Confucius. But there are superstitions associated with chopsticks, too. Finding an uneven pair at your table setting is believed to portend a missed boat, plane or train, or the arrival of a loved one. Dropping chopsticks is said to inevitably bring bad luck, while crossing chopsticks is strictly forbidden – unless done by a *dianxin* (dim sum) waiter to show that the bill has been paid. At the end of the meal, chopsticks should be balanced horizontally across the rim of the bowl or laid on the table beside the dish.

Beverages are not always served at mealtimes by the Chinese. Tea is drunk throughout the day, but with meals clear soup is usually the only liquid provided. When the Chinese are gathered together to drink tea, they are careful to ensure that the spout of the teapot is not pointing towards anyone, but is turned away from the table, preferably in a lucky direction.

This page Individual place settings can include a rice bowl and plates in varied sizes and colours. Eating utensils can be placed alongside the dishes, or poised on ceramic rests. Undecorated white porcelain makes an elegant statement while pieces decorated with motifs and symbols will lend exotic overtones to any cuisine.

Opposite Tableware was often crafted from wood in regions where there was no local clay or kilns. Wooden dishes were painted with vernacular motifs and auspicious symbols, or lacquered to create a durable finish. Nutshells, seashells, horns and even animal bones were transformed into simple eating utensils and serving spoons.

Tea

According to Tang scholars, one of the best ways to delight in the garden was to take tea there. Tea symbolized an earthly purity that united man and nature. Culled from tender shoots that were painstakingly harvested and carefully steeped in hot water, tea was seen as the essence of nature itself – a distillation of the combined elements of the garden. Fragrant teas were made from infusions of lemongrass, geranium, maté or sweet basil. Teas from jasmine flowers and rose petals were highly treasured, but their rich flavours had to be drunk sparingly. Enjoyed as much for their taste as their aromatic properties, herbal teas were also taken as a tonic for good health, digestion and balance of energy. Believing tea to purified by the earth, the Chinese reasoned that its flavour should be treasured in small amounts.

The custom of drinking tea was part of a sophisticated spiritual and scholarly life, presided over by a benign 'tea art' spirit who belonged to the fairies of nature. As a rule, tea would be served in small terracotta teapots, since the full aromas and flavours of the tea were thought to disappear in a large one. The teapots were almost always white – at least on the inner surface – so that the tea drinker could fully appreciate its colour and tone. This tradition was passed down from the the sixteenth-century Ming court, which stipulated that the sensations enjoyed by the tea drinker should be warm and mellow, just like the hospitality offered in a Chinese home.

Below left Because tea was consumed in larger quantities in the West (the Chinese tended to sip it), Chinese craftsmen created teapots large enough to serve several guests.

Page 64 Tea is harvested from young, tender leaves, which are roasted and fermented, turning the dark green leaves reddish-brown. Here, tea leaves have been ground and pressed into decorative moulds to create the 'tea bricks' that make loose tea easier to pack and ship.

Page 65 The ancients identified seven basic daily necessities of life: fuel, rice, oil, salt, soy sauce, vinegar and tea. The custom of drinking tea, though not an elaborate ceremony as in Japan, continues to be an indispensable part of almost every social activity. This form of teapot emerged during the Tang dynasty.

There was a constant dialogue between the interior of the Chinese home and the courtyard. Flowers and plants entered the rooms, and the household furniture was sometimes placed outside. Plants and flowers were considered to be a necessary component of the interior, bringing nature indoors. Fragrant plants, especially summer orchids, were grown in ceramic pots placed on hardwood tables or on cane stands. *Hangchou*, the beguiling plant stands made from lacquered rootstock, provided elegant supports for the plant pots while suggesting that a web of intertwining roots emanated from underneath their base to the floor.

Flowers & Plants

Flower arranging has for centuries been one of the traditional accomplishments of the scholarly class, and there have been many texts published on the subject. Scholars have written at length of the pleasures that can be derived from arranging rocks, flowers and potted orchids. The sensibilities that govern the Chinese interior also direct floral arrangement: trueness to nature, organic structure, rhythmic vitality and expressiveness. Two or three kinds of flowers can feature in each arrangement, provided that they are 'compatible'. Each and every flower has a symbolic association, directing which types of flowers should be grouped together or kept separate. For example, sprays of wintersweet and bamboo can appear together, both being symbols of winter hardiness. A peony, representing opulence and luxury, should never be placed alongside a pine bough, a symbol of austerity and fortitude.

Below, far left
Bamboo grows in a variety of sizes and grains, ranging from trees of immense proportions to lanky, weed-like sprigs.
Below left A hardy branch of cherry blossom against wallpaper.
Opposite As they prepare for the beginning of each festival, the Chinese fill their houses with vases of flowers and foliage. New Year decorations include branches of pussy willow, plum or persimmon, while the Qing Ming Festival celebrates the start of spring with newly blossoming flowers. Year round, the household shrine is adorned with fragrant flowers or bowls of fruit, bamboo shoots or budding plants.

Every flower, branch and leaf should be counted to ensure irregularity; an odd number is preferable since it is meant to convey the dynamic irregularity of the life force itself. Unopened buds should always be included among flowers in bloom, to celebrate life's continuing journey. The colours of the plants should coordinate with the colour of the container, and appear to spill naturally out of it. Arrangements following these principles were recorded in innumerable paintings from the Song dynasty onwards, the arrangements being positioned throughout the house on tables, stands and the shrine. The Chinese never have had anything as formal as the niche in the Japanese home, within which flower arrangements were meant to be placed; the placement of flowers within the Chinese home is much more fluid.

Page 68 The calendar girls of the 1920s and 1930s were icons of style, introducing Chinese women to Westernized fashions, jewellery and hairstyles. Captured in a demure pose, this Shanghai lady cradles a stem of pussy willow, probably heralding the New Year or spring.

Page 69 Displays of flowers in the home have always provided more than just decoration; they inject a note of vitality into the interior and symbolize the life force itself. All flowers and plants are believed to radiate soothing *qi*, counterbalancing the robust energy of the dense stone and heavy timber used to construct traditional Chinese houses.

Wallpaper

The first Chinese wallpaper to reach Europe is thought to have arrived in the 1690s, and wallpaper maintained its popularity throughout the Georgian period. These papers were usually displayed as hanging scrolls in drawing rooms or as paper panels mounted onto screens. As chinoiserie became increasingly fashionable in Europe, many individual 'Chinese rooms' were decorated with imported wallpaper that was pasted directly onto the walls.

Wallpaper in China originated as a product of Ming austerity. Light-coloured paper was applied to mask the rough textures of stone or brick walls, and left undecorated. The paper was sometimes 'whitewashed' using the same technique of brush and paint as was used for decorating screens and scrolls. Wallpaper was never cut from rolls as it is today; it was constructed as panels that were pasted together in a patchwork of overlapping sheets.

Early eighteenth-century chinoiserie wallpaper was hand-painted with scenes or motifs before it left China, often illustrating brooding mandarins or resplendent ladies in elegant robes against a background of exotic flowers and mythological animals. A nickname for these was 'Long Elizas' – an anglicization of *Lange Lijzen*, the Dutch term for the willowy female figures on eighteenth-century Kangxi ceramics. Wallpaper told stories of mystery and charm, of a fairy-tale world among palaces, pagodas, fiery dragons and scrolling clouds. While these large-scale images would never have appeared in the interiors of the Chinese, they illustrated perfectly the eighteenth-century European fascination with Cathay.

Wallpaper was painted by the same method as was used to tint silk for furnishings, with the background washed in a single colour first; the preliminary outlining and final metallic highlighting indicate that the wallpapers and silks were probably painted in the same workshops. Most surviving examples show a mixture of Chinese mythological characters and hunting scenes. These were more to the tastes of Europeans than Chinese, especially since the Chinese had invented wallpaper to give rooms a smooth, uniform white surface rather than a decorative finish.

In the West in recent years, the return to pristine white walls or raw plaster meant that wallpaper was relegated to the margins of interior design. As wallpaper made a comeback with a wave of 1970s graphic motifs and pop art renderings for retro interiors, these were countered by authentic Chinese motifs and chinoiserie floral prints, which provided a soft backdrop for minimal styles. Ottilie Stevenson's chinoiserie range was inspired by a swatch of Chinese silk found in a Paris flea market, while the beautiful silk wallpaper designed by De Gournay recalls the elegant bird-and-flower motifs adorning paintings from earlier dynasties.

Most of the original chinoiserie motifs have been repeated over the years, copied again and again by successive waves of wallpaper and furnishing fabric manufacturers. This is why, unlike the ranges of popular prints that change with every new design wave, these motifs connect the contemporary era with the traditions established in the workshops of Canton three centuries ago. The impact that wallpaper has had on interiors has made it more popular than any other Chinese decorative export, maintaining a presence in Western interior design for centuries.

Though popular today, bird-and-flower motifs continue a painting tradition dating back several thousand years. As early interests in horticulture and botany evolved, the Chinese painted birds and flowers in great detail to record and catalogue native flora and fauna. In the eighteenth and nineteenth centuries, Western botanists collected these beautiful renderings for study, but the delicate beauty of their colours and forms was associated more with fine art than science, and Western designers appropriated their motifs for textiles and wallpaper, silk screens and ceramics.

Top left A simple leaf can capture the essence of a plant, as these feathery renderings illustrate. Their abstract shapes provide a timeless backdrop for antique textiles and furniture, or modern classics.
Bottom left Wallpaper specialists such as De Gournay design large-scale representations of exotic landscapes to create the effect of a hand-painted mural.
Opposite Reversing proportions is an eye-catching and effective device, overturning traditional ideas of scale and symmetry. As the wallpaper magnifies their foliage, these tropical plants become an overgrowth of elegant flora.

Left Geometry played an important role in the decorative arts of the Qing dynasty, when many classical motifs from previous eras were revived and executed in gold leaf against rich hues of red, green and blue. *Opposite* Birds and flowers have always had high aesthetic and decorative value in China. As they became popular in Europe in the eighteenth and nineteenth centuries, the painting studios in China adopted assembly-line methods to keep pace with demand. These chinoiserie styles were gradually developed to complement Western designs; the blend of styles and periods here captures the spirit of chinoiserie at its zenith.

E

Lighting

ast or West, in every culture lighting is a powerful medium, one that highlights and defines the interior and creates both an overall ambience and an instant focal point. Throughout China's long history, lanterns have been an important decorative tradition, featuring in festivals and ceremonies as well as in homes, temples and palaces. They are traditionally made with frames that form a secure base when they are placed on a flat surface, or maintain their shape when hung overhead. Square, oblong or rectangular in shape, lanterns are made from paper or silk stretched around the frame to diffuse the light, and also to deflect the wind if hung outdoors. Circular lanterns were created to be hung overhead, their glowing orbs romantically viewed as representations of the moon.

Paper and cloth lanterns also have ceremonial associations in China. Red lanterns denote festivities of some sort, be it a wedding, a holiday or New Year, and usually have messages of good will written across them in black calligraphy. These decorate the front door and the interior during the celebration. Strung together in a single line, they are draped vertically along a wall or zigzagged across the centre of the room. Sometimes big lanterns are grouped in twos and threes and hung in varying lengths, with long red tassels dangling from each one's base. Traditionally paper lanterns were round or square, but today they can be shaped like hares, birds or dragons to symbolize the auspicious sentiments associated with these creatures.

Table lanterns can be made from glass, bamboo or metal wire, and covered with shades made from paper or silk. Unlike the orb shapes created from paper and silk, glass lanterns are usually square or multi-sided, with bamboo or copper ribs forming the structure of the frame. The panes of glass are often etched with motifs or inscribed with the symbols representing love, peace, joy or harmony, which would also be drawn on the fabric of a silk shade. The candle or light bulb inside is accessed by a hinged door on the side or by a top that can be removed altogether. Chinoiserie table lamps were cast in porcelain and painted in colourful motifs. Symbols were cut into the surface to provide perforations from which soft light could emanate.

Tall lanterns generally mirror the design of table lamps but are secured to a high base or tripod. During the Qing period these bases were elaborately decorated and often richly lacquered. Carved brackets joined the legs and the lantern's base to the stem, but could be detached so they could also be hung from the ceiling. Overhead lanterns were often the most richly detailed, providing the room with a magnificent central feature that even the Qing connoisseur might have considered over the top. Composed of several tiered layers varying in size, their frames were usually octagonal or heptagonal, descending from the largest at the top to the smallest at the bottom. The edges were elaborately ornamented with Baroque-like trim, or supported carvings of dragons and other-wordly creatures poised to frighten away spirits from every direction.

Today there are many more lighting methods available. Even though candles have been unromantically replaced with electric bulbs, Chinese shades still cast dramatic shadows and diffuse light to gently illuminate a room. Despite the fact that their origins are medieval, the simplicity of round paper shades gives them a modern feel. Qing-style lanterns lend an air of fun to any room, if not taking it over altogether.

The rectangular planes of this contemporary lighting display mirror the silhouette of a piece created by an earlier master. Lu Ban, China's legendary fourth-century BC furniture craftsman, designed simple shapes that have been in production ever since. The precise angles and contours used to construct the base and surface of this Ming altar table are attributed to Lu Ban, who set the tone for balance and elegance many centuries earlier. The illuminated walls were designed to evoke the tones of the deep blue visible in the misty landscapes of north China.

This Qing-style lantern combines Manchu ornamentation with superstition. Each paper panel is elaborately trimmed with ornate fretwork and supported by dragons and mythical creatures. Tassels, lucky charms and auspicious characters frighten away any spirits unlucky enough to venture in.

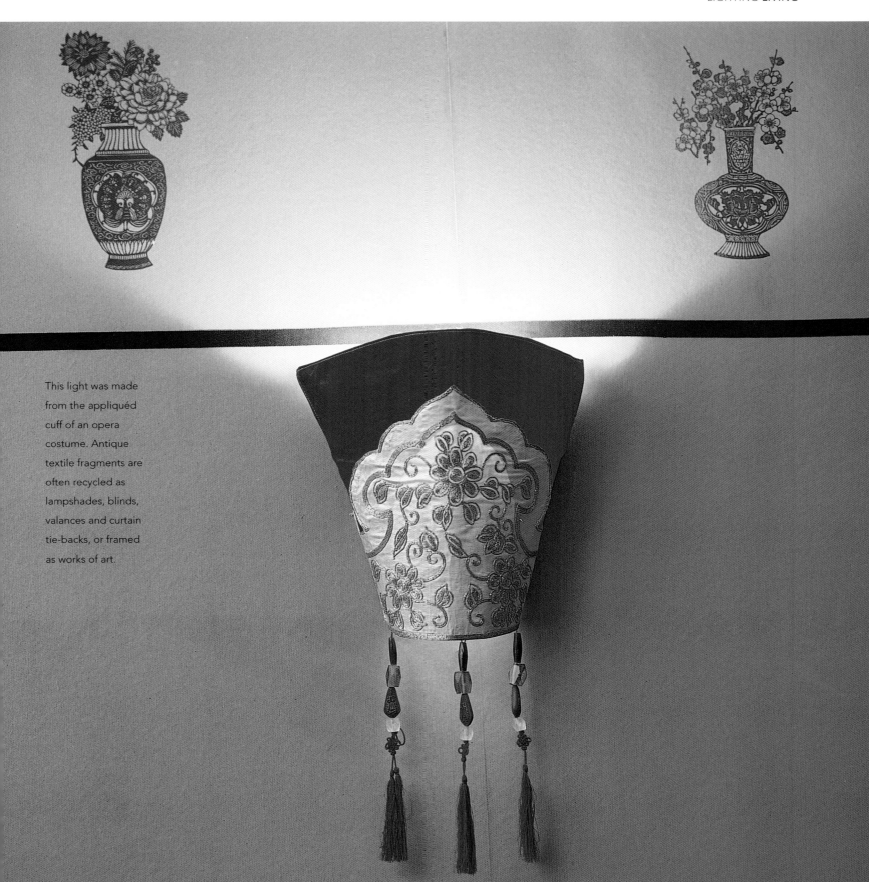

This light was made from the appliquéd cuff of an opera costume. Antique textile fragments are often recycled as lampshades, blinds, valances and curtain tie-backs, or framed as works of art.

Left Paper lanterns are colourful and fun, easy to install and inexpensive to buy. These lanterns were initially strung up as party decorations, but have been left in place to create a festive atmosphere every day.

Opposite Late Qing craftsmen achieved beautifully shaped lanterns made from contoured brackets and sculpted stems, often intricately carved and richly lacquered. This shade recalls the shape of a lotus pod; its brackets and base represent the stem and roots that anchor the lotus to the pond bed beneath it.

Pages 82 & 83 Silk lampshades were traditionally made in rounded shapes to resemble the glow of the moon, as this beautiful light illustrates (left). Square and rectangular shades were not uncommon, but the Chinese regarded them as more functional than decorative. The soft lighting in this contemporary setting (right) updates these principles with a contemporary look, by combining angular shapes to create pillars, overhead lighting and discreet uplighters, concealed behind silk shades to diffuse their glow.

Colour

For a long period in Chinese history colour, especially bright colour, was not an important element of the interior. However, although plain whitewashed walls and natural finishes were celebrated throughout the Ming dynasty, colour was not completely absent. Cinnabar, a volcanic mineral that provided the pigments used to tint lacquers in the distinctive 'Chinese red', was also used to colour boxes, furniture and ornaments in a range of rich hues. Variegated porcelain pieces, flowering plants and arrangements of figurines made from jade, amber, lapis lazuli and other semi-precious stones were alternative sources of vibrant colours throughout the home.

Under the Manchu rulers of the Qing dynasty the Chinese developed a taste for more colourful and exuberant objects and motifs. The trend for elaborate decoration that persisted throughout the Qing dynasty brought dramatic hues of red, gold, turquoise and yellow to the home interior. Though the colour red was especially emblematic of the Manchu reign, it has also symbolized happiness for much of China's history, before and after the Qing dynasty, and still has these associations to the Chinese today. As the Qing dynasty unfolded, the interiors of the late eighteenth and nineteenth centuries became brightly coloured and heavily ornamented, emulating European Baroque and Rococo styles.

Colour symbolism has always been extremely important to the Chinese. In the early dynasties five basic colours were identified and assigned to represent the four cardinal directions of north, south, east and west, plus the central axis between them. They were also correlated with the five elements of water, fire, wood, metal and earth. Theories of yin and yang also provided a basis for the properties of colour, with black symbolizing yin or the female, the moon, water, winter and rejuvenation. Black is also the colour of the north according to the traditional Chinese cardinal points, and it evokes the will to delve deeper within oneself or gain wisdom. The colour red represents yang, or the male, the sun, fire, summer and activity. Red also corresponds to the south and represents the desire to express oneself outwardly.

Yellow symbolizes the earth and the centre, but was also the imperial colour reserved for the emperor, the empress and the dowager empress. Because the earth has a responsibility to sustain mankind, yellow invokes the function of primary sustenance and nutrition, and therefore the emperor's role was to protect and nourish his people. The Chinese described their land as the 'yellow earth'. They also regard the earth as the centre of all their bounty: metals are extracted from the earth's mines and water flows from its wells. The plants they eat sprout from the earth, and it is also where fire breaks out.

The colour green, which relates to the east, is also the colour of the world of plants and nourishment, and a symbol for springtime.

White is the colour of one of the beast-gods, the tiger, whose cardinal direction is west. Often regarded as an ominous colour, white is associated with autumn, death, metal, weapons, war and punishment. The colour has always been a symbol of purity, immortality and mourning in China, with mourners at funerals wearing ceremonial clothing of undyed, unbleached natural white cloth.

Opposite During the Qing dynasty, vibrant colours were injected into the home. The understated ceramics and lacquerware of the Ming period were updated with the vivid colours.

Page 86 Yellow represents the earth and symbolizes nature, much as green does in the West. Yellow was reserved for the emperor and his retinue. Many ceramics, lacquered objects and textiles for the imperial household or the palace temples were coloured yellow.

Page 87 These gilded pebbles rest on a lacquered tray, their sheen reflected in its glossy surface. Gold filigree was often added to lacquer decorations, ebony and onyx to provide a luminous contrast.

Page 88
Contemporary
Chinese designers
often prefer muted
colours or unfinished
surfaces, as in this
vernacular chair,
exquisitely crafted in
light-coloured wooc.
The base echoes the
angular design of a
Ming armchair. The
cushion provides
accents of crimson
and black, visually
softening the square
base of the chair and
adding texture to
counterbalance the
smooth surfaces
around it.
Page 89 Linked with
power and energy,
red is associated with
vitality and passion.
It is also the colour
of happiness.

Left Combined with
subdued lighting,
dark , sombre
colours can create a
relaxing mood, and
transform a room into
a quiet refuge.
Opposite A Western
design, this bed
combines the relaxing
tones of white and
beige associated with
modernism and
minimalism. In China,
white has always been
a symbol of purity,
immortality and
mourning. Classical
Ming interiors and
gardens featured
whitewashed
plaster and chalk-
coloured stones.

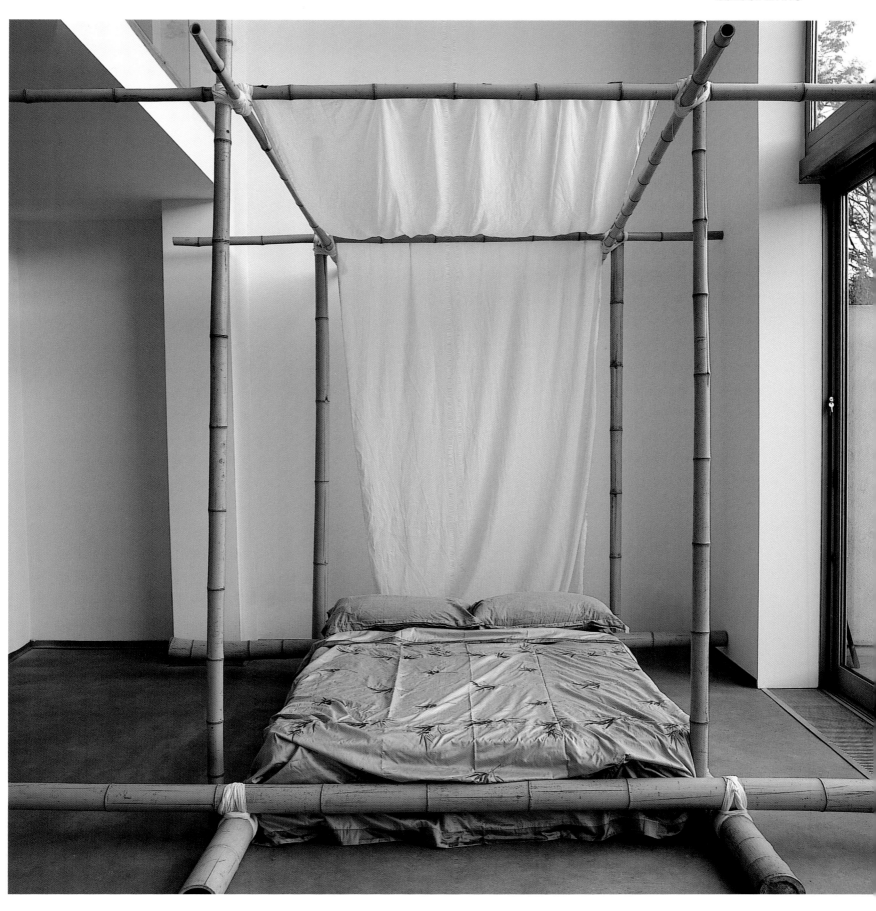

FURNITURE

With the tales of luxury from the East came the lure of a particular type of treasure, which could bestow splendour on any Western interior: furniture. Impassioned collectors waited impatiently for the trading vessels to arrive with their holds full of cabinets, writing bureaux, mirror frames, dressing tables, console tables, stands and toilette cases. The distinctively shaped and decorated desks, screens, cupboards, chairs and beds featured richly lacquered surfaces, elegant curves and elaborate latticework – all exquisitely crafted from precious woods and often inlaid with jewels. The elegance of Ming furniture introduced a graceful simplicity to European homes, while the colourful lacquers and ornamentation of Qing style created an opulent look. Whereas Ming furniture is rarely decorated with auspicious symbols or motifs, the Manchus placed them on every imaginable surface, adorning Qing furniture with the lexicon of an invisible world. To early Western collectors, this mysterious symbolism and exotic imagery gave the works mystic connotations, and they often regarded Chinese furniture as enchanted objects.

Only recently has European furniture been as body conscious as the designs created during the Ming period. Chinese furniture was made according to the same considerations as a fashion garment, providing overall comfort to the body by supporting some areas and facilitating ease of movement in others. Chairs were designed to gently cradle the body, with the chair back curved just enough to support the spine, the chair arms extending to support the elbows and forearms, with the ends rounded into soft contours that embrace the palms of the hands. Most Ming furniture was proportioned to form an invisible box around the body, to centre and

FURNITURE

balance the posture from every direction. Holding oneself erect was believed to be a result of nature rather than of discipline; and correct posture was considered a sign of inner relaxation and health, where the *qi* of nature flowed through the body as it does through the landscape.

While Qing furniture is often described as heavy, elaborate and even garish, Ming pieces are characterized by their refinement and weightlessness. Furniture craftsmanship reached its peak during the Ming dynasty, when the fine quality of the wood and skilled workmanship created an elegance so distinctive that the Chinese refer to this era as the Classical period. Ming furniture continues to appear streamlined and contemporary today, largely because the treatment of the wood and the shape of the pieces seem familiar to modern sensibilities; Westerners are often surprised to learn that the style is over four hundred years old. The lines are so pure that experts in Chinese furniture can determine the age of a piece just by tapping and listening to the vibrations resonating through the wood.

The essence of Ming style was cultivated by scholars, artists and poets, who commissioned craftsmen to produce furniture reflecting their passion for the classical arts of literature, painting, calligraphy and gardening. Both the furniture and the architecture brought nature into an urban setting by emphasizing the processes of nature, its unity with the body and its rhythmic pulse. Wood was never considered to be static: movement was expressed in the subtle curve of each chair leg or armrest.

Throughout Chinese history, furniture has served a decorative and artistic function, indistinguishable from the house itself. The term for architecture is *damugong*, meaning 'large woodwork', while furniture is expressed as *xiaomugong*, or 'small woodwork'. Just as detail is an important aspect of a table or chair, each piece of furniture is considered an element essential to the interior. The walls, windows and doorways of the space, their architectural features and the function of the room are all closely related to the design and structure of the furniture used in the room. Like the house itself, period furniture was rarely constructed with nails, but was crafted instead by tongue-and-groove methods and mortise-and-tenon techniques. Rather than having to pack the furniture when the household moved, it could be taken apart and then reassembled in the new home. Houses, furniture and fine detailing were all crafted from the same woods, creating a harmonious continuity from micro to macro.

Chairs, in the form that we recognize them today, first appeared in China during the rise of the Tang dynasty. They evolved from an object akin to a collapsible camp stool, which had been brought to China in previous dynasties by invading tribes from the steppes of Asia. The Chinese crafted the seat out of woven rattan and adapted it to be carried over the shoulder, making it suitable for travelling or hunting. Over the years it evolved into ceremonial seats for high priests and thrones for emperors, replacing the dais and high platforms where they had traditionally sat.

With the eastward migration of Buddhism from India, chairs and raised platforms began to appear more frequently. The height of seats signified status: great masters would sit on elevated surfaces with their disciples gathered around them on low stools to study and recite scriptures. Hourglass-shaped stools made of straw and basketwork began to appear in the fourth century, and rattan stools made in a similar shape can still be found throughout modern China.

By the beginning of the Tang dynasty, stools and chairs had become common among the elite and those of rank and were starting to be used by the rest of the population. This signalled a turning point in Chinese interiors, which became distinct from those of Japan and the rest of Asia, sharing more similarities with Western homes.

Chairs are often made with seats much broader than those used in the West, to allow the Chinese to sit in the cross-legged 'lotus' position. Of these broad chairs, the *luohan* chair which takes its name from an enlightened Buddhist monk, is characterized by its elegant horseshoe shape. Intended for an aged, wise person, it was traditionally crafted from a single piece of timber, with the wood steamed and bent into a dramatic curve that supported the back and sloped forwards into arm rests. Today *luohan* chairs are generally made from willow wood, which carpenters cut into 7.5cm (3in) planks and steam to bend into the rounded form. Chairs from Shanxi province are characteristically decorated with carvings of landscapes, incense burners, floral motifs and mythic figures that reflect the influence of Buddhism.

The 'official's hat chair' – sometimes referred to as a 'scholar's chair' – is an armchair that takes its name from the similarity between the top horizontal rails protruding over the back posts of the chair, and the winged hats that were part of the formal dress worn by Ming officials.

Page 95 Fine Chinese furniture lends a special presence to a Western home, whether placed in an authentic setting or arranged with other styles. Originally designed to contain scrolls and official documents or store textiles and embroideries, this *maogui*, or cupboard, combines practical storage and understated elegance. Its even lines and muted lacquer finish present a rich contrast to the colourful wallpaper inspired by Chinese painting.

The 'yoke-back chair' is made without armrests, taking its name from the three-tiered rail fitted horizontally across the top of its back. Like the *luohan* chair, the width of the seat allows the legs to be crossed in the lotus position.

The rose chair is designed with a low back that can be placed in front of a latticed window, allowing those seated in it to be cooled by passing breezes or by leaning against the cool marble disc placed in its centre. The rounded carving of the back panel suggests the unfolding leaves of a rose as seen from above, hence the chair's name.

The placement of all furniture reflects the basic principles of architectural orientation, being traditionally arranged on a north–south axis with the most important chair facing south, in the direction of the front gate. This chair was generally large and imposing, and almost ceremonial in its role as the seat occupied by the head of the family. Furniture placement nearly always centred around the position of this important seat; other chairs and stools were aligned symmetrically on either side, with low tables placed between them.

Stools and footstools are made in a variety of shapes and sizes, and they often double as small tables or steps for reaching high shelves and cupboards. *Jiaju*, which literally means 'home tools', is a common word for this or any type of furniture used in a functional context. The cube-shaped stool from the Ming era is a brilliant combination of elegance, functionality and simplicity. Its efficient form gives it a contemporary profile in the West, while in China it has been regarded as a design classic for over five hundred years. The legs, base and top surface all merge together to form continuous lines, broken only by bending at right angles. The top surface is usually wood, but can also be crafted from cane, stone or a ceramic inlay, depending on the region where it is made. Most other types of stool are padded with thin seat cushions.

The height and shape of chairs and stools attest to the regions from which they originate. Low stools reflect the custom of sitting closer to the ground more common to temperate zones in the southern regions, while high chairs and footstools recall the northern climates where people sit well above the cold ground and the draughts blowing over the threshold. In the north of China, stools and footstools are often barrel-shaped and enclosed. Though made of wood, they are sometimes fitted with metal braziers inside, where lumps of burning coal warm those anchored to the seat.

A bed is more than a unique piece of furniture; it is a room within a room. At night it can be draped with fabric to become a private enclosure, and lined with fabric panels of wool or dense felt throughout the winter to block out cold draughts. In daytime the curtains are drawn back and the quilts folded away, and stools and low tables placed alongside for visiting guests.

Traditionally, when women gathered together it was most often in the private area of the home rather than in the formal rooms, where men often conducted business throughout the day and into evening. The bed was the centre of a woman's world, and the place from where she ruled her domain. The most important item in a bride's dowry, it was regarded as a status symbol among wives and concubines. On the wedding night, a small boy would be ritually rolled across the bed before the couple retired, in the hope that the bride would bear many male children during the marriage. The motifs decorating the bed also symbolized the desire for male progeny: depictions of clouds and rain represented sexual intercourse; the dragon, male virility. Because the lotus seedpod continues to grow even when the flower is in bloom, it also symbolized the early arrival of male children. The lotus bloom confirmed the bride's purity, with double lotus-shaped buds symbolizing her promise of chastity. Cross bars are never placed across the centre of the bed's roof in either direction, as an overhead beam is even believed to have the power to split a married couple apart by symbolically invoking the division of their union. The Chinese avoid hanging mirrors facing the bed, where they could drain away the *qi* of those reflected in their sleep.

Like the chair, the bed evolved from a low platform to a dais, and it still retains some of its ceremonial style. Beds are almost always enclosed on three sides of the base, symbolically blocking off space around those sleeping to protect them during the night. Simple railings and low panels of contoured wood are often fitted to the top of the base, rising in a slight arch or humpback shape across their centre. Pieces of intricate latticework stretch between the high posts to form a railing around the bed, and are sometimes fitted underneath the base as decorations or reinforcements. On Qing beds a lattice motif usually extends upwards alongside the posts, joining them together at the top by forming a plinth or a latticework roof.

The *luohan chang*, sometimes known as an opium bed, is undoubtedly the most comfortable piece of furniture in the formal rooms. As its name suggests, it is a long chair for reclining and sitting, similar to the Western *chaise longue*. As the largest and often the most splendid place to sit in the historic home, it made an ideal ceremonial chair for the head of the household. *Luohan chang* were seen as a kind of dais from which the elders could preside over the rest of the family. Qing versions were often elaborately carved and fitted with fretwork railings on three sides, though during the Ming period they were considerably less ornate.

Used primarily for sitting or reclining, some *luohan chang* can also be transformed into low tables by rolling away the cushions and textiles. The surfaces underneath are generally polished to a high gloss, covered in canework or rattan, or cut away altogether and fitted with an inset of woven ropes that form a springlike base. Apart from its pliable support, the woven inset is especially comfortable during the hot summer season. Woven surfaces were common throughout the Ming period and into the early Qing, although the best surviving examples of furniture from these periods are those with wooden panels. Woven seats gave way almost entirely to wooden ones during the eighteenth and nineteenth centuries, as the woven variety was less suited to the opulence of Qing style than to the simplicity of Ming.

The legs and feet of beds and *luohan chang* were generally much stronger than those of tables and chairs, as they had to support the extra weight and girth. If the legs were made of a hardwood they were often rounded and slightly contoured, ending in a horse's hoof or an orb held in the grip of a dragon's claw. If crafted in a softwood, the legs were generally made from slim planks of wood contoured into stylized 'cloud-head' feet, a shape that dates back to the Song dynasty. These mimicked the rolling cloud images featured in paintings and ceramics from this era and were embellished with

This simple daybed is a streamlined version of the opium beds exported to the West in the last century. The daybed has been in use by the Chinese for many centuries. Couch beds were often designated as places of honour where the elders sat as they presided over family life, or were designed with four posts and a canopy roof that transformed them into a room within a room. They were usually constructed with a railing on three sides, or encircled by fretwork or carved wooden panels.

carved or lacquered swirls to suggest movement and depth. This dreamy motif was intended to make the bed appear to be floating in a mist, or soaring among the clouds like a flying carpet.

Traditionally, tables were shaped according to their function, and the literati rarely used them for more than one purpose. Painting, game playing, dining, writing or working is carried out on a table specifically designated for that activity, though in humble homes a single table may fulfil many functions. Round tables were typically made for dining, while long, narrow, rectangular tables were made as altars for the household shrine. The styles of these shrine tables vary from elaborate to simple, but most shrine tables flare sharply upwards on the two outermost edges, creating elegant curves on either side. The leg joins underneath are often concealed by carved brackets to give the top surface the appearance of a plinth. In Western homes, these are popularly used as hall tables today, where their slender width makes them particularly suited to narrow spaces.

Square tables fulfil a variety of functions, serving as desks for bureaucrats, scholars and artists, or as gaming tables for a group of four playing mah jong. When placed in the centre of the room and flanked by high-backed chairs, a square table is used as a gaming table. Pushed directly against a wall, placed under a window or positioned to face the door of the room, it is used as a table for writing or painting. A rectangular shape usually denoted a desk, which is deeper than a shrine but not as long; modern versions are fitted with Western-style shelves and drawers underneath. Side tables vary in size; the low and understated ones provide surfaces on which tea and trays of snacks can be served, while the tallest tables are used as plant stands or pedestals to hold incense burners.

Certain types of low table were constructed especially for use by those seated on the *kang* (a platform for sleeping on at night and reclining on by day), echoing the breakfast-trays used in the West. Though less common today, *kang* tables, desks and trays are made specifically to bridge the folded legs of those seated on the *kang*, and a range of special cabinets and stands are made to complement them. During the winter months in northern China, this type of furniture may completely replace the rest of the tables and chairs in the house, as the *kang*, warmed by the stove underneath, becomes the favourite spot for entertaining, relaxing, eating meals and sleeping. In summer *kang* furniture is taken outside for picnics, and used on boats where its lateral proportions are ideal for the confined space of the hold.

Because cupboards in a traditional Chinese home are seldom built into the architecture, the *maogui* is common to almost every household. Similar to the French armoire, *maogui* are sizeable free-standing cupboards in which folded clothes and textiles are stored. The Chinese name literally means 'hat cupboard', as originally these were where high-ranking officials stored their caps of office, medallions, beads and the many accessories they were required to wear. These are usually among the most treasured pieces found in a Chinese home today, after having been passed down from generation to generation, along with ancestor portraits and dowry beds.

Food cupboards were often built with vents and openings that allowed air to circulate. The term for these translates as 'enraging the cat', because the tiny openings in the surface allowed a cat to see and smell the food within, but not to reach inside.

Folding lacquer screens are the crowning glory of Chinese furniture; the craftsmanship and precious materials are unparalleled. Here, a six-panelled screen (top left) contains inlays of mother-of-pearl in its depiction of a romantic moonlit garden, while on another screen (bottom right) images from the natural world are etched across the lacquer surface in gold leaf. The trim bordering the surface of the *kang* table (top right) is raised to hold objects in place as it is carried from the *kang* to serve food in other parts of the house. The trim on the desk (bottom left) is flush with the surface to allow the scholar to move easily across it while writing or painting.

Wood

The frenzy of construction and furniture-making that resulted from the aesthetically inclined Ming craft movement almost depleted native supplies of luxury hardwoods. After an imperial ban on maritime trade was finally lifted in 1567, most furniture was produced from the tropical hardwoods imported from Burma, Thailand and India into the ports of Shanghai and Canton. It was the use of these heavy, dense woods that accelerated advances in joinery techniques throughout the late Ming and early Qing periods, creating weightless, elegant forms that had been previously unattainable in softwood.

The bulk of the Chinese furniture in today's market is crafted from softwoods typically sourced by local craftsmen. This is why many softwood pieces either are made in a 'vernacular' style – a design typical of a specific region or area – or are based on classical pieces that have been adapted to local sensibilities. Although timber-growing regions are spread far apart, the network of rivers in central and southern China and the rail network in the north make it possible to circulate most precious woods to workshops throughout the country. The provinces of Hubei, Jiangxi and Sichuan are most famous for their hardwoods, but the growing problem of deforestation in these areas means that timber from other parts of South-east Asia continues to be imported in order to meet the demand.

Because hardwood was usually chosen for its durability, its translucency of colour and the satin lustre of its finish, it is associated more with luxury than vernacular style. In this case, hardwood furniture was not necessarily produced in the region where hardwoods grew, as they were harvested for consignment to regions where there were craftsmen skilled enough to work them. This is why the honey-coloured *huanghuali*, or yellow rosewood, furniture was thought to originate from Jiangsu province – despite the fact that the wood itself was probably harvested on the island of Hainan – as specialist craftsmen during the Ming and Qing periods assembled in Jiangsu province to make tables, chairs, panels and screens from it.

The furniture-making of China was superior to that of European craftsmen. While the furniture of great Western cabinetmakers like Chippendale was often merely painted, varnished and adorned with finials, Chinese craftsmen took delight in finishing their work with carvings, patterned inlays, lacquering and metalwork trim. The door jambs of cupboards and cabinets were subtly contoured, and fitted with doors containing panel inlays of exquisite reliefs.

Beds were fenced with fretted palings and intricate latticework, and tables and chairs were buttressed by arched brackets and delicate joints. The frames of tables, chairs and beds were mitred together by joints concealed among subtle moulding carved into the wood.

Woods were celebrated for the natural beauty of their grains and their aromatic properties throughout the whole of the Ming period. The woods chosen for fine furniture were characterized by their natural finishes, which were left untreated but polished to a high sheen. Non-aromatic wood was often coated in clear lacquer to protect it from woodworm, termites, moisture and discoloration. The coloured lacquers applied in the Qing period obscured the grain of the wood altogether, transforming furniture into rich

The detail hidden in this example of Ming fretwork attests to the subtle beauty that characterized carved wood throughout the Ming period. Carefree musicians dance and sing in a forest glade, incorporating representations of harmony and joy into the pattern. The fretwork around them transmutes into gargoyle-like creatures; symbolically poised at the four corners of the earth, they ward off evil from every direction.

Left Nests of tables have been crafted in wood continuously for several millennia. The early nomadic peoples inhabiting the north of China created simple, modular furniture from lightweight softwoods that could be easily stored and quickly assembled. These contemporary nests, shown against a display alcove created by wooden cladding, give a timely update to classical Chinese pieces.

Opposite As well as being crafted into fine pieces of furniture, beautiful woods were used to produce functional items. Robust and hard-wearing, *zhazhen* was often used for chests of drawers (top left) and could be left untreated. This ladder (far right) imitates a functional design, but the black bamboo it is made from transforms its rustic shape into an elegant feature. It was more common to lacquer large tables and chests in black than to make them from wood, and they often had intricate motifs inlaid into their surfaces (bottom left) rather than carvings.

works of baroque splendour. The lacquered surfaces lent themselves to further embellishment, and the furniture from this period was frequently finished with swirling patterns, filigree etchings and auspicious symbols applied in gold leaf.

The Chinese often credit their craft expertise to the guidance of Lu Ban, the patron deity of cabinetmakers and craftsmen, based on the historical figure of Gong Ban, who was a master carpenter in the kingdom of Lu during the fourth century BC. The mythic tales of his adventures portray him as a genius mechanic and craftsman, inventor of the carpenter's sawhorse, the saw, and a variety of other tools and utensils still used today. In art and literature Lu Ban is portrayed as a wandering artisan, mysteriously appearing to bless craftsmen with his advice on how to overcome problems. Legend has it that his blessings extend to those who purchase the final product – they can even call upon Lu Ban to solve the problems of interior decoration after the furniture is taken home!

Precious to Chinese furniture makers are those woods with hues of deep purple, dark red and dense black. Of these, the rare *zitan*, or purple sandalwood, native to southern China has always been especially treasured. The wood is extremely dense, with a deep, fine grain that becomes dark purple in tone when polished to a high sheen. *Zitan* would be sanded and coated in a fine powder to fill any open pores. As it doesn't have the fragrance associated with true sandalwood, it is usually coated with a clear layer of uncoloured lacquer to emphasize its silky shimmer.

Zitan closely resembles *huali*, or rosewood, which rivals it in beauty and lustre. Traditionally, *huali* and *zitan* were cut from the lush tropical forests on the island of Hainan, but today these woods are imported from tropical forests in other parts of South-east Asia. The rich reddish colour and beautiful black markings of the *hongdoumu*, or 'red bean tree', from the Sichuan region are often likened to those of *huali* and *zitan*, but its density makes it more akin to teak. The *hongdoumu* is so dense that it will actually sink in water, meaning it has to be transported overland rather than floated downstream. The variegated *jichimu* wood is unique in having two different textures when cut.

Cypress has been highly prized since the Song dynasty for its lustrous sheen and aromatic fragrance. Its surface has a distinctive waxy or oily feel, its grain is generally quite straight and evenly textured, and the wood is highly resistant to rot and insect infestation. Connoisseurs of fine furniture in the Ming period cited cypress as a favourite. During the Qing dynasty the southern cypress was considered on a par with *nanmu*, which means 'southern wood' and is Chinese cedar; *nanmu* was widely used in the construction of the Yuanmingyuan palaces in Beijing. The heartwood of weeping cypress has a golden-brown tonality, sometimes with reddish streaks. As the cut wood matures, the colour of the heartwood deepens, while the sapwood retains its paler tonalities.

Camphor wood, or *zhangmu*, has a long history of use for wardrobes and storage chests. The strong scent of camphor wood, which repels insects, diminishes very little over time. The interlocking woodgrain produces a contrasting pattern of dark lines against a light background. The hefty wood from its thickest roots was often used to construct cabinets, their dense surfaces polished to a rich lustre. The pale sapwood of camphor is clearly distinguished from the heartwood, whose burgundy-brown colour is typically figured with reddish lines and darker hues.

Wood was highly valued for its grain and colouring, and its beauty was often combined with other materials. This rose chair (top right) has a disc of smooth stone set into the back, while the subtle auburn tones of the latticework screen behind it are offset by the panel of green lacquer it encases. The back, sides and seat of this extraordinary armchair (bottom right) are upholstered with leather, emphasizing the dark grain in the wood of its fan-like 'wings'. This tall cupboard (left), with its intricate lattice insets, displays the dark lustre characteristic of *hongmu*, the wood commonly known as Chinese mahogany.

Lacquer

Lacquerware was developed in China in ancient times, but rose to its peak during the Yuan dynasty, as craftsmen learned to layer the material to unprecedented thickness and give their decorations a sculptural feel. The lacquered objects made during the Ming dynasty often featured intricate designs and subtle motifs, but by the Qing period they depicted complex pictorial scenes and popular auspicious iconography. Europe has imported lacquerwork from Asia from about 1600.

Chinese lacquer, which is a highly polished, opaque varnish applied to wood, comes from the sap extracted from the lacquer tree, *Rhus vernicifera*. This is native to southern and central China and is a close relative of North American poison ivy. Until it has set and dried, the raw lacquer in liquid form is toxic to the skin, creating a reaction similar to that caused by touching poison ivy. The Chinese worked lacquer with special tools to avoid contact. The liquid sap would dry out on the long journey west, making it impossible to export to Europe. Lacquer equivalents were found in parts of southern Europe, but these lacked the lustrous sheen that characterized Chinese lacquerware.

Lacquer has to be applied in thin coats, each of which is allowed to harden and is rubbed smooth before the next is applied. Craftsmen begin with a low-grade lacquer and save the best qualities for the final coats. Lacquer can be coloured by adding pigments, red and black being the most widely used in China.

Its unique properties make lacquer ideal as a protective and decorative coating, and as a malleable surface which can be incised and filled with metal, stone and shell. As early as the twelfth century, lacquered furniture was adorned with pieces of mother-of-pearl cut into shapes and figures, often used with gold foil to construct designs prized for their delicacy and precision.

But lacquer is far more than just a glossy coating for wood; it is also a material that can be shaped, sculpted and carved. Though Japan learned the art of lacquerwork from China, the technique of carving it was unique to Chinese craftsmen. Thick sheets are created for this purpose by applying multiple layers. Because of the time and skill required to prepare raw lacquer, and the labour-intensive processes of layering, burnishing and carving, lacquerware was originally a luxury item found only in wealthy homes.

During the Ming and Qing dynasties, the palace workshops controlled the work of the resident artisan families as well as a large number of craftsmen working in the provinces. The palace lacquers produced during this time were often inscribed with reign titles and cyclical dates, and the imperial symbols continued to be an important characteristic of lacquerware throughout the Ming and Qing dynasties – possibly the earliest form of label chic. As the decorative industries in the coastal ports grew, many craftsmen trained in the palace workshops left to work commercially on export goods. The style of work they did and the decorative motifs they used changed to suit the demands of the West, and some of these hybrid designs were even purchased for the imperial palaces as tokens of 'Europeanoiserie'.

Lacquer screens known as Coromandels were made in China and shipped to Europe via India's Coromandel coast from the seventeenth century. Consisting of up to twelve carved wooden panels coated with a lacquer finish, the screens are delicately engraved, painted and ornamented. They are still produced in China today.

Although the glossy surfaces of this rustic wooden table and leather hatbox resemble black lacquerware, their appearance results from the coats of clear lacquer applied to protect them against infestation and decay. Clear lacquer was often applied to natural wood as a preservative, allowing the beauty of its grain to remain visible beneath its glossy surface.

Bamboo

Throughout Chinese history, scholars and philosophers alike have extolled the virtues of the bamboo, describing it as 'the most humble of woods' and 'the most virtuous of plants'. Just as the poet Tao Qian inspired the literati to romanticize the simple, rustic lifestyle of the peasantry, so too did they learn to revere the aesthetic simplicity of bamboo. Renowned painters chose bamboo as a subject – as they still do today – often depicting it alongside a pool of water, or in the moist terrain in which this woody grass grows. One of the earliest literary references to bamboo was recorded in the *Shijing*, or 'Book of Songs', poetically recounting the beauty of a vibrantly green bamboo tree viewed from across water.

Bamboo has a multitude of purposes: it is flexible enough to be used as fishing rods, strong enough to create ladders and scaffolding, and beautiful enough to craft in fine furniture or to hang exquisite textiles from. The trunk and limbs grow in straight lengths, making it particularly valuable for furniture. Its hollow centre gives it musicality too – bamboo pieces can be played as percussion instruments or made into flutes. Chefs delight in its antibacterial properties, which make it ideal for use as cooking utensils and chopsticks, and its young shoots are even edible.

It has been in use for at least ten thousand years – bamboo objects have been unearthed that date back to the Neolithic period. Even then bamboo was used for both practical purposes and ornamentation: hairpins, arrow sheaths, tools and utensils are among early implements made from it.

Bamboo belongs to a family of evergreen plants of which there are over a thousand varieties. The colour of its wood ranges from light tan to dark brown, reddish-tinted or sometimes deep auburn. Often the wood is darkest around its nodes, with light patches in between them, creating a variegated effect. The bamboo grown in Sichuan is known for its delicate pattern, while the variety found in Hangzhou has been described as deep purple in colour. The bamboo native to Guangdong and Guangxi has palm-like leaves that can be crafted into screens and shutters when dried.

Bamboo furniture is popular in all types of homes, and is used both indoors and outdoors. In southern China, bamboo chairs abound, the most common being the low-seat, high-back type. Their simplicity introduces a rustic element to the homes of the wealthy, where they are placed alongside sophisticated pieces, and over time develop the same luminous patina. The affordability of bamboo makes it the staple furniture of humble homes, especially in rural areas.

Each piece is constructed from lengths of varying thickness, with the broadest pieces used to form the frame, and thinner ones forming slats for the seat and back, or narrow pins that secure the entire frame. Traditionally, the lengths of bamboo are bound together with fibres rather than being nailed.

Like the willow that is steamed and bent to fashion the *luohan* chair (see page 96), bamboo also becomes pliable when heated, to the extent that a single length can be bent into right angles to form a square base or half of the frame. Usually a segment has to be partially cut away to allow the wood to bend into a right angle, creating a recess that doubles as an interlocking join. These steaming techniques mean that fewer cuts and joins are necessary in bamboo furniture.

The versatility of bamboo enables it to assume a multitude of shapes and forms. Here, a vernacular armchair with an integral footstool has been created by bending and steaming the pliable bamboo into shape. The crescent-shaped wall is panelled with the timber harvested from a grove of young bamboo, while the flooring beneath is constructed from narrow planks of mature bamboo to provide a durable and attractive surface.

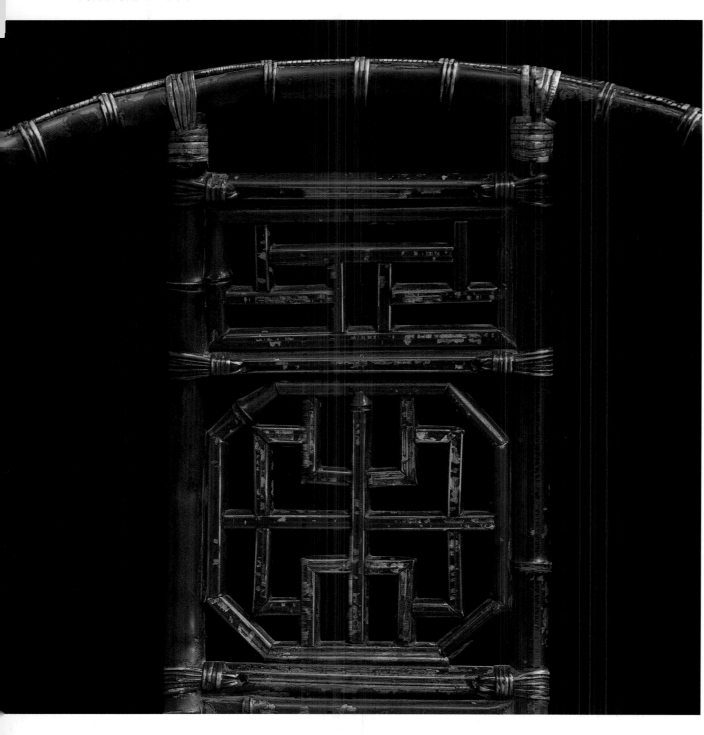

Left Although bamboo is commonly described as light in tone, its wood can be deep purple in colour, as this elaborate chair from southern China illustrates. Its fretwork insets are set into shallow grooves and then wedged permanently in place, while its structural supports are bound together by reeds that have the strength of steel bands.

Opposite This desk and chair are typical examples of the elegant pieces made in Suzhou, a renowned centre for bamboo production not far inland from modern Shanghai. From the sixteenth century, the bamboo furniture produced in its workshops was considered to be the finest in all of China.

Detail

Details play a central role in Chinese furniture. Whether used for practicalities like hinges, handles and corner mounts, or the springy comfort of canework, they were planned into the overall aesthetic at the design stage. The combination of materials became more sophisticated after the ban on imported wood was lifted in the sixteenth century, making great quantities of tropical hardwood available to Chinese craftsmen, who had primarily been working with native softwoods. No longer was it necessary to apply multiple coats of lacquer over the wood for protection and decoration, as had been the case when softwoods were prevalent. The hardness of the wood gave cabinetmakers the perfect material for carving elaborate designs and reliefs. Hardwoods leant themselves to such detailing as inlays of precious stones, tortoiseshell and rare wood, and were strong enough to support mounts made of bronze, brass and other metals used to decorate corners and disguise joints.

Stone was a popular material for decorative panels fitted into chairs, table tops and screens. Marble, serpentine and granite were commonly used; agate, jade, malachite, nephrite and lapis lazuli were more rare. The patterns of nature revealed in these slices of geological time were often regarded as an abstract landscape scene or a vision of the mineral kingdom.

Ceramic panels were sometimes used in table tops in place of stone. These could be left unglazed to mimic coarse stone, or they could be decorated to depict landscapes, figures or motifs.

Metal hardware was commonly used for reinforcement and decoration. Even in ancient times, ironmongery was a specialized guild that had more in common with science than with woodworking. Chinese metalsmiths were skilled in firing decorative hardware to perfection, but were also preoccupied with complex metallurgical formulas to create alloys that had unsurpassed strength and a range of different hues.

The hardware handles made for lattice doors, cupboard doors and drawers depicted a variety of animals, fish and birds. Fish symbolized harmony and freedom during the Ming dynasty. They were heavily romanticized by the philosophers and scholars of the era, who imagined them to be completely content in their underwater kingdom, free of restraint as they followed the course of nature. Fish also featured in the etchings and engravings adorning locks and keys, which were commonly regarded as signs of status and wealth. The keys used by high-ranking officials and members of rich households were beautifully and artistically made, depicting images of *qilins* (the auspicious Chinese unicorn), butterflies, tigers and panthers.

Locksmith craftsmanship reached its peak during the Tang dynasty, when locks were valuable pieces of equipment, and materials like bronze, silver or gold were often used. Tang locks were mostly padlocks that opened by keys or by combinations. Often the keyhole was hidden among tiny crevices decorating the lock's surface so that only the owner could find it immediately. Chinese combination locks were different from those made in the West, as the rotating wheels usually bore symbols rather than numbers, or poetic words that had to form a nonsensical phrase to open. Keys were also a symbol of married women; because married women were designated as the family's 'key-carriers', women who did not have a key fastened to their robes were assumed to be unmarried.

Locks and metal hardware were regarded as signs of status and wealth. Produced in brass alloy, bronze, nickel, silver and gold, they were used to ornament handles and hinges and also to act as decorations. The three plates and set of hinges shown here are cast in *paktong*, a brass alloy containing a small amount of nickel to retard the tarnishing characteristic of pure brass. Set against luminous black and ruby red, *paktong* almost takes on the lustre of gold. The fastenings shown in the top and bottom left-hand pictures can be secured by fitting a lock through the loop. The pull tabs shown in the bottom left-hand picture represent fish, which symbolized harmony and freedom during the Ming era.

TEXTILES

紡織

TEXTILES

The textiles of China have always been considered some of the most resplendent and colourful ever produced, as renowned in the ancient world as they were at the height of chinoiserie. Even before the Chinese began trading ceramics, spices and lacquerware, the sumptuous fabrics acquired by Mediterranean and Middle Eastern traders created a mythology more outlandish than the tall tales of the East India merchants. The Romans traded with a land they called Serica, the land of silk, so remote and mysterious that mere mortals feared to journey beyond its borders, fearing the lithe tigers and fearsome dragons that roamed its motifs.

These legends and mysteries were perpetuated well into the Han dynasty, largely because the Chinese were the only people who possessed the secrets of silk weaving. By that time they had established lucrative export markets to trade directly with Asia and the Middle East. The legendary caravan route that carried goods overland is known today as the Silk Route, following a term coined in the late nineteenth century to describe the trading paths that ran west from China through Central Asia to Turkey and Syria, then by sea to ports in Europe. Silk was but one of the many expensive, sought-after luxuries carried along the Silk Route: elaborate tapestries and intricate embroideries stitched with stories of frivolity and fantasy were sold alongside carpets, brocades and needlework ablaze with crimson and gold.

By the end of the third century, bandit raids threatened these routes; until the seventh century, overland routes to China were too dangerous to attempt without garrison escorts. As Western sea merchants rarely sailed beyond the Black Sea, trade between East and West was sporadic. Not until the thirteenth-century conqueror Genghis Khan re-established links between China and the West did the great mercantile companies of Venice, Pisa and Genoa return to trade with China, mostly in silk.

Bales of silk were regularly exported from China throughout the Yuan dynasty, transported to Europe across Asia and the Middle East. Cloths of gold, silks, delicate embroidery and intricate quilting whetted European appetites for the looms of Cathay. Fabrics adorned with lions, phoenixes and dragons were often used by the Catholic clergy at that time, and these motifs were imitated by weavers in Europe on tapestries and furnishings. Suddenly China closed its doors on foreigners again; the xenophobic policies of the Ming dynasty were virtually to seal China off for another few centuries.

During this long embargo, the demand for silk, embroideries, tapestries and printed cottons continued. European weavers attempted to imitate the splendours of Chinese textiles by producing their own ranges of cloth, which mimicked everything from Buddhist robes to Indian chintzes and Persian carpets. Chintz, the printed cotton exported to Europe from India in the sixteenth and seventeenth centuries, was mistakenly attributed to the chintzes produced in Canton. When imitations were produced in France and England, these were given the generic title of *façon de la Chine*. Indian chintzes popularized the 'Tree of Life' design, and this was later copied in the workshops of Canton at the request of European merchants. They falsely assigned it to the pantheon of chinoiserie motifs as an icon of China.

By the second half of the seventeenth century the East India Company had arrived in England bearing richly embroidered silk hangings stitched with yarns of gleaming gold and silver set amid brilliant jewel colours and soft, gossamer threads. The charter of the East India Company established links with the textile merchants of China through the port of Canton. Ships would anchor at Madras or Bombay on the long journey east, taking Indian fabrics, Buddhist relics and polished jewels on board which they later exchanged for the bolts of silk and embroideries that were to be exported to Europe or back to India.

With the Baroque in full swing in Europe, the brilliance of Chinese fabrics contributed greatly to the extravagance, luxury and romance lavished on the interiors of the period. Chinese embroideries were hung from floor to ceiling in drawing rooms, libraries and ballrooms, draped over bed frames and capped with billowing plumes of feathers. These embroideries and tapestries were often the subject of conversation during the newly fashionable pastime of drinking tea – a ritual which to be complete, required china teapots and lacquered trays.

As the fashion for hanging textiles grew, Chinese fabrics were draped at windows and doors, canopied over settees and hung on the walls. Lengths of painted taffeta were fixed to the wall by stretching them over wooden frameworks, which were then mounted side-by-side as panels, or positioned around the room as though they were overlarge paintings. The most elaborate of these were framed in outlines of faux bamboo or carved trim that mimicked Ming fretwork. The panels of fabric may have decorated the room in a single motif, or each one may have depicted a different design.

Genre scenes of the Chinese emperor and his coterie were popular, as were the brooding mandarins that strolled amid exotic landscapes with umbrella-carrying ladies and their diminutive attendants. These chinoiserie figures seemed preoccupied with drinking tiny pots of tea, smoking pipes of tobacco, catching butterflies and climbing pagodas. The fishing party was to become a favourite theme for chinoiserie fabrics, while arched bridges, bamboo poles and pools of cascading water remained popular throughout the eighteenth century and beyond.

The magic and mystery of Cathay slowly disappeared as the early eighteenth-century looms of London's Spitalfields and Lyon in France produced silk closer to home. Figured silks were among those first woven in Europe, mostly featuring motifs etched in gold or silver thread against a damask background, with foliage and floral designs. The style was set by the active imagination and exquisite draughtsmanship of Jean Pillement, a French *maître d'art* who created hundreds of chinoiserie motifs for hanging textiles and soft furnishings. In the 1750s he set the style for Rococo chinoiserie in London and in Paris, decorating many Rococo rooms with printed linen, or his freehand drawings on cotton and silk. Some of Pillement's most stunning works have been preserved in the staterooms of the sprawling palaces of Oranienbaum, the summer estate of the Russian tsars built on the Gulf of Finland. The fabrics lining the walls of the Glass Bead Room were embroidered with Pillement designs drawn across thick silks. Pillement's willowy trees and giant flowers wind delicately through other-worldly landscapes lavishly covered with two million glass beads coloured in hues of sapphire, ruby and amethyst.

Page 119 The tapestries, brocades and needlework that merchants traded on the Silk Route filled palaces all over the ancient world. The Chinese continue to embrace their rich textile heritage today, with silken wall hangings, cushion covers, embroidered textiles and furniture upholstery. In this Chinese home, a collection of silk cushions featuring embroidered flowers is framed by heavy damask curtains emblazoned with auspicious symbols and lined with Siamoise fabric. A traditional wedding-bed coverlet is stretched across the divan.

Like the ornaments that moved further and further away from the original Chinese designs, chinoiserie textiles also expressed a purely European vision of the mythical Cathay invented by the West. The striped fabric known as Siamoise, a design modelled on the 'Chinese' robes worn by the Siamese ambassadors to the court of Louis XIV, was a favourite of the French and Germans, but far removed from genuine Chinese styles. Pékin, also French, was a brocade with a pattern of Northern European flora woven amidst the alternating matt and shiny bands of the silk. The French textiles known as toiles de Jouy were used to cover chairs, beds and walls, and printed in monochrome using an engraved copper plate. This was the reverse of the Chinese woodblock printing method, as the dye was transferred onto the fabric from the incised areas of the plate rather than from a relief image, as on the woodblock. Featuring pictorial scenes, many of them chinoiserie fantasies, toiles de Jouy were often embellished with festoons of flowers and trailing ribbons that would have been unknown to the Chinese.

European textile artists typically decorated chinoiserie fabrics with elaborate fretwork patterns as background elements, their geometry creating a subtle repeating pattern that circled family crests or classical emblems. Trailing flowers, exotic plants, swirling water, trees with sweeping branches and shrubs with tropical-looking flora and foliage brought nature to life. Vases and ornaments set on carved stands, figures dressed in ceremonial robes and colourful birds were often used as stand-alone motifs, as were, curiously, pineapples. These patterns almost always included architecture of some sort: palaces, shrines, teahouses and pagodas featured in landscapes interspersed with cloud-capped mountains, gnarled trees and zigzag bridges.

It is hard to imagine the reaction of the Chinese if these Western methods and motifs had been brought back to decorate a Chinese home. Textiles in the Chinese interior were used in a different way altogether – although they were often richly embellished, they acted as an accent rather than a decorative feature. It was a common practice in China to drape fabric over wooden furniture in the winter months, and the back rail capping Ming chairs was designed to support an ample width of fabric that would hang over the back and seat before continuing to the floor. In keeping with the motifs characteristic of Ming style, the designs of these fabrics emphasized form and line rather than ornamentation; they were often decorated with little more than a band of contrasting colour around the edges. The textiles used to insulate the walls, windows and doors were hung flush against them, rather than being gathered and draped as was fashionable in Europe. Even the fabrics adorning bed frames were hung with spartan simplicity, providing privacy and insulation rather than decorative swags.

Although the soft furnishings decorating the Chinese home during the Qing period were more elaborate than Ming fabrics, they adorned the interior with the same fluidity, moving from bed frame to chair to window as the weather dictated. On milder days they could be easily packed away. As there were no built-in cupboards, cabinets and chests in many shapes and sizes were used to store fabric. The wardrobes and hat cupboards described on page 100 were comprised of upper and lower units, the doors of each fitted with a removable central stile so that bolts of fabric, folded garments and rolls of bedding could be stored across the entire width of the shelves without wrinkling.

The streamlined elegance of Ming style resurfaced in the late nineteenth/early twentieth century through the textiles of Art Nouveau. Art Nouveau was mostly derived from Gothic and Rococo, which itself had roots in chinoiserie, and from the arts of the East. Much of the enigmatic form, elegance and colour for which Art Nouveau is famous can be related to the spirit of Ming design. Art Nouveau was characterized by stylized patterns and motifs taken primarily from nature, representing a controlled exuberance of form, line and colour that mimicked the balance of Chinese designs. The cresting

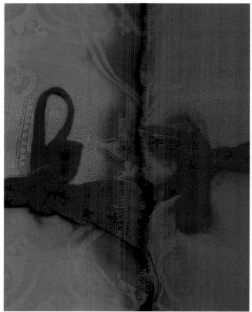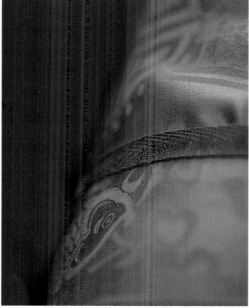

waves, lotus leaves and curvaceous floral motifs were arranged in abstract patterns and repeated on fabrics and wall hangings, or symmetrically arrayed along the edging of upholstery furnishings.

The passion for antique and vintage textiles persists to the present day, and many contemporary interiors feature Chinese textiles as draperies and upholstery, or display antique robes as wall hangings. Today, Chinese furniture, ceramics and works of art are all avidly collected, but textiles are less known and less appreciated. Many 'modern' patterns popular in China today are derived from motifs dating back to the Song and Tang dynasties, but eighteenth-century Qing motifs are by far the most common. North American fabric designers are also beginning to find inspiration in the motifs of China's rich history, depicting them in bright colours against a strong background.

Western textile designers have a long history of finding inspiration in the chinoiserie vogue that thrived on illusion and misrepresentation. This is changing as contemporary textile designers embark on a quest for authenticity unknown to the chinoiserie weavers of previous centuries. Though some designers are recreating the chinoiserie motifs of seventeenth- and eighteenth-century interiors, many others tend to be true to authentic designs, researching and preserving the Chinese motifs of previous eras. While some of these are artfully reworked into new designs, others are painstakingly preserved to reflect the rich tradition that gives them a style of their own.

Below left Colourful Chinese cottons and silks are widely used for home furnishings in the West – many designers travel to fabric fairs in China and ship them home by the roll.

Opposite The image of Chairman Mao, the first chairman of the People's Republic of China, was given pop-art status by Andy Warhol. It was then transformed into a fashion icon by Vivienne Tam, the New York-based fashion designer originally from Hong Kong. More recently, Chairman Mao's portrait has achieved kitsch value, featuring on curtains, cushion covers, book jackets and lampshades.

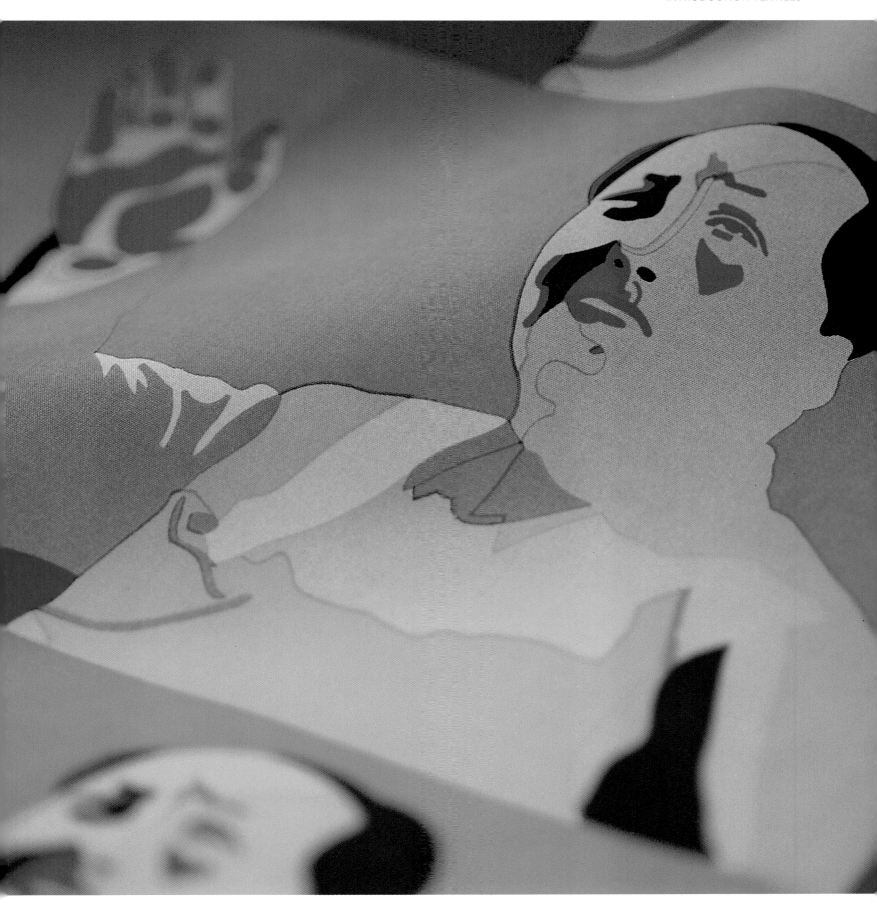

Opposite The European passion for Chinese textiles has persisted through the centuries and continues to the present day. Some enthusiasts claim to sleep in nothing but Chinese silk, collecting antique and vintage bedding like the embroidered textiles shown here. This cushion, set amid silk fabrics (top left), captures two serpentine dragons. The quilted coverlet (top right) is a single piece of hand-stitched cotton, layered over a cotton sheet embroidered with crimson chrysanthemums. Woven silk fabrics (bottom left) have been cut for their next life as cushion covers, while cushions (bottom right) feature foliage embroidery inspired by an autumn sunset.

Above The mystique associated with Chinese fabrics slowly dissipated as European looms produced silk closer to home. Foliage and floral designs, as in the fabric used to upholster these chairs, were among the first types woven in Europe. The early Western chinoiserie textiles were also stretched over a framework of battens and fixed to the walls. This interior replicates the style in the modern day.

Carpets

Chinese carpets have their own distinctive style, characterized by their dense texture, their silky surface and the contours cut into their rug pile to create elegant reliefs. Their long lifespan means that even delicate silk carpets survive their owners by several centuries, improving with age and becoming collectible items. Many nineteenth-century carpets from the Qing dynasty remain in excellent condition today, attributed in part to the practice of removing them from the floor when they were not in use. Carpets were almost never permanent fixtures – they were moved from room to room and from bed to chair, and were often taken with the owners when they travelled.

The bold patterns of Chinese carpets inject energy into the core of any room, whether it is a contemporary setting or a period-style interior. Their patterns range from simple geometric designs and abstract shapes to bold, stylized medallions and familiar floral patterns. Many of the abstract and geometric patterns used by the Chinese were created by the ancient weavers of Central Asia, revealing the influence of primeval symbols from Khotan and the Caucasus. Chequerboard designs, crosses, diagonals and lozenges are combined with figurative images and patterns from nature. Medallion patterns are also derived from the ancient motifs of Central Asia and from similar emblems featured on silk brocades and Chinese porcelain. Traditional floral designs which mimic the motifs of Chinese silk textiles have always been popular. Lotus flowers are popular features, freely combined with dragons, phoenixes, clouds, waves and mountains.

Large carpets, particularly woollen ones, were not used in China until relatively recent times. The early carpets were usually small so that they could be carried easily by the steppe nomads as they were used during the different daily activities. A single carpet provided a sleeping place, a tablecloth, a seat, a base for spiritual or devotional practice and a saddle for riding horseback.

In northern China during the Tang period, small rugs were woven to cover the *kang* (see page 100) and to provide comfortable seating, but sometimes these were extended to cover the whole surface of the *kang*. Most of these carpets were made of felt, yak hair or fine camel down, and typically dyed black and red at the borders. These *kang* carpets are thought to be the earliest surviving examples of authentic Chinese carpets.

By the Ming dynasty, temple floor mats, prayer rugs and decorative carpets were also made in northern China, woven mostly from wool and camel down. Some early Ming carpets still survive today, made in wool pile and woven with Buddhist designs, whose colours still remain bright despite the passage of time. At the height of the trade along the Silk Route, the Chinese provinces bordering it provided carpets to sell to foreign merchants, competing against goods woven in Tibet and Mongolia, both of which were famous for the beauty of their carpets.

China's exportation of carpets slowed down through the centuries as the demand for silk and ceramics increased. In the early 1900s the industry was revitalized, and China continues to export both old and new carpets today. Antique Chinese carpets can be bought in the West at auction or from specialist dealers, who provide certification of provenance and authenticity if the item is valuable. Like a work of art, a carpet is an investment and a treasure – but one that can actually be used as its value increases.

This antique folding chair, also called a hunting chair because of the collapsible design that made it easily transported by a mounted huntsman, rests amidst a multitude of butterflies seemingly hovering above a carpet of interlocking geometric shapes. Butterflies are traditionally depicted in a floral, rather than geometric, environment. The money plant on the chair is considered to be auspicious.

Above In this silken carpet, a flock of chirping swallows lands in a field of poppies. Chinese carpets are often too beautiful to decorate the floor, but on the wall they provide an exotic backdrop that fuels the imagination.

Page 130 A hanging carpet made at the height of Chairman Mao's reign is imbued with patriotic zeal for China's great leap forward. Ceremonial red lanterns hang from the eaves to denote an official holiday, while a red Communist flag flies outside a public building. During the Communist era, China did not halt the production of luxury goods, but replaced many 'decadent' motifs with political imagery.

Page 131 These hanging carpets portray two very different visions of China. The top carpet depicts a public assembly to celebrate Maoist ideology, complete with modern vehicles and Western clothing. The bottom carpet captures the tranquil water garden once enjoyed by a wealthy landowner, representing the beauty of China's artistic heritage.

Opposite While carpets from the Qing dynasty included a broad range of motifs, the dragon was the most popular icon of the era. The fearsome dragon articulated in this design winds its way through an ethereal world laden with auspicious symbolism that appeals to the literati's taste for classical imagery. A grain vessel is filled with a measure of millet in the top left-hand corner, and a pestle and mortar is depicted immediately below it; these are associated with riches and scholarly interests respectively. Butterflies and other insects circle the dragon, while the scrolling clouds below denote its other-worldly status. The wavy motifs at the bottom of the textile are cosmic rays: emanating upwards, they endow the dragon with protective qualities and spiritual harmony.

Hanging Fabrics

Early wall hangings were used to depict religious and ethical teachings in ancient China, and were embroidered with the same auspicious symbols as the ritual objects associated with Taoism, Confucianism and Buddhism. This changed during the Song dynasty, when some tapestries were made for purely decorative purposes. Their designs became richer and more stylized as they were embellished with brushwork and embroidery, making the Song period the golden age of tapestries in China. The tapestries of the Yuan dynasty featured threads of silver and gold for an opulent effect, while Ming tapestries revived the simple, classical designs of Song textiles. By the end of the Ming period, weavers had refined their techniques considerably to create works with detailed compositions and neatly textured surfaces.

Tapestries of the Qing dynasty featured a broader range of motifs than previous eras, and their designs became more complex as they were embellished using embroidery or painting and dyeing techniques. Qing craftsmen repeated the legendary characters popular during the Ming period, depicting the moon goddess, the heavenly maid, the fabled 'Seven Sages of the Bamboo Grove' and the austere 'Twenty-Four Paragons of Filial Piety'. Qing textiles were dominated by a vogue for red. Because red was regarded as the colour of happiness, red tapestries were often presented on festive occasions, featuring the symbols for a happy life. A phoenix was believed to bring joy, the unicorn expressed the hope for noble sons, while the Buddhist lion was a symbol of power and valour. Deer, cranes and peaches symbolized longevity.

The 'cut silk' tapestries known as *kesi* are among the most valuable of all Chinese textiles. Named for the visible slits between colour breaks, the technique was practised during the Han and Tang dynasties but reached its zenith during the Song dynasty. *Kesi* are made through a labour-intensive weaving technique that decorates both sides of the textile, making them reversible for use as hanging screens or room dividers. *Kesi* often depict figures with their features drawn in ink rather than woven or embroidered.

Chinese batik fabrics are also reversible, and hung as screens, curtains and wall coverings. Since ancient times, batik prints have been created by using a resist-dyeing technique, in which designs are stamped on cotton cloth with wax, covering areas of cloth that are not to be dyed. Further layers of wax are added or removed prior to immersing the cloth in other colours of dye. The most beautiful batiks in China are those painted by the tribal Miao people.

Silk banners embroidered in gold and silver thread decorated the home with characters and motifs that conveyed good wishes and welcoming greetings. The banners could be fixed to the walls like scrolls for everyday decoration or they could be hung overhead during festivities.

Silk flags were also hung from above or flown outside, usually as a means of denoting the rank of government officials. Flags were embroidered with blazing red suns, five-toed dragons and a range of symbols and animals. Thousands were produced over the years and, like sleeve bands and textile remnants, these are easily found today in vintage textile boutiques or from antique dealers. The graphic quality of their emblems and symbols brings colour to any interior, whether framed on a wall or flown overhead.

For centuries European craftsmen were unable to rival the intricate stitching for which Chinese needlework was renowned, and magnificent silk embroideries were often displayed in the extravagant interiors of the Baroque period. Chinese embroidered wall hangings depicted genre scenes, deities and elements of the natural world with stunning expression – the vivid colour palette they created was unparalleled in the West. In the silk wall hanging shown here, two pheasants perch in a forest glade where exquisite roses bloom alongside a tranquil pool.

Embroidery

'Fine feathers make the birds', proclaims one ancient Chinese maxim, to highlight the importance of refined detailing in decorative works. Applied to fabrics, this declaration describes the place that works of embroidery hold in the traditional Chinese home, where they embellish household items, furniture, wall hangings and articles of clothing with delicate pastels, rich jewel colours and spectacular motifs. In early centuries the fine stitching and intricate details displayed in Chinese embroidery were revered throughout the ancient world, until they were eclipsed by the silk trade. For centuries afterwards embroidery was regarded as purely a domestic pastime, though many examples of fine needlework were traded along the Silk Route and shipped to the West via textile merchants in Canton.

In China, embroidery even adorned items made for everyday use. Cases made to hold chopsticks, scissors, knives and sets of scales were richly embroidered, as were small receptacles for fans, eyeglasses and money. Household goods like curtains, quilts, tablecloths and pillowcases were often stitched with motifs and decorations, while clothing and accessories were equipped with detachable cuffs and collars crafted from embroidered velvets and silks. Elaborate appliqué borders ornamented both robes and bedding, along with gold braiding and round silk cords made to edge the most elaborate textiles. The Chinese term for this type of trim carries the same meaning as the words for decorative fretwork or railings, making it clear that it was viewed as an integral part of the overall fabric and not merely a decorative afterthought.

The embroidered fabrics prepared for a wedding dowry would furnish the home for generations. Curtains and valances were made not just for windows but also for doors, while pillow covers were made for sets of bedding and soft cushions for the reception rooms. The bride was delivered to her husband's family in a sedan chair along with her embroidered treasures, which included three pairs of silk shoes that she was obliged to make for her new husband and his father and mother. These objects demonstrated the bride's best needlework skills as a means of proving her worth to her husband and his family, showing her usefulness to the household and her willingness to perform the most menial of tasks.

The leisure time of wealthy Chinese families was often spent in industrious activities regarded as cultural pursuits. Men occupied themselves with the scholarly arts while women devoted a large part of their time to making embroideries and decorating textiles. They often based embroideries on the best paintings in the family's collection, creating a type of work now referred to as 'the embroidery of the inner chambers'. This genre takes its name from the rooms in a Chinese home set aside for the exclusive use of the household's women, where they spent their working hours and often their leisure time. Here stitching techniques were passed down from mother to daughter, along with the patterns of classical motifs. Like the images of butterflies sipping nectar from peonies that symbolized a love lasting the joys of passion, the significance of each motif took on a variety of meanings. Other designs depicted courtly ladies in gardens or on moonlit terraces, surrounded by birds and insects, animals, trees and flowers. Chinese women viewed their embroidery as a source of pride and self-esteem, many regarding it as their biggest achievement, apart from bearing sons.

Brocades have been prominent in Chinese textiles since ancient times. The best silk brocades employed gold or silver threads to create the raised figures and motifs characteristic of this technique. These were accentuated by other colours, or were crafted in bold relief by wrapping a fine filament of gold and silver foil around a silk thread. Metallic threads are less commonly used today; although this dragon's head has the luminosity of silver, its form is stitched into the fabric using strands of shimmering silk.

During the Ming and Qing dynasties the domestic art of embroidery was transformed into an industry that existed outside the home. Embroideries were bought by the wealthy to decorate their interiors or present to temples and monasteries as tokens of religious devotion. By the late Qing period the embroidery trade had evolved into a commercial market that continued to produce prestige items for the wealthy, while making everyday items that could be purchased for modest sums. Embroidery shops specialized in goods for the interior, selling the same kind of items as were traditionally presented by a bride to her new family. Brocades also gained currency within this industry, with those featuring raised figures in gold or silver threads especially prized by the Qing court.

Chinese embroideries are renowned for their floral motifs. These can appear in simple outline but are usually stitched from viewpoints that mimic a three-dimensional perspective to make the blooms and foliage more stylized or naturalistic in appearance. Usually they depict as blossoming flowers maturing on climbing vines, or the gentle droop of peonies, azaleas and morning glories. Floral motifs often include other elements from the natural world, depicting rolling waves, scrolling clouds, tropical fruits, butterflies and exotic birds perched on trailing branches. These embroideries adorn household textiles as well as robes, banners and ritual artefacts.

The intricate stitching and exquisite details of sleeve bands have always made them attractive features, whether attached to clothing or not. Certain types of sleeve band were designed with motifs stitched vertically so that they could be viewed as upright images when the wearer folded their arms in front of them. These were often embroidered with characters that illustrated a story told in literature or poetry, or depicted themes ranging from the four seasons to the five virtues. Sleeve bands share characteristics common to tapestries, giving them the feel of miniature tapestries when used as wall hangings. Hanging scrolls were made of similar embroidered silks but were considerably wider and longer.

Imperial Dress

When the Manchus conquered China in 1644 their robes were a hybrid of their own dress and that of the Chinese. As they rose to power they adopted the embroidered sleeve ends of Chinese robes, creating full cuffs with elaborate detailing. Dress in imperial China was always highly codified, with the decorative motifs of court costumes and officials' robes strictly designated by rank. Among the emblems reserved for the emperor's robes were the twelve imperial symbols of the sun, the moon and the constellations; mountains, water and fire; birds, weed and millet, cups and axes, the auspicious *fu* symbol and nine five-clawed dragons. The emperor's dragon robe was worn during religious festivals and periods of fasting – except for a few details in black, white and pale blue, the dragon robe was embroidered in fine gold and silver threads. As well as the standard imperial symbols, the emperor's dragon robe featured clouds, waves and rocky promontories that were symmetrically arranged to represent the order of the cosmos.

As the dragon was the principal motif embroidered on court robes, its poses and styles were varied and complex. The number of dragons allowed on any one garment was an important signifier of the wearer's status. All differences in material, colour and cut of the robes were determined by imperial codes and protocols. At the time of the last Qing emperors, dragon robes were full-length with side fastenings, and structured more like overcoats than loose robes. Dragon robes were also worn by the empress and the women of the imperial household, as well as the wives of the senior officials entitled to wear them. Apart from dragon robes, and needlework roundels on garments, it was unusual for Chinese men to wear embroidered clothing. Embroidered floral motifs, butterflies and garden scenes were more typical of women's robes, while men's robes were usually decorated by patterns woven into the silk on the loom.

The robes of other court officials were embellished with emblems and badges of rank, worn to signify the difference between officials and the wealthy courtiers who were not in service to the emperor. Rank badges were square in shape, often with dark blue backgrounds, and embroidered with a variety of birds, animals or mythological creatures, each symbolizing a different rank within the imperial hierarchy. Protocols in the Ming and Qing dynasties stipulated that a civil official's rank should be a bird: for example, a red-crowned crane, oriole, quail or goose. Animal designs were allocated to military officers, who wore tigers, rhinoceros, leopards and brown bears. The meaning of the emblems changed between the dynasties and rulers as the animals took on new cultural meanings over time.

Sleeve bands were sewn onto robes as cuffs, joined to the fabric at the wrist or elongated to cover the hands as a sign that the wearer did not perform menial tasks. These were generally made in light pastel colours or creams, probably to contrast with the darker background of the robe itself. Because light colours were reserved for mourning, it is unusual to find robes with white backgrounds, even among those made especially for export to the West. Though human figures were rarely embroidered onto the robe itself, sleeve bands depicted warriors and legendary characters from literature and poetry along with deities and the Chinese Immortals. Often the stitching is so fine it is virtually invisible, and the colours so rich that they continue to look vibrant today.

This magnificent robe is indicative of the Manchu imperial style, embroidered with the five-clawed dragon, one of the twelve symbols of imperial sovereignty used in China since the Han dynasty. At the bottom of the robe, representations of invisible cosmic rays and turbulent waves encircle the wearer, along with the other-worldly forms the Chinese believe to exist in the human realm. The dragons move amidst scrolling clouds, with a radiating sun or glowing moon in their centre. The embroidered sleeve bands are shaped in a horse's hoof design and feature miniature versions of the motifs decorating the front and back of the robe.

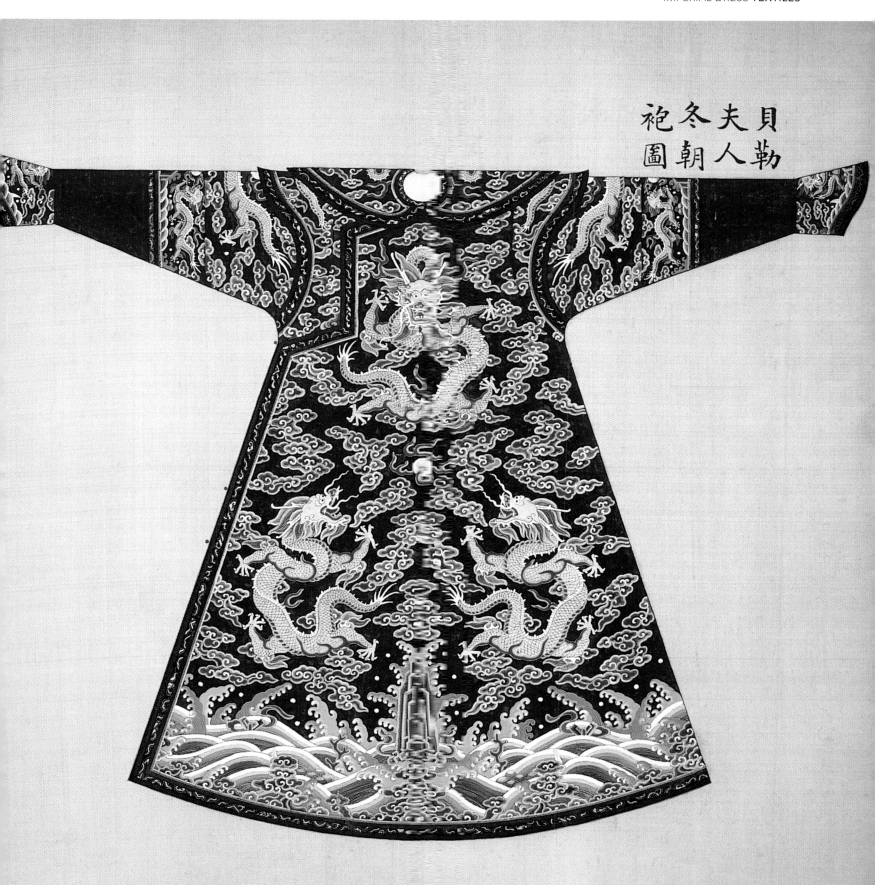

袍冬夫貝
圖朝人勒

DECORATIVE DETAILS

装飾 細節

DECORATIVE DETAILS

Throughout history, the emperors of China retained artists and craftsmen to produce works of subtle beauty and exquisite workmanship. One of the emperor's principal roles was that of arbiter of taste for the empire as a whole, and each dynasty created a powerful aesthetic that would distinguish it from previous dynasties. By the end of the Qing dynasty, the imperial collections had swelled to vast proportions, and thousands of artists still continued to labour in the palace workshops. Works crafted in the precious materials of jade, ivory, silver and gold were produced for the imperial household, along with paintings, portraits and cartouche to line the walls of the palaces. While each object was created to affirm the power and glory of the state and thus the legitimacy of the emperor, they also set the style for the rest of the empire.

Outside the palace, the decorative arts flourished with the support of court patrons. Many private workshops were established during the late sixteenth and early seventeenth centuries to make luxury items for the merchants and scholars living in the south of China. Craftsmen captured beauty in the most unlikely objects: boxes, utensils, cups, books made of stone tablets, scrolls, incense burners and an overwhelming array of ritual and functional items. Motifs ranged from the decorative to the symbolic, usually falling into the themes of protection, virtue, magic and immortality. Thunderclouds and scrolling clouds heralded the arrival of deities, while turbulent waves, rolling waves and cresting waves rolled mysteriously across dry land as well as the sea. Buddhist artefacts and ceremonial objects influenced the colour and design of many decorative items, juxtaposed with vernacular styles and Islamic influences from the Middle East. Calligraphy was elevated to an art form practised on ornamental scrolls and tables to display in the interior.

Traditionally, the Chinese preferred materials that could be worked into a smooth surface with a soft sheen, and items crafted in horn, ivory, precious wood, lacquer resin and stone were carved intricately. The Chinese love of jade is thought to explain their reluctance to cut crystalline stones for their sparkle, preferring always a smooth ground surface. The significance of stone to the Chinese went beyond its form: the slow process of working stone was likened to the onerous process of perfecting the human mind; only through long and unrelenting effort could true character and virtue be achieved. Poems extolled the soft sheen stone takes on when polished, and marvelled that it could be cool to the touch, yet warm when held in the hand. Materials like gilt, painted enamel and metalwork were polished to a rich lustre. The variety of materials and the expertise of the craftsmen from the first centuries through to the early twentieth century attest to the power and importance that the decorative arts gained in China.

China's imperial palace was the heart of an empire that, to the Chinese, was the centre of the aesthetic world. During each dynasty the imperial artists produced paintings with traditional themes such as portraiture, landscapes, still lifes and religious iconography, as well as detailed representations of political ceremonies, military conquests and imperial processions. Representations of nature were depicted in images of clouds and water, mountains, trees and rocks, and flowers such as orchids,

chrysanthemums and plum blossoms. Painters also practised independently of the palace, or painted in a scholarly manner, and they often worked in a looser, more understated style.

The Song dynasty is considered the golden age of Chinese painting. During this era painting evolved from line drawings of figures to highly sophisticated landscapes and flower-and-bird paintings. Landscape paintings have always been held in high esteem by the court and the literati, who contemplated the peaceful calm captured in the paintings of mountains, forests, fields, and gardens to find refuge from the material world. The flowers, trees, grass, stones, animals and birds depicted in the elegant flower-and-bird paintings were widely admired for their highly detailed depictions of flora. They became China's first botanical illustrations as horticulture and botany began to develop. Landscapes, portraits and flower-and-bird paintings continued to be the three main categories of Chinese painting until the contemporary period.

The simplicity of these paintings places emphasis on line, which is often regarded as the basis of all Chinese painting. This characteristic is shared with calligraphy, creating a close relationship between the two. The written character, in itself an abstract form, was of great value to the Chinese eye. The possession of both artistic technique and knowledge was an essential characteristic of the scholarly man, and calligraphy was the means by which the scholar could communicate. Writing enabled the scholar to enter the world of literature and the classics, and from there the world of the literati and the business of the court. Applying brush to silk or paper was an act of expressing skill, knowledge and personal style through the design and sweep of the characters. Using the same tools of brush and ink allowed the artists to represent nature as a concept, an abstraction in black and white.

Monochrome paintings were thought to have a subtle elegance inexpressible in any other paintings. The image resulting from the absence of colour was considered intense, purified by the mind as the essentials of line, shape and space, darkness and light were contemplated. As more scholars began to study painting, a 'literati' school emerged during the Yuan dynasty, characterized by a trend to fuse calligraphy and painting. These artists took inspiration from literature as well as from nature, forming a link between poetry and painting.

Scrolls were hung on walls to display poetry and verse written in elegant calligraphy. Chinese poetry provides a window through which we can observe the emotions that stirred the people of China throughout history. It ranges from the light-hearted to the intense, to deep, dark philosophical truths. Different regions developed distinctive styles of verse, which are divided into historical periods; all of these are categorized into four 'voices' of expression, and comprise a complex tradition that offers poets a broad range of modes for expression.

Early Chinese poetry was commonly believed to represent a rapport with the spirit world; its lines were long and rhapsodic, mingling the spiritual and the physical as they recounted the trance journeys of shamans. Poetry was also written purely in celebration of nature, sweeping across time and space to extol the magnificence of mountain, sea and forest.

Page 143 The decorative arts tradition flourished throughout China's long history. Though styles and aesthetics evolved with each era, the regard for craftsmanship and artistic excellence remained. Craftsmen captured beauty in almost every functional or ritual object, and created exquisite ornaments. This is evident in these hanging scrolls, woodblock prints, ornaments and porcelain figurines.

Music in China can be traced back to distant antiquity. At the time that European music was first coming to life, sophisticated musical instruments and musical theory began appearing in China as a result of the ritual music advocated by Confucius. In the cultural model that the Confucian school laid down, music was considered an integral part of the ceremonial and ritual practices connected with religious rites and ancestor worship – essentially a link between heaven and earth.

From the Han dynasty to the Qing dynasty, court music was played during banquets, ceremonies and dance performances. Court music was much more cosmopolitan than the music played for formal rituals, as it was also influenced by folk songs and music from India and Korea.

The court music of the Qing dynasty included *kunqu* opera, which the scholarly class considered to be the apogee of the dramatic arts. Traditionally *kunqu* was performed in temples, teahouses and private homes, where lattice screens formed the backdrop to the 'stage', and tables and chairs were the only props. This established a tradition for minimal set designs, and today, *kunqu* continues to be performed against a simple backdrop, with a set that includes only a table and chairs. The table might symbolize an official's desk, a dining table, a bridge or even a hill.

Jingju or *jingxi*, which is known to Westerners as the Beijing or Peking opera, is a combination of regional opera styles recognized two hundred years ago by the imperial court and performed in the Mandarin language of the Qing dynasty. The Beijing opera is stylized and abstract, with the lyrics sung in a characteristic pitch that rolls the words liltingly. Cantonese opera is the standard in Hong Kong and the south, and sung rhythmically and poetically.

Above left Tang burial customs dictated that ceramic replicas of animals, people and material possessions be entombed with the dead. These two figures may have been family members or servants intended to serve the deceased in the afterlife.

Above right Lacquerware featured patterns carved into the surface of the lacquer. Here, a bat delineates the rounded handle of a serving ladle.

The singers are always dramatic – the characters become literally larger than life with platform soles, headdresses and hair ornaments that are high and almost architectural in shape. The costumes are based on the style of dress worn four centuries ago during the Ming dynasty, with exaggerated motifs that are ornamented by pennants and badges. Costumes are always colourful and resplendently embroidered, with long, flowing sleeves that trail beyond the feet, bursting into a range of fluttering and waving movements as the singers use them to express emotions. The opera singers, who train their hands to be as expressive as their face or voice, are able to articulate the full spectrum of emotions through hundreds of different hand movements, each one signalling a specific mood. Like the face make-up that creates a mask for each character, the costumes identify the character wearing them.

Gestures and symbols are used to tell the story: performers imitate men on horseback by cantering across the stage as if they were sitting in the saddle, or paddle the air rhythmically to convey a voyage across the ocean. A long stretch of time is expressed by a slow saunter around the stage. In dances, sleeves, fans, and collared satin ribbons are transformed into weapons or tools, and embodied with icon theatrical meaning.

Cross-dressing has characterized Chinese opera for centuries. Beijing opera rarely has female performers, as all the women are traditionally played by men. The most famous opera diva was a man, Mei Lanfang, who became a cultural icon in the early 1900s; his opera roles set the ideal of feminine style and beauty for two generations. At the turn of the last century Mei performed in Europe and in the United States to worldwide acclaim.

Opposite The gentle curves of a stylized Buddha are enveloped within the folds of his robe as he sits in meditation atop a sideboard. Traditionally he would have been placed in the centre of the household shrine as the central focus of religious practice. Today the dignity and serenity of the Buddha introduces the same element of calm to any interior.

Craftsmanship

Dduring the Xia, Shang and Qin dynasties, as the early rulers of northern China forged trade links with the eastern Mediterranean, the Middle East and Central Asia, Chinese craftsmen were influenced by new and different decorative styles and techniques. The shapes and methods that were introduced were adapted to suit Chinese tastes, and traditional Chinese ceremonial and luxury objects began to show signs of Islamic Ottoman, Persian and Greek design.

Silver and goldsmithing techniques were developed by the Chinese during the Tang dynasty. However, a native tradition in silversmithing was not established until the Song dynasty, and it never achieved the sophistication of design and craftsmanship accomplished in works of gold. Gold and silver became popular again during the Yuan dynasty, with new forms and motifs resulting from the influence of the Middle East, but these were mostly works made for the imperial household and the Buddhist temples patronized by the nobility.

By the Han period, bronze was considered rare and precious by the ancient Chinese, who often preferred it to silver and gold. They used bronze to cast large quantities of ritual vessels, weapons and a range of musical instruments that were elegant in form, finely decorated, and inscribed with calligraphy or auspicious motifs. Bronze was also crafted into vases, food dishes and vessels for wine and water. Endless variation is found in both the form and the design of these early pieces, fully demonstrating the rich imagination, creativity and craft techniques of the first Chinese artisans. Dishes and platters for food were cast in many different styles, with scalloped rims and lobed outlines. Vessels for water were generally cast with a circular base to stabilize the belly, while others had a heavy square base added onto the rounded belly to create a dramatic contrast of geometrical forms. Wine vessels were designed so that they could be heated and poured from a single container. Pour spouts and side handles enabled them to be easily decanted, and the tripod base allowed it to be placed directly onto the coals.

Bronze vessels were widely used in banquets and ceremonies held in palaces and temples, and as funerary items for deceased nobility. They featured inlaid patterns in silver, gold, copper and turquoise, crafted into interlocking geometrical shapes based on straight lines and diagonals, or whorled lines and spirals. They also featured motifs depicting animals, dragons, flowers and butterflies. Emperors inscribed vessels with verses honouring the ministers and nobility who made great contributions to the nation or to the sovereign, in order to establish a lasting record for later generations to read.

Incense burners were first cast in bronze during the early Shang and Zhou dynasties, in shapes so refined that they became design classics, repeated for several thousand years. Many of the incense burners made in the Ming and Qing dynasties had finishes to make them resemble the original artefact. Great skill was used to create patinations of rich auburn and tea green, dashed with gold and gilded by fire. This technique suspended the gold in a mercury amalgam and applied it to the bronze; when heated, the mercury ran off the surface, leaving a marbled effect on the incense burner.

Cloisonné was created through firing techniques that fused coloured enamels to the surface of a copper or bronze object. A rudimentary form of cloisonné was introduced to China from the Middle East during the Yuan dynasty, and was perfected as a result of the technical skills of Chinese artisans. The imperial workshops had already developed sophisticated metallurgical technology such as bronze and ceramics, and glaze production techniques were well advanced.

Rich patterns and illustrations could be created by the cloisonné enamels as they were inlaid among brass or copper wires soldered to the surface of the objects. As the ground enamels melted into the metal, they took on a high gloss, and the wires running between them kept them neatly separated. Once they cooled, the wires were polished to a high sheen, giving the appearance of tiny veins of gold threaded through the intricate patterns. More luxurious items had gold plating applied to the wires, the rim and the bottom surface, creating an object that appeared to be made of glass and gold. Cloisonné greatly appealed to Chinese sensibilities – the enamel was as smooth and lustrous as jade, yet glittered like jewellery.

Bronze was a favourite of craftsmen because of its durability and the ease with which it could be cast. From ancient times a variety of tools, utensils and cookware have been cast in bronze, and many of the 'name chops' used by the Chinese throughout the centuries were cast in bronze. From official government papers to private contracts, all business and civil transactions require both a signature and the stamp of the name chop to be legally binding. Each name chop is individually designed, combining the beauty of calligraphy with an individual motif set within a 2cm (½in) square stamp, sometimes also made of stone. Craftsmen, calligraphers and painters stamp their works with their name chops to 'sign' them and provide proof of their authenticity. As the name chop reproduces the same image again and again, it is thought to be a forerunner of Chinese printing.

The skill required to craft ivory went beyond the ability to engrave motifs and carve likenesses; the demand for it in both China and the West called for expertise more advanced than that of many other craft traditions. Even as early as the Song dynasty, ivory was polychromed and gilded, and often more finely detailed than the bronze, wood and stone sculptures made at the time. The development of Buddhist thought in China created a market for images that paid homage to the Buddha and his bodhisattvas, which merged Indian influences with existing Taoist styles. In the late Ming dynasty, Canton had close ties to the Philippines, which had been conquered by the Spanish. The Spaniards, like other Europeans with settlements in the Orient, began to commission devotional figures carved in ivory to decorate their churches in the East.

Chinese ivory figures are primarily representations of divinities, be they influenced by Buddhist, Taoist, Christian or Hindu deities. Other types of figures are usually decorated plaques and ornamental objects, carved in high relief to emphasize the intricate details of their robes and jewellery. Elaborate objects like musical instruments and folding fans were made by craftsmen with special technical skills, while simple articles like brush holders, wrist rests, round boxes and handles could easily be produced in mass quantities. Canton became a second centre for ivory where craftsmen trained in the Qing workshops were relocated to have better access to the material. All ivory was imported from overseas, some coming from as far away as Africa. Although climatic changes caused the elephant to become extinct in China two thousand years ago, it did not interrupt the production of ivory goods, which has continued unabated ever since.

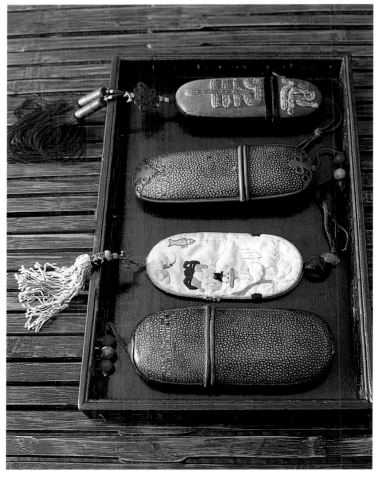

Above left
Ink sticks and ink
stones are among
many functional
objects that have
been appropriated
for their decorative
value today.

Above right Small
cases, such as these
spectacles cases,
were made from a
range of materials,
including
embroidered silk,
tortoiseshell, ivory,
horn and metal.
Fitted with tassels
and handles, they
could be carried like
a small handbag or
tucked deep inside
a sleeve and easily
extracted by pulling
the tassel.

Opposite Chinese
papercuts are a
traditional folk art
that dates back more
than 1,500 years.
Crafted from tissue-
thin rice paper and
hand-painted with
Chinese ink, each
motif is a continuous
piece cut into a
variety of shapes and
figures. The framed
papercuts here create
a colourful display of
flowers, patterns and
mythological figures.

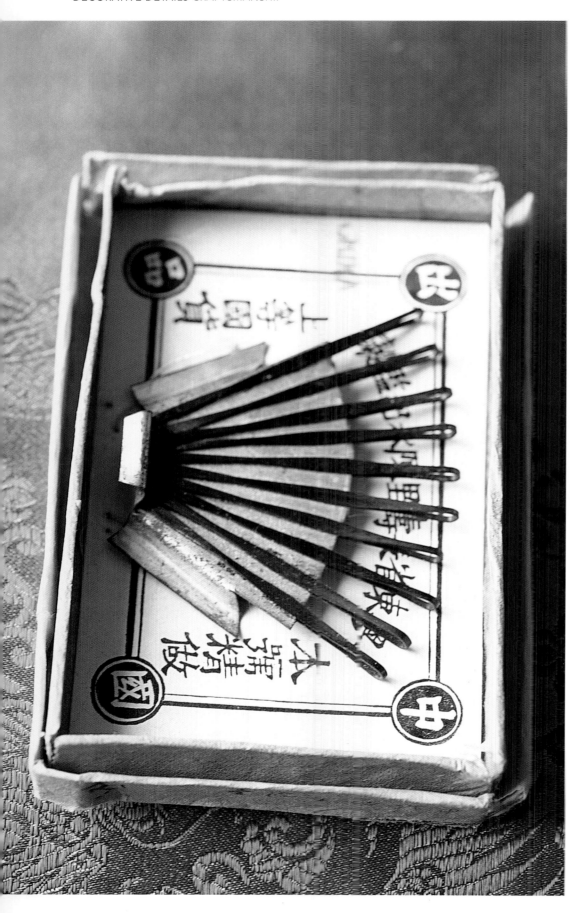

Left Hairgrips like these were essential to create the elaborate hair styles of Chinese women, such as the coiffure worn by the Dowager Empress on page 43. For the Empress, however, hairgrips of jade or precious metals would have been used instead of these factory-made ones.

Opposite Porcelain figurines like these were produced as chinoiserie exports by the ceramic factories of Canton, where they would have been fired by the hundreds. Their style of dress indicates that they may be children or performing artists, and the pose they sit in suggests that they are seated on low three-legged stools, as was the practice throughout most of southern China.

Lacquerware

The lustrous beauty of lacquer and the sophisticated techniques applied to crafting it give lacquered objects a look of luxury. With this in mind, the Chinese coated almost everything imaginable with lacquer to endow it with beauty and value. Musical instruments, writing tools, bowls and utensils for eating and drinking, furniture, funerary objects, weapons and even transportation vehicles were coated in lacquer. Pictures and patterns were carved into the surface of the lacquer, depicting dragons, phoenixes, lotus ponds, waterfowl and other elements of the natural world. Platters, bowls, boxes and furnishings were adorned with festive scenes or depicted fierce warriors, serene deities, groups of children, courtly ladies and huntsmen.

Lacquerware paralleled many articles originally made in the ceramic workshops, imitating the scalloped rims and raised edges of banquet platters and everyday dishes. Ritual objects like incense boxes, three-dimensional cosmic diagrams known as mandalas, ceremonial rice measures and figures of deities were also made in the lacquer workshops for shrines in the temple as well as the home. Lacquered chests and cabinets were sometimes made to create the illusion of several ornate boxes casually stacked together, or several boxes held together by gilt handles mounted as though they could be easily carried away. Real lacquer boxes could be made with compartments to contain delicacies for a picnic, or for use by the scholar to carry scrolls, brushes and inks. Lacquer boxes fitted with basketry panels were used for the presentation of gifts and documents, or as a decorative means of storage in the home.

When lacquered boxes, chests and platters were chosen as gifts, the motifs adorning them were also selected to convey the sentiments appropriate for the occasion. Images of ritual objects like water ewers, incense boxes and grain vessels could be combined with prosperity symbols, such as moulds for minting coins, to create subtle messages. The name for a grain vessel, *fu*, and a coin, *qian*, would form the basis of the expression *fuzai yangqian*, meaning 'happiness is right here'. When the gift was presented, the good wishes expressed in the motif were offered as well.

A style of carved lacquer known as *tixi*, which became popular during the Song dynasty and remained in vogue through the Yuan and Ming dynasties, is characterized by decorative patterns and scenes that are carved in either red or black lacquer. Thin layers of black were applied between the coatings of red – or vice versa – subtly deepening the tone. This effect worked especially well in relief because it enhanced the illusion of depth and foreground that artists used to create several distinct scenes within a flat surface. The motifs found on *tixi* wares are more robust than the delicate works of later centuries; they are charged with a vitality that makes them unique among Chinese lacquerware.

During the Qing dynasty, the development of a moulding technique made it possible to cast figures and ornaments in solid lacquer. This gave the industry tremendous commercial potential, but many of the Chinese eschewed the thought of lacquerware multiples. Most of these were eventually made for export, being early versions of the moulded plastic objects that would make the 'Made in China' sticker an emblem of China in later centuries.

Opposite Lacquer is enjoying a revival as leading designers apply traditional lacquer techniques to new forms. Here, the Chinese-American designer Robert Kuo has crafted a nest of lacquered copper bowls inspired by organic shapes.

Page 156 The Chinese coated a vast range of objects with lacquer to heighten their aesthetic appeal and practicality. Small lacquerware containers (top left) were used to store food, as their lacquered finishes created a watertight surface. These bowls (top right) combine traditional lacquer techniques with early metal-casting methods, using copper to craft these bowls and lacquer to decorate them. A simple bowl (bottom left) is transformed by two contrasting lacquer finishes, and a contemporary lacquerware tray (bottom right) is juxtaposed against an older classic behind it. *Page 157* This collection of modern and vintage pieces illustrates the timeless appeal of lacquered finishes. Antique porcelain, vintage hairgrips, and modern plastic and glass stand on a lacquered surface.

Jade & Precious Stones

Though jade may appear to be merely a beautiful stone with a lustrous green colour, to the Chinese it is 'the essence of heaven and earth'. Jade is found in mountains and riverbeds, places Chinese consider to be sacred and brimming with auspicious *qi*. This is why jade has long been a potent symbol of vitality, protection and immortality throughout Chinese history. It was so popular in ancient times that by 1500 BC some native sources of jade in China began to be depleted, and the stone had to be imported from sources in central Asia and Burma that were thousands of miles away.

Of the semi-precious stones that the Chinese identify as jade, only two are recognized by modern geologists as true jade. Jadeite which is native to Burma, is bright green, and nephrite, which is found near the ancient cities of Khotan and Yarkand in Central Asia, comes in many shades of green, yellow and translucent white. Both stones contain finely variegated colours that lend a sense of texture and patina beneath their soft sheen.

Jade articles were initially crafted as emblems of supernatural and temporal powers. The stone was worked into ceremonial vessels, weapons and talismans by some of China's earliest Neolithic cultures, before becoming widely used for jewellery, furnishings, figures and ornaments. Imperial orders and medallions were crafted in jade and given to the nobility as symbols of their office or authority. When the emperor dispatched a prince, or other high-ranking mandarin for official duty, he might have been given a jade tablet proclaiming the 'divine orders' assigned to him by the ruling 'son of heaven'.

As jade became a part of the decorative arts movement that flourished in China during the late sixteenth and early seventeenth centuries, it was crafted into luxury items for scholars and mandarins living in southern China. Such items included brush holders, brush washers, boxes, small sculptures, wine cups and chimes. Women wore combs, hairpins, bracelets and waist pendants crafted in jade, and they embroidered jade ornaments into their robes, sashes and caps. Each piece exhibited delicate detailing and exquisite workmanship, reflecting the high quality of life aspired to by the Chinese.

At the time of the Emperor Qianlong, who reigned from 1736 to 1796, the imperial workshops made luxury items in amber, agate, lapis lazuli, turquoise, soapstone and malachite, which were often crafted by artisans who had worked in jade. Lapis lazuli and malachite were prized for their veins of blue and green that evoked the tones of jade, and both minerals were ground into pigments for painting.

Amber was also widely used in China during the Tang dynasty, when magical properties were sometimes ascribed to it. Tang scholars identified how its formation occurred over many centuries, and noted that amber occasionally contained embedded insects. Jewellery and furniture inlays were its most popular uses, but it was also carved into small sculptures and figurines.

Soapstone can resemble the golden tones of amber, but while amber has reddish accents, soapstone's accents verge towards brown and it rarely has the translucency of amber. Even so, soapstone could be crafted into beautifully variegated sculptures. Its dense grain made it an ideal representation of a mountain or rock, and it was often used to depict them in sculptures and inlays.

Revered by the Chinese since Neolithic times, jade became more commonplace throughout the decorative arts of the late sixteenth and early seventeenth centuries. When the Han dynasty craftsmen created this jade head and torso, jade was believed to be imbued with supernatural powers that conferred protection and longevity.

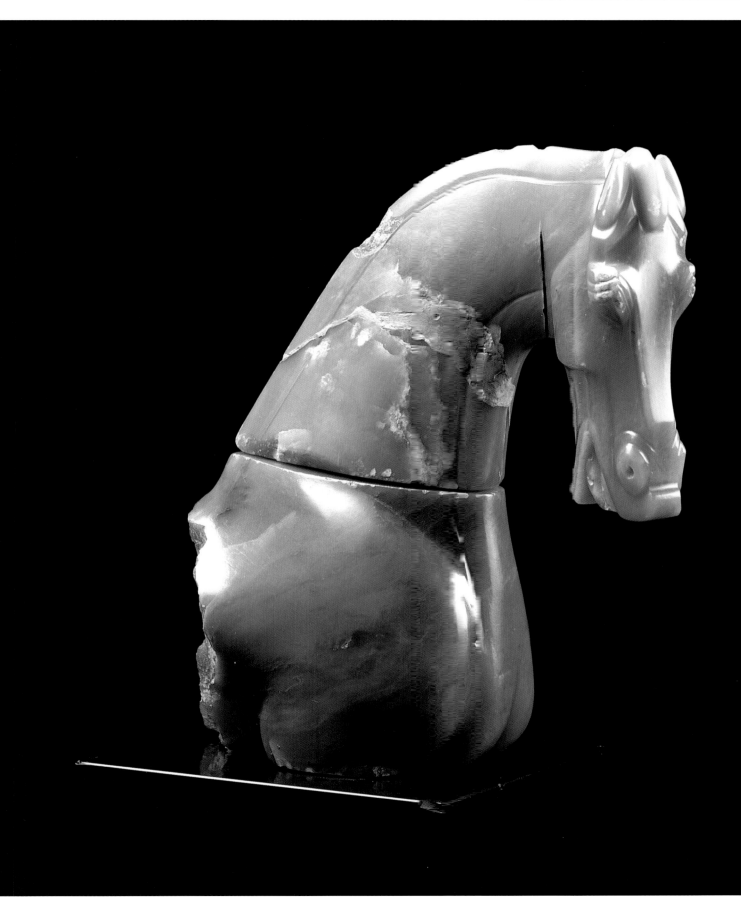

Fans

The fans of imperial China were not only artistic fashion accessories that provided protection from the sun and shielded the face from unwelcome gazes. Fans were also used to intensify the heat of a fire in a stove or brazier, or were fixed to the ceiling to cool the interior during the hot summer. This type of overhanging fan, similar to the Indian *punkah*, is made of cloth or sometimes reed or rattan and became known in southern China as the *chuke*. It was pulled back and forth by strings attached to two floorboards and operated by moving the feet in a pedalling motion. This early version of a ceiling fan was used until the twentieth century, when it was replaced by the electric fan.

Though fans originated as functional items, over time they became a medium for artistic expression, and often bore scenes and motifs painted onto their leaves or the mounts to which they were secured. When these were decorated by well-known painters or exchanged as tokens of friendship, their owners carefully removed them from their mounts and fixed them to individual sheets of paper to preserve them. Fan leaves painted by famous artists were so treasured that they were positioned on album pages, framed and hung on the wall, or fastened to hanging scrolls and fixed to the falls. Fan paintings may feature a bird-and-flower motif, a landscape or pastoral scene, figures, animals or calligraphy. Fans also had significance when captured in portraits. They would denote the status and sensibilities of the portrait sitters, or add a subtle emotive note to the image of women featured in paintings by the way in which they were gesturing with their fans.

The first fans of fashion were invented by the Chinese, and are believed to have emerged in the early Han dynasty. These were typically made with a silk face stretched over a rounded bamboo frame, which was mounted on a long stemmed handle. During the Tang dynasty, artists and scholars were encouraged to demonstrate their writing and painting skills by using fan faces as a medium. The Tang literati gave fans considerable social significance and made them a standard part of the summer costume worn by the scholarly and the elite.

Feather fans were made from all types of bird's feather ranging from the exotic peacock to the ordinary chicken. Goose feathers were a particular favourite, but feathers from pheasants, falcons, cranes and hawks were considered more stylish choices. Hair fans made from the tails of horses and deer were popular during the Han dynasty and were better suited to chasing away unwelcome insects than stirring up a cool breeze. They resembled feather dusters more than typical fans, and were used by officials and noblemen as status symbols. Members of the ruling class were often painted with hair fans in their hands to denote their rank, even in later dynasties.

Folding fans were probably introduced to China from Japan or Korea during the Song dynasty, yet did not achieve widespread popularity until the Ming years. The faces were usually made from fine paper mounted onto thin ribs of bamboo pinned together in a flexible, tier-like structure. Like the fixed fans, these were highly decorated by artists and the literati. The folding fan led in popularity from then until the nineteenth century, when the round fan made a mild comeback. At that time, there was also a vogue for fixing them to walls and furniture as decorative artworks.

Folding fans date back to the Song dynasty, yet were not fully embraced as fashion accessories until the Ming period. The folding fan then led in popularity until the nineteenth century, when the unbendable round fan made a comeback. Embroidered cases like these were made to store the fans when not in use. They remained popular even when folding fans went out of vogue, as they were put to use as holders for chopsticks, scissors and letter openers.

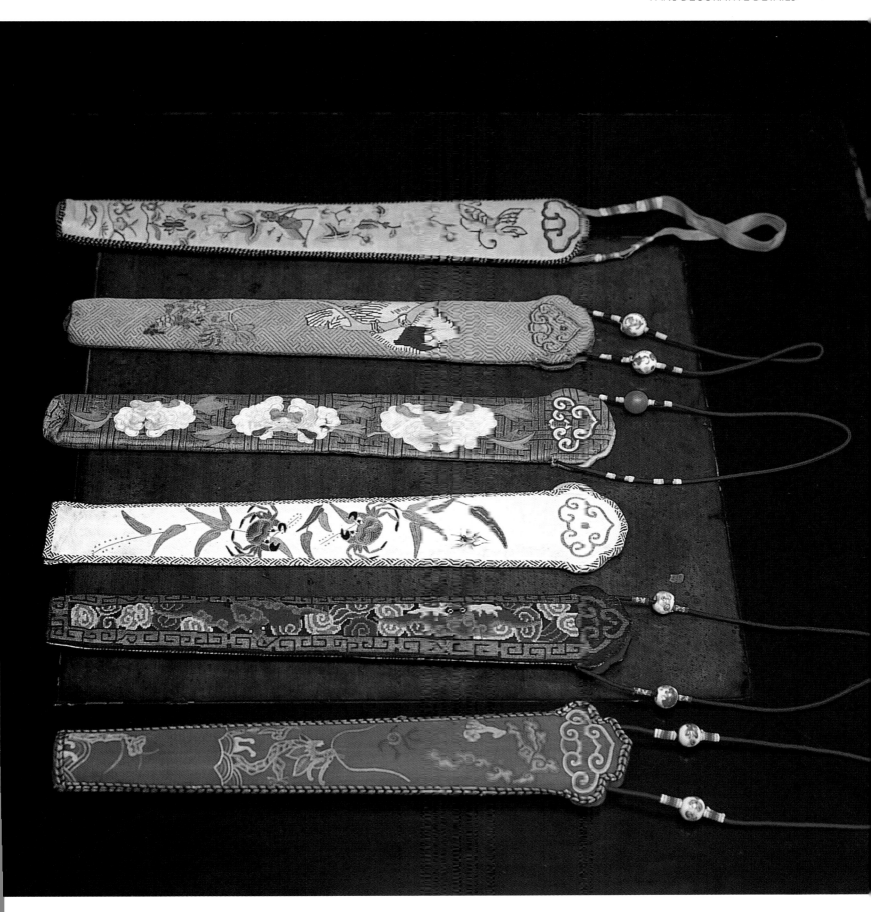

Display

Chinese style is seductive – real enthusiasts often let their passion for Chinese decor take over their living space, colour themes, art collection and choice of furniture. And why not? Chinese art pieces and craftworks bring with them a rich heritage of design and timeless materials that can add colour and exoticism to any interior, without necessarily transforming it into a shrine to Chinese culture.

Often in the West a room is decorated to emphasize the main features, with the decorative details chosen merely to enhance them. The patterns, pictures, ornaments and artefacts adorning the rooms in which the Chinese live and work are carefully considered for their craftsmanship and special qualities. Each object is chosen to convey family values, status, power and spirituality. Colour, whether lavishly used or somewhat understated, is considered in relation to ornaments and artwork, to create a harmony of tone and colour in the interior that give it a sense of completeness. The variety of decorative elements drawn together are recognized by the Chinese as a genre in its own right – the art of the interior.

The art decorating a Chinese home has been chosen not only for its beauty, but also for its references to scholarly knowledge and spiritual awakening. It is often considered to be in effect a portrait of the owners, reflecting their tastes in classicism, their eye for balance, their appreciation of craftsmanship and their regard for the natural world. In previous centuries this reflected the approach of the Chinese scholar, who included art as part of a theoretical and spiritual education. Wealthy mandarins would retire after a short career and devote their fortune to the artistic pursuits of an elegant life, refining the interiors of their homes through collections of art and artefacts, or creating a contemplative garden.

Today, the trend for minimal living and the influence of feng shui has created a modern ethos of living without clutter that recalls the simplicity of the Ming dynasty. Surfaces can be kept bare – as they were then – by confining *objets d'art* to display cabinets or open shelves, or recessing them into a wall niche.

Chinese paintings and hanging scrolls provide the ultimate backdrop to Chinese-inspired collections, as well as filling the interior with beautiful images. These set the tone of the room if they are hung over the mantelpiece or are positioned to be the first thing that is seen when entering a room. The Chinese usually hang scrolls and paintings in pairs or in serried ranks along the walls, sometimes at table height where they can be read at eye level when sitting down. Stone tablets, plaques or antique medallions also make interesting wall hangings, and create a sense of the history behind the millennia of Chinese style.

Every available surface can be appropriated as a display area. Scale is an important consideration – small items like name chops (see page 149), snuff boxes (which can look more like tiny porcelain bottles) and ink stones (see page 168) tend to get lost on a broad surface and are better suited to smaller spaces. For an effective display, combinations of varying heights and contrasting shapes can be grouped together according to similarities in style, function, colour or even period. That said, it can be even more effective to display two or three figures that really stand out, rather than hiding them among a number of less interesting figures.

Opposite A collection of early twentieth-century posters creates an arresting single display.
Page 164 The circular shape of a contemporary lacquerware platter provides an antidote to the sharp angles of a minimal interior. Contoured pieces soften harsh lines: here the rounded lacquerware erases the symmetry of the parallel lines, while the mother-of-pearl mobile above it diffuses the low edges created by the 'floating' ceiling.
Page 165 The irregular shapes provided by a lacquered fretwork screen create the perfect setting for small objects – both front and back are made immediately visible. These late nineteenth-century snuff bottles are made from glass and rock crystal.

Calligraphy

Calligraphy, 'the art of writing', turns a word into a picture, captured in the measured sweep of brush and ink. The meanings contained in each character form a sentence or tell a story, transforming an entire text into a readable work of art. The Chinese alphabet is so rich in imagery that the style of the calligrapher can illustrate the meaning of the story as lavishly as a picture. The calligrapher's brush can also create austere black-and-white landscapes; many generations of artists have used it to translate nature into ink.

The essence of calligraphy lies in its relationship to the Chinese decorative arts. Calligraphy combines the intellectual beauty of what the words mean with the visual beauty of how the words are written. The Chinese believe that written words have mystic meanings, and their calligraphic representations are regarded as magical symbols for health, happiness, wealth or good fortune. These characters feature in the motifs decorating furniture, ceramics, woodwork and textiles, to invoke the protection of the spirit world and sanctify the household and its visitors. So great is their power that the ancients would sit in contemplation of the characters. Like a dreamer awakened, a new sense of the words would unfold, giving insight into their mystic meanings.

Calligraphy is also written to be mounted on decorative scrolls and hung prominently in the formal rooms to greet visitors with messages of good wishes or poetic verse. Carved wooden plaques or stone tablets are etched with Buddhist scriptures or references to countless generations of ancestors. Often crafted from ebony, jade, mother-of-pearl or rich lacquerwork, with the characters outlined in gold leaf or gold powder, these are revered as precious artworks.

The calligrapher works at a writing table, sitting and contemplating the movement of the brush and the surface of the paper before drawing. Getting the feel of the paper is part of the process — he handles the paper and studies its surface, examining its texture and porosity before laying it flat on the table. Identification with the materials is an essential tenet of Taoism and Confucianism, as it is believed to facilitate the expression of spiritual awakening in the act of creation. The calligrapher waits for the *qi* to rise through the body, believing this to be the inspiration behind what is to be transmitted to the paper. A calligrapher sees himself or herself as a tool, not the source, with the brush a conduit for the mysteries of creation.

A topic debated by artists and scholars alike is the merits of various inks. A deep, glossy black ink wash is traditionally based on resinous pine soot and binding gum, mixed inside a deep metal mortar and pounded together with a heavy pestle. Musk, camphor and other fragrances are added to the mixture to mask the odour of the gum just before the ink paste is pressed into wooden moulds. Once the ink cakes set, they are elaborately decorated with symbols or motifs by skilled craftsmen. In the hands of the calligrapher, they are gently rubbed against the coarse surface of an ink stone, which dissolves them into fine powder.

At this stage, water is added, but it has to be done drop by drop, to avoid the extremes of 'too wet' or 'too dry'. 'Wet' characters are looser in form and characterized by sweeping brushstrokes, and spatters or splashes of ink, while 'dry' characters are precise in their shape. The calligrapher's brush itself is a complex and subtle tool. Bristles

As a backdrop for exotic items, the potency of white walls is unrivalled. The crimson colour bordering the calligraphy of this hanging scroll immediately draws the eye across the dazzling white space.

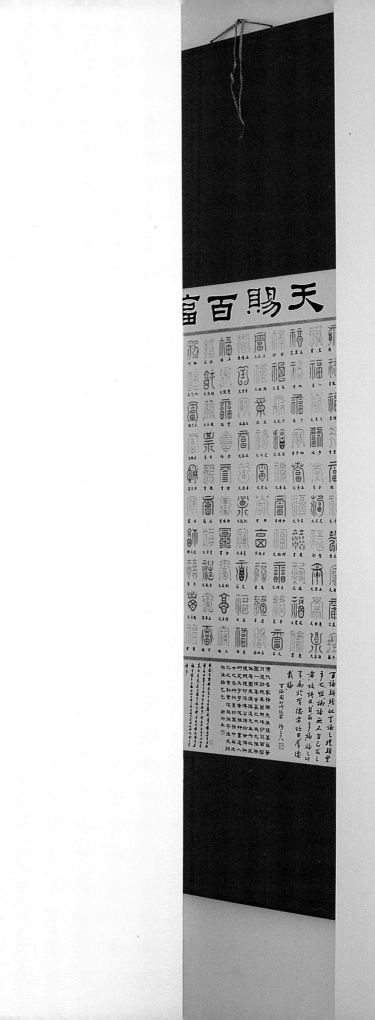

are chosen from among animal hairs, rabbit, badger, hare and weasel being the traditional favourites. Most prized of all are mouse whiskers, which are said to create brush strokes so delicate that they are almost invisible.

Ink sticks, ink stones, brushes and paper of old were crafted with such skill that they were treated as luxury items. They were produced with exquisite stylistic features that carried a strong artistic appeal. Ink stones were the crowning glory of the calligrapher's tools, made from pieces of fine-grained stone or ceramics that were etched, carved or moulded into refined shapes. Sometimes ink stones were moulded from clay that had been repeatedly filtered and washed to sift away the sediment and coarser grains before being cast into shape. An ink stone's surface looks deceptively smooth but is mildly abrasive, sloping into a shallow well into which the calligrapher dips the brush. With these tools and media the calligrapher trained for half a lifetime until he achieved virtuosity worthy of his master's approval.

Calligraphy has played an important role throughout thousands of years of Chinese civilization, when it has been viewed as both an art form and a source of cultural history. Because the legacy of the past is expressed though the written character, there is personal and public reverence for writing, which explains why calligraphy is the most venerated art form in China today. Though Western painting and literature are becoming increasingly popular in China, the passion for calligraphy still persists.

Below left Calligraphy brushes and inks like these are easily obtainable in the West and can be used on paper to imitate Chinese characters or create minimal monochrome landscapes and abstract images. *Opposite* The verbal and the visual are intertwined in the Chinese tradition, where writing is only one step away from painting. Just as Western artists often ground their work in historical techniques, the influence of classical calligraphy enters the work of many contemporary Chinese artists. Here, the double happiness symbol has been drawn in brush strokes charged with a vitality and exhilaration that capture the essence of shared joy.

CERAMICS

Taken from the earth and formed by fire, ceramics are regarded by the Chinese as an expression of nature itself, enhancing the natural elements provided by the wood and stone of the interior. That is not to say that Chinese ceramics are not works of great beauty – in fact, their forms have been perfected over thousands of years to balance their esoteric and aesthetic features against their functional uses.

Simply decorated with birds, animals and flowers, early ceramics celebrated the natural world by reflecting the purity of colours and contours observed in nature. Over the years they evolved into an art form that expressed figures, animals and deities in clay, culminating in the funerary objects of the Tang period. Whether glazed in simple hues of celadon or lavishly decorated with the motifs of the Qing era, Chinese ceramics are charged with a vitality that mirrors that of life itself.

The Chinese trace the history of their ceramics back nine thousand years, when early potters learned to transform the basic elements of fire, earth and water into objects that were both beautiful and functional. The Neolithic Chinese tribes sculpted pottery into slender drinking vessels, and also a type of jug with a handle, a pouring spout and three hollow legs that served as a tripod base, used for heating liquids. The surfaces were marked with simple patterns and geometric designs, or were painted with flowers, fish, animals and human faces, decorations that are still popular in China today.

CERAMICS

The potter's wheel was in use by time of the ancient Longshan culture (c. 2,500 bc), believed to have been the first to make white pottery. Even more spectacular are the black ceramics they produced, the pieces of which are eggshell thin and exquisitely crafted. They were sculpted from clay coiled into ropes and carefully smoothed into shape, then fired in the ground and burnished with pebbles. These black wares are believed to be some of the most beautiful ever produced in China's history, unrivalled until the development of porcelain some three thousand years later. Although porcelain originated in the Han dynasty, the oldest existing porcelain found intact is the ivory-coloured 'white *ding*', which dates back to the seventh century.

The ceramics of the Tang dynasty were cast in rich colours, being the first multi-coloured wares in China. The style was characterized by cylindrical shapes of various proportions, but ceramic production during this period was dominated by the funerary objects entombed with the dead. Tang burial customs dictated that clay replicas of material possessions, animals and people be placed in the tomb to serve the deceased in the afterlife. Human figures representing the deceased's family and servants, sculptures of horses and pets, miniature furniture and even replicas of the house itself were cast in ceramic. The surviving Tang tomb figures are often sculptural in appearance. Camels and horses with grooms and riders, polo players, musicians, overdressed merchants and voluptuous courtesans were crafted in stunning detail. Wide-eyed warriors were made to stand guard against evil spirits, protecting the living from the superstitions that followed them into the afterlife. Most human figures were made standing atop a pedestal, though some were portrayed on horseback or participating in sport. The type of clay used and the colour of the glazes were stipulated by burial laws, and the figures' embroidered

sleeves, long robes, headdress, shoes and office or military emblems would have been made in accordance with court protocol. In keeping with their professional roles, the figures generally bore stern, somewhat remote expressions, their faces shaped with frowning mouths and glaring eyes. Their refinement and realism exemplify the artistic production of the Tang dynasty, an era of political stability and artistic achievement. Many funerary figures from the first dynasties have survived, enabling historians to trace the evolution of styles of dress, furniture and even architecture throughout the centuries.

The size and number of clay objects interred with the dead were not determined by wealth alone; they were stipulated by a complex code of burial laws. The famous life-sized terracotta figures of horses and warriors found at the tomb site of Qin Shihuangdi, the first emperor of China, are the most famous examples – only the emperor was allowed to take an entire army into the afterlife. The scale of the human figures made to represent the dead was also an indication of nobility and rank.

Ceramic funerary figures are thought to be the earliest examples of Chinese three-dimensional figurative art, inspiring the creation of decorative porcelain figurines made in later dynasties. In the early Qing dynasty, ceramic figures were made independently of funerary or religious use, although they still retained the symbolic meanings given to them in Taoism or Buddhism. Tomb figures from the late Ming dynasty later served as models for chinoiserie exports during the late seventeenth and eighteenth centuries, when the figures that were produced during the reign of the Emperor Kangxi became highly prized in the West.

The tones of blue, red and green that characterized Chinese ceramics for centuries appeared during the Song period. Foreign merchants imported a type of blue cobalt that stayed true during firing, creating blue monochrome ceramics and a pigment later used for fine detailing. The lustrous blood-red glazes of this era continued to be popular in successive dynasties, until the secret formula was lost during the sixteenth century. The green Song glazes resulted from attempts to reproduce the colour and texture of jade in ceramic to create a faux jade artefact. This had been a continuing goal of generations of Chinese craftsmen, because the sacred jade was considered a symbol of immortality. These hues of green became known in the West as celadon, and were enormously popular among European collectors throughout the eighteenth century. While the unfired glaze is greyish-green, the final product may be tinged with yellow, aubergine, turquoise or blue.

During the Song dynasty, ceramics were produced for a highly literate and intellectually elite class, resulting in many pieces that are now regarded as classics by the Chinese. With their purity of form and brilliant glazes, they exemplify a perfect balance between vitality and refinement. Monochrome pieces were thought to be especially elegant, introducing a vogue for minimalism that prevailed throughout the Yuan and Ming dynasties. The aesthetic demands of the ruling elite motivated craftsmen to progress and refine their technical skills.

Despite the popularity of coloured glazes, the combination of cobalt blue against a white background that emerged during the Yuan dynasty was to become a classic motif. Blue-and-white wares were exported in huge quantities via the Silk Route

Page 173 Like the rest of modern Chinese design, ceramics are steeped in a rich tradition that continues to draw upon classical pieces, or create expressive abstract shapes as artisans come up with new forms and pioneer new techniques. This incense burner is appliquéd with a gold rose and coated with a high gloss; its lime colour reflects the vibrant palette used in China today.

throughout the Yuan and Ming periods to Arab cultures who believed that the blue-and-white porcelain would reveal the presence of poison by turning the food served in it black. The blue-and-white style survives today, and is undoubtedly one of the oldest continuously produced porcelains ever created.

Chinese porcelain reached its artistic peak in the latter part of the fifteenth century, during the Ming dynasty. This was largely due to the discovery of new glazing techniques that enabled ceramicists to apply pigments after the piece had been fired. Deep monochromes in copper red, charcoal and dark blue followed, given lustre by the application of a clear glaze. The classic trio of yellow, green and burgundy also appeared; examples are referred to today as Ming tricolour wares. Ceramics made in multiple colour combinations are uniformly described as 'five-colour', irrespective of the actual number of colours used. Beautiful two-toned wares were thought to be the height of elegance: green-glazed patterns drawn against a yellow background, yellow glazes juxtaposed with blue, and green glazes fired over deep red were used on a wide variety of designs. The birth of colour during the Ming dynasty fired the imaginations of future artists more than in any other period.

Artistic innovation was less evident in the Qing dynasty, as emphasis was placed on new standards of quality and technical perfection. The imperial kilns in Jingdezhen advanced all forms of ceramics, reproducing the classical wares of previous eras in stronger, thinner porcelain, with perfect glazes and true colours. Porcelain masters began to paint highly detailed pictorial compositions on their wares, replacing the early motifs of flowers and animals with religious scenes, landscapes and still lifes. New technical innovations enabled them to use a wider range of colours and apply them in a variety of tones. As export trade with Europe increased during the Qing dynasty, these fine ceramics came to the attention of the West, influencing the type of porcelain produced in Europe from the mid-eighteenth century onwards.

The enamelled porcelain known in the West as *famille vert* and *famille rose* was produced in the Qing kilns mainly for export from the late seventeenth and the early eighteenth centuries respectively, and is today considered by many to be the highest form of Chinese overglazed porcelain. The polychrome painted decoration was usually floral.

The earthenware produced in China was always described using the Western terms of ceramics, pottery, porcelain and china, which are easily confused. The term 'ceramic' describes the general art of firing clay to create an ornamental or functional object, meaning that all pottery, porcelain and china can be considered ceramics. Pottery generally refers to robust wares made from porous clay that rarely has the strength or refinement of porcelain. Pottery is fired at temperatures ranging from direct sunlight to the heat of a baker's oven, or the intense heat of a kiln reaching 1100°C (about 2000°F). Pigments or colours are generally added before firing, but afterwards pottery usually remains porous enough to absorb colour.

Porcelain, on the other hand, can only be created from fine clays fired at searing temperatures between 1200° and 1400°C (about 2200°–2550°F). This high heat creates a chemical change in the clay that vitrifies it into a white glassy body with roughly the density of glass. Porcelain can be decorated after the initial firing in a range of colours and glazes, then fired again at a low temperature to seal the colour and harden the glaze. Once it has cooled, true porcelain will ring with a sonorous tone when tapped; and if it did not vitrify entirely, it will fracture into smooth pieces.

The 'china' we refer to in the English language initially distinguished fine Chinese porcelain from that manufactured in Europe, but today this distinction is not made. The plates, bowls, cups and vases commonly referred to as china today describe a wide range of everyday items, with the term porcelain often refering to something more luxurious. There are many more distinctions between them, and many different grades of quality within the two categories.

Different grades are determined by a number of factors, the most significant of them being the type of clay. Chinese soil is rich in clay, with large deposits of ochre-coloured loess in the north, referred to by the Chinese as yellow earth. The silt of these deposits washes into the Yellow River, producing its distinctive colour. Historically, ceramicists were restricted to using clay quarried locally as loess is not suitable for ceramics, and this is why the best ceramic workshops were established where the best clay was found. The towns of Yixing and Jingdezhen for example, became the foremost producers of fine porcelain, because there was a plentiful supply of superior-quality clay in the area. Today, high-quality ceramics are made from blends containing several types of clay from different regions, even in the porcelain workshops of Yixing and Jingdezhen.

The most popular clay in these regions is kaolin, or china clay, the hard, white earth that results from the decomposition of granite-bearing rock. Used in China since the seventh century, kaolin is the main ingredient in hard-paste porcelain. Deposits were discovered in Germany and used at Meissen, making it the first factory in Europe to produce true porcelain. In Britain, the pure white porcelain known as bone china takes its name from the added ingredient of bone ash. This is the predominant form of ceramic made in Britain today, based on a formula created at the Spode factory in the late eighteenth century.

With the outbreak of World War II, all kilns were closed and ceramic production ground to a halt until peace was declared in 1945. The state-operated factories in Jingdezhen were reopened and have recently been transformed into private potteries, rapidly regaining some of their former glory. Foreign artists are now flooding into China to study traditional ceramics, as well as painting, calligraphy and sculpture. The fusion of East and West is changing the form and style of China's ceramic tradition, expanding the scope of colour and material used by Chinese ceramicists. Key exhibitions curated in Beijing and Shanghai's major galleries are touring the world to showcase the talent of Chinese ceramicists, to international acclaim. There is now a sculptural dimension in many contemporary Chinese ceramics, inspired by avant-garde and pop art movements in the West, using traditional practices to express contemporary meaning.

Today's industry heralds a renaissance for Chinese ceramics, with reproductions produced to unsurpassed standards, and contemporary Chinese designs gaining recognition throughout the world. Drawing on its rich heritage of ceramics, China is now creating designs that reflect both streamlined decoration and austere functionality, bringing art and history into the mundane aspects of everyday life.

The shapes and forms of Chinese ceramics have changed the throughout China's long decorative history. Many of the shapes shown here remain contemporary today, and these same glazes continue to be reproduced in provincial kilns. Light blue colours and greenish celadon hues are among the oldest glazes used by Chinese ceramicis s they often created a 'washed' effect after firing, as these rustic pieces illustrate. Chinese colouring az s reached their peak in the Qing dynasty when advances in science enabled ceramicists to use minerals that yielded last-g colours and lustrous finishes.

Pattern & Motif

Like the rest of the Chinese decorative arts, the decoration on the ceramics was not to be taken lightly. Before the Qing dynasty, ceramics existed mainly on style and form for aesthetic appeal; the depiction of deities, sacred symbols, mystic signs and mythological animals designated functional ceramics and ritual objects. A Taoist devotee would have displayed a vase depicting the goddess Xiwangmu, the legendary 'Queen Mother of the West', holding a double gourd as a symbol of her ability to foretell the future, to attest to the promise of riches to come. A wine cup depicting a basket of lilies and *lingshi* – a type of fungus associated with immortality or long life – would be a literal means of drinking to one's health. Almost any series of animals portrayed in fives is emblematic of the 'five blessings': long life, riches, peace, love of virtue and a venerated end to one's life. These abound on platters, bowls and vases from the Han dynasty to the present day.

Early eighteenth-century porcelain masters in the West tried to imitate the elegant symbols and motifs of the ceramics made during the reign of Emperor Kangxi, but succumbed to the pervasive pressure of the Baroque. A vogue for the elegant depictions of willowy ladies known as 'Long Elizas' (a corruption of the Dutch term for them, Lange Lijzen) has featured on some eighteenth-century Kangxi blue-and-white porcelain swept through Europe and America, and the designs were copied by Worcester and by manufacturers of delftware. In the nineteenth century, prevailing tastes moved away from chinoiserie and towards Neoclassical designs. It then became possible to make most of these in Europe, since the technical knowledge developed during the Qing era had also been exported to the West. As the industry in Europe grew, the great porcelain factories of Sèvres, Limoges, Staffordshire and Delft became renowned for their sets of china, fine teapots, ceramic tiles and refined vases. Their quality paralleled the works produced in China, but lacked the spirituality fundamental to Chinese ceramics.

East and West were finally bridged at the beginning of the twentieth century by the work of the late Bernard Leach, Britain's leading studio ceramicist and an influential international master. Leach grew up in the Far East; he was born in Hong Kong of British parents and lived in Japan before coming to Britain in 1920. Initially known for his Japanese style, Leach was a purist who combined elements of Eastern and Western practices, designs and glazes. The influence of his work elevated the status of the Western potter to that of an artist rather than a craftsman. Leach charged clay with the feeling and finesse associated with fine art, describing his engagement with the materials as an artistic process. As critics drew parallels between his pieces and sculptural forms, ceramics was established as a discipline of the arts. Leach's works, and those of his wife and son, are today regarded as art pieces and sought after by museums and collectors.

Leach's forte was his ability to paint designs freehand in the traditional Chinese method, using a fine brush to render motifs and to outline the features of the vase. The Chinese also use stencils for ornate detailing like patterns and medallions. Pigments are powdered and blown onto the surface through the stencil using a bamboo tube, then left to dry. The stencil is then removed and further ornamentation applied, painted smoothly and continuously with a brush containing no more paint than can be immediately absorbed. The entire surface is then coated with a clear glaze and fired.

This beautiful gold-rimmed porcelain plate by De Gournay is hand-turned and hand-painted. It features a pseudo tobacco-leaf pattern that imitates the Chinese export porcelain produced in the second half of the eighteenth century. Its 'orange peel' glaze gives it a slightly uneven coating, which makes it look and feel like an antique plate.

Glazes

Chinese glazes are admired throughout the world for their spectacular colours and finishes – not least in China itself where they have been poetically compared to 'the rising moon', 'breaking river ice' and the 'colour of the sky after the rain'. Some Chinese glazes are bright and lustrous in tone, imitating the brilliance of precious gems or shimmering water, while others are deep, multifaceted and subtle, with hues that appear to change along with the ambient light. Glazes could be applied by dipping the entire ceramic into the solution, or washing it with a brush, or slowly dripping it down the sides of the vase so that it stopped just short of the base. Such simple monochromatic glazes were always pleasing to the cultivated Chinese taste.

The story of glazes is also the story of Chinese ceramics itself. The potters of ancient China worked miracles, transforming simple materials into coloured finishes, making high-fired glazed ceramics in beiges and browns. Ding ceramics evolved out of conscious attempts to produce a pure white clay body. White, translucent and unporous, the unfired ding forms easily lent themselves to the application of dense glazes or 'wash' methods. As well as the famous white ding, with its ivory glaze and unglazed rim (usually bound with metal) there were black, purple and red forms. Some of the burnished caramel colours of black ding have surfaces so dark and dense that they glint with the aura of polished ebony. What was initially regarded as the colour 'black' has since proved to be a cunning optical illusion resulting from coating scorched clay with opaque coffee-brown glazes; true black appeared only much later, in the Qing dynasty. Early potters created special effects by spattering the glaze with ash and straw, or painstakingly imitating tortoiseshell patterns, the fine striations of hare's fur and the textured mottling of partridge feathers.

The intense, high-fired glazes used in China today trace their origins all the way back to Bronze Age wares, as high-fired glazes are known to have been used on stoneware as early as the Shang dynasty. Roughly two millennia later the Song dynasty's wonderfully refined monochrome glazes were perfectly complemented by the undecorated earthenware in simple, classic shapes.

The potters of the early Ming dynasty perfected ferrous red and cobalt blue glazes, luring tastes away from the darker, more austere ceramics of old (though dark-glazed ceramics have been making a quiet comeback in the West in recent years).

The body and glaze of the distinctive blue-and-white Ming ceramics gradually changed over the three centuries of the Ming period. The glazed bases of early Ming pieces tend to be mottled and uneven, with thicker forms than those of the mid- and late Ming period. Most glazes appeared heavier and less translucent during the early years of the dynasty, gradually evolving to the transparent glazes of the late Ming period.

The glazes and decorations developed at the imperial kilns of the Qing dynasty were intended to reproduce natural colours by achieving a precise balance of minerals, firing temperature and timing. During the Kangxi reign, copper oxide was introduced as a colorant to create the red hues of the 'sang de boeuf' glaze and the pale pink 'peach bloom' glaze, which darkens and pales like a ripening peach. Also developed during the Kangxi reign, the light blue glaze known as 'clair de lune' has always been one of the most treasured of Qing glazes, and was reserved exclusively for imperial porcelains.

As the use of colour evolved during the Tang dynasty, it created a basic palette for subsequent eras to explore. These Tang wine cups were fired with the *sancai* glaze, later paralleled in the distinctive combination of green, yellow and burgundy that characterized Ming tricolour wares. Though many refined and stylized designs were produced by the Ming kilns, the understated beauty of rustic pieces like these is still appealing today.

Forms

Just as Chinese calligraphy became the world's earliest abstract drawing, by medieval times Chinese ceramics were perhaps the earliest abstract sculptures. Based on the expression of pure form and understated colour, their shapes were borrowed from ancient bronzes dating back thousands of years. These vessels were cast in bold sculptural forms with a functional purpose in mind, and ornamentation and detailing were kept to a minimum. Over time, rich glazes, colours and motifs began to decorate their surfaces, but the striking simplicity of their forms prevailed. The effect created a sense of complex harmony in form rather than a simple balance of decoration; a principle applied to many features of modern design today.

Chinese ceramicists are distinct from their Western counterparts, most markedly in their preservation of classical designs. The Chinese have a long tradition of venerating simple, rounded forms combined with subtle glazes. Though these pieces are essentially functional objects, they can also be appreciated for the sense of balance and precision which they convey.

Modern Chinese ceramics are characterized by the purity and strength associated with classical forms, but their shapes are often abstractly thrown or constructed to suit functional needs. Many of the modern vertical shapes have long, sinuous necks that merge into a broad base, or wide mouths that narrow into a rounded belly. Others can be squarish in shape, with wide necks that sit atop spreading 'shoulders' contoured into the base. Vases may have delicate rims that are flaring or fluted, or distinctive forked mouths. These recall the fine silver and bronze vessels from the Song dynasty that feature complex flower-shaped mouths astride tightly constricted necks. The effect is both delicate and exotic, but notoriously difficult to produce, even today.

The classic ovoid, or egg-shaped, form also emerged during the Song period. The ovoid shape was perfected by highly skilled craftsmen who laboured at the potter's wheel for hours to tease hollow contours out of the bulbous clay. Ovoid shapes were dexterously stretched into a vase or flattened into a dish, and used as decanters and jars. Conical bowls and vases are also associated with this period, many characterized by the deliberate contrasts between their inner and outer surfaces.

Chinese relief decoration on ceramics has always rendered texture and depth, presented contrasts and created a sense of variety. Throughout history it has featured brilliant combinations of imaginary creatures, including coiled dragons, scrolling cloud patterns, breaking waves and pools of water swirling in gentle spirals. Chinese ceramicists deftly applied vertical or spiral ribs of clay in order to create even more strongly contrasting lines and traced the rims and necks of lateral pieces with delicate thread moulding.

Beyond the commercially labelled 'Made in China' ceramics are beautifully crafted one-off, hand-thrown pieces. These ceramics are usually organic in shape and texture, and are crafted as an expression of form rather than as a surface for decoration. Made mostly in provincial workshops, ceramics like these, which are rarely exported, are known mainly among the most esoteric dealers. Their shapes are cool, understated and thoroughly modern, and tend to be of a richer, darker lustre than the light tones that are currently favoured in the West.

The tubed jar (far right) dates from the Song dynasty, its lustre emanating from a China-*pai* glaze applied many centuries ago. The tall urn shown beside it is a Tang amphora; used to hold grain wine or water, it is crafted with handles that transform into dragon's heads as they dip into its spout. The amphora's main body is unadorned except for the ribs of clay applied to define the neck and lip. The vase on its left dates from the Ming dynasty. It was shaped by incising the clay rather than adding ribs, with a cheeky dragon making a whimsical decoration as it winds around the neck of the vase. The symmetry of the crackle-glazed celadon vase (far left) balances two contoured shapes on either side of a hollow orb.

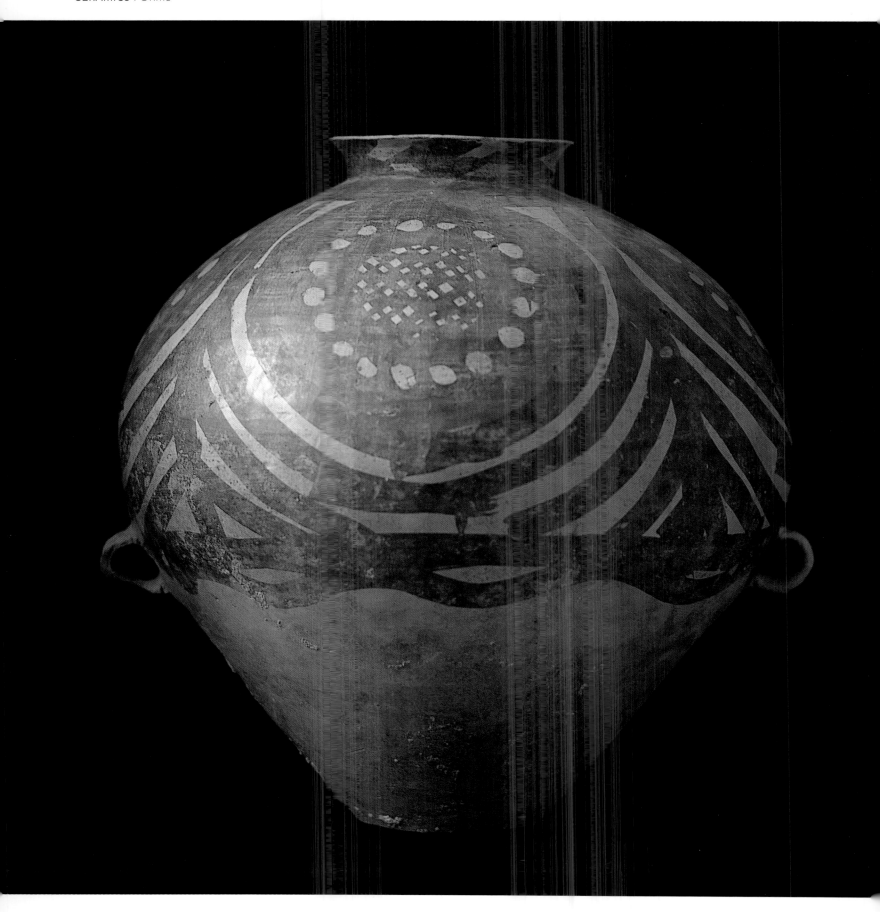

Page 184 Early pottery was sculpted into vessels and jugs with handles and pouring spouts. Their surfaces were simply decorated with birds, animals, flowers and other symbols from the natural world, or with bold patterns. The piece shown here was painted with curving lines that arc around the medallions drawn in their centre. Designs like this have inspired ceramicists today to paint designs freehand, using fine brushes to create motifs and outline the integral features.

Page 185 China produces a wide variety of ceramics, ranging from fine porcelain pieces made in factories to rustic earthenware containers fired in a village kiln. Although pottery generally refers to robust wares made from porous clay, the term is also used to describe the rare, hand-thrown pieces with organic shapes and finishes crafted in provincial workshops, like the bowls shown here.

Above These contemporary white porcelain pieces eschew superfluous decoration and rely upon their streamlined shapes and gentle textures to project a unique aesthetic.

Opposite Rustic pieces provide the perfect elements of contrast in a minimal interior. Set atop a sleek fireplace, their round bowls and wide necks add gentle contours that balance the harsh right angles dominating this part of the room. The white surroundings enhance the subtle tones of blue and grey in their glazes and highlight the shadows cast by their sculptural forms.

Buying antiques

Chinese antiques are often auctioned in the major cities of Europe and North America. Attending auctions is a good way of appraising the market, and auctioneers can sometimes broker deals between collectors on items that have not yet been booked for auction. If you decide to buy a period piece as an investment, it is worth visiting dealers to compare prices and ranges of merchandise. The advantage of buying from dealers is that their antiques are usually sold in pristine condition; if not, they can arrange for a professional conservator to carry out the work needed. But whether buying from an auctioneer or an antique dealer, question the provenance and ask for certificates of authenticity – before handing the money over

Serious collectors travel to Beijing, Shanghai and Hong Kong to look for rare items and competitive prices. All antique dealers must guarantee the quality of their goods in accordance with laws passed to protect the interests of foreign collectors. As buyers are legally obliged to have their purchases appraised by the customs office (which most international shipping companies arrange on their client's behalf), the government can identify any fakes and arrange to take the appropriate action against the dealer. Note that Chinese law currently forbids export of any antique older than three hundred years if it has been crafted from the precious *zitan*, *huanghuali* or *jichimu* woods. As laws change, it is advisable that collectors get advice before purchasing to ensure that they will be allowed to take them home.

Chronology

Xia dynasty	c.1900–c.1550BC	Tang dynasty	618–907
Shang dynasty	c.1550–c.1050BC	Five Dynasties period	907–960
Zhou dynasty	c.1050–256BC	Song dynasty	960–1279
Qin dynasty	221–206BC	Yuan dynasty	1279–1368
Han dynasty	206BC–AD220	Ming dynasty	1368–1644
Three Kingdoms period	220–265	Qing dynasty	1644–1911
Six Dynasties period	265–589	Republic of China established	1912
Sui dynasty	589–618	People's Republic of China established	1949

Index

A

abstract patterns 126
Africa 149
afterlife 42
agate 114, 158
alloys 114
amber 20, 84, 158
America 10, 12, 122,
    178
ancestor worship 28,
    42, 48, 100, 145
antiques 33
    buying 188
    textiles 122, 124,
        132
appliqué 134
Arabia 11, 175
architecture 8, 12, 94
    family life 18–20,
        22, 28
    formal rooms 22–7
    relation to
        furniture 96
    yin and yang 36–9
armchairs 23, 90, 96,
    106, 110
armoires 100
art 8, 28, 34, 52, 94,
    100, 110
Art Deco 14, 26
Art Nouveau 122
artisans 42
Asia 118, 126, 148,
    158

B

Baholyodhin, Ou 7
balance 8, 18, 36
bamboo 56, 57, 67,
    76, 104, 110–13
    faux bamboo 120
banners 132, 136
Baroque 10, 14, 76,

84, 120, 132, 178
basketwork 96
batik 132
bats 44, 46
beams 20, 98
beds 23, 28, 100, 102,
    121
    development 97–8
beige 90
Beijing 14, 34, 106
benches 33
beverages 58
birds 44, 70, 74, 76,
    132, 136
black 12, 48, 84
    symbolism 84
Black Sea 118
blinds 36, 79
blue 74, 174
boats 100
body consciousness 94
Bombay 120
bonsai 34
Book of Changes see
    I Ching
Book of Songs
    (Shijing) 110
brass 114
bridges 34
brocades 118, 120,
    121, 134
bronze 114, 148, 149
brushwork 132
Buddhism 12, 52, 96,
    118, 120, 126, 132,
    142, 146, 148,
    149, 166, 174
burial practices 18,
    146, 172–4
Burma 102, 158
business 22, 42, 97
butterflies 114, 126,
    128, 134, 136

C

cabinets 94, 100, 102,
    106, 121
calligraphy 28, 48, 70,
    94, 100, 142, 144,
    166–9
camel hair 126
camphor 106
candles 36, 76

cane 97, 98, 114
canopies 98, 120
Canton 8, 11, 70, 102,
    118, 120, 134, 149
carpets 118, 126–31
carving 102, 142
cases 134, 150, 160
Cathay 8–11, 42, 70,
    118, 120–1
Catholic Church 118
Caucasus 126
cedar, Chinese 106
celadon 10, 172, 174
Central Asia 118, 126,
    148, 158
ceramics 8, 10, 14, 15,
    118, 126, 172–7
    forms 182–7
    glazes 174, 180–1
    inlays 97, 114
    longevity symbol
        46
    patterns and motifs
        178–9
ceremony 8, 44
chairs 6, 12, 23, 56,
    90, 97, 102, 110
    bamboo 110–13
    development 96
    hunting chairs 126
    official's hat 25, 27,
        39, 96
chaise longue 98
cherry blossom 67
chests 6, 104, 106, 121
China
    emperors 42, 84, 96,
        120, 136, 138–9,
        142–5, 148, 158
    officials 42, 90,
        114, 132, 133
    social structure 42
chinoiserie 10–11, 14,
    70, 74, 76, 118–22,
    124, 174
chintz 118
Chippendale, Thomas
    10, 102
chopsticks 48, 56, 58,
    110
    rests 56, 58, 60
chrysanthemums 44
cinnabar 84

Ci Xi Dowager Empress
    (1831–1908) 42
cloisonné 148–9
    longevity symbol
        46
clothes 42, 48, 66,
    100, 121, 134
    robes 42, 46, 122,
        136, 138–9, 145
coins 44, 46, 98–100,
    126, 128, 136
collecting 122, 124, 126
colour 8, 12–14, 33,
    84–91
    wood 20
columns 20, 22
Communism 128
Confucianism 12, 28, 36,
    48, 132, 145, 166
console tables 94
contrasts 34, 36
cooking utensils 110
copper 76
corner andels 108
cotton 20, 118, 124, 132
courtyards 18, 20, 22,
    34, 66
crabs 44
craftsmanship 8, 12, 80,
    94, 100, 106, 108,
    148–53
    European 10, 132
playing cards 96, 97, 100,
    102, 121
curtains 14, 36, 97, 132,
    134
    tie-backs 79
cushions 90, 97, 98,
    120, 124
cutwork 132
cypress 106

D

dais 76, 98
damask 120
dances 48, 52
daydress 36
De Gournay 70
death 42
decoration 102
desks 28, 100
    bamboo 112

detail 114–15

display 162–5
doors 22, 25, 28, 96
dowries 97, 100, 134
dragons 15, 44, 46, 52,
    76, 78, 98, 118,
    126, 128, 136
    dragon processions
        48
    robes 138–9
dressing tables 94
Drottningholm 11

E

east 18, 84
East India Company
    10, 118, 120
ebony 84
elders 48, 56
elements, five 84
emperors 42, 84, 96,
    120, 136, 142–5,
    148, 158
    dress 138–9
England 10, 12, 118,
    120, 176
etiquette 34, 56
Europe 8–11, 14, 94,
    118–20, 132
    ceramics 176, 178

F

façon de la Chine 118
famille rose 11, 175
famille vert 175
family life 18–20, 22,
    28, 42
    ancestor worship
        28, 42, 48, 100,
        145
    meals 56
fans 8, 134, 160–1
feet 97, 126
feng shui 6, 18
festivals 48–53, 76, 132
fish 44, 114
flags 132
floors 11, 20, 34
flowers 48, 70, 74, 122,
    126, 136
    flower arranging

28, 66
food 48, 52, 56–61,
    100
footstools 97, 110
fragrance 20, 34, 102,
    106
frames 94, 120
France 10, 118, 120, 121
fretwork 20, 98, 102
    patterns 121, 134
furniture 8, 10, 12, 14,
    23, 25, 36, 76, 86,
    90, 94–101
    bamboo 110–13
    kang 100
    longevity symbol
        46
    pairing 31, 52

G

gaming tables 100
gardens 14, 18, 20, 34,
    90
    gardening 94
    tea 62
gates 22, 25, 97
gems 94, 114, 120
Genghis Khan 118
Genoa 118
Germany 11, 121, 176
glass 11, 76, 120
gods and goddesses
    28, 84, 106, 132,
    149, 178
gold 12, 48, 84, 114,
    120, 132, 134, 148
gold leaf 74, 100, 106,
    108
goldfish 34
Gong Ban 106
Gothic 122
granite 20
Greece 148
green 12, 74, 84, 174
    symbolism 84
Guangdong 110
Guangxi 110
Guangzhou see Canton

H

Hainan 102, 106
hairpins 152, 158
hall tables 100

Han dynasty 12, 42, 52, 118, 132, 145, 148, 160
handles 114
hangchou 66
hangings 10, 11, 28, 70, 120, 122, 122–3, 128, 136, 145, 162
Hangzhou 110
hardwood 102, 114
hares 76
harmony 8, 18, 36, 96
headdresses 12, 42
heavenly maid 132
herbal teas 62
hinges 114
homophones 44, 52
Hong Kong 48, 52
hongdoumu 106
hongmu 106
horn 60, 142
house design 12, 20–2, 28, 34, 96
household shrines 67, 100, 146
huali 106
huanghuali 102, 188
Hubei province 102

I
I Ching 18
incense burners 100, 148
India 12, 96, 102, 108, 118, 120, 145, 149
inlays 97, 100, 102, 104, 108, 114, 158
insects 34, 44, 102, 106
insulation 28, 121
ironmongery 114
Islam 142, 148
isolationism 12, 118
ivory 142, 149

J
jade 20, 84, 114, 142, 158–9, 174
Japan 12, 34, 62, 66, 96, 108, 160
jewels 94, 114, 120
jiaju 97
Jiangsu province 102
Jiangxi province 102

jichimu 106, 188
Jingdezhen 175, 176

K
kang 28, 100
    carpets 126
Kangxi 174, 178, 180
kaolin 176
kesi 132
keys 114
Khotan 126, 158
Korea 145, 160
kunqu 145–6

L
lacquer 8, 84, 102–6, 142
lacquerware 6, 10, 57, 76, 80, 84, 94, 100, 108–9, 118, 120, 146, 154–7, 162
lampshades 76, 79, 80
Lantern Festival 48, 52
lanterns 14, 34, 48, 50–1, 54, 76–83, 128
lapis lazuli 84, 114, 158
latticework 20, 22, 25, 34, 94, 97, 102, 106
    beds 98
    walls 34
Leach, Bernard 178
legs (furniture) 98–100
light 20, 36
lighting 76–83
lions 118, 132
    lion dances 48
literature 94
locks 114
longevity 18, 132
    symbol 46
longquan 10
Longshan culture 172
lotus 34, 44, 80, 122, 126
lotus position 96, 97
Lu Ban 76, 106
luohan chairs 96, 97, 110
luohan chang 98

M
Madras 120
mah jong 100
mahogany, Chinese 106
malachite 114, 158

Manchu 12–14, 42, 84, 138–9
mandarins 14, 42, 162
mantis 44
Mao, Chairman 122, 128
maogui 96, 100
marble 20, 97
masks 52
mats 12, 126
medallion patterns 126
Mediterranean 118, 148
Mei Lanfang 146
men 42, 97, 134
Mendoza, Juan Gonzalez de 11
menkan 22, 25
merchants 14, 42
metals 114
    metalwork 76, 102, 142
Miao people 132
Middle East 118, 142, 148
Ming dynasty 6, 11, 12, 14–15, 70, 84, 96, 114, 148, 149, 160
    carpets 126
    ceramics 174–5, 180, 182
    Classical period 94
    domestic architecture 20
    fretwork 102, 120
    furniture 25, 31, 76, 90, 94, 97, 98, 102, 106
    lacquerware 108, 154
    style 26, 27, 33, 38, 122
    textiles 121, 132, 136
minimalism 15, 33, 70, 90, 162, 174
mirrors 11, 94, 98
mitre joints 102
modernism 90
money 48, 52, 134
money plant 126
Mongolia 126
moon 76, 80
mortise-and-tenon 96

mother-of-pearl 100, 108, 162
motifs 8, 12, 70, 75, 94, 118, 120, 121 122, 126, 136
    birds 70, 74, 132 136
    butterflies 114 126 128, 134, 136
    ceramics 173–9
    Chairman Mao 122
    clouds 98–100, 126 128, 135
    dragons 15, 44, 46, 52, 76, 78, 78, 118, 126, 128, 136
    flowers 70, 74, 122 126, 136
    geometrical 74 126
    mountains 126
    symbolism 44–7, 97–8, 128, 132, 134, 142
    waves 44, 120, 126, 128, 136
music 145–6
musical instruments 110

N
nails 96, 110
nanmu 106
natural materials 6, 84, 102
nature 8, 18, 66, 74
necessities of life, seven 62
needlework 118, 120, 132, 134
Neoclassicism 10, 14
nephrite 114, 158
New Year 48, 67, 76
nickel 114
nomads 96, 104, 126
north 18, 22, 84, 97

O
offerings 48, 67
officials 42, 100, 114, 132, 138
onyx 84
opera 145–6
Oranienbaum 120
orchids 66

mother-of-pearl 100, 108, 162
ornamentation 12, 15, 121
Ottoman 148

P
pagodas 34
paintings 11, 52, 110, 142–4, 162
paktong 114
panels 102, 114
panthers 114
paper 48, 76
papercuts 151
patterns 74, 121, 122, 126, 178–9
pavilions 14, 34
paving 34
peaches 132
peasants 42, 110
Pékin 121
penjing 34
peonies 66, 134
Persia 11, 118, 148
persimmon 48, 67
Philippines 149
philosophy 8, 18, 36, 110, 114, 144
phoenix 52, 118, 126, 132
picnics 100
Pillement, Jean 120
pine 66
Pisa 118
place settings 56, 57, 60
plant stands 66, 100
plants 34, 66–9, 126
platforms 96, 98
    kang 100
plum blossom 48, 67
poetry 28, 94, 144
poison ivy 108
Polo, Marco 8
Pompadour, Madame de 10–11
ponds 34
porcelain 8, 56, 76, 84, 153, 174, 175–6
porches 34
posture 94
printed fabrics 118, 121
purple sandalwood 106
pussy willow 48, 66, 67

Q
qi (chi) 18, 66, 94, 98
Qianlong 14, 34, 158
qilin 114
Qin dynasty 148
Qin Shihuangdi 174
Qing dynasty 12–14, 15, 26, 42, 46, 56, 74, 76, 80, 84, 122, 145, 148, 149, carpets 126
    ceramics 15, 172, 174, 175, 180
    furniture 94, 98, 102, 106
    lacquerware 108, 154
    textiles 121, 132, 136
Qing Ming Festival 48, 67
quilting 118
quilts 97, 134

R
railings 98, 134
rain 20, 98
rattan 96, 98
red 12, 48, 74, 174
    Chinese red 84
    lanterns 76, 128
    symbolism 84, 90
    tapestries 132
    weddings 52, 54
red bean tree 106
reeds 112
reliefs 102
Rhus vernicifera 108
robes 42, 46, 122, 136, 145
    dragon 138–9
Rococo 10, 14, 84, 120, 122
Romans 118
rope 98
rose chairs 97, 106
rosewood 6, 106
rugs 20, 126

S
sandalwood 106
scholarship 8, 28, 34, 66, 94, 100, 110, 114, 134, 144, 160

screens 14, 22, 23, 36, 70, 102, 114
  bamboo 110
  batik 132
  Coromandels 108
  lacquer 100
scrolls 11, 57, 70, 144, 162, 166
sculptors 52
semi-precious stones 84
Serica 118
Seven Sages of the Bamboo Grove 132
Shakers 12
Shang dynasty 148
Shanghai 102, 112
Shanxi province 96
shelves 97
Shijing (Book of Songs) 110
shrines 67, 100, 146
shutters 20, 28
  bamboo 110
Siamoise 120, 121
Sichuan province 102, 106, 110
silk 8, 10, 11, 70, 118–20, 124, 126, 132, 134
Silk Route 11, 118, 120, 126, 174–5
silver 114, 120, 132, 134, 148
simplicity 6, 11–12, 121
sleeve bands 136, 138
soapstone 158
softwood 102, 104, 114

Song dynasty 10, 52, 66, 98, 122, 132, 144, 148, 149, 154, 160, 174, 180, 182
soup 58
south 18, 22, 84, 97
Spain 149
spices 118
spirits 22, 25, 48, 76, 78
spirituality 6, 28, 126
spoons 56
stands 66, 94, 100
Stevenson, Ottilie 70
stone 6, 18, 20, 66, 97, 106, 114, 142
stools 56, 58, 110
  development 96, 97
stoves 28, 44, 100
straw 96
studios 20, 22, 28
Suzhou 112
Sweden 11
symbolism 8, 44–7, 76
  clouds 98
  colour 84
  cranes 132
  deer 132
  dragons 52, 98, 128
  fish 114
  imperial 138
  lions 132
  lotus 98
  peaches 132
  phoenix 52, 132
  rain 98
  tea 62
  unicorn 132

water 34
wood 36
  yin and yang 84
symmetry 27, 31
Syria 118

T
table landscapes 34
tables 23, 28, 33, 94, 96, 97, 102, 114
  altar tables 38, 76, 100
  dining 56, 58
  functions 100
  luohan chang 98
taffeta 120
Taiwan 52
Tam, Vivienne 122
Tang dynasty 8, 12, 52, 62, 122, 132, 148, 158, 160
  burial objects 148, 172–4
  ceramics 14, 180–, 182
  furniture 86
  locks 114
Tao Qian (365–427) 42, 110
Taoism 8, 12, 18, 132, 149, 166, 174, 178
tapestries 11, 118, 120, 132, 136
tea 8, 10, 11, 58, 62–5, 120
  tables 100
teak 106

teapots 15, 58, 62, 120
termites 102
terracotta 20
  burial figures 174
  pets 62
  tiles 34
textiles 70, 100, 118–25
  longevity symbol 98
Thailand 102
thresholds 22, 25
Tibet 36
tigers 54, 114, 118
tiles 21, 34
toile de Jouy 121
toilette cases 94
tombs 42, 146, 172–4
tongue-and-groove 96
tortoiseshell 114
trade 11, 14, 100, 148
  export 11, 56, 94, 108, 152
  silk 118–20
trays 60
Tree of Life 118
trompe l'oeil 34
Turkey 118
turquoise 12, 84, 158
The Four Paragons of Filial Piety 132

U
unicorns 114, 132
upholstery 120, 121, 122

V
valances 79, 134

vases 6, 15
Venice 118
vernacular style 102, 110
Versailles 10, 14
views 18, 20, 34
visitors 22, 34, 97, 100

W
wallpaper 8, 10, 70–5
walls 11, 84, 96
  latticework 34
wardrobes 106, 120
Warhol, Andy 122
water 18, 34
waterlilies 34
Watteau, Jean-Antoine 10
waves 44, 120, 126, 128, 136
weaving 132
weddings 52, 54, 76, 134
well-being 6, 18
west 18, 84
white 84, 90
  symbolism 84, 90
windows 20, 21, 28, 96, 97
wintersweet 46
women 42, 97–8, 114, 134
wood 6, 12, 18, 20, 58, 66, 94, 96, 97, 102–7
  bamboo 110
  furniture legs 98–100
  steaming 96, 110
  willow 96, 110

wooden dishes 60
woodworm 102
wool 20, 97, 126
woven seats 96, 98
writing bureaux 94

X
Xia dynasty 48, 148

Y
yak hair 126
Yarkand 158
Yehonala see Cixi
yellow 12, 84
  symbolism 84
yellow rosewood 102
Yijing 18
yin and yang 6, 18, 20, 34, 52
  architecture 36–9
  symbolism 84
Yixing 176
yoke-back chairs 97
Yuan dynasty 15, 108, 118, 132, 144, 148, 154, 174–5
yuan xiao 52
Yuanmingyuan 14, 106

Z
zhangmu 106
zhazhen 104
Zhou dynasty 148
zitan 106, 188
zodiac 44

The author and publisher would like to thank the following for the loan of locations and material for photography:

Agent Provocateur 16 Pont Street, Knightsbridge, London SW1 020 7235 0229 www.agentprovocateur.com **101 top left and bottom right, 124**
Bam-Bou restaurant and bar, 1 Percy Street London W1P 0ET 020 7323 9140 www.bam-bou.co.uk **19, 89, 90**
Eileen Coyne, specialist painter 020 8741 1764: Graham Collins Design 020 8671 5356: **30, 133**
Neisha Crossland: wallpaper **72 top**
De Gournay 112 Old Church Street, London SW3 6EP: curtain **5**, wallpaper **9, 66, 71, 72, bottom 73, 86** wallpaper and china **75, 179** throw **111** china figures **153**
General Trading Company, cafe designed by Spencer Fung **58**
Josette Plismy/Gong **32–33, 81, 99**
Rabhi Hage: furniture **129**
Hakkasan restaurant, designer: Christian Liagre **22, 77**
Kirsten Heckterman: fabric **116–117, 125 top left** cushion **136 left**

Katie Jones 195 Westbourne Grove London W11 2SB, bowls designed by Robert Kuo **55, 156 top right**
Kelaty: carpet **16–17, 130–131**
Mirabelle **72 bottom**
Nom: furniture and television **5** table **85**
Mimmi O'Connell Port of Call 020 7589 4836: **27, 31, 101 top right and bottom left, 146 right** wooden plates **61** trunk **140–141**
Yves Ogier: location and materials posters **68, 163** cushion and chair **88** lacquerware Ivon Ogier, table by Florence Bandoux from Ogier Collection **156 bottom right**
Ormonde Gallery: incense and ink block **150** snuff bottles and display case **65** ceramics **181, 183, 184**
Ornamenta: wallpaper **165 right**
Patara: designer: Ou Baholyodhin **83, 104** Hong Kong chair by Ou Baholyodhin **6**
Sarah Pavey **147**
Phillip Quiggly: cushions **80, 125 bottom right**
Sally Rigg: ceramics **187**
David Robson Architects **129**
Scalamandre: wallpaper **74, 91** fabric and cushion **113**

Shanghai Tang 6a/b Sloane Street, London SW1 9LE www.shanghitang.com: **24, 82, 107** tea pot, cups and tray: **62–63** notebook **109** fabric **122–123**
Shanxi 020 7498 7611: cabinet **2**, vase: **37** furniture **92–93, 95, 105, 112, 113, 115** furniture and hatbox **109** chair **111**
Soo San 598a Kings Road, London SW6 2DX: location and furniture **25** poster **29** carpet **127, 129** location **145, 156 top left, 177** figures **146 left** spectacle cases **150**
Rupert Spira: ceramic **170–171**
Peter Ting: Hiberne Chine 020 7274 8900 **38, 56, 60, 78–79, 119, 143, 151–152, 157, 164, 167** incense burner **173**
Ushida Finlay Architects: **26, 39, 54, 111, 156 bottom left**
Vessel: spoon **179**
Edmund de Wall: ceramics **186**
Linda Wrigglesworth: altar scroll **57** altar cushion **137** fan cases **161**
Bosenquett Yves: carpet **127**

Acknowledgements

I would like to thank those who have influenced the content of this book: Paola Zamperini for her accounts of Qing dynasty urban life; Nancy Berliner for her exhaustive research on Chinese vernacular furniture; Dawn Jacobs for her texts on chinoiserie; Vivienne Tam for her accounts of life in China and Hong Kong; and the American sinologist and historian John S Major, senior lecturer at The China Institute, New York, and author of many books on Chinese history, whose critique vastly improved the manuscript.

I would also like to express my gratitude to the museums and institutions that facilitated my research: the Far Eastern Department at the Victoria and Albert Museum, London especially for providing Craig Clunas' study of classical Chinese furniture and Verity Wilson's texts on Chinese costume and textiles; the librarians, photographic archivists, keepers and curators of the Classical China, Qing China and Lacquer collections, Musée Guimet, Paris; the Far Eastern Department at the Metropolitan Museum of Art, New York, especially for texts on the Astor court and the Chinese Decorative Arts collection; the librarians at the School of Oriental and African Studies, University of London; the Percival David Foundation, University of London; and the History of Art Department, Birkbeck College, University of London.

My thanks to Jan Baldwin for her beautiful photography, Lindsay Milne for her resourcefulness, Megan Smith and Lucy Gowans for their art direction and Alison Wormleighton for her helpful comments. Above all, I would like to thank the editor, Muna Reyal, for her vision, enthusiasm and encouragement. For their support and contributions, I am grateful to Ana Avalon, Bo Madestrand, Deleah Shaffer, Ingela Hedlund Claxton, Hélène Armstrong, Kathryn Earle, Michel Andermatten, Marc Blane, Maria Froerg, Mark Forman, Simon Su, Su Ling Wang and Yeohlee Tan. A special thank you to Kate Haxell for suggesting me in the first place.

The Publisher would like to thank the following photographers and organisations for their kind permission to reproduce the photographs in this book:
10 Christie's Images; 11 Christie's Images; 13 John Thomson, 1869/Wellcome Library, London; 14 Christie's Images; 15 Christie's Images; 21 Hutchison Picture Library; 23 Courtesy of the Trustees of the Victoria and Albert Museum, London; 35 Courtesy of the Trustees of the Victoria and Albert Museum London; 42 Photos12.com – OIP; 139 Christie's Images; 159 Courtesy of the Trustrees of the Victoria and Albert Museum, London

2019
INDEX OF
U.S. MILITARY STRENGTH

DAVIS INSTITUTE FOR NATIONAL SECURITY AND FOREIGN POLICY

The
Heritage Foundation

2019
INDEX OF
U.S. MILITARY STRENGTH

DAVIS INSTITUTE FOR NATIONAL SECURITY AND FOREIGN POLICY

edited by
Dakota L. Wood

We are honored to dedicate the
2019 Index of U.S. Military Strength
to Thomas A. Saunders III.

Contents

Contributors ix

Acknowledgments xi

Preface xiii
Kay Coles James

Introduction 1

Executive Summary 7

Supplying the Manpower That America's National Security Strategy Demands 19
Blaise Misztal and Jack Rametta

Training: The Foundation for Success in Combat 37
Jim Greer, Colonel, U.S. Army (Ret.)

An Overview of the DOD Installations Enterprise 47
John Conger

Winning Future Wars: Modernization and a 21st Century Defense Industrial Base 61
Daniel Gouré, PhD

Logistics: The Lifeblood of Military Power 93
John E. Wissler, Lieutenant General, USMC (Ret.)

Global Operating Environment

    Assessing the Global Operating Environment 107

    Europe 109

    Middle East 153

    Asia 173

    Conclusion: Scoring the Global Operating Environment 201

Threats to U.S. Vital Interests

    Assessing Threats to U.S. Vital Interests 205

    Europe 209

    Middle East 241

    Asia 271

    Conclusion: Global Threat Level 303

U.S. Military Power

    An Assessment of U.S. Military Power 309

    U.S. Army 327

        U.S. Army Modernization Table 335

    U.S. Navy 343

        U.S. Navy Modernization Table 368

    U.S. Air Force 385

        U.S. Air Force Modernization Table 397

    U.S. Marine Corps 409

        U.S. Marine Corps Modernization Table 419

    U.S. Nuclear Weapons Capability 429

    Ballistic Missile Defense 445

    Conclusion: U.S. Military Power 455

Glossary of Abbreviations 459

Methodology 469

Contributors

Heritage Experts

Dakota L. Wood is Senior Research Fellow for Defense Programs in the Center for National Defense, of the Kathryn and Shelby Cullom Davis Institute for National Security and Foreign Policy, at The Heritage Foundation. He served for two decades as an officer in the U.S. Marine Corps, including service as a strategic analyst for the Commandant of the Marine Corps and the Secretary of Defense's Director of Net Assessment.

James Jay Carafano, PhD, is Vice President for the Davis Institute and E. W. Richardson Fellow at The Heritage Foundation. He served for 25 years as a U.S. Army officer and has taught at a number of universities, including the National Defense University.

Thomas W. Spoehr, Lieutenant General, U.S. Army (Ret.), is Director of the Center for National Defense. Before joining The Heritage Foundation, he served America for more than 36 years in the U.S. Army.

Frederico Bartels is Policy Analyst for Defense Budgeting in the Center for National Defense. Before joining The Heritage Foundation, he served for three years as a Policy Analyst with Concerned Veterans for America.

Thomas Callender is Senior Research Fellow for Defense Programs in the Center for National Defense. Following a 20-year career in the U.S. Navy's submarine fleet, he served for five years as Director for Capabilities in the Capabilities and Concepts Directorate of the Office of the Deputy Under Secretary of the Navy for Policy.

Dean Cheng is a Senior Research Fellow in the Asian Studies Center of the Davis Institute. He specializes in China's military and foreign policy.

Luke Coffey is Director of the Douglas and Sarah Allison Center for Foreign Policy of the Davis Institute. He joined Heritage after service as Senior Special Advisor to the Secretary of State for Defence of the United Kingdom.

James DiPane is a Research Assistant in the Center for National Defense. He focuses on foreign security cooperation, maritime security, and the U.S. Coast Guard.

Michaela Dodge is Senior Policy Analyst for Defense and Strategic Policy in the Center for National Defense. She specializes in missile defense, nuclear weapons modernization, and arms control.

Nile Gardiner, PhD, is Director of the Margaret Thatcher Center for Freedom of the Davis Institute. He served as foreign policy researcher in the Private Office of former Prime Minister Margaret Thatcher of the United Kingdom.

Bruce Klingner is Senior Research Fellow for Northeast Asia in the Asian Studies Center. He served for two decades at the Central Intelligence Agency and the Defense Intelligence Agency.

Daniel Kochis is a Policy Analyst in European Affairs in the Margaret Thatcher Center for Freedom, where he specializes in trans-Atlantic security issues including NATO, U.S.–Russia relations, and the Arctic.

Walter Lohman is Director of the Asian Studies Center. He has served on the staff of the Senate Committee on Foreign Relations, in the Office of Senator John McCain, and as Executive Director of the U.S.–ASEAN Business Council.

James Phillips is Senior Research Fellow for Middle Eastern Affairs in the Allison Center. He has also served at the Congressional Research Service and at the East–West Center.

John Venable is Senior Research Fellow for Defense Policy in the Center for National Defense. A 25-year veteran of the U.S. Air Force and F-16 pilot, he served in three combat operations, was commander of the Thunderbirds, and earned the rank of colonel before retiring.

Rachel Zissimos is a Policy Analyst in the Center for National Defense. She focuses on Department of Defense Energy and Industrial Base policy in addition to supporting production of the *Index of U.S. Military Strength*.

External Reviewers and Expert Contributors

John Conger is President of Conger Strategies & Solutions, LLC.

Patrick M. Cronin, PhD, is Senior Director of the Asia–Pacific Security Program at the Center for a New American Security (CNAS).

Lindsey Ford is Director for Political-Security Affairs and Richard Holbrooke Fellow at the Asia Society Policy Institute.

Daniel Gouré, PhD, is Senior Vice President at the Lexington Institute.

Jim Greer, Colonel, U.S. Army (Ret.)

David Isby is a Washington-based defense analyst and consultant.

Roy D. Kamphausen is Senior Vice President for Research at the National Bureau of Asian Research.

Eoin Micheál McNamara is a Junior Research Fellow at the University of Tartu, Estonia.

Blaise Misztal is Director of the National Security Program at the Bipartisan Policy Center.

Thomas C. Moore is an independent consultant.

Jack Rametta is Project Associate for the Bipartisan Policy Center's Economic Policy Project.

Douglas E. Streusand, PhD, is a Professor of International Relations at the U.S. Marine Corps Command and Staff College.

John Wissler, Lieutenant General, USMC (Ret.).

Larry M. Wortzel, PhD, is Senior Fellow for Asian Security at the American Foreign Policy Council.

Acknowledgments

No publication of this type is possible without the contributions of a great many people, but there usually are a few special contributors whose talents, work ethic, and willingness to go the extra mile make it something quite special.

Policy Analyst for National Security and Defense Studies Rachel Zissimos was the linchpin of production success, working with the authors, editors, and graphics and production professionals who made this *Index* a reality, both in print and on the Web. Not only did she substantially smooth and enhance the efficient production of the *Index*, creating additional time and better focus for everyone involved, but she also directly handled the updating of its many framing and explanatory sections. She was supported by Heritage Young Leaders Program interns Matt Bartilotti, Josh Hunter, Hayden Morse, and Matt Ahlquist, who contributed significant research that helped to inform the findings of the *2019 Index*.

As with all past editions, Senior Editor William T. Poole was instrumental not only in maintaining a consistent tone throughout this multi-author document—a challenging feat all its own—but also in checking every reference to ensure accuracy of reporting and coherence throughout the *Index* while also updating text that, though still current, can become stale when carried from one year to the next. He was aided this year by Research Editor Kathleen McCann Scaturro, who edited Blaise Misztal and Jack Rametta's manpower essay with the same attention to detail. Data Graphics Services Manager John Fleming, ably assisted by Data Graphics Specialist and Editorial Associate Luke Karnick, once again gave visual life to text and statistics to convey a message with maximum impact. Senior Designer of Research Projects Jay Simon and Digital Strategy Director Maria Sousa ensured that the presentation of *Index* materials was tuned to account for changes in content delivery as our world becomes increasingly digital, portable, and driven by social media. Finally, Director of Research Editors Therese Pennefather was critical in guiding each of these efforts into place to create a cohesive, finished product.

We believe that this *Index* helps to provide a better informed understanding and wider appreciation of America's ability to "provide for the common defence"—an ability that undergirds The Heritage Foundation's vision of "an America where freedom, opportunity, prosperity, and civil society flourish." Judging by reception of the *Index* during this past year—the work cited and referenced by Congress, the executive branch, officials within the Department of Defense, supporting government agencies, the media, academia, policy institutes, and among the public—we are encouraged that so many Americans are similarly concerned about the state of affairs in and the multitude of factors affecting our country.

The Heritage Foundation seeks a better life for Americans, which requires a stronger economy, a stronger society, and a stronger defense. To help measure the state of the economy, our Institute for Economic Freedom and Opportunity publishes the annual *Index of Economic Freedom*, and to help Americans everywhere more fully understand the state of our defenses, our Kathryn and Shelby Cullom Davis Institute for National Security and Foreign Policy is publishing this fifth annual edition of the *Index of U.S. Military Strength*.

In addition to acknowledging all of those who helped to prepare this edition, very special recognition is due to the Heritage members and donors whose continued support has made this *2019 Index of U.S. Military Strength* possible.

Finally, as always, The Heritage Foundation also expresses its profound appreciation to the members of the U.S. armed forces who continue to protect the liberty of the American people in an increasingly dangerous world.

Preface

Kay Coles James

This 2019 edition marks the fifth anniversary of The Heritage Foundation's *Index of U.S. Military Strength*. For the first time since the initial publication, rebounding budgets and returning end strength point to positive trends for U.S. national defense. However, the damage done over many years will not be undone overnight.

Congress and the President must stay the course.

As the world returns to an era of great-power competition, it is not enough simply to repair and replace aging ships, planes, and tanks. As the U.S. rested on the investments of past Administrations, our competitors and adversaries capitalized on the growing availability of advanced technologies—drawing from global commercial innovation, stealing the intellectual property of American businesses and institutions, and developing indigenous capabilities to counter long-held U.S. advantages in *every* domain of warfare.

The threats we face have grown increasingly sophisticated. According to Secretary of Defense Jim Mattis, "we cannot expect success fighting tomorrow's conflicts with yesterday's weapons and equipment."

U.S. military superiority has bred complacency among a population that has never known military defeat. Our country has largely taken for granted the peace and prosperity won through generations of investment and sacrifice, and we risk learning the hard way that continued superiority is not assured. Retaining a military advantage—particularly under the current pace of technological development—requires an enduring commitment to consistent investment in our country's security. Our history shows that a strong, capable military deters aggression and effectively enhances our ability to engage the world through diplomacy and trade.

The Bipartisan Budget Act of 2018 provided two years of welcome relief from the threat of sequestration. However, decades of continuing resolutions and budgetary uncertainty have left the military hostage to political whims, unable to plan and prepare for challenges on the horizon. Abraham Lincoln eloquently noted that "America will never be destroyed from the outside. If we falter and lose our freedoms, it will be because we destroyed ourselves." With Lincoln's warning in mind, perhaps we should realize that the greatest threat to U.S. military strength is the misconception that America can no longer afford military superiority.

Entitlement costs consume an increasing portion of the federal budget, and Congress continues to blow through debt ceilings. Too many in government have come to see defense as a trade-off rather than as the obligation and responsibility it truly is: a constitutionally mandated function of government to provide for the common defense

The *Index* provides an enduring benchmark for Congress based on what history has shown is necessary to defend national interests. The force for which we advocate will not come cheap, but the costs of weakness and complacency are far greater. Secretary Mattis had a message for Congress this year "America *can* afford survival." In order to ensure future generations the same peace and prosperity that we too often take for granted, Congress must continue to provide for a strong national defense—and remember that there are no permanent victories.

Kay Coles James, President
The Heritage Foundation
October 2018

Introduction

The United States maintains a military force primarily to protect the homeland from attack and to protect its interests abroad. Although there are secondary uses for the military—such as assisting civil authorities in times of emergency or deterring enemies—that amplify other elements of national power such as diplomacy or economic initiatives, America's armed forces exist above all else so that the U.S. can physically impose its will on an enemy and change the conditions of a threatening situation by force or the threat of force.

Each year, The Heritage Foundation's *Index of U.S. Military Strength* gauges the ability of the U.S. military to perform its missions in today's world and assesses how the condition of the military has changed from the preceding year.

The United States prefers to lead through "soft" elements of national power: diplomacy, economic incentives, and cultural exchanges. When soft approaches like diplomacy work, their success often owes much to the knowledge of all involved that U.S. "hard power" stands ready, if silently, in the diplomatic background. Soft approaches cost less in manpower and treasure than military action costs and do not carry the same risk of damage and loss of life, but when confronted by physical threats to U.S. national security interests, soft power cannot substitute for raw military power. In fact, an absence of military power or the perception that one's hard power is insufficient to protect one's interests often invites challenges that soft power is ill-equipped to address. Thus, hard power and soft power are complementary and mutually reinforcing.

The decline of America's military hard power, historically shown to be critical to defending against major military powers and to sustain operations over time against lesser powers or in multiple instances simultaneously, is thoroughly documented and quantified in this *Index*. More difficult to quantify, however, are the growing threats to the U.S. and its allies that are engendered by the perception of American weakness abroad and doubts about America's resolve to act when its interests are threatened.

The anecdotal evidence is consistent with direct conversations between Heritage scholars and high-level diplomatic and military officials from countries around the world: The perception of American weakness is destabilizing many parts of the world and prompting old friends to question their reliance on America's assurances. For decades, the perception of American strength and resolve has served as a deterrent to adventurous bad actors and tyrannical dictators. Regrettably, both that perception and, as a consequence, its deterrent effect are eroding. The result is an increasingly dangerous world threatening a significantly weaker America.

It is therefore critical that we understand the condition of the United States military with respect to America's vital national security interests, the threats to those interests, and the context within which the U.S. might have to use hard power. It is likewise important to know how these three areas—operating environments, threats, and the posture of the U.S. military—change over time, given that such changes can have substantial implications for defense policies and investments.

In the opening paragraph of the U.S. Constitution, "We the People" stated that among their handful of purposes in establishing the Constitution was to "provide for the common defence." The enumeration of limited powers for the federal government in the Constitution includes the powers of Congress "To declare War," "To raise and support Armies," "To provide and maintain a Navy," "To provide for calling forth the Militia," and "To provide for organizing, arming, and disciplining, the Militia" and the power of the President as "Commander in Chief of the Army and Navy of the United States, and of the Militia of the several States, when called into the actual Service of the United States." With such constitutional priority given to defense of the nation and its vital interests, one might expect the federal government to produce a standardized, consistent reference work on the state of the nation's security. Yet no such single volume exists, especially in the public domain, to allow comparisons from year to year. Recently, the Department of Defense has moved to restrict reporting of force readiness even further. Thus, the American people and even the government itself are prevented from understanding whether investments made in defense are achieving their desired results.

What is needed is a publicly accessible reference document that uses a consistent, methodical, repeatable approach to assessing defense requirements and capabilities. The Heritage Foundation's *Index of U.S. Military Strength*, an annual assessment of the state of America's hard power, fills this void, addressing both the geographical and functional environments relevant to the United States' vital national interests and threats that rise to a level that puts or has the strong potential to put those interests at risk.

Any assessment of the adequacy of military power requires two primary reference points: a clear statement of U.S. vital security interests and an objective requirement for the military's capacity for operations that serves as a benchmark against which to measure current capacity. A review of relevant top-level national security documents issued by a long string of presidential Administrations makes clear that three interests are consistently stated:

- Defense of the homeland;

- Successful conclusion of a major war that has the potential to destabilize a region of critical interest to the U.S.; and

- Preservation of freedom of movement within the global commons: the sea, air, outer-space, and cyberspace domains through which the world conducts business.

Every President has recognized that one of the fundamental purposes of the U.S. military is to protect America from attack. While going to war has always been controversial, the decision to do so has been based consistently on the conclusion that one or more vital U.S. interests are at stake.

This *Index* embraces the "two-war requirement"—the ability to handle two major wars or two major regional contingencies (MRCs) successfully at the same time or in closely overlapping time frames—as the most compelling rationale for sizing U.S. military forces. Dr. Daniel Gouré provided a detailed defense of this approach in his essay, "Building the Right Military for a New Era: The Need for an Enduring Analytic Framework," in the *2015 Index*, and it is further elaborated in the military capabilities section. The basic argument, however, is this: The nation should have the ability to engage and defeat one opponent and still have the ability to guard against competitor opportunism (that is, to preclude someone's exploiting the perceived opportunity to move against U.S. interests while America is engaged elsewhere).

The *Index* is descriptive, not prescriptive, reviewing the current condition of its subjects within the assessed year and describing how conditions have changed from the previous year, informed by the baseline condition established by the inaugural *2015 Index*. In short, the *Index* answers the question, "Have conditions improved or worsened during the assessed year?"

This study also assesses the U.S. military against the two-war benchmark and various metrics explained further in the military capabilities section. Importantly, this study measures the hard power needed to win conventional wars rather than the general utility of the military relative to the breadth of tasks it might be (and usually is) assigned to advance U.S. interests short of war.

Assessing the World and the Need for Hard Power

The assessment portion of the *Index* is composed of three major sections that address the aforementioned areas of primary interest: America's military power, the operating environments within or through which it must operate, and threats to U.S. vital national interests. For each of these areas, the *Index* provides context, explaining why a given topic is addressed and how it relates to understanding the nature of America's hard-power requirements.

The authors of this study used a five-category scoring system that ranged from "very poor" to "excellent" or "very weak" to "very strong" as appropriate to each topic. This approach was selected as the best way to capture meaningful gradations while avoiding the appearance that a high level of precision was possible given the nature of the issues and the information that was publicly available.

Some factors are quantitative and lend themselves to discrete measurement; others are very qualitative in nature and can be assessed only through an informed understanding of the material that leads to an informed judgment call.

Purely quantitative measures alone tell only part of the story when it comes to the relevance, utility, and effectiveness of hard power. Assessing military power or the nature of an operating environment using only quantitative metrics can lead to misinformed conclusions. For example, the mere existence of a large fleet of very modern tanks has little to do with the effectiveness of the armored force in actual battle if the employment concept is irrelevant to modern armored warfare. (Imagine, for example, a battle in rugged mountains.) Also, experience and demonstrated proficiency are often decisive factors in war—so much so that numerically smaller or qualitatively inferior but well-trained and experienced forces can defeat a larger or qualitatively superior adversary.

However digital and quantitative the world has become thanks to the explosion of advanced technologies, it is still very much a qualitative place, and judgment calls have to be made in the absence of certainty. We strive to be as objective and evenhanded as possible in our approach and transparent in our methodology and sources of information so that readers can understand why we came to the conclusions we reached and perhaps reach their own. The result will be a more informed debate about what the United States needs in terms of military capabilities to deal with the world as it is. A detailed discussion of scoring is provided in each assessment section.

In our assessment, we begin with the operating environment because it provides the geostrategic stage upon which the U.S. attends to its interests: the various states that would play significant roles in any regional contingency; the terrain that enables or restricts military operations; the infrastructure—ports, airfields, roads, and rail networks (or lack thereof)—on which U.S. forces would depend; and the types of linkages and relationships the U.S. has with a region and major actors within it that cause the U.S. to have interests in the area or that facilitate effective operations. Major actors within each region are identified, described, and assessed in terms of alliances, political stability, the presence of U.S. military forces and relationships, and the maturity of critical infrastructure.

Our assessment focuses on three key regions—Europe, the Middle East, and Asia—because of their importance relative to U.S. vital security interests. This does not mean that we view Latin America and Africa as unimportant. Rather, it means that the security challenges within these regions do not currently rise to the level of direct threats to America's vital security interests as we have defined them. We addressed their current condition in the *2015 Index* and will provide an updated assessment when it is warranted.

Next is a discussion of threats to U.S. vital interests. Here we identify the countries that pose the greatest current or potential threats to U.S. vital interests based on two overarching factors: their behavior and their capability. We accept the classic definition of "threat" as a combination of intent and capability, but while capability has attributes that can be quantified, intent is difficult to measure. We concluded that "observed behavior" serves as a reasonable surrogate for intent because it is the clearest manifestation of intent.

We based our selection of threat countries and non-state actors on their historical behavior and explicit policies or formal statements vis-à-vis U.S. interests, scoring them in two areas: the degree of provocative behavior that they exhibited during the year and their ability to pose a credible threat to U.S. interests irrespective of intent. For example, a state full of bluster but with only a moderate ability to act accordingly poses a lesser threat, while a state that has great capabilities and a pattern of bellicose behavior opposed to U.S. interests still warrants attention even if it is relatively quiet in a given year.

Finally, we address the status of U.S. military power in three areas: capability (or modernity), capacity, and readiness. Do U.S. forces possess operational capabilities that are relevant to modern warfare? Can they defeat the military forces of an opposing country? Do they have a sufficient amount of such capabilities? Is the force sufficiently trained and its equipment materially ready to win in combat? All of these are fundamental to success even if they are not de facto determinants of success (something we explain further in the section). We also address the condition of the United States' nuclear weapons capability, assessing

it in areas that are unique to this military component and critical to understanding its real-world viability and effectiveness as a strategic deterrent, and provide a descriptive overview of current U.S. ballistic missile defense capabilities and challenges.

Topical Essays

Debates about defense matters usually address the use of military power, major procurement programs, and related funding, which is not surprising because they are readily apparent and typically demand a timely decision. By contrast, the foundational elements that make competent, effective military power possible are rarely addressed. Often referred to as Title 10 issues—taken from the section of the U.S. Code that establishes the legal basis for what the U.S. military does and how it is organized, trained, and equipped—these include how the people who comprise the military are brought into the services and handled during their time in uniform; the facilities and resources necessary to host, house, train, and support military forces; the training and education of the military; and the ability to sustain military operations in peacetime and in war.

Our essayists for the *2019 Index* have embraced the challenge of describing each of these areas and their importance to the generation, sustainment, and use of military power.

- Given the centrality of people to the security and defense of the United States, it makes sense to lead these essays with the work of Blaise Misztal and Jack Rametta. In "Supplying the Manpower That America's National Security Strategy Demands," the authors describe the evolution of defense personnel policies from the founding of the U.S. to their most recent revision in 2018 and then go on to explain how changes in U.S. demography, the tools of war, and even how military operations are now conducted are driving the need to revisit long-established approaches to manning the U.S. military and managing the people who contribute their talents.

- Next, Jim Greer, Colonel, U.S. Army (Ret.) tackles "Training: The Foundation for Success in Combat." Colonel Greer walks the reader though the types of training needed to ensure that the military is ready for war. As the author states, "No other activity prepares a military force better for combat than combat itself." Short of that, however, military organizations must train in conditions as close to the reality of combat as possible.

- In "An Overview of the DOD Installations Enterprise," John Conger explains the importance of physical military infrastructure. "Our warfighters cannot do their job without bases from which to fight, on which to train, or in which to live when they are not deployed. The bottom line is that installations support our military readiness." Conger notes that "DOD maintains a global real property portfolio consisting of 568,383 facilities, valued at approximately $1.05 trillion, with more than 2.2 billion square feet of space located on 27.2 million acres of land at over 4,793 sites worldwide." Maintaining this enterprise is expensive but essential.

- Dr. Daniel Gouré looks at the reality of keeping America's military better equipped than those of its competitors. In "Winning Future Wars: Modernization and a 21st Century Defense Industrial Base, " Gouré tracks how the DIB has evolved since the large industrial model of World War II, through conglomeration during the Cold War, to the highly specialized subsectors of the cyber age. He rightly emphasizes that if it is to produce innovative products at acceptable cost, it not only has to be diverse, but also has to be profitable enough for companies to remain viable.

- Wrapping things up, Lieutenant General John E. Wissler, U.S. Marine Corps (Ret.), examines "Logistics: The Lifeblood of Military Power." Drawing from four decades of operational experience, he describes how logistics is not only the "oxygen that allows military muscle to function, grow, and strengthen." It actually determines for the field commander the "freedom of action, endurance, and ability to extend operational reach" that are necessary to succeed in any operational task. Making sure that capabilities are modern and of sufficient capacity is just as important for logistics as it is for the combat forces that the logistics enterprise supports.

Scoring U.S. Military Strength Relative to Vital National Interests

The purpose of this *Index* is to make the national debate about defense capabilities better informed by assessing the ability of the U.S. military to defend against current threats to U.S. vital national interests within the context of the world as it is. Each of the elements can change from year to year: the stability of regions and access to them by America's military forces; the various threats as they improve or lose capabilities and change their behavior; and the United States' armed forces themselves as they adjust to evolving fiscal realities and attempt to balance readiness, capacity (size and quantity), and capability (how modern they are) in ways that enable them to carry out their assigned missions successfully.

Each region of the world has its own set of characteristics that include terrain; man-made infrastructure (roads, rail lines, ports, airfields, power grids, etc.); and states with which the United States has relationships. In each case, these traits combine to create an environment that is either favorable or problematic when it comes to U.S. forces operating against threats in the region.

Various states and non-state actors within these regions possess the ability to threaten—and have consistently behaved in ways that threaten—America's interests. Fortunately for the U.S., these major threat actors are currently few in number and continue to be confined to three regions—Europe, the Middle East, and

Asia—thus enabling the U.S. (if it will do so) to focus its resources and efforts accordingly.

As for the condition of America's military services, they continue to be beset by aging equipment, shrinking numbers, rising costs, and problematic funding. These four elements interact with each other in ways that are difficult to measure in concrete terms and impossible to forecast with any certainty. Nevertheless, the exercise of describing them and characterizing their general condition is worthwhile because it informs debates about defense policies and the allocation of resources that are necessary for the U.S. military to carry out its assigned duties. Further, as seen in this *2019 Index*, noting how conditions have changed from the preceding year help to shed light on the effect that policies, decisions, and actions have on security affairs involving the interests of the United States, its allies and friends, and its enemies.

It should be borne in mind that each annual *Index* assesses conditions as they are for the assessed year. This *2019 Index of U.S. Military Strength* describes changes that occurred during the preceding year, with updates current as of mid-September 2018.

Assessments for U.S. Military Power, Global Operating Environment, and Threats to Vital U.S. Interests are shown in the Executive Summary. Factors that would push things toward "bad" (the left side of the scale) tend to move more quickly than those that improve one's situation, especially when it comes to the material condition of the U.S. military.

Of the three areas measured—U.S. Military Power, Global Operating Environment, and Threats to Vital U.S. Interests—the U.S. can directly control only one: its own military. The condition of the U.S. military can influence the other two because a weakened America arguably emboldens challenges to its interests and loses potential allies, while a militarily strong America deters opportunism and draws partners to its side from across the globe.

Conclusion

During the decades since the end of the Second World War, the United States has underwritten and taken the lead in maintaining a global order that has benefited more people in more ways than at any other period in history. Now, however, that American-led order is under stress, and some have wondered whether it will break apart entirely. Fiscal and economic burdens continue to plague nations; violent, extremist ideologies threaten the stability of entire regions; state and non-state opportunists seek to exploit upheavals; and major states compete to establish dominant positions in their respective regions.

America's leadership role remains in question, and its security interests are under significant pressure. Challenges are growing, old allies are not what they once were, and the U.S. is increasingly beleaguered by debt that constrains its ability to sustain its forces commensurate with its interests.

Informed deliberations on the status of the United States' military power are therefore desperately needed. This *Index of U.S. Military Strength* can help to inform the debate.

Executive Summary

"As currently postured, the U.S. military is only marginally able to meet the demands of defending America's vital national interests."

The United States maintains a military force primarily to protect the homeland from attack and to protect its interests abroad. There are secondary uses—for example, to assist civil authorities in times of emergency or to deter enemies—but this force's primary purpose is to make it possible for the U.S. to physically impose its will on an enemy when necessary.

It is therefore critical that the condition of the United States military with respect to America's vital national security interests, threats to those interests, and the context within which the U.S. might have to use "hard power" be understood. Knowing how these three areas—operating environments, threats, and the posture of the U.S. military—change over time, given that such changes can have substantial implications for defense policies and investment, is likewise important.

Each year, The Heritage Foundation's *Index of U.S. Military Strength* employs a standardized, consistent set of criteria, accessible both to government officials and to the American public, to gauge the U.S. military's ability to perform its missions in today's world. The inaugural 2015 edition established a baseline assessment on which each annual edition builds, assessing the state of affairs for its respective year and measuring how key factors have changed from the previous year.

What the Index Assesses

The *Index of U.S. Military Strength* assesses the ease or difficulty of operating in key regions based on existing alliances, regional political stability, the presence of U. S. military forces, and the condition of key infrastructure. Threats are assessed based on the behavior and physical capabilities of actors that pose challenges to U.S. vital national interests. The condition of America's military power is measured in terms of its capability or modernity, capacity for operations, and readiness to handle assigned missions successfully. This framework provides a single-source reference for policymakers and other Americans who seek to know whether our military power is up to the task of defending our national interests.

Any discussion of the aggregate capacity and breadth of the military power needed to protect U.S. security interests requires a clear understanding of precisely what interests must be defended. Three vital interests have been specified consistently and in various ways by a string of Administrations over the past few decades:

- **Defense** of the homeland;

- **Successful conclusion** of a major war that has the potential to destabilize a region of critical interest to the U.S.; and

- **Preservation** of freedom of movement within the global commons (the sea, air, outer-space, and cyberspace domains) through which the world conducts its business.

To defend these interests effectively on a global scale, the United States needs a military force of sufficient size, or what is known in the Pentagon as capacity. The many factors involved make determining how big the military should be a complex exercise but successive Administrations, Congresses, and Department of Defense staffs have managed to arrive at a surprisingly consistent force-sizing rationale: an ability to handle two major wars or major regional contingencies (MRCs) simultaneously or in closely overlapping time frames. This two-war or two-MRC requirement is embraced in this *Index*.

At the core of this requirement is the conviction that the United States should be able to engage and decisively defeat one major opponent and simultaneously have the wherewithal to do the same with another to preclude opportunistic exploitation by any competitor. Since World War II, the U.S. has found itself involved in a major "hot" war every 15–20 years while simultaneously maintaining substantial combat forces in Europe and several other regions. The size of the total force roughly approximated the two-MRC model, which has the inherent ability to meet multiple security obligations to which the U.S. has committed while also modernizing, training, educating, and maintaining the force. Accordingly, our assessment of the adequacy of today's U.S. military is based on the ability of America's armed forces to engage and defeat two major competitors at roughly the same time.

This *Index*'s benchmark for a two-MRC force is derived from a review of the forces used for each major war that the U.S. has undertaken since World War II and the major defense studies completed by the federal government over the past 30 years. We concluded that a standing (Active Duty component) two-MRC–capable Joint Force would consist of:

- **Army:** 50 brigade combat teams (BCTs);

- **Navy:** 400 battle force ships and 624 strike aircraft;

- **Air Force:** 1,200 fighter/ground-attack aircraft; and

- **Marine Corps:** 36 battalions.

This recommended force does not account for homeland defense missions that would accompany a period of major conflict and are generally handled by Reserve and National Guard forces. Nor does it constitute the totality of the Joint Force, which includes the array of supporting and combat-enabling functions essential to the conduct of any military operation: logistics; transportation (land, sea, and air); health services communications and data handling; and force generation (recruiting, training, and education), to name only a few. Rather, these are combat forces that are the most recognizable elements of America's hard power but that also can be viewed as surrogate measures for the size and capability of the larger Joint Force.

The Global Operating Environment

Looking at the world as an environment in which U.S. forces would operate to protect America's interests, the *Index* focused on three regions—Europe, the Middle East, and Asia—because of the intersection of our vital interests and actors able to challenge them.

Europe. Overall, the European region remains a stable, mature, and friendly operating environment. Russia remains the preeminent threat to the region, both conventionally and nonconventionally, and the impact of the migrant crisis, along with continued economic sluggishness, the terrorist threat, and political fragmentation, increases the potential for internal instability. If the U.S. needs to act in the European region or nearby, there is a history of interoperability with allies and access to key logistical infrastructure that makes the operating environment in Europe more favorable than the environment in other regions in which U.S. forces might have to operate.

The past year saw continued U.S. reengagement with the continent both militarily and politically along with modest increases in European allies' defense budgets and capability investment. Despite allies' initial concerns, the U.S. has increased its investment in Europe, and its military position on the continent is stronger than it has been for some time. NATO's renewed focus on collective defense resulted in a focus on logistics, newly established commands that reflect a changed geopolitical reality, and a robust set of exercises. NATO's biggest challenges derive from continued underinvestment from European members, a tempestuous Turkey, disparate threat perceptions within the alliance, and the need to establish the ability to mount a robust response to both linear and nonlinear forms of aggression.

For Europe, scores this year remained steady, with no substantial changes in any individual categories or average scores. The *2019 Index* again assesses the European Operating Environment as "favorable."

The Middle East. For the foreseeable future, the Middle East region will remain a key focus for U.S. military planners. Once considered relatively stable, the area is now highly unstable and a breeding ground for terrorism. Overall, regional security has deteriorated in recent years. Even though the Islamic State has been seriously weakened, what its successor will be like is unclear. Iraq has restored its territorial integrity after the defeat of ISIS, but relations between Baghdad and the U.S. remain uncertain in the wake of the recent election victory of Muqtada al-Sadr. The regional dispute with Qatar has made U.S. relations in the region even more complex and difficult to manage. The Russian, Iranian, and Turkish interventions in Syria have greatly complicated the fighting there.

Countries like Iraq, Libya, Syria, and Yemen are being challenged by non-state actors that wield influence, power, and resources comparable to those of small states. Decades of U.S. military operations in the Middle East have resulted in an extensive network of bases and substantial operational experience in combatting regional threats. However, many of the United States' partners are hobbled by political instability, economic problems, internal security threats, and mushrooming transnational threats.

Despite an improvement in regional political stability from "very poor" to "unfavorable" as scored in the *2019 Index*, the region (and thus its scores) remains highly volatile. The *2019 Index* accordingly assesses the Middle East Operating Environment as "moderate."

Asia. The Asian strategic environment is extremely expansive, with a variety of political relationships among states that have wildly varying capabilities. The region includes long-standing American allies with relationships dating back to the beginning of the Cold War as well as recently established states and some long-standing adversaries such as North Korea.

American conceptions of the region must therefore start from the physical limitations imposed by the tyranny of distance. Moving forces within the region (never mind to it) will take time and require extensive strategic lift assets as well as sufficient infrastructure, such as sea and aerial ports of debarkation that can handle American strategic lift assets, and political support. At the same time, the complicated nature of intra-Asian relations, especially unresolved historical and territorial issues, means that the United States, unlike Europe, cannot necessarily count on support from all of its regional allies in responding to any given contingency.

For Asia, we therefore arrived at an average score of "favorable."

Summarizing the condition of each region enables us to get a sense of how they compare in terms of the challenge the U.S. would have in projecting military power and sustaining combat operations in each one.

As a whole, the global operating environment currently maintains a score of "favorable," meaning that the United States should be able to project military power anywhere in the world as necessary to defend its interests without substantial opposition or high levels of risk.

Global Operating Environment

VERY POOR	UNFAVORABLE	MODERATE	**FAVORABLE**	EXCELLENT

Operating Environment: Europe

	VERY POOR	UNFAVORABLE	MODERATE	FAVORABLE	EXCELLENT
Alliances				✓	
Political Stability				✓	
U.S. Military Posture			✓		
Infrastructure				✓	
OVERALL				✓	

Operating Environment: Middle East

	VERY POOR	UNFAVORABLE	MODERATE	FAVORABLE	EXCELLENT
Alliances			✓		
Political Stability		✓			
U.S. Military Posture			✓		
Infrastructure			✓		
OVERALL			✓		

Operating Environment: Asia

	VERY POOR	UNFAVORABLE	MODERATE	FAVORABLE	EXCELLENT
Alliances				✓	
Political Stability				✓	
U.S. Military Posture				✓	
Infrastructure				✓	
OVERALL				✓	

Global Operating Environment

	VERY POOR	UNFAVORABLE	MODERATE	FAVORABLE	EXCELLENT
Europe				✓	
Middle East			✓		
Asia				✓	
OVERALL				✓	

Threats to U.S. Interests

Our selection of threat actors discounted troublesome states and non-state entities that lacked the physical ability to pose a meaningful threat to vital U.S. security interests. This reduced the population of all potential threats to a half-dozen that possessed the means to threaten U.S. vital interests and exhibited a pattern of provocative behavior that should draw the focus of U.S. defense planning. This *Index* characterizes their behavior and military capabilities on five-point, descending scales.

All of the six threat actors selected—Russia, China, Iran, North Korea, and terrorist groups in the Middle East and Afghanistan—remained actual or potential threats to U.S. interests over the past year. All amply demonstrated a commitment to expanding their capabilities to pursue their respective interests that directly challenged those of the U.S.

Collectively, the threat to U.S. vital interests remains "high" in the *2019 Index* despite a decrease in the assessed threat level for Af-Pak terrorism from "high" to "elevated." Although this was the only full score change among the six threat actors, scores for both Russia and China come close to being elevated to "severe" from their current "high."

Russia and China continue to be the most worrisome, both because of the ongoing modernization and expansion of their offensive military capabilities and because of the more enduring effect they are having within their respective regions. Russia has maintained its active involvement in the conflict in Ukraine, has been more assertive in the Baltic Sea region, and has reduced its presence in Syria—but only because of its success in salvaging the Bashar al-Assad regime. China's provocative behavior continues to include militarization of islands that it has built in highly disputed

international waters of the South China Sea. China also continues its aggressive naval tactics to intimidate such neighboring countries as Japan and the Philippines and continues to bully other countries that try to exercise their right to navigate international waters in the region.

North Korea maintains its nuclear arsenal, and past tests have hinted at the ability of North Korean missiles to reach targets in the United States. Although little demonstrated progress has been made on denuclearization, Kim Jong-un's regime has decreased the frequency of its missile tests and toned down hostile rhetoric toward the West as it appears to pursue increased engagement with the current U.S. Administration.

Terrorism based in Afghanistan continues to challenge the stability of that country. To the extent that various groups based in the region straddling the border with Pakistan remain potent and active, they also remain a threat to the stability of Pakistan, which is a matter of concern given Pakistan's status as a nuclear power and its sustained frictions with India, also a nuclear power. However, fatalities resulting from terrorist attacks within Pakistan have declined steadily and significantly since 2009.

In addition, Iran's efforts to acquire more advanced military capabilities have been supported by increased cooperation with Russia. Iran's growing military presence in Syria and active support of the various terrorist groups operating in the Middle East continue to undermine regional security conditions and therefore to threaten the regional interests of the U.S.

With these threats taken together, the globalized threat to U.S. vital national interests as a whole during 2018 remained "high."

Threats to U.S. Vital Interests

SEVERE	HIGH	ELEVATED	GUARDED	LOW

Behavior of Threats

	HOSTILE	AGGRESSIVE	TESTING	ASSERTIVE	BENIGN
Russia		✔			
Iran		✔			
Middle East Terrorism	✔				
Af-Pak Terrorism			✔		
China		✔			
North Korea			✔		
OVERALL		✔			

Capability of Threats

	FORMIDABLE	GATHERING	CAPABLE	ASPIRATIONAL	MARGINAL
Russia	✔				
Iran		✔			
Middle East Terrorism			✔		
Af-Pak Terrorism			✔		
China	✔				
North Korea		✔			
OVERALL		✔			

Threats to U.S. Vital Interests

	SEVERE	HIGH	ELEVATED	GUARDED	LOW
Russia		✔			
Iran		✔			
Middle East Terrorism		✔			
Af-Pak Terrorism			✔		
China		✔			
North Korea		✔			
OVERALL		✔			

The Status of U.S. Military Power

Finally, we assessed the military power of the United States in three areas: capability, capacity, and readiness. We approached this assessment by military service as the clearest way to link military force size; modernization programs; unit readiness; and (in general terms) the functional combat power (land, sea, and air) represented by each service. We treated the United States' nuclear capability as a separate entity given its truly unique characteristics and constituent elements, from the weapons themselves to the supporting infrastructure that is fundamentally different from the infrastructure that supports conventional capabilities.

These three areas of assessment (capability, capacity, and readiness) are central to the overarching questions of whether the U.S. has a sufficient quantity of appropriately modern military power and whether military units are able to conduct military operations on demand and effectively.

As reported in all previous editions of the *Index*, the common theme across the services and the U.S. nuclear enterprise is one of force degradation resulting from many years of underinvestment, poor execution of modernization programs, and the negative effects of budget sequestration (cuts in funding) on readiness and capacity in spite of the limited and temporary relief from low budget ceilings imposed by the Budget Control Act of 2011. While the military has been heavily engaged in operations, primarily in the Middle East but elsewhere as well, since September 11, 2001, experience is both ephemeral and context-sensitive. Valuable combat experience is lost as the servicemembers who individually gained experience leave the force, and it maintains direct relevance only for future operations of a similar type: Counterinsurgency operations in Iraq, for example, are fundamentally different from major conventional operations against a state like Iran or China.

Thus, although the current Joint Force is experienced in some types of operations, it lacks experience with high-end, major combat operations toward which it has only begun to redirect its training and planning, and it is still aged and shrinking in its capacity for operations.

We characterized the services and the nuclear enterprise on a five-category scale ranging from "very weak" to "very strong," benchmarked against criteria elaborated in the full report. These characterizations should not be construed as reflecting the competence of individual servicemembers or the professionalism of the services or Joint Force as a whole; nor do they speak to the U.S. military's strength relative to other militaries around the world. Rather, they are assessments of the institutional, programmatic, and material health or viability of America's hard military power.

Our analysis concluded with these assessments:

- **Army as "Marginal."** The Army's score rose from "weak" to "marginal" due to an increased number of ready brigade combat teams. The Army has constrained end strength and modernization to improve readiness. However, accepting risks in these areas has enabled the Army to keep roughly half of its force at acceptable levels of readiness. The Army now relies more consistently on its Army National Guard component to reinforce its ability to respond to crises. While the increased funding for training and readiness is good both for the Guard and for the Total Army, it does reveal shortfalls in the Active Army.

- **Navy as "Marginal."** The Navy's overall score for the *2019 Index* is "marginal," the same as in the *2018 Index*. The Navy's emphasis on restoring readiness and increasing its capacity, enabled by increased funding in 2017 and 2018, signals that its overall score could improve in the near future if needed levels of funding are sustained. However, budget instability resulting from continuing resolutions and a return to Budget Control Act limits will negate these improvements and cause future degradation in the Navy's score. While maintaining a global presence (slightly more than one-third of the fleet is deployed on any given day), the Navy has little ability to surge to meet wartime demands. The Navy's decision to defer maintenance has kept ships at sea but also has affected its ability to deploy. The Navy remained just able to meet operational requirements in 2018. Continuing budget shortfalls in its shipbuilding account will hinder the ability of the service to improve its situation, both materially and quantitatively, for the next several years—an even larger problem considering that the Navy has revised its assessment of how many ships it needs to 355, which is much less than the 400 ships called for in this *Index*.

- **Air Force as "Marginal."** The Air Force is scored as "marginal" overall. This score has trended downward over the past few years largely because of a drop in "capacity" that has not effectively changed and a readiness score of "weak." The shortage of pilots and flying time for those pilots degrades the ability of the Air Force to generate the amount and quality of combat air power that would be needed to meet wartime requirements. Although the Air Force could eventually win a single major regional contingency in any theater, the attrition rates would be significantly higher than those sustained by a ready, well-trained force.

- **Marine Corps as "Weak."** The Corps continues to deal with readiness challenges driven by the combination of high operational tempo and the lingering effects of procurement delays. Aviation remained one of the largest challenges for the Corps in 2018, driven by high demand for Marine Air-Ground Task Forces and sustainment challenges within its legacy fleet of aircraft, and the Corps has cited modernization of its aviation platforms as the single most effective means to increase readiness within the service. Select units and platforms have seen mild readiness improvements as a result of increased funding for spare parts and maintenance requirements. However, Marine operating forces as a whole continue to average a two-to-one deployment-to-dwell ratio. At this pace, readiness is consumed as quickly as it is built,

leaving minimal flexibility to respond to contingencies. Although increased funding for readiness and an emphasis on modernization give strong support to the Corps' readiness recovery efforts, the effects will take time to materialize. The combination of capacity shortfalls and the lack of a "ready bench" maintains the Marine Corps' overall strength score of "weak."

- **Nuclear Capabilities as "Marginal."** The U.S. nuclear complex is "trending toward strong," but this assumes that the U.S. maintains its commitment to modernization and allocates needed resources accordingly. Without this commitment, this overall score will degrade rapidly to "weak." Continued attention to this mission is therefore critical. Although a bipartisan commitment has led to continued progress on U.S. nuclear forces modernization and warhead sustainment, these programs remain threatened by potential future fiscal uncertainties. The infrastructure that supports nuclear programs is aged, and nuclear test readiness has revealed troubling problems within the forces. Additionally, the United States has conducted fewer tests of launch vehicles than in previous years. On the plus side, the 2018 Nuclear Posture Review articulates nuclear weapons policy grounded in realities of international developments and clearly articulates commitment to extended deterrence. The commitment to warhead life-extension programs, the exercise of skills that are critical for the development of new nuclear warheads, and the modernization of nuclear delivery platforms represent a positive trend that should be maintained. Averaging the subscores across the nuclear enterprise in light of our concerns about the future results in an overall score of "marginal."

In the aggregate, the United States' military posture is rated "marginal" and features both positive and negative trends: progress in bringing some new equipment into the force, filling gaps in manpower, and rebuilding some stocks of munitions and repair parts alongside worrisome trends in force readiness, declining strength in key areas like trained pilots, and continued uncertainty across the defense budget.

Overall, the *2019 Index* concludes that the current U.S. military force is likely capable of meeting the demands of a single major regional conflict while also attending to various presence and engagement activities but that it would be very hard-pressed to do more and certainly would be ill-equipped to handle two nearly simultaneous major regional contingencies. The limits imposed on defense spending and the programmatic volatility created by continuing resolutions, passed in lieu of formal budgets approved on schedule, have kept the military services small, aging, and under significant pressure. Essential maintenance continues to be deferred, the availability of fewer units for operational deployments increases the frequency and length of deployments, and old equipment continues to be extended while programmed replacements are either delayed or beset by developmental difficulties.

The military services have continued to prioritize readiness for current operations by shifting funding to deployed or soon-to-deploy units while sacrificing the ability to keep non-deployed units in "ready" condition; delaying, reducing, extending, or canceling modernization programs; and sustaining the reduction in size and number of military units. While Congress and the new Administration took positive steps to stabilize funding for 2018 and 2019 through the Bipartisan Budget Agreement of 2018, they have not overturned the Budget Control Act that otherwise caps defense spending and, absent additional legislative action, will reassert its damaging effects in 2020. Without a real commitment to increases in modernization, capacity, and readiness accounts over the next few years, a significant positive turn in the threat environment, or a reassessment of core U.S. security interests, America's military branches will continue to be strained to meet the missions they are called upon to fulfil.

As currently postured, the U.S. military is only marginally able to meet the demands of defending America's vital national interests.

U.S. Military Power

	VERY WEAK	WEAK	MARGINAL	STRONG	VERY STRONG
Army			✓		
Navy			✓		
Air Force			✓		
Marine Corps		✓			
Nuclear			✓		
OVERALL			✓		

U.S. Military Power: Army

	VERY WEAK	WEAK	MARGINAL	STRONG	VERY STRONG
Capacity		✔			
Capability			✔		
Readiness				✔	
OVERALL			✔		

U.S. Military Power: Navy

	VERY WEAK	WEAK	MARGINAL	STRONG	VERY STRONG
Capacity		✔			
Capability			✔		
Readiness			✔		
OVERALL			✔		

U.S. Military Power: Air Force

	VERY WEAK	WEAK	MARGINAL	STRONG	VERY STRONG
Capacity			✔		
Capability			✔		
Readiness		✔			
OVERALL			✔		

U.S. Military Power: Marine Corps

	VERY WEAK	WEAK	MARGINAL	STRONG	VERY STRONG
Capacity		✔			
Capability			✔		
Readiness		✔			
OVERALL		✔			

U.S. Military Power: Nuclear

	VERY WEAK	WEAK	MARGINAL	STRONG	VERY STRONG
Nuclear Stockpile				✔	
Delivery Platform Reliability			✔		
Warhead Modernization		✔			
Delivery Systems Modernization				✔	
Nuclear Weapons Complex		✔			
National Labs Talent			✔		
Force Readiness			✔		
Allied Assurance				✔	
Nuclear Test Readiness		✔			
OVERALL			✔		

Supplying the Manpower That America's National Security Strategy Demands

Blaise Misztal and Jack Rametta[1]

Introduction

The first mention of the military in our nation's founding document refers, perhaps not surprisingly, to the authority, vested in Congress, to create an armed force in the first place. Article 1, Section 8 of the Constitution imbues the legislative branch with the power to "raise and support Armies." However, the Constitution provides little guidance as to what else Congress should take into account in raising an Army.

Fortunately, George Washington, soon to be our first commander in chief, laid out his vision for the U.S. military. Washington's "Sentiments on a Peace Establishment," written in 1783 three years before he assumed the presidency, might be the first treatise on American strategy.[2] In it, he of course touches on traditional questions of strategy—what threats the Army must defend against, where it should be positioned, or how large it should be—but Washington delves most deeply into questions related to the *who*, not the what or how, of military force: how to recruit troops, how long they should serve, the ideal composition of the military and officer corps, criteria for promoting troops, how to determine pay, and even the appropriateness of providing rum in soldiers' rations (vinegar, it turns out, is better).

As this document was meant for the "Commencement of our Military system," Washington argued that this focus on military personnel was necessary because it was "the proper time to introduce new and beneficial regulations, and to expunge all customs, which from experience have been found unproductive of general good."[3] The questions that Washington raises go beyond concerns about an incipient armed force and are critical to the strength of any military, but particularly one that depends, as the U.S. military does, on voluntary service.

Indeed, one could argue that the unrivaled superiority of the American armed forces over the past 70 years can be attributed in large part to the willingness of lawmakers and defense leaders to revisit and revise how servicemembers are recruited, managed, promoted, paid, and retained. The set of laws and policies that manage these functions, known collectively as the defense personnel system, provides the manpower supply—not just in terms of numbers, but also in terms of rank, skills, and specialties—that America's military needs to execute its mission and America's National Security Strategy demands.[4]

Although there is a surprising degree of continuity between the military envisioned by Washington and the one that exists today, the personnel system has evolved significantly over the past two-and-a-quarter centuries, shifting from volunteer militias to conscription and then finally to an all-volunteer standing force, accompanied by the growth of compensation and benefits and the inclusion of women. Many of these changes have been instituted in the past seven decades and reflect the need to ensure that the force is able to protect American interests as effectively as possible in a changing security environment. The personnel system utilized by today's military, for example, was enshrined in statute shortly after World War II and was updated to address the evolving strategic context of the Cold War.

Given the currently shifting and ambiguous strategic landscape in which threats range from the high end (Russia and China) to the low (non-state actors), and with the military's missions varying from the technological (defending cyberspace) to the personal (security assistance), it might be worth evaluating whether the current personnel system is in need of another update. This sentiment is reflected in the FY 2019 National Defense Authorization Act, which made several statutory changes in the officer promotion system to allow for more flexible military career paths. The questions that should drive such an analysis, U.S. Naval War College Professor Jacquelyn Schneider suggests, include:

- "What does the warrior of the future look like?"

- "What are the roles and missions the United States will need to prepare its people for?"

- "What are the technologies those warriors must master in order to succeed at their mission?"[5]

The greater the variance between the answers to those questions and the servicemembers produced by the current system, the more reform the system might require.

The Evolution of "Up-or-Out": From World War II to DOPMA

World War II: The Origins of "Up-or-Out." While the origins of the modern U.S. military and some of the institutional structures can be traced back to the early years of the Republic, most of today's personnel policy emerged from the World Wars and their aftermath. For example, while conscription has been in use in a variety of different forms since the Revolutionary War,[6] the modern draft originated in World War I (when the phrase "selective service" was first coined).[7] And while basic units of the Army (and later the Navy, Air Force, and Marines), such as officers and enlisted personnel, date from well before the colonial era, the function of those components morphed with the evolution of modern military technology and strategies.

Before World War II began, the Army was ill-prepared (from a personnel perspective) for a large-scale conflict: The total number of officers before the war was only 15,000; older senior officers populated the ranks; and there were limited opportunities for new junior officers to proceed up the ladder.[8] The enlisted force swelled as the United States entered the war, rising from 269,023 in 1940 to 1,462,315 in 1941 to 8,266,373 at its height in 1945.[9] However, there were not enough experienced officers to lead these new troops effectively. At the time, the Army's promotion system was based on seniority, and Congress retained strict control of the number of officers allowed at each rank. This created a significant logjam for promotions between the two world wars. Then Army Chief of Staff and later Secretary of Defense George Marshall gained President Roosevelt's approval to address the issue by culling the Army's senior ranks in 1940.[10] The following year, Congress passed the Army Vitalization Act of 1941,[11] giving Army command further discretion to open senior slots to junior officers for promotion and thereby allowing new officers to be commissioned.

Problems with the seniority system persisted throughout the war because it was nearly impossible to remove officers from the service. Congressional approval was repeatedly required to fix the bloated, aging officer corps. By the end of the war, the Army had more than 385,000 officers,[12] about 19 times more than before the war began. After the war, testifying during hearings on the proposed Officer Personnel Act of 1947, General Dwight D. Eisenhower, then Army Chief of Staff, told the Senate Armed Services Committee that:

I think that no great argument would have to be presented to show that our promotion system [seniority] has been unsatisfactory. Until we got to the grade of general officer, it was absolutely a lock-step promotion; and short of almost crime being committed by an officer, there were ineffectual ways of eliminating a man.[13]

General Eisenhower further explained that:

If you look at General Marshall's difficulties in 1940 and 1941 I believe you will find that of the people he could make division commanders, and corps commanders, and certainly there were not over five of them who went through this war. All the rest of them had to be replaced and gotten out of the way and younger men had to come along and take over the job.

We must keep this corps vital and youthful.[14]

Congress heeded Eisenhower's call and allowed for the drastic expansion of the officer corps.

While congressional action was required to clear the Army's logjams, the Navy operated quite differently. Instead of employing a seniority system for promotions, the Navy relied on an *up-or-out* promotion system, which holds that officers must separate from service after a predetermined length of time if they are passed over for promotion.[15] (In the modern force, with few exceptions, officers passed over twice for promotion must separate from service.) Compared to a seniority system, up-or-out has several advantages.

- First, and most important, it ensures that junior officers have opportunities to climb the ranks, preventing stalwart senior officers from occupying their posts for indefinite periods of time.

- Second, up-or-out is meant to be a meritocratic system that allows talented

servicemembers to steadily climb the ranks, while a system based on seniority merely rewards time in rank.

Given its real and perceived advantages, up-or-out was applied uniformly across the services for permanent promotions after World War II with the passage of the Officer Personnel Act (OPA) of 1947. The services still had flexibility for temporary assignments.[16] The OPA also made a series of other policy changes with the goals of providing uniformity between the Army and the Navy, emphasizing "youth and vigor," and creating a force that could remobilize quickly if necessary.[17]

The 1954 Officer Grade Limitation Act (OGLA) further solidified up-or-out by imposing statutory limitations on the number of regular and reserve officers that could serve at each rank for all grades above major and eliminating the loophole in OPA which did not impose limitations on temporary promotions.[18] The last major change in personnel policy to occur before the end of the draft era in 1973 was the codification of the majority of U.S. military policy into Title X of the U.S. Code after the Korean War. Title X unified most existing permanent statutory military policies, including the OPA and OGLA, under one heading.

At the time, there was widespread agreement among military and civilian experts that up-or-out was a significant improvement. It was designed for the specific security environment in which the United States found itself at the time and for the military strategies it devised to manage that environment. World War II and the Korean War required the services to marshal large and bottom-heavy armies that were quickly assembled through the draft: U.S. peak military personnel was 12,209,238 in 1945 as compared with 458,365 in 1940.[19] These conscripted forces needed the steady leadership of experienced, competent, and energetic officers in order to fight and win the large-scale, industrial ground and naval battles that defined this era of war. Policymakers believed that enlisted and junior-officer personnel, brought in through the draft, could be trained quickly for war but that more experienced commanders needed more time to prepare and could not therefore be recruited swiftly during a crisis. Consequently, the military maintained a much higher percentage of officers than it had previously. "In 1945," according to the Bipartisan Policy Center, "the military had a ratio of approximately 1.3 field-grade officers for every 100 enlisted personnel. Five years later, the ratio stood at 4 to 100."[20]

Moreover, in keeping with the strategic need for officers who could lead fresh recruits into battle, because up-or-out was intended to be meritocratic, the promotion path and criteria created by the post–World War II personnel system emphasized and rewarded the ability to command. Nevertheless:

> It is worth noting that even in 1947 some senators objected to the up-or-out personnel system, correctly noting that the retirement system would incentivize many, if not most, officers to retire from military service in their 40s. Senator Guy Cordon (R–OR) stated his concerns bluntly, saying that for those who reach the rank of colonel, the new personnel system "would mean that the average officer, figuring that he received his commission at age 22, would be forced to retire at 52 years of age. This seems to me to be a most wasteful and illogical requirement, particularly for the technical services." Senator Harry Byrd (D–VA) agreed, saying, "That seems to me mighty early to retire a man, at 52."[21]

Grinding Gears: The Shift to a Professionalized All-Volunteer Force. The era of the all-volunteer force brought significant changes to personnel policy beginning in 1968, when soon-to-be President Richard Nixon made a campaign promise to end conscription. That promise gave rise to the Gates Commission, a group of notable experts chaired by former Secretary of Defense Tom Gates fashioned to examine the viability of an all-volunteer force. On February 20, 1970, the commission officially and unanimously recommended to President Nixon that the United States shift to an all-volunteer force (AVF). Nixon accepted the committee's recommendation, and by 1973, the draft was officially discontinued.[22]

Multiple causes contributed to the demise of the draft, but the evolving strategic context and manpower needs played a role.[23] The Vietnam War showed that servicemembers who had been drafted were much more prone to disciplinary problems, while an AVF was expected to be more professional and motivated to serve. Furthermore, turnover rates were expected to be lower among enlisted service members in an AVF, which would result in longer careers and more experienced personnel.[24]

Several factors were expected to contribute to this evolution, including longer initial enlistments for volunteers, historically higher rates of reenlistment among volunteers, and generally higher pay and morale among volunteers as compared to draftees. In addition, members of an AVF would receive more on-the-job training and were expected, as a result, to be more productive and effective than members of a draft force.[25] All of these factors illustrate the benefit of an AVF over a conscripted force: Its servicemembers are better motivated, better trained, and more likely to serve for longer periods of time, all of which contributes to improved military readiness and efficiency.

There also were strategic reasons for shifting to an AVF at this point in history. Britain, which switched to an AVF in 1957, had simultaneously shifted its defense policies to emphasize nuclear deterrence over the utilization of land troops.[26] The U.S. military was undertaking a similar strategic and political shift in the 1970s away from major set-piece battles and a focus on mobilization toward the possibility of "come-as-you-are" warfare, where troops would quickly mobilize to respond to an immediate threat with little time to conscript fresh recruits.[27]

As the all-volunteer force emerged, policymakers slowly began to realize that in order to retain talent, they would need to compete with the private sector, especially in terms of compensation. This lag occurred even though the final report of the Gates Commission recommended various changes in both the officer and enlisted personnel systems including substantial pay increases and compensation reforms.[28] For the first time in U.S. History, the military began to manage its enlisted personnel *intentionally*.

As analysts at the RAND Corporation note, the history of enlisted personnel policy is a history of responses to immediate events, not long-term policy strategies.[29] For nearly all of American history, enlisted personnel were rapidly conscripted or organized in response to a forthcoming conflict, paid very little, and disbanded quickly following the end of the conflict. Furthermore, the military did not have to compete with the private market for talent because recruits were required to serve either through direct conscription or through the formation of ad hoc regional militias.[30]

DOPMA: One-Size-Fits-All. While the age of the all-volunteer force began in 1973, Congress waited nearly a decade to reform the personnel and promotion systems to account for this shift. Reform finally came in 1981 with the Defense Officer Personnel Management Act (DOPMA) and the Reserve Officer Personnel Management Act (ROPMA). These reforms were notable for a few reasons.

First, DOPMA brought changes to the personnel and promotions systems, including:

- An officer structure simplified and standardized across the services to 10 ranks (O-1 through O-10);

- A standardized promotion system for *regular career officers*;

- A legal *DOPMA grade table* for both permanent and temporary promotion (services previously had greater discretion over temporary promotions);

- A "sliding-scale" grade effect for officers (when the officer corps shrinks, the

number of field-grade (0-4 through 0-6) officers increases).

This standardization of career paths was largely welcomed, with a Member of the House of Representatives observing that "[t]o attract quality officers, we must be able to offer lieutenants and captains a reasonable, reliable career progression."[31] The Assistant Secretary of Defense for Manpower, Reserve Affairs and Logistics at the time, Robert B. Pirie, Jr., also praised the bill as "a viable piece of legislation that on one hand represent[ed] the wishes of the Congress and on the other satisfie[d] the needs of the Department."[32] DOPMA's reforms were a welcome change in a system instituted more than 20 years earlier and were instituted for much the same reason many are advocating for reforms today: the strategic need for high-quality officers.

These changes enshrined the one-size-fits-all military career, particularly for officers. This career, which is about the same length for most officers (regardless of specialty), is highly predictable from a management perspective and gives the services a stable officer corps in peacetime.[33] Still, while DOPMA was a wide-ranging law with significant effects, RAND analysts categorized it as a document that, rather than being truly revolutionary, merely expanded upon the post–World War II status quo.[34] This can be seen in Chart 1, which illustrates how, despite the changes in the OPA framework instituted by DOPMA, the basic system remained largely the same

While DOPMA and ROPMA provided reform for officers, Congress barely touched the enlisted side of the ledger during this period. The policies that govern enlisted personnel mimic the officer side (i.e., strict time-in-grade limitation, up-or-out, etc.), and, unlike officer personnel policy, are largely under DOD's discretion. It is worth noting that DOD does not often pursue radical changes in enlisted policy. Similarly, while ROPMA provided some clarity on the role of reserve officers in the overall structure of the forces, reserve personnel were still not well integrated with the active

CHART 1

Up or Out Promotion Path Pre- and Post-Defense Officer Personnel Management Act

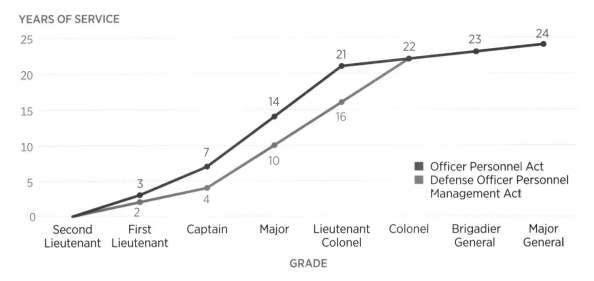

YEARS OF SERVICE

Legend:
- ■ Officer Personnel Act
- ■ Defense Officer Personnel Management Act

GRADE (x-axis): Second Lieutenant, First Lieutenant, Captain, Major, Lieutenant Colonel, Colonel, Brigadier General, Major General

Officer Personnel Act data points: 3, 7, 14, 21, 22, 23, 24
Defense Officer Personnel Management Act data points: 2, 4, 10, 16

SOURCE: H.R. 3800, Officer Personnel Act of 1947, Public Law 381, 61 Stat. 795, 80th Congress, 1st Sess., Title V, §512, https://www.loc.gov/law/help/statutes-at-large/80th-congress/session-1/c80s1ch512.pdf (accessed July 21, 2018).

☎ heritage.org

component—something that remains true today. Many analysts have noted that the reserve component is both culturally segregated and underutilized.[35]

After DOPMA and ROPMA, only one other piece of legislation attempted serious reform: the Goldwater–Nichols Act of 1986.

Goldwater–Nichols: A Push for Interoperability. Goldwater–Nichols was enacted in response to rising frustration that the forces were not sufficiently interoperable—that is, that they were not able to fight efficiently as a joint force. This frustration arose from military engagements in Iran (Operation Desert One); Grenada (Operation Urgent Fury); and Beirut.[36] During Desert One, an operation to extract hostages from Tehran, the U.S. lost eight servicemembers and significant amounts of equipment. The senior commander's description of the operation provides some insight into the causes of its failure: "four commanders at the scene without visible identification, incompatible radios, and no agreed-upon plan."[37]

Operations in Grenada were generally considered to be a success, but groups from the different services still had an extremely difficult time communicating with one another, particularly coordinating fire support. A Senate study of the Grenada mission concluded that "[t]he Services continue to operate as largely independent agencies, even at the level of the unified commands."[38]

In Beirut, where 241 servicemembers were killed in a tragic terrorist bombing, military leaders and policymakers further concluded that a distinct lack of interservice interoperability was to blame and that the combatant commanders still did not have enough direct authority to direct operations in the field.[39] Former Chairman of the Joint Chiefs of Staff Admiral William Crowe stated that:

> Like every other unified [combatant] commander, I could only operate through the Army, Navy, Air Force and Marine component commanders, who stood between me and the forces in the field.... Component commanders reported to their own service chiefs for administration, logistics and training matters, and the service chiefs could use this channel to outflank the unified commander. There was sizeable potential for confusion and conflict.[40]

As a result, Congress added additional requirements to the standard officer career path with the intention of improving the force's overall interoperability, especially regarding the experiences of general and flag officers (GFOs).[41] These policies included a requirement that all officers selected for the rank of GFO must have served in a joint duty assignment and stipulated that GFOs' joint duty assignments would be for two years, compared with three years for other officers. It further required all general/flag officers to attend a joint Capstone course.[42] This was the further evolution of and next logical step in the U.S. military's consistent emphasis on leadership and command ability since World War II.

One consequence of this change was the addition of four to five years to the standard military career. Some, including former DOD Undersecretary for Personnel and Readiness Bernard Rostker, were less than supportive of the change. In 2015, Rostker testified to Congress that Goldwater–Nichols "came at the cost of having less-experienced uniformed managers of the services."[43]

While ensuring that all general and flag officers would have joint force experience was generally accepted as a positive development and was intended to prevent a dangerous fissure from opening between operating forces and command staff without practical field experience, applying the policy uniformly across the officer corps effectively mandated that officers undergo training necessary only for a small subset. Goldwater–Nichols, along with the other reforms of the 1980s, led some to criticize the officer personnel system as "grooming all officers to be chief of staff."[44]

Prior to recent reforms included in the FY 2019 National Defense Authorization Act (NDAA), these were the last major reforms to the active-duty, enlisted, and reserve components, and they led to the structure of the armed forces as it stands today.

Does the System Work? The Challenges Facing America's Future Force

Overall, while the U.S. military personnel and promotions systems have evolved since World War II—thanks to DOPMA, ROPMA, Goldwater–Nichols, and other pieces of reform legislation—their fundamental structure and intent have remained largely the same. Ultimately, the majority of the force, especially ground-combat units, has continued to be made up of young and fit personnel, while officers have been presented with a single, uniform path for advancement with promotions based on and leading to increasingly higher levels of command responsibility.

The military created by this up-or-out, post–World War II personnel system has achieved significant strategic victories: It won the Cold War and protected the nation for 70 years. The system achieved precisely the outcomes that it was designed to achieve. Yet, given the changing security environment and new strategic needs, there are calls from some quarters for a more fundamental reimagining of the personnel system.

While core U.S. national security interests have largely remained constant in the quarter-century since the end of the Cold War, the threats arrayed against those interests are spreading geographically, transforming strategically, and evolving technologically. Once viewed as archaic, the threat of great-power conflict with the resurgence of Russia and rise of China is relevant once again. Add to that the more diffuse threats from malicious non-state actors that have mastered the techniques of unconventional warfare while metastasizing across much of the world. The tremendous technological advances made by rogue nations could allow them to undermine much of the traditional military superiority long enjoyed by U.S. forces,[45] and new domains like cyberspace allow weaker powers to exploit unforeseen vulnerabilities.[46]

New Threats, New Challenges. In this new normal, a military that is designed only to wage conventional war against great powers will likely not be adequate. Success against future enemies on new battlefields will require not only physical strength and vigor, but also (and increasingly) mental agility, technical experience, and rapid innovation. As the 2018 National Defense Strategy states, "a more lethal, resilient, and rapidly innovating Joint Force...will sustain American influence and ensure favorable balances of power that safeguard the free and open international order."[47] Any changes in the strategies the military employs to counter these new threats and keep the nation safe should be reflected in the policies responsible for creating a force capable of executing those strategies, and this most definitely includes policies involving personnel. However, there are differing opinions on whether personnel reforms are necessary and, if they are, how extensive those reforms should be.

The most obvious personnel issue raised by the potential for conflicts waged as much on virtual as on physical battlefields is the need to attract a highly skilled and technologically savvy military workforce. But while constant news of increasingly grave cyber threats and the creation of a Cyber Force presents the most visible manifestation of the role of technology in a 21st century military, the implications are far more widespread and complicated. As Professor Schneider notes, "The defense community needs to do a better job [of] thinking about what this human looks like and how the U.S. military culture can adapt not only to technology, but [to] what we need for the warrior of the future."[48]

Sophisticated networked communications, drone-enabled reconnaissance, and even the integration of electronic warfare are being incorporated into platoon-level infantry tactics.

Autonomous systems will likely press the military to delegate decision-making to lower grades in order to keep up with the speed of warfare.[49]

Perhaps the skills necessary to thrive in this environment can be taught, with updated military training being sufficient to turn recruits into 21st century warriors, but it is also quite possible that, unlike the physical strength and tactics needed for ground combat, some of the qualities the military will prize most in future servicemembers cannot simply be drilled into them. In that case, those with the skills to navigate this high-tech world could well be hotly pursued by private-sector firms that are able to pay many times more than the military and more interested in honing and maintaining their expertise than in commanding troops. If the military is to attract them, it might have to provide a value proposition other than the current one-size-fits-all career path.[50] To address this issue, the 2019 National Defense Authorization Act included provisions to allow for better-qualified officers to be placed at the top of promotion lists and for credit to be awarded to officers for experiences outside of traditional military service.

Another area in which changes in how the military carries out its mission affect how it recruits and manages personnel is train, advise, and assist missions. As the United States looks to other partner nations to share the burden of providing for mutual security, building the capacity of partner forces is likely to become a large part of the U.S. military mission. Traditionally, these operations are given to Special Operations Forces, who are comfortable working and embedding with partner militaries because of their high levels of training and experience. While Special Operations Forces offer impressive and unique capabilities, they have been heavily utilized over the past 15 years of fighting. Many such units have been required to focus their energy on counterterrorism missions, which makes it more challenging to prepare for the train, advise, and assist missions.[51]

To meet the train, advise, and assist demand in the future, the military will have to turn to conventional units to satisfy much of the need. The cadre of mature, experienced, and well-trained personnel required for these missions can be found in the field-grade and non-commissioned officer corps, but the current promotion system also calls on servicemembers in these grades to be checking boxes as they carry out joint and other service-specific key assignments rather than devoting time in the field to teaching partner militaries. While these "check boxes" were initially established with the intent of ensuring that officers had experience with a wide scope of military affairs and operations, expanding security force assistance brigades within the conventional force would most likely require alternative promotion paths and more-flexible career models for both officers and enlisted personnel.

Relatedly, even as the military might increasingly need to rely on its Foreign Area Officers—servicemembers with specific linguistic, political, and cultural understanding of partner nations in which the military operates—there is currently little incentive for the best and brightest to pursue these careers Specializing in a single country instead of commanding forces is currently not the way to advance to senior grades.

Such concerns about whether the current system can attract and retain the skills the military will need to win against 21st century adversaries led the Center for a New American Security's Amy Schafer to argue that "[w]ithout a significant and long-overdue investment in our military's human capital, the United States will struggle to maintain military superiority."[52] But there also are reasons to favor the current system. Mastery of combat arms remains the preeminent demand on the military; changes in military culture that detract from what Secretary of Defense Jim Mattis calls "lethality" or tinkering with career paths, which makes it more difficult for military planners to generate a force that is deployable and ready to fight at a moment's notice, could do more to harm American military strength than to bolster it. Any changes in defense personnel systems must therefore be driven by careful assessment of the strategic environment and the force needed to protect U.S. interests in that environment.

A Whole New World. As the strategic challenges facing the military have evolved, so too have the ambitions, expectations, and lifestyles of U.S. society. In 1960, just over a decade after the passage of the Officer Personnel Act of 1947, only 25 percent of married couples with children had two income earners. In the 1970s, when the draft ended, this figure was around 32 percent.[53] Today, over 60 percent of married couples with children are dual earners.[54] This is a tremendous change and presents a particular challenge for a military system that typically relocates its personnel every two to three years. The operational tempo and ever-present duty requirements of the military often prevent spouses—the majority of whom are women—from holding regular jobs.[55] These challenges are gaining more visibility; in the most recent NDAA, Congress ordered DOD to review the effects of frequent change-of-stations on military families and military readiness.

Another factor to consider is who is serving. A relatively small percentage of the U.S. population serves in the military—"0.4 percent of the population in 2015," according to the Pew Research Center.[56] But military service is neither a duty heeded nor a burden shared by all. "[F]or a growing number of Americans," Defense Secretary Robert Gates warned in 2010, "service in the military, no matter how laudable, is something for other people to do."[57] Furthermore, those who join the military tend to have one thing in common: They come from military families.

A recent Blue Star Family survey shows that nearly three-fifths of servicemembers and their families have at least two other immediate family members who serve or have served in the military. According to a Department of Defense study, roughly 80 percent of new recruits have a military family member. The past 16 years of war, budgetary uncertainty, and troop reductions have exhausted the force. If today's troops are the siblings, parents, aunts, and uncles of our future force, wearing them

TABLE 1

Personnel Cost Per Active-Duty Service Member

DOLLAR FIGURES ARE IN 2016 DOLLARS

	FY 2001	FY 2016	% Change, 2001–2016	FY 2017
Active-Duty End-Strength*	1,386,000	1,311,000	–5%	1,301,000
Pay-Like Compensation	$50,670	$73,038	44%	$74,001
Basic Pay	$33,326	$40,450	21%	$41,299
Retirement Costs	$12,560	$16,635	32%	$15,906
Normal Pension Costs	$12,560	$12,699	1%	$12,102
TRICARE For Life	$0	$3,936	—	$3,804
Defense Health Program	$11,661	$24,940	114%	$25,979
Total Personnel Costs	**$74,890**	**$114,614**	**53%**	**$115,886**

* Not including Reservists or National Guard.
SOURCE: Bipartisan Policy Center, "The Military Compensation Conundrum: Rising Costs, Declining Budgets, and a Stressed Force Caught in the Middle," September 2016, p. 11, https://bipartisanpolicy.org/wp-content/uploads/2016/09/BPC-Defense-Personnel-Compensation.pdf (accessed July 21, 2018).

☎ heritage.org

down could limit tomorrow's recruits. Unfortunately, Blue Star Family data already show a worrying drop in the willingness of military families to recommend service to their children or to any young person.[58]

This illustrates another issue facing America's military: the civilian–military divide, which refers to the disconnect between America's servicemembers and its people at large as a result of cultural, locational, and other differences.[59] As the gap continues to grow, young Americans from nonmilitary families will likely become less inclined to consider volunteering for military service simply because they have no meaningful personal contact with or awareness of it.[60]

Meanwhile, leaning too heavily on one small segment of our population also could weaken our military. Already, because of obesity, a criminal record, or lack of educational achievement, only about a quarter of all 17-to-24-year-olds are eligible to serve. With so few able to serve, the military could struggle to fill its ranks should military families stop handing down their ethic of service.[61]

Experts in the field firmly believe that personnel policies are critical to meeting defense and national security objectives[62] and that defense personnel policy should therefore be driven by the objective of ensuring or improving military effectiveness, not by other social or political goals. It very well might be true that in some circumstances, the armed forces are institutionally stronger, more coherent, better trained and disciplined, and more dedicated to their mission when they stand apart from the general population, but this is not always the case, and the historical record shows several examples of culturally distinct militaries performing worse on the battlefield than their material strength of men and arms would otherwise have predicted.[63]

A responsible and effective personnel system must be mindful of the relation between the military and society, monitoring it for potential problems that could negatively affect the ability to attract sufficient recruits to meet end strength requirements—as the services' personnel chief recently told Congress

CHART 2

How Military Compensation Compares to Private Industry

YEAR-ON-YEAR PERCENT CHANGE IN ACTIVE DUTY BASE PAY AND PRIVATE INDUSTRY COMPENSATION

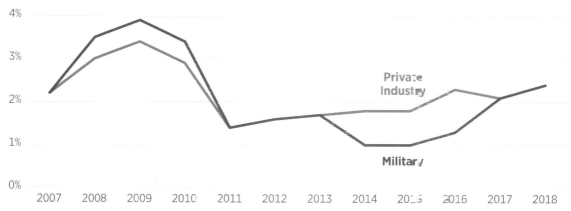

SOURCE: Bipartisan Policy Center, "The Military Compensation Conundrum: Rising Costs, Declining Budgets, and a Stressed Force Caught in the Middle," September 2016, p. 13, https://bipartisanpolicy.org/wp-content/uploads/2016/09/BPC-Defense -Personnel- Compensation.pdf (accessed July 21, 2018).

🏛 heritage.org

is already happening[64]—or to attract those with the skills and talents needed to execute military strategy. According to Representative Mike Coffman (R–CO), Chairman of the House Armed Services Committee's Military Personnel Subcommittee, recruitment and retention challenges are exacerbated "by a lessened overall propensity to serve, reduced pool of qualified candidates and a robust economy."[65] Some feel that this requires a reevaluation of traditional personnel regulations.

In an effort to address this, the 2019 NDAA repealed the age limit on enlisting in the officer corps and took steps to allow for credit to be awarded for nontraditional experiences. Keeping this in mind, closing the civilian–military divide should be the focus of personnel reforms in the coming years.

Budgetary Concerns. Yet another potential barrier to readiness is the increased reliance on fiscal retention bonuses to keep servicemembers in the military. As a result of the Budget Control Act of 2011, caps were placed on most defense spending. These caps

have led to a significant reduction in the defense budget (relative to previous estimates) and cuts in total military end strength and the operations and maintenance budget.[66] This in turn affects military readiness, as there are fewer troops with fewer supplies. In addition to the budget cuts, this issue is exacerbated by the rising costs of military personnel, in part because of the military's very status as an AVF: Servicemembers must be competitively compensated in relation to the private sector, including costs of health care, retirement, and retention bonuses.[67]

However, as Chart 2 shows, military compensation occasionally still lags behind compensation in the private sector. Given this, and given that DOD has only limited funds to spend, many argue that it is time to reevaluate the system to find ways to incentivize servicemember retention without the use of further financial bonuses.[68] These incentives could address quality-of-life issues such as geographic stability, more opportunities for promotions, and longer assignments.[69]

Air Force Pilot Shortage Is Real, and Getting Worse

PERCENTAGE OF ACTUAL STAFFING LEVEL AUTHORIZATIONS

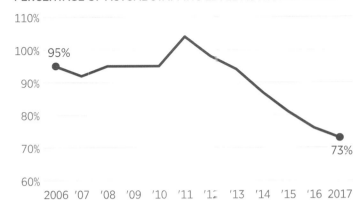

SOURCE: U.S. Government Accountability Office, "Military Personnel: DOD Needs to Reevaluate Fighter Pilot Workforce Requirements," April 11, 2018, p. 11, https://www.gao.gov/products/GAO-18-113 (accessed August 6, 2018).

☎ heritage.org

The Air Force's Recurring Pilot Shortages: A Microcosm

Issues with recruiting and retention affect the service branches in distinct ways. For example, the U.S. military is the world's preeminent air power, yet the Air Force is coming up short on the pilots needed to meet the U.S.'s stated national security objectives. The service is currently short at least 2,000 pilots, and that number is projected to increase substantially in coming years. As with previous shortfalls, the issue is multifaceted. As operations tempo (OPTEMPO) remains high, the service struggles to retain pilots, who feel burned out and overworked. At the same time, because the number of flight hours has decreased, pilots spend less time in the air training and more time on tasks unrelated to combat. Other factors have also contributed to the pilot shortage, including a lack of funding and excessive collateral duties.

Attempts to address the shortage, such as retention bonuses, have failed to stem the tide, and this failure indicates a deeper, structural problem with the Air Force personnel system[70]—a problem that echoes the problems many see in the military's personnel system as a whole. According to Lieutenant General Gina M. Grosso, Air Force Deputy Chief of Staff for Manpower, Personnel and Services,

"Retaining our pilot force goes beyond financial incentives…it's about culture."[71] One fighter pilot who left the service agreed, stating that the reason most pilots leave is the same reason many join in the first place: They want to fly as much as they can, and Air Force pilots are often grounded by excessive administrative work[72] and a lack of available aircraft.[73] A senior Air Force leader has said that fighter pilots average only about 16 flight hours per month.[74]

This disconnect between the needs and wants of airmen and the structure of the Air Force personnel system translates into concrete financial losses for the Pentagon: Lieutenant General Grosso has testified that it costs approximately $11 million "to train a fifth-generation fighter pilot" and that "a 1,200-fighter pilot shortage amounts to a $12 billion capital loss for the Air Force."[75] In addition, in line with the broader historical trends in personnel policy, while the fighter pilot occupation has changed significantly in recent years, the services have not reevaluated fighter squadron requirements.

These changes in the position, which include changes in aircraft technology and tactics, additional training, and the removal of squadron administrative support positions, have led to an unsustainable increase in workload that financial bonuses simply have not alleviated. Air Force officials say these changes have not been incorporated into the assessment of minimum personnel requirements because the Air Force has been prioritizing recapitalizing its fighter aircraft fleet. While the Air Force has attempted to alleviate the pilot workload by hiring contractors, the shortage remains significant.

The pilot shortage illustrates on a smaller scale what the military is experiencing as a whole. Changing strategic needs and technical advancements, as well as increased workload and budget cuts, have caused a troubling decline in U.S. military readiness. To address these problems successfully, we must consider the needs and desires of the servicemembers who are the most fundamental part of American military superiority.

Conclusion

The nation's future national security depends on attracting the service of capable men and women with the necessary skill sets. America's military is nothing without the dedication of those who choose to serve. To ensure that the United States maintains its military advantage over its adversaries, lawmakers and defense leaders will have to evaluate whether the ways in which the military attracts, promotes, and retains servicemembers is contributing to or hindering the creation of a force capable of countering 21st century challenges.

Endnotes

1. The authors wish to acknowledge the contributions to this report made by Mary Farrell, an Intern at the Bipartisan Policy Center.

2. "Washington's Sentiments on a Peace Establishment, 1 May 1783," National Archives, *Founders Online*, last modified June 13, 2018, http://founders.archives.gov/documents/Washington/99-01-02-11202 (accessed August 20, 2018).

3. Ibid.

4. *National Security Strategy of the United States of America*, The White House, December 2017, https://www.whitehouse.gov/wp-content/uploads/2017/12/NSS-Final-12-18-2017-0905.pdf (accessed August 20, 2018).

5. Jacquelyn Schneider, "Blue Hair in the Gray Zone," War on the Rocks, January 10, 2018, https://warontherocks.com/2018/01/blue-hair-gray-zone/ (accessed August 13, 2018).

6. Timothy J. Perri, "The Evolution of Military Conscription in the United States," *The Independent Review*, Vol. 17, No. 3 (Winter 2013), p. 429, http://www.independent.org/pdf/tir/tir_17_03_06_perri.pdf (accessed August 13, 2018).

7. Ibid., p. 432.

8. Bernard Rostker, Harry Thie, James Lacy, Jennifer Kawata, and Susanna Purnell, *The Defense Officer Personnel Management Act of 1980: A Retrospective Assessment* (Santa Monica, CA: RAND Corporation, 1993), p. 3, https://www.rand.org/content/dam/rand/pubs/reports/1993/R4246.pdf (accessed August 21, 2018).

9. U.S. Department of Defense, Directorate for Information Operations and Reports, *Department of Defense Selected Manpower Statistics, Fiscal Year 1997*, 1997, p. 14, http://www.dtic.mil/dtic/tr/fulltext/u2/a347153.pdf#page=20 (accessed August 22, 2018).

10. Rostker, Thie, Lacy, Kawata, and Purnell, *The Defense Officer Personnel Management Act of 1980: A Retrospective Assessment*, pp. 88–89.

11. Ibid., p. 89.

12. Ibid., p. 3.

13. Hearing, *Officer Personnel Act of 1947*, Committee on Armed Services, U.S. Senate, 80th Cong. 1st Sess., July 16, 1947, p. 1, https://babel.hathitrust.org/cgi/pt?id=umn.31951d020979159;view=1up;seq=5 (accessed August 21, 2018).

14. Ibid., p. 10.

15. Bipartisan Policy Center, *Building a F.A.S.T. Force: A Flexible Personnel System for a Modern Military*, March 2017, p. 22, https://cdn.bipartisanpolicy.org/wp-content/uploads/2017/03/BPC-Defense-Building-A-FAST-Force.pdf#page=22 (accessed August 21, 2018).

16. Rostker, Thie, Lacy, Kawata, and Purnell, *The Defense Officer Personnel Management Act of 1980: A Retrospective Assessment*, p. 5.

17. Ibid., p. 91.

18. Colonel Chris Robertson and Lieutenant Colonel Sophie Gainey, "Getting off the Treadmill of Time," *Military Review*, Vol. 89, No. 6 (November–December 2009), p. 105, http://www.armyupress.army.mil/Portals/7/military-review/Archives/English/MilitaryReview_20091231_art016.pdf (accessed August 21, 2018).

19. National World War II Museum, "Research Starters: US Military by the Numbers, US Military Personnel (1939–1945)," https://www.nationalww2museum.org/students-teachers/student-resources/research-starters/research-starters-us-military-numbers (accessed August 21, 2018).

20. Bipartisan Policy Center, *Building a F.A.S.T. Force: A Flexible Personnel System for a Modern Military*, p. 21.

21. Bipartisan Policy Center, *Defense Personnel Systems: The Hidden Threat to a High-Performance Force*, February 2017, p. 8, https://cdn.bipartisanpolicy.org/wp-content/uploads/2017/02/BPC-Defense-Personnel-Systems.pdf (accessed August 21, 2018).

22. Technically, the Selective Service System is still in use, despite the fact that a draft has not been activated in nearly half a century.

23. Bipartisan Policy Center, *Defense Personnel Systems: The Hidden Threat to a High-Performance Force*, p. 9.

24. Congressional Budget Office, *The All-Volunteer Military: Issues and Performance*, July 2007, pp. 7–8, https://www.cbo.gov/sites/default/files/cbofiles/ftpdocs/83xx/doc8313/07-19-militaryvol.pdf (accessed August 21, 2018).

25. Ibid.

26. President's Commission on an All-Volunteer Armed Force, *The Report of the President's Commission on an All-Volunteer Armed Force*, February 1970, pp. 169–170, https://www.rand.org/content/dam/rand/pubs/monographs/MG265/images/webS0243.pdf#page=173 (accessed August 16, 2018).

27. Ibid., p. 13.

28. Ibid., p. 10.

29. Sheila Nataraj Kirby and Harry J. Thie, *Enlisted Personnel Management: A Historical Perspective*, (Santa Monica, CA: RAND Corporation, 1996), http://www.dtic.mil/cti_/tr/fulltext/u2/a321146.pdf (accessed August 22, 2018)

30. Ibid., p. 18.

31. *Congressional Record*, U.S. House of Representatives, 93th Cong., August 5, 1974, p. 26760, https://www.gpo.gov/fdsys/pkg/GPO-CRECB-1974-pt20/pdf/GPO-CRECB-1974-p20-4-2.pdf#page=11 (accessed August 22, 2018).

32. David H. Bent, "DOPMA: An Initial Review," *The Army Lawyer*, Department of the Army Pamphlet 27-50-100, April 1981, p. 3, https://www.loc.gov/rr/frd/Military_Law/pf/04-1981.pdf (accessed August 22, 2018).

33. Rostker, Thie, Lacy, Kawata, and Purnell, *The Defense Officer Personnel Management Act of 1980: A Retrospective Assessment*, p. 12.

34. Ibid., p. v.

35. Bipartisan Policy Center, *Building a F.A.S.T. Force: A Flexible Personnel System for a Modern Military*, p. 60.

36. Kathleen J. McInnis, "Goldwater–Nichols at 30: Defense Reform and Issues for Congress," Congressional Research Service *Report for Members and Committees of Congress*, June 2, 2016, p. 3, https://fas.org/sgp/crs/natsec/R44474.pdf (accessed August 22, 2018).

37. Gregg Garbesi, "U.S. Unified Command," chap. 2 in *America's Viceroys: The Military and U.S. Foreign Policy*, ed. Derek S. Reveron (New York: Palgrave Macmilan, 2004), p. 39, http://library.aceondo.net/ebooks/HISTORY/America%27s_Viceroys_The_Military_and_U_S_Foreign_Policy.pdf (accessed August 22, 2018).

38. McInnis, "Goldwater–Nichols at 30," p. 5.

39. Ibid.

40. Ibid., pp. 5–6.

41. General and flag officers (GFOs) are the most senior military officers (pay grades O–7 to O–10) and hold positions such as members of the Joint Chiefs of Staff, Combatant Commanders, Commander of U.S. Special Operations Command, and Chief of the National Guard, among others. Given their high rank and status, there are certain different personnel regulations that apply specifically to GFOs. See Lawrence Kapp, "General and Flag Officers in the U.S. Armed Forces: Background and Considerations for Congress," Congressional Research Service Report for Members and Committees of Congress, February 18, 2016, https://fas.org/sgp/crs/natsec/R44389.pdf (accessed August 22, 2018).

42. Kristy N. Kamarck, "Goldwater–Nichols and the Evolution of Officer Joint Professional Military Education (JPME)," Congressional Research Service *Report for Members and Committees of Congress*, January 13, 2016, p. 3, https://fas.org/sgp/crs/natsec/R44340.pdf (accessed August 16, 2018).

43. Bernard Rostker, RAND Corporation, "Reforming the American Military Officer Personnel System," testimony presented before the Senate Armed Services Committee on December 2, 2015, p. 5, http://www.rand.org/content/dam/rand/pubs/testimonies/CT400/CT446/RAND_CT446.pdf (accessed August 16, 2018).

44. Bipartisan Policy Center, *Defense Personnel Systems: The Hidden Threat to a High-Performance Force*, p. 11.

45. Robert I. Rotberg, "Repressive, Aggressive, and Rogue Nation-States: How Odious, How Dangerous?" chap. 1 in *Worst of the Worst: Dealing with Repressive and Rogue Nations*, ed. Robert I. Rotberg (Washington: Brookings Institution Press, 2007), pp. 1–39, https://www.brookings.edu/wp-content/uploads/2016/07/worstoftheworst_chapter.pdf (accessed August 22, 2018).

46. Paula Horton, "Weapons of Mass Disrupt o : Dealing with the Asymmetric Threat," SANS Institute *Global Information Assurance Certification Paper*, 2003, https://www.giac.org/paper/gsec/2499/weapons-mass-disruption-dealing-asymmetric-threat/104361 (accessed August 22, 2018).

47. James Mattis, Secretary of Defense, *Summary of the 2018 National Defense Strategy of the United States of America: Sharpening the American Military's Competitive Edge*, p. 1, https://www.defense.gov/Portals/1/Documents/pubs/2018-National-Defense-Strategy-Summary.pdf (accessed August 22, 2018).

48. Schneider, "Blue Hair in the Gray Zone."

49. For example, in a UAV attack, it is necessary to strike quickly, and decision-making may be relegated to the lower-ranking officer manning the drone. Greg Jaffe and Karen DeYoung, "Trump Administration Reviewing Ways to Make it Easier to Launch Drone Strikes," *The Washington Post*, March 13, 2017, https://www.washingtonpost.com/world/national-security/trump-administration-reviewing-ways-to-make-it-easier-to-launch-drone-strikes/2017/03/13/ac39ced0-07f8-11e7-b77c-0047d15a24e0_story.html?utm_term=.211a60aa6f0c (accessed August 21, 2018).

50. Rostker, Thie, Lacy, Kawata, and Purnell, *The Defense Officer Personnel Management Act of 1980: A Retrospective Assessment*, pp. 17–18.

51. Terri Moon Cronk, "Senior Official Outlines U.S. Forces' Missions in Afghanistan," U.S. Department of Defense, May 5, 2016, https://www.defense.gov/News/Article/Article/752718/senior-official-outlines-us-forces-missions-in-afghanistan/ (accessed August 16, 2018).

52. Amy Schafer "Why Military Personnel Reform Matters," War on the Rocks, October 29, 2015, https://warontherocks.com/2015/10/why-military-personnel-reform-matters/ (accessed August 22, 2018).

53. Pew Research Center, "The Rise in Dual Income Households," June 18, 2015, http://www.pewresearch.org/ft_dual-income-households-1960-2012-2/ (accessed August 22, 2018).

54. Ibid.

55. Brooke Goldberg, "Military Spouse Unemployment Rate at Least Four Times Higher Than National Average," Military Officers Association of America, October 6, 2017, http://www.moaa.org/Content/Take-Action/On-Watch/Military-Spouse-Unemployment-Rate-at-Least-Four-Times-Higher-Than-National-Average.aspx (accessed August 16, 2018).

56. Kim Parker, Anthony Cilluffo, and Renee Stepler, "6 Facts About the U.S. Military and Its Changing Demographics," Pew Research Center *FactTank*, April 13, 2017, http://www.pewresearch.org/fact-tank/2017/04/13/6-facts-about-the-u-s-military-and-its-changing-demographics/ (accessed August 22, 2018).

57. Robert M. Gates, "Lecture Delivered at Duke University (All-Volunteer Force)," September 29, 2010, http://archive.defense.gov/Speeches/Speech.aspx?SpeechID=1508 (accessed August 16, 2018).

58. Blue Star Families, *2017 Blue Star Families Military Family Lifestyle Survey: Comprehensive Report*, p. 49, https://bluestarfam.org/wp-content/uploads/2017/03/ComprehensiveReport-33.pdf (accessed August 16, 2018).

59. Robert W. McFarlin IV, "The Overlooked Civilian–Military Divide," *The Hill*, July 15, 2016, http://thehill.com/blogs/congress-blog/presidential-campaign/287817-the-overlooked-civilian-military-divide (accessed August 22, 2018).

60. Ibid.

61. U.S. Department of Defense, Defense Human Resources Activity, Joint Advertising, Market Research & Studies, *Department of Defense Youth Poll Wave 20—December 2010: Overview Report*, JAMRS Report No. 2011-05, September 2011, https://jamrs.defense.gov/Portals/20/Documents/Youth_Poll_20.pdf (accessed August 21, 2013).

62. Radha Iyengar, Brad Carson, Amy Schafer, and John Winkler, "Military Power Is All About People: A Return to Personnel Policy," War on the Rocks, July 27, 2017, https://warontherocks.com/2017/07/military-power-is-all-about-people-a-return-to-personnel-policy/#page=efforts (accessed August 21, 2018).

63. Stephen Peter Rosen, "Military Effectiveness: Why Society Matters," *International Security*, Vol. 9, No. 4 (Spring 1995), pp. 5–31.

64. Lisa Ferdinando, "Military Leaders Highlight Efforts, Challenges in Recruiting, Retention," U.S. Department of Defense, April 13, 2018, https://www.defense.gov/News/Article/Article/1493328/military-leaders-highlight-efforts-challenges-in-recruiting-retention/ (accessed August 16, 2018).

65. Congressional Quarterly, "House Armed Services Subcommittee on Military Personnel Holds Hearing on Fiscal 2019 Military Personnel Posture," CQ Congressional Transcripts, April 13, 2018, http://www.cq.com/doc/congressionaltranscripts-5298857?7 (accessed August 22, 2017).

66. Bipartisan Policy Center, *The Building Blocks of a Ready Military: People, Funding, Tempo*, January 2017, pp. 15–17, https://bipartisanpolicy.org/wp-content/uploads/2017/01/BPC-Defense-Military-Readiness.pdf (accessed August 21, 2018).

67. Bipartisan Policy Center, *The Military Compensation Conundrum: Rising Costs, Declining Budgets, and a Stressed Force Caught in the Middle*, September 2016, p. 16, https://bipartisanpolicy.org/wp-content/uploads/2016/09/BPC-Defense-Personnel-Compensation.pdf (accessed August 16, 2018).

68. Ibid., p. 11.

69. Peter Schirmer, Harry J. Thie, Margaret C. Harrell, and Michael S. Tseng, *Challenging Time in DOPMA: Flexible and Contemporary Military Officer Management* (Santa Monica, CA: RAND Corporation, 2006), p. 2, https://www.rand.org/content/dam/rand/pubs/monographs/2006/RAND_MG451.pdf (accessed August 21, 2018). Prepared for the Office of the Secretary of Defense.

70. U.S. Government Accountability Office, *Military Personnel: DOD Needs to Reevaluate Fighter Pilot Workforce Requirements*, GAO-18-113, April 2018, *passim*, https://www.gao.gov/assets/700/691192.pdf (accessed August 19, 2018).

71. Lieutenant General Gina M. Grosso, Deputy Chief of Staff, Manpower, Personnel and Services, United States Air Force, statement on "Military Pilot Shortage" before the Subcommittee on Personnel, Committee on Armed Services, U.S. House of Representatives, March 29, 2017, p. 7, https://docs.house.gov/meetings/AS/AS02/20170329/105795/HHRG-115-AS02-Wstate-GrossoG-20170329.pdf (accessed August 19, 2018).

72. Zachariah Hughes, "Air Force Faces Pilot Shortage," National Public Radio, July 7, 2018, https://www.npr.org/2018/07/07/626800477/air-force-faces-pilot-shortage (accessed August 19, 2018).

73. U.S. Government Accountability Office, *Military Personnel: DOD Needs to Reevaluate Fighter Pilot Workforce Requirements*, GAO-18-113, April 2018, p. 5.

74. The Honorable Heather Wilson, "A Conversation with the Secretary of the Air Force," remarks at The Heritage Foundation, Washington, D.C., March 1, 2018, https://www.heritage.org/defense/event/conversation-the-secretary-the-air-force (accessed August 22, 2018), and Stephen Losey, "Pilots Are Flying 17 Hours per Month, but It's Still Not Enough, Air Force Secretary Says," *Air Force Times*, March 1, 2018, https://www.airforcetimes.com/news/your-air-force/2018/03/01/secaf-air-force-pilots-are-flying-17-hours-per-month-but-its-still-not-enough (accessed August 23, 2018).

75. Karen Parrish, "Air Force Official Details 'National Aircrew Crisis,'" U.S. Department of Defense, March 23, 2017, https://www.defense.gov/News/Article/Article/1134560/air-force-official-details-national-aircrew-crisis/ (accessed August 21, 2018).

Training: The Foundation for Success in Combat

Jim Greer, Colonel, U.S. Army (Ret.)

In no other profession are the penalties for employing untrained personnel so appalling or so irrevocable as in the military.
—Douglas MacArthur, 1933

It is astounding what well-trained and dedicated Soldiers can accomplish in the face of death, fear, physical privation, and an enemy determined to kill them.
—Lieutenant General Ace Collins, 1978

Death, fear, physical privation, and an enemy determined to kill them: These are the challenges that those who defend our nation face when they go to war. Whether one is a soldier, sailor, airman, or Marine; a brand new private or a grizzled old veteran; a fighter pilot, a submariner, a tanker, a military policeman, a transporter, or a medic, every serviceman and woman must be prepared to make contact with the enemy, survive, and accomplish the mission as a member of the team. That is what training the Armed Forces of the United States is all about: enabling those who serve to fight, win, and come home to their loved ones.

Warfare is always changing, always evolving.

- World War II saw the emergence of blitzkrieg and air operations over land and sea.

- Vietnam demonstrated the power of combinations of enemy regular and insurgent forces.

- The ongoing campaigns in Iraq and Afghanistan have demonstrated how improvised explosive devices can be significant killers on the battlefield.

- In 2006, the Israeli Defense Forces were stymied by Hezbollah's employment of a hybrid approach that combined sophisticated conventional weapons and tactics with terrorism and long-range missiles.[1]

- Most recently, Russia has employed what is termed "New Generation Warfare" to conquer the Crimea, secure the eastern Ukraine, and threaten the Baltic nations.[2]

Military training must therefore change as well. It must continually be forward-thinking, innovative, and aggressive, both in understanding how warfare is evolving and in adapting training to meet those challenges. Today, the Chinese military presents the threat of long-range missiles to deny the U.S. access to the western Pacific Ocean and to our allies such as Japan, South Korea, and Australia. Since the end of World War II, the ability of the U.S. to move freely as it pleases in the Pacific has been assured, but that freedom of action is increasingly at risk as the Chinese military invests in new technologies and capabilities. This growing challenge places a training requirement on all four services to learn how to defeat the threat of such anti-access/area denial tactics.[3]

Training is one of the key functions of each of the services within the Department of Defense (DOD). Others include manning, equipping, organizing, and sustaining, but it is training that wraps all of those functions together to create and maintain effective organizations. Training is so important that each service has its own major subordinate command dedicated to training:

- The Training and Doctrine Command for the Army,[4]

- The Naval Education and Training Command for the Navy,[5]

- The Training and Education Command for the Marine Corps,[6] and

- The Air Education and Training Command for the Air Force.[7]

Each of these commands respectively holds the service responsibility for designing, developing, resourcing, assessing the effectiveness of, and providing command oversight of its service's program. Additionally, for the Joint Force, the Joint Staff J-7 has responsibility for joint oversight, policy, and strategy for training and exercises that bring individual service forces together into a coherent whole.[8]

What Is Training?

The U.S. military defines training as "instruction and applied exercises for acquiring and retaining knowledge, skills, abilities, and attitudes (KSAAs) necessary to complete specific tasks."[9] Generally speaking, military training is divided into two broad categories: individual and collective. Individual training is exactly that: training designed to develop individual skills. Collective training is designed to integrate trained individuals into a cohesive and effective team, whether that team is a tank crew of four or an aircraft carrier crew of 5,000.

Training can be as small as an hour-long class for a four-person team on how to bandage a wound and as large as a multi-week joint exercise including tens of thousands of personnel and units from all four services. It generally occurs in three domains: the institutional domain, which includes the various formal schools in each service; the operational domain, which includes training in units and on ships, whether at home station, deployed, or underway; and the self-development domain, conducted by individuals to address the gaps they see in their own learning.

Training Realism

Their exercises are unbloody battles, and their battles bloody exercises.
—Flavius Josephus, 75 C.E.

No other activity prepares a military force better for combat than combat itself. The environment in which combat is conducted—one of violence, death and destruction, fear and valor, complexity and uncertainty—is one of the most challenging in which any human being or human organization must operate. It is so challenging and unique that it cannot be completely replicated outside of combat itself. Thus, to be effective, military organizations must train under conditions that are as realistic as possible and come as close as possible to placing the individual, the team, the unit, and the crew in the environment and situations they will face in combat. Training realism is one of the key measures of training effectiveness.

Much of the design and innovation in training is aimed at generating realism. Training design generally has three components:

- The *task* itself—the thing an individual or the element is expected to accomplish. An example might be to conduct an attack, conduct resupply of a vessel, or employ electronic warfare to jam an enemy system.

- The *conditions*—the set of circumstances in which the task is expected to be performed. Examples might be day or night, moving or stationary, opposed by an enemy or unopposed, or with full capabilities or some capabilities degraded.

- The *standards*—the level of competence and effectiveness at which the task is expected to be accomplished. Standards might include the speed at which the task is to be performed, the accuracy of hitting a target, or the percentage of operational systems that are ready and available.

Identifying the tasks, conditions, and standards drives training realism. Ultimately, as Flavius Josephus described the training of the Roman army, the goal is for military forces entering combat to have "been there before" so that they know they can fight, win, and survive.

Training Effectiveness

It's not practice that makes perfect; rather, it's perfect practice that makes perfect. It is, after all, the seemingly small disciplines and commitment to high standards that makes us who we are and binds us together as a force, an Army, in peace and in war.

—General Martin Dempsey, 2009

As former Chairman of the Joint Chiefs of Staff General Marty Dempsey's quote implies, the services do not train just for training's sake. They train in order to reach specific measurable levels of performance in specific tasks. Training, then, is both nested and progressive. It is nested because training in specific individual tasks is aggregated to enable training in small elements tasks, which in turn are aggregated into training in progressively larger organization tasks.

Take, for example, a carrier battle group. A carrier battle group consists typically of the carrier; several cruisers, frigates, or destroyers; and perhaps a submarine. On each of those ships, individual crewmembers, petty officers, and officers must be trained on their individual tasks. Those individuals then form teams such as a fire control party or an engineering team. Teams are then combined to make departments, such as the gunnery and engineering departments, which then train together to create an overall crew for the ship that's effective in sailing, attack, defense, or replenishment.

The various ships of the carrier battle group then train together to enable collective attack or defense by the group of ships. At the same time, individuals and organizations are trained progressively under increasingly challenging conditions to increasingly higher standards. All of this must then be assessed for competence and effectiveness.

Because training involves both individual and collective learning, the military uses the standard approach of the educational profession to develop and conduct training. This is known as the ADDIE approach:

- **A**ssess. Organizations assess their training to identify gaps in proficiency or determine new training requirements.

- **D**esign. Training is designed to overcome gaps or to improve proficiency under a variety of conditions.

- **D**evelop. Once designed, training is developed, coordinated, and resourced to enable execution.

- **I**mplement. Developed training is implemented to train the requisite individuals and organizations.

- **E**valuate. Once conducted, training is evaluated for its effectiveness. Individuals and elements are retrained until proficiency goals are achieved.

Training assessments are a critical factor in achieving training effectiveness. On the front end of the ADDIE process, such assessments identify gaps in the achievement of standards, which in turn leads to the design, development, and execution of training to achieve those standards. At the back end of the process, training is evaluated to determine whether standards were met and, if they were not, what further training needs to be conducted to achieve those standards.

The Department of Defense uses the Defense Readiness Reporting System (DRRS)[10] to track readiness, to include training. Under DRRS, each service uses its own readiness reporting system to report training readiness on a monthly basis for all of the elements in its organization. This monthly assessment is used to guide training management to ensure that training is conducted to achieve readiness goals.

Training and Leader Development

Training and leader development are two military functions that go hand in hand. It is of little use to have personnel and units that are well trained if they are not also well led; conversely, the best leader can accomplish little with poorly trained troops. Of course, both training and leader development are forms of learning, and there is significant overlap between the two functions. Consequently, the services invest considerable effort in leader development.

Each service has a Professional Military Education (PME) program for commissioned officers, warrant officers, and non-commissioned officers (NCOs) or petty officers. There is also a Joint Professional Military Education (JPME) program to ensure that officers are qualified to integrate service components into joint headquarters and joint task forces. In each case, PME consists of a progressive series of schools that begin with pre-commissioning education in the military academies, Reserve Officers Training Corps,[11] Marine Corps Platoon Leaders Course, and various officer candidate schools. PME continues with basic, advanced, and specialty education. Each service has a staff college for mid-grade officers and a senior service college, or war college, for senior officers. JPME has a National Defense University system that officers and civilians from all services and partner departments and agencies attend.[12] Within each service, there are parallel PME systems for junior, mid-grade, and senior warrant officers and NCOs.

Leader development represents a significant investment by the Department of Defense. During a 20-year career, a leader is likely to spend between two and four full years in the various PME schools: between 10 and 20 percent of total time served. The investment is necessary because of the unique and complex features of the environment and conduct of warfare. Senior leaders always confront the tension between time in schools and time in operational units. During periods of intense deployment, such as the high points of the Iraq and Afghanistan campaigns in the mid-2000s, attendance at leader development schools is sometimes deferred. When this happens, however, leaders face a challenge: determining whether it is better to have an untrained person present in the unit or a vacancy in the unit while that person is being trained.

Historically, interwar periods—the years between major wars like the 1920s and 1930s between World War I and World War II—have been periods during which leader development flourished and innovation occurred. The military's war colleges, the highest level of leader development, were instituted during interwar periods. Similarly, all of the services' advanced schools, such as the Army's School of Advanced Military Studies, the Marine Corps' School of Advanced Warfare, and the Air Force's School of Advanced Airpower Studies, were started during the Cold War. Clearly, such innovation needs to take place in the post-9/11 environment of seemingly continuous warfare, but how this will happen has not been determined.

Initial Entry Training

Virtually all members of the armed services enter the profession at the ground-floor level. Whether they are recent high school graduates, graduates of a university or one of the service academies, or transitioning from another job or career, they are thrust into an organization whose culture, shaped by the demands of warfare, is significantly different from anything they have previously experienced. At the same time, they are confronted with a myriad of new tasks that they must learn in order to be valued members of the team.

Each of the services has an Initial Entry Training Program, generally divided into two phases: a basic phase, often called "basic" or "boot camp," to develop the foundational skills required of everyone in that specific service and inculcate them into the culture of that service and a more advanced phase to develop specific skills for their chosen or assigned specialty, whether as an intelligence analyst, a dental hygienist, a mechanic, or an air defender.

Initial Entry Training is a significant undertaking. Each year, the U.S. Navy trains approximately 40,000 recruits at Great Lakes Naval Training Center,[13] and the U.S. Air Force trains approximately 35,000 in Basic Military Training at Lackland Air Force Base.[14] The Marine Corps trains approximately 20,000 recruits a year at Parris Island[15] and another 17,000 at San Diego.[16] The U.S. Army trains more than 80,000 recruits each year at Fort Jackson, South Carolina,[17] and three other major training installations. All told, DOD is conducting Initial Entry Training for almost 200,000 young men and women each year.

The design and resourcing of Initial Entry Training always present a challenge. Obviously, senior leaders would like to train new recruits to the maximum extent possible before those soldiers, sailors, airmen, or Marines join their units or their ships, but more training means more time, and each individual has enlisted in the military only for a certain period of time, usually three or four years. As a result, there is a trade-off between time spent in initial training and time spent actually serving in support of a mission.

Another consideration is the investment of more senior, experienced people who serve as the training cadre. The services rightly send their very best to be the first leader under whom a new recruit will serve, but that means that the best leaders, who are limited in number, are not always with the fighting forces.

Command and Staff Training

A central component of training military organizations and units is the training of commanders and staffs. Each of the services has dedicated training programs and resources for such training, which normally employs simulations because it would be wasteful to use large numbers of troops and equipment simply for staff training. Much of this training is aimed at planning, coordination during execution, and decision-making.

- The Army Mission Command Training Program trains the commanders and staffs of large units at the brigade, division, and corps levels.[18]

- The Marine Staff Training Program trains the senior commanders and staffs of Marine Air-Ground Task Forces.[19]

- The Red Flag Series of exercises at Nellis Air Force Base is the U.S. Air Force program for training the commanders and staffs of Expeditionary Air Force elements.[20]

- The U.S. Navy operates several different programs tied to its regional fleets. For example, Carrier Strike Group 15 is responsible for training the commanders and staffs of Pacific-based carrier battle groups, amphibious ready groups, and independent ships.[21]

Another key factor is the training of joint headquarters and joint staffs. U.S. military forces never fight simply as Army, Navy, Air Force, or Marine units. Even if a particular operation is predominantly in one domain, the execution is necessarily joint.

Since 9/11, for example, the U.S. has conducted military operations in Afghanistan. Afghanistan is entirely landlocked, and counterinsurgency and counterterrorism operations are conducted exclusively against targets on the ground against an enemy with no navy and no air force. Yet U.S. military operations in Afghanistan have been completely joint as the Air Force has provided precision attack from the air, the Navy has provided electronic warfare and training for Afghan National Security Forces, and Marine Corps forces have conducted counterinsurgency operations in specific sectors within the country. In addition, special operations forces from all four services have conducted sensitive missions throughout the war.

Previously, training of joint headquarters and staffs was conducted by U.S. Joint Forces Command (USJFCOM) under a comprehensive program that was not unlike the Mission Command Training Program conducted by the Army. However, in 2011, USJFCOM was disestablished, and a very robust capability was lost. Since then, joint staff training has been conducted by the services, by regional Combatant Commands, or to a limited extent by the Joint Staff. Thus far, because the ongoing campaigns in Iraq, Syria, and Afghanistan have not faced multidimensional enemies, the change has not had adverse consequences. However, as the Department of Defense focuses training and readiness on more capable potential enemies such as North Korea, Russia, China, or Iran, the lack of a robust joint training capability will increasingly be an issue.

Training Simulations

Simulators and simulations have a long history of enabling training for military forces. Simulators include capabilities that replicate actual systems in order to maximize training opportunities, reduce cost, promote safety, or preserve equipment for wartime use. Early examples were flight simulators that reproduced the cockpit, wings, and tail of an airplane in order to train pilots in the control, maneuvering, and reaction to emergencies on the ground before they took an airplane up in the air. Other simulators in use today recreate the entire bridge of a navy destroyer so that officers and petty officers can learn to maneuver, fight, and safeguard the ship under tactical conditions.[22]

Simulations enable the training of organizations by creating battlefields or operational environments. Early examples of simulations were tabletop war games in which maps recreated the terrain of a battlefield and markers were used to signify the various units of opposing sides. Participants would fight out battles for training in the art and science of warfare.

Today's simulations are far more sophisticated and often far more integrated. The military uses four general classes of simulation: live, constructive, virtual, and gaming. Each of these classes of simulation has a specific purpose and training audience, and two or more classes of simulations can be integrated to make training of individuals and units even more effective. The goal of much simulation research and development is not just to create the most effective individual simulation, but to create a true *integrated training environment* that combines all four classes to maximize training effectiveness.

- **Live simulations** are the training simulations that most closely represent training as historically conducted with individuals and units using real equipment in training environments that most closely reflect actual combat. This means using actual land, sea, air, space, or cyber terrain; actual weapons using either live or dummy/inert ammunition; and actual vehicles and other equipment, often against an enemy force that is also live and simulated by some portion of the U.S. military.

For example, Red Flag exercises are live training simulations in which Air Force, Navy, and Marine Corps aircraft fight against an enemy portrayed by U.S. aircraft and crews that are trained specifically to represent various enemy capabilities. In a similar manner, Army and Marine Corps ground forces have Combat Training Centers (CTCs) at which large formations of thousands of troops and hundreds of armored and wheeled vehicles and weapons systems fight battles against a well-trained and well-equipped opposing force (OPFOR) and conduct large-scale live-fire training at distances and ranges that they would expect in actual combat.

- **Constructive simulations** are representations of military forces and operational environments, usually aimed at training for large-scale combat involving whole naval fleets, Army Corps, Marine Divisions, or Air Force Wings, to include joint constructive simulations that combine forces from one or more of the services. Originally, constructive simulations were conducted using tabletop war games with pieces representing military units, but today, most constructive simulations are computer-based. Given the size of forces and the fidelity with which military units, ships, and aircraft can be represented, constructive simulations are usually used to train leaders and staffs.

- **Virtual simulations** are computer-based representations of individuals, teams, units, weapons systems, and other capabilities, usually with great fidelity to the operational environment (terrain, weather, urban areas, etc.) to include not only enemies, but also local populations. Virtual simulations are best suited to training individuals, teams, or small units. For example, Conduct of Fire Trainers (COFTs) are used to train individual tank or fighting vehicle crews, and Close Combat Tactical Trainers (CCTTs) are used to train platoon and company-size groupings of tanks or armored fighting vehicles. Virtual simulations have the virtue of training aircrews, ship's combat systems crews, and tank and fighting vehicles crews in many repetitions and situations—in other words, lots of practice—without the large costs for fuel, munitions, and maintenance and without the need for the large spaces that live training requires.

- **Gaming** is the newest class of training simulation. While war games have been used for centuries in the form of board games or tabletop games, the advent of computer gaming brought with it whole new opportunities. The military recognizes that digital games improve rapid decision-making, cognitive processes, and synchronization and integration of

different systems and capabilities while providing almost countless variations of situations and complex problems with almost immediate feedback on performance. The military even uses games to educate new recruits about the military service they have chosen before they actually attend their Initial Entry Training.

Resourcing Training

When personnel are not actually engaged in combat, training dominates military activity in all four services on a daily basis. Soldiers, sailors, airmen, and Marines are trained from the first day they enter the armed forces until the last day of their service. Commanders at every level consider training for future combat and military operations to be one of their primary responsibilities. Institutionally, each service expends significant time, money, and personnel on generating, conducting, and sustaining the most effective training possible for individuals, teams, units, and organizations at every echelon. Failure to conduct such training or conducting training that does not attend to the harsh realities of war will likely lead to failure in battle.

Of all the training resources we have, time is the most precious. Military organizations start the year with 365 days, but with 104 weekend days and a dozen or so holidays, the start point is soon around 250 days. Then training has to compete with other critical events such as maintaining equipment, moving units from one place to another, personnel-related tasks such as medical checkups, and preparation for deployment.

Therefore, in a really good year, a unit might have six months of actual training time. Then commanders must manage that time. How much is devoted to individual training? How much is devoted to collective or unit training? How much is small-unit or individual ship or squadron training, and how much time is spent on large-scale training? How much is live training, and how much time is spent in simulators? Management of the training calendar becomes one of the most important leader tasks.

Providing adequate personnel for training is also a critical resourcing effort. Great training requires great trainers. The basic training that each service provides is only as good as the drill sergeants and other non-commissioned officers who are taken out of combat-ready units and provided to the training base. Similarly, professional military education at all levels requires dedicated and well-educated faculty, both uniformed and civilian. Senior leaders must make strategic decisions about the management of personnel to provide the best support to training while still ensuring that units and ships are adequately manned to go to war if necessary while meeting the needs of ongoing conflicts.

Of course, the most visible resource necessary for training is money. Money pays for all of these capabilities. It pays for training areas, ranges, training ammunition, and fuel. It pays for flight hours for training aircrews, for transporting units to and from training areas, and for the training simulations. The services also must pay for development of future training capabilities such as virtual, constructive, and gaming simulations and for modernization of training forces as the conflict environment and the threats and enemy change. Money also pays the personnel costs associated with training.

Training budgets are very complex across the Department of Defense. Part of the cost of training is contained in a unit's operations and maintenance budget. Other training costs are in infrastructure or base maintenance budgets. Others are found in modernization budgets as the services improve capabilities or field new systems. Some costs are related to pre-deployment training for units that are preparing to go into combat in places like Iraq or Afghanistan. Costs are also spread over several years, or "across the POM" (Program Objective Memorandum) as the five-year DOD budget planning cycle is termed. This means that some training costs are short-term, year-to-year, while others, such as the costs of building training infrastructure, are spread out over several years.

Resourcing training with enough money is a national endeavor, not just a military one. The Department of Defense, in conjunction with other federal departments and agencies, submits budgets to the Administration that include all of the various training requirements. The Administration submits that budget to Congress as part of its overall budget. Congress considers all of the training requirements and costs in crafting an appropriations bill, which eventually is subject to a vote, approved, and signed by the President. At the same time, the various states are developing and approving budgets that include their own defense-related training costs, such as for the Army and Air National Guards and state-level training areas and facilities. And every two years, when Americans vote, the readiness, modernization, and training of the military forces is a consideration.

In other words, military training is every American's business.

Conclusion

Warfare continues to change as new operational methods like hybrid warfare are combined with new technologies such as cyber, drones, and 3-D printing. Military training also must continue to change so that the U.S. military is prepared to confront emerging threats and potential enemies that are growing in strength and ambitions. Training innovation and training resourcing are critical to achieving new and better ways to train the force.

Ultimately, the goal of military training is to ensure that when the nation goes to war or engages in conflicts or military operations short of war, the armed forces of the United States will be able to accomplish strategic, operational, and tactical objectives. The ultimate goal of training is to win battles and engagements and to do so with the lowest cost in terms of national resources and with the lowest loss of life among those who have volunteered to fight to defend the nation.

Endnotes

1. David E. Johnson, *Hard Fighting: Israel in Lebanon and Gaza* (Santa Monica, CA: RAND Corporation, 2001), https://www.rand.org/pubs/monographs/MG1085.html (accessed May 23, 2018).

2. Janis Berzinš, "The New Generation of Russian Warfare," *Aspen Review*, Issue 03 (2014), https://www.aspen.review/article/2017/the-new-generation-of-russian-warfare/ (accessed May 3, 2018).

3. Dean Cheng, "The U.S. Needs an Integrated Approach to Counter China's Anti-Access/Area Denial Strategy," Heritage Foundation *Backgrounder* No. 2927, July 9, 2014, https://www.heritage.org/defense/report/the-us-needs-integrated-approach-counter-chinas-anti-accessarea-denial-strategy.

4. U.S. Army, Training and Doctrine Command Web site, http://tradoc.army.mil/index.asp (accessed May 23, 2018).

5. U.S. Navy, Naval Education and Training Command Web site, https://www.netc.navy.mil/ (accessed May 23, 2018).

6. U.S. Marine Corps, TECOM Training and Education Command Web site, http://www.tecom.marines.mil/ (accessed May 23, 2018).

7. U.S. Air Force, Air Education and Training Command Web site, http://www.aetc.af.mil/ (accessed May 23, 2018).

8. U.S. Department of Defense, Joint Chiefs of Staff, J7 Joint Force Development Web site, http://www.jcs.mil/Directorates/J7-Joint-Force-Development/ (accessed May 23, 2018).

9. U.S. Department of Defense, Joint Chiefs of Staff, "Joint Training Policy for the Armed Forces of the United States," Chairman of the Joint Chiefs of Staff Instruction No. 3500.01H, April 25, 2014, p. A-5, http://www.jcs.mil/Portals/36/Documents/Doctrine/training/cjcsi3500_01h.pdf?ver=2017-12-29-171241-630 (accessed May 23, 2018).

10. R. Derek Trunkey, "Implications of the Department of Defense Readiness Reporting System," Congressional Budget Office *Working Paper* No. 2013-03, May 2013, https://www.cbo.gov/sites/default/files/113th-congress-2013-2014/workingpaper/44127_DefenseReadiness_1.pdf (accessed May 23, 2018).

11. U.S. Department of Defense, "Today's Military: ROTC Programs," https://todaysmilitary.com/training/rotc (accessed May 23, 2018).

12. U.S. Department of Defense, National Defense University Web site, http://www.ndu.edu/ (accessed May 23, 2018).

13. U.S. Navy, Recruit Training Command Web site, http://www.bootcamp.navy.mil/ (accessed May 23, 2018).

14. U.S. Air Force, Air Force Basic Military Training Web site, http://www.basictraining.af.mil/ (accessed May 23, 2018).

15. U.S. Marine Corps, MCRD Parris Island Web site, http://www.mcrdpi.marines.mil/ (accessed May 23, 2018).

16. U.S. Marine Corps, Marine Corps Recruit Depot, Western Recruiting Region Web site, http://www.mcrdsd.marines.mil/ (accessed May 23, 2018).

17. U.S. Army, "Gateway to the Army: Initial Entry Training," https://www.gatewaytothearmy.org/fort-jackson/basic-training (accessed May 3, 2018).

18. U.S. Army, Combined Arms Center, Mission Command Training Program (MCTP) Web site, https://usacac.army.mil/organizations/cact/mctp (accessed May 23, 2018).

19. U.S. Marine Corps, MAGTF Staff Training Program Web site, http://www.tecom.marines.mil/Units/Directorates/MSTP.aspx (accessed May 23, 2018).

20. Fact Sheet, "414th Combat Training Squadron 'Red Flag,'" U.S. Air Force, Nellis Air Force Base, July 6, 2012, https://web.archive.org/web/20150918180334/http://www.nellis.af.mil/library/factsheets/factsheet.asp?id=19160 (accessed May 23, 2018).

21. U.S. Navy, Commander, Carrier Strike Group Fifteen Web site, http://www.ccsg15.navy.mil/ (accessed May 23, 2018).

22. Sam LaGrone, "Navy Makes Training Simulation Based on Fatal USS Fitzgerald Collision," U.S. Naval Institute News, February 21, 2018, https://news.usni.org/2018/02/21/navy-makes-training-simulation-based-fatal-uss-fitzgerald-collision (May 23, 2018).

An Overview of the DOD Installations Enterprise

John Conger

With six aircraft carriers and dozens of cruisers, amphibious assault ships, guided missile destroyers, submarines, and other ships, Naval Station Norfolk is home to the world's largest concentration of naval power. Its ranges extend well into the Atlantic Ocean, offering those forces a place to train and establish their readiness for war. However, without a place to refuel and resupply, a place to repair and maintain its ships, a headquarters for their sailors and their families to live when those ships are not deployed, that incredible concentration of naval power would attenuate, lose its readiness, and become less effective over time.

In contrast with the enormity of Norfolk, the U.S. Army and Marine Corps and allied NATO forces maintain small forward bases across Afghanistan to support ongoing operations. These bases are usually comprised of fortified locations from which our forces can launch. They need to be resupplied continually, but, again, they give U.S. forces a place from which they can project power.

From one end of the spectrum to the other, from domestic locations to those in active combat zones, from the very largest base to the very smallest, installations are critical to maintaining and projecting our warfighting strength. As I testified before Congress many years ago, "Our warfighters cannot do their job without bases from which to fight, on which to train, or in which to live when they are not

deployed. The bottom line is that installations support our military readiness."[1]

Today, however, despite its incredible value to the warfighter, the DOD installations enterprise faces serious challenges. Budget shortfalls (even with recent increases in the overall budget) continue to eat away at its foundations, encroachment challenges impose constraints even as requirements increase, and leaders struggle to build resilience to external impacts like cyber attacks and climate change.

Scope and Scale

To begin to understand the impact and contribution of the Defense Department's installations enterprise, it helps to consider its sheer size. DOD maintains a global real property portfolio consisting of 568,383 facilities, valued at approximately $1.05 trillion, with more than 2.2 billion square feet of space located on 27.2 million acres of land at over 4,793 sites worldwide.[2]

The 568,383 facilities include more than 275,000 buildings, from operational facilities to administrative ones, from barracks to hospitals, from sophisticated research facilities to wastewater treatment plants. They also include a wide range of non-building structures including piers, runways, roads, fuel tanks, and utility lines. For comparison, the General Services Administration—in theory, the real estate manager for the federal government—maintains only 9,600 buildings. DOD's 2.2

TABLE 2

Real Property Managed by Military Service, FY 2016

Military Branch	Buildings	Total Facilities (including structures)	Plant Replacement Value (in billions)	Land (acres)
Army	139,458	278,299	$417.95	13,340,778
Navy	61,368	111,937	$238.50	2,213,663
Air Force	47,738	126,215	$302.58	9,126,467
Marine Corps	26,748	51,112	$79.40	2,504,943
DOD Total	**275,312**	**568,383**	**$1,038.43**	**27,185,851**

NOTE: DOD total excludes Washington Headquarters Service.
SOURCE: U.S. Department of Defense, "Department of Defense Real Property Portfolio," https://www.acq.osd.mil/eie/Downloads/Fast_Facts_2016.pdf (accessed May 23, 2018).

☎ heritage.org

---

billion square feet dwarfs the GSA's 377 million square feet.[3]

DOD's 27.2 million acres is certainly smaller than the acreage held by other federal land-holding agencies such as the Bureau of Land Management or the U.S. Forest Service, which maintain 245 million acres[4] and 193 million acres,[5] respectively, but DOD installations still comprise a land area that is roughly the size of the State of Virginia.

The DOD facilities footprint is dominated by the Army, which maintains about half of the buildings, facilities, and land managed by the department. (See Table 2.)

Another element of DOD's scale is its scope. As the number of buildings implies, there are many different kinds of facilities on DOD bases supporting a wide array of missions.

Consider a base like Fort Hood, Texas, home to the Army's III Corps and the 1st Cavalry Division. Fort Hood alone maintains more than 5,000 facilities on more than 200,000 acres with a value of approximately $9 billion.[6] These buildings include operational facilities like headquarters buildings, motor pools, aircraft hangars and runways, training centers, instrumented training ranges, weapons storage facilities, deployment railheads, and more. They also include the buildings that support the troops and their

families including barracks; family housing; fitness centers; dining halls; a hospital and several medical clinics; exchanges and commissaries; and morale, welfare, and recreation facilities. Moreover, there is the basic infrastructure of the base: miles of roads, utilities infrastructure, fuel lines, dams and bridges, access control points, and fencing. Other federal agencies manage many similar facilities, such as Department of Veterans Affairs hospitals or GSA office buildings, but each DOD installation must contend with diverse arrays of facilities and a concomitant diversity of challenges.

Each base has its own mission and its own specialized facilities, and those facilities are critical to the forces that employ them. Where Fort Hood has motor pools and tank ranges, Norfolk Naval Base has piers and dry docks, and Nellis Air Force Base in Nevada has hangars and runways. A research-focused base like Fort Detrick or Wright-Patterson Air Force Base will have sophisticated lab facilities, intelligence-focused missions will require computer centers and communications equipment, and arsenals and depots will have industrial operations.

A final element of scale in the DOD installations enterprise is its global nature. DOD facilities are located in every state, in multiple

U.S. territories, and in 42 different nations.[7] The largest part of our international footprint is an artifact of World War II and the Cold War, with thousands of U.S. facilities located in East Asia (Japan and South Korea) and Europe (predominantly Germany, the United Kingdom, and Italy). This global presence not only deters aggression, but also allows the United States to respond quickly to regional crises as they emerge.

How Installations Contribute to Military Power

With that context in place, consider how that trillion-dollar portfolio contributes to the military power of the United States. Our installations serve to generate the force, train it, and sustain it. From our bases, these forces can be projected and deployed, and once the mission is complete, they come back to those bases to recover, reconstitute, and ready themselves for redeployment.

Installations may contribute to combat power as power projection platforms, such as Fort Hood or Joint Base Lewis-McChord, which regularly deploy troops to theater, or an Air Force Base like Whiteman AFB, from which B-2 bombers can launch attack operations directly. Some bases conduct operations directly, whether it is a forward operating location in Afghanistan or an airman flying Reaper aircraft over Syria from a facility in the United States. Intelligence operations generally have reachback to critical hubs for processing intelligence and distributing it back out to the field. Transportation and logistics installations are critical elements of that ability to project power, moving people and equipment around the world.

America's global footprint is critical to that power projection capability. Our forces in Japan, for example, provide the ability to reach crises in the Western Pacific much more quickly than forces stationed in the continental United States can reach them. Similarly, Europe is a critical launch point for reaching theaters of operation in the Middle East. The Landstuhl Regional Medical Center in

Germany has been a critical hub for casualties from Iraq and Afghanistan.

In addition to conducting operations and projecting power, installations are essential to building readiness in the first place. Installations from Parris Island, where they make Marines, to Columbus Air Force Base, Mississippi, which specializes in pilot training, are part of the enterprise that provides initial training to the force. Other bases, such as Fort Irwin, California, provide larger-scale maneuver training. In fact, readiness recovery is limited by the throughput capacity (the number of rotations you can schedule in a given year) at bases like this. Readiness is also sustained at logistics bases, whether they be shipyards or depots, where critical military platforms go through regular scheduled maintenance or recovery from battle damage so that they can be available for future operations.

Even as the military services look to equip the force, they turn to critical capabilities at installations. Research centers like Wright-Patterson Air Force Base enable the development of advanced technologies that are fed into new weapons and platforms, and test ranges like Naval Weapons Station China Lake or White Sands Missile Range provide the essential capabilities needed to confirm that our weapons operate as intended. These ranges are some of the most important assets in the installations enterprise, providing capabilities that would be nearly impossible to recreate elsewhere. For example, the pristine spectrum environment (the lack of background signals from cell phones, electronics, or other transmitters that corrupt test results) at a place like Fort Huachuca is a critical ingredient of its Electronic Proving Ground, just as the immense size of the fully instrumented White Sands Missile Range, at 3,200 square miles, makes it possible to test longer-range weapons than cannot be tested anywhere else in our enterprise.

Even the Base Realignment and Closure (BRAC) process evaluates installations based on their "military value." The legally defined definition used in BRAC has several elements, but it is comprised of:

- The current and future mission capabilities of the base and its impact on operational readiness;

- The availability and condition of land, facilities, and airspace;

- The ability to accommodate contingency, mobilization, surge, and future requirements; and

- The cost of operating at that location (in other words, a base that provides a capability cheaply has more military value than one that provides the same capability at a higher price).[8]

Explicit in these criteria is that a base brings military value to the force. It brings mission capabilities, affects operational readiness, provides essential resources such as training land or airspace, and offers the ability to support wartime surges in operations. When we measure military value for an evaluation like this, we recognize the truism that each base contributes military value to the enterprise.

Current and Emerging Challenges

The DOD installations enterprise faces several categories of challenges as it seeks to support the warfighter, generate readiness, and ensure that the force is properly equipped. One recurring challenge is the budget, which even with recent increases continues to be a lower priority than other parts of DOD. Another is encroachment, a problem that emerges when development occurs at the installation-community boundary and negatively affects a unit's ability to train or DOD's ability to test equipment in development. One large category of challenges swirls around questions of resilience: a base's ability to continue to operate or to recover quickly from exterior shocks, whether they be power outages, severe weather damage, or cyberattacks.

Budget Challenges. When trying to maintain more than $1 trillion worth of infrastructure, the sheer scale demands a significant

recurring investment in maintenance, repair, and recapitalization. If infrastructure is not maintained, it will decay and eventually have tangible readiness impacts. New facilities need to be built each year in response to new or growing mission requirements, and as maintenance backlogs grow, recapitalization needs increase.

In general, it is more compelling to speak about the tip of the spear or the tooth versus the tail, which tends to leave support programs like facilities at the back of the funding line. This is not necessarily the wrong choice. With the constraints imposed by the Budget Control Act (BCA), DOD certainly concluded that it made more sense to fund warfighting activities over construction. I testified before Congress that "facilities degrade more slowly than readiness, and in a constrained budget environment, it is responsible to take risk in facilities first."[9] However, that cannot go on indefinitely without affecting that spear tip that we have been fighting so hard to protect.

Reviewing the military construction budget is instructive as we see the historical support for facilities investment. In Chart 4, you can clearly see the increased investment in the most recent BRAC round (2005–2011) and the decrease imposed by the BCA. During the BCA period, DOD has focused its new construction on new mission requirements rather than recapitalizing failing facilities or increasing efficiency. As a result, buildings in poor condition have been retained, imposing higher maintenance costs on the enterprise.

Recent trends are more positive, although the fiscal year (FY) 2018 military construction funding level of $8.4 billion is less than the historical average over the past 30 years, adjusted for inflation. This figure represents less than 1 percent of DOD's aggregate plant value, or a recapitalization rate of about 125 years. While DOD does not currently use a recapitalization rate goal, its historic goal was a 67-year rate.[10]

In addition to military construction, the Defense Department regularly takes risk by underfunding its Facilities Sustainment, Restoration and Modernization account, which

CHART 4

Military Construction Funding

MILITARY CONSTRUCTION TOTAL OBLIGATION AUTHORITY, IN BILLIONS OF FY 2018 DOLLARS

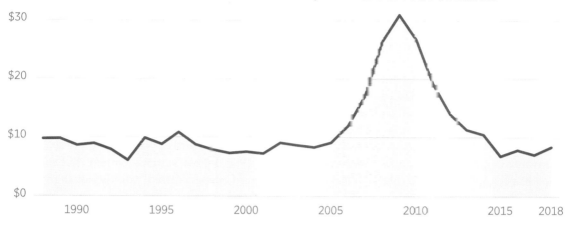

SOURCE: U.S. Department of Defense, Under Secretary of Defense (Comptroller), "National Defense Budget Estimates for FY18," revised August 2017, http://comptroller.defense.gov/Portals/45/Documents/defbudget/fy2018/FY18_Green_Book.pdf (accessed May 22, 2018).

☎ heritage.org

includes regular and emergency maintenance of its buildings and facilities. The department maintains a model that recommends funding levels for this account, but those figures generally are not met except in some specialized accounts like medical facilities, which must be properly maintained to ensure accreditation.

For example, in its FY 2019 budget request, the Navy indicates that it includes 84 percent of the modeled requirement, up from 78 percent in its FY 2018 budget. When funding is short, it must be prioritized, so as it discusses this shortfall, the Navy's budget states, "The Navy continues to take risk in infrastructure funding but mitigates this risk by focusing investments on capabilities directly supporting critical warfighting readiness and capabilities."[11] In other words, the Navy is going to put its funding in runways and piers before fixing administrative facilities, and the other services have similar approaches. Underfunding perpetuates the deferral of preventive maintenance in favor of emergency repairs, a cycle that not only perpetuates itself, but also imposes much larger life-cycle costs on the department.

During the early BCA years, this was even worse. In FY 2013, the year in which sequestration was imposed, facilities accounts were severely curtailed. The U.S. Government Accountability Office reported that the Army, for example, cut back nearly 40 percent of its original budget.[12] Because operations and maintenance funds are relatively flexible, facilities funding could bear more of the burden of sequestration to insulate operations in theater.

As context for how much DOD should be investing in maintenance of its facilities, consider the National Research Council's recommendations on infrastructure maintenance. The NRC recommended funding levels of 2 percent–4 percent of plant replacement value as the appropriate benchmark for facilities maintenance.[13] That would result in a facilities maintenance budget requirement of $21 billion to $42 billion for DOD. In contrast, the FY 2018 appropriation was $9.9 billion.

Years of underfunded facilities maintenance accounts have resulted in widespread condition problems across DOD's facilities portfolio. On April 18, 2018, the department reported that 23 percent of its facilities were in poor condition and another 9 percent were in failing condition. To address these and other maintenance challenges, it faces a maintenance backlog of more than $116 billion.[14]

Funding shortfalls can result in mission or readiness impacts. For example, deteriorating runways have immediate mission impacts, and debris could cause damage to expensive aircraft; burst pipes cause flooding damage with the potential to affect critical electrical systems; and inoperative air conditioning at a minimum can make life miserable for military personnel but could also cause sensitive computers to fail. Of course, mission facilities are prioritized, but that leads to worsening conditions in warehouses, maintenance shops, and other facilities that are not seen as the tip of the spear. Ultimately, failure of those facilities will affect the mission as well.

Base Realignment and Closure. The divestiture of excess infrastructure, saving money without undermining capability, is one of the most important tools that DOD has for reducing costs, particularly when it results in the closure of an entire installation. Due to the highly charged political dynamics that surround the prospect of closing a base and the prospect of losing a regional economic engine, the apolitical process known as BRAC was created. This apolitical, analytical process is focused on assessing excess capacity and realigning units by incorporating them within those installations that have the highest military value, closing those bases with the least military value and then reaping savings.

Through five rounds of BRAC (1988, 1991, 1993, 1995, and 2005), DOD has achieved recurring savings of more than $12 billion[15] that have resulted in 121 major closures, 79 major realignments, and 1,000 minor realignments and closures.[16] The department's most recent proposal for BRAC authority was projected to result in $2 billion in additional annual savings once fully implemented.[17] In theory, those savings could be plowed back into the enterprise to alleviate some of its funding pressures. From a practical perspective, however, the beneficiary of those savings is DOD as a whole, not the installations enterprise. There is no "fencing" of the dollars mandating that savings must be used on other installations requirements.

Despite the fact that BRAC is designed to remove political influence, requiring Congress to vote on an entire package of closures and realignments without making changes, the debate over giving DOD the authority to conduct a round of BRAC is extremely political. Members of Congress assess their prospective risk and generally will oppose even conducting the analysis in the first place for fear that they will be held responsible if the department's recommendations lead to the closure of a base in their district or state. Without question, the department's assessment of 19 percent excess capacity[18] begs for a good-government solution to eliminate waste, but Members of Congress cannot help but weigh the political risk against the prospect of $2 billion in annual savings that comes to fruition six years in the future.

Despite the prohibitions on BRAC, the department was able to conduct a review of its European infrastructure. DOD's 2013–2015 European Infrastructure Consolidation effort did not require congressional approval and did not evoke the same protective instincts that domestic bases evoke. That effort resulted in 26 recommendations designed to save more than $500 million annually when fully implemented without reducing the overall U.S. presence in Europe.

Recent arguments in favor of BRAC have focused on increasing lethality instead of securing savings,[19] harkening back to the 2005 round, which focused on "transformation." Without question, there are important management actions the department can take under BRAC authority that it cannot take otherwise, and many of these actions do not save money. In the 2005 BRAC round, for example, roughly half of the recommendations were never designed to save money. They resulted in $29 billion in costs and only $1 billion in savings but achieved DOD management objectives, such as collocation of law enforcement activities at Quantico

Marine Corps Base or the return of forces from Europe. The efficiency recommendations—the ones designed to save money—cost $6 billion up front but achieved $3 billion in recurring savings.[20] In total, the 2005 BRAC round alone is saving $4 billion every year, allowing $4 billion in other requirements to be funded within the budget caps.

As we consider future arguments about or alternatives to BRAC, particularly if the motivation is budget savings, it is important to recognize what drives those savings: reductions in personnel. While there are some savings to maintenance requirements or utilities from divesting individual buildings, the most significant recurring savings from BRAC are from civilian job cuts, particularly the number of cuts that come from complete closure of a base.

Partnerships and Privatization. Another approach that DOD takes to reducing costs is to find others to take on non-core functions. This might involve privatization, like the Military Housing Privatization Initiative in which DOD divested the preponderance of its family housing to private developers, or it could be as simple as turning to the local community to provide a service like trash collection.

To be a good candidate for privatization, a function should be generally commercial in nature (common in the installations world) and have an associated revenue stream that a private entity can leverage to secure financing. However, the department has taken on these tasks to shore up parts of the enterprise that have been chronically underfunded and is not commonly motivated to explore privatization where things are going well, even if a function is commercial in nature.

All of these factors come into play with the highly touted Military Housing Privatization Initiative. Under authority provided by Congress in 1996, the department has privatized approximately 200,000 housing units on its installations, conveying the homes and providing leases for the underlying land.[21] The families living in that housing receive Basic Allowance for Housing and pay rent just as if they were off base. Developers leveraged the projected income and conveyed assets to secure loans and front-load a huge recapitalization effort, dramatically improving the quality of on-base housing. DOD was able to leverage about $3.4 billion in government investment to generate $31 billion in private capital.[22]

Another successful example is the privatization of utilities. Again in this part of the portfolio, the condition of DOD-owned assets was extremely poor, but electricity, water, and wastewater infrastructure are quite commercial in nature, and monthly utilities bills provide a regular revenue stream. Utilities privatization contractors accept the assets and make capital improvements up front, leveraging the economics of 50-year agreements.

Finally, the degree to which local communities are indispensable to the installations they surround is not always acknowledged. These communities provide a wide range of services to the base that it simply would not have the capacity to provide on its own. In most locations, communities provide utilities infrastructure, housing, education, transportation infrastructure, and a source of civilian employees and contractors. Absorbing those functions back into the base would be cost-prohibitive, and as they look for efficiencies, installations have been looking at more functions to divest to local municipalities. Congress recently provided the department with authority to sign Intergovernmental Service Agreements that allow bases to turn to their local municipalities to provide more services, saving money for both through economies of scale,[23] and the services have been working to leverage the new authority.

Energy Efficiency. Without question, there is inefficiency in the DOD installations enterprise, though it is not always easy to excise. Looking at the foregoing BRAC discussion, macro-level changes and cost reductions involve huge political hurdles, but they are the clearest route to achieving savings in the DOD enterprise. At the installation level, the two largest categories of costs are public works (as noted, maintenance is systematically underfunded) and utilities. Significant effort has been made to reduce energy usage as the department looks to reduce costs.

In 2017, the Department reported that it spent $12.4 billion on energy in FY 2016: $8.7 billion for operational energy (largely fuel), of which $3.7 billion was attributable to installations energy costs, most of which pay for electricity and natural gas.[24] The department has been tracking its energy use since 1975 and has made significant progress over the years, reducing its energy intensity (BTUs per square foot) by 49 percent, but as its *Annual Energy Management and Resilience Report* explains:

> These reductions were a result of substantial low- and no-cost energy efficiency and conservation measures that impacted behavioral changes, and project investments such as insulation or lighting upgrades. As similar, viable low- and no-cost energy efficiency and conservation initiatives continue to diminish, DoD will be challenged to make broad reductions in energy intensity.[25]

This challenge is exacerbated by the underfunding of facility maintenance. To put it bluntly, there is a limit to how much improvement from sophisticated energy management systems is possible when there is a hole in the roof.

Readiness and Encroachment Challenges. Another set of challenges stems from encroachment, which is the negative impact on military readiness and base operations that stems from the growing competition for and limitations on land, sea, air, and even the electromagnetic spectrum that is increasingly crowded by the proliferation of cell phones and Wi-Fi.

Although a case could be made that huge bases like Camp Pendleton, Norfolk Naval Station, or Fort Bragg are the crown jewels of the DOD installations enterprise, the "hidden" gems are the testing and training ranges where our servicemembers have the land, sea, and airspace they need to test new weapons systems and train using the equipment they will bring to war. Mark Twain once said, "Buy land, they're not making it anymore." For DOD, the land that comprises these ranges is priceless.

From bases like Fort Irwin or Twentynine Palms Marine Corps Air Ground Combat Center, where soldiers and Marines practice large-unit operations to prepare for combat, to sophisticated weapons testing ranges like Naval Air Weapons Station China Lake or the White Sands Missile Range, which have sufficient space to conduct realistic testing of new weapons systems, to the pristine spectrum environment at Fort Huachuca's Electronic Proving Ground, DOD counts on its ranges to generate readiness and test its newest weapons systems.

The land, air, sea, and spectrum environments at these ranges have become increasingly constrained. Range managers have been able to use work-arounds to accommodate constraints, but they are exacerbated both by the increased requirements associated with weapons of greater speed and range and by the continual development in the surrounding civilian or commercial communities that creeps closer and closer to installations that once were completely isolated. DOD even set up a separate office to engage with wind companies whose proliferating turbines, if placed in the wrong locations, could affect DOD radars or block aircraft training routes.

DOD's *2017 Sustainable Ranges* report to Congress identifies the encroachment challenges that are of the highest concern:

- Managing threatened or endangered species, which includes requirements that troops ensure that they do not inadvertently affect these populations and that they adhere to the Endangered Species Act. More than 400 endangered species can be found on DOD bases, in no small part because they have held back the surrounding development and species have taken refuge on our bases.

- Commercial development near our ranges and bases, which can have a range of impacts including noise restrictions, constrained munitions activities due to required safety zones, or cell phone signals that corrupt sensitive electronic testing.

- Foreign investment located near sensitive testing and training ranges that require DOD to conceal or change its activities to protect against intelligence gathering.

- Reallocation of electromagnetic spectrum to commercial activities, which forces DOD systems to change their operating parameters.

- Climate impacts such as increased high-heat days, which constrain soldier activities, or drought conditions that block the use of live-fire training or testing because of increased wildfire risk.[26]

The department has developed several ways to meet these challenges, aside from imposing constraints that force testing and training to be less realistic. One key response is the establishment of buffer land around bases, which is done in a variety of ways. In many of the western states, where the surrounding land is controlled by the Bureau of Land Management, the U.S. Forest Service, or the states themselves, DOD is able to collaborate with other government institutions to minimize development in locations that would affect training or testing.

In addition, buffer programs like the Readiness and Environmental Protection Integration (REPI) program leverage unique authorities that allow DOD to share the costs of conservation easements around our bases. In these cases, the department will pay a portion of the costs of an easement, as will a non-governmental conservation organization, and each side gets what it wants—an undeveloped natural resource next to a military installation—for half price or less.

Another key tool is the Joint Land Use Study (JLUS). Under this authority, DOD and local communities work together to inform future development efforts to minimize impacts to the base. Communities are able to pursue compatible development without jeopardizing the local military base, which is usually a principal economic engine.

In recent years, the construction of wind turbines near installations has presented a particular problem. The tip of a turbine blade moves quickly and is often picked up by radar as an aircraft, thereby interfering with radar operations and testing. Moreover, given their height, most commercial turbines present significant obstructions to military training routes. To address this issue, DOD established a DOD Siting Clearinghouse, providing developers and land-use authorities a single point of contact to ask whether a proposed turbine site would affect DOD operations. The clearinghouse reaches into the testing and training expertise of the services and works to mitigate unintended problems.

Resilience Challenges. An emerging category of challenges that the installations leadership is facing today are resilience or mission assurance challenges. Can the installation continue to operate and support its missions, or at least recover quickly, when there is a shock to or disruption of its systems? Recently, this has been focused on energy resilience and ensuring that an installation can continue to operate if the electricity grid is knocked out through severe weather, cyberattack, or even equipment failure. DOD reported 701 utility outages lasting eight hours or more in FY 2016.[27]

The most common way that DOD insulates itself from the impact of electricity outages is through diesel generators. Generators are relatively inexpensive and easy to acquire and for that reason are sometimes purchased by mission owners rather than by installation engineers. However, they are inefficient and are suboptimal solutions for medium-term or long-term outages, and DOD has pursued a more comprehensive strategy.

In addition to backup generators, DOD's energy resilience strategy notes that resilience can be achieved in a number of ways. Recent DOD studies describe increasing energy production on base, installing sophisticated microgrids that can steer power across an installation and insulate key facilities from the impacts of outages, diversifying its fuel supplies, improving testing of its current backup generators, and creating non-energy solutions such as ensuring backup mission facilities at different installations.[28] It is reasonable to expect that the increased attention being paid to these issues will lead to increased investment in these options to ensure energy availability.

Cyberattacks and climate impacts will affect more than just the supply of energy to installations, and DOD has begun to explore the vulnerability of its installations to each of these threats. During his confirmation process, Secretary of Defense James Mattis stated:

> [T]he effects of a changing climate—such as increased maritime access to the Arctic, rising sea levels, desertification, among others—impact our security situation. I will ensure that the department continues to be prepared to conduct operations today and in the future, and that we are prepared to address the effects of a changing climate on our threat assessments, resources, and readiness.[29]

In January 2018, DOD reported that approximately half of its bases reported damage from climate impacts, including flooding and storm surge, wind damage, drought, and wildfires.[30] The Navy, with its preponderance of coastal installations, is already experiencing challenges from sea-level rise at bases like Norfolk or Annapolis,[31] and the Assistant Commandant of the Marine Corps has testified that he is considering a seawall to protect Parris Island.[32]

In many cases, this is about avoiding expenses and reducing risk by selecting where future facilities are placed. An illustrative example of the need to consider climate in planning is the multibillion-dollar radar site on Kwajalein Atoll,[33] which DOD estimates could be unable to support human habitation by as early as 2030.[34] Consideration of climate impacts might have helped planners choose a more enduring site for the investment. Congress has begun to focus on the impacts of climate on national security and has directed DOD to assess its overall vulnerability and develop mitigation plans for its most vulnerable installations.[35]

The cyber threat has received considerable DOD attention and investment, but the vulnerability of installations is only beginning to be understood. Industrial control systems are vulnerable to attack and intrusion, but DOD has no inventory of the systems inside its facilities. New guidance has been issued to govern the cybersecurity of these systems,[36] but installation personnel do not always have the specialized expertise needed to deal with cyber threats. Efforts to hire additional cyber experts will be undermined by the funding problems that DOD's installations face, particularly as they try to meet targets for staff reductions. The staffing challenge makes it even more important to have strong relationships with partners in the cyber community such as those at Cyber Command.

Outside the scope of this discussion but equally critical is the issue of vulnerability to military attack. This is ever-present in the minds of those in our contingency bases in Afghanistan, Iraq, or Niger, but we must begin to consider how to insulate the critical mission that our installations perform and the assets they support when we consider the threat from nations like Russia and China, whose weapons easily possess the range to reach our major enduring installations in Europe and the Western Pacific. Without these bases, our ability to project power in these regions would be severely diminished, and we ignore them at our peril. This is a challenge that the warfighters and the installations communities must address together.

Conclusion

DOD's vast installations enterprise is essential to the military mission in an incredibly diverse number of ways. It faces decay from years of underfunding, tightening constraints from encroachment, and threats from cyberattack and the climate itself, but the men and women of the enterprise continue to make it work and support the warfighter.

I have often been asked about the base of the future and what it would look like, and I have responded that if it continues along its current trajectory, it would be dilapidated, understaffed, underfunded, and underutilized. Just like a car owner who chooses to save money by choosing not to change the oil, the nation will have to pay a much larger price down the line.

The Administration and the Congress have an opportunity and an obligation to change this trajectory. Efficiency and reform are most certainly valuable and even essential when dealing with budgets that are short of the need, but they are not enough to solve the underlying problems that DOD faces. Ultimately the department will need more money for its facilities and a holistic strategy for recovery. It needs to reinvest in its installations or divest them.

Endnotes

1. John Conger, Acting Deputy Under Secretary of Defense (Installations and Environment), statement before the Subcommittee on Military Construction, Veteran Affairs, and Related Agencies, Committee on Appropriations, U.S. Senate, 113th Cong., 2nd Sess., April 2, 2014, p. 1, https://www.appropriations.senate.gov/imo/media/doc/hearings/FINAL%20SAC-M%20%20Posture%20Statement_4_2_14.pdf (accessed May 24, 2018).

2. U.S. Department of Defense, Real Property Assets Database (RPAD), "Department of Defense Real Property Portfolio: 2016 Real Property Fast Facts," February 21, 2017, https://www.acq.osd.mil/eie/Downloads/Fast_Facts_2016.pdf (accessed May 25, 2018).

3. U.S. General Services Administration, "GSA Properties," last reviewed February 16, 2018, https://www.gsa.gov/real-estate/gsa-properties (accessed May 25, 2018).

4. U.S. Department of the Interior, Bureau of Land Management, "What We Manage," https://www.blm.gov/about/what-we-manage/national (accessed May 25, 2018).

5. U.S. Department of Agriculture, U.S. Forest Service, "Budget & Performance," https://www.fs.fed.us/about-agency/budget-performance (accessed May 25, 2018).

6. Table, "Base Structure Report—As of 30 Sept 2014," in U.S. Department of Defense, *Base Structure Report—Fiscal Year 2015 Baseline: A Summary of the Real Property Inventory*, p. 61, https://www.acq.osd.mil/eie/Downloads/BSI/Base%20Structure%20Report%20FY15.pdf (accessed May 25, 2018).

7. U.S. Department of Defense, *Base Structure Report—Fiscal Year 2015 Baseline: A Summary of the Real Property Inventory*, p. 6.

8. 10 U.S. Code §2913 (b)(1), https://www.gpo.gov/fdsys/pkg/USCODE-2011-title10/html/USCODE-2011-title10-subtitleA-partIV-chap159-sec2687.htm (accessed June 4, 2018).

9. John Conger, Performing the Duties of Assistant Secretary of Defense (Energy, Installations and Environment), statement before the Subcommittee on Readiness and Management Support, Committee on Armed Services, U.S. Senate, March 11, 2015, p. 1, https://www.armed-services.senate.gov/imo/media/doc/Conger_%2003-11-15.pdf (accessed May 25, 2018).

10. U.S. Department of Defense, Office of the Deputy Under Secretary of Defense (Installations and Environment), *2007 Defense Installations Strategic Plan*, January 1, 2007, p. 20, http://handle.dtic.mil/100.2/ADA487620 (accessed July 20, 2018).

11. U.S. Department of the Navy, *Fiscal Year (FY) 2019 Budget Estimates: Justification of Estimates, Operation and Maintenance, Navy*, February 2018, p. 7, http://www.secnav.navy.mil/fmc/fmb/Documents/19pres/OMN_Vol1_book.pdf (accessed May 25, 2018).

12. U.S. Government Accountability Office, *Sequestration: Documenting and Assessing Lessons Learned Would Assist DOD in Planning for Future Budget Uncertainty*, GAO-15-470, May 2015, p. 30, https://www.gao.gov/assets/680/670476.pdf (accessed May 25, 2018).

13. National Research Council of the National Academies, *Predicting Outcomes of Investments in Maintenance and Repair of Federal Facilities* (Washington: National Academies Press, 2012). p 15.

14. The Honorable Lucian Niemeyer, Assistant Secretary of Defense (Energy, Installations and Environment), statement on "Fiscal Year 2019 Department of Defense Budget Request for Energy, Installations and Environment" before the Subcommittee on Readiness, Committee on Armed Services, U.S. House of Representatives, April 18, 2018, p. 4, https://docs.house.gov/meetings/AS/AS03/20180418/108135/HHRG-115-AS03-Wstate-NiemeyerL-20180418.PDF (accessed May 25, 2018).

15. Peter Potochney, Acting Assistant Secretary of Defense (Energy, Installations, and Environment), statement on "Fiscal Year 2018 Department of Defense Budget Request for Energy, Installations, and Environment" before the Subcommittee on Military Construction, Veterans Affairs, and Related Agencies, Committee on Appropriations, U.S. Senate, June 6, 2017, p. 16, https://www.appropriations.senate.gov/imo/media/doc/060617-Potochney-Testimony.pdf (accessed May 25, 2018).

16. Brian J. Lepore, Director, Defense Capabilities and Management, U.S. Government Accountability Office, "Military Base Realignments and Closures: Key Factors Contributing to BRAC 2005 Results," testimony before the Subcommittee on Readiness, Committee on Armed Services, U.S. House of Representatives, GAO-12-513T, March 8, 2012, p. 14, https://www.gao.gov/assets/590/589135.pdf (accessed May 25, 2018).

17. Potochney, statement on "Fiscal Year 2018 Department of Defense Budget Request for Energy, Installations, and Environment," June 6, 2017, p. 16.

18. Ibid., p. 15.

19. Aaron Mehta and Joe Gould, "The New BRAC Strategy: Capability over Cost Savings," *Defense News*, December 14, 2017, https://www.defensenews.com/pentagon/2017/12/14/the-new-brac-strategy-capability-over-cost-savings/ (accessed May 25, 2018).

20. Frank Kendall, "A Tale of Two BRACs," *Roll Call*, November 21, 2013, http://www.rollcall.com/news/a_tale_of_two_bracs_commentary-229248-1.html (accessed May 25, 2018).

21. Amaani Lyle, "DoD Housing Pro Describes Privatization Evolution," DoD News, January 26, 2013, https://www.defense.gov/News/Article/Article/603983/dod-housing-pro-describes-privatization-evolution/ (accessed May 25, 2018).

22. Ibid.

23. 10 U.S. Code § 2678, https://www.law.cornell.edu/uscode/text/10/2679 (accessed May 25, 2018).

24. U.S. Department of Defense, Office of the Assistant Secretary of Defense for Energy, Installations and Environment, *Department of Defense Annual Energy Management and Resilience (AEMR) Report: Fiscal Year 2016*, July 2017, p. 15, https://www.acq.osd.mil/eie/Downloads/IE/FY%202016%20AEMR.pdf (accessed May 25, 2018).

25. Ibid., p. 18.

26. U.S. Department of Defense, Secretary of Defense, Under Secretary of Defense (Personnel and Readiness), *Report to Congress: 2017 Sustainable Ranges*, May 2017, p. 2, http://prhome.defense.gov/Portals/52/Documents/RFM/Readiness/docs/2017SRR_FINAL.pdf?ver=2017-07-25-115014-387 (accessed May 25, 2018).

27. U.S. Department of Defense, *Department of Defense Annual Energy Management and Resilience (AEMR) Report: Fiscal Year 2016*, p. 39.

28. U.S. Department of Defense, Office of the Assistant Secretary of Defense (Energy Installations and Environment), *Energy Resilience: Operations, Maintenance, & Testing (OM&T) Strategy and Implementation Guidance*, March 2017, p. 4, https://www.acq.osd.mil/eie/Downloads/IE/2%20-%20Energy%20Resilience%20-%20OM&T%20Guidance%20(v17)%20-%20PR%20Version%20-%20approved.pdf (accessed May 25, 2018).

29. Andrew Revkin, "Trump's Defense Secretary Cites Climate Change as National Security Challenge," ProPublica, March 14, 2017, https://www.propublica.org/article/trumps-defense-secretary-cites-climate-change-national-security-challenge (accessed June 4, 2018).

30. U.S. Department of Defense, Office of the Under Secretary of Defense for Acquisition, Technology, and Logistics, *Climate-Related Risk to DoD Infrastructure: Initial Vulnerability Assessment Survey (SLVAS) Report*, January 2018, p. 2, https://climateandsecurity.files.wordpress.com/2018/01/tab-b-slvas-report-1-24-2018.pdf (accessed May 25, 2018).

31. *Congressional Quarterly*, "Senate Armed Services Subcommittee on Readiness and Management Support Holds Hearing on U.S. Forces Readiness," CQ Congressional Transcripts, February 14, 2018, http://www.cq.com/doc/congressionaltranscripts-5267204?15&search=JFszzkˉn (accessed June 4, 2018).

32. Ibid.

33. Scott Waldman, "Key Missile Defense Installation Will be Uninhabitable in Less Than 20 Years," E&E News, March 1, 2018, https://www.scientificamerican.com/article/key-missile-defense-installation-will-be-uninhabitable-in-ess-than-20-years/ (accessed May 25, 2018).

34. Curt D. Storlazzi, Stephen Gingerich, Peter Swarzenski, Olivia Cheriton, Clifford Voss, Ferdinand Oberle, Joshua Logan, Kurt Rosenberger, Theresa Fregoso, Sara Rosa, Adam Johnson, and Li Erikson (U.S. Geological Survey); Don Field, Greg Piniak, Amit Malhotra, and Mark Finkbeiner (National Oceanic and Atmospheric Administration); Ap van Dongeran, Ellen Quataert, Arnold van Rooijen, Edwin Elias, and Mattijs Gaween (Deltares); and Annamalai Hariharasubramanian, Matthew Widlansky, Jan Hafner, and Chunxi Zhang (University of Hawaii), *The Impact of Sea-Level Rise and Climate Change on Department of Defense Installations on Atolls in the Pacific Ocean (RC-2334)*, Report to the U.S. Department of Defense Strategic Environmental Research and Development Program, August 31, 2017, https://serdp-estcp.org/Program-Areas/Resource-Conservation-and-Resiliency/Infrastructure-Resiliency/Vulnerability-and-Impact-Assessment/RC-2334#factsheet-17382-objective (accessed May 25, 2018).

35. H.R. 2180, National Defense Authorization Act for Fiscal Year 2018, Public Law 115-91, 115th Cong., https://www.congress.gov/115/bills/hr2810/BILLS-115hr2810enr.pdf (accessed May 25, 2018).

36. U.S. Department of Defense, *Unified Facilities Criteria (UFC): Cybersecurity of Facility-Related Control Systems*, UFC 4-010-06, September 19, 2016, https://www.acq.osd.mil/eie/Downloads/IE/UFC_4_010_06.pdf (accessed May 25, 2018).

Winning Future Wars: Modernization and a 21st Century Defense Industrial Base

Daniel Gouré, PhD

Modernization Defined and Theories of Modernization

Former Secretary of Defense Donald Rumsfeld is remembered for (among other statements) his famous comment on military preparedness: "You go to war with the Army you have, not the Army you might want or wish to have at a later time."[1] His insight aptly encompasses the modernization challenge for the U.S. military.

America's military must always be capable of going to war this very day with capabilities on which warfighters can rely, with which they have trained, and for which they have the necessary sustainment. At the same time, the military needs to prepare for future conflicts, to modernize, in anticipation of or in response to changes in threats and technology, seeking capabilities that will be needed in the event of future fights. Finally, the military must ensure that there is sufficient resilience and adaptability in the defense industrial base to respond to unanticipated circumstances and emerging needs, particularly in wartime.

Modernization is one of the four pillars on which U.S. military power rests, along with force structure, readiness, and sustainability. The goals of modernization are to close a capability gap, provide a qualitatively improved capability, and/or reduce costs. Modernization entails the replacement of an existing military technology, generally a platform, weapon, or system, with one that is significantly more capable, even transformational. Modernization is about more than just hardware. To achieve a significant increase in military effectiveness the new item must be married to an appropriate organization, concept of operations, set of tactics, command and control system, and supporting infrastructure.

One of the best historical examples of military modernization involving the interplay of new platforms, organizations, and operational concepts is the United Kingdom's successful effort in the 1930s to create the integrated air defense system that proved victorious during the Battle of Britain. Over a period of years, the British military married advances in technology, most notably radar that could detect hostile aircraft at significant ranges, with a novel command and control network to relay warnings and dispatch interceptors and a family of fighter aircraft, most famously the Hurricane and Spitfire.[2]

It is important to recognize that this achievement owes as much to nontechnical factors as it does to advances in electronics or aircraft design. As one defense analyst has observed, "[t]he revolutionary innovation of British air defense emerged from the confluence of the Royal Air Force reorganization, a revision of strategic assumptions and national strategy, and a small group of pivotal civil-military advocates who championed the integration of emerging technology."[3]

Modernization is qualitatively different from the U.S. military's ongoing efforts to make incremental improvements in individual platforms or weapons systems. This process, termed upgrading, can go on for decades and ultimately involve changing virtually all components or systems on a given piece of military equipment. Often, platforms undergo recapitalization, the process by which they are returned to as-new condition at the same time that they receive upgrades.

Many of the most capable systems that the U.S. military operates today have received repeated upgrades. The current fleet of B-52 bombers, last produced in the late 1950s, has undergone continuous upgrades and is slated to remain in service until around 2040. Similarly, the Abrams main battle tank, first deployed in 1980, has benefitted from an extensive series of upgrades including a new gun; better armor; improved sensors, transmission, command and control capabilities; and, most recently, an active protection system. As a result, the Abrams remains the most lethal main battle tank in the world.

Even the newest platforms and weapons systems undergo continuous incremental improvements. The F-35 Joint Strike Fighter (JSF) has just entered service with the Air Force and Marine Corps; the Navy is a few years behind. Yet the program is beginning early software development and integration for a Block 4 upgrade, scheduled for deployment in the early 2020s, that will allow the employment of additional precision weapons as well as an automatic ground collision avoidance system.[4] Continuous product improvement allows the warfighter to have capabilities in hand while exploiting later advances in tactics and technologies.

Historically, changes in military technologies have often occurred in clusters, reflecting major advances in the sciences, manufacturing processes, the organization of economic activities, and even political structures. Many military historians refer to these as Revolutions in Military Affairs.[5] An RMA is based on the marriage of new technologies with organizational reforms and innovative concepts of operations. The result is often characterized as

a new way of warfare. RMAs require the assembly of a complex mix of tactical, organizational, doctrinal, and technological innovations in order to implement a new conceptual approach to warfare.

There have been a number of RMAs just in the past century.[6] An example is the mechanization of warfare that began in World War I with the introduction of military airpower, aircraft carriers, submarines, and armored fighting vehicles. Out of these advances in technology came independent air forces, strategic bombardment, and large-scale amphibious operations. Another occurred with the invention of nuclear weapons and long-range ballistic missiles, which led to the creation of new organizations such as the now-defunct Strategic Air Command and new concepts such as deterrence. In the 1970s, the advent of information technologies and high-performance computing led to an ongoing RMA based largely on improved intelligence and precision strike weapons. The 1991 Gulf War and Operation Iraqi Freedom in 2003 are considered to be quintessential examples of this RMA.[7]

A variant of the RMA theory that is specifically applicable to U.S. defense planning, Strategic Offsets, was introduced by the Obama Administration in 2014. Senior defense officials argued that since the end of World War II, the United States had twice exploited investments in advanced technologies to offset the military advantages of its major competitors.[8] These strategically driven modernization efforts radically changed the equipment, organization, and operations of America's armed services.

In the 1950s and 1960s, to counter the Soviet Union's quantitative superiority in conventional forces, the United States built a large and sophisticated arsenal of nuclear weapons and delivery systems. This was the First Offset. Once the Soviet Union acquired parity in nuclear forces, the United States reacquired military superiority in the 1970s and 1980s by exploiting the revolutions in electronics and materials and investing in stealth, information technologies, computers, high-resolution/multispectral sensors, and precision navigation. This was the Second Offset. The U.S. military has sought to extend the advantages from this Second Offset for the past 25 years.

Now many believe that the U.S. military must pursue a new modernization effort. This Third Offset is made necessary by the rise of great-power competitors, the loss of the military advantages achieved by the Second Offset, and the development of a host of new technologies, many driven by the private sector rather than by government, that promise to change the way military equipment is designed and built and the way military forces will fight. This new Offset is a function, first and foremost, of the proliferation of sensors and so-called smart devices; the creation of increasingly large, complex, and sophisticated information networks; and the growing potential in automated systems and artificial intelligence.[9] Defense leaders seek to reestablish U.S. military-technological superiority by investing in such new areas as undersea systems, hypersonics, electronic warfare, big data analytics, advanced materials, 3-D printing, energy and propulsion, robotics, autonomy, man-machine interfaces, and advanced sensing and computing.[10]

It is noteworthy that the first two Offset strategies were driven primarily by government, principally defense-related, investments in science and technology. The Third Offset is largely based on advances by the private sector in areas such as electronics, artificial intelligence, information technologies, and networking. The innovation cycle times for many of these new technologies are far faster than those for traditional military programs. In addition, because these advances are the product of commercial development, it is difficult to control access to them by competitors, both great and small. As a result, the U.S. defense establishment is increasingly challenged not only to adopt these advances and integrate them into military systems, but also to adapt to the more rapid pace of change in everything from contracting and budgeting to organization, training, and sustainment.

The centerpiece of the Obama Administration's effort to jump-start a Third Offset was a new Long-Range Research and Development Planning Program (LRRDPP) to help identify, develop, and field breakthroughs in the most cutting-edge technologies and systems, especially in the fields of robotics, autonomous systems, miniaturization, big data, and advanced manufacturing, including 3-D printing.[11] The LRRDPP was a capabilities-based exercise that reflected the generic nature of the Administration's threat assessments.[12] In the absence of a threat-driven research and development (R&D) plan, the best the Pentagon could do was try to speed up the overall introduction of new technologies.

In order to accelerate the acquisition of leading-edge innovations from the commercial sector, then-Secretary of Defense Ashton Carter stood up the Defense Innovation Unit Experimental (DIUx). Located in Silicon Valley and modeled after the CIA's In-Q-Tel, a venture capital firm that provides seed money for innovative commercial companies working in areas of interest to the Intelligence Community,[13] the DIUx provides capital to small and start-up companies that are working on applications of advanced technology that are relevant to long-range Department of Defense (DOD) R&D goals.

The Trump Administration has been even more forceful than its predecessor in stressing the need for a broad-based, strategically driven modernization effort. Great-power competition has returned as a driving force in international relations. While this country spent 20 years in the modernization wilderness, investing in capabilities to defeat low-tech insurgencies and building capacity over capability, competitors targeted modernization efforts intended to undermine U.S. military-technological advantages. According to the Administration's 2017 *National Security Strategy*:

Deterrence today is significantly more complex to achieve than during the Cold War. Adversaries studied the American way of war and began investing in capabilities that targeted our strengths and sought to exploit perceived weaknesses. The spread of accurate and inexpensive weapons and the use of cyber tools have allowed state and non-state competitors to harm the United States across various domains. Such capabilities contest what was until recently U.S. dominance across the land, air, maritime, space, and cyberspace domains. They also enable adversaries to attempt strategic attacks against the United States—without resorting to nuclear weapons—in ways that could cripple our economy and our ability to deploy our military forces.[14]

In addition to the intensification of competition between nations, technological change is also driving the need to modernize the U.S. military. The 2018 *National Defense Strategy* states that the key to future U.S. security lies in the exploitation of these new technologies:

> The security environment is also affected by *rapid technological advancements and the changing character of war*. The drive to develop new technologies is relentless, expanding to more actors with lower barriers of entry, and moving at accelerating speed. New technologies include advanced computing, "big data" analytics, artificial intelligence, autonomy, robotics, directed energy, hypersonics, and biotechnology—the very technologies that ensure we will be able to fight and win the wars of the future.[15]

However, investments in technology are only part of what is required for the United States to engage successfully in the new great-power competition and deter major conflicts. The *National Defense Strategy* takes a broad view of what must be done to modernize U.S. national security capabilities and institutions. In particular, it proposes expanding the competitive space in ways that position areas of U.S. comparative advantage against those where our adversaries are relatively weak:

> A long-term strategic competition requires the seamless integration of multiple elements of national power—diplomacy, information, economics, finance, intelligence, law enforcement, and military. More than any other nation, America can expand the competitive space, seizing the initiative to challenge our competitors where we possess advantages and they lack strength. A more lethal force, strong alliances and partnerships, American technological innovation, and a culture of performance will generate decisive and sustained U.S. military advantages.[16]

It is difficult to question the fundamental assumption in current U.S. national security planning: that this nation must pursue comprehensive, rapid modernization of its military capabilities. The rapid evolution of the international security environment, the growing military-technological sophistication of both state and non-state adversaries, and the intensifying rate of global technological change, much of it driven by the private sector, necessitate such an effort. While inevitably costly, the alternative—the loss of U.S. military superiority—would entail far greater costs to this country.

Challenges to U.S. Military Modernization in the 21st Century

Today, U.S. national security may be under greater stress than at any time since the early days of the Cold War. The number of geostrategic threats to U.S. global interests and allies has increased, and the ways and means of modern warfare are evolving with remarkable speed. Competitors are engaged in an intensive and broad-based arms race intended, first, to deny the United States its hard-won military advantages and, second, to establish their own military superiority. Advanced military and dual-use technologies are proliferating widely. The defense industrial base has shrunk to the point that there are numerous instances of single suppliers of critical items. The national security innovation base is under stress from within and attack from without.

Senior defense officials and military leaders have identified five evolving strategic challenges to U.S. security: Russia, China, North Korea, Iran, and terrorism. The first two are engaged in major military modernization programs, investing in capabilities designed to counter long-held U.S. military-technological advantages. According to Army Major General Eric Wesley, "some analysts have said of 10 major capabilities that we use for warfighting that by the year 2030, Russia will have exceeded our capability in six, will have parity in three, and the United States will dominate in one."[17]

In a number of ways, Russia has made the greatest strides in the shortest period of time. Compare Russia's problematic campaign against Georgia in 2008 with the much better-planned and better-executed operations in Crimea and Ukraine a short six years later. Moscow's operations in Ukraine allowed the world to observe the gains Russian ground forces have made in both technologies and combat techniques. Russian forces have demonstrated advances in armored combat vehicles; electronic warfare (EW); long-range massed fires coupled with drone-provided intelligence, surveillance, and reconnaissance (ISR); mobile, high-performance air defenses; and air assault.[18] A respected expert on this new generation of Russian military capabilities has described one engagement:

> In a 3-minute period...a Russian fire strike wiped out two mechanized battalions [with] a combination of top-attack munitions and thermobaric warheads.... If you have not experienced or seen the effects of thermobaric warheads, start taking a hard look. They might soon be coming to a theater near you.[19]

The impact of Russian investments in a new generation of ground combat capabilities has been amply demonstrated by operations over the past several years in Ukraine and Syria. The combination of drone-based ISR, communications jamming, and the application of long-range firepower with advanced warheads has proved to be especially lethal.

Russian advances in EW have been particularly noteworthy and have resulted in the deployment of systems that can challenge one of the central features of modern U.S. military capabilities: the ability to link sensors to shooters in a manner that provides a near real-time ability to conduct long-range and multidomain fires. Ukrainian separatist forces equipped with Russian EW systems have demonstrated a highly sophisticated ability to jam communications systems, deny access to GPS, and interfere with the operation of sensor platforms. Recently, it has been reported that U.S.-made tactical drones operated by Ukrainian security forces were being jammed and hacked by the Ukrainian rebels.[20] Russian forces in Syria were reported to have jammed U.S. intelligence/psychological operations aircraft operating in the western portion of that country.[21]

"Given [the Russian military's] modernization, the pace that it's on," Army General Curtis M. Scaparrotti, Supreme Allied Commander, Europe, has warned. "we have to maintain our modernization...so that we can remain dominant in the areas that we are dominant today." Otherwise, "I think that their pace would put us certainly challenged in a military domain in almost every perspective by, say, 2025."[22]

China is equally intent on developing military capabilities that pose a direct challenge to the United States and its allies. According to Defense Department's 2017 *Annual Report to Congress: Military and Security Developments Involving the People's Republic of China*:

> China's leaders remain focused on developing the capabilities to deter or defeat adversary power projection and counter third-party intervention—including by the United States—during a crisis or conflict....
>
> China's military modernization is targeting capabilities with the potential to degrade core U.S. military-technological advantages. To support this modernization, China uses a variety of methods to acquire foreign military and dual-use

technologies, including cyber theft, targeted foreign direct investment, and exploitation of the access of private Chinese nationals to such technologies....[23]

In its 2017 report to Congress, the U.S.–China Economic and Security Review Commission identified a number of specific capabilities that the People's Liberation Army is developing for the purposes of targeting U.S. military forces and countering advanced U.S. capabilities:

The weapons and systems under development and those that are being fielded by China's military—such as intermediate-range ballistic missiles, bombers with long-range precision strike capabilities, and guided missile nuclear attack submarines—are intended to provide China the capability to strike targets further from shore, such as Guam, and potentially complicate U.S. responses to crises involving China in the Indo-Pacific....

China's increasingly accurate and advanced missile forces are intended to erode the ability of the United States to operate freely in the region in the event of a conflict and are capable of holding U.S. forces in the region at risk.

China's continued focus on developing counter space capabilities indicates Beijing seeks to hold U.S. intelligence, surveillance, and reconnaissance satellites at risk in the event of conflict.[24]

More and more, the strategic competition with Russia and China will be in the exploitation of advanced technologies with military applications. In her statement before the Senate Armed Services Committee, Lisa J. Porter, nominee to be Deputy Under Secretary of Defense for Research and Engineering, observed that:

[N]ot only do we face a diversity of threats, we also face a diversity of technological approaches being employed against us, which range from innovative uses of existing technologies in ways we have not always anticipated, to the employment of cutting edge capabilities ranging from space systems to cyber attacks to machine learning to hypersonics to biotechnology.[25]

Outgoing Commander of U.S. Pacific Command (PACOM) Admiral Harry Harris has warned explicitly that the United States is in danger of losing the next arms race with China:

I am also deeply concerned about China's heavy investments into the next wave of military technologies, including hypersonic missiles, advanced space and cyber capabilities, and artificial intelligence—if the U.S. does not keep pace, USPACOM will struggle to compete with the People's Liberation Army (PLA) on future battlefields. China's ongoing military modernization is a core element of China's stated strategy to supplant the U.S. as the security partner of choice for countries in the Indo-Pacific.[26]

In addition, Russia and China are providing advanced conventional military hardware to a growing number of states. According to a senior U.S. Army source, "If the Army goes into ground combat in the Middle East, we will face equipment from Russia, Iran and in some cases China."[27] Russia is a major defense exporter. It sells advanced aircraft, air defense systems, radar, and ships to China and India; recently began to deliver the S-300 air defense system to Iran; and has reentered the Egyptian market, selling Egypt 50 Kamov Ka-52 Alligator combat helicopters.

Regional challengers like North Korea and Iran are investing in such asymmetric military capabilities as ballistic missiles, advanced air defense systems, and even nuclear weapons. Both nation-states and non-state terrorist groups are able to access advanced military equipment provided not only by Russia and

China, but by Western countries as well. Iran has received advanced air defense systems from Russia and land-based anti-ship cruise missiles from China. Capabilities once viewed as restricted to peer competitors are increasingly within the arsenals of local adversaries and terrorist groups.

The Army's latest operating concept describes the challenge in stark terms:

> As new military technologies are more easily transferred, potential threats emulate U.S. military capabilities to counter U.S. power projection and limit U.S. freedom of action. These capabilities include precision-guided rockets, artillery, mortars and missiles that target traditional U.S. strengths in the air and maritime domains. Hostile nation-states may attempt to overwhelm defense systems and impose a high cost on the U.S. to intervene in a contingency or crisis. State and non-state actors apply technology to disrupt U.S. advantages in communications, long-range precision fires and surveillance.[28]

Even terrorist groups are deploying advanced weaponry. A recent YouTube video that went viral shows the destruction of an Iraqi M-1 Abrams, basically the same kind operated by the U.S. military, by an Islamic State (ISIS)-fired, Russian-made Kornet anti-tank guided missile.[29] Since 2003, the U.S. military and its coalition allies have lost vehicles of all kinds to rocket-propelled grenades. U.S. Navy ships operating in the Gulf of Aden have been attacked repeatedly by Yemeni Islamist rebels armed with Chinese-made anti-ship cruise missiles.[30] It has been discovered that ISIS set up industrial-scale facilities to produce improvised explosive devices (IEDs) and other military equipment.[31]

A new global arms race is heating up. It does not involve nuclear weapons, advanced fighter aircraft, robotic tanks, or long-range missiles. It is a race between terrorists weaponizing commercially available drones and

efforts by the world's most technologically advanced militaries to deploy effective, low-cost countermeasures.

In the hands of groups like ISIS, Hezbollah, and Hamas, drones constitute the ultimate hybrid threat. For the first time in history, non-state terrorists and insurgencies have an air force. ISIS, for example, now routinely employs commercially available drones to perform many of the missions that the U.S. military performs with large, sophisticated, and expensive aircraft: ISR, targeting for indirect fire systems, weapons delivery, and information operations. ISIS is reported to use drones to help direct vehicle-borne IED attacks.[32]

It is evident that both nation-states and terrorist groups are making enormous efforts to negate the U.S. military's long-held technological advantages. Some challengers are developing a comprehensive suite of countervailing capabilities; others are deploying available technologies, sometimes based on commercial systems adapted for military purposes. All however, are creating forces that are intended to counter or even defeat U.S. ground forces.

The consequence of investments by adversaries in systems to counter and even exceed the capabilities deployed by the U.S. military is the progressive loss of tactical overmatch. Challengers generally—but the Russian military in particular—have invested in asymmetric capabilities such as EW, air defenses, anti-armor weapons, improved combat vehicles, and advanced artillery and missiles precisely for the purpose of denying tactical overmatch to U.S. and allied ground forces.

The Department of Defense has created the dangerous illusion of undiminished U.S. military prowess by ensuring the readiness of deploying forces at the expense of force size, modernization, infrastructure recapitalization, and training. In fairness to those in uniform and their civilian counterparts, they had no other choice. It made no sense to prepare for the next war while losing the ones you were currently fighting. In addition, for most of the past century, the risk of major conflict with a regional power or near-peer was judged to be extremely low. But that is no longer the case.

Decades of declining U.S. defense budgets and a 20-year focus on low-intensity conflicts has resulted in a U.S. military that is simultaneously unready for today's conflicts; unfit to conduct the high-end, high intensity wars of the future; and worn out after nearly two decades of continuous combat. According to Secretary of Defense James Mattis:

> Our military remains capable, but our competitive edge has eroded in every domain of warfare—air, land, sea, space, and cyber. The combination of rapidly changing technology, the negative impact on military readiness resulting from the longest continuous period of combat in our Nation's history, and a prolonged period of unpredictable and insufficient funding, created an overstretched and under-resourced military.[33]

Senior members of the military made the obligatory pilgrimage to Capitol Hill last year to testify as to the state of the armed forces. In virtually every case, the message was the same: As a consequence of years of underfunding, the U.S. military is at the breaking point—and this is in the absence of a major conflict.

- According to the Army representatives, in order to maintain enough ready forces, the service has "accepted considerable risk by reducing end-strength and deferring modernization programs and infrastructure investments" in "trade-offs [that] reflect constrained resources, not strategic insight.... [O]ur restored strength must be coupled with sufficient and sustained funding to avoid creating a hollow force."[34]

- The Navy representatives acknowledged that the effort to ensure that deployed forces are ready has come at the expense of the rest of the service: "[W]hile our first team on deployment is ready, our bench—the depth of our forces at home—is thin. It has become clear to us that the Navy's overall readiness has reached its lowest level in many years."[35]

- Air Force leaders joined this somber chorus, pointing out that "[s]ustained global commitments combined with continuous fiscal turmoil continue to have a lasting impact on readiness, capacity, and capability for a full-spectrum fight against a near-peer adversary."[36]

All of the services have credible plans to repair the damage done over the past decades, but funding limitations are forcing them to modernize at a pace that is both uneconomical and irrelevant to the growing threat. For example, at current production rates, the Air Force, Navy, and Marine Corps will not receive their full complements of F-35 fighters until approximately 2037. The Army's plan is to modernize its fleets of tanks, armored fighting vehicles, artillery, and rocket launchers over a period of decades. Even with additional funding, the Navy will not achieve its goal of 355 ships until the 2030s.

The U.S. military is at an inflection point. It must address readiness shortfalls for a force that could be called on to fight at any time. However, decades of deferred modernization have resulted in a force that is obsolescing. Maintaining fleets of aging planes, ships, and tanks is becoming prohibitively expensive. In addition, new threats and a quickening pace of technological progress make modernization an imperative. The challenge confronting DOD is the need to lay out a long-term investment strategy that replaces aging systems with new ones that incorporate advanced technologies to provide greater lethality, improved maintainability, and lower operating costs.

The same underfunding that hollowed out the U.S. military over the past several decades also affected the industrial base that is necessary for a credible national defense. In the future, that industrial base may not have sufficient capacity and capability to meet the needs of a nation engaged in a long-term strategic competition with multiple adversaries.

The United States fought and won the Cold War on the basis of a unique set of political, economic, industrial, and technological advantages. By the end of World War II, this country had learned how to harness its industrial might and scientific talent to produce more and, in many cases, better military equipment than any other country was capable of producing.[37] In the decades that followed, the United States continued to depend on its superiority in science and technology and the capabilities of its aerospace and defense industries to turn the products of government-sponsored research and development into advanced military systems.

The end of the Cold War marked the beginning of the end for the system of technological and industrial investment that had sustained U.S. military preeminence for more than four decades. Protracted periods of declining defense budgets caused a sharp contraction in the aerospace and defense sector.[38] A period of rapid vertical and horizontal integration in this sector led to the concentration of critical manufacturing and R&D capabilities in a handful of major defense companies, the so-called primes, and a hollowing out of the supplier base on which these large companies relied for parts, components, and even major systems.

As a result, the once vaunted Arsenal of Democracy withered. The demand of national security no longer would drive investments in science and technology or in productive capacity. The number of companies specializing in aerospace and defense goods shrank precipitously through mergers and exiting of the sector. "We will have American industry providing for national defense," opined Norman Augustine, then chairman of one of the new defense primes, Lockheed Martin, itself a product of the merger of Lockheed and Martin Marietta. "But we will not have a national defense industry. This is not the best of all worlds. We'll have to draw on our industrial base rather than having the defense capability of the past."[39]

The decline of the defense industrial base as a driver of the overall economy is reflected in the *Fortune* 500 listings. In 1961, 15 defense companies were among the top 100 companies listed. In 2017, only four aerospace and defense companies were ranked above 100. Of these, only two—Lockheed Martin and General Dynamics—were primarily defense companies. The other two—Boeing, the highest ranking of the four at 24, and United Technologies—are major providers of defense products but receive a large percentage of their total revenues from commercial sales.[40]

The change in the ranking of defense and aerospace companies in the *Fortune* 500 reflects two critical factors. The first is the long-term decline in U.S. defense spending. Even as the overall revenues and earnings of the top 100 companies increased about sevenfold over the past five decades, those of the aerospace and defense companies only doubled.[41] This decline translated into a reduced demand for unique defense items, which in turn resulted in a collapse in the resources available to aerospace and defense companies to sustain, much less upgrade or modernize, their productive capacities.

The impact of declining defense spending on the output of defense-related goods and products has been exacerbated by the overall deindustrialization of the U.S. economy. From basic commodities such as steel and aluminum to the major subsectors such as shipbuilding and even textiles, the United States has seen the decline of domestic production and increased reliance on offshore suppliers, including such competitors as China.[42] Survival of the commercial U.S. shipbuilding, ship repair, and maritime workforce now depends almost entirely on the requirements imposed by the Jones Act.[43]

The globalization and offshoring of critical industries challenge the U.S. industrial base to produce sufficient quantities of major end items even in peacetime. In the event of war, the U.S. military could rapidly run out of munitions, spare parts, and even critical consumables. Even in major industrial sectors such as automobiles, there is no longer the domestic capacity to support a major, protracted high-end conflict. "In not just World War II, but Korea and Vietnam and the Cold War, you were able to draw from this manufacturing industrial base that was dual use. You had a vibrant automotive industry for instance," an Administration official has said. "Today, the manufacturing capacity is just not there on the civilian side."[44]

Consequently, the U.S. military faces a problem both of capability, the product of modernization, and capacity, the result of insufficient productive means. According to Marine Corps General Joseph Dunford, Chairman of the Joint Chiefs of Staff, the combination of disinvestment and deindustrialization has limited the ability of the U.S. industrial base to meet the demands of a high-end conflict: "Aging logistics infrastructure (i.e. roads, rails, ports, bases), along with an increasingly brittle defense industrial base have long-term consequences that limit our ability to sustain a protracted or simultaneous conflict."[45]

The second factor behind the defense and aerospace companies' changed *Fortune* 500 rankings is the change in the composition of defense goods and services. Increasingly, advances in defense capabilities, whether they result from upgrades or from modernization, are due to the introduction of technologies developed by private companies for the commercial market. Many of these companies provide goods and services to the military, but for the majority, the Department of Defense is but one of many customers. This is particularly the case with respect to IT products, logistics services, and activities critical to the sustainment of military forces and operations. For example, in order to save money and improve functionality, the Pentagon is shuttering its own data centers and increasingly buying cloud services from commercial suppliers. In Operations Iraqi Freedom and Enduring Freedom, much of the flow of supplies into the theater, as well as the sustainment of military forces, was conducted by such private companies as UPS, FedEx, KBR, and Agility.

Defense leaders are increasingly aware that the impetus for innovation for much of the next generation of military equipment, both hardware and software, will come from the commercial sector and that this sector is increasingly globalized. This is particularly true with respect to information technologies, software development, artificial intelligence, robotics, and the biological sciences.

This has created a host of challenges for U.S. defense modernization. The primary challenge is the defense acquisition system, which has a set of standards, practices, timelines, and incentives that are orthogonal to those that operate in the commercial world. The increasingly globalized nature of advanced R&D and production requires a different approach to exploiting cutting-edge commercial advances ahead of potential adversaries. According to Under Secretary of Defense for Research and Engineering Michael Griffin, the key is rapid innovation:

> The technology playing field is changing. Important technology breakthroughs in many fields are now driven by commercial and international concerns. Our strategy acknowledges the imperative of a global, networked and full-spectrum joint force. It responds to the new fiscal environment and emphasizes new ways of operating and partnering. In a world where all have nearly equal access to open technology, innovation is a critical discriminator in assuring technology superiority.[46]

Defense R&D and acquisition officials are struggling to reconcile two very different approaches to the development, production, and support of goods and services. It often takes 15 or 20 years for major defense programs to go from initial concept to full-rate production. In the commercial world, it can take only two years. It is recognized by DOD's leadership that the current acquisition system is too slow at fielding new capabilities. In the words of Under Secretary Griffin:

> We need to think again, as we have really not since the 1980s, about our approach to acquisition. Government acquisition

across the board—not restricted to space—is a mess. We take far longer to buy things that we need on behalf of the taxpayers, and we spend more money trying to prevent a mistake than the cost of the mistake. We're far out of balance on checks and balances in terms of government acquisition.[47]

When it comes to software, the contrast between defense and commercial practices is even starker. It can take the Pentagon two years to write a request for proposal for a new software system and another two years to award a contract. In the commercial world, six months can be a long time for the delivery of software. Will Roper, former head of DOD's Strategic Capabilities Office and now Assistant Secretary of the Air Force for Acquisition, Technology and Logistics (AT&L), has reportedly warned that "[t]he Defense Department's decades-old acquisition system, which was created to build things like aircraft and submarines, simply doesn't work for software, because by the time the service actually takes ownership of the software it's no longer relevant."[48]

More broadly, the argument made by critics of the current defense acquisition system is that it lacks the characteristics that enable agile and innovative organizations like those in Silicon Valley. According to one account, Lisa Porter has aptly described the difference between the two cultures: "'We have to reset the culture at the Pentagon' to allow for failure, learn from it and move on.... To Silicon Valley entrepreneurs, 'risk aversion is anathema,' but that is the practice in the Defense Department."[49]

The Trump Administration is the first to identify the American ability to innovate as critical to the nation's security and economic well-being. The 2017 *National Security Strategy* specifically calls for the protection of the National Security Innovation Base

We must defend our National Security Innovation Base (NSIB) against competitors. The NSIB is the American network of knowledge capabilities, and people—including academia, National Laboratories, and the private sector—that turns ideas into innovations, transforms discoveries into successful commercial products and companies, and protects and enhances the American way of life. The genius of creative Americans, and the free system that enables them is critical to American security and prosperity.[50]

Congress has recognized the need to make the Pentagon's acquisition system more agile and innovative. To that end, the 2017 National Defense Authorization Act (NDAA) mandated that the office of Under Secretary for AT&L, the organization that oversees the entire Pentagon acquisition system from basic science and technology to sustainment of existing capabilities and demilitarization of retiring platforms and systems be split into two smaller offices: Under Secretary of Defense for Research and Engineering and Under Secretary for Acquisition and Sustainment.[51] The primary objectives of this reorganization are to achieve greater innovation in the pursuit of advanced military technologies, more rapid transition of new technologies into acquisition programs, and more expeditious fielding of new capabilities.

Beyond achieving the goal of greater innovation, defense modernization also depends on the ability to produce advanced military capabilities and related software rapidly and in volume. The ability to respond to changing demands from the field and to increase the production of defense end items is limited by the state of the defense industrial base and by cumbersome acquisition processes.

Perhaps the clearest acknowledgement of the current acquisition system's inadequacies was the creation by DOD and the services of special offices with unique authorities expressly for the purpose of leveraging technology development efforts across DOD and expanding or repurposing existing operational capabilities. In 2012, the Pentagon created the Strategic Capabilities Office (SCO). According to then-Secretary of Defense Ashton Carter, "The

SCO is particularly focused on taking weapons systems that we now have. It has been one of the things—places where it's been more creative...and giving them new missions."[52]

Each of the military services has created its own rapid capabilities office (RCO). These organizations have demonstrated that improved capabilities that address critical capability gaps can be fielded more rapidly. The first was the Air Force's RCO, responsible for (among other programs) initial development of the X-37B space plane and B-21 bomber.[53] The Navy's Maritime Accelerated Capabilities Office has been instrumental in accelerating that service's MQ-25A unmanned tanker, Large Displacement Unmanned Undersea Vehicle, and Standard Missile-2 Block 3 system.[54] Similarly, the Army's RCO has begun to address deficiencies in electronic warfare, long-range fires, and non-GPS-based position, navigation, and targeting systems.[55]

Several important features of the SCO/RCO approach are relevant to the overall reform of the services' acquisition systems. These offices:

- Focus on what can be deployed in the near term (one or two years) based on available technology;

- Do not have to pursue full and open competitions;

- Are not only R&D organizations, but also have the ability to procure and field real capabilities; and

- Have a close working relationship with the warfighters that enables the rapid collection of feedback to improve their offerings.

The Army is taking its RCO to a new level by reorganizing it into a Program Executive Office. There will be two program managers under the new structure, one for rapid prototyping and one responsible for rapid acquisition.[56] The rapid prototyping program manager will support the cross-functional teams (CFTs)

and, logically, the new Futures Command. The RCO also is working very closely with Army program managers to ensure that the latter benefits from the insights and data that the former develops.

The successes of the SCO and RCOs provide a template for reform of the services' acquisition systems. In essence, they have proven that there is an alternative approach to acquisition, one that is agile, creative, willing to take risks, and able to pull ideas from traditional defense companies, large commercial ventures, start-ups, government laboratories, and academia.

However, the work of both the SCO and service-based rapid capability offices is more about adaptation than innovation. They are working to fill critical capability gaps largely by repurposing or modifying existing systems. Their work does not require significant changes in organizations or operating concepts. Modernization—the transition to a new generation of capabilities with possibly revolutionary effects—is a more involved, complex, and time-consuming activity.

The current difficulty of maintaining adequate stockpiles of precision munitions is an excellent example of the problems facing today's defense industrial base. The Air Force has been rapidly depleting its stockpiles of smart munitions in order to meet the demands of the fight against ISIS. According to DOD's *Fiscal Year 2017 Annual Industrial Capabilities Report to Congress*, this is a result of decades of inconsistent funding, the lack of investment in new designs reflecting changes in component technologies, the loss of domestic suppliers, and a growing dependence on foreign sources for raw materials and components. The effects of these various challenges could be nothing short of catastrophic for the nation's security:

The loss of this design and production capability could result in costly delays, unanticipated expense, and a significant impact to many current and future missile programs, damaging the readiness of the Department [of Defense] and negatively impacting a foundational national defense priority by placing the ballistic missile production capability at risk.[57]

In some instances, where foreign producers have the best products, it makes sense to acquire designs, components, and even entire platforms from foreign sources. This has been the case with Active Protection Systems for armored vehicles, light attack aircraft, and the Marine Corps' Amphibious Combat Vehicle Increment 1.1. In the case of the F-35 Joint Strike Fighter, eight foreign allies are part of the consortium to develop and build the aircraft.

However, over the past half century, more and more production of items that go into U.S. defense goods comes from foreign countries, including those that are our main competitors. It is difficult for DOD even to track the sourcing of many components that end up in U.S. weapons systems. There have been numerous reports of faulty and even fraudulent parts from China showing up in U.S. military systems.[58] Recently, the Pentagon banned the sale or use on U.S. military bases of telecommunications devices made by the Chinese companies Huawei and ZTE.[59] Under Secretary of Defense for Acquisition and Sustainment Ellen Lord has warned that U.S. dependence on China for materials and components that are essential to high-end defense products is "quite alarming." According to Lord, "We have an amazing amount of dependency on China, and we are sole sourced for rare earth minerals, energetics, different things. This is a problem for us as we move forward."[60]

Finally, the defense acquisition system and companies engaged in defense-related production and sustainment face a critical workforce shortage. The secular decline in manufacturing has resulted in a loss both of aerospace and defense workers and of the skilled technicians and artisans that produce the machines and tools needed to construct next-generation weapons systems. DOD's *Fiscal Year 2017 Annual Industrial Capabilities Report to Congress* identifies weaknesses in the workforce as a serious threat to the ability of the aerospace and defense industrial base to support military requirements:

A&D [aerospace and defense] companies are being faced with a shortage of qualified workers to meet current demands as well as needing to integrate a younger workforce with the right skills, aptitude, experience, and interest to step into the jobs vacated by senior-level engineers and skilled technicians" as they exit the workforce.[61]

The retirement of the Baby Boomer generation and the lack of sufficient opportunities for technical education are also exacerbating the workforce problem. "Throughout our defense industrial base, talented workers in these critically important trades are retiring and not being replaced in sufficient numbers to support our defense needs," according to White House National Trade Council Director Peter Navarro. "Shipyards, vehicle manufacturing and aircraft facilities are particularly hard-hit. Training the next generation of skilled trade workers will be essential to our military's future success."[62]

An additional workforce issue is the backlog in security clearances. The number of engineers, scientists, and even procurement officers awaiting clearances has grown exponentially over the past several years. Major defense programs are being hampered by the inability to get critical technical personnel cleared expeditiously. As one longtime observer of the aerospace and defense industry has observed, this shortfall also acts like a tax on defense procurement:

The government is not keeping up with the demand for clearances. As of last month [April 2017], the National Background Investigations Bureau within the Office of Personnel Management—which performs 95% of federal background checks—had accumulated a backlog of 570,000 applications. Delays in granting initial Top Secret clearances are averaging over 500 days. Average time required to receive an initial Confidential/Secret clearance, one of the least demanding in terms of required background checks, is 262 days.

These delays have been particularly hard on industry, because it is difficult to attract and retain talent when new employees may have to cool their heels for a year or longer before beginning work on classified programs. One big contractor reports that as of April, 72% of the clearances it has requested since January of 2016 were still awaiting initial clearance determinations. Another contractor reported 75% of requests for background checks or periodic reinvestigations were still pending after 18 months; 10% were still pending after 24 months.

The hidden cost to taxpayers of these long delays is huge. An engineer hired at a defense contractor for $100,000 per year will cost the company $725 per day in salary and benefits, which gets added to overhead if they cannot work on the project for which they were hired. If the wait to receive an initial clearance determination is 300 days, it will cost the company $217,500—which then gets billed to the government as a price of doing business....

But the waste does not end there. When clearances take a year or longer to process, programs are delayed, workers are under-employed, and holding on to the people who are most in demand becomes a challenge. Nobody rigorously tracks what all this inefficiency costs the government, but over time it is undoubtedly in the billions of dollars....[63]

Modernization and Innovation

In discussing the 2018 *National Defense Strategy*'s key messages, Secretary of Defense Mattis has made a particular point of the need to accelerate the pace at which weapons systems, military organizations, and concepts of operations are evolved to meet future threats.

To meet this need, DOD "will transition to a culture of performance and affordability that operates at the speed of relevance" because "[s]uccess does not go to the country that develops a new technology first, but rather, to the one that better integrates it and more swiftly adapts its way of fighting."[64]

This formulation stands the traditional metrics of DOD's acquisition system on its head. Procurement programs must always balance performance against affordability or cost. The most noteworthy phrase used by the Defense Secretary is "the speed of relevance." Every current senior DOD leader has stressed the need to develop and deploy new capabilities faster, first to fill capability gaps and then to reestablish military superiority. The Secretary of Defense recently provided a very clear example of what he means by relevance and why speed in modernizing U.S. military capabilities is so vital:

I want to repeat here that we have no God-given right to victory on the battlefield. And in that regard, make no mistake that our adversaries are right now making concentrated efforts to erode our competitive edge. You know it, I know it. We can see it in the world around us. And I would say, too, that by contesting our supremacy in every domain, we can see it working against us in aggregate....

So our air, naval, ground, and logistics bases today are also under threat of precision, all-weather, day/night guided munition bombardment, which will complicate our operations, and make passive and active base defense absolutely critical in the future. So if we fail to adapt... at the speed of relevance, then our forces, military forces, our air force, will lose the very technical and tactical advantage that we've enjoyed since World War II.[65]

The other important part of Secretary Mattis's formulation is that new and advanced weapons systems are not enough to ensure military superiority. Seeming to borrow from the theory of RMAs, Mattis asserts that reestablishment of meaningful military advantage in future conflicts requires changes to organizations and employment concepts.

But in order to allow the services to undertake the required change in organizations, operational concepts, and tactics, it is important to get new capabilities in the hands of the warfighter speedily. There is general agreement among defense experts that once soldiers, sailors, and airmen are able to work with new platforms and systems, they identify ways to improve performance and employ these capabilities. These ideas and suggestions from the field often were not envisioned by the developers or those writing the requirements.

The approach to modernization laid out by Secretary Mattis is orthogonal to the way the existing acquisition system has pursued modernization. The established acquisition system has rightly been criticized as excruciatingly slow, risk-averse, unable to transition new technologies from the R&D to fieldable systems, overly focused on costs at the expense of performance, and preferring process at the expense of results. The belief that adversaries are innovating more rapidly than the U.S. military has therefore sent DOD on the hunt for the magic elixir that will make its own acquisition system more agile and creative. The Office of the Secretary of Defense and the services are looking to cutting-edge commercial firms both for advanced technologies with military applications and as a source for the "spark" of innovation.

The Pentagon is using the Defense Innovation Unit Experimental to connect defense organizations that have critical capability requirements to private companies that offer potential solutions. Not surprisingly, the site for DIUx's first office was Silicon Valley. DIUx provides relatively small amounts of capital in exchange for commercial products that solve national defense problems. It currently is focused on five areas in which the commercial marketplace is leading in technology innovation: artificial intelligence; autonomy;

information technology (IT); human systems; and space.[66]

DIUx has pioneered the use of other transaction authorities (OTAs) to access nontraditional technology providers and speed the process of awarding contracts. It also has created Commercial Solutions Opening agreements. DIUx solicits solutions to warfighters' problems, ultimately awarding contracts for prototypes based on OTA. A prototype contract can reach $250 million, must use a nontraditional defense contractor and have all of its participants be small businesses, or have at least a third of its total cost paid by parties other than the government.[67]

Seeking to replicate the DIUx model, the Air Force stood up the Air Force innovation incubator (AFWERX). AFWERX is exploring ways to develop an entrepreneurial commercial business base of companies that understand national security problems and are able to work with the Pentagon's acquisition system by running multiple programs and familiarizing companies with national security problems and how they can engage effectively with the government. The AFWERX methodology also includes so-called challenge events that bring together small businesses, entrepreneurs, and academia to provide innovative solutions to urgent service requirements.[68]

The Office of Naval Research has taken a similar approach by creating the Naval Innovation Process Adoption (NIPA) to exploit the opportunities created by new contracting mechanisms to connect with small, innovative companies and speed the development of militarily relevant technologies.[69] NIPA is embracing Hacking for Defense (H4D), a program designed by Steve Blank, an adjunct professor at Stanford University, and retired Colonel Pete Newell, former head of the Army's Rapid Equipping Force, of BMNT. H4D began at Stanford University and is now operating at 10 additional colleges and universities. It organizes teams of students at major U.S. universities to help solve difficult problems facing DOD. The goal is to produce a "minimum viable product." Among the problems currently under investigation by H4D are detecting nuclear, biological, and chemical weapons in tunnels; identifying objects in U-2 high-resolution imagery; and battlefield energy self-sufficiency.[70]

One of the key barriers to innovation and faster delivery of relevant new military capabilities to the warfighter is the current acquisition system's requirements-driven approach. It can take up to a decade for a service to develop a fully validated requirement for a new capability. Too often in the past, the requirements developers did so without significant input from technologists, industry, or logisticians. As a senior corporate officer at Alphabet Inc. observed during an Air Force conference, the requirements-driven acquisition process is "more than inefficient, it's become dangerous."[71]

Testifying before the Senate Armed Services Committee in December 2017, Ellen Lord, then Under Secretary of Defense for AT&L, underscored the importance of reducing the upfront time it took to award a contract for major new procurement:

> I have placed priority across the Defense Acquisition System on reducing the time required to award contracts once the requisite funds are authorized and appropriated by Congress. Having reviewed data measuring the typical lead time following validation of a warfighter requirement until awarding the resulting major weapon systems contract, I've concluded that we have the ability to reduce this procurement lead time by as much as 50 percent; significantly reducing our costs while accelerating our timelines for fielding major capability.[72]

Each of the military services is engaged in an effort to respond to Secretary Mattis's initiative by making its acquisition process both faster and more relevant. The most radical reforms have been initiated by the Army. More than the other services, the Army is in dire need of modernization. As current Vice Chief of Staff General James McConville recently

acknowledged, "we are at an inflection point where we can no longer afford to defer modernizing our capabilities and developing new ones without eroding competitive advantages of our technology and weapon systems."[73] For this reason, the Army's current modernization efforts deserve particular attention.

Army Secretary Mark Esper and Chief of Staff General Mark Milley have set ambitious goals for a revamped acquisition system. Secretary Esper has spoken of reducing the time it takes to formulate requirements from an average of five years to just one. General Milley wants new capabilities that are 10 times more lethal than those they replace. Getting there, he suggested in a recent speech, is as much about attitude and culture as it is about technology:

> I'm not interested in a linear progression into the future. That will end up in defeat on a future battlefield. If we think that if we just draw a straight line into the future and simply make incremental improvements to current systems, then we're blowing smoke up our collective fourth point of contact....[74]

The leadership of the U.S. Army has locked arms and is advancing like the proverbial phalanx on a single objective: to make that service's acquisition system faster and more effective. Rather than take the usual incremental approach to change, Army leaders are going big and bold. Even if only a partial success, the reform effort could produce an Army acquisition system that is speedier, more agile, less costly, and more likely to produce better outcomes than is possible under the current system.

As described by Army Secretary Esper in recent testimony before the Senate Armed Services Committee, the reform effort consists of five interrelated initiatives:

- Establishing a Futures Command;

- Streamlining and improving ongoing acquisition activities such as contracting, sustainment, and testing;

- Creating cross-functional teams focused on rapidly defining requirements for programs that address the Army's six modernization priorities;

- Refocusing science and technology priorities and investment; and

- Changing oversight and decision-making related to major acquisition programs.

The Army hopes that just by using CFTs it can reduce the time needed to develop requirements "from up to 60 months to 12 months or less."[75] "The overall goal," according to Secretary Esper, "is to shorten the acquisition cycle to between 5 and 7 years."[76]

But how fast can any acquisition system be when asked to come up with cutting-edge capabilities that can operate in any environment, survive combat, and last for decades? The history of Army programs shows wide variation in acquisition timelines. A review of successful major acquisition programs over the past half-century suggests that they take a minimum of a decade and more often 15–20 years to go from concept development to initial operating capability (IOC).[77] The history of the Army's vaunted Big Five modernization programs—the Abrams tank, Bradley infantry fighting vehicle, Blackhawk and Apache helicopters, and Patriot surface-to-air missile system—illustrates the challenges facing Army acquisition even after current reform initiatives are implemented.

Army planners recognize that in an environment short of national mobilization, true modernization of their service will take time—in reality, decades. In recent written testimony before the Senate Armed Services Committee, four senior Army leaders laid out a three-phase modernization strategy:

In the near-term, the Army will invest in capabilities that address critical gaps and improve lethality to expand and maintain overmatch against peer competitors. In the mid-term, the Army will develop,

procure, and field next generation capabilities to fight and win in Multi-Domain Battle. In the far-term, we will build an Army for a fundamentally different conflict environment—one that will require us to exercise mission command across dispersed and decentralized formations, leverage disruptive technologies at the small unit level, and operate with and against autonomous and artificial intelligence systems, all at an accelerated speed of war.[78]

The Army's proposed acquisition reforms are intended to eliminate the false starts and bets on immature technologies that marred a number of Army acquisition programs, but in many cases, these errors allowed technologies to mature and requirements to be refined. Prior programs could have been executed more efficiently but not necessarily much faster. The reality is that fielding next-generation capabilities inevitably takes a lot of time. The Army has been working on most of its modernization priorities for at least a decade. Even with the use of CFTs and implementation of the other reforms, it is unlikely that new capabilities will be fielded in less than another decade.

Like the Army, the Air Force is putting a great deal of emphasis on reforming the front end of the acquisition process. Secretary of the Air Force Heather Wilson has described her service's vision of acquisition reform in testimony before the Senate Armed Services Committee:

The acquisition enterprise is currently optimized for industrial-age procurement of large weapons systems with extensive requirement development, military specifications and resultant long acquisition timelines. We must shift to align with modern industry practices in order to get cost-effective capabilities from the lab to the warfighter faster. We are changing the culture in the Air Force to focus on innovation, speed and risk acceptance while meeting cost, schedule and performance metrics.[79]

The Air Force is examining ways to improve the process of formulating requirements including by the increased use of prototyping and experimentation. According to the head of Air Force Materiel Command, General Ellen Pawlikowski:

> We have to truly embrace this idea of experimentation in prototyping. Recognizing that we will spend money to build things that we will never buy because we will find out early it doesn't do what we really want.... Money spent on things that we try and don't adopt—that will be more than recouped.[80]

Given the centrality of software in all of its platforms and systems, the Air Force is particularly concerned about changing the acquisition system to reflect the fast-paced evolution of this vital technology. This challenge is made all the more difficult by the reality that when it comes to software, DOD cannot shape the market. Unlike the market for fighter aircraft, tanks, or nuclear-powered attack submarines, when it comes to software, the Pentagon is dependent on commercial providers. Moreover, the commercial market operates under different rules with timelines and incentive structures that are unlike many of those in the traditional defense industrial base. As Secretary Wilson has observed:

> There are areas where the Air Force is still struggling to be exceptionally good buyers. Software is one. We need to improve the development and deployment of software-intensive national security and business information technology systems. As we move toward industry practices and standards, the line[s] between development, procurement, and sustainment for software are blurred. Development cycles of 3–5 years or longer do not align with the pace of technological advancement. They contribute to failures in software-intensive programs and cause cost and schedule overruns. We have initiated

pathfinder efforts and are working to improve the speed of software development. Likewise, we are continuing efforts with Open Mission Systems architecture, and initiatives with Defense Digital Services, Air Force Digital Services, and Defense Innovation Unit Experimental, in addition to our organic development capabilities, to improve software agility, development, and performance.[81]

The Navy is pursuing multiple approaches to making its acquisition system more agile and innovative. It has established the Accelerated Acquisition Board chaired by the service chiefs and its Service Acquisition Executive. It has created specialized approaches to accelerate the system's response to urgent needs. One of these is the Maritime Accelerated Capability Office (MACO), which is tasked with addressing priority needs where a suitable material solution has been identified and a formal program can be established. In the absence of a clear material solution to a priority need, the Navy will pursue a Rapid Prototyping, Experimentation and Demonstration (RPED) project.[82]

The effort to encourage greater innovation makes sense up to a point. Unfortunately, there is a growing tendency for Pentagon officials and defense experts alike to view innovation and efficiency as increasingly the domains of commercial companies and to minimize and occasionally even disparage the U.S. defense industry's ability to produce cutting-edge capabilities. The reason for this is a growing tendency among Pentagon officials and defense experts to conflate advances in basic technologies with innovation in military capabilities. While it is true that more new technology today comes from commercial rather than government investment, innovation in high-end defense products remains almost the exclusive domain of defense companies.

The wars in Iraq and Afghanistan witnessed a veritable explosion of innovation, including platforms and systems, tactics, techniques, and procedures. This also is the same period when innovation by commercial companies was increasing almost exponentially. In a number of instances, new military capabilities were based on commercial innovations, but the creation of entire suites of capabilities to counter IEDs or provide real-time, multispectral tactical ISR and to integrate them on a wide range of platforms was due to the skills and even genius of the public and private defense industrial bases.

Defense companies continue to demonstrate a capacity for innovation that far outstrips that of any commercial entity, not just in the United States but globally. The case of the F-35 Joint Strike Fighter illustrates this point. According to DOD's former Director of Cost Assessment and Program Evaluation (CAPE), Dr. Christine Fox, "from a CAPE perspective, the JSF is not over-cost, it's over-dreamed."[83] While it is true that the plan for the JSF was overly optimistic and underresourced, the program has been remarkably successful in meeting those dreams. Virtually everyone in the military who has been involved with the program over the years has declared it to be a "game changer."[84] The F-35 demonstrates that the defense industrial base can still make dreams come true.

Admittedly, there is one technology area that does pose a serious challenge for the acquisition system: information technology. The entire U.S. defense enterprise, from individual weapons systems to platforms, individual units, and command and control elements to supporting infrastructure, is becoming increasingly information-centric. The result is an orders-of-magnitude improvement in the U.S. military's ability to conduct the full range of missions. Much of the technology underpinning this revolution in military capabilities is commercial in nature. Moreover, the breadth and speed of innovation in commercial IT completely confound the traditional defense acquisition process.

This is even more the case when it comes to cyber security. It is clear that entirely new approaches to the acquisition of cyber capabilities and the management of military networks will be required if the Defense Department is to have any hope of staying abreast of the threat. If the U.S. military cannot successfully defend its systems and networks against this ever-changing threat, current efforts at innovation, which are largely based on IT, will be for naught.

Without question, commercial companies of all types will have a greater role to play in defense innovation during the coming decades than they have had in the past, but the ability of traditional U.S. defense companies to take the products of commercial innovation and create the systems, platforms and capabilities that ensure U.S. military dominance will continue to be determinative.

Modernization and Procurement: How to Buy as Important as What to Buy

Most of the military services' reform efforts have been focused on the front end of the acquisition process: R&D, prototyping, and the formulation of requirements. As part of its effort to stand up the new Futures Command, the Army has focused to a great extent on where to locate its new headquarters. The desire is to imbed the command in an environment of technological and commercial innovation similar to Silicon Valley. The other services are similarly focused on injecting innovation and speed into the front-end or technology-development portion of the acquisition process.

Even more time is consumed by the complex and cumbersome processes of developing, testing, and producing new capabilities. Moreover, because the military acquires platforms and systems in relatively small quantities per year, continuing the current approach means that it will take decades to modernize the force even once new capabilities are developed.

Although the Army talks about having reached an inflection point and needing to rapidly counter the loss of overmatch vis-à-vis great-power competitors, recent programmatic and budgetary decisions suggest that when it comes to putting new capabilities in the field, not much has changed. In fact, some priority modernization programs actually appear to be moving more slowly than they were before being highlighted as essential to national security.

According to documents submitted in support of its fiscal year (FY) 2019 budget request, the Army appears to be increasing the time it will take to field the Future Vertical Lift (FVL) replacement for current rotary-wing systems.[85] Despite having spent years conducting research and producing prototypes in FVL's precursor program, the Joint Multi-Role Technology Demonstrator, the Army still does not plan to field the system before 2030.

Similarly, a year appears to have been added to the development phase of the Long Range Precision Fires (LRPF) program.[86] The additional time will be used to assess the current state of technology and conduct analyses of key price drivers that could affect life-cycle cost estimates and force the program down an alternative path. Both of these factors suggest that further delays in the LRPF program could be coming.

For the Air Force, modernization is here and now. The Air Force currently has major modernization programs underway for virtually all of its aircraft fleets, the nuclear deterrent, space launch, and military satellites. As Secretary Wilson noted in a speech at an Air Force Association conference:

> The average age of our aircraft is 28 years old. We have to be able to evolve faster, to respond faster than our potential adversaries. We've got a bow wave of modernization coming across the board for the Air Force over the next 10 years—it's bombers, it's fighters, it's tankers, it's satellites, it's helicopters and it's our nuclear deterrent.[87]

The key to Air Force modernization is the rate at which it can bring new capabilities online. Unfortunately, current annual production rates for the major platforms on which the Air Force's modernization plan relies are too low. At 48 F-35As per year in FY 2019 and 54 per year in FY 2020–FY 2023, it will take more than 30 years for the Air Force to reach its acquisition goal of 1,700 Joint Strike Fighters. The current acquisition target for the KC-46A tanker is 15 aircraft per year. At this rate, the target of 187 new tankers will not be realized for 12 years. Even then, the Air Force will have to keep flying more than 200 obsolescent KC-135s.

The Air Force's acquisition reform initiatives do not address the fundamental problem of procurement numbers that are simply too low. This reality led one eminent defense expert to warn that:

> There's nothing wrong with pursuing the various leap-ahead ideas that the Air Force has recently embraced in its pursuit of future air dominance. But none of the leap-ahead ideas is likely to come to fruition anytime soon, including the B-21 bomber. One lesson of the Reagan buildup and similar spending surges in the postwar period is that new programs begun in the midst of a buildup tend to falter for lack of funding or feasibility long before they reach the force. It's a lot easier and faster to buy more of what is already being produced.[88]

For the Navy, there is an inherent tension between the desire to be more innovative, to invest in advanced technologies, and the need to increase the overall size of the fleet. It has long been recognized that the Navy is too small to fulfill all of its missions. Now a larger Navy is the law of the land. Section 1025 of the 2018 NDAA states, "It shall be the policy of the United States to have available, as soon as practicable, not fewer than 355 battle force ships...."[89]

The key words in the NDAA are "as soon as practicable." It takes years to build a warship. It also takes lots of money. Then there is the ability of the industrial base, including shipyards but also all of the mid-sized and smaller companies, to expand to meet the demand for more warships. The Navy plans to spend billions to upgrade the four public shipyards so that they can build additional warships and improve maintenance activities.[90] Finally, of course, the size and quality of the workforce that builds the ships and their systems are crucial. Ensuring a continuing, predictable flow of work allows shipbuilders and their suppliers to improve the management and training of their workforces.

One proven way to make procurement of new warships more rapid while simultaneously lowering their cost is to buy them in bulk. The Navy currently purchases several of its most important platforms in groups, either as multiyear procurements or as block buys. The longest-running and most successful example of this approach is for the *Virginia*-class nuclear-powered fast attack submarine (SSN), which is now on its third multiyear procurement.[91] The Navy is preparing to issue its second multiyear procurement for the DDG-51 *Arleigh Burke*–class destroyer. The second multiyear, for as many as 10 advanced Flight III *Arleigh Burkes*, is expected to yield savings of up to $1.8 billion across the planned buy.[92] Block-buy contracts that encompass two providers with different designs are also being used to procure the Littoral Combat Ship (LCS).

Achieving the goal of a 12–aircraft carrier force as part of a 355-ship Navy means shortening the interval between the start of construction, currently five years, as well as finding ways to reduce their cost.[93] The acquisition strategy that has been employed successfully to procure surface combatants and submarines could also be applied to buying aircraft carriers. The Navy bought the first two *Ford*-class carriers, CVNs 78 and 79, as single ships. Initiating a block-buy procurement for the next several ships could help to reduce the interval between construction starts, shorten the overall length of time needed to complete construction, and save money. The only shipyard in the nation that can build nuclear-powered aircraft carriers, Newport News, believes that it could save $1.5 billion on a three-ship block buy and shorten the average construction time by up to two years.[94]

There is a recognition by the Pentagon that it must address industrial base issues in order to modernize. According to senior Army officials:

The past trends of constrained resources in the Army's modernization account have led to significant challenges for the Defense Industrial Base (DIB), especially for companies that cannot leverage commercial sales and for small companies that must diversify quickly to remain viable. When developing our equipment modernization strategy, we have carefully assessed risk across all portfolios to ensure balanced development of new capabilities, incremental upgrades to existing systems, and protection of critical capabilities in the commercial and organic elements of the DIB.[95]

Weaknesses in the defense industrial base are only one of the challenges confronting military modernization. All of the services raise the challenge of moving good ideas from development to procurement. This transition is often referred to as "the valley of death." The DOD R&D establishment annually pursues hundreds of projects. Only a handful ever become programs of record.

Toward a 21st Century Defense Industrial Base

The Department of Defense needs a new model for the defense industrial base. In World War II, we created industrial enterprises modeled on the public arsenals and shipyards. During the Cold War, we encouraged the development of defense conglomerates. Over the past two decades DOD managed the DIB's decline by supporting the development of a small number of relatively specialized defense giants. Today, the Pentagon needs an acquisition system that allows it to innovate rapidly in new areas, including those where commercial companies are leading, and manage large defense programs with very long life cycles.

The Department of Defense is in love with the idea of getting cutting-edge commercial companies to become part of a new defense industrial base. During the Obama Administration, the Pentagon pursued an acquisition reform initiative called Better Buying Power

(BBP). One of its key tenets was the need to leverage commercial technologies to achieve dominant capabilities while controlling life-cycle costs. In pursuit of the innovative spirit, former Defense Secretary Ashton Carter made a pilgrimage to Silicon Valley where he gushed about the IT sector's ability to achieve "boundless transformation, progress, opportunity and prosperity" while simultaneously making "many things easier, cheaper and safer."[96]

In recent years, Congress has sought to inject greater flexibility and speed into the acquisition system. The FY 2016 NDAA included a set of reforms focused on improving the system's efficiency and agility. DOD is now allowed to use rapid acquisition authority to meet urgent operation needs identified by the warfighter or to acquire critical national security capabilities. The FY 2016 NDAA also directed DOD to develop a rapid acquisition strategy for so-called middle-tier programs intended for completion in two to five years.[97]

In 2017, Congress gave DOD additional flexibility with respect to acquisitions. The FY 2017 NDAA expands on earlier acquisition reform efforts. It explicitly establishes the authority for prototype projects in response to a high-priority warfighter need resulting from a capability gap. It also permits DOD to initiate a prototype project when an opportunity exists to use commercial technology to develop new components for major weapon systems so long as the technology is expected to be mature enough to prototype within three years and there is an opportunity to reduce sustainment costs.[98]

What is being created today is a bifurcated defense acquisition system. One part of it centers on small, special organizations such as the Rapid Equipping Force, DIUx, SCO, RCO, and CFTs and employs alternative contracting approaches, accounting standards, and funding mechanisms. The primary goals of this acquisition "sub-system" are the rapid identification of promising technologies, exploration of their application for military purposes, and development of prototypes that can serve as the basis for a program of record. This sub-system seeks to tap into the entrepreneurial character of commercial companies, particularly small and start-up businesses. Its features include the willingness to take risks, acceptance of failure, ability to connect nontraditional sources of ideas, and capacity to bring new products and processes to market expeditiously.

The other part of the acquisition system, representing the overwhelming number of programs and the vast preponderance of expenditures, operates according to a set of complex, fairly restrictive rules set down in the Defense Federal Acquisition Regulations. This system is often accused of being risk averse. While this is true to an extent, its cautious behavior with respect to new and unproven technologies also reflects the reality that standards for the performance and sustainment of military equipment are of necessity much more stringent than those for commercial systems. Moreover, the Pentagon's fleets of aircraft, vehicles, and ships are required to operate under more stressful conditions and to be serviceable far longer than is the case with respect to almost any commercial equivalents.

The notion that DOD can convert its acquisition system to mirror the behavior of the commercial marketplace is largely without merit. At its heart, the difference between the agility and risk-taking culture of a Silicon Valley and the more deliberate, long-term perspective of the defense acquisition system also exists in the commercial world. It is the difference between the attitude, values, and behavior of so-called entrepreneurs at the head of small, start-up companies and the leadership of large, complex, and established businesses. The former are focused on creation; the latter, on production and maintenance. The entrepreneurial spirit driving Tesla would be misplaced in a company like General Motors. This is largely the reason why major commercial companies pursue innovation through acquisitions of or partnerships with smaller cutting-edge firms.

An outstanding response to this unrequited love that defense officials have for commercial companies was provided by Wes Bush, Chief

Operating Officer of Northrop Grumman, one of our leading defense companies. In a speech at the Center for Strategic and International Studies, Bush warned that "commercial solutions—while an important ingredient [in] much of what gets done—in and of themselves are not the answer for our national security and our technological superiority and therefore should not be used as an excuse for further reductions in R&D."[99]

Bush went on to point out that because commercial technologies are available to all, including U.S. adversaries, they will not provide any unique advantages to the U.S. military. Military systems, regardless of the degree to which they rely on commercial technologies, address a unique class of requirements and demand the application of the special skills and knowledge possessed by long-established defense companies.

Defense companies have demonstrated what can be achieved with rapid and innovative product development when not under the system's thumb.

So far, the discussion regarding leveraging advances in the commercial sector to support DOD has focused almost exclusively on developing technologies and producing new capabilities, but there are two fundamental acquisition challenges. One is to acquire dominant capabilities, and the other is to control sustainment and life-cycle costs. It is in the ability to control costs that commercial companies have the most to offer DOD. The revolution in supply chain management, epitomized by the concept of just-in-time manufacturing and delivery, has been every bit as transformational globally as has the invention of the smartphone. Moreover, the Pentagon can avail itself of the advantages of importing best-of-breed commercial supply chain management and sustainment practices more readily than it can adapt commercial technologies to achieve dominant military capabilities.

The Pentagon spends some $200 billion annually on logistics and sustainment. When one adds to this number those support and training functions such as military communications and pilot training that countries like the U.K. have privatized the number could be as high as $300 billion, or nearly three times the current procurement budget. If DOD wants real budget savings and improved warfighting outcomes, it needs to adopt proven commercial-derived logistics and sustainment practices. Where it has done so, costs have gone down and aircraft availability has increased. Similarly, commercial logistics providers have spent more than a decade providing affordable logistics support to U.S forces in Iraq and Afghanistan. Privatizing non-core military functions could save tens of billions of dollars and free hundreds of thousands of uniformed personnel and government civilians for more important tasks.

Acquisition officials are trying to figure out how to get commercial companies to be part of the acquisition system and behave like traditional defense firms. This approach is not likely to be successful. However, one way to fulfill this wish is to allow traditional defense companies to serve as middlemen between the commercial vendors and DOD. Long-standing defense companies have all of the right contracting, accounting, and reporting systems in place.

DOD has resisted the widespread use of commercial best practices in logistics and sustainment because it means giving up some control of resources, people, and even equipment. What Pentagon officials, particularly program managers, have to realize is that the key to successful cost reduction is giving up control of much of the process and relying instead on the incentives of a free market–oriented approach with properly written contracts to drive the desired behavior by the private sector.

A proven way to reduce sustainment costs is by applying commercial best practices to defense acquisition and sustainment. One of these best practices when it comes to managing the maintenance, repair, and overhaul of major weapons systems and platforms is performance-based logistics (PBL). Unlike traditional fee-for-service or time-and-materials contracts, PBL works by specifying outcomes, not activities. The contractor commits to meeting a specified level of performance, such as the percentage of a fleet of vehicles or aircraft available for operations, for a price that is usually below what the government was paying previously.

DOD has had some notable successes with PBL-based sustainment contracts. They are particularly useful in the management of aircraft fleets. There are PBL contracts in place to help support the C-17 Globemaster, MV-22 Osprey, CH-47 Chinook, AH-44 Apache, and MH-60R Seahawk.[100]

A similar situation is developing in the area of networking and software. Increasingly, the commercial world is focused on cloud computing and fee-for-service delivery of capabilities. This approach allows for the rapid advancement of applications, high-speed access to data, effective security, and reduced costs.

The federal government is beginning the transition to the new approach to managing its network and computing needs. The 17 members of the Intelligence Community (IC) are benefitting from a new contract with the private sector for cloud services managed by the CIA and NSA. This is essentially a public cloud on private property, a government facility built to IC security standards.[101] DOD is considering a number of large contracts with commercial cloud providers, such as the Defense Enterprise Office Solutions (DEOS) cloud-based e-mail and messaging contract and the Joint Enterprise Defense Infrastructure (JEDI), which is intended to support core DOD services, data management, and advanced analytics.[102]

There is a simple truth to all defense contracting: Private companies require appropriate incentives for innovating or improving production processes. Investments in R&D and infrastructure are costs that a company, at a minimum, must believe it can recoup once its invention hits the market. If a company is really lucky, it might even make a profit from its efforts.

The constraints of profits imposed on government contracts is a major barrier to commercial firms doing business with the Pentagon. For many high-tech commercial companies, particularly those involved in IT and software, pretax profits can be twice what is earned in the aerospace and defense sector.[103] By many standard measures, private companies have little incentive to do business with the Defense Department.

Every company that innovates, from the "lowly" inventor of an app for a smartphone to biotechnology and pharmaceutical companies looking for the next breakthrough drug and the makers of vehicles, ships, airplanes, and satellites, invest in new products or processes for one reason only: to make money. Wall Street severely punishes publicly held companies that behave in any other way.

Then there is the practice of structuring contracts based on the standard of the Lowest Price Technically Acceptable (LPTA) proposal.[104] Companies bidding on LPTA-type contracts have to demonstrate only the minimum level of proficiency. Providing a better product and high-quality service or proposing a more innovative solution does not increase a bidder's chance of success. In fact, any investments made to attract highly qualified personnel or expenditures made to develop a new solution increase costs for the vender, and thus for the product offered, and reduce the chances of winning.

The combination of declining defense budgets and increasing regulation and oversight has had a suffocating effect on the propensity of defense and aerospace companies to spend on R&D or infrastructure. Without procurements (in other words, purchases by the government), companies have struggled just to recover their costs and earn profits. It makes no sense for them to invest more in R&D when there is no prospect of increased revenues. As the head of a major profit and loss center for one of the largest U.S. defense companies made clear, "I cannot convince my senior management to invest any of our money without the clear prospect of a procurement program at the end of the day and incoming revenues."[105]

The good news is that recent commitments by the federal government to spend more on defense, driven especially by Secretary Mattis's 2018 *National Defense Strategy* that emphasizes the reemergence of great-power competition, has led defense companies once again to spend their own money on R&D and capital improvements. In a recent series of earnings calls and discussions with Wall Street analysts, a number of defense firms announced that they were increasing their spending on R&D, facilities, and manufacturing capacity. In most cases, these firms are spending their own resources before higher defense budgets have materialized or contracts have been won.[106]

There are two reasons for this. The more obvious one is the Trump Administration's commitment to increase defense spending. While much of this increase inevitably will be used to improve readiness and even increase the size of the military, DOD has made it clear that it intends to buy more ships, aircraft, vehicles, missiles, and munitions.

An equally significant reason for defense companies to commit more resources to this effort is the apparent change in DOD's attitude toward the defense industry. In particular, there is a willingness to treat industry as a partner rather than as an adversary and to incentivize increased investment in innovation and manufacturing by increasing procurement. "If we can give industry some reassurance that there will be a contract on the other end, that there are dollars committed behind it, then I think you will see a lot more industry putting their dollars into the game and getting us there quickly," observed Army Secretary Esper recently. "What we are trying to do is improve collaboration with industry. That is how we see it moving forward."[107]

The Pentagon's top acquisition official, Ellen Lord, has proposed incentivizing industry to respond to proposals in 60 days or less and to reduce by half the time it takes for the government to review proposals and award a contract.[108] Since time really is money for these companies, a speedier contracting process matters.

Another roadblock to DOD's ability to access commercial technologies is the government's treatment of intellectual property (IP). There has long been tension between the government and private companies over the former's desire to acquire the rights to the latter's IP. At issue are the government's right to IP that is produced solely with private funds, the extent to which a contract with a defense prime allows the government access to the IP of subcontractors, and the ability of the government to protect that IP from competitors.[109]

DOD leaders have acknowledged that the way the Pentagon addresses the IP concerns of all companies involves serious difficulties. According to Assistant Secretary of the Army for Acquisition, Logistics and Technology Bruce Jette, the Army needs both to find new ways to conduct fair and open competitions that do not force companies to expose their best ideas to potential competitors and to ensure that it is clear who owns which IP.[110]

A 21st century U.S. defense industrial base must also be international. The pace of globalization in the aerospace and defense industry is quickening. In part, this reflects the great expense involved in many large aerospace programs. The Eurofighter and JSF programs are examples of countries pooling their resources and sharing the work involved in building new fighter aircraft. Russia is believed to have joined with India in developing the T-50, a stealthy competitor for the F-22 fighter.

In part, this also reflects the reality that many foreign countries, particularly U.S. allies in Europe and Asia, now possess critical design skills, production capabilities, and products. For example, several of the teams competing for the new Air Force trainer are offering a foreign-designed or foreign-made airframe. The two teams that competed for the Marine Corps' Amphibious Combat Vehicle 1.1 were providing a vehicle made overseas. U.S. Army tanks are being equipped with an Israeli-made active protection system. In many areas, including night vision systems, naval radar, sonar, air-to-air missiles, and even space systems, foreign companies' technologies and products are equal to or better than those provided by U.S. companies.

The fundamental challenge to military modernization in the 21st century is the need to change DOD's acquisition culture in order to incentivize both government and the private sector. Without a major change in DOD's own culture, the effort to make the acquisition system more efficient is more likely than not to enhance inefficiency. In particular, it will almost certainly engender a more combative relationship between DOD and the private sector.

The defense industry has repeatedly shown that it is willing to adapt to meet changes in the way the Pentagon decides to conduct itself. Whether it is fixed-price versus cost-plus contracts,[111] the use of commercial items, basic ordering agreements, small-business and minority set-aside, performance-based logistics, contractor logistics support arrangements, or systems engineering and technical assistance support, the private sector has responded to every invention and notion that the bureaucrats have devised and has continued to support the warfighters.

Conclusion

The U.S. military's ability to defeat its opponents in battle depends largely, though not exclusively, on the equipment, weapons, and supporting capabilities that it possesses. In turn, these depend on an industrial base that is viable and healthy enough to produce them and the relative effectiveness of new capabilities that spring from competition in design. All of this implies some level of competitive redundancy among manufacturers that can come only from a defense funding stream that is large enough and consistent enough to keep companies that produce the wherewithal of America's military power in business. To be clear: This is not some form of corporate welfare. It is an investment in the nation's fundamental security.

Modernization requires the ability of the military to keep place with the technological evolution of the battlefield. A force able to modernize in turn requires an industrial base healthy and diverse enough to develop and apply emerging technologies that are relevant to war. Failure in either area—a weak, moribund defense industrial base or obsolete forces—means failure in war and the fatal compromise of the nation's security. Conversely, a healthy and effective force, made possible by a healthy and relevant industrial base, means a secure and prosperous country.

The latter is clearly better than the former, and the country would be wise to view defense expenditures accordingly.

Endnotes

1. Eric Schmitt, "Iraq Bound Troops Confront Rumsfeld over Lack of Armor," *The New York Times*, December 8, 2004, https://www.nytimes.com/2004/12/08/international/middleeast/iraqbound-troops-confront-rumsfeld-over-lack-of.html (accessed June 15, 2018).

2. Allan R. Millet, "Patterns of Military Innovation in the Interwar Period," Chapter 9 in *Military Innovation in the Interwar Period*, ed. Williamson Murray and Allan R. Millett (New York: Cambridge University Press, 1996), pp. 329–368.

3. Austin M. Duncan, "Innovation Determinants of the World's First Integrated Air Defense System," *The Bridge*, May 3, 2018, https://thestrategybridge.org/the-bridge/2018/5/3/innovation-determinants-of-the-worlds-first-integrated-air-defense-system?utm_source=The+Bridge&utm_campaign=c256af813f-RSS_EMAIL_CAMPAIGN&utm_medium=email&utm_term=0_bcf191ca0f-c256af813f-29639622 (accessed June 14, 2018).

4. Kris Osborn, "Air Force Preps 'Block 4' Variant of the F-35—New Weapons & Tech for the 2020s," *Warrior Maven*, April 30, 2018, https://www.themaven.net/warriormaven/air/air-force-preps-block-4-variant-of-the-f-35-new-weapons-tech-for-2020s-QyxrwVC61EK7KB3L74A7EA/ (accessed June 14, 2018).

5. There is an extensive literature on MTRs and RMAs. See, for example, Benjamin Huebschman, "Historical Lessons Applied to the Current Technical Revolution in Military Affairs," Association of the United States Army, March 14, 2012, https://www.ausa.org/publications/historical-lessons-applied-current-technical-revolution-military-affairs (accessed June 14, 2018), and Steven Metz and James Kievit, "Strategy and the Revolution in Military Affairs: From Theory to Policy," U.S. Army War College, Strategic Studies Institute, June 27, 1995, https://ssi.armywarcollege.edu/pdffiles/PUB236.pdf (accessed June 14, 2018).

6. Andrew F. Krepinevich, Jr., *The Military–Technical Revolution: A Preliminary Assessment*, Center for Strategic and Budgetary Assessments, 2002, http://csbaonline.org/uploads/documents/2002.10.02-Military-Technical-Revolution.pdf (accessed June 14, 2018).

7. Metz and Kievit, "Strategy and the Revolution in Military Affairs: From Theory to Policy."

8. Chuck Hagel, Secretary of Defense, "Reagan National Defense Forum Keynote," address delivered at Ronald Reagan Presidential Library, Simi Valley, California, November 15, 2014, https://www.defense.gov/News/Speeches/Speech-View/Article/606635/ (accessed June 14, 2018).

9. Yuna Huh Wong, "Approaching Future Offsets," *The Hill*, December 20, 2016, http://thehill.com/blogs/congress-blog/economy-budget/311129-approaching-future-offsets (accessed June 15, 2018).

10. Robert Work, Deputy Secretary of Defense, "The Third U.S. Offset Strategy and its Implications for Partners and Allies," speech delivered at Center for a New American Security meeting, Washington, DC, January 16, 2015, https://www.defense.gov/News/Speeches/Speech-View/Article/606641/the-third-us-offset-strategy-and-its-implications-for-partners-and-allies/ (accessed June 15, 2018).

11. Chuck Hagel, Secretary of Defense, memorandum for Deputy Secretary of Defense; Secretaries of the Military Departments; Chairman of the Joint Chiefs of Staff; Under Secretaries of Defense; Deputy Chief Management Officer; Chiefs of the Military Services; Chief of the National Guard Bureau; Director, Cost Assessment and Program Evaluation; Director, Operational Test and Evaluation; General Counsel of the Department of Defense; Inspector General of the Department of Defense; Assistant Secretaries of Defense; Department of Defense Chief Information Officer; Assistants to the Secretary of Defense; Directors of the Defense Agencies; and Directors of the DOD Field Activities, "Subject: The Defense Innovation Initiative," November 15, 2014, http://archive.defense.gov/pubs/OSD013411-14.pdf (accessed June 15, 2018).

12. Ben Fitzgerald, "Technology Strategy Then and Now—The Long Range Research and Development Planning Program," *War on the Rocks*, October 21, 2014, https://warontherocks.com/2014/10/technology-strategy-then-and-now-the-long-range-research-and-development-planning-program/ (accessed June 15, 2018).

13. Fred Kaplan, "The Pentagon's Innovation Experiment," *MIT Technology Review*, December 19, 2016, https://www.technologyreview.com/s/603084/the-pentagons-innovation-experiment/ (accessed June 15, 2018).

14. *National Security Strategy of the United States of America*, The White House, December 2017, p. 27, https://www.whitehouse.gov/wp-content/uploads/2017/12/NSS-Final-12-18-2017-0905.pdf (accessed June 15, 2018).

15. James Mattis, Secretary of Defense, *Summary of the 2018 National Defense Strategy of the United States of America: Sharpening the American Military's Competitive Edge*, p. 3, https://www.defense.gov/Portals/1/Documents/pubs/2018-National-Defense-Strategy-Summary.pdf (accessed June 15, 2018). Emphasis in original.

16. Ibid.

17. Courtney McBride, "Wesley: Russia Offers 'Pacing Threat' for Army Modernization Effort," *Inside the Army*, Vol. 28, No. 44 (November 7, 2016), pp. 4–5.

18. Phillip Karber and Joshua Thibeault, "Russia's New-Generation Warfare," Association of the United States Army, May 20, 2016, https://www.ausa.org/articles/russia%E2%80%99s-new-generation-warfare (accessed June 15, 2018).

19. Phillip Karber, President, Potomac Foundation, quoted in Patrick Ticker, "How the Pentagon Is Preparing for a Tank War with Russia," *DefenseOne*, May 19, 2016, http://www.defenseone.com/technology/2016/05/how-pentagon-preparing-tank-war-russia/128460/ (accessed June 15, 2018).

20. Mark Pomerleau, "Threat from Russian UAV Jamming Real, Officials Say," *C4ISRNET*, December 20, 2016, https://www.c4isrnet.com/unmanned/uas/2016/12/20/threat-from-russian-uav-jamming-real-officials-say/ (accessed June 15, 2018).

21. Joseph Trevithick, "American General Says 'Adversaries' Are Jamming AC-130 Gunships in Syria," *The Drive*, April 25, 2018, http://www.thedrive.com/the-war-zone/20404/american-general-says-adversaries-are-jamming-ac-130-gunships-in-syria (accessed June 15, 2018).

22. Patrick Tucker, "Russia Will Challenge US Military Superiority in Europe by 2025: US General," *DefenseOne*, March 8, 2018, https://www.defenseone.com/threats/2018/03/russia-will-challenge-us-military-superiority-europe-2025-us-general/146523/ (accessed June 15, 2018).

23. U.S. Department of Defense, Office of the Secretary of Defense, *Annual Report to Congress: Military and Security Developments Involving the People's Republic of China 2017*, May 15, 2017, p. ii, https://www.defense.gov/Portals/1/Documents/pubs/2017_China_Military_Power_Report.PDF (accessed June 15, 2018).

24. U.S.–China Economic and Security Review Commission, *2017 Report to Congress of the U.S.–China Economic and Security Review Commission*, 115th Cong., 1st Sess., November 2017, pp. 9–10, https://www.uscc.gov/sites/default/files/annual_reports/2017_Annual_Report_to_Congress.pdf (accessed June 15, 2018).

25. Lisa J. Porter, statement before the Committee on Armed Services, U.S. Senate, May 10, 2018, p. 1, https://www.armed-services.senate.gov/imo/media/doc/Porter_05-10-18.pdf (accessed June 15, 2018).

26. Admiral Harry B. Harris Jr., U.S. Navy, Commander, U.S. Pacific Command, statement on "U.S. Pacific Command Posture" before the Committee on Armed Services, U.S. House of Representatives, February 14, 2018, p. 4, https://docs.house.gov/meetings/AS/AS00/20180214/106847/HHRG-115-AS00-Wstate-HarrisJrH-20180214.pdf (accessed June 15, 2018).

27. Kris Osborne, "How the U.S. Army Plans to Go to War Against Russia, China and Iran (Their Weapons, That Is)," *The National Interest*, February 13, 2017, http://nationalinterest.org/blog/the-buzz/how-the-us-army-plans-go-war-against-russia-china-iran-their-19415 (accessed June 15, 2018).

28. U.S. Army, Training and Doctrine Command, *The U.S. Army Operating Concept, Win in a Complex World, 2020–2040*, TRADOC Pamphlet 525-3-1, October 31, 2014, p. 10, http://www.tradoc.army.mil/tpubs/pams/tp525-3-1.pdf (accessed June 15, 2018).

29. Russia Today, "RAW: Iraqi M1 Abrams Tank Hit by ISIS Kornet Guided Missile Near Mosul," YouTube, October 25, 2016, https://www.youtube.com/watch?v=y5xKCzdhAC8 (accessed June 15, 2018).

30. Emilyn Tuomala, "Houthis," Missile Defense Advocacy Alliance, June 2018, http://missiledefenseadvocacy.org/missile-threat-and-proliferation/todays-missile-threat/non-state-actors/houthis/ (accessed June 15, 2018).

31. John Ismay, Thomas Gibbons-Neff, and C. J. Chivers, "How ISIS Produced Its Cruel Arsenal on an Industrial Scale," *The New York Times*, December 10, 2017, https://www.nytimes.com/2017/12/10/world/middleeast/isis-bombs.html (Accessed June 15, 2018).

32. Robert Windrem, "U.S. Fears New Threat from ISIS Drones," NBC News, May 24, 2017, https://www.nbcnews.com/storyline/isis-terror/u-s-fears-new-threat-isis-drones-n764246 (accessed June 15, 2018).

33. James Mattis, Secretary of Defense, "Written Statement for the Record" before the Subcommittee on Defense, Committee on Appropriations, U.S. Senate, May 9, 2018, p. 4, https://www.appropriations.senate.gov/imo/media/doc/050918%20-%20FY19%20DoD%20Mattis%20Testimony.pdf (accessed June 15, 2018).

34. Lieutenant General John M. Murray, Deputy Chief of Staff of the Army, G-8, and Lieutenant General Joseph Anderson, Deputy Chief of Staff of the Army, G-3/5/7, statement on "The Effect of Sequestration and Continuing Resolutions on Modernization and Readiness" before the Subcommittee on Tactical Air and Land Forces, Committee on Armed Services, U.S. House of Representatives, 115th Cong., 1st Sess., March 16, 2017, p. 2, https://docs.house.gov/meetings/AS/AS25/20170316/105700/HHRG-115-AS25-Wstate-AndersonJ-20170316.pdf (accessed June 15, 2018).

35. Vice Admiral Joseph P. Mulloy, Deputy Chief of Naval Operations for Integration of Capabilities and Resources; Vice Admiral Philip H. Cullom, Deputy Chief of Naval Operations for Fleet Readiness and Logistics; and Vice Admiral Luke M. Cullom, Chief of Navy Reserve, Commander Navy Reserve Force, statement on "U.S. Navy Readiness" before the Subcommittee on Readiness, Committee on Armed Services, U.S. House of Representatives, March 16, 2017, p. 1, https://docs.house.gov/meetings/AS/AS03/20170316/105690/HHRG-115-AS03-Wstate-CullomP-20170316.pdf (accessed June 15, 2018).

36. Lieutenant General Scott Rice, Director Air National Guard, Headquarters, U.S. Air Force; Lieutenan General Maryanne Miller, Chief of Air Force Reserve, Headquarters, U.S. Air Force; and Major General Scott West, Director of Current Operations, Deputy Chief of Staff for Operations, Headquarters, U.S. Air Force, statement on "Total Force Readiness" before the Subcommittee on Readiness, Committee on Armed Services, U.S. House of Representatives, March 22, 2017, p. 3, https://docs.house.gov/meetings/AS/AS03/20170322/105747/HHRG-115-AS03-Wstate-MillerUSAFRM-20170322.pdf (accessed June 15, 2018).

37. Victor Davis Hanson, "Why America Was Indispensable to the Allies' Winning World War II," *National Review*, May 14, 2015, https://www.nationalreview.com/2015/05/why-america-was-indispensable-allies-winning-world-war-ii-victor-davis-hanson/ (accessed June 15, 2018).

38. Lynn M. Williams, Heidi M. Peters, and Jason A. Purdy, "Defense Primer: U.S. Defense Industrial Base," Congressional Research Service *In Focus* No. 10548, April 20, 2018, https://fas.org/sgp/crs/natsec/IF10548.pdf (accessed June 15, 2018).

39. Leslie Wayne, "The Shrinking Military Complex; After the Cold War, the Pentagon Is Just Another Customer," *The New York Times*, February 27, 1998, https://www.nytimes.com/1998/02/27/business/shrinking-military-complex-after-cold-war-pentagon-just-another-customer.html (accessed June 15, 2018).

40. *Fortune* 500, 2018, http://fortune.com/fortune500/list/ (accessed June 15, 2018).

41. M. Thomas Davis, "The Incredible Shrinking Defense Industrial Base," *Signal*, June 16, 2015, https://www.afcea.org/content/Blog-incredible-shrinking-defense-industrial-base (accessed June 15, 2018).

42. Michael Snyder, "19 Facts About the Deindustrialization of America That Will Make You Weep," *Business Insider*, September 27, 2010, http://www.businessinsider.com/deindustrialization-factory-closing-2010-9 (accessed June 15, 2018).

43. Dan Goure, "The Jones Act Is Needed Now More Than Ever," *The National Interest*, March 6, 2018, http://nationalinterest.org/blog/the-buzz/the-jones-act-needed-now-more-ever-24770 (accessed June 15, 2018).

44. Sydney J. Freedberg Jr., "Industrial Base Too 'Brittle' for Big War: Dunford," *Breaking Defense*, September 26, 2017, https://breakingdefense.com/2017/09/industrial-base-too-brittle-for-big-war-dunford/ (accessed June 15, 2018).

45. Committee on Armed Services, U.S. Senate, "Advance Policy Questions for General Joseph Dunford, USMC Nominee for Reconfirmation as Chairman of the Joint Chiefs of Staff," September 26, 2017, p. 4, http://www.armed-services.senate.gov/imo/media/doc/Dunford_APQs_09-26-17.pdf (accessed June 15, 2018).

46. Mike Griffin, Under Secretary of Defense for Research and Engineering, statement on "Technology Transfer and the Valley of Death" before the Subcommittee on Emerging Threats and Capabilities, Committee on Armed Services, U.S. Senate, 116th Cong., 2nd Sess., April 18, 2018, p. [3], https://www.armed-services.senate.gov/imo/media/doc/Griffin_04-18-18.pdf (accessed June 15, 2018).

47. Sandra Erwin and Jeff Faust, "Pentagon Nominee Griffin: Procurement a 'Mess,' U.S. Losing Edge in Aviation, Space," *Space News*, October 28, 2017, http://spacenews.com/pentagon-nominee-griffin-procurement-a-mess-u-s-losing-edge-in-aviation-space/ (accessed June 15, 2018).

48. Amy McCullough, "Roper: Fixing Software Development Necessary for Future Success," *Air Force Magazine*, April 29, 2018, http://www.airforcemag.com/Features/Pages/2018/April%202018/Roper-Fixing-Software-Development-Necessary-For-Future-Success.aspx (accessed June 15, 2018).

49. John Grady, "Pentagon Research Chief Nominee: China, Russia Racing to Develop Next Generation Weapon Technology," U.S. Naval Institute News, May 11, 2018, https://news.usni.org/2018/05/11/pentagon-research-chief-nominee-china-russia-racing-develop-next-generation-weapon-technology?utm_source=USNI+News&utm_campaign (accessed June 15, 2018).

50. *National Security Strategy of the United States of America*," p. 21.

51. Aaron Mehta, "This Is the Pentagon's New Acquisition Structure," *Defense News*, August 2, 2017, https://www.defensenews.com/breaking-news/2017/08/02/this-is-the-pentagons-new-acquisition-structure/ (accessed June 15, 2018).

52. Dave Majumdar, "The Pentagon's Strategic Capabilities Office (SCO) Takes Center Stage," *The National Interest*, November 17, 2016, http://nationalinterest.org/blog/the-buzz/the-pentagons-strategic-capabilities-office-sco-takes-center-18435 (accessed June 19, 2018).

53. Valerie Insinna, "Air Force Wants to Apply Success of Rapid Capabilities Office to Other Weapons Programs," *Defense News*, October 12, 2017, https://www.defensenews.com/air/2017/10/12/air-force-wants-to-apply-success-of-rapid-capabilities-office-to-other-weapons-programs/ (accessed June 15, 2018).

54. Justin Katz, "Navy Admiral: MACO Accelerating IOC by Three Years on Several Programs," *Inside Defense*, December 5, 2017, https://insidedefense.com/insider/navy-admiral-maco-accelerating-ioc-three-years-several-programs (accessed June 15, 2018).

55. U.S. Army, Army Rapid Capabilities Office, "Experiment, Evolve and Deliver," last modified May 31, 2017, http://rapidcapabilitiesoffice.army.mil/ (accessed June 15, 2018).

56. Jen Judson, "The Next Army Program Executive Office Will Be the Rapid Capabilities Office," *C4ISRNET,* March 26, 2018, https://www.c4isrnet.com/digital-show-dailies/global-force-symposium/2018/03/26/the-next-army-program-executive-office-will-be-the-rapid-capabilities-office/ (accessed June 15, 2018).

57. U.S. Department of Defense, Office of the Under Secretary of Defense for Acquisition and Sustainment, Office of the Deputy Assistant Secretary of Defense for Manufacturing and Industrial Base Policy, *Fiscal Year 2017 Annual Industrial Capabilities Report to Congress*, March 2018, p. 47, http://www.businessdefense.gov/Portals/51/Documents/Resources/2017%20AIC%20RTC%2005-17-2018%20-%20Public%20Release.pdf?ver=2018-05-17-224631-340 (accessed June 18, 2018). See also Aaron Mehta, "The US Is Running Out of Bombs—and It May Soon Struggle to Make More," *Defense News*, May 22, 2018, https://www.defensenews.com/pentagon/2018/05/22/the-us-is-running-out-of-bombs-and-it-may-soon-struggle-to-make-more/ (accessed June 15, 2018).

58. Ian Simpson, "Flood of Fake Chinese Parts in US Military Gear—Report," Reuters, May 22, 2012, https://www.reuters.com/article/usa-defense-counterfeit/flood-of-fake-chinese-parts-in-us-military-gear-report-idUSL1E8GMMCV20120522 (accessed June 15, 2018).

59. Hamza Shaban, "Pentagon Tells U.S. Military Bases to Stop Selling ZTE, Huawei Phones," *The Washington Post*, May 2, 2018, https://www.washingtonpost.com/news/the-switch/wp/2018/05/02/pentagon-tells-u-s-military-bases-to-stop-selling-zte-huawei-phones/?utm_term=.468920 (accessed June 1, 2018).

60. Adam Behsudi, "NAFTA Negotiators Work Around the Clock; Thorny Issues Remain," Politico, April 25, 2018, https://www.politico.com/newsletters/morning-trade/2018/04/25/nafta-negotiators-work-around-the-clock-thorny-issues-remain-182788 (accessed September 6, 2019).

61. U.S. Department of Defense, Office of the Under Secretary of Defense for Acquisition and Sustainment, Office of the Deputy Assistant Secretary of Defense for Manufacturing and Industrial Base Policy, *Fiscal Year 2017 Annual Industrial Capabilities Report to Congress*, p. 47. See also Aaron Mehta, "America's Industrial Base Is at Risk, and the Military May Feel the Consequences," *Defense News*, May 22, 2018, https://www.defensenews.com/pentagon/2018/05/22/americas-industrial-base-is-at-risk-and-the-military-may-feel-the-consequences/ (accessed June 15, 2018).

62. Joe Gould, "Navarro: Trump Ordered US Defense-Industrial Base Study to Help 'Rebuild' Military," *Defense News*, July 24, 2017, https://www.defensenews.com/home/2017/07/24/navarro-trump-ordered-us-defense-industrial-base-study-to-help-rebuild-military/ (accessed June 15, 2018).

63. Loren B. Thompson, "One-Year Waits for Security Clearances Are Costing Washington Billions," *Forbes*, May 23, 2017, https://www.forbes.com/sites/lorenthompson/2017/05/23/one-year-waits-for-security-clearances-are-costing-washington-billions/#579904066205 (accessed June 15, 2018).

64. News Transcript, "Remarks by Secretary Mattis on the National Defense Strategy," U.S. Department of Defense, January 19, 2018, https://www.defense.gov/News/Transcripts/Transcript-View/Article/1420042/remarks-by-secretary-mattis-on-the-national-defense-strategy/ (accessed June 15, 2018).

65. James N. Mattis, Secretary of Defense, remarks delivered at Air Force Association 2017 Air, Space, and Cyber Conference, National Harbor, Maryland, September 20, 2017, https://www.defense.gov/News/Speeches/Speech-View/Article/1318960/air-force-association-2017-air-space-and-cyber-conference/ (accessed June 15, 2018).

66. Defense Innovation Unit Experimental, "Five Focus Areas," https://diux.mil/team (accessed June 15, 2018).

67. Defense Innovation Unit Experimental, "DIUx Commercial Solutions Opening: How-to Guide," November 30, 2017, p. 4, https://diux.mil/download/datasets/740/CSOhowtoguide.pdf (accessed June 15, 2018).

68. AFWERX, "AFWERX Fusion," http://afwerxdc.org/ (accessed June 15, 2018).

69. Scott Maucione, "Office of Naval Research Is DoD's Newest Organization to Set Up Innovation Cell," Federal News Radio, April 3, 2018, https://federalnewsradio.com/defense-main/2018/04/office-of-naval-research-is-dods-newest-organization-to-set-up-innovation-cell/ (accessed June 15, 2018).

70. Stanford University, "Hacking 4 Defense (H4D)," http://hacking4defense.stanford.edu/ (accessed June 15, 2018).

71. Gideon Grudo, "Alphabet Executive: USAF Wasting Opportunities for Future Innovation," *Air Force Magazine*, February 22, 2018, http://www.airforcemag.com/Features/Pages/2018/February%202018/Alphabet-Executive-USAF-Wasting-Opportunities-for-Future-Innovation.aspx (accessed June 15, 2018).

72. The Honorable Ellen M. Lord, Under Secretary of Defense, Acquisition, Technology and Logistics, statement on "Current State of Defense Acquisition and Associated Reforms" before the Committee on Armed Services, U.S. Senate, 115th Cong., 1st Sess., December 7, 2017, p. 4, https://www.armed-services.senate.gov/imo/media/doc/Lord_12-07-17.pdf (accessed June 18, 2018).

73. General James C. McConville, Vice Chief of Staff, United States Army, statement "On Readiness" before the Subcommittee on Readiness and Management Support, Committee on Armed Services, U.S. Senate, 115th Cong., 2nd Sess., February 14, 2018, p. 2, https://www.armed-services.senate.gov/imo/media/doc/McConville_02-14-18.pdf (accessed June 15, 2018).

74. "Army Chief of Staff Milley Talks New Army Rifle at AUSA Breakfast," *Tactical-Life,* January 22, 2013, https://www.tactical-life.com/news/new-army-rifle/ (accessed June 15, 2018).

75. The Honorable Mark T. Esper, Secretary of the Army, statement "On the Current State of Department of Defense Acquisition Enterprise and Associated Reforms" before the Committee on Armed Services, U.S. Senate, December 7, 2017, p. 2, https://www.armed-services.senate.gov/imo/media/doc/Esper_12-07-17.pdf (accessed June 15, 2018).

76. Daniel Gouré, "Will Proposed Reforms Really Make Army Acquisition Faster?" *The National Interest*, December 20, 2017, https://www.realcleardefense.com/2017/12/20/will_proposed_reforms_really_make_army_acquisition_faster_299131.html (accessed June 15, 2018).

77. See, for example, J. Ronald Fox, *Defense Acquisition Reform, 1960–2009: An Elusive Goal,* U.S. Army, Center of Military History, 2011, pp. xii and 215, https://history.army.mil/html/books/051/51-3-1/CMH_Pub_51-3-1.pdf (accessed June 15, 2018).

78. Lieutenant General John M. Murray, Deputy Chief of Staff of the Army, G-8; Lieutenant General Joseph Anderson, Deputy Chief of Staff of the Army, G-3/5/7; Lieutenant General Paul A. Ostrowski, Military Deputy to the Assistant Secretary of the Army for Acquisition, Logistics and Technology; and Major General Robert M. Dyess, Jr., Acting Director, Army Capabilities Integration Center, U.S. Army Training and Doctrine Command, statement on "Army Modernization" before the Subcommittee on Airland, Committee on Armed Services, U.S. Senate, 115th Cong., 2nd Sess., February 7, 2018, p. 6, https://www.armed-services.senate.gov/imo/media/doc/Murray-Anderson-Ostrowski-Dyess_02-07-18.pdf (accessed June 15, 2018).

79. The Honorable Heather Wilson, "Acquisition Enterprise and Associated Reforms," testimony before Committee on Armed Services, U.S. Senate, December 7, 2017, p. [3], https://www.armed-services.senate.gov/imo/media/doc/Wilson_12-07-17.pdf (accessed June 15, 2018).

80. Lauren C. Williams, "Acquisition Reform Requires Cultural Change, Air Force Commander Says," *Washington Technology*, March 15, 2018, https://washingtontechnology.com/articles/2018/03/15/usaf-otas-culture.aspx (accessed June 15, 2018).

81. Wilson, "Acquisition Enterprise and Associated Reforms," p. [3].

82. The Honorable James F. Geurts, Assistant Secretary of the Navy, Research, Development and Acquisition, statement on "Department of Defense Acquisition Enterprise and Associated Reforms" before the Committee on Armed Services, U.S. Senate, December 7, 2017, p. 1, https://www.armed-services.senate.gov/imo/media/doc/Geurts_12-07-17.pdf (accessed June 15, 2018).

83. The Honorable Christine Fox, speech on "Defense Acquisition Reform" at Lexington Institute Capitol Hill Defense Acquisition Reform Event, June 24, 2015, https://www.youtube.com/watch?v=1l2ihYcgtD4 (accessed June 20, 2018).

84. See, for example, Robbin F. Laird, "Game Changer: The F-35 and the Pacific," *The Diplomat*, April 25, 2013, https://thediplomat.com/2013/04/game-changer-the-f-35-and-the-pacific/ (accessed June 19, 2018); Dave Majumdar, "Game Changer: Combining Lockheed Martin's F-35 and AEGIS Missile Defense," The National Interest, September 13, 2015, http://nationalinterest.org/blog/the-buzz/game-changer-combining-lockheed-martins-f-35-aegis-missle-17695 (accessed June 8, 2018); "An Overview of the F-35 as a Game Changer," Second Line of Defense, October 11, 2016, https://sldinfo.com/whitepapers/an-overview-of-the-f-35-as-a-game-changer/ (accessed June 19, 2018); and Alex Lockie, "Top US Generals on the F-35: We Have a 'War Winner on Our Hands,'" *Business Insider*, February 17, 2017, http://www.businessinsider.com/f-35-war-winner-game-changer-bogdan-2017-2 (accessed June 19, 2018).

85. Jen Judson, "Development for Future Vertical-lift Aircraft Slow-rolled in Army Budget Plans," *Defense News*, February 27, 2018, https://www.defensenews.com/land/2018/02/27/development-for-future-vertical-lift-aircraft-slow-rolled-in-army-budget-plans/ (accessed June 15, 2018).

86. Jen Judson, "Army Pushes Long-Range Precision Fires Development Out by a Year," *Defense News*, June 9, 2017, https://www.defensenews.com/land/2017/06/09/army-pushes-long-range-precision-fires-development-out-by-a-year/ (accessed June 15, 2018).

87. Cheryl Pellerin, "Air Force Secretary Outlines Forward-Looking Changes, Priorities," U.S. Department of Defense, September 18, 2017, https://www.defense.gov/News/Article/Article/1315169 (accessed June 1, 2018).

88. Loren Thompson, "The Air Force Is Missing Its Best Opportunity to Replace Aging Aircraft," RealClearDefense, February 21, 2018, https://www.realcleardefense.com/articles/2018/02/21/the_air_force_is_missing_its_best_opportunity_to_replace_aging_aircraft_113086.html (accessed June 15, 2018).

89. Report No. 115-404, *National Defense Authorization Act for Fiscal Year 2018*, Conference Report to Accompany H.R. 2810, 115th Cong., 1st Sess., November 9, 2017, p. 269, https://www.congress.gov/115/crpt/hrpt404/CRPT-115hrpt404.pdf (accessed June 15, 2018).

90. Megan Eckstein, "NAVSEA: FY 2019 Navy Budget Request Will Include More Shipbuilding, Life Extensions to Help Grow Fleet," U.S. Naval Institute News, January 2, 2018, https://news.usni.org/2018/01/02/navys-fy-2019-budget-request-will-include-new-shipbuilding-life-extensions-help-grow-fleet (accessed June 15, 2018).

91. Ibid.

92. Megan Eckstein, "DDG-51 Program Office Preparing RFP for Next Multiyear Buy; Will Include Options for Additional Ships," U.S. Naval Institute News, updated December 20, 2017, https://news.usni.org/2017/12/19/30117 (accessed June 15, 2018).

93. Ronald O'Rourke, "Navy Ford (CVN-78) Class Aircraft Carrier Program: Background and Issues for Congress, Congressional Research Service *Report for Members and Committees of Congress*, April 17, 2018, https://fas.org/sgp/crs/weapons/RS20643.pdf (accessed June 15, 2018).

94. Brock Vergakis, "Buying 3 Carriers at Once Could Save $1.5 Billion, Cut 2 Years off Production, Shipyard Says," *The Virginian-Pilot*, May 19, 2017, https://pilotonline.com/news/military/local/article_21d37f42-c638-558c-b81f-2f48df4c158f.html (accessed June 16, 2018).

95. Murray, Anderson, Ostrowski, and Dyess, statement on "Army Modernization," February 7, 2018, pp. 8–9.

96. Ashton Carter, Secretary of Defense, "Rewiring the Pentagon: Charting a New Path on Innovation and Cybersecurity," speech delivered at Stanford University, Palo Alto, California, April 23, 2015, https://www.defense.gov/News/Speeches/Speech-View/Article/606666/ (accessed June 11, 2018).

97. Moshe Schwartz and Heidi M. Peters, "Acquisition Reform in the FY2016–FY2018 National Defense Authorization Acts (NDAAs)," Congressional Research Service *Report for Members and Committees of Congress*, January 19, 2018, p. 2, https://fas.org/sgp/crs/natsec/R45068.pdf (accessed June 11, 2018).

98. Ibid.

99. Sydney J. Freedberg Jr., "Big Primes Don't Cry: Wes Bush Defends Defense Contractors," *Breaking Defense*, May 26, 2015, https://breakingdefense.com/2015/05/big-primes-dont-cry-wes-bush-defends-defense-contractors/ (accessed June 11, 2018).

100. Dan Goure, "Pentagon & Industry Show the Value of Performance-Based Logistics," *The National Interest*, March 15, 2017, http://nationalinterest.org/blog/the-buzz/pentagon-industry-show-the-value-performance-based-logistics-19792 (accessed June 11, 2018).

101. Frank Konkel, "Daring Deal," *Government Executive*, July 9, 2014, https://www.govexec.com/magazine/features/2014/07/daring-deal/88207 (accessed June 11, 2018).

102. Lauren C. Williams, "The Thinking Behind DISA's $8 Billion DEOS Contract," *Federal Computer Week*, May 21, 2018, https://fcw.com/articles/2018/05/21/deos-contract-disa.aspx (accessed June 11, 2018), and Lauren C. Williams, "DOD Details Its Plans for JEDI Cloud Contract," *Federal Computer Week*, March 7, 2018, https://fcw.com/articles/2018/03/07/cloud-jedi-dod-contract.aspx (accessed June 11, 2018).

103. Loren Thompson, "Five Reasons Why Silicon Valley Won't Partner with the Pentagon," *Forbes*, April 27, 2015, https://www.forbes.com/sites/lorenthompson/2015/04/27/five-reasons-why-silicon-valley-wont-partner-with-the-pentagon/#6acc850e4de9 (accessed June 11, 2018).

104. 48 Code of Federal Regulations 1—Federal Acquisition Regulation, https://www.law.cornell.edu/cfr/text/48/chapter-1 (accessed June 16, 2018).

105. Daniel Gouré, "Incentivizing a New Defense Industrial Base," Lexington Institute, September 2015, p. 1, www.lexingtoninstitute.org/wp-content/uploads/2015/10/Incentivizing-a-New-Defense-Industrial-Base.pdf (accessed June 11, 2018).

106. Ben Werner, "Defense Firms Tell Wall Street They're Gearing Up for More Contracts," U.S. Naval Institute News, January 31, 2018, https://news.usni.org/2018/01/31/31041 (accessed June 16, 2018).

107. Jen Judson, "US Army Looks to Cut Typical Acquisition Timeline in Half," *Defense News*, December 7, 2017, https://www.defensenews.com/land/2017/12/07/army-looks-to-cut-typical-acquisition-timeline-in-half/ (accessed June 11, 2018).

108. Aaron Mehta, "Here's How Ellen Lord Will Reduce Acquisition Time by 50 Percent," *Defense News*, December 8, 2017, https://www.defensenews.com/pentagon/2017/12/08/heres-how-ellen-lord-will-reduce-acquisition-time-by-50-percent/ (accessed June 11, 2018).

109. U.S. Government Accountability Office, *Military Acquisitions: DOD Is Taking Steps to Address Challenges Faced by Certain Companies*, GAO-17-644, July 2017, https://www.gao.gov/assets/690/686012.pdf (accessed June 11, 2018).

110. Jared Serbu, "Army Acquisition Chief Wants Clearer Lines Between Government, Industry Intellectual Property," Federal News Radio, April 3, 2018, https://federalnewsradio.com/dod-reporters-notebook-jared-serbu/2018/04/army-acquisition-chief-wants-clearer-lines-between-government-industry-intellectual-property/ (accessed June 11, 2018).

111. U.S. Department of Defense, Acquisition, Technology and Logistics, Table, "Comparison of Major Contract Types," https://www.acq.osd.mil/dpap/ccap/cc/jcchb/Files/Topical/Contract_Type_Comparison_Table/resources/contract_type_table.docx (accessed June 16, 2018).

Logistics: The Lifeblood of Military Power

John E. Wissler, Lieutenant General, USMC (Ret.)

The end for which a soldier is recruited, clothed, armed, and trained, the whole objective of his sleeping, eating, drinking, and marching is simply that he should fight at the right place and the right time.
—Major-General Carl von Clausewitz, *On War*

The term "logistics" was not commonly used until shortly before World War II, but the concept and understanding of logistics have been around since the earliest days of warfare. In Clausewitz's words, getting the force to the "fight at the right place and the right time"[1] is the true essence of military logistics.

The Merriam-Webster online dictionary defines logistics as "the aspect of military science dealing with the procurement, maintenance, and transportation of military materiel, facilities, and personnel."[2] The Joint Chiefs of Staff's *Logistics* elaborates on this definition and quotes Rear Admiral Henry E. Eccles's 1959 statement that "Logistics is the bridge between the economy of the Nation and the tactical operations of its combat forces. Obviously then, the logistics system must be in harmony, both with the economic system of the Nation and with the tactical concepts and environment of the combat forces."[3]

This simple two-sentence statement effectively captures both the complexity and far-reaching implications of military logistics. From the farthest tactical edge to the economic system of the nation, military logistics has far-reaching implications for the nation and the military element of national power and therefore affects every aspect of organizing, training, equipping, deploying, and employing the force.

Logistics is perhaps the most complex and interrelated capability provided by today's military. Unfortunately, to those unfamiliar with its intellectual and technological breadth, depth, and complexity, it can be considered an assumed capability—something that simply happens—or, worse yet, a "back office" function that is not connected to warfighting capability.

The success of military logistics during the past 16-plus years of overseas combat operations is partly to blame for anyone's assumption that continued logistical success in the ever-changing national security environment is a given across the entirety of the military logistics enterprise. This dangerous assumption tends to exclude logistics from the conversation regarding the nation's current and future warfighting needs. As a result, the logistics enterprise is rarely debated outside the logistics profession with the same intensity as other more publicized warfighting needs, especially the need to regain our military technological advantage over major competitors like China and Russia, are debated. Failure to understand the implications of not modernizing logistics in a time of great technological change potentially spells doom for the success of the modernized force.

In addition to ensuring that modernized logistics capabilities are appreciated as central to regaining our military advantage, logistics capabilities must be considered in the ongoing discussion of solutions to overcome the current readiness shortfalls of today's military. Logistics is nearly absent from the recent testimonies by military leaders, members of congress, and industry.[4] While all of the testimonies highlight the need to modernize the U.S. military in order to regain our technological advantage, few specifically highlight the need for modernized logistics capabilities.

Alan Estevez, former Principal Deputy Under Secretary of Defense for Acquisition, Technology and Logistics and a career Department of Defense Senior Executive Service logistics leader, recently stated, "Logistics isn't rocket science...it's much harder!"[5] Logistics is fundamental to the readiness of the entire Joint force—those at home, deployed in operational settings, and permanently stationed abroad—given that it must operate around the world and across every domain of activity in spite of enemy efforts to frustrate its operations. Consequently, it is far more complex than even the most sophisticated global business enterprises.

The Logistics Enterprise

You will not find it difficult to prove that battles, campaigns, and even wars have been won or lost primarily because of logistics.
— General Dwight D. Eisenhower

Logistics touches every aspect of military strength and is the sum of the capabilities brought to bear by all of the U.S. military services and those of a wide array of international partners.[6]

The core functions within logistics are supply, maintenance, deployment and distribution, health services, logistic services, engineering, and operational contract support (OCS).[7] Logistics includes planning and executing the movement and support of forces as well as those aspects of military operations that deal with:

- The acquisition, storage, distribution, use, maintenance, and disposal of materiel;

- Medical services including patient movement, evacuation, and hospitalization for U.S. and partner personnel as well as indigenous personnel affected by operations;

- Facilities and infrastructure acquisition, construction, use, and disposition;

- Provision of food, water, and operational hygiene and sanitation support;

- Operational contract support including contract management;

- Infrastructure assessment, repairs, and maintenance;

- Common-user logistics support to other U.S. government entities, intergovernmental and nongovernmental organizations, and other nations;

- Establishing and sustaining large-scale and enduring detention compounds;

- Planning, coordinating, and integrating host-nation support from overseas partners;

- Disposal operations that deal with the removal and remediation of waste and unusable military property;

- In-transit visibility of sustainment and asset visibility of all major military end items; and

- Engineering support including horizontal and vertical construction of ports, airfields, and other military support infrastructure.[8]

Thus, military logistics' defining attributes—agility, survivability, responsiveness, and effectiveness—are measured by the breadth and depth of these core functions, which affect the military from force generation to training to the readiness of units stationed at home and abroad.

Logistics is the oxygen that allows military muscle to function, grow, and strengthen. Just as DNA represents "the fundamental and distinctive characteristics or qualities of someone or something,"[9] logistics planning and modernization define the distinctive characteristics or qualities of the military force and ultimately provide the military commander the freedom of action, endurance, and ability to extend operational reach that are necessary to achieve success. Logistics is the foundation for the success of military operations from entry-level training to the most complex operations across the spectrum of conflict. From providing the facilities that house the members of the force and the ranges where they train, to sustaining the equipment warriors operate and wear, to providing fuel and ammunition in operations and training, the interconnectedness of logistics inextricably links logistics to military combat power.

U.S. Transportation Command (US-TRANSCOM) provides daily examples of what it takes to keep U.S. forces and their sustainment moving around the world. US-TRANSCOM conducts more than 1,900 air missions during an average week and has 25 ships underway and 10,000 ground shipments operating in 75 percent of the world's countries. It does this with a total wartime personnel capability of 45,945 active-duty soldiers, sailors, airmen, Marines, and Coast Guardsmen; 73,058 Reserve and Guard personnel; and 19,104 DOD civilian personnel—numbers that do not include the significant contributions of USTRANSCOM's commercial partners or the contributions of foreign entities.[10]

Utilizing its people, trucks, trains, railcars, aircraft, ships, information systems, and distribution infrastructure, as well as commercial partners' 1,203 aircraft in the Civil Reserve Air Fleet (CRAF) and 379 vessels in the Voluntary Intermodal Sealift Agreement (VISA), USTRANSCOM provides the U.S. military with highly responsive strategic mobility.[11] Its handoff to service logistics personnel around the globe creates a distribution pipeline that moves critical sustainment from the factory to the tactical edge of U.S. military operations.

In coordination with USTRANSCOM's distribution functions, the actions of the Defense Logistics Agency (DLA) as supplier for the military are equally staggering in scope and scale. During fiscal year (FY) 2017, DLA provided more than $35 billion in goods and services, coordinating the actions of 25,000 military, civilian, and contract personnel who provided food, clothing, fuel, repair parts, and other items across nine supply chains distributing approximately 5 million distinct consumable, expendable, and reparable items. DLA's activity is spread across 48 U.S. states and in 28 different countries.[12]

These are far from "back office" functions and are truly what sustain the force and support its warfighting readiness. The criticality of logistics is not a new phenomenon, however; logistics has a significantly more complex nature today because of its integration across air, land, sea, space, and the information and cyber environments.

The Timelessness and Ever-Changing Nature of Logistics

Amateurs think about tactics, but professionals think about logistics.
—General Robert H. Barrow, USMC

Alexander the Great noted with dark humor the importance and complexity of logistics during his campaigns of conquest nearly 2,400 years ago: "My logisticians are a humorless lot...they know if my campaign fails, they are the first ones I will slay."[13] Alexander's ability to move a force from Greece to India and back, conquering adversaries in Europe, Africa, the Middle East, and Central Asia and leaving functioning outposts along the way, attests to his logistical prowess.

In the modern era, the appreciation of logistics by Admiral Ernest J. King, Commander in Chief of the United States Fleet and Chief of Naval Operations during World War II, is equally telling: "I don't know what the hell this 'logistics' is that [General George C.] Marshall is always talking about, but I want some of it."[14] Similarly, in his timeless treatise on warfighting, *Defeat into Victory*, British Field Marshal Viscount Slim commented that building his theater's logistical infrastructure and supply reserves and maintaining his army's health were two of the three "foundations of victory" in his campaign in Burma and India. The third foundation, the morale of his troops, was directly affected by the first two.[15] Slim's ability to innovate in planning, organizing, and sustaining his logistics enterprise was critical to his logistics success.

These historically rooted truths of the centrality of logistics to success in war are reflected in the 2018 National Defense Strategy (NDS) in which Secretary of Defense James Mattis notes the criticality of logistical preparation to the resilience and agility of U.S. forces in any setting. For the U.S. to be able to sustain effective combat operations in the modern era, it must "prioritize prepositioned forward stocks and munitions, strategic mobility assets, partner and allied support, as well as non-commercially dependent distributed logistics and maintenance to ensure logistics sustainment while under persistent multi-domain attack."[16]

Demands of Today and Tomorrow

Logistics is critical not only to employing the force, but also (and perhaps even more importantly) to building the everyday readiness of the force. At the tactical level, one need only look at the various elements of readiness reporting reviewed by senior leaders to discern that the fundamentals of logistics directly affect the majority of elements that define readiness across the services—personnel, equipment, and supply readiness—which in turn directly affect the ability of the services to meet the recurring needs of ongoing deployments and generate the forces needed for war.

For example, Secretary of Defense Mattis's recently announced intention to reduce non-deployable personnel is one aspect of force readiness that is affected by the health services component of logistics.[17] Large numbers of non-deployable personnel reduce the available strength of military units, and without the full complement of personnel, teams cannot be trained effectively, whether they are ground units, ship's crews, or aviation formations. Personnel readiness is also affected by other logistics-related issues such as the lack of training throughput caused by insufficient, inadequate, or nonfunctional training facilities or the disruption caused by manpower transitions across the force that limit the availability of ready personnel.

Equipment readiness is another area of concern. Military units cannot perform their mission without the equipment needed to do so. Availability and delivery of parts and spare components, maintenance capability and the capacity to surge increased maintenance volume on short notice, the ability to contract additional support when necessary—all of these logistical elements are essential to military effectiveness.

Within logistics, the supply function is critical to equipment readiness. Simply stated, supply readiness is the ability to have the right types and amount of equipment available for a ground unit, a ship, or an aviation unit. Perhaps not so obvious is the interconnectedness of supply readiness to all other aspects of unit readiness. Without the right equipment, units cannot train to the full complement of their mission sets. Lacking something as simple as power generation capability on a ship, on the ground, or on an aircraft can prevent a unit from establishing the command and control capabilities that are vital to modern warfighting. As cyber and electronic warfare capabilities are introduced to the forward edge of the battlespace, individual capabilities represented by on-hand quantities of various technologies and trained personnel will truly define a unit's ability to execute the mission-essential tasks demanded in the complex warfighting environment of a peer adversary.

Supply readiness has been the subject of various testimonies to Congress regarding the readiness of the force on land, in the air, or on the sea. Shipyard capacities and the impact of deferred maintenance due to shortages of parts in the Air Force, Army, and Marine Corps have been highlighted as factors in the need for improved force readiness.[18]

The impact of logistics beyond readiness grows exponentially when taken in the context of the larger complexities of strategic logistics capabilities such as national and international highway, rail, port, and sealift capacities. Reductions in the size and capability of the industrial base, limitations on our national sealift capacity, and aging of the infrastructure needed to move personnel, weapons systems, ammunition, and fuel all directly challenge the ability of the United States to project military power.

Port facilities capable of handling critical munitions movements are critical to force deployment and sustainment. The U.S. has only 23 designated Strategic Seaports—17 commercially operated and six under military control—that make it possible to sustain overseas forces daily and keep them sustained during wartime. Airlift, composed of the Civil Reserve air and cargo fleets[19] and thus a critical capability that directly affects our ability to move large portions of our force and their associated sustainment to points of crisis around the globe, is similarly limited.

At first glance, the challenges of military logistics may appear to be the same as, or at least very similar to, those experienced by FEDEX, Walmart, Amazon, DHL, or any other major supply chain operation supporting vast numbers of customers both internationally and across the United States. On deeper inspection, however, the differences are profound.

- Military logistics involves the interaction of military and government entities with private, commercial, foreign, and multinational organizations worldwide.

- Unlike commercial companies with global distribution operations, the military faces conflicts that usually erupt with very little warning and immediately create enormous demands for support akin to the Christmas rush, the Black Friday crush, and Cyber Monday rolled into one.

- Unlike commercial firms that can prepare by the calendar, the military must operate without knowing when the date of each event occurs and still have the ability to respond to a sudden change in the "latest hot item" within hours, if not minutes.

- Military forces must receive such support regardless of how limited or intermittent their access to the Internet may be, and supporting logistics forces must meet the demand while an enemy is trying to kill the customers, both at home and in the parking lot, and is destroying the delivery fleet at every opportunity.

To say the least, the challenges of military logistics are unique. Although many of industry's best practices and technologies are relevant and even vital to the modernization of military logistics, the agility, survivability, responsiveness, and effectiveness of military logistics require another level of integrated innovation in technology and operational concepts.

The Challenge

To appreciate the challenge confronting America's logistical capabilities, imagine having to execute a future operation similar in scale to the major deployment of U.S. combat power to Kuwait in preparation for Operation Iraqi Freedom (OIF) in March 2003. Now imagine doing this in an environment devoid of modern infrastructure in a manner that defeats an adversary's desire to prevent our use of air, land, sea, space, and cyberspace to project military power, all in consonance within the complex interrelationships and intricacies that support current collective defense arrangements. Imagine further that this must be accomplished against a force that has near-parity with our technological capabilities and the ability to engage us from fixed, friendly facilities with engagement timed on their terms.

While significant force-protection requirements affected the deployment of military capability to Kuwait for combat operations in Iraq, the U.S. and partner-nation forces did not have to "fight their way to the fight" in Kuwait. Additionally, U.S. and partner-nation forces had significant time to deploy military capability, ultimately using a single point of entry with mature facilities and infrastructure and Internet access.

In preparation for combat operations in Iraq, logisticians had six months to deploy the force and its associated sustainment. U.S. forces initiated the deployment with Military Sealift Command (MSC), a USTRANSCOM subordinate command, prepositioning assets moving to Kuwait beginning in October 2002, with the off-load of increased military capability beginning in earnest in January 2003 and wrapping up in April 2003, completing the six-month force buildup.

Six months may seem a long time, but the volume of activity was immense. According to one account:

In January 2003, MSC began the build-up for what would become Operation Iraqi Freedom. In January 2003 momentum was really gaining and APS-3 downloaded several ships of equipment into theater. In late March 2003 MSC reached a peak of 167 ships in the "Steel Bridge of Democracy", carrying "the torch of freedom to the Iraqi people" in the words of Rear Admiral D. L. Brewer III, Commander, Military Sealift Command.

The span of that bridge was literally a ship every 72 miles from the US to Kuwait. That was more than 78 percent of the total MSC active fleet of 214 ships that day—ships dedicated to supporting the US forces.... The mix of ships encompassed all four of MSC's programs, and included the U.S. Maritime Administration's Ready Reserve Force, and more than four times the normal daily number of commercial ships. Twenty-five of 33 Naval Fleet Auxiliary Force ships were providing combat logistics for the carrier strike groups and amphibious strike groups involved in Operation Iraqi Freedom. Three of 25 Special

Mission ships were directly supporting Navy combatants with telemetric, hydrographic and acoustic data....

During the height of Operation Iraqi Freedom, MSC had 167 of its 214 active ships directly supporting the war. Of these ships, 26 were operated by federally employed mariners and 141, or 84 percent, were crewed by merchant mariners employed by commercial companies under contract with MSC. Of the 141 ships, 127 ships were carrying combat equipment and cargo from the U.S. or Europe into the theater of operations or were en route to load cargo for the operation.[20]

The same account further reflects that from January 2003 through the end of April 2003, MSC delivered more than 21 million square feet of warfighting equipment and supplies, 260 million gallons of fuel, and 95,000 tons of ammunition to the Persian Gulf area for the Army, Marine Corps, Air Force, and Navy warfighters involved in Operation Iraqi Freedom. More than 90 percent of the military cargo to support OIF was delivered by MSC ships. While 10 percent of the cargo was delivered by other means, primarily aircraft, understanding the magnitude and significance of sea-based sustainment is critical to understanding what it takes to deploy and employ the U.S. military.

At the same time, Naval Fleet Auxiliary Force oilers pumped more than 117 million gallons of fuel to Navy combat ships for bunkering and aircraft fuel. Of the 42 ships in the Prepositioning Program, 33 were underway or had already off-loaded gear for warfighting forces in the Persian Gulf area.

In the MSC Sealift Program, 106 of 115 ships, including government-owned surge sealift ships, Maritime Administration Ready Reserve Fleet ships, and chartered commercial ships, were carrying equipment and supplies for the Army's 3rd and 4th Infantry Divisions, 82nd and 101st Airborne Divisions, and V Corps and the Marine Corps' I and II Marine Expeditionary Forces. Additionally, two of the three Maritime Prepositioning squadrons supporting the U.S. Marine Corps were unloaded at the Ash Shuayba Port in Kuwait. By late April 2003, more than 150 MSC ships had off-loaded in Kuwaiti ports.[21]

It should be noted, however, that in the years since these tremendous accomplishments, the size of the force available to execute these missions has shrunk considerably.

Admiral Brewer put these accomplishments into context: "The amount of cargo we delivered could fill all 119 Division 1-A college football fields three times over."[22] Specifically:

From November 2002 to May 2003, nearly 85,000 pieces of cargo and 4,000 containers of ammunition, requiring 16 million square feet of cargo space, were loaded aboard MSC ships under MSC Atlantic's operational control. This was enough military cargo to fill the deck space of 58 Nimitz class aircraft carriers.

These figures comprised equipment loaded in Texas, Georgia and Florida for the U.S. Army's 3rd and 4th Infantry Divisions and 101st Airborne Division, which included thousands of Abrams main battle tanks, Bradley fighting vehicles, humvees and helicopters....

In February, MSC Pacific provided direct support in the activation of 10 MSC cargo ships at various West Coast ports. They also coordinated the loading of another 10 MSC ships at Tacoma, Wash., and San Diego, Calif., which resulted in the movement of over 1 million square feet of military equipment for the U.S. Marine Corps 1st Marine Expeditionary Force and the U.S. Army's 101st Airborne Division....

MSC normally operates 120 civilian-crewed, non-combatant ships for a variety of missions around the world. The number of ships expanded to about 214 in mid-March as additional ships were activated from reduced operating status or chartered for the command's support of U.S. forces in OIF.[23]

While the immensity of this undertaking is staggering, it pales in comparison to the requirement laid out for the future military force in the National Defense Strategy (NDS). The future fight will require significantly greater responsiveness and diversity in the face of a greater threat. The NDS requires a military that will "be able to strike diverse targets inside adversary air and missile defense networks to destroy mobile power-projection platforms. This will include capabilities to enhance close combat lethality in complex terrain."[24] With regard to mobility and resilience, our military will be required to field "ground, air, sea, and space forces that can *deploy*, survive, *operate*, maneuver, and *regenerate* in all domains while under attack. Transitioning from large, centralized, urhardened infrastructure to smaller, dispersed, resilient, adaptive basing that includes active and passive defenses will also be prioritized."[25]

These challenges become infinitely harder when considering the vastness of the Pacific or the intricacies of meeting challenges across the depth and breadth of Europe. The force of tomorrow must be ready to defeat a peer competitor in a broad battlespace that requires security for each logistics movement, the ability to off-load across various widely distributed locations, with minimal infrastructure, and in a communications-degraded environment.

The ability to meet the NDS requirements requires a significantly more agile force. It must be able to dictate the time and tempo of its buildup and control the massive capabilities of the U.S. military. It must coordinate with allies and partners to place combined force capabilities against the adversary's weakness and develop and sustain a broad array of overseas advanced bases that will change frequently and provide the responsiveness and effectiveness needed to prevail despite enemy efforts to prevent U.S. forces from getting to or operating within the theater of combat. The U.S. military has not had to "fight its way to the fight" since World War II. Equally absent since that time has been the need to apply combat power to preserve logistics capabilities.

Given the evolution of competitors' abilities to threaten the logistical underpinnings of U.S. combat power, force logistics planning now requires innovation in both technology and operational concepts. In a time of constrained fiscal resources, this means doing differently with less. There is no option to fail, and there is no hope of unlimited resources. The combination of innovation and new technology is therefore critical to maintaining the competitive logistical advantage that U.S. forces have enjoyed since World War II.

The NDS focuses on investments needed to improve the ability of forces deployed abroad to maneuver against an enemy and ensure that the posture of those forces (how they are arrayed in theater) has resilience (the ability to sustain losses and remain effective). Not explicitly addressed in the NDS but fundamentally implied is the equally daunting challenge of winning the "home games" by having the critical military–industry partnerships and dedicated infrastructure that serve as the preparation and launching pads for our forces.

The shrinking military–industrial base that provides the wherewithal of national power faces significant challenges because of unpredictable budgets and inconsistent program funding. During World War II, from 1939 to 1945, the United States delivered 1,089 warfighting ships to the fleet that today would be classified as battle force ships. These 1,089 ships included 32 carriers, 10 battleships, 62 cruisers, 442 destroyers, and 563 frigates and destroyer escorts.[26] Compare this to the Navy's *Report to Congress on the Annual Long-Range Plan for Construction of Naval Vessels for Fiscal Year 2019*, which proposes the construction of 54 battle force ships during the five years from 2019 to 2024.[27]

It should be noted that the current shipbuilding plan projects 11 more battle force ships than were projected in the 2017 plan. This trend is very similar across the industrial capacity capabilities that produce aircraft and major land-component warfighting systems.

While procurement is not exclusively a function of logistics, the country's industrial capacity affects the availability of spare parts, the availability of technical support for contract maintenance, and the ability to replace warfighting platforms that are well beyond their service life, be they ships, aircraft, or major land-component systems (tanks, artillery, reconnaissance vehicles, personnel carriers, radars, ground vehicles, etc.).

When the instability of funding that results from continuing resolutions and an inability to pass budgets on time is added to these challenges, one can see that the problems confronting the industrial base are magnified at a time when they most need to be reduced so that our ability to supply the force is responsive and resilient. Perhaps counterintuitively, a constrained ability to build "new iron" (ships, aircraft, and major ground weapons systems) actually increases the logistical burden and budget because the cost of maintaining older systems necessarily increases.

The problem is made worse by the complexity of dealing with both old and new technologies in a single logistics enterprise. Add to these challenges the reduction of skilled manpower in the active and reserve forces, the increased difficulty of retaining seasoned military personnel, and a decreasing number of civilian and contractor artisans in the logistics workforce, and the need for modernizing the logistics force, from training to developing new concepts, becomes even more obvious.

Modernizing "home game" infrastructure must also include improved, state-of-the-art ranges and maintenance facilities, which are critical to supporting the readiness of new platforms that are being acquired in every service. Such facilities must also be made resilient in the face of cyber challenges, now a common feature of modern conflict. Integrating simulators and virtual reality capabilities into range design will also help to reduce the logistical impact of home-station training and generate much-needed efficiencies in major range training opportunities while also improving overall warfighting readiness.

Success Now and in the Future

New principles must be embraced to achieve the requirements for successful logistics capabilities in support of operational commanders and the National Defense Strategy. Many have written on the challenges of logistics in the 21st century, but Lieutenant General Michael Dana, Marine Corps Deputy Commandant for Installations and Logistics, has captured the requirement succinctly in his term "hybrid logistics," which he defines as the era "where 'old' meets 'new.'"[28] This is a period in logistics operations in which the combination of old and new technology and innovative concepts will provide precise logistics support to a widely distributed force instead of a large logistics footprint that delivers through a central hub.

The hybrid logistics attributes that Dana describes are a mixture of legacy and evolving technologies. They are delivered from the sea by means of modern connectors, platforms, processes, and concepts with the flexibility to enable multi-domain fires and maneuver. They are innovative in thought and practice, with a command and control architecture that is immunized against cyber and electronic warfare threats, and data-driven through predictive analytics. They also are applicable across the entire U.S. military from the strategic level to the tactical level. Ultimately, the effectiveness of any logistics capability is determined at the tactical level, but sustained success at the tactical level requires effectiveness further upstream at the operational and strategic levels.

Success at the operational level requires the integration of logistics capabilities contributed by all entities involved in military affairs, to include service, coalition-partner, interagency, governmental, private/commercial, and host-nation capabilities. The operational integration of these various capabilities provides the linkage between the tactical and strategic levels: a means to leverage the "Arsenal of Democracy"[29] in the hands of the men and women who serve in harm's way around the globe.

In assessing the true value of logistics, however, one needs to distinguish between efficiency and effectiveness, even though the former certainly affects the latter. Effectiveness is ultimately what matters at the tactical edge. Efficiencies should be pursued to free resources for use elsewhere, but those efficiencies must never be taken at the expense of the soldiers, sailors, airmen, or Marines who have been committed to battle. Many logistical challenges will remain unchanged in the near future because of the sheer physics of distributing ammunition and bulk liquids and the requirement to move major ground warfighting equipment and personnel. Nevertheless, changes that positively influence the agility, survivability, responsiveness, and effectiveness of logistics systems can and must be made.

Change must be made that ensures logistics agility by designing procedures and acquiring systems that adjust to changing requirements across a widely distributed force constantly and with domain-wide visibility, highlighting the needs, resources, and capabilities of the force. An understanding of the changing requirements must be achieved in the absence of direct input from the supported force through predictive capabilities that are enabled through improved artificial intelligence and machine learning capabilities.

Future logistics command and control systems can ensure agility by operating despite an enemy's efforts to disrupt communications through cyber and electronic warfare. This can be done by developing the means to transfer logistics data systems seamlessly from digital-based processes to analog-based processes and back. This requires both technological and training/conceptual change across the force, not exclusively in the logistics enterprise.

The use of unmanned platforms will be critical to the future of agile logistics. Unmanned platforms that support ground distribution will complement unmanned aerial platforms that deliver vital sustainment to widely distributed forces. In addition, unmanned platforms that can evacuate the injured from the point of injury without sacrificing high-cost combat platforms and additional combat capability will be critical in the dispersed battlefield. Every facet of military logistics must embrace unmanned platforms, from unmanned sea-based ship-to-shore connectors to platforms for the refueling of ships to the use of unmanned platforms for aerial refueling.

Logistics survivability upgrades can achieve reduced targetability of the logistics force through development of manageable electronic signatures, a reduced logistics footprint, and improved distribution with reduced static inventory. Static inventory is distribution moving at zero miles per hour, and anything that is static on the modern battlefield has little chance of remaining survivable.

The ability to make the force more survivable requires both technological improvements that reduce the need for large footprints in bulk liquids and ammunition and refocused training and logistics concepts. Technologies such as additive manufacturing, improved man–machine interfaces, and advanced robotics will contribute significantly to improved survivability. Ultimately, change must ensure both speed and reliability of logistics systems that build trust from the tactical level to the strategic level. Improvements in munitions and energy systems will directly improve the speed and reliability of the force and, thus, its logistical survivability and effectiveness.

Responsiveness can be improved by leveraging industrial-base support from the point of manufacture to the tactical edge forces. Improved responsiveness through domain-wide visibility and predictive logistics capabilities driven by improved artificial intelligence capabilities will provide sustainment based on finely tuned metrics that eliminate the need to request support. In short, we need to have the ability to autonomously anticipate the needs of the commander, not simply respond faster to bottom-up needs identification.

Improvements in logistics effectiveness require improved integrated capabilities and authorities that allow logistics challenges to be resolved at the lowest levels, leveraging shared awareness, and focused on effectiveness. The ability to measure effectiveness against

efficient performance is critical. This focus on effectiveness will prioritize the force's critical logistics needs by evaluating all requirements against mission success and differentiating the critical requirements from the multitude of inputs: in essence, providing the nail at the right time and place that prevents having to build a complete inventory of shoes, horses, and riders in order to win the battle.[30]

Conclusion

Logistics is critical to success on the battlefield. To remain a vital contributor to military success, logistics must adapt continuously so that it bridges old systems and capabilities while embracing new technologies and concepts. In addition, the success of every new system and concept, every new technology and military organization, must be evaluated against the commensurate evolution and revolution in logistics sustainability.

While not a new consideration in designing a force for tomorrow that remains relevant today, the development of integrated, agile, technologically advanced, and effective logistics systems that drive efficiencies into every corner of the military is increasingly essential in today's dynamic, fast-paced, and ever-changing national security environment. The shift in our military focus to competing in an era of great-power competition demands an even greater understanding of logistics and highlights the breadth of the requirement to support the entirety of the force in innovative ways, from training in the United States to deploying far from home.

Whether the unit engaging the enemy is in the air, on land, at sea, or in space or cyberspace, it must embrace innovation in logistics that not only integrates new technology, but also innovates in the "hybrid" environment of old and new in order to retain our military's true advantage as the world's only force that can "prevail in conflict and preserve peace through strength,"[31] both today and well into the future.

Endnotes

1. Carl von Clausewitz, *On War*, ed. Michael Howard and Peter Paret (Princeton, NJ: Princeton University Press, 1989), p. 95.

2. "Logistics," *Merriam-Webster.com*, www.merriam-webster.com/dictionary/logistics (accessed May 29, 2018).

3. U.S. Department of Defense, Joint Chiefs of Staff, *Logistics*, Joint Publication 4-0, October 16, 2017, p. I-1, http://www.jcs.mil/Portals/36/Documents/Doctrine/pubs/jp4_0.pdf (accessed May 29, 2018).

4. See, for example, The Honorable Mark T. Esper, Secretary of the Army, and General Mark A. Milley, Chief of Staff, U.S. Army, statement "On the Posture of the United States Army" before the Committee on Armed Services, U.S. Senate, 115th Cong., 2nd Sess., April 12, 2018, https://www.armed-services.senate.gov/imo/media/doc/Esper-Milley_04-12-18.pdf (accessed May 30, 2018); The Honorable Richard V. Spencer, Secretary of the Navy, statement on "Fiscal Year 2019 Department of the Navy Budget" before the Committee on Armed Services, U.S. Senate, April 19, 2018, https://www.armed-services.senate.gov/imo/media/doc/Spencer_04-19-18.pdf (accessed May 30, 2018); Admiral John M. Richardson, Chief of Naval Operations, statement on "Fiscal Year 2019 Navy Budget" before the Committee on Armed Services, U.S. Senate, April 19, 2018, https://www.armed-services.senate.gov/imo/media/doc/Richardson_04-19-18.pdf (accessed May 30, 2018); General Robert B. Neller, Commandant of the Marine Corps, statement on "The Posture of the United States Marine Corps" before the Committee on Armed Services, U.S. Senate, April 19, 2018, https://www.armed-services.senate.gov/imo/media/doc/Neller_04-19-18.pdf (accessed May 30, 2018); and The Honorable Dr. Heather Wilson, Secretary of the Air Force, and General David L. Goldfein, Chief of Staff, U.S. Air Force, "USAF Posture Statement: Fiscal Year 2019," Department of the Air Force presentation to the Committee on Armed Services, U.S. Senate, 115th Cong., 2nd Sess., April 24, 2018, https://www.armed-services.senate.gov/imo/media/doc/Wilson-Goldfein_04-24-18.pdf (accessed May 30, 2018).

5. The Honorable Alan Estevez, remarks at Marine Corps Association and Foundation 14th Annual Ground Logistics Awards Dinner, Arlington, Virginia, March 22, 2018.

6. U.S. Department of Defense, Joint Chiefs of Staff, *Logistics*, pp. I-5–I-6.

7. Ibid., p. I-2.

8. Ibid.

9. "DNA," *Oxford Living Dictionaries*, https://en.oxforddictionaries.com/definition/dna (accessed May 29, 2018).

10. U.S. Department of Defense, U.S. Transportation Command, "About USTRANSCOM," https://www.ustranscom.mil/cmd/aboutustc.cfm (accessed May 29, 2018).

11. General Darren W. McDew, U.S. Air Force, Commander, U.S. Transportation Command, statement "On the State of the Command" before the Committee on Armed Services, U.S. Senate, April 10, 2018, pp. 10–21, https://www.armed-services.senate.gov/imo/media/doc/McDew_04-10-18.pdf (accessed May 29, 2018).

12. U.S. Department of Defense, Defense Logistics Agency, "DLA at a Glance, http://www.dla.mil/At-a-Glance.aspx (accessed May 29, 2018).

13. Naval Supply Systems Command, "Logistics Quotations," http://www.au.af.mil/au/awc/awcgate/navy/log_quotes_navsup.pdf (accessed May 30, 2018).

14. Ibid.

15. Field Marshal Viscount Slim, *Defeat into Victory: Battling Japan in Burma and India, 1942–1945* (New York: Cooper Square Press, 2000), pp. 169–180.

16. James Mattis, Secretary of Defense, *Summary of the 2018 National Defense Strategy of the United States of America: Sharpening the American Military's Competitive Edge*, U.S. Department of Defense, p. 7, https://www.defense.gov/Portals/1/Documents/pubs/2018-National-Defense-Strategy-Summary.pdf (accessed May 29, 2018).

17. Robert L. Wilke, Under Secretary of Defense, Personnel and Readiness, memorandum, "DOD Retention Policy for Non-Deployable Service Members," February 14, 2018, https://news.usni.org/2018/02/16/new-pentagon-separation-policy-non-deployable-service-members (accessed May 29, 2018).

18. See Esper and Milley, statement "On the Posture of the United States Army," April 12, 2018; Spencer, statement on "Fiscal Year 2019 Department of the Navy Budget," April 19, 2018; Richardson, statement on "Fiscal Year 2019 Navy Budget," April 19, 2018; Neller, statement on "The Posture of the United States Marine Corps," April 19, 2018; and Wilson and Goldfein, "USAF Posture Statement: Fiscal Year 2019," April 24, 2018.

19. Fact Sheet, "Civil Reserve Air Fleet," U.S. Air Force, July 28, 2014, http://www.af.mil/About-Us/Fact-Sheets/Display/Article/104583/civil-reserve-air-fleet/ (accessed May 29, 2018).

20. Global Security.org, "Sealift in Operation Iraqi Freedom," last modified July 7, 2011, https://www.globalsecurity.org/military/systems/ship/sealift-oif.htm (accessed May 30, 2018).

21. Ibid.

22. Press release, "MSC Area Commands Provide a World of Service to Military Forces in Middle East," U.S. Navy, Military Sealift Command, July 23, 2003, http://www.msc.navy.mil/publications/pressrel/press03/press34.htm (accessed May 29, 2018).

23. Ibid.

24. Mattis, *Summary of the 2018 National Defense Strategy of the United States of America*, p. 6.

25. Ibid. Emphasis added.

26. Shipbuilding History, "Large Naval Ships and Submarines," http://www.shipbuildinghistory.com/navalships.htm (accessed July 27, 2018).

27. U.S. Department of Defense, Office of the Chief of Naval Operations, Deputy Chief of Naval Operations (Warfare Systems) (N9), *Report to Congress on the Annual Long-Range Plan for Construction of Naval Vessels for Fiscal Year 2019*, February 2018, p. 3, https://news.usni.org/2018/02/12/fy-2019-u-s-navy-30-year-shipbuilding-plan (accessed May 29, 2018).

28. Lieutenant General Michael G. Dana, USMC, "21st Century Logistics: Designing and Developing Capabilities," *Marine Corps Gazette*, Vol. 101, Issue 10 (October 2017), https://www.mca-marines.org/gazette/2017/10/21st-century-logistics (accessed May 29, 2018).

29. Franklin Delano Roosevelt, "The Great Arsenal of Democracy," address delivered December 29, 1940, http://www.americanrhetoric.com/speeches/fdrarsenalofdemocracy.html, (accessed May 29, 2018).

30. "For the want of a nail the shoe was lost, / For the want of a shoe the horse was lost, / For the want of a horse the rider was lost, / For the want of a rider the battle was lost, / For the want of a battle the kingdom was lost, / And all for the want of a horseshoe-nail." Benjamin Franklin, *Poor Richards Almanack*, https://www.goodreads.com/quotes/tag/poor-richard-s-almanac (accessed May 30, 2018).

31. Mattis, *Summary of the 2018 National Defense Strategy of the United States of America*, p. 1.

Global Operating Environment

Assessing the Global Operating Environment

Measuring the "strength" of a military force—the extent to which that force can accomplish missions—requires examination of the environments in which the force operates. Aspects of one environment may facilitate military operations, but aspects of another may work against them. A favorable operating environment presents the U.S. military with obvious advantages; an unfavorable operating environment may limit the effect of U.S. military power. The capabilities and assets of U.S. allies, the strength of foes, the geopolitical environment of the region, and the availability of forward facilities and logistics infrastructure all factor into whether an operating environment is one that can support U.S. military operations.

When assessing an operating environment, one must pay particular attention to any treaty obligations the United States has with countries in the region. A treaty defense obligation ensures that the legal framework is in place for the U.S. to maintain and operate a military presence in a particular country. In addition, a treaty partner usually yields regular training exercises and interoperability as well as political and economic ties.

Additional factors—including the military capabilities of allies that might be useful to U.S. military operations; the degree to which the U.S. and allied militaries in the region are interoperable and can use, for example, common means of command, communication, and other systems; and whether the U.S. maintains key bilateral alliances with nations in the region—also affect the operating environment. Likewise, nations where the U.S. has already stationed assets or permanent bases and countries from which the U.S. has launched military operations in the past may provide needed support to future U.S. military operations. The relationships and knowledge gained through any of these factors would undoubtedly ease future U.S. military operations in a region and contribute greatly to a positive operating environment.

In addition to U.S. defense relations within a region, additional criteria—including the quality of the local infrastructure, the political stability of the area, whether or not a country is embroiled in any conflicts, and the degree to which a nation is economically free—should also be considered.

Each of these factors contributes to an informed judgment as to whether a particular operating environment is favorable or unfavorable to future U.S. military operations. The operating environment assessment is meant to add critical context to complement the threat environment and U.S. military assessments that are detailed in subsequent sections of the *Index*.

This *Index* refers to all disputed territories by the name employed by the United States Department of State and should not be seen as reflecting a position on any of these disputes.

Europe

Over the past year, America's reengagement with Europe continued. The resurgence of Russia, brought into starkest relief in Ukraine, and the continued fight against the Islamic State (IS) in Iraq, Syria, and Libya brought Europe back into the top tier of U.S. international interests, and the U.S. increased its financial and military investment in support of European deterrence. The 51 countries in the U.S. European Command (EUCOM) area of responsibility include approximately one-fifth of the world's population, 10.7 million square miles of land, and 13 million square miles of ocean.

Some of America's oldest (France) and closest (the United Kingdom) allies are found in Europe. The U.S. and Europe share a strong commitment to the rule of law, human rights, free markets, and democracy. During the 20th century, millions of Americans fought alongside European allies in defense of these shared ideals—the foundations on which America was built.

America's economic ties to the region are likewise important. A stable, secure, and economically viable Europe is in America's economic interest. For more than 70 years, the U.S. military presence has contributed to regional security and stability, economically benefiting both Europeans and Americans. The economies of the member states of the European Union (EU), now 28 but soon to be 27,[1] along with the United States, account for approximately half of the global economy. The U.S. and the members of the EU are also each other's principal trading partners.

Europe is also important to the U.S. because of its geographical proximity to some of the world's most dangerous and contested regions. From the eastern Atlantic Ocean to the Middle East, up to the Caucasus through Russia, and into the Arctic, Europe is enveloped by an arc of instability. The European region also has some of the world's most vital shipping lanes, energy resources, and trade choke points.

European basing for U.S. forces provides the ability to respond robustly and quickly to challenges to U.S. economic and security interests in and near the region. Russian naval activity in the North Atlantic and Arctic has necessitated a renewed focus on regional command and control and has led to increased U.S. and allied air and naval assets operating in the Arctic. In addition, Russia's strengthened position in Syria has led to a resurgence of Russian naval activity in the Mediterranean that has contributed to "congested" conditions.[2]

Threats to Internal Stability. In recent years, Europe has faced turmoil and instability brought about by high government debt, high unemployment, the threat of terrorist attacks, and a massive influx of migrants. Political fragmentation resulting from these pressures, disparate views on how to solve them, and a perceived lack of responsiveness among politicians threaten to erode stability even further, as centrist political parties and government institutions are seen as unable to deal effectively with the public's concerns.

Economic Factors. While Europe may finally have turned a corner with reasonable growth in 2017 (the eurozone grew by 2.5 percent), growth slowed again in the first quarter of 2018.[3] Unemployment across the 19-country eurozone bloc stands at 8.5 percent; for all 28

EU members, it averages 7.1 percent.[4] Greece has the EU's highest unemployment rate: 20.6 percent; Spain's is 16.1 percent, and Italy's is 11 percent.[5] Average youth unemployment across the eurozone is even greater, standing at 17.3 percent.[6]

In addition to jobless youth, income disparities between older and younger Europeans have widened. A January 2018 International Monetary Fund report noted that "[i]nequality across generations...erodes social cohesion and polarizes political preferences, and may ultimately undermine confidence in political institutions."[7] High government debt is another obstacle to economic vitality.[8] Italy's debt-to-GDP ratio is 131.8 percent. Greece's is even higher at 178.6 percent, and Portugal's is 125.7 percent. In addition, Europe's banking sector is burdened by $1.17 trillion in nonperforming loans.[9] The Italian banking sector's woes are especially troubling, followed by those of French and Spanish banks.[10]

The interconnectedness of the global economy and global financial system means that any new economic crisis in Europe will have profound impacts in the U.S. as well. Asked whether things were going in the right direction in the European Union, 49 percent of Europeans responded that they are going in the wrong direction, and 35 percent responded that they are headed in the right direction.[11]

Migrant Crisis. The biggest political issue in Europe and the most acute threat to stability is migration. An Ipsos Institute poll released in September 2017 found that 78 percent of Turks, 74 percent of Italians, 66 percent of Swedes, 65 percent of Germans, and 58 percent of French citizens believed that the number of migrants in their nations had become too large over the previous five years.[12] Conflicts in Syria and Iraq, as well as open-door policies adopted by several European nations—importantly, Germany and Sweden in 2015—led large numbers of migrants from across Africa, Asia, and the Middle East to travel to Europe in search of safety, economic opportunity, and the benefits of Europe's most generous welfare states. Russia also sought to weaponize migrant flows by intentionally targeting civilians in Syria "in an attempt to overwhelm European structures and break European resolve."[13]

Germany registered 890,000 asylum seekers in 2015, 280,000 in 2016, and 186,644 in 2017.[14] Today, one in eight people living in Germany is a foreign national, and half are from non-EU nations.[15] Other European nations such as Austria, Italy, and Sweden have also taken in large numbers of migrants. Italy, for instance, has seen 500,000 migrants arrive since 2014.[16]

The impact of the migrant crisis is widespread and will continue for decades to come. Specifically, it has buoyed fringe political parties in some European nations and has imposed steep financial, security, and societal costs. The impact on budgets is significant. Germany reportedly plans to "spend close to $90 billion to feed, house and train refugees between 2017 and 2020."[17] The costs of this crisis, which affect both federal and state governments in Germany, include processing asylum applications, administrative court costs, security, and resettlement for those migrants who accept; in Germany, families receive up to $3,540 to resettle back in their home countries.[18] For a host of reasons, integrating migrants into European economies has fallen flat.[19] "In Sweden and Norway, foreigners are three times more likely to be jobless than local people."[20]

A tenuous agreement with Turkey in March 2016 has largely capped migrant flows through the Balkans and Greece, but arrivals have not stopped altogether. Rather, they have decreased and shifted to the central and western Mediterranean. In May 2018, the EU Commission proposed that the EU's border force be increased from 1,200 to 10,000.[21] Austria, Denmark, France, Germany, Norway, and Sweden have reintroduced and continue to maintain temporary border controls.[22] An April 2018 YouGuv survey that asked "What are the top two issues facing the EU right now?" found immigration to be the top issue for people in Denmark, Finland, France, Germany, Greece, Italy, Lithuania, Poland, Sweden, and the United Kingdom, with terrorism the second most important issue cited in every country but Italy.[23]

A perceived lack of responsiveness from political elites has led to a loss of support among established political parties in many European countries.

- In France, in the first round of 2017's presidential elections, about half of voters cast their ballots for candidates espousing anti-EU views. In the second round, 9 percent cast a blank ballot (a protest vote), the highest level in the history of the Fifth Republic.[24]

- In Austria, Sebastian Kurz of the People's Party became prime minister in December 2017 promising tighter immigration controls.

- In Germany, Chancellor Angela Merkel's center-right Christian Democratic Union/Christian Social Union (CDU/CSU) coalition and the center-left Social Democrats (SPD) lost seats in Parliament following elections in September 2017.[25] The nationalist, anti-immigrant AFD entered Parliament for the first time, winning 94 seats.[26] Nearly 1 million former CDU/CSU voters and nearly 500,000 SPD voters voted for the AFD.[27]

- In Italy, the trend of eroding established parties continued in the March parliamentary elections, which saw the populist Five Star Movement emerge as the largest single party, followed by the nationalist Lega party, which campaigned heavily on the issue of immigration.

The migrant crisis has had a direct impact on NATO resources as well. In February 2016, Germany, Greece, and Turkey requested NATO assistance to deal with illegal trafficking and illegal migration in the Aegean Sea.[28] That month, NATO's Standing Maritime Group 2 deployed to the Aegean to conduct surveillance, monitoring, and reconnaissance of smuggling activities, and the intelligence gathered was sent to the Greek and Turkish coast guards and to Frontex, the European Border and Coast Guard Agency.[29] NATO Strategic Direction South, a new NATO hub in Naples with a focus on threats emanating from the Middle East and North Africa region, was scheduled to become operational in July 2018.[30]

Terrorism. Terrorism remains all too familiar in Europe, which has experienced a spate of terrorist attacks in the past two decades. March 2018 attacks in Carcassonne and Trèbes, France cost four innocent lives[31] and left 15 injured.[32] The migrant crisis has increased the risk and exacerbated the already significant workload of European security services. In Germany alone, the estimated number of Salafists has doubled to 11,000 in just five years.[33] In May 2017, the U.S. Department of State took the rare step of issuing a travel alert for all of Europe, citing the persistent threat from terrorism.[34] Today, the State Department warns Americans to exercise increased caution in a number of Western European countries.[35]

Although terrorist attacks may not pose an existential threat to Europe, they do affect security and undermine U.S. allies by increasing instability, forcing nations to spend more financial and military resources on counterterrorism operations, and jeopardizing the safety of U.S. servicemembers, their families, and facilities overseas. In 2017, noting the challenges presented by an increasingly complex and fluid security situation in Europe, the International Institute for Strategic Studies (IISS) concluded that "[a]s a result of this blending of internal and external security tasks, the requirement for closer cooperation between civilian and military actors emerged as a more comprehensive challenge for domestic security than was anticipated."[36]

U.S. Reinvestment in Europe. Continued Russian aggression has caused the U.S. to turn its attention back to Europe and reinvest military capabilities on the continent. General Curtis M. Scaparrotti, Supreme Allied Commander and EUCOM Commander, has described the change as "returning to our historic role as a warfighting command focused on deterrence and defense."[37]

In April 2014, the U.S. launched Operation Atlantic Resolve (OAR), a series of actions meant to reassure U.S. allies in Europe, particularly those bordering Russia. Under OAR and funded through the European Deterrence Initiative (EDI), the U.S. has increased its forward presence in Europe, invested in European basing infrastructure and prepositioned stocks and equipment and supplies, engaged in enhanced multinational training exercises, and negotiated agreements for increased cooperation with NATO and Baltic states.

European Deterrence Initiative. As cataloged by The Heritage Foundation, "Initial funding for the EDI in FY 2015 [when it was known as the European Reassurance Initiative] was $985 million." Funding was renewed in FY 2016, but "the $789 million authorization was $196 million less than in FY 2015." The Obama Administration asked for a substantial increase in FY 2017, and funding "jumped to $3.4 billion for the year." Under the Trump Administration, funding once again rose significantly to nearly $4.8 billion in FY 2018, and the DOD requested $6.5 billion for FY 2019.[38]

Testifying in March 2018, General Scaparrotti was clear about the importance of EDI funding in returning to a posture of deterrence:

These resources, in addition to the base budget funding that supports USEUCOM, enable our headquarters and Service components to: 1) increase presence through the use of rotational forces; 2) increase the depth and breadth of exercises and training with NATO allies and theater partners; 3) preposition supplies and equipment to facilitate rapid reinforcement of U.S. and allied forces; 4) improve infrastructure at key locations to improve our ability to support steady state and contingency operations; and 5) build the capacity of allies and partners to contribute to their own deterrence and defense.[39]

Forward Presence. In September 2017, the 2nd Armored Brigade Combat Team, 1st Infantry Division, replaced the outgoing BCT in a "heel to toe" rotation schedule. The BCT deployed to sites across Bulgaria, Germany, Hungary, Poland, and Romania, with the largest portion of the forces stationed in Poland.

In November 2017, Army Chief of Staff General Mark Milley emphasized the value of ground forces in deterrence: "The air [and] maritime capabilities are very important, but I would submit that ground forces play an outsize role in conventional deterrence and conventional assurance of allies. Because your physical presence on the ground speaks volumes."[40]

In addition to back-to-back rotations of armor, the U.S. has maintained a rotational aviation brigade in Europe since February 2017.[41] Although the brigade is based in Illesheim, Germany, five Black Hawk helicopters and 80 soldiers were forward deployed to Lielvarde Air Base in Latvia, five Black Hawks and 50 soldiers were forward deployed to Mihail Kogalniceanu Air Base in Romania, and 100 soldiers along with four Black Hawks and four Apache helicopters were forward deployed to Powidz, Poland, as of October 2017.[42] The 4th Combat Aviation Brigade, 4th Infantry Division, was scheduled to take over the aviation brigade in August 2018.[43]

In addition to rotational armored and aviation brigades, the U.S. has beefed up its presence in Norway. A 330-Marine rotational deployment will remain in Vaernes, Norway, through the end of 2018 to train and exercise with Norwegian forces.[44] In June, the Norwegian government invited the U.S. to increase its presence to 700 Marines beginning in 2019, deploying on a five-year rotation and basing in the Inner Troms region in the Arctic rather than in central Norway.[45] Operation Atlantic Resolve's naval component has consisted in part of increased deployments of U.S. ships to the Baltic and Black Seas. Additionally, the Navy has taken part in bilateral and NATO exercises. In May 2018, the Navy announced the reestablishment of the Second Fleet, covering the northern Atlantic, including the GIUK gap, formerly disbanded in 2011.[46]

Prepositioned Stocks. The U.S. Army has prepositioned additional equipment across Europe as part of Operation Atlantic Resolve. A prepositioning site in Eygelshoven, Netherlands, opened in December 2016 and will store 1,600 vehicles including "M1 Abrams Tanks, M109 Paladin Self-Propelled Howitzers and other armored and support vehicles."[47] A second site in Dülmen, Germany, opened in May 2017 and will hold equipment for an artillery brigade.[48] Other prepositioning sites include Zutendaal, Belgium; Miesau, Germany; and Powidz, Poland. The Polish site, which has been selected by the Army for prepositioned armor and artillery, is expected to cost $200 million (funded by NATO) and will open in 2021.[49]

Equipment and ammunition sufficient to support a division will continue to arrive in Europe through 2021.[50] The U.S. Air Force, Special Forces, and Marine Corps are beefing up prepositioned stocks; the Marine Corps Prepositioning Program in Norway is emphasizing cold-weather equipment.[51]

Infrastructure Investments. The U.S. plans to use $214.2 million of FY 2018 EDI funds to upgrade air bases in Europe.[52] The U.S. plans additional temporary deployments of fifth-generation aircraft to European air bases. According to EUCOM, "we continuously look for opportunities for our fifth-generation aircraft to conduct interoperability training with our allies and partners in the European theater."[53] Construction of hangers at Naval Air Station Keflavik in Iceland for U.S. P-8 sub-hunter aircraft will constitute a $14 million investment.[54] The U.S. has stated that it still has no plans for permanent basing of forces in Iceland and that the P-8s, while frequently rotating to Keflavik, will remain permanently based at Sigonella in Italy.[55]

Multinational Training. In FY 2017, according to General Scaparrotti, "USEUCOM conducted over 2,500 military-to-military engagements, including over 700 State Partnership Program events in 22 countries, and under Section 1251 authority, USEUCOM trained nine allies in 22 exercises."[56] The combat training center at Hohenfels, Germany, is one of a very few located outside of the continental United States at which large-scale combined-arms exercises can be conducted, and more than 60,000 U.S. and allied personnel train there annually.

U.S.–European training exercises further advance U.S. interests by developing links between America's allies in Europe and National Guard units back in the U.S. At a time when most American servicemembers do not recall World War II or the Cold War, cementing bonds with allies in Europe is a vital task. Currently, 22 nations in Europe have a state partner in the U.S. National Guard.[57]

In addition to training with fellow NATO member states, the U.S Joint Multinational Training Group–Ukraine (JMTG–U) will train up to five Ukrainian battalions a year through 2020.[58] Canada, Estonia, Latvia, Lithuania, and the U.K. also participate in JMTG-U.[59]

U.S. Nuclear Weapons in Europe. It is believed that until the end of the Cold War, the U.S. maintained approximately 2,500 nuclear warheads in Europe. Unofficial estimates put the current figure at between 150 and 200 warheads based in Italy, Turkey, Germany, Belgium, and the Netherlands.[60]

All of these weapons are free-fall gravity bombs designed for use with U.S. and allied dual-capable aircraft. The bombs are undergoing a Life Extension Program that is expected to add at least 20 years to their life span.[61] In 2018, the U.S. will carry out tests of a new B61-12 gravity bomb, which Paul Waugh, Director of Air-Delivered Capabilities at the Air Force's nuclear division, says "ensures the current capability for the air-delivered leg of the U.S. strategic nuclear triad well in to the future for both bombers and dual-capable aircraft supporting NATO."[62] The B61-12, according to U.S. officials, is intended to be three times more accurate than earlier versions.[63]

Important Alliances and Bilateral Relations in Europe

The United States has a number of important multilateral and bilateral relationships

TABLE 3

Initial Correlation of Ground Forces in the Vicinity of the Baltic States, 2017

	NATO Forces in Baltic States	Russian Federation, Western Military District
Major formations Brigade (BDE) equivalents*	2 armored/mechanized (NATO EFP** and U.S. armored BDE) 6 infantry/motorized (Baltic states and U.S. Stryker BDE)	~ 8 motor rifle ~ 4 tank 6 airborne/air assault 3 artillery 1 rocket artillery

Weapon Systems (estimated)	NATO	Russia	Ratio (NATO : Russia)
Main battle tanks	129	757	1 : 5.9
Infantry fighting vehicles	280	1,276	1 : 4.6
Self-propelled howitzers	32	342	1 : 10.7
Rocket artillery	0	270	0 : 270

* Russian motor rifle, tank, and airborne/air assault regiments are considered equivalent to brigades.
** Enhanced Forward Presence.
NOTE: These figures are estimates of forces available in the initial days and weeks of a conventional fight. They include active units in the Western Military District and forces available in defense of the Baltic States.
SOURCE: RAND Corporation, "Assessing the Conventional Force Imbalance in Europe — Implications for Countering Russian Local Superiority," p. 9, Table 1, https://www.rand.org/pubs/research_reports/RR2402.html (accessed August 8, 2018).

☎ heritage.org

in Europe. First and foremost is NATO, the world's most important and arguably most successful defense alliance.

The North Atlantic Treaty Organization. NATO is an intergovernmental, multilateral security organization that was designed originally to defend Western Europe from the Soviet Union. It anchored the U.S. firmly in Europe, solidified Western resolve during the Cold War, and rallied European support following the terrorist attacks on 9/11. Since its creation in 1949, NATO has been the bedrock of transatlantic security cooperation, and it is likely to remain so for the foreseeable future.

The past year saw continued focus on military mobility and logistics in line with NATO's 2014 Readiness Action Plan (RAP). The RAP was designed to reassure nervous member states and put in motion "longer-term changes to NATO's forces and command structure so that the Alliance will be better able to react swiftly and decisively to sudden crises."[64]

NATO Response Force. Following the 2014 Wales summit, NATO announced the creation of a Very High Readiness Joint Task Force (VJTF) as part of the RAP to enhance the NATO Response Force (NRF).[65] The VJTF is "a new Allied joint force that will be able to deploy within a few days to respond to challenges that arise, particularly at the periphery of NATO's territory."[66] A rotational plan for the VJTF's land component was established to maintain this capability through 2023.[67]

The VJTF also represents a significant improvement in deployment time. Part of the VJTF can deploy within 48 hours, which is a marked improvement over the month that its predecessor, the Immediate Response Force, needed to deploy.[68] According to an assessment

TABLE 4

NATO Capability to Gain Control of the Air Over Baltic States, 2017

Aircraft	NATO	Russia
Fourth generation	**5,094** 2,928 U.S., 2,529 non-U.S.	**1,251**
Fifth generation	**363** 159 F–22A (U.S. only), 20 B–2 (U.S. only), ~175 F–35A/B/C*	—
Air Missile Defense		
Advanced long-range SAMs	—	17 regiments of SA-20/21 and SA-23 (approximately 272 launchers)
Advanced medium-range SAMs	—	3 brigades of SA-11/17 (approximately 72 launchers)
Advanced short-range SAMs	—	24+ battalions (approximately 288 launchers)

* May not yet be combat-ready.
NOTE: These figures are estimates of forces available in the initial days and weeks of a conventional fight. They include active units in the Western Military District and forces available in defense of the Baltic States.
SOURCE: RAND Corporation, "Assessing the Conventional Force Imbalance in Europe — Implications for Countering Russian Local Superiority," p. 9, Table 2, https://www.rand.org/pubs/research_reports/RR2402.html (accessed August 8, 2018).

⌨ heritage.org

published by the Norwegian Institute of International Affairs, the entire NRF will undergo "a much more rigorous and demanding training program than the old NRF. Future NRF rotations will see many more snap-exercises and short notice inspections."[69]

This does not mean, however, that the VJTF and NRF are without their problems. Readiness remains a concern. For instance, NATO reportedly believes that the VJTF would be too vulnerable during its deployment phase to be of use in Poland or the Baltics.[70] Another concern is the 26,000-strong Initial Follow-on Forces Group (IFFG), which makes up the rest of the NRF and would deploy following the VJTF. The IFFG reportedly would need 30–45 days to deploy in the event of a conflict.[71]

Denmark, France, Italy, Germany, the Netherlands, Norway, Poland, Spain, and the United Kingdom have a combined 334 battalions, but only nine (three British, three French, and three German) could be combat ready within 30 days, and only five battalions from Italy (which is leading the land component of the NRF in 2018)[72] could be combat ready within 10 days.[73]

Enhanced Forward Presence. The centerpiece of NATO's renewed focus on collective defense is the four multinational battalions stationed in Poland and the Baltic States as part of the alliance's Enhanced Forward Presence (EFP).

- The U.S. serves as the framework nation in Orzysz, Poland, near the Suwalki Gap. The U.S.-led battlegroup consists of 795 American troops[74] augmented by 72 from Croatia, 120 from Romania, and 130 from the United Kingdom.[75]

- In Estonia, the United Kingdom serves as the framework nation with 800 troops in an armored infantry battalion along with main battle tanks and artillery and 200 troops from Denmark and one Coast Guard officer from Iceland.[76]

- In Latvia, Canada is the framework nation with 450 troops and armored fighting vehicles augmented by 18 troops from Albania, 160 from Italy, 169 from Poland, 49 from Slovenia, 322 from Spain, and two headquarters staff officers from Slovakia.[77]

- In Lithuania, Germany serves as the framework nation with 699 troops augmented by another 187 from Croatia, 266 from France, 224 from the Netherlands, and 28 from Norway.[78]

EFP troops are under NATO command and control; a Multinational Division Headquarters Northeast located in Elblag, Poland, coordinates the four battalions.[79] In February 2017, the Baltic States signed an agreement to facilitate the movement of NATO forces among the countries.[80]

In addition, NATO has established eight Force Integration Units located in Sofia, Bulgaria; Tallinn, Estonia; Riga, Latvia; Vilnius, Lithuania; Bydgoszcz, Poland; Bucharest, Romania; Szekesfehervar, Hungary; and Bratislava, Slovakia.[81] These new units "will help facilitate the rapid deployment of Allied forces to the Eastern part of the Alliance, support collective defence planning and assist in coordinating training and exercises."[82]

At the Warsaw summit, NATO also agreed to create a multinational framework brigade based in Craiova, Romania, under the control of Headquarters Multinational Division Southeast in Bucharest.[83] The HQ became operational in June 2017.[84] Reportedly, "the force will initially be built around a Romanian brigade of up to 4,000 soldiers, supported by troops from nine other NATO countries, and complementing a separate deployment of 900 U.S. troops who are already in place."[85] Unfortunately, the U.S. and allied naval presence in the Black Sea has declined significantly since 2014.

In February 2018, Canada announced that it was rejoining the NATO Airborne Warning and Control System (AWACS), which it had announced it was leaving in 2011, "with operational standdown coming in 2014."[86] Addressing a NATO capability gap, Belgium, Germany, Luxembourg, the Netherlands, and Norway are jointly procuring eight A330 air-to-air refueling aircraft, to be deployed from 2020–2024.[87]

This past year has seen a significant refocusing on logistics issues within the alliance. An internal alliance assessment in 2017 reportedly concluded that NATO's "ability to logistically support rapid reinforcement in the much-expanded territory covering SACEUR's (Supreme Allied Commander Europe) area of operation has atrophied since the end of the Cold War."[88] NATO established two new commands in 2018: a joint force command for the Atlantic and a logistics and military mobility command.[89] These commands consist of a combined total of 1,500 personnel, with the logistics headquartered in Ulm, Germany.[90]

In recent years, the shortfalls in the alliance's ability to move soldiers and equipment swiftly and efficiently have occasionally been glaring. In January 2018, German border guards stopped six U.S. M109 Paladin howitzers en route from Poland to multinational exercises in Bavaria because the trucks being used to transport the artillery were allegedly too wide and heavy for German roadways. In addition, contractors driving the trucks were missing paperwork and trying to transport the howitzers outside of the allowed 9:00 p.m.–5:00 a.m. window.

Training Exercises. In order to increase interoperability and improve familiarity with allied warfighting capabilities, doctrines, and operational methods, NATO conducts frequent joint training exercises. NATO has increased the number of these exercises from 108 in 2017 to 180 in 2018.[91]

The broad threat that Russia poses to Europe's common interests makes military-to-military cooperation, interoperability, and overall preparedness for joint warfighting especially important in Europe, yet they are not implemented uniformly. For example, day-to-day interaction between U.S. and allied officer corps and joint preparedness exercises have been more regular with Western European militaries than with frontier allies in Central Europe, although the situation has improved markedly since 2014.

Cyber Capabilities. Another key area in which NATO is seeking to bolster its capabilities is development of a robust response to increasing cyber threats and threats from space. In 2017, senior NATO officials stated that the alliance plans to spend $3.24 billion "to upgrade its satellite and computer technology over the next three years."[92] The alliance is seeking ways to work more closely with the EU on cyber issues, but "despite political-level agreement to work together, EU–NATO cyber cooperation remains difficult and the institutional options often limited."[93]

Nevertheless, cyber is recognized as a critical area of competition, and NATO is expanding its efforts to gain greater expertise and capability in this area. In 2018, Japan and Australia became the first non-NATO countries outside of the EU to join the Cooperative Cyber Defence Centre of Excellence (CCDCOE) in Tallinn.[94]

Ballistic Missile Defense. NATO announced the initial operating capability of the Ballistic Missile Defense (BMD) system in 2016.[95] An Aegis Ashore site in Deveselu, Romania, became operational in May 2016.[96] Other components include a forward-based early-warning BMD radar at Kürecik, Turkey, and BMD-capable U.S. Aegis ships forward deployed at Rota, Spain.[97] A second Aegis Ashore site in Redzikowo, Poland, which broke ground in May 2016, was expected to be operational in 2017,[98] but Poland announced in March 2018 that construction of the site would be delayed two years, which means that it would not become operational until 2020.[99] Ramstein Air Base in Germany hosts a command and control center.[100]

In January 2017, the Russian embassy in Norway threatened that if Norway contributes ships or radar to NATO BMD, Russia "will have to react to defend our security."[101] Denmark, which agreed in 2014 to equip at least one frigate with radar to contribute to NATO BMD and made further progress in 2016 toward this goal, was threatened by Russia's ambassador in Copenhagen, who stated, "I do not believe that Danish people fully understand the consequences of what may happen if Denmark joins the American-led missile defense system. If Denmark joins, Danish warships become targets for Russian nuclear missiles."[102] A new Danish Defence Agreement announced in early 2018 reiterated the nation's planned contribution to BMD.[103]

The Dutch will equip four *Iver Huitfeldt*-class frigates with a SMART-L Multi-Mission/Naval (MM/N) D-band long-range radar, which is "capable of detecting exo-atmospheric targets up to 2,000 kilometers away."[104] In December 2016, the German Navy announced plans to upgrade radar on three F124 *Sachsen*-class frigates in order to contribute sea-based radar to NATO BMD.[105]

The U.K. operates a BMD radar at RAF Fylingdales in England. In November 2015, the U.K. stated that it plans to build new ground-based BMD radar as a contribution.[106] It expects the new radar to be in service by the mid-2020s.[107] The U.K. reportedly will also "investigate further the potential of the Type 45 Destroyers to operate in a BMD role."[108]

It also has been reported that Belgium intends to procure M-class frigates that "will be able to engage exo-atmospheric ballistic missiles."[109] Belgium and the Netherlands are jointly procuring the frigates.

In October 2017, the U.S. and allies from Canada, France, Germany, Italy, the Netherlands, Spain, and the United Kingdom took part in a three-and-a-half-week BMD exercise Formidable Shield off the Scottish Coast.[110] It is intended that Formidable Shield will be a yearly exercise.[111]

Quality of Armed Forces in the Region

As an intergovernmental security alliance, NATO is only as strong as its member states. A

CHART 5

Few NATO Members Follow Defense Spending Guidelines

NATO members are expected to spend at least 2 percent of their GDP on defense, and at least 20 percent of their defense spending is supposed to go to equipment. Only the U.S. and the U.K. do both, though Estonia and Poland nearly meet both guidelines.

DEFENSE SPENDING AS A SHARE OF GDP, 2017

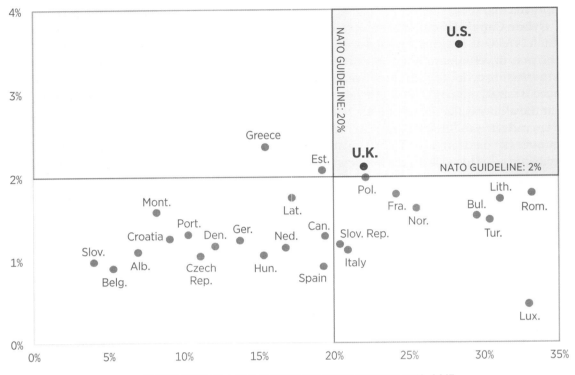

EQUIPMENT AS A SHARE OF DEFENSE EXPENDITURES, 2017

NOTES: Figures are estimates for 2017. Iceland is not listed because it has no military.
SOURCE: NATO, "Defence Expenditures of NATO Countries (2010–2017)," March 15, 2018, https://www.nato.int/cps/ic/natohq/news_152830.htm (accessed July 16, 2018).

☎ heritage.org

2017 RAND report found that France, Germany, and the U.K. would face difficulty in quickly deploying armored brigades to the Baltics in the event of a crisis. The report concludes that getting "deployments up to brigade strength would take…a few weeks in the French case and possibly more than a month in the British or German case" and that "[a] single armored brigade each appears to represent a maximum sustainable effort." In addition, there are "questions regarding their ability to operate at the level required for a conflict with the Russians, whether because of training cutbacks, neglected skills, or limited organic support capabilities." The report further states that "the faster British, French, and German forces needed to get to the Baltics, the more direct assistance they would need from the United States in the form of strategic airlift."[112]

Belgium, Britain, France, Germany, Luxembourg, Spain, and Turkey are procuring A400M air transports from Airbus; however, a report published in February 2018 noted an agreement that Airbus had signed to allow it to negotiate deals with individual nations to opt out of including features deemed too difficult to include.[113] Additionally, "the agreement recognizes that Airbus needs more time to deliver the plane than originally planned and paves the way for negotiations over a new delivery schedule."[114]

Article 3 of the 1949 North Atlantic Treaty, NATO's founding document, states that at a minimum, members "will maintain and develop their individual and collective capacity to resist armed attack."[115] Regrettably, only a handful of NATO members are living up to their Article 3 commitment. In 2017, four countries spent the required 2 percent of gross domestic product (GDP) on defense—Estonia (2.08 percent); Greece (2.36 percent); the United Kingdom (2.12 percent); and the United States (3.57 percent)—and Poland spent almost the required amount (1.99 percent).[116] During the past year, however, NATO defense spending continued to trend upward:

> In 2017, the trend continued, with European Allies and Canada increasing their defence expenditure by almost 5%. Many Allies have put in place national plans to reach 2% [cf GDP] by 2024 and are making progress towards that goal. In real terms, defence spending among European Allies and Canada increased by 4.87% from 2016 to 2017, with an additional cumulative spending increase of USD 46 billion for the period from 2015 to 2017, above the 2014 level.[117]

Germany. Germany remains an economic powerhouse that punches well below its weight in terms of defense. In 2017, it spent only 1.24 percent of GDP on defense and 13.75 percent of its defense budget on equipment.[118] In February 2018, German Defense Minister Ursula von der Leyen stated, "We will need significantly more funds in coming years so the Bundeswehr (armed forces) can accomplish the missions and assignments that parliament gives

it."[119] However, lackluster defense spending is unlikely to change; Germany plans to "lift its defence budget from €38.75bn this year to €42.65bn in 2021. With the economy set for continued expansion, military spending would still account for less than 1.5 per cent of GDP four years from now."[120]

Federal elections in September 2017 led to months of negotiations on forming a coalition. The resulting three-party coalition made up of the Christian Democratic Union, Christian Social Union, and Social Democratic Party will not mean a significant change in terms of defense spending.[121] Although Germany is beginning to take on a larger role within NATO as the framework nation for the NATO EFP in Lithuania and has taken some decisions to strengthen its military capabilities, its military remains underfunded and underequipped. An April 2017 RAND report stated that Germany "has only two battalions with equipment modern enough to serve as a worthy battlefield adversary for Russia." [122]

In addition to stationing troops in the Baltics, Germany is the second largest contributor to NATO's Kosovo Force (KFOR) mission[123] and the second largest contributor to the Resolute Support Mission in Afghanistan.[124] In March 2018, the Bundestag approved a bill that increased the maximum number of German troops that can deploy in support of Resolute Support by one-third, raising it to 1,300.[125] The Bundestag also extended the mandate for Germany's participation in NATO's Sea Guardian maritime security operation, as well as deployments in support of the U.N. peacekeeping mission in Mali and South Sudan and participation in the counter-ISIS coalition.[126]

In March 2018, the German government also announced that it was planning to cut the number of German troops fighting ISIS in Iraq from 1,200 to 800 and expand its military training mission to include the Iraqi Army in addition to the Peshmerga.[127] In addition to training, through the summer of 2017, Germany supplied Kurdish Peshmerga forces with 1,200 anti-tank missiles and 24,000 assault rifles as they fought against ISIS.[128]

German troops contribute to NATO's Very High Readiness Joint Task Force, as well as to Baltic Air Policing.[129] Germany will take over the rotating head of the VJTF in January 2019. However, an ominous internal Ministry of Defense report leaked in February 2018 questioned the readiness and ability of the brigade that will lead the VJTF, citing a lack of equipment. According to reports, "the brigade had only nine of 44 Leopard 2 tanks, and three of the 14 Marder armored personnel carriers that it needs. It is also missing night vision goggles, support vehicles, winter clothing and body armor."[130]

The myriad examples of the deleterious state of Germany's armed forces are worrisome. At one point in late 2017 and early 2018, the German Navy had no working submarines; all six of its Type 212 class submarines were in dry-dock awaiting repairs or not ready for active service.[131] In December 2017, Germany's F-125 *Baden-Württemberg*–class frigate failed sea trials because of "software and hardware defects."[132] In addition, the frigate reportedly had "problems with its radar, electronics and the flameproof coating on its fuel tanks. The vessel was also found to list to the starboard,"[133] and lacked sufficiently robust armaments, as well as the ability to add them.[134] Germany returned the ship to the shipbuilder following delivery.[135]

The Luftwaffe faces similar problems. At the end of 2017, for instance, none of the German air force's 14 transport aircraft were available for deployment.[136] In 2017, according to a report from the German Defense Ministry, only 39 of 128 Eurofighters on average were available, usually for lack of spare parts and long maintenance periods.[137] An even grimmer report in a German magazine in May 2018 found that a lack of missiles and problems with the Eurofighter air defense systems, which alerts pilots to potential attacks,[138] meant that only four are ready for actual combat missions.[139] Among other examples, only 26 of 93 Tornadoes are ready for action.[140]

Germany's army is similarly ill equipped and understaffed, with 21,000 vacant positions in its officer corps.[141] In February 2018, only 95 of 244 Leopard 2 tanks were in service.[142] In December 2017, the Army outsourced helicopter training to a private company because the condition of its own helicopters prevented pilots from getting enough flight time.[143] In 2017, one-tenth of Germany's military helicopter pilots lost their licenses for lack of adequate flying time.[144]

Germany is seeking a replacement for its 90 Tornado aircraft, set to be retired in 2030. In April 2018, three companies submitted bids to deliver the replacement, which the Luftwaffe plans will "enter service in about 2025."[145] The Tornado replacement will need to be able to carry both nuclear and conventional weapons, as the Tornadoes are dual-capable aircraft equipped to carry B61 tactical nukes in addition to conventional payloads.[146]

Germany's military faces institutional challenges to procurement that include an understaffed procurement office with 1,300 vacancies, which is equal to 20 percent of its entire workforce,[147] and the need for special approval by a parliamentary budget committee for any expenditure of more than €25 million.[148]

In February 2017, Germany and Norway announced joint development and procurement of naval anti-surface missiles.[149] In October 2017, Germany announced plans to purchase five corvettes for its Navy at a total cost of €1.5 billion.[150]

The Bundeswehr plans to add 5,000 new soldiers to its ranks along with 1,000 civilians and 500 reservists by 2024.[151] In April 2017, the Bundeswehr established a new cyber command, which initially will consist of 260 staff but will number around 13,500 by the time it becomes fully operational in 2021.[152]

In February 2017, Germany decided to replace its short-range air defense systems. Once complete, this upgrade, which could cost as much as €3.3 billion by 2030, will help to close a gap in Europe's short-range air defense weapons that was identified in 2016.[153] Continued problems with the procurement of A400M cargo aircraft have raised questions about whether Germany will have replacement transport aircraft ready before its C-160 fleet is due to be retired in 2021. According to one account, a "confidential German military report said there was a 'significant risk' that the A400M would not meet all its tactical requirements" in time to replace the aging C-160.[154]

France. France sees itself as a global power, remains one of the most capable militaries within the NATO alliance, and retains an independent nuclear deterrent capability. Although France rejoined NATO's Integrated Command Structure in 2009, it remains outside the alliance's nuclear planning group. France spent 1.79 percent of GDP on defense in 2017 and 24.17 percent of defense spending on equipment, attaining one of two NATO benchmarks.[155] The outlook for defense investment has improved following initial defense cuts under President Emmanuel Macron that led the Chief of Defense to resign in protest.

In July 2018, President Macron signed a law increasing defense spending over six years, including a $2.1 billion increase for the current year, with France spending 2 percent of GDP on defense by 2025. One-third of the planned increases will not take effect until 2023, after the next French general election. Much of the increased spending will be used for intelligence and military procurement, including "the acquisition of more than 1,700 armored vehicles for the Army as well as five frigates, four nuclear-powered attack submarines and nine offshore patrol vessels for the Navy." Procurements for the Air Force would include "12 in-flight refueling tankers, 28 Rafale fighter jets and 55 upgraded Mirage 2000 fighters."[156]

France is upgrading its sea-based and air-based nuclear deterrent. "It is estimated the cost of this process will increase from $4.4bn in 2017 to $8.6bn per year in 2022–2025," according to the IISS, "but decrease thereafter—with these outlays likely to come at the expense of conventional procurements."[157] France opened a cyber-operational command in December 2016. The Army plans to employ 2,600 cyber soldiers supported by 600 cyber experts, along with 4,400 reservists, and to invest €1 billion in this effort by 2019.[158]

France withdrew the last of its troops from Afghanistan at the end of 2014, although all French combat troops had left in 2012. As of April 2017, France had 1,100 soldiers deployed in the campaign against the Islamic State, along with 10 Rafale fighter jets and four CAESAR self-propelled howitzers.[159] By September 2017, French planes operating from bases in Jordan, the United Arab Emirates, and occasional maritime platforms had flown 7,136 missions, including 1,375 strikes and 2,152 targets neutralized.[160] French artillery has taken part in supporting the ground offensive against the IS since September 2016,[161] and France has helped to train Iraqi forces. Around 40 French Special Operations Forces on the ground are actively engaged in tracking down and locating some of the 1,700 French nationals that have joined ISIS.[162]

The September 2017 death of a Special Forces soldier was the first combat death in Operation Chammal (French operations in Iraq).[163] In April 2018, France joined the U.S. and U.K. in targeting the Assad regime over its use of chemical weapons.[164] According to French Air Force Chief of Staff Andre Lanata, the pace of Operation Chammal is having a deleterious impact on French forces. In addition to such other problems as a shortage of drones and refueling tankers, Lanata has stated that he is "having a hard time (recruiting and retaining personnel) in a number of positions, from plane mechanics to intelligence officers, image analysts and base defenders."[155]

In Europe, France's deployment of 266 troops, along with armored fighting vehicles, to Lithuania[166] contributes to NATO's Enhanced Forward Presence. The French military is very active in Africa, with over 4,000 troops taking part in anti-terrorism operations in Burkina Faso, Chad, Mali, Mauritania, and Niger as part of Operation Barkhane.[167] France also has over 1,450 troops in Djibouti and troops in Côte d'Ivoire, Gabon, and Senegal.[168] In addition, France has a close relationship with the United Arab Emirates and stations 850 troops in the UAE; a 15-year defense agreement between the countries came into force in 2012.[169]

France recently added 11,000 soldiers to its Army.[170] Operation Sentinelle, launched in January 2015 to protect the country from terrorist attacks, is the largest operational commitment of French forces and accounts for some 13,000 troops.[171] Operation Sentinelle soldiers helped to foil an attack near the Louvre museum in February 2017 and an attempted attack on a soldier patrolling Orly Airport in March 2017.[172] In October, Sentinelle soldiers killed a terrorist who had killed two people at a train station in Marseille.[173]

Frequent deployments, especially in Operation Sentinelle, have placed significant strains on French forces and equipment.[174] "In early September 2017," according to the IISS, "the chief of defense staff declared that the French armed forces have been used to '130% of their capacities and now need time to regenerate.'"[175] To counteract the strain on soldiers, the government both extended deployment pay to soldiers taking part in and created a new "medal for Protection of the Territory" for troops deployed for 60 days in Operation Sentinelle.[176]

The United Kingdom. America's most important bilateral relationship in Europe is the Special Relationship with the United Kingdom.

In his famous 1946 "Sinews of Peace" speech—now better known as his "Iron Curtain" speech—Winston Churchill described the Anglo–American relationship as one that is based first and foremost on defense and military cooperation. From the sharing of intelligence to the transfer of nuclear technology, a high degree of military cooperation has helped to make the Special Relationship between the U.S. and the U.K. unique. U.K. Prime Minister Margaret Thatcher made clear the essence of the Special Relationship between the U.K. and the U.S. when she first met U.S.S.R. President Mikhail Gorbachev in 1984: "I am an ally of the United States. We believe the same things, we believe passionately in the same battle of ideas, we will defend them to the hilt. Never try to separate me from them."[177]

In 2015, the U.K. conducted a Strategic Defence and Security Review (SDSR), the results of which have driven a modest increase in defense spending and an effort to reverse some of the cuts that had been implemented pursuant to the previous review in 2010. Through 2015, defense spending had dropped to 2.08 percent of GDP,[178] and U.K. forces suffered as a consequence. In 2016, the U.K. moved to repair the damage in capability and capacity by increasing spending to 2.17 percent of GDP, with 22.56 percent of this devoted to equipment purchases.[179] In 2017, the U.K. spent 2.14 percent of GDP on defense and 22.03 percent of GDP on equipment.[180] In recent years, it has increased funding for its highly respected Special Forces.

Funding procurement is an issue. As noted by the Royal United Services Institute, "The 2015 SDSR bridged the gap between a 5% increase in the total budget and a 34% increase in procurement spending by promising substantial efficiency savings over its first five years."[181] Those efficiencies were insufficient, and this led to a funding gap of £4.9 billion and £21 billion for the Ministry of Defence's decade-long procurement plans.[182] A widely anticipated defense review, the Defence Modernisation Programme, is due out in mid-2018 and will take a fresh look at U.K. capabilities, requirements, and funding.

Though its military is small in comparison to the militaries of France and Germany, the U.K. maintains one of the most effective armed forces in European NATO. Former Defense Secretary Michael Fallon stated in February 2017 that the U.K. will have an expeditionary force of 50,000 troops by 2025.[183] However, an April 2018 report from the National Audit Office found that the military was 8,200 people (5.7 percent) short of its required level, a shortfall that it will take at least five years to rectify.[184] The same report also found a gap of 26 percent for intelligence analysts.[185]

By 2020, if funding is sustained, the Royal Air Force (RAF) will operate a fleet of F-35 and Typhoon fighter aircraft, the latter being upgraded to carry out ground attacks. While the U.K. is committed to purchasing 138 F-35s, rising acquisition costs and defense budget pressure have led some, including the Deputy

Chief of the U.K. Defence Staff, to raise the possibility that the number of F-35s acquired might have to be cut.[186]

The RAF recently brought into service a new fleet of air-to-air refuelers, which is particularly noteworthy because of the severe shortage of this capability in Europe. With the U.K., the U.S. produced and has jointly operated an intelligence-gathering platform, the RC-135 Rivet Joint aircraft, that has already seen service in Mali, Nigeria, and Iraq and is now part of the RAF fleet.

The U.K. operates seven C-17 cargo planes and has started to bring the European A400M cargo aircraft into service after years of delays. The 2015 SDSR recommended keeping 14 C-130Js in service even though they initially were going to be removed from the force structure. The Sentinel R1, an airborne battlefield and ground surveillance aircraft, originally was due to be removed from the force structure in 2015, but its service is being extended to at least 2025, and the U.K. will soon start operating the P-8 Poseidon maritime patrol aircraft (MPA). The U.K. has procured nine P-8A maritime patrol aircraft, which will come into service in 2019.[187] A £132 million facility to house the P-8s is under construction at RAF Lossiemouth in Scotland,[188] to be completed in 2020.[189] In the meantime, the U.K. has relied on allied MPAs to fill the gap. In 2017, 17 MPAs from the U.S., Canada, France, Germany, and Norway deployed to RAF Lossiemouth.[190]

The Royal Navy's surface fleet is based on the new Type-45 Destroyer and the older Type-23 Frigate. The latter will be replaced by the Type-26 Global Combat Ship sometime in the 2020s. In total, the U.K. operates only 19 frigates and destroyers, which most experts agree is dangerously low for the commitment asked of the Royal Navy (in the 1990s, the fleet numbered nearly 60 surface combatants). In December, 12 of 13 Type-23 Frigates and all six Type-45 Destroyers were in port, leaving only one Royal Navy frigate on patrol.[191]

The U.K. will not have an aircraft carrier in service until the first Queen Elizabeth-class carrier enters service in the 2020s. This will be the largest carrier operated in Europe. Two of her class will be built, and both will enter service. The Queen Elizabeth underwent sea trials in June 2017[192] and was commissioned in December.[193] By the end of 2017, the U.K. had taken delivery of 14 F-35Bs, the variant that will be operated jointly by the RAF and the Royal Navy.[194] Additionally, the Royal Navy is introducing seven Astute-class attack submarines as it phases out its older Trafalgar-class. Crucially, the U.K. maintains a fleet of 13 Mine Counter Measure Vessels (MCMVs) that deliver world-leading capability and play an important role in Persian Gulf security contingency planning.

Perhaps the Royal Navy's most important contribution is its continuous-at-sea, submarine-based nuclear deterrent based on the Vanguard-class ballistic missile submarine and the Trident missile. In July 2016, the House of Commons voted to renew Trident and approved the manufacture of four replacement submarines to carry the missile. However, the replacement submarines are not expected to enter service until 2028 at the earliest.[195] In March 2018, Prime Minister Theresa May announced a £600m increase for procurement of the new Dreadnought-class submarines, stating that the extra funds "will ensure the work to rebuild the UK's new world-class submarines remains on schedule."[196]

The U.K. remains a leader inside NATO, serving as framework nation for NATO's EFP in Estonia and as a contributing nation for the U.S.-led EFP in Poland. In March, the U.K. announced the first operational deployment of four Lynx Wildcat reconnaissance helicopters to Estonia for a period of four months.[197] The Royal Air Force has taken part in Baltic Air Policing four times, including most recently from April–August 2016.[198] Four RAF Typhoons were deployed to Romania for four months in May 2017 to support NATO's Southern Air Policing mission,[199] and another four were deployed from May–September 2018.[200] "In the face of an increasingly assertive Russia," U.K. Defence Minister Gavin Williamson has stated, "the UK has significantly stepped up its commitment to Europe and today I can confirm a further package of support, showing how we remain at the forefront on European security."[201]

The U.K. also maintains a sizeable force of 500 troops in Afghanistan[202] as part of NATO's Resolute Support mission and contributes to NATO's Kosovo Force,[203] Standing NATO Maritime Group 2, and Mine Countermeasures Group Two.[204] U.K. forces are an active part of the anti-ISIS coalition, and the U.K. joined France and the U.S. in launching airstrikes against the Assad regime in April 2018 over its use of chemical weapons against civilians.[205]

Turkey. Turkey remains an important U.S. ally and NATO member, but the increasingly autocratic presidency of Recep Tayyip Erdogan and a recent thaw in relations between Turkey and Russia have introduced troubling challenges. Turkey has been an important U.S. ally since the closing days of World War II. During the Korean War, it deployed a total of 15,000 troops and suffered 721 killed in action and more than 2,000 wounded. Turkey joined NATO in 1952, one of only two NATO members (the other was Norway) that had a land border with the Soviet Union. Today, it continues to play an active role in the alliance, but not without difficulties.

Turkey is vitally important to Europe's energy security. It is the gateway to the resource-rich Caucasus and Caspian Basin and controls the Bosporus, one of the world's most important shipping straits. Several major gas and oil pipelines run through Turkey. As new oilfields are developed in the Central Asian states, and given Europe's dependence on Russian oil and gas, Turkey can be expected to play an increasingly important role in Europe's energy security.

On July 15, 2016, elements of the Turkish armed forces reportedly attempted a coup d'état against the increasingly Islamist-leaning leadership of President Erdogan. This was the fourth coup attempt since 1960 (the fifth if one counts the so-called postmodern coup in 1997). In each previous case, the military was successful, and democracy was returned to

the people; in this case, however, Erdogan immediately enforced a state of emergency and cracked down on many aspects of government, the military, and civil society. Following the failed coup attempt, thousands of academics, teachers, journalists, judges, prosecutors, bureaucrats, and soldiers were fired or arrested. As of April 2018, "More than 150,000 people have been detained and 110,000 civil servants dismissed since the coup attempt."[206]

The post-coup crackdown has had an especially negative effect on the military. In April 2018, Erdogan announced the firing of an additional 3,000 military officers; more than 11,000 military members have been fired since the 2016 coup attempt.[207] Turkey's military is now suffering from a loss of experienced generals and admirals as well as an acute shortage of pilots, and NATO Supreme Allied Commander General Scaparrotti has stated that Erdogan's military purges have "degraded" NATO's capabilities.[208]

The failed plot has enabled Erdogan to consolidate more power. A referendum that was approved by a narrow margin in April 2017 granted the president's office further powers—such as eliminating the position of prime minister in the government—that came into effect following the June 2018 general election.[209] An interim report by election observers from the Organization for Security and Co-operation in Europe found an "unlevel playing field" and stated that the two sides of the campaign "did not have equal opportunities."[210] Erdogan's response to the coup has further eroded Turkey's democracy, once considered a model for the region.

Senior government officials' erratic and at times hyperbolic statements alleging U.S. involvement in the coup, combined with Erdogan's rapprochement with Russian President Vladimir Putin, have brought U.S.–Turkish relations to an all-time low. In December 2017, Turkey signed a $2.5 billion agreement with Russia to purchase S-400 air defense systems.[211] In April 2018, President Erdogan announced that delivery of the S-400s would be brought forward from 2020 to July 2019 and raised the possibility of additional defense co-operation with Russia.[212]

In April 2017, former Turkish Defense Minister and current Deputy Prime Minister Fikri Işık stated that no S-400s would be integrated into the NATO air defense systems.[213] U.S. officials pointed out the ineffectiveness of older Russian-made air defenses in Syria, which failed to intercept any of the 105 missiles launched by U.S. and allied forces in retaliation for the Assad regime's use of chemical weapons in April 2018.[214] Radars on Russia's newer S-400 systems deployed to Syria were active but did not engage the incoming strikes.[215] Turkey, however, has stated that the purchase of the S-400s is a "done deal."[216]

Also in April 2018, construction began on a $20 billion nuclear power plant in Mersin Province on Turkey's south central coast. The plant is being built by the Russian state corporation Rosatom. In March 2018, Turkey condemned the poisoning of a former Russian spy on British soil[217] but demurred from either naming Russia as the perpetrator or expelling Russian diplomats from Turkey.[218] Despite warmed relations, Turkish and Russian interests do not always neatly align, especially in Syria, where Turkey remains very much the junior player. In February 2018, for instance, Russia was assisting the Assad regime's targeting of forces that were supported by Turkey.[219]

The U.S. decision in May 2017 to arm Syrian Kurds of the People's Protection Units (YPG) further angered Turkey, which considers the YPG to be connected to the Kurdistan Workers Party (PKK), long viewed by Ankara as its primary threat.[220] In January 2018, Turkey launched a major offensive military operation near the Syrian city of Afrin. At issue was the creation of a "30,000-strong border security force in north-east Syria, built around the SDF [Syrian Democratic Forces]. In Ankara's eyes, this offers the YPG permanent title to the land it has carved out. Mr. Erdogan vowed to 'drown' and/or 'strangle' this 'army of terror before it is born.'"[221] U.S. officials have expressed public consternation at Turkey's military engagement in Syria and coordination with Russia. In

April, Assistant Secretary of State for European and Eurasian Affairs Wess Mitchell voiced that uneasiness: "The ease with which Turkey brokered arrangements with the Russian military to facilitate the launch of its Operation Olive Branch in Afrin District, arrangements to which America was not privy, is gravely concerning."[222]

Nevertheless, U.S. security interests in the region lend considerable importance to America's relationship with Turkey. Turkey is home to Incirlik Air Base, a major U.S. and NATO air base, but it was reported early in 2018 that U.S. combat operations at Incirlik had been significantly reduced and that the U.S. was considering permanent reductions.[223] In January, the U.S. relocated an A-10 squadron from Incirlik to Afghanistan to avoid operational disruptions. According to U.S. officials, "Turkey has been making it harder to conduct air operations at the base, such as requesting the U.S. suspend operations to allow high-ranking Turkish officials to use the runway. Officials said this sometimes halts U.S. air operations for more than a day."[224]

In addition to a drawdown in operations in the Middle East, Germany's decision to leave the base also has soured American views on Incirlik,[225] although U.S. officials sought to downplay tensions with Turkey after reports surfaced. An official at EUCOM, for example, stated that "Incirlik still serves as [a] forward location that enables operational capabilities and provides the U.S. and NATO the strategic and operational breadth needed to conduct operations and assure our allies and partners."[226]

One cause for optimism has been NATO's decision to deploy air defense batteries to Turkey and increased AWACS flights in the region after the Turkish government requested them in late 2015.[227] In January 2018, deployments of NATO air defense batteries to Incirlik were extended until June.[228] In addition, after an initial period of vacillation in dealing with the threat from the Islamic State, a spate of IS attacks that rocked the country has led Turkey to play a bigger role in attacking the terrorist group, with NATO AWACS aircraft, for

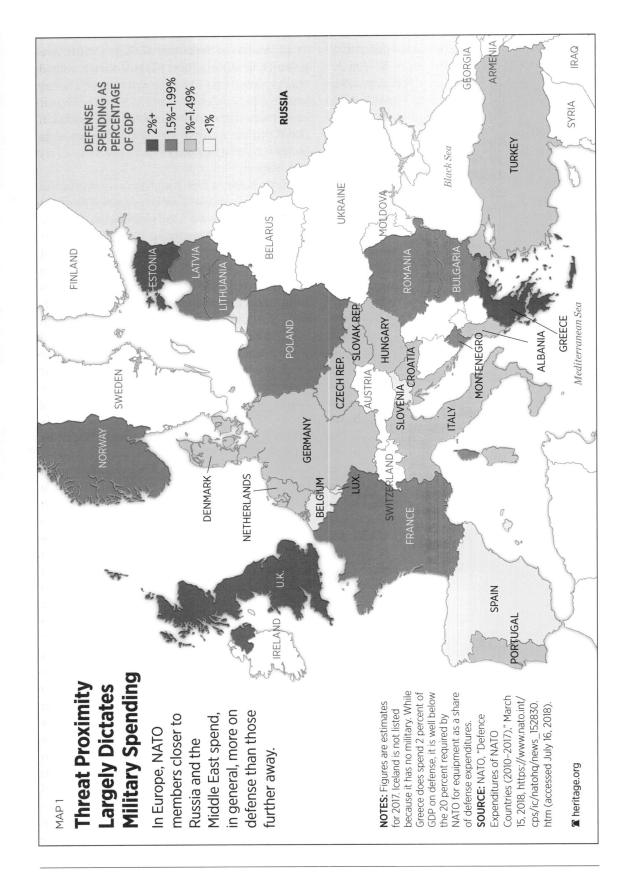

MAP 1

Threat Proximity Largely Dictates Military Spending

In Europe, NATO members closer to Russia and the Middle East spend, in general, more on defense than those further away.

DEFENSE SPENDING AS PERCENTAGE OF GDP

- 2%+
- 1.5%–1.99%
- 1%–1.49%
- <1%

NOTES: Figures are estimates for 2017. Iceland is not listed because it has no military. While Greece does spend 2 percent of GDP on defense, it is well below the 20 percent required by NATO for equipment as a share of defense expenditures.

SOURCE: NATO, "Defence Expenditures of NATO Countries (2010–2017)," March 15, 2018, https://www.nato.int/cps/ic/natohq/news_152830.htm (accessed July 16, 2018).

🔥 heritage.org

example, that are taking part in counter-ISIS operations flying from Turkey's Konya Air Base.[229] Turkey also hosts a crucial radar at Kurecik, which is part of NATO's BMD.[230]

While visiting Turkey in April, NATO Secretary General Jens Stoltenberg stated that "Turkey is a highly valued NATO Ally, and Turkey contributes to our shared security, our collective defence, in many different ways."[231] Stoltenberg also referenced the significant financial investment NATO was making in the upgrading of Turkey's military infrastructure.[232] The U.S. reportedly designated $6.4 million to build out a second undisclosed site (site K) near Malatya, which is home to an AN/TPY-2 radar with a range of up to 1,800 miles.[233]

The Turks have deployed thousands of troops to Afghanistan and have commanded the International Security Assistance Force (ISAF) twice since 2002. Turkey continues to maintain more than 500 troops in Afghanistan as part of NATO's Resolute Support Mission, making it the sixth-largest troop contributor out of 39 nations.[234] The Turks also have contributed to a number of peacekeeping missions in the Balkans, still maintain 307 troops in Kosovo,[235] and have participated in counterpiracy and counterterrorism missions off the Horn of Africa in addition to deploying planes, frigates, and submarines during the NATO-led operation in Libya.

Turkey has a 355,200-strong active-duty military,[236] making it NATO's second largest after that of the United States. Major current procurement programs include up to 250 new Altay main battle tanks, 350 T-155 Fırtına 155mm self-propelled howitzers, six Type-214 submarines, and more than 50 T-129 attack helicopters.[237] Turkish submarine procurement has faced six-year delays, and the first submarine will not be delivered until 2021.[238] Turkey has also upgraded its M60A3 main battle tanks and its M60T tanks.[239] M60Ts taking part in Operation Olive Branch near Afrin were reportedly "equipped with laser warning receivers, situational awareness systems, and remotely operated weapon stations forming part of an indigenous upgrade package."[240]

In February, President Erdogan expressed a desire to utilize internal military procurements and upgrades, declaring that Turkey "will not buy any defence products, software, and systems from abroad that can be designed, produced, and developed in the country except those required urgently."[241]

Geographically and geopolitically, Turkey remains a key U.S. ally and NATO member. It has been a constructive and fruitful security partner for decades, and maintaining the relationship is in America's interest. The challenge for U.S. and NATO policymakers will be to navigate Erdogan's increasingly autocratic leadership, discourage Ankara's warming relations with Russia, and square differing goals in Syria without alienating Turkey.

The Baltic States. The U.S. has a long history of championing the sovereignty and territorial integrity of the Baltic States that dates back to the interwar period of the 1920s. Since regaining their independence from Russia in the early 1990s, the Baltic States have been staunch supporters of the transatlantic relationship. Although small in absolute terms, the three countries contribute significantly to NATO in relative terms.

Estonia. Estonia has been a leader in the Baltics in terms of defense spending and was one of five NATO members to meet the 2 percent of GDP spending benchmark in 2017.[242] Although the Estonian armed forces total only 6,600 active-duty service personnel (including the army, navy, and air force),[243] they are held in high regard by their NATO partners and punch well above their weight inside the alliance. Between 2003 and 2011, 455 served in Iraq. Perhaps Estonia's most impressive deployment has been to Afghanistan: more than 2,000 troops deployed between 2003 and 2014, sustaining the second-highest number of deaths per capita among all 28 NATO members.

In 2015, Estonia reintroduced conscription for men ages 18–27, who must serve eight or 11 months before being added to the reserve rolls.[244] The number of Estonian conscripts will increase from 3,200 to 4,000 by 2026.[245]

Estonia has demonstrated that it takes defense and security policy seriously, focusing on improving defensive capabilities at home while maintaining the ability to be a strategic actor abroad. Procurements are expected to rise to $210 million by 2020.[246] One recent joint procurement is with neighboring Finland to acquire 12 South Korean–built howitzers by 2021.[247] Estonia has purchased 44 used infantry fighting vehicles from the Netherlands, the last of which were delivered in 2018.[248] In June 2018, Estonia signed a $59 million deal to purchase short-range air defenses, with Mistral surface-to-air missiles to be delivered starting in 2020.[249] According to Estonia's National Defence Development Plan for 2017–2026, "the size of the rapid reaction structure will increase from the current 21,000 to over 24,400."[250]

Estonia has a Cyber Defence League, a reserve force that relies heavily on expertise found in the civilian sector, and is planning "to create our own full spectrum cyber command, from defence to offence."[251] In 2017, Estonia and the U.S. strengthened their bilateral relationship by signing a defense cooperation agreement that builds on the NATO–Estonia Status of Forces Agreement to further clarify the legal framework for U.S. troops in Estonia.[252] In 2019, the U.S. "intends to spend more than $15 million to improve working conditions for special operations forces on missions in the Baltics" by upgrading operations and training facilities at an undisclosed site in Estonia.[253]

Latvia. Latvia's recent military experience also has been centered on operations in Iraq and Afghanistan alongside NATO and U.S. forces. Latvia has deployed more than 3,000 troops to Afghanistan and between 2003 and 2008 deployed 1,165 troops to Iraq. In addition, it has contributed to a number of other international peacekeeping and military missions. These are significant numbers considering that only 5,310 of Latvia's troops are full-time servicemembers; the remainder are reserves.[254] In 2018, Latvia added 710 soldiers to its armed forces.[255]

Latvia's 2016 National Defense Concept clearly defines Russia as a threat to national security and states that "[d]eterrence is enhanced by the presence of the allied forces in Latvia."[256] The concept aims to strengthen the operational capability of the armed forces through "further integration of the National Guard within the Armed Forces, strengthening the Special Tasks Unit (special operations forces), as well as boosting early-warning capabilities, airspace surveillance and air defense."[257]

Latvia plans that a minimum of 8 percent of its professional armed forces will be deployed at any one time but will train to ensure that no less than 50 percent will be combat-ready to deploy overseas if required. In 2018, Latvia met the NATO benchmark of 2 percent of GDP spent on defense, and it will also spend 43 percent of its defense budget on procurement in 2018.[258] Also in 2018, Latvia received the first of three TPS-77 Multi-Role radars,[259] along with two unmanned aircraft systems, from the U.S.[260] In addition, Latvia is procuring "second-hand M109 self-propelled artillery pieces from Austria and has selected the *Stinger* man-portable air-defense system."[261] In January, Latvia announced plans to invest $61.7 million through 2021 on military infrastructure, including the expansion of training areas.[262]

Lithuania. Lithuania is the largest of the three Baltic States, and its armed forces total 18,350 active-duty troops.[263] It reintroduced conscription in 2015.[264] Lithuania has also shown steadfast commitment to international peacekeeping and military operations. Between 2003 and 2011, it sent 930 troops to Iraq. Since 2002, around 3,000 Lithuanian troops have served in Afghanistan, a notable contribution that is divided between a special operations mission alongside U.S. and Latvian Special Forces and command of a Provisional Reconstruction Team (PRT) in Ghor Province, making Lithuania one of only a handful of NATO members to have commanded a PRT. Lithuania continues to contribute to NATO's KFOR and Resolute Support Missions.[265]

In 2018, Lithuania reached the NATO benchmark of 2 percent GDP devoted to spending on defense.[266] The government's 2018 National Threat Assessment clearly identifies Russia as the main threat to the nation.[267] Lithuania is dedicating significant resources to procurement with a focus on land maneuver, indirect fire support, air defense radars, anti-tank weapons systems, and ground-based air defense.[268]

Prime Minister Saulius Skvernelis has identified modernization as the armed forces' "number-one priority."[269] Specifically, "Lithuania's government aims to acquire Boxer infantry fighting vehicles, PzH 2000 self-propelled howitzers and the Norwegian Advanced Surface to Air Missile System" by 2021 and "is also mulling plans to purchase transport and perhaps combat [helicopters]."[270] In 2016, Lithuania reached an agreement to acquire 88 Boxer Infantry Fighting Vehicles, to be delivered by 2021.[271]

Lithuania has also taken steps to mitigate the threat from Russia by reducing its dependence on Russian energy. Its decision to build a liquefied natural gas (LNG) import facility at Klaipėda has begun to pay dividends, breaking Russia's natural gas monopoly in the region. In 2016, Norway overtook Russia as the top exporter of natural gas to Lithuania.[272] In June 2017, a Lithuanian energy company signed an agreement to buy LNG directly from the U.S.[273] In May 2017, the Baltic States agreed to connect their power grids (currently integrated with Belarus and Russia) with Poland's with the goal of creating a link to the rest of Europe and decreasing dependence on Russian energy.[274]

Russian cyber aggression against Lithuania in 2018 targeted "Lithuanian state institutions and the energy sector. In addition to these traditional cyber activities, a new phenomenon has been observed—a large-scale spread of ransomware programmes."[275]

Poland. Situated in the center of Europe, Poland shares a border with four NATO allies, a long border with Belarus and Ukraine, and a 144-mile border with Russia alongside the Kaliningrad Oblast. Poland also has a 65-mile border with Lithuania, making it the only NATO member state that borders any of the Baltic States, and NATO's contingency plans for liberating the Baltic States in the event of a Russian invasion reportedly rely heavily on Polish troops and ports.[276]

Poland has an active military force of 105,000, including a 61,200-strong army with 937 main battle tanks.[277] In November 2016, Poland's Parliament approved a new 53,000-strong territorial defense force to protect infrastructure and provide training in "unconventional warfare tactics."[278] The new force will be established by 2019[279] and is the fifth branch of the Polish military, subordinate to the Minister of Defense.[280] The territorial defense force will tackle hybrid threats, linking "the military closely to society, so that there will be someone on hand in the event of an emergency to organize our defenses at the local level."[281]

The prioritization of this new force has ignited controversy in Polish defense circles.[282] Ninety percent of General Staff leadership and 80 percent of Army leadership left or were replaced following military reforms in 2016, introducing a measure of volatility into defense planning.[283]

In 2017, Poland spent 1.99 percent of GDP on defense and 22.14 percent on equipment, essentially reaching both NATO benchmarks.[284] In April, the Ministry of National Defence stated that its goal is to raise defense spending to 2.5 percent of GDP by 2030.[285] Poland is looking at major equipment purchases and is planning to spend an additional $55 billion on modernization over the next 14 years.[286]

In March 2018, Poland signed a $4.75 billion deal for two Patriot missile batteries, the largest procurement contract in the nation's history.[287] In addition, "Warsaw is negotiating with Washington to buy more Patriots, a new 360-degree radar and a low-cost interceptor missile as part of a second phase of modernization."[288] In February, Poland joined an eight-nation "coalition of NATO countries seeking to jointly buy a fleet of maritime surveillance aircraft."[289] Additionally, Warsaw has "established a fund to bolster the defence-modernisation ambitions of neighbors under the Regional Security Assistance Program."[290]

Although Poland's focus is territorial defense, it has 247 troops deployed in Afghanistan as part of NATO's Resolute Support Mission.[291] In 2016, Polish F-16s began to fly reconnaissance missions out of Kuwait as part of the anti-IS mission Operation Inherent Resolve.[292] Approximately 60 soldiers deployed to Iraq in 2015 as trainers.[293] Poland's air force has taken part in Baltic Air Policing seven times since 2006, most recently from September 2017.[294] Poland also is part of NATO's EFP in Latvia and has 262 troops taking part in NATO's KFOR mission.[295]

Current U.S. Military Presence in Europe

Former head of U.S. European Command General Philip Breedlove has aptly described the role of U.S. basing in Europe:

> The mature network of U.S. operated bases in the EUCOM AOR provides superb training and power projection facilities in support of steady state operations and contingencies in Europe, Eurasia, Africa, and the Middle East. This footprint is essential to TRANSCOM's global distribution mission and also provides critical basing support for intelligence, surveillance, and reconnaissance assets flying sorties in support of AFRICOM, CENTCOM, EUCOM, U.S. Special Operations Command, and NATO operations.[296]

At its peak in 1953, because of the Soviet threat to Western Europe, the U.S. had approximately 450,000 troops in Europe operating across 1,200 sites. During the early 1990s, both in response to a perceived reduction in the threat from Russia and as part of the so-called peace dividend following the end of the Cold War, U.S. troop numbers in Europe were slashed. Today, around 65,000 active U.S. forces remain in Europe,[297] an 85 percent decrease in personnel and 75 percent reduction in basing from the height of the Cold War.[298]

Until 2013, the U.S. Army had two heavy brigade combat teams in Europe, the 170th and 172nd BCTs in Germany; one airborne Infantry BCT, the 173rd Airborne Brigade in Italy; and one Stryker BCT, the 2nd Armored Cavalry Regiment in Germany, permanently based in Europe. Deactivation of the 170th BCT in October 2012, slightly earlier than the planned deactivation date of 2013, marked the end of a 50-year period during which U.S. combat soldiers had been stationed in Baumholder, Germany. Deactivation of the 172nd BCT took place in October 2013. In all, this meant that more than 10,000 soldiers were removed from Europe. The U.S. has returned one armored BCT to Europe as part of continuous rotations; according to General Breedlove, "[t]he challenge EUCOM faces is ensuring it is able to meet its strategic obligations while primarily relying on rotational forces from the continental United States."[299]

As of April 2014, according to General Breedlove, the U.S. had only 17 main operating bases left in Europe,[300] primarily in Germany, Italy, the United Kingdom, Turkey, and Spain. In April 2017, EUCOM announced that additional closures proposed under the 2015 European Infrastructure Consolidation effort have been postponed while EUCOM conducts a review of U.S. force posture and future requirements.[301] Currently, the U.S. Army is scouting sites in lower Saxony in northern Germany for the potential basing of an additional 4,000 troops.[302]

EUCOM's stated mission is to conduct military operations, international military partnering, and interagency partnering to enhance transatlantic security and defend the United States as part of a forward defensive posture. EUCOM is supported by four service component commands and one subordinate unified command: U.S. Naval Forces Europe (NAVEUR); U.S. Army Europe (USAREUR); U.S. Air Forces in Europe (USAFE); U.S. Marine Forces Europe (MARFOREUR); and U.S. Special Operations Command Europe (SOCEUR).

U.S. Naval Forces Europe. NAVEUR is responsible for providing overall command, operational control, and coordination for maritime assets in the EUCOM and Africa Command (AFRICOM) areas of responsibility. This includes more than 20 million square nautical miles of ocean and more than 67 percent of the Earth's coastline.

This command is currently provided by the U.S. Sixth Fleet based in Naples and brings critical U.S. maritime combat capability to an important region of the world. Some of the more notable U.S. naval bases in Europe include the Naval Air Station in Sigonella, Italy; the Naval Support Activity Base in Souda Bay, Greece; and the Naval Station at Rota, Spain. Naval Station Rota is home to four capable Aegis-equipped destroyers.[303]

In 2017, the U.S. allocated over $21 million to upgrade facilities at Keflavik Air Station in Iceland to enable operations of P-8 Poseidon aircraft in the region.[304] With a combat radius of 1,200 nautical miles, the P-8 is capable of flying missions over the entirety of the GIUK (Greenland, Iceland, and United Kingdom) Gap, which has seen an increase in Russian submarine activity. The U.S. Navy expects to complete the replacement of P-3s with P-8s by FY 2019.[305]

The U.S. Navy also keeps a number of submarines in the area that contribute to EUCOM's intelligence, surveillance, and reconnaissance (ISR) capacities, but with increased Russian naval activity, more are needed. Testifying in March 2018, General Scaparrotti stated that Russia's Arctic buildup and naval investments could put it in a position to control northern sea-lanes within three years.[306] General Scaparrotti testified in 2017 that he did "not have the carrier or the submarine capacity that would best enable me" to address EUCOM requirements.[307]

U.S.–U.K. military cooperation helps the U.S. to keep submarine assets integrated into the European theater. The British Overseas Territory of Gibraltar, for example, frequently hosts U.S. nuclear-powered submarines. Docking U.S. nuclear-powered submarines in Spain is problematic and bureaucratic, making access to Gibraltar's Z berths vital. Gibraltar is the best place in the Mediterranean to carry out repair work. U.S. nuclear submarines also frequently surface in Norwegian waters to exchange crew or take on supplies.

In addition, last year saw a significant uptick in U.S. and allied nuclear submarine portcalls in Norway, with the number of submarines reaching "3 to 4 per month."[308] The U.S. Navy also has a fleet of Maritime Patrol Aircraft and Reconnaissance Aircraft that operate from U.S. bases in Italy, Greece, Spain, and Turkey and complement the ISR capabilities of U.S. submarines.

U.S. Army Europe USAREUR was established in 1952. Then, as today, the U.S. Army formed the bulk of U.S. forces in Europe. At the height of the Cold War, 277,000 soldiers and thousands of tanks, armored personnel carriers, and tactical nuclear weapons were positioned at the Army's European bases. USAREUR also contributed to U.S. operations in the broader region, such as the U.S intervention in Lebanon in 1985 when it deployed 8,000 soldiers for four months from bases in Europe. In the 1990s, after the fall of the Berlin Wall, USAREUR continued to play a vital role in promoting U.S. interests in the region, especially in the Balkans.

USAREUR is headquartered in Wiesbaden, Germany. Its core is formed around the permanent deployment of two BCTs: the 2nd Cavalry Regiment, based in Vilseck, Germany, and the 173rd Airborne Brigade in Italy, with both units supported by the 12th Combat Aviation Brigade out of Ansbach, Germany. In addition, the U.S. Army's 21st Theater Sustainment Command has helped the U.S. military presence in Europe to become an important logistics hub in support of Central Command.

The 2nd Cavalry Regiment Field Artillery Squadron began training on a Q-53 radar system in 2017. The radar has been described as a "game changer."[309] The unit is the first in the European theater to acquire this system, which is expected to help the army monitor the border between NATO and Russia more effectively. In April 2018, the U.S. deployed the National Guard's 678th Air Defense Artillery Brigade to Europe, the first such unit since drawdowns following the end of the Cold War.[310]

U.S. Air Forces in Europe. USAFE provides a forward-based air capability that can support a wide range of contingency operations. USAFE originated as the 8th Air Force in 1942 and flew strategic bombing missions over the European continent during World War II.

Headquartered at Ramstein Air Base, USAFE has seven main operating bases along with 88 geographically separated locations.[311] The main operating bases are the RAF bases at Lakenheath and Mildenhall in the U.K., Ramstein and Spangdahlem Air Bases in Germany, Lajes Field in the Azores, Incirlik Air Base in Turkey, and Aviano Air Base in Italy. These bases provide benefits beyond the European theater. For example, U.S. Air Force Colonel John Dorrian has said that "any actions by Turkey to shut down or limit U.S. air operations out of Incirlik would be disastrous for the U.S. anti-ISIS campaign." Incirlik is "absolutely invaluable," and "the entire world has been made safer by the operations that have been conducted there."[312] Approximately 39,000 active-duty, reserve, and civilian personnel are assigned to USAFE along with 200 aircraft.[313]

The 2018 EUCOM posture statement describes the value of EDI funding for USAFE:

> In the air domain, we leverage EDI to deploy theater security packages of bombers as well as 4th and 5th generation fighter aircraft to execute deterrence missions and train with ally and partner nation air forces. We are building prepositioned kits for the Air Force's European Contingency Air Operation Sets (ECAOS) and making improvements to existing Allied airfield infrastructure, which will afford us the ability to rapidly respond with air power in the event of a contingency.[314]

U.S. Marine Forces Europe. MARFOREUR was established in 1980. It was originally a "designate" component command, meaning that it was only a shell during peacetime but could bolster its forces during wartime. Its initial staff was 40 personnel based in London. By 1989, it had more than 180 Marines in 45 separate locations in 19 countries throughout the European theater. Today, the command is based in Boeblingen, Germany, and 140 of the 1,500 Marines based in Europe are assigned to MARFOREUR.[315] It was also dual-hatted as Marine Corps Forces, Africa (MARFORAF), under U.S. Africa Command in 2008.

In the past, MARFOREUR has supported U.S. Marine units deployed in the Balkans and the Middle East. It also supports the Norway Air Landed Marine Air Ground Task Force, the Marine Corps' only land-based prepositioned stock. The Marine Corps has enough prepositioned stock in Norway to "to equip a fighting force of 4,600 Marines, led by a colonel, with everything but aircraft and desktop computers,"[316] and the Norwegian government covers half of the costs of the prepositioned storage. The stores have been utilized for Operation Iraqi Freedom and current counter-ISIS operations, as well as humanitarian and disaster response.[317] The prepositioned stock's proximity to the Arctic region makes it of particular geostrategic importance. In 2016, 6,500 pieces of equipment from the stock were utilized for the Cold Response exercise.[318] The U.S. is currently studying whether equipment for 8,000 to 16,000 Marines could be stored in Norway and whether equipment could be stored in ways that would make it possible to deploy it more rapidly.[319] Norway must approve any U.S. request to increase the amount of prepositioned material in the country.[320]

Crucially, MARFOREUR provides the U.S. with rapid reaction capability to protect U.S. embassies in North Africa. The Special-Purpose Marine Air-Ground Task Force–Crisis Response–Africa (SPMAGTF) is currently located in Spain, Italy, and Romania and provides a response force of 1,550 Marines. Six of the unit's 12 Ospreys and three of its C-130s were sent back to the U.S. to bolster Marine capabilities in the U.S.[321] Marine Corps General Joseph Dunford, current Chairman of the Joints Chief of Staff, said in 2016 that this reduction in strength "does reduce the [unit's]

CHART 6

U.S. Presence in Europe Has Declined

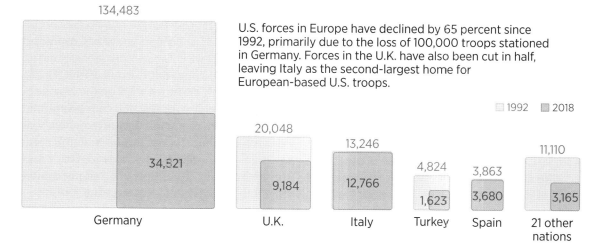

U.S. forces in Europe have declined by 65 percent since 1992, primarily due to the loss of 100,000 troops stationed in Germany. Forces in the U.K. have also been cut in half, leaving Italy as the second-largest home for European-based U.S. troops.

☐ 1992 ☐ 2018

	1992	2018
Germany	134,483	34,521
U.K.	20,048	9,184
Italy	13,246	12,766
Turkey	4,824	1,623
Spain	3,863	3,680
21 other nations	11,110	3,165

NOTE: 2018 figures are as of March.
SOURCES: U.S. Department of Defense, Defense Manpower Data Center, "DoD Personnel, Workforce Reports & Publications: Historical Reports–Military Only–1950, 1953–1999," https://www.dmdc.osd.mil/appj/dwp/dwp_reports.jsp (accessed August 10, 2018), and U.S. Department of Defense, Defense Manpower Data Center, "DoD Personnel, Workforce Reports & Publications: Military and Civilian Personnel by Service/Agency by State/Country," https://www.dmdc.osd.mil/appj/dwp/dwp_reports.jsp (accessed August 10, 2018).

☎ heritage.org

flexibility, it reduces the depth."[322] The SP-MAGTF helped with embassy evacuations in Libya and South Sudan and conducts regular drills with embassies in the region.

In July 2015, Spain and the United States signed the Third Protocol of Amendment to the U.S.–Spanish Agreement for Defense and Cooperation, which allows the U.S. Marine Corps to station up to 2,200 military personnel, 21 aircraft, and 500 nonmilitary employees permanently at Morón Air Base. The Defense Department stated that "a surge capability was included in the amendment of another 800 dedicated military crisis-response task force personnel and 14 aircraft at Morón, for a total of 3,500 U.S. military and civilian personnel and 35 aircraft."[323]

The Marine Corps also maintains a Black Sea Rotational Force (BSRF) composed of approximately 400 Marines, based in Romania, that conduct training events with regional partners.

U.S. Special Operations Command Europe. SOCEUR is the only subordinate unified command under EUCOM. Its origins are in the Support Operations Command Europe, and it was initially based in Paris. This headquarters provided peacetime planning and operational control of special operations forces during unconventional warfare in EUCOM's area of responsibility. SOCEUR has been headquartered in Panzer Kaserne near Stuttgart, Germany, since 1967. It also operates out of RAF Mildenhall. In June 2018, U.S. Special Operations Command Chief General Tony Thomas stated that the U.S. plans to "move tactical United States special operations forces from the increasingly crowded and encroached Stuttgart installation of Panzer Kaserne to the more open training grounds of Baumholder,"[324] a move that is expected to take a few years.

Due to the sensitive nature of special operations, publicly available information is scarce. However, it has been documented that SOCEUR elements participated in various capacity-building missions and civilian evacuation operations in Africa; took an active role in the Balkans in the mid-1990s and in combat operations in the Iraq and Afghanistan wars; and most recently supported AFRICOM's Operation Odyssey Dawn in Libya. SOCEUR also plays an important role in joint training with European allies; since June 2014, it has maintained an almost continuous presence in the Baltic States and Poland in order to train special operations forces in those countries.

The FY 2019 DOD budget request included just under $200 million for various special operations programs and functions through EDI.[325] This funding is intended to go to such projects as enhancement of special operations forces' staging capabilities and prepositioning in Europe, exercise support, enhancement of intelligence capabilities and facilities, and partnership activities with Eastern and Central European allies' special operations forces.

EUCOM has played an important role in supporting other combatant commands such as CENTCOM and AFRICOM. Of the 65,000 U.S. troops based in Europe, almost 10,000 are there to support other combatant commands. The facilities available in EUCOM allowed the U.S. to play a leading role in combating Ebola in western Africa during the 2014 outbreak.

In addition to CENTCOM and AFRICOM, U.S. troops in Europe have worked closely with U.S. Cyber Command (CYBERCOM) to implement Department of Defense cyber policy in Europe and to bolster the cyber defense capabilities of America's European partners. This work has included hosting a number of cyber-related conferences and joint exercises with European partners.

Cyber security in Europe has improved. This improvement includes operationalization of EUCOM's Joint Cyber Center in 2017. EUCOM has also supported CYBERCOM's work inside NATO by becoming a full member of the NATO Cooperative Cyber Defense Center of Excellence in Tallinn, Estonia.

Key Infrastructure and Warfighting Capabilities

One of the major advantages of having U.S. forces in Europe is the access to logistical infrastructure that it provides. For example, EUCOM supports the U.S. Transportation Command (TRANSCOM) with its array of air bases and access to ports throughout Europe. EUCOM supported TRANSCOM with work on the Northern Distribution Network (NDN), which supplied U.S. troops in Afghanistan during major combat operations there. Today, Mihail Kogalniceanu Air Base in Romania is a major logistics and supply hub for U.S. equipment and personnel traveling to the Middle East region.[326]

Europe is a mature and advanced operating environment. America's decades-long presence in Europe means that the U.S. has tried and tested systems that involve moving large numbers of matériel and personnel into, inside, and out of the continent. This offers an operating environment that is second to none in terms of logistical capability. For example, there are more than 166,000 miles of rail line in Europe (not including Russia), and an estimated 90 percent of roads in Europe are paved. The U.S. enjoys access to a wide array of airfields and ports across the continent.

EDI has supported infrastructure improvements across the region. One major EDI-funded project is a replacement hospital at Landstuhl in Germany. When completed in 2022, the new permanent facility "will provide state-of the-art combat and contingency medical support to service members from EUCOM, AFRICOM and CENTCOM."[327] EDI funds are also contributing to creation of the Joint Intelligence Analysis Center, which will consolidate intelligence functions formerly spread across multiple bases and "strengthen EUCOM, NATO and UK intelligence relationships."[328]

Some of the world's most important shipping lanes are also in the European region. In fact, the world's busiest shipping lane is the English Channel, through which pass 500 ships a day, not including small boats and pleasure craft. Approximately 90 percent of the world's trade travels by sea. Given the high volume of maritime traffic in the European region, no U.S. or NATO military operation can be undertaken without consideration of how these shipping lanes offer opportunity—and risk—to America and her allies. In addition to the English Channel, other important shipping routes in Europe include the Strait of Gibraltar; the Turkish Straits (including the Dardanelles and the Bosporus); the Northern Sea Route; and the Danish Straits.

The biggest danger to infrastructure assets in Europe would be any potential NATO conflict with Russia in one or more of NATO's eastern states. In such a scenario, infrastructure would be heavily targeted in order to deny or delay the alliance's ability to move the significant numbers of manpower, matériel, and equipment that would be needed to retake any territory lost during an initial attack.

Conclusion

Overall, the European region remains a stable, mature, and friendly operating environment. Russia remains the preeminent threat to the region, both conventionally and nonconventionally, and the impact of the migrant crisis, continued economic sluggishness, threat from terrorism, and political fragmentation increase the potential for internal instability. The threats emanating from the previously noted arc of instability that stretches from the eastern Atlantic Ocean to the Middle East and up to the Caucasus through Russia and into the Arctic have spilled over into Europe itself in the form of terrorism and migrants arriving on the continent's shores.

America's closest and oldest allies are located in Europe. The region is incredibly important to the U.S. for economic, military, and political reasons. Perhaps most important, the U.S. has treaty obligations through NATO to defend the European members of that alliance. If the U.S. needs to act in the European region or nearby, there is a history of interoperability with allies and access to key logistical infrastructure that makes the operating environment in Europe more favorable than the environment in other regions in which U.S. forces might have to operate.

The past year saw continued U.S. reengagement with the continent both militarily and politically along with modest increases in European allies' defense budgets and capability investment. Despite initial concerns by allies, the U.S. has increased its investment in Europe, and its military position on the continent is stronger than it has been for some time. NATO's renewed focus on collective defense resulted in a focus on logistics, newly established commands that reflect a changed geopolitical reality, and a robust set of exercises. NATO's biggest challenges derive from continued underinvestment from European members, a tempestuous Turkey, disparate threat perceptions within the alliance, and the need to establish the ability to mount a robust response to both linear and nonlinear forms of aggression.

Scoring the European Operating Environment

As noted at the beginning of this section, various considerations must be taken into account in assessing the regions within which the U.S. may have to conduct military operations to defend its vital national interests. Our assessment of the operating environment utilized a five-point scale, ranging from "very poor" to "excellent" conditions and covering four regional characteristics of greatest relevance to the conduct of military operations:

1. **Very Poor.** Significant hurdles exist for military operations. Physical infrastructure is insufficient or nonexistent, and the region is politically unstable. The U.S. military is poorly placed or absent, and alliances are nonexistent or diffuse.

2. **Unfavorable.** A challenging operating environment for military operations is marked by inadequate infrastructure,

weak alliances, and recurring political instability. The U.S. military is inadequately placed in the region.

3. **Moderate.** A neutral to moderately favorable operating environment is characterized by adequate infrastructure, a moderate alliance structure, and acceptable levels of regional political stability. The U.S. military is adequately placed.

4. **Favorable.** A favorable operating environment includes good infrastructure, strong alliances, and a stable political environment. The U.S. military is well placed in the region for future operations.

5. **Excellent.** An extremely favorable operating environment includes well-established and well-maintained infrastructure; strong, capable allies; and a stable political environment. The U.S. military is exceptionally well placed to defend U.S. interests.

The key regional characteristics consist of:

a. **Alliances.** Alliances are important for interoperability and collective defense, as allies would be more likely to lend support to U.S. military operations. Various indicators provide insight into the strength or health of an alliance. These include whether the U.S. trains regularly with countries in the region, has good interoperability with the forces of an ally, and shares intelligence with nations in the region.

b. **Political Stability.** Political stability brings predictability for military planners when considering such things as transit, basing, and overflight rights for U.S. military operations. The overall degree of political stability indicates whether U.S. military actions would be hindered or enabled and considers, for example, whether transfers of power in the region are generally peaceful and whether there have been any recent instances of political instability in the region.

c. **U.S. Military Positioning.** Having military forces based or equipment and supplies staged in a region greatly facilitates the United States' ability to respond to crises and, presumably, achieve successes in critical "first battles" more quickly. Being routinely present in a region also assists in maintaining familiarity with its characteristics and the various actors that might try to assist or thwart U.S. actions. With this in mind, we assessed whether or not the U.S. military was well positioned in the region. Again, indicators included bases, troop presence, prepositioned equipment, and recent examples of military operations (including training and humanitarian) launched from the region.

d. **Infrastructure.** Modern, reliable, and suitable infrastructure is essential to military operations. Airfields, ports, rail lines, canals, and paved roads enable the U.S. to stage, launch operations from, and logistically sustain combat operations. We combined expert knowledge of regions with publicly available information on critical infrastructure to arrive at our overall assessment of this metric.

For Europe, scores this year remained steady, with no substantial changes in any individual categories or average scores. The *2018 Index* again assesses the European Operating Environment as "favorable":

- Alliances: **4—Favorable**

- Political Stability: **4—Favorable**

- U.S. Military Positioning: **3—Moderate**

- Infrastructure: **4—Favorable**

  Leading to a regional score of: **Favorable**

Operating Environment: Europe

	VERY POOR	UNFAVORABLE	MODERATE	FAVORABLE	EXCELLENT
Alliances				✓	
Political Stability				✓	
U.S. Military Posture			✓		
Infrastructure				✓	
OVERALL				✓	

Endnotes

1. On March 29, 2017, Great Britain began a two-year process of formal withdrawal from the EU by invoking Article 50 of the Treaty on European Union.

2. Trisha Thomas, "NATO: Russia Uses Syrian War to Boost Mediterranean Presence," Associated Press, May 8, 2018, https://www.military.com/daily-news/2018/05/08/nato-russia-uses-syrian-war-boost-mediterranean-presence.html (accessed June 25, 2018).

3. Clare Downey, "European Union Economy Records Fastest Economic Growth in a Decade," Sky News, February 14, 2018, https://news.sky.com/story/european-union-economy-records-fastest-economic-growth-in-a-decade-11250315 (accessed June 25, 2018); Deutsche Welle, "Eurozone: Slower Growth, Stagnant Unemployment," May 2, 2018, http://www.dw.com/en/eurozone-slower-growth-stagnant-unemployment/a-43618515 (accessed June 25, 2018).

4. News release, "Euro Area Unemployment at 8.5%," Eurostat, May 2, 2018, p. 1, http://ec.europa.eu/eurostat/documents/2995521/8853183/3-02052018-AP-EN.pdf/ab3f9296-2449-4816-b1db-1faf6a15b79a (accessed June 25, 2018).

5. Ibid.

6. Ibid., p. 2.

7. Paul Hannon, "IMF Urges Action on Europe's Generation Gap," *The Wall Street Journal*, January 24, 2018, https://www.wsj.com/articles/imf-urges-action-on-europes-generation-gap-1516784401 (accessed June 25, 2018).

8. William Horobin and Paul Hannon, "Europe's Economic Growth, Aided by France, Outpaces U.S.," *The Wall Street Journal*, January 30, 2018, https://www.wsj.com/articles/french-economy-accelerates-at-fastest-pace-in-six-years-1517303003 (accessed June 25, 2018).

9. Nicholas Comfort, Giovanni Salzano, and Sonia Sirletti, "Five Charts That Explain How European Banks Are Dealing With Their Bad-Loan Problem," Bloomberg, February 13, 2018, https://www.bloomberg.com/news/articles/2018-02-14/get-a-grip-on-europe-s-bad-loan-problem-with-these-five-charts (accessed June 25, 2018).

10. Ibid.

11. European Commission, *Public Opinion in the European Union*, Standard Eurobarometer 88, Autumn 2017, p. 63, http://ec.europa.eu/commfrontoffice/publicopinion/index.cfm/Survey/getSurveyDetail/instruments/STANDARD/surveyKy/2143 (accessed August 21, 2018).

12. Kalina Oroschakoff, "We've Got Too Many Migrants: Survey," Politico, September 16, 2018, https://www.politico.eu/article/we-got-too-many-migrants-survey-europe-migration/ (accessed June 29, 2018).

13. Deutsche Welle, "NATO Commander: Russia Uses Syrian Refugees as 'Weapon' Against West," March 2, 2016, http://www.dw.com/en/nato-commander-russia-uses-syrian-refugees-as-weapon-against-west/a-19086285 (accessed June 23, 2017).

14. Deutsche Welle, "Refugee Numbers in Germany Dropped Dramatically in 2017," January 16, 2018, http://www.dw.com/en/refugee-numbers-in-germany-dropped-dramatically-in-2017/a-42162223 (accessed June 29, 2018).

15. Reuters, "Number of Migrants in Germany Hits Record High," April 12, 2018, https://uk.reuters.com/article/uk-germany-immigration/number-of-migrants-in-germany-hits-record-high-idUKKBN1HJ2BQ (accessed June 29, 2018).

16. Steve Scherer, "Italy's Homeless, Jobless Migrants Shunned by Politicians," Reuters, January 24, 2018, https://mobile.reuters.com/article/amp/idUSKBN1FD2BD?__twitter_impression=true (accessed June 29, 2018).

17. Harriet Torry, "Are Migrants a Burden or Boon to the German Economy? It Could Depend on the Skills Gap," *The Wall Street Journal*, April 4, 2017, https://blogs.wsj.com/economics/2017/04/04/are-migrants-a-burden-or-boon-to-the-german-economy-it-could-depend-on-the-skills-gap/ (accessed June 29, 2018).

18. Rebecca Seales, "Migrants in Germany: Should They Be Paid to Go Home?" BBC News, December 15, 2017, http://www.bbc.com/news/world-europe-42235232 (accessed June 29, 2018).

19. Friedrich Geiger, "Germany's Efforts to Integrate Migrants Into Its Workforce Falter," *The Wall Street Journal*, updated September 15, 2016, https://www.wsj.com/articles/germanys-efforts-to-integrate-migrants-into-its-workforce-falter-1473948135 (accessed June 29, 2018).

20. Richard Milne, "Sweden's Immigrants Struggle with Jobs and Integration," *Financial Times*, March 26, 2017, https://www.ft.com/content/838d60c2-0961-11e7-97d1-5e720a26771b (accessed June 29, 2018).

21. Simon Nixon, "Limbo Lingers for the European Union," *The Wall Street Journal*, May 9, 2018, https://www.wsj.com/articles/limbo-lingers-for-the-european-union-1525900286?mod=nwsrl_corrections&cx_refModule=nwsrl (accessed June 29, 2018).

22. European Commission, Migration and Home Affairs, "Temporary Reintroduction of Border Control," last updated June 29, 2018, https://ec.europa.eu/home-affairs/what-we-do/policies/borders-and-visas/schengen/reintroduction-border-control_en (accessed June 29, 2018).

23. Matthew Goodwin, Twitter Post, May 11, 2018, 4:09 AM, https://twitter.com/goodwinmj/status/994897239003844608?lang=en (accessed June 29, 2018).

24. Eliza Mackintosh and Judith Vonberg, "A Record Number of French Voters Cast Their Ballots for Nobody," CNN, May 8, 2017, http://www.cnn.com/2017/05/08/europe/french-voters-spoiled-ballots-abstained/index.html?sr=twCNN050817french-voters-spoiled-ballots-abstained0442PMVODtopLink&linkId=37346306 (accessed June 1, 2017).

25. "Germany's Election Results in Charts and Maps," *Financial Times*, September 25, 2017, https://www.ft.com/content/e7c7d918-a17e-11e7-b797-b61809486f2 (accessed May 11, 2018).

26. Ibid.

27. Ibid.

28. North Atlantic Treaty Organization, "Assistance for the Refugee and Migrant Crisis in the Aegean Sea," last updated June 27, 2016, http://www.nato.int/cps/en/natohq/topics_128746.htm (accessed July 10, 2017).

29. News release, "Statement by the NATO Secretary General on NATO Support to Assist with the Refugee and Migrant Crisis," North Atlantic Treaty Organization, February 25, 2016, http://www.nato.int/cps/en/natohq/opinions_128372.htm?selectedLocale=en (accessed June 1, 2017).

30. John Vandiver, "NATO's New Southern Hub in Italy to Be Fully Operational in July," *Stars and Stripes*, June 11, 2018, https://www.stripes.com/news/nato-s-new-southern-hub-in-italy-to-be-fully-operational-in-july-1.532131#.WyCv884yNNc.twitter (accessed June 29, 2018).

31. Hilary Clarke and Nicole Chavez, "French Officer Who Swapped Places with a Hostage in Terror Attack Dies," CNN, March 24, 2018, https://www.cnn.com/2018/03/24/europe/france-trebes-officer-dead/index.html (accessed June 29, 2018).

32. "Attaques terroristes dans l'Aude : revivez le fil de cette journée dramatique" (Terrorist attacks in Aude: relive the thread of this dramatic day), *LeParisien*, March 23, 2018, http://www.leparisien.fr/faits-divers/direct-coups-de-feu-sur-un-crs-et-prise-d-otages-dans-un-super-u-de-l-aude-23-03-2018-7624818.php (accessed June 29, 2018).

33. Deutsche Welle, "Number of Salafists in Germany Has Doubled in Past Five Years," April 4, 2018, http://m.dw.com/en/number-of-salafists-in-germany-has-doubled-in-past-five-years/a-43243111?maca=en-Twitter-sharing&xtref=https%253A%252F%252Ft.co%252FY7NKV83ETU%253Famp%253D1sharing&xtref=https%253A%252F%252Ft.co%252FY7NKV83ETU%253Famp%253D1 (accessed July 3, 2018).

34. U.S. Department of State, Bureau of Consular Affairs, U.S. Passports and International Travel, "Europe Travel Alert: The Department of State Alerts U.S. Citizens to the Continued Threat of Terrorist Attacks Throughout Europe," updated May 1, 2017, https://travel.state.gov/content/passports/en/alertswarnings/Europe.html (accessed July 12, 2017).

35. Alexis Flynn, "ISIS Sympathizer Found Guilty of Planning Attack Against U.S. Military in U.K.," *The Wall Street Journal*, April 1, 2016, http://www.wsj.com/articles/isis-sympathizer-found-guilty-of-planning-attack-against-u-s-military-in-u-k-1459514064 (accessed June 1, 2017).

36. International Institute for Strategic Studies, *The Military Balance 2017: The Annual Assessment of Global Military Capabilities and Defence Economics* (London: Routledge, 2017), p. 65.

37. Stenographic transcript of *Hearing to Receive Testimony on United States European Command*, Committee on Armed Services, U.S. Senate, March 23, 2017, p. 14, https://www.armed-services.senate.gov/imo/media/doc/17-24_03-23-17.pdf (accessed August 8, 2017).

38. Frederico Bartels and Daniel Kochis, "Congress Should Transform the European Deterrence Initiative into an Enduring Commitment," Heritage Foundation *Backgrounder* No. 3319, May 29, 2018, pp. 5–6, https://www.heritage.org/sites/default/files/2018-05/BG3319_2.pdf.

39. General Curtis M. Scaparrotti, U.S. Army, Commander, United States European Command, statement on EUCOM posture before the Committee on Armed Services, U.S. Senate, March 8, 2018, http://www.eucom.mil/mission/eucom-posture-statement-2018 (accessed June 29, 2018).

40. Caroline Houck, "Army Chief: The US Needs More Troops in Europe," *Defense One*, November 15, 2017, https://www.defenseone.com/threats/2017/11/army-chief-us-needs-more-troops-europe/142580/ (accessed June 29, 2018).

41. This was announced early in 2016. See Reuters, "U.S. to Deploy Armored Brigade Combat Teams to Europe," March 30, 2016, https://www.reuters.com/article/us-usa-military-europe-idUSKCN0WW23P (accessed August 21, 2018). In early 2017, the Army initiated a program to rotate units from CONUS to Europe and back, emphasizing the heel-to-toe aspect, meaning that the replacing unit would arrive before departure of the current unit so as to achieve a constant presence in Europe. The program began in January 2017 with the 10th CAB, followed by the 1st CAB in November 2017 and the 4th CAB in June 2018. See Specialist Thomas Skaggs, "10th Combat Aviation Brigade Returns from Successful Rotation in Europe," U.S. Army, November 15, 2017, https://www.army.mil/article/196979/10th_combat_aviation_brigade_returns_from_successful_rotation_in_europe (accessed August 21, 2018), and Staff Sergeant Adrian Patoka, "Third Atlantic Resolve Aviation Brigade Arrives in Europe," U.S. Department of Defense, June 22, 2018, https://www.defense.gov/News/Article/Article/1558059/third-atlantic-resolve-aviation-brigade-arrives-in-europe/ (accessed August 21, 2018).

42. Fact Sheet, "1st Air Cavalry Brigade, 1st Cavalry Division," U.S. Army Europe Public Affairs Office, October 17, 2017.

43. Racheal Wardwell, "Fort Carson Announces 2018 Summer Deployment," KOAA News 5, April 18, 2018, http://www.koaa.com/story/37988139/fort-carson-announces-2018-summer-deployment (accessed June 29, 2018).

44. Tara Copp, "Norway Extends Marine Corps Rotations to 2018," *Stars and Stripes*, June 21, 2017, https://www.stripes.com/news/norway-extends-marine-corps-rotations-to-2018-1.474667 (accessed June 22, 2018).

45. Gwladys Fouche, "Norway to Invite More U.S. Marines, for Longer and Closer to Russia" Reuters, June 12, 2018, https://www.reuters.com/article/us-norway-us-russia/norway-to-invite-more-u-s-marines-for-longer-and-closer-to-russia-idUSKBN1J8149?utm_campaign=trueAnthem:+Trending+Content&utm_content=5b1fd69a04d30124f2870dac&utm_medium=trueAnthem&utm_source=twitter (accessed June 21, 2018).

46. Idrees Ali, "With an Eye on Russia, U.S. Navy Re-Establishing Its Second Fleet," Reuters, May 4, 2018, https://www.reuters.com/article/us-usa-defense-navy-russia/with-an-eye-on-russia-u-s-navy-re-establishing-its-second-fleet-idUSKBN1I152CJ (accessed June 22, 2018).

47. Sgt. 1st Class Jacob McDonald, "Prepositioned Equipment Site Officially Opens in Netherlands," U.S. Army, December 16, 2016, https://www.army.mil/article/179831/prepositioned_equipment_site_officially_opens_in_netherlands (accessed June 5, 2017).

48. Sgt. 1st Class Jacob A. McDonald, "Ribbon Cut on Second Prepositioned Equipment Site," U.S. Army, May 11, 2017, https://www.army.mil/article/187565/ (accessed July 12, 2017).

49. Dan Stoutamire, "Army to Move Brigade's Worth of Firepower into Poland," *Stars and Stripes*, April 26, 2017, https://www.stripes.com/news/army-to-move-brigade-s-worth-of-firepower-into-poland-1.465372#.WQyodoWcHcv (accessed July 12, 2017).

50. U.S. Army Europe, "Army Prepositioned Stock–Europe," August 3, 2017, https://www.army.mil/standto/2017-08-03 (accessed June 29, 2018).

51. U.S. Department of Defense, Office of the Secretary of Defense (Comptroller), *Department of Defense Budget Fiscal Year (FY) 2019: European Deterrence Initiative*, February 2018, pp. 12, 13, and 23, http://comptroller.defense.gov/Portals/45/Documents/defbudget/fy2019/fy2019_EDI_JBook.pdf (accessed June 29, 2018).

52. Shawn Snow, "US Plans $200 Million Buildup of European Air Bases Flanking Russia," *Air Force Times*, December 17, 2017, https://www.airforcetimes.com/flashpoints/2017/12/17/us-plans-200-million-buildup-of-european-air-bases-flanking-russia/ (accessed June 29, 2018).

53. Ibid.

54. Ibid.

55. Nancy Montgomery, "No Permanent Basing for Navy Sub Hunters in Iceland Despite Construction Projects," *Stars and Stripes*, January 9, 2018, https://www.stripes.com/news/no-permanent-basing-for-navy-sub-hunters-in-iceland-despite-construction-projects-1.505835 (accessed June 29, 2018).

56. Scaparrotti, statement on EUCOM posture, March 8, 2018.

57. U.S. Department of Defense, National Guard Bureau, "State Partnership Program," June 2018, http://www.nationalguard.mil/Portals/31/Documents/J-5/InternationalAffairs/StatePartnershipProgram/SPP%20Partnership%20Map_Jun%202018.png (accessed August 21, 2018).

58. United States Army Europe, 7th Army Training Command, "Joint Multinational Training Group–Ukraine: Train on Defense," http://www.7atc.army.mil/JMTGU/ (accessed August 21, 2018).

59. General Curtis M. Scaparrotti, Commander, United States European Command, statement before the Committee on Armed Services, U.S. Senate, March 23, 2017, p. 17, https://www.armed-services.senate.gov/imo/media/doc/Scaparrotti_03-23-17.pdf (accessed June 29, 2018).

60. Malcolm Chalmers and Simon Lunn, "NATO's Tactical Nuclear Dilemma," Royal United Services Institute *Occasional Paper*, March 2010, p. 1, https://rusi.org/sites/default/files/201003_op_natos_tactical_nuclear_dilemma.pdf (accessed September 6, 2016).

61. Geoff Ziezulewicz, "B61-12 Life Extension Program Receives NNSA Approval," United Press International, August 2, 2016, http://www.upi.com/Business_News/Security-Industry/2016/08/02/B61-12-life-extension-program-receives-NNSA-approval/3261470147434/ (accessed June 29, 2018).

62. Tom O'Connor, "The U.S. Is Building a Nuclear Bomb That's More Accurate Than Ever," *Newsweek*, April 18, 2017, http://www.newsweek.com/us-build-better-nuclear-missile-585686 (accessed June 5, 2017).

63. Oriana Pawlyk, "Air Force Advances Testing of New Nuclear Gravity Bomb: General," Military.com, May 1, 2018, https://www.military.com/dodbuzz/2018/05/01/air-force-advances-testing-new-nuclear-gravity-bomb-general.html (accessed June 29, 2018).

64. North Atlantic Treaty Organization, "Readiness Action Plan," last updated September 21, 2017, http://www.nato.int/cps/on/natohq/topics_119353.htm (accessed June 29, 2018).

65. North Atlantic Treaty Organization, "NATO Response Force," last updated January 16, 2017, https://www.nato.int/cps/ua/natohq/topics_49755.htm (accessed June 29, 2018).

66. News release, "Wales Summit Declaration," North Atlantic Treaty Organization, September 5, 2014, http://www.nato.int/cps/en/natohq/official_texts_112964.htm (accessed June 6, 2016).

67. North Atlantic Treaty Organization, *The Secretary General's Annual Report: 2016*, p. 14, http://www.nato.int/nato_static_fl2014/assets/pdf/pdf_2017_03/20170313_SG_AnnualReport_2016_en.pdf#page=13 (accessed July 12, 2017).

68. Jens Ringsmose and Sten Rynning, "Can NATO's New Very High Readiness Joint Task Force Deter?" Norwegian Institute of International Affairs *Policy Brief* No. 15/2016, 2016, p. 2, https://brage.bibsys.no/xmlui/bitstream/handle/11250/2392132/NUPI_Policy_Brief_15_16_Ringmose_Rynning.pdf (accessed July 14, 2017).

69. Ibid.

70. Sam Jones, "NATO Rapid Unit Not Fit for Eastern Europe Deployment, Say Generals," *Financial Times*, May 15, 2016, https://www.ft.com/content/7ac5075c-1a96-11e6-b286-cddde55ca122 (accessed June 6, 2016).

71. Ringsmose and Rynning, "Can NATO's New Very High Readiness Joint Task Force Deter?" p. 2.

72. Italian Ministry of Defence, "NATO: Italy Takes the Lead of NRF Land Component," January 10, 2018, https://www.difesa.it/EN/Primo_Piano/Pagine/so.aspx (accessed June 29, 2018).

73. Julian E. Barnes, "NATO Fears Its Forces Not Ready to Confront Russian Threat," *The Wall Street Journal*, March 28, 2018, https://www.wsj.com/articles/nato-moves-toward-readying-more-troops-to-confront-russian-threat-1522290156 (accessed June 29, 2018).

74. Fact Sheet, "NATO's Enhanced Forward Presence," North Atlantic Treaty Organization, February 2018, https://www.nato.int/nato_static_fl2014/assets/pdf/pdf_2018_02/20180213_1802-factsheet-efp.pdf (accessed June 29, 2018).

75. North Atlantic Treaty Organization, "Boosting NATO's Presence in the East and Southeast," last updated March 2, 2018, https://www.nato.int/cps/er/natohq/topics_136388.htm?selectedLocale=enhttps://www.nato.int/nato_static_fl2014/assets/pdf/pdf_2018_02/20180213_1802-factsheet-efp.pdf (accessed June 29, 2018).

76. Fact Sheet, "NATO's Enhanced Forward Presence."

77. Ibid.

78. Ibid.

79. North Atlantic Treaty Organization, Multinational Division North East, "Landcom Soldiers in Elblag," February 22, 2018, https://mndne.wp.mil.pl/en/articlesnews-u/2018-02-226-landcom-soldiers-in-elblag/ (accessed June 29, 2018).

80. Baltic News Service, "Baltic Countries Sign Agreement on Fast Movement of NATO Forces," Latvian Information Agency, February 15, 2017, http://www.leta.lv/eng/defence_matters_eng/defence_matters_eng/news/CEB6CED4-EA2D-404C-8814-A8765D6BA915/ (accessed July 12, 2017).

81. North Atlantic Treaty Organization, Allied Joint Force Command, "NATO Force Integration Unit (NFIT) Fact Sheet," https://jfcbs.nato.int/page5725819/nato-force-integration-units/nato-force-integration-units-fact-sheet (accessed June 29, 2018).

82. Ibid.

83. Boris Toucas, "NATO and Russia in the Black Sea: A New Confrontation?" Center for Strategic and International Studies, March 6, 2017, https://www.csis.org/analysis/nato-and-russia-black-sea-new-confrontation (accessed June 6, 2017); news release, "Warsaw Summit Communiqué Issued by the Heads of State and Government Participating in the Meeting of the North Atlantic Council in Warsaw 8–9 July 2016," North Atlantic Treaty Organization, July 9, 2016, http://www.nato.int/cps/en/natohq/official_texts_133169.htm (accessed July 11, 2017).

84. Fergus Kelly, "NATO Launches New Multinational Division in Romania," The Defense Post, October 9, 2017, https://thedefensepost.com/2017/10/09/nato-romania-multinational-division-southeast/ (accessed June 29, 2018).

85. Robin Emmott, "NATO Launches Black Sea Force as Latest Counter to Russia," Reuters, October 9, 2017, https://www.reuters.com/article/us-russia-nato/nato-launches-black-sea-force-as-latest-counter-to-russia-idUSKBN1CE0MJ (accessed June 29, 2018).

86. David Pugliese and Aaron Mehta, "NATO's Tanks, AWACS Programs See Membership Increase," Defense News, February 14, 2018, https://www.defensenews.com/smr/munich-security-forum/2018/02/14/natos-tanker-awacs-programs-see-membership-increase/ (accessed June 29, 2018).

87. Ibid.

88. Christopher Woody, "A Convoy of US Army Howitzers Got Stopped by German Police, and It Points to a Major Problem NATO Has in Europe," Business Insider, January 12, 2018, http://www.businessinsider.com/us-army-howitzers-stopped-in-germany-nato-logistics-problems-2018-1 (accessed June 29, 2018).

89. North Atlantic Treaty Organization, "NATO Defence Ministers Take Decisions to Strengthen the Alliance," last updated February 15, 2018, https://www.nato.int/cps/ua/natohq/news_152125.htm (accessed June 29, 2018).

90. Reuters, "Germany Chooses Ulm for New Proposed NATO Logistics Command," March 20, 2018, https://www.reuters.com/article/us-nato-germany/germany-chooses-ulm-for-new-proposed-nato-logistics-command-idUSKBN1GW1QM (accessed June 29, 2018).

91. Fact Sheet, "Key NATO and Allied Exercises in 2018," North Atlantic Treaty Organization, June 2018, https://www.nato.int/nato_static_fl2014/assets/pdf/pdf_2018_04/20180425_1804-factsheet_exercises_en.pdf (accessed June 29, 2018).

92. Robin Emmott, "NATO to Spend 3 Billion Euros on Satellite, Cyber Defenses," Reuters, March 27, 2017, http://mobile.reuters.com/article/idUSKBN16Y0P5 (accessed June 6, 2017).

93. Bruno Lete and Piret Pernik, "EU–NATO Cybersecurity and Defense Cooperation: From Common Threats to Common Solutions," German Marshall Fund of the United States Policy Brief No. 38, December 2017, p. 3, http://www.gmfus.org/publications/eu-nato-cybersecurity-and-defense-cooperation-common-threats-common-solutions (accessed June 29, 2018).

94. Defence Connect, "Australia Joins NATO Cyber Centre," May 3, 2018, https://www.defenceconnect.com.au/intel-cyber/2240-australia-joins-nato-cyber-centre (accessed June 29, 2018).

95. News release, "Warsaw Summit Communiqué."

96. Robin Emmott, "U.S. Activates Romanian Missile Defense Site, Angering Russians," Reuters, May 12, 2016, http://www.reuters.com/article/us-nato-shield-idUSKCN0Y30JX (accessed June 6, 2017).

97. Fact Sheet, "NATO Ballistic Missile Defence," North Atlantic Treaty Organization, July 2016, http://www.nato.int/nato_static_fl2014/assets/pdf/pdf_2016_07/20160630_1607-factsheet-bmd-en.pdf (accessed June 6, 2017).

98. Lisa Ferdinando, "Work Joins Groundbreaking for Ballistic Missile Defense Site in Poland," U.S. Department of Defense, May 13, 2016, https://www.defense.gov/News/Article/Article/759662/work-joins-groundbreaking-for-ballistic-missile-defense-site-in-poland/ (accessed August 8, 2017).

99. Marcin Goclowski and Lidia Kelly, "Poland Says U.S. Missile Shield Site Delayed Until 2020," Reuters, March 22, 2018, https://www.reuters.com/article/us-poland-defence-usa/poland-says-u-s-missile-shield-site-delayed-until-2020-idUSKBN1GY2RE (accessed June 29, 2018).

100. Fact Sheet, "NATO Ballistic Missile Defence."

101. Russian Embassy in Norway and Norway Today, "Russia Threatens Norway to Stay out of NATO Missile Defense," Atlantic Council, March 21, 2017, http://www.atlanticcouncil.org/blogs/natosource/russia-threatens-norway-to-stay-out-of-nato-missile-defense (accessed June 6, 2017).

102. Gerard O'Dwyer, "Denmark Progresses in NATO Ballistic Missile Defense Role," Defense News, April 22, 2016, http://www.defensenews.com/story/defense/air-space/strike/2016/04/22/denmark-progresses-nato-ballistic-missile-defense-role/83391868/ (accessed June 6, 2017).

103. Danish Ministry of Defence, "Agreement for Danish Defence 2018–2023," last updated March 16, 2018, http://www.fmn.dk/eng/allabout/Pages/danish-defence-agreement.aspx (accessed June 30, 2018).

104. "Ballistic Missile Defense Exercise Begins off Scotland," *Naval Today*, September 25, 2017, https://navaltoday.com/2017/09/25/ballistic-missile-defense-exercise-begins-off-scotland/ (accessed June 30, 2018).

105. "German Navy to Modernize Its Sachsen-Class Frigates with New Radar to Join NATO BMD," *Navy Recognition*, December 23, 2016, http://www.navyrecognition.com/index.php/news/defence-news/2016/december-2016-navy-naval-forces-defense-industry-technology-maritime-security-global-news/4719-german-navy-to-modernize-its-f124-sachsen-class-frigates-with-new-radar-to-join-nato-bmd.html (accessed July 12, 2017).

106. Fact Sheet, "NATO Ballistic Missile Defence."

107. George Allison, "UK Looks to Industry for New Ground-Based Ballistic Missile Defence Radar Capability," *UK Defence Journal*, July 18, 2017, https://ukdefencejournal.org.uk/uk-issues-request-information-industry-new-ground-based-ballistic-missile-defence-radar/ (accessed June 30, 2018).

108. Ibid.

109. "Future Belgian Navy Frigates May Have Ballistic Missile Defense Capabilities," *Navy Recognition*, January 5, 2017, http://www.navyrecognition.com/index.php/news/defence-news/2017/january-2017-navy-naval-forces-defense-industry-technology-maritime-security-global-news/4766-future-belgian-navy-frigates-may-have-ballistic-missile-defense-capabilities.html (accessed June 30, 2018).

110. Megan Eckstein, "Navy, NATO Forces Conduct Integrated Air and Missile Defense Exercise off Scotland," U.S. Naval Institute News, October 16, 2017, https://news.usni.org/2017/10/16/navy-nato-forces-conduct-integrated-air-missile-defense-exercise-off-scotland (accessed June 30, 2018).

111. Ibid.

112. Michael Shurkin, "The Abilities of the British, French, and German Armies to Generate and Sustain Armored Brigades in the Baltics," RAND Corporation *Research Report* No. 1629-A, 2017, pp. 1 and 9, https://www.rand.org/content/dam/rand/pubs/research_reports/RR1600/RR1629/RAND_RR1629.pdf (accessed July 11, 2017).

113. Tim Hepher and Andrea Shalal, "Exclusive: Europe's A400M Army Plane May See Some Features Axed," Reuters, February 12, 2018, https://www.reuters.com/article/us-airbus-a400m-exclusive/exclusive-europes-a400m-army-plane-may-see-some-features-axed-idUSKBN1FW1TR?utm_campaign=trueAnthem:+Trending+Content&utm_content=5a81ca6f04d301505b09c4bb&utm_medium=trueAnthem&utm_source=twitter (accessed June 30, 2018).

114. Ibid.

115. The North Atlantic Treaty, Article 3, April 4, 1949, last updated April 9, 2018, http://www.nato.int/cps/en/SID-857936BB-66246E10/natolive/official_texts_17120.htm (accessed June 30, 2018).

116. News release, "Defence Expenditure of NATO Countries (2010–2017)," North Atlantic Treaty Organization, March 15, 2018, p. 3, https://www.nato.int/nato_static_fl2014/assets/pdf/pdf_2018_03/20180315_180315-pr2018-16-en.pdf (accessed June 30, 2018).

117. North Atlantic Treaty Organization, *The Secretary General's Annual Report: 2017*, March 15, 2018, p. 32, https://www.nato.int/nato_static_fl2014/assets/pdf/pdf_2018_03/20180315_SG_AnnualReport_en.pdf (accessed June 30, 2018).

118. News release, "Defense Expenditure of NATO Countries (2010–2017)," p. 3.

119. Andrea Shalal and Sabine Siebold, "Less than Half of German Submarines and Warplanes Ready for Use," Reuters, February 27, 2018, https://www.reuters.com/article/us-germany-military/less-than-half-of-german-submarines-and-warplanes-ready-for-use-idUSKCN1GB27B (accessed June 30, 2018).

120. Tobias Buck, "German Military: Combat Ready?" *Financial Times*, February 15, 2018, https://www.ft.com/content/36e2cd40-0fdf-11e8-940e-08320fc2a277 (accessed April 24, 2018).

121. Ibid.

122. John Vandiver, "Report: Europe's Armies Too Slow for a Baltic Clash," *Stars and Stripes*, April 13, 2017, http://www.military.com/daily-news/2017/04/13/report-europes-armies-too-slow-baltic-clash.html (accessed June 6, 2017).

123. North Atlantic Treaty Organization, *The Secretary General's Annual Report: 2017*, p. 103,

124. North Atlantic Treaty Organization, Resolute Support Mission, "Resolute Support Mission (RSM): Key Facts and Figures," April 2018, https://www.nato.int/nato_static_fl2014/assets/pdf/pdf_2018_04/20180425_2018-04-RSM-Placemat.pdf (accessed June 30, 2018).

125. Radio Free Europe/Radio Liberty, "German Lawmakers Approve Troop Increase for Afghanistan," March 22, 2018, https://www.rferl.org/a/germany-approves-troop-increase-afghanistan/29116022.html (accessed June 30, 2018).

126. Associated Press, "Germany Extends Military Missions in Iraq, Afghanistan, Mali," *U.S. News & World Report*, March 7, 2018, https://www.usnews.com/news/world/articles/2018-03-07/germany-extends-military-missions-in-iraq-afghanistan-mali (accessed June 30, 2018).

127. Deutsche Welle, "Berlin Wants to Expand Bundeswehr Training Mission in Iraq," March 15, 2018, http://www.dw.com/en/berlin-wants-to-expand-bundeswehr-training-mission-in-iraq/a-42988772 (accessed June 30, 2018).

128. Ibid.

129. North Atlantic Treaty Organization, Allied Air Command, "Germany Continues Augmenting Baltic Air Policing," January 6, 2017, https://ac.nato.int/archive/2017/germany-continues-augmenting-baltic-air-policing (accessed June 30, 2018).

130. Andrea Shalal, "Equipment Shortages Impair German Military Ahead of Key NATO Mission," Reuters, February 19, 2018, https://www.reuters.com/article/us-germany-military/equipment-shortages-impair-german-military-ahead-of-key-nato-mission-idUSKCN1G31PX (accessed June 30, 2018).

131. Sean Gallagher, "Das boot Ist Kaputt: German Navy Has Zero Working Subs," Ars Technica, December 19, 2017, https://arstechnica.com/tech-policy/2017/12/das-boot-ist-kaputt-german-navy-has-zero-working-subs/ (accessed June 30, 2018).

132. Tyler Rogoway, "The German Navy Decided to Return Their Bloated News Frigate to Ship Store This Christmas," The War Zone, December 23, 2017, http://www.thedrive.com/the-war-zone/17185/the-german-navy-has-decided-to-return-their-new-frigate-to-the-ship-store-this-christmas (accessed June 30, 2018).

133. William Wilkes, "German Engineering Yields New Warship That Isn't Fit for Sea," *The Wall Street Journal*, January 12, 2018, https://www.wsj.com/articles/german-engineering-yields-new-warship-that-isnt-fit-for-sea-1515753000 (accessed June 30, 2018).

134. Ibid.

135. "Germany Returns Lead F125 Frigate to Builder, Report," *Naval Today*, December 22, 2017, https://navaltoday.com/2017/12/22/germany-returns-lead-f125-frigate-to-builder-report/ (accessed June 30, 2018).

136. Deutsche Welle, "Germany's Lack of Military Readiness 'Dramatic,' Says Bundeswehr Commissioner," February 20, 2018, http://www.dw.com/en/germanys-lack-of-military-readiness-dramatic-says-bundeswehr-commissioner/a-42663215 (accessed June 30, 2018).

137. Shalal and Siebold, "Less than Half of German Submarines and Warplanes Ready for Use."

138. Christopher Woody, "Germany Has a 'Massive Problem' That Has Reportedly Knocked Almost All of Its Eurofighter Typhoon Fighter Jets out of Commission," *Business Insider*, May 4, 2018, http://www.businessinsider.com/german-military-fighters-jets-not-ready-for-combat-2018-5 (accessed June 30, 2018).

139. Matthias Gebauer, "Luftwaffe hat nur vier kampfbereite 'Eurofighter'" (German air force only has four fight-ready Eurofighters), *Spiegel Online*, May 2, 2018, http://www.spiegel.de/politik/deutschland/bundeswehr-luftwaffe-hat-nur-vier-kampfbereite-eurofighter-a-1205641.html (accessed July 2, 2018),

140. Niall McCarthy, "The German Military Is Woefully Unprepared for Action," Statista, February 28, 2018, https://www.statista.com/chart/13077/the-german-military-is-woefully-unprepared-for-action/ (accessed June 30, 2018).

141. Ibid.

142. Christopher Woody, "Germany's Military Is Falling Behind, and the US Is Putting It on Notice," *Business Insider*, February 3, 2018, http://www.businessinsider.com/german-military-falls-behind-the-us-puts-it-on-notice-2018-2 (accessed June 30, 2018).

143. Nicholas Fiorenza, "Bundeswehr Outsources Helicopter Training," Jane's 360, January 9, 2018, http://www.janes.com/article/76919/bundeswehr-outsources-helicopter-training (accessed June 30, 2018).

144. Alexander Pearson, "1 in 10 German Military Pilots Lost Helicopter Licenses for Lack of Flight Time," Deutsche Welle, May 3, 2018, http://www.dw.com/en/1-in-10-german-military-pilots-lost-helicopter-licenses-for-lack-of-flight-time/a-43646369 (accessed June 30, 2018).

145. Gareth Jennings, "ILA 2018: All Industry Bids for German Tornado-Replacement Submitted," Jane's 360, April 26, 2018, http://www.janes.com/article/79599/ila-2018-all-industry-bids-for-german-tornado-replacement-submitted (accessed July 1, 2018).

146. Douglas Barrie, "Dogfight over Berlin: Germany's Tornado Replacement Aspirations," International Institute for Strategic Studies, Military Balance Blog, December 21, 2017, https://www.iiss.org/blogs/military-balance/2017/12/berlin (accessed June 29, 2018).

147. Reuters, "Report Shows 1,300 Unfilled Jobs, Strain for German Defense Procurement," December 13, 2017, https://www.reuters.com/article/us-germany-military/report-shows-1300-unfilled-jobs-strain-for-german-defense-procurement-idUSKBN1E72IW (accessed July 1, 2018).

148. Konstantin von Hammerstein and Peter Müller, "U.S. Pressures Germany to Increase Defense Spending," *Spiegel Online*, February 17, 2017, http://www.spiegel.de/international/world/pressure-on-germany-to-increase-defense-spending-for-nato-a-1135192.html?utm_source=dlvr.it&utm_medium=twitter#ref=rss (accessed July 2, 2018).

149. German Government, "Germany and Norway to Extend Naval Forces Cooperation," *Defence Talk*, February 15, 2017, https://www.defencetalk.com/germany-and-norway-to-extend-naval-forces-cooperation-69124/ (accessed July 1, 2018).

150. Reuters, "Germany to Spend 1.5 Bln Euros for More Navy Ships—Navy," October 14, 2016, http://www.reuters.com/article/german-navy-idUSL8N1CK4QI (accessed June 6, 2017).

151. Reuters, "Germany to Increase Army to 198,000 by 2024 Amid NATO Spending Row," February 21, 2017, http://www.reuters.com/article/germany-army-idUS_8N1G65BZ (accessed June 6, 2017).

152. Nina Werkhäuser, "German Army Launches New Cyber Command," Deutsche Welle, April 1, 2017, http://www.dw.com/en/german-army-launches-new-cyber-command/a-38246517 (accessed July 11, 2017).

153. Andrea Shalal, "Germany to Move Ahead on New Short-Range Air Defense System," Reuters, February 2, 2017, http://www.reuters.com/article/us-germany-military-idUSKBN15H1Z9 (accessed June 6, 2017).

154. Sabine Siebold, "Exclusive: Germany Raises Fears over Capabilities of Airbus A400M Aircraft," Reuters, March 29, 2018, https://www.reuters.com/article/us-airbus-a400m-germany-exclusive/exclusive-germany-raises-fears-over-capabilities-of-airbus-a400m-aircraft-idUSKBN1H51CX (accessed July 1, 2018).

155. News release, "Defence Expenditure of NATO Countries (2010–2017)," March 15, 2018, p. 3.

156. Pierre Tran, "Macron Signs French Military Budget into Law. Here's What the Armed Forces Are Getting," *Defense News*, July 17, 2018, https://www.defensenews.com/global/europe/2018/07/16/macron-signs-french-military-budget-into-law-heres-what-the-armed-forces-are-getting/ (accessed August 21, 2018).

157. International Institute for Strategic Studies, *The Military Balance 2018: The Annual Assessment of Global Military Capabilities and Defence Economics* (London: Routledge, 2018), p. 74.

158. Reuters, "FEATURE—Under Threat, France Grooms Army Hackers for Cyberwarfare," April 5, 2017, http://uk.reuters.com/article/france-cyber-idUKL5N1HC2XQ (accessed June 6, 2017).

159. Republic of France, Minstere Des Armées, "Cartes (maps): Opéracion Chammal," updated April 12, 2017, https://www.defense.gouv.fr/english/operations/operations/irak-syrie/cartes/cartes (accessed July 1, 2018).

160. Emmanuel Huberdeau, "French Forces Mark Three Years of Operation Chammal," Air & Cosmos International, September 25, 2017, http://www.aircosmosinternational.com/french-forces-mark-three-years-of-operation-chammal-100671 (accessed July 1, 2018).

161. Chad Garland, "Paratrooper Becomes France's First Combat Death in Anti-ISIS Coalition," *Stars and Stripes*, September 23, 2017, https://www.stripes.com/news/middle-east/paratrooper-becomes-france-s-first-combat-death-in-anti-isis-coalition-1.489322 (accessed July 1, 2018).

162. Tamer El-Ghobashy, Maria Abi-Habib, and Benoit Faucon, "France's Special Forces Hunt French Militants Fighting for Islamic State," *The Wall Street Journal,* May 29, 2017, https://www.wsj.com/articles/frances-special-forces-hunt-french-militants-fighting-for-islamic-state-1496090116 (accessed July 1, 2018).

163. Garland, "Paratrooper Becomes France's First Combat Death in Anti-ISIS Coalition."

164. Nancy A. Youseff and Michael C. Bender, "U.S., U.K. and France Launch Strikes Against Syria," *The Wall Street Journal*, updated April 14, 2018, https://www.wsj.com/articles/u-s-u-k-launch-strikes-against-syria-1523668212 (accessed July 1, 2018).

165. i24NEWS, "France Has Dropped Twice as Many Bombs on IS as in Libya: Airforce Chief," January 30, 2017, https://www.i24news.tv/en/news/international/136413-170130-france-has-dropped-twice-as-many-bombs-on-is-as-in-libya-airforce-chief (accessed July 1, 2018).

166. Fact Sheet, "NATO's Enhanced Forward Presence."

167. Republic of France, Ministere Des Armées, "Cartes des operations et mission militaires (Map of military operations and missions)," updated May 14, 2018, https://www.defense.gouv.fr/english/operations/rubriques_complementaires/carte-des-operations-et-missions-militaires (accessed July 1, 2018).

168. Republic of France, Ministere Des Armées, "Le forces francaises stationnées a Djibouti (French forces stationed in Djibouti)," updated September 20, 2016. http://www.defense.gouv.fr/ema/forces-prepositionnees/djibouti/dossier/les-forces-francaises-stationnees-a-djibouti (accessed July 1, 2018).

169. Republic of France, Ministry for Europe and Foreign Affairs, "France and the United Arab Emirates," https://www.diplomatie.gouv.fr/IMG/pdf/17_2978_2979_en_texte_infographie_ang_accessibleversion_cle04fd3b.pdf (accessed July 1, 2018).

170. Jim Garamone, "France Deploys Globally in Counter-Extremism Fight," U.S. Department of Defense, January 17, 2017, https://www.defense.gov/News/Article/Article/1050644/france-deploys-troops-globally-in-counter-extremism-fight (accessed June 7, 2017).

171. Republic of France, Ministere Des Armées, "Cartes des operations et mission militaires."

172. Laura Smith-Spark and Laura Goehler, "Louvre Knife Attack: Soldier Shoots Assailant Near Paris Museum," CNN, February 3, 2017, http://www.cnn.com/2017/02/03/europe/france-paris-louvre-incident/ (accessed July 13, 2017); Alissa J. Rubin and Benoît Morenne, "Gunman Is Killed in Orly Airport in France After Attacking a Soldier," *The New York Times*, March 18, 2017, https://www.nytimes.com/2017/03/18/world/europe/orly-airport-france-shooting.html (accessed July 13, 2017).

173. Marc Leras and Emmanuel Jarry, "Knifeman Yelling 'Allahu Akbar' Shot Dead After Killing Two in France," Reuters, October 1, 2017, https://www.reuters.com/article/us-france-security-marseille/knifeman-yelling-allahu-akbar-shot-dead-after-killing-two-in-france-idUSKCN1C61DC (accessed July 1, 2018).

174. International Institute for Strategic Studies, *The Military Balance 2018*, p. 102.

175. Ibid., p. 74.

176. "On the Frontline with Operation Sentinelle," *Politico*, December 29, 2016, http://www.politico.eu/interactive/french-soldiers-deployed-operation-sentinelle-paris-terror-attacks/ (accessed June 7, 2017).

177. Transcript of Geoffrey Smith interview with Margaret Thatcher, Margaret Thatcher Foundation, January 8, 1990, http://www.margaretthatcher.org/document/109324 (accessed June 7, 2017).

178. News release, "Defence Expenditure of NATO Countries (2010–2017)," North Atlantic Treaty Organization, June 29, 2017, p. 8, http://www.nato.int/nato_static_fl2014/assets/pdf/pdf_2017_06/20170629_170629-pr2017-111-en.pdf (accessed July 1, 2018).

179. News release, "Defence Expenditures of NATO Countries (2009–2016)," North Atlantic Treaty Organization, March 13, 2017, p. 3, https://www.nato.int/nato_static_fl2014/assets/pdf/pdf_2017_03/20170313_170313-pr2017-045.pdf (accessed July 1, 2018).

180. News release, "Defence Expenditure of NATO Countries (2010–2017)," June 29, 2017, p. 8.

181. Malcolm Chalmers, "The UK Defence Modernisation Programme: A Risk and Opportunity," Royal United Services Institute *Commentary*, January 25, 2018, https://rusi.org/commentary/uk-defence-modernisation-programme-risk-and-opportunity (accessed July 1, 2018).

182. Peggy Hollinger, "MoD Faces Funding Gap of up to £21bn, Says UK Spending Watchdog," *Financial Times*, January 31, 2018, https://www.ft.com/content/980de9de-0683-11e8-9650-9c0ad2d7c5b5 (accessed May 2, 2018).

183. Steve McCarthy, "Britain's Defense Capabilities and the Future of Transatlantic Security," Atlantic Council, February 28, 2017, http://www.atlanticcouncil.org/blogs/natosource/britain-s-defense-capabilities-and-the-future-of-transatlantic-security (accessed June 7, 2017).

184. Rajeev Syal, "Armed Forces Facing Biggest Shortfall in Staff for a Decade—Report," *The Guardian*, April 17, 2018, https://www.theguardian.com/uk-news/2018/apr/18/armed-forces-facing-biggest-shortfall-in-staff-for-a-decade-report (accessed July 1, 2018).

185. Ibid.

186. David Bond, "UK Military Chief 'Sympathetic' to Cut in F-35 Fighter Jet Order," *Financial Times*, November 21, 2017, https://www.ft.com/content/696be98e-cec8-11e7-b781-794ce08b24dc (accessed May 2, 2018).

187. Tim Ripley, "UK Aims to Certify P-8 by Early 2019," Jane's 360, November 24, 2017, http://www.janes.com/article/75940/uk-aims-to-certify-p-8-by-early-2019 (accessed July 1, 2018).

188. Shephard Media, "New Facility for RAF's P-8 Poseidon Fleet," April 24, 2018, https://www.shephardmedia.com/news/mil-log/new-facility-rafs-p-8-poseidon-fleet/ (accessed July 1, 2018).

189. Naval Technology, "UK and Norway Advance Cooperation on Maritime Patrol Aircraft," May 4, 2018, https://www.naval-technology.com/news/uk-norway-advance-cooperation-maritime-patrol-aircraft/ (accessed July 1, 2018).

190. Lizzie Dearden, "UK Military Forced to Borrow Nato Planes to Monitor Increasing Activity by Russian Submarines, Shows New Figures," *The Independent*, January 10, 2018, https://www.independent.co.uk/news/uk/home-news/uk-russia-submarines-patrol-planes-nimrod-poseidon-p8-nato-monitor-activity-navy-air-force-security-a8151931.html (accessed July 1, 2018).

191. Joseph Trevithick, "Almost All of the UK's Surface Combatants Are in Port While Germany Has No Working Subs," The War Zone, December 20, 2017, http://www.thedrive.com/the-war-zone/17140/almost-all-of-the-uks-surface-combatants-are-in-port-while-germany-has-no-working-subs (accessed July 1, 2018).

192. BBC News, "HMS Queen Elizabeth Sets Sail from Rosyth for Sea Trials," June 27, 2017, https://www.bbc.com/news/uk-scotland-edinburgh-east-fife-40402153 (accessed July 2, 2018).

193. BBC News, "HMS Queen Elizabeth: UK's Biggest Warship Commissioned," December 7, 2017, http://www.bbc.com/news/av/uk-england-hampshire-42267110/hms-queen-elizabeth-uk-s-biggest-warship-commissioned (accessed July 1, 2018).

194. British Royal Navy, "UK Takes Delivery of Final F-35B Lightning of This Year," December 18, 2017, https://www.royalnavy.mcd.uk/news-and-latest-activity/news/2017/december/18/171218-uk-takes-delivery-of-final-f-35b-lightning-of-this-year (accessed July 2, 2018).

195. Reuters, "Trident: UK Parliament Backs Nuclear-Armed Submarine Fleet Renewal," Australian Broadcasting Corporation News, July 18, 2016, http://www.abc.net.au/news/2016-07-19/uk-parliament-backs-trident-nuclear-submarine-renewal/7640150 (accessed July 2, 2018).

196. David Bond, "May Pledges £600m Boost for Nuclear Submarines," *Financial Times*, March 28, 2018, https://www.ft.com/content/2e74f8e8-3296-11e8-ac48-10c6fdc22f03 (accessed May 2, 2018).

197. Tim Ripley, "British Army to Deploy Lynx Wildcat Helicopters to Estonia," Jane's 360, March 7, 2017, http://www.janes.com/article/78422/british-army-to-deploy-lynx-wildcat-helicopters-to-estonia#.WqFkLQR1uhM.twitter (accessed July 2, 2018).

198. North Atlantic Treaty Organization, Allied Air Command, "Baltic Air Policing Augmenting Nations Pass Baton at Ämari, Estonia," August 31, 2016, https://ac.nato.int/archive/2016/baltic-air-policing-augmenting-nations-pass-baton-at-amari--estonia (accessed July 13, 2017).

199. News release, "UK's NATO Southern Air Policing Mission to Begin in May," U.K. Ministry of Defence and The Rt. Hon. Sir Michael Fallon MP, March 27, 2017, https://www.gov.uk/government/news/uks-nato-southern-air-policing-mission-to-begin-in-may (accessed July 2, 2018).

200. George Allison, "Typhoons Return to Black Sea NATO Air Policing Mission," *UK Defence Journal*, April 25, 2018, https://ukdefencejournal.org.uk/typhoons-return-to-black-sea-nato-air-policing-mission/ (accessed July 2, 2018).

201. Press TV, "UK Committing Jets, Troops to Deter 'Assertive Russia,'" November 9, 2017, http://www.presstv.com/Detail/2017/11/09/541565/UK-Williamson-NATO-Russia-Romania-Typhoon-jets (accessed July 2, 2018).

202. North Atlantic Treaty Organization, Resolute Support Mission, "Resolute Support Mission (RSM): Key Facts and Figures."

203. North Atlantic Treaty Organization, *The Secretary General's Annual Report: 2017*, p. 103.

204. North Atlantic Treaty Organization, Allied Maritime Command, "Standing NATO Mine Countermeasures Group Two (SNMCMG2)," https://mc.nato.int/snmcmg2.aspx (accessed July 2, 2018).

205. Helene Cooper, Thomas Gibbons-Neff, and Ben Hubbard, "U.S., Britain and France Strike Syria over Suspected Chemical Weapons Attack," *The New York Times*, April 13, 2018, https://www.nytimes.com/2018/04/13/world/middleeast/trump-strikes-syria-attack.html (accessed July 2, 2018).

206. Hannah Lucinda Smith, "Erdogan Orders Fresh Purge on Military Before Elections as Economic Slump Looms," *The Times*, April 20, 2018, https://www.thetimes.co.uk/article/erdogan-orders-fresh-purge-on-military-before-elections-as-economic-slump-looms-pl6j5jvfq (accessed May 9, 2018).

207. Ibid.

208. Peter Müller and Maximilian Popp, "Purges Have Weakened Once Mighty Turkish Military," *Spiegel Online*, January 18, 2017, http://www.spiegel.de/international/world/purges-have-weakened-once-mighty-turkish-military-a-1130494.html (accessed July 13, 2017)

209. Tulay Karadeniz and Tuvan Gumrukcu, "Turkey's Erdogan Sworn in with New Powers, Names Son-in-Law Finance Minister," Reuters, July 8, 2018, https://www.reuters.com/article/us-turkey-politics-erdogan/turkeys-erdogan-sworn-in-with-new-powers-names-son-in-law-finance-minister-idUSKBN1JY10S (accessed August 20, 2018).

210. Organization for Security and Co-operation in Europe, Office for Democratic Institutions and Human Rights, and Council of Europe, Parliamentary Assembly, "International Referendum Observation Mission, Republic of Turkey—Constitutional Referendum, 16 April 2017: Statement of Preliminary Findings and Conclusions," p. 1, http://www.csce.org/odihr/elections/turkey/311721?download=true (accessed July 13, 2017).

211. Reuters, "Turkey Says Russian S-400 Missile Delivery Brought Forward to July 2019," April 4, 2018, https://www.reuters.com/article/us-russia-turkey-missiles/turkey-says-russian-s-400-missile-delivery-brought-forward-to-july-2019-idUSKCN1HB0IU (accessed July 2, 2018).

212. Ibid.

213. "S-400 Missile System Purchase at Final Stage: Turkish Defense Minister," *Daily Sabah*, April 13, 2017, https://www.dailysabah.com/diplomacy/2017/04/13/s-400-missile-system-purchase-at-final-stage-turkish-defense-minister (accessed June 7, 2017).

214. Jamie McIntyre, "US to Turkey: You Can Buy Russian Air Defenses, but They Really Suck," *Washington Examiner*, April 19, 2018, https://www.washingtonexaminer.com/policy/defense-national-security/us-to-turkey-you-can-buy-russian-air-defenses-but-they-really-suck (accessed July 2, 2018).

215. Ibid.

216. Radio Free Europe/Radio Liberty, "Turkey Dismisses U.S. Warning Against Buying Russian Missile System," April 28, 2018, https://www.rferl.org/a/turkey-cavusoglu-dismisses-us-warning-against-buying-russian-2-400-missile-system-pompeo-done-deal/29197261.html (accessed July 2, 2018).

217. "Turkey Condemns Poison Attack on Ex-spy in UK," *Hurriyet Daily News*, March 27, 2018, http://www.hurriyetdailynews.com/turkey-condemns-poison-attack-on-ex-spy-in-uk-129378 (accessed July 2, 2018).

218. Suzan Fraser and Ayse Wieting, "Turkey, Russia Deepen Ties Amid Troubled Relations with West," *Chicago Tribune*, April 2, 2018, http://www.chicagotribune.com/news/nationworld/ct-turkey-russia-ties-20180402-story.html (accessed July 2, 2018).

219. Sune Engel Rasmussen, "Behind Turkey's Action in Syria: A Fear of Waning Influence," *The Wall Street Journal*, February 16, 2018, https://www.wsj.com/articles/behind-turkeys-actions-in-syria-a-fear-of-waning-influence-1518810799 (accessed July 2, 2018).

220. Radio Free Europe/Radio Liberty, "Erdogan Urges U.S. to Reverse Decision on Arming Syrian Kurds," last updated May 10, 2017, https://www.rferl.org/a/turkey-protests-us-arming-syria-kurds/28477965.html (accessed July 13, 2017).

221. David Gardner, Turkey's Action in Syria Threatens Fragile Alliance," *Financial Times*, January 24 2018, https://www.ft.com/content/f7c3808a-fa19-11e7-9b32-d7d59aace167 (accessed May 9, 2018).

222. McIntyre, "US to Turkey: You Can Buy Russian Air Defenses, but They Really Suck."

223. Gordon Lubold, Felicia Schwartz, and Nancy A. Youssef, "U.S. Pares Back Use of Turkish Base Amid Strains with Ankara," *The Wall Street Journal*, updated March 11, 2018, https://www.wsj.com/articles/u-s-pares-back-use-of-turkish-base-amid-strains-with-ankara-1520766121?mod=e2twp (accessed July 2, 2018).

224. Ibid.

225. Ibid.

226. Oriana Pawlyk, "Air Force General Downplays Possible Restrictions at Incirlik," Military.com, March 18, 2018, https://www.military.com/daily-news/2018/03/18/air-force-general-plays-down-possibility-restrictions-incirlik.htm (accessed July 2, 2018).

227. North Atlantic Treaty Organization, *The Secretary General's Annual Report: 2016*, p. 14; Deutsche Welle, "NATO Discussing Request for AWACS Surveillance Aircraft in Syrian Anti-'IS' Fight," January 22, 2016, http://www.dw.com/en/nato-discussing-request-for-awacs-surveillance-aircraft-in-syrian-anti-is-fight/a-18998325 (accessed June 7, 2017).

228. Ozgenur Sevinç, "Term of Spanish Patriot Missile in Turkey Extended Until June," *Daily Sabah*, January 8, 2018, https://www.dailysabah.com/politics/2018/01/09/term-of-spanish-patriot-missiles-in-turkey-extended-until-june (accessed July 2, 2018).

229. North Atlantic Treaty Organization, "Joint Press Conference with NATO Secretary General Jens Stoltenberg and the Minister of Foreign Affairs of Turkey, Mevlüt Çavuşoğlu," last updated April 17, 2018, https://www.nato.int/cps/en/natohq/opinions_153695.htm (accessed July 2, 2018).

230. North Atlantic Treaty Organization, "NATO Ballistic Missile Defense Architecture as of 2017," https://www.nato.int/nato_static_fl2014/assets/pictures/2016_07_160711a-infographics-bmd/20170907_170907-bmd03.jpg (accessed July 2, 2018).

231. North Atlantic Treaty Organization, "Joint Press Conference with NATO Secretary General Jens Stoltenberg and the Minister of Foreign Affairs of Turkey, Mevlüt Çavuşoğlu."

232. Ibid.

233. Joseph Trevithick. "The U.S. Army Wants to Expand a Secretive Missile Defense Site in Turkey," The War Zone, May 25, 2107, http://www.thedrive.com/the-war-zone/10638/the-u-s-army-wants-to-expand-a-secretive-missile-defense-site-in-turkey (accessed July 2, 2018).

234. North Atlantic Treaty Organization, Resolute Support Mission, "Resolute Support Mission (RSM): Key Facts and Figures."

235. North Atlantic Treaty Organization, *The Secretary General's Annual Report: 2017*, p. 103.

236. International Institute for Strategic Studies, *The Military Balance 2018*, p. 157.

237. International Institute for Strategic Studies, *The Military Balance 2016: The Annual Assessment of Global Military Capabilities and Defence Economics* (London: Routledge, 2016), pp. 147–148.

238. "Turkey Starts Construction of Third Reis-Class Submarine," *Naval Today*, February 27, 2018, https://navaltoday.com/2018/02/27/turkey-starts-construction-of-third-reis-class-submarine/ (accessed July 2, 2018).

239. Samuel Cranny-Evans and Lale Sariibrahimoglu," Turkey Upgrades M60A3 in Addition to M60T," Jane's 360, April 4, 2018, http://www.janes.com/article/79000/turkey-upgrades-m60a3-in-addition-to-m60t (accessed July 2, 2019).

240. Ibid.

241. Lale Sariibrahimoglu, "Turkey to No Longer Buy Foreign Defence Systems Except in Urgent Cases." Jane's 360, February 7, 2018, http://www.janes.com/article/77708/turkey-to-no-longer-buy-foreign-defence-systems-except-in-urgent-cases (accessed July 2, 2018).

242. News release, "Defence Expenditure of NATO Countries (2010–2017)," June 29, 2017, p. 8.

243. International Institute for Strategic Studies, *The Military Balance 2018*, p. 98.

244. Simon Newton, "Why NATO's Military Might Is Focused on Estonia," Forces Network, November 5, 2015, http://forces.tv/54579182 (accessed July 13, 2017).

245. Republic of Estonia, Ministry of Defence, and Republic of Estonia, Defence Forces, "National Defence Development Plan (2017–2026)," http://www.kaitseministeerium.ee/riigikaitse2026/arengukava/eng/ (accessed July 12, 2018).

246. Richard Tomkins, "Estonia Consolidates Military Procurement Process," United Press International, January 3, 2017, http://www.upi.com/Defense-News/2017/01/03/Estonia-consolidates-military-procurement-process/9171483458417/ (accessed July 2, 2018).

247. Jarolsław Adamowski, "Estonia Joins Finland in Howitzer Procurement," *Defense News*, February 6, 2017, http://www.defensenews.com/articles/estonia-joins-finland-in-howitzer-procurement (accessed June 7, 2017).

248. Tomkins, "Estonia Consolidates Military Procurement Process."

249. Associated Press, "Estonia to Buy Missiles, Air Defense System in $59M Deal," *Defense News*, June 12, 2018, https://www.defensenews.com/air/2018/06/12/estonia-to-buy-missiles-air-defense-system-in-50m-deal/ (accessed July 2, 2018).

250. Republic of Estonia, Ministry of Defence, and Republic of Estonia, Defence Forces, "National Defence Development Plan (2017–2026)."

251. Brooks Tigner, "Estonia to Incorporate Offensive Capabilities into Its Future Cyber Command," Jane's 360, December 1, 2017, http://www.janes.com/article/76115/estonia-to-incorporate-offensive-capabilities-into-its-future-cyber-command (accessed July 2, 2018).

252. U.S. Embassy in Estonia, "Signing of Defense Cooperation Agreement—Remarks by Ambassador James D. Melville," Tallinn, Estonia, January 17, 2017, https://ee.usembassy.gov/signing-defense-cooperation-agreement-remarks-ambassador-james-d-melville/ (accessed July 13, 2017).

253. John Vandiver, "US Special Ops to Get a Boost for Baltic Mission," *Stars and Stripes*, March 14, 2018, https://www.stripes.com/news/us-special-ops-to-get-a-boost-for-baltic-mission-1.516689 (accessed July 2, 2018).

254. International Institute for Strategic Studies, *The Military Balance 2018*, p. 122.

255. Latvian Public Broadcasting, "Latvia to Invest Annual €50m in Military Infrastructure 2018–2021," January 25, 2018, https://eng.lsm.lv/article/society/defense/latvia-to-invest-annual-50m-in-military-infrastructure-2018-2021.a265564/ (accessed July 2, 2018).

256. Raimonds Bergmanis, Minister of Defence, Republic of Latvia, "The National Defence Concept," approved by Cabinet of Ministers May 24, 2016, and adopted by Parliament June 16, 2016, p. 8, http://mepoforum.sk/wp-content/uploads/2017/01/Latvia-national-defence-concept-2016-en.pdf (accessed July 2, 2018).

257. Olevs Nikers, "Inside Latvia's New State Defense Concept: Riga Declares Its Military Ambitions Ahead of NATO Summit," Jamestown Foundation, *Eurasia Daily Monitor*, Vol. 13, Issue 104 (May 28, 2016), https://jamestown.org/program/inside-latvias-new-state-defense-concept-riga-declares-its-military-ambitions-ahead-of-nato-summit/ (accessed June 7, 2017).

258. Nicholas Fiorenza, "Latvia Plans to Spend EUR234 Million on Defence Procurement in 2018," Jane's 360, February 27, 2018, http://www.janes.com/article/78210/latvia-plans-to-spend-eur234-million-on-defence-procurement-in-2018 (accessed July 2, 2018),

259. Robin Hughes, "Latvia Takes Delivery of First TPS-77 MMR," Jane's 360, March 20, 2018, http://www.janes.com/article/78702/latvia-takes-delivery-of-first-tps-77-mmr (accessed July 2, 2018).

260. Gareth Jennings, "Latvia to Receive Puma UASs from US," Jane's 360, March 27, 2018, http://www.janes.com/article/78886/latvia-to-receive-puma-uass-from-us (accessed July 2, 2018).

261. International Institute for Strategic Studies, *The Military Balance 2018*, p. 122.

262. Remigiusz Wilk, "Latvia Invests in Military Infrastructure," Jane's 360, February 7, 2018, http://www.janes.com/article/77679/latvia-invests-in-military-infrastructure (accessed July 2, 2018).

263. International Institute for Strategic Studies, *The Military Balance 2018*, p. 124.

264. "Lithuania's Defence Budget: Expanded and Expanding," *The Baltic Times*, February 28, 2018, https://www.baltictimes.com/lithuania_s_defence_budget__expanded_and_expanding/ (accessed July 2, 2018).

265. North Atlantic Treaty Organization, *The Secretary General's Annual Report: 2017*, pp. 102–103.

266. "Lithuania's 2018 Defense Budget Should Be 2.06 pct of GDP," *The Baltic Times*, October 11, 2017, https://www.baltictimes.com/lithuania_s_2018_defense_budget_should_be_2_06_pct_of_gdp/ (accessed July 2, 2018).

267. State Security Department of the Republic of Lithuania and Second Investigation Department under the Ministry of National Defence, *National Threat Assessment 2018*, Vilnius, 2018, https://kam.lt/download/61270/eng.pdf (accessed July 2, 2018).

268. Republic of Lithuania, Ministry of National Defence, *Lithuanian Defense Policy*, White Paper, 2017, https://kam.lt/en/defence_policy_1053/important_documents/the_white_paper_on_lithuanian_defence_policy.html (accessed August 21, 2018).

269. "Lithuania PM Says Army Modernization Now More Important than Universal Conscription," *The Baltic Times*, February 8, 2018, https://www.baltictimes.com/lithuanian_pm_says_army_modernization_now_more_important_than_universal_conscription/ (accessed July 2, 2018).

270. Jaroslaw Adamowski, "Fear Factor: As Russia Looms Large, Baltics Up Military Capacity," *Defense News*, August 28, 2017, https://www.defensenews.com/smr/european-balance-of-power/2017/08/28/fear-factor-as-russia-looms-large-baltics-up-military-capacity/ (accessed July 2, 2018).

271. "1st Two Boxers Arrive in Lithuania," *The Baltic Times*, December 15, 2017, https://www.baltictimes.com/1st_two_boxers_arrive_in_lithuania/ (accessed July 2, 2018).

272. Reuters, "Norway to Surpass Russia as Lithuania's Top Gas Supplier in 2016," February 8, 2016, http://mobile.reuters.com/article/idUSL8N15N1UF (accessed June 9, 2017).

273. Reuters, "Lithuania Signs First Deal for U.S. LNG," June 26, 2017, http://mobile.reuters.com/article/amp/idUSKBN19H14M (accessed June 29, 2017).

274. Reuters, "Baltic States Agree to Link Their Power Grids to EU via Poland," May 8, 2017, http://www.voanews.com/a/baltic-states-to-link-power-grids-to-eu-via-poland/3843362.html?utm_source=dlvr.it&utm_medium=twitter (accessed June 9, 2017).

275. State Security Department of the Republic of Lithuania and Second Investigation Department under the Ministry of National Defence, *National Threat Assessment 2018*, p. 4.

276. Daniel Kochis, "Poland: The Lynchpin of Security on NATO's Front Lines," Heritage Foundation *Issue Brief* No. 4455, August 17, 2015, http://www.heritage.org/research/reports/2015/08/poland-the-lynchpin-of-security-on-natos-front-lines.

277. International Institute for Strategic Studies, *The Military Balance 2018*, p. 135.

278. Christian Davies, "New Polish Military Force Worries Political Opposition," *Politico*, November 15, 2016, http://www.politico.eu/article/new-polish-military-force-worries-political-opposition/ (accessed June 9, 2017).

279. International Institute for Strategic Studies, *The Military Balance 2018*, p. 135.

280. Charlie Gao, "This Is How Poland Plans to Fight Russia in a War," *The National Interest*, March 3, 2018, http://nationalinterest.org/blog/the-buzz/how-poland-plans-fight-russia-war-24731 (accessed July 2, 2018).

281. John R. Schindler, "Poland's Defense Minister Answers the Question: What Does Putin Want?" *Observer*, November 14, 2017, http://observer.com/2017/11/interview-polish-defense-minister-antoni-macierewicz-on-russia-nato/ (accessed July 2, 2018).

282. Gao, "This Is How Poland Plans to Fight Russia in a War."

283. Marek Strzelecki, "Poland Guts Military Command on NATO Front Line," *Stars and Stripes*, February 23, 2017, https://www.stripes.com/news/europe/poland-guts-military-command-on-nato-front-line-1.455528#.WRHPh4WcHcs (accessed June 9, 2017).

284. News release, "Defence Expenditure of NATO Countries (2010–2017)," March 15, 2018, p. 3.

285. Radio Poland, "Poland to Increase Defence Spending," April 25, 2017, http://www.thenews.pl/1/9/Artykul/304138,Poland-to-increase-defence-spending (accessed June 9, 2017).

286. Lidia Kelly, "Poland to Allocate Additional $55 Billion on Defense by 2032: Deputy Minister," Reuters, August 23, 2017, https://www.reuters.com/article/us-poland-military-spending-idUSKCN1B31AB (accessed July 2, 2018).

287. Lidia Kelly, "Poland Signs $4.75 Billion Deal for U.S. Patriot Missile System Facing Russia," Reuters, March 25, 2018, https://www.reuters.com/article/us-raytheon-poland-patriot/poland-united-states-sign-4-75-billion-deal-on-patriot-missiles-idUSKBN1H417S (accessed July 2, 2018).

288. Ibid.

289. Aaron Mehta, "Poland, Canada Join NATO Members in Potential Maritime Surveillance Aircraft Buy," *Defense News*, February 15, 2018, https://www.defensenews.com/smr/munich-security-forum/2018/02/15/poland-canada-join-nato-members-in-potential-maritime-surveillance-aircraft-buy/ (accessed July 2, 2018).

290. International Institute for Strategic Studies, *The Military Balance 2018*, p. 135.

291. North Atlantic Treaty Organization, Resolute Support Mission, "Resolute Support Mission (RSM): Key Facts and Figures."

292. Air Force Master Sgt. Benjamin Wilson, "Weather Station Supports Intelligence, Surveillance, Reconnaissance Mission," U.S. Central Command, May 1, 2017, http://www.centcom.mil/MEDIA/NEWS-ARTICLES/News-Article-View/Article/1168329/weather-station-supports-intelligence-surveillance-reconnaissance-mission/ (accessed July 3, 2018).

293. Kurdistan Regional Government, Representation in Poland, "Poland Sent F-16 Fighter Aircraft, 200 Soldiers to Iraq and Kuwait," June 20, 2016, http://poland.gov.krd/polski-polska-wysyla-sily-zbrojne-do-walki-z-isis/ (accessed July 3, 2018).

294. "Poland Taking over NATO Air-Policing Mission at Lithuanian Air Base from Netherlands," *The Baltic Times*, May 2, 2017, http://www.baltictimes.com/poland_taking_over_nato_air-policing_mission_at_lithuanian_air_base_from_netherlands/ (accessed July 3, 2018).

295. North Atlantic Treaty Organization, *The Secretary General's Annual Report: 2017*, pp. 13 and 104.

296. General Philip Breedlove, Commander, U.S. Forces Europe, statement before the Committee on Armed Services, U.S. Senate, March 1, 2016, pp. 18–19, https://www.armed-services.senate.gov/imo/media/doc/Breedlove_03-01-16.pdf (accessed July 13, 2017).

297. Steven Beardsley, "Hopeful for More Troops, US Scouts Basing Option in Germany," Deutsche Welle, March 9, 2017, http://www.dw.com/en/hopeful-for-more-troops-us-scouts-basing-options-in-germany/a-37871968 (accessed July 3, 2018).

298. U.S. European Command, Communication and Engagement Directorate, Media Operations Division, "U.S. Military Presence in Europe (1945–2016)," current as of May 26, 2016.

299. Breedlove, statement before the Committee on Armed Services, March 1, 2016, p. 20.

300. General Philip Breedlove, Commander, U.S. Forces Europe, statement prepared for the Committees on Armed Services, U.S. Senate and U.S. House of Representatives, April 1, 2014, p. 27.

301. John Vandiver, "EUCOM Gives 'Another Look' at Planned Base Closures," *Stars and Stripes*, April 17, 2017, http://www.military.com/daily-news/2017/04/17/eucom-gives-another-look-planned-base-closures.html (accessed June 12, 2017).

302. "US Army Considers New Base in Northern Germany," *The Local*, March 10, 2017, https://www.thelocal.de/20170310/us-army-to-deploy-more-soldiers-to-germany?utm_content=buffer59ce7&utm_medium=social&utm_source=twitter.com&utm_campaign=buffer (accessed June 12, 2017).

303. "US Destroyer Begins Third Forward Deployed Patrol from Spain," *Naval Today*, March 17, 2017, http://navaltoday.com/2017/03/17/us-destroyer-begins-third-forward-deployed-patrol-from-spain/ (accessed June 12, 2017).

304. Deutsche Welle, "Iceland Agrees to the Return of American Troops," June 30, 2016, http://www.dw.com/en/iceland-agrees-to-the-return-of-american-troops/a-19369461 (accessed July 12, 2017).

305. "U.S. Navy Receives 50th P-8A Poseidon," *Naval Today*, January 6, 2017, http://navaltoday.com/2017/01/06/u-s-navy-receives-50th-p-8a-poseidon/ (accessed June 12, 2017).

306. John Vandiver, "EUCOM Chief: 'We Are Not Keeping Pace' with Russia in Balkans, Arctic," *Stars and Stripes*, March 8, 2018, https://www.stripes.com/news/eucom-chief-we-are-not-keeping-pace-with-russia-in-balkans-arctic-1.515661 (accessed July 3, 2018).

307. *Hearing to Receive Testimony on United States European Command*, p. 41.

308. Thomas Nilsen, "Nuclear Submarines Inshore Norway 3 to 4 Times Monthly," *The Barents Observer*, January 27, 2018, https://thebarentsobserver.com/en/security/2018/01/nuclear-submarines-inshore-norway-3-4-times-monthly#.Wm9cD0kuCDM.twitter (accessed July 3, 2018).

309. Martin Egnash, "New Radar Extends Army's Vision in Europe as Eyes Turn to Russia," *Stars and Stripes*, April 7, 2017, https://www.stripes.com/news/new-radar-extends-army-s-vision-in-europe-as-eyes-turn-to-russia-1.462469#.WQyaeYWcHct (accessed June 12, 2017).

310. John Vandiver, "Army Air Defense Brigade Back in Europe in a Post-Cold War First," *Stars and Stripes*, April 2, 2017, https://www.stripes.com/news/army-air-defense-brigade-back-in-europe-in-a-post-cold-war-first-1.520007 (accessed July 3, 2018).

311. U.S. Air Force, U.S. Air Forces in Europe & Air Forces Africa, "Units," http://www.usafe.af.mil/units/ (accessed July 10, 2017).

312. Richard Sisk, "Turkey Hints at Shuttering Incirlik to US Air Operations," Military.com, January 4, 2017, https://www.military.com/daily-news/2017/01/04/turkey-hints-shuttering-incirlik-us-air-operations.html (accessed July 3, 2018).

313. U.S. European Command, "Our Forces: U.S. Air Forces in Europe," http://www.eucom.mil/about/organization/our-forces/u-s-air-forces-in-europe (accessed July 10, 2017).

314. Scaparrotti, statement on EUCOM posture, March 8, 2018.

315. U.S. European Command, "Our Forces: U.S. Marine Forces Europe," http://www.eucom.mil/about/organization/our-forces/u-s-marine-forces-europe (accessed July 12, 2017).

316. Hope Hodge Seck, "Marines May Move Even More Combat Gear into Norwegian Caves," Military.com, June 16, 2017, https://www.military.com/defensetech/2017/06/16/marines-combat-gear-norwegian-caves (accessed July 3, 2019).

317. Ibid.

318. Ryan Browne, "U.S. Stationing Tanks and Artillery in Classified Norwegian Caves," CNN, updated February 19, 2016, http://edition.cnn.com/2016/02/18/politics/u-s-tanks-artillery-norwegian-caves/ (accessed July 12, 2017).

319. Seck, "Marines May Move Even More Combat Gear into Norwegian Caves."

320. Ibid.

321. Hope Hodge Seck, "With MEU Delayed by Hurricane, Task Force Alone for Africa Response," Military.com, January 18, 2018, https://www.military.com/daily-news/2018/01/18/meu-delayed-hurricane-task-force-alone-africa-response.html (accessed July 3, 2018).

322. Michael S. Darnell, "Marines Cutting 6 Ospreys from Crisis Response Task Force," *Stars and Stripes*, May 4, 2016, https://www.stripes.com/news/marines-cutting-6-ospreys-from-crisis-response-task-force-1.407781#.WRs8CmgrLcs (accessed June 12, 2017).

323. Cheryl Pellerin, "U.S., Spain Agree to Make U.S. Crisis Force Deployment Permanent," U.S. Department of Defense, June 18, 2015, http://www.defense.gov/News/Article/Article/604842 (accessed June 12, 2017).

324. John Vandiver, "Special Forces, SEAL Units to Join Mix of Elite Troops at Rural Baumholder," *Stars and Stripes*, June 13, 2018, https://www.stripes.com/news/special-forces-seal-units-to-join-mix-of-elite-troops-at-rural-baumholder-1.532491 (accessed June 22, 2018).

325. U.S. Department of Defense, Office of the Secretary of Defense (Comptroller), *Department of Defense Budget Fiscal Year (FY) 2019: European Deterrence Initiative*, pp. 21–25.

326. Dan Stoutamire, "Romanian Air Base Proving Crucial as US Hub Ahead of Major Exercises," *Stars and Stripes*, April 18, 2017, https://www.stripes.com/news/romanian-air-base-proving-crucial-as-us-hub-ahead-of-major-exercises-1.464105#.WPZirOR1rcs (accessed June 12, 2017).

327. General Curtis M. Scaparrotti, Commander, United States European Command, statement before the Subcommittee on Military Construction, Veterans Affairs, and Related Agencies, Committee on Appropriations, U.S. Senate, May 2, 2017, unclassified "Resource Requirements—Addendum," p. [1], (accessed June 29, 2018).

328. Ibid., p. [2].

Middle East

Strategically situated at the intersection of Europe, Asia, and Africa, the Middle East has long been an important focus of United States foreign policy. U.S. security relationships in the region are built on pragmatism, shared security concerns, and economic interests, including large sales of U.S. arms to countries in the region that are seeking to defend themselves. The U.S. also maintains a long-term interest in the Middle East that is related to the region's economic importance as the world's primary source of oil and gas.

The region is home to a wide array of cultures, religions, and ethnic groups, including Arabs, Jews, Kurds, Persians, and Turks, among others. It also is home to the three Abrahamic religions of Judaism, Christianity, and Islam, in addition to many smaller religions like the Bahá'í, Druze, Yazidi, and Zoroastrian faiths. The region contains many predominantly Muslim countries as well as the world's only Jewish state.

The Middle East is deeply sectarian, and these long-standing divisions, exacerbated by religious extremists that are constantly vying for power, are central to many of the challenges that the region faces today. In some cases, these sectarian divides go back centuries. Contemporary conflicts, however, have less to do with these histories than they do with modern extremist ideologies and the fact that modern-day borders often do not reflect the region's cultural, ethnic, or religious realities. Today's borders are often the results of decisions taken by the British, French, and other powers during and soon after World War I as they dismantled the Ottoman Empire.[1]

In a way not understood by many in the West, religion remains a prominent fact of daily life in the modern Middle East. At the heart of many of the region's conflicts is the friction within Islam between Sunnis and Shias. This friction dates back to the death of the Prophet Muhammad in 632 AD.[2] Sunni Muslims, who form the majority of the world's Muslim population, hold power in most of the Arab countries in the Middle East.

Viewing the Middle East's current instability through the lens of a Sunni–Shia conflict, however, does not show the full picture. The cultural and historical division between Arabs and Persians has reinforced the Sunni–Shia split. The mutual distrust of many Arab/Sunni powers and the Persian/Shia power (Iran), compounded by clashing national and ideological interests, has fueled instability, including in Bahrain, Iraq, Lebanon, Syria, and Yemen. Sunni extremist organizations such as al-Qaeda and the Islamic State (IS) have exploited sectarian and ethnic tensions to gain support by posing as champions of Sunni Arabs, Syria's Alawite-dominated regime, and other non-Sunni governments and movements.

Current regional demographic trends also are destabilizing factors. The Middle East contains one of the world's youngest and fastest-growing populations. In most of the West, this would be viewed as an advantage, but not in the Middle East. Known as "youth bulges," these demographic tsunamis have overwhelmed the inadequate political, economic, and educational infrastructures in many countries, and the lack of access to education, jobs, and meaningful political participation fuels discontent. Because more than 60 percent of the region's inhabitants are less than 25 years old, this demographic bulge will continue to have a substantial effect on political stability across the region.

The Middle East contains more than half of the world's oil reserves and is the world's chief oil-exporting region. As the world's biggest oil consumer, the U.S. has a vested interest in maintaining the free flow of oil and gas from the region, even though the U.S. actually imports relatively little of its oil from the Middle East.[3] Oil is a fungible commodity, and the U.S. economy remains vulnerable to sudden spikes in world oil prices.

Because many U.S. allies depend on Middle East oil and gas, there is also a second-order effect for the U.S. if supply from the Middle East is reduced or compromised. For example, Japan (the world's third largest economy) is the world's largest liquefied natural gas (LNG) importer, accounting for 32 percent of the global market share of LNG demand.[4] The U.S. itself might not be dependent on Middle East oil or LNG, but the economic consequences arising from a major disruption of supplies would ripple across the globe.

Financial and logistics hubs are also growing along some of the world's busiest transcontinental trade routes. One of the region's economic bright spots in terms of trade and commerce is found in the Persian Gulf. The emirates of Dubai and Abu Dhabi in the United Arab Emirates (UAE), along with Qatar, are competing to become the region's top financial center. Although many oil-exporting countries recovered from the 2008 financial crisis and subsequent recession, they have since experienced the deepest economic downturn since the 1990s as a result of falling oil prices.[5] Various factors such as weak demand, infighting within the Organization of the Petroleum Exporting Countries (OPEC), and increased U.S. domestic oil production have contributed to these plunging oil prices.[6]

The economic situation in the Middle East is part of what drives the political environment. The lack of economic freedom was an important factor leading to the 2011 Arab Spring uprisings, which disrupted economic activity, depressed foreign and domestic investment, and slowed economic growth.

The political environment has a direct bearing on how easily the U.S. military can operate in a region. In many Middle Eastern countries, the political situation remains fraught with uncertainty. The Arab Spring uprisings that began in early 2011 formed a regional sandstorm that eroded the foundations of many authoritarian regimes, erased borders, and destabilized many countries in the region. Even so, the popular uprisings in Tunisia, Libya, Egypt, Bahrain, Syria, and Yemen did not usher in a new era of democracy and liberal rule, as many in the West were hoping. At best, these uprisings made slow progress toward democratic reform. At worst, they added to political instability, exacerbated economic problems, and contributed to the rise of Islamist extremists. Six years later, the economic and political outlooks remain bleak.[7]

There is no shortage of security challenges for the U.S. and its allies in this region. Using the breathing space and funding afforded to it by the Joint Comprehensive Plan of Action (JCPOA), Iran has exacerbated Shia–Sunni tensions to increase its influence on embattled regimes and undermine adversaries in Sunni-led states. In May 2018, the Trump Administration left the JCPOA after European allies failed to address many of the serious flaws in the deal like the sunset clauses. U.S. economic sanctions have been restored to pre-JCPOA levels and in some cases have been expanded. While many of America's European allies publicly denounced the Administration's decision to withdraw, privately, most officials agree that the JCPOA was flawed and needs to be fixed. America's allies in the Middle East, including Israel and most Gulf Arab states, supported the U.S. decision and welcomed a harder line against the Iranian regime.

Tehran attempts to run an unconventional empire by exerting great influence on sub-state entities like Hamas (Palestinian territories); Hezbollah (Lebanon); the Mahdi movement

(Iraq); and the Houthi insurgents (Yemen). In Afghanistan, Tehran's influence on some Shiite groups is such that thousands have volunteered to fight for Bashar al-Assad in Syria.[8] Iran also provided arms to the Taliban after it was ousted from power by a U.S.-led coalition[9] and has long considered the Afghan city of Herat, near the Afghan–Iranian border, to be within its sphere of influence.

Iran already looms large over weak and divided Arab rivals. Iraq and Syria have been destabilized by insurgencies and civil war and may never fully recover. Egypt is distracted by its own internal problems, economic imbalances, and the Islamist extremist insurgency in the Sinai Peninsula. Jordan has been inundated by a flood of Syrian refugees and is threatened by the spillover of Islamist extremist groups from Syria. Meanwhile, Tehran has continued to build up its missile arsenal (now the largest in the Middle East) and has intervened to prop up the Assad regime in Syria and reinforced Shiite Islamist revolutionaries in Yemen and Bahrain.[10]

In Syria, the Assad regime's brutal repression of peaceful demonstrations in early 2011 ignited a fierce civil war that has led to the deaths of more than half a million people[11] and displaced more than 5 million refugees in Turkey, Lebanon, Jordan, Iraq, and Egypt. Around 6.1 million people are internally displaced within Syria, which is down slightly from 6.3 million last year.[12] Among the destabilizing spillover effects of this civil war is the creation of large refugee populations that could become a reservoir of potential recruits for extremist groups. Thanks to the power vacuum created by the ongoing civil war in Syria, Islamist extremist groups, including the Islamists Hay'at Tahrir al-Sham (formally known as the al-Qaeda–affiliated Jabhat Fateh al-Sham and before that as al-Nusra Front) and the self-styled Islamic State, formerly known as ISIS or ISIL and before that as al-Qaeda in Iraq, carved out extensive sanctuaries where they built proto-states and trained militants from a wide variety of other Arab countries, Central Asia, Russia, Europe, Australia, and the United States. At the height of its power, with a sophisticated Internet and social media presence and by capitalizing on the civil war in Syria and sectarian divisions in Iraq, the IS was able to recruit over 25,000 fighters from outside the region to join its ranks in Iraq and Syria. These foreign fighters included over 4,500 citizens from Western nations, including approximately 250 U.S. citizens.[13]

On September 10, 2014, the U.S. announced the formation of a broad international coalition to defeat the Islamic State. Since then, the IS has been substantially reduced. The self-proclaimed caliphate lost its final major redoubt in Iraq's second largest city, Mosul, in July 2017 and then lost its so-called capital city located in Raqqa, Syria, in October. Today, thanks to the international coalition led by the U.S., the IS controls less than 2 percent of the territory it once dominated.

Arab–Israeli tensions are another source of instability in the region. The repeated breakdown of Israeli–Palestinian peace negotiations has created an even more antagonistic situation. Hamas, the Palestinian branch of the Muslim Brotherhood that has controlled Gaza since 2007, seeks to transform the conflict from a national struggle over sovereignty and territory into a religious conflict in which compromise is denounced as blasphemy. Hamas invokes jihad in its struggle against Israel and seeks to destroy the Jewish state and replace it with an Islamic state.

Important Alliances and Bilateral Relations in the Middle East

The U.S. has strong military, security, intelligence, and diplomatic ties with several Middle Eastern nations, including Israel, Egypt, Jordan, and the members of the Gulf Cooperation Council (GCC).[14] Since the historical and political circumstances that led to the creation of NATO have largely been absent in the Middle East, the region lacks a similarly strong collective security organization. Middle Eastern countries traditionally have preferred to maintain bilateral relationships with the U.S. and generally have shunned multilateral arrangements because of the lack of trust among Arab states.

This lack of trust manifested itself in June 2017 when the Kingdom of Saudi Arabia, the United Arab Emirates, Bahrain, Egypt, and several other Muslim-majority countries cut or downgraded diplomatic ties with Qatar. All commercial land, air, and sea travel between Qatar and these nations has been severed, and Qatari diplomats and citizens have been evicted.

This is the best example of how regional tensions can transcend the Arab–Iranian or Israeli–Palestinian debate. Qatar has long supported Muslim Brotherhood groups, as well as questionable Islamist factions in Syria and Libya, and has often been seen as being too close to Iran, a major adversary of Sunni Arab states in the Gulf.

This is not the first time that something like this has happened, albeit on a much smaller scale. In 2014, a number of Arab states recalled their ambassadors to Qatar to protest Doha's support for Egypt's Muslim Brotherhood movement. It took eight months to resolve this dispute before relations could be fully restored.

Bilateral and multilateral relations in the region, especially with the U.S. and other Western countries, are often made more difficult by their secretive nature. The opaqueness of these relationships sometimes creates problems for the U.S. when it tries to coordinate defense and security cooperation with European allies (mainly the U.K. and France) that are active in the region.

Military training is an important part of these relationships. The principal motivation behind these exercises is to ensure close and effective coordination with key regional partners, demonstrate an enduring U.S. security commitment to regional allies, and train Arab armed forces so that they can assume a larger share of responsibility for regional security. In 2017, the U.S. Naval Forces Central Command launched the largest maritime exercise ever launched across the Middle East to demonstrate global resolve in maintaining freedom of navigation and the free flow of maritime commerce.[15] This has been followed by subsequent, smaller, maritime exercises.

Kuwait, Bahrain, the UAE, Saudi Arabia, and Qatar have participated in, and in some cases have commanded, Combined Task Force-152, formed in 2004 to maintain maritime security in the Persian Gulf. The commander of the U.S. Central Command (CENTCOM) noted that Middle Eastern partners have begun to take the threat from transnational Islamist extremist groups more seriously, especially as ISIS has gained momentum, increased in strength, and expanded its international influence.[16] Middle Eastern countries have also participated further afield in Afghanistan; since 2001, Jordan, Egypt, Bahrain, and the UAE have supplied troops to the U.S.-led mission there. During the 2011 NATO-led operation in Libya, U.S. allies Qatar, Jordan, and the UAE participated to varying degrees.

Israel. America's most important bilateral relationship in the Middle East is with Israel. Both countries are democracies, value free-market economies, and believe in human rights at a time when many Middle Eastern countries reject those values. Israel has been designated as a Major Non-NATO ally (MN-NA)[17] because of its close ties to the U.S. With support from the United States, it has developed one of the world's most sophisticated air and missile defense networks.[18] No significant progress on peace negotiations with the Palestinians or on stabilizing Israel's volatile neighborhood is possible without a strong and effective Israeli–American partnership.[19]

After years of strained relations during the Obama Administration, ties between the U.S. and Israel have improved significantly since President Donald Trump took office. In May 2018, the U.S. moved its embassy from Tel Aviv to a location in western Jerusalem.

Saudi Arabia. After Israel, the U.S. military relationship is deepest with the Gulf States, including Saudi Arabia, which serves as de facto leader of the GCC. America's relationship with Saudi Arabia is based on pragmatism and is important for both security and economic reasons. The Saudis enjoy huge influence across the

Muslim world, and roughly 2 million Muslims participate in the annual Hajj pilgrimage to the holy city of Mecca. Riyadh has been a key partner in efforts to counterbalance Iran. The U.S. is also the largest provider of arms to Saudi Arabia and regularly, if not controversially, sells munitions needed to resupply stockpiles expended in the Saudi-led campaign against the Houthis in Yemen. President Trump recently approved a $110 billion arms sale to the Saudis.

Gulf Cooperation Council. The countries of the GCC (Bahrain, Kuwait, Oman, Qatar, Saudi Arabia, and the UAE) are located close to the Arab–Persian fault line, making them strategically important to the U.S.[20] The root of the Arab–Iranian tensions in the Gulf is Tehran's ideological drive to export its Islamist revolution and overthrow the traditional rulers of the Arab kingdoms. This ideological clash has further amplified long-standing sectarian tensions between Shia Islam and Sunni Islam. Tehran has sought to radicalize Shia Arab minority groups to undermine Sunni Arab regimes in Saudi Arabia, Kuwait, and Bahrain. It also sought to incite revolts by the Shia majorities in Iraq against Saddam Hussein's regime and in Bahrain against the Sunni al-Khalifa dynasty. Culturally, many Iranians look down on the Gulf States, many of which they see as artificial entities carved out of the former Persian Empire and propped up by Western powers.

The GCC often has difficulty agreeing on a common policy on matters of security. This reflects both the organization's intergovernmental nature and its members' desire to place national interests above those of the GCC. The recent dispute regarding Qatar illustrates this difficulty. Another source of disagreement involves the question of how best to deal with Iran. On one end of the spectrum, Saudi Arabia, Bahrain, and the UAE take a hawkish view of the threat from Iran. Oman and Qatar, both of which share natural gas fields with Iran, view Iran's activities in the region as less of a threat and maintain cordial relations with Tehran. Kuwait tends to fall somewhere in the middle. Inter-GCC relations also can be problematic.

Egypt. Egypt is another important U.S. military ally. As one of only two Arab countries (the other being Jordan) that maintain diplomatic relations with Israel, Egypt is closely enmeshed in the Israeli–Palestinian conflict and remains a leading political, diplomatic, and military power in the region.

Relations between the U.S. and Egypt have been problematic since the 2011 downfall of President Hosni Mubarak after 30 years of rule. The Muslim Brotherhood's Mohamed Morsi was elected president in 2012 and used the Islamist-dominated parliament to pass a constitution that advanced an Islamist agenda. Morsi's authoritarian rule, combined with rising popular dissatisfaction with falling living standards, rampant crime, and high unemployment, led to a massive wave of protests in June 2013 that prompted a military coup in July. The leader of the coup, Field Marshal Abdel Fattah el-Sisi, pledged to restore democracy and was elected president in 2014 and again in 2018 in elections that many considered to be neither free nor fair.[21] His government faces major political, economic, and security challenges.

Quality of Armed Forces in the Middle East

The quality and capabilities of the region's armed forces are mixed. Some countries spend billions of dollars each year on advanced Western military hardware, and others spend very little. Due to the drop in global oil prices, defense spending decreased in 2017 for oil-producing countries in the region while increasing for the non–oil-producing countries. For example, Saudi Arabia was by far the region's largest military spender despite dropping from $81.9 billion in 2015 to $76.79 billion in 2016—a decrease of 7 percent. On the other side of the Persian Gulf, defense spending in Iran has increased by 40 percent since implementation of the JCPOA.[22]

Historically, figures on defense spending for the Middle East have been very unreliable, but the lack of data has worsened. For 2017, there were no available data for Kuwait, Qatar, Syria, the United Arab Emirates, and Yemen according to the Stockholm International Peace Research Institute.[23]

Different security factors drive the degree to which Middle Eastern countries fund, train, and arm their militaries. For Israel, which fought and defeated Arab coalitions in 1948, 1956, 1967, 1973, and 1982, the chief potential threats to its existence are now posed by an Iranian regime that has called for Israel to be "wiped from the map."[24] States and non-state actors in the region have responded to Israel's military dominance by investing in asymmetric and unconventional capabilities to offset its military superiority.[25] For the Gulf States, the main driver of defense policy is the Iranian military threat combined with internal security challenges. For Iraq, the internal threat posed by insurgents and terrorists drives defense policy. In many ways, the Obama Administration's engagement with Tehran united Israel and its Arab neighbors against the shared threat of Iran.

The Israel Defense Forces (IDF) are widely considered the most capable military force in the Middle East. On a conventional level, the IDF consistently surpasses other regional military forces.[26] Other countries, such as Iran, have developed asymmetric tactics and have built up the military capabilities of proxy groups to close the gap in recent years, but the IDF's quality and effectiveness remain unparalleled with regard to both technical capacity and personnel. This was demonstrated by Israel's 2014 military operations against Hamas in the Gaza Strip: After weeks of conflict, the IDF mobilized over 80,000 reservists, demonstrating the depth and flexibility of the Israeli armed forces.[27]

Israel funds its military sector heavily and has a strong national industrial capacity supported by significant funding from the U.S. Combined, these factors give Israel a regional advantage despite limitations of manpower and size. In particular, the IDF has focused on maintaining its superiority in missile defense, intelligence collection, precision weapons, and cyber technologies.[28] The Israelis regard their cyber capabilities as especially important.

Cyber technologies are used for a number of purposes, including defending Israeli cyberspace, gathering intelligence, and carrying out attacks.[29] Israel maintains its qualitative superiority in medium-range and long-range missile capabilities.[30] It also fields effective missile defense systems, including Iron Dome and Arrow, both of which the U.S. helped to finance.[31]

Israel also has a nuclear weapons capability (which it does not publicly acknowledge) that increases its strength relative to other powers in the region. Israel's nuclear weapons capability has helped to deter adversaries as the gap in conventional capabilities has been reduced.

After Israel, the most technologically advanced and best-equipped armed forces are found in the Gulf Cooperation Council. Previously, the export of oil and gas meant that there was no shortage of resources to devote to defense spending, but the collapse of crude oil prices may force oil-exporting countries to adjust their defense spending patterns. At present, however, GCC nations still have the best-funded, although not necessarily the most effective, Arab armed forces in the region.

All GCC members boast advanced defense hardware with a preference for U.S., U.K., and French equipment. Saudi Arabia maintains the most capable military force in the GCC. It has an army of 75,000 soldiers and a National Guard of 100,000 personnel reporting directly to the king. The army operates 900 main battle tanks including 370 U.S.-made M1A2s. Its air force is built around American and British-built aircraft and consists of more than 338 combat-capable aircraft including F-15s, Tornados, and Typhoons.[32]

In fact, air power is the strong suit of most GCC members. Oman operates F-16s and has purchased 12 Typhoons, which entered service in 2017. According to *Defense Industry Daily*, "The UAE operates the F-16E/F Desert Falcon, which holds more advanced avionics than any F-16 variant in the US inventory."[33] Qatar operates French-made Mirage fighters and recently bought 24 Typhoons from the UK.[34] The UAE and Qatar deployed fighters to participate in NATO-led operations over Libya in 2011 (although they did not participate in strike operations). Beginning in early fall 2014, all six GCC members joined the U.S.-led anti-ISIS coalition, with the UAE contributing the most in terms of air power.[35] Air strikes in Syria by members of the GCC ended in 2017. The navies of the GCC members rarely deploy beyond their Exclusive Economic Zones, but all members (other than Oman) have participated in regional combined task forces led by the U.S.[36] In 2016, Oman and Britain launched a multimillion-dollar joint venture to develop Duqm as a strategic Middle Eastern port in the Indian Ocean to improve defense security and prosperity agendas.[37]

With 438,500 active personnel and 479,000 reserve personnel, Egypt has the largest Arab military force in the Middle East.[38] It possesses a fully operational military with an army, air force, air defense, navy, and special operations forces. Until 1979, when the U.S. began to supply Egypt with military equipment, Cairo relied primarily on less capable Soviet military technology.[39] Since then, its army and air force have been significantly upgraded with U.S. military weapons, equipment, and warplanes.

Egypt has struggled with increased terrorist activity in the Sinai Peninsula, including attacks on Egyptian soldiers, attacks on foreign tourists, and the October 2015 bombing of a Russian airliner departing from the Sinai, for all of which the Islamic State's "Sinai Province" terrorist group has claimed responsibility. The government's response to the uptick of violence has been severe: arrests of thousands of suspected Islamist extremists and restrictive measures such as a law criminalizing media reporting that contradicts official reports.[40]

Jordan is a close U.S. ally with small but effective military forces. The principal threats to its security include ISIS, turbulence in Syria and Iraq, and the resulting flow of refugees. Jordan is currently home to more than 1.4 million registered and unregistered Syrian refugees. While Jordan faces few conventional threats from its neighbors, its internal security is threatened by Islamist extremists returning from fighting in the region who have

been emboldened by the growing influence of al-Qaeda and other Islamist militants. As a result, Jordan's highly professional armed forces have been focused in recent years on border and internal security.

Considering Jordan's size, its conventional capability is significant. Jordan's ground forces total 74,000 soldiers and include 390 British-made Challenger 1 tanks. The backbone of its air force is comprised of 43 F-16 Fighting Falcons.[41] Jordan's special operations forces are highly capable, having benefitted from extensive U.S. and U.K. training. Jordanian forces have served in Afghanistan and in numerous U.N.-led peacekeeping operations.

Iraq has fielded one of the region's most dysfunctional military forces. After the 2011 withdrawal of U.S. troops, Iraq's government selected and promoted military leaders according to political criteria. Shiite army officers were favored over their Sunni, Christian, and Kurdish counterparts. Then-Prime Minister Nouri al-Maliki chose top officers according to their political loyalties. Politicization of the armed forces also exacerbated corruption within many units, with some commanders siphoning off funds allocated for "ghost soldiers" who never existed or had been separated from the army for various reasons.

The promotion of incompetent military leaders, poor logistical support due to corruption and other problems, limited operational mobility, and weaknesses in intelligence, reconnaissance, medical support, and air force capabilities have combined to weaken the effectiveness of the Iraqi armed forces. In June 2014, for example, the collapse of up to four divisions, which were routed by vastly smaller numbers of Islamic State fighters, led to the fall of Mosul. Since then, the U.S. and its allies have undertaken a massive training program for the Iraqi military, which led to the liberation of Mosul on July 9, 2017.

Current U.S. Military Presence in the Middle East

The United States maintained a limited military presence in the Middle East before

1980, chiefly a small naval force based at Bahrain since 1958. The U.S. "twin pillar" strategy relied on prerevolutionary Iran and Saudi Arabia to take the lead in defending the Persian Gulf from the Soviet Union and its client regimes in Iraq, Syria, and South Yemen,[42] but the 1979 Iranian revolution demolished one pillar, and the December 1979 Soviet invasion of Afghanistan increased the Soviet threat to the Gulf. President Jimmy Carter proclaimed in January 1980 that the United States would take military action to defend oil-rich Persian Gulf States from external aggression, a commitment known as the Carter Doctrine. In 1980, he ordered the creation of the Rapid Deployment Joint Task Force (RDJTF), the precursor to USCENTCOM, which was established in January 1983.[43]

Up until the late 1980s, a possible Soviet invasion of Iran was considered to be the most significant threat facing the U.S. in the Middle East.[44] After the collapse of the Soviet Union, Saddam Hussein's Iraqi regime became the chief threat to regional stability. Iraq invaded Kuwait in August 1990, and the United States responded in January 1991 by leading an international coalition of more than 30 nations to expel Saddam's forces from Kuwait. CENTCOM commanded the U.S. contribution of more than 532,000 military personnel to the coalition's armed forces, which totaled at least 737,000.[45] This marked the peak U.S. force deployment in the Middle East.

Confrontations with Iraq continued throughout the 1990s as a result of Iraqi violations of the 1991 Gulf War cease-fire. Baghdad's failure to cooperate with U.N. arms inspectors to verify the destruction of its weapons of mass destruction and its links to terrorism led to the U.S. invasion of Iraq in 2003. During the initial invasion, U.S. forces reached nearly 150,000, joined by military personnel from coalition forces. Apart from the "surge" in 2007, when President George W. Bush deployed an additional 30,000 personnel, American combat forces in Iraq fluctuated between 100,000 and 150,000.[46] In December 2011, the U.S. officially completed its withdrawal of troops, leaving

only 150 personnel attached to the U.S. embassy in Iraq.[47] In the aftermath of IS territorial gains in Iraq, the U.S. has redeployed thousands of troops to the country. Today, approximately 5,000 U.S. troops operate in Iraq.

In addition, the U.S. continues to maintain a limited number of forces in other locations in the Middle East, primarily in GCC countries. Currently, tens of thousands of U.S. troops are serving in the region. Their exact disposition is not made public because of political sensitivities,[48] but information gleaned from open sources reveals the following:

- **Kuwait.** Approximately 15,000 U.S. personnel are based in Kuwait and are spread among Camp Arifjan, Ahmed Al Jaber Air Base, and Ali Al Salem Air Base.[49] A large depot of prepositioned equipment and a squadron of fighters and Patriot missile systems are also deployed to Kuwait.

- **UAE.** In 2017, the U.S. and the UAE signed a new defense accord expanding the level of cooperation.[50] About 5,000 U.S. personnel, mainly from the U.S. Air Force, are stationed in the UAE, primarily at Al Dhafra Air Base.[51] Their main mission in the UAE is to operate fighters, unmanned aerial vehicles (UAVs), refueling aircraft, and surveillance aircraft. The United States also has regularly deployed F-22 Raptor combat aircraft to Al Dhafra.[52] Patriot missile systems are deployed for air and missile defense.

- **Oman.** In 1980, Oman became the first Gulf State to welcome a U.S. military base. Today, it provides important access in the form of over 5,000 aircraft overflights, 600 aircraft landings, and 80 port calls annually. The number of U.S. military personnel in Oman has fallen to about 200, mostly from the U.S. Air Force. According to the Congressional Research Service, "the United States reportedly can use—with advance notice and for specified purposes—Oman's military airfields in Muscat (the capital), Thumrait, and Masirah Island."[53]

- **Bahrain.** Today, some 7,000 U.S. military personnel are based in Bahrain.[54] Bahrain is home to the Naval Support Activity Bahrain and the U.S. Fifth Fleet, so most U.S. military personnel there belong to the U.S. Navy. A significant number of U.S. Air Force personnel operate out of Shaykh Isa Air Base, where F-16s, F/A-18s, and P-3 surveillance aircraft are stationed.[55] U.S. Patriot missile systems also are deployed to Bahrain. The deep-water port of Khalifa bin Salman is one of the few facilities in the Gulf that can accommodate U.S. aircraft carriers.

- **Saudi Arabia.** The U.S. withdrew the bulk of its forces from Saudi Arabia in 2003. Little information on the number of U.S. military personnel currently based there is available. However, the six-decade-old United States Military Training Mission to the Kingdom of Saudi Arabia, the four-decade-old Office of the Program Manager of the Saudi Arabian National Guard Modernization Program, and the Office of the Program Manager–Facilities Security Force are based in Eskan Village Air Base approximately 13 miles south of the capital city of Riyadh.[56]

- **Qatar.** Approximately 10,000 U.S. personnel, mainly from the U.S. Air Force, are deployed in Qatar.[57] The U.S. operates its Combined Air Operations Center at Al Udeid Air Base, which is one of the most important U.S. air bases in the world. It is also the base from which the anti-ISIS campaign is headquartered. Heavy bombers, tankers, transports, and ISR aircraft operate from there. Al Udeid Air Base also serves as the forward headquarters of CENTCOM. The base also houses prepositioned U.S. military equipment and is defended by U.S. Patriot missile systems. So far, the recent diplomatic moves by Saudi Arabia and other Arab states against Doha have not affected the United States' relationship with Qatar.

- **Jordan.** According to CENTCOM, Jordan "is one of our strongest and most reliable partners in the Levant sub-region."[58] Although there are no U.S. military bases in Jordan, the U.S. has a long history of conducting training exercises in the country. Due to recent events in neighboring Syria, approximately 2,300 troops, a squadron of F-16s, a Patriot missile battery, and M142 High Mobility Artillery Rocket Systems have been deployed in Jordan.[59]

CENTCOM's stated mission is to promote cooperation among nations; respond to crises; deter or defeat state and non-state aggression; support economic development; and, when necessary, perform reconstruction in order to establish the conditions for regional security, stability, and prosperity. Execution of this mission is supported by four service component commands and one subordinate unified command: U.S. Naval Forces Middle East (USNAVCENT); U.S. Army Forces Middle East (USARCENT); U.S. Air Forces Middle East (USAFCENT); U.S. Marine Forces Middle East (MARCENT); and U.S. Special Operations Command Middle East (SOCCENT).

- **U.S. Naval Forces Central Command** is the maritime component of USCENTCOM. With its forward headquarters in Bahrain, it is responsible for commanding the afloat units that rotationally deploy or surge from the United States, in addition to other ships that are based in the Gulf for longer periods. USNAVCENT conducts persistent maritime operations to advance U.S. interests, deter and counter disruptive countries, defeat violent extremism, and strengthen partner nations' maritime capabilities in order to promote a secure maritime environment in an area encompassing about 2.5 million square miles of water.

- **U.S. Army Forces Central Command** is the land component of USCENTCOM. Based in Kuwait, USARCENT is responsible for land operations in an area encompassing 4.6 million square miles (1.5 times larger than the continental United States).

- **U.S. Air Forces Central Command** is the air component of USCENTCOM. Based in Qatar, USAFCENT is responsible for air operations and for working with the air forces of partner countries in the region. It also manages an extensive supply and equipment prepositioning program at several regional sites.

- **U.S. Marine Forces Central Command** is the designated Marine Corps service component for USCENTCOM. Based in Bahrain, USMARCENT is responsible for all Marine Corps forces in the region.

- **U.S. Special Operations Command Central** is a subordinate USCENTCOM unified command. Based in Qatar, SOC-CENT is responsible for planning special operations throughout the USCENTCOM region, planning and conducting peacetime joint/combined special operations training exercises, and orchestrating command and control of peacetime and wartime special operations.

In addition to the American military presence in the region, two U.S. allies—the United Kingdom and France—play an important role that should not be overlooked.

The U.K.'s presence in the Middle East is a legacy of British imperial rule. The U.K. has maintained close ties with many countries over which it once ruled and has conducted military operations in the region for decades. Approximately 1,200 British service personnel are based throughout the Gulf.

The British presence in the region is dominated by the Royal Navy. In terms of permanently based naval assets, there are four mine hunters and one Royal Fleet Auxiliary supply ship. Generally, there also are frigates or destroyers in the Gulf or Arabian Sea performing maritime security duties. Although such matters are not the subject of public discussion, U.K. attack submarines also operate in the area. As a sign of its long-term maritime presence in the region, the U.K. opened its first overseas military base in the Middle East in more than four decades in Bahrain.[60] The U.K. has also made a multimillion-dollar investment in modernization of the Duqm Port complex in Oman to accommodate the new U.K. *Queen Elizabeth*-class aircraft carriers.[61]

The U.K. also has a sizeable Royal Air Force (RAF) presence in the region, mainly in the UAE and Oman. A short drive from Dubai, Al-Minhad Air Base is home to a small contingent of U.K. personnel. The U.K. also operates small RAF detachments in Oman that support U.K. and coalition operations in the region. Although considered to be in Europe, the U.K.'s Sovereign Base Areas of Akrotiri and Dhekelia in Cyprus have supported U.S. military and intelligence operations in the past and will continue to do so in the future.

The British presence in the region extends beyond soldiers, ships, and planes. A British-run staff college operates in Qatar, and Kuwait chose the U.K. to help run its own equivalent of the Royal Military Academy at Sandhurst.[62] The U.K. also plays a very active role in training the Saudi Arabian and Jordanian militaries.

The French presence in the Gulf is smaller than the U.K.'s but is still significant. France opened its first military base in the Gulf in 2009, in Abu Dhabi in the UAE. This was the first foreign military installation built by the French in 50 years.[63] In total, the French have 650 personnel based in the country along with eight Rafale fighter jets.[64] French ships have access to the Zayed Port, which is big enough to handle every ship in the French Navy except the aircraft carrier *Charles De Gaulle*.

Another important actor in Middle East security is the small East African country of Djibouti. It sits on the Bab el-Mandeb Strait, through which an estimated 4.8 million barrels of oil a day transited in 2016 (the most recent year for which U.S. Energy Administration data are available) and which is a choke point on the route to the Suez Canal. An increasing number of countries recognize Djibouti's value as a base from which to project maritime power and launch counterterrorism operations. It is home to the U.S.'s only permanent military base in Africa, Camp Lemonnier, with its approximately 4,000 personnel. In 2017, China chose Djibouti as the location for its first permanent overseas base, which can house 10,000 troops and which Chinese marines have used to stage live-fire exercises featuring armored combat vehicles and artillery. Saudi Arabia also announced in 2016 that it would build a base in Djibouti. France, Italy, Germany, and Japan already have presences of varying strength there.

Key Infrastructure and Warfighting Capabilities

The Middle East is critically situated geographically. Two-thirds of the world's population lives within an eight-hour flight from the Gulf region, making it accessible from most of the globe. The Middle East also contains some of the world's most critical maritime choke points, such as the Suez Canal and the Strait of Hormuz.

Although infrastructure is not as developed in the Middle East as it is in North America or Europe, a decades-long presence means that the U.S. has tried-and-tested systems that involve moving large numbers of matériel and personnel into and out of the region. For example, according to the Department of Defense, at the height of U.S. combat operations in Iraq during the Second Gulf War, the U.S. presence included 165,000 servicemembers and 505 bases. Moving personnel and equipment out of the country was an enormous undertaking—"the largest logistical drawdown since World War II"[65]—and included the redeployment of "the 60,000 troops who remained in Iraq at the time and more than 1 million pieces of equipment ahead of their deadline."[66]

The condition of roads in the region varies from country to country. For example, 100 percent of the roads in Israel, Jordan, and the UAE are paved. Other nations, such as Oman (49.3 percent), Saudi Arabia (21.5 percent), and Yemen (8.7 percent), have poor paved road coverage according to the most recent information available.[67] Rail coverage is also poor. For instance, Saudi Arabia has only 563 miles of railroads.[68] By comparison, New Hampshire, which is roughly 1 percent the size of Saudi Arabia, had 489 freight rail miles alone in 2015 (the most recent year for which Association of American Railroads data are available).[69] In Syria, years of civil war have wreaked havoc on the rail system.[70]

The U.S. has access to several airfields in the region. The primary air hub for U.S. forces is at Al Udeid Air Base in Qatar. Other airfields include Ali Al Salem Air Base, Kuwait; Al Dhafra, UAE; Al Minhad, UAE; Isa, Bahrain; Eskan Village Air Base, Saudi Arabia; Muscat, Oman; Thumrait, Oman; and Masirah Island, Oman, in addition to the commercial airport at Seeb, Oman. In the past, the U.S. has used major airfields in Iraq, including Baghdad International Airport and Balad Air Base, as well as Prince Sultan Air Base in Saudi Arabia. Just because the U.S. has access to a particular air base today, however, does not mean that it will be made available for a particular operation in the future. For example, it is highly unlikely that Qatar and Oman would allow the U.S. to use air bases in their territory for strikes against Iran.

The U.S. has access to ports in the region, perhaps most importantly in Bahrain. The U.S. also has access to a deep-water port, Khalifa bin Salman, in Bahrain and naval facilities at Fujairah, UAE.[71] The UAE's commercial port of Jebel Ali is open for visits from U.S. warships and prepositioning of equipment for operations in theater.[72]

Approximately 90 percent of the world's trade travels by sea, and some of the busiest and most important shipping lanes are located in the Middle East. For example, tens of thousands of cargo ships travel through the Strait of Hormuz and the Bab el-Mandeb Strait each year.[73] Given the high volume of maritime traffic in the region, no U.S. military operation can be undertaken without consideration of how these shipping lanes offer opportunity and risk to America and her allies. The major shipping routes include:

- **The Suez Canal.** In 2017, more than 1 billion tons of cargo transited the canal, averaging 48 ships each day.[74] Considering that the canal itself is 120 miles long but only 670 feet wide, this is an impressive amount of traffic. The Suez Canal is important for Europe in terms of oil transportation. The canal also serves as an important strategic asset, as it is used routinely by the U.S. Navy to move surface combatants between the Mediterranean Sea and the Red Sea.

  Thanks to a bilateral arrangement between Egypt and the United States, the U.S. Navy enjoys priority access to the canal. However, the journey through the narrow waterway is no easy task for large surface combatants. The canal was not constructed with the aim of accommodating 90,000-ton aircraft carriers and therefore exposes a larger ship to attack. For this reason, different types of security protocols are followed, including the provision of air support by the Egyptian military.[75]

- **Strait of Hormuz.** The Strait of Hormuz is a critical oil-supply bottleneck and the world's busiest passageway for oil tankers. The strait links the Persian Gulf with the Arabian Sea and the Gulf of Oman. "The Strait of Hormuz is the world's most important oil chokepoint," according to the U.S. Energy Information Administration, "because its daily oil flow of about 17 million barrels per day in 2015, accounted for 30% of all seaborne-traded crude oil and other liquids. The volume that traveled through this vital choke point increased to 18.5 million b/d in 2016." Most of these crude oil exports go to Asian markets, particularly Japan, India, South Korea, and China.[76]

The shipping routes through the Strait of Hormuz are particularly vulnerable to disruption, given the extreme narrowness of the passage and its proximity to Iran. Tehran has repeatedly threatened to close the strategic strait if Iran is attacked. While attacking shipping in the strait would drive up oil prices, Iran would also lose, both because it depends on the Strait of Hormuz to export its own crude oil and because such an attack would undermine Tehran's relations with such oil importers as China, Japan, and India. Tehran also would pay a heavy military price if it provoked a U.S. military response.

- **Bab el-Mandeb Strait.** The Bab el-Mandeb Strait is a strategic waterway located between the Horn of Africa and Yemen that links the Red Sea to the Indian Ocean. Exports from the Persian Gulf and Asia destined for Western markets must pass through the strait en route to the Suez Canal. In 2016, oil tankers transported approximately 4.8 million barrels of oil per day through the strait.[77] The Bab el-Mandeb Strait is 18 miles wide at its narrowest point, limiting passage to two channels for inbound and outbound shipments.[78]

Maritime Prepositioning of Equipment and Supplies. The U.S. military has deployed non-combatant maritime prepositioning ships (MPS) containing large amounts of military equipment and supplies in strategic locations from which they can reach areas of conflict relatively quickly as associated U.S. Army or Marine Corps units located elsewhere arrive in the areas. The British Indian Ocean Territory of Diego Garcia, an island atoll, hosts the U.S. Naval Support Facility Diego Garcia, which supports prepositioning ships that can supply Army or Marine Corps units deployed for contingency operations in the Middle East.

Conclusion

For the foreseeable future, the Middle East region will remain a key focus for U.S. military planners. Once considered relatively stable, mainly due to the ironfisted rule of authoritarian regimes, the area is now highly unstable and a breeding ground for terrorism. Overall, regional security has deteriorated in recent years. Even though the Islamic State appears to have been seriously weakened, what its successor will be like is unclear. While Iraq has restored its territorial integrity after the defeat of ISIS, the political situation and future relations between Baghdad and the U.S. remain uncertain in the wake of the recent election victory of Muqtada al-Sadr. The regional dispute with Qatar has made U.S. relations in the region even more complex and difficult to manage, although it has not stopped the U.S. military from operating. The Russian, Iranian, and Turkish interventions in Syria have greatly complicated the fighting there.

Many of the borders created after World War I are under significant stress. In countries like Iraq, Libya, Syria, and Yemen, the supremacy of the nation-state is being challenged by non-state actors that wield influence, power, and resources comparable to those of small states. The main security and political challenges in the region are linked inextricably to the unrealized aspirations of the Arab Spring, surging transnational terrorism, and the potential threat of Iran. These challenges are made more difficult by the Arab–Israeli conflict, Sunni–Shia sectarian divides, the rise of Iran's Islamist revolutionary nationalism, and the proliferation of Sunni Islamist revolutionary groups.

Thanks to decades of U.S. military operations in the Middle East, the U.S. has tried-and-tested procedures for operating in the region. Bases and infrastructure are well established. The logistical processes for maintaining a large force forward deployed thousands of miles away from the homeland are well in place. Unlike in Europe, all of these processes have recently been tested in combat. The personal links between allied armed forces are also present. Joint training exercises improve interoperability, and U.S. military educational courses regularly attended by officers (and often royals) from the Middle East allow the U.S. to influence some of the region's future leaders.

America's relationships in the region are based pragmatically on shared security and economic concerns. As long as these issues remain relevant to both sides, the U.S. is likely to have an open door to operate in the Middle East when its national interests require that it do so.

Scoring the Middle East Operating Environment

As noted at the beginning of this section, various aspects of the region facilitate or inhibit the ability of the U.S. to conduct military operations to defend its vital national interests against threats. Our assessment of the operating environment utilizes a five-point scale, ranging from "very poor" to "excellent" conditions and covering four regional characteristics of greatest relevance to the conduct of military operations:

1. **Very Poor.** Significant hurdles exist for military operations. Physical infrastructure is insufficient or nonexistent, and the region is politically unstable. In addition, the U.S. military is poorly placed or absent, and alliances are nonexistent or diffuse.

2. **Unfavorable.** A challenging operating environment for military operations is marked by inadequate infrastructure, weak alliances, and recurring political instability. The U.S. military is inadequately placed in the region.

3. **Moderate.** A neutral to moderately favorable operating environment is characterized by adequate infrastructure, a moderate alliance structure, and acceptable levels of regional political stability. The U.S. military is adequately placed.

4. **Favorable.** A favorable operating environment includes good infrastructure, strong alliances, and a stable political

environment. The U.S. military is well placed for future operations.

5. **Excellent.** An extremely favorable operating environment includes well-established and well-maintained infrastructure, strong and capable allies, and a stable political environment. The U.S. military is exceptionally well placed to defend U.S. interests.

The key regional characteristics consist of:

a. **Alliances.** Alliances are important for interoperability and collective defense, as allies would be more likely to lend support to U.S. military operations. Various indicators provide insight into the strength or health of an alliance. These include whether the U.S. trains regularly with countries in the region, has good interoperability with the forces of an ally, and shares intelligence with nations in the region.

b. **Political Stability.** Political stability brings predictability for military planners when considering such things as transit, basing, and overflight rights for U.S. military operations. The overall degree of political stability indicates whether U.S. military actions would be hindered or enabled and considers, for example, whether transfers of power in the region are generally peaceful and whether there have been any recent instances of political instability.

c. **U.S. Military Positioning.** Having military forces based or equipment and supplies staged in a region greatly facilitates the ability of the United States to respond to crises and, presumably, achieve success in critical "first battles" more quickly. Being routinely present in a region also assists in maintaining familiarity with its characteristics and the various actors that might assist or thwart U.S. actions. With this in mind, we assessed whether or not the U.S. military was well positioned in the region. Again, indicators included bases, troop presence, prepositioned equipment, and recent examples of military operations (including training and humanitarian) launched from the region.

d. **Infrastructure.** Modern, reliable, and suitable infrastructure is essential to military operations. Airfields, ports, rail lines, canals, and paved roads enable the U.S. to stage, launch, and logistically sustain combat operations. We combined expert knowledge of regions with publicly available information on critical infrastructure to arrive at our overall assessment of this metric.[79]

In summary, the U.S. has developed an extensive network of bases in the region and has acquired substantial operational experience in combatting regional threats, but many of its allies are hobbled by political instability, economic problems, internal security threats, and mushrooming transnational threats. Although the overall score remains "moderate," as it was last year, it is in danger of falling to "poor" because of political instability and growing bilateral tensions with allies over the security implications of the nuclear agreement with Iran and how best to fight the Islamic State.

With this in mind, we arrived at these average scores for the Middle East (rounded to the nearest whole number):

- Alliances: **3—Moderate**

- Political Stability: **2—Unfavorable**

- U.S. Military Positioning: **3—Moderate**

- Infrastructure: **3—Moderate**

  Leading to a regional score of: **Moderate**

Operating Environment: Middle East

	VERY POOR	UNFAVORABLE	MODERATE	FAVORABLE	EXCELLENT
Alliances			✓		
Political Stability		✓			
U.S. Military Posture			✓		
Infrastructure			✓		
OVERALL			✓		

Endnotes

1. For example, Sir Mark Sykes, Britain's lead negotiator with the French on carving up the Ottoman Empire in the Middle East, during a 1916 meeting in Downing Street pointed to the map and told the Prime Minister that for Britain's sphere of influence in the Middle East, "I should like to draw a line from the *e* in Acre [modern-day Israel] to the last *k* in Kirkuk [modern-day Iraq]." See James Barr, *A Line in the Sand: Britain, France, and the Struggle That Shaped the Middle East* (London: Simon & Schuster U.K., 2011), pp. 7–20. See also Margaret McMillan, *Paris 1919: Six Months That Changed the World* (New York: Random House, 2003).

2. S.B., "What Is the Difference Between Sunni and Shia Muslims?" *The Economist*, May 29, 2013, http://www.economist.com/blogs/economist-explains/2013/05/economist-explains-19/ (accessed June 8, 2018).

3. U.S. net imports of oil equaled roughly 19 percent of U.S. consumption in 2017. Of this, 17 percent came from Persian Gulf countries. Since 2005, U.S. oil imports have decreased year on year. See U.S. Department of Energy, Energy Information Administration, "Oil: Crude and Petroleum Products Explained: Oil Imports and Exports," last updated May 1, 2018, https://www.eia.gov/energyexplained/index.cfm?page=oil_imports (accessed June 8, 2018).

4. U.S. Department of Energy, Energy Information Administration, "Country Analysis Brief: Japan," last updated February 2, 2017, https://www.eia.gov/beta/international/analysis_includes/countries_long/Japan/japan.pdf (accessed June 8, 2018).

5. Clifford Krauss, "Oil Prices: What to Make of the Volatility," *The New York Times*, updated June 14, 2017, http://www.nytimes.com/interactive/2016/business/energy-environment/oil-prices.html?_r=0 (accessed June 8, 2018).

6. Tim Bowler, "Falling Oil Prices: Who Are the Winners and Losers?" BBC News, January 19, 2015, http://www.bbc.com/news/business-29643612 (accessed June 8, 2018).

7. "The Arab Winter," *The Economist*, January 9, 2016, http://www.economist.com/news/middle-east-and-africa/21685503-five-years-after-wave-uprisings-arab-world-worse-ever (accessed June 8, 2018).

8. Sune Engel Rasmussen and Zahra Nader, "Iran Covertly Recruits Afghan Shias to Fight in Syria," *The Guardian*, June 30, 2016, https://www.theguardian.com/world/2016/jun/30/iran-covertly-recruits-afghan-soldiers-to-fight-in-syria (accessed June 8, 2018).

9. BBC News, "Hague Fury as 'Iranian Arms' Bound for Taliban Seized," March 9, 2011, http://www.bbc.com/news/uk-12694266 (accessed June 8, 2018).

10. Ibid.

11. Bethan McKernan, "Past Month 'Deadliest on Record' for Syrian Civilians Killed in US-Led Air Strikes," *Independent*, May 23, 2017, http://www.independent.co.uk/news/world/middle-east/syria-war-us-air-strikes-civilian-death-toll-deadliest-on-record-isis-donald-trump-a7751911.html (accessed June 8, 2018).

12. U.N. Office for the Coordination of Humanitarian Affairs, "Middle East and North Africa Displacement Snapshot, January–December 2017," March 28 2018, https://reliefweb.int/sites/reliefweb.int/files/resources/OCHA-ROMENA-Displacement%20Snapshot-2017.pdf (accessed June 8, 2018).

13. Lisa Curtis, ed., "Combatting the ISIS Foreign Fighter Pipeline: A Global Approach," Heritage Foundation *Special Report* No. 180, January 6, 2016, http://www.heritage.org/middle-east/report/combatting-the-isis-foreign-fighter-pipeline-global-approach.

14. Bahrain, Kuwait, Oman, Qatar, Saudi Arabia, and the United Arab Emirates.

15. News release, "World's Largest Maritime Exercise Underway in Middle East," U.S. Naval Forces Central Command, April 4, 2016, http://www.navy.mil/submit/display.asp?story_id=93996 (accessed June 8, 2018).

16. General Lloyd J. Austin III, Commander, U.S. Central Command, statement on "The Posture of U.S. Central Command" before the Committee on Armed Services, U.S. Senate, March 8, 2016, p. 6, https://www.armed-services.senate.gov/imo/media/doc/Austin_03-08-16.pdf (accessed June 8, 2018).

17. The MNNA designation was established during the dying days of the Cold War in 1989 to acknowledge American partners that contribute to U.S. security, defense, and broader geopolitical goals but are not members of NATO. The first tranche of countries to become MNNAs included South Korea, Israel, Egypt, Australia, and Japan. The country most recently awarded this title is Afghanistan, designated in 2012 by President Barack Obama.

18. Pieter D. Wezeman, "Conventional Strategic Military Capabilities in the Middle East," EU Non-Proliferation Consortium *Background Paper*, July 2011, https://www.sipri.org/sites/default/files/2016-03/Conventional-strategic-military-capabilities-in-the-Middle-East.pdf (accessed June 8, 2018).

19. James Phillips, "Threats Demand U.S., Israeli Partnership," Heritage Foundation *Commentary*, July 7, 2010, http://www.heritage.org/middle-east/commentary/threats-demand-us-israeli-partnership.

20. Created in 1981, the GCC was founded to offset the threat from Iran, which became hostile to Sunni-led Arab states after its 1979 revolution.

21. Declan Walsh and Nour Youssef, "For as Little as $3 a Vote, Egyptians Trudge to Election Stations," *The New York Times*, March 27, 2018, https://www.nytimes.com/2018/03/27/world/middleeast/egypt-election-sisi.html (accessed June 8, 2018).

22. Max Greenwood, "Trump: Iran's Military Budget Proves Nuclear Deal Was "a Big Lie," *The Hill*, May 12, 2018, http://thehill.com/homenews/administration/387448-trump-irans-military-budget-proves-nuclear-deal-was-a-big-lie (accessed June 8, 2018).

23. Fact Sheet, "Trends in World Military Expenditure, 2017," Stockholm International Peace Research Institute, May 2018, https://www.sipri.org/sites/default/files/2018-05/sipri_fs_1805_milex_2017.pdf (accessed June 8, 2018).

24. Nazila Fathi, "Wipe Israel 'Off the Map' Iranian Says," *The New York Times*, October 27, 2005, http://www.nytimes.com/2005/10/26/world/africa/26iht-iran.html?_r=0 (accessed June 8, 2018).

25. Ibid.

26. International Institute for Strategic Studies, *The Military Balance 2017: The Annual Assessment of Global Military Capabilities and Defence Economics* (London: Routledge, 2017), p. 382.

27. Voice of America News, "Israel Calls up 16,000 More Reservists," GlobalSecurity.org, July 31, 2014, http://www.globalsecurity.org/military/library/news/2014/07/mil-140731-voa01.htm (accessed June 8, 2018).

28. T. S. Allen, "Here Is How Israel's Military Dominates the Battlefield," *The National Interest*, February 27, 2018, http://nationalinterest.org/blog/the-buzz/here-how-israels-military-dominates-the-battlefield-24679 (accessed July 20, 2018).

29. See, for example, Christopher P. Skroupa, "Cyber Warfare—Reasons Why Israel Leads the Charge," *Forbes*, September 7, 2017, https://www.forbes.com/sites/christopherskroupa/2017/09/07/cyber-warfare-reasons-why-israel-leads-the-charge/#2f9ba2c6e366 (accessed July 20, 2018), and "Israel Is a Small Country, but a Cyber Superpower, Says Ex-CIA Director at CyberTech 2018," NoCamels, January 20, 2018, http://nocamels.com/2018/01/israel-cyber-superpower-cia-cybertech-2018/ (accessed 20, 2018).

30. Ruth Eglash and William Booth, "Israel to Launch One of the Most Advanced Missile Defense Systems in the World, with U.S. Help," *The Washington Post*, March 3, 2016, https://www.washingtonpost.com/world/middle_east/israel-to-launch-one-of-the-most-advanced-missile-defense-systems-in-the-world-with-us-help/2016/03/03/6383cb88-dfd5-11e5-8c00-8aa03741dced_story.html (accessed June 8, 2018).

31. GlobalSecurity.org, "Iron Dome," last modified September 18, 2016, http://www.globalsecurity.org/military/world/israel/iron-dome.htm (accessed June 3, 2028).

32. International Institute for Strategic Studies, *The Military Balance 2018: The Annual Assessment of Global Military Capabilities and Defence Economics* (London: Routledge, 2018), pp. 358–360.

33. Defense Industry Daily Staff, "Top Falcons: The UAE's F-16 Block 60/61 Fighters," *Defense Industry Daily*, January 26, 2014, http://www.defenseindustrydaily.com/the-uaes-f-16-block-60-desert-falcon-fleet-04538/ (accessed June 8, 2018).

34. Reuters, "Qatar Goes Ahead with $6.7 Billion Typhoon Combat Jets Deal with UK's BAE Systems," December 10, 2017, https://www.reuters.com/article/us-britain-qatar-typhoons/qatar-goes-ahead-with-6-7-billion-typhoon-combat-jets-deal-with-uks-bae-systems-idUSKBN1E40QM (accessed June 8, 2018).

35. Helene Cooper and Anne Barnard, "Jordan and Emirates Carry Out Airstrikes in Syria Against ISIS," *The New York Times*, February 10, 2015, www.nytimes.com/2015/02/11/world/middleeast/united-arab-emirates-resume-airstrikes-against-isis.html (accessed June 8, 2018).

36. Combined Maritime Forces, "CTF-152: Gulf Maritime Security," http://combinedmaritimeforces.com/ctf-152-gulf-security-cooperation/ (accessed June 8, 2018).

37. U.K. Ministry of Defence and The Rt. Hon. Sir Michael Fallon, MP, "Multi-Million Pound Joint Venture Announced Between Britain and Oman," March 30, 2016 https://www.gov.uk/government/news/multi-million-pound-joint-venture-announced-between-britain-and-oman (accessed June 8, 2018).

38. International Institute for Strategic Studies, *The Military Balance 2018*, p. 329.

39. GlobalSecurity.org, "Egypt: Introduction," last modified April 4, 2012, http://www.globalsecurity.org/military/world/egypt/intro.htm (accessed June 8, 2018).

40. Jared Malsin, "Egypt Is Struggling to Cope with Its ISIS Insurgency," *Time*, July 23, 2015, http://time.com/3969596/egypt-isis-sinai/ (accessed June 8, 2018).

41. International Institute for Strategic Studies, *The Military Balance 2018*, pp. 343–344.

42. During 1967 and 1990, South Yemen, officially known as the People's Democratic Republic of Yemen, was a socialist state in the southeastern provinces of the present-day Republic of Yemen.

43. U.S. Central Command, "U.S. Central Command History," http://www.centcom.mil/ABOUT-US/HISTORY/ (accessed June 8, 2018).

44. Ibid.

45. Lieutenant Colonel Joseph P. Englehardt, *Desert Shield and Desert Storm: A Chronology and Troop List for the 1990–1991 Persian Gulf Crisis*, U.S. Army War College, Strategic Studies Institute *Special Report* AD-A234 743, March 25, 1991, p. 5, http://www.dtic.mil/dtic/tr/fulltext/u2/a234743.pdf (accessed June 8, 2018).

46. BBC News, "Iraq War in Figures," December 14, 2011, http://www.bbc.com/news/world-middle-east-11107739 (accessed June 8, 2018).

47. Reuters, "Timeline: Invasion, Surge, Withdrawal; U.S. Forces in Iraq," December 18, 2011, http://www.reuters.com/article/2011/12/18/us-iraq-usa-pullout-idUSTRE7BH08E20111218 (accessed June 8, 2018).

48. Julia Zorthian and Heather Jones, "This Graphic Shows Where U.S. Troops Are Stationed Around the World," *Time*, October 16, 2015, http://time.com/4075458/afghanistan-drawdown-obama-troops/ (accessed June 8, 2018).

49. Daniel Brown and Sky Gould, "The US Has 1.3 Million Troops Stationed Around the World—Here Are the Major Hotspots," *Business Insider*, August 31, 2017, http://www.businessinsider.com/us-military-deployments-may-2017-5 (accessed June 11, 2018).

50. Phil Stewart, "U.S. Signs New Defense Accord with Gulf Ally UAE," Reuters, May 16, 2017, https://www.reuters.com/article/us-usa-emirates-military-idUSKCN18C1TN (accessed June 8, 2018).

51. Kenneth Katzman, "The United Arab Emirates (UAE): Issues for U.S. Policy," Congressional Research Service *Report for Members and Committees of Congress*, January 25 , 2018, p. 20, https://www.hsdl.org/?view&did=807913 (accessed June 8, 2018).

52. Ibid.

53. Kenneth Katzman, "Oman: Reform, Security, and U.S. Policy," Congressional Research Service *Report for Members and Committees of Congress*, March 8, 2018, p. 14, https://fas.org/sgp/crs/mideast/RS21534.pdf (accessed June 8, 2018).

54. Kenneth Katzman, "Bahrain: Reform, Security, and U.S. Policy," Congressional Research Service *Report for Members and Committees of Congress*, February 15, 2018, p. 2, https://fas.org/sgp/crs/mideast/95-1013.pdf (accessed June 8, 2018).

55. Ibid., pp. 17–18.

56. Captain Marie Harnley, "Wing Leadership Visits Eskan Village," U.S. Air Forces Central Command, July 5, 2013, http://www.afcent.af.mil/Units/379thAirExpeditionaryWing/News/Display/tabid/5382/Article/350180/wing-leadership-visits-eskan-village.aspx (accessed June 8, 2018).

57. General Joseph L. Votel, Commander, U.S. Central Command, statement on "The Posture of U.S. Central Command" before the Committee on Armed Services, U.S. Senate, March 13, 2018, p. 31, http://www.centcom.mil/Portals/6/Documents/Transcripts/Votel_03-13-18.pdf (accessed June 8, 2018).

58. U.S. Army Central, "Eager Lion," April 11, 2018, U.S. Army STAND-TO! https://www.army.mil/standto/2018-04-11 (accessed June 8, 2018).

59. Jeremy Sharp, "Jordan: Background and U.S. Relations" Congressional Research Service *Report for Members and Committees of Congress*, February 16, 2018, https://fas.org/sgp/crs/mideast/RL33546.pdf (accessed June 8, 2018).

60. Associated Press, "U.K. Opens Persian Gulf Military Base in Bahrain," Bloomberg, https://www.bloomberg.com/news/articles/2018-04-05/uk-opens-persian-gulf-naval-base-in-bahrain (accessed June 8, 2018).

61. U.K. Ministry of Defence and Rt. Honorable Sir Michael Fallon, "Multi-Million Pound Joint Venture Announced Between Britain and Oman."

62. Frank Gardner, "'East of Suez': Are UK Forces Returning?" BBC News, April 29, 2013, http://www.bbc.com/news/uk-22333555 (accessed June 10, 2018).

63. Harriet Alexander, "Where Are the World's Major Military Bases?" *The Telegraph*, July 11, 2013, http://www.telegraph.co.uk/news/uknews/defence/10173740/Where-are-the-worlds-major-military-bases.html (accessed June 10, 2018).

64. International Institute for Strategic Studies, *The Military Balance 2018*, p. 107.

65. Donna Miles, "Centcom Undertakes Massive Logistical Drawdown in Afghanistan," U.S. Department of Defense, June 21, 2013, http://archive.defense.gov/news/newsarticle.aspx?id=120348 (accessed June 10, 2018).

66. Ibid.

67. U.S. Central Intelligence Agency, *The World Factbook 2018*, "Field Listing: Roadways: Country Comparison to the World," https://www.cia.gov/library/publications/the-world-factbook/fields/2085.html (accessed July 20, 2018).

68. World Bank, "Rail Lines (Total Route-km)," 1980–2016, http://data.worldbank.org/indicator/IS.RRS.TOTL.KM/countries?display=default (accessed June 10, 2018).

69. Association of American Railroads, "U.S. Freight Railroad Industry Snapshot," https://www.aar.org/data-center/railroads-states#state/NH (accessed June 10, 2018).

70. Anne Barnard, "Once Bustling, Syria's Fractured Railroad Is a Testament to Shattered Ambitions," *The New York Times*, May 25, 2014, http://www.nytimes.com/2014/05/26/world/middleeast/damascus-syria-hejaz-railway-station.html (accessed June 10, 2018).

71. Katzman, "Bahrain: Reform Security, and U.S. Policy."

72. Ibid.

73. In 2014, for example, it was estimated that a combined total of more than 65,000 cargo ships travel through the Strait of Hormuz and the Bab el-Mandeb Strait every year. See Combined Maritime Forces, "CMF Commanders Speak on Maritime Security at Doha Maritime Defence Exhibition," April 1, 2014, http://combinedmaritimeforces.com/2014/04/01/cmf-commanders-speak-on-maritime-security-at-doha-maritime-defence-exhibition/ (accessed June 22, 2017).

74. Suez Canal Authority, "Navigation Statistics," https://www.suezcanal.gov.eg/English/Navigation/Pages/NavigationStatistics.aspx (accessed May 24, 2018).

75. Associated Press, "US Carrier Crosses Suez Canal into Red Sea," *The Times of Israel*, November 8, 2013, http://www.timesofisrael.com/us-carrier-crosses-suez-canal-into-red-sea/ (accessed June 26, 2017).

76. U.S. Department of Energy, Energy Information Administration, "World Oil Transit Chokepoints," last updated July 25, 2017, p. 4, http://www.eia.gov/beta/international/analysis_includes/special_topics/World_Oil_Transit_Chokepoints/wotc.pdf (accessed June 10, 2018). Punctuation as in original.

77. Ibid., p. 11.

78. Ibid.

79. See, for example, World Bank, "Logistics Performance Index: Quality of Trade and Transport-Related Infrastructure (1=Low to 5=High)," 2007–2016, http://data.worldbank.org/indicator/LP.LPI.INFR.XQ (accessed June 10, 2018).

Asia

Since the founding of the American republic, Asia has been a key area of interest for the United States for both economic and security reasons. One of the first ships to sail under an American flag was the aptly named *Empress of China*, which inaugurated America's participation in the lucrative China trade in 1784. In the more than 200 years since then, the United States has worked under the strategic assumption that it was inimical to American interests to allow any single nation to dominate Asia. Asia constituted too important a market and was too great a source of key resources for the United States to be denied access. Thus, beginning with U.S. Secretary of State John Hay's "Open Door" policy toward China in the 19th century, the United States has worked to prevent the rise of a regional hegemon in Asia, whether it was imperial Japan or the Soviet Union.

In the 21st century, Asia's importance to the United States will continue to grow. Already, approximately 40 percent of U.S. trade in goods is in Asian markets.[1] Asia is a key source of vital natural resources and a crucial part of the global value chain in areas like electronic components. It is America's second largest trading partner in services.[2] Disruption in Asia, as occurred with the March 2011 earthquake in Japan, affects the production of things like cars, aircraft, and computers around the world, as well as the global financial system.

Asia is of more than just economic concern, however. Several of the world's largest militaries are in Asia, including those of China, India, North and South Korea, Pakistan, Russia, and Vietnam. The United States also maintains a network of treaty alliances and security partnerships, as well as a significant military presence, in Asia. Five Asian states (China, North Korea, India, Pakistan, and Russia) possess nuclear weapons.

The region is a focus of American security concerns both because of the presence of substantial military forces and because of its legacy of conflict. Both of the two major "hot" wars fought by the United States during the Cold War (Korea and Vietnam) were fought in Asia. Moreover, the Asian security environment is unstable. For one thing, the Cold War has not ended in Asia. Of the four states divided between Communism and democracy by the Cold War, three (China, Korea, and Vietnam) were in Asia. Neither the Korean situation nor the China–Taiwan situation was resolved despite the fall of the Berlin Wall and the collapse of the Soviet Union.

The Cold War itself was an ideological conflict layered atop long-standing—and still lingering—historical animosities. Asia is home to several major territorial disputes, among them:

- Northern Territories/Southern Kuriles (Japan and Russia);

- Senkakus/Diaoyutai/Diaoyu Dao (Japan, China, and Taiwan);

- Dok-do/Takeshima (Korea and Japan);

- Paracels/Xisha Islands (Vietnam, China, and Taiwan);

- Spratlys/Nansha Islands (China, Taiwan, Vietnam, Brunei, Malaysia, and the Philippines);

- Kashmir (India and Pakistan); and

- Aksai Chin and parts of the Indian state of Arunachal Pradesh (India and China).

Even the various names applied to the disputed territories reflect the fundamental differences in point of view, as each state refers to the disputed areas under a different name. Similarly, different names are applied to the various major bodies of water: for example, "East Sea" or "Sea of Japan" and "Yellow Sea" or "West Sea." China and India do not even agree on the length of their disputed border, with Chinese estimates as low as 2,000 kilometers and Indian estimates generally in the mid-3,000s.

These disputes over names also reflect the broader tensions rooted in historical animosities that still scar the region. Most notably, Japan's actions leading up to and during World War II remain a major source of controversy, particularly in China and South Korea, where debates over issues such as what is incorporated in textbooks and governmental statements prevent old wounds from completely healing. Similarly, a Chinese claim that much of the Korean Peninsula was once Chinese territory aroused reactions in both Koreas. The end of the Cold War did little to resolve any of these underlying disagreements.

It is in this light and in light of the regional states' reluctance to align with great powers that one should consider the lack of a political–security architecture. There is no equivalent of NATO in Asia, despite an ultimately failed mid-20th century effort to forge a parallel multilateral security architecture through the Southeast Asia Treaty Organization (SEATO). Regional security entities like the Five Power Defence Arrangement (involving the United Kingdom, Australia, New Zealand, Malaysia, and Singapore in an "arrangement" rather than an alliance) or discussion forums like the ASEAN Regional Forum and the ASEAN Defense Ministers-Plus Meeting have been far weaker. In addition, there is no Asian equivalent of the Warsaw Pact. Instead, Asian security has been marked by a combination of bilateral alliances,

mostly centered on the United States, and individual nations' efforts to maintain their own security. In recent years, these core aspects of the regional security architecture have been supplemented by "mini-lateral" consultations like the U.S.–Japan–Australia and India–Japan–Australia trilaterals and the quadrilateral security dialogue.

Nor is there much of an architecture undergirding East Asia. Despite substantial trade and expanding value chains among the various Asian states, as well as with the rest of the world, formal economic integration is limited. There is no counterpart to the European Union or even to the European Economic Community, just as there is no parallel with the European Coal and Steel Community, the precursor to European economic integration.

The Association of Southeast Asian Nations (ASEAN) is a far looser agglomeration of disparate states, although they have succeeded in expanding economic linkages among themselves over the past 50 years through a range of economic agreements like the ASEAN Free Trade Area (AFTA). Less important to regional stability has been the South Asia Association of Regional Cooperation (SAARC), which includes Afghanistan, Bangladesh, Bhutan, India, Maldives, Nepal, Pakistan, and Sri Lanka. The SAARC is largely ineffective, both because of the lack of regional economic integration and because of the historical rivalry between India and Pakistan.

With regard to Asia-wide free trade agreements, the 11 countries remaining in the Trans-Pacific Partnership (TPP) after U.S. withdrawal subsequently modified and signed it. The Regional Comprehensive Economic Partnership—the ASEAN-centric agreement that includes China, Japan, South Korea, India, Australia, and New Zealand—has gone through 22 rounds of negotiations. When implemented, these agreements will help to remedy the lack of regional integration.

Important Alliances and Bilateral Relations in Asia

For the United States, the keys to its position in the Western Pacific are its alliances with Japan, the Republic of Korea (ROK), the Philippines, Thailand, and Australia. These five alliances are supplemented by very close security relationships with New Zealand and Singapore and evolving relationships with other nations with interests in the region like India, Vietnam, Malaysia, and Indonesia. The U.S. also has a robust unofficial relationship with Taiwan. In South Asia, American relationships with Afghanistan and Pakistan are critical to establishing peace and security.

The United States also benefits from the interoperability that results from sharing common weapons and systems with many of its allies. Many nations, for example, have equipped their ground forces with M-16/M-4–based infantry weapons (and share the 5.56mm caliber ammunition); field F-15 and F-16 combat aircraft; and employ LINK-16 data links. Australia, Japan, and South Korea are partners in the production of the F-35 Joint Strike Fighter; Australia and Japan have already taken delivery of aircraft, and South Korea is due to take delivery next year. Consequently, in the event of conflict, the various air, naval, and even land forces will be able to share information in such key areas as air defense and maritime domain awareness. This advantage is further expanded by the constant ongoing range of both bilateral and multilateral exercises, which acclimate various forces to operating together and familiarize both American and local commanders with each other's standard operating procedures (SOPs), as well as training, tactics, and (in some cases) war plans.

Japan. The U.S.–Japan defense relationship is the linchpin in the American network of relations in the Western Pacific. The U.S.–Japan Treaty of Mutual Cooperation and Security, signed in 1960, provided for a deep alliance between two of the world's largest economies and most sophisticated military establishments, and changes in Japanese defense policies are now enabling an even greater level of cooperation on security issues between the two allies and others in the region.

Since the end of World War II, Japan's defense policy has been distinguished by Article 9 of the Japanese constitution. This article, which states in part that "the Japanese people forever renounce war as a sovereign right of the nation and the threat or use of force as means of settling international disputes,"[3] in effect prohibits the use of force by Japan's governments as an instrument of national policy. It also has led to several other associated policies.

One such policy is a prohibition on "collective self-defense." Japan recognized that nations have a right to employ their armed forces to help other states defend themselves (i.e., to engage in collective defensive operations) but rejected that policy for itself: Japan would employ its forces only in defense of Japan. This changed, however, in 2015. The U.S. and Japan revised their defense cooperation guidelines, and the Japanese passed legislation to enable their military to exercise limited collective self-defense in certain cases involving threats to both the U.S. and Japan, as well as in multilateral peacekeeping operations.

A similar policy decision was made in 2014 regarding Japanese arms exports. For a variety of economic and political reasons, Tokyo had chosen until then to rely on domestic or licensed production to meet most of its military requirements while essentially banning defense-related exports. The relaxation of these export rules in 2014 enabled Japan, among other things, to pursue (ultimately unsuccessfully) an opportunity to build new state-of-the-art submarines in Australia for the Australians and a seemingly successful effort to sell amphibious search and rescue aircraft to the Indian navy.[4] Japan has also supplied multiple patrol vessels to the Philippine and Vietnamese Coast Guards and is exploring various joint development opportunities with the U.S. and a few other nations.

Tokyo relies heavily on the United States for its security. In particular, it depends on the United States to deter both conventional and nuclear attacks on the home islands. The combination of the pacifist constitution and Japan's past (i.e., the atomic bombings of Hiroshima and Nagasaki) has forestalled much public interest in obtaining an independent nuclear deterrent. Similarly, throughout the Cold War, Japan relied on the American conventional and nuclear commitment to deter Soviet and Chinese aggression.

As part of its relationship with Japan, the United States maintains some 54,000 military personnel and another 8,000 Department of Defense civilian employees in Japan under the rubric of U.S. Forces Japan (USFJ).[5] These forces include, among other things, a forward-deployed carrier battle group centered on the USS *Ronald Reagan*; an amphibious assault ship at Sasebo; and the bulk of the Third Marine Expeditionary Force (III MEF) on Okinawa. U.S. forces exercise regularly with their Japanese counterparts, and this collaboration has expanded in recent years from air and naval exercises to practicing amphibious operations together.

The American presence is supported by a substantial American defense infrastructure throughout Japan, including Okinawa. The array of major bases provides key logistical and communications support for U.S. operations throughout the Western Pacific, cutting travel time substantially compared with deployments from Hawaii or the West Coast of the United States. They also provide key listening posts to monitor Russian, Chinese, and North Korean military operations. This is supplemented by Japan's growing array of space systems, including new reconnaissance satellites.

The Japanese government provides "nearly $2 billion per year to offset the cost of stationing U.S. forces in Japan."[6] These funds cover a variety of expenses, including utility and labor costs at U.S. bases, improvements to U.S. facilities in Japan, and the cost of relocating training exercises away from populated areas in Japan. Japan is also covering nearly all of the expenses related to relocation of the Futenma Marine Corps Air Station from its crowded urban location to a less densely populated part of the island and facilities in Guam to accommodate some Marines being moved off the island.

At least since the 1990 Gulf War, the United States had sought to expand Japanese participation in international security affairs. Japan's political system, grounded in Japan's constitution, legal decisions, and popular attitudes, generally resisted this effort. Attempts to expand Japan's range of defense activities, especially away from the home islands, have also often been vehemently opposed by Japan's neighbors, especially China and South Korea, because of unresolved differences on issues ranging from territorial claims and boundaries to historical grievances, including visits by Japanese leaders to the Yasukuni Shrine. Even with the incremental changes allowing for broader Japanese defense contributions, these issues will doubtless continue to constrain Japan's contributions to the alliance.

These historical issues have been sufficient to torpedo efforts to improve defense cooperation between Seoul and Tokyo, a fact highlighted in 2012 by South Korea's last-minute decision not to sign an agreement to share sensitive military data, including details about the North Korean threat to both countries.[7] In December 2014, the U.S., South Korea, and Japan signed a military data-sharing agreement limited to information on the North Korean military threat and requiring both allies to pass information through the United States military. This was supplemented in 2016 by a Japan–ROK bilateral agreement on sharing military intelligence. Similar controversies, rooted in history as well as in contemporary politics, have also affected Sino–Japanese relations and, to a lesser extent, Japanese ties to some Southeast Asian states.

Republic of Korea. The United States and the Republic of Korea signed their Mutual Defense Treaty in 1953. That treaty codified the relationship that had grown from the Korean War, when the United States dispatched troops to help South Korea defend itself against invasion by Communist North Korea. Since then, the two states have forged an enduring alliance supplemented by a substantial trade and economic relationship that includes a free trade agreement.

As of March 2018, the United States had some 24,915 troops in Korea,[8] the largest concentration of American forces on the Asian mainland. This presence is centered mainly on the U.S. 2nd Infantry Division, rotating brigade combat teams, and a significant number of combat aircraft.

The U.S.–ROK defense relationship involves one of the more integrated and complex command-and-control structures. A United Nations Command (UNC) established in 1950 was the basis for the American intervention and remained in place after the armistice was signed in 1953. UNC has access to a number of bases in Japan in order to support U.N. forces in Korea. In concrete terms, however, it only oversaw South Korean and American forces as other nations' contributions were gradually withdrawn or reduced to token elements.

In 1978, operational control of frontline South Korean and American military forces passed from UNC to Combined Forces Command (CFC). Headed by the American Commander of U.S. Forces Korea, who is also Commander, U.N. Command, CFC reflects an unparalleled degree of U.S.–South Korean military integration. Similarly, the system of Korean Augmentees to the United States Army (KATUSA), which places South Korean soldiers into American units assigned to Korea, allows for an atypical degree of tactical-level integration and cooperation.

Current command arrangements for the U.S. and ROK militaries are for CFC to exercise operational control (OPCON) of all forces on the peninsula in time of war; peacetime control rests with respective national authorities, although the U.S. exercises peacetime OPCON over non-U.S., non-ROK forces located on the peninsula. In 2003, South Korean President Roh Moo-hyun, as agreed with the U.S., began the process of transferring wartime operational control from CFC to South Korean commanders, thereby establishing the ROK military as fully independent of the United States. This decision engendered significant opposition within South Korea and raised serious military questions about the transfer's impact on unity of command. Faced with various North Korean provocations, including a spate of missile tests as well as attacks on South

Korean military forces and territory in 2010, Washington and Seoul agreed in late 2014 to postpone wartime OPCON transfer.[9]

The domestic political constraints under which South Korea's military operates are less stringent than those that govern the operations of the Japanese military. Thus, South Korea rotated several divisions to fight alongside Americans in Vietnam. In the first Gulf War, the Iraq War, and Afghanistan, South Korea limited its contributions to noncombatant forces and monetary aid. The focus of South Korean defense planning remains on North Korea, especially as Pyongyang has deployed its forces in ways that optimize a southward advance and has carried out several penetrations of ROK territory over the years by ship, submarine, commandos, and drones. The sinking of the South Korean frigate *Cheonan* and shelling of Yongpyeong-do in 2010, which together killed 48 military personnel, wounded 16, and killed two civilians, have only heightened concerns about North Korea.

Over the past several decades, the American presence on the peninsula has slowly declined. In the early 1970s, President Richard Nixon withdrew the 7th Infantry Division, leaving only the 2nd Infantry Division on the peninsula. Those forces have been positioned farther back so that few Americans are now deployed on the Demilitarized Zone (DMZ).

Washington is officially committed to maintaining 28,500 American troops in the ROK. These forces regularly engage in major exercises with their ROK counterparts, including the Key Resolve and Foal Eagle series, both of which involve the actual deployment of a substantial number of forces and are partly intended to deter Pyongyang, as well as to give U.S. and ROK forces a chance to practice operating together. The ROK government also provides substantial resources to defray the costs of U.S. Forces–Korea. It pays approximately half of all non-personnel costs for U.S. forces stationed in South Korea, amounting to $821 million in 2016, and "is paying $9.74 billion for the relocation of several U.S. bases within the country and construction of new military facilities."[10]

With new governments in place in both the U.S. and South Korea, the health of the alliance at the political level will need to be monitored closely for impact on the operational levels. The two could diverge on issues such as North Korea sanctions policy, the timing of engagement with North Korea, deployment of the Terminal High-Altitude Area Defense (THAAD) system, and ROK–Japan relations.

The Philippines. America's oldest defense relationship in Asia is with the Philippines. The United States seized the Philippines from the Spanish over a century ago as a result of the Spanish–American War and a subsequent conflict with Philippine indigenous forces. Unlike other colonial states, however, the U.S. also put in place a mechanism for the Philippines to gain its independence, transitioning through a period as a commonwealth until the archipelago was granted full independence in 1946. Just as important, substantial numbers of Filipinos fought alongside the United States against Japan in World War II, establishing a bond between the two peoples. Following World War II and after assisting the newly independent Filipino government against the Communist Hukbalahap movement in the 1940s, the United States and the Philippines signed a mutual security treaty.

For much of the period between 1898 and the end of the Cold War, the largest American bases in the Pacific were in the Philippines, centered on the U.S. Navy base in Subic Bay and the complex of airfields that developed around Clark Field (later Clark Air Base). While the Philippines have never had the ability to provide substantial financial support for the American presence, the unparalleled base infrastructure provided replenishment and repair facilities and substantially extended deployment periods throughout the East Asian littoral.

These bases, being reminders of the colonial era, were often centers of controversy. In 1991, a successor to the Military Bases Agreement between the U.S. and the Philippines was submitted to the Philippine Senate for ratification. The Philippines, after a lengthy debate, rejected the treaty, compelling American withdrawal from Philippine bases. Coupled with the effects of the 1991 eruption of Mount Pinatubo, which devastated Clark Air Base and damaged many Subic Bay facilities, and the end of the Cold War, closure of the bases was not seen as fundamentally damaging to America's posture in the region.

Moreover, despite the closing of the American bases and consequent slashing of American military assistance, U.S.–Philippine military relations remained close, and assistance began to increase again after 9/11 as U.S. forces assisted the Philippines in countering Islamic terrorist groups, including the Abu Sayyaf Group (ASG), in the south of the archipelago. From 2002–2015, the U.S. rotated 500–600 special operations forces regularly through the Philippines to assist in counterterrorism operations. That operation, Joint Special Operations Task Force–Philippines (JSOTF–P), closed during the first part of 2015. The U.S. presence in Mindanao continued at a reduced level until the Trump Administration, alarmed by the terrorist threat there, began Operation Pacific Eagle–Philippines. The presence of these 200–300 American advisers proved very valuable to the Philippines in its 2017 battle against Islamist insurgents in Marawi.[11]

The Philippines continues to have serious problems with Islamist insurgencies and terrorists in its South. This affects the government's priorities and, potentially, its stability. Although not a direct threat to the American homeland, it also bears on the U.S. military footprint in the Philippines and the type of cooperation that the two militaries undertake. In addition to the current threat from ISIS-affiliated groups like the ASG, trained ISIS fighters returning to the Philippines could pose a threat similar to that of the "mujahedeen" who returned from Afghanistan after the Soviet war there in the 1980s.

Thousands of U.S. troops participate in combined exercises with Philippine troops, most notably as a part of the annual Balikatan exercises. In all, 261 activities with the Philippines are planned for 2018, "slowly expanding parameters of military-to-military cooperation."[12]

In 2014, the United States and the Philippines announced a new Enhanced Defense Cooperation Agreement (EDCA) that allows for an expanded American presence in the archipelago,[13] and in early 2016, they agreed on five specific bases that are subject to the agreement. Under the EDCA, U.S. forces will rotate through these locations on an expanded basis, allowing for a more regular presence (but not new, permanent bases) in the islands and more joint training with the Armed Forces of the Philippines (AFP). The agreement also facilitates the provision of humanitarian assistance and disaster relief. The United States also agreed to improve the facilities it uses and to transfer and sell more military equipment to the AFP to help it modernize. In 2018, construction began on facilities at one of the bases covered, Basa Air Base in Pampanga, central Luzon, the main Philippine island.[14]

One long-standing difference between the U.S. and the Philippines involves the application of the U.S.–Philippine Mutual Defense Treaty to disputed islands in the South China Sea. The U.S. has long maintained that the treaty does not extend American obligations to disputed areas and territories, but Filipino officials occasionally have held otherwise.[15] The EDCA does not settle this question, but tensions in the South China Sea, including in recent years at Scarborough Shoal, have highlighted Manila's need for greater support from and cooperation with Washington. Moreover, the U.S. government has long been explicit that any attack on Philippine government ships or aircraft, or on the Philippine armed forces, would be covered under the treaty, "thus separating the issue of territorial sovereignty from attack on Philippine military and public vessels."[16]

In 2016, the Philippines elected a very unconventional President, Rodrigo Duterte, to a six-year term. His rhetorical challenges to current priorities in the U.S.–Philippines alliance have raised questions about the trajectory of the alliance and initiatives that are important to it. With the support of the Philippine government at various levels, however, the two militaries continue to work together with some adjustment in the size and purpose of their cooperation.[17]

Thailand. The U.S.–Thai security relationship is built on the 1954 Manila Pact, which established the now-defunct SEATO, and the 1962 Thanat–Rusk agreement. These were supplemented by the 2012 Joint Vision Statement for the Thai–U.S. Defense Alliance.[18] In 2003, Thailand was designated a "major, non-NATO ally," giving it improved access to American arms sales.

Thailand's central location has made it an important component of the network of U.S. alliances in Asia. During the Vietnam War, a variety of American aircraft were based in Thailand, ranging from fighter-bombers and B-52s to reconnaissance aircraft. In the first Gulf War and again in the Iraq War, some of those same air bases were essential for the rapid deployment of American forces to the Persian Gulf. Access to these bases remains critical to U.S. global operations.

U.S. and Thai forces exercise together regularly, most notably in the annual Cobra Gold exercises, first begun in 1982. This builds on a partnership that began with the dispatch of Thai forces to the Korean War, where over 1,200 Thai troops died out of some 6,000 deployed. The Cobra Gold exercises are among the world's largest multilateral military exercises. In 2018, after a brief period of reduced U.S. commitment due to objections over Thailand's 2014 coup, the U.S. doubled the size of its troop deployment.

U.S.–Thai relations have been strained in recent years as a result of domestic unrest and two coups in Thailand. This strife has limited the extent of U.S.–Thai military cooperation, as U.S. law prohibits U.S. funding for many kinds of assistance to a foreign country in which a military coup deposes a duly elected head of government. Nonetheless, the two states continue to cooperate, including in joint military exercises and counterterrorism. The Counter Terrorism Information Center (CTIC) continues to allow the two states to share vital information about terrorist activities in Asia. Among other things, the CTIC reportedly played a key role in the capture of Jemaah Islamiyah leader Hambali (Riduan Isamuddin) in 2003.[19]

Thailand has also been drawing closer to the People's Republic of China (PRC). This process, underway since the end of the Vietnam War, is accelerating partly because of expanding economic relations between the two states. Today, China is Thailand's leading trading partner.[20] Relations are also expanding because of complications in U.S.–Thai relations arising from the Thai coups in 2014 and 2016.

Relations between the Thai and Chinese militaries also have improved over the years. Intelligence officers began formal meetings in 1988. Thai and Chinese military forces have engaged in joint naval exercises since 2005, joint counterterrorism exercises since 2007, and joint marine exercises since 2010 and conducted their first joint air force exercises in 2015.[21] The Thais have been buying Chinese military equipment for many years. Recent purchases include two significant buys of battle tanks as well as armored personnel carriers.[22]

In 2017, Thailand made the first of three planned submarine purchases in one of the most expensive arms deals in its history.[23] Submarines could be particularly critical to Sino–Thai relations because the training and maintenance required will entail greater Chinese military presence at Thai military facilities. For a number of years, there has been discussion of a joint arms factory in Thailand and Chinese repair and maintenance facilities needed to service Chinese-made equipment.[24]

Australia. Australia is one of America's most important allies in the Asia–Pacific. U.S.–Australia security ties date back to World War I, when U.S. forces fought under Australian command on the Western Front in Europe. These ties deepened during World War II when, after Japan commenced hostilities in the Western Pacific (and despite British promises), Australian forces committed to the North Africa campaign were not returned to defend the continent. As Japanese forces attacked the East Indies and secured Singapore, Australia turned to the United States to bolster its defenses, and American and Australian forces subsequently cooperated closely in the Pacific War. Those ties and America's role as the main external supporter for Australian security were codified in the Australia–New Zealand–U.S. (ANZUS) pact of 1951.

A key part of the Obama Administration's "Asia pivot" was to rotate additional United States Air Force units and Marines through northern Australia.[25] Eventually expected to total some 2,500 troops by 2020, a record number of more than 1,500, along with Osprey aircraft and howitzers, have been deployed in 2018. During the six months they are in Australia, "the rotation will include additional equipment and assets such as AH-1W Super Cobra helicopters, UH-1Y Venom helicopters, F/A-18 Hornet aircraft and MC-130 Hercules aircraft."[26]

The U.S. and Australia are also working to upgrade air force and naval facilities in the area to "accommodate stealth warplanes and long-range maritime patrol drones" as well as provide refueling for visiting warships.[27] The Air Force has deployed F-22 fighter aircraft to northern Australia for joint training exercises, and there have been discussions about rotational deployments of other assets to that part of the country as well.[28] Meanwhile, the two nations engage in a variety of security cooperation efforts, including joint space surveillance activities. These were codified in 2014 with an agreement that allows the sharing of space information data among the U.S., Australia, the U.K., and Canada.[29]

The two nations' chief defense and foreign policy officials meet annually in the Australia–United States Ministerial (AUSMIN) process to address such issues of mutual concern as security developments in the Asia–Pacific region, global security and development, and bilateral security cooperation.[30] Australia has also granted the United States access to a number of joint facilities, including space surveillance facilities at Pine Gap and naval communications facilities on the North West Cape of Australia.[31]

Australia and the United Kingdom are two of America's closest partners in the defense industrial sector. In 2010, the United States approved Defense Trade Cooperation Treaties with Australia and the U.K. that allow for the expedited and simplified export or transfer of certain defense services and items between the U.S. and its two key partners without the need for export licenses or other approvals under the International Traffic in Arms Regulations. This also allows for much greater integration among the American, Australian, and British defense industrial establishments.[32]

Singapore. Although Singapore is not a security treaty ally of the United States, it is a key security partner in the region. Their close defense relationship was formalized in 2005 with the Strategic Framework Agreement (SFA) and expanded in 2015 with the U.S.–Singapore Defense Cooperation Agreement (DCA).

The 2005 SFA was the first agreement of its kind since the end of the Cold War. It built on the 1990 Memorandum of Understanding Regarding United States Use of Facilities in Singapore, as amended, which allows for U.S. access to Singaporean military facilities.[33] The 2015 DCA establishes "high-level dialogues between the countries' defense establishments" and a "broad framework for defense cooperation in five key areas, namely in the military, policy, strategic and technology spheres, as well as cooperation against non-conventional security challenges, such as piracy and transnational terrorism."[34] Singapore trains 1,000 service personnel a year on American-produced equipment like F-15SG and F-16C/D fighter aircraft and CH-47 Chinook and AH-64 Apache helicopters.[35]

New Zealand. For much of the Cold War, U.S. defense ties with New Zealand were similar to those between America and Australia. As a result of controversies over U.S. Navy employment of nuclear power and the possible deployment of U.S. naval vessels with nuclear weapons, the U.S. suspended its obligations to New Zealand under the 1951 ANZUS Treaty.

Defense relations improved, however, in the early 21st century as New Zealand committed forces to Afghanistan and dispatched an engineering detachment to Iraq. The 2010 Wellington Declaration and 2012 Washington Declaration, while not restoring full security ties, allowed the two nations to resume high-level defense dialogues.[36]

In 2013, U.S. Secretary of Defense Chuck Hagel and New Zealand Defense Minister Jonathan Coleman announced the resumption of military-to-military cooperation,[37] and in July 2016, the U.S. accepted an invitation from New Zealand to make a single port call, reportedly with no change in U.S. policy to confirm or deny the presence of nuclear weapons on the ship.[38] At the time of the visit in November 2016, both sides claimed to have satisfied their respective legal requirements.[39] The Prime Minister expressed confidence that the vessel was not nuclear-powered and did not possess nuclear armaments, and the U.S. neither confirmed nor denied this. The visit occurred in a unique context, including an international naval review and relief response to the Kaikoura earthquake, but the arrangement may portend a longer-term solution to the nuclear impasse between the two nations.

Taiwan. When the United States shifted its recognition of the government of China from the Republic of China (on Taiwan) to the People's Republic of China (the mainland), it declared certain commitments concerning the security of Taiwan. These commitments are embodied in the Taiwan Relations Act (TRA) and the subsequent "Six Assurances."

The TRA is an American law and not a treaty. Under the TRA, the United States maintains programs, transactions, and other relations with Taiwan through the American Institute in Taiwan (AIT). Except for the Sino–U.S. Mutual Defense Treaty, which had governed U.S. security relations with Taiwan, all other treaties and international agreements made between the Republic of China and the United States remain in force. (President Jimmy Carter terminated the Sino–U.S. Mutual Defense Treaty following the shift in recognition to the PRC.)

Under the TRA, it is the policy of the United States "to provide Taiwan with arms of a defensive character." The TRA also states that the U.S. will "make available to Taiwan such defense articles and services in such quantity as may be necessary to enable Taiwan to maintain a sufficient self-defense capability." The U.S. has implemented these provisions of the TRA through sales of weapons to Taiwan.

The TRA states that it is U.S. policy to "consider any effort to determine the future of Taiwan by other than peaceful means, including by boycotts or embargoes, a threat to the peace and security of the Western Pacific area and of grave concern to the United States." It also states that it is U.S. policy to "maintain the capacity of the United States to resist any resort to force or other forms of coercion that would jeopardize the security, or the social or economic system, of the people on Taiwan."[40]

The TRA requires the President to inform Congress promptly of "any threat to the security or the social or economic system of the people on Taiwan and any danger to the interests of the United States arising therefrom." It then states: "The President and the Congress shall determine, in accordance with constitutional processes, appropriate action by the United States in response to any such danger."

Supplementing the TRA are the "Six Assurances" issued by President Ronald Reagan in a secret July 1982 memo, later publicly released and the subject of a Senate hearing. These assurances were intended to moderate the third Sino–American communiqué, itself generally seen as one of the "Three Communiqués" that form the foundation of U.S.–PRC relations. These assurances of July 14, 1982, were that:

> In negotiating the third Joint Communiqué with the PRC, the United States:
> 1. *has not agreed to set a date for ending arms sales to Taiwan;*
> 2. *has not agreed to hold prior consultations with the PRC on arms sales to Taiwan;*
> 3. *will not play any mediation role between Taipei and Beijing;*
> 4. *has not agreed to revise the Taiwan Relations Act;*
> 5. *has not altered its position regarding sovereignty over Taiwan;*
> 6. *will not exert pressure on Taiwan to negotiate with the PRC.*[41]

Although the United States sells Taiwan a variety of military equipment and sends observers to its major annual exercises, it does not engage in joint exercises with the Taiwan armed forces. Some Taiwan military officers, however, attend professional military education institutions in the United States. There also are regular high-level meetings between senior U.S. and Taiwan defense officials, both uniformed and civilian.

The United States does not maintain any bases in Taiwan. In 2017, however, the U.S. Congress authorized the U.S. Department of Defense to consider ship visits to Taiwan as part of the FY 2018 National Defense Authorization Act. Coupled with the Taiwan Travel Act passed in 2018, this could lead to a significant increase in the number and/or grade of American military officers visiting Taiwan in the coming years.

Vietnam, Malaysia, and Indonesia. The U.S. has security relationships with several key Southeast Asian countries. None of these relationships is as extensive and formal as its relationship with Singapore and its treaty allies, but all are of growing significance. The U.S. "rebalance" to the Pacific incorporated a policy of "rebalance within the rebalance" that included efforts to expand relations with this second tier of America's security partners and diversify the geographical spread of forward-deployed U.S. forces.

Since shortly after the normalization of diplomatic relations between the two countries in 1995, the U.S. and Vietnam also have gradually normalized their defense relationship. The relationship was codified in 2011 with a Memorandum of Understanding "advancing bilateral defense cooperation" that covers five areas of operations, including maritime security, and was updated with the 2015 Joint Vision

Statement on Defense Cooperation, which includes a reference to "cooperation in the production of new technologies and equipment."[42]

The most significant development in security ties over the past several years has been the relaxation of the ban on sales of arms to Vietnam. The U.S. lifted the embargo on maritime security-related equipment in the fall of 2014 and then lifted the ban completely when President Barack Obama visited Hanoi in 2016. This full embargo had long served as a psychological obstacle to Vietnamese cooperation on security issues, but lifting it does not necessarily change the nature of the articles likely to be sold. The only transfer to have been announced is the provision under the Foreign Assistance Act of a decommissioned *Hamilton*-class Coast Guard cutter.[43] Others, including P-3 maritime patrol aircraft, discussed since the relaxation of the embargo three years ago have yet to be concluded. However, lifting the embargo does expand the potential of the relationship and better positions the U.S. to compete with Chinese and Russian positions in Vietnam.

The Joint Statement from President Obama's visit also memorialized a number of other improvements in the U.S.–Vietnam relationship, including the Cooperative Humanitarian and Medical Storage Initiative (CHAMSI), which will advance cooperation on humanitarian assistance and disaster relief by, among other things, prepositioning related American equipment in Danang, Vietnam.[44] During Vietnamese Prime Minister Nguyen Xuan Phuc's visit to Washington in 2017, the U.S. and Vietnam recommitted to this initiative, and it is being implemented.

There has been an increase in cooperation between the two nations' coast guards as well. In March 2018, the U.S. Embassy and Consulate in Hanoi announced an "official transfer at Region 4 Station on Phu Quoc Island" that "comprises 20 million dollars' worth of infrastructure and equipment including a training center, a maintenance facility, a boat lift, vehicles, a navigation simulator, and six brand-new fast-response Metal Shark boats—capable of reaching up to 50 knots."[45] In early 2018, the USS *Carl Vinson* visited Da Nang with its escort ships, marking the first port call by a U.S. aircraft carrier since the Vietnam War.

There remain significant limits on the U.S.–Vietnam security relationship, including a Vietnamese defense establishment that is very cautious in its selection of defense partners, party-to-party ties between the Communist Parties of Vietnam and China, and a foreign policy that seeks to balance relationships with all major powers. The U.S., like others among Vietnam's security partners, remains officially limited to one port call a year, with an additional one to two calls on Vietnamese bases being negotiable.

The U.S. and Malaysia "have maintained steady defense cooperation since the 1990s" despite occasional political differences. Each year, they participate jointly in dozens of bilateral and multilateral exercises to promote effective cooperation across a range of missions.[46] The U.S. occasionally flies P-3 and/or P-8 patrol aircraft out of Malaysian bases in Borneo. During former Prime Minister Najib Razak's 2017 visit to Washington, he and President Trump committed to strengthening their two countries' bilateral defense ties, including in the areas of "maritime security, counterterrorism, and information sharing between our defense and security forces." They also "committed to pursu[ing] additional opportunities for joint exercises and training."[47] To this end, in 2018, Malaysia for the first time sent a warship to participate in U.S.-led RIMPAC exercises.[48] Close U.S.–Malaysia defense ties can be expected to continue quietly under Malaysia's new government.

The U.S.–Indonesia defense relationship was revived in 2005 following a period of estrangement caused by American concerns about human rights. It now includes regular joint exercises, port calls, and sales of weaponry. Because of their impact on the operating environment in and around Indonesia, as well as the setting of priorities in the U.S.–Indonesia relationship, the U.S. is also working closely with Indonesia's defense establishment to institute reforms in Indonesia's strategic defense planning processes.

The United States carried through on the transfer of 24 refurbished F-16s to Indonesia under its Excess Defense Articles program in 2018 and is talking with Indonesian officials about recapitalizing its aging and largely Russian-origin air force with new F-16s.[49] Indonesia has also begun to take delivery of eight Apache helicopters bought in 2012. The U.S. plans more than 200 cooperative military activities with Indonesia in 2018 and is looking for a way to resume its training of Indonesia's special forces (KOPASSUS).[50]

The U.S. is working across the board at modest levels of investment to help build Southeast Asia's maritime security capacity.[51] Most notable in this regard is the Maritime Security Initiative (MSI) announced by Secretary of Defense Ashton Carter in 2015.[52]

Afghanistan. On October 7, 2001, U.S. forces invaded Afghanistan in response to the September 11, 2001, attacks on the United States. This marked the beginning of Operation Enduring Freedom to combat al-Qaeda and its Taliban supporters. The U.S., in alliance with the U.K. and the anti-Taliban Afghan Northern Alliance forces, ousted the Taliban from power in December 2001. Most Taliban and al-Qaeda leaders fled across the border into Pakistan's Federally Administered Tribal Areas, where they regrouped and started an insurgency in Afghanistan in 2003.

In August 2003, NATO joined the war in Afghanistan and assumed control of the International Security Assistance Force (ISAF). At the height of the war in 2011, there were 50 troop-contributing nations and nearly 150,000 NATO and U.S. forces on the ground in Afghanistan.

On December 28, 2014, NATO formally ended combat operations and relinquished responsibility to the Afghan security forces, which numbered around 352,000 (including army and police).[53] After Afghan President Ashraf Ghani signed a bilateral security agreement with the U.S. and a Status of Forces Agreement with NATO, the international coalition launched Operation Resolute Support to train and support Afghan security forces. As

of May 2018, more than 15,600 U.S. and NATO forces were stationed in Afghanistan. Most U.S. and NATO forces are stationed at bases in Kabul, with tactical advise-and-assist teams located there and in Mazar-i-Sharif, Herat, Kandahar, and Laghman.[54]

In August 2017, while declining to announce specific troop levels, President Trump recommitted America to the effort in Afghanistan and announced that "[c]onditions on the ground—not arbitrary timetables—will guide our strategy from now on."[55] According to the most recent available public information, the U.S. currently has almost 8,500 troops in Afghanistan,[56] roughly the same level left in place by President Obama

Pakistan. During the war in Afghanistan, the U.S. and NATO relied heavily on logistical supply lines running through Pakistan to resupply coalition forces in Afghanistan. Supplies and fuel were carried on transportation routes from the port at Karachi to Afghan–Pakistani border crossing points at Torkham in the Khyber Pass and Chaman in Baluchistan province. During the initial years of the Afghan war, about 80 percent of U.S. and NATO supplies traveled through Pakistani territory. This amount decreased to around 50 percent–60 percent as the U.S. shifted to northern routes and when U.S.–Pakistan relations deteriorated significantly because of U.S. drone strikes, continued Pakistani support to Taliban militants, and the fallout surrounding the U.S. raid on Osama bin Laden's hideout in Abbottabad on May 2, 2011.

From October 2001 until December 2011, the U.S. leased Pakistan's Shamsi Airfield southwest of Quetta in Baluchistan province and used it as a base from which to conduct surveillance and drone operations against terrorist targets in Pakistan's tribal border areas. Pakistan ordered the U.S. to vacate the base shortly after NATO forces attacked Pakistani positions along the Afghanistan border, killing 24 Pakistani soldiers, on November 26, 2011.

Since 2001, Pakistan has received over $30 billion in military aid and "reimbursements" from the U.S. in the form of coalition support funds (CSF) for its military deployments and operations along the border with Afghanistan. Pakistan has periodically staged offensives into the Federally Administered Tribal Areas (FATA), though its operations have tended to target anti-Pakistan militant groups like the Pakistani Taliban rather than those targeting Afghanistan and U.S.-led coalition forces operating there. In recent years, frustration with Pakistan's inaction toward such groups has led the U.S. to withhold ever-larger sums of reimbursement and support funds. In 2016, reflecting a trend of growing congressional resistance to military assistance for Pakistan, Congress blocked funds for the provision of eight F-16s to Pakistan.

Meanwhile, U.S. aid appropriations and military reimbursements have fallen continuously since 2013, from $2.60 billion that year to $2.18 billion in 2014, $1.60 billion in 2015, $1.19 billion in 2016, an estimated $0.53 billion in 2017, and $0.35 billion requested for 2018.[57] As frustration with Pakistan has coalesced on Capitol Hill, the Trump Administration has signaled a series of measures designed to hold Pakistan to account for its "double game."[58] "We can no longer be silent about Pakistan's safe havens for terrorist organizations," President Trump declared in August 2017. "We have been paying Pakistan billions and billions of dollars at the same time they are housing the very terrorists that we are fighting. But that will have to change and that will change immediately."[59] Aside from withholding additional support funds, the Administration has supported both Pakistan's addition to the Financial Action Task Force (FATF) "grey list" for failing to fulfil obligations to prevent the financing of terrorism and its designation on a special watch list for violations of religious freedom.

India. During the Cold War, U.S.–Indian military cooperation was minimal, except for a brief period during the Sino–Indian border war in 1962 when the U.S. sided with India and supplied it with arms and ammunition. The rapprochement was short-lived, however, and mutual suspicion continued to mark the Indo–U.S. relationship because of India's robust relationship with Russia and the U.S. provision of military aid to Pakistan, especially during the 1970s under the Nixon Administration. America's ties with India hit a nadir during the 1971 Indo–Pakistani war when the U.S. deployed the aircraft carrier USS *Enterprise* toward the Bay of Bengal in a show of support for Pakistani forces.

Military ties between the U.S. and India have improved significantly over the past decade as the two sides have moved toward establishment of a strategic partnership based on their mutual concern about rising Chinese military and economic influence and converging interests in countering regional terrorism. The U.S. and India have completed contracts worth approximately $14 billion for the supply of U.S. military equipment to India, including C-130J and C-17 transport aircraft and P-8 maritime surveillance aircraft.

Defense ties between the two countries are poised to expand further as India moves forward with an ambitious military modernization program. In 2015, the U.S. and India agreed to renew and upgrade their 10-year Defense Framework Agreement. During Prime Minister Narendra Modi's visit to the U.S. in June 2016, the two governments finalized the text of a logistics and information-sharing agreement that would allow each country to access the other's military supplies and refueling capabilities through ports and military bases. The signing of the agreement, formally called the Logistics Exchange Memorandum of Agreement (LEMOA), marks a milestone in the Indo–U.S. defense partnership. During that visit, the U.S. also designated India a "major defense partner," a designation unique to India that is intended to ease its access to American defense technology. The Trump Administration subsequently reaffirmed this status.[60]

New Delhi and Washington regularly hold joint military exercises across all services, including the annual Malabar naval exercise that added Japan as a regular participant in 2012. The Indian government and Trump Administration are currently negotiating several prospective arms sales and military cooperation agreements, including the sale of armed drones to India and the completion of two outstanding "foundational agreements," the Basic Exchange and Cooperation Agreement (BECA) and Communications and Information Security Memorandum of Agreement (CISOMA).

Quality of Allied Armed Forces in Asia

Because of the lack of an integrated, regional security architecture along the lines of NATO, the United States partners with most of the nations in the region on a bilateral basis. This means that there is no single standard to which all of the local militaries aspire; instead, there is a wide range of capabilities that are influenced by local threat perceptions, institutional interests, physical conditions, historical factors, and budgetary considerations.

Moreover, the lack of recent major conflicts in the region makes assessing the quality of Asian armed forces difficult. Most Asian militaries have limited combat experience, particularly in high-intensity air or naval combat. Some (e.g., Malaysia) have never fought an external war since gaining independence in the mid-20th century. The Indochina wars, the most recent high-intensity conflicts, are now 30 years in the past. It is therefore unclear how well Asian militaries have trained for future warfare and whether their doctrine will meet the exigencies of wartime realities.

Based on examinations of equipment, however, it is assessed that several Asian allies and friends have substantial potential military capabilities supported by robust defense industries and significant defense spending. Japan's, South Korea's, and Australia's defense budgets are estimated to be among the world's 15 largest. Each of their military forces fields some of the world's most advanced weapons, including F-15s in the Japan Air Self Defense Force and ROK Air Force; airborne early warning (AEW) platforms; Aegis-capable surface combatants and modern diesel-electric submarines; and third-generation main battle tanks. As noted, all three nations are involved in the production and purchase of F-35 fighters.

At this point, both the Japanese and Korean militaries are arguably more capable than most European militaries, at least in terms of conventional forces. Japan's Self Defense Forces, for example, field more tanks, principal surface combatants, and combat-capable aircraft (690, 47, and 542, respectively) than their British opposite numbers (227, 19, and 258, respectively).[61] Similarly, South Korea fields a larger military of tanks, principal surface combatants, and combat-capable aircraft (more than 2,514, 25, and 587, respectively) than their German counterparts (236, 14, and 211, respectively).[62]

Both the ROK and Japan are also increasingly interested in developing missile defense capabilities, including joint development and coproduction in the case of Japan. After much negotiation and indecision, South Korea deployed America's THAAD missile defense system on the peninsula in 2017. It is also pursuing an indigenous missile defense capability. As for Japan, its Aegis-class destroyers are equipped with SM-3 missiles, and it decided in 2017 to install the Aegis ashore missile defense system to supplement its Patriot missile batteries.[63]

Singapore's small population and physical borders limit the size of its military, but in terms of equipment and training, it has the largest defense budget among Southeast Asia's countries[64] and fields some of the region's highest-quality forces. For example, Singapore's ground forces can deploy third-generation Leopard II main battle tanks, and its fleet includes four conventional submarines, including one with air-independent propulsion systems, as well as six frigates and six missile-armed corvettes. Its air force not only has F-15E Strike Eagles and F-16s, but also has one of Southeast Asia's largest fleets of airborne early warning and control aircraft (G550-AEW aircraft) and a squadron of KC-130 tankers that can help to extend range or time on station.[65]

At the other extreme, the Armed Forces of the Philippines are among the region's weakest military forces. Having long focused on waging counterinsurgency campaigns while relying on the United States for its external security, the AFP has one of the lowest budgets in the region—and one of the most extensive coastlines to defend. With a defense budget of only $2.8 billion[66] and forced to deal with a number of insurgencies, including the Islamist Abu Sayyaf and New People's Army, Philippine defense resources have long been stretched thin. The most modern ships in the Philippine navy are three former U.S. *Hamilton*-class Coast Guard cutters. In 2017, however, South Korea completed delivery of 12 TA light attack fighter aircraft to the Philippines. The Philippine air force had possessed no jet fighter aircraft since 2005, when the last of its F-5s were decommissioned. The Duterte government has expressed interest in supplementing its current fleet with a follow-on purchase of 12 more.[67]

Current U.S. Presence in Asia

U.S. Indo-Pacific Command. Established in 1947 as U.S. Pacific Command (PACOM), USINDOPACOM is the oldest and largest of America's unified commands. According to its Web site:

> USINDOPACOM protects and defends, in concert with other U.S. Government agencies, the territory of the United States, its people, and its interests. With allies and partners, USINDOPACOM is committed to enhancing stability in the Asia-Pacific region by promoting security cooperation, encouraging peaceful development, responding to contingencies, deterring aggression, and, when necessary, fighting to win. This approach is based on partnership, presence, and military readiness.[68]

USINDOPACOM's area of responsibility (AOR) includes the expanses of the Pacific, but also Alaska and portions of the Arctic, South Asia, and the Indian Ocean. It includes 36 nations holding more than 50 percent of the world's population, two of the three largest economies, and nine of the 10 smallest; the most populous nation (China); the largest democracy (India); the largest Muslim-majority nation (Indonesia); and the world's smallest republic

(Nauru). The region is a vital driver of the global economy and includes the world's busiest international sea-lanes and nine of its 10 largest ports. By any meaningful measure, the Asia–Pacific is also the most militarized region in the world, with seven of its 10 largest standing militaries and five of its declared nuclear nations.[69]

Under INDOPACOM are a number of component commands, including:

- **U.S. Army Pacific.** USARPAC is the Army's component command in the Pacific. It is comprised of 80,000 soldiers and supplies Army forces as necessary for various global contingencies. It administers (among others) the 25th Infantry Division headquartered in Hawaii, U.S. Army Japan, and U.S. Army Alaska.[70]

- **U.S. Pacific Air Force.** PACAF is responsible for planning and conducting defensive and offensive air operations in the Asia–Pacific region. It has three numbered air forces under its command: 5th Air Force in Japan; 7th Air Force in Korea; and 11th Air Force, headquartered in Alaska. These air forces field two squadrons of F-15s, two squadrons of F-22s, five squadrons of F-16s, and a single squadron of A-10 ground attack aircraft, as well as two squadrons of E-3 early-warning aircraft, tankers, and transports.[71] Other forces that regularly come under PACAF command include B-52, B-1, and B-2 bombers.

- **U.S. Pacific Fleet.** PACFLT normally controls all U.S. naval forces committed to the Pacific, which usually represents 60 percent of the Navy's fleet. It is organized into Seventh Fleet, headquartered in Japan, and Third Fleet, headquartered in California. Seventh Fleet comprises the forward-deployed element of PACFLT and includes the only American carrier strike group (CTF-70) and amphibious group (CTF-76) home-ported abroad, ported at Yokosuka and Sasebo, Japan, respectively. The Third Fleet's AOR spans

The Tyranny of Distance

Steam times are in parentheses.

RUSSIA

Arctic
Ocean

Alaska

Bering
Sea

Gulf of
Alaska

U.S.

40°N

San Diego
6,700 miles
(13–21 days)

CHINA

JAPAN

Tokyo
1,700 miles

Okinawa
1,000 miles (2–3 days)

160°E

180°

160°W

140°W

20°N

Hawaii
5,000 miles
(10–16 days)

South
China
Sea

Guam
1,700 miles
(3–5 days)

0°

Pacific Ocean

1,900 miles *Darwin*

20°S

AUSTRALIA

SOURCE: Heritage Foundation estimates based on data from Shirley A. Kan, "Guam: U.S. Defense Deployments," Congressional Research Service, April 29, 2014, Table 1, https://www.hsdl.org/?view&did=752725 (accessed January 13, 2015).

☎ heritage.org

the West Coast of the United States to the International Date Line and includes the Alaskan coastline and parts of the Arctic. In recent years, this boundary between the two fleets' areas of operation has been blurred under a concept called "Third Fleet Forward." This has eased the involvement of the Third Fleet's five carrier strike groups in the Western Pacific.

Beginning in 2015, the conduct of Freedom of Navigation Operations (FONOPS) that challenge excessive maritime claims, a part of the Navy's mission since 1979, has assumed a higher profile as a result of several well-publicized operations in the South China Sea. Under the Trump Administration, the frequency of these operations has increased significantly.

- **U.S. Marine Forces Pacific.** With its headquarters in Hawaii, MARFORPAC controls elements of the U.S. Marine Corps operating in the Asia–Pacific region. Because of its extensive responsibilities and physical span, MARFORPAC controls two-thirds of Marine Corps forces: the I Marine Expeditionary Force (MEF), centered on the 1st Marine Division, 3rd Marine Air Wing, and 1st Marine Logistics Group, and the III Marine Expeditionary Force, centered on the 3rd Marine Division, 1st Marine Air Wing, and 3rd Marine Logistics Group. The I MEF is headquartered at Camp Pendleton, California, and the III MEF is headquartered on Okinawa, although each has various subordinate elements deployed at any time throughout the Pacific on exercises, maintaining presence, or engaged in other activities. MARFORPAC is responsible for supporting three different commands: It is the U.S. Marine Corps component of USINDOPACOM, provides the Fleet Marine Forces to PACFLT, and provides Marine forces for U.S. Forces Korea (USFK).[72]

- **U.S. Special Operations Command Pacific.** SOCPAC has operational control of various special operations forces, including Navy SEALs; Naval Special Warfare units; Army Special Forces (Green Berets); and Special Operations Aviation units in the Pacific region, including elements in Japan and South Korea. It supports the Pacific Command's Theater Security Cooperation Program as well as other plans and contingency responses. SOCPAC forces support various operations in the region other than warfighting, such as counterdrug operations, counterterrorism training, humanitarian assistance, and demining activities.

- **U.S. Forces Korea and U.S. Eighth Army.** Because of the unique situation on the Korean Peninsula, two subcomponents of USINDOPACOM, U.S. Forces Korea (USFK) and U.S. Eighth Army, are based in Korea. USFK, a joint headquarters led by a four-star U.S. general, is in charge of the various U.S. military elements on the peninsula. U.S. Eighth Army operates in conjunction with USFK as well as with the United Nations presence in the form of United Nations Command.

Other forces, including space capabilities, cyber capabilities, air and sealift assets, and additional combat forces, may be made available to USINDOPACOM depending on requirements and availability.

U.S. Central Command—Afghanistan. Unlike the U.S. forces deployed in Japan and South Korea, there is no permanent force structure committed to Afghanistan; instead, forces rotate through the theater under the direction of USINDOPACOM's counterpart in that region of the world, U.S. Central Command (CENTCOM). As of January 2017, these forces included:

- **Resolute Support Mission,** including U.S. Forces Afghanistan.

- **Special Operations Joint Task Force—Afghanistan.** This includes a Special Forces battalion, based out of Bagram Airfield, and additional allied special operations forces at Kabul.

- **9th Air and Space Expeditionary Task Force.** This includes the 155th Air Expeditionary Wing, providing air support from Bagram Airfield; the 451st Air Expeditionary Group and 455th Expeditionary Operations Group, operating from Kandahar and Bagram Airfields, respectively, providing air support and surveillance operations over various parts of Afghanistan; and the 421st Expeditionary Fighter Squadron, providing close air support from Bagram Airfield.

- **Combined Joint Task Force for Operation Freedom's Sentinel,** centered on Bagram Airfield. This is the main U.S. national support element. It includes seven battalions of infantry, air defense artillery for counter-artillery missions, and explosive ordnance disposal across Afghanistan. It also includes three Army aviation battalions, a combat aviation brigade headquarters, and two additional joint task forces to provide nationwide surveillance support.[73]

- **Five Train, Advise, Assist Commands** in Afghanistan, each of which is a multinational force tasked with improving local capabilities to conduct operations.[74]

Key Infrastructure That Enables Expeditionary Warfighting Capabilities

Any planning for operations in the Pacific will be dominated by the "tyranny of distance." Because of the extensive distances that must be traversed in order to deploy forces, even Air Force units will take one or more days to deploy, and ships measure steaming time in weeks. For instance, a ship sailing at 20 knots requires nearly five days to get from San Diego to Hawaii. From there, it takes a further seven days to get to Guam, seven days to Yokosuka, Japan; and eight days to Okinawa—if ships encounter no interference along the journey.[75]

China's growing anti-access/area denial (A2/AD) capabilities, ranging from an expanding fleet of modern submarines to anti-ship ballistic and cruise missiles, increase the operational risk for deployment of U.S. forces in the event of conflict. China's capabilities not only jeopardize American combat forces that would flow into the theater for initial combat, but also would continue to threaten the logistical support needed to sustain American combat power for the subsequent days, weeks, and months.

American basing structure in the Indo–Pacific region, including access to key allied facilities, is therefore both necessary and increasingly at risk.

American Facilities

Much as in the 20th century, Hawaii remains the linchpin of America's ability to support its position in the Western Pacific. If the United States cannot preserve its facilities in Hawaii, both combat power and sustainability become moot. The United States maintains air and naval bases, communications infrastructure, and logistical support on Oahu and elsewhere in the Hawaiian Islands. Hawaii is also a key site for undersea cables that carry much of the world's communications and data, as well as satellite ground stations.

The American territory of Guam is located 4,600 miles farther west. Obtained from Spain as a result of the Spanish–American War, Guam became a key coaling station for U.S. Navy ships. Seized by Japan in World War II, it was liberated by U.S. forces in 1944 and after the war became an unincorporated, organized territory of the United States. Key U.S. military facilities on Guam include U.S. Naval Base Guam, which houses several attack submarines and possibly a new aircraft carrier berth, and Andersen Air Force Base, one of a handful of facilities that can house B-2 bombers. U.S. task forces can stage out of Apra Harbor, drawing weapons from the Ordnance Annex in the island's South Central Highlands. There is also a communications and data relay facility on the island.

Guam's facilities have improved steadily over the past 20 years. B-2 bombers, for example, began operating from Andersen Air Force Base in 2005.[76] These improvements have been accelerated and expanded even as China's A2/AD capabilities have raised doubts about the ability of the U.S. to sustain operations in the Asian littoral. The concentration of air and naval assets as well as logistical infrastructure, however, makes the island an attractive potential target in the event of conflict. The increasing reach of Chinese and North Korean ballistic missiles reflects this growing vulnerability.

The U.S. military has noncombatant maritime prepositioning ships (MPS), which contain large amounts of military equipment and supplies, in strategic locations from which they can reach areas of conflict relatively quickly as associated U.S. Army or Marine Corps units located elsewhere arrive in the areas. U.S. Navy units on Guam and in Saipan, Commonwealth of the Northern Marianas, support prepositioning ships that can supply Army or Marine Corps units deployed for contingency operations in Asia.

Allied and Friendly Facilities

For the United States, access to bases in Asia has long been a vital part of its ability to support military operations in the region. Even with the extensive aerial refueling and replenishment skills of the U.S. Air Force and U.S. Navy, it is still essential for the United States to retain access to resupply and replenishment facilities, at least in peacetime. The ability of those facilities to survive and function will directly influence the course of any conflict in the Western Pacific region. Moreover, a variety of support functions, including communications, intelligence, and space support, cannot be accomplished without facilities in the region.

At the present time, it would be extraordinarily difficult to maintain maritime domain awareness or space situational awareness without access to facilities in the Asia–Pacific region. The American alliance network is therefore a matter both of political partnership and of access to key facilities on allied soil.

Japan. In Japan, the United States has access to over 100 different facilities, including communications stations, military and dependent housing, fuel and ammunition depots, and weapons and training ranges, in addition to major bases such as air bases at Misawa, Yokota, and Kadena and naval facilities at Yokosuka, Atsugi, and Sasebo. The naval facilities support the USS *Ronald Reagan* carrier strike group (CSG), which is home-ported in Yokosuka, and a Marine Expeditionary Strike Group (ESG) centered on the USS *Wasp*, home-ported at Sasebo. Additionally, the skilled workforce at places like Yokosuka is needed to maintain American forces and repair equipment in time of conflict. Replacing them would take years, if not decades.

This combination of facilities and workforce, in addition to physical location and political support, makes Japan an essential part of any American military response to contingencies in the Western Pacific. Japanese financial support for the American presence also makes these facilities some of the most cost-effective in the world.

The status of one critical U.S. base has been a matter of public debate in Japan for many years. The U.S. Marine Corps' Third Marine Expeditionary Force, based on Okinawa, is the U.S. rapid reaction force in the Pacific. The Marine Air-Ground Task Force, comprised of air, ground, and logistics elements, enables quick and effective response to crises or humanitarian disasters. To improve the political sustainability of U.S. forces by reducing the impact on the local population in that densely populated area, the Marines are relocating some units to Guam and less-populated areas of Okinawa. The latter includes moving a helicopter unit from Futenma to a new facility in a more remote location in northeastern Okinawa. Because of local resistance, construction of the Futenma Replacement Facility at Camp Schwab will not be complete until 2025, but the U.S. and Japanese governments have affirmed their support for the project.

South Korea. The United States also maintains an array of facilities in South Korea, with a larger Army footprint than in Japan, as the United States and South Korea remain focused on deterring North Korean aggression and preparing for any possible North Korean contingencies. The Army maintains four major facilities (which in turn control a number of smaller sites) at Daegu, Yongsan in Seoul, and Camps Red Cloud/Casey and Humphreys. These facilities support the U.S. 2nd Infantry Division, which is based in South Korea. Other key facilities include air bases at Osan and Kunsan and a naval facility at Chinhae near Pusan.

The Philippines. In 1992, The United States ended nearly a century-long presence in the Philippines when it withdrew from its base in Subic Bay as its lease there ended. Clark Air Base had been closed earlier due to the eruption of Mount Pinatubo; the costs of repairing the facility were deemed too high to be worthwhile. In 2014, however, with the growing Chinese assertiveness in the South China Sea, including against Philippine claims such as Mischief Reef (seized in 1995) and Scarborough Shoal (2012), the U.S. and the Philippines negotiated the Enhanced Defense Cooperation Agreement, which will allow for the rotation of American forces through Philippine military bases.

In 2016, the two sides agreed on an initial list of five bases in the Philippines that will be involved. Geographically distributed across the country, they are Antonio Bautista Air Base in Palawaan, closest to the Spratlys; Basa Air Base on the main island of Luzon and closest to the hotly contested Scarborough Shoal; Fort Magsaysay, also on Luzon and the only facility on the list that is not an air base; Lumbia Air Base in Mindanao, where Manila remains in low-intensity combat with Islamist insurgents; and Mactan-Benito Ebuen Air Base in the central Philippines.[77] Work at Basa Air Base is progressing.

It remains unclear precisely which forces would be rotated through the Philippines as a part of this agreement, which in turn affects the kinds of facilities that would be most needed. The base upgrades and deployments pursuant to the EDCA are part of a broader expansion of U.S.–Philippines defense ties, which most recently included the U.S. leaving behind men and matériel at Clark Air Base following annual exercises,[78] as well as joint naval patrols and increased levels of assistance under the Maritime Security Initiative (MSI). Since July 2016, the Duterte government has shed doubt on the future of U.S.–Philippines military cooperation, but it continues to be robust at the operational level.

Singapore. The United States does not have bases in Singapore, but it is allowed access to several key facilities that are essential for supporting American forward presence. Since the closure of its facilities at Subic Bay, the United States has been allowed to operate the principal logistics command for the Seventh Fleet out of the Port of Singapore Authority's Sembawang Terminal. The U.S. Navy also has access to Changi Naval Base, one of the few docks in the world that can handle a 100,000-ton American aircraft carrier. In addition, a small U.S. Air Force contingent operates out of Paya Lebar Air Base to support U.S. Air Force combat units visiting Singapore and Southeast Asia, and Singapore hosts Littoral Combat Ships (LCS) and a rotating squadron of F-16 fighter aircraft.

Australia. A much-discussed element of the "Asia pivot" has been the 2011 agreement to deploy U.S. Marines to Darwin in northern Australia. While planned to amount to 2,500 Marines, the rotations fluctuate and have not yet reached that number. "In its mature state," according to the Australian Department of Defence, "the Marine Rotational Force–Darwin (MRF–D) will be a Marine Air-Ground Task Force...with a variety of aircraft, vehicles and equipment."[79] The Marines do not constitute a permanent presence in Australia, in keeping with Australian sensitivities about permanent American bases on Australian soil.[80] Similarly, the United States jointly staffs the Joint Defence Facility Pine Gap and the Joint Geological and Geophysical Research Station at Alice Springs and has access to the Harold E. Holt Naval Communication Station in western Australia, including the space surveillance radar system there.[81]

Finally, the United States is granted access to a number of facilities in Asian states on a contingency or crisis basis. Thus, U.S. Air Force units transited Thailand's U-Tapao Air Base and Sattahip Naval Base during the first Gulf War and during the Iraq War, but they do not maintain a permanent presence there. Additionally, the U.S. Navy conducts hundreds of port calls throughout the region.

Diego Garcia. The American facilities on the British territory of Diego Garcia are vital to U.S. operations in the Indian Ocean and Afghanistan and provide essential support for operations in the Middle East and East Asia. The island is home to the 12 ships of Maritime Prepositioning Squadron-2 (MPS-2), which can support a Marine brigade and associated

Navy elements for 30 days. Several elements of the U.S. global space surveillance and communications infrastructure, as well as basing facilities for the B-2 bomber, are also on the island.

Conclusion

The Asian strategic environment is extremely expansive, as it includes half the globe and is characterized by a variety of political relationships among states that have wildly varying capabilities. The region includes long-standing American allies with relationships dating back to the beginning of the Cold War as well as recently established states and some long-standing adversaries such as North Korea.

American conceptions of the region must therefore start from the physical limitations imposed by the tyranny of distance. Moving forces within the region (never mind to it) will take time and require extensive strategic lift assets as well as sufficient infrastructure, such as sea and aerial ports of debarkation that can handle American strategic lift assets, and political support. At the same time, the complicated nature of intra-Asian relations, especially unresolved historical and territorial issues, means that the United States, unlike Europe, cannot necessarily count on support from all of its regional allies in responding to any given contingency.

Scoring the Asia Operating Environment

As with the operating environments of Europe and the Middle East, we assessed the characteristics of Asia as they would pertain to supporting U.S. military operations. Various aspects of the region facilitate or inhibit America's ability to conduct military operations to defend its vital national interests against threats. Our assessment of the operating environment utilized a five-point scale, ranging from "very poor" to "excellent" conditions and covering four regional characteristics of greatest relevance to the conduct of military operations:

1. **Very Poor.** Significant hurdles exist for military operations. Physical infrastructure is insufficient or nonexistent, and the region is politically unstable. The U.S. military is poorly placed or absent, and alliances are nonexistent or diffuse.

2. **Unfavorable.** A challenging operating environment for military operations is marked by inadequate infrastructure, weak alliances, and recurring political instability. The U.S. military is inadequately placed in the region.

3. **Moderate.** A neutral to moderately favorable operating environment is characterized by adequate infrastructure, a moderate alliance structure, and acceptable levels of regional political stability. The U.S. military is adequately placed in the region.

4. **Favorable.** A favorable operating environment includes good infrastructure, strong alliances, and a stable political environment. The U.S. military is well placed in the region for future operations.

5. **Excellent.** An extremely favorable operating environment includes well-established and well-maintained infrastructure, strong and capable allies, and a stable political environment. The U.S. military is exceptionally well placed to defend U.S. interests.

The key regional characteristics consisted of:

a. **Alliances.** Alliances are important for interoperability and collective defense, as allies would be more likely to lend support to U.S. military operations.

Various indicators provide insight into the strength or health of an alliance. These include whether the U.S. trains regularly with countries in the region, has good interoperability with the forces of an ally, and shares intelligence with nations in the region.

b. **Political Stability.** Political stability brings predictability for military planners when considering such things as transit, basing, and overflight rights for U.S. military operations. The overall degree of political stability indicates whether U.S. military actions would be hindered or enabled and considers, for example, whether transfers of power in the region are generally peaceful and whether there have been any recent instances of political instability in the region.

c. **U.S. Military Positioning.** Having military forces based or equipment and supplies staged in a region greatly facilitates the ability of the United States to respond to crises and, presumably, achieve successes in critical "first battles" more quickly. Being routinely present in a region also assists in maintaining familiarity with its characteristics and the various actors that might act to assist or thwart U.S. actions. With this in mind, we

assessed whether or not the U.S. military was well positioned in the region. Again, indicators included bases, troop presence, prepositioned equipment, and recent examples of military operations (including training and humanitarian) launched from the region.

d. **Infrastructure.** Modern, reliable, and suitable infrastructure is essential to military operations. Airfields, ports, rail lines, canals, and paved roads enable the U.S. to stage, launch operations from, and logistically sustain combat operations. We combined expert knowledge of regions with publicly available information on critical infrastructure to arrive at our overall assessment of this metric.[82]

For Asia, we arrived at these average scores:

- Alliances: **4—Favorable**

- Political Stability: 4—**Favorable**

- U.S. Military Positioning: **4—Favorable**

- Infrastructure: **4—Favorable**

Aggregating to a regional score of: **Favorable**

Operating Environment: Asia

	VERY POOR	UNFAVORABLE	MODERATE	FAVORABLE	EXCELLENT
Alliances				✓	
Political Stability				✓	
U.S. Military Posture				✓	
Infrastructure				✓	
OVERALL				✓	

Endnotes

1. U.S. Department of Commerce, Bureau of Economic Analysis, *International Trade & Investment: U.S. International Trade in Goods and Services*, August 3, 2018, https://www.bea.gov/data/intl-trade-investment/international-trade-goods-and-services (accessed August 20, 2018).

2. Shari A. Allen and Alexis N. Grimm, *U.S. International Services: Trade in Services in 2016 and Services Supplied Through Affiliates in 2015*, U.S. Department of Commerce, Bureau of Economic Analysis, *Survey of Current Business*, October 2017, p. 4, https://www.bea.gov/scb/pdf/2017/10-October/1017-international-services.pdf (accessed July 24, 2018).

3. "Aspiring sincerely to an international peace based on justice and order, the Japanese people forever renounce war as a sovereign right of the nation and the threat or use of force as means of settling international disputes. In order to accomplish the aim of the preceding paragraph, land, sea, and air forces, as well as other war potential, will never be maintained. The right of belligerency of the state will not be recognized." Constitution of Japan, Article 9, promulgated November 3, 1946, came into effect May 3, 1947, http://japan.kantei.go.jp/constitution_and_government_of_japan/constitution_e.html (accessed August 10, 2017).

4. Purnendra Jain, "A New High: India–Japan Defense Links," Lowy Institute, *The Interpreter*, April 17, 2018, https://www.lowyinstitute.org/the-interpreter/new-high-india-japan-defence-links (accessed July 24, 2018).

5. U.S. Forces, Japan, "About USFJ," http://www.usfj.mil/AboutUSFJ.aspx (accessed June 1, 2018).

6. Emma Chanlett-Avery, Mark E. Manyin, Rebecca M. Nelson, Brock R. Williams, and Taishu Yamakawa, "Japan–U.S. Relations: Issues for Congress," Congressional Research Service *Report for Members and Committees of Congress*, February 16, 2017, p. 23, https://mansfieldfdn.org/mfdn2011/wp-content/uploads/2014/02/USJ.Feb14.RL33436.pdf (accessed July 24, 2018).

7. K. J. Kwon, "South Korea and Japan Put Military Intelligence Pact on Hold After Outcry," CNN, updated June 29, 2012, http://www.cnn.com/2012/06/29/world/asia/south-korea-japan-pact/index.html (accessed July 24, 2018).

8. U.S. Department of Defense, Defense Manpower Data Center, DoD Personnel, Workforce Reports & Publications, Military and Civilian Personnel by Service/Agency by State/Country (Updated Quarterly), "Number of Military and DoD Appropriated Fund (APF) and Civilian Personnel Permanently Assigned By Duty Location and Service/Component As of March 1, 2018," https://www.dmdc.osd.mil/appj/dwp/rest/download?fileName=DMDC_Website_Location_Report_1803.xlsx&groupName=milRegionCountry (accessed August 10, 2017). The total includes 24,915 "Active Duty" and 316 "National Guard/Reserve" personnel. If the 2,956 in the "APF DOD Civilian" category are added, the total comes to 28,187.

9. For further details, see Bruce Klingner, "The U.S. and South Korea Should Focus on Improving Alliance Capabilities Rather Than the OPCON Transition," Heritage Foundation *Backgrounder* No. 2935, August 7, 2014, https://www.heritage.org/global-politics/report/the-us-and-south-korea-should-focus-improving-alliance-capabilities-rather.

10. Mark E. Manyin, Emma Chanlett-Avery, Mary Beth D. Nikitin, Brock R. Williams, and Jonathan R. Corrado, "U.S.–South Korea Relations," Congressional Research Service *Report for Members and Committees of Congress*, May 23, 2017, p. 23, https://fas.org/sgp/crs/row/R41481.pdf (accessed August 14, 2017).

11. U.S. Department of Defense, Office of Inspector General; U.S. Department of State, Office of Inspector General; and U.S. Agency for International Development, Office of Inspector General, *Overseas Contingency Operations: Operation Inherent Resolve, Operation Pacific Eagle–Philippines*, Lead Inspector General Report to the United States Congress, October 1, 2017–December 31, 2017, pp. 99–100, https://mronline.org/wp-content/uploads/2018/02/FY2018_LIG_OCO_OIR_Q1_12222017_2.pdf (accessed July 24, 2018).

12. Admiral Harry B. Harris Jr., U.S. Navy, Commander, U.S. Pacific Command, statement "On U.S. Pacific Command Posture" before the Committee on Armed Services, U.S. House of Representatives, February 14, 2018, p. 41, https://docs.house.gov/meetings/AS/AS00/20180214/106847/HHRG-115-AS00-Wstate-HarrisJrH-20180214.pdf (accessed July 24, 2018).

13. The White House, "Fact Sheet: United States–Philippines Bilateral Relations," April 28, 2014, http://www.whitehouse.gov/the-press-office/2014/04/28/fact-sheet-united-states-philippines-bilateral-relations (accessed July 28, 2018).

14. Prashanth Parameswaran, "Why the New US–Philippines Military Pact's First Project Launch Matters," *The Diplomat*, April 19, 2018, https://thediplomat.com/2018/04/why-the-new-us-philippines-military-pacts-first-project-launch-matters/ (accessed July 24, 2018).

15. Ben Dolven, Mark E. Manyin, and Shirley A. Kan, "Maritime Territorial Disputes in East Asia: Issues for Congress," Congressional Research Service *Report for Members and Committees of Congress*, May 14, 2014, p. 31, https://fas.org/sgp/crs/row/R42930.pdf (accessed August 10, 2017).

16. Walter Lohman, "Scarborough Shoal and Safeguarding American Interests," Heritage Foundation *Issue Brief* No. 3603, May 14, 2012, p. 2, http://www.heritage.org/research/reports/2012/05/south-china-sea-dispute-between-china-and-the-philippines-safeguarding-americas-interests.

17. Seth Robson, "US–Philippines Relations on an Uptick Ahead of Annual Balikatan Drills," *Stars and Stripes*, April 24, 2017, https://www.stripes.com/news/us-philippines-relations-on-an-uptick-ahead-of-annual-balikatan-drills-1.465104#.WSXN72jyu70 (accessed August 10, 2017).

18. News release, "2012 Joint Vision Statement for the Thai–U.S. Defense Alliance," U.S. Department of Defense, November 15, 2012, http://archive.defense.gov/releases/release.aspx?releaseid=15685 (accessed July 25, 2018).

19. Emma Chanlett-Avery, Ben Dolven, and Wil Mackey, "Thailand: Background and U.S. Relations," Congressional Research Service *Report for Members and Committees of Congress*, July 29, 2015, p. 8, http://fas.org/sgp/crs/row/RL32593.pdf (accessed July 24, 2018).

20. Association of Southeast Asian Nations, *ASEAN Community in Figures (ACIF) 2016*, p. 18, http://www.aseanstats.org/wp-content/uploads/2017/01/25Content-ACIF.pdf (accessed August 10, 2017).

21. Phuong Nguyen and Brittany Billingsley, "China's Growing Military-to-Military Engagement with Thailand & Myanmar," Center for Strategic and International Studies, Asia Program, cogitASIA blog, September 12, 2013, http://cogitasia.com/chinas-growing-military-to-military-engagement-with-thailand-and-myanmar/ (accessed August 10, 2017); Patpicha Tanakasempipat and Jutarat Skulpichetrat, "China, Thailand Joint Air Force Exercise Highlights Warming Ties," Reuters, November 14, 2015, https://uk.reuters.com/article/uk-china-thailand-military-idUKKBN0TD0CB20151124 (accessed July 24, 2018).

22. Mike Yeo, "Thailand to Buy More Chinese Tanks, Reportedly for $58M," *Defense News*, April 4, 2017, http://www.defensenews.com/articles/thailand-to-buy-more-chinese-tanks-reportedly-for-58m (accessed August 10, 2017); Reuters, "Thailand in $67-M Deal to Buy Armored Personnel Carriers from China," June 14, 2017, https://www.reuters.com/article/us-thailand-china-defence-idUSKBN1950IH (accessed July 24, 2018).

23. Reuters, "Thailand Approves $393-Mln Purchase of Chinese Submarines," April 24, 2017, http://in.reuters.com/article/thailand-china-idINKBN17Q15O (accessed July 24, 2018); Prashanth Parameswaran, "When Will Thailand's First China Submarine Arrive?" *The Diplomat*, January 31, 2017, http://thediplomat.com/2017/01/will-thailand-seal-its-china-submarine-deal-this-year/ (accessed August 10, 2017).

24. Panu Wongcha-um, "Thailand Plans Joint Arms Factory with China," Reuters, November 16, 2017, https://www.reuters.com/article/us-thailand-defence/thailand-plans-joint-arms-factory-with-china-idUSKBN1DG0U4 (accessed July 24, 2018).

25. Australian Government, Department of Defence, "United States Force Posture Initiatives in Australia," http://defence.gov.au/usfpi/ (accessed July 24, 2018).

26. Media release, "Expanded Force Posture Initiatives in Northern Australia," Australian Government, Department of Defence, March 23, 2018, https://www.minister.defence.gov.au/minister/marise-payne/media-releases/expanded-force-posture-initiatives-northern-australia (accessed July 24, 2018).

27. Rob Taylor, "Darwin Evolves: U.S. Military Turns Australian Outpost into Asia Launchpad," *The Wall Street Journal*, May 24, 2018, https://www.wsj.com/articles/darwin-evolves-u-s-military-turns-australian-outpost-into-asia-launchpad-1527154203 (accessed July 11, 2018).

28. "USAF F-22s Arrive in Australia for Joint Training Exercises with the RAAF," *Australian Aviation*, February 10, 2017, http://australianaviation.com.au/2017/02/usaf-f-22s-head-to-australia-for-joint-training-exercises-with-the-raaf/ (accessed July 24, 2018); Andrew Greene, "Long-Range Heavy Bombers Could Be Based in Australia, US General Reveals," ABC News, updated March 8, 2016, http://www.abc.net.au/news/2016-03-08/long-range-bombers-could-rotate-through-nt-general-says/7231098 (accessed August 10, 2017).

29. Gene Blevins, "Canada Formalizes Joint Space Operations with Australia, U.S. and U.K.," *The Globe and Mail*, September 22, 2014, updated May 12, 2018, https://www.theglobeandmail.com/news/national/canada-formalizes-joint-space-operations-with-australia-us-and-uk/article20735843/ (accessed July 24, 2018).

30. Bruce Vaughn and Thomas Lum, "Australia: Background and U.S. Relations," Congressional Research Service *Report for Members and Committees of Congress*, December 14, 2015, pp. 1–3, https://fas.org/sgp/crs/row/RL33010.pdf (accessed July 24, 2018).

31. Stephen Smith, Minister of Defence and Deputy Leader of the House, Ministerial Statement on "Full Knowledge and Concurrence," Commonwealth of Australia, Parliamentary Debates, House of Representatives, June 26, 2013, pp. 7071–7075, http://parlinfo.aph.gov.au/parlInfo/genpdf/chamber/hansardr/4d60a662-a538-4e48-b2d8-9e97b8276c77/0016/hansard_frag.pdf;fileType=application%2Fpdf (accessed July 24, 2018).

32. U.S. Department of State, "Fact Sheet: U.S. Defense Trade Cooperation Treaties with the United Kingdom and Australia," September 30, 2010, https://2009-2017.state.gov/r/pa/prs/ps/2010/09/148478.htm (accessed July 24, 2018).

33. Emma Chanlett-Avery, "Singapore: Background and U.S. Relations," Congressional Research Service *Report for Congress*, July 26, 2013, pp. 3–4, https://www.fas.org/sgp/crs/row/RS20490.pdf (accessed July 24, 2018).

34. News release, "Carter, Singapore Defense Minister Sign Enhanced Defense Cooperation Agreement," U.S. Department of Defense, December 7, 2015, https://www.defense.gov/News/Article/Article/633243/carter-singapore-defense-minister-sign-enhanced-defense-cooperation-agreement/ (accessed July 24, 2018).

35. "Joint Statement by the United States of America and the Republic of Singapore," The White House, October 24, 2017, https://sg.usembassy.gov/remarks-president-trump-prime-minister-lee-singapore-joint-statements-october-23-2017/ (accessed July 24, 2018).

36. See "Text of the Wellington Declaration," November 5, 2005, http://usnzcouncil.org/us-nz-issues/wellington-declaration/ (accessed July 25, 2018), and "Text of the Washington Declaration on Defense Cooperation Between the Department of Defense of the United States of America and the Ministry of Defense of New Zealand and the New Zealand Defense Force," June 19, 2012, http://usnzcouncil.org/us-nz-issues/washington-declaration/ (accessed July 25, 2018).

37. Nick Simeone, "U.S., New Zealand Announce Expanded Defense Cooperation," U.S. Department of Defense, October 28, 2013, http://archive.defense.gov/news/newsarticle.aspx?id=121016 (accessed August 10, 2017).

38. David B. Larter, "In Port Visit, New Zealand and U.S. Seek to Bolster Military Ties," *Navy Times*, July 22, 2016, http://www.navytimes.com/story/military/2016/07/22/port-visit-new-zealand-and-us-seek-bolster-military-ties/87450022/ (accessed August 10, 2017).

39. Associated Press, "US Warship to Visit New Zealand as USS Sampson's Arrival Ends Stalemate on Nuclear Vessels," ABC News, October 18, 2016, http://www.abc.net.au/news/2016-10-18/new-zealand-to-end-stalemate-on-us-warships/7943252 (accessed August 10, 2017).

40. Taiwan Relations Act, Public Law 96-8, 96th Cong., January 1, 1979, 22 U.S.C. §§ 3301–3316, https://www.ait.org.tw/our-relationship/policy-history/key-u-s-foreign-policy-documents-region/taiwan-relations-act/ (accessed August 10, 2017).

41. Shirley A. Kan, "China/Taiwan: Evolution of the 'One China' Policy—Key Statements from Washington, Beijing, and Taipei," Congressional Research Service *Report for Members and Committees of Congress*, October 10, 2014, pp. 43–44, https://www.fas.org/sgp/crs/row/RL30341.pdf (accessed August 10, 2017). Emphasis in original.

42. Aaron Mehta, "New US–Vietnam Agreement Shows Growth, Challenges," *Defense News*, June 1, 2015, http://www.defensenews.com/story/defense/policy-budget/budget/2015/06/01/us-vietnam-joint-vision-statement-signed-in-hanoi/28291963/ (accessed August 10, 2017).

43. Jon Grevatt, "Vietnam to Acquire USCG Cutter," Jane's 360, April 21, 2017, http://www.janes.com/article/69742/vietnam-to-acquire-uscg-cutter (accessed August 10, 2017).

44. U.S. Indo-Pacific Command, "Joint Statement: Between the United States of America and the Socialist Republic of Vietnam," May 23, 2016, http://www.pacom.mil/Media/News/News-Article-View/Article/779376/joint-statement-between-the-united-states-of-america-and-the-socialist-republic/ (accessed July 24, 2018).

45. U.S. Embassy and Consulate in Vietnam, "The United States Transfers Six Metal Shark Patrol Boats to Vietnam," March 29, 2018, https://vn.usembassy.gov/prC3292018/ (accessed July 24, 2018).

46. Ian E. Rinehart, "Malaysia: Background and U.S. Relations," Congressional Research Service *Report for Members and Committees of Congress*, November 19, 2015, p. 15, https://www.fas.org/sgp/crs/row/R43505.pdf (accessed August 10, 2017).

47. "Joint Statement for Enhancing the Comprehensive Partnership Between the United States of America and Malaysia," The White House, September 13, 2017, https://www.whitehouse.gov/briefings-statements/joint-statement-enhancing-comprehensive-partnership-united-states-america-malaysia/ (accessed July 24, 2018).

48. Prashanth Parameswaran, "A First: Malaysia to Deploy Warship for RIMPAC 2018," *The Diplomat*, April 20, 2018, https://thediplomat.com/2018/04/a-first-malaysia-to-deploy-warship-for-rimpac-2018/ (accessed July 11, 2018).

49. Admiral Harry B. Harris Jr., U.S. Navy, Commander, U.S. Pacific Command, statement "On U.S. Pacific Command Posture" before the Committee on Armed Services, U.S. House of Representatives, February 14, 2018, pp. 43–44, https://docs.house.gov/meetings/AS/AS00/20180214/106847/HHRG-115-AS00-Wstate-HarrisJrH-20180214.pdf (accessed July 24, 2018).

50. Alex Horton, "Secretary Mattis Seeks Ties with Once-Brutal Indonesia Special Forces Unit, with an Eye on China," *The Washington Post*, January 23, 2018, https://www.washingtonpost.com/news/checkpoint/wp/2018/01/23/secretary-mattis-seeks-ties-with-once-brutal-indonesia-special-forces-unit-with-an-eye-on-china/?utm_term=.a9724f6e0695 (accessed July 24, 2018).

51. "Fact Sheet: U.S. Building Maritime Capacity in Southeast Asia," The White House, November 17, 2015, https://www.whitehouse.gov/the-press-office/2015/11/17/fact-sheet-us-building-maritime-capacity-southeast-asia (accessed July 24, 2018).

52. Prashanth Parameswaran, "US Kicks Off New Maritime Security Initiative for Southeast Asia," *The Diplomat*, April 10, 2016, http://thediplomat.com/2016/04/us-kicks-off-new-maritime-security-initiative-for-southeast-asia/ (accessed August 26, 2016).

53. U.S. Department of Defense, *Enhancing Security and Stability in Afghanistan*, December 2016, p. 33, https://www.defense.gov/Portals/1/Documents/pubs/Afghanistan-1225-Report-December-2016.pdf (accessed August 10, 2017).

54. North Atlantic Treaty Organization, Resolute Support Mission, "Resolute Support Mission (RSM): Key Facts and Figures," May 2018 https://www.nato.int/nato_static_fl2014/assets/pdf/pdf_2018_05/20180502_2018-05-RSM-Placemat.pdf (accessed July 24, 2018).

55. "Remarks by President [Donald] Trump on the Strategy in Afghanistan and South Asia," Fort Myer, Arlington, Virginia, August 21, 2017, https://www.whitehouse.gov/the-press-office/2017/08/21/remarks-president-trump-strategy-afghanistan-and-south-asia (accessed September 8, 2017).

56. North Atlantic Treaty Organization, Resolute Support Mission, "Resolute Support Mission (RSM): Key Facts and Figures."

57. Jeff M. Smith, Twitter Post, November 28, 2017, 9:10 AM, https://t.co/YpJSCLfhck (accessed July 25, 2018).

58. Rosie Perper, "Nikki Haley Accuses Pakistan of Playing 'Double Game' with the US, Vows to Withhold $255 Million in Aid," *Business Insider*, January 2, 2018, https://www.businessinsider.com/us-to-withhold-255-million-in-aid-to-pakistan-2018-1 (accessed July 26, 2018), and Zalmay Khalilzad, "It's Time to End Pakistan's Double Game," *The National Interest*, January 3, 2018, https://nationalinterest.org/feature/its-time-end-pakistans-double-game-23919 (accessed July 26, 2018).

59. "Remarks by President [Donald] Trump on the Strategy in Afghanistan and South Asia."

60. Vivek Raghuvanshi, "Trump Administration Reaffirms India as Major Defense Partner," *Defense News*, April 19, 2017, http://www.defensenews.com/articles/trump-administration-reaffirms-india-as-major-defense-partner (accessed August 10, 2017).

61. International Institute for Strategic Studies, *The Military Balance 2018: The Annual Assessment of Global Military Capabilities and Defence Economics* (London: Routledge, 2018), pp. 160–165 and 270–274.

62. Ibid., pp. 108–209 and 278–279.

63. Marie Yamaguchi, "Japan to Buy Aegis Ashore Missile Defense Systems," *Defense News*, December 19, 2017, https://www.defensenews.com/land/2017/12/19/japan-to-buy-aegis-ashore-missile-defense-systems/ (accessed July 11, 2018).

64. Stockholm International Peace Research Institute, "Military Expenditure by Country, in Constant (2016) US$ m., 1998–2008," 2018, https://www.sipri.org/sites/default/files/1_Data%20for%20all%20countries%20from%201988%E2%80%932017%20in%20constant%20%282016%29%20USD.pdf (accessed July 25, 2018).

65. International Institute for Strategic Studies, *The Military Balance 2018*, pp. 298–299.

66. RG Cruz, "House Ratifies P3.7-Trillion 2018 Budget," ABS-CBN News, December 12, 2017, http://news.abs-cbn.com/news/12/12/17/house-ratifies-p37-trillion-2018-budget (accessed July 25, 2018).

67. Jun Hyun-Suk, "Philippines President Visits Korea," *The Chosunilbo*, June 4, 2018, http://english.chosun.com/site/data/html_dir/2018/06/04/2018060401451.html (accessed July 11, 2018).

68. U.S. Indo–Pacific Command, "About USINDOPACOM," http://www.pacom.mil/About-USINDOPACOM/ (accessed July 25, 2018).

69. Ibid. and U.S. Pacific Command, "USPACOM Strategy," https://jsou.blackboard.com/bbcswebdav/library/Library%20Content/JSOU%20References/SOPC/USPACOM%20Strategy.pdf (accessed August 27, 2016).

70. United States Army, U.S. Army Pacific, "About Us," https://www.usarpac.army.mil/about.asp (accessed June 5, 2018).

71. International Institute for Strategic Studies, *The Military Balance 2018*, pp. 298–299.

72. U.S. Marine Corps, "U.S. Marine Corps Forces, Pacific (MARFORPAC)," https://www.globalsecurity.org/military/agency/usmc/marforpac.htm (accessed July 25, 2018).

73. Wesley Morgan, "Afghanistan Order of Battle: Coalition Combat and Advisory Forces in Afghanistan," Institute for the Study of War, January 1, 2017, p. 1, http://www.understandingwar.org/sites/default/files/ORBAT%20January%202017.pdf (accessed August 20, 2018).

74. U.S. Central Command, "Resolute Support," http://www.centcom.mil/operations-and-exercises/resolute-support/ (accessed August 11, 2017).

75. These steaming times were calculated using Marine Vessel Traffic, "Sea Distance Calculator," 2016, http://www.marinevesseltraffic.com/2013/07/distance-calculator.html (accessed August 27, 2016).

76. Airforce-Technology.com, "B-2 Spirit Stealth Bomber, United States of America," http://www.airforce-technology.com/projects/b2/ (accessed August 11, 2017).

77. News release, "Sixth United States–Philippines Bilateral Strategic Dialogue Joint Statement," U.S. Department of State, March 18, 2016, https://2009-2017.state.gov/r/pa/prs/ps/2016/03/254833.htm (accessed July 27, 2016).

78. Eric Haun, "US Ramps up Military Presence in the Philippines," Marine Link, April 14, 2016, http://www.marinelink.com/news/military-presence-ramps408137.aspx (accessed July 27, 2016).

79. Australian Government, Department of Defence, "United States Force Posture Initiatives in Australia."

80. Wyatt Olson, "Deal to Bring More US Assets to Australia," *Stars and Stripes*, June 21, 2014, http://www.military.com/daily-news/2014/06/21/deal-likely-to-bring-more-us-military-assets-to-australia.html (accessed August 23, 2016).

81. Smith, Ministerial Statement on "Full Knowledge and Concurrence."

82. For an example of a very accessible database, see World Bank, "Logistics Performance Index: Quality of Trade and Transport-Related Infrastructure (1=Low to 5=High)," http://data.worldbank.org/indicator/LP.LPI.INFR.XQ (accessed August 11, 2017).

Conclusion: Scoring the Global Operating Environment

The United States is a global power with global security interests, and threats to those interests can emerge from any region. Consequently, the U.S. military must be ready to operate in any region when called upon to do so and must account for the range of conditions that it might encounter when planning for potential military operations. This informs its decisions about the type and amount of equipment it purchases (especially to transport and sustain the force); the location or locations from which it might operate; and how easy (or not) it will be to project and sustain combat power when engaged with the enemy.

Aggregating the three regional scores provides a Global Operating Environment score.

Global Operating Environment:

FAVORABLE

Global Operating Environment

	VERY POOR	UNFAVORABLE	MODERATE	FAVORABLE	EXCELLENT
Europe				✓	
Middle East			✓		
Asia				✓	
OVERALL				✓	

Scoring of the Global Security Environment remained "favorable" for the *2019 Index of U.S. Military Strength*, although scores increased for Asia and the Middle East in the political stability subcategory.

Global Operating Environment

VERY POOR	UNFAVORABLE	MODERATE	**FAVORABLE**	EXCELLENT

The Middle East Operating Environment remained "moderate" in the *2019 Index*. However, the score for regional political stability rose to "unfavorable" from "poor." This shift reflects the continued decline of ISIS, the Assad regime's consolidation of control over much of Syria, the ebbing flow of refugees out of Syria, and a common regional commitment to counter the destabilizing influence of Iran and its proxies.

The Europe Operating Environment did not see categorical changes in any of its scores and remains "favorable." The migrant crisis, economic sluggishness, and political fragmentation increase the potential for instability, but the region remains generally stable and friendly to U.S. interests.

Overall scoring for the Asia Operating Environment remained at "favorable" from the *2018 Index* to the *2019 Index*. The political stability score returned to "favorable" following the conclusion of South Korea's presidential election.

Threats to U.S. Vital Interests

Assessing Threats to U.S. Vital Interests

The United States is a global power with global interests. Scaling its military power to threats requires judgments with regard to the importance and priority of those interests, whether the use of force is the most appropriate and effective way to address the threats to those interests, and how much and what types of force are needed to defeat such threats.

This *Index* focuses on three fundamental, vital national interests:

- Defense of the homeland;

- Successful conclusion of a major war that has the potential to destabilize a region of critical interest to the U.S.; and

- Preservation of freedom of movement within the global commons: the sea, air, and outer space domains through which the world conducts business.

The geographical focus of the threats in these areas is further divided into three broad regions: Asia, Europe, and the Middle East.

This is not to say that these are America's only interests. Among many others, the U.S. has an interest in the growth of economic freedom in trade and investment, the observance of internationally recognized human rights, and the alleviation of human suffering beyond our borders. None of these interests, however, can be addressed principally and effectively by the use of military force, nor would threats to these interests result in material damage to the foregoing vital national interests. These additional American interests, however important

they may be, therefore are not used in this assessment of the adequacy of current U.S. military power.

Throughout this *Index*, we reference two public sources as a mechanism with which to check our work against that of other recognized professional organizations in the field of threat analysis: *The Military Balance*, published annually by the London-based International Institute for Strategic Studies,[1] and the annual *Worldwide Threat Assessment of the US Intelligence Community* (WWTA).[2] The latter serves as a reference point produced by the U.S. government against which each threat assessment in this *Index* was compared. We note any differences between assessments in this *Index* and the work of the two primary references in summary comments.

The juxtaposition of our detailed, reviewed analysis against both *The Military Balance* and the WWTA revealed two stark limitations in these external sources.

- *First, The Military Balance* is an excellent, widely consulted source, but it is only a count of military hardware without context in terms of equipment capability, maintenance and readiness, training, manpower, integration of services, doctrine, or the behavior of competitors— those that threaten the national interests of the U.S. as defined in this *Index*.

- *Second*, the WWTA omits many threats, and its analysis of those that it does address is limited. Moreover, it does not reference underlying strategic dynamics

Threat Categories

Behavior	HOSTILE	AGGRESSIVE	TESTING	ASSERTIVE	BENIGN
Capability	FORMIDABLE	GATHERING	CAPABLE	ASPIRATIONAL	MARGINAL

that are key to the evaluation of threats and that may be more predictive of future threats than is a simple extrapolation of current events.

We suspect that this is a consequence of the U.S. intelligence community's withholding from public view its very sensitive assessments, which are derived from classified sources and/or result from analysis of unclassified, publicly available documents, with the resulting synthesized insights becoming classified by virtue of what they reveal about U.S. determinations and concerns. Given the need to avoid compromising sources, methods of collection, and national security findings, such a policy is understandable, but it also causes the WWTA's threat assessments to be of limited value to policymakers, the public, and analysts working outside of the government. Perhaps surprisingly, The Heritage Foundation's *Index of U.S. Military Strength* may actually serve as a useful correction to the systemic deficiencies that we found in these open sources.

Measuring or categorizing a threat is problematic because there is no absolute reference that can be used in assigning a quantitative score. Two fundamental aspects of threats, however, are germane to this *Index*: the threatening entity's desire or intent to achieve its objective and its physical ability to do so. Physical ability is the easier of the two to assess; intent is quite difficult. A useful surrogate for intent is observed behavior, because this is where intent becomes manifest through action. Thus, a provocative, belligerent pattern of behavior that seriously threatens U.S. vital interests would be very worrisome. Similarly, a comprehensive ability to accomplish objectives even in the face of U.S. military power would cause serious concern for U.S. policymakers, while

weak or very limited abilities would lessen U.S. concerns even if an entity behaved provocatively vis-à-vis U.S. interests.

Each categorization used in the *Index* conveys a word picture of how troubling a threat's behavior and set of capabilities have been during the assessed year. The five ascending categories for observed behavior are:

* Benign,

* Assertive,

* Testing,

* Aggressive, and

* Hostile.

The five ascending categories for physical capability are:

* Marginal,

* Aspirational,

* Capable,

* Gathering, and

* Formidable.

These characterizations—behavior and capability—form two halves of an overall assessment of the threats to U.S. vital interests.

As noted, the following assessments are arranged by region (Europe, Middle East, and Asia) to correspond with the flow of the chapter on operating environments and then by U.S. vital interest (threat posed by an actor to the U.S. homeland, potential for regional war, and freedom of global commons) within each region. Each actor is then discussed in terms of how and to what extent its behavior and physical capabilities posed a challenge to U.S. interests in the assessed year.

Endnotes

1. International Institute for Strategic Studies, *The Military Balance 2014: The Annual Assessment of Global Military Capabilities and Defence Economics* (London: Routledge, 2014); *The Military Balance 2015: The Annual Assessment of Global Military Capabilities and Defence Economics* (London: Routledge, 2015); *The Military Balance 2016: The Annual Assessment of Global Military Capabilities and Defence Economics* (London: Routledge, 2016); *The Military Balance 2017: The Annual Assessment of Global Military Capabilities and Defence Economics* (London: Routledge, 2017); and *The Military Balance 2018: The Annual Assessment of Global Military Capabilities and Defence Economics* (London: Routledge, 2018).

2. James R. Clapper, Director of National Intelligence, "Worldwide Threat Assessment of the US Intelligence Community," statement before the Select Committee on Intelligence, U.S. Senate, January 29, 2014, http://www.dni.gov/files/documents/Intelligence%20Reports/2014%20WWTA%20%20SFR_SSCI_29_Jan.pdf; James R. Clapper, Director of National Intelligence, "Worldwide Threat Assessment of the US Intelligence Community," statement before the Committee on Armed Services, U.S. Senate, February 26, 2015, http://www.armed-services.senate.gov/imo/media/doc/Clapper_02-26-15.pdf; James R. Clapper, Director of National Intelligence, "Worldwide Threat Assessment of the US Intelligence Community," statement before the Committee on Armed Services, U.S. Senate, February 9, 2016, https://www.armed-services.senate.gov/imo/media/doc/Clapper_02-09-16.pdf; Daniel R. Coats, Director of National Intelligence, "Worldwide Threat Assessment of the US Intelligence Community," statement before the Select Committee on Intelligence, U.S. Senate, May 11, 2017, https://www.dni.gov/files/documents/Newsroom/Testimonies/SSCI%20Unclassified%20SFR%20-%20Final.pdf; and Daniel R. Coats, Director of National Intelligence, "Worldwide Threat Assessment of the US Intelligence Community," statement before the Select Committee on Intelligence, U.S. Senate, February 13, 2018, https://www.dni.gov/files/documents/Newsroom/Testimonies/2018-ATA---Unclassified-SSCI.pdf.

Europe

Russia remains an acute and formidable threat to the U.S. and its interests in Europe. From the Arctic to the Baltics, Ukraine, the South Caucasus, and increasingly the Mediterranean Sea, Russia continues to foment instability in Europe. Despite economic problems, Russia continues to prioritize the rebuilding of its military and funding for its military operations abroad. Russia's military and political antagonism toward the United States continues unabated, and its efforts to undermine U.S. institutions and the NATO alliance are serious and troubling. Russia uses its energy position in Europe along with espionage, cyberattacks, and information warfare to exploit vulnerabilities and seeks to drive wedges into the transatlantic alliance and undermine people's faith in government and societal institutions.

Overall, Russia has significant conventional and nuclear capabilities and remains the top threat to European security. Its aggressive stance in a number of theaters, including the Balkans, Georgia, Syria, and Ukraine, continues both to encourage destabilization and to threaten U.S. interests.

Russian Military Capabilities. According to the International Institute for Strategic Studies (IISS), among the key weapons in Russia's inventory are 313 intercontinental ballistic missiles; 2,780 main battle tanks; and more than 5,140 armored infantry fighting vehicles, more than 6,100 armored personnel carriers, and more than 4,328 pieces of artillery. The navy has one aircraft carrier; 62 submarines (including 13 ballistic missile submarines); five cruisers; 15 destroyers; 13 frigates; and 100 patrol and coastal combatants. The air force has 1,176 combat-capable aircraft. The IISS counts 280,000 members of the army. Russia also has a total reserve force of 2,000,000 for all armed forces.[1] Russian deep-sea research vessels include converted ballistic missile submarines, which hold smaller auxiliary submarines that can operate on the ocean floor.[2]

To avoid political blowback from military deaths abroad, Russia has increasingly deployed paid private volunteer troops trained at Special Forces bases and often under the command of Russian Special Forces. Russia has used such volunteers in Libya, Syria, and Ukraine because "[t]hey not only provide the Kremlin with plausible political deniability but also apparently take casualties the Russian authorities do not report."[3] In December 2017, it was reported that 3,000 mercenaries from one private company, the Wagner Group, which is closely tied to Russian President Vladimir Putin, have fought in Syria since 2015.[4]

In July 2016, Putin signed a law creating a 340,000-strong (both civilian and military) National Guard over which he has direct control.[5] He created his National Guard, which is responsible for "enforcing emergency-situation regimes, combating terrorism, defending Russian territory, and protecting state facilities and assets,"[6] by amalgamating "interior troops and various law-enforcement agencies."[7] Although Putin could issue a directive to deploy the force abroad,[8] forces are more likely to be used to stifle domestic dissent.

Hamstrung by low oil prices, economic sanctions, and deep structural issues, Russia's economy is projected to produce only tepid growth of 1.5 percent–2.0 percent in 2018.[9] Though Russia cut defense spending by 20 percent from $70 billion in 2016 to $66.3 billion in 2017,[10] it has invested heavily in modernization of its armed forces. In January 2018, Chairman of the Joint Chiefs of Staff and U.S. Marine Corps General Joseph Dunford noted that "[t]here is not a single aspect of the Russian armed forces that has not received some degree of modernization over the past decade."[11]

In early 2018, Russia introduced the new State Armament Program 2018–2027, a $306 billion investment in new equipment and force modernization. However, according to Chatham House, "as inflation has eroded the value of the rouble since 2011, the new programme is less ambitious than its predecessor in real terms."[12] A Swedish Defense Research Agency brief notes that the new armaments program is likely to be distributed more evenly between military branches and that "the emphasis of the 2018–2027 programme is on procurement of high-precision weapons for air, sea and land battle—including hypersonic missiles—unmanned air strike complexes, individual equipment for servicemen and advanced reconnaissance, communication and electronic warfare systems."[13] The new state armaments program will also focus on development of unmanned vehicles and robotics.[14]

Russia's counterspace and countersatellite capabilities are formidable. In February 2018, Director of National Intelligence Daniel R. Coats testified that "[b]oth Russia and China continue to pursue anti-satellite (ASAT) weapons as a means to reduce US and allied military effectiveness."[15]

Russia's nuclear arsenal has been progressively modernized. According to the IISS:

> The Strategic Rocket Force (RVSN) continues to progressively rearm, with a number of regiments continuing to receive new Yars missiles and launchers in 2016. Meanwhile, tests of the heavy Sarmat liquid fuel intercontinental ballistic missile (ICBM) have been postponed several times due to technical difficulties,

and these are now expected to resume towards the end of 2017. Ejection tests of the rail-mobile Barguzin ICBM were first carried out in November 2016, but the future of the system has yet to be decided.[16]

Russia has announced that the new RS-28 ballistic missile, commissioned in 2011, will come into service in 2018 as planned. Russia also plans to deploy the RS-28 (Satan 2) ICBM by 2021 as a replacement for the RS-36, which is being phased out in the 2020s.[17]

The armed forces also continue to undergo process modernization, which was begun by Defense Minister Anatoly Serdyukov in 2008.[18] Partially because of this modernization, U.S. Deputy Assistant Secretary of Defense for Strategy and Force Development Elbridge Colby stated in January 2018 that the U.S. military advantage over Russia is eroding.[19] Russia has invested heavily in military modernization over the past decade and projects that 70 percent of its military equipment will have been modernized by 2020.[20] In March 2017, Russia announced life-extension programs for its *Akula*-class and *Oscar II*-class nuclear-powered submarines, which operate in both the Northern and Pacific Fleets.[21] However, problems remain:

> The naval shipbuilding industry has suffered from years of neglect and under investment; while the Ukraine crisis and the imposition of sanctions is starting to have an effect. The refurbishment of existing naval vessels is progressing, albeit at a slower, and more expensive, pace than originally envisaged. Although several new frigates, corvettes and submarines have already entered service, delivery of new vessels is behind schedule.[22]

Following years of delays, the commissioning of the *Admiral Gorshkov* stealth guided missile frigate was delayed until the end of summer 2018.[23] The second *Admiral Gorshkov*-class frigate, the *Admiral Kasatonov*, began sea trials in 2018; however, according to some analysts, tight budgets and an inability to procure parts from Ukrainian industry (importantly, gas turbine engines) make it difficult for Russia to build the three additional *Admiral Gorshkov*-class frigates as planned.[24] In April, Russia announced that its only aircraft carrier would be out of service until 2021 for modernization and repair.[25] Russia plans to procure eight *Lider*-class guided missile destroyers for its Northern and Pacific fleets, but procurement has faced consistent delay, and construction will not begin until 2025 at the earliest.[26]

Russia's naval modernization continues to prioritize submarines, including upgrades to its diesel electric *Kilo*-class subs.[27] According to one analyst:

> [R]einvigorating submarine construction has been one of the visible accomplishments of the Russian Navy's modernization program for 2011–2020. Russia has built three new SSBNs of the Borei class (Project 955) and recently launched the second SSGN in the Yasen class (Project 885M)—an upgraded version of the well-known Severodvinsk—and it intends to build five more Borei-class SSBNs by 2021 and another four or five SSGNs of the Yasen class by 2023.[28]

Russia also has expressed ambitions to produce a fifth-generation stealth nuclear-powered submarine by 2030[29] and to arm it with Zircon hypersonic missiles, which have a reported speed of from Mach 5 to Mach 6.[30]

Transport remains a nagging problem, and Russia's Defense Minister has stressed the paucity of transport vessels. In 2017, Russia reportedly needed to purchase civilian cargo vessels and use icebreakers to transport troops and equipment to Syria at the beginning of major operations in support of the Assad regime.[31]

Although budget shortfalls have hampered modernization efforts overall, analysts believe that Russia will continue to focus on developing high-end systems such as the S-500 surface-to-air missile system and Su-57 fighter and the T-14 Armata main battle tank.[32] In May, it was reported that Russian testing of the S-500 system struck a target 299 miles away. If true, this is the longest surface-to-air missile test ever conducted, and the S-500's range could have significant implications for European security when the missile becomes operational.[33]

Russian Exercises. Russian military exercises, especially snap exercises, are a source of serious concern because they have masked real military operations in the past. In 2013, Russia reintroduced snap exercises, which are conducted with little or no warning and often involve thousands of troops and pieces of equipment.[34] In February 2017, for example, Russia ordered snap exercises involving 45,000 troops, 150 aircraft, and 200 anti-aircraft pieces.[35] These exercises often encompass multiple military districts, police forces, and the new National Guard. For instance, "in March 2015, the armed forces conducted a major snap exercise of the northern fleet and its reinforcement with elements from the Central, Southern, Western and Eastern Military Districts. This was followed by a major policing exercise, Zaslon 2015."[36]

Snap exercises have been used for military campaigns as well. According to General Curtis Scaparrotti, NATO Supreme Allied Commander and Commander, U.S. European Command (EUCOM), "the annexation of Crimea took place in connection with a snap exercise by Russia."[37]

Snap exercises also provide Russian leadership with a hedge against unpreparedness or corruption. "In addition to affording combat-training benefits," the IISS reports, "snap inspections appear to be of increasing importance as a measure against corruption or deception. As a result of a snap inspection in the Baltic Fleet in June 2016, the fleet's commander, chief of staff and dozens of high-ranking officers were dismissed."[38]

In September 2017, Russia and Belarus conducted Zapad 2017, a massive exercise in Russia's Western Military District, Kaliningrad, and Belarus, the most recent iteration of which had taken place in 2013. While Russia claimed that only 12,700 troops took part, which is 300 fewer than the 13,000 threshold that would require monitoring by the Organization for Security and Co-operation in Europe (OSCE) under the Vienna Document,[39] the actual total was 60,000–70,000, with 12,000 exercises across Belarus and the rest in Russia.[40] In addition to underreporting troop numbers in its exercises, "Russia simply compartmentalizes its large-scale exercises into chunks small enough to evade Vienna Document requirements."[41] Zapad 2017 was smaller than Zapad 13 because it "focused on strengthening Command and Control (C2) and integrating forces, rather than emphasising troop displacements."[42]

While Zapad 17 was ostensibly a counter-terrorism exercise, one NATO staff officer wrote that:

> The "terrorist" formations confronting the combined Russian and Belorussian forces were of sufficient size and strength to require three days of operations by combined-arms and armoured land forces with extensive fixed and rotary-wing air support, large-scale aerospace operations and engagement by the Baltic Fleet and coastal defence units.[43]

Estonian Defense Forces Commander Riho Terras stated plainly that the exercise "simulated a large-scale military attack against Nato."[44] In addition to exercises in the Western Military District, Russia exercised simultaneously in every other military district as well, including live firings of Iskander missiles deployed outside the Western Military District, and a simulated defense of Moscow by S-400s from a large-scale cruise missile attack.[45] Zapad 17 also featured Russian exercises in the Arctic region.[46]

During Zapad 17, Russia deployed Iskander missiles near the northern Norwegian border, nine miles from the town of Korpfjell.[47] Russian signal jamming during the exercise interfered with GPS signals over 150 miles from the Russian border and disrupted commercial aircraft and fishing and shipping vessels in Norway.[48]

Russian exercises in the Baltic Sea in April 2018, a day after the leaders of the three Baltic nations met with President Donald Trump in Washington, were meant as a message. Twice in April, Russia stated that it planned to conduct three days of live-fire exercises in the Exclusive Economic Zone of Latvia, which forced a rerouting of commercial aviation as Latvia closed some of its airspace.[49] Sweden issued warnings to commercial aviation and sea traffic.[50] Russia did not actually fire any live missiles,[51] and the event was described by the Latvian Ministry of Defense as "a show of force, nothing else."[52] The exercises took place near the Karlskrona Naval Base, the Swedish Navy's largest base.[53]

Threats to the Homeland

Russia is the only state adversary in the region that possesses the capability to threaten the U.S. homeland with both conventional and nonconventional means. Although there is no indication that Russia plans to use its capabilities against the United States absent a broader conflict involving America's NATO allies, the plausible potential for such a scenario serves to sustain the strategic importance of those capabilities.

Russia's National Security Strategy describes NATO as a threat to the national security of the Russian Federation:

> The buildup of the military potential of the North Atlantic Treaty Organization (NATO) and the endowment of it with global functions pursued in violation of the norms of international law, the galvanization of the bloc countries' military activity, the further expansion of the alliance, and the location of its military infrastructure closer to Russian borders are creating a threat to national security.[54]

The document also clearly states that Russia will use every means at its disposal to achieve its strategic goals: "Interrelated political,

MAP 3

U.S., Russian Troops Near NATO Nations

The U.S. maintains a permanent active-duty force of about 65,000 troops in Europe. Following its recent actions in Georgia, Syria, and Ukraine, Russia has about 61,000 troops outside its borders on NATO's perimeter.

● U.S. troops   ● Russian troops   ● Russian troops in occupied territories   ☐ NATO member

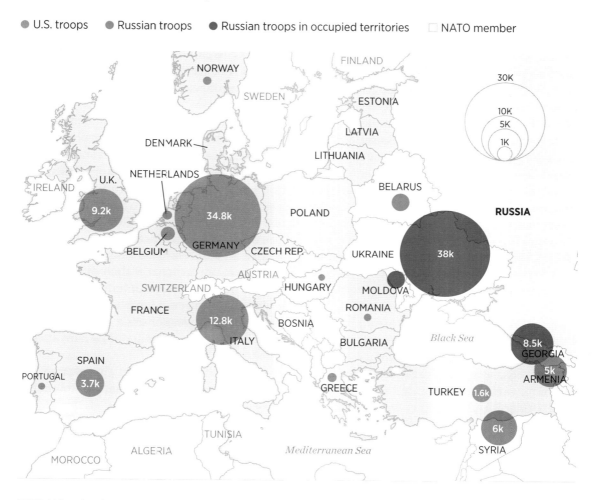

NOTE: U.S. active-duty troops in 15 NATO nations with levels below 200 are not represented.
SOURCE: U.S. Department of Defense, Defense Manpower Data Center, and Heritage Foundation research.

☎ heritage.org

military, military-technical, diplomatic, economic, informational, and other measures are being developed and implemented in order to ensure strategic deterrence and the prevention of armed conflicts."[55] In December 2014, Putin signed a new version of Russia's military doctrine emphasizing the claimed threat of NATO and global strike systems to Russia.[56]

Russian Strategic Nuclear Threat. Russia possesses the largest arsenal of nuclear weapons among the nuclear powers (when short-range nuclear weapons are included). It is one of the few nations with the capability to destroy many targets in the U.S. homeland and in U.S.-allied nations and to threaten and prevent free access to the commons by other nations. Russia has both intercontinental-range and short-range ballistic missiles and a varied nuclear weapons arsenal that can be delivered by sea, land, and air. It also is investing significant resources in modernizing its arsenal and maintaining the skills of its workforce, and nuclear triad modernization will remain a top priority under the new State Armaments Program.[57] However, an aging nuclear workforce could hamper modernization: "[A]lthough Russia's strategic-defence enterprises appear to have preserved some of their expertise, problems remain, for example, in transferring the necessary skill sets and experience to the younger generation of engineers."[58]

Russia is currently relying on its nuclear arsenal to ensure its invincibility against any enemy, intimidate European powers, and deter counters to its predatory behavior in its "near abroad," primarily in Ukraine but also concerning the Baltic States.[59] This arsenal serves as a protective umbrella under which Russia can modernize its conventional forces at a deliberate pace. While its nuclear deterrent protects it from a large-scale attack, Russia also needs a modern and flexible military to fight local wars such as those against Georgia in 2008 and the ongoing war against Ukraine that began in 2014. Under Russian military doctrine, the use of nuclear weapons in conventional local and regional wars is seen as de-escalatory because it would cause an enemy to concede defeat. In May 2017, for example, a Russian parliamentarian threatened that nuclear weapons might be used if the U.S. or NATO were to move to retake Crimea or defend eastern Ukraine.[60]

General Scaparrotti discussed the risks presented by Russia's possible use of tactical nuclear weapons in his March 23, 2017, EUCOM posture statement: "Most concerning...is Moscow's substantial inventory of non-strategic nuclear weapons in the EUCOM AOR [Area of Responsibility] and its troubling doctrine that calls on the potential use of these weapons to escalate its way out of a failing conflict."[61]

Particularly worrisome are Moscow's plans for rail-based nuclear-armed missiles, which are very difficult to detect. The missiles are scheduled to begin testing in 2019 and to become operational in 2020. Russia reportedly plans to deploy five regiments with a total of 30 railroad ICBMs: six missiles per regiment.[62] The Defense Ministry states that the new armed forces structure is being created with the goal of increased flexibility, mobility, and readiness for combat in limited-scale conflicts. Strategic Rocket Forces are the first line of defense (and offense) against Russia's great-power counterparts.[63]

Russia has two strategies for nuclear deterrence. The first is based on a threat of massive launch-on-warning and retaliatory strikes to deter a nuclear attack; the second is based on a threat of limited demonstration and "de-escalation" nuclear strikes to deter or terminate a large-scale conventional war.[64] Russia's reliance on nuclear weapons is based partly on their small cost relative to conventional weapons, especially in terms of their effect, and on Russia's inability to attract sufficient numbers of high-quality servicemembers. Thus, Russia sees its nuclear weapons as a way to offset the lower quantity and quality of its conventional forces.

Moscow has repeatedly threatened U.S. allies in Europe with nuclear deployments and even preemptive nuclear strikes.[65] The Russians justify their aggressive behavior by pointing to deployments of U.S. missile defense systems in Europe even though these systems are not scaled or postured to mitigate Russia's advantage in ballistic missiles and nuclear weapons to any significant degree.

Russia continues to violate the Intermediate-Range Nuclear Forces (INF) Treaty, which bans the testing, production, and possession of intermediate-range missiles.[66] In early 2017, Russia fully deployed the SSC-X-8 Cruise Missile in violation of the INF treaty. One battalion with the cruise missile remains at a missile test site in southern Russia, and another battalion with the missile deployed to an operational base in December 2016. U.S. officials acknowledge that the banned cruise missiles are no longer in the testing phase and now consider them to be fully operational.[67] In March 2017, Joint Chiefs of Staff Vice Chairman and U.S. Air Force General Paul Selva testified that Russia's cruise missile deployment "violates the spirit and intent of the Intermediate Nuclear Forces Treaty" and "presents a risk to most of our facilities in Europe."[68] In December 2017, the U.S. announced new diplomatic, military, and economic measures "intended to induce the Russian Federation to return to compliance and to deny it any military advantage should it persist in its violation."[69]

Summary: The sizable Russian nuclear arsenal remains the only threat to the existence of the U.S. homeland emanating from Europe and Eurasia. While the potential for use of this arsenal remains low, the fact that Russia continues to threaten Europe with nuclear attack demonstrates that it will continue to play a central strategic role in shaping both Moscow's military and political thinking and its level of aggressive behavior beyond its borders.

Threat of Regional War

In the view of many U.S. allies, Russia poses a genuine threat. At times, this threat is of a military nature. At other times, Russia uses less conventional tactics such as cyberattacks, utilization of energy resources, and propaganda. Today as in Imperial times, Russia's influence is exerted by both the pen and the sword. Organizations like the Collective Security Treaty Organization (CSTO) or Eurasia Economic Union attempt to bind regional capitals to Moscow through a series of agreements and treaties.

Espionage is another tool that Russia uses in ways that are damaging to U.S. interests. In May 2016, a Russian spy was sentenced to prison for gathering intelligence for the Russia's Foreign Intelligence Service (SVR) while working as a banker in New York. The spy specifically transmitted intelligence on "potential U.S. sanctions against Russian banks and the United States' efforts to develop alternative energy resources."[70] In May 2016, a senior intelligence official from Portugal working for the Portuguese Security Intelligence Service was arrested for passing secrets, especially classified NATO intelligence and material, to the Russian Federation.

On March 4, 2018, Sergei Skripal, a former Russian GRU colonel who was convicted in 2006 of selling secrets to the United Kingdom and freed in a spy swap between the U.S. and Russia in 2010,[71] and his daughter Yulia were poisoned with Novichok nerve agent by Russian security services in Salisbury, U.K. Hundreds of residents of Salisbury could have been contaminated,[72] including a police officer who was exposed to the nerve agent after responding.[73] The physical cleanup of Salisbury is ongoing as of this writing, and businesses in the city are struggling with mounting losses.[74] On March 15, France, Germany, the UK, and the U.S. issued a joint statement condemning Russia's use of the nerve agent: "This use of a military-grade nerve agent, of a type developed by Russia, constitutes the first offensive use of a nerve agent in Europe since the Second World War."[75]

In response to Russia's actions, two dozen countries expelled over 150 Russian intelligence agents operating under diplomatic cover; the U.S., for its part, expelled 60 Russian diplomats whom it had identified as intelligence agents and shuttered the Russian consulate in Seattle.[76] Russia retaliated by expelling 60 American diplomats and closing the U.S. consulate in St. Petersburg[77] in addition to expelling another 59 diplomats from 23 other nations.[78] In May, the suspected perpetrators of the poisoning were reported to be back in Russia.[79] Skripal, who survived the attack (along with his daughter), has continued to assist Western security services, including those of the Czech Republic and Estonia.[80] U.S. intelligence officials have reportedly linked Russia to the deaths of 14 people in the U.K. alone, many of them Russians who ran afoul of the Kremlin.[81]

Russian intelligence operatives are reportedly mapping U.S. telecommunications infrastructure around the United States, focusing especially on fiber optic cables.[82] In March 2017, the U.S. charged four people, including two Russian intelligence officials, with directing hacks of user data involving Yahoo and Google accounts.[83] In December 2016, the U.S. expelled 35 Russian intelligence operatives, closed two compounds in Maryland and New York that were used for espionage, and levied additional economic sanctions against individuals who took part in interfering in the 2016 U.S. election.[84]

Russia has also used its relations with friendly nations—especially Nicaragua—for espionage purposes. In April 2017, Nicaragua began using a Russian-provided satellite station at Managua that—even though the Nicaraguan government denies it is intended for spying—is of concern to the U.S.[85] The Russian-built "counter-drug" center at Las Colinas that opened in November 2017 will likely be "supporting Russian security engagement with the entire region."[86] Russia also has an agreement with Nicaragua, signed in 2015, that allows access to Nicaraguan ports for its naval vessels.[87]

Russian Pressure on Central and Eastern Europe. Moscow poses a security challenge to members of NATO that border Russia. Although a conventional Russian attack against a NATO member is unlikely, primarily because it would trigger a NATO response, it cannot be entirely discounted. Russia continues to use nonconventional means to apply pressure to sow discord among NATO member states. Russia continues to utilize cyberattacks, espionage, its significant share of the European energy market, and propaganda to undermine the alliance. The Estonian Foreign Intelligence Service's *International Security and Estonia 2018* report states clearly that "[t]he only existential threat to the sovereignty of Estonia and other Baltic Sea states emanates from Russia. However, the threat of a direct Russian military attack on NATO member states in 2018 is low."[88]

Due to decades of Russian domination, the countries in Central and Eastern Europe factor Russia into their military planning and foreign policy formulation in a way that is simply unimaginable in many Western European countries and North America. Estonia and Latvia have sizable ethnic Russian populations, and there is concern that Russia might exploit the situation as a pretext for aggression. This view is not without merit, considering Moscow's irredentist rhetoric and Russia's use of this technique to annex Crimea.

The Estonian Foreign Intelligence Service report also predicted that Russian propaganda and fake think tanks would seek to "tarnish and diminish" events and celebrations surrounding the 100th anniversary of the Baltic States' independence.[89] In 2017, Lithuanian Defense Minister Raimundas Karoblis stated that Russian propaganda claims that the cities of Vilnius and Klaipeda did not belong to Lithuania may be groundwork for future "kinetic operations."[90] "There are real parallels with Crimea's annexation" by Russia, said Karoblis. "We are speaking of a danger to the territorial integrity of Lithuania."[91] Similar Russian efforts have sought to undermine the statehood and legitimacy of the other two Baltic States; in January 2018, for example, Putin signed a decree renaming an air force regiment the "Tallinn Regiment" to "preserve holy historical military traditions" and "raise [the] spirit of military obligation."[92]

General Scaparrotti testified in March 2017 that Russian propaganda and disinformation should be viewed as an extension of Russia's military capabilities: "The Russians see this as part of that spectrum of warfare, it's their asymmetric approach."[93] Russia has sought to use misinformation to undermine NATO's Enhanced Forward Presence in the Baltics. In April 2017, Russian hackers planted a false story about U.S. troops being poisoned by mustard gas in Latvia on the Baltic News Service's website.[94] Similarly, Lithuanian parliamentarians and media outlets began to receive e-mails in February 2017 containing a false story that German soldiers had sexually assaulted an underage Lithuanian girl.[95] U.S. troops stationed in Poland for NATO's EFP have been the target of similar Russian misinformation campaigns.[96] A fake story that a U.S. Army vehicle had hit and killed a Lithuanian boy during Saber Strike 2018 in June was meant to undermine public support for NATO exercises.[97]

Russia has also demonstrated a willingness to use military force to change the borders of modern Europe. When Kremlin-backed Ukrainian President Viktor Yanukovych failed to sign an Association Agreement with the European Union (EU) in 2013, months of street demonstrations led to his ouster early in 2014. Russia responded by violating Ukraine's territorial integrity, sending troops, aided by pro-Russian local militia, to occupy the Crimean Peninsula under the pretext of "protecting Russian people." This led to Russia's eventual annexation of Crimea, the first such forcible annexation of territory in Europe since the Second World War.[98]

Russia's annexation of Crimea has effectively cut Ukraine's coastline in half, and Russia has claimed rights to underwater resources off the Crimean Peninsula.[99] In May 2018, Russia inaugurated the first portion of a $7.5 billion 11.8-mile bridge connecting Russia with Kerch in occupied Crimea. The project will be fully completed in 2023.[100] Russia has deployed 28,000 troops to Crimea and has embarked on a major program to build housing, restore airfields, and install new radars there.[101] In addition, control of Crimea has allowed Russia to use the Black Sea as a platform to launch and support naval operations in the Gulf of Aden and the Eastern Mediterranean.[102] Russia has allocated $1 billion to modernize the Black Sea fleet by 2020 and has stationed additional warships there, including two frigates equipped with Kaliber-NK long-range cruise missiles.[103] Kaliber cruise missiles have a range of at least 2,500km, placing cities from Rome to Vilnius within range of Black Sea–based cruise missiles.[104]

In August 2016, Russia deployed S-400 air defense systems with a potential range of around 250 miles to Crimea;[105] a second deployment occurred in January 2018.[106] In addition, "local capabilities have been strengthened by the Pantsir-S1 (SA-22 Greyhound) short-to-medium-range surface-to-air missile (SAM) and anti-aircraft artillery weapons system, which particularly complements the S-400."[107]

In eastern Ukraine, Russia has helped to foment and sustain a separatist movement. Backed, armed, and trained by Russia, separatist leaders in eastern Ukraine have declared the so-called Lugansk People's Republic and Donetsk People's Republic. Russia has backed separatist factions in the Donbas region of eastern Ukraine with advanced weapons, technical and financial assistance, and Russian conventional and special operations forces. Around 3,000 Russian soldiers are operating in Ukraine.[108] Russian-backed separatists daily violate the September 2014 and February 2015 cease-fire agreements, known respectively as Minsk I and Minsk II.[109] The Minsk cease-fire agreements have led to the de facto partition of Ukraine and have created a frozen conflict that remains both deadly and advantageous for Russia. The war in Ukraine has cost 11,000 lives and displaced 1.7 million people.[110]

In Moldova, Russia supports the breakaway enclave of Transnistria, where yet another frozen conflict festers to Moscow's liking. According to EUCOM's 2017 posture statement:

> Russia has employed a decades-long strategy of indirect action to coerce, destabilize, and otherwise exercise a malign influence over other nations. In neighboring states, Russia continues to fuel "protracted conflicts." In Moldova, for example, Russia has yet to follow through on its 1999 Istanbul summit commitments to withdraw an estimated 1,500 troops— whose presence has no mandate—from the Moldovan breakaway region of Transnistria. Russia asserts that it will remove its force once a comprehensive settlement to the Transnistrian conflict has been reached. However, Russia continued to undermine the discussion of a comprehensive settlement to the Transnistrian conflict at the 5+2 negotiations.[111]

Russia's permanent stationing of Iskander missiles in Kaliningrad in 2018 occurred a year to the day after NATO's EFP deployed to Lithuania.[112] Russia reportedly has deployed tactical nuclear weapons, the S-400 air defense system, and P-800 anti-ship cruise missiles to Kaliningrad.[113] It also has outfitted a missile brigade in Luga, Russia, a mere 74 miles from the Estonian city of Narva, with Iskander missiles.[114] Iskanders have been deployed to the Southern Military District at Mozdok near Georgia and Krasnodar near Ukraine as well,[115] and Russian military officials have reportedly asked manufacturers to increase the Iskander missiles' range and improve their accuracy.[116]

Moreover, Russia is not deploying missiles only in Europe. In November 2016, Russia announced that it had stationed Bal and Bastion missile systems on the Kurile islands of Iturup and Kunashir, which are also claimed by Japan.[117] In February 2018, Russia approved the deployment of warplanes to an airport on Iturup, one of the largest islands.[118]

Russia has deployed additional troops and capabilities near its western borders. Bruno Kahl, head of the German Federal Intelligence Service, stated in March 2017 that "Russia has doubled its fighting power on its Western border, which cannot be considered as defensive against the West."[119] In January 2017, Russia's Ministry of Defence announced that four S-400 air defense systems would be deployed to the Western Military District.[120] In January 2016, Commander in Chief of Russian Ground Forces General Oleg Salyukov announced the formation of four new ground divisions, three of them based in the Western Military District, allegedly in response to "intensified exercises of NATO countries."[121] According to an assessment published by the Carnegie Endowment for International Peace, "The overall effect is to produce a line of substantial Russian combat forces along the western border, including opposite Belarus. By contrast with the ad hoc arrangements of the early stages of the conflict with Ukraine, these new forces are permanently established."[122]

Summary: Russia represents a real and potentially existential threat to NATO member countries in Eastern and Central Europe. Considering Russia's aggression in Georgia and Ukraine, a conventional attack against a NATO member by Russia, while unlikely, cannot be ruled out entirely. In all likelihood, Russia will continue to use nonlinear means in an effort to pressure and undermine both these nations and the NATO alliance.

Militarization of the High North. The Arctic region is home to some of the world's roughest terrain and harshest weather. Increasingly, the melting of Arctic ice during the summer months is causing new challenges for the U.S. in terms of Arctic security. Many of the shipping lanes currently used in the Arctic are a considerable distance from search and rescue (SAR) facilities, and natural resource exploration that would be considered routine in other locations is complex, costly, and dangerous in the Arctic.

The U.S. is one of five littoral Arctic powers and one of only eight countries with territory located above the Arctic Circle, the area just north of 66 degrees north latitude that includes portions of Norway, Sweden, Finland, Russia, Canada, Greenland, Iceland, and the United States.

Arctic actors take different approaches to military activity in the region. Although the security challenges currently faced in the Arctic are not yet military in nature, there is still a requirement for military capability in the region that can support civilian authorities. For example, civilian SAR and response to natural disasters in such an unforgiving environment can be augmented by the military.

Russia has taken steps to militarize its presence in the region. In March 2017, a decree signed by Russian President Putin gave the Federal Security Service (FSB) additional powers to confiscate land "in areas with special objects for land use, and in the border areas."[123] Russia's Arctic territory is included within this FSB-controlled border zone. The Arctic-based Northern Fleet accounts for two-thirds of the Russian Navy. A new Arctic command was established in 2015 to coordinate all Russian military activities in the Arctic region.[124] Two Arctic brigades have been formed, and Russia is planning to form Arctic Coastal Defense divisions,[125] which will be under the command of

CHART 7

Russia's Icebreaker Fleet Dominates the Arctic

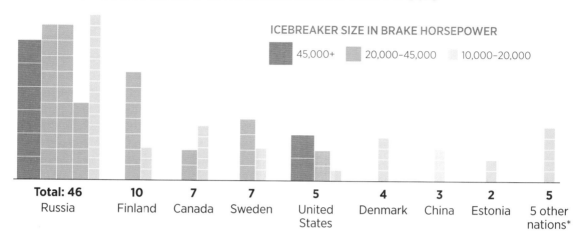

ICEBREAKER SIZE IN BRAKE HORSEPOWER

45,000+   20,000–45,000   10,000–20,000

Total: 46	**10**	**7**	**7**	**5**	**4**	**3**	**2**	**5**
Russia	Finland	Canada	Sweden	United States	Denmark	China	Estonia	5 other nations*

* Norway, Germany, Latvia, Japan, and South Korea.

NOTE: List includes both government-owned and privately owned icebreakers. List excludes icebreakers for southern hemisphere countries Chile, Australia, South Africa, and Argentina.

SOURCE: Ronald O'Rourke, "Coast Guard Polar Icebreaker Program: Background and Issues for Congress," Congressional Research Service *Report* RL34391, July 9, 2018, p. 10, https://fas.org/sgp/crs/weapons/RL34391.pdf (accessed August 1, 2018).

heritage.org

the Northern Fleet and stationed in the Kola Peninsula and in Russia's eastern Arctic.[126]

Russia is also investing in Arctic bases. Its base on Alexandra Land, commissioned in 2017, can house 150 soldiers autonomously for up to 18 months.[127] In addition, old Soviet-era facilities have been reopened. The airfield on Kotelny Island, for example, was reactivated in 2013 for the first time in 20 years and "will be manned by 250 personnel and equipped with air defense missiles."[123] In 2018, Russia plans to open an Arctic airfield at Nagurskoye[129] that "will be equipped with a 2,500 meter long landing strip and a fleet of MiG-31 or Su-34" Russian fighters.[130]

In fact, air power in the Arctic is increasingly important to Russia, which has 14 operational airfields in the region along with 16 deep-water ports.[131] In January, the Northern Fleet announced that it would "significantly expand the geography of the Arctic flights."[132] These flights are often aggressive. In March 2017, nine Russian bombers simulated an attack on the U.S.-funded, Norwegian-run radar installation at Vardø, Norway, above the Arctic Circle.[133] In May 2017, 12 Russian aircraft simulated an attack against NATO naval forces taking part in the EASTLANT17 exercise near Tromsø, Norway, and later that month, Russian aircraft targeted aircraft from 12 nations, including the U.S., that took part in the Arctic Challenge 2017 exercise near Bodø.[134] In April 2018, Maritime Patrol Aircraft from Russia's Pacific Fleet for the first time exercised locating and bombing enemy submarines in the Arctic, while fighter jets exercised repelling an air invasion in the Arctic region.[135]

The 45th Air Force and Air Defense Army of the Northern Fleet was formed in December 2015, and Russia reportedly has placed radar and S-300 missiles on the Arctic bases at Franz Joseph Land, New Siberian Islands, Novaya Zemlya, and Severnaya Zemlya.[136] In 2017, Russia activated a new radar complex on Wrangel Island.[137] Beginning in 2019, Russia plans to lay a nearly 8,000-mile fiber optic cable across its Arctic coast, linking military installations along the way from the Kola Peninsula through Vladivostok.[138]

Russia's ultimate goal is to have a combined Russian armed force deployed in the Arctic by 2020,[139] and it appears that Moscow is on track to accomplish this. Russia is developing equipment optimized for Arctic conditions like the Mi-38 helicopter[140] and three new nuclear icebreakers to add to the 40 icebreakers already in service (six of which are nuclear).[141] Admiral Paul F. Zukunft, former Commandant of the U.S. Coast Guard, has expressed concern that "Russia probably is going to launch two icebreaking corvettes with cruise missiles on them over the course of the next several years."[142]

In July 2017, Russia released a new naval doctrine that cited an alleged threat from the "ambition of a range of states, and foremost the United States of America and its allies, to dominate the high seas, including in the Arctic, and to press for overwhelming superiority of their naval forces."[143] In May 2017, Russia announced that its buildup of the Northern Fleet's nuclear capacity is intended "to phase 'NATO out of [the] Arctic.'"[144]

Russia's Northern Fleet is also building newly refitted submarines, including a newly converted Belgorod nuclear-powered submarine that will be commissioned in 2018 or 2019 to carry out "special missions."[145] Construction on the vessel had been suspended in 2000 when the *Kursk*, its sister submarine, sank. According to Russian media reports, the submarine "will be engaged in studying the bottom of the Russian Arctic shelf, searching for minerals at great depths, and also laying underwater communications."[146] In January 2018, Russia established a deep-water division, based in Gadzhiyevo in the Murmansk region, that is directly subordinate to the Minister of Defense.[147]

Summary: Russia continues to develop and increase its military capabilities in the Arctic region. The likelihood of armed conflict remains low, but physical changes in the region mean that the posture of players in the Arctic will continue to evolve. It is clear that Russia

intends to exert a dominant influence. In the words of EUCOM's 2018 posture statement:

> In the Arctic, Russia is revitalizing its northern fleet and building or renovating military bases along their Arctic coast line in anticipation of increased military and commercial activity.... Although the chances of military conflict in the Arctic are low in the near-term, Russia is increasing its qualitative advantage in Arctic operations, and its military bases will serve to reinforce Russia's position with the threat of force.[148]

Russian Destabilization in the South Caucasus. The South Caucasus sits at a crucial geographical and cultural crossroads and has proven to be strategically important, both militarily and economically, for centuries. Although the countries in the region (Armenia, Georgia, and Azerbaijan) are not part of NATO and therefore do not receive a security guarantee from the United States, they have participated to varying degrees in NATO and U.S.-led operations. This is especially true of Georgia, which aspires to join NATO.

Russia views the South Caucasus as part of its natural sphere of influence and stands ready to exert its influence in the region by force if necessary. In August 2008, Russia invaded Georgia, coming as close as 15 miles to the capital city of Tbilisi. Seven years later, several thousand Russian troops occupied the two Georgian provinces of South Ossetia and Abkhazia.

In 2015, Russia signed so-called integration treaties with South Ossetia and Abkhazia. Among other things, these treaties call for a coordinated foreign policy, creation of a common security and defense space, and implementation of a streamlined process for Abkhazians and South Ossetians to receive Russian citizenship.[149] The Georgian Foreign Ministry criticized the treaties as a step toward "annexation of Georgia's occupied territories,"[150] both of which are still internationally recognized as part of Georgia. In January 2018,

Russia ratified an agreement with the de facto leaders of South Ossetia to create a joint military force, which the U.S. condemned.[151]

In November 2017, the U.S. State Department approved an estimated $75 million sale of Javelin missiles to Georgia.[152] Russia has based 7,000 soldiers in Abkhazia and South Ossetia[153] and is regularly expanding its "creeping annexation" of Georgia.[154] Towns are split in two and families are separated as a result of Russia's occupation and imposition of an internal border. In 2017 alone, over 514 people were detained by Russian border guards for "illegal" crossings into South Ossetia.[155]

Today, Moscow continues to exploit ethnic divisions and tensions in the South Caucasus to advance pro-Russian policies that are often at odds with America's or NATO's goals in the region, but Russia's influence is not restricted to soft power. In the South Caucasus, the coin of the realm is military might. It is a rough neighborhood surrounded by instability and insecurity reflected in terrorism, religious fanaticism, centuries-old sectarian divides, and competition for natural resources.

Russia maintains a sizable military presence in Armenia based on an agreement giving Moscow access to bases in that country for 49 years.[156] The bulk of Russia's forces, consisting of 3,300 soldiers, dozens of fighter planes and attack helicopters, 74 T-72 tanks, and S-300 and Buk M01 air defense systems, are based around the 102nd Military Base.[157] In 2015, Russia and Armenia signed a Combined Regional Air Defense System agreement. In March 2018, Russia signed a new $100 million defense loan with Armenia.[158] Around the same time, nationwide protests arose in Armenia that led to the election of a new prime minister, Nikol Pashinyan.[159] Once elected, Pashinyan met with Russian President Putin and declared that he "favored closer political and military ties with Russia."[160]

Another source of regional instability is the Nagorno–Karabakh conflict, which began in 1988 when Armenia made territorial claims to Azerbaijan's Nagorno–Karabakh Autonomous Oblast.[161] By 1992, Armenian forces and Armenian-backed militias had occupied 20 percent of Azerbaijan, including the Nagorno–Karabakh region and seven surrounding districts. A cease-fire agreement was signed in 1994, and the conflict has been described as frozen since then. Since August 2014, violence has increased noticeably along the Line of Contact between Armenian and Azerbaijani forces. Intense fighting in April 2016 left 200 dead.[162] In addition, Azerbaijani forces recaptured some of the territory lost to Armenia in the early 1990s, the first changes in the Line of Contact since 1994.[163] Recently, tensions have escalated, with the Azerbaijani army declaring its full preparation for large-scale military operations against Armenia.[164]

This conflict offers another opportunity for Russia to exert malign influence and consolidate power in the region. While its sympathies lie with Armenia, Russia is the largest supplier of weapons to both Armenia and Azerbaijan.[165] As noted by the late Dr. Alexandros Petersen, a highly respected expert on Eurasian security, it is no secret "that the Nagorno–Karabakh dispute is a Russian proxy conflict, maintained in simmering stasis by Russian arms sales to both sides so that Moscow can sustain leverage over Armenia, Azerbaijan and by its geographic proximity Georgia."[166]

Following the outbreak of fighting, Russia expanded its influence in the region by brokering a shaky cease-fire that has largely held. By the time the OSCE Minsk Group, created in 1995 to find a peaceful solution to the Nagorno–Karabakh conflict, met, the Russian-brokered cease-fire was already in place.[167]

The South Caucasus might seem distant to many American policymakers, but the spillover effect of ongoing conflict in the region can have a direct impact both on U.S. interests and on the security of America's partners, as well as on Turkey and other countries that are dependent on oil and gas transiting the region.

Summary: Russia views the South Caucasus as a vital theater and uses a multitude of tools that include military aggression, economic pressure, and the stoking of ethnic tensions to exert influence and control, usually

MAP 4

The Ganja Gap

To bypass Russia or Iran for overland trade between Asia and Europe there is only one option: Azerbaijan. Armenia's occupation of almost 20 percent of Azerbaijan's territory means that there is only a narrow 60-mile-wide chokepoint for trade. This is the Ganja Gap.

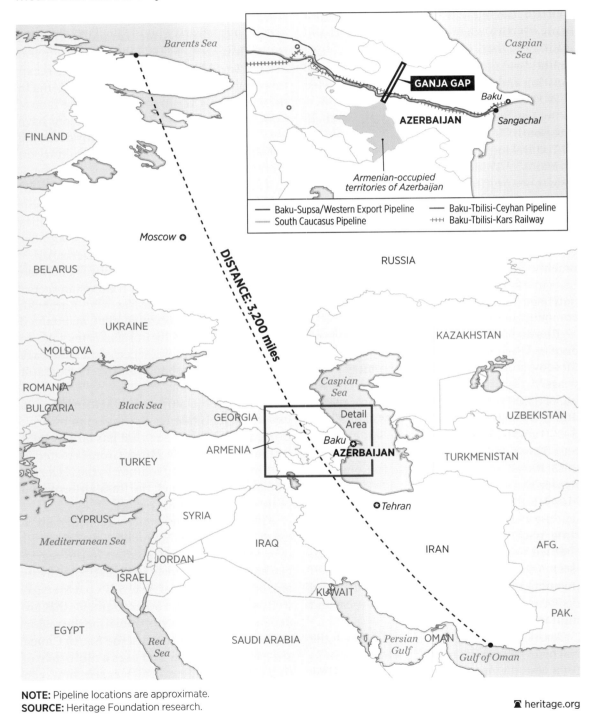

NOTE: Pipeline locations are approximate.
SOURCE: Heritage Foundation research.

🏠 heritage.org

to promote outcomes that are at odds with U.S. interests.

Increasingly Active Mediterranean. Although Russia has had a military presence in Syria for decades, in September 2015, it became the decisive actor in Syria's ongoing civil war, having saved Bashar al-Assad from being overthrown and strengthened his hand militarily, thus enabling government forces to retake territory lost during the war. In January 2017, Russia signed an agreement with the Assad regime to expand the naval facility at Tartus (Russia's only naval base on the Mediterranean) "under a 49-year lease that could automatically renew for a further 25 years." The planned expansion reportedly would "provide simultaneous berthing for up to 11 warships, including nuclear-powered vessels, more than doubling [the facility's] present known capacity."[168] Russia is expanding the Tartus base to include a submarine maintenance facility.[169]

The agreement with Syria also includes upgrades to the Hmeymim air base at Latakia, including repairs to a second runway.[170] Russia deployed the S-400 anti-aircraft missile system to Hmeymim in late 2015.[171] In addition to the S-400 system, Russia has deployed the Pantsir S1 system. "The two systems working in tandem provide a 'layered defense,'" according to one account, "with the S-400 providing long-ranged protection against bombers, fighter jets, and ballistic missiles, and the Pantsir providing medium-ranged protection against cruise missiles, low-flying strike aircraft, and drones."[172]

Russia is using Syria as a testing ground for new weapons systems while obtaining valuable combat experience for its troops. According to Lieutenant General Ben Hodges, former Commander, U.S. Army Europe, Russia has used its intervention in Syria as a "live-fire training opportunity."[173] In February 2017, Russian Defense Minister Sergei Shoigu claimed that Russia had tested 162 weapons systems in Syria.[174] Despite this display of Russian arms in Syria, however, Russian weapons exports have remained flat, in part because India and China are developing more weapons systems domestically.[175] In 2016, Russian arms exports rose slightly to $15 billion, up from $14.5 billion in 2015 but still lower than $15.7 billion in 2013.[176]

Russia's activities in Syria have allowed Assad to stay in power and have made achievement of a peaceful political settlement with rebel groups nearly impossible. They also have undermined American policy in the Middle East, including by frequently targeting U.S.-backed forces. A study of Russian airstrikes in Syria from September 2015 to March 2018 found that only 14 percent targeted ISIS and that Russian airstrikes were "particularly concentrated in areas where the Islamic State had little or no operational presence."[177]

Russian pilots have occasionally acted dangerously in the skies over Syria. In May 2017, for example, a Russian fighter jet intercepted a U.S. KC-10 tanker, performing a barrel roll over the top of the KC-10.[178] That same month, Russia stated that U.S. and allied aircraft would be banned from flying over large areas of Syria because of a deal agreed to by Russia, Iran, and Turkey. The U.S. responded that the deal does not "preclude anyone from going after terrorists wherever they may be in Syria."[179] The U.S. and Russia have a deconfliction hotline to avoid mid-air collisions and incidents.

In November 2018, Russia sought to solidify its relations with Egypt, approving a five-year agreement for the two countries to use each other's air bases.[180] Russia has also greatly stepped up its military operations in the Mediterranean, often harassing U.S. and allied vessels taking part in counter-IS operations. In April 2018, for example, a fully armed Russian Su-24M Fencer and Su-30SM Flanker fighter aircraft flew aggressively low over the *Aquitaine*, a French frigate operating in the eastern Mediterranean.[181] That same month, one or two improved *Kilo*-class submarines, two Russian frigates, and Russian anti-submarine aircraft pursued a British *Astute*-class attack submarine operating in the Mediterranean near Syria. The British sub received assistance from U.S. P-8As operating in the region.[182]

In addition, the U.S., along with British, Dutch, and Spanish allies, tracked the *Krasnodar*, a *Kilo*-class submarine, as it sailed from the Baltic Sea to a Russian base in occupied Crimea from April–August 2017. The submarine stopped twice in the eastern Mediterranean to launch cruise missiles into Syria and conducted drills in the Baltic Sea and off the coast of Libya. It was one of the first times since the Cold War that the U.S. and NATO allies had tracked a Russian submarine during combat operations.[183]

Summary: Russia's entrenched position in Syria, including its expanded area-access/area-denial capabilities and increased submarine presence, underscores the growing importance of the Mediterranean theater in ensuring Europe's security.

The Balkans. Security has improved dramatically in the Balkans since the 1990s, but violence based on religious and ethnic differences remains an ongoing possibility. These tensions are exacerbated by sluggish economies, high unemployment, and political corruption.

Russia's interests in the Western Balkans are at odds with the desire of the U.S. and our European allies to continue to assist the region in forging closer ties to the transatlantic community. Russia seeks to sever the transatlantic bond forged with the Western Balkans by sowing instability, chiefly by inflaming preexisting ethnic, historic, and religious tensions. Russian propaganda magnifies this toxic ethnic and religious messaging, fans public disillusionment with the West as well as institutions inside the Balkan nations, and misinforms the public about Russia's intentions and interests in the region.[184]

Senior members of the Russian government have cited NATO enlargement in the Balkans as one of the biggest threats to Russia.[185] In June 2017, Montenegro became NATO's 29th member state, joining Albania and Croatia as NATO member states in the Balkans. Russia stands accused of being behind a failed plot to break into Montenegro's parliament on election day in 2016, assassinate its former prime minister, and install a pro-Russian government. The trial of 14 people accused of taking part in the coup plot began in July 2017. Two Russian nationals believed to be the masterminds behind the plot are being tried in absentia.[186]

After Russia annexed Crimea, the Montenegrin government backed European sanctions against Moscow and even implemented its own sanctions. Nevertheless, Russia has significant economic influence in Montenegro and in 2015 sought unsuccessfully to gain access to Montenegrin ports for the Russian navy to refuel and perform maintenance. Today, Russia accounts for one-third of foreign direct investment in Montenegro, and Russian nationals or companies own 40 percent of the nation's real estate as well as almost one-third of all Montenegrin companies.[187]

Serbia in particular has long served as Russia's foothold in the Balkans:

> Russia's influence in the Balkans centers on Serbia, a fellow religiously orthodox nation with whom it enjoys a close economic, political, and military relationship. Serbia and Russia have an agreement in place allowing Russian soldiers to be based at Niš airport in Serbia. The two countries signed a 15-year military cooperation agreement in 2013 that includes sharing of intelligence, officer exchanges, and joint military exercises. In October, Russia gave Serbia six MiG-29 fighters (which while free, will require Serbia to spend $235 million to have them overhauled). Additionally, Russia plans to supply Serbia with helicopters, T-72 tanks, armored vehicles, and potentially even surface-to-air missile systems.[188]

The so-called Russian–Serbian Humanitarian Center at Niš—widely believed to be a Russian spy base—is only 58 miles from NATO's Kosovo Force mission based in Pristina.[189]

Serbia and Russia have signed a strategic partnership agreement focused on economic issues. Russia's inward investment is focused on the transport and energy sectors. Except for those in the Commonwealth of Independent States, Serbia is the only country in Europe that has a free trade deal with Russia. Russia dealt a blow to Serbia in 2014 when it cancelled plans to build the South Stream Pipeline. The pipeline's proposed route through the Western Balkans would have been lucrative to Serbia and would have greatly strengthened Russia's energy grip on the region.

However, Serbia still exercises far more without Russia than with Russia: "In 2016, out of 26 training exercises only two are with Russia. Out of 21 multinational training drills in 2015, the Serbian military participated in only two with Russia."[190] Like Russia, Serbia is a member of NATO's Partnership for Peace program. Additionally, Serbia has been part of the U.S. National Guard's State Partnership Program, partnering with the State of Ohio since 2006.

Russia is also active in Bosnia and Herzegovina—specifically, the ethnically Serb Republika Srpska, one of two substate entities inside Bosnia and Herzegovina that emerged from that country's civil war in the 1990s. Moscow knows that the easiest way to prevent Bosnia and Herzegovina from entering the transatlantic community is by exploiting internal ethnic and religious divisions among the country's Bosniak, Croat, and Serb populations.

Republika Srpska's leader, Milorad Dodik, has long advocated independence for the region and has enjoyed a very close relationship with the Kremlin. Recent events in Ukraine, especially the annexation of Crimea, have inspired more separatist rhetoric in Republika Srpska.

In many ways, Russia's relationship with Republika Srpska is akin to its relationship with Georgia's South Ossetia and Abkhazia autonomous regions: more like a relationship with another sovereign state than a relationship with a semiautonomous region inside Bosnia and Herzegovina. When Putin visited Serbia in October 2014, Dodik was treated like a head of state and invited to Belgrade to meet with him. More recently, in September 2016, Dodik was treated as a head of state on a visit to Moscow just days before a referendum that chose January 9 as Republika Srpska's "statehood day," a date filled with religious and ethnic symbolism for the Serbs.[191] Republika Srpska hosted its "statehood day" in defiance of a ruling by Bosnia's federal constitutional court that both the celebration and the referendum establishing it were illegal.[192] The U.S. sanctioned Dodik in January 2017, saying that "by obstructing the Dayton accords, Milorad Dodik poses a significant threat to the sovereignty and territorial integrity of Bosnia–Herzegovina."[193]

On January 9, 2018, Bosnian Serbs again held "statehood day."[194] Joining in this year's celebrations was a delegation from the breakaway region of South Ossetia in Georgia.[195] Dodik and the self-proclaimed leaders of South Ossetia "signed a memorandum on cooperation between the 'states.'"[196] Russia has reportedly trained a Republika Srpska paramilitary force in Russia at the nearby Niš airbase to defend the Serbian entity. It has been reported that "[s]ome of its members fought as mercenaries alongside the Kremlin's proxy separatists in Ukraine."[197]

Russia does not want to see Kosovo as a successful nation pointed toward the West. Rather, it seeks to derail Kosovo's efforts to integrate into the West, often utilizing grievances of the Serbian minority to cause problems. In the most jarring example, in January 2017, a train traveling from Belgrade to Mitrovica, a heavily Serb town in Kosovo, was stopped at the Kosovar border. The Russian-made train was "painted in the colors of the Serbian flag and featured pictures of churches, monasteries, and medieval towns, as well as the words 'Kosovo is Serbian' in 21 languages."[198]

Macedonia's accession to NATO remains on hold because of opposition by Greece. In January 2018, Greece and Macedonia agreed to renew talks to find a settlement of the name dispute, and the talks are ongoing. The decade-long denial of Macedonia's admission to NATO is having a deleterious impact on the public's perception of the alliance. While support for membership remains high, public support is beginning to decline.[199]

Russia's destabilizing influence may be partly to blame for this decline. Leaked reports of a memo prepared for the Director of Macedonia's Administration for Security and Counterintelligence detail Russia's decades-long efforts to destabilize Macedonia through espionage and propaganda. According to one excerpt, "it is evaluated that in the past nine years, the Republic of Macedonia has been undergoing strong subversive propaganda and intelligence activity implemented through the Embassy of the RF (Russian Federation)."[200] Russia has also sought to gain influence in Macedonia by constructing Orthodox churches and creating so-called friendship associations.[201]

In addition to Russia's destabilizing influence, the region faces threats from Islamist terrorism, rising Chinese investment and influence, and the potentially negative impacts of Turkish economic, cultural, and religious ties. The U.S. has invested heavily in the Balkans since the end of the Cold War. Tens of thousands of U.S. servicemembers have served in the Balkans, and the U.S. has spent billions of dollars in aid there, all in the hope of creating a secure and prosperous region that will someday be part of the transatlantic community.

Summary: The foremost external threat to the Balkans is Russia. Russia's interests in the Balkans are at odds with the U.S. goal of encouraging the region to progress toward the transatlantic community. Russia seeks to sever the transatlantic bond forged with the Western Balkans by sowing instability and increasing its economic, political, and military footprint in the region.

Threats to the Commons

Other than cyberspace and (to some extent) airspace, the commons are relatively secure in the European region. Despite periodic Russian aggressive maneuvers near U.S. and NATO vessels, this remains largely true with respect to the security of and free passage through shipping lanes: The maritime domain is heavily patrolled by the navies and coast guards of NATO and NATO partner countries; except in remote areas in the Arctic Sea, search and rescue capabilities are readily available; maritime-launched terrorism is not a significant problem; and piracy is virtually nonexistent.

Sea. On February 10, 2017, the USS *Porter*, a destroyer operating in international waters in the Black Sea, was buzzed by two Russian Su-24 fighters, followed by a solo Su-24 and finally by a Russian IL-38. The aircraft were flying with their transponders switched off and did not respond to radio requests to stop. A spokesperson for EUCOM said that such buzzing incidents are "always concerning because they could result in miscalculation or accident."[202] In April 2018, a fully armed Russian jet buzzed a French frigate operating in the eastern Mediterranean.[203]

Russian threats to the maritime theater also include activity near undersea fiber optic cables. In December 2017, Rear Admiral Andrew Lennon, Commander Submarines NATO, stated, "We are now seeing Russian underwater activity in the vicinity of undersea cables that I don't believe we have ever seen."[204] On any given day, undersea cables "carry some $10 trillion of financial transfers and process some 15 million financial transactions," to say nothing of the breadth of nonfinancial information and communications that they carry.[205] The *Yantar*, a mother ship to two Russian mini submersibles,[206] is often seen near undersea cables, which it is capable of tapping or cutting, and has been observed collecting intelligence near U.S. naval facilities, including the submarine base at Kings Bay, Georgia.[207] The Russian spy ship *Viktor Leonov* was spotted collecting intelligence within 20 miles of Kings Bay in March 2017 and within 30 miles of Groton, Connecticut, in February 2018.[208]

Airspace. Russia has continued its provocative military flights near U.S. and European airspace over the past year. In January 2018, a Russian Su-27 fighter intercepted a U.S. surveillance aircraft operating over the Black Sea, forcing the surveillance aircraft to return to base. "This interaction was determined to be unsafe," according to a statement from the U.S. 6th Fleet, "due to the SU-27 closing to within five feet and crossing directly through the EP-3's flight path, causing the EP-3 to fly through the SU-27's jet wash."[209] In November 2017, a Russian Su-30 fighter flew within 50 feet of a U.S. P-8A flying over the Black Sea in a 24-minute intercept that the U.S. also called "unsafe." Specifically, "the aircraft crossed in front of the US plane from right to left while engaging its afterburners, forcing the P-8 to enter its jet wash, an action that caused the US plane to experience 'a 15-degree roll and violent turbulence,'" according to a Pentagon spokeswoman[210] In another incident in January 2018, Belgian and British fighters scrambled to intercept two Russian TU-160 Blackjack bombers flying in NATO airspace over the North Sea.[211]

Aggressive Russian flying has also occurred near U.S. airspace. In May 2018, U.S. F-22s intercepted two Tu-95 Bear Bombers, which flew into the American Air Defense Identification Zone near Alaska.[212]

Russian flights have also targeted U.S. ally Japan. In April 2017, three Russian Tu-95 Bear Bombers and an IL-20 surveillance aircraft flew within 36 miles of the Japanese coast, and 14 Japanese fighters were scrambled to intercept them.[213] A similar incident occurred in January 2017 when three Russian Bear bombers, three refueling IL-78 aircraft, and two radar and communications A-50 AWACS flew near Japan. The bombers flew around Japan, and the incident caused NORAD to increase its threat posture from 5 to 4.[214] In November, two Tu-95 bombers flew within 80 miles of the USS *Ronald Reagan* aircraft carrier operating in the Sea of Japan before being escorted away by American F-18 fighters.[215]

The main threat from Russian airspace incursions, however, remains near NATO territory in Eastern Europe, specifically the Black Sea and Baltic regions. In April 2018, NATO jets taking part in Baltic Air Policing intercepted two Russian Su-35 fighters and one Su-24 attack aircraft that were flying over the Baltic Sea. "The Russian aircraft had their onboard transponders off, kept no radio contact with the regional air traffic control center, and hadn't submitted a flight plan."[216] In the Baltics, NATO

aircraft intercepted Russian military aircraft 120 times in 2017, an increase over the 110 intercepts recorded in 2016 but still less than the 2015 high of 160.[217]

That the provocative and hazardous behavior of the Russian armed forces or Russian-sponsored groups poses a threat to civilian aircraft in Europe was demonstrated by the July 2014 downing of Malaysia Airlines Flight MH17, killing all 283 passengers and 15 crewmembers, over the skies of southeastern Ukraine. In addition, there have been several incidents involving Russian military aircraft flying in Europe without using their transponders. In February 2015, for example, civilian aircraft in Ireland had to be diverted or were prevented from taking off when Russian bombers flying with their transponders turned off flew across civilian air lanes.[218] Similarly, in March 2014, Scandinavian Airlines plane almost collided with a Russian signals intelligence (SIGINT) plane, the two coming within 90 meters of each other.[219] In a December 2014 incident, a Cimber Airlines flight from Copenhagen to Poznan nearly collided with a Russian intelligence plane that was flying with its transponder turned off.[220]

Summary: Russia's violation of the sovereign airspace of NATO member states is a probing and antagonistic policy that is designed both to test the defense of the alliance and as practice for potential future conflicts. Similarly, Russian antagonistic behavior in international waters is a threat to freedom of the seas. Russia's reckless aerial activity in the region remains a threat to civilian aircraft flying in European airspace.

Cyber. Russian cyber capabilities are sophisticated and active, regularly threatening economic, social, and political targets around the world. Even more, Moscow appears to be increasingly aggressive in its use of digital techniques, often employing only the slightest veneer of deniability in an effort to intimidate targets and openly defy international norms and organizations. Russia clearly believes that these online operations will be essential to its domestic and foreign policy for the foreseeable future. As former Chief of the Russian General Staff General Yuri Baluyevsky, has observed, "[cyber-attacks are] much more important than victory in a classical military conflict, because it is bloodless, yet the impact is overwhelming and can paralyze all of the enemy state's power structures."[221]

Relatedly, the 2018 Worldwide Threat Assessment of the U.S. Intelligence Community (WWTA) identifies the cyber threat as one of our nation's top concerns and cites Russia specifically:

> We expect that Russia will conduct bolder and more disruptive cyber operations during the next year, most likely using new capabilities against Ukraine. The Russian Government is likely to build on the wide range of operations it is already conducting, including disruption of Ukrainian energy distribution networks, hack-and-leak influence operations, distributed denial-of-service attacks, and false flag operations. In the next year, Russian intelligence and security services will continue to probe US and allied critical infrastructures, as well as target the United States, NATO, and allies for insights into US policy.[222]

In June 2018, the U.S. Treasury Department sanctioned five Russian entities and three Russian individuals for "malign and destabilizing" cyber activities, including "the destructive NotPetya cyber-attack; cyber intrusions against the U.S. energy grid to potentially enable future offensive operations; and global compromises of network infrastructure devices, including routers and switches, also to potentially enable disruptive cyber-attacks."[223] These sanctions built on a joint assessment by the Department of Homeland Security and the FBI that Russian hackers were behind a series of attacks against American network infrastructure devices and the U.S. energy and critical infrastructure sectors.[224]

But the United States is not Russia's only target. In April 2018 alone, Germany's head of domestic intelligence accused Moscow of attacking his government's computer networks, and the U.K.'s National Cyber Security Center warned that Russian hackers were targeting Britain's critical infrastructure supply chains. Russia continues to employ cyber as a key tool in manipulating and undermining democratic elections in Europe and elsewhere.

In addition to official intelligence and military cyber assets, Russia continues to employ allied criminal organizations (so-called patriotic hackers) to help it engage in cyber aggression. Using these hackers gives Russia greater resources and can help to shield their true capabilities. Patriotic hackers also give the Russian government deniability when it is desired. In June 2017, for example, Putin stated that "[i]f they (hackers) are patriotically-minded, they start to make their own contribution to what they believe is the good fight against those who speak badly about Russia. Is that possible? Theoretically it is possible."[225]

Summary: Russia's cyber capabilities are advanced and are a key tool in realizing the state's strategic aims. Russia has used cyber-attacks to further the reach and effectiveness of its propaganda and disinformation campaigns, and its ongoing cyber-attacks against election processes in the U.S. and European countries are designed to undermine citizens' belief in the veracity of electoral outcomes and erode support for democratic institutions in the longer term. Russia also has used cyber-attacks to target physical infrastructure, including electrical grids, air traffic control, and gas distribution systems. Russia's increasingly bold use of cyber capabilities, coupled with their sophistication and Moscow's willingness to use them aggressively, presents a challenge to the U.S. and its interests abroad.

Conclusion

Overall, the threat to the U.S. homeland originating from Europe remains low, but the threat to America's interests and allies in the region remains significant. Behind this threat lies Russia. Although Russia has the military capability to harm and (in the case of its nuclear arsenal) to pose an existential threat to the U.S., it has not conclusively demonstrated the intent to do so.

The situation is different when it comes to America's allies in the region. Through NATO, the U.S. is obliged by treaty to come to the aid of the alliance's European members. Russia continues its efforts to undermine the NATO alliance and presents an existential threat to U.S. allies in Eastern Europe. NATO has been the cornerstone of European security and stability ever since its creation in 1949, and it is in America's interest to ensure that it maintains both the military capability and the political will to fulfill its treaty obligations.

While Russia is not the threat to U.S. global interests that the Soviet Union was during the Cold War, it does pose challenges to a range of America's interests and those of its allies and friends closest to Russia's borders. Russia possesses a full range of capabilities from ground

forces to air, naval, space, and cyber. It still maintains the world's largest nuclear arsenal, and although a strike on the U.S. is highly unlikely, the latent potential for such a strike still gives these weapons enough strategic value vis-à-vis America's NATO allies and interests in Europe to keep them relevant.

Russian provocations much less serious than any scenario involving a nuclear exchange pose the most serious challenge to American interests, particularly in Central and Eastern Europe, the Arctic, the Balkans, and the South Caucasus. The 2018 WWTA states that "Moscow will use a range of relatively low-cost tools to advance its foreign policy objectives, including influence campaigns, economic coercion, cyber operations, multilateral forums, and measured military force."[226] For these reasons, this *Index* continues to assess the threat from Russia as "aggressive" and "formidable."

Threats: Russia

Behavior	HOSTILE	AGGRESSIVE	TESTING	ASSERTIVE	BENIGN
		✓			

Capability	FORMIDABLE	GATHERING	CAPABLE	ASPIRATIONAL	MARGINAL
	✓				

Endnotes

1. International Institute for Strategic Studies, *The Military Balance 2018: The Annual Assessment of Global Military Capabilities and Defence Economics* (London: Routledge, 2018), pp. 192–206.

2. Michael Birnbaum, "Russian Submarines Are Prowling Around Vital Undersea Cables. It's Making NATO Nervous," *The Washington Post*, December 22, 2017, https://www.washingtonpost.com/world/europe/russian-submarines-are-prowling-around-vital-undersea-cables-its-making-nato-nervous/2017/12/22/d4c1f3da-e5d0-11e7-927a-e72eac1e73b6_story.html?utm_term=.bd78ff119ead (accessed June 13, 2018).

3. Pavel Felgenhauer, "Private Military Companies Forming Vanguard of Russian Foreign Operations," Jamestown Foundation, *Eurasia Daily Monitor*, Vol. 14, Issue 36 (March 16, 2017), https://jamestown.org/program/private-military-companies-forming-vanguard-russian-foreign-operations/ (accessed July 17, 2017).

4. Nataliya Vasilyeva, "Thousands of Russian Private Contractors Fighting in Syria," Associated Press, December 12, 2017, https://apnews.com/7f9e63cb14a54dfa9148b6430d89e873 (accessed July 13, 2018).

5. International Institute for Strategic Studies, *The Military Balance 2017: The Annual Assessment of Global Military Capabilities and Defence Economics* (London: Routledge, 2017), p. 186.

6. Radio Free Europe/Radio Liberty, "Putin Creates National Guard Force," July 4, 2016, https://www.rferl.org/a/putin-national-guard-dissent-riots/27836301.html (accessed July 10, 2017).

7. International Institute for Strategic Studies, *The Military Balance 2017*, p. 169.

8. Ibid., p. 186.

9. Andrey Ostroukh and Gabrielle Tétrault-Farber, "World Cup Economic Boost May Fall Short of Russian Hopes," Reuters, May 31, 2018, https://www.reuters.com/article/us-soccer-worldcup-russia-impact/world-cup-to-have-little-impact-on-russias-economy-moodys-idUSKCN1IW11K?il=0 (accessed July 13, 2018).

10. David Brennan, "Why Is Russia Cutting Military Spending?" *Newsweek*, May 2, 2018, http://www.newsweek.com/why-russia-cutting-military-spending-908069 (accessed June 15, 2018).

11. Damien Sharkov, "Russia's Military Expansion Makes It Greatest Threat to Europe and NATO Must Defend It, Says U.S. General," *Newsweek*, January 16, 2018, http://www.newsweek.com/russias-military-expansion-makes-it-greatest-threat-europe-nato-782114 (accessed June 15, 2018).

12. Richard Connolly and Mathieu Boulègue, "Russia's New State Armament Programme: Implications for the Russian Armed Forces and Military Capabilities to 2027," Royal Institute of International Affairs, Chatham House, *Research Paper*, May 2018, p. 2, https://www.chathamhouse.org/sites/default/files/publications/research/2018-05-10-russia-state-armament-programme-connolly-boulegue-final.pdf (accessed July 13, 2018).

13. Tomas Malmlöf, "Russia's New Armament Programme—Leaner and Meaner," Swedish Defense Research Agency, *RUFS Briefing* No. 42, March 2018, p. [1], https://www.foi.se/report-search/pdf?fileName=D%3A%5CReportSearch%5CFiles%5C4ca7f16e-cf73-40db-87fc-85e946cfcf7b.pdf (accessed July 13, 2018).

14. International Institute for Strategic Studies, *The Military Balance 2017*, p. 177.

15. Daniel R. Coats, Director of National Intelligence, "Worldwide Threat Assessment of the US Intelligence Community," statement before the Select Committee on Intelligence, U.S. Senate, February 13, 2018, p. 13, https://www.dni.gov/files/documents/Newsroom/Testimonies/2018-ATA---Unclassified-SSCI.pdf (accessed July 18, 2018).

16. International Institute for Strategic Studies, *The Military Balance 2017*, p. 175.

17. Franz-Stefan Gady, "Russia's Most Powerful Intercontinental Ballistic Missile to Enter Service in 2021," *The Diplomat*, March 30, 2018, https://thediplomat.com/2018/03/russias-most-powerful-intercontinental-ballistic-missile-to-enter-service-in-2021/ (accessed July 13, 2018).

18. International Institute for Strategic Studies, *The Military Balance 2017*, p. 159.

19. Tom Bowman, "U.S. Military Advantage over Russia and China 'Eroding,' Pentagon Says," National Public Radio, January 19, 2018, https://www.npr.org/2018/01/19/579088536/u-s-military-advantage-over-russia-and-china-eroding-says-pentagon (accessed July 2, 2018).

20. International Institute for Strategic Studies, *The Military Balance 2018*, p. 178.

21. Thomas Nilsen, "Russian Navy Upgrades Multi-Purpose Submarines," *The Independent Barents Observer*, March 20, 2017, https://thebarentsobserver.com/en/security/2017/03/russian-navy-upgrades-multi-purpose-submarines (accessed July 10, 2017).

22. Claire Mills, "Russia's Rearmament Programme," House of Commons Library *Briefing Paper* No. 7877, January 24, 2017, p. 6, http://researchbriefings.parl ament.uk/ResearchBriefing/Summary/CBP-7877#fullreport (accessed June 28, 2018).

23. TASS, "Commissioning of Russian Frigate Admiral Gorshkov Delayed Until End of Summer," *Navy Recognition*, March 18, 2018, http://www.navyrecognition.com/index.php/news/defence-news/2018/march-2018-navy-naval-defense-news/6062-commissioning-of-russian-frigate-admiral-gorshkov-delayed-until-end-of-summer.html (accessed July 14, 2018).

24. Franz-Stefan Gady, "Russia's Latest Stealth Frigate to Commence Sea Trials in 2018," *The Diplomat*, November 15, 2017, https://thediplomat.com/2017/11/russias-latest-stealth-frigate-to-commence-sea-trials-in-2018/ (accessed June 15, 2018).

25. Mykhailo Samus, "Russia Postpones Future Aircraft Carrier Program," Jamestown Foundation, *Eurasia Daily Monitor*, Vol. 15, Issue 69 (May 7, 2018), https://jamestown.org/program/russia-postpones-future-aircraft-carrier-program/ (accessed July 14, 2018).

26. Thomas Nilsen, "Russian Navy Gets Go-ahead for Design of New Nuclear Powered Destroyers," *The Barents Observer*, August 28, 2017, https://thebarentsobserver.com/en/security/2017/08/russian-navy-gets-go-ahead-design-new-nuclear-powered-destroyers (accessed June 15, 2018).

27. International Institute for Strategic Studies, *The Military Balance 2017*, p. 174.

28. Michael Kofman, "Russia's Fifth-Generation Sub Looms," Russia Military Analysis, October 9, 2017, https://russianmilitaryanalysis.wordpress.com/2017/10/09/russias-fifth-generation-sub-looms/ (accessed July 26, 2018). Reprinted from U.S. Naval Institute *Proceedings*, Vol. 143, No. 10 (October 2017).

29. Sputnik, "What Is Known About Russia's 5th Gen Husky-Class Stealth Subs," December 20, 2017, https://sputniknews.com/military/201712201060172180-russia-husky-submarines-missiles/ (accessed July 14, 2018).

30. Michael Peck, "Russia Wants to Arm Its New Husky-Class Submarines with Hypersonic Missiles," *The National Interest,* May 31, 2018, http://nationalinterest.org/blog/the-buzz/russia-wants-arm-its-new-husky-class-submarines-hypersonic-26063 (accessed June 18, 2018).

31. Reuters, "Russia Expands Military Transport Fleet to Move Troops Long Distances," March 7, 2017, http://www.reuters.com/article/russia-navy-expansion-idUSL5N1GK470 (accessed July 10, 2017).

32. International Institute for Strategic Studies, *The Military Balance 2017*, pp. 173 and 192.

33. Amanda Macias, "Russia Quietly Conducted the World's Longest Surface-to-Air Missile Test," CNBC, May 24, 2018, https://www.cnbc.com/2018/05/24/russia-quietly-conducted-the-worlds-longest-surface-to-air-missile-test.html?__source=twitter%7Cmain (accessed July 14, 2018).

34. Colonel Tomasz K. Kowalik and Dominik P. Jankowski, "The Dangerous Tool of Russian Military Exercises," Center for European Policy Analysis, StratCom Program, May 9, 2017, http://cepa.ecms.pl/EuropesEdge/The-dangerous-tool-of-Russian-military-exercises (accessed July 14, 2018).

35. Damien Sharkov, "Putin Cals 45,000 Troops to Snap Air Drill," *Newsweek*, February 8, 2017, http://www.newsweek.com/putin-called-45000-troops-snap-air-drill-554312 (accessed July 10, 2017).

36. International Institute for Strategic Studies, *The Military Balance 2018*, p. 171.

37. U.S. Strategic Command, "Remarks by Gen. Curtis M. Scaparrotti at the 2016 Deterrence Symposium," La Vista, Nebraska, July 27, 2016, http://www.stratcom.mil/Media/Speeches/Article/986470/2016-deterrence-symposium/ (accessed July 17, 2017).

38. International Institute for Strategic Studies, *The Military Balance 2017*, p. 187.

39. Ariana Rowberry, "The Vienna Document, the Open Skies Treaty and the Ukraine Crisis," Brookings Institution Up Front, April 10, 2014, https://www.brookings.edu/blog/up-front/2014/04/10/the-vienna-document-the-open-skies-treaty-and-the-ukraine-crisis/ (accessed July 14, 2018).

40. Dave Johnson, "ZAPAD 2017 and Euro-Atlantic Security," *NATO Review Magazine*, December 14, 2017, https://www.nato.int/docu/review/2017/also-in-2017/zapad-2017-and-euro-atlantic-security-military-exercise-strategic-russia/EN/index.htm (accessed July 14, 2018).

41. Ibid.

42. Mathieu Boulègue, "Five Things to Know About the Zapad-2017 Military Exercise," Royal Institute of International Affairs, Chatham House, September 25, 2017, https://www.chathamhouse.org/expert/comment/five-things-know-about-zapad-2017-military-exercise (accessed July 14, 2018).

43. Johnson, "ZAPAD 2017 and Euro-Atlantic Security."

44. Samuel Osborne, "Russia 'Simulated Full-Scale War' Against Nato, Says Military Commander," *The Independent,* January 7, 2018, https://www.independent.co.uk/news/world/europe/russia-nato-zapad-simulated-full-scale-war-against-west-vladimir-putin-riho-terras-commander-estonia-a8146296.html (accessed July 14, 2018).

45. Johnson, "ZAPAD 2017 and Euro-Atlantic Security."

46. Michael Kofman, "Michael Kofman: What Actually Happened During Zapad 2017," Estonian Public Broadcasting, December 23, 2017, https://news.err.ee/650543/michael-kofman-what-actually-happened-during-zapad-2017 (accessed July 15, 2018).

47. Thomas Nilsen, "Russian Bombers Simulated an Attack Against This Radar on Norway's Barents Sea Coast," *The Barents Observer*, March 5, 2018, https://thebarentsobserver.com/en/security/2018/03/russian-bombers-simulated-attack-against-radar-norways-barents-sea-coast (accessed June 18, 2018).

48. Bruce Jones, "Norway's Defence Minister Downplays GPS Jamming, Spoofing Threat," Jane's 360, December 20, 2017, http://www.janes.com/article/76565/norway-s-defence-minister-downplays-gps-jamming-spoofing-threat (accessed June 18, 2018).

49. Olevs Nikers, "Russia's Offshore 'Missile Tests': Psychologically Undermining the Economic Security of the Baltics," Jamestown Foundation, *Eurasia Daily Monitor*, Vol. 15, Issue 74 (May 15, 2018), https://jamestown.org/program/russias-offshore-missile-tests-psychologically-undermining-the-economic-security-of-the-baltics/ (accessed July 15, 2018); Michael Birnbaum, "Russia Tests Missiles in the Baltic Sea, a Day After Baltic Leaders Met with Trump," *The Washington Post*, April 4, 2018, https://www.washingtonpost.com/world/europe/russia-tests-missiles-in-the-baltic-sea-a-day-after-baltic-leaders-met-with-trump/2018/04/04/0a35e222-380d-11e8-af3c-2123715f78df_story.html?utm_term=.8f8c10f97f62 (accessed June 20, 2018).

50. Samuel Osborne, "Russian Live Missile Tests Force Latvia to Close Airspace over Baltic Sea: 'It's Hard to Comprehend,'" *The Independent*, April 5, 2018, https://www.independent.co.uk/news/world/europe/russia-latvia-missile-tests-baltic-sea-airspace-donald-trump-baltic-leaders-white-house-a8289451.html (accessed June 18, 2018).

51. Nikers, "Russia's Offshore 'Missile Tests': Psychologically Undermining the Economic Security of the Baltics."

52. Birnbaum, "Russia Tests Missiles in the Baltic Sea, a Day After Baltic Leaders Met with Trump."

53. Osborne, "Russian Live Missile Tests Force Latvia to Close Airspace over Baltic Sea."

54. Vladimir Putin, "On the Russian Federation's National Security Strategy," Presidential Edict 683, December 31, 2015, http://www.ieee.es/Galerias/fichero/OtrasPublicaciones/Internacional/2016/Russian-National-Security-Strategy-31Dec2015.pdf (accessed July 11, 2017).

55. Ibid.

56. Pavel Podvig, "New Version of the Military Doctrine," Russian Strategic Nuclear Forces blog, December 26, 2014, http://russianforces.org/blog/2014/12/new_version_of_the_military_do.shtml (accessed July 15, 2018).

57. Connolly and Boulègue, "Russia's New State Armament Programme: Implications for the Russian Armed Forces and Military Capabilities to 2027."

58. International Institute for Strategic Studies, *The Military Balance 2017*, p. 15.

59. Ibid.

60. Tom O'Connor, "Russia Conflict with NATO and U.S. Would Immediately Result in Nuclear War, Russian Lawmaker Warns," *Newsweek*, May 30, 2017, http://www.newsweek.com/russia-politician-nuclear-weapons-us-nato-crimea-617613 (accessed July 11, 2017).

61. General Curtis M. Scaparrotti, Commander, United States European Command, statement on EUCOM posture before the Committee on Armed Services, U.S. Senate, March 23, 2017, p. 5, https://www.armed-services.senate.gov/imo/media/doc/Scaparrotti_03-23-17.pdf (accessed July 16, 2018).

62. Kyle Mizokami, "All Aboard Russia's Nuclear Weapon Apocalypse Train," *Popular Mechanics*, February 27, 2017, http://www.popularmechanics.com/military/weapons/a25423/all-aboard-russias-apocalypse-train/ (accessed July 11, 2017).

63. Mikhail Barabanov, Konstantin Makienko, and Ruslan Pukhov, "Military Reform: Toward the New Look of the Russian Army," Valdai Discussion Club *Analytical Report*, July 2012, p. 14, http://vid1.rian.ru/ig/valdai/Military_reform_eng.pdf (accessed July 11, 2017).

64. Barry D. Watts, *Nuclear-Conventional Firebreaks and the Nuclear Taboo*, Center for Strategic and Budgetary Assessments, 2013, http://csbaonline.org/publications/2013/04/nuclear-conventional-firebreaks-and-the-nuclear-taboo/ (accessed July 11, 2017).

65. Shaun Waterman, "Russia Threatens to Strike NATO Missile Defense Sites," *The Washington Times*, May 3, 2012, http://www.washingtontimes.com/news/2012/may/3/russia-threatens-strike-nato-missile-defense-sites/?page=all (accessed July 11, 2017).

66. Michael R. Gordon, "U.S. Says Russia Tested Missile, Despite Treaty," *The New York Times*, January 29, 2014, http://www.nytimes.com/2014/01/30/world/europe/us-says-russia-tested-missile-despite-treaty.html (accessed July 11, 2017).

67. Michael R. Gordon, "Russia Deploys Missile, Violating Treaty and Challenging Trump," *The New York Times*, February 14, 2017, https://www.nytimes.com/2017/02/14/world/europe/russia-cruise-missile-arms-control-treaty.html?_r=1 (accessed May 23, 2017).

68. Testimony of General Paul Selva, Vice Chairman of the Joint Chiefs of Staff, in "Transcript of Hearing on Military Assessment of Nuclear Deterrence Requirements," Committee on Armed Services, U.S. House of Representatives, March 8, 2017, p. 10, https://www.defense.gov/Portals/1/features/2017/0917_nuclear-deterrence/docs/Transcript-HASC-Hearing-on-Nuclear-Deterrence-8-March-2017.pdf (accessed July 18, 2018).

69. U.S. Department of State, "Bureau of Arms Control, Verification and Compliance Factsheet INF Treaty: At a Glance," December 8, 2017, https://www.state.gov/t/avc/rls/2017/276361.htm (accessed July 15, 2018).

70. News release, "Russian Banker Sentenced in Connection with Conspiracy to Work for Russian Intelligence," U.S. Department of Justice, May 25, 2016, https://www.justice.gov/opa/pr/russian-banker-sentenced-connection-conspiracy-work-russian-intelligence (accessed July 13, 2017).

71. BBC, "Sergei Skripal: Who Is the Former Russian Intelligence Officer?" March 29, 2018, http://www.bbc.com/news/world-europe-43291394 (accessed July 15, 2018).

72. Martin Evans and Victoria Ward, "Salisbury Nerve Agent Backlash: Residents Outraged as 500 Told They May Be at Risk a Week After Spy Attack," The Telegraph, March 12, 2018, https://www.telegraph.co.uk/news/2018/03/11/salisbury-public-warned-wash-clothes-nerve-agent-attack/ (accessed July 15, 2018).

73. Ella Wills, "Police Officer Discharged from Hospital After Salisbury Spy Poisoning Speaks Out: 'Life Will Probably Never Be the Same,'" Evening Standard, March 22, 2018, https://www.standard.co.uk/news/uk/police-officer-discharged-from-hospital-after-salisbury-spy-poisoning-speaks-out-for-first-time-life-a3797041.html (accessed July 15, 2018).

74. BBC, "Salisbury Spy Attack: City Gets £1m to Boost Trade After Poisoning," BBC, March 27, 2018, http://www.bbc.com/news/uk-england-wiltshire-43556787 (accessed July 15, 2018).

75. News release, "Statement from the United States, France, Germany, and the United Kingdom on the Attack in Salisbury," The White House, March 15, 2018, https://www.whitehouse.gov/briefings-statements/statement-united-states-france-germany-united-kingdom-attack-salisbury/ (accessed June 18, 2018).

76. Jeremy Diamond, Allie Malloy, and Angela Dewan, "Trump Expelling 60 Russian Diplomats in Wake of UK Nerve Agent Attack," CNN, updated March 26, 2018, https://www.cnn.com/2018/03/26/politics/us-expel-russian-diplomats/index.html (accessed July 16, 2018).

77. Al Jazeera News, "Russia Expels 60 US Diplomats, Closes American Consulate," March 30, 2018, https://www.aljazeera.com/news/2018/03/russia-expels-60-diplomats-closes-american-consulate-180329185734965.html (accessed July 16, 2018).

78. Al Jazeera News, "Russia Expels Diplomats from 23 Countries as Spy Row Worsens," March 30, 2018, https://www.aljazeera.com/news/2018/03/russia-expels-diplomats-23-countries-spy-row-worsens-180330192725390.html (accessed July 16, 2018).

79. Rob Price, "Police Have Reportedly Identified Suspects Believed to Be Behind the Sergei Skripal Poisoning," Business Insider, April 20, 2018, http://www.businessinsider.com/police-identify-suspects-sergei-skripal-nerve-agent-poisoning-report-2018-4 (accessed June 18, 2018).

80. Michael Schwirtz and Ellen Barry, "Sergei Skripal Was Retired, but Still in the Spy Game. Is That Why He Was Poisoned?" The New York Times, May 14, 2018, https://www.nytimes.com/2018/05/14/world/europe/sergei-skripal-spying-russia-poisoning.html (accessed May 16, 2018).

81. Heidi Blake, Tom Warren, Richard Holmes, Jason Leopold, Jane Bradley, and Alex Campbell, "From Russia with Blood," BuzzFeed News, June 15, 2017 (including June 16, 2017, update), https://www.buzzfeed.com/heidiblake/from-russia-with-blood-14-suspected-hits-on-british-soil?utm_term=.dtzm1n1mZB#.po1WlrIWp0 (accessed July 16, 2018).

82. Ali Watkins, "Russia Escalates Spy Games After Years of U.S. Neglect," Politico, June 1, 2017, http://www.politico.com/story/2017/06/01/russia-spies-espionage-trump-239003 (accessed July 13, 2017).

83. BBC, "US Charges Russian Spies over Yahoo Breach," March 15, 2017, http://www.bbc.com/news/technology-39281063 (accessed July 16, 2018).

84. Katie Bo Williams, "US Sanctions Russia over Hacking, Expels 35 Officials," The Hill, December 29, 2016, http://thehill.com/policy/national-security/312119-us-announces-sanctions-on-russia (accessed July 13, 2017).

85. Cristina Silva, "New Cold War: Is Russia Spying on the U.S. from a Nicaragua Military Compound?" Newsweek, May 22, 2017, http://www.newsweek.com/new-cold-war-russia-spying-us-nicaragua-military-compound-613427 (accessed July 13, 2017).

86. Evan Ellis, "Russian Engagement in Latin America: An Update," Center for Strategic and International Studies, December 19, 2017, https://www.csis.org/analysis/russian-engagement-latin-america-update (accessed July 16, 2018).

87. Brett Forrest, "In Cold War Echo, Russia Returns to U.S.'s Backyard," The Wall Street Journal, January 31, 2018, https://www.wsj.com/articles/russia-returns-to-u-s-s-backyard-1517403600 (accessed July 16, 2018).

88. Estonian Ministry of Defence, Foreign Intelligence Service, *International Security and Estonia 2018*, p. 18, https://www.valisluureamet.ee/pdf/raport-2018-ENG-web.pdf (accessed July 16, 2018).

89. Ibid., p 48.

90. Christopher Woody, "Baltic States Think Russia Is Laying the Groundwork for Looming 'Kinetic Operations,'" *Business Insider,* April 3, 2017, http://www.businessinsider.com/russia-propaganda-in-lithuania-attack-on-the-baltics-2017-4 (accessed June 18, 2018).

91. Ibid.

92. Per Olaf Salming, "Kremlin Intimidation: Putin Renames Air Force Regiment 'Tallinn Regiment,'" *UpNorth*, January 30, 2018, https://upnorth.eu/kremlin-intimidation-putin-renames-air-force-regiment-tallinn-regiment/ (accessed July 16, 2018).

93. Bill Gertz, "Russia Waging Information Warfare, General Says," *The Washington Free Beacon*, March 24, 2017, http://freebeacon.com/national-security/russia-waging-information-warfare-general-says/ (accessed July 14, 2017).

94. BNS/TBT Staff, "Fake News About US Troops Posted on BNS Website and Cyber Attack Suspected," *The Baltic Times*, April 13, 2017, http://www.baltictimes.com/fake_news_about_us_troops_posted_on_bns_website_and_cyber_attack_suspected/ (accessed July 14, 2017).

95. Deutsche Welle, "NATO: Russia Targeted German Army with Fake News Campaign," February 16, 2017, http://www.dw.com/en/nato-russia-targeted-german-army-with-fake-news-campaign/a-37591978 (accessed July 14, 2017).

96. Bill Gertz, "Russia Steps Up Anti-U.S. Military Propaganda," *The Washington Free Beacon*, April 27, 2017, http://freebeacon.com/national-security/russia-steps-anti-u-s-military-propaganda/ (accessed July 14, 2017).

97. Andrius Sytas, "Lithuania Sees Fake News Attempt to Discredit NATO Exercises," Reuters, June 13, 2018, https://uk.reuters.com/article/uk-nato-russia/lithuania-sees-fake-news-attempt-to-discredit-nato-exercises-idUKKBN1J92GS (accessed June 19, 2018).

98. Kathrin Hille, Neil Buckley, Courtney Weaver, and Guy Chazan, "Vladimir Putin Signs Treaty to Annex Crimea," *Financial Times*, March 18, 2014, http://www.ft.com/cms/s/0/d93e4c7c-ae6d-11e3-8e41-00144feab7de.html (accessed July 13, 2017).

99. Janusz Bugajski and Peter B. Doran, "BLACK SEA RISING: Russia's Strategy in Southeast Europe," Center for European Policy Analysis *Black Sea Strategic Report* No. 1, February 2016, p. 8, https://docs.wixstatic.com/ugd/644196_29f8496cc1934185865b81480c4561b5.pdf (accessed July 16, 2018).

100. Neil MacFarquhar, "Putin Opens Bridge to Crimea, Cementing Russia's Hold on Neighbor," *The New York Times*, May 15, 2018, https://www.nytimes.com/2018/05/15/world/europe/putin-russia-crimea-bridge.html (accessed June 1, 2018).

101. International Institute for Strategic Studies, *The Military Balance 2018*, p. 214; Reuters, "In Crimea, Russia Signals Military Resolve with New and Revamped Bases," November 1, 2016, http://www.reuters.com/investigates/special-report/russia-crimea/ (accessed July 13, 2017).

102. Bugajski and Doran, "BLACK SEA RISING: Russia's Strategy in Southeast Europe," p. 3.

103. Sam Jones and Kathrin Hille, "Russia's Military Ambitions Make Waves in the Black Sea," *Financial Times*, May 13, 2016, https://next.ft.com/content/1b9c24d8-1819-11e6-b197-a4af20d5575e (accessed July 13, 2017); Radio Free Europe/Radio Liberty, "Russia Adds Cruise-Missile Ships to Black Sea Force," December 12, 2015, http://www.rferl.org/content/russia-black-sea-fleet-cruise-missile-ships/27422679.html (accessed July 13, 2017).

104. "Russia: SSGN Severodvinsk to Get Caliber Cruise Missiles," *Naval Today*, August 16, 2012, http://navaltoday.com/2012/08/16/russia-ssgn-severodvinsk-to-get-caliber-cruise-missiles/ (accessed July 13, 2017); Jones and Hille, "Russia's Military Ambitions Make Waves in the Black Sea."

105. Reuters, "Russia Deploys Advanced S-400 Air Missile System to Crimea: Agencies," August 12, 2016, http://www.reuters.com/article/us-ukraine-crisis-crimea-missiles-idUSKCN10N1H4 (accessed July 17, 2017); Sebastien Roblin, "Syria and the S-400: The Most Dangerous Game of Cat and Mouse on Earth," *The National Interest*, April 15, 2017, http://nationalinterest.org/blog/the-buzz/syria-the-s-400-the-most-dangerous-game-cat-mouse-earth-20200 (accessed July 17, 2017).

106. Phil Stewart, "U.S. Warily Eyeing New Russian Air Defenses in Crimea," Reuters, January 16, 2018, https://www.reuters.com/article/us-usa-russia-crimea/u-s-warily-eyeing-new-russian-air-defenses-in-crimea-idUSKBN1F521E (accessed June 19, 2018)

107. Sergey Sukhankin, "Russia Pours More Military Hardware into 'Fortress Crimea,'" Jamestown Foundation, *Eurasia Daily Monitor*, Vol. 14, Issue 147 (November 14, 2017), https://jamestown.org/program/russia-pours-military-hardware-fortress-crimea/ (accessed July 16, 2018).

108. Nolan Peterson, "NATO Braces for Putin's Next Military Move in Eastern Europe," The Daily Signal, March 26, 2018, https://www.dailysignal.com/2018/03/26/nato-braces-putins-next-military-move-eastern-europe/.

109. Meetings coverage, "Situation in Eastern Ukraine Remains 'Tense and Volatile' Despite Post-Ceasefire Reduction in Fighting, Security Council Told During Briefing," U.N. Security Council, December 11, 2015, https://www.un.org/press/en/2015/sc12154.doc.htm (accessed July 14, 2017).

110. Peterson, "NATO Braces for Putin's Next Military Move in Eastern Europe."

111. Scaparrotti, statement on EUCOM posture, March 23, 2017, pp. 5–6.

112. Sergey Sukhankin, "Kaliningrad: From Boomtown to Battle-Station," European Council on Foreign Relations, March 27, 2017, https://www.ecfr.eu/article/commentary_kaliningrad_from_boomtown_to_battle_station_7256 (accessed July 16, 2018).

113. Michael Krepon and Joe Kendall, "Beef Up Conventional Forces; Don't Worry About a Tactical Nuke Gap," *Breaking Defense*, March 28, 2016, http://breakingdefense.com/2016/03/beef-up-conventional-forces-dont-worry-about-a-tactical-nuke-gap/ (accessed July 14, 2017); Sukhankin, "Kaliningrad: From Boomtown to Battle-Station."

114. Kalev Stoicescu and Henrik Praks, "Strengthening the Strategic Balance in the Baltic Sea Area," International Centre for Defence and Security *Report*, March 2016, p. 14, https://icds.ee/wp-content/uploads/2016/Kalev_Stoicescu__Henrik_Praks_-_Strengthening_the_Strateg c_Balance_in_the_Baltic_Sea_Area.pdf (accessed July 16, 2018).

115. International Institute for Strategic Studies, *The Military Balance 2017*, p. 216.

116. Damien Sharkov, "Russian Military Asks Weapons Makers to Extend Range and Precision of Nuclear-Capable Iskander Missiles," *Newsweek*, May 19, 2017, http://www.newsweek.com/russia-military-weapons-maker-nato-arms-missiles-iskander-nuclear-capable-612409 (accessed July 14, 2017).

117. Radio Free Europe/Radio Liberty, "Russia Deploys Coastal Missile Systems on Disputed Kurile Islands," November 22, 2016, https://www.rferl.org/a/russia-deploys-coastal-missile-systems-on-disputed-kurile-islands/28133041.html (accessed July 17, 2017).

118. Andrew Osborn, "Russia Approves Warplane Deployment on Disputed Island Near Japan," Reuters, February 2, 2018, https://uk.reuters.com/article/uk-japan-russia-islands-military/russia-approves-warplane-deployment-on-disputed-island-near-japan-idUKKBN1FM179 (accessed June 20, 2018).

119. Roland Oliphant, "British Troops Arrive in Estonia as German Spy Chief Warns of Russian Troop Build Up," *The Telegraph*, March 18, 2017, http://www.telegraph.co.uk/news/2017/03/18/british-troops-arrive-estonia-german-spy-chief-warns-russian/ (accessed July 14, 2017).

120. TASS, "Russia's Western Military District to Get Four S-400 Missile Systems This Year," January 13, 2017, http://tass.com/defense/924840 (accessed July 16, 2018).

121. Radio Free Europe/Radio Liberty, "Russia to Create New Military Divisions in Response to NATO," January 22, 2016, http://www.rferl.org/content/russia-new-military-divisions-nato/27503176.html (accessed June 27, 2016).

122. Keir Giles, "Assessing Russia's Reorganized and Rearmed Military," Carnegie Endowment for International Peace, Task Force on U.S. Policy Toward Russia, Ukraine, and Eurasia, May 3, 2017, p. 9, https://carnegieendowment.org/files/5.4.2017_Keir_Giles_RussiaMilitary.pdf (accessed July 14, 2017).

123. Thomas Nilsen, "FSB Gets Right to Confiscate Land from People," *The Barents Observer*, May 16, 2017, https://thebarentsobserver.com/en/security/2017/05/fsb-gets-right-confiscate-land-people#.WR3YvGBXtZy.twitter (accessed July 16, 2018).

124. Dave Majumdar, "Russia to Standup New Arctic Command," U.S. Naval Institute News, February 18, 2014, http://news.usni.org/2014/02/18/russia-standup-new-arctic-command (accessed July 16, 2018).

125. Reuters, "Putin Instigating Biggest Russian Arctic Military Buildup Since Soviet Fall," *The Japan Times*, January 31, 2017, http://www.japantimes.co.jp/news/2017/01/31/world/putin-instigating-biggest-russian-arctic-military-buildup-since-soviet-fall/#.WSMOIoWcHcs (accessed July 14, 2017).

126. MarEx, "New Forces to Guard Northern Sea Route," *The Maritime Executive*, January 20, 2017, http://www.maritime-executive.com/article/new-forces-to-guard-northern-sea-route (accessed July 14, 2017).

127. Elizabeth McLaughlin, "The Race for the Arctic: As New Frontier Opens, Russia Leaves US in Its Wake," ABC News, May 10, 2017, http://abcnews.go.com/International/race-arctic-frontier-opens-russia-leaves-us-wake/story?id=47304875 (accessed July 14, 2017); Andrew Osborn, "Putin's Russia in Biggest Arctic Military Push Since Soviet Fall," Reuters, January 30, 2017, http://mobile.reuters.com/article/idUSKBN15E0W0 (accessed July 14, 2017).

128. Jacek Siminski, "Russia Reactivates Military Airfield in the Arctic Region After 20 Years," The Aviationist, December 8, 2013, https://theaviationist.com/2013/12/08/russia-arctic-base/ (accessed July 16, 2018); Osborn, "Putin's Russia in Biggest Arctic Military Push Since Soviet Fall."

129. Bruce Jones, "Shoigu Details Russian Military Expansion in the Arctic," Jane's 360, January 5, 2018, http://www.janes.com/article/76825/shoigu-details-russian-military-expansion-in-the-arctic (accessed July 16, 2018).

130. Atle Staalesen, "Russian Navy Announces It Will Significantly Expand Arctic Air Patrols," *The Barents Observer*, January 2, 2018, https://thebarentsobserver.com/en/security/2018/01/russian-navy-announces-it-will-significantly-increase-arctic-air-patrols (accessed July 16, 2018).

131. Robbie Gramer, "Here's What Russia's Military Build-Up in the Arctic Looks Like," *Foreign Policy*, January 25, 2017, http://foreignpolicy.com/2017/01/25/heres-what-russias-military-build-up-in-the-arctic-looks-like-trump-oil-military-high-north-infographic-map/?utm_content=buffer12641&utm_medium=social&utm_source=twitter.com&utm_campaign=buffer (accessed June 2, 2017).

132. Staalesen, "Russian Navy Announces It Will Significantly Expand Arctic Air Patrols."

133. Nilsen, "Russian Bombers Simulated an Attack Against This Radar on Norway's Barents Sea Coast."

134. Thomas Nilsen, "Arctic Challenge 2017 Set for Take Off," *The Barents Observer*, May 16, 2017, https://thebarentsobserver.com/en/security/2017/05/arctic-challenge-2017-set-take (accessed June 20, 2018); Nilsen, "Russian Bombers Simulated an Attack Against This Radar on Norway's Barents Sea Coast."

135. TASS, "Russian Pacific Fleet Il-38N MPA Practice ASW in Arctic," *Navy Recognition*, April 2, 2018, https://www.navyrecognition.com/index.php/news/defence-news/2018/april-2018-navy-naval-defense-news/6109-russian-pacific-fleet-il-38n-mpa-practice-asw-in-arctic.html (accessed July 16, 2018).

136. Trude Pettersen, "Northern Fleet Gets Own Air Force, Air Defense Forces," *The Barents Observer*, February 1, 2016, https://thebarentsobserver.com/en/security/2016/02/northern-fleet-gets-own-air-force-air-defense-forces (accessed July 16, 2018).

137. Damien Sharkov, "Russia Deploys Air Radar on Arctic Wrangel Island," *Newsweek*, January 4, 2017, http://www.newsweek.com/russia-deploys-air-radar-arctic-wrangel-island-538527 (accessed July 16, 2018).

138. Thomas Nilsen, "Russia Plans to Lay Trans-Arctic Fiber Cable Linking Military Installations," *The Barents Observer*, April 24, 2018, https://thebarentsobserver.com/en/security/2018/04/russia-slated-lay-military-trans-arctic-fibre-cable#.Wt-EVDOjlWl.twitter (accessed June 20, 2018).

139. RIA Novosti, "Russian Commandos Train for Arctic Combat," Sputnik, October 14, 2013, https://sputniknews.com/military/20131014/184143129/Russian-Commandos-Train-for-Arctic-Combat.html (accessed July 14, 2017).

140. Stephen Blank, "Russia's New Arctic Base Continue[s] the Militarization of the High North," Jamestown Foundation, *Eurasia Daily Monitor*, Vol. 12, Issue 202 (November 6, 2015), http://www.jamestown.org/single/?tx_ttnews%5Btt_news%5D=44572&no_cache=1#.VxqCwfkrJph (accessed July 14, 2017).

141. Osborn, "Putin's Russia in Biggest Arctic Military Push Since Soviet Fall."

142. Richard R. Burgess, "Russia Developing Missile-Armed Icebreakers, Coast Guard Commandant Says," *Seapower*, May 3, 2017, http://seapowermagazine.org/stories/20170503-Russia.html (accessed July 14, 2017).

143. Dmitry Gorenburg, "Russia's New and Unrealistic Naval Doctrine," *War on the Rocks*, July 26, 2017, https://warontherocks.com/2017/07/russias-new-and-unrealistic-naval-doctrine/ (accessed July 16, 2018).

144. Daniel Brown, "Russia's NATO Northern Fleet Beefs Up Its Nuclear Capabilities to Phase 'NATO Out of Arctic,'" *Business Insider*, June 1, 2017, http://www.businessinsider.com/russias-northern-fleet-beefs-up-its-nuclear-capabilities-phase-nato-out-arctic-2017-6 (accessed July 14, 2017).

145. TASS, "Russian Northern Fleet Creates Submarine Division for Deep-Water Operations," *Navy Recognition*, April 27, 2018, http://www.navyrecognition.com/index.php/news/defence-news/2018/april-2018-navy-naval-defense-news/6169-russian-northern-fleet-creates-submarine-division-for-deep-water-operations.html (accessed July 16, 2018); Sputnik, "Russia to Convert Belgorod Submarine for Special Missions," February 9, 2012, https://sputniknews.com/military/20120209171227695/ (accessed July 14, 2017).

146. Sputnik, "Russian Navy to Receive Biggest and Most Unique Nuclear Submarine in the World," April 23, 2017, https://sputniknews.com/military/201704231052905471-russia-navy-biggest-sub/ (accessed July 14, 2017).

147. TASS, "Russian Northern Fleet Creates Submarine Division for Deep-Water Operations."

148. United States European Command, "EUCOM Posture Statement 2018," March 8, 2018, http://www.eucom.mil/mission/eucom-posture-statement-2018 (accessed July 16, 2018).

149. Civil Georgia, "Moscow, Sokhumi Endorse Final Text of New Treaty," November 22, 2014, http://www.civil.ge/eng/article.php?id=27841 (accessed May 30, 2018).

150. Civil Georgia, "Tbilisi Condemns Russia's Move to Sign New Treaty with Sokhumi," November 22, 2014, http://www.civil.ge/eng/article.php?id=27842 (accessed May 30, 2018).

151. Radio Free Europe/Radio Liberty, "U.S. Condemns Russian Military Deal with Georgian Breakaway Region," January 26, 2018, https://www.rferl.org/a/u-s-condemns-russian-ossetia-military-deal-georgia/29000754.html (accessed July 16, 2018); Press statement, "Russia's Violations of Georgian Sovereignty," U.S. Department of State, January 26, 2018, https://www.state.gov/r/pa/prs/ps/2018/01/277705.htm (accessed May 24, 2018).

152. News release, "Georgia—Javelin Missiles and Command Launch Units," U.S. Department of Defense, Defense Security Cooperation Agency, November 20, 2017, http://www.dsca.mil/major-arms-sales/georgia-javelin-missiles-and-command-launch-units (accessed July 16, 2018).

153. International Institute for Strategic Studies, *The Military Balance 2017*, p. 188.

154. Adrian Croft, "Georgia Says Russia Bent on 'Creeping Annexation' of Breakaway Regions," Reuters, February 26, 2015, http://www.reuters.com/article/us-georgia-russia-idUSKBN0LU2M020150226 (accessed May 30, 2018); Luke Coffey, "NATO Membership for Georgia: In U.S. and European Interest," Heritage Foundation *Special Report* No. 199, January 29, 2018, p. 10, https://www.heritage.org/defense/report/nato-membership-georgia-us-and-european-interest.

155. Agenda.ge, "514 People Illegally Detained at Occupation Line in 2017," January 20, 2018, http://agenda.ge/news/94166/eng (accessed May 24, 2018).

156. Andrew Osborn, "Russia to Beef Up Military Presence in Former Soviet Space," *The Telegraph*, August 18, 2010, http://www.telegraph.co.uk/news/worldnews/europe/russia/7952433/Russia-to-beef-up-military-presence-in-former-Soviet-space.html (accessed May 30, 2018).

157. International Institute for Strategic Studies, *The Military Balance 2018*, p. 182.

158. Panorama.am, "Russia to Start Arms Supplies to Armenia Under New $100 Mln Defense Loan in 2018," March 29, 2018, https://www.panorama.am/en/news/2018/03/29/Russia-arms-supplies-Armenia/1926232 (accessed May 24, 2018).

159. Bradley Jardine and Joshua Kucera, "Armenia Elects Protest Leader as Prime Minister," Eurasianet, May 8, 2018, https://eurasianet.org/s/armenia-elects-protest-leader-as-prime-minister (accessed July 16, 2018).

160. Denis Pinchuk and Andrew Osborn, "New Armenian PM Tells Putin He Wants Closer Ties with Russia," Reuters, May 14, 2018, https://www.reuters.com/article/us-russia-armenia-putin-pashinyan/new-armenian-pm-tells-putin-he-wants-closer-military-ties-with-russia-idUSKCN1IF1A3 (accessed May 24, 2018).

161. In 1991, the Azerbaijan SSR Parliament dissolved the Nagorno–Karabakh Autonomous Oblast and divided the area among five rayons (administrative regions) in Azerbaijan.

162. Reuters, "Armenia, Azerbaijan Closer to War over Nagorno–Karabakh Than at Any Time Since 1994—ICG," June 1, 2017, http://www.reuters.com/article/armenia-azerbaijan-conflict-idUSL8N1IY402 (accessed July 16, 2018).

163. Deutsche Welle, "Ceasefire Holds in Contested Armenia–Azerbaijan Border Region," April 6, 2016, http://www.dw.com/en/ceasefire-holds-in-contested-armenia-azerbaijan-border-region/a-19170371 (accessed May 30, 2018).

164. Radio Free Europe/Radio Liberty, "Azerbaijan Warns Armenia It's Ready for 'Large-Scale Military Operations,'" May 12, 2018, https://www.rferl.org/a/azerbaijan-warns-armenia-it-s-ready-for-large-scale-military-operations-/29223151.html (accessed July 16, 2018).

165. Jack Farchy, "Russia Senses Opportunity in Nagorno–Karabakh Conflict," *Financial Times*, April 19, 2016, https://next.ft.com/content/3d485610-0572-11e6-9b51-0fb5e65703ce (accessed May 24, 2018); Nurlan Aliyev, "Russia's Arms Sales: A Foreign Policy Tool in Relations with Azerbaijan and Armenia," Jamestown Foundation, *Eurasia Daily Monitor*, Vol. 15, Issue 47 (March 28, 2018), https://jamestown.org/program/russias-arms-sales-foreign-policy-tool-relations-azerbaijan-armenia/ (accessed July 16, 2018).

166. Alexandros Petersen, "Russia Shows Its Hand on Karabakh," *EUobserver*, November 8, 2013, https://euobserver.com/opinion/122032 (accessed July 16, 2018).

167. Farchy, "Russia Senses Opportunity in Nagorno–Karabakh Conflict."

168. Rod Nordland, "Russia Signs Deal for Syria Bases; Turkey Appears to Accept Assad," *The New York Times*, January 20, 2017, https://mobile.nytimes.com/2017/01/20/world/middleeast/russia-turkey-syria-deal.html?_r=1&referer=https://t.co/T1Cwr3UdJi (accessed July 14, 2017).

169. Julian E. Barnes, "A Russian Ghost Submarine, Its U.S. Pursuers and a Deadly New Cold War," *The Wall Street Journal*, October 20, 2017, https://www.wsj.com/articles/a-russian-ghost-submarine-its-u-s-pursuers-and-a-deadly-new-cold-war-1508509841 (accessed July 16, 2018).

170. Reuters, "Russia to Upgrade Its Naval, Air Bases in Syria: Interfax," January 15, 2017, http://www.reuters.com/article/us-mideast-crisis-syria-russia-base-idUSKBN14Z0FQ (accessed July 14, 2017).

171. Jonathan Marcus, "Russia S-400 Syria Missile Deployment Sends Robust Signal," BBC, December 1, 2015, http://www.bbc.com/news/world-europe-34976537 (accessed July 14, 2017).

172. Ben Brimelow, "Russia's Newest Anti-Air Defenses Are in Syria—and the US Should Be Worried," *Business Insider*, April 11, 2018, http://www.businessinsider.com/pantsir-s1-makes-russian-air-defenses-stronger-2018-2 (accessed July 16, 2018).

173. BBC, "Russia Used Syria as Live-Fire Training—US General," December 22, 2016, http://www.bbc.com/news/world-europe-38402506 (accessed July 16, 2018).

174. Lucian Kim, "Russian Defense Minister Says His Military Has Tested 162 Weapons in Syria," National Public Radio, February 23, 2017, http://www.npr.org/sections/parallels/2017/02/23/516895124/russian-defense-minister-says-his-military-has-tested-162-weapons-in-syria (accessed July 14, 2017).

175. Tobin Harshaw, "Putin's Arms Bazaar Is in a Serious Sales Slump," Bloomberg, April 25, 2017, https://www.bloomberg.com/view/articles/2017-04-25/putin-s-arms-bazaar-is-in-a-serious-sales-slump (accessed July 14, 2017).

176. Marcus Weisgerber, "Russia's Arms Export Boom Stalls; Wisconsin Shipbuilding and Trump; Mattis Meets Industry Leaders; and a Lot More," *Defense One*, April 20, 2017, http://www.defenseone.com/business/2017/04/global-business-brief-april-20-2017/137185/ (accessed July 19, 2017).

177. Agence France-Presse, "Study: Russian Support Gave Assad Half of Syria," Voice of America, May 15, 2018, https://www.voanews.com/amp/russian-support-gave-assad-half-of-syria-study-says/4394613.html?__twitter_impression=true (accessed June 20, 2018).

178. Ryan Browne, "US Official: Russia Apologized After Russian Jet Performed Barrel Roll over US Plane," CNN, updated May 25, 2017, http://www.cnn.com/2017/05/25/politics/russia-us-aircraft-barrel-roll/ (accessed July 16, 2018)

179. Anne Barnard, "Russia Says Deal Bars American Jets from Much of Syria's Skies. U.S. Says No," *The New York Times*, May 5, 2017, https://www.nytimes.com/2017/05/05/world/middleeast/syria-deescalation-zones-russia-iran-turkey.html (accessed July 14, 2017).

180. Vladimir Isachenkov, "Russia Negotiates Deal for Its Warplanes to Use Egypt Bases," Associated Press, November 30, 2017, https://apnews.com/bdfae4502ca74c1eacdbf6d32252e8f4 (accessed July 16, 2018).

181. Ukrainian Independent Information Agency, "Russian Jet Makes Aggressive Move over French Frigate in Eastern Mediterranean," April 10, 2018, https://www.unian.info/world/10075277-russian-jet-makes-aggressive-move-over-french-frigate-in-eastern-mediterranean.html (accessed July 16, 2018).

182. Christopher Woody, "A British Sub Was Reportedly Tracked by Russian Subs in a 'Cat-and-Mouse' Pursuit Before the Latest Strikes in Syria," *Business Insider,* April 16, 2018, http://www.businessinsider.com/uk-submarine-russia-tracked-before-syria-strikes-2018-4 (accessed June 20, 2018).

183. Barnes, "A Russian Ghost Submarine, Its U.S. Pursuers and a Deadly New Cold War."

184. Daniel Kochis, "A Roadmap for Strengthened Transatlantic Pathways in the Western Balkans," Heritage Foundation *Backgrounder* No. 3286, March 16, 2018, https://www.heritage.org/global-politics/report/roadmap-strengthened-transatlantic-pathways-the-western-balkans.

185. Leonid Bershidsky, "Russia Re-Enacts the Great Game in the Balkans," Bloomberg, January 19, 2017, https://www.bloomberg.com/view/articles/2017-01-19/russia-re-enacts-the-great-game-in-the-balkans (accessed July 14, 2017).

186. Kochis, "A Roadmap for Strengthened Transatlantic Pathways in the Western Balkans."

187. Ibid.

188. Ibid.

189. Ibid.

190. Aleksandar Vasovic, "Serbia Hosts Joint Military Exercises with Russia," Reuters, November 3, 2016, http://www.reuters.com/article/us-serbia-defence-russia-idUSKBN12Y1JX (accessed July 14, 2017).

191. Radio Free Europe/Radio Liberty, "Tensions Rise as Bosnian Serbs Vote in Banned Referendum," last updated September 25, 2016, https://www.rferl.org/a/balkan-tensions-rise-as-bosnian-serbs-push-ahead-with-banned-referendum/28010813.html (accessed July 19, 2017); Gordana Knezevic, "Russia's Fingers in Bosnia's Pie," Radio Free Europe/Radio Liberty, September 28, 2016, https://www.rferl.org/a/russia-putin-republika-srpska-bosnia-dodik-referendum-statehood-day/28018362.html (accessed July 19, 2017).

192. Andrew Byrne, "Bosnian Serb Forces Take Part in Illegal 'Statehood Day' Parade," *Financial Times*, January 9, 2017, https://www.ft.com/content/5ffff694-d66f-11e6-944b-e7eb37a6aa8e (accessed July 14, 2017).

193. Radio Free Europe/Radio Liberty, "U.S. Imposes Sanctions on Republika Srpska's President Dodik," January 17, 2017, https://www.rferl.org/a/dodik-republika-srpska-united-states-sanctions/28239895.html (accessed July 19, 2017).

194. Radio Free Europe/Radio Liberty, "Defying Court Ban, Republika Srpska Goes Ahead with 'Statehood Day,'" last updated January 9, 2018, https://www.rferl.org/a/republika-srpska-statehood-day-defying-court-ban/28964699.html (accessed July 16, 2018).

195. Byrne, "Bosnian Serb Forces Take Part in Illegal 'Statehood Day' Parade."

196. Thea Morrison, "Georgia's Breakaway S.Ossetia Signs Agreements with Republika Srpska," *Georgia Today*, January 11, 2018, http://georgiatoday.ge/news/8733/Georgia%E2%80%99s-Breakaway-S.Ossetia-Signs-Agreements-with-Republika-Srpska (accessed July 16, 2018).

197. Ibid.

198. Radio Free Europe/Radio Liberty, "Serbia Stops 'Promo Train' to Kosovo's North," last updated January 14, 2017, https://www.rferl.org/a/28233304.html (accessed July 16, 2018).

199. Kochis, "A Roadmap for Strengthened Transatlantic Pathways in the Western Balkans."

200. Luke Harding, Aubrey Belford, and Saska Cvetkovska, "Russia Actively Stoking Discord in Macedonia Since 2008, Intel Files Say," *The Guardian*, June 4, 2017, https://www.theguardian.com/world/2017/jun/04/russia-actively-stoking-discord-in-macedonia-since-2008-intel-files-say-leak-kremlin-balkan-nato-west-influence (accessed July 17, 2018).

201. Kochis, "A Roadmap for Strengthened Transatlantic Pathways in the Western Balkans."

202. Bill Gertz, "Russian Jets Buzzed U.S. Destroyer," *The Washington Free Beacon*, February 14, 2017, http://freebeacon.com/national-security/russian-jets-buzzed-u-s-destroyer/ (accessed July 14, 2017).

203. Reuters, "As Syria Tensions Surge, Russian Fighter Jet Buzzes French Warship in Breach of International Law," *The Japan Times*, April 11, 2018, https://www.japantimes.co.jp/news/2018/04/11/world/syria-tensions-surge-russian-fighter-jet-buzzes-french-warship-breah-international-law/#.Wx_gGIpKjcs (accessed June 20, 2018).

204. Birnbaum, "Russian Submarines Are Prowling Around Vital Undersea Cables."

205. Rishi Sunak, *Undersea Cables: Indispensable, Insecure*, Policy Exchange, December 4, 2017, p. 5, https://policyexchange.org.uk/wp-content/uploads/2017/11/Undersea-Cables.pdf (accessed July 17, 2018).

206. Kyle Mizokami, "What Is a Russian Spy Ship Doing in the Eastern Mediterranean?" *Popular Mechanics*, September 19, 2017, https://www.popularmechanics.com/military/navy-ships/a28276/yantar-spy-ship-eastern-mediterranean/ (accessed June 20, 2018).

207. Deb Reichmann, "Russia May Be Targeting Undersea Internet Cables. Here's Why That's Bad," *Time*, March 30, 2018, https://www.yahoo.com/news/russia-may-targeting-undersea-internet-213130980.html (accessed July 17, 2018).

208. Ryan Browne and Zachary Cohen, "Russian Spy Ship Spotted 100 Miles off North Carolina Coast," CNN, January 22, 2018, https://www.cnn.com/2018/01/22/politics/russia-spy-ship-us-coast/index.html?sr=twCNNp012218russia-spy-ship-us-coast0253PMStory&CNNPolitics=Tw (accessed July 17, 2018).

209. Ben Werner, "Russian Su-27 Fighter Buzzes U.S. Navy EP-3 Aries over Black Sea," U.S. Naval Institute News, January 29, 2018, https://news.usni.org/2018/01/29/30987 (accessed July 17, 2018).

210. Ryan Browne, "Russian Jet Makes 'Unsafe' Intercept of US Navy Aircraft," CNN, November 27, 2017, https://www.cnn.com/2017/11/27/politics/russia-us-unsafe-intercept/index.html (accessed July 17, 2018).

211. Janene Peters, "Russia Bombers Intercepted by Belgian Jets Above Netherlands," *NL Times*, January 15, 2018, https://nltimes.nl/2018/01/15/russian-bombers-intercepted-belgian-jets-netherlands (accessed July 17, 2018).

212. Bill Gertz, "Russian Nuclear Bombers Intercepted Near Alaska," *The Washington Free Beacon*, May 11, 2018, http://freebeacon.com/national-security/russian-nuclear-bombers-intercepted-near-alaska/ (accessed July 17, 2018).

213. Lucas Tomlinson, "Russian Nuclear-Capable Bombers Fly Near Japan, US Officials Say," Fox News, April 12, 2017, http://www.foxnews.com/world/2017/04/12/russian-nuclear-capable-bombers-fly-near-japan-us-officials-say.html (accessed July 20, 2017).

214. Lucas Tomlinson, "NORAD Responds After Russian Bombers Zoom Around Japan," Fox News, January 25, 2017, http://www.foxnews.com/us/2017/01/25/norad-responds-after-russian-bombers-zoom-around-japan.html (accessed July 20, 2017).

215. Barbara Starr and Zachary Cohen, "Russian Bombers Escorted Away from US Aircraft Carrier," CNN, updated November 21, 2017, https://www.cnn.com/2017/10/31/politics/us-jets-escort-russian-bombers-uss-ronald-reagan/index.html (accessed July 17, 2018).

216. Baltic News Service, "NATO Jets Intercept Three Russian Fighter Aircraft," Estonian Public Broadcasting, April 30, 2018, https://news.err.ee/827681/nato-jets-intercept-three-russian-fighter-aircraft (accessed June 20, 2018).

217. LETA/TBT Staff, "NATO's Intercepts of Russian Aircraft Increased in 2017 from 2016," *The Baltic Times*, January 6, 2018, https://www.baltictimes.com/nato_s_intercepts_of_russian_aircraft_increased_in_2017_from_2016/ (accessed June 20, 2018).

218. Sean O'Riordan, "Passenger Planes Dodged Russian Bombers," *Irish Examiner*, March 3, 2015, http://www.irishexaminer.com/ireland/passenger-planes-dodged-russian-bombers-315623.html (accessed July 14, 2017).

219. "SAS Flight in Russian Spy Plane Near Miss," *The Local*, May 8, 2014, http://www.thelocal.se/20140508/sas-plane-in-russian-spy-plane-near-miss (accessed July 20, 2017).

220. David Cenciotti, "Russian Spy Plane Nearly Collided with Airliner off Sweden. Again," The Aviationist, December 14, 2014, http://theaviationist.com/2014/12/14/near-collision-off-sweden/ (accessed July 14, 2017).

221. BBC, "Russian Military Admits Significant Cyber-War Efforts," February 23, 2017, http://www.bbc.com/news/world-europe-39062663 (accessed July 15, 2017).

222. Coats, "Worldwide Threat Assessment of the US Intelligence Community," February 13, 2018, p. 6. Emphasis in original.

223. Press release, "Treasury Sanctions Russian Federal Security Service Enablers," U.S. Department of the Treasury, June 11, 2018, https://home.treasury.gov/news/press-releases/sm0410 (accessed July 18, 2018).

224. U.S. Department of Homeland Security, U.S. Computer Emergency Readiness Team, "Grizzly Steppe – Russian Malicious Cyber Activity," https://www.us-cert.gov/GRIZZLY-STEPPE-Russian-Malicious-Cyber-Activity (accessed on July 18, 2018).

225. Denis Pinchuk, "Patriotic Russians May Have Staged Cyber Attacks on Own Initiative: Putin," Reuters, June 1, 2017, http://www.reuters.com/article/us-russia-economic-forum-putin-cyber-idUSKBN18S56Y (accessed July 14, 2017).

226. Coats, "Worldwide Threat Assessment of the US Intelligence Community," February 13, 2018, p. 23.

Middle East

Threats to the Homeland

Radical Islamist terrorism in its many forms remains the most immediate global threat to the safety and security of U.S. citizens at home and abroad, and most of the actors posing terrorist threats originate in the greater Middle East. More broadly, threats to the U.S. homeland and to Americans abroad include terrorist threats from non-state actors such as al-Qaeda that use the ungoverned areas of the Middle East as bases from which to plan, train, equip, and launch attacks; terrorist threats from state-supported groups such as Hezbollah; and the developing ballistic missile threat from Iran.

Terrorism Originating from al-Qaeda, Its Affiliates, and the Islamic State (IS). Although al-Qaeda has been damaged by targeted strikes that have killed key leaders in Pakistan, including Osama bin Laden, the terrorist network has evolved in a decentralized fashion, and regional affiliates continue to pose potent threats to the U.S. homeland. The regional al-Qaeda groups share the same long-term goals as the parent organization, but some have developed different priorities related to their local conflict environments.

Al-Qaeda in the Arabian Peninsula (AQAP), based in Yemen, has emerged as one of the leading terrorist threats to homeland security since the al-Qaeda high command was forced into hiding. Yemen has long been a bastion of support for militant Islamism in general and al-Qaeda in particular. Many Yemenis who migrated to Saudi Arabia to find work during the 1970s oil boom were exposed to radicalization there. Yemenis made up a disproportionate number of the estimated 25,000 foreign Muslims who flocked to Afghanistan to join the war against the Soviet occupation in the 1980s. They also make up a large segment of al-Qaeda, which was founded by foreign veterans of that war to expand the struggle into a global revolutionary campaign.

Al-Qaeda's first terrorist attack against Americans occurred in Yemen in December 1992, when a bomb was detonated in a hotel used by U.S. military personnel involved in supporting the humanitarian food relief flights to Somalia. Al-Qaeda launched a much deadlier attack in Yemen in October 2000 when it attacked the USS *Cole* in the port of Aden with a boat filled with explosives, killing 17 American sailors.[1]

Yemen was a site for the radicalization of American Muslims such as John Walker Lindh, who traveled there to study Islam before being recruited to fight in Afghanistan. Seven Yemeni Americans from Lackawanna, New York, were recruited by al-Qaeda before 9/11. Six were convicted of supporting terrorism and sent to prison, and the seventh became a fugitive who later surfaced in Yemen.

Following crackdowns in other countries, Yemen became increasingly important as a base of operations for al-Qaeda. In September 2008, al-Qaeda launched a complex attack on the U.S. embassy in Yemen that killed 19 people, including an American woman. Yemen's importance to al-Qaeda increased further in January 2009 when al-Qaeda members who had been pushed out of Saudi Arabia merged with the Yemeni branch to form Al-Qaeda in the Arabian Peninsula.

AQAP's Anwar al-Aulaqi, a charismatic American-born Yemeni cleric, reportedly incited several terrorist attacks on U.S. targets before being killed in a drone air strike in 2011. He inspired Major Nidal Hassan, who perpetrated the 2009 Fort Hood shootings that killed 13 soldiers,[2] and Umar Farouk Abdulmutallab, the failed suicide bomber who sought to destroy an airliner bound for Detroit on Christmas Day 2009.[3] Aulaqi is also suspected of playing a role in the November 2010 AQAP plot to dispatch parcel bombs to the U.S. in cargo planes. After Aulaqi's death, his videos on the Internet continued to radicalize and recruit young Muslims, including the perpetrators of the April 2013 bombing of the Boston Marathon that killed three people; the July 2015 fatal shootings of four Marines and a Navy sailor at a military recruiting office in Chattanooga, Tennessee; the December 2015 terrorist attack in San Bernardino, California, that killed 14 people; and the June 2016 shootings of 49 people in a nightclub in Orlando, Florida.[4]

AQAP, estimated to have had as many as 4,000 members in 2016,[5] has greatly expanded in the chaos of Yemen's civil war, particularly since the overthrow of Yemen's government by Iran-backed Houthi rebels in 2015. AQAP has exploited alliances with powerful, well-armed Yemeni tribes (including the Aulaq tribe from which Osama bin Laden and the radical cleric Aulaqi claimed descent) to establish sanctuaries and training bases in Yemen's rugged mountains. This is similar to al-Qaeda's *modus operandi* in Afghanistan before 9/11. In April 2015, AQAP seized the city of al Mukalla and expanded its control of rural areas in southern Yemen; after it withdrew in April 2016, the city was recaptured by pro-government Yemeni troops and troops from the United Arab Emirates (UAE), a member of the Saudi-led coalition that intervened in March 2015 in support of the Yemeni government. Nevertheless, AQAP remains a potent force that could capitalize on the anarchy of Yemen's multi-sided civil war to seize new territory.

The Islamic State (IS), formerly known as the Islamic State of Iraq and Syria (ISIS) or the Islamic State in Iraq and the Levant (ISIL) and before that as the Islamic State of Iraq and Al-Qaeda in Iraq, emerged as an al-Qaeda splinter group but has outstripped its parent organization in terms of its immediate threats to U.S. national interests. Although the Islamic State has been decimated in Iraq and Syria, it still is expanding in Africa and Asia. Moreover, it has attracted more recruits and self-radicalized followers in Western countries than al-Qaeda ever did. In the short run, the Islamic State's greater appeal for young Muslims in the West makes it a more immediate threat to the U.S. homeland than Al-Qaeda, although the older terrorist network may pose a greater long-term threat.

The Islamic State seeks to overthrow the governments of Iraq, Syria, Lebanon, and Jordan and establish a nominal Islamic state governed by a harsh and brutal interpretation of Islamic law that is an existential threat to Christians, Shiite Muslims, Yazidis, and other religious minorities. Its long-term goals are to launch what it considers a jihad (holy war) to drive Western influence out of the Middle East; destroy Israel; diminish and discredit Shia Islam, which it considers apostasy; and become the nucleus of a global Sunni Islamic empire.

By mid-2018, the Islamic State had been decimated and pushed out of most of its self-declared "caliphate." The U.S.-backed Syrian Democratic Forces militia liberated Raqqah, the IS capital city, in October 2017. In February 2018, the Commander of U.S. Central Command (CENTCOM) estimated that the Islamic State had lost more than 98 percent of the territory it had formerly held in Iraq and Syria.[6] IS forces, estimated to number about 1,000 to 3,000 fighters in June 2018, retreated to the Iraq–Syria border area, where they continue to pose a local terrorist threat.[7]

The IS began as a branch of al-Qaeda before it broke away from the core al-Qaeda leadership in 2013 in a dispute over leadership of the jihad in Syria. The IS shares a common ideology with its al-Qaeda parent organization but differs with respect to how to apply that ideology. It now rejects the leadership of bin Laden's successor, Ayman al-Zawahiri, who criticized its extreme brutality, which has alienated many Muslims. This is a dispute about tactics and strategies, however, not long-term goals. The schism also was fueled by a personal rivalry between Zawahiri and IS leader Abu Bakr al-Baghdadi, who sees himself as bin Laden's true successor and the leader of a new generation of jihadists. Baghdadi also declared the formation of a caliphate with himself as the leader in June 2014, a claim that al-Qaeda and almost all Muslim scholars rejected as illegitimate.

Although the IS has been defeated militarily in Iraq and Syria, it has continued to expand elsewhere, particularly in Afghanistan, Bangladesh, Egypt, Indonesia, Libya, Pakistan, the Philippines, and Yemen. Boko Haram, the Nigeria-based Islamist terrorist group, also pledged allegiance to the IS in March 2015.

The Islamic State primarily poses a regional terrorist threat. It has launched terrorist attacks inside Afghanistan, Egypt, Jordan, Kuwait, Lebanon, Libya, Saudi Arabia, Tunisia, Turkey, and Yemen, among other countries. It also claimed responsibility for the October 31, 2015, downing of a Russian passenger jet over Egypt's Sinai Peninsula that killed 224 people. The Islamic State also is known to have used chemical weapons in Syria and Iraq and to have the capability to make small amounts of crude mustard agent, which it has used along with captured Syrian mustard munitions.

The Islamic State's early success in attracting the support of foreign militants, including at least 4,500 from Western countries and at least 250 specifically from the United States, has amplified its potential threat as these foreign volunteers, many of whom received military training, return home.[8] IS foreign fighters teamed with local Islamist militants to launch terrorist attacks that killed 130 people in Paris, France, in November 2015 and 32 people in Brussels, Belgium, in March 2016, as well as a string of smaller attacks. The IS also has inspired self-radicalized individuals to use vehicles as battering rams in terrorist attacks. A terrorist in a truck killed 86 people at

a Bastille Day celebration in July 2016 in Nice, France; another truck attack killed 12 people at a Christmas market in Berlin, Germany, in December 2016; and in June 2017, three men in a van killed eight people on or near London Bridge in London, England, by running them over or stabbing them. In May 2017, a terrorist with proven links to the Islamic State killed 22 people in a suicide bombing at a concert in Manchester, England. A Moroccan-born French national who declared himself to be an IS supporter killed four people before being killed by police in Trebes, France, in March 2018.

IS leader al-Baghdadi threatened to strike "in the heart" of America in July 2012.[9] The IS reportedly has tried to recruit Americans who have joined the fighting in Syria and would be in a position to carry out this threat after returning to the United States.[10] It also has inspired several terrorist attacks by self-radicalized "stray dogs" or "lone wolves" who have acted in its name, such as the foiled May 3, 2015, attack by two Islamist extremists who were fatally shot by police before they could commit mass murder in Garland, Texas; the July 16, 2015, shootings that killed four Marines and a sailor in Chattanooga, Tennessee; the December 2, 2015, shootings that killed 14 people in San Bernardino, California; the June 12, 2016, shootings at a nightclub in Orlando, Florida, that killed 49 people, and the October 31, 2017, vehicle attack by a self-radicalized Uzbek immigrant who killed eight people with his truck on a New York City bicycle path. Such terrorist attacks, incited but not directed by the IS, are likely to continue for the foreseeable future.

Hayat Tahrir al-Sham (HTS—Organization for the Liberation of the Levant), al-Qaeda's official affiliate in Syria, is a front organization formed in January 2017 in a merger between Jabhat Fateh al-Sham (Front for the Conquest of Syria), formerly known as the al-Nusra Front, and several other Islamist extremist movements. HTS was estimated to have 12,000 to 14,000 fighters in March 2017.[11] Before the merger, al-Nusra had an estimated

5,000 to 10,000 members and had emerged as one of the top two or three rebel groups fighting Syria's Assad dictatorship.[12] Al-Nusra was established as an offshoot of Al-Qaeda in Iraq (now renamed the Islamic State) in late 2011 by Abu Muhammad al-Julani, a lieutenant of AQI leader Abu Bakr al-Baghdadi.[13] It has adopted a more pragmatic course than its extremist parent organization and has cooperated with moderate Syrian rebel groups against the Assad regime, as well as against the Islamic State.

When Baghdadi unilaterally proclaimed the merger of his organization and al-Nusra in April 2013 to form the Islamic State of Iraq and Syria, Julani rejected the merger and renewed his pledge to al-Qaeda leader Ayman al-Zawahiri. The two groups have clashed repeatedly and remain bitter enemies.

HTS, like its previous incarnation al-Nusra, has focused its attention on overthrowing the Syrian regime and has not emphasized its hostility to the United States, but that will change if it consolidates power within Syria. It already poses a potential threat because of its recruitment of foreign Islamist militants, including some from Europe and the United States. According to U.S. officials, al-Qaeda leader al-Zawahiri dispatched a cadre of experienced al-Qaeda operatives to Syria, where they were embedded with al-Nusra and charged with organizing terrorist attacks against Western targets. Many members of the group, estimated to number in the dozens, were veterans of al-Qaeda's operations in Afghanistan and Pakistan (part of what was called Khorasan in ancient times) and were referred to as the "Khorasan group" by U.S. officials.[14]

An American Muslim recruited by al-Nusra, Moner Mohammad Abusalha, conducted a suicide truck bombing in northern Syria on May 25, 2014, that was the first reported suicide attack by an American in that country.[15] At least five men have been arrested inside the United States for providing material assistance to al-Nusra, including Abdirahman Sheik Mohamud, a naturalized U.S. citizen born in Somalia who was arrested in April 2015 after returning from training in Syria, possibly to launch a terrorist attack inside the United States.[16] The Khorasan group was targeted by a series of U.S. air strikes in 2014–2015 that degraded its capacity to organize terrorist attacks in Western countries. By mid-2015, the FBI assessed that the Islamic State had eclipsed al-Nusra as a threat to the U.S. homeland.[17] In September 2017, testifying before the Senate Homeland Security and Government Affairs Committee, FBI Director Christopher Wray identified "the Islamic State... and homegrown violent extremists as the main terrorism threats to the Homeland."[18]

Al-Qaeda in the Islamic Maghreb (AQIM), one of al-Qaeda's weaker franchises before the onset of the Arab Spring uprisings in 2011, has flourished in recent years in North Africa and is now one of al-Qaeda's best-financed and most heavily armed elements. The overthrow of Libyan dictator Muammar Qadhafi in 2011 opened a Pandora's box of problems that AQIM has exploited to bolster its presence in Algeria, Libya, Mali, Morocco, and Tunisia. AQIM accumulated large quantities of arms, including man-portable air defense systems (MANPADS), looted from Qadhafi's huge arms depots.

The fall of Qadhafi also led hundreds of heavily armed Tuareg mercenaries formerly employed by his regime to cross into Mali, where they joined a Tuareg separatist insurgency against Mali's weak central government. In November 2011, they formed the separatist National Movement for the Liberation of Azawad (MNLA) and sought to carve out an independent state. In cooperation with AQIM and the Islamist movement Ansar Dine, they gained control of northern Mali, a territory as big as Texas and the world's largest terrorist sanctuary until the January 2013 French military intervention dealt a major setback to AQIM and its allies.

AQIM is estimated to have several hundred militants operating in Algeria, Libya, Mali, Niger, and Tunisia.[19] Many AQIM cadres pushed out of Mali by the French intervention have regrouped in southwestern Libya and remain committed to advancing AQIM's self-declared long-term goal of transforming the Sahel "into one vast, seething, chaotic Somalia."[20]

The September 11, 2012, attack on the U.S. diplomatic mission in Benghazi underscored the extent to which Islamist extremists have grown stronger in the region, particularly in eastern Libya, a longtime bastion of Islamic fervor. The radical Islamist group that launched the attack, Ansar al-Sharia, has links to AQIM and shares its violent ideology. Ansar al-Sharia and scores of other Islamist militias have flourished in post-Qadhafi Libya because the weak central government has been unable to tame fractious militias, curb tribal and political clashes, or dampen rising tensions between Arabs and Berbers in the West and Arabs and the Toubou tribe in the South.

AQIM does not pose as much of a threat to the U.S. homeland as other al-Qaeda offshoots pose, but it does threaten regional stability and U.S. allies in North Africa and Europe, where it has gained supporters and operates extensive networks for the smuggling of arms, drugs, and people.

WWTA: The WWTA assesses that "Sunni violent extremists—most notably ISIS and al-Qa'ida—pose continuing terrorist threats to US interests and partners worldwide" and that "[h]omegrown violent extremists (HVEs) will remain the most prevalent and difficult-to-detect Sunni terrorist threat at home, despite a drop in the number of attacks in 2017."[21]

Summary: Although the al-Qaeda core group has been weakened, the Islamic State and al-Qaeda franchises based in the Middle East pose a continuing threat to the U.S. homeland as a result of the recruitment of Muslim militants from Western countries, including the United States, and their efforts to inspire terrorist attacks by homegrown Islamist extremists.

Hezbollah Terrorism. Hezbollah (Party of God), the radical Lebanon-based Shiite revolutionary movement, poses a clear terrorist threat to international security. Hezbollah terrorists have murdered Americans, Israelis, Lebanese, Europeans, and citizens of many other nations. Originally founded with support from Iran in 1982, this Lebanese group has evolved from a local menace into a global terrorist network that is strongly backed by regimes in Iran and Syria, assisted by a political wing that has dominated Lebanese politics and funded by Iran and a web of charitable organizations, criminal activities, and front companies.

Hezbollah regards terrorism not only as a useful tool for advancing its revolutionary agenda, but also as a religious duty as part of a "global jihad." It helped to introduce and popularize the tactic of suicide bombings in Lebanon in the 1980s, developed a strong guerrilla force and a political apparatus in the 1990s, provoked a war with Israel in 2006, intervened in the Syrian civil war after 2011 at Iran's direction, and has become a major destabilizing influence in the ongoing Arab–Israeli conflict.

Hezbollah murdered more Americans than any other terrorist group before September 11, 2001. Despite al-Qaeda's increased visibility since then, Hezbollah remains a bigger, better equipped, better organized, and potentially more dangerous terrorist organization, in part because it enjoys the support of the two chief state sponsors of terrorism in the world today: Iran and Syria. Hezbollah's demonstrated capabilities led former Deputy Secretary of State Richard Armitage to dub it "the A-Team of Terrorists."[22]

Hezbollah has expanded its operations from Lebanon to regional targets in the Middle East and then far beyond. It now is a global terrorist threat that draws financial and logistical support from its Iranian patrons as well as from the Lebanese Shiite diaspora in the Middle East, Europe, Africa, Southeast Asia, North America, and South America. Hezbollah fundraising and equipment procurement cells have been detected and broken up in the United States and Canada. Europe is believed to contain many more of these cells.

Hezbollah has been implicated in numerous terrorist attacks against Americans, including:

- The April 18, 1983, bombing of the U.S. embassy in Beirut, which killed 63 people including 17 Americans;

- The October 23, 1983, suicide truck bombing of the Marine barracks at Beirut Airport, which killed 241 Marines and other personnel deployed as part of the multinational peacekeeping force in Lebanon;

- The September 20, 1984, suicide truck bombing of the U.S. embassy annex in Lebanon, which killed 23 people including two Americans; and

- The June 25, 1996, Khobar Towers bombing, which killed 19 American servicemen stationed in Saudi Arabia.

Hezbollah also was involved in the kidnapping of several dozen Westerners, including 14 Americans, who were held as hostages in Lebanon in the 1980s. The American hostages eventually became pawns that Iran used as leverage in the secret negotiations that led to the Iran–Contra affair in the mid-1980s.

Hezbollah has launched numerous attacks outside of the Middle East. It perpetrated the two deadliest terrorist attacks in the history of South America: the March 1992 bombing of the Israeli embassy in Buenos Aires, Argentina, which killed 29 people, and the July 1994 bombing of a Jewish community center in Buenos Aires that killed 96 people. The trial of those who were implicated in the 1994 bombing revealed an extensive Hezbollah presence in Argentina and other countries in South America.

Hezbollah has escalated its terrorist attacks against Israeli targets in recent years as part of Iran's intensifying shadow war against Israel. In 2012, Hezbollah killed five Israeli tourists and a Bulgarian bus driver in a suicide bombing near Burgas, Bulgaria. Hezbollah terrorist plots against Israelis were foiled in Thailand and Cyprus during that same year.

In 2013, Hezbollah admitted that it had deployed several thousand militia members to fight in Syria on behalf of the Assad regime. By 2015, Hezbollah forces had become crucial in propping up the Assad regime after the Syrian army was hamstrung by casualties, defections,

and low morale. Hezbollah also deployed personnel to Iraq after the 2003 U.S. intervention to assist pro-Iranian Iraqi Shia militias that were battling the U.S.-led coalition. In addition, Hezbollah has deployed personnel in Yemen to train and assist the Iran-backed Houthi rebels.

Although Hezbollah operates mostly in the Middle East, it has a global reach and has established a presence inside the United States. Hezbollah cells in the United States generally are focused on fundraising, including criminal activities such as those perpetrated by over 70 used-car dealerships identified as part of a scheme to launder hundreds of millions of dollars of cocaine-generated revenue that flowed back to Hezbollah.[23]

Covert Hezbollah cells could morph into other forms and launch terrorist operations inside the United States. Given Hezbollah's close ties to Iran and past record of executing terrorist attacks on Tehran's behalf, there is a real danger that Hezbollah terrorist cells could be activated inside the United States in the event of a conflict between Iran and the U.S. or Israel. On June 1, 2017, two naturalized U.S. citizens were arrested and charged with providing material support to Hezbollah and conducting preoperational surveillance of military and law enforcement sites in New York City and at Kennedy Airport, the Panama Canal, and the American and Israeli embassies in Panama.[24]

Nicholas Rasmussen, Director of the National Counterterrorism Center, noted at an October 10, 2017, briefing that the June arrests were a "stark reminder" of Hezbollah's global reach and warned that Hezbollah posed a potential threat to the U.S. homeland: "It's our assessment that Hizballah is determined to give itself a potential homeland option as a critical component of its terrorism playbook, and that is something that those of us in the counterterrorism community take very, very seriously."[25]

WWTA: The WWTA assesses that "Lebanese Hizballah has demonstrated its intent to foment regional instability by deploying thousands of fighters to Syria and by providing weapons, tactics, and direction to militant and terrorist groups." In addition, "Hizballah probably also emphasizes its capability to attack US, Israeli, and Saudi Arabian interests."[26]

Summary: Hezbollah operates mostly in the Middle East, but it has established cells inside the United States that could be activated, particularly in the event of a military conflict with Iran, Hezbollah's creator and chief backer.

Palestinian Terrorist Threats. A wide spectrum of Palestinian terrorist groups threaten Israel, including Fatah (al-Aqsa Martyrs Brigade); Hamas; Palestinian Islamic Jihad; the Popular Front for the Liberation of Palestine (PFLP); the Popular Front for the Liberation of Palestine–General Command (PFLP–GC); the Palestine Liberation Front; and the Army of Islam. Most of these groups are also hostile to the United States, which they denounce as Israel's primary source of foreign support.

Although they are focused more on Israel and regional targets, these groups also pose a limited potential threat to the U.S. homeland, particularly should the Israeli–Palestinian peace process break down completely and the Palestinian Authority be dissolved. In the event of a military confrontation with Iran, Tehran also might seek to use Palestinian Islamic Jihad, the PFLP–GC, or Hamas as surrogates to strike the United States. Jihadist groups based in Gaza, such as the Army of Islam, also could threaten the U.S. homeland even if a terrorist attack there would set back Palestinian national interests. In general, however, Palestinian groups present a much bigger threat to Israel, Jordan, Egypt, and other regional targets than they do to the United States.

WWTA: The WWTA does not reference the potential threat of Palestinian terrorist attacks on the U.S. homeland.

Summary: Palestinian terrorist groups are focused primarily on Israeli targets and potentially on Egypt and Jordan, which are perceived as collaborating with Israel. They also, however, pose a limited potential threat to the U.S. homeland because of the possibility that if the Israeli–Palestinian peace process broke down completely or Iran became involved in a military conflict with the U.S., Palestinian

surrogates could be used to target the U.S. homeland.

Iran's Ballistic Missile Threat. Iran has an extensive missile development program that has received key assistance from North Korea and more limited support from Russia and China until sanctions were imposed by the U.N. Security Council. Although the U.S. intelligence community assesses that Iran does not have an ICBM capability (an intercontinental ballistic missile with a range of 5,500 kilometers or about 2,900 miles), Tehran could develop one in the future. Iran has launched several satellites with space launch vehicles that use similar technology, which could also be adapted to develop an ICBM capability.[27]

Although Tehran's missile arsenal primarily threatens U.S. bases and allies in the region, Iran eventually could expand the range of its missiles to include the continental United States. In its January 2014 report on Iran's military power, the Pentagon assessed that "Iran continues to develop technological capabilities that could be applicable to nuclear weapons and long-range missiles, which could be adapted to deliver nuclear weapons, should Iran's leadership decide to do so."[28]

WWTA: The WWTA assesses that "Iran's ballistic missile programs give it the potential to hold targets at risk across the region, and Tehran already has the largest inventory of ballistic missiles in the Middle East." Moreover, "Tehran's desire to deter the United States might drive it to field an ICBM." In this connection, the WWTA warns that "[p]rogress on Iran's space program, such as the launch of the Simorgh SLV in July 2017, could shorten a pathway to an ICBM because space launch vehicles use similar technologies."[29]

Summary: Iran's ballistic missile force poses a significant regional threat to the U.S. and its allies, and Tehran eventually could expand the range of its missiles to threaten the continental United States.

Threat of Regional War

The Middle East region is one of the most complex and volatile threat environments faced

MAP 5

Iran's Ballistic Missile Ranges

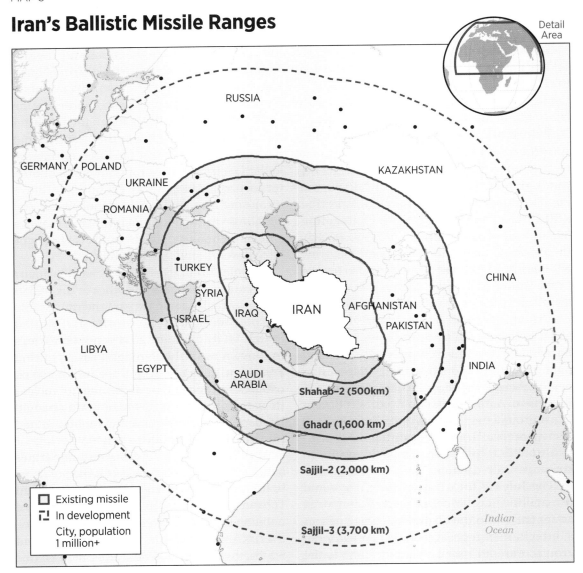

Detail Area

RUSSIA

GERMANY POLAND

KAZAKHSTAN

UKRAINE

ROMANIA

TURKEY

CHINA

SYRIA

IRAQ   IRAN   AFGHANISTAN

ISRAEL   PAKISTAN

LIBYA

INDIA

EGYPT

SAUDI ARABIA

Shahab–2 (500km)

Ghadr (1,600 km)

☐ Existing missile

⌐⌐ In development

City, population 1 million+

Sajjil–2 (2,000 km)

Sajjil–3 (3,700 km)

Indian Ocean

SOURCES: International Institute for Strategic Studies, *The Military Balance 2014* (London: Routledge, 2014), and Michael Elleman, "Iran's Ballistic Missile Program," United States Institute of Peace, http://iranprimer.usip.org/resource/irans-ballistic-missile-program (accessed August 25, 2015).

📞 heritage.org

by the United States and its allies. Iran, various al-Qaeda offshoots, Hezbollah, Arab–Israeli clashes, and a growing number of radical Islamist militias and revolutionary groups in Egypt, Gaza, Iraq, Jordan, Lebanon, Libya, Syria, and Yemen pose actual or potential threats both to America's interests and to those of its allies.

Iranian Threats in the Middle East. Iran is an anti-Western revolutionary state that seeks to tilt the regional balance of power in its favor by driving out the Western presence, undermining and overthrowing opposing governments, and establishing its hegemony over the oil-rich Persian Gulf region. It also seeks

CHART 8

Iran Defense Spending on Rise Since 2014

**SPENDING IN BILLIONS OF
CONSTANT 2016 DOLLARS**

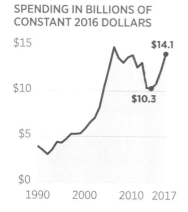

**SPENDING AS SHARE
OF GDP**

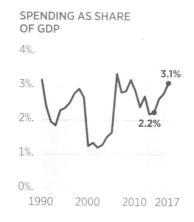

**SPENDING AS A SHARE OF
GOVERNMENT SPENDING**

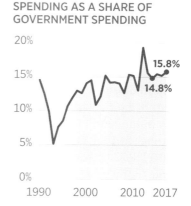

SOURCE: Stockholm International Peace Research Institute,
https://www.sipri.org/ (accessed August 8, 2018).

☎ heritage.org

to radicalize Shiite communities and advance their interests against Sunni rivals. Iran has a long record of sponsoring terrorist attacks against American allies and other interests in the region. With regard to conventional threats, Iran's ground forces dwarf the relatively small armies of the other Gulf States, and its formidable ballistic missile forces pose significant threats to its neighbors.

The July 14, 2015, Iran nuclear agreement, which lifted nuclear-related sanctions on Iran in January 2016, gave Tehran access to about $100 billion in restricted assets and allowed Iran to expand its oil and gas exports, the chief source of its state revenues. Relief from the burden of sanctions boosted Iran's economy and enabled Iran to enhance its strategic position, military capabilities, and support for surrogate networks and terrorist groups. Tehran announced in May 2016 that it was increasing its military budget for 2016–2017 to $19 billion—a 90 percent increase over the previous year.[30]

The lifting of sanctions also has allowed Tehran to emerge from diplomatic isolation and strengthen strategic ties with Russia that will allow it to purchase advanced arms and modernize its military forces. Russian

President Vladimir Putin traveled to Iran in November 2015 to meet with Ayatollah Khamenei, Iran's Supreme Leader, and other officials. Both regimes called for enhanced military cooperation. During Iranian President Hassan Rouhani's visit to Russia in March 2017, Putin proclaimed his intention to raise bilateral relations to the level of a "strategic partnership."[31] Putin met with Rouhani again on June 9, 2018, on the sidelines of the Shanghai Cooperation Organization (SCO) summit, where he noted that Iran and Russia were "working well together to settle the Syrian crisis" and promised to support Iran's entry into the SCO.[32]

This growing strategic relationship has strengthened Iran's military capabilities. Tehran announced in April 2016 that Russia had started deliveries of up to five S-300 Favorit long-range surface-to-air missile systems, which can track up to 100 aircraft and engage six of them simultaneously at a range of 200 kilometers.[33] Moscow also began negotiations to sell Iran T-90 tanks and advanced Sukhoi Su-30 Flanker fighter jets.[34] The warplanes will significantly improve Iran's air defense and long-range strike capabilities.

After the nuclear agreement, Iran and Russia escalated their strategic cooperation in propping up Syria's embattled Assad regime. Iran's growing military intervention in Syria was partly eclipsed by Russia's military intervention and launching of an air campaign against Assad's enemies in September 2015, but Iran's Islamic Revolutionary Guard Corps (IRGC) and surrogate militia groups have played the leading role in spearheading the ground offensives that have retaken territory from Syrian rebel groups and tilted the military balance in favor of the Assad regime. By October 2015, Iran had deployed an estimated 7,000 IRGC troops and paramilitary forces in Syria, along with an estimated 20,000 foreign fighters from Iran-backed Shiite militias from Lebanon, Iraq, Afghanistan, and Pakistan.[35] Iran, working closely with Russia, then expanded its military efforts and helped to consolidate a costly victory for the Assad regime.

Iran's growing military presence in Syria and continued efforts to provide advanced weapons to Hezbollah through Syria have fueled tensions with Israel. Israel has launched over one hundred air strikes against Hezbollah and Iranian forces to prevent the transfer of sophisticated arms and prevent Iran-backed militias from deploying near Israel's border. On February 10, 2018, Iranian forces in Syria launched an armed drone that penetrated Israeli airspace before it was shot down. Israel responded with air strikes on IRGC facilities in Syria. Iranian forces in Syria later launched a salvo of 20 rockets against Israeli military positions in the Golan Heights on May 9, 2018, provoking Israel to launch ground-to-ground missiles, artillery salvos, and air strikes against all known Iranian bases in Syria.[36] Although Russia has sought to calm the situation, another clash could quickly escalate into a regional conflict.

Terrorist Attacks. Iran has adopted a political warfare strategy that emphasizes irregular warfare, asymmetric tactics, and the extensive use of proxy forces. The Islamic Revolutionary Guard Corps has trained, armed, supported, and collaborated with a wide variety of radical Shia and Sunni militant groups, as well as Arab, Palestinian, Kurdish, and Afghan groups that do not share its radical Islamist ideology. The IRGC's elite Quds (Jerusalem) Force has cultivated, trained, armed, and supported numerous proxies, particularly the Lebanon-based Hezbollah; Iraqi Shia militant groups; Palestinian groups such as Hamas and Palestinian Islamic Jihad; and groups that have fought against the governments of Afghanistan, Bahrain, Egypt, Israel, Iraq, Jordan, Kuwait, Morocco, Saudi Arabia, Turkey, the United Arab Emirates, and Yemen.

Iran is the world's foremost state sponsor of terrorism and has made extensive efforts to export its radical Shia brand of Islamist revolution. It has found success in establishing a network of powerful Shia revolutionary groups in Lebanon and Iraq; has cultivated links with Afghan Shia and Taliban militants; and has stirred Shia unrest in Bahrain, Iraq, Lebanon, Saudi Arabia, and Yemen. In recent years, Iranian arms shipments have been intercepted regularly by naval forces off the coasts of Bahrain and Yemen, and Israel has repeatedly intercepted arms shipments, including long-range rockets, bound for Palestinian militants in Gaza.

Mounting Missile Threat. Iran possesses the largest number of deployed missiles in the Middle East.[37] In June 2017, Iran launched mid-range missiles from its territory that struck opposition targets in Syria. This was the first such operational use of mid-range missiles by Iran in almost 30 years, but it was not as successful as Tehran might have hoped. It was reported that of the five missiles launched, three missed Syria altogether and landed in Iraq, and the remaining two landed in Syria but missed their intended targets by miles.[38]

The backbone of the Iranian ballistic missile force is the Shahab series of road-mobile surface-to-surface missiles, which are based on Soviet-designed Scud missiles. The Shahab missiles are potentially capable of carrying nuclear, chemical, or biological warheads in addition to conventional high-explosive warheads. Their relative inaccuracy (compared to NATO ballistic missiles) limits their effectiveness unless they are employed against large, soft targets such as cities.

Iran's heavy investment in such weapons has fueled speculation that the Iranians intend eventually to replace the conventional warheads on their longer-range missiles with nuclear warheads. As the Nuclear Threat Initiative has observed, "Iran's rapidly improving missile capabilities have prompted concern from international actors such as the United Nations, the United States and Iran's regional neighbors."[39]

Iran is not a member of the Missile Technology Control Regime, and it has sought aggressively to acquire, develop, and deploy a wide spectrum of ballistic missile, cruise missile, and space launch capabilities. During the 1980–1988 Iran–Iraq war, Iran acquired Soviet-made Scud-B missiles from Libya and later acquired North Korean–designed Scud-C and No-dong missiles, which it renamed the Shahab-2 (with an estimated range of 500 kilometers or 310 miles) and Shahab-3 (with an estimated range of 900 kilometers or 560 miles). It now can produce its own variants of these missiles as well as longer-range Ghadr-1 and Qiam missiles.

Iran's Shahab-3 and Ghadr-1, which is a modified version of the Shahab-3 with a smaller warhead but greater range (about 1,600 kilometers or 1,000 miles), are considered more reliable and advanced than the North Korean No-dong missile from which they are derived. In 2014, then-Defense Intelligence Agency Director Lieutenant General Michael T. Flynn warned that:

> Iran can strike targets throughout the region and into Eastern Europe. In addition to its growing missile and rocket inventories, Iran is seeking to enhance lethality and effectiveness of existing systems with improvements in accuracy and warhead designs. Iran is developing the Khalij Fars, an anti-ship ballistic missile which could threaten maritime activity throughout the Persian Gulf and Strait of Hormuz.[40]

Iran's ballistic missiles pose a major threat to U.S. bases and allies from Turkey, Israel, and Egypt in the west to Saudi Arabia and the other Gulf States to the south and Afghanistan and Pakistan to the east. However, it is Israel, which has fought a shadow war with Iran and its terrorist proxies, that is most at risk from an Iranian missile attack. In case the Israeli government had any doubt about Iran's implacable hostility, the Revolutionary Guards displayed a message written in Hebrew on the side of one of the Iranian missiles tested in March 2016: "Israel must be wiped off the earth."[41] The development of nuclear warheads for Iran's ballistic missiles would significantly degrade Israel's ability to deter attacks, an ability that the existing (but not officially acknowledged) Israeli monopoly on nuclear weapons in the Middle East currently provides.

For Iran's radical regime, hostility to Israel, which Iran sometimes calls the "little Satan," is second only to hostility to the United States, which the leader of Iran's 1979 revolution, Ayatollah Khomeini, dubbed the "great Satan." But Iran poses a greater immediate threat to Israel than it does to the United States: Israel is a smaller country with fewer military capabilities, is located much closer to Iran, and already is within range of Iran's Shahab-3 missiles. Moreover, all of Israel can be hit with the thousands of shorter-range rockets that Iran has provided to Hezbollah in Lebanon and to Hamas and Palestinian Islamic Jihad in Gaza.

Weapons of Mass Destruction. Tehran has invested tens of billions of dollars since the 1980s in a nuclear weapons program concealed within its civilian nuclear power program. It built clandestine, but subsequently discovered, underground uranium-enrichment facilities near Natanz and Fordow and a heavy-water reactor near Arak that would give it a second potential route to nuclear weapons.[42]

Before the 2015 nuclear deal, Iran had accumulated enough low-enriched uranium to build eight nuclear bombs if enriched to weapons-grade levels, and it could enrich enough uranium to arm one bomb in less than two months.[43] Clearly, the development of a nuclear bomb would greatly amplify the threat posed by Iran. Even if Iran did not use a nuclear weapon or pass it on to one of its terrorist surrogates to use, the regime in Tehran could become emboldened to expand its support for terrorism, subversion, and intimidation, assuming that its nuclear arsenal would protect it from retaliation as has been the case with North Korea.

On July 14, 2015, President Barack Obama announced that the United States and Iran, along with China, France, Germany, Russia, the United Kingdom, and the European Union High Representative for Foreign Affairs and Security Policy, had reached a "comprehensive, long-term deal with Iran that will prevent it from obtaining a nuclear weapon."[44] The short-lived agreement, however, did a much better job of dismantling sanctions against Iran than it did of dismantling Iran's nuclear infrastructure. This flaw led President Donald Trump to withdraw the U.S. from the agreement on May 8, 2018, and reimpose sanctions.

In fact, the agreement did not require that any of Iran's covertly built facilities would have to be dismantled. The Natanz and Fordow uranium-enrichment facilities were allowed to remain in operation, although the latter facility was to be repurposed at least temporarily as a research site. The heavy-water reactor at Arak was also retained with modifications that will reduce its yield of plutonium. All of these facilities, built covertly and housing operations prohibited by multiple U.N. Security Council resolutions, were legitimized by the agreement.

The Iran nuclear agreement marked a risky departure from more than five decades of U.S. nonproliferation efforts under which Washington opposed the spread of sensitive nuclear technologies, such as uranium enrichment, even for allies. Iran got a better deal on uranium enrichment under the agreement than such U.S. allies as the United Arab Emirates, South Korea, and Taiwan have received from Washington in the past. In fact, the Obama Administration gave Iran better terms on uranium enrichment than President Gerald Ford's Administration gave the Shah of Iran, a close U.S. ally before the 1979 revolution.

President Trump's decision to exit the nuclear agreement marks a return to long-standing U.S. nonproliferation policy. Iran, Britain, France, Germany, and the European Union (EU) have announced that they will try to salvage the agreement, but this is unlikely, given the strength of the U.S. sanctions that are slated to be fully reimposed by November 4, 2018, after a 180-day wind-down period.

Iran is a declared chemical weapons power that claims to have destroyed all of its chemical weapons stockpiles. U.S. intelligence agencies have assessed that Iran maintains "the capability to produce chemical warfare (CW) agents and 'probably' has the capability to produce some biological warfare agents for offensive purposes, if it made the decision to do so."[45] Iran also has threatened to disrupt the flow of Persian Gulf oil exports by closing the Strait of Hormuz in the event of a conflict with the U.S. or its allies.

WWTA: The WWTA assesses that "Iran will seek to expand its influence in Iraq, Syria, and Yemen, where it sees conflicts generally trending in Tehran's favor," and "will exploit the fight against ISIS to solidify partnerships and translate its battlefield gains into political, security, and economic agreements." It also notes that "Iran continues to develop and improve a range of new military capabilities to target US and allied military assets in the region, including armed UAVs, ballistic missiles, advanced naval mines, unmanned explosive boats, submarines and advanced torpedoes, and antiship and land-attack cruise missiles." Tehran has the Middle East's "largest ballistic missile force... and can strike targets up to 2,000 kilometers from Iran's borders," and "Russia's delivery of the SA-20c SAM system in 2016 has provided Iran with its most advanced long-range air defense system."[46]

Summary: Iran poses a major potential threat to U.S. bases, interests, and allies in the Middle East by virtue of its ballistic missile capabilities, continued nuclear ambitions, long-standing support for terrorism, and extensive support for Islamist revolutionary groups.

Arab Attack on Israel. In addition to threats from Iran, Israel faces the constant threat of attack from Palestinian, Lebanese, Egyptian, Syrian, and other Arab terrorist groups. The threat posed by Arab states, which lost four wars against Israel in 1948, 1956, 1967, and 1973 (Syria and the PLO lost a fifth war in 1982 in Lebanon), has gradually declined. Egypt and Jordan have signed peace treaties with Israel, and Iraq, Libya, Syria, and Yemen are bogged down by increasingly brutal civil wars. Although the conventional military threat to Israel from Arab states has declined, unconventional military and terrorist threats, especially from an expanding number of sub-state actors, have risen substantially.

Iran has systematically bolstered many of these groups even when it did not necessarily share their ideology. Today, Iran's surrogates, Hezbollah and Palestinian Islamic Jihad, along with more distant ally Hamas, pose the chief immediate threats to Israel. After Israel's May 2000 withdrawal from southern Lebanon and the September 2000 outbreak of fighting between Israelis and Palestinians, Hezbollah stepped up its support for such Palestinian extremist groups as Hamas, Palestinian Islamic Jihad, the al-Aqsa Martyrs' Brigades, and the Popular Front for the Liberation of Palestine. It also expanded its own operations in the West Bank and Gaza and provided funding for specific attacks launched by other groups.

In July 2006, Hezbollah forces crossed the Lebanese border in an effort to kidnap Israeli soldiers inside Israel, igniting a military clash that claimed hundreds of lives and severely damaged the economies on both sides of the border. Hezbollah has since rebuilt its depleted arsenal with help from Iran and Syria. Israeli officials have estimated that Hezbollah has amassed around 150,000 rockets, including a number of long-range Iranian-made missiles capable of striking cities throughout Israel.[47]

Since Israel's withdrawal from the Gaza Strip in 2005, Hamas, Palestinian Islamic Jihad, and other terrorist groups have fired more than 11,000 rockets into Israel, sparking wars in 2008–2009, 2012, and 2014.[48] Over 5 million Israelis out of a total population of 8.1 million live within range of rocket attacks from Gaza, although the successful operation of the Iron Dome anti-missile system greatly mitigated this threat during the Gaza conflict in 2014. In that war, Hamas also unveiled a sophisticated tunnel network that it used to infiltrate Israel to launch attacks on Israeli civilians and military personnel.

Israel also faces a growing threat of terrorist attacks from Syria. Islamist extremist groups fighting the Syrian government, including the al-Qaeda–affiliated Hayat Tahrir al-Sham (formerly al-Nusra Front), have attacked Israeli positions in the Golan Heights, which Israel captured in the 1967 Arab–Israeli war.

WWTA: The WWTA does not reference Arab threats to Israel.

Summary: The threat posed to Israel by Arab states has declined in recent years as a result of the overthrow or weakening of hostile Arab regimes in Iraq and Syria. However, there is a growing threat from sub-state actors such as Hamas, Hezbollah, the Islamic State, and other terrorist groups in Egypt, Gaza, Lebanon, and Syria. Given the region's inherent volatility, the general destabilization that has occurred as a consequence of Syria's civil war, the growth of the Islamic State as a major threat actor, and the United States' long-standing support for Israel, any concerted attack on Israel would be a major concern for the U.S.

Terrorist Threats from Hezbollah. Hezbollah is a close ally of, frequent surrogate for, and terrorist subcontractor for Iran's revolutionary Islamist regime. Iran played a crucial role in creating Hezbollah in 1982 as a vehicle for exporting its revolution, mobilizing Lebanese Shia, and developing a terrorist surrogate for attacks on its enemies.

Tehran provides the bulk of Hezbollah's foreign support: arms, training, logistical support, and money. The Pentagon has estimated that Iran provides up to $200 million in annual financial support for Hezbollah; other estimates, made before the 2015 nuclear deal offered Tehran substantial relief from sanctions, ran as high as $350 million annually.[49]

After the nuclear deal boosted Iran's financial health, Tehran increased its aid to Hezbollah, providing as much as $800 million per year, according to Israeli officials.[50] Tehran has lavishly stocked Hezbollah's expensive and extensive arsenal of rockets, sophisticated land mines, small arms, ammunition, explosives, anti-ship missiles, anti-aircraft missiles, and even unmanned aerial vehicles that Hezbollah can use for aerial surveillance or remotely piloted terrorist attacks. Iranian Revolutionary Guards have trained Hezbollah terrorists in Lebanon's Bekaa Valley and in Iran.

Iran has used Hezbollah as a club to hit not only Israel and Tehran's Western enemies, but also many Arab countries. Tehran's revolutionary ideology has fueled Iran's hostility to other Middle Eastern states, many of which it seeks to overthrow and replace with radical allies. During the Iran–Iraq war, Iran used Hezbollah to launch terrorist attacks against Iraqi targets and against Arab states that sided with Iraq. Hezbollah launched numerous terrorist attacks against Saudi Arabia and Kuwait, which extended strong financial support to Iraq's war effort, and participated in several other terrorist operations in Bahrain and the United Arab Emirates.

Iranian Revolutionary Guards conspired with the branch of Hezbollah in Saudi Arabia to conduct the 1996 Khobar Towers bombing in Saudi Arabia. Hezbollah collaborated with the IRGC's Quds Force to destabilize Iraq after the 2003 U.S. occupation and helped to train and advise the Mahdi Army, the radical anti-Western Shiite militia led by militant Iraqi cleric Moqtada al-Sadr. Hezbollah detachments also have cooperated with IRGC forces in Yemen to train and assist the Houthi rebel movement.

Hezbollah threatens the security and stability of the Middle East and Western interests in the Middle East on a number of fronts. In addition to its murderous actions against Israel, Hezbollah has used violence to impose its radical Islamist agenda and subvert democracy in Lebanon. Some experts believed that Hezbollah's participation in the 1992 Lebanese elections and subsequent inclusion in Lebanon's parliament and coalition governments would moderate its behavior, but political inclusion did not lead it to renounce terrorism.

Hezbollah also poses a potential threat to America's NATO allies in Europe. Hezbollah established a presence inside European countries in the 1980s amid the influx of Lebanese citizens seeking to escape Lebanon's civil war and took root among Lebanese Shiite immigrant communities throughout Europe. German intelligence officials estimate that roughly 900 Hezbollah members live in Germany alone. Hezbollah also has developed an extensive web of fundraising and logistical support cells throughout Europe.[51]

France and Britain have been the principal European targets of Hezbollah terrorism, in part because both countries opposed Hezbollah's agenda in Lebanon and were perceived as enemies of Iran, Hezbollah's chief patron. Hezbollah has been involved in many terrorist attacks against Europeans, including:

- The October 1983 bombing of the French contingent of the multinational peacekeeping force in Lebanon (on the same day as the U.S. Marine barracks bombing), which killed 58 French soldiers;

- The December 1983 bombing of the French embassy in Kuwait;

- The April 1985 bombing of a restaurant near a U.S. base in Madrid, Spain, which killed 18 Spanish citizens;

- A campaign of 13 bombings in France in 1986 that targeted shopping centers and railroad facilities, killing 13 people and wounding more than 250; and

- A March 1989 attempt to assassinate British novelist Salman Rushdie that failed when a bomb exploded prematurely, killing a terrorist in London.

Hezbollah attacks in Europe trailed off in the 1990s after Hezbollah's Iranian sponsors accepted a truce in their bloody 1980–1988 war with Iraq and no longer needed a surrogate to punish states that Tehran perceived as supporting Iraq. Significantly, the participation of European troops in Lebanese peacekeeping operations, which became a lightning rod for Hezbollah terrorist attacks in the 1980s, could become an issue again if Hezbollah attempts to revive its aggressive operations in southern Lebanon. Troops from EU member states may someday find themselves attacked by Hezbollah with weapons financed by Hezbollah supporters in their home countries.

Hezbollah operatives have been deployed in countries throughout Europe, including Belgium, Bulgaria, Cyprus, France, Germany, and Greece.[52]

WWTA: The WWTA assesses that "Lebanese Hizballah has demonstrated its intent to foment regional instability by deploying thousands of fighters to Syria and by providing weapons, tactics, and direction to militant and terrorist groups." In addition, "Hizballah probably also emphasizes its capability to attack US, Israeli, and Saudi Arabian interests."[53]

Summary: Hezbollah poses a major potential terrorist threat to the U.S. and its allies in the Middle East and Europe.

Al-Qaeda and the Islamic State: Continuing Regional Threats. The Arab Spring uprisings that began in 2011 created power vacuums that al-Qaeda, the Islamic State, and other Islamist extremist groups have exploited to advance their revolutionary agendas. The al-Qaeda network has taken advantage of failed or failing states in Iraq, Libya, Mali, Syria, and Yemen. The fall of autocratic Arab regimes and the subsequent factional infighting within the ad hoc coalitions that ousted them created anarchic conditions that have enabled al-Qaeda franchises to expand the territories that they control. Rising sectarian tensions resulting from conflicts in Iraq, Syria, and Yemen also have presented al-Qaeda and other Sunni extremist groups with major opportunities to expand their activities.

Jonathan Evans, Director General of the British Security Service (MI5), warned presciently in 2012 that "parts of the Arab world [had] once more become a permissive environment for al-Qaeda."[54] In Egypt, Libya, Syria, Tunisia, and Yemen, the collapse or purge of intelligence and counterterrorism organizations removed important constraints on the growth of al-Qaeda and similar Islamist terrorist groups. Many dangerous terrorists were released or escaped from prison. Al-Qaeda and other revolutionary groups were handed new opportunities to recruit, organize, attract funding for, train, and arm a new wave of followers and to consolidate safe havens from which to mount future attacks.

The Arab Spring uprisings were a golden opportunity for al-Qaeda, coming at a time when its sanctuaries in Pakistan were increasingly threatened by U.S. drone strikes. Given al-Qaeda's Arab roots, the Middle East and North Africa provide much better access to potential Arab recruits than is provided by the more distant and remote regions along the Afghanistan–Pakistan border, to which many al-Qaeda cadres fled after the fall of Afghanistan's Taliban regime in 2001. The countries destabilized by the Arab uprisings also could provide easier access to al-Qaeda's Europe-based recruits, who pose dangerous threats to the U.S. homeland by virtue of their European passports and greater ability to blend into Western societies.

WWTA: The WWTA assesses that "Al-Qa'ida almost certainly will remain a major actor in global terrorism because of the combined staying power of its five affiliates" and that "[t]he primary threat to US and Western interests from al-Qa'ida's global network through 2018 will be in or near affiliates' operating areas." Specifically, "[n]ot all affiliates will have the intent and capability to pursue or inspire attacks in the US homeland or elsewhere in the West" and "probably will continue to dedicate most of their resources to local activity, including participating in ongoing conflicts in Afghanistan, Somalia, Syria, and Yemen, as well as attacking regional actors and populations in other parts of Africa, Asia, and the Middle East."[55]

The WWTA also assesses that "ISIS is likely to focus on regrouping in Iraq and Syria, enhancing its global presence, championing its cause, planning international attacks, and encouraging its members and sympathizers to attack in their home countries" and that its "claim of having a functioning caliphate that governs populations is all but thwarted." Efforts by "ISIS core" to conduct "a robust insurgency in Iraq and Syria as part of a long-term strategy to...enable the reemergence of its so-called caliphate...will challenge local CT efforts against the group and threaten US interests in the region."[56]

Summary: The al-Qaeda network and the Islamic State have exploited the political turbulence of the Arab Spring to expand their strength and control of territory in the Middle East. Although the Islamic State has been rolled back in Iraq and Syria, it continues to pose regional threats to the U.S. and its allies.

Growing Threats to Jordan. Jordan, a key U.S. ally, faces external threats from Syria's Assad regime and from Islamist extremists, including the Islamic State, who maintain terrorist and insurgent operations in neighboring Syria and Iraq. Jordan's cooperation with the United States, Saudi Arabia, and other countries in the air campaign against the IS in Syria and in supporting moderate elements of the Syrian opposition has angered both the Assad regime and Islamist extremist rebels. Damascus could retaliate for Jordanian support for Syrian rebels with cross-border attacks, air strikes, ballistic missile strikes, or the use of terrorist attacks by such surrogates as Hezbollah or the PFLP–GC.

The Islamic State is committed to overthrowing the government of Jordan and replacing it with an Islamist dictatorship. In its previous incarnation as al-Qaeda in Iraq, the IS mounted attacks against targets in Jordan that included the November 2005 suicide bombings at three hotels in Amman that killed 57 people.[57] The IS also burned to death a Jordanian Air Force pilot captured in Syria after his plane crashed and released a video of his grisly murder in February 2015. Jordan also faces threats from Hamas and from Jordanian Islamist extremists, particularly some based in the southern city of Maan who organized pro-IS demonstrations in 2014. Although Jordanian security forces have foiled several IS terrorist plots, six Jordanian border guards were killed by a car bomb on June 21, 2016, prompting Jordan to close the border. IS terrorists also killed 14 people in a December 18, 2016, terrorist attack in the city of Karak.

Jordan is a prime target for terrorist attacks because of its close cooperation with the U.S.-led anti-terrorism coalition, its long and permeable borders, and the nearby presence of Islamic State diehards who seek to demonstrate their continued relevance. An estimated 2,000 Jordanians joined the Islamic State, and Jordan hosts up to a million Syrian refugees, some of whom may support the IS agenda.

The large refugee population also has strained Jordan's already weak economy and scarce resources. Government austerity measures and tax hikes provoked popular protests that led to the June 4, 2018, resignation of Prime Minister Hani al-Mulki, who was replaced by economist Omar Razaz. Jordan's new government must address the country's chronic economic problems, which have been exacerbated by the influx of Syrian refugees.

WWTA: The WWTA does not reference threats to Jordan.

Summary: Jordan faces significant security threats from the Islamic State, based in neighboring Syria and Iraq, as well as from home-grown extremists. Because Jordan is one of the very few Arab states that maintain a peaceful relationship with Israel and has been a key regional partner in fighting Islamist terrorism, its destabilization would be a troubling development.

Terrorist Attacks on and Possible Destabilization of Egypt. The overthrow of President Hosni Mubarak's regime in 2011 undermined the authority of Egypt's central government and allowed disgruntled Bedouin tribes, Islamist militants, and smuggling networks to grow stronger and bolder in Egypt's Sinai Peninsula. President Mohamed Morsi's

Muslim Brotherhood–backed government, elected to power in 2012, took a relaxed attitude toward Hamas and other Gaza-based Islamist extremists, enabling Islamist militants in the Sinai to grow even stronger with support from Gaza. They carved out a staging area in the remote mountains of the Sinai that they have used as a springboard for attacks on Israel, Egyptian security forces, tourists, the Suez Canal, and a pipeline carrying Egyptian natural gas to Israel and Jordan.

The July 2013 coup against Morsi resulted in a military government that took a much harder line against the Sinai militants, but it also raised the ire of more moderate Islamists, who sought to avenge Morsi's fall. Terrorist attacks, which had been limited to the Sinai, expanded in lethality and intensity to include bomb attacks in Cairo and other cities by early 2014. In November 2014, the Sinai-based terrorist group Ansar Bayt al-Maqdis (Supporters of Jerusalem) declared its allegiance to the Islamic State and renamed itself the Sinai Province of the Islamic State. It has launched a growing terrorist campaign against Egypt's army, police, and other government institutions, as well as the country's Christian minority, and has claimed responsibility for the October 31, 2015, bombing of a Russian passenger plane flying to Saint Petersburg from Sharm-el-Sheikh that killed 224 people.

The Islamic State–Sinai Province has fiercely resisted military operations and has launched a series of terrorist attacks that have taken a heavy toll. A car bomb killed at least 23 people at a police checkpoint near Gaza on July 7, 2017; an estimated 40 IS gunmen slaughtered 311 people at a Sufi mosque in the northern Sinai on November 24, 2017, the deadliest terrorist attack in Egyptian history; and 14 IS militants wearing bomb belts killed at least eight soldiers at an army base in Sinai on April 14, 2018.

Egypt also faces potential threats from Islamist militants and al-Qaeda affiliates based in Libya. The Egyptian air force bombed Islamic State targets in Libya on February 16, 2015, the day after the terrorist organization released a video showing the decapitation of 21 Egyptian Christians who had been working in Libya. Cairo has stepped up security operations along the border with Libya to block the smuggling of arms and militants into Egypt. It also has supported Libyans fighting Islamist extremists in eastern Libya.

During the 2014 conflict between Hamas and Israel, Egypt closed tunnels along the Gaza–Sinai border that have been used to smuggle goods, supplies, and weapons into Gaza. It has continued to uncover and destroy tunnels to disrupt an important source of external support for Sinai Province terrorists. Egypt has continued to uphold its peace treaty with Israel and remains an important ally against Islamist terrorist groups.

WWTA: The WWTA does not reference threats to Egypt.

Summary: Egypt is threatened by Islamist extremist groups that have established bases in the Sinai Peninsula, Gaza, and Libya. Left unchecked, these groups could foment greater instability not only in Egypt, but also in neighboring countries.

Threats to Saudi Arabia and Other Members of the Gulf Cooperation Council. Saudi Arabia and the five other Arab Gulf States—Bahrain, Kuwait, Oman, Qatar, and the United Arab Emirates—formed the Gulf Cooperation Council (GCC) in 1981 to deter and defend against Iranian aggression. Iran remains the primary external threat to their security. Tehran has supported groups that launched terrorist attacks against Bahrain, Kuwait, Saudi Arabia, and Yemen. It sponsored the Islamic Front for the Liberation of Bahrain, a surrogate group that plotted a failed 1981 coup against Bahrain's ruling Al Khalifa family, the Sunni rulers of the predominantly Shia country. Iran also has long backed Bahraini branches of Hezbollah and the Dawa Party.

However, in recent years, some members of the GCC, led mainly by Saudi Arabia, have shown concern over Qatar's support for the Muslim Brotherhood and its perceived coziness with Iran, with which Doha shares a major gas field in the Gulf. This led to the breakdown of diplomatic relations between many Arab states and Qatar in June 2017 and the imposition of economic sanctions as part of a diplomatic standoff that shows no signs of ending.[58]

When Bahrain was engulfed in a wave of Arab Spring protests in 2011, its government charged that Iran again exploited the protests to back the efforts of Shia radicals to overthrow the royal family. Saudi Arabia, fearing that a Shia revolution in Bahrain would incite its own restive Shia minority, led a March 2011 GCC intervention that backed Bahrain's government with about 1,000 Saudi troops and 500 police from the UAE.

Bahrain has repeatedly intercepted shipments of Iranian arms, including sophisticated bombs employing explosively formed penetrators (EFPs). The government withdrew its ambassador to Tehran when two Bahrainis with ties to the IRGC were arrested after their arms shipment was intercepted off Bahrain's coast in July 2015. Iranian hardliners have steadily escalated pressure on Bahrain. In March 2016, a former IRGC general who is a close adviser to Ayatollah Khamenei stated that "Bahrain is a province of Iran that should be annexed to the Islamic Republic of Iran."[59] After Bahrain stripped a senior Shiite cleric, Sheikh Isa Qassim, of his citizenship, General Qassim Suleimani, commander of the IRGC's Quds Force, threatened to make Bahrain's royal family "pay the price and disappear."[60]

Saudi Arabia has criticized Iran for supporting radical Saudi Shiites, intervening in Syria, and supporting Shiite Islamists in Lebanon, Iraq, and Yemen. In January 2016, Saudi Arabia executed a Shiite cleric charged with sparking anti-government protests and cut diplomatic ties with Iran after Iranian mobs enraged by the execution attacked and set fire to the Saudi embassy in Tehran.

Saudi Arabia also faces threats from Islamist extremists, including al-Qaeda offshoots in Iraq and Yemen that have attracted many Saudi recruits. Al-Qaeda launched a series of bombings and terrorist attacks inside the kingdom in 2003 and a major attack on the vital Saudi oil facility in Abqaiq in 2006, but a security crackdown drove many of its members out of the country by the end of the decade. Many of them joined Al-Qaeda in the Arabian Peninsula in neighboring Yemen. AQAP has flourished, aided by the instability fostered by Arab Spring protests and the ouster of the Yemeni government by Iran-backed Houthi rebels in early 2015.

In addition to terrorist threats and possible rebellions by Shia or other disaffected internal groups, Saudi Arabia and the other GCC states face possible military threats from Iran. Because of their close security ties with the United States, Tehran is unlikely to launch direct military attacks against these countries, but it has backed Shiite terrorist groups like Saudi Hezbollah within GCC states and has supported the Shiite Houthi rebels in Yemen. In March 2015, Saudi Arabia led a 10-country coalition that launched a military campaign against Houthi forces and provided support for ousted Yemeni President Abdu Rabu Mansour Hadi, who took refuge in Saudi Arabia. The Saudi Navy also established a blockade of Yemeni ports to prevent Iran from aiding the rebels. The Houthis have retaliated by launching Iranian-supplied missiles at military and civilian targets in Saudi Arabia and the UAE.

WWTA: The WWTA assesses that "[i]n Yemen, Iran's support to the Huthis further escalates the conflict and poses a serious threat to US partners and interests in the region." Continued Iranian support also "enables Huthi attacks against shipping near the Bab al Mandeb Strait and land-based targets deep inside Saudi Arabia and the UAE, such as the 4 November and 19 December ballistic missile attacks on Riyadh and an attempted 3 December cruise missile attack on an unfinished nuclear reactor in Abu Dhabi."[61]

Summary: Saudi Arabia and other members of the Gulf Cooperation Council face continued threats from Iran as well as rising threats from Islamist extremist groups such as al-Qaeda, the Islamic State, and Houthi militias in Yemen. Saudi citizens and Islamic charities have supported Islamist extremist groups, and the Saudi government promulgates the religious views of the fundamentalist Wahhabi sect of Sunni Islam, but the Saudi government also serves to check radical Islamist groups like the Islamic State and is a regional counterbalance to Iran.

Threats to the Commons

The United States has critical interests at stake in the Middle Eastern commons: sea, air, space, and cyber. The U.S. has long provided the security backbone in these areas, which in turn has supported the region's economic development and political stability.

Maritime. Maintaining the security of the sea lines of communication in the Persian Gulf, Arabian Sea, Red Sea, and Mediterranean Sea is a high priority for strategic, economic, and energy security purposes. The Persian Gulf region contains approximately 50 percent of the world's oil reserves and is a crucial source of oil and gas for energy-importing states, particularly China, India, Japan, South Korea, and many European countries. The flow of that oil could be interrupted by interstate conflict or terrorist attacks.

Bottlenecks such as the Strait of Hormuz, Suez Canal, and Bab el-Mandeb Strait are potential choke points for restricting the flow of oil, international trade, and the deployment of U.S. Navy warships. The chief potential threat to the free passage of ships through the Strait of Hormuz, one of the world's most important maritime choke points, is Iran. Approximately 18.5 million barrels of oil a day—more than 30 percent of the seaborne oil traded worldwide—flowed through the strait in 2016.[62]

Iran has trumpeted the threat that it could pose to the free flow of oil exports from the Gulf if it is attacked or threatened with a cutoff of its own oil exports. Iran's leaders have threatened to close the Strait of Hormuz, the jugular vein through which most Gulf oil exports flow to Asia and Europe. Although the United States has greatly reduced its dependence on oil exports from the Gulf, it still would sustain economic damage in the event of a spike in world oil prices, and many of its European and Asian allies and trading partners import a substantial portion of their oil needs from the region. Iran's Supreme Leader, Ayatollah Ali Khamenei, has repeatedly played up Iran's threat to international energy security, proclaiming in 2006 that "[i]f the Americans make a wrong move toward Iran, the shipment of energy will definitely face danger, and the Americans would not be able to protect energy supply in the region."[63]

Iran has established a precedent for attacking oil shipments in the Gulf. During the Iran–Iraq war, each side targeted the other's oil facilities, ports, and oil exports. Iran escalated attacks to include neutral Kuwaiti oil tankers and terminals and clandestinely laid mines in Persian Gulf shipping lanes while its ally Libya clandestinely laid mines in the Red Sea. The United States defeated Iran's tactics by reflagging Kuwaiti oil tankers, clearing the mines, and escorting ships through the Persian Gulf, but a large number of commercial vessels were damaged during the "Tanker War" from 1984 to 1987.

Iran's demonstrated willingness to disrupt oil traffic through the Persian Gulf in the past to place economic pressure on Iraq is a red flag to U.S. military planners. During the 1980s Tanker War, Iran's ability to strike at Gulf shipping was limited by its aging and outdated weapons systems and the arms embargo imposed by the U.S. after the 1979 revolution. However, since the 1990s, Iran has been upgrading its military with new weapons from North Korea, China, and Russia, as well as with weapons manufactured domestically.

Today, Iran boasts an arsenal of Iranian-built missiles based on Russian and Chinese designs that pose significant threats to oil tankers as well as warships. Iran is well stocked with Chinese-designed anti-ship cruise missiles, including the older HY-2 Seersucker and the more modern CSS-N-4 Sardine and CSS-N-8 Saccade models. It also has reverse engineered Chinese missiles to produce its own anti-ship cruise missiles, the Ra'ad and Noor. More recently, Tehran has produced and deployed more advanced anti-ship cruise missiles, the Nasir and Qadir.[64] Shore-based missiles deployed along Iran's coast would be augmented by aircraft-delivered laser-guided bombs and missiles, as well as by television-guided bombs.

Iran has a large supply of anti-ship mines, including modern mines that are far superior to the simple World War I–style contact mines that it used in the 1980s. They include the Chinese-designed EM-52 "rocket" mine, which remains stationary on the sea floor and fires a homing rocket when a ship passes overhead. In addition, Iran can deploy mines or torpedoes from its three *Kilo*-class submarines, which would be effectively immune to detection for brief periods when running silent and remaining stationary on a shallow bottom just outside the Strait of Hormuz,[65] and also could deploy mines by mini-submarines, helicopters, or small boats disguised as fishing vessels.

Iran's Revolutionary Guard naval forces have developed swarming tactics using fast attack boats and could deploy naval commandos trained to attack using small boats, mini-submarines, and even jet skis. The Revolutionary Guards also have underwater demolition teams that could attack offshore oil platforms and other facilities.

On April 28, 2015, the Revolutionary Guard naval force seized the *Maersk Tigris*, a container ship registered in the Marshall Islands, near the Strait of Hormuz. Tehran claimed that it seized the ship because of a previous court ruling ordering the Maersk Line, which charters the ship, to make a payment to settle a dispute with a private Iranian company. The ship was later released after being held for more than a week.[66] On May 14, 2015, an oil tanker flagged in Singapore, the *Alpine Eternity*, was surrounded and attacked by Revolutionary Guard gunboats in the strait when it refused to be boarded. Iranian authorities alleged that it had damaged an Iranian oil platform in March, although the ship's owners maintained that it had hit an uncharted submerged structure.[67] The Revolutionary Guard's aggressive tactics in using commercial disputes as pretexts for illegal seizures of transiting vessels prompted the U.S. Navy to escort American and British-flagged ships through the Strait of Hormuz for several weeks in May before tensions eased.

The July 2015 nuclear agreement did not alter the confrontational tactics of the Revolutionary Guards in the Gulf.[68] IRGC naval forces have frequently challenged U.S. naval forces in a series of incidents in recent years. IRGC missile boats launched rockets within 1,500 yards of the carrier *Harry S. Truman* near the Strait of Hormuz in late December 2015, flew drones over U.S. warships, and detained and humiliated 10 American sailors in a provocative January 12, 2016, incident. Despite the fact that the two U.S. Navy boats carrying the sailors had drifted inadvertently into Iranian territorial waters, the vessels had the right of innocent passage, and their crews should not have been disarmed, forced onto their knees, filmed, and exploited in propaganda videos.

Iran halted the harassment of U.S. Navy ships in 2017 for unknown reasons. According to U.S. Navy reports, Iran instigated 23 "unsafe and/or unprofessional" interactions with U.S. Navy ships in 2015, 35 in 2016, and 14 in the first eight months of 2017, with the last incident occurring on August 14, 2017.[69] Although this is a welcome development, the provocations could resume suddenly if U.S.–Iran relations were to deteriorate.

Finally, Tehran could use its extensive client network in the region to sabotage oil pipelines and other infrastructure or to strike oil tankers in port or at sea. Iranian Revolutionary Guards deployed in Yemen reportedly played a role in the unsuccessful October 9 and 12, 2016, missile attacks launched by Houthi rebels against the USS *Mason*, a U.S. Navy warship, near the Bab el-Mandeb Strait in the Red Sea.[70] The Houthis denied that they launched the missiles, but they did claim responsibility for an October 1, 2016, attack on a UAE naval vessel and the suicide bombing of a Saudi warship in February 2017. Houthi irregular forces have deployed mines along Yemen's coast, used a remote-controlled boat packed with explosives in an unsuccessful attack on the Yemeni port of Mokha in July 2017, and launched several unsuccessful naval attacks against ships in the Red Sea. Houthi gunboats also attacked and damaged a Saudi oil tanker near the port of Hodeidah on April 3, 2018.

Terrorists also pose a potential threat to oil tankers and other ships. Al-Qaeda strategist Abu Mus'ab al-Suri has identified four strategic choke points that should be targeted for disruption: the Strait of Hormuz, the Suez Canal, the Bab el-Mandeb Strait, and the Strait of Gibraltar.[71] In 2002, al-Qaeda terrorists attacked and damaged the French oil tanker *Limbourg* off the coast of Yemen. Al-Qaeda also almost sank the USS *Cole*, a guided-missile destroyer, in the port of Aden, killing 17 American sailors with a suicide boat bomb in 2000. An Egyptian patrol boat was attacked in November 2014 by the crews of small boats suspected of smuggling arms to Islamist terrorists in Gaza. In July 2015, the Islamic State–Sinai Province claimed responsibility for a missile attack on an Egyptian coast guard vessel.

Terrorists have targeted the Suez Canal as well. In two incidents on July 29 and August 31, 2013, ships in the waterway were attacked with rocket-propelled grenades. The attacks were claimed by a shadowy Islamist extremist group called the Furqan Brigades, which operated in Egypt's Sinai Peninsula.[72] The vessels reportedly escaped major damage. More important, the canal was not forced to close, which would have disrupted global shipping operations, ratcheted up oil prices, and complicated the deployment of U.S. and NATO naval vessels responding to potential crises in the Middle East, Persian Gulf, and Horn of Africa.

Over the past decade, piracy off the coast of Somalia has threatened shipping near the Bab el-Mandeb Strait and the Gulf of Aden. After more than 230 pirate attacks off the coast of Somalia in 2011, the number of attacks fell off steeply because of security precautions such as the deployment of armed guards on cargo ships and increased patrols by the U.S. Navy and other navies.[73] Then, after a four-year lull, pirate attacks surged in 2016 with 27 incidents, although no ships were hijacked. Between January and May 2017, three commercial vessels were hijacked, the first to be taken since 2012.[74] In 2017, the number of pirate incidents off the coast of East Africa doubled to 54.[75] Somali criminal networks apparently have exploited a decline in international naval patrols and the complacency of some shipping operators who have failed to deploy armed guards on ships in vulnerable shipping lanes.

WWTA: The WWTA assesses that "Iran continues to provide support that enables Huthi attacks against shipping near the Bab al Mandeb Strait and land-based targets deep inside Saudi Arabia and the UAE."[76]

Summary: Iran poses the chief potential threat to shipping in the Strait of Hormuz and has boosted the Houthi naval threat in the Red Sea. Various terrorist groups pose the chief threats to shipping in the Suez Canal and the Bab el-Mandeb Strait. Although pirate attacks off the coast of Somalia declined steeply between 2011 and 2016, there was a spike in attacks in 2017.

Airspace. The Middle East is particularly vulnerable to attacks on civilian aircraft. Large quantities of arms, including man-portable air defense systems, were looted from Libyan arms depots after the fall of Muammar Qadhafi's regime in 2011. Although Libya is estimated to have had up to 20,000 MANPADS (mostly old Soviet models), only about 10,000 have been accounted for, and an unknown number may have been smuggled out of Libya, which is a hotbed of Islamist radicalism.[77]

U.S. intelligence sources have estimated that at least 800 MANPADS fell into the hands of foreign insurgent groups after being moved out of Libya.[78] Libyan MANPADS have turned up in the hands of AQIM, the Nigerian Boko Haram terrorist group, and Hamas in Gaza. At some point, one or more could be used in a terrorist attack against a civilian airliner. Insurgents or terrorists also could use anti-aircraft missile systems captured from regime forces in Iraq, Syria, and Yemen. In January 2015, a commercial airliner landing at Baghdad International Airport was hit by gunfire that injured a passenger and prompted a temporary suspension of flights to Baghdad.

Al-Qaeda also has used MANPADS in several terrorist attacks. In 2002, it launched two SA-7 MANPADS in a failed attempt to bring down an Israeli civilian aircraft in Kenya. In 2007, the al-Qaeda affiliate al-Shabaab shot down a Belarusian cargo plane in Somalia, killing 11 people.[79] Al-Qaeda's al-Nusra Front and the Islamic State have acquired substantial numbers of MANPADS from government arms depots in Iraq and Syria. Although such weapons may pose only a limited threat to modern warplanes equipped with countermeasures, they pose a growing threat to civilian aircraft in the Middle East and could be smuggled into the United States and Europe to threaten aircraft there.

The Islamic State–Sinai Province claimed responsibility for a bomb that destroyed Metrojet Flight 9268, a Russian passenger jet en route from Sharm el-Sheikh, Egypt, to Saint Petersburg, Russia, on October 31, 2015. The incident claimed the lives of 224 people on the plane, one of the biggest death tolls in a terrorist attack in recent years. The May 19, 2016, crash of EgyptAir flight MS804, which killed 66 people flying from Paris, France, to Cairo, Egypt, has been attributed to a fire, but the cause of that onboard fire has not been determined.

WWTA: The WWTA makes no mention of the terrorist threat to airspace in the Middle East.

Summary: Al-Qaeda, the Islamic State, and other terrorists have seized substantial numbers of anti-aircraft missiles from military bases in Iraq, Libya, and Syria, and these missiles pose potential threats to safe transit of airspace in the Middle East, North Africa, and elsewhere.

Space. Iran has launched satellites into orbit, but there is no evidence that it has an offensive space capability. Tehran successfully launched three satellites in February 2009, June 2011, and February 2012 using the Safir space launch vehicle, which uses a modified Ghadr-1 missile for its first stage and has a second stage that is based on an obsolete Soviet submarine-launched ballistic missile, the R-27.[80] The technology probably

was transferred by North Korea, which built its BM-25 missiles using the R-27 as a model.[81] Safir technology could be used to develop long-range ballistic missiles.

Iran claimed that it launched a monkey into space and returned it safely to Earth twice in 2013.[82] Tehran also announced in June 2013 that it had established its first space tracking center to monitor objects in "very remote space" and to help manage the "activities of satellites."[83] On July 27, 2017, Iran tested a Simorgh (Phoenix) space launch vehicle that it claimed could place a satellite weighing up to 250 kilograms (550 pounds) in an orbit of 500 kilometers (311 miles).[84]

WWTA: The WWTA assesses that "[p]rogress on Iran's space program, such as the launch of the Simorgh SLV in July 2017, could shorten a pathway to an ICBM because space launch vehicles use similar technologies."[85]

Summary: Iran has launched satellites into orbit successfully, but there is no evidence that it has yet developed an offensive space capability that could deny others the use of space or exploit space as a base for offensive weaponry.

Cyber Threats. Iranian cyber capabilities present a significant threat to the U.S. and its allies. Iran has developed offensive cyber capabilities as a tool of espionage and sabotage and claims "to possess the 'fourth largest' cyber force in the world—a broad network of quasi-official elements, as well as regime-aligned 'hacktivists,' who engage in cyber activities broadly consistent with the Islamic Republic's interests and views."[86]

The creation of the "Iranian Cyber Army" in 2009 marked the beginning of a cyber offensive against those whom the Iranian government regards as enemies. A hacking group dubbed the Ajax Security Team, believed to be operating out of Iran, has used malware-based attacks to target U.S. defense organizations and has successfully breached the Navy Marine Corps Intranet. The group also has targeted dissidents within Iran, seeding versions of anti-censorship tools with malware and gathering information about users of those programs.[87] Iran has invested heavily in cyber activity, reportedly spending "over $1 billion on its cyber capabilities in 2012 alone."[88]

Hostile Iranian cyber activity has increased significantly since the beginning of 2014 and could threaten U.S. critical infrastructure, according to an April 2015 report released by the American Enterprise Institute. The Islamic Revolutionary Guard Corps and Sharif University of Technology are two Iranian institutions that investigators have linked to efforts to infiltrate U.S. computer networks, according to the report.[89]

Iran allegedly has used cyber weapons to engage in economic warfare, most notably the sophisticated and debilitating "denial-of-service (DDoS) attacks against a number of U.S. financial institutions, including the Bank of America, JPMorgan Chase, and Citigroup."[90] In February 2014, Iran launched a crippling cyberattack against the Sands Casino in Las Vegas, owned by Sheldon Adelson, a leading supporter of Israel who is known to be critical of the Iranian regime.[91] In 2012, Tehran was suspected of launching both the "Shamoon" virus attack on Saudi Aramco, the world's largest oil-producing company—an attack that destroyed approximately 30,000 computers—and an attack on Qatari natural gas company Rasgas's computer networks.[92]

U.S. officials warned of a surge of sophisticated computer espionage by Iran in the fall of 2015 that included a series of cyberattacks against State Department officials.[93] In March 2016, the Justice Department indicted seven Iranian hackers for penetrating the computer system that controlled a dam in the State of New York.[94]

The sophistication of these and other Iranian cyberattacks, together with Iran's willingness to use these weapons, has led various experts to characterize Iran as one of America's most cyber-capable opponents. Iranian cyber forces have gone so far as to create fake online personas in order to extract information from U.S. officials through accounts such as LinkedIn, YouTube, Facebook, and Twitter.[95] Significantly, the FBI sent the following cyber alert to American businesses on May 22, 2018:

The FBI assesses [that] foreign cyber actors operating in the Islamic Republic of Iran could potentially use a range of computer network operations—from scanning networks for potential vulnerabilities to data deletion attacks—against U.S.-based networks in response to the U.S. government's withdrawal from the Joint Comprehensive Plan of Action (JCPOA).[96]

WWTA: The WWTA assesses that "Iran will continue working to penetrate US and Allied networks for espionage and to position itself for potential future cyberattacks, although its intelligence services primarily focus on Middle Eastern adversaries—especially Saudi Arabia and Israel." Iran "probably views cyberattacks as a versatile tool to respond to perceived provocations, despite [its] recent restraint from conducting cyberattacks on the United States or Western allies," and its "cyber attacks against Saudi Arabia in late 2016 and early 2017 involved data deletion on dozens of networks across government and the private sector."[97]

Summary: Iranian cyber capabilities present significant espionage and sabotage threats to the U.S. and its allies, and Tehran has shown both willingness and skill in using them.

Threat Scores

Iran. Iran represents by far the most significant security challenge to the United States, its allies, and its interests in the greater Middle East. Its open hostility to the United States and Israel, sponsorship of terrorist groups like Hezbollah, and history of threatening the commons underscore the problem it could pose. Today, Iran's provocations are mostly a concern for the region and America's allies, friends, and assets there. Iran relies heavily on irregular (to include political) warfare against others in the region and fields more ballistic missiles than any of its neighbors. The development of its ballistic missiles and potential nuclear capability also mean that it poses a long-term threat to the security of the U.S. homeland.

According to the International Institute for Strategic Studies' *Military Balance 2018,* among the key weapons in Iran's inventory are 22-plus MRBM launchers, 18-plus SRBM launchers, 334 combat-capable aircraft, 1,513-plus main battle tanks, 640-plus armored personnel carriers, 21 tactical submarines, seven corvettes, and 12 amphibious landing ships. There are 523,000 personnel in the armed forces, including 350,000 in the Army, 125,000-plus in the Islamic Revolutionary Guard Corps, and 18,000 in the Navy. With regard to these capabilities, the IISS assesses that:

> Iran continues to rely on a mix of ageing combat equipment, reasonably well-trained regular and Islamic Revolutionary Guard Corps (IRGC) forces, and its ballistic-missile inventory to underpin the security of the state. The IRGC, including senior military leaders, has been increasingly involved in the civil war in Syria, supporting President Bashar al-Assad's regular and irregular forces; it was first deployed to Syria in an "advisory" role in 2012, deployments of the army began in 2013....
>
> The armed forces continue to struggle with an ageing inventory of primary combat equipment that ingenuity and asymmetric warfare techniques can only partially offset.[98]

This *Index* assesses the overall threat from Iran, considering the range of contingencies, as "aggressive." Iran's capability score holds at "gathering."

Threats: Iran

	HOSTILE	AGGRESSIVE	TESTING	ASSERTIVE	BENIGN
Behavior		✓			

	FORMIDABLE	GATHERING	CAPABLE	ASPIRATIONAL	MARGINAL
Capability		✓			

Greater Middle East–Based Terrorism

Collectively, the varied non-state actors in the Middle East that are vocally and actively opposed to the United States are the closest to being rated "aggressive" with regard to the degree of provocation they exhibit. These groups, from the Islamic State to al-Qaeda and its affiliates, Hezbollah, and the range of Palestinian terrorist organizations in the region, are primarily a threat to America's allies, friends, and interests in the Middle East. Their impact on the American homeland is mostly a concern for American domestic security agencies, but they pose a challenge to the stability of the region that could result in the emergence of more dangerous threats to the United States.

The IISS *Military Balance* addresses only the military capabilities of states. Consequently, it does not provide any accounting of such entities as Hezbollah, Hamas, al-Qaeda, or the Islamic State.

This *Index* assesses the overall threat from greater Middle East–based terrorism, considering the range of contingencies, as "hostile" and "capable." The increase from "aggressive" to "hostile" reflects the growing assertiveness of Iranian-controlled Shia militias in Iraq and Syria.[99]

Threats: Middle East Terrorism

Behavior	HOSTILE	AGGRESSIVE	TESTING	ASSERTIVE	BENIGN
	✔				

Capability	FORMIDABLE	GATHERING	CAPABLE	ASPIRATIONAL	MARGINAL
			✔		

Endnotes

1. James Phillips, "The Yemen Bombing: Another Wake-up Call in the Terrorist Shadow War," Heritage Foundation *Executive Memorandum* No. 773, October 25, 2000, http://www.heritage.org/middle-east/report/the-yemen-bombing-another-wake-call-the-terrorist-shadow-war.

2. Stephen F. Hayes and Thomas Joscelyn, "Connecting the Dots," *The Weekly Standard*, November 23, 2009, https://www.weeklystandard.com/stephen-f-hayes-and-thomas-joscelyn/connecting-the-dots-271303 (accessed July 28, 2018).

3. Peter Finn, "Al-Awlaki Directed Christmas 'Underwear Bomber' Plot, Justice Department Memo Says," *The Washington Post*, February 10, 2012, http://www.washingtonpost.com/world/national-security/al-awlaki-directed-christmas-underwear-bomber-plot-justice-department-memo-says/2012/02/10/gIQArDOt4Q_story.html (accessed June 22, 2017).

4. Scott Shane, "The Enduring Influence of Anwar al-Awlaki in the Age of the Islamic State," Combating Terrorism Center at West Point, *CTC Sentinel*, Vol. 9, Issue 7 (July 2016), pp. 15–19, https://www.ctc.usma.edu/v2/wp-content/uploads/2016/08/CTC-SENTINEL_Vol9Iss710.pdf https://ctc.usma.edu/the-enduring-influence-of-anwar-al-awlaki-in-the-age-of-the-islamic-state/ (accessed July 29, 2018).

5. U.S. Department of State, Bureau of Counterterrorism, "Foreign Terrorist Organizations," Chapter 6 in *Country Reports on Terrorism 2016*, July 2017, https://www.state.gov/j/ct/rls/crt/2016/272238.htm (accessed July 30, 2018).

6. General Joseph L. Votel, Commander, U.S. Central Command, statement on "The Posture of U.S. Central Command: Terrorism and Iran: Defense Challenges in the Middle East," before the Committee on Armed Services, U.S. House of Representatives, February 27, 2018, p. 2, http://www.centcom.mil/Portals/6/Documents/Transcripts/HASCVotel20180227.pdf (accessed July 29, 2018).

7. News transcript, "Department of Defense Press Briefing by Colonel Veale via Teleconference from Baghdad, Iraq," U.S. Department of Defense, June 5, 2018, http://www.centcom.mil/MEDIA/Transcripts/Article/1543988/department-of-defense-press-briefing-by-colonel-veale-via-teleconference-from-b/ (accessed July 29, 2018).

8. Lisa Curtis, ed., "Combatting the ISIS Foreign Fighter Pipeline: A Global Approach," Heritage Foundation *Special Report* No. 180, January 6, 2016, p. 5, https://www.heritage.org/middle-east/report/combatting-the-isis-foreign-fighter-pipeline-global-approach (accessed July 30, 2018).

9. Brian Bennett, "Al Qaeda in Iraq Threatens Attacks in U.S.," *Los Angeles Times*, July 25, 2012, http://articles.latimes.com/2012/jul/25/nation/la-na-qaeda-us-20120726 (accessed July 30, 2018).

10. James Phillips and Cassandra Lucaccioni, "Al-Qaeda Recruits Americans in Syria," The Daily Signal, January 10, 2014, http://dailysignal.com/2014/01/10/al-qaeda-seeks-american-recruits-syria/.

11. Charles Lister, "Al -Qaeda Is Starting to Swallow the Syrian Opposition," *Foreign Policy*, March 15, 2017, http://foreignpolicy.com/2017/03/15/al-qaeda-is-swallowing-the-syrian-opposition/ (accessed July 30, 2018).

12. Eric Schmitt, "Al Qaeda Turns to Syria, With a Plan to Challenge ISIS," *The New York Times*, May 15, 2016, http://www.nytimes.com/2016/05/16/world/middleeast/al-qaeda-turns-to-syria-with-a-plan-to-challenge-isis.html?_r=0 (accessed July 28, 2018).

13. U.S. Department of State, Office of the Coordinator for Counterterrorism, "Foreign Terrorist Organizations," Chapter 6 in *Country Reports on Terrorism 2012*, May 30, 2013, http://www.state.gov/j/ct/rls/crt/2012/209989.htm (accessed July 30, 2018).

14. James Phillips, "The Rise of Al-Qaeda's Khorasan Group: What It Means for U.S. National Security," Heritage Foundation *Issue Brief* No. 4281, October 6, 2014, http://www.heritage.org/middle-east/report/the-rise-al-qaedas-khorasan-group-what-it-means-us-national-security.

15. Adam Goldman, Greg Miller, and Nicole Rodriquez, "American Who Killed Himself in Syria Suicide Attack Was from South Florida," *The Washington Post*, May 31, 2014, http://www.washingtonpost.com/world/national-security/american-who-killed-himself-in-syria-suicide-attack-was-from-south-florida-official-says/2014/05/30/03869b6e-e7f4-11e3-a86b-362fd5443d19_story.html (accessed June 22, 2017).

16. Adam Goldman, "Ohio Man Who Trained with Jabhat al-Nusra Is Indicted on Terrorism Charges," *The Washington Post*, April 16, 2015, http://www.washingtonpost.com/world/national-security/ohio-man-who-trained-with-jabhat-al-nusra-is-indicted-on-terrorism-charges/2015/04/16/8e8ded08-e455-11e4-b510-962fcfabc310_story.html (accessed June 22, 2017).

17. Evan Perez and Tom LoBianco, "FBI Head: Khorasan Group Diminished; ISIS Bigger Threat than al Qaeda," CNN, July 23, 2015, http://www.cnn.com/2015/07/22/politics/fbi-james-comey-isis-khorasan-group/ (accessed June 22, 2017).

18. Christopher Wray, Director, Federal Bureau of Investigation, "Current Threats to the Homeland," statement before the Committee on Homeland Security and Government Affairs, U.S. Senate, September 27, 2017, https://www.fbi.gov/news/testimony/current-threats-to-the-homeland (accessed July 30, 2018).

19. U.S. Department of State, Bureau of Counterterrorism, *Country Reports on Terrorism 2016*.

20. William Maclean, "Insight—Local Wars Blur al-Qaeda's Threat to West," Reuters, July 5, 2012, http://uk.reuters.com/article/2012/07/05/uk-security-qaeda-idUKBRE86408B20120705 (accessed June 22, 2017).

21. Daniel R. Coats, Director of National Intelligence, "Worldwide Threat Assessment of the US Intelligence Community," statement before the Committee on Intelligence, U.S. Senate, February 13, 2018, pp. 9 and 10, https://www.dni.gov/files/documents/Newsroom/Testimonies/2018-ATA---Unclassified-SSCI.pdf (accessed August 3, 2018). Cited hereafter as 2018 WWTA.

22. Rebecca Leung, "Hezbollah: 'A-Team of Terrorists,'" CBS News, April 18, 2003, http://www.cbsnews.com/news/hezbollah-a-team-of-terrorists/ (accessed June 22, 2017).

23. Suzanne Kelly, "Experts: Hezbollah Positioned for Attack in U.S.," CNN, March 21, 2012, http://security.blogs.cnn.com/2012/03/21/house-panel-hears-testimony-on-hezbollah-in-u-s/ (accessed June 22, 2017).

24. Ellie Kaufman, "2 Americans Led Double Lives as Hezbollah Agents, Officials Say," CNN, June 9, 2017, http://www.cnn.com/2017/06/08/us/americans-accused-hezbollah-agents/ (accessed July 30, 2018).

25. Nathan A. Sales, Ambassador-at-Large and Coordinator for Counterterrorism, and Nicholas J. Rasmussen, National Counterterrorism Center Director, "Briefing on U.S. Efforts to Counter Hizballah," U.S. Department of State, October 10, 2017, https://www.state.gov/r/pa/prs/ps/2017/10/274726.htm (accessed July 30, 2018).

26. 2018 WWTA, p. 10.

27. Kenneth Katzman, "Iran's Foreign and Defense Policies," Congressional Research Service *Report for Members and Committees of Congress*, July 18, 2018, pp. 12–13, https://fas.org/sgp/crs/mideast/R44017.pdf (accessed July 30, 2018).

28. U.S. Department of Defense, unclassified "Annual Report on Military Power of Iran: Executive Summary," January 2014, p. [1], http://freebeacon.com/wp-content/uploads/2014/07/Iranmilitary.pdf (accessed July 30, 2018).

29. 2018 WWTA, p. 8.

30. Saeed Ghasseminejad, "Iran Doubles Down on Its Military Budget," Foundation for Defense of Democracies *Policy Brief*, June 3, 2016, http://www.defenddemocracy.org/media-hit/saeed-ghasseminejad-iran-doubles-down-on-its-military-budget/ (accessed June 22, 2017).

31. Sima Shine and Zvi Magen, "President Rouhani's Visit to Russia: A New Level of Relations?" Tel Aviv University, Institute for National Security Studies, *INSS Insight* No. 914, April 5, 2017, http://www.inss.org.il/publication/president-rouhanis-visit-russia-new-level-relations/ (accessed June 22, 2017).

32. President of Russia, Events, "Meeting with President of Iran Hassan Rouhani," June 9, 2018, http://en.kremlin.ru/events/president/news/57710 (accessed July 30, 2018).

33. Reuters, "Iran Says Russia Delivers First Part of S-300 Defense System," April 11, 2016, http://www.reuters.com/article/us-russia-iran-arms-idUSKCN0X80MM?elqTrackId=e02d5aca6d48418984d902ced0c33d77&elq=39fecef381094e0cbc6de535feb74a3c&elqaid=17334&elqat=1&elqCampaignId=10743 (accessed June 22, 2017).

34. Farzin Nadimi, "Iran and Russia's Growing Defense Ties," Washington Institute for Near East Policy *PolicyWatch* No. 2563, February 18, 2016, http://www.washingtoninstitute.org/policy-analysis/view/iran-and-russias-growing-defense-ties (accessed June 22, 2017).

35. Sam Dagher and Asa Fitch, "Iran Expands Role in Syria in Conjunction with Russia's Airstrikes," *The Wall Street Journal*, October 2, 2015, http://www.wsj.com/articles/iran-expands-role-in-syria-in-conjunction-with-russias-airstrikes-1443811030 (accessed June 22, 2017).

36. Oren Lieberman, Salma Abdelaziz, and James Masters, "Netanyahu Says Iran 'Crossed a Red Line' After Israel Pounds Iranian Targets in Syria," CNN, May 11, 2018, https://www.cnn.com/2018/05/09/middleeast/israel-rockets-syria/index.html (accessed July 30, 2018).

37. Nuclear Threat Initiative, "Iran: Missile," last updated July 2017, http://www.nti.org/country-profiles/iran/delivery-systems/ (accessed July 30, 2018).

38. Amos Harel and Associated Press, "Iran's Missile Attack on Syria Failed: 5 Missed, 3 Landed in Iraq," *Haaretz*, June 21, 2017, http://www.haaretz.com/middle-east-news/1.796836 (accessed July 30, 2018).

39. Nuclear Threat Initiative, "Iran: Missile."

40. Lieutenant General Michael T. Flynn, U.S. Army, Director, Defense Intelligence Agency, "Annual Threat Assessment," statement before the Committee on Armed Services, U.S. Senate, February 11, 2014, p. 20, http://www.dia.mil/Portals/27/Documents/News/2014_DIA_SFR_SASC_ATA_FINAL.pdf (accessed June 26, 2017).

41. Tim Hume and Alireza Hajihosseini, "Iran Fires Ballistic Missiles a Day After Test; U.S. Officials Hint at Violation," CNN, March 9, 2016, http://www.cnn.com/2016/03/09/middleeast/iran-missile-test/ (accessed June 22, 2017).

42. James Phillips, "Iran's Nuclear Program: What Is Known and Unknown," Heritage Foundation *Backgrounder* No. 2393, March 26, 2010, http://www.heritage.org/research/reports/2010/03/iran-s-nuclear-program-what-is-known-and-unknown, and Nuclear Threat Initiative, "Arak Nuclear Complex," last updated July 11, 2017, http://www.nti.org/learn/facilities/177/ (accessed July 30, 2018).

43. Valerie Lincy and Gary Milhollin, "Iran's Nuclear Timetable," Wisconsin Project for Nuclear Arms Control, *Iran Watch*, June 17, 2015, http://www.iranwatch.org/our-publications/articles-reports/irans-nuclear-timetable (accessed June 22, 2017).

44. News release, "Statement by the President on Iran," The White House, July 14, 2015, https://www.whitehouse.gov/the-press-office/2015/07/14/statement-president-iran (accessed June 22, 2017).

45. Kenneth Katzman, "Iran, Gulf Security, and U.S. Policy," Congressional Research Service *Report for Members and Committees of Congress*, August 19, 2016, p. 25, http://www.parstimes.com/history/crs_august_16.pdf (accessed August 5, 2018).

46. 2018 WWTA, p. 19.

47. Avi Issacharoff, "Israel Raises Hezbollah Rocket Estimate to 150,000," *The Times of Israel*, November 12, 2015, http://www.timesofisrael.com/israel-raises-hezbollah-rocket-estimate-to-150000/ (accessed June 22, 2017).

48. Israel Defense Forces, "4 Reasons Why Hamas Is a Terror Organization," June 12, 2017, https://www.idf.il/en/minisites/hamas/4-reasons-why-hamas-is-a-terror-organization/ (accessed August 13, 2018).

49. Matthew Levitt, "A Proxy for Iran," Washington Institute for Near East Policy *Cipher Brief*, July 14, 2016, http://www.washingtoninstitute.org/policy-analysis/view/a-proxy-for-iran (accessed June 26, 2017).

50. Yaya J. Fanusie and Alex Entz, "Hezbollah: Financial Assessment," Foundation for Defense of Democracies, Center on Sanctions and Illicit Finance, *Terror Finance Briefing Book*, September 2017, p. 8, http://www.defenddemocracy.org/content/uploads/documents/CSIF_TFBB_Hezbollah.pdf (accessed July 30, 2018).

51. James Phillips, "Hezbollah's Terrorist Threat to the European Union," testimony before the Subcommittee on Europe, Committee on Foreign Affairs, U.S. House of Representatives, June 20, 2007, http://www.heritage.org/research/testimony/hezbollahs-terrorist-threat-to-the-european-union.

52. Matthew Levitt, "Inside Hezbollah's European Plots," Washington Institute for Near East Policy *Policy Analysis*, July 20, 2015, https://www.washingtoninstitute.org/policy-analysis/view/inside-hezbollahs-european-plots (accessed June 22, 2017).

53. 2018 WWTA, p. 10.

54. "The Olympics and Beyond: Address at the Lord Mayor's Annual Defence and Security Lecture by the Director General of the Security Service, Jonathan Evans," London, MI5 Security Service, June 25, 2012, https://www.mi5.gov.uk/home/about-us/who-we-are/staff-and-management/director-general/speeches-by-the-director-general/the-olympics-and-beyond.html (accessed July 30, 2018).

55. 2018 WWTA, p. 10.

56. Ibid., p. 9.

57. James Phillips, "Zarqawi's Amman Bombings: Jordan's 9/11," Heritage Foundation *WebMemo* No. 919, November 18, 2005, http://www.heritage.org/research/reports/2005/11/zarqawis-amman-bombings-jordans-9-11.

58. For more information on the inter-Arab dispute with Qatar, see "Assessing the Global Operating Environment," *supra*.

59. Middle East Media Research Institute, "Former IRGC General Close to Supreme Leader Khamenei: 'Bahrain Is a Province of Iran That Should Be Annexed to [It],'" *Special Dispatch* No. 6358, March 23, 2016, http://www.memri.org/report/en/0/0/0/0/0/0/9090.htm (accessed June 26, 2017).

60. Maayan Groisman, "Iranian Commander Threatens to Make Bahrain's Royal Family 'Disappear,'" *The Jerusalem Post*, June 21, 2016, http://www.jpost.com/Middle-East/Iran-News/Iranian-Quds-Force-commander-threatens-to-make-Bahrains-royal-family-disappear-457354 (accessed July 30, 2018).

61. 2018 WWTA, p. 19.

62. U.S. Department of Energy, Energy Information Administration, "World Oil Transit Chokepoints," July 25, 2017, p. 2, https://www.eia.gov/beta/international/regions-topics.php?RegionTopicID=WOTC (accessed July 30, 2018).

63. Thom Shanker, "Rice Dismisses Iranian Cleric's Warning on Oil," *The New York Times*, June 5, 2006, http://www.nytimes.com/2006/06/05/world/middleeast/05diplo.html?_r=0 (accessed June 22, 2017).

64. Tom O'Connor, "Iran's Military Fires New Cruise Missiles Amid Gulf Tensions with U.S.," *Newsweek*, April 26, 2017, https://www.newsweek.com/iran-military-fire-cruise-missiles-gulf-tensions-us-590462 (accessed July 30, 2018), and Editor, "Iranian Navy Test-Fires Long-Range Qadir Cruise Missile During Drills," DefenceTalk.com, January 26, 2018, https://www.defencetalk.com/iranian-navy-test-fires-long-range-qadir-cruise-missile-during-drills-71175/ (accessed July 30, 2018).

65. Michael Knights, *Troubled Waters: Future U.S. Security Assistance in the Persian Gulf*, Washington Institute for Near East Policy *Focus*, 2006, p. 71, http://www.washingtoninstitute.org/uploads/Documents/pubs/TroubledWaters.pdf.pdf (accessed July 30, 2018).

66. Asa Fitch, "Iranian Authorities Release Maersk Tigris," *The Wall Street Journal*, May 7, 2015, http://www.wsj.com/articles/iranian-authorities-release-maersk-tigris-1430991500 (accessed June 22, 2017).

67. Jonathan Saul, "Tanker Attacked by Iranian Craft Collided with Iran Oil Platform in March: Owner," Reuters, May 15, 2015, https://www.reuters.com/article/us-gulf-iran-ship/tanker-attacked-by-iranian-craft-collided-with-iran-oil-platform-in-march-owner-idUSKBN0O01F620150515 (accessed August 13, 2018).

68. James Phillips, "The Dangerous Regional Implications of the Iran Nuclear Agreement," Heritage Foundation *Backgrounder* No. 3124, May 9, 2016, http://www.heritage.org/middle-east/report/the-dangerous-regional-implications-the-iran-nuclear-agreement.

69. Robert Burns, "US Military Official: Iran Naval Forces Have Deliberately Halted 'Provocations,'" *Chicago Tribune*, March 16, 2018, http://www.chicagotribune.com/news/nationworld/sns-bc-ml--mideast-mattis-20180315-story.html (accessed July 30, 2018).

70. Paul Bucala, Caitlin Shayda Pendleton, Christopher Harmer, Emily Estelle, and Marie Donovan, "Iranian Involvement in Missile Attacks on the USS Mason," American Enterprise Institute, Critical Threats Project, October 19, 2016, https://www.criticalthreats.org/analysis/iranian-involvement-in-missile-attacks-on-the-uss-mason (accessed July 31, 2018).

71. Niklas Anziger, "Jihad at Sea—Al Qaeda's Maritime Front in Yemen," Center for International Maritime Security, February 25, 2014, http://cimsec.org/jihad-sea-yemen-al-qaedas-new-frontier (accessed June 22, 2017).

72. Steven Starr, "Attacks in the Suez: Security of the Canal at Risk?" Combating Terrorism Center at West Point, *CTC Sentinel*, Vol. 7, Issue 1 (January 15, 2014), https://www.ctc.usma.edu/posts/attacks-in-the-suez-security-of-the-canal-at-risk (accessed June 22, 2017).

73. Thomas Gibbons-Neff, "Piracy Back on the Rise off Somalia, U.S. Military Says," *Chicago Tribune*, April 23, 2017, http://www.chicagotribune.com/news/nationworld/ct-piracy-somali-waters-20170423-story.html (accessed June 22, 2017).

74. Lisa Otto, "Has Somali Piracy Returned?" *The Maritime Executive*, May 22, 2017, http://maritime-executive.com/editorials/has-somali-piracy-returned (accessed June 22, 2017).

75. Oceans Beyond Piracy, "Piracy and Armed Robbery Against Ships in East Africa 2017," http://oceansbeyondpiracy.org/reports/sop/east-africa (accessed July 30, 2018).

76. 2018 WWTA, p. 19.

77. Scott Stewart, "The Continuing Threat of Libyan Missiles," Stratfor Worldview *On Security*, May 3, 2012, http://www.stratfor.com/weekly/continuing-threat-libyan-missiles#axzz39ABWqV00 (accessed July 31, 2018).

78. David Ignatius, "Libyan Missiles on the Loose," *The Washington Post*, May 8, 2012, http://www.washingtonpost.com/opinions/libyan-missiles-on-the-loose/2012/05/08/gIQA1FCUBU_story.html (accessed June 22, 2017).

79. Matt Schroeder, "New Information on Somali MANPADS," Federation of American Scientists, July 27, 2007, https://fas.org/blogs/security/2007/07/new_information_on_somali_manp/ (accessed June 22, 2017).

80. Nuclear Threat Initiative, "Iran: Missile."

81. Duncan Gardham, "WikiLeaks: Iran 'Obtains North Korea Missiles Which Can Strike Europe,'" *The Telegraph*, November 28, 2017, https://www.telegraph.co.uk/news/worldnews/8166848/WikiLeaks-Iran-obtains-North-Korea-missiles-which-can-strike-Europe.html (accessed July 31, 2018).

82. Lateef Mungin, "Iran Claims 2nd Launch of Monkey into Space and Back," CNN, December 14, 2013, http://www.cnn.com/2013/12/14/world/meast/iran-monkey-space/ (accessed September 17, 2014).

83. Nasser Karimi, "Iran Says It Sets up Space Monitoring Center," Associated Press, June 9, 2013, http://news.yahoo.com/iran-says-sets-space-monitoring-center-072742942.html (accessed June 27, 2017).

84. Reuters, "U.S. Says Iran Rocket Test Breaches U.N. Resolution," July 27, 2017, https://www.reuters.com/article/us-iran-satellite/u-s-says-iran-rocket-test-breaches-u-n-resolution-idUSKBN1AC1YY (accessed July 31, 2018).

85. 2018 WWTA, p. 8.

86. Ilan Berman, Vice President, American Foreign Policy Council, "The Iranian Cyber Threat, Revisited," statement before the Subcommittee on Cybersecurity, Infrastructure Protection, and Security Technologies, Committee on Homeland Security, U.S. House of Representatives, March 20, 2013, p. 3, https://homeland.house.gov/hearing/subcommittee-hearing-cyber-threats-china-russia-and-iran-protecting-american-critical/ (accessed July 31, 2018).

87. Nart Villeneuve, Ned Moran, Thoufique Haq, and Mike Scott, "Operation Saffron Rose 2013," FireEye *Special Report*, 2014, https://www.fireeye.com/content/dam/fireeye-www/global/en/current-threats/pdfs/rpt-operation-saffron-rose.pdf (accessed July 31, 2018).

88. Ian Bremmer, "These 5 Facts Explain the State of Iran," *Time*, March 27, 2015, http://time.com/3761786/5-facts-explain-iran-nuclear-talks-sanctions/ (accessed August 5, 2018). Israel's Institute for National Security Studies similarly reported in October 2012 that "[i]n order to realize the goals of its strategy, Iran has allocated about $1 billion to develop and acquire technology and recruit and train experts." Gabi Siboni and Sami Kronenfeld, "Iran's Cyber Warfare," Institute for National Security Studies *Insight* No. 375, October 15, 2012, http://www.inss.org.il/publication/irans-cyber-warfare/ (accessed August 5, 2018).

89. Frederick W. Kagan and Tommy Stiansen, *The Growing Cyberthreat from Iran: The Initial Report of Project Pistachio Harvest*, American Enterprise Institute Critical Threats Project and Norse Corporation, April 2015, https://www.aei.org/publication/growing-cyberthreat-from-iran/ (accessed June 27, 2017).

90. Berman, "The Iranian Cyber Threat, Revisited," p. 3.

91. Tony Capaccio, David Lerman, and Chris Strohm, "Iran Behind Cyber-Attack on Adelson's Sands Corp., Clapper Says," Bloomberg, February 26, 2015, http://www.bloomberg.com/news/articles/2015-02-26/iran-behind-cyber-attack-on-adelson-s-sands-corp-clapper-says (accessed July 31, 2018).

92. Christopher Bronk and Eneken Tikk-Ringas, "The Cyber Attack on Saudi Aramco," *Survival: Global Politics and Strategy*, Vol. 55, No. 2 (April/May 2013), pp. 81–96, https://www.tandfonline.com/doi/full/10.1080/00396338.2013.784468 (accessed August 13, 2018); Saudi Aramco, "Oil Production," http://www.saudiaramco.com/en/home/our-business/upstream/oil-production.html (accessed August 13, 2018).

93. David E. Sanger and Nicole Perlroth, "Iranian Hackers Attack State Dept. via Social Media Accounts," *The New York Times*, November 24, 2015, http://www.nytimes.com/2015/11/25/world/middleeast/iran-hackers-cyberespionage-state-department-social-media.html?_r=0 (accessed June 22, 2017).

94. Ellen Nakashima and Matt Zapotosky, "U.S. Charges Iran-Linked Hackers with Targeting Banks, N.Y. Dam," *The Washington Post*, March 24, 2016, https://www.washingtonpost.com/world/national-security/justice-department-to-unseal-indictment-against-hackers-linked-to-iranian-goverment/2016/03/24/9b3797d2-f17b-11e5-a61f-e9c95c06edca_story.html (accessed June 22, 2017).

95. David E. Sanger, "Iran Hackers Dangle a Familiar Name to Fish for Data," *The New York Times*, May 30, 2014, http://www.nytimes.com/2014/05/31/world/middleeast/iran-hackers-dangle-a-familiar-name-to-fish-for-data.html?_r=2 (accessed June 22, 2017).

96. Bill Gertz, "FBI: Iran to Launch New Cyber Attacks," *The Washington Free Beacon*, May 24, 2018, http://freebeacon.com/national-security/fbi-iran-launch-new-cyber-attacks/ (accessed July 30, 2018).

97. 2018 WWTA, p. 6.

98. International Institute for Strategic Studies, *The Military Balance 2018: The Annual Assessment of Global Military Capabilities and Defence Economics* (London: Routledge, 2018), pp. 333–337.

99. This *Index* scores threat capability as it relates to the vital national interests of the U.S. and the role and utility of U.S. military forces. Terrorist groups clearly have the ability to conduct attacks using improvised explosive devices (IEDs), firearms, and even hijacked airplanes. The bombing of the Boston Marathon in April 2013, an attempted car bomb attack in New York City's Times Square in May 2010, and al-Qaeda's attacks on September 11, 2001, are stark examples. Often, the U.S. has handled terrorism as a law enforcement and intelligence collection matter, especially within the United States and when it presents a threat to particular U.S. interests in other countries. Compared to the types of threats posed by states such as China or Russia, terrorism is a lesser sort of threat to the security and viability of the U.S. as a global power. This *Index* does not dismiss the deaths, injuries, and damage that terrorists can inflict on Americans at home and abroad; it places the threat posed by terrorism in context with substantial threats to the U.S. homeland, the potential for major regional conflict, and the potential to deny U.S. access to the global commons. With this in mind, terrorist groups seldom have the physical ability either to accomplish the extreme objectives they state or to present a physical threat that rises to a level that threatens U.S. vital security interests. Of course, terrorist organizations can commit acts of war on a continuing basis, as reflected in their conduct in the war against al-Qaeda and its associates in which the United States has been engaged for more than a decade.

Asia

Threats to the Homeland

Threats to the U.S. homeland that stem from Asia include terrorist threats from non-state actors resident in ungoverned areas of South Asia, an active and growing North Korean ballistic missile capability, and a credible Chinese nuclear missile capability that supports other elements of China's national power.

Terrorism Originating from Afghanistan and Pakistan (AfPak). Terrorist groups operating from Pakistan and Afghanistan continue to pose a direct threat to the U.S. homeland. Pakistan is home to a host of terrorist groups that keep the region unstable and contribute to the spread of global terrorism. The killing of Osama bin Laden at his hideout in Abbottabad, Pakistan, in May 2011 and an intensive drone campaign in Pakistan's tribal areas bordering Afghanistan from 2010–2012 have helped to degrade the al-Qaeda threat, but the residual presence of al-Qaeda and the emergence of ISIS in Afghanistan remain serious concerns. This is a deadly region. According to General John W. Nicholson, then commander of U.S. and NATO forces in Afghanistan, "there are 98 U.S.-designated terrorist groups globally. Twenty of them are in the AfPak region. This represents the highest concentration of terrorist groups anywhere in the world...13 in Afghanistan, seven in Pakistan."[1]

ISIS efforts to make inroads into Pakistan and Afghanistan have met with only limited success, most likely because of al-Qaeda's well-established roots in the region, ability to maintain the loyalty of the various South Asian terrorist groups, and careful nurturing of its relationship with the Afghan Taliban. The Afghan Taliban views ISIS as a direct competitor for financial resources, recruits, and ideological influence. This competition was evident in a June 16, 2015, letter sent by the Taliban to ISIS leader Abu Bakr al-Baghdadi, urging his group not to take actions that could lead to "division of the Mujahideen's command."[2] There also have been reports of clashes between ISIS militants and the Taliban in eastern and southern Afghanistan.

Reports of an ISIS presence in Afghanistan first began to surface in 2014, and the group has slowly gained a small foothold in the country. Though its actual numbers remain modest, its high-profile, high-casualty terrorist attacks have helped it to attract followers. In 2017 and 2018, several high-profile attacks in the Afghan capital and elsewhere targeted cultural centers, global charities, voter registration centers, and Afghan military and intelligence facilities, although they still pale in comparison to the number of attacks launched by the Taliban.

In April 2017, the U.S. military claimed there were 700 ISIS fighters in Afghanistan; in November, however, General Nicholson said that 1,600 ISIS fighters had been "remov[ed]" from the battlefield since March.[3] In June 2017, a U.S. airstrike killed the head of ISIS-Khorasan, Abu Sayed.

Experts believe there is little coordination between the ISIS-Khorasan branch operating in Afghanistan and the central command structure of the group located in the Middle East. Instead, it draws recruits from disaffected members of the Pakistani Taliban and other radicalized Afghans and has frequently found itself at odds with the Afghan Taliban, with which it competes for resources, territory, and recruits.

Pakistan's continued support for terrorist groups that have links to al-Qaeda undermines U.S. counterterrorism goals in the region. Pakistan's military and intelligence leaders maintain a short-term tactical approach of fighting some terrorist groups that are deemed to be a threat to the state while supporting others that are aligned with Pakistan's goal of extending its influence and curbing India's.

A December 16, 2014, terrorist attack on a school in Peshawar that killed over 150 people, mostly children, shocked the Pakistani public and prompted the government led by Prime Minister Nawaz Sharif to introduce a National Action Plan (NAP) to reinvigorate the country's fight against terrorism. The action plan includes steps like lifting the moratorium on the death penalty for terrorists, establishing special military courts to try terrorists, curbing the spread of extremist literature and propaganda on social media, freezing the assets of terrorist organizations, and forming special committees of army and political leaders in the provinces to implement the NAP. The NAP has been criticized for being poorly implemented, but in the summer of 2018, the leaders of the PPP and PTI opposition parties, Bilawal Bhutto and Imran Khan, called for the NAP to be strengthened and extended across the country.

Implementation of the NAP and the Pakistani military's operations against TTP (Pakistani Taliban) hideouts in North Waziristan have helped to reduce Pakistan's internal terrorist threat to some degree. According to the India-based South Asia Terrorism Portal, total terrorist attack fatalities inside Pakistan have been on a steady decline since 2009, when they peaked at 11,704. Since then, they have fallen to 5,496 in 2014, 1,803 in 2016, 1,260 in 2017, and just 281 in the first half of 2018.[4]

There are few signs that Pakistan's crackdown on terrorism extends to groups that target India, such as the Lashkar-e-Taiba (LeT), which was responsible for the 2008 Mumbai attacks, and the Jaish-e-Mohammed (JeM), which carried out an attack on the Indian airbase at Pathankot on January 2, 2016. In early April 2015, Pakistan released on bail the mastermind of the Mumbai attacks, Zakiur Rehman Lakhvi, who had been in Pakistani custody since 2009.

In April 2012, the U.S. issued a $10 million reward for information leading to the arrest or conviction of LeT founder Hafez Muhammad Saeed. The LeT has engaged in recruitment and fundraising activities in the U.S. In September 2011, for instance, U.S. authorities arrested Jubair Ahmad, an American permanent resident born in Pakistan, for providing material support to the LeT by producing LeT propaganda and uploading it to the Internet. Ahmad reportedly attended an LeT training camp in Pakistan before moving to the U.S. in 2007.[5]

The U.S. trial of Pakistani American David Coleman Headley, who was arrested in Chicago in 2009 for his involvement in the 2008 Mumbai attacks, led to striking revelations about the LeT's international reach and close connections to Pakistani intelligence. Headley had traveled frequently to Pakistan, where he received terrorist training from the LeT, and to India, where he scouted the sites of the Mumbai attacks. In four days of testimony and cross-examination, Headley provided details about his meetings with a Pakistani intelligence officer, a former army major, and a navy frogman who were among the key players in orchestrating the Mumbai assault.[6]

The possibility that terrorists could gain effective access to Pakistani nuclear weapons is contingent on a complex chain of circumstances. In terms of consequence, however, it is the most dangerous regional threat scenario. Concern about the safety and security of Pakistan's nuclear weapons increases when India–Pakistan tensions increase. During the 1999 Kargil crisis, for example, U.S. intelligence indicated that Pakistan had made "nuclear preparations," and this spurred greater U.S. diplomatic involvement in defusing the crisis.[7]

If Pakistan were to move around its nuclear assets or, worse, take steps to mate weapons with delivery systems, the likelihood of terrorist theft or infiltration would increase.

Increased reliance on tactical nuclear weapons (TNWs) is of particular concern because launch authorities for TNWs are typically delegated to lower-tier field commanders far from the central authority in Islamabad. Another concern is the possibility that miscalculations could lead to regional nuclear war if top Indian leaders were to lose confidence that nuclear weapons in Pakistan are under government control or, conversely, were to assume that they were under Pakistani government control after they ceased to be.

There is concern that Islamist extremist groups with links to the Pakistan security establishment could exploit those links to gain access to nuclear weapons technology, facilities, and/or materials. The realization that Osama bin Laden stayed for six years within a half-mile of Pakistan's premier defense academy has fueled concern that al-Qaeda can operate relatively freely in parts of Pakistan and might eventually gain access to Pakistan's nuclear arsenal. The Nuclear Threat Initiative (NTI) *Nuclear Security Index* ranks 24 countries with "weapons useable nuclear material" for their susceptibility to theft. Pakistan's weapons-grade materials are the 22nd least secure, with only Iran's and North Korea's ranking lower. In the NTI's broader survey of 44 countries with nuclear power and related facilities, Pakistan ranks 36th least secure against sabotage.[8]

There is the additional, though less likely, scenario of extremists gaining access through a collapse of the state. While Pakistan remains unstable because of its weak economy, regular terrorist attacks, sectarian violence, civil–military tensions, and the growing influence of religious extremist groups, it is unlikely that the Pakistani state will collapse altogether. The country's most powerful institution, the 550,000-strong army that has ruled Pakistan for almost half of its existence, would almost certainly intervene and take charge once again if the political situation began to unravel. The potential breakup of the Pakistani state would have to be preceded by the disintegration of the army, which currently is not plausible.[9]

WWTA: The 2018 Worldwide Threat Assessment of the U.S. Intelligence Community (WWTA) does not reference any threat to the homeland from AfPak-based terrorism. The 2017 assessment, however, cited "[p]lotting against the US homeland" by individual members within terrorist groups.[10]

Summary: The threat to the American homeland emanating from Afghanistan and Pakistan is diverse, complex, and mostly indirect, largely involving non-state actors. The intentions of non-state terrorist groups like the TTP, al-Qaeda, and ISIS toward the U.S. are demonstrably hostile. Despite the broad and deep U.S. relationships with Pakistan's governing elites and military, however, it is likely that the political–military interplay in Pakistan and instability in Afghanistan will continue to result in an active threat to the American homeland.

Missile Threat: North Korea and China. The two sources of the ballistic missile threat to the U.S. (North Korea and China) are very different in terms of their sophistication and integration into broader strategies for achieving national goals. The threats from these two countries are therefore very different in nature.

North Korea. In 2017, North Korea conducted three successful tests of two variants of road-mobile intercontinental ballistic missiles (ICBMs). All launches were flown in an elevated trajectory so as not to fly over Japan and to allow testing of a reentry vehicle to protect a nuclear warhead during an attack. Experts assess that the Hwasong-14 ICBM has the capability to fly 10,000 or perhaps 11,000 kilometers. At that range, Los Angeles, Denver, and Chicago (and possibly New York City, Boston, and Washington, D.C.) are within range.[11] The Hwasong-15 has a range of 13,000 kilometers and could reach the entire continental United States. North Korea conducted its fourth and fifth nuclear tests in 2016 and its most recent —the first test of a much more powerful hydrogen bomb—in 2017.

North Korea has declared that it already has a full nuclear strike capability, even altering its constitution to enshrine itself as a nuclear-armed state.[12] In late 2017, Kim Jong-un

MAP 6

North Korean Missiles

North Korean missiles can target South Korea, Japan, and U.S. bases in Guam and now can reach the United States.

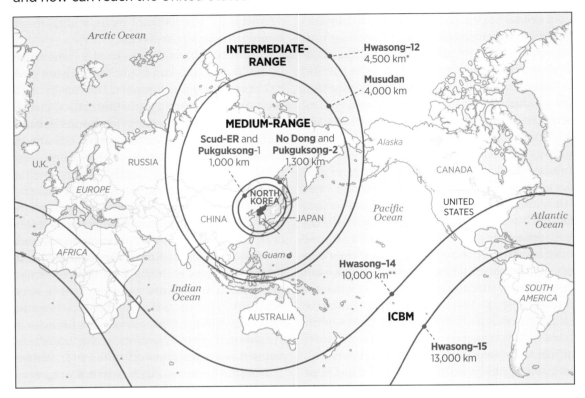

* First tested May 2017.   ** First tested July 2017.
SOURCES: Heritage Foundation research and media reports.   ☎ heritage.org

declared that North Korea had completed development of a nuclear ICBM to threaten the American homeland and vowed to "bolster up the nuclear force in quality and quantity."[13] Among North Korea's many direct verbal threats to the U.S., the regime warned in March 2016 that it would "reduce all bases and strongholds of the U.S. and South Korean warmongers for provocation and aggression into ashes in a moment, without giving them any breathing spell."[14]

The United States and South Korea have revised their estimates and now see a more dire North Korean threat. In January 2018, then-CIA Director Mike Pompeo assessed that North Korea would attain an ICBM capability within a "handful of months."[15] Vice Admiral James Syring, then head of the U.S. Missile Defense Agency, has testified that "[i]t is incumbent on us to assume that North Korea today can range the United States with an ICBM carrying a nuclear warhead."[16] In April 2016, Admiral William Gortney, head of U.S. Northern Command, stated that "[i]t's the prudent decision on my part to assume that North Korea has the capability to miniaturize a nuclear weapon and put it on an ICBM."[17]

Most non-government experts assess that North Korea has perhaps 30 or more nuclear weapons. However, an April 2017 assessment by David Albright of the Institute for Science and International Security concluded that

Pyongyang could have had "13–30 nuclear weapons as of the end of 2016, based on the estimates of North Korea's production and use of plutonium and WGU [weapon-grade uranium]," and "is currently expanding its nuclear weapons at a rate of about 3–5 weapons per year."[18] An earlier study by Joel S. Witt and Sun Young Ahn that was published in February 2015 by the Korea Institute at Johns Hopkins University's Nitze School of Advanced International Studies included a worst-case scenario in which Pyongyang could have "100 [nuclear] weapons by 2020."[19]

In 2016 and 2017, North Korea had breakthrough successes with many missiles in development. It successfully test-launched the Hwasong 12 intermediate-range ballistic missile (IRBM), which can target critical U.S. bases in Guam, and both the Pukguksong-2 road-mobile medium-range ballistic missile (MRBM) and the Pukguksong-1 submarine-launched ballistic missile (SLBM). In June 2017, in written testimony before the House Armed Services Committee, Secretary of Defense James Mattis called North Korea "the most urgent and dangerous threat to peace and security."[20]

In June 2018, President Donald Trump met with Kim Jong-un in Singapore and subsequently declared both that "[t]here is no longer a Nuclear Threat from North Korea"[21] and that "total denuclearization…has already started taking place."[22] The Singapore Communique may be the first step toward North Korea's denuclearization after eight failed diplomatic attempts during the past 27 years, but as of July 2018, there has been no decrease in North Korea's WMD arsenal or production capabilities. To the contrary, the U.S. Intelligence Community assessed that Pyongyang had increased production of fissile material for nuclear weapons, and satellite imagery showed upgrades to missile, reentry vehicle, missile launcher, and nuclear weapon production facilities.[23]

China. Chinese nuclear forces are the responsibility of the People's Liberation Army Rocket Forces (PLARF), one of three new services created on December 31, 2015. China's nuclear ballistic missile forces include land-based missiles with a range of 13,000 kilometers that can reach the U.S. (CSS-4) and submarine-based missiles that can reach the U.S. when the submarine is deployed within missile range.

The PRC became a nuclear power in 1964 when it exploded its first atomic bomb as part of its "two bombs, one satellite" effort. In quick succession, China then exploded its first thermonuclear bomb in 1967 and orbited its first satellite in 1970, demonstrating the capability to build a delivery system that can reach the ends of the Earth. China chose to rely primarily on a land-based nuclear deterrent instead of developing two or three different basing systems as the United States did.

Furthermore, unlike the United States or the Soviet Union, China chose to pursue only a limited nuclear deterrent. The PRC fielded only a small number of nuclear weapons, with estimates of about 100–150 weapons on MRBMs and about 60 ICBMs. Its only ballistic missile submarine (SSBN) conducted relatively few deterrence patrols (perhaps none),[24] and its first-generation SLBM, the JL-1, if it ever attained full operational capability, had limited reach.

While China's nuclear force remained stable for several decades, it has been part of the modernization effort of the past 20 years. The result has been modernization and some expansion of the Chinese nuclear deterrent. The core of China's ICBM force today is the DF-31 series, a solid-fueled, road-mobile system, along with a growing number of longer-range DF-41 missiles (also rail mobile) that may be in the PLA operational inventory. The DF-41 may be deployed with multiple independently targetable reentry vehicles (MIRVs). China's medium-range nuclear forces have similarly shifted to mobile, solid-rocket systems so that they are both more survivable and more easily maintained.

Notably, the Chinese are expanding their ballistic missile submarine fleet. Replacing the one Type 092 *Xia*-class SSBN are several Type 094 *Jin*-class SSBNs, four of which are already operational. These are expected to be equipped with the new, longer-range JL-2 SLBM. Such a system would give the PRC a "secure second-strike" capability, substantially enhancing its nuclear deterrent. There is also some possibility that the Chinese nuclear arsenal now contains land-attack cruise missiles. The CJ-20, a long-range, air-launched cruise missile carried on China's H-6 bomber, may be nuclear tipped, although there is not much evidence that China has pursued such a capability. China is also believed to be working on a cruise missile submarine that, if equipped with nuclear cruise missiles, would further expand the range of its nuclear attack options.[25]

As a result of its modernization efforts, China's nuclear forces appear to be shifting from a minimal deterrent posture (one suited only to responding to an attack and even then with only limited numbers) to a more robust but still limited deterrent posture. While the PRC will still likely field fewer nuclear weapons than either the United States or Russia, it will field a more modern and diverse set of capabilities than India or Pakistan (or North Korea), its nuclear-armed neighbors, are capable of fielding. If there are corresponding changes in doctrine, modernization will enable China to engage in limited nuclear options in the event of a conflict.

China has also been working on an array of hypersonic weapons. Undersecretary of Defense Michael Griffin and General John Hyten, head of U.S. Strategic Command, have testified that China and Russia are working aggressively to develop hypersonic weapons. Both have warned that China is at or ahead of the American level of development. General Hyten, for example, warned that "we don't have any defense that could deny the employment of such a weapon against us, so our response would be our deterrent force, which would be the triad and the nuclear capabilities that we have to respond to such a threat."[26]

WWTA: The language of the WWTA has changed slightly in its description of the North Korean nuclear threat, from a "serious threat to US interests and to the security environment in East Asia"[27] to "among the most volatile and confrontational WMD threats to the United States."[28] However, it again reports that North Korea is "committed to developing a long-range, nuclear-armed missile that is capable of posing a direct threat to the United States."[29] With respect to the broader threat from North Korea's "weapons of mass destruction program, public threats, defiance of the international community, confrontational military posturing, cyber activities, and potential for internal instability," the WWTA warns that they "pose a complex and increasing threat to US national security and interests."[30] Last year, it described this same mix of factors as an "increasingly grave threat."[31]

The WWTA's assessment of the Chinese nuclear missile threat is unchanged from 2016 and 2017: China "continues to modernize its nuclear missile force by adding more survivable road-mobile systems and enhancing its silo-based systems. This new generation of missiles is intended to ensure the viability of China's strategic deterrent by providing a second-strike capability."[32] The 2018 assessment adds the observation that the Chinese are intent on forming a "triad by developing a nuclear-capable next generation bomber."[33]

Summary: The respective missile threats to the American homeland from North Korea and China are very different. China has many more nuclear weapons, multiple demonstrated and tested means of delivery, and more mature systems, but it is a more stable actor with a variety of interests, including relations with the United States and its extensive interaction with the international system. North Korea has fewer weapons and questionable means of delivery, but it is less stable and less predictable, with a vastly lower stake in the international system. There is also a widely acknowledged difference in intentions: China seeks a stable second-strike capability and, unlike North Korea, is not actively and directly threatening the United States.

Threat of Regional War

America's forward-deployed military at bases throughout the Western Pacific, five treaty allies, security partners in Taiwan and Singapore, and growing security partnership with India are keys to the U.S. strategic footprint in Asia. One of its critical allies, South Korea, remains under active threat of attack and invasion from the North, and Japan faces both intimidation attacks intended to deny the U.S. its base access to Japan and nuclear attacks on U.S. bases in the case of conflict on the Korean Peninsula.[34] Taiwan is under a long-standing, well-equipped, purposely positioned, and increasingly active military threat from China. Japan, Vietnam, and the Philippines, by virtue of maritime territorial disputes, are under paramilitary, military, and political pressure from China.

In South Asia, India is geographically positioned between two major security threats: Pakistan to its west and China to its northeast. From Pakistan, India faces the additional threat of terrorism, whether state-enabled or carried out without state knowledge or control.

North Korean Attack on American Bases and Allies. North Korea's conventional and nuclear missile forces threaten U.S. bases in South Korea, Japan, and Guam. Beyond its nuclear weapons programs, North Korea poses additional risks to its neighbors. North Korea has an extensive ballistic missile force. Pyongyang has deployed approximately 800 Scud short-range tactical ballistic missiles, 300 No-dong medium-range missiles, and 50 Musudan intermediate-range ballistic missiles. The Scud missiles threaten South Korea, the No-dong can target all of Japan and South Korea, and the Musudan and Hwasong-12 IRBMs can hit U.S. bases on Okinawa and Guam. Pyongyang continues its development of several different ICBMs with enough range to hit the continental U.S.[35]

North Korea has approximately 1 million people in its military, with reserves numbering several million more. Pyongyang has forward-deployed 70 percent of its ground forces within 90 miles of the Demilitarized Zone (DMZ), making it possible to attack with little or no warning. This is of particular concern because South Korea's capital, Seoul, is only 30

miles south of the DMZ.[36] In addition to three conventional corps alongside the DMZ, Pyongyang has deployed two mechanized corps, an armor corps, and an artillery corps.[37]

The April 2018 inter-Korean summit led to bilateral pledges of nonaggression and mutual force reduction. However, similar pledges were contained in the 1972, 1992, 2000, and 2007 joint statements, all of which Pyongyang subsequently violated or abrogated.

In the Panmunjom Declaration that marked the 2018 summit, South Korean President Moon Jae-in and North Korean leader Kim Jong-un committed their countries to "completely cease all hostile acts against each other." The two leaders "pledged that 'there will be no more war on the Korean Peninsula and thus a new era of peace has begun.'"[38] In 1972, however, the Koreas futilely agreed to "implement appropriate measures to stop military provocation which may lead to unintended armed conflicts."[39] In 1992, they vowed that they would "not use force against each other" and would "not undertake armed aggression against each other."[40] And in 2007, Seoul and Pyongyang agreed to "adhere strictly to their obligation to nonaggression."[41]

None of those pledges prevented North Korea from conducting assassination attempts on the South Korean president, terrorist acts, military and cyber-attacks, and acts of war. For this reason, as of July 2018, there have been no changes in either North Korea's or South Korea's force posture.

After the June 2018 U.S.–North Korea summit, Washington and Seoul unilaterally canceled the annual Ulchi Freedom Guardian joint exercise, as well as South Korea's Taeguk command-post exercise, and suspended the joint Marine Exercise Program.[42] North Korea did not announce any reciprocal suspensions of its conventional military exercises, including its large-scale annual Winter and Summer Training Cycles.

South Korea remains North Korea's principal target. In 2005, South Korea initiated a comprehensive defense reform strategy to transform its military into a smaller but more capable force to deal with the North Korean threat and a predicted shortfall of 18 year olds by 2025 to fully staff the military. The defense reform program has gone through a number of iterations but remains a goal in 2018. Overall, South Korean military manpower would be reduced approximately 25 percent, from 681,000 to 500,000. The army would face the largest cuts, disbanding four corps and 23 divisions and cutting troops from 560,000 in 2004 to 370,000 in 2020. Seoul planned to compensate for decreased troop levels by procuring advanced fighter and surveillance aircraft, naval platforms, and ground combat vehicles.[43] Some Moon Jae-in administration advisers have suggested that force levels could be reduced further if progress is made in improving inter-Korean relations.

That North Korea's conventional forces are a very real threat to South Korea was clearly demonstrated by two deadly attacks in 2010. In March, a North Korean submarine sank the South Korean naval corvette *Cheonan* in South Korean waters, killing 46 sailors. In November, North Korean artillery shelled Yeonpyeong Island, killing four South Koreans.

Since the North Korean military is predominantly equipped with older ground force equipment, Pyongyang has prioritized deployment of strong asymmetric capabilities, including special operations forces, long-range artillery, and missiles. As noted, North Korea has deployed hundreds of Scud short-range ballistic missiles that can target all of South Korea with explosive, chemical, and biological warheads. The land and sea borders between North and South Korea remain unsettled, heavily armed, and actively subject to occasional, limited armed conflict.

North Korea's September 2017 hydrogen bomb test—in excess of 150 kilotons—demonstrated a thermonuclear hydrogen bomb capability. It is unknown whether the warhead has been miniaturized for an ICBM, but then-CIA Director Michael Pompeo said in January 2018 that North Korea would have the ability to carry out a nuclear attack on the mainland U.S. in a mere "handful of months."[44] North

Korea is already assessed as having the ability to target South Korea and Japan with nuclear-capable missiles.

In March 2016, the Korean Central News Agency declared that Pyongyang has a "military operation plan...to liberate south Korea and strike the U.S. mainland," that "offensive means have been deployed to put major strike targets in the operation theatres of south Korea within the firing range," and that "the powerful nuclear strike means targeting the U.S. imperialist aggressor forces bases in the Asia–Pacific region and the U.S. mainland are always ready to fire."[45]

In May 2018, North Korea blew up the entrance adits to its Punggye-ri nuclear test site. Foreign reporters were able to confirm the explosive closure of the entrances to six test tunnels but could not confirm overall damage to the tunnels. In April 2018, Kim Jong-un had declared that "under the proven condition of complete nuclear weapons, we no longer need any nuclear tests, mid-range and intercontinental ballistic rocket tests" and that "the nuclear test site in [the] northern area has also completed its mission."[46]

WWTA: The WWTA specifically cites Pyongyang's "serious and growing threat to South Korea and Japan" and the expanded "conventional strike options...that improve North Korea's ability to strike regional US and allied targets with little warning."[47]

Summary: North Korean forces arrayed against American allies in South Korea and Japan are substantial, and North Korea's history of provocation is a consistent indicator of its intent to achieve its political objectives by threat of force.

Chinese Threat to Taiwan. China's long-standing threat to end the de facto independence of Taiwan and ultimately to bring it under the authority of Beijing—if necessary, by force—is both a threat to a major American security partner and a threat to the American interest in peace and stability in the Western Pacific.

After easing for eight years, tensions across the Taiwan Strait resumed as a result of Beijing's reaction to the outcome of Taiwan's 2016 presidential election. Regardless of the state of the relationship at any given time, however, Chinese leaders from Deng Xiaoping and Mao Zedong to Xi Jinping have consistently emphasized the importance of ultimately reclaiming Taiwan. The island, along with Tibet, is the clearest example of a geographical "core interest" in Chinese policy. China has never renounced the use of force, and it continues to employ political warfare against Taiwan's political and military leadership.

For the Chinese leadership, the failure to effect unification, whether peacefully or through the use of force, would reflect fundamental political weakness in the PRC. For this reason, there is no realistic means by which any Chinese leadership can back away from the stance of having to unify the island with the mainland. As a result, the island remains an essential part of the People's Liberation Army's "new historic missions," shaping PLA acquisitions and military planning.

Two decades of double-digit increases in China's announced defense budget have produced a significantly more modern PLA, much of which remains focused on a Taiwan contingency. This modernized force includes more than 1,000 ballistic missiles, a modernized air force, and growing numbers of modern surface combatants and diesel-electric submarines capable of mounting a blockade. As the 1995–1996 Taiwan Strait crisis demonstrated, Beijing is prepared at least to use open displays of force. Accordingly, over the last year, the Chinese have sought to intimidate Taiwan with a growing number of military exercises, including live-fire drills and bomber flights around the island.[48] In the absence of a strong American presence, it might be willing to go farther than this.

It is widely posited that China's counter-intervention strategy—the deployment of an array of overlapping capabilities, including anti-ship ballistic missiles (ASBMs), submarines, and long-range cruise missiles, satellites, and cyber weapons, that Americans refer to as an anti-access/area-denial (A2/AD) strategy—is aimed largely at forestalling American intervention in support of friends and allies in the Western Pacific, including Taiwan. By holding at risk key American platforms and systems such as aircraft carriers, the Chinese seek to delay or even deter American intervention in support of key friends and allies, allowing the PRC to achieve a fait accompli. The growth of China's military capabilities is specifically oriented toward countering America's ability to assist in the defense of Taiwan.

Chinese efforts to reclaim Taiwan are not limited to overt military means. The doctrine of "three warfares"[49] highlights Chinese political warfare methods, including legal warfare/lawfare, public opinion warfare, and psychological warfare. The PRC employs such approaches to undermine both Taiwan's will to resist and America's willingness to support Taiwan. The Chinese goal would be to "win without fighting"—to take Taiwan without firing a shot or with only minimal resistance before the United States could organize an effective response.

WWTA: The WWTA does not reference the threat that China poses to Taiwan but does again reference Beijing's "firm stance" with regard to Taipei.[50]

Summary: The Chinese threat to Taiwan is a long-standing one. After an extended lull in apparent tensions, its reaction to the new government in Taipei has once again brought the threat to the fore. China's ability to execute a military action against Taiwan, albeit at high economic, political, and military cost, is improving. Its intent to unify Taiwan with the mainland under the full authority of the PRC central government and to end the island's de facto independence has been consistent over time.

Major Pakistan-Backed Terrorist Attack on India Leading to Open Warfare Between India and Pakistan. An India–Pakistan conflict would jeopardize multiple U.S. interests in the region and potentially increase the threat of global terrorism if Pakistan were destabilized. Pakistan would rely on militant non-state actors to help it fight

India, potentially creating a more permissive environment in which various terrorist groups could operate freely. The potential for a nuclear conflict would threaten U.S. businesses in the region and disrupt investment and trade flows, mainly between the U.S. and India, whose bilateral trade in goods and services currently totals well over $100 billion annually.[51] A conflict would also potentially strain America's ties with one or both of the combatants at a time when Pakistan–U.S. ties are already under severe stress and America is trying to build a stronger partnership with India. The effects of an actual nuclear exchange—both the human lives lost and the long-term economic damage—would be devastating.

Meanwhile, India and Pakistan are engaged in a nuclear competition that threatens stability throughout the subcontinent. Both countries tested nuclear weapons in 1998, establishing themselves as overtly nuclear weapons states, although India first conducted a "peaceful" nuclear weapons test in 1974. Both countries also are developing naval nuclear weapons and already possess ballistic missile and aircraft-delivery platforms.[52]

Pakistan has been said to have "the world's fastest-growing nuclear stockpile."[53] Islamabad currently has an estimated 140 nuclear weapons and "has lowered the threshold for nuclear weapons use by developing tactical nuclear weapons capabilities to counter perceived Indian conventional military threats."[54] This in turn affects India's nuclear use threshold, which could affect China and possibly others.

The broader military and strategic dynamic between India and Pakistan remains volatile and has arguably grown more so since the May 2014 election of Bharatiya Janata Party (BJP) leader Narendra Modi as India's prime minister. While Modi initially sought to extend an olive branch by inviting Pakistani Prime Minister Nawaz Sharif to his swearing-in ceremony, he subsequently called off foreign secretary–level talks that were scheduled for August 2014 to express anger over a Pakistani official's meeting with Kashmiri separatist leaders. During the same month, the two sides engaged in intense firing and shelling along their international border (called the working boundary) and across the Line of Control (LoC) that divides Kashmir. The director of India's Border Security Force noted that the firing across the international border was the worst it had been since the war between India and Pakistan in 1971. A similar escalation in border tensions occurred again in December 2014 when a series of firing incidents over a one-week period resulted in the deaths of at least five Pakistani soldiers and one Indian soldier.

On December 25, 2015, a meeting did occur when Prime Minister Modi made an impromptu visit to Lahore to meet with Pakistani Prime Minister Sharif, the first visit to Pakistan by an Indian leader in 12 years. The visit created enormous goodwill between the two countries and raised hope that official dialogue would soon resume. Again, however, violence marred the new opening. Six days after the meeting, JeM militants attacked the Indian airbase at Pathankot, killing seven Indian security personnel. India has provided information on the attackers to Pakistan and has demanded action against JeM, but to no avail.

As a result, official India–Pakistan dialogue remains deadlocked even though the two sides are reportedly communicating quietly through their foreign secretaries and national security advisers. Since 2015, there has also been an uptick in cross-border firing between the Indian and Pakistani militaries, raising questions about whether a cease-fire that has been in place since 2003 is being rendered ineffective.

As noted, Pakistan continues to harbor terrorist groups like Lashkar-e-Taiba and Jaish-e-Mohammed. The latter was responsible for a January 2, 2016, attack on an Indian airbase at Pathankot, as well as a February 2018 attack on an Indian army camp in Jammu.[55] Media reports indicate that some JeM leaders were detained in Pakistan following the Pathankot attack, but no charges were filed.

Hafez Muhammed Saeed, LeT's founder and the leader of its front organization Jamaat-ud-Dawa (JuD), has periodically been placed under arrest, only to be later released. Previously, he had operated freely in Pakistan, often holding press conferences and inciting violence against India during large public rallies. In December 2014, Saeed held a two-day conclave in Lahore that received support from the Pakistani government, including security from 4,000 police officers and government assistance in transporting attendees to the gathering of more than 400,000. India condemned the Pakistani government's support for the gathering as "blatant disregard" of global norms against terrorism.[56]

There is some concern about the impact on Indian–Pakistani relations of an international troop drawdown in Afghanistan. Such a drawdown could enable the Taliban and other extremist groups to strengthen their grip in the region, further undermining stability in Kashmir and raising the chances of another major terrorist attack against India. Afghan security forces thwarted an attack on the Indian consulate in Herat, Afghanistan, in May 2014. However, a successful future attack on Indian interests in Afghanistan along the lines of the bombing of the Indian embassy in Kabul in 2008 would sharpen tensions between New Delhi and Islamabad.

With terrorist groups operating relatively freely in Pakistan and maintaining links to the country's military and intelligence services, there is a moderate risk that the two countries might climb the military escalation ladder and eventually engage in all-out conflict. Pakistan's nuclear weapons capability appears to have acted as a deterrent against Indian military escalation both during the 2001–2002 military crisis and following the 2008 Mumbai attacks, but the Indian government would be under great pressure to react strongly in the face of another major terrorist provocation. Pakistan's recent focus on incorporating tactical nuclear weapons into its warfighting doctrine has also raised concern that if conflict does break out, there is now a higher risk of nuclear exchange.[57]

WWTA: The 2018 WWTA does not reference the threat to American interests from a Pakistani attack on India and potential escalation, but it does refer to "tense" relations between the two countries and the "risk of escalation" in the event of "another high-profile terrorist attack in India or an uptick in violence on the Line of Control."[58] It also calls attention to the production of "new types of nuclear weapons [that] will introduce new risks for escalation dynamics and security in the region."[59] More broadly, there is significant new language specifying that "Pakistan will continue to threaten US interests by deploying new nuclear weapons capabilities, maintaining its ties to militants, restricting counterterrorism cooperation, and drawing closer to China."[60]

Summary: Indian military retaliation against a Pakistan-backed terrorist strike against India could include targeted air strikes on terrorist training camps inside Pakistan. This would likely lead to broader military conflict with some prospect of escalating to a nuclear exchange. Neither side desires another general war. Both countries have limited objectives and have demonstrated their intent to avoid escalation, but this is a delicate calculation.

Threat of China–India Conflict. The possibility of armed conflict between India and China, while currently remote, poses an indirect threat to U.S. interests because it could disrupt the territorial status quo and raise nuclear tensions in the region. It would also risk straining the maturing India–U.S. partnership if the level of U.S. support and commitment in a conflict scenario did not meet India's expectations. Meanwhile, a border conflict between India and China could prompt Pakistan to try to take advantage of the situation, further contributing to regional instability.

The Chinese continue to enjoy an advantage over India in terms of military infrastructure and along the Line of Actual Control (LAC) that separates Indian-controlled territory from Chinese-controlled territory and continue to expand a network of road, rail, and air links in the border areas. To meet these challenges, the government of Prime Minister Modi has committed to expanding infrastructure development along India's disputed border with China, especially in the Indian states of Arunachal Pradesh and Sikkim, but progress has been slow. Although China currently holds a decisive military edge over India, New Delhi is engaged in an ambitious military modernization program.

Long-standing border disputes that led to a Sino–Indian War in 1962 have been heating up again in recent years. India claims that China occupies more than 14,000 square miles of Indian territory in the Aksai Chin along its northern border in Kashmir, and China lays claim to more than 34,000 square miles of India's northeastern state of Arunachal Pradesh. The issue is also closely related to China's concern for its control of Tibet and the presence in India of the Tibetan government in exile and Tibet's spiritual leader, the Dalai Lama.

In April 2013, Chinese troops settled for three weeks several miles inside northern Indian territory on the Depsang Plains in Ladakh, marking a departure from the several hundred minor transgressions reported along the LAC every year, which are generally short-lived. A visit to India by Chinese President Xi Jinping in September 2014 was overshadowed by another flare-up in border tensions when hundreds of Chinese PLA forces reportedly set up camps in the mountainous regions of Ladakh, prompting Indian forces to deploy to forward positions in the region. The border standoff lasted three weeks and was defused when both sides agreed to pull their troops back to previous positions.

The Border Defense and Cooperation Agreement (BDCA) signed during then-Prime Minister Manmohan Singh's visit to China in October 2013 affirms that neither side will use its military capabilities against the other, proposes a hotline between the two countries' military headquarters, institutes meetings between border personnel in all sectors, and ensures that neither side tails the other's patrols along the LAC.[61] The agreement also includes language stipulating that in the event the two sides come face-to-face, they "shall exercise maximum self-restraint, refrain from any provocative actions, not use force or threaten

to use force against the other side, treat each other with courtesy and prevent exchange of armed conflict."[62]

However, the agreement failed to reduce border tensions or restore momentum to border negotiations that have been largely stalled since the mid-2000s. Some analysts have even contended that the Chinese intend to buy time on their border disputes with India through the BDCA while focusing on other territorial claims in the Asia–Pacific.[63]

In the summer of 2017, China and India engaged in a tense and unprecedented standoff in the Doklam Plateau region near the tri-border area linking Bhutan, China, and India. An attempt by Chinese forces to extend a road south into Bhutanese territory claimed by China prompted an intervention by nearby Indian forces to halt construction. As with other recent border incidents, no shots were fired, but tensions ran high, with Chinese officials and media outlets levying unusually direct threats at India and demanding a full Indian withdrawal from "Chinese territory" with no preconditions. Quiet diplomacy eventually produced a mutual phased withdrawal, but Chinese troops remain encamped nearby, expanding local infrastructure and planning for a more permanent presence.

In early 2018, the two sides sought to reduce tensions, and an informal summit between President Xi and Prime Minister Modi was held in April. Despite this nominal charm offensive, however, the two sides face a growing divide along several key geopolitical fault lines.

The first major opponent of China's Belt and Road Initiative (BRI), India continues to oppose China's grand infrastructure initiative because one of its subcomponents, the China–Pakistan Economic Corridor (CPEC), traverses Indian-claimed Kashmir. Meanwhile, China has significantly expanded its economic, political, and military footprint in the Indian Ocean and South Asia, contributing to a sense of encirclement in Delhi. Beijing has achieved major diplomatic breakthroughs and landmark investments in Nepal, Sri Lanka, and the

MAP 7

China's Belt and Road Initiative

Through its Belt and Road Initiative (BRI), China endeavors to reshape the economic and geopolitical landscape of Eurasia and the Indian Ocean with an unprecedented wave of infrastructure investments.

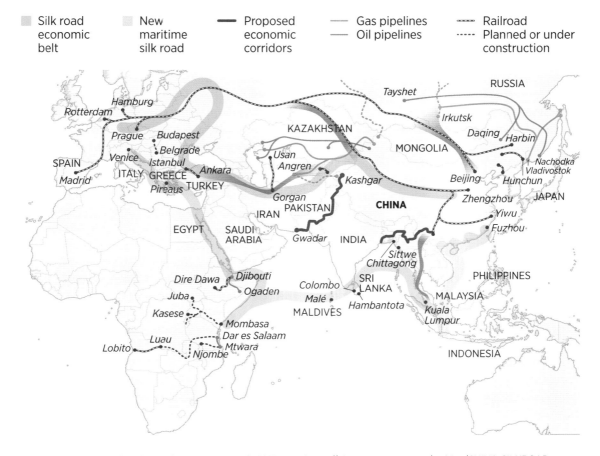

Legend:
- Silk road economic belt
- New maritime silk road
- Proposed economic corridors
- Gas pipelines
- Oil pipelines
- Railroad
- Planned or under construction

SOURCES: "Reviving the Silk Road," Reuters, May 10, 2017, map, https://pictures.reuters.com/archive/CHINA-SILKROAD--C-ET1ED5A1MD43P.html (accessed July 3, 2018), and Heritage Foundation research.

☎ heritage.org

Maldives, and the PLA Navy has begun regular conventional and nuclear submarine patrols in the Indian Ocean, complementing the anti-piracy naval task force it regularly rotates through the Indian Ocean. China opened its first "overseas logistics supply facility," which closely resembles a full military base, in Djibouti in 2017 and reportedly has expressed interest in building a naval base in Pakistan near the Chinese-operated Gwadar port.

WWTA: Unlike the 2016 and 2017 WWTAs, which were silent with respect to India–China relations, the 2018 WWTA assesses that "relations between India and China [are expected] to remain tense and possibly to deteriorate further, despite the negotiated settlement to their three-month border standoff in August, elevating the risk of unintentional escalation."[64]

Summary: American interest in India's security is substantial and expanding. Both

India and China apparently want to avoid allowing minor incidents to escalate into a more general war. The Chinese seem to use border tensions for limited diplomatic and political gain vis-à-vis India, and India responds in ways that are intended to contain minor incursions and maximize reputational damage to China. Despite limited aims, however, the unsettled situation and gamesmanship along the border could result in miscalculation, accidents, or overreaction.

Threats to the Commons

The U.S. has critical direct interests at stake in the East Asia and South Asia commons that include sea, air, space, and cyber interests. These interests include an economic interest in the free flow of commerce and the military use of the commons to safeguard America's own security and contribute to the security of its allies and partners.

Washington has long provided the security backbone in these areas, which in turn has supported the region's remarkable economic development. However, China is taking increasingly assertive steps to secure its own interests in these areas independent of U.S. efforts to maintain freedom of the commons for all in the region. It cannot be assumed that China shares either a common conception of international space with the United States or an interest in perpetuating American predominance in securing the commons.

Moreover, this concern extends beyond its immediate region. In addition to the aforementioned facility in Djibouti and the possibility of naval access to Gwadar, Chinese submarines have called at Sri Lankan ports, demonstrating China's growing ability to operate far from its shores.

Maritime and Airspace Commons. The aggressiveness of the Chinese navy, maritime law enforcement forces, and air forces in and over the waters of the East China Sea and South China Sea, coupled with ambiguous, extralegal territorial claims and assertion of control there, poses an incipient threat to American and overlapping allied interests.

East China Sea. Since 2010, China has intensified its efforts to assert claims of sovereignty over the Senkaku Islands of Japan in the East China Sea. Beijing asserts not only exclusive economic rights within the disputed waters, but also recognition of "historic" rights to dominate and control those areas as part of its territory.

Chinese coast guard vessels and military aircraft regularly challenge Japanese administration of the waters surrounding the Senkakus by sailing into and flying over them, prompting reaction from Japanese Self Defense Forces. This raises the potential for miscalculation and escalation into a military clash. In the summer of 2016, China began to deploy naval units into the area.

In November 2013, China declared an Air Defense Identification Zone (ADIZ) in the East China Sea that largely aligned with its claimed maritime Exclusive Economic Zone (EEZ). The government declared that it would "adopt defensive emergency measures to respond to aircraft that do not cooperate in the identification or refuse to follow the instructions."[65] The announcement was a provocative act—an attempt to change the status quo unilaterally.

The ADIZ declaration is part of a broader Chinese pattern of using intimidation and coercion to assert expansive extralegal claims of sovereignty and/or control incrementally. In June 2016, a Chinese fighter made an "unsafe" pass near a U.S. RC-135 reconnaissance aircraft in the East China Sea area. In March 2017 Chinese authorities warned the crew of an American B-1B bomber operating in the area of the ADIZ that they were flying illegally in PRC airspace. In response to the incident, the Chinese Foreign Ministry called for the U.S. to respect the ADIZ.[66] In May 2017, the Chinese intercepted an American WC-135, also over the East China Sea,[67] and in July, they intercepted an EP-3 surveillance plane.[68]

South China Sea. Roughly half of global trade in goods, a third of trade in oil, and over half of global liquefied natural gas shipments pass through the South China Sea, which also accounts for approximately 10 percent of global fish catch and may contain massive potential reserves of oil and natural gas. The U.S. Navy also operates in the area and requires access to meet its security and treaty obligations in the region most effectively.

The South China Sea is hotly contested by six countries, including Taiwan. Incidents between Chinese law enforcement vessels and other claimants' fishing boats occur there on a regular basis, as do other Chinese assertions of administrative authority. The most serious intraregional incidents have occurred between China and the Philippines and between China and Vietnam.

In 2012, a Philippine naval ship operating on behalf of the country's coast guard challenged private Chinese poachers in waters around Scarborough Shoal. The resulting escalation left Chinese government ships in control of the shoal, which in turn led the Philippines to bring a wide-ranging case before the Permanent Court of Arbitration (PCA) disputing Chinese activities (not its territorial claims) in the waters around the Spratlys, not limited to Scarborough. The Philippines won the case in July 2016 when the PCA invalidated China's sweeping claims to the waters and found its "island" reclamation to be in violation of commitments under the U.N. Convention on the Law of the Sea (UNCLOS).

Although the Chinese have never accepted the authority of the proceedings, they have allowed Filipino fishermen access to Scarborough Shoal in accordance with the PCA award and have refrained from reclaiming land around it. In exchange, the new Duterte government in the Philippines has chosen to set the ruling aside in pursuit of warmer relations with Beijing. This tacit agreement has lowered tensions over the past two years, although Chinese missile deployments to islands in 2018 provoked debate in Manila and a strengthening of Filipino rhetoric.[69] The government's reaction also revealed that the Philippines has formally protested Chinese activity dozens of times during Duterte's presidency.

China–Vietnam tensions in the South China Sea were on starkest display in 2014 when state-owned China National Offshore Oil Corporation (CNOOC) deployed an oil rig inside Vietnam's EEZ. The Chinese platform was accompanied by dozens of ships including naval vessels. The resulting escalation saw Chinese ships ramming Vietnamese law enforcement ships and using water cannon against the crews of Vietnamese ships. It also resulted in massive and sometimes violent demonstrations in Vietnam. The oil rig was ultimately withdrawn, and relations were restored, but the occasional reappearance of the same rig has served to underscore the continuing volatility of this issue, which involves the same area over which China and Vietnam engaged in armed battle in 1974. As recently as 2018, the Chinese were still pressing their advantages in areas contested with Vietnam with widely publicized bomber deployments to the Paracel Islands.[70] They also successfully pressured Vietnam to cancel "major oil development" projects in the South China Sea in July 2017 and again in March 2018.[71]

The U.S. presence also has become an object of Chinese attention, beginning with confrontations with the ocean surveillance ship USNS *Impeccable* and the destroyer USS *John McCain* in 2009. In addition, the Chinese routinely and vigorously protest routine U.S. Navy operations and American "freedom of navigation" operations in the area, which have increased in frequency and intensity during the course of the Trump Administration.

Differences between the U.S. and China in the South China Sea have expanded significantly with Chinese reclamation of land features in the Spratlys that began in 2013. China has reclaimed territory at seven of these man-made islands and has built airstrips on three, thereby expanding the potential reach of its navy. In 2017 and 2018, the Chinese deployed surface-to-air missiles and anti-ship cruise missiles on the "islands" despite a 2015 promise by President Xi to President Barack Obama not to "militarize" them.[72]

In his February 14, 2018, posture statement to the House Committee on Armed Services, Admiral Harry Harris, Commander, U.S. Pacific

Command, listed the structures on each of the three largest of these islands:

- 10,000 foot runways capable of launching and recovering all military aircraft;

- Fighter aircraft hangers;

- Large aircraft hangars, capable of supporting larger aircraft such as bombers, AWACS, and transports;

- Protected air defense launcher sheds;

- Protected anti-ship missile launcher sheds;

- Water and fuel storage tank farms;

- Barracks, communication systems, deep water pier facilities, military radars.[73]

Admiral Harris went on to say that "[t]hese bases appear to be forward military outposts, built for the military, garrisoned by military forces and designed to project Chinese military power and capability across the breadth of China's disputed South China Sea claims."[74] Most dramatically, in responding to a series of "Advance Policy Questions" in connection with his confirmation hearing in April, Admiral Philip Davidson, who had been nominated to replace Admiral Harris, said that "China is now capable of controlling the South China Sea in all scenarios short of war with the United States."[75]

The Chinese could use their current position as a basis for declaring an ADIZ above the South China Sea. This would cause major tensions in the region and could lead to conflict. There also are concerns that in the event of a downturn in its relationship with the Philippines, China will take action against vulnerable targets like Philippines-occupied Second Thomas Shoal or Reed Bank, which are not among the seven reclaimed "islands" but which the PCA determined are part of the Philippines EEZ and continental shelf. Proceeding

with reclamation at Scarborough is another destabilizing possibility, as it would facilitate the physical assertion of Beijing's claims and cross what the Philippine government has called a "red line."

In 2018, the situation involving continued militarization of the Spratlys led the U.S. to disinvite China from participation in biannual RIMPAC exercises.[76] In his first visit to China as Secretary of Defense, James Mattis also publicly criticized the Chinese for the militarization and made a point of raising it in his conversations with President and Communist Party General Secretary Xi Jinping.[77]

Airpower. Although China is not yet in a position to enforce an ADIZ consistently in either area, the steady improvement of the PLA Air Force (PLAAF) and naval aviation over the past two decades will eventually provide the necessary capabilities. Chinese observations of recent conflicts, including wars in the Persian Gulf, the Balkans, and Afghanistan, have emphasized the growing role of airpower and missiles in conducting "non-contact, non-linear, non-symmetrical" warfare.

China also seems to have made a point of publicizing its air force modernization, unveiling new aircraft prototypes, including two new stealth fighters, on the eve of visits by American Secretaries of Defense. (Secretary Chuck Hagel's visit in 2014 was preceded by the unveiling of the J-15 naval fighter.) Those aircraft have been flown much more aggressively, with Chinese fighters flying very close to Japanese aircraft in China's East China Sea ADIZ and conducting armed combat air patrols in the skies over Tibet.[78]

The PLA has shed most of its 1960s-era aircraft, replacing them with much more modern systems. Today's PLAAF is dominated by fourth-generation and 4.5th-generation fighter aircraft. These include the domestically designed and produced J-10 and the Su-27/Su-30/J-11 system, which is comparable to the F-15 or F-18 and dominates both the fighter and strike missions.[79] Older airframes such as the J-7 are steadily being retired from the fighter inventory. China is also believed to be preparing to field two stealth fifth-generation fighter designs. The J-20 is the larger aircraft, resembling the American F-22 fighter. The J-31 appears to resemble the F-35 but with two engines rather than one. The production of advanced combat aircraft engines remains one of the greatest challenges to Chinese fighter design.

China fields some long-range strike aircraft, largely the H-6 bomber based on the Soviet-era Tu-16 Badger. This aircraft has little prospect of penetrating advanced air defenses but is suitable as a cruise missile carrier. China also has used the H-6 as the basis for initial efforts to develop an aerial tanker fleet and seems to be examining other options as well. As it deploys more tankers, China will extend the range and loiter time of its fighter aircraft and be better equipped to enforce its declared East China Sea Air Defense Identification Zone and any possible future South China Sea ADIZ.

A variety of modern support aircraft have also entered the PLAAF inventory, including airborne early warning (AEW), command and control (C2), and electronic warfare (EW) aircraft. At the Zhuhai Air Show, Chinese companies have displayed a variety of unmanned aerial vehicles (UAVs) that reflect substantial investments and research and development efforts. Chinese drone systems include the CH-5 (Rainbow-5) drone, described in DOD's 2017 report on *Military and Security Developments Involving the People's Republic of China* as China's most heavily armed drone (carrying 16 air-to-surface munitions),[80] and the stealthy Lijian.

China's air defenses, which are controlled by the PLAAF, have also been modernizing steadily. China has acquired the advanced S-300 surface-to-air missile (SAM) system (SA-10B/SA-20), which is roughly analogous to the American Patriot SAM system, and is developing its own advanced SAM, the HQ-9, which is deployed both on land and at sea. Early in 2018, Russia delivered to China the first of four to six S-400 SAM systems under a contract concluded between the two governments in 2014. This marks a substantial improvement in PLAAF air defense capabilities.[81] China has deployed these SAM systems in a dense, overlapping belt along its coast, protecting the nation's economic center of gravity. Key industrial and military centers such as Beijing are also heavily defended by SAM systems. Some of these systems have reportedly been deployed to the Paracel Islands in the South China Sea.

A third component of the PLAAF is China's airborne forces. The 15th Airborne Corps is part of the PLAAF and is now organized in approximately six brigades.[82] These are not believed to be assigned to any of the Chinese military regions but are instead a strategic reserve as well as a rapid reaction force. They are believed to be deployed mainly in the Central War Zone. In 2009, in the military review associated with the 60th anniversary of the founding of the PRC, Chinese airborne units paraded through Tiananmen Square with ZBD-03 mechanized airborne combat vehicles. These vehicles provide Chinese airborne forces with tactical mobility as well as some degree of protected fire support from their 30mm autocannon and HJ-73 anti-tank missile (a domestic version of the AT-3 Sagger)—something that American airborne forces continue to lack.

Sea Power. As the world's foremost trading state, China depends on the seas for its economic well-being. China's factories are increasingly powered by imported oil, and Chinese diets include a growing percentage of imported food. China relies on the seas to move its products to markets. At the same time, because its economic center of gravity is now in the coastal region, China has to emphasize maritime power to defend key assets and areas. Consequently, China has steadily expanded its maritime power, including its merchant marine and maritime law enforcement capabilities, but especially the People's Liberation Army Navy (PLAN).

The PLAN is no longer an unsophisticated coastal defense force. Instead, since the end of the Cold War, China's navy has moved away from reliance on mass toward incorporating advanced platforms and weapons. Most notably, the Chinese navy is the first in East Asia to deploy its own aircraft carrier since World War II and is now the first to deploy a home-built aircraft carrier. Both *Liaoning* and its Chinese-made sister ship are expected to carry a mixed air group of J-15 fighters (based on the navalized Su-27) and helicopters. China is also reportedly working on a third carrier with a modern flat-top design.

Many obsolete vessels have been decommissioned, including scores of older, missile-armed, fast attack craft. In their place, China has produced a range of more capable combatants and is building each class in significant numbers. These range from the Type 022 *Houbei* missile-armed catamaran, which is armed with sea-skimming supersonic anti-ship cruise missiles, to the Type-052C *Luyang-II* destroyer, which is equipped with a phased-array radar for its HQ-9 SAM system. The HQ-9, with its ability to combat most air-breathing systems and a limited anti–ballistic missile capability, is believed to be comparable to early model Patriot missiles. China is also apparently producing a new class of cruisers, the Type 055, which will carry both anti-aircraft and anti-missile systems. Although these new ships are not replacing older Chinese surface combatants on a one-for-one basis, the overall capability of the PLAN surface force is steadily improving.

The PLAN has similarly been modernizing its submarine force. Since 2000, the PLAN has consistently fielded between 50 and 60 diesel-electric submarines, but the age and capability of the force has been improving as older boats, especially 1950s-vintage *Romeo*-class boats, are replaced with newer designs. These include a dozen *Kilo*-class submarines purchased from Russia and domestically designed and manufactured *Song* and *Yuan* classes. All of these are believed to be capable of firing anti-ship cruise missiles as well as torpedoes. The Chinese have also developed variants of the *Yuan* with an air-independent propulsion (AIP) system that reduces the boats' vulnerability by removing the need to use noisy diesel engines to recharge batteries.

The PLAN has been augmenting its aerial maritime strike capability as well. In addition to more modern versions of the H-6 twin-engine bombers (a version of the Soviet/Russian Tu-16 Badger), the PLAN's Naval Aviation force has added a range of other strike aircraft to its inventory. These include the JH-7/FBC-1 Flying Leopard, which can carry between two and four YJ-82 anti-ship cruise missiles, and the Su-30 strike fighter. Within Chinese littoral waters, the PLAN Air Force can bring a significant amount of firepower to bear.

Finally, the PLAN has been working to improve its "fleet train." The 2010 PRC defense white paper noted the accelerated construction of "large support vessels." It also specifically noted that the navy is exploring "new methods of logistics support for sustaining long-time maritime missions."[83] Since then, the Chinese have expanded their fleet of logistics support ships, including underway replenishment oilers and cargo ships. Chinese submarine tenders have accompanied submarines into the Indian Ocean, allowing Chinese subs to remain on station longer.

As with other aspects of PLA modernization, even as the PLAN is upgrading its weapons, it is also improving its doctrine and training, including increased emphasis on joint operations and the incorporation of electronic warfare into its training regimen. Such improvements suggest that PLA Air Force assets, space and cyber operations, and even PLA Rocket Force units might support naval aviation strikes. The new anti-ship ballistic missile forces, centered on the DF-21D anti-ship ballistic missile (now reportedly at initial operational capability) and possibly the longer-range DF-26, should be seen as part of joint Chinese efforts to control the seas, complementing PLAAF and PLAN air, surface, and sub-surface forces.

Escalation of Territorial Disputes or Incidents at Sea. Because the PRC and other countries in the region see active disputes over the East and South China Seas not as differences regarding the administration of the commons, but rather as matters of territorial sovereignty, there exists the threat of armed conflict between China and American allies who are also claimants, particularly Japan and the Philippines.

Beijing prefers to accomplish its objectives quietly and through nonmilitary means. In both the East and South China Seas, China has sought to exploit "gray zones," gaining control incrementally and deterring others without resort to the lethal use of force. It uses military and economic threats, bombastic language, and enforcement through military bullying. Chinese paramilitary-implemented, military-backed encroachment in support of expansive extralegal claims could lead to an unplanned armed clash.

Rising nationalism is exacerbating tensions, making geostrategic relations in Asia increasingly complex and volatile. In the face of persistent economic challenges, nationalist themes are becoming an increasingly strong undercurrent and affecting policymaking. Although the nationalist phenomenon is not new, it is gaining force and complicating efforts to maintain regional stability.

Governments may choose to exploit nationalism for domestic political purposes, but they also run the risk of being unable to control the genie that they have released. Nationalist rhetoric is mutually reinforcing, which makes countries less likely to back down than in the past. The increasing power that the Internet and social media provide to the populace, largely outside of government control, add elements of unpredictability to future clashes.

In case of armed conflict between China and the Philippines or between China and Japan, either by intention or as a result of an accidental incident at sea, the U.S. could be required to exercise its treaty commitments.[84] Escalation of a direct U.S.–China incident is likewise not unthinkable. Keeping an inadvertent incident from escalating into a broader military confrontation would be difficult. This is particularly true in the East and South China Seas, where naval as well as civilian law enforcement vessels from both China and the U.S. operate in what the U.S. considers to be international waters.

WWTA: The WWTA does not address threats to the maritime and airspace commons, but it does say that "China will continue to pursue an active foreign policy" in the region that is "highlighted by [among other things] a firm stance on competing territorial claims in the East China Sea (ECS) and South China Sea (SCS)."[85] Unlike last year's assessment, the 2018 WWTA does not reference Chinese construction in the South China Sea and offers no judgment with respect to the threat that this poses to American interests or whether large-scale conventional conflict in the region is likely to result from Chinese activity.

Summary: In both the air and maritime domains, China is ever more capable of challenging American dominance and disrupting the freedom of the commons that benefits the entire region. Both territorial disputes related to what the U.S. and its allies consider the commons and accidental incidents could draw the U.S. into conflict. China probably does not intend to engage in armed conflict with its neighbors, particularly American treaty allies, or with the U.S. itself. However, it will continue to press its territorial claims at sea in ways that, even if inadvertent, cause incidents that could escalate into broader conflict.

Space. One of the key force multipliers for the United States is its extensive array of space-based assets. Through its various satellite constellations, the U.S. military can track opponents, coordinate friendly forces, engage in precision strikes against enemy forces, and conduct battle-damage assessments so that its munitions are expended efficiently.

The American military is more reliant than many others on space-based systems because it is also an expeditionary military (meaning that its wars are conducted far distant from the homeland). Consequently, it requires global rather than regional reconnaissance, communications and data transmission, and meteorological information and support. At this point, only space-based systems can provide this sort of information on a real-time basis. The U.S. can leverage space in ways that no other country can, and this is a major advantage, but this heavy reliance on space systems is also a key American vulnerability.

China fields an array of space capabilities, including its own navigation and timing satellites, the Beidou/Compass system, and has claimed a capacity to refuel satellites.[86] It has three satellite launch centers, and a fourth is under construction. China's interest in space dominance includes not only accessing space, but also denying opponents the ability to do the same. As one Chinese assessment notes, space capabilities provided 70 percent of battlefield communications, over 80 percent of battlefield reconnaissance and surveillance, and 100 percent of meteorological information for American operations in Kosovo. Moreover, 98 percent of precision munitions relied on space for guidance information. In fact, "It may be said that America's victory in the Kosovo War could not [have been] achieved without fully exploiting space."[87]

The PLA has therefore been developing a range of anti-satellite capabilities that include both hard-kill and soft-kill systems. The former include direct-ascent kinetic-kill vehicles (DA-KKV) but also more advanced systems that are believed to be capable of reaching targets in medium earth orbit (MEO) and even geostationary earth orbit (GEO).[88] The latter include anti-satellite lasers for either dazzling or blinding purposes.[89] This is consistent with PLA doctrinal writings, which emphasize the need to control space in future conflicts. "Securing space dominance has already become the prerequisite for establishing information, air, and maritime dominance," according to one Chinese teaching manual, "and will directly affect the course and outcome of wars."[90]

Soft-kill attacks need not come only from dedicated weapons, however. The case of Galaxy-15, a communications satellite owned by Intelsat Corporation, showed how a satellite could effectively disrupt communications simply by being in "switched on" mode all of the time.[91] Before it was finally brought under control, it had drifted through a portion of the geosynchronous belt, forcing other satellite owners to move their assets and juggle frequencies. A deliberate such attempt by China (or any other country) could prove far harder to handle, especially if conducted in conjunction with attacks by kinetic systems or directed-energy weapons.

China has created a single service, the PLA Strategic Support Force (PLASSF), with authority over its space, electronic warfare, and network warfare capabilities. In essence, this is a service that is focused on fighting in the information domain, striving to secure what the PLA terms "information dominance" for itself while denying it to others. This service will probably combine electronic warfare, cyber warfare, and physical attacks against adversary space and information systems in order to deny them the ability to gather, transmit, and exploit information.

WWTA: The WWTA assesses that China "would justify attacks against US and allied satellites as necessary to offset any perceived US military advantage derived from military, civil, or commercial space systems." China "continue[s] to pursue a full range of anti-satellite (ASAT) weapons as a means to reduce US and allied military effectiveness" and "aim[s] to have nondestructive and destructive counterspace weapons available for use during a potential future conflict." In addition, "[m]ilitary reforms...in the past few years indicate an increased focus on establishing operational forces designed to integrate attacks against space systems and services with military operations in other domains." China's "destructive ASAT weapons probably will reach initial operating capability in the next few years," and China is "advancing directed-energy weapons technologies for the purpose of fielding ASAT weapons that could blind or damage sensitive space-based optical sensors, such as those used for remote sensing or missile defense."[92]

Summary: The PRC poses a challenge to the United States that is qualitatively different from the challenge posed by any other potential adversary in the post–Cold War environment. It is the first nation to be capable of accessing space on its own while also jeopardizing America's ability to do the same. This appears to be its intent.

Cyber. Threats in this area derive primarily from China and North Korea, and the threats posed by both countries are serious.

China. In 2013, the Verizon Risk Center found that China was responsible for the largest percentage (30 percent) of external breaches in which "the threat actor's country of origin was discoverable" and that "96% of espionage cases were attributed to threat actors in China and the remaining 4% were unknown."[93] Given the difficulties of attribution, country of origin should not necessarily be conflated with the perpetrator, but forensic efforts have identified at least one Chinese military unit with cyber intrusions.[94] Similarly, the Verizon report concluded that China was the source of 95 percent of state-sponsored cyber-espionage attacks. Since the 2015 Xi–Obama summit at which the two sides reached an understanding to reduce cyber economic espionage, Chinese cyber trends have been difficult to discern. While Chinese economic cyber-espionage is reported to have declined, the overall level of cyber activity appears to have remained relatively constant. On the other hand, FireEye, a cyber-security consulting firm, has observed an increase in attacks against U.S. companies in attempts to obtain sensitive business information and warns that this may be due to Chinese activity.[95]

China's cyber-espionage efforts are often aimed at economic targets, reflecting the much more holistic Chinese view of both security and information. Rather than creating an artificial dividing line between military security and civilian security, much less information, the PLA plays a role in supporting both and seeks to obtain economic intellectual property as well as military electronic information.

This is not to suggest, however, that the PLA has not emphasized the military importance of cyber warfare. Chinese military writings since the 1990s have emphasized a fundamental transformation in global military affairs (*shijie junshi gaige*). Future wars will be conducted through joint operations involving multiple services rather than through combined operations focused on multiple branches within a single service. These future wars will span not only the traditional land, sea, and air domains, but also outer space and cyberspace. The latter two arenas will be of special importance because warfare has shifted from an effort to establish material dominance (characteristic of Industrial Age warfare) to establishing information dominance (*zhi xinxi quan*). This is due to the rise of the information age and the resulting introduction of information technology into all areas of military operations.

Consequently, according to PLA analysis, future wars will most likely be "local wars under informationized conditions." That is, they will be wars in which information and information technology not only will be widely applied, but also will be a key basis of victory. The ability to gather, transmit, analyze, manage, and exploit information will be central to winning such wars: The side that is able to do these things more accurately and more quickly will be the side that wins. This means that future conflicts will no longer be determined by platform-versus-platform performance and not even by system against system (*xitong*). Rather, conflicts are now clashes between rival arrays of systems of systems (*tixi*).[96]

Chinese military writings suggest that a great deal of attention has been focused on developing an integrated computer network and electronic warfare (INEW) capability. This would allow the PLA to reconnoiter a potential adversary's computer systems in peacetime, influence opponent decision-makers by threatening those same systems in times of crisis, and disrupt or destroy information networks and systems by cyber and electronic warfare means in the event of conflict. INEW capabilities would complement psychological warfare and physical attack efforts to secure "information dominance," which Chinese military writings emphasize as essential for fighting and winning future wars.

Attacks on computer networks in particular have the potential to be extremely disruptive. The 2014 indictment of five serving PLA officers on the grounds of cyber espionage highlights how active the Chinese military is in this realm.[97]

Since then, the major Chinese military reform announced at the end of 2015 included the establishment of the PLA Strategic Support Force (PLASSF), which brings together China's space, electronic warfare, and network warfare (which includes cyber) forces. This reflects the importance that the PLA is likely placing on computer network operations.

It is essential to recognize, however, that the PLA views computer network operations as part of the larger body of information operations (*xinxi zuozhan*), or information combat. Information operations are specific operational activities that are associated with striving to establish information dominance. They are conducted in both peacetime and wartime, with the peacetime focus on collecting information, improving its flow and application, influencing opposing decision-making, and effecting information deterrence.

Information operations involve four mission areas:

- **Command and Control Missions.** An essential part of information operations is the ability of commanders to control joint operations by disparate forces. Thus, command, control, communications, computers, intelligence, surveillance, and reconnaissance structures constitute a key part of information operations, providing the means for collecting, transmitting, and managing information.

- **Offensive Information Missions.** These are intended to disrupt the enemy's battlefield command and control systems and communications networks, as well as to strike the enemy's psychological defenses.

- **Defensive Information Missions.** Such missions are aimed at ensuring the survival and continued operation of information systems. They include deterring an opponent from attacking one's own information systems, concealing information, and combating attacks when they do occur.

- **Information Support and Information-Safeguarding Missions.** The ability to provide the myriad types of information necessary to support extensive joint operations and to do so on a continuous basis is essential to their success.[98]

Computer network operations are integral to all four of these overall mission areas. They can include both strategic and battlefield network operations and can incorporate both offensive and defensive measures. They also include protection not only of data, but also of information hardware and operating software.

Computer network operations will not stand alone, however, but will be integrated with electronic warfare operations, as reflected in the phrase "network and electronics unified [*wangdian yiti*]." Electronic warfare operations are aimed at weakening or destroying enemy electronic facilities and systems while defending one's own.[99] The combination of electronic and computer network attacks will produce synergies that affect everything from finding and assessing the adversary to locating one's own forces to weapons guidance to logistical support and command and control. The creation of the PLASSF is intended to integrate these forces and make them more complementary and effective in future "local wars under informationized conditions."

North Korea. In April 2018, North Korea was suspected in a cyber-attack on a Turkish bank as part of a hacking campaign identified as Operation GhostSecret that spanned 17 countries and numerous industries. North Korean hackers were believed to be seeking information from several critical infrastructure sectors, including telecommunications and health care.[100]

In February 2016, North Korea conducted the first government-sponsored digital bank robbery. North Korean hackers gained access to the Society for Worldwide Interbank Financial Telecommunication (SWIFT), the system used by central banks to authorize monetary transfers, to steal $81 million. The regime had attempted to send money transfer requests of

$951 million from the Central Bank of Bangladesh to banks in the Philippines, Sri Lanka, and other parts of Asia.[101] North Korean hackers have also targeted the World Bank, the European Central Bank, 20 Polish banks, and large American banks such as Bank of America,[102] as well as financial institutions in Costa Rica, Ecuador, Ethiopia, Gabon, India, Indonesia, Iraq, Kenya, Malaysia, Nigeria, Poland, Taiwan, Thailand, and Uruguay.[103]

In 2014, North Korea conducted the largest cyber-attack on U.S. soil, targeting Sony Pictures in retaliation for the studio's release of a satirical film depicting the assassination of Kim Jong-un. The cyber-attack was accompanied by physical threats against U.S. theaters and citizens. Contrary to the perception of North Korea as a technologically backward nation, the regime has an active cyber warfare capability. As far back as 2009, North Korea declared that it was "fully ready for any form of high-tech war."[104]

The Reconnaissance General Bureau, North Korea's intelligence agency, oversees Unit 121 with approximately 6,000 "cyber-warriors" dedicated to attacking Pyongyang's enemies. Defectors from the unit have told South Korean intelligence officials that hackers are sent to other countries for training as well as to conduct undercover operations. The unit's hackers never operate primarily within North Korea, and this makes both attribution and retaliation more difficult.[105] North Korea has been "expanding both the scope and sophistication of its cyberweaponry, laying the groundwork for more-devastating attacks," according to a February 2018 report by cybersecurity firm FireEye.[106]

Seoul concluded that North Korea was behind cyber-attacks using viruses or distributed denial-of-service tactics against South Korean government agencies, businesses, banks, and media organizations in 2009, 2011, 2012, and 2013. The most devastating attack, launched in 2013 against South Korean banks and media outlets, deleted the essential Master Boot Record from 48,000 computers.[107] North Korea also jammed GPS signals in 2012,

putting hundreds of airplanes transiting Seoul's Incheon airport at risk. Lieutenant General Bae Deag-sig, head of South Korea's Defense Security Command, stated that "North Korea is attempting to use hackers to infiltrate our military's information system to steal military secrets and to incapacitate the defense information system."[108]

WWTA: The WWTA gives the cyber threat from China and North Korea a new level of priority: "Russia, China, Iran, and North Korea will pose the greatest cyber threats to the United States over the next year."[109] It assesses that "China will continue to use cyber espionage and bolster cyber attack capabilities to support national security priorities" but also characterizes the volume of cyber activity as "significantly lower than before the bilateral US–China cyber commitments of September 2015."[110] It further assesses that North Korea can be expected to use cyber operations to "raise funds and to gather intelligence or launch attacks on South Korea and the United States" And that North Korea "probably" has the ability to "achieve a range of offensive effects with little or no warning."[111]

Summary: With obvious implications for the U.S., the PLA emphasizes the need to suppress and destroy an enemy's information systems while preserving one's own, as well as the importance of computer and electronic warfare in both the offensive and defensive roles. Methods to secure information dominance would include establishing an information blockade; deception, including through electronic means; information contamination; and information paralysis.[112] China sees cyber as part of an integrated capability for achieving strategic dominance in the Western Pacific region. For North Korea, cyber security is an area in which even its limited resources can directly support discrete political objectives.

Threat Scores

AfPak-Based Terrorism. A great deal of uncertainty surrounds the threat from the AfPak region. For the U.S., Pakistan is both a security partner and a security challenge.

Pakistan provides a home and support to terrorist groups that are hostile to the U.S., other U.S. partners in South Asia like India, and the fledgling government of Afghanistan. Afghanistan is particularly vulnerable to destabilization efforts. Both Pakistan and Afghanistan are already among the world's most unstable states, and the instability of the former, given its nuclear arsenal, has a direct bearing on U.S. security.

The IISS *Military Balance* addresses the military capabilities of states. It no longer contains a section on the capabilities of non-state actors. The 2018 edition contains no reference to the possibility that Pakistani nuclear weapons might fall into hands that would threaten the American homeland or interests more broadly. The 2014 edition stated that Pakistan's "nuclear weapons are currently believed to be well-secured against terrorist attack."[113] Pakistan's Army Strategic Forces Command has 30 medium-range ballistic missiles, 30 short-range ballistic missiles, and land-attack cruise missiles.[114] Previous editions of the *Military Balance* have also cited development of "likely nuclear capable" artillery. Pakistan also has "1–2 squadrons of F-16A/B or Mirage 5 attack aircraft that may be assigned a nuclear strike role."[115]

This *Index* assesses the overall threat from AfPak-based terrorists, considering the range of contingencies, as "testing" for level of provocation of behavior and "capable" for level of capability.

Threats: Af-Pak Terrorism

	HOSTILE	AGGRESSIVE	TESTING	ASSERTIVE	BENIGN
Behavior			✔		

	FORMIDABLE	GATHERING	CAPABLE	ASPIRATIONAL	MARGINAL
Capability			✔		

China. China presents the United States with the most comprehensive security challenge in the region. It poses various threat contingencies across all three areas of vital American national interests: homeland; regional war (extending from attacks on overseas U.S. bases or against allies and friends); and the global commons. China's provocative behavior is well documented: It is challenging the U.S. and U.S. allies like Japan at sea and in cyberspace, it has raised concerns on its border with India, and it is a standing threat to Taiwan. While there may be a lack of official transparency, publicly available sources shed considerable light on China's fast-growing military capabilities.

According to the IISS *Military Balance*, among the key weapons in China's inventory are 70 Chinese ICBMs; 162 medium-range and intermediate-range ballistic missiles; four SSBNs with up to 12 missiles each; 77 satellites; 6,740 main battle tanks; 58 tactical submarines; 83 principal surface combatants (including one aircraft carrier and 23 destroyers); and 2,397 combat-capable aircraft in its air force. There are about two million active duty members of the People's Liberation Army.[116]

The Chinese launched their first homegrown aircraft carrier during the past year and are fielding large numbers of new platforms for their land, sea, air, and outer space forces. The PLA has been staging larger and more comprehensive exercises, including live-fire exercises in the East China Sea near Taiwan, which are improving the Chinese ability to operate their plethora of new systems. It has also continued to conduct probes of both the South Korean and Japanese air defense identification zones, drawing rebukes from both Seoul and Tokyo.

In addition, there is little evidence that Chinese cyber espionage and computer network exploitation have abated. The 2018 *Military Balance* cites "significant amounts of old equipment [remaining in] service," as well as questions about the quality of domestically produced equipment, but also notes that "the restructuring process may see outdated designs finally withdrawn over the next few years."[117]

This *Index* assesses the overall threat from China, considering the range of contingencies, as "aggressive" for level of provocation of behavior and "formidable" for level of capability.

Threats: China

	HOSTILE	AGGRESSIVE	TESTING	ASSERTIVE	BENIGN
Behavior		✓			

	FORMIDABLE	GATHERING	CAPABLE	ASPIRATIONAL	MARGINAL
Capability	✓				

....

North Korea. In the first instance, North Korea poses the most acute security challenge for American allies and bases in South Korea. However, it is also a significant challenge to U.S. allies in Japan and American bases there and in Guam.

North Korean authorities are very actively and vocally provocative toward the United States. While North Korea has used its missile and nuclear tests to enhance its prestige and importance—domestically, regionally, and globally—and to extract various concessions from the United States in negotiations over its nuclear program and various aid packages, such developments also improve North Korea's military posture. North Korea likely has already achieved warhead miniaturization, the ability to place nuclear weapons on its medium-range missiles, and an ability to reach the continental United States with a missile.

According to the IISS *Military Balance*, key weapons in North Korea's inventory include 3,500-plus main battle tanks, 560-plus light tanks, and 21,100 pieces of artillery. The navy has 73 tactical submarines, three frigates, and 383 patrol and coastal combatants.[118] The air force has 545 combat-capable aircraft (58 fewer than 2014), including 80 H-5 bombers. The IISS counts 1,100,000 active-duty members of the North Korean army, a reserve of 600,000, and 189,000 paramilitary personnel, as well as 5,700,000 in the "Worker/Peasant Red Guard." Regarding the missile threat in particular, the 2018 *Military Balance* lists six-plus ICBMs, 12 IRBMs, 10 MRBMs, and 30-plus submarine-launched ballistic missiles. It points out, however, that although the higher frequency of testing in 2016 and 2017 "reveal[ed] four new successfully tested road-mobile systems"—including those listed above—other ICBMs remain untested.[119] With respect to conventional forces, the 2018 *Military Balance* includes a caveat that they "remain reliant on increasingly obsolete equipment with little evidence of widespread modernization across the armed services."[120]

This *Index* assesses the overall threat from North Korea, considering the range of contingencies, as "testing" for level of provocation of behavior and "gathering" for level of capability.

Threats: North Korea

	HOSTILE	AGGRESSIVE	TESTING	ASSERTIVE	BENIGN
Behavior			✔		

	FORMIDABLE	GATHERING	CAPABLE	ASPIRATIONAL	MARGINAL
Capability		✔			

Endnotes

1. Transcript, "Department of Defense Press Briefing by General Nicholson in the Pentagon Briefing Room," U.S. Department of Defense, December 2, 2016, https://www.defense.gov/News/Transcripts/Transcript-View/Article/1019029/department-of-defense-press-briefing-by-general-nicholson-in-the-pentagon-brief/ (accessed July 27, 2018). See also General John W. Nicholson, Commander, U.S. Forces–Afghanistan, statement on "The Situation in Afghanistan" before the Committee on Armed Services, U.S. Senate, February 9, 2017, p. 1, https://www.armed-services.senate.gov/imo/media/doc/Nicholson_02-09-17.pdf (accessed July 27, 2018).

2. Sudarsan Raghavan, "Taliban in Afghanistan Tells Islamic State to Stay out of Country," *The Washington Post*, June 16, 2016, https://www.washingtonpost.com/world/asia_pacific/taliban-warns-islamic-state-to-stay-out-of-afghanistan/2015/06/16/a88bafb8-1436-11e5-8457-4b431bf7ed4c_story.html?utm_term=.4f4de593d5e9 (accessed July 31, 2018). See also Mirwais Harooni and Kay Johnson, "Taliban Urge Islamic State to 'Interference' in Afghanistan," Reuters, June 16, 2015, https://www.reuters.com/article/us-afghanistan-islamicstate-idUSKBN0OW19220150616 (accessed July 31, 2018), and Aaron Y. Zelin, "Letter from the Taliban to Abu Bakr al-Baghdadi from the Head of the Shura Council," Lawfare, June 27, 2015, https://www.lawfareblog.com/letter-taliban-abu-bakr-al-baghdadi-head-shura-council (accessed July 31, 2018).

3. Transcript, "Department of Defense Press Briefing by General Nicholson via Teleconference from Kabul, Afghanistan," U.S. Department of Defense, November 28, 2017, https://www.defense.gov/News/Transcripts/Transcript-View/Article/1382901/department-of-defense-press-briefing-by-general-nicholson-via-teleconference-fr/ (accessed July 27, 2018).

4. Institute for Conflict Management, South Asia Terrorism Portal, "Fatalities in Terrorist Violence in Pakistan 2000–2018," http://www.satp.org/satporgtp/countries/pakistan/database/casualties.htm (accessed July 27, 2018).

5. Reuters, "Pakistani Man Arrested on U.S. Terrorism Charges," September 2, 2011, http://www.reuters.com/article/2011/09/02/us-pakistan-usa-arrest-idUSTRE7815M920110902 (accessed June 29, 2017).

6. Abha Shankar, "Trial's First Week Reinforces Pakistani Intelligence Suspicions," Investigative Project on Terrorism, May 27, 2011, http://www.investigativeproject.org/2919/trial-first-week-reinforces-pakistani (accessed July 27, 2018).

7. Peter R. Lavoy, ed., *Asymmetric Warfare in South Asia: The Causes and Consequences of the Kargil Conflict* (Cambridge, UK: Cambridge University Press, 2009), p. 10.

8. Nuclear Threat Initiative, *NTI Nuclear Security Index, Theft/Sabotage: Building a Framework for Assurance, Accountability, and Action, Third Edition*, January 2016, p. 30, https://www.nti.org/media/pdfs/NTI_2016_Index_FINAL.pdf (accessed July 27, 2018).

9. Stephen P. Cohen, "The Future of Pakistan," The Brookings Institution, South Asia Initiative, January 2011, p. 51, https://www.brookings.edu/wp-content/uploads/2016/06/01_pakistan_cohen.pdf (accessed June 29, 2017).

10. Daniel R. Coats, Director of National Intelligence, "Worldwide Threat Assessment of the US Intelligence Community," statement before the Select Committee on Intelligence, U.S. Senate, May 11, 2017, p. 24, https://www.dni.gov/files/documents/Newsroom/Testimonies/SSCI%20Unclassified%20SFR%20-%20Final.pdf (accessed July 19, 2018). Cited hereafter as 2017 WWTA.

11. David Wright, "North Korean ICBM Appears Able to Reach Major US Cities," Union of Concerned Scientists, July 28, 2017, http://allthingsnuclear.org/dwright/new-north-korean-icbm (accessed August 14, 2017).

12. Yonhap News Agency, "N.K. Calls Itself 'Nuclear-Armed State' in Revised Constitution," May 30, 2012, http://english.yonhapnews.co.kr/northkorea/2012/05/30/76/0401000000AEN20120530005200315F.HTML (accessed June 29, 2017).

13. Lee Sung-eun and Jeon Yong-soo, "Nuke Program Complete, Claims Kim Jong-un," *Korea JoongAng Daily*, December 14, 2017, http://koreajoongangdaily.joins.com/news/article/Article.aspx?aid=3042044 (accessed July 19, 2018).

14. Anna Fifield, "North Korea's Making a Lot of Threats These Days. How Worried Should We Be?" *The Washington Post*, March 11, 2016, https://www.washingtonpost.com/news/worldviews/wp/2016/03/11/north-koreas-making-a-lot-of-threats-these-days-how-worried-should-we-be/ (accessed June 29, 2017).

15. Yonhap News Agency, "N. Korea 'Handful of Months' Away from Ability to Nuke U.S.: CIA Chief," January 23, 2018, http://english.yonhapnews.co.kr/news/2018/01/23/0200000000AEN20180123000200315.html (accessed July 19, 2018).

16. Reuters, "Head of U.S. Missile Defense Agency Says North Korea Missile Advances a 'Great Concern,'" June 7, 2017, http://www.reuters.com/article/us-usa-northkorea-missiles-idUSKBN18Y2XA (accessed July 4, 2017).

17. Dan Goure, "Why Trump Needs to Deploy Missile Defenses to Counter North Korea and Iran," *The National Interest*, February 20, 2017, http://nationalinterest.org/blog/the-buzz/why-trump-needs-deploy-missile-defenses-counter-north-korea-19510 (accessed July 4, 2017).

18. David Albright, "North Korea's Nuclear Capabilities: A Fresh Look," Institute for Science and International Security, April 28, 2017, p. [1], http://isis-online.org/uploads/isis-reports/documents/North_Korea_Nuclear_Capability_Estimates_Summary_28Apr2017_Final.pdf (accessed July 27, 2018).

19. Joel S. Wit and Sun Young Ahn, "North Korea's Nuclear Futures: Technology and Strategy," Johns Hopkins University, Paul H. Nitze School of Advanced International Studies, U.S.–Korea Institute, North Korea's Nuclear Futures Series, February 2015, p. 8, http://38north.org/wp-content/uploads/2015/02/NKNF-NK-Nuclear-Futures-Wit-0215.pdf (accessed June 29, 2017).

20. James Mattis, Secretary of Defense, "Written Statement for the Record" on the President's budget request for FY 2018 before the Committee on Armed Services, U.S. House of Representatives, June 12, 2017, p. 4, http://docs.house.gov/meetings/AS/AS00/20170612/106090/HHRG-115-AS00-Bio-MattisJ-20170612.pdf (accessed July 27, 2018).

21. Eileen Sullivan, "Trump Says 'There Is No Longer a Nuclear Threat' After Kim Jong-un Meeting," *The New York Times*, June 13, 2018, https://www.nytimes.com/2018/06/13/us/politics/trump-north-korea-nuclear-threat-.html (accessed July 27, 2018).

22. David Brunnstrom and James Oliphant, "Trump: North Korea 'Total Denuclearization' Started; Officials See No New Moves," Reuters, June 21, 2018, https://www.reuters.com/article/us-northkorea-usa-sites/trump-north-korea-total-denuclearization-started-officials-see-no-new-moves-idUSKBN1JH2QX (accessed July 27, 2018).

23. Jonathan Cheng, "North Korea Expands Key Missile-Manufacturing Plant," *The Wall Street Journal*, July 1, 2018, https://www.wsj.com/articles/north-korea-expands-key-missile-manufacturing-plant-1530486907 (accessed July 27, 2018); Courtney Kube, Ken Dilanian, and Carol E. Lee, "North Korea Has Increased Nuclear Production at Secret Sites, Say U.S. Officials," NBC News, updated June 30, 2018, https://www.nbcnews.com/news/north-korea/north-korea-has-increased-nuclear-production-secret-sites-say-u-n887926 (accessed July 27, 2018); Frank V. Pabian, Joseph S. Bermudez Jr., and Jack Liu, "Infrastructure Improvements at North Korea's Yongbyon Nuclear Research Facility," Henry L. Stimson Center, 38 North, June 26, 2018, https://www.38north.org/2018/06/yongbyon062618/ (accessed July 27, 2018); Ankit Panda, "Exclusive: North Korea Has Continued Ballistic Missile Launcher Production in 2018, Per US Intelligence," *The Diplomat*, June 30, 2018, https://thediplomat.com/2018/07/exclusive-north-korea-has-continued-ballistic-missile-launcher-production-per-us-intelligence/ (accessed July 19, 2018).

24. Andrew S. Erickson and Michael S. Chase, "China's SSBN Forces: Transitioning to the Next Generation," Jamestown Foundation, *China Brief*, Vol. 9, Issue 12 (June 12, 2009), http://www.jamestown.org/single/?no_cache=1&tx_ttnews[tt_news]=35120#.U5G0OSjb5NQ (accessed June 29, 2017).

25. For more information on China's cruise missile program, see Dennis M. Gormley, Andrew S. Erickson, and Jingdong Yuan, *A Low-Visibility Force Multiplier: Assessing China's Cruise Missile Ambitions* (Washington: National Defense University Press, 2014), http://ndupress.ndu.edu/Portals/68/Documents/Books/force-multiplier.pdf (accessed July 27, 2018). Published for the Center for the Study of Chinese Military Affairs of the NDU's Institute for National Strategic Studies.

26. Barbara Starr, "US General Warns of Hypersonic Weapons Threat from Russia and China," CNN, March 27, 2018, https://www.cnn.com/2018/03/27/politics/general-hyten-hypersonic-weapon-threat/index.html (accessed July 19, 2018).

27. 2017 WWTA, p. 7.

28. Daniel R. Coats, Director of National Intelligence, "Worldwide Threat Assessment of the US Intelligence Community," statement before the Select Committee on Intelligence, U.S. Senate, February 13, 2018, p. 8, https://www.dni.gov/files/documents/Newsroom/Testimonies/2018-ATA---Unclassified-SSCI.pdf (accessed July 27, 2018). Cited hereafter as 2018 WWTA.

29. Ibid.

30. Ibid., p. 18.

31. 2017 WWTA, p. 16.

32. 2018 WWTA, p. 7.

33. Ibid.

34. North Korea Leadership Watch, "Kim Jong-un Supervises Missile Drill," March 6, 2017, http://www.nkleadershipwatch.org/2017/03/06/kim-jong-un-supervises-missile-drill/ (accessed August 14, 2017).

35. International Crisis Group, "North Korea's Nuclear and Missile Programs," *Asia Report* No. 168, June 18, 2009, https://www.crisisgroup.org/asia/north-east-asia/korean-peninsula/north-korea-s-nuclear-and-missile-programs (accessed June 29, 2017).

36. U.S. Department of Defense, Office of the Secretary of Defense, *Military and Security Developments Involving the Democratic People's Republic of Korea 2013*, Annual Report to Congress, 2014, http://www.defense.gov/Portals/1/Documents/pubs/North_Korea_Military_Power_Report_2013-2014.pdf (accessed June 29, 2017).

37. Bruce E. Bechtol, Jr., "Understanding the North Korean Military Threat to the Security of the Korean Peninsula and Northeast Asia: Declined or Evolved?" *Korea Observer*, Vol. 40, No. 1 (Spring 2009), p. 115–154.

38. Chung-in Moon, "A Real Path to Peace on the Korean Peninsula," *Foreign Affairs*, April 30, 2018, https://www.foreignaffairs.com/articles/north-korea/2018-04-30/real-path-peace-korean-peninsula (accessed July 28, 2018).

39. "July 4th North–South Joint Statement," July 4, 1992, http://www2.law.columbia.edu/course_00S_L9436_001/North%20 Korea%20materials/74js-en.htm (accessed July 28, 2018).

40. "Agreement on Reconciliation, Nonagression [*sic*] and Exchanges and Cooperation Between the South and the North," February 19, 1992, https://2001-2009.state.gov/t/ac/rls/or/2004/31012.htm (accessed July 28, 2018).

41. Bruce Klingner, "Nice Try, North Korea and South Korea, but Your Pledges Are Airy, Empty Confections," *Los Angeles Times*, May 1, 2018, http://www.latimes.com/opinion/op-ed/la-oe-klingner-north-korea-declaration-is-mostly-empty-promises-20180501-story. html (accessed July 23, 2018).

42. Tara Copp, "South Korea, US Cancel Ulchi Freedom Guardian Exercise for 2018," *Military Times*, June 18, 2018, https://www.militarytimes.com/news/your-air-force/2018/06/18/south-korea-us-cancel-ulchi-freedom-guardian-exercise-for-2018/ (accessed July 23, 2018).

43. Bruce W. Bennett, "A Brief Analysis of the Republic of Korea's Defense Reform Plan," RAND Corporation *Occasional Paper* No. OP-165-OSD, 2006, http://www.rand.org/content/dam/rand/pubs/occasional_papers/2006/RAND_OP165.pdf (accessed June 29, 2017).

44. Yonhap News Agency, "N. Korea 'Handful of Months' Away from Ability to Nuke U.S.: CIA Chief."

45. Victor Morton, "North Korea Threatens Pre-emptive Nuclear Strikes Against U.S., South Korea," *The Washington Times*, March 6, 2016, http://www.washingtontimes.com/news/2016/mar/6/north-korea-threatens-nuclear-strike-against-us-so/ (accessed July 28, 2018).

46. Sophie Jeong, Will Ripley, and Euan McKirdy, "Kim Jong UN: North Korea No Longer Needs Nuclear Tests," CNN, April 22, 2018, https://www.cnn.com/2018/04/20/asia/north-korea-closes-nuclear-site/index.html (accessed July 19, 2018).

47. 2018 WWTA, p. 18.

48. Agence France-Presse–Jiji Press, "Tensions Surge as China Flies Bombers Around Taiwan, Holds Live-Fire Drills," *The Japan Times*, April 20, 2018, https://www.japantimes.co.jp/news/2018/04/20/asia-pacific/tensions-surge-china-flies-bombers-around-taiwan-holds-live-fire-drills/#.W0N5W6dKi70 (accessed July 28, 2018).

49. Peter Navarro, "China's Non-Kinetic 'Three Warfares' Against America," *The National Interest*, January 5, 2016, https://nationalinterest.org/blog/the-buzz/chinas-non-kinetic-three-warfares-against-america-14808 (accessed July 28, 2018).

50. 2018 WWTA, p. 18.

51. Office of the United States Trade Representative, "India: U.S.–India Bilateral Trade and Investment," last updated March 22, 2017, https://ustr.gov/countries-regions/south-central-asia/india (accessed August 13, 2018).

52. International Institute for Strategic Studies, *Strategic Survey 2013: The Annual Review of World Affairs* (London: Routledge, 2013), p. 32.

53. Nuclear Threat Initiative, "Pakistan: Nuclear," last updated April 2016, http://www.nti.org/learn/countries/pakistan/nuclear/ (accessed July 28, 2018).

54. Fact Sheet, "Nuclear Weapons: Who Has What at a Glance," Arms Control Association, updated June 2018, https://www.armscontrol.org/factsheets/Nuclearweaponswhohaswhat (accessed July 28, 2018).

55. Ravi Krishnan Khajuria, "Jammu Army Camp Attack: Two Soldiers Killed as JeM Militants Storm into Sunjuwan Base," *Hindustan Times*, February 10, 2018, https://www.hindustantimes.com/india-news/terrorists-attack-army-camp-in-jammu-soldier-and-daughter-injured/story-20ILSRP8tuSE6UM2nvxt1O.html (accessed July 19, 2018).

56. "India Condemns Pak Support to Hafiz Saeed's Rally in Lahore," *India Today*, December 4, 2014, http://indiatoday.intoday.in/story/hafiz-saeed-pakistan-lahore-rally-26-11-mumbai-attacks-jud-al-qaeda/1/405036.html (accessed July 28, 2018).

57. International Institute for Strategic Studies, *Strategic Survey 2013*, p. 31.

58. 2018 WWTA, p. 23.

59. Ibid., p. 8.

60. Ibid., p. 22.

61. N. C. Bipindra, "India, China Skid on Visa, Ink Border Pact," *The New Indian Express*, October 24, 2013, http://newindianexpress.com/nation/India-China-skid-on-visa-ink-border-pact/2013/10/24/article1852361.ece (accessed July 28, 2018).

62. Nirupama Subramanian, "India, China Not to Use Force in Case of Face-offs," *The Hindu*, October 24, 2013, http://www.thehindu.com/todays-paper/india-china-not-to-use-force-in-case-of-faceoffs/article5266608.ece (accessed July 28, 2018).

63. Major General P. J. S. Sandhu (Retd.), "Border Defence Cooperation Agreement—What Next?" United Service Institution of India, October 28, 2013, http://www.usiofindia.org/Article/?pub=Strategic%20Perspective&pubno=38&ano=2003 (accessed July 23, 2018).

64. 2018 WWTA, p. 23.

65. Madison Park, "Why China's New Air Zone Incensed Japan, U.S.," CNN, November 27, 2013, http://www.cnn.com/2013/11/25/world/asia/china-japan-island-explainer/ (accessed July 28, 2018).

66. Jason Le Miere, "China Claims U.S. Military Plane 'Illegally' Entered Chinese Air Defense Zone," *Newsweek*, March 24, 2017, http://www.newsweek.com/china-claims-us-military-plane-illegally-entered-chinese-air-defense-zone-573711 (accessed July 23, 2018).

67. Hans Nichols and Courtney Kube, "Two Chinese Fighter Jets Intercept U.S. Plane Over East China Sea, Officials Say," NBC News, May 18, 2017, http://www.nbcnews.com/news/us-news/two-chinese-fighter-jets-intercept-u-s-plane-officials-say-n761931 (accessed July 23, 2018).

68. Idrees Ali, "Chinese Jets Intercept US Surveillance Plane in East China Sea," *Business Insider*, July 24, 2017, http://www.businessinsider.com/r-chinese-jets-intercept-us-surveillance-plane-us-officials-2017-7 (accessed July 19, 2018).

69. Anne Barker, "China's Missiles in the South China Sea Put the United States and Australia in a Difficult Position," ABC News, May 4, 2018, http://www.abc.net.au/news/2018-05-05/china-missile-deployment-will-force-the-us-hand/9729460 (accessed July 28, 2018), and Patricia Lourdes Viray, "Philippines, China Draw 'Red Lines' in South China Sea Dispute," *Philstar Global*, May 29, 2018, https://www.philstar.com/headlines/2018/05/29/1819745/philippines-china-draw-red-lines-south-china-sea-dispute (accessed July 19, 2018)..

70. Center for Strategic and International Studies, Asia Maritime Transparency Initiative, "China Lands First Bomber on South China Sea Island," May 18, 2018, https://amti.csis.org/china-lands-first-bomber-south-china-sea-island/ (accessed July 28, 2018).

71. Reuters, "Vietnam Scraps South China Sea Oil Drilling Project Under Pressure from Beijing–BBC," March 23, 2018, https://www.reuters.com/article/southchinasea-vietnam/vietnam-scraps-south-china-sea-oil-drilling-project-under-pressure-from-beijing-bbc-idUSL3N1R451F (accessed July 28, 2018).

72. Amanda Macias, "China Quietly Installed Defensive Missile Systems on Strategic Spratly Islands in Hotly Contested South China Sea," CNBC, May 2, 2018, https://www.cnbc.com/2018/05/02/china-added-missile-systems-on-spratly-islands-in-south-china-sea.html (accessed July 19, 2018), and Thomas Gibbons-Neff, "New Satellite Images Show Reinforced Chinese Surface-to-Air Missile Sites Near Disputed Islands," *The Washington Post*, February 23, 2017, https://www.washingtonpost.com/news/checkpoint/wp/2017/02/23/new-satellite-images-show-reinforced-chinese-surface-to-air-missile-sites-near-disputed-islands/?utm_term=.37c6062fd16b (accessed July 19, 2018).

73. Admiral Harry B. Harris Jr., U.S. Navy, Commander, U.S. Pacific Command, statement on "U.S. Pacific Command Posture" before the Committee on Armed Services, U.S. House of Representatives, February 14, 2018, p. 12, https://docs.house.gov/meetings/AS/AS00/20180214/106847/HHRG-115-AS00-Wstate-HarrisJrH-20180214.pdf (accessed July 28, 2018). End punctuation added.

74. Ibid.

75. Committee on Armed Services, U.S. Senate, "Advance Policy Questions for Admiral Philip Davidson, USN, Expected Nominee for Commander, U.S. Pacific Command," April 17, 2018, p. 18, https://www.armed-services.senate.gov/imo/media/doc/Davidson_APQs_04-17-18.pdf (accessed July 28, 2018).

76. Megan Eckstein, "China Disinvited from Participating in 2018 RIMPAC Exercise," U.S. Naval Institute News, May 23, 2018, https://news.usni.org/2018/05/23/china-disinvited-participating-2018-rimpac-exercise (accessed July 19, 2018).

77. Ben Bland, "Mattis Attacks Beijing for 'Coercion' in South China Sea," *Financial Times*, June 2, 2018, https://www.ft.com/content/e35a488c-6615-11e8-90c2-9563a0613e56 (accessed July 23, 2018), and Bill Gertz, "Mattis Hits South China Sea Military Buildup in Talks with Xi," *The Washington Free Beacon*, June 27, 2018, http://freebeacon.com/national-security/mattis-hits-south-china-sea-military-buildup-talks-xi/ (accessed July 19, 2018).

78. Tim Hume, "Close Call as China Scrambles Fighter Jets on Japanese Aircraft in Disputed Territory," CNN, updated May 26, 2014, http://www.cnn.com/2014/05/26/world/asia/china-japan-jets-scramble/ (accessed July 23, 2018).

79. International Institute for Strategic Studies, *The Military Balance 2014: The Annual Assessment of Global Military Capabilities and Defence Economics* (London: Routledge, 2014), p. 292.

80. U.S. Department of Defense, Office of the Secretary of Defense, *Military and Security Developments Involving the People's Republic of China 2017*, Annual Report to Congress, 2017, p. 29, https://www.defense.gov/Portals/1/Documents/pubs/2017_China_Military_Power_Report.PDF (accessed July 28, 2018).

81. Franz-Stefan Gady, "Russia Delivers 1st S-400 Missile Defense Regiment to China," *The Diplomat*, April 3, 2018, https://thediplomat.com/2018/04/russia-delivers-1st-s-400-missile-defense-regiment-to-china (accessed July 19, 2018).

82. U.S. Marine Corps Tactics and Operations Group, "China's Airborne Corps," *The Sand Table*, Vol. 1, Issue 5 (March 2018), p. 2, https://www.mca-marines.org/sites/default/files/THE_SAND_TABLE_Vol1_Iss5_Mar18_Final.pdf (accessed August 13, 2018).

83. Xinhua, "Full Text: China's National Defense in 2010," March 31, 2011, http://www.nti.org/media/pdfs/1_1a.pdf?_=1316627912 (accessed July 23, 2018).

84. While it has long been a matter of U.S. policy that Philippine territorial claims in the South China Sea lie outside the scope of American treaty commitments, the treaty does apply in the event of an attack on Philippine "armed forces, public vessels or aircraft in the Pacific." Mutual Defense Treaty Between the United States and the Republic of the Philippines, August 30, 1951, Article V, http://avalon.law.yale.edu/20th_century/phil001.asp (accessed June 29, 2017). In any event, Article IV of the treaty obligates the U.S. in case of such an attack to "meet the common dangers in accordance with its constitutional processes." Regardless of formal treaty obligations, however, enduring U.S. interests in the region and perceptions of U.S. effectiveness and reliability as a check on growing Chinese ambitions would likely spur the U.S. to become involved.

85. 2018 WWTA, p. 16.

86. Xinhua, "China Announces Success in Technology to Refuel Satellites in Orbit," June 30, 2016, http://news.xinhuanet.com/english/2016-06/30/c_135479061.htm (accessed July 23, 2018).

87. Mei Lianju, *Space Operations Teaching Materials* (Beijing, PRC: Academy of Military Sciences Publishing House, 2013), p. 65.

88. Brian Weeden, "Through a Glass, Darkly: Chinese, American, and Russian Anti-Satellite Testing in Space," Secure World Foundation, March 17, 2014, https://swfound.org/media/167224/through_a_glass_darkly_march2014.pdf (accessed July 23, 2018).

89. Ian Easton, "The Great Game in Space: China's Evolving ASAT Weapons Programs and Their Implications for Future U.S. Strategy," Project 2049 Institute, 2009, pp. 4–5.

90. Mei Lianju, *Space Operations Teaching Materials*, p. 69.

91. Peter B. de Selding, "Runaway Zombie Satellite Galaxy 15 Continues to Pose Interference Threat," Space.com, October 15, 2010, http://www.space.com/9340-runaway-zombie-satellite-galaxy-15-continues-pose-interference-threat.html (accessed July 23, 2018).

92. 2018 WWTA, p. 13.

93. Verizon, *2013 Data Breach Investigations Report*, pp. 21–22, http://www.verizonenterprise.com/resources/reports/rp_data-breach-investigations-report-2013_en_xg.pdf (accessed August 13, 2018). See also Elise Ackerman, "New Verizon Security Report Finds a Growing Number of Attacks by China's Hacker Army," *Forbes*, April 23, 2013, https://www.forbes.com/sites/eliseackerman/2013/04/23/new-verizon-security-report-finds-a-growing-number-of-attacks-by-chinas-hacker-army/#11429f622c49 (accessed August 13, 2018), and Lucian Constantin, "Verizon: One in Five Data Breaches Are the Result of Cyberespionage," *PC World*, April 23, 2013, http://www.pcworld.com/article/2036177/one-in-five-data-breaches-are-the-result-of-cyberespionage-verizon-says.html (accessed August 13, 2018).

94. Dan McWhorter, "Mandiant Exposes APT1—One of China's Cyber Espionage Units & Releases 3,000 Indicators," Mandiant, February 18, 2013, https://www.mandiant.com/blog/mandiant-exposes-apt1-chinas-cyber-espionage-units-releases-3000-indicators/ (accessed June 28, 2018).

95. FireEye, *M-Trends 2018*, p. 49, https://www.fireeye.com/content/dam/collateral/en/mtrends-2018.pdf (accessed July 28, 2018).

96. Bai Bangxi and Jiang Lijun, "'Systems Combat' Is Not the Same as 'System Combat,'" *China National Defense Newspaper*, January 10, 2008, cited in Dean Cheng, "U.S.–China Competition in Space," testimony before the Subcommittee on Space, Committee on Science, Space, and Technology, U.S. House of Representatives, September 27, 2016, https://docs.house.gov/meetings/SY/SY16/20160927/105387/HHRG-114-SY16-Wstate-ChengD-20160927.pdf (accessed July 28, 2018).

97. News release, "U.S. Charges Five Chinese Military Hackers for Cyber Espionage Against U.S. Corporations and a Labor Organization for Commercial Advantage," U.S. Department of Justice, May 19, 2014, http://www.justice.gov/opa/pr/us-charges-five-chinese-military-hackers-cyber-espionage-against-us-corporations-and-labor (accessed July 23, 2018).

98. Guo Ruobing, *Theory of Military Information Security* (Beijing, PRC: National Defense University Publishing House, 2013), pp. 12–21.

99. Tan Rukan, Building Operational Strength Course Materials (Beijing, PRC: Academy of Military Sciences Publishing House, 2012), p. 204.

100. Timothy W. Martin, "'Operation GhostSecret': North Korea Is Suspected in Intensifying Global Cyberattack," *The Wall Street Journal*, April 25, 2018, https://www.wsj.com/articles/operation-ghostsecret-north-korea-is-suspected-in-intensifying-global-cyberattack-1524629807 (accessed July 19, 2018).

101. Krishna N. Das and Jonathan Spicer, "How the New York Fed Fumbled over the Bangladesh Bank Cyber-Heist," Reuters, July 21, 2016, https://www.reuters.com/investigates/special-report/cyber-heist-federal/ (accessed August 2, 2018).

102. Paul Mozur and Choe Sang-hun, "North Korea's Rising Ambition Seen in Bid to Breach Global Banks," *The New York Times*, March 25, 2017, https://www.nytimes.com/2017/03/25/technology/north-korea-hackers-global-banks.html (accessed July 23, 2018).

103. Jose Pagliery, "North Korea-linked Hackers Are Attacking Banks Worldwide," CNN, April 4, 2017, http://www.cnn.com/2017/04/03/world/north-korea-hackers-banks/ (accessed July 23, 2018).

104. "Cyber Attack Retaliation Against Seoul's Move to Join 'Cyber Storm,'" *The Korea Herald*, July 7, 2009, http://www.koreaherald.com/common_prog/newsprint.php?ud=20090710000075&dt=2 (accessed July 23, 2018).

105. David E. Sanger, David D. Kirkpatrick, and Nicole Perlroth, "The World Once Laughed at North Korean Cyberpower. No More," *The New York Times*, October 15, 2017, https://www.nytimes.com/2017/10/15/world/asia/north-korea-hacking-cyber-sony.html (accessed August 13, 2018).

106. Anna Fifield, "North Korea Poised to Launch Large-Scale Cyberattacks, Says New Report," *The Washington Post*, February 20, 2018, https://www.washingtonpost.com/world/north-korea-poised-to-launch-large-scale-cyberattacks-says-new-report/2018/02/20/7f52196a-160a-11e8-942d-16a950029788_story.html?utm_term=.d8adc463761a (accessed July 20, 2018).

107. Kelly Beaucar Vlahos, "Special Report: The Cyberwar Threat from North Korea," Fox News, February 14, 2014, http://www.foxnews.com/tech/2014/02/14/cyberwar-experts-question-north-korea-cyber-capabilities/ (accessed July 23, 2018).

108. Choi He-suk, "N.K. Third for Cyber War Capabilities," *The Korea Herald*, June 7, 2012, http://www.koreaherald.com/view.php?ud=20120607001276 (accessed July 23, 2018).

109. 2018 WWTA, p. 5.

110. Ibid., p. 6.

111. Ibid.

112. Yuan Wenxian, *Joint Campaign Information Operations Teaching Materials* (Beijing, PRC: National Defense University Press, 2009), pp. 109–112.

113. International Institute for Strategic Studies, *The Military Balance 2014*, p. 220.

114. International Institute for Strategic Studies, *The Military Balance 2018: The Annual Assessment of Global Military Capabilities and Defence Economics* (London: Routledge, 2018), p. 291.

115. Ibid.

116. Ibid., pp. 249–259.

117. Ibid., p. 249.

118. Ibid., p. 267.

119. Ibid., p. 275.

120. Ibid.

Conclusion: Global Threat Level

America and its interests face challenges around the world from countries and organizations that have:

- Interests that conflict with those of the U.S.;

- Sometimes hostile intentions toward the U.S.; and

- In some cases, growing military capabilities.

The government of the United States constantly faces the challenge of employing, sometimes alone but more often in concert with allies, the right mix of diplomatic, economic, public information, intelligence, and military capabilities to protect and advance U.S. interests.

In Europe, Russia remains the primary threat to American interests. The *2019 Index* again assesses the threat emanating from Russia as a behavior score of "aggressive" and a capability score of "formidable," the highest category on the scale. Moscow continues to engage in massive pro-Russia propaganda campaigns in Ukraine and other Eastern European countries, regularly performs provocative military exercises and training missions, and continues to sell and export arms to countries hostile to U.S. interests. It also has increased its investment in modernizing its military and has gained significant combat experience while continuing to sabotage U.S. and Western policy in Syria and Ukraine.

In the Middle East, Iran remains the state actor that is most hostile to American interests. The *2019 Index* assesses Iran's behavior as "aggressive" and its capability as "gathering." In the years since publication of the *2015 Index*, Iran has methodically moved closer to becoming a nuclear power, and it continues to enhance its capabilities relating to ICBMs, missile defense, and unmanned systems. Iran also continues to perpetuate and exploit instability to expand its influence in the region—both in its direct involvement in regional engagements and through its proxies, particularly in Syria.

Also in the Middle East, a broad array of terrorist groups, most notably the Iran-sponsored Hezbollah, remain the most hostile of any of the global threats to America examined in the *Index*. As of mid-2018, the Islamic State had been essentially decimated, having lost more than 98 percent of previously held territory, but it has not been completely eliminated and has made efforts to reassert itself in the region. Despite the declining strength of ISIS forces, the growing assertiveness of Iranian-backed Shia militias contributes to a scoring inflation from "aggressive" to "hostile" in level of behavior. Fortunately, Middle East terrorist groups also are evaluated as being among the least capable of the threats facing the U.S.

In Asia, China returned to "aggressive" in the scope of its provocative behavior from "testing" in the *2018 Index*. The People's Liberation Army continues to extend its reach and military activity beyond its immediate region and engages in larger and more comprehensive exercises, including live-fire exercises in the East China Sea near Taiwan. It has also continued to conduct probes of the South Korean and Japanese air defense identification zones, drawing rebukes from both Seoul and Tokyo. There is also little evidence that Chinese cyber espionage and computer network exploitation have abated.

North Korea's level of behavior fell to "testing" from the *2018 Index* to the *2019 Index*. In a 2018 summit, South Korean President Moon Jae-in and North Korean leader Kim Jong-un committed to mutual nonaggression and force reduction. Kim Jung-un also declared that North Korea no longer needed to conduct nuclear and intercontinental ballistic missile tests. Both statements would appear to contribute to a positive appearance of cooperation and an improved level of behavior, but they could also reflect North Korea's improved confidence in its nuclear capabilities as opposed to being a sign of genuinely good faith. North Korea's capability level has also remained at "gathering" as Pyongyang continues to develop and refine its missile technology, especially in the area of submarine-launched ballistic missiles.

Finally, the terrorist threats emanating from the Afghanistan–Pakistan region dropped to "testing" in the *2019 Index*. Fatalities attributed to terrorism inside of Pakistan continue to fall as various terrorist groups within the region find themselves in competition with each other for recruits, territory, and resources.

Just as there are American interests that are not covered by this *Index*, there may be additional threats to American interests that are not identified here. The *Index* focuses on the more apparent sources of risk and those in which the risk is greater.

Compiling the assessments of these threat sources, the *2019 Index* again rates the overall global threat environment as "aggressive" and "gathering" in the areas of threat actor behavior and material ability to harm U.S. security interests, respectively, leading to an aggregated threat score of "high."

Behavior of Threats

	HOSTILE	AGGRESSIVE	TESTING	ASSERTIVE	BENIGN
Russia		✓			
Iran		✓			
Middle East Terrorism	✓				
Af-Pak Terrorism			✓		
China		✓			
North Korea			✓		
OVERALL		✓			

Capability of Threats

	FORMIDABLE	GATHERING	CAPABLE	ASPIRATIONAL	MARGINAL
Russia	✓				
Iran		✓			
Middle East Terrorism			✓		
Af-Pak Terrorism			✓		
China	✓				
North Korea		✓			
OVERALL		✓			

Threats to U.S. Vital Interests

	SEVERE	HIGH	ELEVATED	GUARDED	LOW
Russia		✔			
Iran		✔			
Middle East Terrorism		✔			
Af-Pak Terrorism			✔		
China		✔			
North Korea		✔			
OVERALL		✔			

Our combined score for threats to U.S. vital interests can be summarized as:

Threats to U.S. Vital Interests

SEVERE	HIGH	ELEVATED	GUARDED	LOW

U.S. Military Power

An Assessment of U.S. Military Power

America is a global power with global interests. Its military is meant first and foremost to defend America from attack. Beyond that, it is meant to protect Americans abroad, allies, and the freedom to use international sea, air, and space while retaining the ability to engage in more than one major contingency at a time. America must be able not only to defend itself and its interests, but also to deter enemies and opportunists from taking action that would challenge U.S. interests, a capability that includes preventing the destabilization of a region and guarding against threats to the peace and security of America's friends.

As noted in the four preceding editions of the *Index*, however, the U.S. does not have the necessary force to meet a two–major regional contingency (two-MRC) requirement and is not ready to carry out its duties effectively. Consequently, as we have seen during the past few years, the U.S. risks seeing its interests increasingly challenged and the world order it has led since World War II undone.

How to Think About Sizing Military Power

Military power begins with the people and equipment used to conduct war: the weapons, tanks, ships, airplanes, and supporting tools such as communications systems that make it possible either for one group to impose its will on another or to prevent such an outcome from happening.

However, simply counting the number of people, tanks, or combat aircraft that the U.S. possesses would be insufficient because it would lack context. For example, the U.S. Army might have 100 tanks, but to accomplish a specific military task, 1,000 or more might be needed or none at all. It might be that the terrain on which a battle is fought is especially ill-suited to tanks or that the tanks one has are inferior to the enemy's. The enemy could be quite adept at using tanks, or his tank operations might be integrated into a larger employment concept that leverages the supporting fires of infantry and airpower, whereas one's own tanks are poorly maintained, the crews are ill-prepared, or one's doctrine is irrelevant.

Success in war is partly a function of matching the tools of warfare to a specific task and employing those tools effectively in the conditions of the battle. Get these wrong—tools, objective, competence, or context—and you lose.

Another key element is the military's capacity to conduct operations: how many of the right tools—people, tanks, planes, or ships—it has. One might have the right tools and know how to use them effectively but not have enough to win. Given that one cannot know with certainty beforehand just when, where, against whom, and for what reason a battle might be fought, determining how much capability is needed is an exercise of informed but not certain judgment.

Further, two different combatants can use the same set of tools in radically different ways to quite different effects. The concept of employment matters. Concepts are developed to account for numbers, capabilities, material readiness, and all sorts of other factors that enable or constrain one's actions, such as whether one fights alone or alongside allies, on familiar or strange terrain, or with a large, well-equipped force or a small, poorly equipped force.

All of these factors and a multitude of others bear upon the outcome of any military contest. Military planners attempt to account for them when devising requirements, developing training and exercise plans, formulating war plans, and providing advice to the President in his role as Commander in Chief of U.S. military forces.

Measuring hard combat power in terms of its capability, capacity, and readiness to defend U.S. vital interests is difficult, especially in such a limited space as this *Index*, but it is not impossible. Regardless of the difficulty of determining the adequacy of one's military forces, the Secretary of Defense and the military services have to make such decisions every year when the annual defense budget request is submitted to Congress.

The adequacy of hard power is affected most directly by the resources the nation is willing to apply. Although that decision is informed to a significant degree by an appreciation of threats to U.S. interests and the ability of a given defense portfolio to protect U.S. interests against such threats, it is not informed solely by such considerations; hence the importance of clarity and honesty in determining just what is needed in terms of hard power and the status of such power from year to year.

Administrations take various approaches in determining the type and amount of military power needed and, by extension, the amount of money and other resources to commit to it. After defining the national interests to be protected, the Department of Defense can use worst-case scenarios to determine the maximum challenges the U.S. military might have to overcome. Another way is to redefine what constitutes a threat. By taking a different view of whether major actors pose a meaningful threat and of the extent to which friends and allies have the ability to assist the U.S. in meeting security objectives, one can arrive at different conclusions about necessary military strength.

For example, one Administration might view China as a rising belligerent power bent on dominating the Asia–Pacific region. Another Administration might view China as an inherently peaceful rising economic power, with the expansion of its military capabilities a natural occurrence commensurate with its strengthening status. The difference between these views can have a dramatic impact on how one thinks about U.S. defense requirements. So, too, can policymakers amplify or downplay risk to justify defense budget decisions.

There also can be strongly differing views on requirements for operational capacity.

- Does the country need enough for two major combat operations (MCOs) at roughly the same time or just enough for a single major operation and some number of lesser cases?

- To what extent should "presence" tasks—the use of forces for routine engagement with partner countries or simply to be on hand in a region for crisis response—be in addition to or a subset of a military force sized to handle two major regional conflicts?

- How much value should be assigned to advanced technologies as they are incorporated into the force?

Where to Start

There are two major references that one can use to help sort through the variables and arrive at a starting point for assessing the adequacy of today's military posture: government studies and historical experience. The government occasionally conducts formal reviews that are meant to inform decisions on capabilities and capacities across the Joint Force relative to the threat environment (current and projected) and evolutions in operating conditions, the advancement of technologies, and aspects of U.S. interests that may call for one type of military response over another.

The 1993 Bottom-Up Review (BUR) conducted by then-Secretary of Defense Les Aspin is one such frequently cited example. Secretary

Aspin recognized that "the dramatic changes that [had] occurred in the world as a result of the end of the Cold War and the dissolution of the Soviet Union" had "fundamentally altered America's security needs" and were driving an imperative "to reassess all of our defense concepts, plans, and programs from the ground up."[1]

The BUR formally established the requirement that U.S. forces should be able "to achieve decisive victory in two nearly simultaneous major regional conflicts and to conduct combat operations characterized by rapid response and a high probability of success, while minimizing the risk of significant American casualties."[2] Thus was formalized the two-MRC standard.

Dr. Daniel Gouré, in his 2015 *Index* essay "Building the Right Military for a New Era: The Need for an Enduring Analytic Framework," noted that various Administrations have redefined force requirements based on their perceptions of what was necessary to protect U.S. interests.[3] In an attempt to formalize the process, and perhaps to have a mechanism by which to influence the executive branch in such matters, Congress mandated that each incoming Administration must conduct a comprehensive strategic review of the global security environment, articulate a relevant strategy suited to protecting and promoting U.S. security interests, and recommend an associated military force posture.[4]

The Quadrennial Defense Reviews (QDRs) have been conducted since 1997, accompanied in 1997, 2010, and 2014 by independent National Defense Panel (NDP) reports that have reviewed and commented on them. Both sets of documents purport to serve as key assessments, but analysts have come to minimize their value, regarding them as justifications for executive branch policy preferences (the QDR reports) or overly broad generalized commentaries (the NDP reports) that lack substantive discussion about threats to U.S. interests, a credible strategy for dealing with them, and the actual ability of the U.S. military to meet national security requirements.

Correlation of Forces as a Factor in Force Sizing

During the Cold War, the U.S. used the Soviet threat as its primary reference in determining its hard-power needs. At that time, the correlation of forces—a comparison of one force against another to determine strengths and weaknesses—was highly symmetrical. U.S. planners compared tanks, aircraft, and ships against their direct counterparts in the opposing force. These comparative assessments drove the sizing, characteristics, and capabilities of fleets, armies, and air forces.

The evolution of guided, precision munitions and the rapid technological advancements in surveillance and targeting systems, however, made comparing combat power more difficult. What was largely a platform v. platform model has shifted somewhat to a munitions v. target model.

The proliferation of precise weaponry increasingly means that each round, bomb, rocket, missile, and even (in some instances) individual bullet can hit its intended target, thus decreasing the number of munitions needed to prosecute an operation. It also means that the lethality of an operating environment increases significantly for the people and platforms involved. We are now at the point where one must consider how many "smart munitions" the enemy has when thinking about how many platforms and people are needed to win a combat engagement instead of focusing primarily on how many ships or airplanes the enemy can bring to bear against one's own force.[5]

In one sense, increased precision and the technological advances now being incorporated into U.S. weapons, platforms, and operating concepts make it possible to do far more with fewer assets than ever before.

- Platform signature reduction (stealth) makes it harder for the enemy to find and target them, and the increased precision of weapons makes it possible for fewer platforms to hit many more targets.

- The ability of the U.S. Joint Force to harness computers, modern telecommunications, space-based platforms—such as for surveillance, communications, and positioning-navigation-timing (PNT) support from GPS satellites—and networked operations potentially means that in certain situations, smaller forces can have far greater effect in battle than at any other time in history (although these same advances also enable enemy forces).

- Certain military functions—such as seizing, holding, and occupying territory—may require a certain number of soldiers, no matter how state-of-the-art their equipment may be. For example, securing an urban area where line of sight is constrained and precision weapons have limited utility requires the same number of squads of infantry as were needed in World War II.

With smaller forces, each individual element of the force represents a greater percentage of its combat power. Each casualty or equipment loss therefore takes a larger toll on the ability of the force to sustain high-tempo, high-intensity combat operations over time, especially if the force is dispersed across a wide theater or across multiple theaters of operation.

As advanced technology has become more affordable, it has become more accessible for nearly any actor, whether state or non-state. Consequently, it may be that the outcomes of future wars will depend on the skill of the forces and their capacity to sustain operations over time far more than it depends on some great disparity in technology. If so, readiness and capacity will take on greater importance than absolute advances in capability.

All of this illustrates the difficulties of and need for exercising judgment in assessing the adequacy of America's military power. Yet without such an assessment, all that remains are the defense strategy reviews, which are subject to filtering and manipulation to suit policy interests; annual budget submissions, which typically favor desired military programs at presumed levels of affordability and are therefore necessarily budget-constrained; and leadership posture statements, which often simply align with executive branch policy priorities.

The U.S. Joint Force and the Art of War

This section of the *Index*, on military capabilities, assesses the adequacy of the United States' defense posture as it pertains to a conventional understanding of "hard power," defined as the ability of American military forces to engage and defeat an enemy's forces in battle at a scale commensurate with the vital national interests of the U.S. While some hard truths in military affairs are appropriately addressed by math and science, others are not. Speed, range, probability of detection, and radar cross-section are examples of quantifiable characteristics that can be measured. Specific future instances in which U.S. military power will be needed, the competence of the enemy, the political will to sustain operations in the face of mounting deaths and destruction, and the absolute amount of strength needed to win are matters of judgment and experience, but they nevertheless affect how large and capable a force one might need.

In conducting the assessment, we accounted for both quantitative and qualitative aspects of military forces, informed by an experience-based understanding of military operations and the expertise of external reviewers. The authors of these military sections bring a combined total of over a hundred years of uniformed military experience to their analysis.

Military effectiveness is as much an art as it is a science. Specific military capabilities represented in weapons, platforms, and military units can be used individually to some effect. Practitioners of war, however, have learned that combining the tools of war in various ways and orchestrating their tactical employment in series or simultaneously can dramatically amplify the effectiveness of the force that is committed to battle.

Employment concepts are exceedingly hard to measure in any quantitative way, but their value as critical contributors in the conduct of war is undeniable. How they are utilized is very much an art-of-war matter that is learned through experience over time.

What Is Not Being Assessed

In assessing the current status of the military forces, this *Index* uses the primary references used by the military services themselves when they discuss their ability to employ hard combat power. The Army's unit of measure is the brigade combat team (BCT), while the Marine Corps structures itself by battalions. For the Navy, it is the number of ships in its combat fleet, and the most consistent reference for the Air Force is total number of aircraft, sometimes broken down into the two primary subtypes of fighters and bombers.

Obviously, this is not the totality of service capabilities, and it certainly is not everything needed for war, but these measures can be viewed as surrogate measures that subsume or represent the vast number of other things that make these "units of measure" possible and effective in battle. For example, combat forces depend on a vast logistics system that supplies everything from food and water to fuel, ammunition, and repair parts. Military operations require engineer support, and the force needs medical, dental, and administrative capabilities. The military also fields units that transport combat power and its sustainment wherever they may be needed around the world.

The point is that the military spear has a great deal of shaft that makes it possible for the tip to locate, close with, and destroy its target, and there is a rough proportionality between shaft and spear tip. Thus, in assessing the basic units of measure for combat power, one can get a sense of what is likely needed in the combat support, combat service support, and supporting establishment echelons. The scope of this *Index* does not extend to analysis of everything that makes hard power possible; it focuses on the status of the hard power itself.

This assessment also does not assess the Reserve and National Guard components of the services, although they account for roughly one-third of the U.S. military force[6] and have been essential to the conduct of operations since September 2001. Consistent assessment of their capability, readiness, and operational role is a challenge because each service determines the balance among its Active, Reserve, and National Guard elements differently (only the Army and Air Force have Guard elements; the Navy and Marine Corps do not). This balance can change from year to year and is based on factors that include cost of the respective elements, availability for operational employment, time needed to respond to an emergent crisis, allocation of roles between the elements, and political considerations.[7]

As with other elements essential to the effective employment of combat power—logistics, medical support, strategic lift, training, etc.—the U.S. military could not handle a major conflict without the Reserve and Guard forces. Nevertheless, to bound the challenge of annually assessing the status of U.S. military strength using consistent metrics over time, this *Index* looks at the baseline requirement for a given amount of combat power that is readily available for use in a major combat operation, something that is usually associated with the Active components of each service. There are exceptions, however. For example, in this edition of the *Index*, four Army National Guard BCTs are counted as "available" for use because of the significant amounts of additional resources that have been dedicated specifically to these formations to raise their readiness levels.

The Defense Budget and Strategic Guidance

When it comes to the defense budget, how much we spend does not automatically determine the posture or capacity of the U.S. military. As a matter of fact, simply looking at how much is allocated to defense does not tell us much about the capacity, modernity, or readiness of the forces. Proper funding is a necessary condition for a capable, modern, and ready force, but it is not sufficient by itself. It is possible that a larger defense budget could be associated with less military capability if the money were allocated inappropriately or spent wastefully. That said, however, the budget does reflect the importance assigned to defending the nation and its interests in the prioritization of federal spending.

Absent a significant threat to the survival of the country, the U.S. government will always balance expenditures on defense with spending in all of the other areas of government activity that are deemed necessary or desirable. Some have argued that a defense budget indexed to a percent of gross domestic product (GDP) is a reasonable reference. However, a fixed percentage of GDP does not accurately reflect national security requirements *per se* any more than the size of the budget alone correlates to levels of capability. Additionally, the fact that the economy changes over time does not necessarily mean that defense spending should increase or decrease in lockstep by default.

Ideally, defense requirements are determined by identifying national interests that might need to be protected with military power; assessing the nature of threats to those interests, what would be needed to defeat those threats, and the costs associated with that capability; and then determining what the country can afford or is willing to spend. *Any difference between assessed requirements and affordable levels of spending on defense would constitute a risk to U.S. security interests.*

This *Index* enthusiastically adopts this approach: interests, threats, requirements, resulting force, and associated budget. Spending less than the amount needed to maintain a two-MRC force results in policy debates about where to accept risk: force modernization, the capacity to conduct large-scale or multiple simultaneous operations, or force readiness.

The National Defense Strategy released in late January 2018 by the Department of Defense (DOD) is the department's current effort to establish the connection among interests, threats, requirements, and resources.[8]

It serves to orient how DOD intends to prepare the country's defense and, importantly, establishes a public baseline of mission and associated requirements against which the country can measure its defense efforts. When discussing resources, the strategy calls for an increased, sustained, and predictable budget as the necessary precondition for its execution—something that has proved elusive in the current budgetary climate of two-year deals designed to circumvent the Budget Control Act of 2011 (BCA).

The decision to fund national defense commensurate with interests and prevailing threats reflects our national priorities and risk tolerance. This *Index* assesses the ability of the nation's military forces to protect vital national security interests within the world *as it is* so that the debate about the level of funding for hard power is better informed.

The fiscal year (FY) 2018 base discretionary budget for defense was $629 billion.[9] This represents the resources allocated to pay for the forces (manpower, equipment, training); enabling capabilities (things like transportation, satellites, defense intelligence, and research and development); and institutional support (bases and stations, facilities, recruiting, and the like). The base budget does not pay for the cost of major ongoing overseas operations, which is captured in supplemental funding known as OCO (overseas contingency operations).

The debate over how much funding to allocate to defense has been framed by the current Administration's campaign promise to rebuild the military, an objective that is generally supported by Congress. Despite repeated emphasis on the importance of investing more to fix obvious readiness, capacity, and modernization problems, the debate was determined once again by larger political dynamics that pitted those who wanted to see an overall reduction in federal spending against those who advocate higher levels of defense spending and those who want to see any increase in defense spending matched by commensurate increases in domestic spending.

FY 2018 was marred from the beginning by multiple continuing resolutions (CRs) that temporarily funded the federal government and the Department of Defense at roughly FY 2017 levels. This funding mechanism is inherently inefficient and often wasteful because of the limitations it places on how funds can be used and the start-and-stop disruption that CRs introduce into defense planning and program execution.[10] Passage of the Bipartisan Budget Act of 2018 (BBA) in early February 2018 brought CR volatility to an end and raised the BCA caps for FY 2018 and FY 2019.[11] The legislation raised the cap by $71 billion to $629 billion in FY 2018 and by $69 billion to $647 billion in FY 2019. This provided substantial budgetary relief for DOD and, given its two-year coverage, a modicum of stability.

Unfortunately, because the legislation did not alter the caps for 2020 and 2021, the restrictions placed on defense spending by the BCA continue to be a major concern of the military service chiefs, who have testified consistently about the damage these restrictions are causing to readiness, modernization, and capacity for operations.

In testimony before the House Armed Services Committee, for example, Secretary of Defense James Mattis and Chairman of the Joint Chiefs of Staff General Joseph Dunford emphasized the need for sustained budget growth so that U.S. forces can maintain a competitive advantage over likely adversaries.[12] "We know now," General Dunford testified, "that continued growth in the base budget of at least 3 percent *above inflation* is the floor necessary to preserve just the competitive advantage we have today, and we can't assume our adversaries will remain still."[13] The BCA limits the increases to little over inflation, and the current budget request projects increases that are slightly below the inflationary rate.[14]

President Barack Obama's 2012 defense budget, the last sent to Congress before passage of the BCA, proposed $673 billion in defense spending for FY 2019, $26 billion more than the temporary increase provided by the 2018 BBA. A bipartisan consensus, as seen in the National Defense Panel report in 2014, identified the so-called Gates budget (named after then-Secretary of Defense Robert Gates) as the "minimal baseline for appropriate defense spending in the future."[15] It recommended a topline of $661 billion for 2018 and $673 billion for 2019, $32 billion and $26 billion more than the 2018 BBA, respectively. As seen in Chart 9, despite consistent pushes toward a higher topline, the current and projected defense budget still trails this minimum.

Purpose as a Driver in Force Sizing

The Joint Force is used for a wide range of purposes, only one of which is major combat operations. Fortunately, such events have been rare (but consistent), averaging roughly 15–20 years between occurrences.[16] In between (and even during) such occurrences, the military is used to support regional engagement, crisis response, strategic deterrence, and humanitarian assistance, as well as to support civil authorities and U.S. diplomacy.

The U.S. Unified Geographic Combatant Commands, or COCOMS—Northern Command (NORTHCOM); European Command (EUCOM); Central Command (CENTCOM); Indo-Pacific Command (INDOPACOM); Southern Command (SOUTHCOM); and Africa Command (AFRICOM)—all have annual and long-term plans through which they engage with countries in their assigned regions. These engagements range from very small unit training events with the forces of a single partner country to larger bilateral and sometimes multilateral military exercises. Such events help to foster working relationships with other countries, acquire a more detailed understanding of regional political–military dynamics and on-the-ground conditions in areas of interest, and signal U.S. security interests to friends and competitors.

To support such COCOM efforts, the services provide forces that are based permanently in respective regions or that operate in them temporarily on a rotational basis. To make these regional rotations possible, the

CHART 9

Defense Spending to Receive Long-Overdue Boost

Long hindered by the Budget Control Act, defense spending is projected to approach
levels requested by former Secretary of Defense Robert Gates back in 2012.

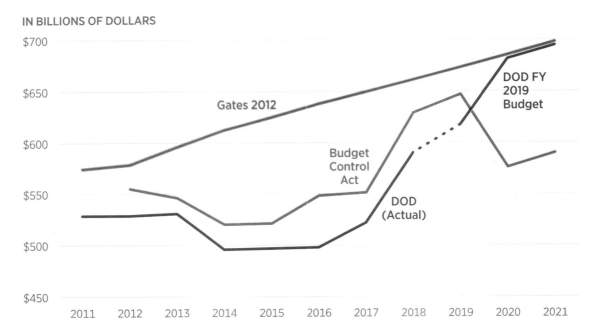

IN BILLIONS OF DOLLARS

- Gates 2012
- Budget Control Act
- DOD (Actual)
- DOD FY 2019 Budget

(x-axis: 2011, 2012, 2013, 2014, 2015, 2016, 2017, 2018, 2019, 2020, 2021)
(y-axis: $450, $500, $550, $600, $650, $700)

SOURCES:

- Gates 2012: White House, Office of Management and Budget, *Fiscal Year 2012 Budget of the U.S. Government, Analytical Perspectives*, February 2011, https://www.gpo.gov/fdsys/search/pagedetails.action?collectionCode=BUDGET&granuleId=&packageId=BUDGET-2012-PER (accessed July 31, 2017).
- Budget Control Act: Brendan W. McGarry, "The Defense Budget and the Budget Control Act: Frequently Asked Questions," Congressional Research Service *Report* R44039, July 13, 2018, https://fas.org/sgp/crs/natsec/R44039.pdf (accessed August 8, 2018).
- Department of Defense: U.S. Department of Defense, "National Defense Budget Estimates for FY 2019," April 2018, https://comptroller.defense.gov/Portals/45/Documents/defbudget/fy2019/FY19_Green_Book.pdf (accessed August 8, 2018), and U.S. Department of Defense, "Defense Budget Overview," February 13, 2018, http://comptroller.defense.gov/Portals/45/Documents/defbudget/fy2019/FY2019_Budget_Request_Overview_Book.pdf (accessed August 8, 2018).

☎ heritage.org

services must maintain a base force that is sufficiently large to train, deploy, support, receive back, and make ready again a stream of units that ideally is enough to meet validated COCOM demand.

The ratio between time spent at home and time spent away on deployment for any given unit is known as OPTEMPO (operational tempo), and each service attempts to maintain a ratio that both gives units enough time to educate, train, and prepare their forces and allows the individuals in a unit to maintain some semblance of a healthy home and family life. This ensures that units are fully prepared for the next deployment cycle and that service-members do not become "burned out" or suffer adverse consequences in their personal lives because of excessive deployment time.

Experience has shown that a ratio of at least 3:1 (three periods of time at home for every period deployed) is sustainable. If a unit is to be out for six months, for example, it will be home for 18 months before deploying again. Obviously, a service needs enough people, units, ships, and planes to support such a ratio. If peacetime engagement were the primary focus for the Joint Force, the services could size their forces to support these forward-based and forward-deployed demands.

Thus, the size of the total force must necessarily be much larger than any sampling of its use at any point in time.

In contrast, sizing a force for major combat operations is an exercise informed by history—how much force was needed in previous wars—and then shaped and refined by analysis of current threats, a range of plausible scenarios, and expectations about what the U.S. can do given training, equipment, employment concept, and other factors. The defense establishment must then balance "force sizing" between COCOM requirements for presence and engagement and the amount of military power (typically measured in terms of combat units and major combat platforms, which inform total end strength) that is thought necessary to win in likely war scenarios.

Inevitably, compromises are made that account for how much military the country is willing to buy. Generally speaking:

- **The Army** sizes to major warfighting requirements.

- **The Marine Corps** focuses on crisis response demands and the ability to contribute to one major war.

- **The Air Force** attempts to strike a balance that accounts for historically based demand across the spectrum because air assets are shifted fairly easily from one theater of operations to another ("easily" being a relative term when compared to the challenge of shifting large land forces), and any peacetime engagement typically requires some level of air support.

- **The Navy** is driven by global presence requirements. To meet COCOM requirements for a continuous fleet presence at sea, the Navy must have three to four ships in order to have one on station. A commander who wants one U.S. warship stationed off the coast of a hostile country, for example, needs the use of four ships from the fleet: one on station, one that left station and is traveling home, one that just left home and is traveling to station, and one that is otherwise unavailable due to major maintenance or modernization work.

This *Index* focuses on the forces required to win two major wars as the baseline force-sizing metric. The military's effectiveness, both as a deterrent against opportunistic competitor states and as a valued training partner in the eyes of other countries, derives from its effectiveness (proven or presumed) in winning wars.

Our Approach

With this in mind, we assessed the state of military affairs for U.S. forces as it pertains to their ability to deliver hard power against an enemy in three areas:

- Capability,

- Capacity, and

- Readiness.

Capability. Examining the capability of a military force requires consideration of:

- The proper tools (material and conceptual) of sufficient design, performance characteristics, technological advancement, and suitability needed for the force to perform its function against an enemy force successfully.

- The sufficiency of armored vehicles, ships, airplanes, and other equipment and weapons to win against the enemy.

- The appropriate variety of options to preclude strategic vulnerabilities in the force and give flexibilities to battlefield commanders.

- The degree to which elements of the force reinforce each other in covering potential vulnerabilities, maximizing strengths, and gaining greater effectiveness through synergies that are not possible in narrowly stovepiped, linear approaches to war.

The capability of the U.S. Joint Force was on ample display in its decisive conventional war victory over Iraq in liberating Kuwait in 1991 and later in the conventional military operation in Iraq to depose Saddam Hussein in 2003. Aspects of its capability have also been seen in numerous other operations undertaken since the end of the Cold War. While the conventional combat aspect at the "pointy end of the spear" of power projection has been more moderate in places like Yugoslavia, Somalia, Bosnia and Serbia, and Kosovo, and even against the Taliban in Afghanistan in 2001, the fact that the U.S. military was able to conduct highly complex operations thousands of miles away in austere, hostile environments and sustain those operations as long as required is testament to the ability of U.S. forces to do things that the armed forces of few if any other countries can do.

A modern-day "major combat operation"[17] along the lines of those upon which Pentagon planners base their requirements would feature a major opponent possessing modern integrated air defenses; naval power (surface and undersea); advanced combat aircraft (to include bombers); a substantial inventory of short-range, medium-range, and long-range missiles; current-generation ground forces (tanks, armored vehicles, artillery, rockets, and anti-armor weaponry); cruise missiles; and (in some cases) nuclear weapons. Such a situation involving an actor capable of threatening vital national interests would present a challenge that is comprehensively different from the challenges that the U.S. Joint Force has faced in past decades.

During 2018, the military community reenergized its debate over the extent to which the U.S. military is ready for major conventional warfare, given its focus on counterinsurgency, stability, and advise-and-assist operations since 2004 and Secretary Mattis's directive to prepare for conflict in an era of great-power competition.[18] The Army in particular has noted the need to reengage in training and exercises that feature larger-scale combined arms maneuver operations, especially to ensure that its higher headquarters elements are up to the task.

This *Index* ascertains the relevance and health of military service capabilities by looking at such factors as average age of equipment, generation of equipment relative to the current state of competitor efforts as reported by the services, and the status of replacement programs that are meant to introduce more updated systems as older equipment reaches the end of its programmed service life. While some of the information is quite quantitative, other factors could be considered judgment calls made by acknowledged experts in the relevant areas of interest or as addressed by senior service officials when providing testimony to Congress or addressing specific areas in other official statements.

It must be determined whether the services possess capabilities that are relevant to the modern combat environment.

Capacity. The U.S. military must have a sufficient quantity of the right capability or capabilities. When speaking of platforms such as planes and ships, there is a troubling and fairly consistent trend that characterizes the path from requirement to fielded capability within U.S. military acquisition. Along the way to acquiring the capability, several linked things happen that result in far less of a presumed "critical capability" than supposedly was required.

- The manufacturing sector attempts to satisfy the requirements articulated by the military.

- "Unexpected" technological hurdles arise that take longer and much more money to solve than anyone envisioned.

- Programs are lengthened, and cost overruns are addressed (usually with more money).

- Then the realization sets in that the country either cannot afford or is unwilling to pay the cost of acquiring the total number of platforms originally advocated. The acquisition goal is adjusted downward (if not canceled), and the military finally fields fewer platforms (at a higher cost per unit) than it originally said it needed to be successful in combat.

As deliberations proceed toward a decision on whether to reduce planned procurement, they rarely focus on and quantify the increase in risk that accompanies the decrease in procurement.

Something similar happens with force structure size: the number of units and total number of personnel the services say they need to meet the objectives established by the Commander in Chief and the Secretary of Defense in their strategic guidance. The Marine Corps has stated that it needs 27 infantry battalions to fully satisfy the validated requirements of the regional Combatant Commanders, yet it currently fields only 24. In 2012, the Army was building toward 48 brigade combat teams, but incremental budget cuts reduced that number over time to 31—less than two-thirds the number that the Army originally thought was necessary.

Older equipment can be updated with new components to keep it relevant, and commanders can employ fewer units more expertly for longer periods of time in an operational theater to accomplish an objective. At some point, however, sheer numbers of updated, modern equipment and trained, fully manned units are going to be needed to win in battle against a credible opponent when the crisis is profound enough to threaten a vital interest.

Capacity (numbers) can be viewed in at least three ways: compared to a stated objective for each category by each service, compared to amounts required to complete various types of operations across a wide range of potential missions as measured against a potential adversary, and as measured against a set benchmark for total national capability. This *Index* employs the two-MRC metric as a benchmark.

The two-MRC benchmark for force sizing is the *minimum* standard for U.S. hard-power capacity because one will never be able to employ 100 percent of the force at the same time. Some percentage of the force will always be unavailable because of long-term maintenance overhaul (for Navy ships in particular); unit training cycles; employment in myriad engagement and small-crisis response tasks that continue even during major conflicts; and the need to keep some portion of the force uncommitted to serve as a strategic reserve.

The historical record shows that the U.S. Army commits 21 BCTs on average to a major conflict; thus, a two-MRC standard would require 42 BCTs available for actual use. But an Army built to field only 42 BCTs would also be an Army that could find itself entirely committed to war, leaving nothing back as a strategic reserve, to replace combat losses, or to handle other U.S. security interests.

Again, this *Index* assesses only the Active component of the services, though with full awareness that the Army also has Reserve and National Guard components that together account for half of the total Army. The additional capacity needed to meet these "above two-MRC requirements" could be handled by these other components or mobilized to supplement Active-component commitments. In fact, this is how the Army thinks about meeting operational demands and is at the heart of the long-running debate within the total Army about the roles and contributions of the various Army components. A similar situation exists with the Air Force and Marine Corps.

The balance among Active, Reserve, and Guard elements is beyond the scope of this

TABLE 5

Historical U.S. Force Allocation

Troop figures are in thousands.

	Korean War	Vietnam War	Persian Gulf War	Operation Iraqi Freedom
ARMY				
Total Troop Deployment During Engagement	206.3	219.3	267.0	99.7
Divisions*	6	7	4	1
Reserve Component Divisions Total for Strategic Documents	n/a	n/a	n/a	n/a
Total Army End Strength During Engagement, During Year of Strategy Document Active	1,313.8	1,113.3	738.0	499.0
Total Active End Strength Recommendations	n/a	n/a	n/a	n/a
NAVY				
Total Fleet During Engagement	904	770	529	297
Aircraft Carriers	6	5	6	5
Carrier Air Wings	6	5	6	5
Large Surface Combatants	37	14	30	23
Small Surface Combatants	16	47	16	9
Attack Submarines	4	0	12	12
Amphibious Vessels	34	26	21	7
Combat Logistics and Support Ships	28	29	45	42
Fighter/Attack Squadrons	21	43	22	24
MARINE CORPS				
Total Troop Deployment During Engagement	33.5	44.7	90.0	66.2
Active Divisions*	1	2	2	1
Reserve Divisions	n/a	n/a	n/a	n/a
Marine Expeditionary Force	1	1	1	2
Air Wings Active/Reserve	1	1	1	1
Total Marine Corps End Strength During Engagement by Year of Strategy Document	187.0	289.0	196.3	178.0
Total Recommended End Strength	n/a	n/a	n/a	n/a
AIR FORCE				
Bombers or Bomber Squadrons**	21	23	3	4
Fighter Squadrons	26		30	30
Active Fighter Wings	7	8	10	10
Reserve Fighter Wings				
Airlift/Tankers	239	167	388	293

* Figures for engagements are numbers deployed; figures for documents are totals.
** Figures for Air Force bombers for Korean War, Vietnam War, Persian Gulf War, and Iraq are bomber squadrons. All other figures are bombers.
*** 2014 QDR prescribed nine heavy bomber squadrons, equaling 96 aircraft.

	1993 BUR	1997 QDR	2001 QDR	2006 QDR	2010 QDR	2010 Indep. Panel	2-MRC Paper	2014 QDR	2014 NDP
ARMY									
Total Troop Deployment During Engagement	n/a	n/a	n/a	n/a	n/a	n/a	n/a	n/a	n/a
Divisions*	10	10	10	11		11	10	10	n/a
Reserve Component Divisions Total for Strategic Documents	n/a	5	8	8	18	7	8	8	n/a
Total Army End Strength During Engagement, During Year of Strategy Document Active	572.0	492.0	481.0	505.0	566.0	566.0	550.0	490.0	490.0
Total Active End Strength Recommendations	n/a	n/a	n/a	482.4	n/a	1,106.0	600.0	450.0	490.0
NAVY									
Total Fleet During Engagement	346	310	n/a	n/a	n/a	346	350	n/a	346
Aircraft Carriers	12	12	12	11	11	11	11	11	n/a
Carrier Air Wings	12	11	11	n/a	10	10	10	10	n/a
Large Surface Combatants	124	116	116	n/a	84–88	n/a	120	92	n/a
Small Surface Combatants				n/a	14–28	n/a	n/a	43	n/a
Attack Submarines	55	50	55	n/a	53–55	55	50	51	n/a
Amphibious Vessels	41	36	36	n/a	29–31	n/a	38	33	n/a
Combat Logistics and Support Ships	65	n/a	n/a	n/a	58	n/a	75	n/a	n/a
Fighter/Attack Squadrons	33	30	30	n/a	30	30	30	30	n/a
MARINE CORPS									
Total Troop Deployment During Engagement	n/a	n/a	n/a	n/a	n/a	n/a	n/a	n/a	n/a
Active Divisions*	4	3	3	n/a	3	n/a	n/a	3	n/a
Reserve Divisions	1	1	1	n/a	1	n/a	n/a	1	n/a
Marine Expeditionary Force	3	3	3	n/a	3	3	3	2	n/a
Air Wings Active/Reserve	n/a	4	4	n/a	4	n/a	n/a	4	n/a
Total Marine Corps End Strength During Engagement by Year of Strategy Document	174.0	174.0	173.0	180.0	202.0	202.0	196.0	182.0	182.0
Total Recommended End Strength	n/a	n/a	n/a	175.0	n/a	243.0	202.0	182.0	182.0
AIR FORCE									
Bombers or Bomber Squadrons**	200	187	112	n/a	96	180	200	96***	n/a
Fighter Squadrons	54	54	46	n/a	42	66	54	48	n/a
Active Fighter Wings	13	12+	15	n/a	n/a	20	20	9	n/a
Reserve Fighter Wings	7	8	12	n/a	n/a	n/a		7	n/a
Airlift/Tankers	n/a	n/a	n/a	n/a	1023	1023	1,000	954	n/a

study. Our focus here is on establishing a minimum benchmark for the capacity needed to handle a two-MRC requirement.

We conducted a review of the major defense studies (1993 BUR, QDR reports, and independent panel critiques) that are publicly available,[19] as well as modern historical instances of major wars (Korea, Vietnam, Gulf War, Operation Iraqi Freedom), to see whether there was any consistent trend in U.S. force allocation. The results of our review are presented in Table 5. To this we added 20 percent, both to account for forces and platforms that are likely to be unavailable and to provide a strategic reserve to guard against unforeseen demands.

Summarizing the totals, this *Index* concluded that a Joint Force capable of dealing with two MRCs simultaneously or nearly simultaneously would consist of:

- **Army:** 50 BCTs.

- **Navy:** at least 400 ships and 624 strike aircraft.

- **Air Force:** 1,200 fighter/attack aircraft.

- **Marine Corps:** 36 battalions.

America's security interests require that the services have the capacity to handle two major regional conflicts successfully.

Readiness. The consequences of the sharp reductions in funding mandated by sequestration have caused military service officials, senior DOD officials, and even Members of Congress to warn of the dangers of recreating the "hollow force" of the 1970s when units existed on paper but were staffed at reduced levels, minimally trained, and woefully ill-equipped.[20] To avoid this, the services have traded quantity/capacity and modernization to ensure that what they do have is "ready" for employment.

Supplemental funding in FY 2017 and a higher topline in FY 2018 have helped to stop the bleeding and have enabled the services to plan and implement readiness recovery efforts. Although the return of further cuts under the BCA could threaten to undo these gains, readiness reporting has been largely optimistic compared to recent years. For example:

- Secretary of the Army Mark T. Esper testified in March 2018 that FY 2017 and FY 2018 appropriations funded additional manning requirements and combat training center rotations. "As a result, the number of brigade combat teams (BCTs) in the highest state of personnel readiness has more than doubled."[21]

- In April 2018, Secretary of the Air Force Heather A. Wilson testified that in 2017, the Air Force "started to turn the corner" and that "additional resources added by the Congress in fiscal year 2018 are helping us to start to climb out of a readiness deficit...."[22]

- Admiral John Richardson, Chief of Naval Operations, reported similar trends, testifying in March 2018 that "[i]n FY17 [the Navy] arrested readiness decline with the Request for Additional Appropriations, and the FY18 and FY19 budget requests further restore readiness while beginning to increase warfighting capacity and capability."[23]

- General Robert Neller, Commandant of the Marine Corps, agreed in April 2018 that additional appropriations for readiness in FY 2017 "provided the investment needed to arrest this decline, and the PB18 and PB19 budget submissions provide the resources needed to accelerate our readiness recovery."[24]

It is one thing to have the right capabilities to defeat the enemy in battle. It is another thing to have enough of those capabilities to sustain operations over time and many battles against an enemy, especially when attrition or dispersed operations are significant factors. But sufficient numbers of the right capabilities are rather meaningless if the force is unready to engage in the task.

U.S. Military Power: Five-Grade Scale

VERY WEAK	WEAK	MARGINAL	STRONG	VERY STRONG

Scoring. In our final assessments, we tried very hard not to convey a higher level of precision than we think is achievable using unclassified, open-source, publicly available documents; not to reach conclusions that could be viewed as based solely on assertions or opinion; and not to rely solely on data and information that can be highly quantified, since simple numbers do not tell the whole story.

We believe that the logic underlying our methodology is sound. This *Index* drew from a wealth of public testimony from senior government officials, from the work of recognized experts in the defense and national security analytic community, and from historical instances of conflict that seemed most appropriate to this project. It then considered several questions, including:

- How does one place a value on the combat effectiveness of such concepts as Air-Sea Battle, Multi-Domain Operations, Littoral Operations in a Contested Environment, Distributed Maritime Operations, Network-centric Operations, or Joint Operational Access?

- Is it entirely possible to assess accurately (1) how well a small number of newest-generation ships or aircraft will fare against a much larger number of currently modern counterparts when (2) U.S. forces are operating thousands of miles from home, (3) orchestrated with a particular operational concept, and (4) the enemy is leveraging a "home field advantage" that includes strategic depth and much shorter and perhaps better protected lines of communication and (5) might be pursuing much dearer national objectives than the

U.S. so that the political will to conduct sustained operations in the face of mounting losses might differ dramatically?

- How does one neatly quantify the element of combat experience, the erosion of experience as combat operation events recede in time and those who participated in them leave the force, the health of a supporting workforce, the value of "presence and engagement operations," and the related force structures and deployment/employment patterns that presumably deter war or mitigate its effects if it does occur?

This *Index* focused on the primary purpose of military power—to defeat an enemy in combat—and the historical record of major U.S. engagements for evidence of what the U.S. defense establishment has thought was necessary to execute a major conventional war successfully. To this we added the two-MRC benchmark, on-the-record assessments of what the services themselves are saying about their status relative to validated requirements, and the analysis and opinions of various experts in and out of government who have covered these issues for many years.

Taking it all together, we rejected scales that would imply extraordinary precision and settled on a scale that conveys broader characterizations of status that range from very weak to very strong. Ultimately, any such assessment is a judgment call informed by quantifiable data, qualitative assessments, thoughtful deliberation, and experience. We trust that our approach makes sense, is defensible, and is repeatable.

U.S. Military Power

	VERY WEAK	WEAK	MARGINAL	STRONG	VERY STRONG
Army			✔		
Navy			✔		
Air Force			✔		
Marine Corps		✔			
Nuclear			✔		
OVERALL			✔		

Endnotes

1. Les Aspin, Secretary of Defense, *Report on the Bottom-Up Review*, U.S. Department of Defense, October 1993, p. iii, http://www.google.com/url?sa=t&rct=j&q=&esrc=s&source=web&cd=2&ved=0CCUQFjAB-ahUKEwjj4dWf6N3HAhVEmh4KHdG1Cdg&url=http%3A%2F%2Fwww.dtic.mil%2Fcgi-bin%2FGetTRDoc%3FAD%3DADA359953&usg=AFQjCNFvzw730XRz7YRxpc5BNr5_UdfMiQ (accessed August 6, 2018).

2. Ibid., p. 8.

3. Daniel Gouré, "Building the Right Military for a New Era: The Need for an Enduring Analytic Framework," in *2015 Index of U.S. Military Strength*, ed. Dakota L. Wood (Washington: The Heritage Foundation, 2015), pp. 27–36, http://index.heritage.org/militarystrength/important-essays-analysis/building-right-military-new-era/.

4. John Y. Schrader, Leslie Lewis, and Roger Allen Brown, *Quadrennial Defense Review 2001: Lessons on Man-aging Change in the Department of Defense* (Santa Monica, CA: RAND Corporation, National Defense Research Institute, 2003), http://www.rand.org/content/dam/rand/pubs/documented_briefings/2005/DB379.pdf (accessed August 1, 2017).

5. The United States has not had to contend in combat with any credible air force since the Vietnam War, but U.S. Air Force planners are increasingly concerned about an enemy's ground-based, anti-air missile capability. For naval planners, ship-based, air-based, and shore-based anti-ship cruise missiles are of much greater concern than is the number of conventional surface combatants armed with large-caliber guns that an enemy navy has. Likewise, ground force planners have to consider the numbers and types of guided anti-armor weapons that an enemy possesses and whether an opposing force has guided artillery, mortar, or rocket capabilities. Guided/precision weapons are typically less expensive (by orders of magnitude) than the platforms they target, which means that countries can produce far more guided munitions than primary weapons platforms. Some examples: Harpoon ASCM ($2 million)/DDG-51 *Arleigh Burke*–Class destroyer ($2 billion); AT4 anti-armor weapon ($1,500)/M1A1 Abrams main battle tank ($9 million); 120mm guided mortar round ($10,000) or 155mm guided artillery round ($100,000)/M198 155mm howitzer ($500,000); S-300 anti-air missile ($1 million)/F/A-18 Hornet ($60 million) or F-35A Lightning II ($180 million).

6. For a complete discussion of this force, see Richard J. Dunn III, "America's Reserve and National Guard Components: Key Contributors to U.S. Military Strength," 2016 Index of U.S. Military Strength (Washington: The Heritage Foundation, 2015), pp. 61–73, https://s3.amazonaws.com/ims-2016/PDF/2016_Index_of_US_Military_Strength_FULL.pdf. For the percentage of U.S. military capability that resides in the Guard/Reserve, see ibid., p. 63.

7. One example of balancing the forces was the Army's Aviation Restructuring Initiative, in which the active-duty force sought to redistribute certain rotorcraft platforms among the active-duty Army and the National Guard, a plan that the Guard has contended would reduce the capabilities it has gained during recent combat engagements, such as its pilots' proficiency in flying Apache helicopters. For more on this issue, see U.S. Government Accountability Office, *Force Structure: Army's Analyses of Aviation Alternatives*, GAO–15–430R, April 27, 2015, http://www.gao.gov/assets/670/669857.pdf (accessed August 6, 2018).

8. James Mattis, U.S. Secretary of Defense, *Summary of the 2018 National Defense Strategy of the United States of America: Sharpening the American Military's Competitive Edge*, U.S. Department of Defense, https://www.defense.gov/Portals/1/Documents/pubs/2018-National-Defense-Strategy-Summary.pdf (accessed August 6, 2018).

9. H.R. 1892, Bipartisan Budget Act of 2018, Public Law 115-123, 115th Cong., February 9, 2018, https://www.congress.gov/bill/115th-congress/house-bill/1892/text (accessed August 6, 2018).

10. Frederico Bartels, "Continuing Resolutions Invariably Harm National Defense," Heritage Foundation *Issue Brief* No. 4819, February 21, 2018, https://www.heritage.org/defense/report/continuing-resolutions-invariably-harm-national-defense.

11. Budget Control Act of 2011, Public Law 112-25, 112th Cong., August 2, 2011, https://www.congress.gov/112/plaws/publ25/PLAW-112publ25.pdf (accessed August 6, 2018).

12. James Mattis, U.S. Secretary of Defense, statement on President's budget request for FY 2018 before the Committee on Armed Services, U.S. House of Representatives, June 12, 2017, https://docs.house.gov/meetings/AS/AS00/20170612/106090/HHRG-115-AS00-Bio-MattisJ-20170612.pdf (accessed August 6, 2018).

13. Aaron Mehta, "DoD Needs 3–5 Percent Annual Growth 2023, Top Officials Say," *Defense News,* June 13, 2017, http://www.defensenews.com/pentagon/2017/06/13/dod-needs-3-5-percent-annual-growth-through-2023-top-officials-say/ (accessed July 24, 2017). Emphasis added.

14. For future year projections, see U.S. Department of Defense, Office of the Under Secretary of Defense (Comptroller)/Chief Financial Officer, *United States Department of Defense Fiscal Year 2019 Budget Request: Defense Budget Overview*, revised February 13, 2018, https://comptroller.defense.gov/Portals/45/Documents/defbudget/fy2019/FY2019_Budget_Request_Overview_Book.pdf (accessed August 13, 2018); for future inflationary rate, see U.S. Department of Defense, Office of the Under Secretary of Defense (Comptroller), *National Defense Budget Estimates for FY 2019*, April 2018, https://comptroller.defense.gov/Portals/45/Documents/defbudget/fy2019/FY19_Green_Book.pdf (accessed August 13, 2018).

15. See *Ensuring a Strong U.S. Defense for the Future: The National Defense Panel Review of the 2014 Quadrennial Defense Review*, Advance Copy, U.S. Institute of Peace, released July 31, 2014, p. 4, http://www.usip.org/sites/default/files/Ensuring-a-Strong-U.S.-Defense-for-the-Future-NDP-Review-of-the-QDR_0.pdf (accessed August 6, 2018).

16. Since World War II, the U.S. has fought four major wars: the Korean War (1950–1953); the Vietnam War (1965–1973); the Gulf War/Operation Desert Shield/Desert Storm (1990–1991); and the Iraq War/Operation Iraqi Freedom (2003–2011).

17. Defense references to war have varied over the past few decades from "major combat operation" (MCO) and "major theater war" (MTW) to the current "major regional contingency" (MRC). Arguably, there is a supporting rationale for such shifts as planners attempt to find the best words to describe the scope and scale of significant military efforts, but the terms are basically interchangeable.

18. Mattis, *Summary of the 2018 National Defense Strategy of the United States of America*, p. 4.

19. The Department of Defense, through the Joint Staff and Geographic Combatant Commanders, manages a relatively small set of real-world operational plans (OPLANS) focused on specific situations where the U.S. feels it is most likely to go to war. These plans are reviewed and updated regularly to account for changes in the Joint Force or with the presumed enemy. They are highly detailed and account not only for the amount of force the U.S. expects that it will need to defeat the enemy, but also for which specific units would deploy; how the force would actually flow into the theater (the sequencing of units); what ports and airfields it would use; how much ammunition, fuel, and other supplies it would need at the start; how much transportation or "lift" would be needed to get the force there (by air, sea, trucks, or rail); and the basic plan of attack. The Pentagon also routinely develops, explores, and refines various notional planning scenarios in order to better understand the implications of different sorts of contingencies, which approaches might be more effective, how much of what type of force might be needed, and the regional issue or issues for which there would have to be an accounting. These types of planning events inform service efforts to develop, equip, train, and field military forces that are up to the task of defending national security interests. All of these efforts and their products are classified national security information and therefore not available to the public.

20. For more on the potential for a hollow force, see Association of the United States Army, "Preventing a Hollow Force Is Army's Top Priority," May 25, 2017, https://www.ausa.org/news/preventing-hollow-force-army%E2%80%99s-top-priority (accessed August 6, 2018), and J. V. Venable, "America's Air Force Is in Bad Shape," *National Review*, June 13, 2017, http://www.nationalreview.com/article/448556/us-air-force-weakened-funding-cuts-shrinking-workforce-aging-fleet-hurt-preparedness (accessed July 31, 2017).

21. The Honorable Mark T. Esper, Secretary of the Army, statement on "The Posture of the United States Army" before the Committee on Armed Services, U.S. House of Representatives, 115th Cong., 2nd Sess., March 20, 2018, p. 3, https://docs.house.gov/meetings/AS/AS00/20180320/108047/HHRG-115-AS00-Wstate-EsperM-20180320.pdf (accessed July 12, 2018).

22. Testimony of The Honorable Heather A. Wilson, Secretary of the Air Force, in stenographic transcript of *Hearing to Receive Testimony on the Posture of the Department of the Air Force in Review of the Defense Authorization Request for Fiscal Year 2019 and The Future Years Defense Program*, Committee on Armed Services, U.S. Senate, April 24, 2018, p. 9, https://www.armed-services.senate.gov/imo/media/doc/18-43_04-24-18.pdf (accessed August 6, 2018).

23. Admiral John Richardson, Chief of Naval Operations, statement on "Fiscal Year 2019 Navy Budget" before the Subcommittee on Defense, Committee on Appropriations, U.S. House of Representatives, March 7, 2018, p. 2, http://www.navy.mil/navydata/people/cno/Richardson/Speech/07MAR18_HAC-D_FY19_DON_Posture.pdf (accessed July 12, 2018).

24. General Robert B. Neller, Commandant of the Marine Corps, statement on "The Posture of the United States Marine Corps" before the Committee on Armed Services, U.S. Senate, April 19, 2018, p. 12, https://www.armed-services.senate.gov/imo/media/doc/Neller_04-19-18.pdf (accessed August 6, 2018).

U.S. Army

The U.S. Army is America's primary land warfare component. Although it addresses all types of operations across the range of ground force employment, its chief value to the nation is its ability to defeat and destroy enemy land forces in battle.

Secretary of Defense James Mattis has warned that a decade of combat operations and a lack of reliable and predictable funds have left the U.S. military in "a position where we are losing or eroding our competitive edge."[1] Fiscal challenges have similarly strained the ability of the Army to meet the national security requirements outlined in the Defense Planning Guidance as it works to balance readiness, modernization, and end strength.

Secretary of the Army Mark Esper and Army Chief of Staff General Mark Milley have testified that "strong support" from Congress "has enabled the Army to halt the decline in our warfighting readiness,"[2] but despite the inclusion of additional Army end strength in the 2018 National Defense Authorization Act (NDAA) and increased funding in the omnibus Consolidated Appropriations Act, 2018, issues of inadequate size, readiness, modernization, and high operational tempo remain to be addressed.

- General Milley has testified that the Army is too small and needs to grow to "north of 500,000...in the regular Army" to accomplish the missions outlined in the National Security and Defense Strategies.[3]

- Secretary Esper and General Milley have further testified that the Army "can no longer afford to delay modernization without risking overmatch on future battlefields."[4]

- Although the Army's internal goal is to have 66 percent of its brigade combat teams considered ready at any given time, the number considered ready today is only "in the range of the 50 percent mark."[5] (This is an improvement over 2017 when only one-third were considered ready.[6])

- Of the 15 of 31 Active BCTs considered "ready," only eight are considered "fully ready,"[7] which limits options for the President. According to Vice Chief of Staff General Daniel Allyn, the Army considers a unit fully ready if it "needs no additional people, no additional training, and no additional equipment."[8]

In fiscal year (FY) 2018, the Army's authorized active-duty end strength was 483,500, down from 566,000 as recently as FY 2011.[9] The Obama Administration had planned to cut Active Army end strength further still to 450,000 by 2018,[10] but President Trump's election forestalled those cuts. Although the Bipartisan Budget Act of 2018 has provided a period of stability in 2018–2019 for the Department of Defense (DOD), unless Congress acts, the return of the Budget Control Act (BCA) in 2020 and beyond will serve to reverse recent hard-fought gains in readiness.[11] Army leaders have testified that if BCA-mandated budget caps return in FY 2020, the Army will be able to conduct at best platoon-level training and that "squad and platoon training an Army does not make."[12]

Operationally, the Army has approximately 178,000 soldiers forward stationed across 140 countries. Of the total number of U.S. forces deployed globally, according to Army Deputy Chief of Staff Lieutenant General Joseph Anderson, "[t]he U.S. Army currently fills 50 percent of Combatant Command base force demand and 70 percent of emergent force demand,"[13] which highlights the oversized role that the Army plays in the nation's defense.

Capacity

The 2018 NDAA increased Army authorized end strength to 1,026,500 soldiers: 483,500 in the Regular Army, 199,500 in the Army Reserve, and 343,500 in the Army National Guard, reversing years of reductions.[14] As noted, General Milley has testified that the Army is too small for the missions it has been assigned and that the Army is "shooting to get north of 500,000...in the regular Army."[15] He has previously testified that he believes that the Active Army should number from 540,000 to 550,000, the Army National Guard from 350,000 to 355,000, and the Army Reserve from 205,000 to 209,000.[16]

The Army normally refers to its capacity in terms of brigade combat teams. BCTs are the basic building blocks for employment of Army combat forces. They are usually employed within a larger framework of U.S. land operations but are equipped and organized so that they can conduct independent operations as circumstances demand.[17] A BCT averages 4,500 soldiers depending on its variant: Stryker, Armored, or Infantry. A Stryker BCT is a mechanized infantry force organized around the Stryker combat vehicle. Armored BCTs are the Army's primary armored units and principally employ the M1 Abrams main battle tank and the M2 Bradley fighting vehicle. An Infantry BCT is a highly maneuverable motorized unit. Variants of the Infantry BCT are the Airmobile BCT (optimized for helicopter assault) and the Airborne BCT (optimized for parachute forcible entry operations).

The Army also has a separate air component organized into combat aviation brigades (CABs), which can operate independently.[18] CABs are made up of Army rotorcraft, such as the AH-64 Apache, and perform various roles including attack, reconnaissance, and lift.

CABs and Stryker, Infantry, and Armored BCTs make up the Army's main combat forces, but they do not make up the entirety of the Army. About 90,000 troops form the Institutional Army and provide such forms of support as preparing and training troops for deployments, carrying out key logistics tasks, and overseeing military schools and Army educational institutions. The troops constituting the Institutional Army cannot be reduced at the same ratio as BCTs or CABs, and the Army endeavors to insulate these soldiers from drawdown and restructuring proposals in order to "retain a slightly more senior force in the Active Army to allow growth if needed."[19] In addition to the Institutional Army, a great number of functional or multifunctional support brigades (amounting to approximately 13 percent of the active component force based on historical averages[20]) provide air defense; engineering; explosive ordnance disposal (EOD); chemical/biological/radiological and nuclear protection; military police; military intelligence; and medical support among other types of battlefield support for BCTs.

While end strength is a valuable metric in understanding Army capacity, the number of BCTs is a more telling measure of actual hard power. In preparation for the reduction of its end strength to 460,000, the planned level for FY 2017,[21] the Active Army underwent brigade restructuring that decreased the number of BCTs from 38 to 31. When Congress reversed the reduction in end strength and authorized growth starting in 2017 and reaching an active-duty level of 483,500 for 2018, instead of "re-growing" BCTs, the Army chose primarily to "thicken" the force and raise the manning levels within the individual BCTs to increase unit readiness.[22] The Army recently reported that 21 of its 31 BCTs are now manned at 100 percent.[23]

The 2015 NDAA established a National Commission on the Future of the Army to conduct a comprehensive study of Army structure. To meet the threat posed by a resurgent Russia and others, the commission recommended that the Army increase its numbers of Armored BCTs.[24] The Army converted one Infantry BCT to Armored in 2018, and the FY 2019 budget supports the conversion of another Infantry BCT to Armored, marking the creation of the Army's 16th Armored BCT.[25]

In 2017, in a major initiative personally shepherded by General Milley, the Army established the first of six planned Security Force Assistance Brigades (SFABs). These units, composed of about 530 personnel each, are designed specifically to train, advise, and mentor other partner-nation military units. The Army had been using regular BCTs for this mission, but because train-and-assist missions typically require senior officers and noncommissioned officers, a BCT comprised predominantly of junior soldiers is a poor fit. The Army envisions that these SFABs will be able to reduce the stress on the service.[26] The Army activated its second SFAB in January 2018 at Fort Bragg, North Carolina. It also plans to activate a third Regular Army and first National Guard unit later in 2018 and the final two SFABs in 2019. The first SFAB is currently in Afghanistan.[27]

The number of Army aviation units also has been reduced. In May 2015, the Army deactivated one of its 12 Combat Aviation Brigades (CABs),[28] leaving only 11 in the Regular Army.[29]

The reductions in end strength since 2011 have had a disproportionate effect on BCTs. Authorized end strength for the Active Army has decreased from 45 BCTs (552,100 soldiers) in FY 2013 to 31 BCTs (483,500 soldiers) in FY 2019.[30] Put another way, a 14 percent reduction in troop numbers has led to a 31 percent reduction in BCTs.

In addition to the increased strategic risk, the result of fewer BCTs and a reduced Army end strength, combined with an undiminished daily global demand, has been a sustained level of operational tempo (OPTEMPO). Despite a reduction in large unit deployments,

particularly to Iraq and Afghanistan, Army units continue to experience sustained demand. General Robert Abrams, Commander of Army Forces Command, recently put it bluntly: "[T]he deployment tempo has not slowed down." Recent Army Forces Command data reflect that division headquarters are deploying every 14 to 16 months, Armored Brigade Combat Teams every 15 months, and Stryker and Infantry BCTs every 12–14 months.[31]

Included in these deployments are the rotations of Armored BCTs to and from Europe and Korea. Rather than relying on forward-stationed BCTs, the Army now rotates Armored BCTs to Europe and Korea on a "heel-to-toe" basis. There is an ongoing debate whether the rotational BCT or the forward-stationed BCT represents the best option. Proponents of rotational BCTs argue that the BCTs arrive fully trained and remain at a high state of readiness throughout a typical nine-month overseas rotation; those who favor forward-stationed forces point to a lower cost, forces that typically are more familiar with the operating environment, and a more reassuring presence for our allies.[32]

In the past 24 months, the Army has made a deliberate decision to increase the integration and readiness of select Army National Guard and Reserve formations so that they can be employed more easily when needed. In March 2016, the Army initiated an Associated Units pilot program to link select Regular Army and Reserve component units. As one such example, Georgia's National Guard 48th Infantry BCT was associated with the Regular Army's 3rd Infantry Division at Fort Stewart, Georgia. Twenty-seven units across the country are participating in the pilot program, which will be evaluated in March 2019 to determine whether it should be made permanent.[33]

Additionally, the Army is resourcing select Army National Guard BCTs and other units with additional numbers of training days, moving from the standard number of 39 training days to as many as 63 per year to increase readiness levels. Under a concept called "Army National Guard 4.0," the National Guard is implementing a multi-year training cycle to build readiness over time. As part of this concept, the Army has increased the number of Army Reserve/National Guard (ARNG) BCTs participating in a Combat Training Center (CTC) rotation from two to four starting in FY 2019.[34]

As a result of this change in strategy and the increased investment in the National Guard, the 2019 *Index of U.S. Military Strength* counts four ARNG BCTs in the overall Army BCT capacity count, reflecting their ability to be employed on a dramatically shortened timeline as a result of their training at a Combat Training Center and the increased number of training days.

Capability

The Army's main combat platforms are ground vehicles and rotorcraft. The Abrams Main Battle Tank (latest version: M1A2 SEPv3, service entry date 2017) and Bradley Fighting Vehicle (latest version: M2A4, service entry date 2012) are found primarily in Armored BCTs.[35] Also in Armored BCTs, the venerable M113 personnel carrier is scheduled to be replaced by the new Armored Multi-Purpose Vehicle (AMPV), which is entering its late testing phase.[36] Stryker BCTs are equipped with Stryker vehicles. In response to an Operational Needs Statement, the Stryker BCT in Europe is receiving Strykers fitted with a 30mm cannon to provide an improved anti-armor capability. Fielding began in 2017.[37] Infantry BCTs have fewer vehicles and rely on lighter platforms such as trucks and High Mobility Multipurpose Wheeled Vehicles (HMMWVs) for mobility. Airborne BCTs are scheduled to receive a new platform, the Ground Mobility Vehicle (GMV), starting in 2019 to increase their speed and mobility.[38] Finally, CABs are composed of Army helicopters including AH-64 Apaches, UH-60 Black Hawks, and CH-47 Chinooks.

Overall, the Army's equipment inventory, while increasingly dated, is well maintained. Despite high usage in Afghanistan and Iraq, because the Army deliberately undertook a "reset" plan, most Army vehicles are relatively "young" because recent remanufacture programs for the Abrams and Bradley vehicles have extended the service life of both vehicles beyond FY 2028.[39]

While the current equipment is well maintained and has received several incremental upgrades, Abrams and Bradley fighting vehicles first entered service in the early 1980s, making them 38 years old in many cases.

The Army has also been methodically upgrading the oldest variants of its rotorcraft. Today, the UH-60M, the newest version of the UH-60, makes up approximately two-thirds of the total UH-60 inventory. Similarly, the CH-47F Chinook, a rebuilt variant of the Army's CH-47D heavy lift helicopter, is expected to "remain the Army's heavy lift helicopter for the next several decades."[40] Despite major plus-ups to Army procurement in 2019, the 2019 budget request for aircraft procurement, at $2.8 billion,[41] is $172 million less than the FY 2018 President's budget, reflecting that the Army has beefed up procurement programs other than aviation.

In addition to the viability of today's equipment, the military must ensure the health of future programs. Although future modernizing programs are not current hard-power capabilities that can be applied against an enemy force today, they are a significant indicator of a service's overall fitness for future sustained combat operations. The service may be able to engage an enemy but be forced to do so with aging equipment and no program in place to maintain viability or endurance in sustained operations.

The U.S. military services are continually assessing how best to stay a step ahead of competitors: whether to modernize the force today with currently available technology or wait to see what investments in research and development produce years down the road. Technologies mature and proliferate, becoming more accessible to a wider array of actors over time.

After years of a singular focus on counterinsurgency due to the wars in Iraq and Afghanistan, followed by a concentration on the readiness of the force, the Army is now playing catch-up in the area of equipment modernization. Army leaders have testified that "a combination of strategic, technological, institutional, and budgetary trends places at risk the Army's competitive edge over near-peer competitors in the next fight."[42]

Secretary of the Army Mark Esper has established a new four-star headquarters, Army Futures Command, to manage modernization. It achieved initial operating capability (IOC) in the summer of 2018.[43] Additionally, the Army has established eight cross-functional teams (CFTs) to better manage its top modernization priorities.[44] Army leadership, in particular the Under Secretary and Vice Chief of Staff of the Army, are said to be devoting an extraordinary amount of time to issues of equipment modernization, but only time will tell whether the new structures, commands, and emphasis will result in long-term improvement in modernization posture. When asked to summarize the situation with respect to Army modernization in November 2016, Major General Eric Wesley, Commanding General, U.S. Army Maneuver Center of Excellence, repeated an assessment that "of 10 major capabilities that we use for warfighting, by the year 2030, Russia will have exceeded our capacity in six, we will have parity in three, and the United States will dominate in one."[45] This assessment has not materially changed since then.

The anemic nature of the Army's modernization program is best illustrated by the fact that its highest-profile Major Defense Acquisition Program (MDAP) is a *truck* program, the Joint Light Tactical Vehicle (JLTV). Intended to combine the protection offered by Mine Resistant Ambush Protected Vehicles (MRAPs) with the mobility of the original unarmored HMMWV, the JLTV is a follow-on to the HMMWV (also known as the Humvee) and features design improvements that will increase its survivability against anti-armor weapons and improvised explosive devices (IEDs). The Army plans to procure 49,099 vehicles over the life of the program, replacing only a portion of the current HMMWV fleet. The program is heavily focused on vehicle survivability and is not intended as a one-for-one replacement of the HMMWV. In fact, the JLTV is intended to take on high-risk missions traditionally tasked to the HMMWV, to include scouting and troop transport in adverse environments, guerrilla ambushes, and artillery bombardment.[46]

FY 2019 Base Procurement of $1.3 billion supports 3,390 JLTVs of various configurations to fulfill the requirements of multiple mission roles and minimize ownership costs for the Army's Light Tactical Vehicle fleet.[47]

Other notable Army procurements requested in the FY 2019 budget include the M1A2 Abrams SEPv3 upgrade (135); M2 Bradley modifications (210); M109A6 Paladin 155mm Howitzers (Paladin Integrated Management) (36); and munitions including the Guided Multiple Launch Rocket System (GMLRS) (9,450) and a large number of 155mm artillery projectiles (148,287).[48]

Similar to the rest of their modernization programs, the Army's rotorcraft modernization programs do not include any new platform designs. Instead, the Army is upgrading current rotorcraft to account for more advanced systems.

The Army's main modernization programs are not currently encumbered by any major problems, but there is justifiable concern about the lack of new development programs underway. "The Army is engaged in a protracted struggle to out-innovate future competitors," in the words of the two senior Army officers directly responsible for equipment modernization, "and right now, we are not postured for success. If the Army does not modernize its force to expand and maintain overmatch, we face the potential of being out-matched in high-end conventional combat."[49]

Readiness

The combined effects of the Budget Control Act of 2011, the unrelenting global demand for forces, and reductions in end strength have caused Army readiness to decline to the point where only half of Active Army BCTs are now considered "ready" and only eight are considered "fully ready."[50] The Chief of Staff of the Army has testified that the Army's goal is to have two-thirds of Active Army BCTs ready.[51]

As part of the $700 billion provided for defense in the 2018 omnibus appropriations bill,

FIGURE 1

Army Readiness: Brigade Combat Teams

Based on historical force requirements, Heritage experts assess that the Army needs a total of 50 Brigade Combat Teams (BCTs). In addition to active-duty forces, the Army National Guard has four BCTs that operate at a high level of readiness.

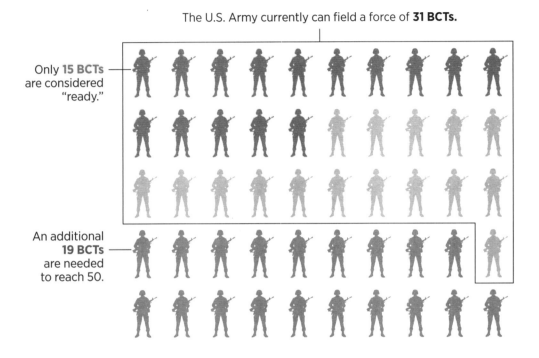

The U.S. Army currently can field a force of **31 BCTs.**

Only **15 BCTs** are considered "ready."

An additional **19 BCTs** are needed to reach 50.

SOURCES: *Congressional Quarterly*, "House Armed Services Committee Holds Hearing on the State of the Military," CQ Congressional Transcripts, February 7, 2017, https://plus.cq.com/doc/congressionaltranscripts-5036905?7 (accessed May 23, 2018), and Heritage Foundation research.

☎ heritage.org

Congress provided much-needed relief to the Army by appropriating approximately $164 billion. Combined with the total increase of 12,334 soldiers in all components of Army end strength authorized in the 2018 NDAA, this provided critical resources needed to rebuild Army readiness.

In the FY 2019 budget request, training activities are relatively well resourced. When measuring training resourcing, the Army uses training miles and flying hours, which reflect the number of miles that formations are resourced to drive their primary vehicles and

aviators can fly their helicopters.[52] According to the Department of the Army's budget justification exhibits, "[t]he FY 2019 budget funds 1,279 annual Operating Tempo Full Spectrum Training Miles and 10.8 flying hours per crew, per month for an expected overall training proficiency of BCT(–)."[53] These are higher than resourced levels of 1,188 miles and 10.6 hours in FY 2018.[54]

Nonetheless, structural readiness problems summarized by too small a force attempting to satisfy too many global presence requirements and Operations Plan (OPLAN) warfighting requirements have led to a force that is both unable to achieve all required training events and overly stressed. As a result, the Army reports that "[d]espite increased funding in 2017 and 2018, the Army remains at high military risk of not meeting the demands of current operations while also responding to two near-simultaneous contingencies."[55] As a result of years of high operational tempos and sustained budget cuts, the Army now does not expect to return to desired levels of "full spectrum readiness" until 2022.[56]

These reduced levels of readiness mean that only a select number of BCTs are available and ready for decisive action. As a function of resources, time, and available force structure, this has resulted in approximately one-half of the 31 Active BCTs being ready for contingency operations in FY 2018 compared to a desired readiness level of two-thirds, although this is still an improvement over 2017, when only one-third of the Active BCTs were judged "ready."[57]

As part of its new Sustainable Readiness Model (SRM),[58] the Army uses Combat Training Centers (CTCs) to train its forces to desired levels of proficiency. Specifically, the CTC program's mission is to "provide realistic Joint and combined arms training" to approximate actual combat and increase "unit readiness for deployment and warfighting."[59] The Army requested resources for 20 CTC rotations in FY 2019, including four for the Army National Guard.[60] Another change in the Army's training model involves the implementation of a system of Objective T metrics that seeks to remove the subjectivity behind unit commander evaluations of training. Under the Objective T program, the requirements that must be met for a unit to be assessed as fully ready for combat are to be made clear and quantitative.[61]

The ongoing challenge for the Army remains a serious one: Despite increased levels of funding for training and modernization, if the size of the Army remains the same and global demand does not diminish, the Army risks consuming readiness as fast as it builds it, which means that the date by which Army leaders hope to regain full spectrum readiness (2022) could continue to be pushed back, prolonging strategic risk for the nation.

Another key factor in readiness is available quantities of munitions. The Army's chief logistician, Lieutenant General Aundre Piggee, Deputy Chief of Staff, G-4, testified in 2017 about shortages of "preferred munitions—Patriot, THAAD, Hellfire and our Excalibur which are howitzer munitions," adding that "if we had to surge, if we had a contingency operation, and if there...continue to be emerging threats which we see around the world, I am very concerned with our current stockage of munitions."[62] These shortages have persisted into 2018.

Scoring the U.S. Army

Capacity Score: Weak

Historical evidence shows that, on average, the Army needs 21 brigade combat teams to fight one major regional conflict. Based on a conversion of roughly 3.5 BCTs per division, the Army deployed 21 BCTs in Korea, 25 in Vietnam, 14 in the Persian Gulf War, and around four in Operation Iraqi Freedom—an average of 16 BCTs (or 21 if the much smaller Operation Iraqi Freedom initial invasion operation is excluded). In the 2010 Quadrennial Defense Review, the Obama Administration recommended a force capable of deploying 45 Active BCTs. Previous government force-sizing documents discuss Army force structure in terms of divisions; they consistently advocate for 10–11 divisions, which equates to roughly 37 Active BCTs.

Considering the varying recommendations of 35–45 BCTs and the actual experience of nearly 21 BCTs deployed per major engagement, our assessment is that 42 BCTs would be needed to fight two MRCs.[63] Taking into account the need for a strategic reserve, the Army force should also include an additional 20 percent of the 42 BCTs.

Because of the investment the Army has made in National Guard readiness, this *Index* counts four additional ARNG BCTs in the Army's overall BCT count, giving them 35 (31 Regular Army plus four ARNG), but 35 is still not enough to meet the two-MRC construct. The service's overall capability score therefore remains unchanged from 2018.

- **Two-MRC Benchmark:** 50 brigade combat teams.

- **Actual 2018 Level:** 35 (31 active + four ARNG) brigade combat teams.

The Army's current BCT capacity meets 70 percent of the two-MRC benchmark and thus is scored as "weak."

Capability Score: Marginal

The Army's aggregate capability score remains "marginal." This aggregate score is a result of "marginal" scores for "Age of Equipment," "Size of Modernization Programs," and "Health of Modernization Programs." More detail on these programs can be found in the equipment appendix following this section. The Army scored "weak" for "Capability of Equipment."

In spite of modest progress with the JLTV and AMPV, and in spite of promising developments in the form of announcements regarding Army Futures Command, CFTs, and new modernization priorities, Army equipment programs are largely still in the planning stage

and have not entered procurement phases and thus are not yet replacing legacy platforms. These planned procurements are highly sensitive to any turbulence or reduction in funding.

Readiness Score: Strong

About half of Active BCTs were ready according to the Army Chief of Staff in April 2018.[64] The Army has 31 Active BCTs; therefore, roughly 15 of the Active Army BCTs were considered ready. The Army's internal requirement for Active BCT readiness is 66 percent, or 20.5 BCTs ready. Using the assessment methods of this *Index*, this results in a percentage of service requirement of 73 percent, or "strong." However, it should be noted that Lieutenant General Joseph Anderson, the Army Operations Officer, also reported in April 2018 that of the 15 BCTs considered "ready," only eight were considered "fully ready," meaning that they needed no additional training, personnel or equipment.[65]

Overall U.S. Army Score: Marginal

The Army's overall score is calculated based on an unweighted average of its capacity, capability, and readiness scores. The average score was 3; thus, the overall Army score is "marginal." This was derived from the aggregate score for capacity ("weak"); capability ("marginal"); and readiness ("strong"). This score is an increase over the assessment of the 2018 *Index*, which rated the Army as "weak." The increase was driven by increased BCT readiness.

U.S. Military Power: Army

	VERY WEAK	WEAK	MARGINAL	STRONG	VERY STRONG
Capacity		✔			
Capability			✔		
Readiness				✔	
OVERALL			✔		

ARMY SCORES

Main Battle Tank

PLATFORM	Age Score	Capability Score	MODERNIZATION PROGRAM	Size Score	Health Score
M1A1/2 Abrams Inventory: **775/1,609** Fleet age: **28/7.5** Date: **1980** The Abrams is the main battle tank used by the Army in its armored brigade combat teams (BCTs). The Abrams went through a remanufacture program to extend its life to 2045.	④	④	**Next Generation Combat Vehicles (NGCV)** The NGCV program is intended to replace the Bradley fighting vehicle and the Abrams tank, and is number two among the Army's "Big Six" modernization priorities.		

Infantry Fighting Vehicle

PLATFORM	Age Score	Capability Score	MODERNIZATION PROGRAM	Size Score	Health Score
M2 Bradley Inventory: **6,547** Fleet age: **13** Date: **1981** The Bradley is a tracked infantry fighting vehicle (IFV) meant to transport infantry and provide covering fire. The Bradley complements the Abrams tank in armored BCTs. Originally intended to be replaced by the Ground Combat Vehicle (now canceled), the Bradley underwent a remanufacture program to extend the life of the platform. The Army plans to keep the Bradley in service until 2045.	④	②	**Next Generation Combat Vehicles (NGCV)** The NGCV program is intended to replace the Bradley fighting vehicle and the Abrams tank, and is number two among the Army's "Big Six" modernization priorities.		

Armored Fighting Vehicle

PLATFORM	Age Score	Capability Score	MODERNIZATION PROGRAM	Size Score	Health Score
Stryker Inventory: **3,892** Fleet age: **12** Date: **2002** The Stryker is a wheeled armored fighting vehicle that makes up the Stryker BCTs. The program was considered an interim vehicle to serve until the arrival of the Future Combat System (FCS), but that program was cancelled due to technology and cost hurdles. The Stryker is undergoing modifications to receive a double-v hull (DVH) to increase survivability. The Stryker is expected to remain in service for 30 years.	④	③	None		

See Methodology for descriptions of scores.   Fleet age—Average age of fleet   Date—Year fleet first entered service

ARMY SCORES

Armored Personnel Carrier

PLATFORM	Age Score	Capability Score	MODERNIZATION PROGRAM	Size Score	Health Score
M113 Armored Personnel Carrier Inventory: **3,000** Fleet age: **19** Date: **1960** The M113 is a tracked APC that plays a supporting role for armored BCTs and infantry BCTs. The APC was also to be replaced by the GCV. Plans are to use the platform until 2045.	③	❶	**Armored Multi-Purpose Vehicle (AMPV)** Timeline: **2018–2035** The AMPV will be adapted from an existing vehicle design which allowed the program to bypass the technology development phase. Initial operation capability is not expected until 2022.	②	❺

PROCUREMENT

42   2,894

SPENDING ($ millions)

$739 $13,036

Light Wheeled Vehicle

PLATFORM	Age Score	Capability Score	MODERNIZATION PROGRAM	Size Score	Health Score
HMMWV Inventory: **150,000** Fleet age: **10.5** Date: **1985** The HMMWV is a light wheeled vehicle used to transport troops under some level of protection. The expected life span of the HMMWV is 15 years. Some HMMWVs will be replaced by the Joint Light Tactical Vehicle (JLTV).	②	❶	**Joint Light Tactical Vehicle (JLTV)** Timeline: **2015–2036** Currently in development, the JLTV is a vehicle program meant to replace some of the HMMWVs and improve reliability and survivability of vehicles. So far the program has experienced a one-year delay due to changes in vehicle requirements. This is a joint program with USMC. IOC is anticipated at the end of 2019 for the Army.	❶	④

PROCUREMENT

4,800   44,299

SPENDING ($ millions)

$3,001 $25,028

See Methodology for descriptions of scores.   Fleet age—Average age of fleet   Date—Year fleet first entered service

ARMY SCORES

Attack Helicopter

PLATFORM	Age Score	Capability Score	MODERNIZATION PROGRAM	Size Score	Health Score
AH-64 D Apache Inventory: **400** Fleet age: **13** Date: **1984** The Apache is an attack helicopter that makes up the Army Combat Aviation Brigades. The expected life cycle is about 20 years.	❶		**AH-64E Reman** Timeline: **2010–2024** The AH-64E Reman is a program to remanufacture old Apache helicopters into the more advanced AH-64E version. The AH-64E will have more modern and interoperable systems and be able to carry modern munitions. **PROCUREMENT** 341 / 298 **SPENDING** (\$ millions) \$8,500 / \$6,048	②	④
		②			
AH-64E Inventory: **203** Fleet age: **4** Date: **2013** The AH-64E variant of the Apache is a remanufactured version with substantial upgrades in powerplant, avionics, communications, and weapons capabilities. The expected life cycle is about 20 years.	❺		**AH-64E New Build** Timeline: **2013–2028** The AH-64E New Build pays for the production of new Apaches. The program is meant to modernize and sustain the current Apache inventory. The AH-64E will have more modern and interoperable systems and be able to carry modern munitions. FY 2019 defense appropriation support increased procurement quantities to address national guard shortfalls. **PROCUREMENT** 58 **SPENDING** (\$ millions) \$1,528	②	④

Medium Lift

PLATFORM	Age Score	Capability Score	MODERNIZATION PROGRAM	Size Score	Health Score
UH-60A Black Hawk Inventory: **802** Fleet age: **25** Date: **1979** The Black Hawk UH-60A is a medium-lift utility helicopter. The expected life span is about 25 years. This variant of the Black Hawk is now being replaced by the newer UH-60M variant.	❶		**UH-60M Black Hawk** Timeline: **2005–2030** The UH-60Ms, currently in production, are intended to modernize and replace current Black Hawk inventories. The newer M variant will improve the Black Hawk's range and lift by upgrading the rotor blades, engine, and computers. **PROCUREMENT** 926 / 444 **SPENDING** (\$ millions) \$18,149 / \$9,290	⑤	④
		③			
UH-60M Black Hawk Inventory: **621** Fleet age: **9** Date: **2006** The Black Hawk UH-60M is a medium-lift utility helicopter that is a follow-on to the UH-60A. As the UH-60A is retired, the M variant will be the main medium-lift rotorcraft used by the Army. Expected to remain in service until 2030.	④				

See Methodology for descriptions of scores.   Fleet age—Average age of fleet   Date—Year fleet first entered service

ARMY SCORES

Heavy Lift

PLATFORM	Age Score	Capability Score	MODERNIZATION PROGRAM	Size Score	Health Score
CH-47D Chinook Inventory: **60** Fleet age: **28** Date: **1962** The Chinook is a heavy-lift helicopter. It has an expected life cycle of 20 years. The CH-47Ds were originally upgraded from earlier variants of the CH-47s.	①		**CH-47F** Timeline: **2003–TBD**	⑤	④
CH-47F Chinook Inventory: **390** Fleet age: **4.4** Date: **2001** CH-47F is "a remanufactured version of the CH-47D with a new digital cockpit and modified airframe to reduce vibrations." It also includes a common aviation architecture cockpit and advanced cargo-handling capabilities. The expected life span is 35 years.	⑤	⑤ ⑤	Currently in production, the CH-47F program is intended to keep the fleet of heavy-lift rotorcraft healthy as older variants of the CH-47 are retired. The program includes both remanufactured and new builds of CH-47s. The F variant has engine and airframe upgrades to lower the maintenance requirements. Total procurement numbers include the MH-47G configuration for U.S. Special Operations Command (67 total). FY2018 funding exceeded stated acquisition objectives, citing "emergency requirements."		

PROCUREMENT	SPENDING ($ millions)
548	$15,077

Intelligence, Surveillance, and Reconnaissance (ISR)

PLATFORM	Age Score	Capability Score	MODERNIZATION PROGRAM	Size Score	Health Score
MQ-1C Gray Eagle Inventory: **125** Fleet age: **3** Date: **2009** The Gray Eagle is a medium-altitude long-endurance (MALE) unmanned aerial vehicle (UAV) used to conduct ISR missions. The use of MALE UAVs is a new capability for the Army. The Gray Eagle is currently in production.	⑤	⑤	**MQ-1C Gray Eagle** Timeline: **2010–2016** The MQ-1C UAV provides Army reconnaissance, surveillance, and target acquisition capabilities. The army is continuing to procure MQ1Cs to replace combat losses.	⑤	④

PROCUREMENT	SPENDING ($ millions)	
204	$5,761	$146

SOURCE: Heritage Foundation research using data from government documents and websites. See also Dakota L. Wood, ed., *2019 Index of U.S. Military Strength* (Washington, DC: The Heritage Foundation, 2018), http://index.heritage.org/militarystrength/.

See Methodology for descriptions of scores.   Fleet age—Average age of fleet   Date—Year fleet first entered service

Endnotes

1. Congressional Quarterly, "Senate Appropriations Subcommittee on Defense Holds Hearing on the Fiscal 2019 Budget Request for the Defense Department," CQ Financial Transcripts, May 9, 2018, https://plus.cq.com/doc/financialtranscripts-5314019?6 (accessed June 2, 2018).

2. The Honorable Mark T. Esper, Secretary of the Army, and General Mark A. Milley, Chief of Staff, U.S. Army, statement "On the Posture of the United States Army" before the Committee on Armed Services, U.S. Senate, 115th Cong., 2nd Sess., April 12, 2018, p. 1, https://www.armed-services.senate.gov/imo/media/doc/Esper-Milley_04-12-18.pdf (accessed June 2, 2018).

3. Congressional Quarterly, "Senate Armed Services Committee Holds Hearing on the Fiscal 2019 Budget Request for the Army Department," CQ Financial Transcripts, April 12, 2018, https://plus.cq.com/doc/financialtranscripts-5297588?5 (accessed June 5, 2018).

4. Esper and Milley, statement "On the Posture of the United States Army," April 12, 2018, p. 4.

5. Congressional Quarterly, "Senate Armed Services Committee Holds Hearing on the Fiscal 2019 Budget Request for the Army Department," April 12, 2018.

6. General Daniel Allyn, Vice Chief of Staff, U.S. Army, statement on "Current State of Readiness of the U.S. Forces" before the Subcommittee on Readiness and Management Support, Committee on Armed Services, U.S. Senate, 115th Cong., 1st Sess., February 8, 2017, p. 4, https://www.armed-services.senate.gov/imo/media/doc/Allyn_02-08-17.pdf (accessed May 22, 2018).

7. Congressional Quarterly, "House Armed Services Committee Subcommittee on Readiness Holds Hearing on Army Readiness Posture," CQ Congressional Transcripts, April 19, 2018, https://plus.cq.com/doc/congressionaltranscripts-5302905?9 (accessed May 15, 2018).

8. Congressional Quarterly, "House Armed Services Committee Holds Hearing on the State of the Military," CQ Congressional Transcripts, February 7, 2017, https://plus.cq.com/doc/congressionaltranscripts-5036905?7 (accessed May 23, 2018).

9. Major General Paul A. Chamberlain, Director, Army Budget, and Davis S. Welch, Deputy Director, Army Budget, *Army FY 2019 Budget Overview*, February 2018, p. 6, https://www.asafm.army.mil/documents/BudgetMaterial/FY2019/Army%20FY%20 2019%20Budget%20Overview.pdf (accessed June 5, 2018).

10. Michelle Tan, "Army Lays out Plan to Cut 40,000 Soldiers," *Army Times*, July 10, 2015, http://www.armytimes.com/story/military/pentagon/2015/07/09/army-outlines-40000-cuts/29923339/ (accessed May 23, 2018).

11. Congressional Quarterly, "Senate Armed Services Committee Holds Hearing on the Fiscal 2019 Budget Request for the Army Department," April 12, 2018.

12. Ibid.

13. Congressional Quarterly, "House Armed Services Committee Subcommittee on Readiness Holds Hearing on Army Readiness Posture," April 19, 2018.

14. Chamberlain and Welch, *Army FY 2019 Budget Overview*, p. 6.

15. Congressional Quarterly, "Senate Armed Services Committee Holds Hearing on the Fiscal 2019 Budget Request for the Army Department," April 12, 2018.

16. Congressional Quarterly, "Senate Appropriations Subcommittee on Defense Holds Hearing on the U.S. Army Fiscal 2018 Budget," CQ Congressional Transcripts, June 7, 2017, http://www.cq.com/doc/congressionaltranscripts-5117288?33#speakers (accessed June 5, 2018).

17. U.S. Department of the Army, Field Manual 3-96, *Brigade Combat Team*, October 2015, http://www.apd.army.mil/epubs/DR_pubs/DR_a/pdf/web/fm3_96.pdf (accessed July 26, 2017).

18. Ibid., p. 3-31.

19. Andrew Feickert, "Army Drawdown and Restructuring: Background and Issues for Congress," Congressional Research Service *Report for Members and Committees of Congress*, February 28, 2014, p. 18, https://www.fas.org/sgp/crs/natsec/R42493.pdf (accessed July 18, 2017).

20. The 13 percent estimate is based on a review of historical figures as referenced in U.S. Government Accountability Office, *Army Planning: Comprehensive Risk Assessment Needed for Planned Changes to the Army's Force Structure*, GAO–16–327, April 2016, p. 12, http://www.gao.gov/assets/680/676516.pdf (accessed June 21, 2016).

21. U.S. Department of Defense, Office of the Under Secretary of Defense (Comptroller), *National Defense Budget Estimates for FY 2017*, March 2016, p. 260, http://comptroller.defense.gov/Portals/45/Documents/defbudget/fy2017/FY17_Green_Book.pdf (accessed July 19, 2017).

22. Congressional Quarterly, "House Armed Services Committee Subcommittee on Readiness Holds Hearing on Army Readiness Posture," April 19, 2018.

23. Ibid.

24. National Commission on the Future of the Army, *Report to the President and the Congress of the United States*, January 28, 2016, p. 52, http://www.ncfa.ncr.gov/sites/default/files/NCFA_Full%20Final%20Report_0.pdf (accessed July 19, 2017).

25. Chamberlain and Welch, *Army FY 2019 Budget Overview*, p. 8.

26. C. Todd Lopez, "Security Force Assistance Brigades to Free Brigade Combat Teams from Advise, Assist Mission," U.S. Army, May 18, 2017, https://www.army.mil/article/188004/security_force_assistance_brigades_to_free_brigade_combat_teams_from_advise_assist_mission (accessed July 19, 2017).

27. Congressional Quarterly, "House Armed Services Committee Subcommittee on Readiness Holds Hearing on Army Readiness Posture," April 19, 2018.

28. General Daniel Allyn, Vice Chief of Staff, U.S. Army, statement on "Current State of Readiness of the U.S. Forces in Review of the Defense Authorization Request for Fiscal Year 2017 and the Future Years Defense Program" before the Subcommittee on Readiness and Management Support, Committee on Armed Services, U.S. Senate, 114th Cong., 2nd Sess., March 15, 2016, p. 2, http://www.armed-services.senate.gov/imo/media/doc/Allyn_03-15-16.pdf (accessed June 26, 2016).

29. U.S. Department of the Army, *Department of Defense Fiscal Year (FY) 2018 Budget Estimates, Volume I, Operation and Maintenance, Army: Justification of Estimates*, May 2017, p. 120, https://www.asafm.army.mil/documents/BudgetMaterial/fy2018/oma-v1.pdf (accessed July 18, 2017).

30. Chamberlain and Welch, *Army FY 2019 Budget Overview*, p. 6.

31. Todd South, "Army Works to Balance High Operations Tempo with Increased Training," *Army Times*, October 8, 2017, https://www.armytimes.com/news/your-army/2017/10/08/army-works-to-balance-high-operations-tempo-with-increased-training/ (accessed June 5, 2018).

32. See Andrew Gregory, "Maintaining a Deep Bench: Why Armored BCT Rotations in Europe and Korea Are Best for America's Global Security Requirements," Modern War Institute, July 31, 2017, https://mwi.usma.edu/maintaining-deep-bench-armored-bct-rotations-europe-korea-best-americas-global-security-requirements/ (accessed June 5, 2018), and Daniel Kochis and Thomas Spoehr, "It's Time to Move US Forces Back to Europe," Heritage Foundation *Commentary*, September 15, 2017, https://www.heritage.org/defense/commentary/its-time-move-us-forces-back-europe.

33. David Vergun, "Associated Units Concept Improving Readiness, says MG Jarrard," U.S. Army, November 2, 2017, https://www.army.mil/article/196318/associated_units_concept_improving_readiness_says_mg_jarrard (accessed June 5, 2018).

34. Technical Sergeant Erich B. Smith, "Readiness Enhanced with Army National Guard 4.0 Initiative," U.S. Army, February 26, 2018, https://www.army.mil/article/201131/readiness_enhanced_with_army_national_guard_40_initiative (accessed June 5, 2018).

35. Andrew Feickert, "The Army's M-1 Abrams, M-2/M-3 Bradley, and M-1126 Stryker: Background and Issues for Congress," Congressional Research Service *Report for Members and Committees of Congress*, April 5, 2016, p. 9, https://www.fas.org/sgp/crs/weapons/R44229.pdf (accessed July 26, 2017), and Ashley Givens, "Army Rolls Out Latest Version of Iconic Abrams Main Battle Tank," U.S. Army, October 9, 2017, https://www.army.mil/article/194952/army_rolls_out_latest_version_of_iconic_abrams_main_battle_tank (accessed June 5, 2018).

36. Allen Cone, "BAE Delivers Armored Multi-Purpose Vehicles to Army for Testing," United Press International, April 4, 2018, https://www.upi.com/BAE-delivers-Armored-Multi-Purpose-Vehicles-to-Army-for-testing/5181522850392/ (accessed June 5, 2018).

37. Kyle Rempfer, "New Upgunned Stryker Arrives in Europe," *Army Times*, December 19, 2017, https://www.armytimes.com/news/2017/12/19/new-upgunned-stryker-arrives-in-europe/ (accessed June 5, 2018).

38. Nancy Montgomery, "Flyer-based Vehicle to give 173rd Airborne Troops Speed on the Ground," *Stars and Stripes*, May 10, 2018, https://www.stripes.com/news/flyer-based-vehicle-to-give-173rd-airborne-troops-speed-on-the-ground-1.526208 (accessed June 5, 2018).

39. Feickert, "The Army's M-1 Abrams, M-2/M-3 Bradley, and M-1126 Stryker," p. 1.

40. U.S. Department of the Army, *Department of Defense Fiscal Year (FY) 2019 Budget Estimates, Army: Justification Book of Aircraft Procurement, Army*, February 2018, p. 73, https://www.asafm.army.mil/documents/BudgetMaterial/FY2019/aircraft.pdf (accessed June 5, 2018).

41. U.S. Department of the Army, Assistant Secretary of the Army (Financial Management and Comptroller, *FY 2019 President's Budget Highlights*, February 2018, p. 20, https://www.asafm.army.mil/documents/BudgetMaterial/FY2019/Army%20FY%202019%20Budget%20Highlights.pdf (accessed June 5, 2018).

42. Lieutenant General John M. Murray, Deputy Chief of Staff of the Army, G-8, and Lieutenant General Paul A. Ostrowski, Military Deputy to the Assistant Secretary of the Army for Acquisition, Logistics and Technology, statement on "Army Modernization" before the Subcommittee on Tactical Air and Land Forces, Committee on Armed Services, U.S. House of Representatives, 115th Cong., 2nd Sess., April 18, 2018. p. 2, https://docs.house.gov/meetings/AS/AS25/20180418/108159/HHRG-115-AS25-Wstate-MurrayJ-20180418.pdf (accessed June 5, 2018).

43. Andrew Feickert, "Army Futures Command (AFC)," Congressional Research Service *Insight*, July 16, 2018, https://fas.org/sgp/crs/natsec/IN10889.pdf (accessed July 20, 2018).

44. U.S. Army, Training and Doctrine Command, Army Capability Integration Center, "U.S. Army Modernization Strategy," June 6, 2018, https://www.army.mil/standto/archive_2018-06-06 (accessed July 20, 2018).

45. Courtney McBride, "Wesley: Russia Offers 'Pacing Threat' for Army Modernization Efforts," *Inside Defense*, November 1, 2016, https://insidedefense.com/daily-news/wesley-russia-offers-pacing-threat-army-modernization-efforts (accessed July 18, 2017).

46. U.S. Department of the Army, *Department of Defense Fiscal Year (FY) 2019 Budget Estimates, Army: Justification Book of Other Procurement, Army: Tactical and Support Vehicles, Budget Activity 1*, February 2018, p. 42, https://www.asafm.army.mil/documents/BudgetMaterial/FY2019/opa1.pdf (accessed June 7, 2018).

47. Ibid., p. 43.

48. Chamberlain and Welch, *Army FY 2019 Budget Overview*, p. 8.

49. Murray and Ostrowski, statement on "Army Modernization," April 18, 2018, p. 3.

50. Congressional Quarterly, "Senate Armed Services Committee Holds Hearing on the Fiscal 2019 Budget Request for the Army Department," April 12, 2018, and Congressional Quarterly, "House Armed Services Committee Subcommittee on Readiness Holds Hearing on Army Readiness Posture," April 19, 2018.

51. Ibid.

52. G3/5/7, "OPTEMPO and Full-Spectrum Operations Training," U.S. Army STAND-TO! January 26, 2011, https://www.army.mil/article/50883/optempo_anc_full_spectrum_operations_training (accessed June 7, 2018).

53. U.S. Department of the Army, *Department of the Army Fiscal Year (FY) 2019 Budget Estimates, Volume 1, Operation and Maintenance, Army: Justification of Estimates*, February 2018 (Revised), p. 2, https://www.asafm.army.mil/documents/BudgetMaterial/FY2019/oma-v1.pdf (accessed June 5, 2018).

54. U.S. Department of the Army, *Department of the Army Fiscal Year (FY) 2018 Budget Estimates, Volume 1, Operation and Maintenance, Army: Justification of Estimates*, May 2017, p. 2, https://www.asafm.army.mil/documents/BudgetMaterial/fy2018/oma-v1.pdf (accessed June 5, 2018).

55. U.S. Department of the Army, *Department of Defense Fiscal Year (FY) 2019 Budget Estimates, Volume I, Operation and Maintenance, Army: Justification of Estimates*, February 2018 (Revised), p. 1, https://www.asafm.army.mil/documents/BudgetMaterial/FY2019/oma-v1.pdf (accessed June 5, 2018).

56. Esper and Milley, statement "On the Posture of the United States Army," April 12, 2018, p. 3.

57. Meghann Myers, "Only a Third of the Army's BCTs Are Ready to Deploy. Here's How the Service Plans to Fix That," *Army Times*, May 21, 2018, https://www.armytimes.com/news/your-army/2018/05/21/only-a-third-of-the-armys-bcts-are-ready-to-deploy-heres-how-the-service-plans-to-fix-that/ (accessed July 20, 2018).

58. Army G-3/5/7, "Army Readiness Guidance," U.S. Army STAND-TO! May 19, 2016, https://www.army.mil/standto/2016-05-19 (accessed June 5, 2018).

59. U.S. Department of the Army, "Combat Training Center Program," Army Regulation 350–50, April 3, 2013, p. 1, https://armypubs.army.mil/epubs/DR_pubs/DR_a/pdf/web/ARN8650_AR350_50_Final.pdfhttp://www.apd.army.mil/epubs/DR_pubs/DR_a/pdf/web/r350_50.pdf (accessed August 8, 2017).

60. Chamberlain and Welch, *Army FY 2019 Budget Overview*, p. 8.

61. Michelle Tan, "'Objective T': The Army's New Mission to Track Training," *Army Times*, October 11, 2016, https://www.armytimes.com/articles/objective-t-the-armys-new-mission-to-track-training (accessed June 7, 2018).

62. Congressional Quarterly, "House Armed Services Subcommittee on Readiness Holds Hearing on Current State of U.S. Army Readiness," March 8, 2017, http://www.cq.com/doc/congressionaltranscripts-5057103?2 (accessed June 7, 2018).

63. Note that the first figures derive from an average BCT size of 4,500 and average division size of 15,000. The second set of numbers derives from the current average of around 3.5 BCTs per division and analysis of the structure of each Army division.

64. Congressional Quarterly, "Senate Armed Services Committee Holds Hearing on the Fiscal 2019 Budget Request for the Army Department," April 12, 2018.

65. Congressional Quarterly, "House Armed Services Committee Subcommittee on Readiness Holds Hearing on Army Readiness Posture," April 19, 2018, https://plus.cq.com/doc/congressionaltranscripts-5302905?9 (accessed May 15, 2018).

U.S. Navy

In *A Design for Maintaining Maritime Superiority, Version 1.0,* issued in January 2016, Chief of Naval Operations Admiral John M. Richardson describes the U.S. Navy's mission as follows:

> The United States Navy will be ready to conduct prompt and sustained combat incident to operations at sea. Our Navy will protect America from attack and preserve America's strategic influence in key regions of the world. U.S. naval forces and operations—from the sea floor to space, from deep water to the littorals, and in the information domain—will deter aggression and enable peaceful resolution of crises on terms acceptable to the United States and our allies and partners. If deterrence fails, the Navy will conduct decisive combat operations to defeat any enemy.[1]

The March 2015 update to *A Cooperative Strategy for 21st Century Seapower* provided the basis for understanding the key functions necessary to accomplish this mission.[2]

For much of the post–Cold War period, the Navy, Marine Corps, and Coast Guard (known collectively as the sea services) have enabled the U.S. to project power across the oceans, control activities on the seas when and where needed, provide for the security of coastlines and shipping in maritime areas of interest, and thereby enhance America's deterrent capability without opposition from competitors. However, the ability of competitors to contest U.S. actions has improved, forcing the sea services to revisit their assumptions about gaining access to key regions.

Together, these functional areas—power projection, sea control, maritime security, deterrence, and domain access—constitute the basis for the Navy's strategy. Achieving and sustaining the ability to excel in these functions drives Navy thinking and programmatic efforts.

As the U.S. military's primary maritime arm, the Navy provides the enduring forward global presence that enables the United States to respond quickly to crises around the world. Unlike land forces (or even, to a large extent, air forces), which are tethered to a set of fixed, larger-scale support bases that require consent from host nations, the U.S. Navy can operate freely across the globe and shift its presence wherever needed without any other nation's permission. As a result, naval forces are often the first U.S. forces to respond to a crisis and, through their persistent forward deployments, continue to preserve U.S. security interests long after conflict formally ends. In addition to the ability to project combat power rapidly anywhere in the world, the Navy's peacetime forward presence supports missions that include securing sea lines of communication for the free flow of goods and services, assuring U.S. allies and friends, deterring adversaries, and providing a timely response to crises short of war.

A few key documents inform the Navy's day-to-day fleet requirements:

- The 2018 National Defense Strategy (NDS);[3]

- The Global Force Management Allocation Plan (GFMAP);[4]

- The 2015 update to *A Cooperative Strategy for 21st Century Seapower*; and

- The 2016 *Design for Maintaining Maritime Superiority, Version 1.0.*

The 2018 NDS issued by the Secretary of Defense describes 11 Department of Defense (DOD) objectives for the Navy and the other branches of the U.S. military including "defending the homeland from attack; sustaining Joint Force military advantages, both globally and in key regions; deterring adversaries from aggression against our vital interests; and ensuring common domains remain open and free."[5] The NDS also directs the building of a more lethal, resilient, and agile force to deter and defeat aggression by great-power competitors and adversaries in all warfare domains and across the spectrum of military operations.[6]

In addition, the U.S. Navy must meet forward presence requirements laid out in the fiscal year (FY) 2017 GFMAP, which specifies the force presence needed around the world as determined by the combatant commanders (COCOMs) and the Secretary of Defense. To meet the objectives of the NDS and GFMAP, "the Navy and Marine Corps primary combat force contributors are two Carrier Strike Groups (CSGs) and two Amphibious Ready Groups (ARGs) forward [deployed] at all times, and keeping three additional CSGs and ARGs in a ready use or surge status (2+3) to deploy within 30 days."[7]

The Navy's maritime manifestation of the NDS, the *Navy the Nation Needs (NNN)*, stresses that credible and effective naval power is based on six key pillars—Readiness, Capability, Capacity, Manning, Networks, and Operating Concepts—and that:

These six pillars must remain balanced and scalable in order to field the needed credible naval power, guarding against over-investment in one area that might disadvantage another. This disciplined approach ensures force structure growth accounts for commensurate, properly phased investments across all six pillars—a balanced warfighting investment strategy to fund the total ownership cost of the Navy (manning, support, training, infrastructure, etc.).[8]

This *Index* focuses on three of these pillars—capacity, capability, and readiness—as the primary means to measure U.S. naval strength.

- Sufficient capacity is required both to defeat adversaries in major combat operations and to provide a credible peacetime forward global presence to maintain freedom of the global shipping lanes and deter aggression.

- Naval ships, submarines, and aircraft must also possess the most modern warfighting capabilities including weapons, radar, and command and control systems to maintain a competitive advantage over potential adversaries.

- Finally, these naval platforms must be properly maintained and their sailors must be adequately trained to ensure that they are "ready to fight tonight."

Failure in any one of these critical performance measures drastically increases the risk that the U.S. Navy will not be able to succeed in its mission and ensure the security of the nation and its global interests. For example, if the fleet is sufficiently large but has out-of-date equipment and weapons, and if its sailors are not proficient at warfighting, the Navy will fail to deter adversaries and succeed in battle.

Capacity

The Navy measures capacity by the number of ships rather than the number of sailors, and it does not count all ships equally. The Navy focuses mainly on the size of its "battle force," which is composed of ships it considers to be directly related to its combat missions.[9]

FIGURE 2

Carrier Strike Group

A Carrier Strike Group (CSG) is a principal element of U.S. power projection, conducting missions such as sea control, offensive strike, and air warfare.

Aircraft Carrier (CVN)
Capable of supporting combat operations for a carrier air wing of at least 70 aircraft, providing sea-based air combat and power projection capabilities that can be deployed anywhere in international waters.

Guided Missile Destroyer (DDG)
Surface combatant capable of conducting integrated IAMD, AAW, ASuW, and ASW.

Guided Missile Cruiser (CG)
Large surface combatant (LSC) capable of conducting integrated air and missile defense (IAMD), anti-air warfare (AAW), anti-surface warfare (ASuW), and anti-submarine warfare (ASW). CGs are the preferred platform for serving as the Air and Missile Defense Commander.

Guided-Missile Frigate FFG(x)
Multi-mission small surface combatant (SSC) designed to complement the ASuW and ASW capabilities of the CSG as well as serve as a force multiplier for air defense capable DDGs.

Attack Submarine (SSN)
Multi-mission capable submarines capable of performing ASW and ASuW in defense of the CSG.

Logistics Ship
Provides fuel, dry-stores, and ammunition in support of CSG operations.

SOURCE: The Heritage Foundation research.

☎ heritage.org

The first edition of this *Index* established a benchmark of 346 ships for the minimum battle force fleet required to "fight and win two MRCs and a 20 percent margin that serves as a strategic reserve" as well as maintain a peacetime global forward presence to deter potential aggressors and assure our allies and maritime partners that the nation remains committed to defending its national security interests and alliances. The groundwork for this year's *Index* included an independent review of previous force structure assessments, historical naval combat operations, Navy and Marine Corps guidance on naval force composition, current and near-future maritime threats, U.S. naval strategy, and enduring naval missions to determine whether the *Index* benchmark should be updated.

To provide the 13 carrier strike groups and 12 expeditionary strike groups (ESGs) required to meet the simultaneous two-MRC construct, meet the historical steady-state demand of approximately 100 ships constantly forward deployed, and ensure that ships and aircraft are properly maintained and sailors are adequately trained to "fight tonight," this *Index* assesses that the U.S. requires a minimum of 400 ships. While this represents a significant increase both from the previous benchmark of 346 ships and from the language of the FY 2018 National Defense Authorization Act (NDAA), which specified an official U.S. policy of "not fewer than 355 battle force ships,"[10] the Navy's recent fleet readiness issues and the 2018 NDS's focus on the "reemergence of long-term strategic competition"[11] point to the need for a much larger and more capable fleet.

The vast distances of the world's oceans and the relatively slow average transit speeds of naval warships (15 knots) require that the U.S. Navy maintain sufficient numbers of ships constantly forward deployed in key regions around the world to respond quickly to crises and deter potential aggression. This larger fleet not only includes additional small surface combatants (SSCs) to support the strike groups, but also a significant increase in combat logistics force (CLF) ships to ensure that distributed forces deployed in peacetime and in combat operations can receive timely fuel, food, and ammunition resupply.

On average, four ships in the fleet are required to maintain one ship forward deployed. Most important, the fleet must be large enough to provide the requisite number of CSGs and ESGs when called upon as the primary elements of naval combat power during an MRC operation. Although a 400-ship fleet may be difficult to achieve based on current DOD fiscal constraints and the present shipbuilding industrial base capacity, this *Index* benchmark is budget agnostic and based strictly on assessed force-sizing requirements.

The Navy currently sails 284 vessels as part of its battle force fleet,[12] up from 276 in 2017[13] but still well below both the Navy's goal of 355 ships and the 400-ship fleet required to fight and win two MRCs. The FY 2018 NDAA provides $23.8 billion for the construction of 14 new ships, including one additional Littoral Combat Ship (LCS); accelerates the procurement of the first LPD Flight II and one additional Expeditionary Fast Transport (T-EPF); and adds one ocean survey ship (T-AGS).[14] The Navy has requested the procurement of 10 ships in FY 2019. This is two fewer than recommended in the Congressional Budget Office (CBO) assessment of the average annual ship procurement needed to achieve a 355-ship fleet by 2037.[15]

On average, depending on the ship class, a ship is commissioned and joins the fleet three to five years after it is purchased by the Navy. The Navy plans to commission six additional ships and submarines by the end of 2018[16] and 11 ships and submarines in FY 2019.[17] It also will retire one *Los Angeles*-class nuclear attack submarine (SSN) in FY 2019.[18] The number of ships decommissioned will increase significantly over the next five years as additional *Los Angeles*-class SSNs and mine countermeasure ships (MCMs) reach the end of their service life, slowing the pace at which fleet size can grow.[19] The Navy recently completed a technical evaluation of the "feasibility of extending the service life of selected non-nuclear vessels" and may decide to extend the life of numerous ship classes from seven to 17 years depending on the funding available and shipyard capacity to achieve and maintain a 355-ship Navy more rapidly by reducing ships lost to decommissioning.[20]

The largest proportional shortfall in the Navy fleet assessed in the *2019 Index* is the same as in past editions: small surface combatants.[21] The Navy's current SSC inventory include 13 Littoral Combat Ships and 11 MCM ships for a total of 24 SSCs,[22] 28 below the

FIGURE 3

Expeditionary Strike Group

An Expeditionary Strike Group (ESG) is the primary element of
U.S. amphibious warfare and expeditionary operations.

Amphibious Assault Ship LHA or LHD
A landing helicopter assault ship (LHA) or landing helicopter
dock (LHD). Capable of supporting short take-off vertical
landing (STOVL) operations for embarked Marine strike
aircraft squadron as well as tilt-rotor and helicopter
squadrons. Some of these ships possess a well deck to launch
landing craft to support ship to shore transport of Marines.

**Amphibious Transport Dock (LPD), and
Amphibious Dock Landing Ship (LSD)**
Embarked landing craft and amphibious
assault vehicles (AAV) augmented by
helicopters and tilt-rotor aircraft use LPDs
and LSDs to transport and land Marines,
and their equipment and supplies.

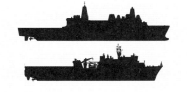

Guided Missile Destroyer (DDG)
LSC capable of conducting integrated
IAMD, AAW, ASuW, and ASW.

Logistics Ship
Provides fuel, dry-stores, and ammunition
in support of CSG operations.

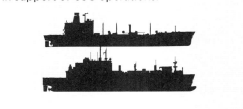

Guided-Missile Frigate FFG(x)
Multi-mission small surface combatant
(SSC) designed to complement the ASuW
and ASW capabilities of the CSG as well as
serve as a force multiplier for air defense
capable DDGs.

SOURCE: The Heritage Foundation research.   ☎ heritage.org

objective requirement of 52 established by
the Navy[23] and 47 less than the 2018 Heritage
Foundation requirement of 71.[24]

The next largest shortfall occurs in CLF
ships. The Navy's current CLF inventory is
comprised of 12 *Lewis and Clark*-class dry cargo and ammunition ships (T-AKE); 15 *Henry J.
Kaiser*-class fleet replenishment oilers (T-AO);

and two *Supply*-class fast combat support ships
(T-AOE), for a total of 29 CLF ships.[25] This is
three below the Navy requirement of 32 ships
and 25 less than the *Index* requirement of 54.[26]

The aircraft carrier force suffers a capacity
shortfall of two hulls: 11 are currently in the
fleet, and the two-MRC construct requires 13.[27]
Current U.S. law requires the Navy to maintain

FIGURE 4

The Case for 13 Carriers

The U.S. Navy carrier fleet is a critical element of U.S. power projection and supports a constant presence in regions of the world where permanent basing is limited. To properly handle this large mission, Heritage Foundation experts recommend a fleet of 13 carriers.

3
The U.S. goal is to maintain one carrier in each of the major regions of the world.

ATLANTIC

PACIFIC

MEDITERRANEAN/ MIDDLE EAST

+9
To be operationally realistic, and to ensure ships, aircraft, and crew are healthy and effective, three additional carriers are needed for each carrier deployed.

RETURNING FROM DEPLOYMENT

UNDERGOING MAINTENANCE

PREPARING FOR DEPLOYMENT

+1
One carrier is almost always undergoing an extensive mid-life overhaul.

☎ heritage.org

a force of "not less than 11 operational aircraft carriers."[28] Representative K. Michael Conaway (R–TX) introduced an amendment to H.R. 5515, the National Defense Authorization Act (NDAA) for Fiscal Year 2019, that would have amended U.S. Code, Title 10, § 5062(b), effective September 30, 2022, to require a minimum of "12 operational aircraft carriers," that the U.S. Navy "expedite delivery of 12 aircraft carriers," and that "an aircraft carrier should be authorized every three years" to keep pace with the loss of carriers as they are retired.[29] The final version of the NDAA as enacted specifies only that "It is the sense of Congress that the United States should accelerate the production of aircraft carriers to rapidly achieve the Navy's goal of having 12 operational aircraft carriers."[30]

The Congressional Research Service (CRS) has assessed that "increasing aircraft carrier procurement from the currently planned rate of one ship every five years...to a rate of one ship every three years...would achieve a 12-carrier force on a sustained basis by about 2030...."[31] The Navy has stated that with its current fleet of only 11 carriers, it cannot meet the requirement to maintain two carriers deployed at all times and three ready to surge deploy within 30 days.[32]

The carrier force fell to 10 from December 2012 until July 2017. During the first week of January 2017, for the first time since World War II, no U.S. aircraft carriers were deployed.[33] The USS *Gerald R. Ford* (CVN-78) was commissioned on July 22, 2017, returning the Navy's carrier force to 11 ships. While the *Ford* is now part of the fleet battle force, it will not be ready for routine flight operations until 2020 and will not operationally deploy until 2022.[34] In addition, through 2037, one *Nimitz*-class carrier at a time will be in a four-year refueling and complex overhaul (RCOH) to modernize the ship and refuel the reactor to support its full 50-year service life. Although the carrier in RCOH will count as a battle force ship, it will not be operationally deployable during this four-year period. The combination of these two factors means that only nine aircraft carriers will be operationally available until 2022.

In December 2016, the U.S. Navy released its latest study of forecasted fleet requirements. The Navy Force Structure Assessment (FSA) was developed to determine the correct balance of existing forces for "ever-evolving and increasingly complex maritime security threats."[35] The Navy concluded that a 653-ship force would be necessary to address all of the demands registered in the FY 2017 Global Force Management (GFM) system. A fleet of 459 ships, 200 fewer than the ideal fleet but thought still to be too expensive given current and projected limits on defense spending, would meet warfighting requirements but accept risk in providing continual presence missions.[36] The Navy's final force objective of 355 ships as recommended by the FSA is based on a minimum force structure that "complies with current defense planning guidance," "meets approved Day 0 and warfighting response timelines," and "delivers future steady state and warfighting requirements with an acceptable degree of risk."[37]

The final recommendation for a 355-ship force is an increase of 47 in the minimum number of ships from the previous requirement of 308. The most significant increases are:

- Aircraft carriers, from 11 to 12;

- Large surface combatants (guided missile destroyers (DDG) and cruisers (CG)), from 88 to 104 "to deliver increased air defense and expeditionary BMD [ballistic missile defense] capacity and provide escorts for the additional Aircraft Carrier";

- Attack submarines (SSNs), from 48 to 66 to "provide the global presence required to support national tasking and prompt warfighting response"; and

- Amphibious ships, from 34 to 38.[38]

Section 1025 of the FY 2018 National Defense Authorization Act states in part that "[i]t shall be the policy of the United States to have available, as soon as practicable, not fewer than 355 battle force ships, comprised of the optimal mix of platforms, with funding subject to the availability of appropriations or other funds."[39] According to the CBO:

> [O]ver the next 30 years, meeting the 355-ship objective would cost the Navy an average of about $26.6 billion (in 2017 dollars) annually for ship construction, which is more than 60 percent above the average amount the Congress has appropriated each year for that purpose over the past 30 years and 40 percent more than the amount appropriated for 2016.[40]

The Navy's SCN (Shipbuilding and Conversion, Navy) request for FY 2019 totaled approximately $21.8 billion,[41] well below the level that the CBO has assessed is necessary to reach fleet goals. As noted, this includes funding for procurement of only 10 battle force ships during this fiscal year, which will make it difficult to increase the fleet size.

The seeming anomaly of increased funding for shipbuilding without a corresponding increase in fleet force structure is due in part to the fact that a significant portion of this funding is dedicated to advanced procurement of the next-generation ballistic missile submarine program (SSBN(X) *Columbia*-class).[42] Additionally, the CRS has estimated that "roughly 15,000 additional sailors and aviation personnel would be needed at sea to operate those 47 additional ships."[43] Although the Department of Defense updated the NDS in early 2018, the Navy has not formally announced any intention to update its 2016 FSA to reflect this new guidance.

The Navy released its *Report to Congress on the Annual Long-Range Plan for the Construction of Naval Vessels for Fiscal Year 2019* (or the 30-year shipbuilding plan) in February

CHART 10

Rate of U.S. Navy Ship Commissionings Nearly Cut in Half

The U.S. Navy must commission an average of 14 ships annually to reach a 400-ship navy by the late-2030s. Its current commissioning rate is about 5 ships annually.

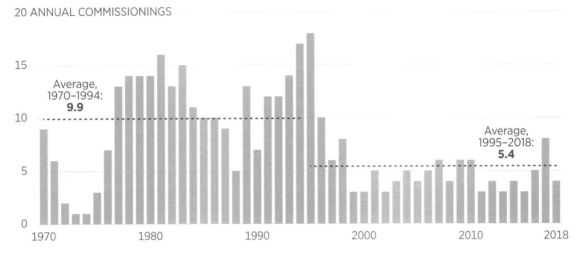

20 ANNUAL COMMISSIONINGS

Average, 1970–1994: **9.9**

Average, 1995–2018: **5.4**

SOURCE: Shipbuilding History, "Large Naval Ships and Submarines," http://www.shipbuildinghistory.com/navalships.htm (accessed August 8, 2018).

☎ heritage.org

2018. This updated plan provides the foundation for building the *Navy the Nation Needs* and ultimately achieving the congressionally mandated requirement for 355 battle force ships. While this plan includes 54 ships within the Future Years Defense Program (FYDP) FY 2019–FY 2023 and 301 ships over the next 30 years, it fails to achieve a 355-ship Navy until beyond 2050. Of significant note, the plan will only reach the 2016 FSA requirements for attack submarines, ballistic submarines, and combat logistics force ships by 2048.[44] The plan averages 10 new ships per year, two fewer than the average number of new ships per year that the CBO assesses is required to reach 355 ships by 2037.[45]

The 30-year shipbuilding plan also includes plans for service life extensions (SLEs) for qualified candidate vessels. The Navy's FY 2019 budget submission includes SLEs for six *Ticonderoga*-class cruisers, four mine countermeasure ships, and the first of potentially five improved *Los Angeles*-class attack submarines.[46] On April 12, 2018, Vice Admiral William

Merz, Deputy Chief of Naval Operations for Warfare Systems, informed the House Armed Services Committee's Seapower and Force Projection Subcommittee that the Navy will extend the entire *Arleigh Burke* destroyer class to a service life of 45 years, enabling the Navy to achieve 355 ships by 2036 or 2037.[47] This destroyer class extension will not provide the required mix of ships per the 2016 FSA, but it will provide additional fleet capacity.

Taken alone, total fleet size can be a misleading statistic; related factors must also be taken into account when considering numbers of ships. One such important factor is the number of ships that are forward deployed to meet operational demands. On average, the Navy maintains approximately one-third of the total fleet deployed at any given time (90–100 ships). The type or class of ship is also important. Operational commanders must have the proper mix of capabilities deployed to enable a timely and effective response to emergent crises.

Not all ships in the battle force are at sea at the same time. The majority of the fleet is

CHART 11

Length of Service Since Commissioning

The number and types of ships commissioned by the U.S. Navy has decreased over the past 20 years. The procurement holiday of the 1990s and decreased emphasis on modernization in a time of fiscal constraints has resulted in a fleet of increasing age.

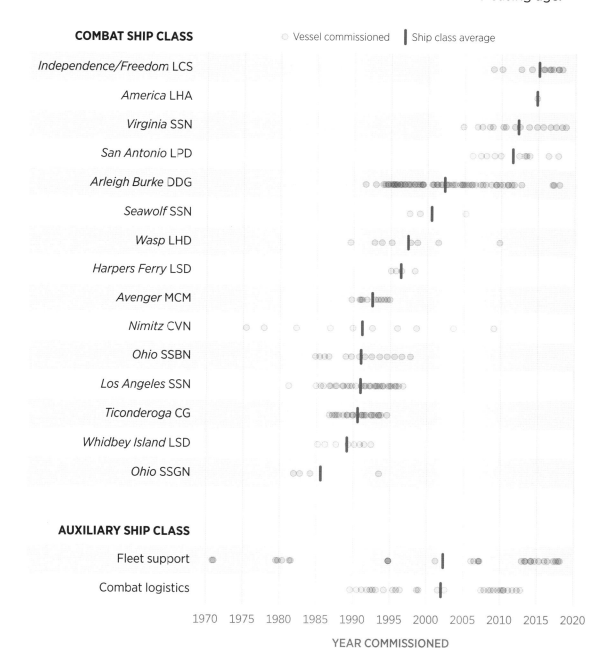

COMBAT SHIP CLASS

○ Vessel commissioned | Ship class average

Independence/Freedom LCS
America LHA
Virginia SSN
San Antonio LPD
Arleigh Burke DDG
Seawolf SSN
Wasp LHD
Harpers Ferry LSD
Avenger MCM
Nimitz CVN
Ohio SSBN
Los Angeles SSN
Ticonderoga CG
Whidbey Island LSD
Ohio SSGN

AUXILIARY SHIP CLASS

Fleet support
Combat logistics

1970 1975 1980 1985 1990 1995 2000 2005 2010 2015 2020

YEAR COMMISSIONED

NOTE: Data are current as of July 30, 2018.
SOURCE: Naval Sea Systems Command, Naval Vessel Register, "Fleet Size,"
http://www.nvr.navy.mil/NVRSHIPS/ FLEETSIZE.HTML (accessed August 6, 2018).

☎ heritage.org

based in the continental United States (CONUS) to undergo routine maintenance and training, as well as to limit deployment time for sailors. However, given the COCOMs' requirements for naval power presence in each of their regions, there is an impetus to have as many ships forward deployed as possible.

In November 2014, the Navy established an Optimized Fleet Response Plan (OFRP) "to ensure continuous availability of manned, maintained, equipped, and trained Navy forces capable of surging forward on short notice while also maintaining long-term sustainability of the force."[48] The plan incorporates four phases of ship availability/maintenance, resulting in a basic ratio of 4:1 for CONUS-based force structure required for deployed platforms. The OFRP is on track to achieve the Navy's goal of "2 deployed and 3 surge ready" carrier strike groups just beyond 2021.[49]

In 2017, the Navy had 104 ships deployed globally (including submarines): 38 percent of the total battle force fleet and an increase from the 94 deployed in 2016.[50] As of August 17, 2018, the Navy had 89 "Deployed Battle Force Across the Fleet Including Forward Deployed Submarines."[51] A primary factor in this decrease is the Navy's improved focus on restoring surface fleet material and mission proficiency readiness following the deadly Seventh Fleet collisions of 2017. While the Navy remains committed to deploying roughly a third of its fleet at all times, capacity shortages have caused the current fleet to fall below the levels needed to fulfill both the Navy's stated forward presence requirements and below the levels needed for a fleet that is capable of projecting power at the two-MRC level.

The Navy has attempted to increase forward presence by emphasizing non-rotational deployments (having a ship "homeported" overseas or keeping it forward stationed):[52]

- **Homeported:** The ships, crew, and their families are stationed at the port or based abroad.

- **Forward Stationed:** Only the ships are based abroad while crews are rotated out to the ship.[53] This deployment model is currently used for LCS and SSGNs manned with rotating blue and gold crews, effectively doubling the normal forward deployment time.

Both of these non-rotational deployment options require formal agreements and cooperation from friends and allies to permit the Navy's use of their facilities, as well as U.S. investment in additional facilities abroad. However, these options allow one ship to provide a greater level of presence than four ships based in CONUS and in rotational deployment because they offset the time needed to deploy ships to distant theaters.[54] The Navy's GFM planning assumptions assume a forward deployed presence rate of 19 percent for a CONUS-based ship compared to a 67 percent presence rate for an overseas-homeported ship.[55]

Capability

Scoring the U.S. Navy's overall ability to protect U.S. interests globally is not simply a matter of counting the fleet. The quality of the battle force is also important in determining naval strength.

A comprehensive measure of platform capability would involve a comparison of each ship and its weapons systems relative to the military capabilities of other nations. For example, a complete measure of naval capabilities would have to assess not only how U.S. platforms would match up against an enemy's weapons, but also whether formal operational concepts would be effective in a conflict, after which the assessment would be replicated for each potential conflict. This is a necessary exercise and one in which the military currently engages, but it is beyond the scope of this *Index* because such details and analysis are routinely classified.

Capability can be usefully assessed based on the age of ships, modernity of the platform, payloads and weapons systems carried by

CHART 12

An Aging U.S. Navy

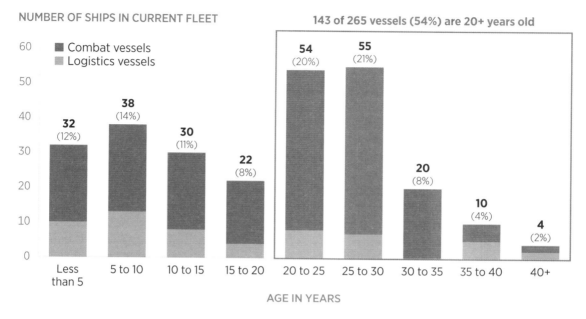

NUMBER OF SHIPS IN CURRENT FLEET

143 of 265 vessels (54%) are 20+ years old

- Combat vessels
- Logistics vessels

32 (12%) | 38 (14%) | 30 (11%) | 22 (8%) | 54 (20%) | 55 (21%) | 20 (8%) | 10 (4%) | 4 (2%)

Less than 5 | 5 to 10 | 10 to 15 | 15 to 20 | 20 to 25 | 25 to 30 | 30 to 35 | 35 to 40 | 40+

AGE IN YEARS

NOTE: Data are current as of August 15, 2018.
SOURCE: Naval Sea Systems Command, Naval Vessel Register, "Fleet Size," http://www.nvr.navy.mil/NVRSHIPS/FLEETSIZE.HTML (accessed August 15, 2018).

☎ heritage.org

ships, and ability of planned modernization programs to maintain the fleet's technological edge. The Navy has several classes of ships that are nearing the end of their life spans, and this will precipitate a consolidation of ship classes in the battle force.

The Navy retired the last of its *Oliver Hazard Perry*-class guided missile frigates in 2015 and since then has been without a multi-mission SSC that can perform anti-submarine warfare (ASW), surface warfare (SuW), and local air defense in support of CSGs and ESGs and as a logistic fleet escort. The Littoral Combat Ship is the only current SSC in the fleet other than the MCM ships.[56] The LCS concept of operations has been modified several times since its original design. The Navy's current plan calls for three divisions on each coast of the United States, each with ships dedicated to a specific mission: ASW, SuW, or MCM.[57]

Planned capability upgrades to give the LCS fleet frigate-like capabilities include "[o]ver-the-horizon surface to surface missile and additional weapon systems and combat system upgrades" and "increased survivability… achieved by incorporating additional self-defense capabilities and increased hardening of vital systems and vital spaces."[58] The Navy recently awarded Raytheon the LCS's over-the-horizon anti-ship (OTH) weapon contract to provide an unspecified number of the Kongsberg-designed Naval Strike Missiles.[59] This encapsulated anti-ship and land attack missile has a range of up to 100 nautical miles and will provide a significant increase in the LCS's offensive capabilities.[60]

Critics of the LCS program have continued to express concerns about "past cost growth, design and construction issues with the first LCSs"; "the survivability of LCSs (i.e., their ability to withstand battle damage)"; "whether LCSs are sufficiently armed and would be able to perform their stated missions effectively"; and "the development and testing of the modular mission packages for LCSs."[61] The annual report from DOD's Director, Operational Test and Evaluation (DOT&E), has contained numerous comments, many of them extremely critical, regarding LCS operational performance and LCS mission modules.[62]

The Administration's FY 2019 budget request includes funding for one LCS. Congress authorized the procurement of three LCSs in the FY 2018 NDAA, meeting the LCS requirement for 32 ships. The Navy has stated that the one additional LCS requested in FY 2019 provides sufficient workload, coupled with the 21 LCSs currently under construction or planned, to "allow [two] shipbuilders to maintain stability and be competitive for the FFG(X) award in FY 2020."[63] Both Austal USA and Lockheed Martin disagreed with the Navy's assessment. Austal responded that "funding one LCS in the FY19 budget is not sufficient to support the Shipbuilding Industrial Base" and that "[a]ny reduction in [production] volume would negatively impact the shipbuilding industrial base, including our suppliers (local and national), as well as the ability to efficiently transition to Frigate."[64] Lockheed Martin countered that with its production rate of two LCS per year, "our current production backlog is insufficient to maintain the employment and efficiency levels required for our team to remain competitive for Frigate."[65]

The Navy projects that the LCS deployable force will reach 16 LCSs by the end of FY 2018 and reach 20 ships by the end of FY 2019.[66] This is still well below the fleet size of 71 small surface combatants necessary to fulfill the Navy's global responsibilities, even when combined with the 11 remaining mine countermeasure vessels in the fleet.

In July 2017, the Navy released a Request for Information to the shipbuilding industry with the goal of building a new class of 20 ships, currently referred to as the future Guided Missile Frigate (FFG(X)), beginning in FY 2010.[67] The Navy stated that:

The purpose of this type of ship is to (1) fully support Combatant and Fleet Commanders during conflict by supplementing the fleet's undersea and surface warfare capabilities, allow for independent operations in a contested environment, extend the fleet tactical grid, and host and control unmanned systems; and (2) relieve large surface combatants from stressing routine duties during operations other than war.[68]

The notional FFG(X) procurement plan would purchase 20 ships over 11 years.[69] The Navy's desire to award the FFG(X) detailed design and construction contract in FY 2020 did not provide sufficient time for a completely new design, instead driving it to build FFG(X) based an existing SSC ship design that can be modified to meet the FFG(X)'s specific capability requirements.[70] On February 16, 2018, the Navy awarded five FFG(X) conceptual design contracts to Austal USA; Huntington Ingalls Industry/Ingalls Shipbuilding (HII/Ingalls); Lockheed Martin; Fincantieri/Marinette Marine (F/MM); and General Dynamics/Bath Iron Works (GD/BIW).[71] The Navy will select one shipbuilder in FY 2020.[72]

The Navy possesses 22 *Ticonderoga*-class cruisers.[73] To save operating expenses, it has been pursuing a plan to put half of this fleet into temporary layup status in order to extend this class's fleet service time into the 2030s—even though these ships are younger than their expected service lives (in other words, have been used less than planned). Under the FY 2015 National Defense Authorization Act:

Congress...directed the Navy to implement the so-called "2-4-6" program for modernizing the 11 youngest Aegis cruisers. Under the 2-4-6 program no more than two of the cruisers are to enter the modernization program each year, none of the cruisers is to remain in a reduced status for modernization for more than four years, and no more than six of the cruisers are to be in the program at any given time....[74]

In FY 2019, the Navy will continue to execute the "2-4-6" plan on seven of 11 cruisers, with the remaining four BMD-capable cruisers to receive scheduled modernization to their hull and support systems throughout their service life.[75] The Navy currently has six cruisers inducted in the modernization program. Along with the USS *Anzio*, inducted in May 2017, the program includes USS *Cape St. George*, inducted in March 2017; USS *Chosin* and USS *Vicksburg*, inducted in FY 2016; and USS *Cowpens* and USS *Gettysburg*, inducted in FY 2015.[76]

The Navy's FY 2019 budget request includes "$276 million for guided missile cruiser modernization and $79 million to upgrade eight cruisers to AEGIS Baseline 9, enabling them to perform critical Integrated Air and Missile Defense (IAMD) and Ballistic Missile Defense (BMD) operations simultaneously."[77] It also requests $5.6 billion for three DDG 51 Flight III destroyers as part of a 10-ship Multi-Year Procurement (MYP), bringing the class size to 82 ships.[78] The Flight III provides a significant capability upgrade to the Navy's integrated air and missile defense with the incorporation of the Air and Missile Defense Radar.

The DDG-1000 *Zumwalt*-class is a "multi-mission destroyer designed with a primary mission of naval surface fire support (NSFS) and operations in littoral (i.e., near-shore) waters."[79] The *Zumwalt*-class has been plagued by cost overruns, schedule delays, and the exorbitant cost of the projectile for its advanced gun system. In July 2008, the Navy announced that it would end procurement of DDG-1000s after the initial three ships because it had "reevaluated the future operating environment and determined that its destroyer program must emphasize three missions: open-ocean antisubmarine warfare (ASW), countering anti-ship cruise missiles (ASCMs), and countering ballistic missiles."[80] The stealthy DDG-1000 hull design cannot support the required ballistic defense capabilities without significant modifications.

In December 2017, the Navy announced that because of changes in global security threats and resulting shifts in Navy mission requirements since the original DDG-1000's missions were established in 1995, it was updating the DDG-1000's primary mission to better reflect the current needs of the Navy and the ship's stealth and other advanced capabilities. The DDG-1000's primary mission will shift from an emphasis on naval gunfire support for Marines on shore to an emphasis on surface strike (the use of missiles to attack surface ships and possibly land targets).[81] The Navy's FY 2019 budget requests $89.7 million to convert the *Zumwalt*-class destroyers by integrating Raytheon's multi-mission SM-6 anti-air and anti-surface missile, as well as the Maritime Strike variant of the Tomahawk missile.[82]

The Navy's 12 landing ships (LSDs), the *Whidbey Island*-class and *Harpers Ferry*-class amphibious vessels, are currently scheduled to reach the end of their 40-year service lives in 2025. The 13-ship LPD-17 Flight II program, previously known as the LX(R) program, will replace these legacy landing ships. The Flight II was designed to be a less costly and subsequently less capable alternative to the LPD-17 Flight I *San Antonio*-class design.[83] Although the first Flight II ship was planned for FY 2020, Congress directed the Navy to accelerate it to FY 2018.[84]

Most of the Navy's battle force fleet consists of legacy platforms. Of the 20 classes of ships in the Navy, only eight are currently in production. For example, 64 percent of the Navy's attack submarines are *Los Angeles*-class submarines, an older platform that is being replaced with a more modern and capable *Virginia*-class.[85]

The 30-year shipbuilding plan is not limited to programs of record and assumes procurement programs that have yet to materialize. Some of the Navy's ship designs in recent years, such as the *Gerald R. Ford*-class aircraft carrier, the *San Antonio*-class amphibious ship, and the Littoral Combat Ship, have proven to be substantially more expensive to build than the Navy originally estimated.[86] The first ship of any class is typically more expensive than early estimates project, which is

CHART 13

Combat Fleets Pushing Limits of Life Expectancy

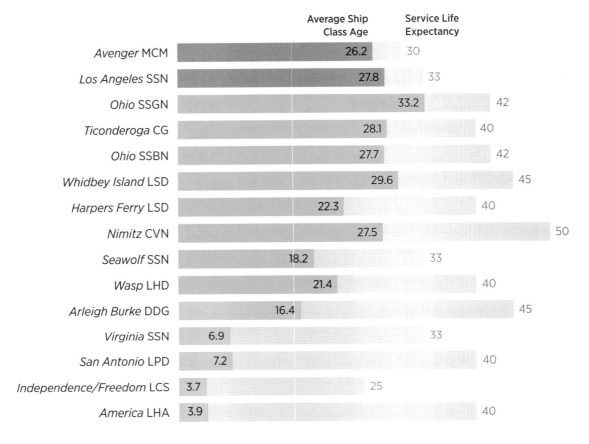

AVERAGE SHIP CLASS AGE AS PERCENTAGE OF SERVICE LIFE EXPECTANCY: ▪ <50% ▪ 50%–75% ▪ 75%+

	Average Ship Class Age	Service Life Expectancy
Avenger MCM	26.2	30
Los Angeles SSN	27.8	33
Ohio SSGN	33.2	42
Ticonderoga CG	28.1	40
Ohio SSBN	27.7	42
Whidbey Island LSD	29.6	45
Harpers Ferry LSD	22.3	40
Nimitz CVN	27.5	50
Seawolf SSN	18.2	33
Wasp LHD	21.4	40
Arleigh Burke DDG	16.4	45
Virginia SSN	6.9	33
San Antonio LPD	7.2	40
Independence/Freedom LCS	3.7	25
America LHA	3.9	40

NOTE: Average Ship Class Age is as of October 2018.
SOURCE: Heritage Foundation research based on data from the U.S. Department of the Navy, U.S. Department of Defense, U.S. Government Publishing Office, and other sources.

☎ heritage.org

not entirely surprising given the technology assumptions and cost estimates that must be made several years before actual construction begins. Although the CBO has reported that only two of the last 11 lead ships have been delivered over budget, the trend has been downward for the most recent classes.[87] In addition, the Navy is acting to ensure that critical technologies are fully mature (T-AO 205 *John Lewis*-class Fleet Replenishment Oiler) before incorporation into ship design and requiring greater design completion (83

percent for *Columbia* ballistic missile submarine) before actual production.[88]

Many consider the 30-year shipbuilding plan to be optimistic based on recent history. For example, the Navy received $24 billion more in shipbuilding funding than planned yet purchased 50 fewer ships than outlined in the 2007 long-range shipbuilding plan.[89]

The goal of 355 ships stated in the Navy's most recent 30-year plan includes an objective for 12 *Columbia*-class nuclear ballistic missile submarines (SSBNs) to replace the legacy *Ohio*-class SSBN. Production of these 12 *Columbia*-class submarines will require a significant portion of the Navy's shipbuilding funding if the overall budget is not increased.

The Navy's FY 2013 budget deferred procurement of the lead boat from FY 2019 to FY 2021, with the result that "the Navy's SSBN force will drop to 11 or 10 boats for the period FY2029–FY2041."[90] This is something that the Navy will continue to have difficulty maintaining as it struggles to sustain, overhaul, modernize, and eventually retire the remainder of its legacy SSBN fleet. The *Columbia*-class SSBN is "the Navy's top priority program"[91] and has been allocated $3 billion—almost 15 percent of its total shipbuilding budget—in the Navy's FY 2019 request for "detail design efforts, continuous missile tube production, and Advanced Construction of major hull components and propulsion systems."[92]

The Navy's long-range strike capability derives from its ability to launch various missiles and combat aircraft. Naval aircraft are much more expensive and difficult to modernize as a class than missiles are. Until the 1980s, the Navy operated several models of strike aircraft that included the F-14 Tomcat, A-6 Intruder, A-4 Skyhawk, and F/A-18 Hornet. The last of the A-6, A-4, and F-14 aircraft were retired, respectively, in 1997, 2003, and 2006.

Over the past 20 years, this variety has been winnowed to a single model: the F/A-18. The F/A-18A-D Legacy Hornet has served since 1983; it is out of production and currently flown by 13 Marine Corps squadrons, the Naval Aviation Warfighting Development Center, and the Blue Angels. The last Navy legacy Hornet squadron completed its final operational deployment in April 2018.[93] By the end of 2018, all Navy squadrons will have transitioned to more capable and modern F/A-18E/F Super Hornets.[94]

The F/A-18E/F Super Hornet has better range, greater weapons payload, and increased survivability than the F/A-18A-D Legacy Hornet.[95] The Navy is implementing efforts to extend the life of some of the older Super Hornet variants until the F-35C is fully fielded in the mid-2030s, ensuring that the F/A-18E/F "will be the numerically predominant aircraft in CVWs into the mid-late 2030s."[96] The Navy's FY 2019 budget request includes $1.99 billion for 24 F/A-18E/F Super Hornets, and it plans to buy 110 Block III Super Hornets over the next five years in an attempt to mitigate shortfalls in its strike aircraft inventory.[97]

The EA-18G Growler is the U.S. Navy's primary electronic attack aircraft, providing tactical jamming and suppression of enemy air defenses. The final EA-18G aircraft will be delivered in FY 2018, bringing the total to 160 aircraft and fulfilling "current Navy requirements for Airborne Electronic Attack (AEA) for nine CVWs and five expeditionary squadrons plus one reserve squadron."[98] The FY 2019 budget requests "$147.4 million for research, development, testing, and evaluation (RDT&E) for additional modernization" to ensure that the EA-18G maintains its technical advantage over adversary electronic warfare and air defense systems.[99]

The Navy has been addressing numerous incidents, or physiological episodes (PEs), of dizziness and blackouts by F/A-18 aircrews over the past five years. There were 57 such incidents in 2012 and 114 in 2016, and 52 were reported during the first half of 2017.[100] Of the 588 F/A-18 PE incidents analyzed to date:

> 212 involved ECS [Environmental Control System] component failures, 194 were attributed to breathing gas issues, including 51 OBOGS [Onboard Oxygen Generation System] component failures and 13 breathing gas delivery component failures, 92 involved human factors, and 87 were inconclusive or involved another aircraft system failure.[101]

Only six T-45 training aircraft PEs were reported after the planes returned from an operational pause and modifications to their OBOG system in July 2017, and only one of these PEs has been attributed to the aircraft's breathing systems. The remaining five events "have all been linked to other human factors."[102]

The Navy's Physiological Episode Action Team (PEAT) "considers hypoxia and decompression events [to be] the two most likely causes of recent physiological episodes in aviators," but as physical symptoms related to "pressure fluctuations, hypoxia and contamination overlap, discerning of a root cause is a complex process."[103]

The Navy has implemented numerous corrective actions to address PEs in F/A-18F/F and EA-18G aircraft. These include "new maintenance rules for handling the occurrence of specific ECS built-in test faults;" "revised and expanded emergency procedures;" "forward deployment of transportable recompression systems to immediately treat aircrew in the event they experience pressure related symptoms"; and "annual hypoxia awareness and biennial dynamic training using a Reduced Oxygen Breathing Device (ROBD) to experience and recognize hypoxia symptoms while operating an aircraft simulator."[104] Even with the Navy's focus on identifying and correcting the causes of these events, PEs continue to be a significant concern for the naval aviation community and have further reduced the operational availability of its strike fighter and electronic attack aircraft.

The F-35C is the Navy's largest aviation modernization program. This fifth-generation fighter (all F/A-18 variants are considered fourth-generation) has greater stealth capabilities and state-of-the-art electronic systems, allowing it to sense its tactical environment and communicate with multiple other platforms more effectively. The Department of the Navy plans to purchase 273 Navy F-35Cs and 67 Marine Corps F-35Cs.[105] The F-35 is supposed to be a more capable aircraft relative to the F/A-18, but at planned procurement levels of 260 aircraft, it will not be enough to make up for the Hornets that the Navy will need to replace. The Navy now plans for future carrier air wings to include a combination of both F/A-18E/Fs and F-35Cs. In addition, like the other F-35 variants, the F-35C has faced development problems. The system has been grounded because of engine problems, and software development issues have threatened further delay. The aircraft also has grown more expensive through the development process.

As evidence of continued program issues, in March 2018, the Department of Defense stopped accepting new F-35s "pending resolution of a dispute with [the builder], Lockheed Martin, over who should pay to repair identified issues with corrosion on F-35s." As of April 12, 2018, the delivery of "five aircraft had been deferred."[106] The F-35 program's delay of the Initial Operations Test and Evaluation (IOT&E) until September 2018 appears to be jeopardizing the F-35C's scheduled initial operational capability of February 2018. According to Rear Admiral Dale Horan, Director of Joint Strike Fighter Fleet Integration:

> The whole F-35 enterprise's IOT&E starts in September, so it's not Navy F-35C that's holding up IOC, it's that we're tied to IOT&E and need to see the demonstration and capabilities. We need to really see the 3F capability demonstrated in IOT&E and there's just not going to be enough time to see enough of that before Feb. 2019.[107]

This delay in the F-35C's IOC is not expected to affect the first F-35C operational deployment in 2021.[108]

The Navy is investing in cruise missile modernization and new missile programs to provide increased range, survivability, and effectiveness in modern Anti-Access/Area Denial (A2/AD) environments. The Navy's FY 2019 budget requests $282.4 million in RDT&E and $98.6 million in weapons procurement to develop and procure 112 A2/AD capability upgrades as well as to develop an improved warhead and an anti-ship maritime strike version of the Tactical Tomahawk (TACTOM) Block IV cruise missile.[109] It also requests $143.1 million for development and testing of the Long Range Anti-Ship Missile (LRASM) and $81.2 million to purchase 25 LRASM weapons that will provide the "ability to conduct anti-surface warfare (ASuW) operations against high-value surface combatants protected by Integrated Air Defense Systems with long-range

Surface-to-Air-Missiles and deny adversaries sanctuary of maneuver against 2018–2020 threats."[110] The LRASM is "scheduled to achieve Early Operational Capability on the... Navy F/A-18E/F by the end of FY 2019."[111]

Readiness

Although the Navy states that it can still deploy forces in accordance with GFMAP requirements, various factors indicate a continued decline in readiness over the past year. Admiral William Moran, Vice Chief of Naval Operations, testified before the Senate Armed Services Readiness Subcommittee in February 2018 that:

> At the height of the Cold War, approximately one in six ships were deployed on any given day, today almost one in three are deployed on any given day.... [N]ational demands for your Navy far exceed its capacity, driving operational tempo [OPTEMPO] to unsustainable levels....
>
> The readiness of Naval Forces is a function of three components; people, material and time. Buying all the people, ships and aircraft will not produce a ready Navy without the time to maintain hardware and time for our people to train and operate. Too much time operating and not maintaining degrades our material and equipment readiness. Conversely, too much time for maintenance has a negative impact on meeting planned training and operational schedules, and the corresponding negative impact on the readiness of our Sailors to fight. This is a vicious cycle that Continuing Resolutions and insufficient funding create by disrupting the balance we need to maintain readiness, and our ability to grow capability and capacity.[112]

Over the past nine years, "Continuing Resolutions have averaged 106 days per fiscal year," forcing the Navy to operate under reduced spending levels and severely limiting the ability to complete required ship and aircraft

maintenance and training.[113] The FY 2018 Appropriations Act did not become law until March 23, 2018, effectively forcing the Navy to plan and execute 12 months of maintenance and training within the final six months of the fiscal year. "In a six month Continuing Resolution," according to Admiral Moran, "we will delay up to six ship maintenance periods, suffer delays in aircraft maintenance and repair parts, delay our munitions contracts, and...will not award three ship contracts."[114] The cycle of annual continuing resolutions continues to hamper and delay the ability of the U.S. Navy to restore readiness. Admiral John Richardson, Chief of Naval Operations, testified before the Senate Armed Services Committee in April 2018 that it would take until 2021 or 2022 to restore fleet readiness to an "acceptable" level but that the continued lack of "stable and adequate funding" would delay these efforts.[115]

The $1.7 billion provided by Congress as part of the FY 2017 Request for Additional Appropriations did help to reverse some of the Navy's "most critical readiness problems by executing 13 more ship maintenance availabilities, restoring 35 additional air frames to flight, and providing 18,000 flying hours to train 900 pilots," all of which "gained back two ship deployments and a combined one year of carrier operations and surge capability."[116]

Like the other services, the Navy has had to dedicate readiness funding to the immediate needs of various engagements around the globe, which means that the maintenance and training for non-deployed ships and sailors are not prioritized. Deferral of ship and aircraft depot maintenance because of inadequate funding or because public shipyards do not have sufficient capacity has had a ripple effect on the whole fleet. When ships and aircraft are finally able to begin depot maintenance, their material condition is worse than normal because of the delay and high OPTEMPO of the past 15 years. This in turn causes maintenance to take longer than scheduled, which leads to further delays in fleet depot maintenance and increases the demands placed on ships and aircraft that are still operational. Even with the hiring of additional shipyard workers over the past two years, the public (government-owned) shipyards are still undermanned for the amount of work they need to do.

Correcting these maintenance backlogs will require sufficient and stable funding to defray the costs of ship maintenance and further expand the workforce of the public shipyards. These maintenance and readiness issues also affect the Navy's capacity by significantly reducing the numbers of operational ships and aircraft available to support the combatant commanders. For example, between 2011 and 2016, ship maintenance overruns resulted in the loss of 1,103 aircraft carrier; 6,603 large surface combatant (cruiser and destroyers); and 6,220 submarine operational days.[117] This is the equivalent of losing 0.5 aircraft carriers, 3.0 large surface combatants, and 2.8 submarines from fleet operations for a year.

The FY 2019 budget seeks to increase the public shipyard workforce by 3,187 workers and to provide additional funding to private yards for submarine maintenance in order to lessen the workload on government shipyards.[118] In FY 2019, funding ship maintenance at the maximum executable capacity of both public and private shipyards can address only 96 percent of the required maintenance, and funding aviation maintenance at the maximum executable level of the depots can meet only 92 percent of the requirement.[119] The Navy has commenced a $21 billion, 20-year public shipyard optimization plan to increase shipyard capacity by updating equipment, improving workflow, and modernizing dry docks to accommodate new ship and submarine classes.[120]

Ship and aircraft operations and training are just as critical to fleet readiness as maintenance is. The Navy's FY 2019 budget supports the OFRP and forward deployed presence requirements by funding ship operations for deployed and non-deployed forces at a rate of 58 days and 24 days underway per quarter, respectively.[121] In addition, flight hours are funded to achieve a T-rating of 2.0 for nine Navy carrier air wings.[122] T-rating is measured on a scale of 1.0–4.0 and "describes a unit's capability to execute its mission essential tasks (METs)." A T-rating of 2.0

means that a squadron or air wing is "able to complete 80 percent of its METs."[123]

The Navy's aviation readiness is also suffering because of deferred maintenance, delayed modernization, and high OPTEMPO. An April 2018 *Military Times* report revealed that naval aviation mishaps for F/A-18E/F Super Hornets had increased 108 percent over the past five years, while across the entire aviation fleet, mishaps rose 82 percent. While analysis showed numerous causes behind individual accidents, this abrupt rise began after 2013, the first year that Budget Control Act (BCA) sequestration limits took effect. The Navy made cuts in aviation maintenance and spare parts to meet budget caps while operational demand was simultaneously increasing. For example, F/A-18E/F Super Hornets "conducted 18,000 more flight hours in 2017 than in 2013."[124]

The naval aviation community has made extreme efforts to gain every bit of readiness possible with the existing fleet, but even these efforts cannot solve the problems of too little money, too few usable assets, and too much work. Consistent with its policy of "supporting deployed and next to deploy forces, the Navy was forced to cannibalize aircraft, parts and people" to ensure deploying squadrons had sufficient operational aircraft and personnel operate safely and effectively.[125] Moreover, "to properly man the required Carrier Air Wings either on deployment or on preparing to deploy at mandated levels of 95%, there are not enough sailors left to fill the two remaining Air Wings in their maintenance phase."[126]

Vice Admiral Troy Shoemaker, Commander, Naval Air Forces, made the operational impact of this aviation readiness decline starkly clear when he testified in November 2017 that "in our Super Hornet community alone, only half of our total inventory of 542 aircraft were flyable, or mission capable, and only 170 or 31% of the total inventory were fully mission capable and ready to 'fight tonight.'"[127]

During the summer of 2017, the U.S. Navy experienced the worst peacetime surface ship collisions in over 41 years when the USS *John S. McCain* (DDG 56) and USS *Fitzgerald* (DDG 62) collided with commercial vessels, claiming the lives of 17 sailors during two unrelated routine "independent steaming" operations in the western Pacific Ocean. These tragic incidents, coupled with the USS *Antietam* (CG 54) grounding and the USS *Lake Champlain* (CG 57) collision earlier in 2017, raised significant concerns about the readiness and operational proficiency of the U.S. Navy's surface fleet. Admiral Richardson responded by ordering a "service wide operational pause" to review practices throughout the fleet.[128] The Department of the Navy conducted two major reviews to examine root causes and recommended corrective actions both for the surface fleet and fleet-wide.

In October 2017, at the direction of the Vice Chief of Naval Operations, Admiral Phil Davidson, then Commander, Fleet Forces Command, completed a *Comprehensive Review of Recent Surface Force Incidents* to determine the improvements or changes needed to make the surface force safer and more effective. The *Comprehensive Review* addressed training and professional development; "operational and mission certification of deployed ships with particular emphasis on ships based in Japan"; "deployed operational employment and risk management"; "material readiness of electronic systems to include navigation equipment, surface search radars, propulsion and steering systems"; and "the practical utility and certification of current navigation and combat systems equipment including sensors, tracking systems, displays and internal communication systems."[129] The report recommended 58 actions to correct deficiencies across the "Doctrine, Organization, Training, Material, Leadership and Education, Personnel, and Facilities (DOTMLPF)" spectrum.[130]

The Secretary of the Navy directed a team of senior civilian executives and former senior military officers to conduct a *Strategic Readiness Review* examining issues of governance, accountability, operations, organizational structure, manning, and training over the past three-plus decades to identify trends and contributing factors that have compromised performance and readiness of the fleet.[131] The report identifies four broad strategic recommendations that the Navy must address to arrest the erosion of readiness and reverse the "normalization-of-deviation" that led to a gradual degradation of standards:

- "The creation of combat ready forces must take equal footing with meeting the immediate demands of Combatant Commanders."

- "The Navy must establish realistic limits regarding the number of ready ships and sailors and, short of combat, not acquiesce to emergent requirements with assets that are not fully ready."

- "The Navy must realign and streamline its command and control structures to tightly align responsibility, authority, and accountability."

- "Navy leadership at all levels must foster a culture of learning and create the structures and processes that fully embrace this commitment."[132]

In short, Navy readiness levels are problematic and will take several years to correct. It is also worth noting again that the Navy's own readiness assessments are based on the ability to execute a strategy that assumes a force-sizing construct that is smaller than the one prescribed by this *Index*.

Scoring the U.S. Navy

Capacity Score: Weak

The Navy is unusual relative to the other services in that its capacity requirements must meet two separate objectives. First, during peacetime, the Navy must maintain a global forward presence both to deter potential aggressors from conflict and to assure our allies and maritime partners that the nation remains committed to defending its national security interests and alliances. This enduring peacetime requirement to maintain a sufficient quantity of ships constantly forward deployed around the world is the driving force behind ship force structure requirements: enough ships to ensure that the Navy can provide the necessary global presence.

On the other hand, the Navy also must be able to fight and win wars. In this case, the expectation is to be able to fight and win two simultaneous or nearly simultaneous MRCs. When thinking about naval combat power in this way, the defining metric is not necessarily a total ship count, but rather the carrier strike groups, amphibious ships, and submarines deemed necessary to win both the naval component of a war and the larger war effort by means of strike missions inland or cutting off the enemy's maritime access to sources of supply. An accurate assessment of Navy capacity takes into account both sets of requirements and scores to the larger requirement.

It should be noted that the scoring in this *Index* includes the Navy's fleet of ballistic missile and fast attack submarines to the extent that they contribute to the overall size of the battle fleet and with general comment on the status of their respective modernization programs. Because of their unique characteristics and the missions they perform, their detailed readiness rates and actual use in peacetime and planned use in war are classified. Nevertheless, the various references consulted are fairly consistent, both with respect to the numbers recommended for the overall fleet and with respect to the Navy's shipbuilding plan.

The role of SSBNs (fleet ballistic missile submarines) as one leg of America's nuclear triad capability is well known; perhaps less well known are the day-to-day tasks undertaken by the SSN force, whose operations, which can include collection, surveillance, and support to the special operations community, often take place far from the operations of the surface Navy.

Two-MRC Requirement. This *Index* uses the Navy's fleet size required "to meet a simultaneous or nearly simultaneous two-war or two–major regional contingency (MRC)" as the benchmark against which to measure service capacity. This benchmark consists of the force necessary to "fight and win two MRCs and a 20 percent margin that serves as a strategic reserve." The primary elements of naval combat power during an MRC operation derive from carrier strike groups (which include squadrons of strike and electronic warfare aircraft as well as support ships) and amphibious assault capacity. Since the Navy maintains a constantly deployed global peacetime presence, many of its fleet requirements are beyond the scope of the two-MRC construct, but it is nevertheless important to observe the historical context of naval deployments during a major theater war.

Thirteen Deployable Carrier Strike Groups. The average number of aircraft carriers deployed in major U.S. military operations since the end of the Cold War, such as the conflicts in Kuwait in 1991,[133] Afghanistan in 2001,[134] and Iraq in 2003,[135] was between five and seven. An operational fleet of 11 carriers would ensure that five are available to deploy within 30 days for a crisis or conflict. (The rest would be undergoing scheduled maintenance or taking part in training exercises and would not be ready for combat.) Within 90 days, the Navy would generally have seven carriers available.[136] This correlates with the recommendations of numerous force-sizing assessments, from the 1993 Bottom-Up Review (BUR)[137] to the Navy's 2016 Force Structure Assessment,[138] each of which recommended at least 11 aircraft carriers.

Assuming that 11 aircraft carriers are required to engage simultaneously in two MRCs, and assuming that the Navy ideally should have a 20 percent strategic reserve in order to avoid having to commit 100 percent of its carrier groups and account for scheduled maintenance, the Navy should maintain 13 CSGs. Several Navy-specific metrics regarding fleet readiness and deployment cycles support a minimum of at least a 20 percent capacity margin above fleet operational requirements.[139]

The November 2017 Chief of Naval Operations Instruction 3501.316C, "Force Composition of Afloat Navy and Naval Groups," provides the most current guidance on CSG baseline capabilities and force mix:

- "[F]ive to seven air and missile defense–capable large surface combatant ships (guided missile cruiser (CG) or guided missile destroyer (DDG)) to combat the advent of highly capable anti-ship ballistic missiles and anti-ship cruise missiles" and conduct "simultaneous ballistic missile defense and anti-air warfare" operations.

- "A naval integrated fire control-counter air capable cruiser," which "is the preferred ship for the [air and missile defense commander]."

- "No less than three cruise missile land attack capable (e.g. Tomahawk land attack missile or follow on weapon) capable large surface combatant ships."

- "No less than three [surface warfare] cruise missile (e.g. Harpoon or follow-on weapon) capable large surface combatant ships."

- "No less than four multi-functional tactical towed array systems."

- "One fast combat support (T-AOE) or equivalent dry cargo and ammunition (T-AKE) or fleet replenishment oiler (T-AO) pair combat logistics force ship(s)," which, "while not a part of the CSG, are usually assigned to support CSG operations."[140]

Although not mentioned in this instruction, at least one SSN is typically assigned to a CSG.[141]

Therefore, this *Index* defines the nominal CSG engaged in an MRC as follows: one nuclear-powered aircraft carrier (CVN); one carrier air wing (CVW); one CG; four DDGs; two FFGs; two SSNs; and one T-AOE or one T-AO and one T-AKE. Until the new FFG(X) becomes operational, this nominal CSG will consist of six in place of four DDGs.

Thirteen Carrier Air Wings. Each carrier deployed for combat operations was equipped with a carrier air wing, meaning that five to six air wings were necessary for each of those four major contingencies listed. The strategic documents differ slightly in this regard because each document suggests one less carrier air wing than the number of aircraft carriers.

A carrier air wing customarily includes four strike fighter squadrons.[142] Twelve aircraft typically comprise one Navy strike fighter squadron, so at least 48 strike fighter aircraft are required for each carrier air wing. To support 13 carrier air wings, the Navy therefore needs a minimum of 624 strike fighter aircraft.[143]

Forty-Five Amphibious Ships. The 1993 BUR recommended a fleet of 41 large amphibious vessels to support the operations of 2.5 Marine Expeditionary Brigades (MEBs).[144] Since then, the Marine Corps has expressed a need to be able to perform two MEB-level operations simultaneously, which would require a fleet of 38 amphibious vessels.[145] The number of amphibious vessels required in combat operations has declined since the Korean War, which employed 34 amphibious vessels; 26 were deployed in Vietnam, 21 in the Persian Gulf War, and only seven supported Operation Iraqi Freedom (which did not require as large a sea-based expeditionary force).[146] The Persian Gulf War is the most pertinent example for today because similar vessels were employed, and the modern requirements for an MEB most closely resemble this engagement.[147]

The Marine Corps' *Expeditionary Force 21, Marine Expeditionary Brigade Informational Overview* describes an MEB Amphibious Assault Task Force (AATF) as consisting of five amphibious transport dock ships (LPDs); five dock landing ships (LSDs); and five amphibious assault ships, either landing ship assault (LHA) or landing helicopter dock (LHD).[148] In conjunction with the Navy's Expeditionary

TABLE 6

Navy Force Structure Assessment

Ship Type/Class	Current Fleet	2016 Force Structure Assessment	*2019 Index* Recommendation
Ballistic Missile Submarines	14	12	12
Aircraft Carriers	11	12	13
Large Surface Combatants	90	104	105
Small Surface Combatants	24	52	71
Attack Submarines	50	66	65
Guided Missile Submarines	4	0	0
Amphibious Warships	32	38	45
Combat Logistics Force	29	32	54
Command and Support	30	39	35
Total	**284**	**355**	**400**

SOURCE: U.S. Department of Defense, U.S. Navy, Naval Vessel Register, "Fleet Size," http://www.nvr.navy.mil/NVRSHIPS/FLEETSIZE.HTML (accessed August 8, 2018). For more information, see footnote 169.

☎ heritage.org

Strike Group definition, five ESGs compose one MEB AATF.[149] Based on these requirements and definitions, this *Index* defines the nominal ESG engaged in an MRC as follows: one LHA or LHD; one LPD/LX(R); one LSD; two DDGs; two FFGs; and one T-AOE or one T-AO and one T-AKE. Two simultaneous MEB-level operations therefore require a minimum of 10 ESGs or 30 operational amphibious warships. The 1996 and 2001 QDRs each recommended 12 "amphibious ready groups."

While the Marine Corps has consistently advocated a fleet of 38 amphibious vessels to execute its two-MEB strategy,[150] it is more prudent to field a fleet of at least 45 amphibious ships. This incorporates a more conservative assumption that 12 ESGs could be required in a two-MRC scenario against near-peer adversaries as well as ensuring a strategic reserve of 20 percent.

Total Ship Requirement. The bulk of the Navy's battle force ships are not directly supporting a CSG or ESG during peacetime operations. Many surface vessels and attack submarines deploy independently, which is often why their requirements exceed those of a CSG. The same can be said of the ballistic missile submarine (nuclear missiles) and guided missile submarine (conventional cruise missiles), which operate independently of an aircraft carrier.

This *Index*'s benchmark of 400 battle force ships is informed by previous naval force structure assessments and government reports as well as independent analysis incorporating the simultaneous two-MRC requirement, CSG and ESG composition, and other naval missions and requirements. This analysis did not consider unmanned systems or ship classes that are not current programs of record. While unmanned systems offer the promise to improve the effectiveness and reach of ships and submarines, they have not matured sufficiently to replace a manned ship or submarine in the battle force.

The most significant differences in this updated total ship requirement compared to the Navy's 2016 FSA are in SSC and CLF ships. The increase in SSC from the Navy requirement of 52 to 71 is driven primarily by the assessed CSG and ESG compositions, which include two FFGs per strike group. The two-MRC ESG and CSG demand alone requires 56 FFGs plus the continued requirement for a combination of least 15 MCM ships and MIW LCS. Similarly, the CLF requirement of 54 ships is dependent on the logistics demands of the two-MRC requirement of 13 operational CSGs and 12 ESGs. Since the Navy possesses only two T-AOEs that can each support the fuel and ammunition needs of a strike group, a pair of single-purpose T-AOs and T-AKEs is required for each CSG and ESG.

While a 400-ship fleet is significantly larger than the Navy's current 355-ship requirement, it should be noted that the final 2016 FSA requirement of 355 ships was based on the previous Administration's "Defeat/Deny" Defense Planning Guidance and "delivers future steady state and warfighting requirements with an acceptable degree of risk."[151] The Navy's analysis determined that a 459-ship force was "needed to achieve the Navy's mission with reasonable expectations of success without incurring significant losses" but that it was "unreasonable for Navy to assume we would have the resources to aspire to a force of this size with this mix of ships."[152] Finally, this FSA has not been updated to address the 2018 National Defense Strategy, which reestablished long-term strategic competition with China and long-term strategic competition with Russia as the principal Department of Defense priorities.[153]

The numerical values used in the score column refer to the five-grade scale explained earlier in this section, where 1 is "very weak" and 5 is "very strong." Taking the *Index* requirement for Navy ships as the benchmark, the Navy's current battle forces fleet capacity of 284 ships, planned fleet of 289 ships by the end of FY 2018, and revised fleet size (implied by both the 2018 NDS, which highlights great-power competition, and analysis of the Navy's history of employment in major conflicts) result in a score of "weak," down from its *2017 Index* score of "marginal." Depending on the Navy's

ability to fund more aggressive growth options and service life extensions as identified in the FY 2019 30-year shipbuilding plan, and in view of the *Columbia*-class ballistic missile submarine program that could cost nearly half of the current shipbuilding budget per hull, the Navy's capacity score could fall further in the "weak" category in the near future.

Capability Score: Marginal

The overall capability score for the Navy is "marginal," an increase over its score of "weak" in the *2018 Index*. This was consistent across all four components of the capability score: "Age of Equipment," "Capability of Equipment," "Size of Modernization Program," and "Health of Modernization Programs." Given the number of programs, ship classes, and types of aircraft involved, the details that informed the capability assessment are more easily presented in a tabular format as shown in the Appendix.

Readiness Score: Marginal

The Navy's readiness score remained "marginal." This assessment combines two major elements of naval readiness: the ability to provide the required levels of presence around the globe and surge capacity on a consistent basis. As elaborated below, the Navy's ability to maintain required presence in key regions is "strong," but its ability to surge to meet combat requirements ranges from "weak" to "very weak" depending on how one defines the requirement. In both cases—presence and surge—the Navy has sacrificed long-term readiness to meet current operational demands for many years. Although it has prioritized restoring readiness through increased maintenance and training in 2017 and 2018, as Admiral Richardson has stated, it will take at least until 2022 for the Navy to restore its readiness to required levels.[154] To improve personnel readiness, the Navy is adding 7,500 sailors in FY 2019 "to address [manpower] gaps at sea."[155]

The Navy has reported that it continues to meet GFMAP goals but at the cost of future readiness. The U.S. Government Accountability Office (GAO) reported in May 2016 that "[t]o meet heavy operational demands over the past decade, the Navy has increased ship deployment lengths and has reduced or deferred ship maintenance"[156] The GAO further found that the Navy's efforts to provide the same amount of forward presence with an undersized fleet have "resulted in declining ship conditions across the fleet" and have "increased the amount of time that ships require to complete maintenance in the shipyards."[157]

Though the Navy has been able to maintain approximately a third of its fleet globally deployed, and while the OFRP has improved readiness for individual hulls by restricting deployment increases, demand still exceeds the supply of ready ships needed to meet requirements sustainably. Admiral Moran expressed deep concern about the Navy's ability to meet the nation's needs in a time of conflict in this exchange with Senator Joni Ernst (R–IA) in 2016:

> Senator Ernst: ...If our Navy had to answer to two or more of the so-called four-plus-one threats today, could we do that?

> Admiral Moran: ... [W]e are at a point right now...that our ability to surge beyond our current force that's forward is very limited, which should give you a pretty good indication that it would be challenging to meet the current guidance to defeat and deny in two conflicts.[158]

Three surface ship collisions and one grounding that resulted in the loss of 17 sailors in the Pacific during 2017 revealed how significant the Navy's and specifically its surface fleet's readiness crisis had become. Navy leadership responded quickly. The Chief of Naval Operations, Admiral Richardson, directed that "an operational pause be taken in all fleets around the world and that a comprehensive review be launched that examines the training and certification of forward-deployed forces as well as a wide span of factors that may have contributed to the recent costly incidents."[159]

The Government Accountability Office also conducted its own readiness reviews. One of its most disturbing findings was a lack of formal dedicated training and deployment certification time for the Japan-based ships compared to the CONUS-based ships whose OFRP cycle ensures that all ships are properly trained and mission certified before being forward deployed. Since the Japan-based ships are in a permanently deployed status, and in an effort to meet the ever-increasing demand, these ships were not provided any dedicated training time, and by June 2017, 37 percent of their warfare certifications were expired.[160] Pacific Fleet leadership had increasingly waived these expired certifications to deploy these ships, and the GAO discovered that these waivers increased fivefold between 2015 and 2017.[161]

Another critical find was the lack of basic seamanship proficiency, not just among the crews of USS *John S. McCain* and USS *Fitzgerald*, but across the surface warfare community. Recently completed Surface Warfare Officer School seamanship competency checks of 196 first sea tour Officer of the Deck–qualified junior officers revealed that evaluations of almost 84 percent of these officers revealed "some concerns" or "significant concerns."[162]

The readiness reviews presented numerous corrective actions to improve the material condition of its ships as well as the professional training and operational proficiency of its crews. For example:

- Cancellation of all risk-assessment mitigation plans and waivers for expired mission certifications.[163]

- A new 24-month force generation plan for all Japan-based ships that includes 18 weeks of dedicated training time and seven months of maintenance time.[164]

- Ready for Sea Assessments on Japan-based cruisers and destroyers, with the exception of those completing or in maintenance, in order to rebaseline mission certifications.[165]

- A redesigned Surface Warfare Officer (SWO) career path that increases professional and seamanship training, adds individual proficiency assessments, and increases at-sea time.[166]

A Readiness Reform Oversight Council to oversee not only implementation of the recommended actions, but also the ongoing impact of these actions to ensure that they achieve their desired results now and in the future.[167]

The Navy's FY 2019 budget request includes $79 million for FY 2019 and $600 million across the FY 2019–FY 2023 Future Years Defense Program "to address training, manning and equipment issues and recommendations identified in the [Comprehensive and Strategic Readiness Reviews]."[168] The Navy's readiness as it pertains to providing global presence is rated as "marginal." The level of COCOM demand for naval presence and the fleet's ability to meet that demand is similar to that found in the *2018 Index* but is still challenged by the range of funding problems noted in this section. The Navy maintains its ability to forward deploy approximately one-third of its fleet and has been able to stave off immediate readiness challenges through the OFRP.

However, the Navy's readiness corrective actions, coupled with an inadequate fleet size, have resulted in a reduction in its ability to respond to COCOM requirements for sustained presence, crisis support, and surge response in the event of a major conflict. Since COCOM demand signals have been become insatiable in recent years, recent actions by the Navy to prioritize maintenance and training over peacetime deployments have created a more realistic and sustainable OPTEMPO for missions short of major conflict. While the Navy's actions to improve training and efficiency for the fleet and specifically for the surface warfare community will help to correct the systemic issues that led to severely degraded ship-driving skills, it will be several years before they can fully change the culture and raise the fleet's overall professional knowledge and experience.

Even with prioritized investments for ship and aircraft maintenance at the maximum executable levels of the Navy's ship and aircraft depots, the Navy still cannot meet the maintenance requirement for FY 2019.

Without increased and sustained funding to meet the Navy's fleet recapitalization requirements and improvements in shipyard maintenance capacity, the readiness of the Navy's fleet will remain compromised. Although the Navy has made strides in arresting its readiness decline since Admiral Moran expressed his concerns about the Navy's ability to handle two major crises over one year ago, the gains have not been sufficient to assume that his concerns do not still hold true today.

Overall U.S. Navy Score: Marginal

The Navy's overall score for the *2018 Index* is "marginal," the same as it was in the *2018 Index*. This was derived by aggregating the scores for capacity ("weak"); capability ("marginal"); and readiness ("marginal"). The Navy's prioritization of restoring readiness and increasing its capacity, matched by increased funding in 2017 and 2018, suggests that its overall score could improve in the near future. Continuation of unstable funding as the result of future continuing resolutions and a return to BCA sequestration-level funding will negate these improvements and instead cause future degradation in the Navy's score.

U.S. Military Power: Navy

	VERY WEAK	WEAK	MARGINAL	STRONG	VERY STRONG
Capacity		✓			
Capability			✓		
Readiness			✓		
OVERALL			✓		

NAVY SCORES

Weakest ⟵⟶ Strongest

Procurement and Spending ■ Through FY 2018 ▫ Pending

Aircraft Carrier

PLATFORM	Age Score	Capability Score	MODERNIZATION PROGRAM	Size Score	Health Score
Nimitz-Class Aircraft Carrier (CVN-68) Inventory: **10** Fleet age: **27.5** Date: **1975** The expected life of the _Nimitz_-class nuclear aircraft carrier is 50 years. The class will start retiring in the mid-2020s and will be replaced by the _Ford_-class carriers.	③	③	**_Ford_-Class Aircraft Carrier (CVN-78)** Timeline: **2008–2018** Currently in production, the _Ford_-class will replace the current Nimitz-class aircraft carriers. The _Ford_-class will increase aircraft sorties by 25 percent, require a crew of several hundred fewer sailors, and be able to handle more advanced weapon systems. Program cost increases reflect an increased acquisition objective from 3 to 4 ships.	❶	❷
Ford-Class Aircraft Carrier (CVN-21) Inventory: **1** Fleet age: **1** Date: **2017** The expected life of the _Ford_-class nuclear aircraft carrier is 50 years.	❺				

PROCUREMENT

3   1

SPENDING (_$ millions_)

$32,707 $25,932

See Methodology for descriptions of scores.   Fleet age—Average age of fleet   Date—Year fleet first entered service

NAVY SCORES

Large Surface Combatant

PLATFORM	Age Score	Capability Score	MODERNIZATION PROGRAM	Size Score	Health Score
Ticonderoga-Class Cruiser (CG-47)			**Zumwalt-Class Destroyer (DDG-1000)**	①	①
Inventory: **22**			Timeline: **2007–2009**		
Fleet age: **28** Date: **1983**					
The *Ticonderoga*-class guided missile cruiser has a life expectancy of 40 years. There are plans to lay up half of the cruiser fleet to modernize it and extend its life into the 2030s. There are no replacements currently planned.	②		The DDG-1000 was designed to be a new-generation destroyer capable of handling more advanced weapon systems with modern gun systems and a hull design aimed to reduce radar detectability. The DDG-1000 program was intended to produce a total of 32 ships, but this number has been reduced to 3. The first DDG-1000 was commissioned in October 2016.		

PROCUREMENT

3

SPENDING (*$ millions*)

$22,292 $1,200

PLATFORM	Age Score	Capability Score	MODERNIZATION PROGRAM	Size Score	Health Score
Zumwalt-Class Destroyer					
Inventory: **1**					
Fleet age: **2** Date: **2016**					
Although the ship has passed sea trials, it continues to experience problems with its combat systems. The second ship of the Zumwalt class is expected to commission in January 2019.	⑤	④			
Arleigh Burke-Class Destroyer (DDG-51)			**Arleigh Burke-Class Destroyer (DDG-51)**	④	④
Inventory: **66**			Timeline: **1985–2024**		
Fleet age: **16.3** Date: **1991**					
The *Arleigh Burke*-class guided missile destroyer is the only operating class of large surface combatant currently in production. The Navy plans to extend the service life of the entire class to 45 years from its original life expectancy of 35 years.	③		The DDG-51 was restarted in FY 2013 to make up for the reduction in DDG-1000 acquisitions. Future DDG-51s will be upgraded to a Flight III design, which will include the Advanced Missile Defense Radar (AMDR), a more capable missile defense radar. Cost growth reflects a procurement increase to 95 ships.		

PROCUREMENT

80   15

SPENDING (*$ millions*)

$90,566 $31,182

See Methodology for descriptions of scores.   Fleet age—Average age of fleet   Date—Year fleet first entered service

① ② ③ ④ ⑤
Weakest ⟵ ⟶ Strongest

Procurement ■ Through FY 2018
and Spending ▪ Pending

Small Surface Combatant

PLATFORM	Age Score	Capability Score	MODERNIZATION PROGRAM	Size Score	Health Score
Littoral Combat Ship (LCS) Inventory: **12** Fleet age: **3.6**　Date: **2008** The Littoral Combat Ship includes two classes: the *Independence*-class and the *Freedom*-class, both of which are in the early phases of production. The ship is expected to have a service life of 25 years. The LCS is designed to meet multiple missions and make up the entirety of the small surface combatant requirement. LCS 14 was commissioned in May 2018.	⑤	②	**Littoral Combat Ship (LCS)** Timeline: **2009–2025** The LCS is intended to fulfil the mine countermeasure, antisubmarine warfare, and surface warfare roles for the Navy. It will be the only small surface combatant in the fleet once the Navy's MCM ships retire. Procurement of 3 additional LCSs in FY2019 will exceed the planned procurement of 32. A new program called the FFG(x) will fill out the remaining 20-ship small surface combatant requirement.	②	①
***Avenger*-Class Mine Counter Measure (MCM-1)** Inventory: **11** Fleet age: **26.1**　Date: **1987** Designed for mine sweeping and hunting/killing, 11 of the 14 *Avenger*-class ships built are still active. The class has a 30-year life span. The remaining MCMs are expected to be decommissioned throughout the 2020s. There is no replacement in production for this class of ship, but the Navy plans to fill its mine countermeasure role with the LCS.	①				

PROCUREMENT	SPENDING *($ millions)*
▬▬▬	▬▬▬▬▬▬▬▬▬
32	$21,953

SSGN Cruise Missile Submarine

PLATFORM	Age Score	Capability Score	MODERNIZATION PROGRAM	Size Score	Health Score
***Ohio*-Class (SSGN-726)** Inventory: **4** Fleet age: **33.1**　Date: **1981** Rather than retiring the four oldest *Ohio*-class ballistic missile submarines early, the Navy converted them to SSGN-726 guided missile submarines, equipping them with conventional Tomahawk cruise missiles rather than Trident ballistic missiles tipped with nuclear warheads. The SSGNs provide the Navy with a large stealthy strike capability. The conversion began in 2002 and was completed in 2007. Since the conversion, they are expected to be retired in the late 2020s. The Navy has no planned replacement for the SSGNs once they retire.	②	④	None		

See Methodology for descriptions of scores.　　Fleet age—Average age of fleet　　Date—Year fleet first entered service

Attack Submarines

PLATFORM	Age Score	Capability Score	MODERNIZATION PROGRAM	Size Score	Health Score
Seawolf-Class (SSN-21)			**Virginia-Class (SSN–774)**	⑤	④
Inventory: **3** Fleet age: **18.1** Date: **1997**			Timeline: **1998–2021**		
Larger and equipped with more torpedo tubes than the U.S. Navy's other current nuclear-powered attack submarines, the class was cancelled after three submarines were purchased due to budget constraints in the 1990s. The *Seawolf*-class submarines are expected to be retired by 2030. Meant to replace the *Los Angeles*-class, the *Seawolf* has been replaced by the *Virginia*-class attack submarine.	③		In 2017, the Navy increased the official acquistion objective from 30 to 48.		

Virginia-Class (SSN–774)

⑤ ④

Timeline: **1998–2021**

In 2017, the Navy increased the official acquistion objective from 30 to 48.

PROCUREMENT	SPENDING ($ millions)
▬▬▬▬▬▬▬▬▬ ▨▨▨	▬▬▬▬▬▬▬▬ ▨▨▨▨
28 20	$84,133 $80,073

Los Angeles-Class (SSN-688)

Inventory: **31**
Fleet age: **27.2** Date: **1976**

Capability Score: ④
Age Score: ❶

The *Los Angeles*-class comprises the largest portion of the Navy's attack submarine fleet. The class has a 33 year service life. Of the 62 built, 28 have been decommissioned and three have been inactivated awaiting decommissioning. The last *Los Angeles*-class submarine is expected to retire in the late 2020s. The *Virginia*-class is replacing this submarine class.

Virginia-Class (SSN-774)

Inventory: **15**
Fleet age: **6.8** Date: **2004**

Age Score: ④

The *Virginia*-class is the U.S. Navy's next-generation attack submarine. The life expectancy of the *Virginia*-class is 33 years. The *Virginia*-class is in production and will replace the *Los Angeles*-class and *Seawolf*-class attack submarines as they are decommissioned.

See Methodology for descriptions of scores.   Fleet age—Average age of fleet   Date—Year fleet first entered service

NAVY SCORES

❶ ❷ ③ ④ ❺
Weakest ◄——► Strongest

Procurement ■ Through FY 2018
and Spending ▨ Pending

SSBN Ballistic Missile Submarine

PLATFORM	Age Score	Capability Score	MODERNIZATION PROGRAM	Size Score	Health Score
Ohio-Class (SSBN) Inventory: **14** Fleet age: **27.6** Date: **1984**	❷	④	**Columbia-Class (SSBN-826)** Inventory: **n/a** Fleet age: **26.7** Date: **1984**	❺	❺

The SSBN Ohio-class is one of the three legs of the U.S. military's nuclear triad. The Ohio-class's expected service life is 42 years. The Ohio-class fleet will begin retiring in 2027 at an estimated rate of one submarine per year until 2039. The Navy plans to replace the Ohio-class with the SSBN(X) or next-generation "Ohio replacement program."

In January 2017, the SSBN Columbia-class was designated a major defense acquisition program. This also marks the entry of the program into the engineering and manufacturing development phase. The ships will begin construction in FY 2021, and are expected to remain in service until 2080.

PROCUREMENT	SPENDING ($ millions)	
12	$9,534	$117,340

Amphibious Warfare Ship

PLATFORM	Age Score	Capability Score	MODERNIZATION PROGRAM	Size Score	Health Score
Wasp-Class Amphibious Assault Ship (LHD-1) Inventory: **8** Fleet age: **21.3** Date: **1989**	③	③	**America-class (LHA-6)** Timeline: **2007–2017**	❶	❶

The Wasp-class is the Navy's current amphibious landing helicopter deck, meant to replace the Tarawa-class LHA. This ship has a 40-year life span. This class is no longer in production and will be replaced by the new America-class.

America-Class Amphibious Assault Ship (LHA-6)

Inventory: **1**
Fleet age: **3.8**   Date: **2014**   ❺

The America-class, the Navy's new class of large-deck amphibious assault ships, is meant to replace the retiring Wasp-class LHDs. The lead ship was delivered in April 2014. The America-class is designed to accommodate the Marine Corps's F-35Bs.

The America-class is in production with all three LHA-6s already procured. There has been significant cost growth in this program resulting in a Nunn–McCurdy cost breach. The program is also experiencing a 19-month delay because of design problems. One problem was caused by the level of heat from the F-35B STOVL's exhaust. The LHA-7 will follow designs from the LHA-6; FY2017 funded the procurement of the third and final America-Class LHA.

PROCUREMENT	SPENDING ($ millions)	
3	$10,748	$509

See Methodology for descriptions of scores.   Fleet age—Average age of fleet   Date—Year fleet first entered service

NAVY SCORES

Amphibious Warfare Ship

PLATFORM	Age Score	Capability Score	MODERNIZATION PROGRAM	Size Score	Health Score
San Antonio-Class Amphibious Transport Dock (LPD-17) Inventory: **11** Fleet age: **7.1** Date: **2006** The *San Antonio*-class is the replacement for the *Austin*-class LPD and makes up most of the LPD inventory. The LPDs have well decks that allow the USMC to transfer the vehicles and supplies carried by the ship to the shore via landing craft. The LPD can also carry 4 CH-46s or 2 MV-22s. The class has a 40-year life expectancy.	⑤		**San Antonio-Class Amphibious Transport Dock (LPD-17)** Timeline: **1996–2016** The LPD-17s are replacements for the *San Antonio*-class LPDs. All 13 LPD-17s have been procured.	⑤	④

PROCUREMENT ■■■■■■■■■■■■■ 13

SPENDING (*$ millions*) ■■■■■■■■■■■■■ $22,464 $195

Whidbey Island-Class Dock Landing Ship (LSD-41) Inventory: **8** Fleet age: **29.5** Date: **1985** The *Whidbey Island*-class is a dock landing ship that transports Marine Corps units, equipment, and supplies for amphibious operations through use of its large stowage and well decks. The *Whidbey Island*-class and *Harpers Ferry*-class ships are to be replaced by LPD–117 Flight II program, which began procurement in FY2018.	③	③			

| **Harpers Ferry-Class Dock Landing Ships (LSD-49)**

Inventory: **4**
Fleet age: **22.2**   Date: **1995**

A follow-on to the *Whidbey Island*-class, the *Harpers Ferry*-class LSDs have a larger well deck with more space for vehicle stowage and landing craft. Like the *Whidbey Island*-class, these ships should remain in service until 2038. The *Whidbey Island*-class and *Harpers Ferry*-class ships are planned to be replaced by the LPD–17 Flight II, which began procurement in FY2018. | ③ | | **LPD-17 Flight II**

Timeline: **2018–TBD**

Previously known as LX(R), the LPD–17 Flight II program will procure 13 ships to replace the Navy's LSD-type ships. The Navy originally planned to procure the first Flight II ships in 2020, however accelerated procurement funding enabled procurement of the first LPD-17 Flight II in 2018. A procurement timeline remains in development. | ⑤ | ⑤ |

PROCUREMENT ■▨▨▨▨▨▨ 1   12

SPENDING (*$ millions*) ■■■■■■■■■■ $1,800

See Methodology for descriptions of scores.   Fleet age—Average age of fleet   Date—Year fleet first entered service

Airborne Early Warning

PLATFORM	Age Score	Capability Score	MODERNIZATION PROGRAM	Size Score	Health Score
E-2C Hawkeye Inventory: **50** Fleet age: **32** Date: **1964** The E-2C Hawkeye is a battle management and airborne early warning aircraft. While still operational, the E-2C is nearing the end of its service life and is being replaced by the E-2D Advanced Hawkeye. The E-2C fleet received a series of upgrades to mechanical and computer systems around the year 2000.	①	④	**E-2D Advanced Hawkeye** Timeline: **2009–2024** Meant to replace the E-2C, the E-2D Hawkeye is in production. The original plan was to purchase five per year until 2023.	⑤	④
E-2D Advanced Hawkeye Inventory: **30** Fleet age: **3** Date: **2013** A more advanced version of the E-2C, the E-2D provides improved battle management capabilities.	⑤				

PROCUREMENT
51   24

SPENDING *($ millions)*
$14,805 $6,652

Electronic Attack Aircraft

PLATFORM	Age Score	Capability Score	MODERNIZATION PROGRAM	Size Score	Health Score
EA-18G Growler Inventory: **131** Fleet age: **4** Date: **2010** The EA-18G electronic warfare aircraft replaced the legacy EA-6B Prowlers. The platform is still in production and is relatively new.	⑤	⑤	**EA-18G Growler** Timeline: **2006–2016** The EA-18G Growler has been in production for several years, with few current acquisition problems. The program total of 160 is an increase from previous years, which estimated the Navy would purchase 88. All 160 have been procured.	⑤	④

PROCUREMENT
160

SPENDING *($ millions)*
$15,031 $377

See Methodology for descriptions of scores.   Fleet age—Average age of fleet   Date—Year fleet first entered service

NAVY SCORES

Fighter/Attack Aircraft

PLATFORM	Age Score	Capability Score
F/A-18 A-D Hornet Inventory: **139** Fleet age: **25.5** Date: **1983** The F/A-18 is the Navy's older carrier-based fighter and strike attack aircraft. The Navy has been trying to extend the life of the later variants (C-D) from 6,000 flight hours to potentially 10,000. In 2019, the Navy plans to transfer its remaining F/A–18 A–Ds to the Marine Corps to help maintain its fleet through 2030.	①	③
F/A-18 E/F Super Hornet Inventory: **561** Fleet age: **15** Date: **2001** The F/A-18 E/F Super Hornet is a newer, more capable version of the Hornet. The Navy is aiming to have a combination of Super Hornets and F-35Cs make up their carrier-based strike capability. The F/A-18E-F has an expected service life of 20 years.	②	

MODERNIZATION PROGRAM	Size Score	Health Score
F-35C Joint Strike Fighter Timeline: **2009–2033**	①	①

The F-35C is the Navy's variant of the Joint Strike Fighter. The Joint Strike Fighter faced many issues during its developmental stages, including engine problems, software development delays, cost overruns incurring a Nunn–McCurdy breach, and structural problems. The F-35C variant was always scheduled to be the last one to reach IOC, which repeatedly has been and is currently planned for 2019.

PROCUREMENT		SPENDING ($ millions)	
75	185	$133,099	$273,122

NOTES: The total program dollar value reflects the full F–35 joint program, including engine procurement. The Navy is also procuring 67 F-35Cs for the Marine Corps. Age of fleet is calculated from date of commissioning to January 2016.
SOURCE: Heritage Foundation research using data from government documents and websites. See also Dakota L. Wood, ed., *2018 Index of U.S. Military Strength* (Washington, DC: The Heritage Foundation, 2018), http://index.heritage.org/militarystrength/.

See Methodology for descriptions of scores.   Fleet age—Average age of fleet   Date—Year fleet first entered service

Endnotes

1. Admiral John M. Richardson, "A Design for Maintaining Maritime Superiority, Version 1.0," January 2016, p. 1, http://www.navy.mil/cno/docs/cno_stg.pdf (accessed August 11, 2018).

2. U.S. Marine Corps, U.S. Navy, and U.S. Coast Guard, *A Cooperative Strategy for 21st Century Seapower*, March 2015, p. 2, http://www.navy.mil/local/maritime/150227-CS21R-Final.pdf (accessed August 12, 2018).

3. James Mattis, U.S. Secretary of Defense, *Summary of the 2018 National Defense Strategy of the United States of America: Sharpening the American Military's Competitive Edge*, U.S. Department of Defense, January 2018, https://www.defense.gov/Portals/1/Documents/pubs/2018-National-Defense-Strategy-Summary.pdf (accessed August 11, 2018).

4. The Global Force Management Allocation Plan (GFMAP) is a classified document that specifies forces to be provided by the services for use by operational commanders. It is an extension of a reference manual maintained by the Joint Staff, *Global Force Management Allocation Policies and Procedures* (CJCSM 3130.06B), which is also a classified publication. See U.S. Department of Defense, Joint Chiefs of Staff, "Adaptive Planning and Execution Overview and Policy Framework," Chairman of the Joint Chiefs of Staff Guide 3130, May 29, 2015, p. B-2, http://www.jcs.mil/Portals/36/Documents/Library/Handbooks/g3130.pdf?ver=2016-02-05-175741-677 (accessed July 3, 2018), and U.S. Department of Defense, Joint Chiefs of Staff, "Current list of CJCSG/I/M/Ns," May 4, 2018, p. 17, http://www.jcs.mil/Portals/36/Documents/Library/SupportDocs/CJCS%20Reports/CJCS%20CURRENT%20DIRECTIVES%20-%204%20May%202018v2.pdf?ver=2018-05-10-130109-313 (accessed August 12, 2018).

5. Mattis, *Summary of the 2018 National Defense Strategy*, p.4.

6. Ibid., pp. 4–7.

7. U.S. Department of the Navy, Office of Budget, *Highlights of the Department of the Navy FY 2019 Budget*, 2018, pp. 1-1 and 1-2, http://www.secnav.navy.mil/fmc/fmb/Documents/19pres/Highlights_book.pdf (accessed August 12, 2018).

8. U.S. Navy, Office of the Chief of Naval Operations, Deputy Chief of Naval Operations (Warfare Systems) (N9), *Report to Congress on the Annual Long-Range Plan for Construction of Naval Vessels for Fiscal Year 2019*, February 2018, p. 4, http://www.secnav.navy.mil/fmc/fmb/Documents/19pres/LONGRANGE_SHIP_PLAN.pdf (accessed August 12, 2018). See also Admiral John Richardson, Chief of Naval Operations, transcript of speech delivered at program on "The Navy Our Nation Needs" at The Heritage Foundation, Washington, D.C., February 1, 2018, http://www.navy.mil/navydata/people/cno/Richardson/Speech/180201_CNORichardson_Heritage_Speech.pdf (accessed August 12, 2018).

9. U.S. Department of Defense, Department of the Navy, Office of the Secretary, "General Guidance for the Classification of Naval Vessels and Battle Force Ship Counting Procedures," SECNAV Instruction 5030.8C, June 14, 2016, pp. 1–2, http://www.nvr.navy.mil/5030.8C.pdf (accessed August 12, 2018).

10. Ronald O'Rourke, "Navy Force Structure and Shipbuilding Plans: Background and Issues for Congress," Congressional Research Service *Report for Members and Committees of Congress*, July 31, 2018, p. 2, https://fas.org/sgp/crs/weapons/RL32665.pdf (accessed August 12, 2018).

11. Mattis, *Summary of the 2018 National Defense Strategy*, p. 2.

12. U.S. Department of Defense, Naval Vessel Register, "Fleet Size," last updated August 7, 2018, http://www.nvr.navy.mil/NVRSHIPS/FLEETSIZE.HTML (accessed August 12, 2018).

13. "An Assessment of U.S. Military Power: U.S. Navy," in *2018 Index of U.S. Military Strength*, ed. Dakota L. Wood (Washington: The Heritage Foundation, 2017), p. 334, https://www.heritage.org/sites/default/files/2017-10/2018_IndexOfUSMilitaryStrength-2.pdf.

14. Senate Committee on Appropriations, "Department of Defense Appropriations Bill, 2018: Omnibus Agreement Summary," https://www.appropriations.senate.gov/imo/media/doc/FY18-OMNI-DEFENSE-SUM.pdf (accessed August 12, 2018).

15. Congressional Budget Office, *Costs of Building a 355-Ship Navy*, April 2017, p. 6, https://www.cbo.gov/system/files/115th-congress-2017-2018/reports/52632-355shipnavy.pdf (accessed August 13, 2018).

16. Navy League of the United States, "Upcoming US Navy Commissionings," last updated August 2, 2018, https://www.navycommissionings.org/ (accessed August 12, 2018).

17. U.S. Department of the Navy, Office of Budget, *Highlights of the Department of the Navy FY 2019 Budget*, p. 3-3.

18. Ibid.

19. Table A6-1, "Ships Planned for Decommissioning or to Be Placed Out of Service During the FYDP," in U.S. Navy, Office of the Chief of Naval Operations, Deputy Chief of Naval Operations (Warfare Systems) (N9), *Report to Congress on the Annual Long-Range Plan for Construction of Naval Vessels for Fiscal Year 2019*, p. 20.

20. U.S. Department of the Navy, Naval Sea Systems Command, memorandum on "Surface Ship Life Extensions," April 25, 2018, https://2.bp.blogspot.com/-B3as-Uf3EuM/WwK9lEVRthI/AAAAAAAANBI/aOx4hOANKB4EN5tVyYufTHDHGsInxyiGACLcBGAs/s1600/shiplife.jpeg (accessed August 18, 2018).

21. "An Assessment of U.S. Military Power: U.S. Navy," *2018 Index of U.S. Military Strength*, p. 334.

22. U.S. Department of Defense, Naval Vessel Register, "Ship Battle Forces," http://www.nvr.navy.mil/NVRSHIPS/SHIPBATTLEFORCE.HTML (accessed August 12, 2018).

23. U.S. Navy, "Executive Summary: 2016 Navy Force Structure Assessment (FSA)," December 14, 2016, p. 1, https://news.usni.org/wp-content/uploads/2016/12/FSA_Executive-Summary.pdf (accessed August 12, 2018). The full FSA was not released to the public.

24. The *2019 Index* SSC requirement is 71 ships, which includes 56 FFGs and 15 mine warfare (MIW) LCS.

25. U.S. Department of Defense, Naval Vessel Register, "Ship Battle Forces."

26. The Heritage Foundation CLF requirement of 56 ships includes two T-AOE, 26 T-AKE, and 26 T-AO.

27. U.S. Department of Defense, Naval Vessel Register, "Ship Battle Forces."

28. U.S. Code, Title 10, § 5062(b), https://www.gpo.gov/fdsys/pkg/USCODE-2010-title10/pdf/USCODE-2010-title10-subtitleC-partI-chap507-sec5062.pdf (accessed July 3, 2018).

29. See H.R. 941, 12 Carrier Act, 115th Cong., 1st Sess., February 7, 2017, https://www.congress.gov/115/bills/hr941/BILLS-115hr941ih.pdf (accessed August 14, 2018).

30. Section 123, "Sense of Congress on Accelerated Production of Aircraft Carriers," in H.R. 5515, John S. McCain National Defense Authorization Act for Fiscal Year 2019, 115th Cong., 2nd Sess., passed by Congress August 4, 2018, and signed into law August 13, 2018, p. 28, https://www.gpo.gov/fdsys/pkg/BILLS-115hr5515enr/pdf/BILLS-115hr5515enr.pdf (accessed August 14, 2018).

31. Ronald O'Rourke, "Navy Ford (CVN-78) Class Aircraft Carrier Program: Background and Issues for Congress," Congressional Research Service *Report for Members and Committees of Congress*, July 31, 2018, p. 2, https://fas.org/sgp/crs/weapons/RS20643.pdf (accessed August 13, 2018).

32. U.S. Department of the Navy, Office of Budget, *Highlights of the Department of the Navy FY 2019 Budget*, p. 1-2.

33. Lucas Tomlinson, "No U.S. Aircraft Carrier at Sea Leaves Gap in Middle East," Fox News, December 30, 2016, http://www.foxnews.com/us/2016/12/30/no-us-carrier-at-sea-leaves-gap-in-middle-east.html (accessed July 5, 2018).

34. Mike Fabey, "The U.S. Navy's Most Advanced Aircraft Carrier Will Soon Face Its Greatest Challenge," *The National Interest*, June 27, 2017, http://nationalinterest.org/blog/the-buzz/the-us-navys-most-advanced-aircraft-carrier-will-soon-face-21336 (accessed July 5, 2018).

35. U.S. Navy, "Executive Summary: 2016 Navy Force Structure Assessment (FSA)," p. 1.

36. Ibid., p. 2.

37. Ibid., pp. 2–3.

38. Ibid., pp. 3–4.

39. O'Rourke, "Navy Force Structure and Shipbuilding Plans," p. 2.

40. Congressional Budget Office, *Costs of Building a 355-Ship Navy*, p. 1.

41. U.S. Department of the Navy, Office of Budget, *Highlights of the Department of the Navy FY 2019 Budget*, p. 1-8.

42. Ibid., p. 4-3.

43. O'Rourke, "Navy Force Structure and Shipbuilding Plans," p. 8. For a detailed breakout of sailors per type and number of ships, see ibid., note 22.

44. U.S. Navy, Office of the Chief of Naval Operations, Deputy Chief of Naval Operations (Warfare Systems) (N9), *Report to Congress on the Annual Long-Range Plan for Construction of Naval Vessels for Fiscal Year 2019*, pp. 3 and 12.

45. Congressional Budget Office, *Costs of Building a 355-Ship Navy*, p. 6.

46. U.S. Navy, Office of the Chief of Naval Operations, Deputy Chief of Naval Operations (Warfare Systems) (N9), *Report to Congress on the Annual Long-Range Plan for Construction of Naval Vessels for Fiscal Year 2019*, p. 5.

47. Megan Eckstein. "Navy Will Extend All DDGs to a 45-Year Service Life; 'No Destroyer Left Behind' Officials Say," U.S. Naval Institute News, April 12, 2018, https://news.usni.org/2018/04/12/navy-will-extend-ddgs-45-year-service-life-no-destroyer-left-behind-officials-say (accessed July 5, 2018).

48. U.S. Department of Defense, Department of the Navy, Office of the Chief of Naval Operations, "Optimized Fleet Response Plan," OPNAV Instruction 3000.15A, November 10, 2014, p. 1, https://doni.documentservices.dla.mil/Directives/03000%20Naval%20Operations%20and%20Readiness/03-00%20General%20Operations%20and%20Readiness%20Support/3000.15A.pdf (accessed August 14, 2018).

49. U.S. Department of Defense, Office of the Under Secretary of Defense (Comptroller)/Chief Financial Officer, *United States Department of Defense Fiscal Year 2018 Budget Request: Defense Budget Overview*, May 2017, p. 2-5, http://comptroller.defense.gov/Portals/45/Documents/defbudget/fy2018/fy2018_Budget_Request_Overview_Book.pdf (accessed July 5, 2018).

50. "An Assessment of Military Power: U.S. Navy, *2018 Index of U.S. Military Strength*, p. 336.

51. U.S. Department of the Navy, "Status of the Navy" as of August 14, 2018, http://www.navy.mil/navydata/nav_legacy.asp?id=146 (accessed August 14, 2018).

52. Rotational deployments involve a ship sailing to a location for a set amount of time and returning to the United States, usually to be replaced by another ship although not always providing an overlapping or unbroken presence.

53. U.S. Navy, U.S. Marine Corps, and U.S. Coast Guard, *Naval Operations Concept 2010: Implementing the Maritime Strategy*, p. 26, https://fas.org/irp/doddir/navy/noc2010.pdf (accessed August 14, 2018).

54. On average, rotational deployments require four ships for one ship to be forward deployed. This is necessary because one ship is sailing out to a designated location, one is at location, one is sailing back to the CONUS, and one is in the CONUS for maintenance.

55. Figure 4, "Comparison of Forward-Presence Rates Provided on an Annual Basis for Ships Homeported in the United States and Overseas," in U.S. Government Accountability Office, *Navy Force Structure: Sustainable Plan and Comprehensive Assessment Needed to Mitigate Long-Term Risks to Ships Assigned to Overseas Homeports*, GAO-15-329, May 2015, p.13, https://www.gao.gov/assets/680/670534.pdf (accessed August 14, 2018).

56. U.S. Department of Defense, Naval Vessel Register, "Ship Battle Forces."

57. Ronald O'Rourke, "Navy Littoral Combat Ship (LCS) Program: Background and Issues for Congress," Congressional Research Service *Report for Members and Committees of Congress*, July 31, 2018, p. 6, https://fas.org/sgp/crs/weapons/RL33741.pdf (accessed August 14, 2018).

58. Ronald O'Rourke, "Navy Littoral Combat Ship (LCS)/Frigate Program: Background and Issues for Congress," Congressional Research Service *Report for Members and Committees of Congress*, June 12, 2015, p. 15, https://news.usni.org/wp-content/uploads/2015/06/RL33741_2.pdf#viewer.action=download (accessed July 5, 2018).

59. Sam LaGrone, "Raytheon Awarded LCS Over-the-Horizon Anti-Surface Weapon Contract; Deal Could be Worth $848M," U.S. Naval Institute News, May 31, 2018, https://news.usni.org/2018/05/31/raytheon-awarded-lcs-horizon-anti-surface-weapon-contract-deal-worth-848m (accessed August 14, 2018).

60. Raytheon, "Naval Strike Missile: 5th Gen Over-the-Horizon Tech. Ready Now," *Raytheon*, https://www.raytheon.com/capabilities/products/naval-strike-missile-over-the-horizon-solution (accessed August 14, 2018).

61. O'Rourke, "Navy Littoral Combat Ship (LCS) Program," p. 3.

62. U.S. Department of Defense, Office of the Secretary of Defense, Director, Operational Test and Evaluation, *FY 2017 Annual Report*, January 2018, pp. 187-191, http://www.dote.osd.mil/pub/reports/FY2017/pdf/other/2017DOTEAnnualReport.pdf (accessed August 14, 2018).

63. Megan Eckstein, "Shipbuilders Worried about Navy Plan for 1 LCS in 2019 Ahead of Frigate Transition," U.S. Naval Institute News, March 2, 2018, https://news.usni.org/2018/03/02/shipbuilders-worried-about-navy-plans-for-1-lcs-in-2019-ahead-of-frigate-transition (accessed August 14, 2018).

64. Ibid.

65. Ibid.

66. Figure 17, "DON Battle Force Ships," in U.S. Department of the Navy, Office of Budget, *Highlights of the Department of the Navy FY 2019 Budget*, p. 3-3.

67. Megan Eckstein, "Navy Slowing Frigate Procurement to Allow Careful Requirements Talks; Contract Award Set for FY2020," U.S. Naval Institute News, May 3, 2017, https://news.usni.org/2017/05/03/navy-slowing-frigate-procurement-to-allow-careful-requirements-talks-contract-award-set-for-fy2020 (accessed August 14, 2018).

68. U.S. Department of the Navy, Naval Sea Systems Command, "Request for Information: FFG(X)—U.S. Navy Guided Missile Frigate Replacement Program," Solicitation Number N0002418R2300, July 10, 2017, https://www.fbo.gov/index?s=opportunity&mode=form&id=cdf24447b8015337e910d330a87518c6&tab=core&tabmode=list& (accessed August 14, 2018).

69. Program Executive Office Littoral Combat Ships, Frigate Program Office, "FFG(X) Industry Day," July 25, 2017, pp. 8–9, https://www.fbo.gov/utils/view?id=73a65bb953f970ae10c1fa82b1030493 (accessed August 14, 2018).

70. U.S. Department of the Navy, Naval Sea Systems Command, "Request for Information: FFG(X)—U.S. Navy Guided Missile Frigate Replacement Program."

71. David B. Larter, "Navy Awards Design Contracts for Future Frigate," *Defense News*, February 16, 2018, https://www.defensenews.com/naval/2018/02/16/navy-awards-design-contracts-for-for-future-frigate/ (accessed July 5, 2018)

72. Lee Hudson, "Navy to Downselect to One Vendor for Future Frigate Competition," Inside Defense, January 9, 2018, https://insidedefense.com/daily-news/navy-downselect-one-vendor-future-frigate-competition (accessed August 14, 2018).

73. Figure 17, "DON Battle Force Ships," in U.S. Department of the Navy, Office of Budget, *Highlights of the Department of the Navy FY 2019 Budget*, p. 3-3.

74. Ronald O'Rourke, "Navy Aegis Ballistic Missile Defense (BMD) Program: Background and Issues for Congress," Congressional Research Service *Report for Members and Committees of Congress*, October 25, 2016, p. 1, https://www.history.navy.mil/content/dam/nhhc/research/library/online-reading-room/technology/bmd/navyaegis_ballistic.pdf (accessed August 14, 2018).

75. The Honorable James F. Geurts, Assistant Secretary of the Navy for Research, Development and Acquisition ASN (RD&A); Vice Admiral William R. Merz, USN, Deputy Chief of Naval Operations for Warfare Systems (OPNAV N9); and Vice Admiral Thomas J. Moore, USN, Commander, Naval Sea Systems Command, statement on "355-Ship Navy: Delivering the Right Capabilities" before the Subcommittee on Seapower and Projection Forces, Committee on Armed Services, U.S. House of Representatives, April 12, 2018, p. 8, https://docs.house.gov/meetings/AS/AS28/20180412/108060/HHRG-115-AS28-Wstate-GeurtsJ-20180412.pdf (accessed August 14, 2018).

76. U.S. Navy, "Cruisers–CG," U.S. Navy *Fact File*, last updated January 9, 2017, http://www.navy.mil/navydata/fact_display.asp?cid=4200&tid=800&ct=4 (accessed July 5, 2018).

77. Admiral John M. Richardson, Chief of Naval Operations, statement on "Fiscal Year 2019 Navy Budget" before the Subcommittee on Defense, Committee on Appropriations, U.S. House of Representatives, March 7, 2018, p. 2, https://docs.house.gov/meetings/AP/AP02/20180307/106932/HHRG-115-AP02-Wstate-RichardsonJ-20180307.PDF (accessed August 14, 2018).

78. Ronald O'Rourke, "Navy DDG-51 and DDG-1000 Destroyer Programs: Background and Issues for Congress," Congressional Research Service *Report for Members and Committees of Congress*, July 31, 2018, "Summary," https://www.everycrsreport.com/files/20180518_RL32109_54ee63399206f53fcb78c1548cdab75207d72ff0.pdf (accessed August 14, 2018).

79. Ibid., p. 8.

80. Ibid., pp. 8–10.

81. Megan Eckstein, "New Requirements for DDG-1000 Focus on Surface Strike," U.S. Naval Institute News, December 4, 2017, https://news.usni.org/2017/12/04/navy-refocus-ddg-1000-surface-strike (accessed August 14, 2018).

82. David B. Larter, "The Navy's Stealth Destroyers to Get New Weapons and a New Mission: Killing Ships," *Defense News*, February 15, 2018, https://www.defensenews.com/naval/2018/02/15/its-official-the-navys-new-stealth-destroyers-will-be-ship-killers/ (accessed July 5, 2018).

83. Ronald O'Rourke, "Navy LPD-17 Flight II (LX[R]) Amphibious Ship Program: Background and Issues for Congress," Congressional Research Service *Report for Members and Committees of Congress*, August 1, 2018, p. 5, https://fas.org/sgp/crs/weapons/R43543.pdf (accessed August 12, 2018).

84. Ibid., p. 1.

85. This is based on a calculation of the total number of attack submarines (which includes three different classes), which was 50 as of publication, and the number of *Los Angeles*-class submarines, which was 32 as of publication.

86. Stephen J. Ilteris, "Build Strategic Fast Attack Submarines," U.S. Naval Institute *Proceedings*, Vol. 142/10/1,364 (October 2016), https://www.usni.org/magazines/proceedings/2016-10/build-strategic-fast-attack-submarines (July 5, 2018).

87. Figure 1, "Navy Lead Ships Consistently Cost More Than Initially Budgeted," in U.S. Government Accountability Office, *Navy Shipbuilding: Past Performance Provides Valuable Lessons for Future Investments*, GAO-18-238SP, June 2018, p. 8, https://www.gao.gov/assets/700/692331.pdf (accessed August 12, 2018).

88. "Q&A with Rear Adm. Goggins," *Undersea Warfare Magazine*, Issue No. 64 (Winter 2018), pp. 10–12, http://www.public.navy.mil/subfor/underseawarfaremagazine/Issues/PDF/USW_Winter_2018.pdf (accessed July 5, 2018).

89. U.S. Government Accountability Office, *Navy Shipbuilding: Past Performance Provides Valuable Lessons for Future Investments*, p. 1.

90. Ronald O'Rourke, "Navy Columbia Class (Ohio Replacement) Ballistic Missile Submarine (SSBN[X]) Program: Background and Issues for Congress," Congressional Research Service *Report for Members and Committees of Congress*, May 12, 2017, p. 6, https://www.hsdl.org/?view&did=801023 (accessed August 12, 2018).

91. Ibid., p. 1.

92. U.S. Department of the Navy, Office of Budget, *Highlights of the Department of the Navy FY 2019 Budget*, p. 4-3.

93. Tyler Rogoway, "Navy F/A-18 Legacy Hornets Have Taken Their Last Cruise Aboard a U.S. Aircraft Carrier," The War Zone, April 14, 2018, http://www.thedrive.com/the-war-zone/20119/navy-f-a-18-legacy-hornets-have-taken-their-last-cruise-aboard-a-u-s-aircraft-carrier (accessed August 12, 2018).

94. Vice Admiral Paul Grosklags, Representing the Assistant Secretary of the Navy (Research, Development And Acquisition); Lieutenant General Steven Rudder, Deputy Commandant for Aviation; and Rear Admiral Scott Conn, Director, Air Warfare, statement on "Department of the Navy's Aviation Programs" before the Subcommittee on Tactical Air and Land Forces, Committee on Armed Services, U.S. House of Representatives, April 12, 2018, p. 3, https://docs.house.gov/meetings/AS/AS25/20180412/108078/HHRG-115-AS25-Wstate-GrosklagsP-20180412.pdf (accessed July 5, 2018).

95. Vice Admiral Paul Grosklags, Representing Assistant Secretary of the Navy (Research, Development and Acquisition); Lieutenant General Jon Davis, Deputy Commandant for Aviation; and Rear Admiral Michael C. Manazir, Director, Air Warfare, statement on "Department of the Navy's Aviation Programs" before the Subcommittee on Seapower, Committee on Armed Services, U.S. Senate, April 20, 2016, p. 9, http://www.armed-services.senate.gov/imo/media/doc/Grosklags-Davis-Manazir_04-20-16.pdf (accessed July 5, 2018).

96. Vice Admiral Paul Grosklags, Representing Assistant Secretary of the Navy (Research, Development and Acquisition); Lieutenant General Steven Rudder, Deputy Commandant for Aviation; and Rear Admiral Scott Conn, Director, Air Warfare, statement on "Department of the Navy's Aviation Programs" before the Subcommittee on Seapower, Committee on Armed Services, U.S. Senate, March 6, 2018, pp. 3 and 5, https://www.armed-services.senate.gov/imo/media/doc/Grosklags_Rudder_Conn_03-06-18.pdf (accessed August 14, 2018).

97. Figure 30, "Aircraft Programs," in U.S. Department of the Navy, Office of Budget, *Highlights of the Department of the Navy FY 2019 Budget*, p. 4-5.

98. Grosklags, Rudder, and Conn, statement on "Department of the Navy's Aviation Programs," April 12, 2018, p. 6.

99. Ibid.

100. Zachary Cohen, "US Navy Fighter Pilot Deaths Tied to Oxygen Issues," CNN, June 17, 2017, http://www.cnn.com/2017/06/16/politics/us-navy-aircraft-pilot-deaths-oxygen-issues/index.html (accessed July 5, 2018).

101. Rear Admiral Sara Joyner, Physiological Episode Action Team Lead, statement on "Physiological Episodes Within Naval Aviation" before the Subcommittee on Tactical Air and Land Forces, Committee on Armed Services, U.S. House of Representatives, February 6, 2018, p. 5, https://docs.house.gov/meetings/AS/AS25/20180206/106824/HHRG-115-AS25-Wstate-JoynerS-20180206.pdf (accessed August 12, 2018).

102. Ibid.

103. Ibid., p. 6.

104. Ibid., pp. 6–9.

105. Jeremiah Gertler, "F-35 Joint Strike Fighter (JSF) Program," Congressional Research Service *Report for Members and Committees of Congress*, April 23, 2018, p. 14, https://fas.org/sgp/crs/weapons/RL30563.pdf (accessed July 5, 2018).

106. Ibid., p. 8.

107. Ben Werner, "Schedule at Risk for Navy F-35C Fighters to be Combat Ready by End of Year," U.S. Naval Institute News, March 29, 2018, https://news.usni.org/2018/03/29/current-schedule-risk-navy-f-35c-fighters-combat-ready-end-year (accessed August 12, 2018).

108. Ibid.

109. Grosklags, Rudder, and Conn, statement on "Department of the Navy's Aviation Programs," April 12, 2018, pp. 17–18, https://docs.house.gov/meetings/AS/AS25/20180412/108078/HHRG-115-AS25-Wstate-GrosklagsP-20180412.pdf (accessed July 5, 2018).

110. Ibid., p. 18.

111. Ibid.

112. Admiral William F. Moran, Vice Chief of Naval Operations, statement on "Current Readiness of U.S. Forces" before the Subcommittee on Readiness, Committee on Armed Services, U.S. Senate, February 14, 2018, pp. 2–4, https://www.armed-services.senate.gov/imo/media/doc/Moran_02-14-18.pdf (accessed August 12, 2018).

113. Ibid., p. 3.

114. Ibid., p. 5.

115. Congressional Quarterly, "Senate Armed Services Committee Holds Hearing on Navy Posture," CQ Congressional Transcripts, April 19, 2018, http://www.cq.com/doc/congressionaltranscripts-5302843?3 (accessed August 12, 2018).

116. Moran, statement on "Current Readiness of U.S. Forces," February 14, 2018, p. 2, https://www.armed-services.senate.gov/imo/media/doc/Moran_02-14-18.pdf (accessed July 5, 2018).

117. John H. Pendleton, Director, Defense Capabilities and Management, U.S. Government Accountability Office, "Navy Readiness: Actions Needed to Address Persistent Maintenance, Training, and Other Challenges Affecting the Fleet," GAO-17-809T, testimony before the Committee on Armed Services, U.S. Senate, September 19, 2017, p. 14, https://www.gao.gov/assets/690/687224.pdf (accessed August 12, 2018).

118. U.S. Department of the Navy, Office of Budget, *Highlights of the Department of the Navy FY 2019 Budget*, pp. 2-12 and 3-5.

119. Ibid., pp. 3-6 and 3-10.

120. Megan Eckstein, "Navy Plans to Spend $21B over 20 Years to Optimize, Modernize Public Shipyards," U.S. Naval Institute News, April 17, 2018, https://news.usni.org/2018/04/17/navy-plans-spend-21b-20-years-optimize-modernize-public-shipyards (accessed August 12, 2018).

121. U.S. Department of the Navy, Office of Budget, *Highlights of the Department of the Navy FY 2019 Budget*, p. 3-4.

122. Ibid., p. 3-9.

123. U.S. Department of the Navy, *Naval Aviation Vision 2016–2025*, p. 12, http://www.navy.mil/strategic/Naval_Aviation_Vision.pdf (accessed August 12, 2018).

124. Tara Copp, "Navy's Spike in Aviation Mishaps Is the Military's Worst, up 82 Percent," *Military Times*, April 8, 2018, https://www.militarytimes.com/news/your-military/2018/04/08/navys-spike-in-aviation-mishaps-is-the-militarys-worst-up-82-percent/ (accessed August 11, 2018).

125. Vice Admiral Troy M. Shoemaker, Commander, Naval Air Forces, statement on "Aviation Readiness" before the Subcommittee on Readiness, Committee on Armed Services, U.S. House of Representatives, November 9, 2017, p. 3, https://armedservices.house.gov/legislation/hearings/aviation-readiness-whats-flight-plan (accessed August 11, 2018).

126. Ibid., p. 4.

127. Ibid., p. 5.

128. Corey Dickstein, "CNO Orders Navy-wide Pause, Broad Review After 2nd Pacific Collision in 2 Months," *Stars and Stripes*, August 21, 2017, https://www.stripes.com/news/pacific/cno-orders-navy-wide-pause-broad-review-after-2nd-pacific-collision-in-2-months-1.483806#.WZxmGumQyUk (accessed July 5, 2018).

129. U.S. Department of the Navy, Fleet Forces Command, *Comprehensive Review of Recent Surface Force Incidents*, October 26, 2017, p. 6, http://s3.amazonaws.com/CHINFO/Comprehensive+Review_Final.pdf (accessed July 5, 2018).

130. Ibid., pp. 6–7 and 107–114.

131. U.S. Department of the Navy, *Strategic Readiness Review 2017*, http://s3.amazonaws.com/CHINFO/SRR+Final+12112017.pdf (accessed August 11, 2018).

132. Ibid., pp. 4–5.

133. U.S. Navy, Naval History and Heritage Command, "Naval Aviation Units Involved in the Persian Gulf War (16 January–27 February 1991)," July 8, 2014, https://www.history.navy.mil/research/histories/naval-aviation-history/involvement-by-conflict/gulf-war-carrier-deployments.html (accessed August 11, 2018).

134. Gregory Bereiter, "The US Navy in Operation Enduring Freedom, 2001–2002," U.S. Navy, Naval History and Heritage Command, August 18, 2017, https://www.history.navy.mil/research/library/online-reading-room/title-list-alphabetically/u/us-navy-operation-enduring-freedom-2001-2002.html (accessed August 11, 2018).

135. U.S. Navy, Naval History and Heritage Command, "Operation Iraqi Freedom," November 6, 2017, https://www.history.navy.mil/browse-by-topic/wars-conflicts-and-operations/terrorism/operation-iraqi-freedom.html (accessed August 11, 2018).

136. Congressional Budget Office, *The U.S. Military's Force Structure: A Primer*, July 2016, p. 53, https://www.cbo.gov/publication/51535 (accessed August 11, 2018).

137. This requirement is derived from the BUR's requirement for four–five carrier strike groups per MRC; however, this *Index* finds that this number is low by historical accounts and therefore recommends one additional carrier per MRC.

138. The 2016 Force Structure Assessment established a requirement for "[a] minimum of 12 Aircraft Carriers...to meet the increased warfighting response requirements of the Defense Planning Guidance Defeat/Deny force sizing direction." U.S. Navy, "Executive Summary: 2016 Navy Force Structure Assessment (FSA)," p. 3.

139. The Navy's Optimized Fleet Response Plan dictates a 36-month cycle of maintenance, training, and forward deployment. The OFRP allows for six months of shipyard maintenance, eight months of basic and integrated training, and a seven-month deployment followed by a 15-month sustainment period in which the CSG will be at its homeport but maintaining a deployed-force level of proficiency. If we assume that the carrier and its escort ships are not available during their maintenance cycle for even a 30-day surge, this equates to just over 19 percent unavailability in the 36-month cycle. The seven-month deployment per each cycle also equates to five CVNs required for a 1.0 continuous CVN presence.

140. U.S. Department of the Navy, Office of the Chief of Naval Operations, "Force Composition of Afloat Navy and Naval Groups," OPNAV INSTRUCTION 3501,316C, November 10, 2017, Enclosure (1), "Carrier Strike Group," p. 2. https://doni.documentservices. dla.mil/Directives/03000%20Naval%20Operations%20and%20Readiness/03-500%20Training%20and%20Readiness%20 Services/3501.316C.pdf (accessed August 15, 2018).

141. Table 1.1, "Notional Configuration for a Carrier Battle Group," in U.S. General Accounting Office, *Navy Carrier Battle Groups: The Structure and Affordability of the Future Force*, GAO/NSIAD-93-94, February 1993, p. 18, https://www.gao.gov/assets/160/152948. pdf (accessed August 11, 2018).

142. U.S. Navy, "The Carrier Air Wing," http://www.navy.mil/navydata/ships/carriers/powerhouse/airwing.asp (accessed July 5, 2018).

143. The full array of aircraft comprising a carrier air wing also includes one EA-18G Growler electronic attack squadron, one E-2D Hawkeye airborne early warning squadron, two SH-60 Seahawk helicopter squadrons, and one C-2 Greyhound logistics support squadron.

144. Table E-1, "Comparison of Navy's 355-Ship Goal, 346-Ship Navy Goal from 1993 BUR, and 346-Ship Navy Goal from 2010 QDR Review Panel," in O'Rourke, "Navy Force Structure and Shipbuilding Plans," p. 62.

145. U.S. Navy, "Executive Summary: 2016 Navy Force Structure Assessment (FSA)," p. 1.

146. The size and capability of amphibious ships also have grown over time, with smaller amphibious ships like the old landing ship tank (LST) replaced by the much larger LSD and LPD classes. Consequently, fewer ships are required to lift the same or an even larger amphibious force.

147. U.S. Marine Corps, Concepts and Programs, "Types of MAGTFs," http://www.candp.marines.mil/Organization/MAGTF/Types-cf-MAGTFs/ (accessed August 18, 2018). See especially the included graphic, "Notional Laydown of a Marine Expeditionary Brigade (MEB)."

148. Ibid.

149. The Navy's "Force Composition of Afloat Navy and Naval Groups" defines the requirements for an ESG as follows: "[a] minimum of three amphibious ships" based on Combatant Commander requirements and missions, including "[a]t least one amphibious assault ship, multi- or general purpose ship (landing ship assault (LHA) [or] landing helicopter dock (LHD))"; "[a]t least one amphibious transport dock (LPD)"; and "[at] least one amphibious dock landing ship (LSD)." "[O]ther forces assigned (surface combatants and auxiliary support vessels will be similar to those assigned to a CSG dependent on the threat and capabilities of the ships assigned)." U.S. Department of the Navy, Office of the Chief of Naval Operations, "Force Composition of Afloat Navy and Naval Groups," OPNAVINST 3501.316C, Enclosure (2), "Amphibious Ready Group and Marine Expeditionary Unit," p. 1, and Enclosure (3), "Expeditionary Strike Group," p. 1.

150. Congressional Budget Office, *An Analysis of the Navy's Amphibious Warfare Ships for Deploying Marines Overseas*, November 2011, p. 1, http://www.cbo.gov/sites/default/files/cbofiles/attachments/11-18-AmphibiousShips.pdf (accessed July 5, 2018).

151. U.S. Navy, "Executive Summary: 2016 Navy Force Structure Assessment (FSA)," p. 3.

152. Ibid., p. 2.

153. Mattis, *Summary of the 2018 National Defense Strategy*, p. 4.

154. Congressional Quarterly, "Senate Armed Services Committee Holds Hearing on Navy Posture," April 19, 2018.

155. Vice Admiral Luke M. McCollum, Chief of Navy Reserve, Commander, Navy Reserve Force; Vice Admiral William K. Lescher, Deputy Chief of Naval Operations for Integration of Capabilities and Resources; and Vice Admiral Andrew L. Lewis, Deputy Chief of Naval Operations for Operations, Plans and Strategy, statement on "U.S. Navy Readiness" before the Subcommittee on Readiness of the House Committee on Armed Services, U.S. House of Representatives, March 20, 2018, p. 6, https://docs.house. gov/meetings/AS/AS03/20180320/108020/HHRG-115-AS03-Wstate-LescherW-20180320.pdf (accessed August 12, 2018).

156. U.S. Government Accountability Office, *Military Readiness: Progress and Challenges in Implementing the Navy's Optimized Fleet Response Plan*, GAO-16-466R, May 2, 2016, p. 1, https://www.gao.gov/assets/680/676904.pdf (accessed August 12, 2018).

157. Ibid., p. 8.

158. Stenographic transcript of *Hearing to Receive Testimony on the Current Readiness of U.S. Forces*, Subcommittee on Readiness and Management Support, Committee on Armed Services, U.S. Senate, February 8, 2016, pp. 44–45, https://www.armed-services.senate.gov/imo/media/doc/17-07_02-08-17.pdf (accessed August 12, 2018).

159. Hope Hodge Seck, "CNO Orders Operational Pause, Review After Latest Ship Collision," Military.com, August 21, 2017, https://www.military.com/daily-news/2017/08/21/cno-orders-operational-pause-review-after-latest-ship-collision.html (accessed August 11, 2018).

160. Pendleton, "Navy Readiness: Actions Needed to Address Persistent Maintenance, Training, and Other Challenges Affecting the Fleet," p. 8, https://www.gao.gov/assets/690/687224.pdf (accessed July 5, 2018).

161. Ibid.

162. David B. Larter, "Troubling US Navy Review Finds Widespread Shortfalls in Basic Seamanship," *Defense News*, June 6, 2018, https://www.defensenews.com/naval/2018/06/06/troubling-us-navy-review-finds-widespread-shortfalls-in-basic-seamanship/ (accessed August 11, 2018).

163. Congressional Quarterly, "House Armed Services Subcommittees on Readiness and Seapower and Projection Forces Holds [*sic*] Joint Hearing on Surface Warfare," CQ Congressional Transcripts, January 18, 2018, http://www.cq.com/doc/congressionaltranscripts-5250864?2 (accessed August 17, 2018).

164. David B. Larter, "In Japan, a Hard-Hit US Navy Fleet Is Steadying on a New Course," *Defense News*, April 10, 2018, https://www.defensenews.com/digital-show-dailies/navy-league/2018/04/10/in-japan-a-hard-hit-fleet-is-steadying-on-a-new-course/ (accessed August 11, 2018).

165. Department of the Navy, Admiral John Richardson, Chief of Naval Operations, statement on "Surface Warfare at a Crossroads" before the Subcommittee on Readiness and Subcommittee on Seapower and Projection Forces, Committee on Armed Services, U.S. House of Representatives, January 18, 2018, p. 2, https://docs.house.gov/meetings/AS/AS03/20180118/106784/HHRG-115-AS03-Wstate-RichardsonJ-20180118.pdf (accessed August 12, 2018).

166. Commander, Naval Surface Forces (COMNAVSURFOR), message on "Surface Warfare Officer Career Path and Training Continuum," June 15, 2018, https://news.usni.org/2018/06/28/new-career-path-surface-warfare-officers-stresses-fundamentals-training-first-ship-time-sea (accessed August 12, 2018).

167. Navy News Service, "Navy Stands Up Readiness Reform and Oversight Council," February 2, 2018, http://www.navy.mil/submit/display.asp?story_id=104212 (accessed August 12, 2018).

168. McCollum, Lescher, and Lewis, statement on "U.S. Navy Readiness," March 20, 2018, p. 8.

169. "Current Fleet" numbers taken from the Naval Vessel Registry as of July 16, 2018. U.S. Department of the Navy recommendations come from the 2016 Navy Force Structure Assessment. 12 Columbia-class nuclear-powered ballistic missile submarines (SSBN) can provide the same at-sea presence requirements as 14 Ohio-class SSBNs due to condensed timelines for midlife maintenance overhauls. Numbers for large surface combatants include guided missile destroyers (DDG) and guided missile cruisers (CG). Large surface combatant requirement driven by carrier strike group (CSG), expeditionary strike group (ESG), and ballistic missile defense (BMD) requirements. Numbers for small surface combatants include littoral combat ships (LCS), guided missile frigates (FFG), and mine countermeasure ships (MCM). Nuclear-powered guided missile submarines (SSGNs) were not considered in recommended force structure since all SSGNS will be retired by 2028 and the soonest the Navy could field a replacement would be approximately 2040. *2019 Index* recommendation of 45 large deck amphibious ships represents a minimum requirement. New Marine Corps requirements for distributed expeditionary operations could demand additional smaller/non-traditional amphibious support ships. If the current fleet of single mission fleet oilers (T-AO) and dry cargo/ammunition ships (T-AKE) in the Navy's combat logistics force were replaced by a more capable class of logistics ships, this number could be reduced. Command and support ships include amphibious command ships (LCC), expeditionary fast transport ships (EPF), expeditionary mobile base ships (ESB), expeditionary transfer dock (ESD), submarine tenders (AS), ocean surveillance ships (T-AGOS), and salvage and submarine rescue mission support (T-ATS).

U.S. Air Force

The U.S. Air Force (USAF) is the youngest of the four branches of the U.S. military, having been born out of the Army Signal Corps to become its own service in 1947. The USAF's mission set has expanded significantly over the years, and this is reflected in the organizational changes in its structure. Initially, Air Force operations were divided among four major components—Strategic Air Command, Tactical Air Command, Air Defense Command, and Military Air Transport Service—that collectively reflected the "fly, fight, and win" nature of the service. Space's rise to prominence began in the early 1950s, and with it came a host of faculties that would help to expand the impact (and mission set) of this service.

Today, the Air Force focuses on five principal missions:

- Air and space superiority;

- Intelligence, surveillance, and reconnaissance (ISR);

- Mobility and lift;

- Global strike; and

- Command and control (C2).

These missions, while all necessary, put an even greater squeeze on the resources available to the Air Force in an incredibly strained and competitive fiscal environment. Using the 2012 Defense Strategic Guidance (DSG) as its framework for determining investment priorities and posture, the Air Force intentionally traded size for quality by aiming to be a "smaller, but superb, force that maintains the agility, flexibility, and readiness to engage a full range of contingencies and threats."[1]

There can be no doubt that the Air Force has become smaller. Testifying before the Senate Armed Services Committee in 2017, Secretary of the Air Force Heather Wilson and Air Force Chief of Staff General David Goldfein stated flatly that the Air Force "is too small for the missions demanded of it." Even with its reduced size, the funding available through fiscal year (FY) 2017 did not allow the service to acquire enough aircraft to reverse the downward spiral of aircraft availability or the level of flying time that pilots need to sustain more than a marginal level of readiness.[2] Appearing before the same committee in 2018, Secretary Wilson and General Goldfein testified that "[t]he projected mismatch between demand and available resources has widened."[3]

Sequestration has forced General Goldfein to make strategic trades in capability, capacity, and readiness to meet the current operational demands of the war on terrorism and prepare for the future. Budgetary uncertainty over the five years of sequestration has had many detrimental effects on the USAF's ability to sustain the war on terrorism, remain ready for a full-spectrum war, and modernize its aging fleet of aircraft. Presidential budgets during the sequestration years of the Obama Administration always proved aspirational, and those trades among capability, capacity, and readiness failed to keep pace with the demands placed on the service. When funding did arrive, it was through continuing resolutions well into the year of execution, which prevented any real form of strategic planning.[4]

The Obama Administration's FY 2017 budget would have continued that decline if Congress had not delivered a $5.6 billion topline increase through a request for additional appropriations that was approved in the spring of 2018. The additional appropriations allowed the Air Force to bring on an additional 4,000 active-duty personnel and fully fund its flying hour program, arresting the decline in people, equipment, and training.[5] The President's budget will increase the Air Force topline from $132.2 billion in FY 2017 to $146.3 billion in FY 2018 and $156.2 in FY 2019. Used prudently, these funding levels will enable the Air Force to reverse downward trends in capacity, capability, and readiness, all three of which are under stress.

Capacity

The tradeoff in capacity has seen near-term reductions in lift, command and control, and fourth-generation fighter aircraft to ensure that the Air Force's top three modernization programs—the F-35A, Long-Range Strike Bomber (LRS-B), and KC-46A—are preserved.[6] Unlike some of the other services, the Air Force did not expand in numbers during the post-9/11 buildup. Rather, it got smaller as programmed retirement dates for older aircraft were not offset by programmed retirements. Successive delays in F-35 and KC-46 development have carried over into production, leaving both fighter and tanker fleets short of the ready numbers required to train for and execute their respective missions.

Air Force capacity in terms of the number of aircraft had been on a constant downward slope since 1952.[7] The President's budget for FY 2018 had projected a decrease from 5,517 aircraft in 2017 to 5,416 in 2018,[8] but over the course of the year, the inventory slipped to 5,373. The President's budget for FY 2019 ends the slide and adds 53 aircraft to the roster for a projected total of 5,426 at the end of FY 2019.[9] Totals for specific platforms can be found in Table 7.

Adversaries are modernizing and innovating faster than the Air Force is, jeopardizing America's technological advantage in air and space. Before 1991, the Air Force bought approximately 510 aircraft per year. Over the past 20 years, it has acquired an average of only 96 new aircraft per year. Today, the average age of our aircraft is over 28 years, yet the Air Force—even with the budget increases for FY 2018 and FY 2019—has no plans to raise the acquisition rates for the F-35 or KC-46 to buy down that average.[10] The decades-long trend of steadily declining aircraft numbers, coupled with the fleet's ever-growing average age, may be lulling senior leaders into the belief that the service can be fixed sometime in the future, but the numbers tell a different story.

The combination of downsizing following the end of the Cold War and Budget Control Act of 2011 (BCA) spending caps has caused the Air Force to shrink from 70 combat-coded[11] active-duty fighter squadrons during Desert Storm[12] to just 55 across the whole of the active-duty, guard, and reserve force today. Only 32 of those squadrons are part of the active-duty Air Force.[13]

For the purpose of assessing capacity and readiness, this *Index* refers to combat-coded aircraft and units maintained within the Active component of the U.S. Air Force. "Combat-coded" aircraft and related squadrons are aircraft and units assigned a wartime mission. The numbers exclude units and aircraft assigned to training, operational test and evaluation, and other missions. The software and munitions carriage/delivery capability of aircraft in these units renders them incompatible with or less survivable than combat-coded versions of the same aircraft. For example, all F-35As may appear to be ready for combat, but training wings and test and evaluation jets have hardware and software limitations that would severely limit their utility in combat. While those jets may be slated for upgrades, hardware updates sideline jets for several months to manifest, and training wings and certain test organizations will be the last to receive those upgrades.

TABLE 7

Total Active-Duty Aircraft Inventory

	2016	2017	2018	End 2019 Total
A-10	143	143	143	143
AC-130J	29	28	35	41
B-1	61	62	62	62
B-2	20	20	20	20
B-52	58	58	58	58
C-130H	13	4	3	0
C-130J	85	94	104	105
C-5	36	33	36	36
C-12	28	28	28	28
C-17	170	147	154	146
C-20	5	0	—	0
C-21	17	17	19	19
C-32	4	4	4	4
C-37	12	12	12	12
C-40	4	4	4	4
CV-22	49	50	50	50
E-3	31	31	31	31
E-4	4	4	4	4
E-9	2	2	2	2
E-11A	—	—	4	4
EC-130H	14	14	14	13
F-15	317	313	316	316
F-16	570	570	557	548
F-22	165	166	166	166
F-35	102	123	161	212
HC-130J	19	19	19	23
HC-130N	2	2	0	0
HH-60	78	86	82	89
KC-10	59	59	59	53*
KC-135	156	155	147	146*
KC-46	11	16	28	34*
MC-130H	13	16	16	15
MC-130J	35	37	37	41
MQ-9	228	225	220	228
NC-135	1	1	1	1
OC-135	2	2	2	2
RC-135	22	22	22	22
RQ-4	7	33	36	36
T-1	178	178	178	178
T-6	445	445	444	444
T-38	506	505	504	504
T-41	4	4	3	3
T-51	3	3	3	3
T-53	25	24	24	24
TC-135	3	3	3	3
TG-15	5	5	5	5
TG-16	19	19	19	19
TH-1	28	28	28	28
TU-2	5	5	5	4
U-2	27	27	27	26
UH-1	68	68	68	68
UV-18B	3	3	3	3
VC-25	2	2	2	2
WC-135	2	2	2	2

* FY 2019 total numbers are contingent upon acquisition of six KC-46 aircraft.
SOURCE: Headquarters U.S. Air Force response to query by The Heritage Foundation.

☎ heritage.org

CHART 14

Air Force Attack and Fighter Aircraft

Total aircraft inventory (including training and replacement aircraft) has declined by 57 percent over 30 years. Although two new aircraft have been added to the inventory in the past two decades, their procurement rates have barely offset the retirement of legacy systems.

TOTAL AIR FORCE INVENTORY OF ATTACK AND FIGHTER AIRCRAFT

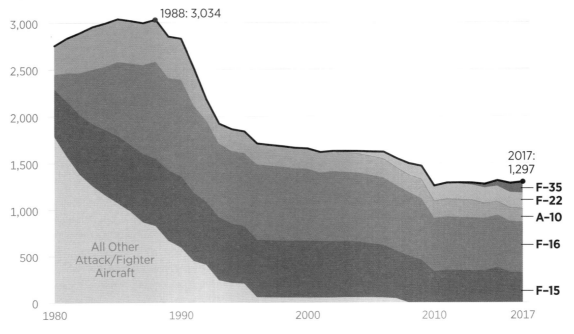

NOTE: These figures differ slightly from figures found elsewhere in this *Index*. The *Index* only assesses combat-coded aircraft (capable of executing operational missions).

SOURCES:

- Pre-1996: James C. Ruehrmund Jr. and Christopher J. Bowie, "Arsenal of Airpower: USAF Aircraft Inventory 1950–2009," The Mitchell Institute, November 2010, https://higherlogicdownload.s3.amazonaws.com/AFA/6379b747-7730-4f82-9b45-a1c80d6c8fdb/UploadedImages/Mitchell%20Publications/Arsenal%20of%20Airpower.pdf (accessed August 6, 2018).
- 1996–current: *Air Force Magazine*, "Air Force Magazine Almanacs Archive," 1997–2018, http://www.airforcemag.com/Almanacs/Pages/default.aspx (accessed August 6, 2018).

🏠 heritage.org

The Heritage *Index of U.S. Military Strength* assesses that a force of 1,200 fighter aircraft is required to execute a two–major regional contingency (two-MRC) strategy, a number that is also reflected in a 2011 study conducted by the Air Force.[14] In 2015, pressured by a third year of budget caps dictated by the BCA, the service acknowledged that it could reduce the 1,200 fighter requirement by 100 jets by assuming more risk.[15]

Of the 5,426 manned and unmanned aircraft projected to be in the USAF's inventory at the end of FY 2019, 1,385 are active-duty fighters, and 924 of these are combat-coded aircraft.[16] This number includes all active-duty backup inventory aircraft as well as attrition reserve spares.[17]

The number of fighters and fighter squadrons available to deploy to contingency

TABLE 8

Precision Munitions Expenditures and Acquisitions

NUMBER OF MUNITIONS

	Expended FY 2017	Expended FY 2018 (est.)	FY 2019 Acquisitions
JDAM	21,628	5,462	36,000
HELLFIRE	2,990	2,110	4,354
SDB-I	2,871*	749*	6,853
SDB-II			510
APKWS	0	0	7,279
JASSM-ER	0	19*	360
LGB	1,660	276	0
TOTAL	**29,149**	**8,597**	**56,105**

* Figures not broken out.
SOURCE: Headquarters U.S. Air Force response to query by The Heritage Foundation.   ☏ heritage.org

operations does not just affect wartime readiness; it also affects retention. The constant churn of overseas deployments and stateside temporary duty (TDY) assignments is one of the primary reasons cited by pilots for separating from the service. The only two ways to solve that problem are to decrease operational tempo and/or increase capacity. When the order to deploy assets comes from the President, the Air Force must answer that call with assets capable of executing the mission no matter what the effects on morale or retention might be, which means that reducing operational tempo is not an option for Air force leadership. This leaves increasing capacity as the only fix, and that option has not been brought up as a possibility by the Chief of Staff, much less through actual Air Force budgetary commitment.

The funding that facilitated the Reagan build-up of the 1980s was available for just a few years, and the assets acquired during that period are now aging out. Even the most stalwart defense hawks are forecasting an end to the current defense plus-up in FY 2020, and unless Congress intervenes, the opportunity to increase capacity beyond its current marginal level may be lost.

Capacity also relies on the stockpile of available munitions and the production capacity of the munitions industry. The actual number of munitions within the U.S. stockpile is classified, but there are indicators that render an assessment of the overall health of this vital area. The inventory for precision-guided munitions (PGM) has been severely stressed by nearly 17 years of sustained combat operations and budget actions that limited the service's ability to procure replacements and increase stockpiles. In 2017, the Air Force alone expended 29,149 precision-guided munitions. While Overseas Contingency Operations (OCO) funding has provided some relief, there is typically a delay of 24–36 months between conclusion of a contract and delivery of these weapons, which means that munitions are often replaced three years after they were expended.

During the past three years, however, funding has improved significantly, and the preferred munitions are starting to recover to pre-war levels.[18] Table 8 depicts recent expenditures as well as inventory replenishments.

Capability

The risk assumed with a marginal level of capacity has placed an ever-growing burden on the capability of the assets within the Air Force portfolio. The ensuing capability-over-capacity strategy centers on the idea of developing and maintaining a *more*-capable force that can win against advanced fighters and surface-to-air missile systems now being developed by top-tier potential adversaries like China and Russia that are also increasing their capacity.

Any assessment of capability includes not only the incorporation of advanced technologies, but also the overall health of the inventory. Most aircraft have programmed life spans of 20 to 30 years, based on a programmed level of annual flying hours. The bending and flexing of airframes over time in the air generates predictable levels of stress and metal fatigue. The average age of Air Force aircraft is 28 years, and some fleets, such as the B-52 bomber, average 56 years. In addition, KC-135s comprise 87 percent of the Air Force's tankers and are over 56 years old on average, and the average age of the F-15C fleet is over 34 years, leaving less than 8 percent of its useful service life remaining.[19] That same fleet comprises 44 percent of USAF air superiority platforms.[20] An unknown number of F-15s will likely receive airframe modifications through service life extension programs (SLEPs) that will keep them in service at least through 2030.

The fleet of F-16Cs are 27 years old on average,[21] and the service has used up nearly 82 percent of its expected life span. The Air Force recently announced its intent to extend the service lives of 300 F-16s with a plan to keep those jets flying through 2050.[22] Although SLEPs can lengthen the useful life of airframes, the dated avionics of those airframes become increasingly expensive to maintain. Those modifications are costly, and the added expense consumes available funding and reduces the amount the services have to invest in modernization, which is critical to ensuring future capability.

The Air Force's ISR and lift capabilities face similar problems in specific areas that affect both capability and capacity. The majority of the Air Force's ISR aircraft are now unmanned aerial vehicles (UAVs),[23] but even here the numbers fell in 2018 from 371[24] to 220 with the complete retirement of the MQ-1 Predator weapons system.[25] The RQ-4 Global Hawk is certainly one of the more reliable of those platforms, but gross weight restrictions limit the number of sensors that it can carry, and the warfighter still needs the capability of the U-2, which is now 35 years old on average with no scheduled retirement currently on the books.[26]

The E-8 Joint Surveillance Target Attack Radar System (J-STARS) and the RC-135 Rivet Joint are critical ISR platforms, and each was built on the Boeing 707 platform, the last one of which was constructed in 1979. The reliability of the Air Force fleet is at risk because of the challenges linked to aircraft age and flight hours, and the fleet needs to be modernized. In the 2019 NDAA, Congress elected not to recapitalize the J-STARS fleet, in line with the service's belief that that platform could not survive in a modern high-threat environment. In its stead, the Air Force is working on an incremental approach for a J-STARS replacement that focuses on advanced and disaggregated sensors, along with enhanced and hardened communications links. The Air Force refers to this solution as the Advanced Battle Management System, envisioned as an all-encompassing approach to both airborne and ground Battle Management Command and Control (BMC2) that is designed to allow the Air Force to fight and support joint and coalition partners in the high-end fight of tomorrow.[27]

A service's investment in modernization ensures that future capability remains healthy. Investment programs aim not only to procure enough to fill current capacity requirements, but also to advance future capabilities with advanced technology. The Air Force's number one priority remains the F-35A. It is the next-generation fighter scheduled to replace all legacy multirole and close air support aircraft. The rationale for the Air Force's program of record of 1,763 aircraft is to replace every F-117, F-16, and A-10 aircraft on a one for one basis.[28] The Defense Department made draconian cuts in the original plan to purchase 750 F-22A program of record aircraft,[29] reducing it to a final program of record of just 183 total active, guard, and reserve fighters.[30] Even so,

Heritage Foundation experts find a requirement for 1,200 combat-coded fighters, and given the service's intent to retain hundreds of fourth-generation fighters in its fleet for the foreseeable future, the programmed purchase of F-35As should be reduced to 1,260 aircraft.[31]

The Active Air Force currently has just 96 F-15Cs left in its fleet, and the concerns about what platform will fill this role when the F-15C is retired have now manifested into a significant gap. Even with their superior technology, 166 combat-coded F-22As from the active and guard inventory would be unable to fulfill the wartime requirement for air superiority fighters for even a single major regional contingency.[32] The F-35A's multirole design favors the air-to-ground mission, but its fifth-generation faculties will allow it also to be dominant in an air-to-air role,[33] which will allow it to augment the F-22A in many scenarios.[34]

Fulfilling the operational need for air superiority fighters will be further strained in the near term because the F-22 retrofit—a mix of structural alterations to the fleet of aircraft needed for the airframe to reach its promised service life—has been forecasted to run through 2021. As a result of the retrofit, only 62 percent (103 of 166) of the active duty mission fleet of F-22As are currently available.[35]

As with the other Joint Strike Fighter variants, the F-35A has experienced a host of developmental problems that resulted in its initial operating capability (IOC) date being pushed from 2013 to 2016. This system of systems relies heavily on software, and the 3F software that enables full operating capability (FOC) is currently being fielded.[36] The updated software and required hardware modifications are already incorporated in jets coming off the production line.[37] The F-35 has endured several delays and controversies, but experienced fighter pilots now flying the jet have a great deal of confidence in their new fighter.[38]

A second top priority for the USAF is the KC-46A air refueling tanker aircraft. Although the KC-46 has experienced a series of delays, it reached a milestone in August 2016 that enabled low-rate initial production.[39] The Air

Force awarded the contract for 19 initial aircraft in August 2016 and has programmed delivery of 70 aircraft by FY 2020.[40] It expects to have all 179 of these new tankers in service by 2028. The Pegasus "will replace less than half of the current tanker fleet and will leave the Air Force with over 200 aging KC-135s awaiting recapitalization."[41]

The third major priority for the USAF from an acquisition perspective is the B-21 Raider, formerly called the Long-Range Strike Bomber (LSRB). As of May 2017, the capacity of the Air Force bomber fleet had fallen from 290 aircraft in 1991 to 156 B-1s, B-2s, and B-52s, and "[t]he current number [was] insufficient to meet Defense Planning Guidance and nuclear guidance while sustaining current operational demands and maintaining sufficient training and readiness capacity."[42]

The USAF awarded Northrop Grumman the B-21 contract to build the Engineering and Manufacturing Development (EMD) phase, which includes associated training and support systems and initial production lots. The program completed an Integrated Baseline Review for the overall B-21 development effort, as well as the jet's Preliminary Design Review. The Air Force is committed to a minimum of 100 B-21s at an average cost of $564 million per plane.[43]

With the budget deal that was reached for FY 2018 and FY 2019, the Secretary of the Air Force announced the service's intent to retire all B-1s and B-2s and sustain a fleet comprised of 100 B-21s and 71 B-52s.[44]

The B-21 is programmed to begin replacing portions of the B-52 and B-1B fleets by the mid-2020s.[45] In the interim, the Air Force continues to execute a SLEP on the entire fleet of 62 B-1s in the inventory to restore all 289 B-1 engines to their original specifications. The Air Force plans to modernize the B-2's Defense Management System, Stores Management Operational Flight Program, and Common Very-Low-Frequency/Low Frequency Receiver Program to ensure that this penetrating bomber remains viable in highly contested environments, keeping it fully viable until it is replaced by the B-21.

Modernization efforts are also underway for the B-52. The FY 2018 budget funds the re-engineering of this fleet. The jet was designed in the 1950s. The current fleet entered service in the 1960s and will remain in the inventory through 2050.

The Air Force's strategy of capability over capacity is encumbered by the requirement to sustain ongoing combat operations in Afghanistan, Iraq, and Syria. While operations are down in Syria and Iraq, they are likely to accelerate in Afghanistan during the next two years.

Readiness

During testimony before the Senate Armed Services Committee in 2017, the Secretary of the Air Force and the Chief of Staff informed Congress that "[w]e are at our lowest state of full spectrum readiness in our history."[46] While the Department of Defense has seemingly stifled open conversations or testimony about readiness, there are plenty of facts and ancillary evidence to support a conclusion that their statement and other 2017 general officer testimony still apply in 2018.

Full-spectrum operations include the seamless conduct of nuclear deterrence operations, continued support of counterterrorism (CT) operations, and readiness for potential conflict with a near-peer competitor. During testimony before the House Armed Services Committee Subcommittee on Readiness, Major General Scott West informed Congress that the Air Force was "able to conduct nuclear deterrence operations and support CT operations, [but] operations against a near-peer competitor would require a significant amount of training" because readiness is out of balance "at a time when the Air Force is small, old, and heavily tasked."[47]

The Air Force used five areas or "levers" of readiness to inform the FY 2018 budget request:

- Flying Hour Program (FHP), which includes funding sortie production;

- Critical Skills Availability (Pilot/Maintenance specialty level training);

- Weapons System Sustainment (Aircraft availability production);

- Training Resource Availability (Funding for Ranges, Live/Virtual Construct);

- Deploy to Dwell (Funding for force capacity to meet current taskings).

Flying Hour Program and Critical Skills Availability. A shortage of aircraft maintenance personnel (maintainers) limited the ability of the Air Force to generate sorties through 2017. The Air Force was short 3,400 aircraft maintainers at the close of 2016,[48] and senior leaders cited this shortfall as the principal reason why fighter pilots who once averaged over 200 hours per year were fortunate to fly 120 hours in 2014.[49] The average was said to have risen above 150 hours a year in 2017,[50] but data provided by the Air Force organization charged with tracking these details revealed that fighter pilots received an average of 11.8 hours per month in 2017, and the average has fallen to just 11.6 hours per month for the first five months of 2018. Pilots are flying less than seven sorties per month, less than two times a week on average. If that rate holds for the rest of the year, pilots will receive just 139 hours in 2018.

F-35A pilots received the lowest number of hours and sorties of any other major weapons system in the fighter community, averaging just 6.3 hours and 6.3 sorties per month—an annualized rate of just 76 hours and 76 sorties per year.[51] These low sortie rates are happening in spite of the fact that maintenance manning levels have almost fully recovered from the shortfalls suffered in previous years.

In June 2016, responding to written questions posed as part of the hearing on his confirmation as Chief of Staff of the Air Force, General David Goldfein stated that his service could not surge enough combat-ready forces to execute a single MRC and still meet the remaining demand for global combat-ready forces. He went on to say that less than 50 percent of combat units are ready for "full spectrum"

TABLE 9

Maintenance Skill Level Manning

Skill Level	Authorized Level	Actual Manning	Manning Percentage
3–Level (Apprentice)	14,525	17,331	119%
5–Level (Journeyman)	16,857	16,225	91%
7–Level (Craftsman)	33,492	32,152	96%

NOTE: Figures are current as of June 2018.
SOURCE: Headquarters U.S. Air Force response to query by The Heritage Foundation.   ☎ heritage.org

---

(high-threat, high-intensity) combat.[52] Nearly a year later, on March 29, 2017, Lieutenant General Mark Nowland, Air Force Deputy Chief of Staff for Operations, testified that only four of the Air Force's 55 total (Active, Reserve, and National Guard) fighter squadrons were at the very highest levels of readiness and that fewer than half were in the top two readiness tiers.[53] There is no evidence of any real improvement since then.

The current state of Air Force fighter readiness has many intangibles, but the things that can be measured such as average sortie per aircraft/month and total flying time point to a readiness level that has not improved over 2017. These sortie/hour rates remain below those of the hollow force experienced during the Carter Administration in the late 1970s.

Weapons System Sustainment. Nearly constant deployments and a shortage of maintenance personnel have severely limited aircraft availability and sortie production. Maintenance manning shortfalls have almost fully recovered from the previous year, but manning for pilots has continued to fall.

On March 29, 2017, Lieutenant General Gina M. Grosso, Air Force Deputy Chief of Staff for Manpower, Personnel, and Services, testified that at the end of FY 2016, the Air Force had a shortfall of 1,555 pilots across all mission areas (608 active, 653 guard, 294 reserve). Of this amount, the total force was short 1,211 fighter pilots (873 active, 272 guard, 66 reserve).[54] The numbers continued to fall, and at the end of FY 2017, the Air Force was short

more than 2,000 pilots, of which 1,300 are empty fighter pilot billets across the Total Force (All Active/Guard/Reserve requirements). Although the Air Force no longer breaks these numbers out by Active Guard and Reserve, the total pilot shortfall has grown by 29 percent, and 9 percent for the fighter community over the previous year.[55]

The pipeline for pilots is also suffering. After a rash of hypoxia incidents, the Air Force grounded its fleet of T-6 trainers, effectively shutting down the pilot training pipeline for a month in February 2018.[56] The Air Force had projected that it would graduate 1,200 pilots in 2018, but the grounding will reduce that number by at least 82 for a total of 1,118 pilots in 2018.[57] The projections for 2019 increase pilot production to 1,300. However, both numbers rely on a 100 percent graduation rate for every pilot training class. In 2016, the rate was 93 percent, and in 2017, the rate was 98 percent,[58] but the expectation for 100 percent graduation means that the quality of those respective year groups will be even lower.

Training Resource Availability (Funding for Ranges, Live/Virtual Construct). To prepare for full-spectrum combat in peacetime, pilots require the opportunity to engage high-end air-to-air and surface-to-air missile platforms and simulators on a regular basis. The two effective methods for giving aircrew the repetitions they need to sharpen these perishable skills are live, large force exercises (LFEs) over well-equipped ranges or a live/virtual construct.

The three exercises/ranges that have the airspace and assets required for a live high-threat training are the Red Flag exercises at Nellis Air Force Base, Nevada, and Elmendorf Air Force Base, Alaska. The Air Force funded seven of these large force exercises in 2018,[59] and the same number will be executed in FY 2019.[60]

The live/virtual construct attempts to fill the gaps between deployments to Nellis and Elmendorf through networked simulators as well as plug-and-play simulations that feed a virtual scenario and the accompanying threats into the software/cockpit displays of fighters flying "local" missions out of their home airfields. While these systems show genuine progress, the number of opportunities offered does not offset the drought in sorties, and the pilots themselves do not regard them as replacements for actual flying time.[61]

Deploy to Dwell. The last of the five Air Force levers or areas of readiness is the deploy-to-dwell ratio. The projected dwell time for active-duty personnel in the FY 2019 President's budget request is 1:2 dwell (or better) for active-duty members and a 1:5 dwell (or better) for Guard and Reserve personnel. On paper, these look healthy enough, but the major deployments do not include shorter-term dispatch to schools, exercises, and other non-elective temporary duty assignments, and those career specialties that find themselves in the 3 percent to 4 percent that do not meet the established goals for dwell are in such great demand that they generally do not even come close to the target dwell.

Wartime Readiness Materials. An additional consideration in assessing Air Force readiness is the availability of wartime readiness materials (WRM) like munitions. Funding limitations have not allowed restocking of all WRM accounts. Munitions have been used faster than they have been replaced. While programmed purchases for 2019 will begin to reverse that trend, the air-to-surface weapons that offer stand-off, direct attack, and penetrators are short of current inventory objectives.[62] The concurrent shortage of air-to-air weapons could lead to an increase in the time needed to gain and maintain air superiority in future environments,[63] particularly highly contested ones.

The Air Force has rapidly been depleting its wartime inventory levels of precision-guided munitions. Over 87,000 missiles and bomb-related munitions have been used since August 2014,[64] significantly drawing down stockpiles, and the rate of expenditure has only grown with time. Even with the current buy plan for 2018 and 2019, absent sustained and increased funding, the ongoing depletion of our munition stockpiles will continue to reduce Air Force readiness and jeopardize America's ability to meet its national security objectives.[65]

Space. The classified nature of deployed space assets and their capabilities makes any assessment of this mission area challenging. That said, the United States constellation of ISR, navigation, and communication satellites is arguably unrivaled by any other nation-state. This array allows the Air Force and its sister services to find, fix, and target virtually any terrestrial or sea-based threat anywhere, anytime.

Unfortunately, the United States' historically unchecked dominance in space has facilitated an environment of overreliance on the domain and an underappreciation of the vulnerabilities of its capabilities.[66] Some space assets represent nearly single-point failures in which a loss caused by either a system failure or an attack could cripple a linchpin capability. Because of U.S. dominance of and nearly complete reliance on assets based in space for everything from targeting to weapons guidance, other state actors have every incentive to target those assets.[67]

Adversaries will capture and hold the initiative by leveraging surprise and every asymmetric advantage that they possess while denying those warfighting elements to their opponents. Since Operation Desert Storm, the world and every American near-peer competitor therein have watched the United States employ satellite-enabled precision targeting to profound effect on the battlefield. That ability depends almost entirely on the kinetic end of the strike system: precision-guided munitions.[68]

China and Russia are investing heavily in ground-based anti-satellite (ASAT) missiles;[69] orbital ASAT programs that can deliver a kinetic blow;[70] or co-orbital robotic interference to alter signals, mask denial efforts, or even pull adversary satellites out of orbit.[71] If near-peer competitors were able to degrade regional GPS signals or blind GPS receivers, they could neutralize the PGMs that the U.S. uses to conduct virtually every aspect of its kinetic strike capability.

As General John Hyten, former Commander of Air Force Space Command, has clearly indicated, the vulnerability of the U.S. space constellation is in its design.[72] Every satellite we currently rely on costs millions of dollars and takes years to design, build, and launch into orbit. Until the Air Force shortens that time span or diversifies its ability to precisely find, fix, and destroy targets, space will remain both a dominant and an incredibly vulnerable domain for the U.S. Air Force.

The omnibus appropriations deal reached in March 2018 included funding for the Air Force to increase the unclassified budget for space combat operations and space procurement over FY 2017 levels[73] by a total of 34 percent in FY 2018 and 23 percent for FY 2019.[74] While there certainly are increases for Air Force space assets in the classified funding streams, these are substantial increases that will allow this service to increase both the capability and survivability of U.S. Air Force satellite constellations.

Scoring the U.S. Air Force

Capacity Score: Marginal

One of the key elements of combat power in the U.S. Air Force is its fleet of fighter aircraft. In responding to major combat engagements since World War II, the Air Force has deployed an average of 28 fighter squadrons, based on an average of 18 aircraft per fighter squadron. That equates to a requirement of 500 active component fighter aircraft to execute one MRC. Based on government force-sizing documents that count fighter aircraft, squadrons, or wings, an average of 55 squadrons (990 aircraft) is required to field a two-MRC–capable force (rounded up to 1,000 fighter aircraft to simplify the numbers). This *Index* looks for 1,200 active fighter aircraft to account for the 20 percent reserve necessary when considering availability for deployment and the risk of employing 100 percent of fighters at any one time.

- **Two-MRC Level:** 1,200 fighter aircraft.

- **Actual 2018 Level:** 924 fighter aircraft.

Based on a pure count of combat-coded fighter/attack platforms that have achieved IOC, the USAF currently is at 77 percent of the two-MRC benchmark, and even that low number should be taken with a few caveats. The F-35 will become a highly advanced and capable multirole platform, but the 210 aircraft that have entered the USAF inventory to date[75] are only IOC and do not yet field many of the capabilities that would constitute full-spectrum readiness.

The 924 figure yields a capacity level well within the methodology's range of "marginal." Aircraft require pilots to fly them and maintainers to launch, recover, and fix them. With a fighter pilot shortage of over 1,200, the ability of the Air Force to meet the wartime manning requirements for fighter cockpits continues to wane. Those factors, coupled with the dismally low flying hours that those pilots are receiving, has kept the rating at "marginal." As noted, given shortfalls in personnel and flying time, the Air Force capacity score continues to trend toward "weak."

Capability Score: Marginal

The Air Force's capability score is "marginal," the result of being scored "strong" in "Size of Modernization Program," "marginal" for "Age of Equipment" and "Health of Modernization Programs," but "weak" for "Capability of Equipment." These scores have not changed from the *2018 Index*'s assessment. However, with new F-35 and KC-46 aircraft continuing to roll off their respective production lines, the Air Force should slowly begin to turn this corner.

Readiness Score: Weak

The Air Force scores "weak" in readiness in the *2019 Index*, a grade lower than it received in the *2018 Index*. The Air Force's growing deficit of pilots and a systemic drought of sorties and flying hours for those pilots since 2012 are the principal reasons for the drop in this assessment.[76] The Air Force should be prepared to respond quickly to an emergent crisis and retain full readiness of its combat airpower, but it has been suffering from degraded high-end combat readiness since 2003, and implementation of BCA-imposed budget cuts in FY 2012 cut flying hours and sortie rates to the bone.

Fighter pilots should receive an average of three sorties a week and 200 hours a year to have the skill sets to survive in combat but have averaged less than two sorties a week and 150 hours of flight time a year for the past five years. Even with the greatly improved maintenance manning/experience levels and the increased funding for FY 2018, there has been no improvement. This fact and the ever-growing exodus of experienced pilots from the ranks of the active-duty force are very troubling indicators. Both factors have already strained the service and, unless reversed in the near term, will lead to a death spiral for both retention and readiness challenges in the very near future.

Overall U.S. Air Force Score: Marginal

The Air Force is scored as "marginal" overall. This is an unweighted average of its capacity score of "marginal," capability score of "marginal," and readiness score of "weak." This score has trended downward since the *2018 Index* largely because of two factors: a drop in "capacity" that has not effectively changed and a readiness score of "weak." The shortage of pilots and flying time for those pilots degrades the ability of the Air Force to generate the amount and quality of combat air power that would be needed to meet wartime requirements. While the Air Force could eventually win a single major regional contingency in any theater, the attrition rates would be significantly higher than those sustained by a ready, well-trained force.

U.S. Military Power: Air Force

	VERY WEAK	WEAK	MARGINAL	STRONG	VERY STRONG
Capacity			✓		
Capability			✓		
Readiness		✓			
OVERALL			✓		

AIR FORCE SCORES

Weakest ⟵⟶ Strongest

Strategic Bomber

PLATFORM	Age Score	Capability Score	MODERNIZATION PROGRAM	Size Score	Health Score
B-52 Inventory: **58** Fleet age: **56** Date: **1955** The B-52, the oldest of the bombers, can provide global strike capabilities with conventional or nuclear payloads, although it largely has made up the core of the strategic bomber force. The aircraft entered service in 1955 and was in production until 1962.	❶		The B-21 is intended to replace the Air Force bomber fleet. Initial conventional capability is enhanced for the mid-2020s. The program completed primary design review in early 2017.		
B-1 Inventory: **61** Fleet age: **30** Date: **1986** The B-1, originally designed to carry nuclear weapons, was reconfigured for conventional weapons in the early 1990s. The program entered service in 1986 and completed production in 1988. The B-1B will remain in service until 2040.	③	❶			
B-2 Inventory: **20** Fleet age: **23** Date: **1997** The B-2 bomber provides the USAF with global strike capabilities. It can carry both nuclear and conventional payloads. Initially deployed in 1997, the aircraft communication modules are being upgraded. It is expected to remain in service until 2058.	④				

See Methodology for descriptions of scores.   Fleet age—Average age of fleet   Date—Year fleet first entered service

AIR FORCE SCORES

① ② ③ ④ ⑤
Weakest ⟵⟶ Strongest

Procurement
and Spending

■ Through FY 2018
▨ Pending

Ground Attack/Multi-Role Aircraft

PLATFORM	Age Score	Capability Score	MODERNIZATION PROGRAM	Size Score	Health Score
A-10 Thunderbolt II Inventory: **141** Fleet age: **36** Date: **1977** The A-10 is the only USAF platform designed primarily for close air support, which it provides usng a variety of conventional munitions. The USAF has proposed retiring the aircraft earlier than the planned 2028 date for budget reasons.	②	①	**F-35A** Timeline: **2007–2038** The F-35A is the Air Force variant of the Joint Strike Fighter program, a multirole fixed-wing aircraft. It is currently in early stages of production. The program has faced many issues including a Nunn–McCurdy cost breach during development, grounding due to engine problems, and software development problems. The F-35A achieved IOC on August 2, 2016.	⑤	①
F-16 Inventory: **570** Fleet age: **27** Date: **1978** The F-16 is a multirole aircraft that was built between 1976 and 1999. It has received various upgrade blocks over that time. The aircraft was expected to last about 30 years.	②	①			
F-35A Inventory: **122** Fleet age: **2.6** Date: **2016** See Ground Attack Modernization Program entry. The USAF has received a small portion of a projected 1,763 total aircraft for the program.	⑤				

For the F-35A modernization program:

PROCUREMENT		SPENDING *($ millions)*	
234	1,529	$132,461	$273,670

Fighter Aircraft

PLATFORM	Age Score	Capability Score	MODERNIZATION PROGRAM	Size Score	Health Score
F-15 Inventory: **317** Fleet age: **30** Date: **1979** The F-15 is a legacy fighter that performs air superiority missions. It is no longer in production. The newer F-15E Strike Eagle variant is to operate until 2025 to supplement the F-22.	①	②	None		
F-22 Inventory: **166** Fleet age: **10** Date: **2005** The F-22 is the preeminent air superiority fighter aircraft. The stealth aircraft completed production in 2009 after a dramatic cut of its overall order from 750 to 187. It is currently being modified.	⑤				

See Methodology for descriptions of scores.   Fleet age—Average age of fleet   Date—Year fleet first entered service

AIR FORCE SCORES

Weakest ⟵ ⟶ Strongest

Procurement and Spending ■ Through FY 2018 ▨ Pending

Tanker

PLATFORM	Age Score	Capability Score	MODERNIZATION PROGRAM	Size Score	Health Score
KC-10 Inventory: **59** Fleet age: **33** Date: **1981** An aerial refueling tanker supporting the USAF's Mobility and Lift mission, the KC-10 was deployed in 1981. The aircraft was purchased to increase the number of tankers available, which the Air Force posited did not meet current requirements. The aircraft is no longer in production, but is planned to remain in inventory until 2040.	③	①	**KC-46** Timeline: **2015–2027** The KC-46 is meant to replace the KC-135. The program entered low rate initial production in August 2016 after having been delayed by a year due to "design changes and late parts." The first delivery is anticipated in October 2018.	①	③
KC-135 Inventory: **156** Fleet age: **57** Date: **1956** The KC-135 supports the mobility and lift mission by providing the joint force aerial refueling capability. The KC-135 makes up the bulk of the aerial refueling capability. The aircraft was initially deployed in 1956, completing production in 1965. The aircraft has undergone several modifications, mainly engine upgrades to improve reliability. It is expected to be in service until 2040, but excessive usage has created many reliability issues due to problems from wear and tear, such as corrosion and fuel bladder leaks.	①				

PROCUREMENT 55 124

SPENDING (*$ millions*) $15,712 $28,106

Heavy Lift

PLATFORM	Age Score	Capability Score	MODERNIZATION PROGRAM	Size Score	Health Score
C–5M Inventory: **35** Fleet age: **30** Date: **1970** The C-5 is the USAF's largest mobility and lift aircraft, enabling it to transport a greater amount of cargo (270,000 pounds) compared with other transport aircraft. Originally deployed in 1970, the aircraft has undergone three modification cycles. The latest started in 2009 to upgrade the platform to a C-5M. Funding is now completed for the modernization program.	②	⑤	None		

See Methodology for descriptions of scores.   Fleet age—Average age of fleet   Date—Year fleet first entered service

AIR FORCE SCORES

Heavy Lift

PLATFORM	Age Score	Capability Score	MODERNIZATION PROGRAM	Size Score	Health Score
C-17 Inventory: **162** Fleet age: **14** Date: **1993** The C-17 is a large fixed-wing transport aircraft in support of USAF's mobility and lift mission. The aircraft can lift 170,900 pounds and land on short runways. The aircraft entered service in 1995. The program was expanded from 120 aircraft to 223 aircraft. The procurement program for the C-17 was recently completed. The aircraft was originally planned to last 30 years, but more frequent usage may shorten that life span.	③	⑤	None		

Medium Lift

PLATFORM	Age Score	Capability Score	MODERNIZATION PROGRAM	Size Score	Health Score
C-130J Inventory: **87** Fleet age: **8.8** Date: **1956** The C-130J aircraft supports the USAF's tactical mobility and lift capability. Unlike the other transport aircraft, the C-130s can land on rough dirt strips. It can carry about 42,000 pounds and is expected to last 25 years. The air force active component completed transition to the C-130J in October 2017.	⑤	⑤	**C-130J** Timeline: **1994–2023** The program provides the Air Force with an upgraded medium-lift capability. The C-130J can lift over 40,000 pounds of cargo. The frame supports various other types of aircraft, such as the USMC tanker KC-130J. There are few issues with the current acquisition of C-130Js.	④	④

PROCUREMENT

████████████████   168   2

SPENDING *($ millions)*

██████████████ $14,124 $110

See Methodology for descriptions of scores.   Fleet age—Average age of fleet   Date—Year fleet first entered service

AIR FORCE SCORES

Weakest ← → Strongest

Procurement and Spending ■ Through FY 2018 ▨ Pending

Intelligence, Surveillance, and Reconnaissance (ISR)

PLATFORM	Age Score	Capability Score	MODERNIZATION PROGRAM	Size Score	Health Score
RQ-4 Global Hawk Inventory: **29** Fleet age: **6.6** Date: **2011** The RQ-4 is an unmanned aerial vehicle (UAV) that supports the USAF's ISR mission. Unlike the MQ-1 or MQ-9, the RQ-4 is a high-altitude, long-endurance (HALE) UAV, which in addition to higher altitude has a longer range than medium-altitude, long-endurance (MALE) UAVs.	④		None		
MQ-9 A/B Inventory: **200** Fleet age: **4.4** Date: **2007** The MQ-9 Reaper replaced the MQ-1 Predator to fulfill the USAF's ISR mission. The UAV is in production. The expected life span of the MQ-9 is 20 years.	④	④	**MQ-9** Timeline: **2002–2017** The MQ-9 is in production. It has experienced delays due to manufacturing and testing problems. The Air Force continues to increase planned acquistion objectives for the MQ-9.	⑤	③
RC-135 Rivet Joint Inventory: **22** Fleet age: **54** Date: **1964** The RC-135 is a manned ISR aircraft. It was originally fielded in 1964. The Air Force plans to keep the system in service through 2018.	❶		None		
U-2 Inventory: **27** Fleet age: **34** Date: **1956** Initially deployed in 1956, this manned ISR aircraft can operate at high altitudes and long ranges. The U-2 has undergone a series of modification programs since 1967 to extend the life of the aircraft.	③				

For MQ-9 modernization program:

PROCUREMENT		SPENDING ($ millions)	
363	73	$8,947	$4,215

See Methodology for descriptions of scores.   Fleet age—Average age of fleet   Date—Year fleet first entered service

The Heritage Foundation | heritage.org/Military

401

AIR FORCE SCORES

1 ② ③ ④ **5**
Weakest ←——→ Strongest

Procurement **■** Through FY 2018
and Spending ▪ Pending

Command and Control

PLATFORM	Age Score	Capability Score	MODERNIZATION PROGRAM	Size Score	Health Score
E-3 AWACS Inventory: **31** Fleet age: **39** Date: **1978** The E-3 is an airborne warning and control system (AWACS) that provides USAF with command and control and battle management capabilities. The aircraft entered service in 1978. No longer in production, the current inventory is undergoing modifications to upgrade computing systems. The fleet is currently intended to remain in service until 2025.	**1**	②	None		
E-8 JSTARS Inventory: **16** Fleet age: **17** Date: **1997** The E-8 is a newer command and control aircraft that provides battle management and C4ISR capabilities, mainly by providing ground surveillance to various air and ground commanders in theater. The aircraft first entered service in 1997 and is not currently in production. The Air Force plans to retire the JSTARs in the early 2030s.	②				

SOURCE: Heritage Foundation research using data from government documents and websites. See also Dakota L. Wood, ed., *2018 Index of U.S. Military Strength* (Washington, DC: The Heritage Foundation, 2018), http://index.heritage.org/militarystrength/.

See Methodology for descriptions of scores.   Fleet age—Average age of fleet   Date—Year fleet first entered service

Endnotes

1. The Honorable Michael B. Donley, Secretary of the Air Force, and General Mark A. Welsh III, Chief of Staff, United States Air Force, "Fiscal Year 2014 Air Force Posture Statement," statement before the Committee on Armed Services, U.S. House of Representatives, April 12, 2013, p. 2, http://www.au.af.mil/au/awc/awcgate/af/posture_usaf_12apr2013.pdf (accessed August 8, 2018).

2. The Honorable Heather A. Wilson, Secretary of the Air Force, and General David L. Goldfein, Chief of Staff of the Air Force, statement on "Air Force Budget Posture" before the Committee on Armed Services, U.S. Senate, June 6, 2017, p. 2, https://www.armed-services.senate.gov/imo/media/doc/Wilson-Goldfein_06-06-17.pdf (accessed August 8, 2018), and Congressional Quarterly, "Senate Armed Services Committee Holds Hearing on Posture of the Department of the Air Force," CQ Congressional Transcripts, June 6, 2017, http://www.cq.com/doc/congressionaltranscripts-5116113?3 (accessed July 25, 2017).

3. The Honorable Dr. Heather Wilson, Secretary of the Air Force, and General David L. Goldfein, Chief of Staff, United States Air Force, "USAF Posture Statement Fiscal Year 2019," statement before the Committee on Armed Services, U.S. Senate, 115th Cong., 2nd Sess., April 24, 2018, p. 1, https://www.armed-services.senate.gov/imo/media/doc/Wilson-Goldfein_04-24-18.pdf (accessed May 24, 2018).

4. General David Goldfein, U.S. Air Force, "Rebuilding Air Force Readiness," remarks at The Heritage Foundation, Washington, D.C., April 12, 2017, http://www.heritage.org/defense/event/rebuilding-air-force-readiness (accessed July 25, 2017).

5. General Stephen W. Wilson, Vice Chief of Staff of the Air Force, statement on "Current Readiness of U.S. Forces" before the Subcommittee on Readiness and Management Support, Committee on Armed Services, U.S. Senate, February 14, 2018, p. 2, https://www.armed-services.senate.gov/imo/media/doc/Wilson_02-14-18.pdf (accessed August 9, 2018).

6. U.S. Department of Defense, Office of the Under Secretary (Comptroller)/Chief Financial Officer, *United States Department of Defense Fiscal Year 2018 Budget Request: Defense Budget Overview*, May 2017, pp. 2-9, 3-14, and 7-21, http://comptroller.defense.gov/Portals/45/Documents/defbudget/fy2018/fy2018_Budget_Request_Overview_Book.pdf (accessed August 9, 2018).

7. Technological advances in aircraft materials and structure greatly extended the service life of USAF equipment. As a result, the USAF was able to sustain its force structure while procuring fewer aircraft. See Colonel James C. Ruehrmund Jr. and Christopher J. Bowie, *Arsenal of Airpower: USAF Aircraft Inventory 1950–2009*, Mitchell Institute for Airpower Studies, November 2010), p. 8, http://higherlogicdownload.s3.amazonaws.com/AFA/6379b747-7730-4f82-9b45-a1c80d6c8fdb/UploadedImages/Mitchell%20Publications/Arsenal%20of%20Airpower.pdf (accessed July 25, 2017).

8. U.S. Department of Defense, Secretary of the Air Force, Office of Financial Management and Budget (SAF/FMB), *United States Air Force Fiscal Year 2018 Budget Overview*, May 2017, p. 15, http://www.saffm.hq.af.mil/LinkClick.aspx?fileticket=m3vZOmfR368%3d&portalid=84 (accessed August 6, 2017).

9. U.S. Department of Defense, Secretary of the Air Force, Office of Financial Management and Budget (SAF/FMB), *United States Air Force Fiscal Year 2019 Budget Overview*, February 2018, p. 5, https://www.saffm.hq.af.mil/Portals/84/documents/FY19/FY19_BOB_FINAL_v3.pdf?ver=2018-02-13-150300-757 (accessed August 9, 2018).

10. The Honorable Heather A. Wilson, "A Conversation with the Secretary of the Air Force," The Heritage Foundation, March 1, 2018, https://www.heritage.org/defense/event/conversation-the-secretary-the-air-force (accessed June 6, 2018).

11. See Report No. 112–329, *National Defense Authorization Act for Fiscal Year 2012*, Conference Report to Accompany H.R. 1540, U.S. House of Representatives, 112th Cong, 1st Sess., December 12, 2011, p. 25, https://www.gpo.gov/fdsys/pkg/CRPT-112hrpt329/pdf/CRPT-112hrpt329-pt1.pdf (accessed August 9, 2018).

12. "The Air Force in Facts and Figures," U.S. Air Force Almanac 1996, *Air Force Magazine*, Vol. 79, No. 5 (May 1996), p. 59, http://www.airforcemag.com/MagazineArchive/Magazine%20Documents/1996/May%201996/0596facts_figures.odf (accessed August 26, 2016). The Air Force uses a variety of categorizations to describe or refer to its inventory of aircraft and units. This can make assessing Air Force capacity a challenging exercise.

13. "Assessment of Military Power: U.S. Air Force," in *2018 Index of U.S. Military Strength*, ed. Dakota L. Wood (Washington: The Heritage Foundation, 2017, p. 356, https://www.heritage.org/sites/default/files/2017-10/2018_IndexOfUSMilitaryStrength-2.pdf.

14. Dr. William A. LaPlante, Assistant Secretary of the Air Force (Acquisition); Lieutenant General James M. "Mike" Holmes, Deputy Chief of Staff (Strategic Plans and Requirements); and Lieutenant General Tod D. Wolters, Deputy Chief of Staff (Operations), "Fiscal Year 2016 Air Force, Force Structure and Modernization Programs," statement before the Subcommittee on Airland Forces, Committee on Armed Services, U.S. Senate, March 19, 2015, p. 8, http://www.armed-services.senate.gov/imo/media/doc/LaPlante_Holmes_Wolters_03-19-15.pdf (accessed August 9, 2018).

15. Ibid.

16. The numbers of Total Aircraft Inventory (TAI) and Combat Coded aircraft for the active-duty Air Force were derived through review of U.S. Department of Defense, Secretary of the Air Force, Office of Financial Management and Budget (SAF/FMB), *United States Air Force Fiscal Year 2019 Budget Overview*, and International Institute for Strategic Studies, *The Military Balance 2018: The Annual Assessment of Global Military Capabilities and Defence Economics* (London: Routledge, 2018), pp. 54–56. Where the two publications were in conflict for TAI, the SAF/FMB numbers were adopted. Neither document specifies the number of active-duty Combat Coded aircraft. That number was derived by tallying the total number of fighters by type and dividing that number by the total number of active-duty squadrons flying that type of aircraft. The number and type of aircraft associated with Weapons Squadrons, Adversary Tactics, Test, OT&E, and other units are not standard/determinable and could not be assessed. The associated error is minimized by totaling all like fighter aircraft (F-16, F-15C, etc.); dividing them by the total number of squadrons flying that aircraft; and spreading the error equally across all combat-coded fighter and training units. The total number of fighters associated with non–Fighter Training Unit (FTU) squadrons was counted as "combat coded."

17. The numbers here are complicated. Air Force formulas contained in Adam J. Herbert, "The Fighter Numbers Flap," *Air Force Magazine*, Vol. 91, No. 4 (April 2008), p. 26, http://www.airforcemag.com/MagazineArchive/Documents/2008/April%20 2008/0408issue.pdf (accessed August 11, 2018), convey how the service estimates this number, but it is merely an estimate. Using this formula on an AF/A8XC-provided (as of June 9, 2018) figure of 689 PMAI fighters renders a total of 1,198 total Air Force active-duty fighters, a number that is well short of the 1,385 carried on the Air Force roster. This calls for the use of a different method to determine the actual number of combat-coded fighters as detailed in note 16, *supra*.

18. Headquarters U.S. Air Force, A8XC/A5RW, written response to Heritage Foundation request for information on Air Force PGM expenditures and programmed replenishments, June 10, 2018.

19. "The Air Force in Facts & Figures," U.S. Air Force Almanac 2018, *Air Force Magazine*, Vol. 100, No. 6 (June 2018), p. 52, http://www.airforcemag.com/MagazineArchive/Magazine%20Documents/2018/June%202018/Air%20Force%20Magazine%20 2018%20USAF%20Almanac.pdf (accessed August 10, 2018). Age "[a]s of Sept. 30, 2017." Ten months were added due to time between the publication of the 2018 *USAF Almanac* and this edition of the *Index*.

20. Comparison made between U.S. Department of Defense, Secretary of the Air Force, Office of Financial Management and Budget (SAF/FMB), *United States Air Force Fiscal Year 2019 Budget Overview*, p. 37, and International Institute for Strategic Studies, *The Military Balance 2018* (London: Routledge, 2018), pp. 54–56.

21. "The Air Force in Facts & Figures," U.S. Air Force Almanac 2018, p. 52.

22. Micah Garbarino, "F-16 Service Life Extension Program a 'Great Deal' for Department of Defense, Taxpayers," Air Force Materiel Command, March 3, 2018, http://www.afmc.af.mil/News/Article-Display/Article/1512449/f-16-service-life-extension-program-a-great-deal-for-department-of-defense-taxp/ (accessed August 10, 2018).

23. Comparison made between U.S. Department of Defense, Secretary of the Air Force, Office of Financial Management and Budget (SAF/FMB), *United States Air Force Fiscal Year 2019 Budget Overview*, and International Institute for Strategic Studies, *The Military Balance 2018*, pp. 54–55.

24. U.S. Department of Defense, Secretary of the Air Force, Office of Financial Management and Budget (SAF/FMB), *United States Air Force Fiscal Year 2019 Budget Overview*, p. 37.

25. Comparison made between U.S. Department of Defense, Secretary of the Air Force, Office of Financial Management and Budget (SAF/FMB), *United States Air Force Fiscal Year 2019 Budget Overview*, p. 37, and International Institute for Strategic Studies, *The Military Balance 2018*, pp. 54–56.

26. "The Air Force in Facts & Figures," U.S. Air Force Almanac 2018, p. 52.

27. Headquarters U.S. Air Force, A8XC/A5RW, written response to Heritage Foundation request for information on Air Force PGM expenditures and programmed replenishments, June 10, 2018.

28. See Colonel Michael W. Pietrucha, U.S. Air Force, "The Comanche and the Albatross: About Our Neck Was Hung," *Air & Space Power Journal*, Vol. 28, No. 3 (May–June 2014), pp. 133–156, https://www.airuniversity.af.mil/Portals/10/ASPJ/journals/Volume-28_Issue-3/F-Pietrucha.pdf (accessed August 20, 2018).

29. Jeremiah Gertler, "Air Force F-22 Fighter Program," Congressional Research Service *Report for Congress*, July 11, 2013, p. 7, https://www.fas.org/sgp/crs/weapons/RL31673.pdf (accessed July 26, 2017).

30. Rebecca Grant and Loren Thompson, "Losing Air Dominance? The Air Force and Its Future Roles," presentation at Air Force Association Air & Space Conference, Washington, D.C., September 16, 2008, p. 3, https://secure.afa.org/Mitchell/presentations/091608LosingAirDominance_tnx.pdf (accessed August 19, 2018).

31. Thomas W. Spoehr and Rachel Zissimos, eds., "Preventing a Defense Crisis: The 2018 National Defense Authorization Act *Must* Begin to Restore U.S. Military Strength," Heritage Foundation *Backgrounder* No. 3205, March 29, 2017, p. 8, https://www.heritage.org/sites/default/files/2017-03/BG3205.pdf.

32. Gertler, "Air Force F-22 Fighter Program," p. 7. The total number of F-22As increased from 159 in the 2018 *Index* to 166 in the current year as a result of updated numbers in U.S. Department of Defense, Secretary of the Air Force, Office of Financial Management and Budget (SAF/FMB), *United States Air Force Fiscal Year 2019 Budget Overview*, p. 37.

33. Venable, "Independent Capability Assessment of the U.S Air Force Reveals Readiness Level Below Carter Administration Hollow Force," Heritage Foundation *Backgrounder* No. 3208, April 17, 2017, p. 2, https://www.heritage.org/sites/default/files/2017-04/BG3208.pdf.

34. Dave Majumdar, "Can the F-35 Win a Dogfight?" War Is Boring, December 17, 2013, p. 1, https://warisboring.com/can-the-f-35-win-a-dogfight-95462ccd6745#.5pvpajaos (accessed July 26, 2017).

35. James Drew, "F-22 Raptor Retrofit to Take Longer, but Availability Hits 63%," FlightGlobal, July 6, 2015, http://www.flightglobal.com/news/articles/f-22-raptor-retrofit-to-take-longer-but-availability-hits-414341/ (accessed July 26, 2017).

36. Kris Osborn, "Air Force: F-35 3F Software Drop Challenges Resolved," *Defense Systems*, May 17, 2017, https://defensesystems.com/articles/2017/05/17/f35.aspx (accessed July 26, 2017).

37. Lara Seligman, "F-35 Full Combat Capability Will Be Four Months Late," *Defense News*, March 23, 2016, http://www.defensenews.com/story/defense/air-space/2016/03/23/f-35-full-combat-capability-four-months-late/82187648/ (accessed August 26, 2016).

38. John Venable, "Operational Assessment of the F-35A Argues for Full Program Procurement and Concurrent Development Process," Heritage Foundation *Backgrounder* No. 3140, August 4, 2016, pp. 8–10, https://www.heritage.org/defense/report/operational-assessment-the-f-35a-argues-full-program-procurement-and-concurrent.

39. Aaron Mehta, "KC-46 Tanker Cleared for Production," *Defense News*, August 12, 2016, http://www.defensenews.com/training-sim/2016/08/12/kc-46-tanker-cleared-for-production/ (accessed July 26, 2017).

40. Colin Clark, "Boeing Wins $2.8B for KC-4 Tanker Low Rate Production," *Breaking Defense*, August, 18, 2016, http://breakingdefense.com/2016/08/boeing-wins-2-5b-for-kc-46-tanker-low-rate-production/ (accessed July 26, 2017), and U.S. Department of Defense, Office of the Under Secretary of Defense (Comptroller)/Chief Financial Officer, *United States Department of Defense Fiscal Year 2016 Budget Request: Overview*, February 2015, p. 8-17, http://comptroller.defense.gov/Portals/45/Documents/defbudget/fy2016/FY2016_Budget_Request_Overview_Book.pdf (accessed August 10, 2018).

41. Lieutenant General Arnold W. Bunch, Jr., Military Deputy, Office of the Assistant Secretary of the Air Force (Acquisition); Lieutenant General Jerry D. Harris, Deputy Chief of Staff (Strategic Plans and Requirements); and Major General Scott A. Vander Hamm, Assistant Deputy Chief of Staff (Operations), statement on "Air Force Bomber/Tanker/Airlift Acquisition Programs" before the Subcommittee on Seapower and Projection Forces, Committee on Armed Services, U.S. House of Representatives, May 25, 2017, p. 10, http://docs.house.gov/meetings/AS/AS28/20170525/106013/HHRG-115-AS28-Wstate-BunchA-20170525.pdf (accessed July 26, 2017).

42. Lieutenant General Jerry "JD" Harris, Jr., Deputy Chief of Staff (Strategic Plans, Programs and Requirements); Lieutenant General Arnold W. Bunch, Jr., Military Deputy, Office of the Assistant Secretary of the Air Force (Acquisition); and Lieutenant General Mark C. Nowland, Deputy Chief of Staff (Operations), statement on "Air Force, Force Structure and Modernization Programs" before the Subcommittee on Airland Forces, Committee on Armed Services, U.S. Senate, March 29, 2017, p. 13, https://www.armed-services.senate.gov/imo/media/doc/Harris-Bunch-Nowland_03-29-17.pdf (accessed August 10, 2018).

43. Ibid. and Lieutenant General James M. "Mike" Holmes, Deputy Chief of Staff (Strategic Plans and Requirements), and Lieutenant General Arnold W. Bunch, Jr., Military Deputy, Office of the Assistant Secretary of the Air Force (Acquisition), statement on "Air Force Bomber/Tanker/Airlift Acquisition Programs" before the Subcommittee on Seapower and Projection Forces, Committee on Armed Services, U.S. House of Representatives, March 1, 2016, p. 4, http://docs.house.gov/meetings/AS/AS28/20160301/104353/HHRG-114-AS28-Wstate-BunchA-20160301.pdf (accessed August 10, 2018).

44. Small group discussion with the Honorable Heather Wilson, Secretary of the Air Force, February 9, 2018.

45. Holmes and Bunch, statement on "Air Force Bomber/Tanker/Airlift Acquisition Programs," March 1, 2016, pp. 2–3.

46. Wilson and Goldfein, statement on "Fiscal Year 2018 Air Force Posture," June 6, 2017, p. 3.

47. Major General Scott West, Director of Current Operations, Deputy Chief of Staff for Operations, Headquarters, U.S. Air Force, statement on "Military Aviation Readiness and Safety" before the Subcommittee on Readiness, Committee on Armed Services, U.S. House of Representatives, July 6, 2016, p. 2, http://docs.house.gov/meetings/AS/AS03/20160706/105159/HHRG-114-AS03-Wstate-WestS-20160706.pdf (accessed August 10, 2018).

48. 2016 maintainer shortage statistic provided by Headquarters U.S. Air Force, Deputy Chief of Staff for Logistics, Engineering, and Force Protection (HAF A4), on April 13, 2017.

49. Julian E. Barnes, "Warning Sounded on Cuts to Pilot Training," *The Wall Street Journal*, December 19, 2013, http://www.wsj.com/articles/SB10001424052702304773104579268651994849572 (accessed July 26, 2017).

50. Wilson, "A Conversation with the Secretary of the Air Force."

51. Headquarters U.S. Air Force, Deputy Chief of Staff for Operations, written response to Heritage Foundation request for information on Air Force flying hours and manning levels, June 10, 2018.

52. Committee on Armed Services, U.S. Senate, "Advance Policy Questions for General David L. Goldfein, USAF, Nominee for the Position of Chief of Staff of the U.S. Air Force," June 16, 2016, pp. 7–8, http://www.armed-services.senate.gov/hearings/16-06-16-nomination_-goldfein (accessed August 10, 2018).

53. Courtney Albon, "Air Force: 1,900 Fighter Jets Is Low-end Requirement; Service Likely Needs About 2,100," *Inside Defense*, March 30, 2017, https://insidedefense.com/daily-news/air-force-1900-fighter-jets-low-end-requirement-service-likely-needs-about-2100 (accessed April 11, 2017).

54. Lieutenant General Gina M. Grosso, Deputy Chief of Staff Manpower, Personnel and Services United States Air Force, statement on "Military Pilot Shortage" before the Subcommittee on Personnel, Committee on Armed Services, U.S. House of Representatives, March 29, 2017, p. 2, http://docs.house.gov/meetings/AS/AS02/20170329/105795/HHRG-115-AS02-Wstate-GrossoG-20170329.pdf (accessed August 10, 2018).

55. Headquarters U.S. Air Force, Deputy Chief of Staff for Operations, written response to Heritage Foundation request for information on Air Force manning levels, June 10, 2018.

56. Stephen Losey, "Air Force's Grounded T-6 Trainers Could Fly Again Next Week," *Air Force Times*, February 23, 2018, https://www.airforcetimes.com/news/your-air-force/2018/02/23/air-forces-grounded-t-6-trainers-could-fly-again-next-week/ (accessed August 10, 2018).

57. Lara Seligman, "USAF T-6 Grounding Has Cost 82 New Pilots So Far," *Aeropsace Daily & Defense Report*, Aviation Week, February 16, 2018, http://aviationweek.com/awindefense/usaf-t-6-grounding-has-cost-82-new-pilots-so-far (last accessed August 10, 2018).

58. Headquarters U.S. Air Force, Deputy Chief of Staff for Operations, written response to Heritage Foundation request for information on Air Force manning levels, June 10, 2018.

59. The *2018 Index of U.S. Military Strength* listed 16 LFEs as published in U.S. Department of Defense, Office of the Under Secretary (Comptroller)/Chief Financial Officer, *United States Department of Defense Fiscal Year 2018 Budget Request: Defense Budget Overview*, p. 2-11. Green Flag is no longer an LFE; it is now a joint exercise at Fort Irwin, California, the focus of which is low-intensity close air support employing markedly smaller forces. See U.S. Air Force, Nellis Air Force Base, "Exercises & Flight Operations," http://www.nellis.af.mil/Home/Flying-Operations/ (accessed on August 10, 2018).

60. U.S. Department of Defense, Office of the Under Secretary of Defense (Comptroller)/Chief Financial Officer, *United States Department of Defense Fiscal Year 2019 Budget Request: Defense Budget Overview*, February 2018, p. 3-22, https://www.defense.gov/Portals/1/Documents/pubs/FY2019-Budget-Request-Overview-Book.pdf (accessed August 10, 2018).

61. Venable, "Independent Capability Assessment of the U.S. Air Force Reveals Readiness Level Below Carter Administration Hollow Force," p. 4.

62. LaPlante, Holmes, and Wolters, "Fiscal Year 2016 Air Force, Force Structure and Modernization Programs," p. 16.

63. Ibid., p. 17.

64. This number is calculated by adding the numbers received from Headquarters U.S. Air Force, Deputy Chief of Staff for Operations, in 2018 to numbers in U.S. Department of Defense, Secretary of the Air Force, Office of Financial Management and Budget (SAF/FMB), *United States Air Force Fiscal Year 2018 Budget Overview*, May 10, 2017, p. 4, https://www.saffm.hq.af.mil/Portals/84/documents/FY2018%20Air%20Force%20Budget%20Overview%20Book%20(updated%20June).pdf?ver=2017-07-03-114127-010 (accessed August 10, 2018).

65. Bunch, Harris, and Vander Hamm, "Air Force Bomber/Tanker/Airlift Acquisition Programs," p. 14.

66. Air Force Space Command Public Affairs, "Hyten Announces Space Enterprise Vision," U.S. Air Force, April 13, 2016, http://www.af.mil/News/Article-Display/Article/719941/hyten-announces-space-enterprise-vision/ (accessed August 10, 2018).

67. Colin Clark, "Space Command Readies for War with 'Space Enterprise Vision,'" *Breaking Defense*, June 20, 2016 http://breakingdefense.com/2016/06/space-command-readies-for-war-with-space-enterprise-vision/ (accessed July 26, 2017).

68. Venable, "Independent Capability Assessment of the U.S. Air Force Reveals Readiness Level Below Carter Administration Hollow Force," p. 10.

69. Bill Gertz, "China Tests Anti-Satellite Missile," *The Washington Free Beacon*, November 9, 2015, http://freebeacon.com/national-security/china-tests-anti-satellite-missile/ (accessed July 26, 2017).

70. Weston Williams, "Russia Launches Anti-Satellite Weapon: A New Warfront in Space?" *The Christian Science Monitor*, December 22, 2016, http://www.csmonitor.com/USA/Military/2016/1222/Russia-launches-anti-satellite-weapon-A-new-warfront-in-space (accessed April 11, 2017).

71. Brid-Aine Parnell, "Mystery Russian Satellite: Orbital Weapon? Sat Gobbler? What?" *The Register*, November 18, 2014, http://www.theregister.co.uk/2014/11/18/russia_secret_satellite_kosmos_2499/ (accessed August 10, 2018).

72. Air Force Space Command Public Affairs, "Hyten Announces Space Enterprise Vision."

73. For FY 2017 levels, see Major General Jim Martin, SAF/FMB, *United States Air Force Fiscal Year 2017 Budget Overview* Brief, U.S. Air Force, February 2016, pp. 11 (space combat forces) and 14 (space procurement), http://www.saffm.hq.af.mil/Portals/84/documents/FY17/AFD-160209-037.pdf?ver=2016-08-24-102126-717 (accessed August 10, 2018).

74. Calculated based on data in Major General [John M.] Pletcher, SAF/FMB, *United States Air Force Fiscal Year 2019 Budget Overview* Brief, February 2018, pp. 8–11, http://www.saffm.hq.af.mil/Portals/84/documents/FY19/SuppDoc/FY19%20PB%20Rollout%20Brief_v35.pdf?ver=2018-02-14-144850-200 (accessed August 10, 2018).

75. U.S. Department of Defense, Secretary of the Air Force, Office of Financial Management and Budget (SAF/FMB), *United States Air Force Fiscal Year 2019 Budget Overview*, p. 37.

76. Venable, "Independent Capability Assessment of the U.S. Air Force Reveals Readiness Level Below Carter Administration Hollow Force."

U.S. Marine Corps

The U.S. Marine Corps (USMC) is the nation's expeditionary armed force, positioned and ready to respond to crises around the world. Marine units assigned aboard ships ("soldiers of the sea") or at bases abroad stand ready to project U.S. power into crisis areas. Marines also serve in a range of unique missions, from combat defense of U.S. embassies under attack abroad to operating the President's helicopter fleet.

Although Marines have a wide variety of individual assignments, the focus of every Marine is on combat: Every Marine is first a rifleman. The USMC has positioned itself for crisis response and has evolved its concepts to leverage its equipment more effectively to support operations in a heavily contested maritime environment such as the one found in the Western Pacific.

As of February 2018, 35,200 Marines (roughly one-third of Marine Corps operating forces)[1] were deployed around the world "to assure our allies and partners, to deter our adversaries, and to respond when our...citizens and interests are threatened."[2] In 2017, "Marines executed approximately 104 operations, 87 security cooperation events with partners and allies, and participated in 61 major exercises" in addition to providing substantial support to civil authorities in "Texas, Florida, Puerto Rico and the U.S. Virgin Islands after recent Hurricanes Harvey, Irma and Maria wreaked havoc on the homeland."[3]

Pursuant to the Defense Strategic Guidance (DSG), maintaining the Corps' crisis response capability is critical. Thus, given the fiscal constraints imposed, the Marines have prioritized "near-term readiness" at the expense of other areas such as capacity, capability, modernization, home station readiness, and infrastructure.[4] However, the President's fiscal year (FY) 2019 budget request states that the service will now "prioritize modernization."[5] This is consistent with and central to its readiness-recovery efforts and represents a shift to a longer-term perspective. Recapitalization and repair of legacy systems is no longer sufficient to sustain current operational requirements. According to General Glenn Walters, Assistant Commandant of the Marine Corps:

> After years of prioritizing readiness to meet steady-state requirements, our strategy now defines readiness as our ability to compete, deter and win against the rising peer threats we face. We define readiness by whether we possess the required capabilities and capacity we need to face the threats outlined in the NDS.[6]

Capacity

The measures of Marine Corps capacity in this *Index* are similar to those used to assess the Army's: end strength and units (battalions for the Marines and brigades for the Army). The Marine Corps' basic combat unit is the infantry battalion, which is composed of approximately 900 Marines and includes three rifle companies, a weapons company, and a headquarters and service company.

In 2011, the Marine Corps maintained 27 infantry battalions in its active component at an authorized end strength of 202,100.[7] As budgets declined, the Corps prioritized readiness through managed reductions in capacity, including a drawdown of forces, and delays or reductions in planned procurement levels. After the Marine Corps fell to a low of 23 active component infantry battalions in FY 2015,[8] Congress began to fund gradual increases in end strength, returning the Marine Corps to 24 infantry battalions.

President Donald Trump's FY 2019 budget request would increase the size of the active component Marine Corps by only 1,500 over the congressionally authorized level of 185,000 in FY 2018.[9] Despite increases in active component end strength, the President's FY 2019 budget provides enough support for only 24 infantry battalions. Additional manpower will backfill existing units and help the Marine Corps to recruit and retain individuals with critical skillsets and specialties.

One impact of reduced capacity is a strain on Marines' dwell time. Cuts in capacity—the number of units and individual Marines—enabled the Marine Corps to disperse the resources it did receive among fewer units, thus maintaining higher readiness levels throughout a smaller force. However, without a corresponding decrease in operational requirements, demand for Marine Corps units and assets has resulted in unsustainable deployment rates.[10] For example, as a result of sustained engagement in the Middle East, diminished capacity, and increased operational tempo (OPTEMPO), Marine Corps tactical aviation units have been operating under a surge condition (in excess of a 1:2 deployment-to-dwell ratio) "for more than fifteen years."[11] This increased deployment frequency has exacerbated the degradation of readiness as people and equipment are used more frequently with less time to recover between deployments.

The stated ideal deployment-to-dwell (D2D) time ratio is 1:3 (seven months deployed for every 21 months at home).[12] This leaves more time available for training and recovery and provides support for a "ready bench," without which readiness investments are immediately consumed. Current budget constraints support only "an approximate 1:2 D2D ratio in the aggregate."[13] A return to BCA-level budget caps could reduce capacity even further, and the dwell ratio for the Marine Corps could fall to 1:1.[14] The same problems are present across the Marine Corps' aviation units and amphibious assets.

Infantry battalions serve as a surrogate measure for the Corps' total force. As the first to respond to many contingencies, the Marine Corps requires a large degree of flexibility and self-sufficiency, and this drives its approach to organization and deployment of operational formations that, although typically centered on infantry units, are composed of ground, air, and logistics elements. Each of these assets and capabilities is critical to effective deployment of force, and any one of them can be a limiting factor in the conduct of training and operations.

Aviation. Marine aviation has been particularly stressed by insufficient funding. Although operational requirements have not decreased, fewer Marine aircraft are available for tasking or training. For example, according to its *2018 Marine Aviation Plan*, the USMC currently fields 18 tactical fighter squadrons,[15] compared to 19 in 2017[16] and around 28 during Desert Storm.[17] This is a decrease from 2017, but the Marine Corps has begun to increase quantities of aircraft in some of its legacy squadrons. In 2016, "shortages in aircraft availability due to increased wear on aging aircraft and modernization delays" led the Corps to reduce the requirement of aircraft per squadron for the F/A-18, CH-53E, and AV-8B temporarily in order to provide additional aircraft for home station training.[18] As availability of legacy aircraft has slowly improved—the result of increased funding for spare parts and implementation of recommendations from independent readiness reviews—the Marine Corps has increased unit "flight line entitlements for F/A-18s and AV-8Bs back to 12 and 16, respectively."[19]

Although budget increases have yielded incremental improvements, however, the Marine Corps remains "20% short of the required aircraft to meet Congress' [readiness requirements]."[20] The transfer of legacy Hornets from the Navy will contribute to existing inventory, and increased funding for spare parts will increase availability within the current inventory, but meaningful capacity increases in Marine aviation will depend on procurement of new systems. For example, the Corps' heavy-lift capability is filled by the CH-53E, of which it maintains only 143 airframes, only 37 percent of which are considered flyable. [21] The Corps began a reset of the CH-53E in 2016 to bridge the procurement gap and aims to "reset...the entire 143-aircraft fleet by FY20,"[22] but this will still leave the service 57 aircraft short of the stated heavy-lift requirements of 200 airframes, and the Marine Corps will not have enough helicopters to meet its heavy-lift requirement without the transition to the CH-53K.[23]

According to the *2018 Marine Aviation Plan*, the transition to the Osprey is 80 percent complete, with 15 fully operational squadrons in the active component and the 18th (and final) squadron planned for activation in FY 2019.[24] However, the procurement objective could increase to 380 aircraft pending the results of an ongoing requirements-based analysis.[25] The Osprey has been called "our most in-demand aircraft,"[26] and with only a year of planned procurement remaining, the Marine Corps will have to reconcile high OPTEMPOs with the objective of maintaining the platform in inventory "for at least the next 40 years."[27]

Shallow acquisition ramps for the F-35 pose similar problems for the service's fighter fleet. As the F-35 enters into service and legacy platforms reach the end of their service lives, the Marine Corps expects a near-term inventory challenge due to a combination of reduced Joint Strike Fighter (JSF) procurement, increasing tactical aircraft utilization rates, and shortfalls in F/A-18A-D and AV-8B depot facility production.[28] Any reduction in Marine aviation capability has a direct effect on overall combat capability, as the Corps usually fights with its ground and aviation forces integrated as Marine Air-Ground Task Forces (MAGTFs).

Although amphibious ships are assessed as part of the Navy's fleet capacity, Marines operate and train aboard naval vessels, making "the shortage of amphibious ships...the quintessential challenge to amphibious training."[29] The Navy currently operates only 32 ships and is projected to continue operating short of the 38-ship requirement until FY 2033, thus limiting what the Marine Corps can do in operational, training, and experimentation settings.[30] Because of this chronic shortfall in amphibious ships, the USMC has relied partially on land-based Special Purpose Marine Air-Ground Task Forces (SPMAGTFs). While SPMAGTFs have enabled the Corps to meet Joint Force requirements, land-based locations "lack the full capability, capacity and strategic and operational agility that results when Marine Air-Ground Task Forces (MAGTFs) are embarked aboard Navy amphibious ships."[31]

The USMC continues to invest in the recapitalization of legacy platforms in order to extend platform service life and keep aircraft and amphibious vehicles in the fleet, but as these platforms age, they also become less relevant to the evolving modern operating environment. Thus, while they do help to maintain capacity, programs to extend service life do not provide the capability enhancements that modernization programs provide. The result is an older, less-capable fleet of equipment that costs more to maintain.

Capability

The nature of the Marine Corps' crisis response role requires capabilities that span all domains. The USMC ship requirement is managed by the Navy and is covered in the Navy's section of the *Index*. The Marine Corps is focusing on "essential modernization" and emphasizing programs that "underpin our core competencies," making the Amphibious Combat Vehicle (ACV) and F-35 JSF programs its top two priorities.[32] However, modernization spending still accounts for only 14 percent of the Marine Corps' proposed FY 2019 budget,[33] compared to 21 percent for the Army, 47 percent for the Air Force, and 45 percent for the Navy.[34] The Corps' aircraft, tanks, and ground combat vehicles are some of the oldest in the entire U.S. inventory.

Of the Marine Corps' current fleet of vehicles, its amphibious vehicles—specifically, the Assault Amphibious Vehicle (AAV-7A1) and Light Armored Vehicle (LAV)—are the oldest, with the AAV-7A1 averaging over 40 years old and the LAV averaging 26 years old.[35] The AAV-7A1 is undergoing survivability upgrades. Following the successful test and evaluation of 10 initial prototype vehicles in 2016, the DOD awarded Science Applications International Corporation (SAIC) a low-rate initial production contract for the AAV Survivability Upgrade (AAV SU) in August 2017.[36] The AAV SU is slated to reach full-rate production in FY 2019.[37] The Marine Corps has procured 48 vehicles to-date.[38] These upgrades will help to bridge the capability gap until the fielding of the ACV and keep the AAV SU in service until 2035.[39] In the meantime, the Marine Corps will "continue to spend limited fiscal resources to sustain legacy systems as a result of deferred modernization" and "risk steadily losing our capability advantage against potential adversaries."[40]

Though not yet in development, service testimony notes that the Marine Corps is "beginning to look at a replacement" for the LAV, which will "help accelerate movement to the acquisition phase within the next four to five years."[41] As noted, the average age of the LAV is 26 years. Comparatively, the Corps' M1A1 Abrams inventory is 28 years old with an estimated 33-year life span,[42] while the newest HMMWV variant has already consumed half of a projected 15-year service life.[43]

All of the Corps' main combat vehicles entered service in the 1970s and 1980s, and while service life extensions, upgrades, and new generations of designs have allowed the platforms to remain in service, these vehicles are quickly becoming poorly suited to the changing threat environment. The President's FY 2019 budget seeks to provide "a balanced level of attainment and maintenance of inventory in order to meet mission requirements"[44] and plans to invest "approximately 29 percent of its modernization resources into GCTV [ground combat tactical vehicle] systems within the FYDP."[45]

The age profiles of the Corps' aircraft are similar to those of the Navy's. As of 2018, the USMC had 251 F/A-18A-Ds (including one reserve squadron)[46] and six EA-6Bs in its primary mission aircraft inventory,[47] and both aircraft have already surpassed their originally intended life spans. The Marine Corps began to retire its EA-6B squadrons in FY 2016 with the decommissioning of Marine Tactical Electronic Warfare Squadron 1, followed by deactivation of a second squadron in May 2018.[48] The last remaining EA-6B squadron will begin deactivation in October 2018.[49]

Unlike the Navy, the Corps did not acquire the newer F/A-18 E/F Super Hornets; thus, a portion of the older F/A-18 Hornets are going through a service life extension program to extend their life span to 10,000 flight hours from the original 6,000 hours.[50] This was intended to bridge the gap until the F-35Bs and F-35Cs enter service to replace the Harriers and most of the Hornets. However, delays in the service life extension program and "increased wear on aging aircraft" have further limited availability of the F/A-18A-D and AV-8B.[51]

As the Navy accelerates its transition to the Super Hornet, it plans to transfer some of its "best of breed" aircraft from its F/A-18A-D inventory to the Marine Corps and scrap the remaining for parts to help maintain the Corps' legacy fleet through FY 2030.[52] The AV-8B Harrier, designed to take off from the LHA and LHD amphibious assault ships, will be retired from Marine Corps service by 2026.[53] The AV-8B received near-term capability upgrades in 2015, which continued in 2017 in order to maintain its lethality and interoperability[54] until the F-35 transition is completed in FY 2022.[55] The Corps declared its first F-35B squadron operationally capable on July 31, 2015, after it passed an "Operational Readiness Inspection" test.[56] To date, three F-35B squadrons have been delivered to the Marine Corps, including two operational squadrons and one fleet replacement squadron, totaling 57 aircraft.[57]

The Marine Corps has two Major Defense Acquisition (MDAP) vehicle programs: the

FIGURE 5

Marine Corps Combat Vehicles

All of the Marine Corps' current combat vehicle fleets first entered service before 1990. Upgrades have extended the fleets, and two new vehicles are expected to enter service around 2020.

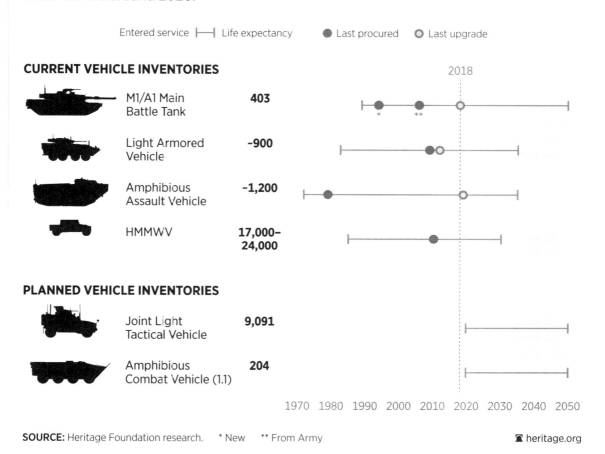

Entered service ⊢–⊣	Life expectancy	● Last procured	○ Last upgrade

CURRENT VEHICLE INVENTORIES

Vehicle	Count
M1/A1 Main Battle Tank	403
Light Armored Vehicle	~900
Amphibious Assault Vehicle	~1,200
HMMWV	17,000–24,000

PLANNED VEHICLE INVENTORIES

Vehicle	Count
Joint Light Tactical Vehicle	9,091
Amphibious Combat Vehicle (1.1)	204

1970 1980 1990 2000 2010 2020 2030 2040 2050

SOURCE: Heritage Foundation research.   * New   ** From Army   ☎ heritage.org

Joint Light Tactical Vehicle (JLTV) and Amphibious Combat Vehicle.[58] The JLTV is a joint program with the Army to acquire a more survivable light tactical vehicle to replace a percentage of the older HMMWV fleet, originally introduced in 1985. The Army retains overall responsibility for JLTV development through its Joint Program Office.[59]

Following FY 2015 plans for the JLTV, the program awarded a low-rate initial production contract, which includes a future option of producing JLTVs for the Marine Corps, to defense contractor Oshkosh.[60] Congressional testimony indicates that if its budget permits it to do so, the USMC may be interested in procuring a larger quantity in the long term than originally intended. Despite a delay in the program's full-rate production decision and reduced procurement quantities in FY 2016 and FY 2017, in June 2017, the Corps had still expected to complete its prior acquisition objective of 5,500 by FY 2023.[61] Reductions in annual procurement quantities reflect prioritization of the ACV within the USMC's ground force.[62]

The President's budget request for FY 2018 would fund the final year of low-rate initial production for the JLTV, including 1,642 vehicles for the Marine Corps and limited procurement quantities for the Air Force.[63] Because the JLTV will not be a one-for-one replacement of the HMMWV, there are concerns that limited procurement will create a battlefield mobility gap for some units.[64] Although the Marine Corps reached a decision to increase its acquisition objective from 7,241 to 9,091,[65] this will still only partially offset the inventory of 17,000 HMMWVs.[66] The service is considering what percent of the fleet should be replaced by the JLTV and what percent of the requirement might be filled by lighter wheeled vehicles.[67] As end strength and combat units return to each of the services, this could further affect JLTV requirements and result in additional procurement demand.

The Corps has procured 844 JLTVs through FY 2018.[68] The lack of operational detail in the Army's Tactical Wheeled Vehicle Strategy could affect future USMC JLTV procurement and modernization plans.[69] The USMC expected the program to reach initial operational capability (IOC) in the fourth quarter of 2018, but this has been delayed to the first quarter of 2020 because of program disruption caused by bid protests and scheduled testing delays.[70] "Marines are expected to start receiving JLTVs for operational use in FY 2019," along with a full-rate production decision.[71] The increased acquisition objective will extend the program's procurement timeline through FY 2023.[72]

The Marine Corps intends to replace the AAV-7A1 with the ACV, planned "to enter the acquisition cycle at Milestone B (Engineering and Manufacturing Development) in FY2016, award prototype contracts leading to a down select to one vendor in FY2018, and [then] enter low-rate initial production."[73] The ACV, which took the place of the Expeditionary Fighting Vehicle (EFV), "has been structured to provide a phased, incremental capability."[74] The AAV-7A1 was to be replaced by the EFV, a follow-on to the cancelled Advanced AAV, but the EFV was also cancelled in 2011 as a result of technical obstacles and cost overruns. Similarly, the Corps planned to replace the LAV inventory with the Marine Personnel Carrier (MPC), which would serve as a Light Armored Vehicle with modest amphibious capabilities but would be designed primarily to provide enhanced survivability and mobility once ashore.[75] However, budgetary constraints led the Corps to shelve the program, leaving open the possibility that it might be resumed in the future.

After restructuring its ground modernization portfolio, the Marine Corps determined that it would combine its efforts by upgrading 392 of its legacy AAVs and continuing development of the ACV to replace part of the existing fleet and complement the upgraded AAVs.[76] This would help the Corps to meet its requirement of armored lift for 10 battalions of infantry.[77] In June 2018, BAE Systems won the contract award to build the ACV 1.1, and it is expected to deliver the first 30 vehicles by the fall of 2019.[78] The Marine Corps plans to field 204 vehicles in the first increment—enough to support lift requirements for two infantry battalions.[79]

The ACV 1.1 platform is notable because it is an amphibious wheeled vehicle instead of a tracked vehicle, capable of traversing open water only with the assistance of Navy shore connectors such as Landing Craft, Air Cushion Vehicles (LCAC). Development and procurement of the ACV program will be phased so that the new platforms can be fielded incrementally alongside a number of modernized AAVs.[80] Plans call for a program of record of 694 vehicles (a combination of upgraded AAVs and ACVs), with the first battalion to reach IOC in FY 2020, and for modernizing enough of the current AAV fleet to outfit six additional battalions, two in the first increment and four in the second. The AAV survivability upgrade program will modernize the remaining four battalions, allowing the Corps to meet its armored lift requirement for 10 battalions.[81]

Regarding aviation, Lieutenant General Brian Beaudreault, Marine Corps Deputy Commandant for Plans, Policies, and Operations, has testified that "[t]he single most effective way to meet our NDS responsibilities, improve overall readiness, and gain the competitive advantage required for combat against state threats is through the modernization of our aviation platforms."[82] The F-35B remains the Marine Corps' largest investment program in FY 2019. The Corps announced IOC of the F-35B variant in July 2015.[83] Total procurement will consist of 420 F-35s (353 F-35Bs and 67 F-35Cs). AV-8Bs and F/A-18A-Ds continue to receive interoperability and lethality enhancements in order to extend their useful service lives during the transition to the F-35, and the Corps continues to seek opportunities to accelerate procurement.[84]

Today, the USMC MV-22 Osprey program is operating with few problems and nearing completion of the full acquisition objective of 360 aircraft.[85] The Marine Corps added one squadron to its active component over the past year, bringing the total to 15 fully operational squadrons in the active component.[86] Two additional squadrons are expected to stand up in FY 2018, followed by the final active component squadron in FY 2019.[87] The MV-22's capabilities are in high demand from the Combatant Commanders (COCOMS), and the Corps is adding capabilities such as fuel delivery and use of precision-guided munitions to the MV-22 to enhance its value to the COCOMs.

The Corps continues to struggle with sustainment challenges in the Osprey fleet. Since the first MV-22 was procured in 1999, the fleet has developed more than 70 different configurations.[88] This has resulted in increased logistical requirements, as maintainers must be trained to each configuration and spare parts are not all shared. The Marine Corps has developed a plan to consolidate the inventory to a common configuration at a rate of "2–23 aircraft installs per year" beginning in FY 2018.[89]

The USMC's heavy-lift replacement program, the CH-53K, conducted its first flight on October 27, 2015.[90] The CH-53K will replace the Corps' CH-53E, which is now 28 years old. Although "unexpected redesigns to critical components" delayed a low-rate initial production decision,[91] the program achieved Milestone C in April 2017, and the President's FY 2019 budget requests $1,601.8 million for the procurement of eight aircraft in its second year

of low-rate initial production.[92] The helicopter is predicted to reach IOC in 2019, almost four years later than initially anticipated.[93] This is of increasing concern as the Marine Corps maintains only 139 CH-53Es[94] and will not have enough helicopters to meet its heavy-lift requirement of 200 aircraft without the transition to the CH-53K.[95]

The Corps began a reset of the CH-53E in 2016 to bridge the procurement gap, but as of November 2017, it had completed the reset of only 13 CH-53Es.[96] The DOD plans to complete fielding of the CH-53K by FY28, but continuing resolutions "have resulted in shallow acquisition ramps" and could further delay this transition.[97] The FY 2019 request would continue to fund procurement totals of 194 CH-53K aircraft.[98]

Readiness

The Marine Corps' first priority is to be the crisis response force for the military, which is why investment in immediate readiness has been prioritized over capacity and capability. Although this is sustainable for a short time, future concerns when the Budget Control Act was passed are rapidly becoming impediments in the present. Modernization is now a primary inhibitor of readiness as keeping aging platforms in working order becomes increasing challenging and aircraft are retired before they can be replaced, leaving a smaller force available to meet operational requirements and further increasing the use of remaining platforms.

With respect to training, the Marine Corps continues to prioritize training for deploying and next-to-deploy units. Marine operating forces as a whole continue to average a two-to-one deployment-to-dwell ratio.[99] At this pace, readiness is consumed as quickly as it is built, leaving minimal flexibility to respond to contingencies. As a result, the USMC has maintained support for current operations but "may not have the required capacity—the 'ready bench'—to respond to larger crises at the readiness levels and timeliness required" or to support sustained conflict.[100]

Marine Corps guidance identifies multiple levels of readiness that can affect the ability to conduct operations:

> Readiness is the synthesis of two distinct but interrelated levels. a. unit readiness—The ability to provide capabilities required by the combatant commanders to execute their assigned missions. This is derived from the ability of each unit to deliver the outputs for which it was designed. b. joint readiness—The combatant commander's ability to integrate and synchronize ready combat and support forces to execute his or her assigned missions.[101]

The availability of amphibious ships, although funded through the Navy budget, has a direct impact on the Marine Corps' joint readiness. For example, while shore-based MAGTFs can maintain unit-level readiness and conduct training for local contingencies, a shortfall in amphibious lift capabilities leaves these units without "the strategic flexibility and responsiveness of afloat forces and...constrained by host nation permissions."[102]

In December 2017, a U.S. Government Accountability Office (GAO) official testified that while deploying units completed all necessary pre-deployment training for amphibious operations, the Marine Corps was "unable to fully accomplish...home-station unit training to support contingency requirements, service-level exercises, and experimentation and concept development for amphibious operations."[103] A shortage of available amphibious ships was identified as the primary factor in training limitations. Of the 32 amphibious ships currently in the U.S. fleet, only 16 are considered "available to support current or contingency operations."[104] While infantry battalions can maintain unit-level readiness requirements, their utility depends equally on their ability to deploy in defense of U.S. interests.

Marine aviation in particular is experiencing significant readiness shortfalls. The *2018 Marine Aviation Plan* found that "[a]cross all of Marine aviation, readiness is below steady state requirements."[105] With a smaller force structure and fewer aircraft available for training, aviation units are having difficulty keeping up with demanding operational requirements. According to Lieutenant General Stephen Rudder, Marine Corps Deputy Commandant for Aviation, most Marine aviation squadrons "still lack the required number of ready aircraft required to 'fight tonight.'"[106]

As of November 2017, approximately half of the Marine Corps' tactical aircraft were considered flyable.[107] This is a slight increase over FY 2018 readiness figures and has helped to improve the D2D ratio from 1:2 to 1:2.6 across the TACAIR fleet. Through investments in modernization and adequate funding for spare parts, the Marine Corps has managed to increase readiness by roughly 15 percent in the modern fleet and 10 percent in the legacy fleet.[108]

However, readiness gains have begun to plateau.[109] The Marine Corps received funding for spare parts at the "maximum executable levels" in FY 2017 and even higher levels in FY 2018.[110] In FY 2017, the Corps added only six ready basic aircraft to the fleet, compared to 44 in FY 2016,[111] yielding only modest increases in flight hours of two per crew per month in 2017. Although the Marine Corps is working to maximize their utilization, as long as it continues to rely on legacy systems, the amount of time committed to maintenance and access to spare parts will constrain aircraft availability.

Readiness rates remain particularly stressed within certain high-demand communities (including the MV-22, F/A-18, and F-35) that lack necessary numbers of available aircraft, pilots, and maintainers.[112] Although the MV-22 is a relatively new platform and is operating with few problems, high demand has held its readiness rates at 48 percent and forced the Marine Corps to put these aircraft "into operation as fast as they were coming off the line."[113] As is the case with the Corps' infantry battalions, this leaves little capacity available to support a "ready bench," and immediate demand challenges efforts to reduce the platform to a common configuration.

Availability of spare parts remains "the primary degrader of Marine aviation readiness."[114] Although adequate funding for spare parts and maintenance will help to maintain current numbers of ready basic aircraft, the Marine Corps recognizes that "modernization of [its] legacy fleet is the true key to regaining readiness."[115] The transition to modern systems will increase capacity, dispersing some of the strain from high utilization rates and offsetting costs from legacy platforms, which require more time and money to maintain.

For FY 2018, the Department of the Navy chose to prioritize immediate readiness by accepting "risk in facilities [and] weapons capacity," "delay[ing] certain modernization programs,"[116] and "protect[ing] near-term operational readiness of its deployed and next-to-deploy units" while struggling to maintain a "ready bench."[117] According to former Marine Corps Assistant Commandant General John M. Paxton, "[b]y degrading the readiness of these bench forces to support those forward deployed, we are forced to accept increased risk in our ability to respond to further contingencies, our ability to assure we are the most ready when the nation is least ready."[118] In looking beyond immediate readiness, the USMC FY 2019 budget request aims to support a "comprehensive aviation recovery plan that, *if sufficiently resourced and supported by our industrial base*, recovers the force to an acceptable readiness level by FY20 with a ready bench by FY22."[119]

The Marines Corps' Ground Equipment Reset Strategy, developed to recover from the strain of years of sustained operations in Iraq and Afghanistan, is nearing completion after being delayed from the end of FY 2017 to FY 2019. As of March 2018, the Marine Corps had reset approximately 99 percent of its ground equipment, compared to 90 percent in the prior year.[120] Reconstituting equipment and ensuring that the Corps' inventory can meet operational requirements are critical aspects of readiness.

Scoring the U.S. Marine Corps

Capacity Score: Weak

Based on the deployment of Marines across major engagements since the Korean War, the Corps requires roughly 15 battalions for one MRC.[121] This translates to a force of approximately 30 battalions to fight two MRCs simultaneously. The government force-sizing documents that discuss Marine Corps composition support this. Though the documents that make such a recommendation count the Marines by divisions, not battalions, they are consistent in arguing for three Active Marine Corps divisions, which in turn requires roughly 30 battalions. With a 20 percent strategic reserve, the ideal USMC capacity for a two-MRC force-sizing construct is 36 battalions.

More than 33,000 Marines were deployed in Korea, and more than 44,000 were deployed in Vietnam. In the Persian Gulf, one of the largest Marine Corps missions in U.S. history, some 90,000 Marines were deployed, and approximately 66,000 were deployed for Operation Iraqi Freedom. As the Persian Gulf War is the most pertinent example for this construct, an operating force of 180,000 Marines is a reasonable benchmark for a two-MRC force, not counting Marines that would be unavailable for deployment (assigned to institutional portions of the Corps) or that are deployed elsewhere. This is supported by government documents that have advocated a force as low as 174,000 (1993 Bottom-Up Review) and as high as 202,000 (2010 Quadrennial Defense Review), with an average end strength of 185,000 being recommended. However, as recent increases in end strength have not corresponded with deployable combat power, these government recommendations may have to be reassessed.

- **Two-MRC Level:** 36 battalions.

- **Actual 2018 Level:** 24 battalions.

Despite an increase in manpower, the Corps continues to operate with less than 67 percent of the number of battalions relative to the two-MRC benchmark. Marine Corps capacity is therefore scored as "weak" again in 2018.

Capability Score: Marginal
The Corps receives scores of "weak" for "Capability of Equipment," "marginal" for "Age of Equipment" and "Health of Modernization Programs," but "strong" for "Size of Modernization Program." Therefore, the aggregate score for Marine Corps capability is "marginal." Excluded from the scoring are various ground vehicle programs that have been cancelled and are now being reprogrammed.

Readiness Score: Weak
In FY 2018, the Marine Corps again prioritized next-to-deploy units. As the nation's crisis response force, the Corps requires that all units, whether deployed or non-deployed, be ready. However, since most Marine Corps ground units are meeting readiness requirements only immediately before deployment and the Corps' "ready bench" would "not be as capable as necessary" if deployed on short notice, USMC readiness is sufficient to meet ongoing commitments only at reported deployment-to-dwell ratios of 1:2. This means that only a third of the force—the deployed force—could be considered fully ready. Furthermore, as of November 2017, the USMC reported that only half of its tactical aircraft were considered flyable.

Marine Corps officials have not been clear as to the status of ground component readiness during FY 2018, but in testimony to Congress during the year, as noted, they have highlighted concerns about shortfalls in service readiness to mobilize for larger-scale operational commitments. Due to the lack of a "ready bench" and a further decline in readiness levels among the USMC aircraft fleet, the *2019 Index* assesses Marine Corps readiness levels as "weak."

Overall U.S. Marine Corps Score: Weak
Although 2018 congressional testimony strikes an optimistic note and increased funding for readiness and an emphasis on modernization give strong support to the Corps' readiness-recovery efforts, the effects will take time to materialize. As a result, the Marine Corps maintains an overall score of "weak" in the *2019 Index*.

U.S. Military Power: Marine Corps

	VERY WEAK	WEAK	MARGINAL	STRONG	VERY STRONG
Capacity		✓			
Capability			✓		
Readiness		✓			
OVERALL		✓			

MARINE CORPS SCORES

Weakest ← → Strongest

Procurement　■ Through FY 2018
and Spending　▨ Pending

Main Battle Tank

PLATFORM	Age Score	Capability Score	MODERNIZATION PROGRAM	Size Score	Health Score
M1A1 Abrams Inventory: **447** Fleet age: **28**　Date: **1989** The M1A1 Abrams Main Battle Tank provides the Marine Corps with heavy-armor direct fire capabilities. It is expected to remain in service beyond 2028.	②	❶	None		

Light Wheeled Vehicle

PLATFORM	Age Score	Capability Score	MODERNIZATION PROGRAM	Size Score	Health Score
HMMWV Inventory: **17,000** Fleet age: **10**　Date: **1985** The HMMWV is a light wheeled vehicle used to transport troops with some measure of protection against light arms, blast, and fragmentation. The expected life span of the HMMWV is 15 years. Some HMMWVs will be replaced by the Joint Light Tactical Vehicle (JLTV).	②	❶	**Joint Light Tactical Vehicle (JLTV)** Timeline: **2015–2023** Currently in development, the JLTV is a vehicle program meant to replace some of the HMMWVs and improve reliability, survivability, and strategic and operational transportability. So far the program has experienced a one-year delay due to changes in vehicle requirements. This is a joint program with Army. The Marine Corps has increased its acquistion objective by 1,850 vehicles, bringing the total planned procurement to 9,091 and extending the timeline procurement through 2023.	②	❺

PROCUREMENT
■
850　　8,511

SPENDING (*$ millions*)
■
$3,001　　$25,028

NOTE: JLTV spending figures reflect the full joint program spending.

See Methodology for descriptions of scores.　　Fleet age—Average age of fleet　　Date—Year fleet first entered service

Amphibious Assault Vehicle

PLATFORM	Age Score	Capability Score	MODERNIZATION PROGRAM	Size Score	Health Score
AAV Inventory: ~1,200 Fleet age: **40** Date: **1972** The Amphibious Assault Vehicle transports troops and cargo from ship to shore. The AAV is undergoing a survivability upgrade to extend its life through 2035. The Marine Corps has procured 48 upgraded vehicles to-date. It will upgrade 392 in total.	①	①	**Amphibious Combat Vehicle (ACV) 1.1** Timeline: **2014–2021** The Amphibious Combat Vehicle is now a major defense acquisition program. The ACV is intended to replace the aging AAV. ACV 1.1 will procure 204 vehicles. Delivery of the first 30 vehicles are anticipated for 2019.	③	⑤
LAV-25 Inventory: ~900 Fleet age: **26** Date: **1983** The LAV is a wheeled light armor vehicle with modest amphibious capability used for armored reconnaissance and highly mobile fire support. It has undergone several service life extensions (most recently in 2012) and will be in service until 2035.	②	①	**PROCUREMENT** 26 178 **SPENDING** (*$ millions*) $619 $1,271		

Attack Helicopters

PLATFORM	Age Score	Capability Score	MODERNIZATION PROGRAM	Size Score	Health Score
AH-1W Cobra Inventory: **77** Fleet age: **26** Date: **1986** The Super Cobra is an attack helicopter that provides the Marines with close air support and armed reconnaissance. The Super Cobra will remain in service until 2021, when it will be replaced with the AH-1Z.	①		**AH-1Z** Timeline: **2004–2020** The new AH-1Z Viper program is part of a larger modification program to the H-1 platform. The new H-1 rotorcraft will have upgraded avionics, rotor blades, transmissions, landing gear, and structural modifications to enhance speed, maneuverability, and payload. The AH-1Z started out as a remanufacture program, but that was later changed to a New Build program because of concerns over existing airframes. While costs have increased, the program has not met the APB breach threshold.	⑤	③
AH-1Z Viper Inventory: **76** Fleet age: **4** Date: **2010** The AH-1Z Viper is the follow on to the AH-1W Cobra attack helicopter. The Viper will have greater speed, payload, and range, as well as a more advanced cockpit. It is expected that the AH-1Z will fully replace the AH-1W Cobra in 2021. The expected operational life span of the Viper is 30 years.	⑤	②	**PROCUREMENT** 148 41 **SPENDING** (*$ millions*) $11,554 $731		

See Methodology for descriptions of scores.   Fleet age—Average age of fleet   Date—Year fleet first entered service

MARINE CORPS SCORES

Airborne Electronic Attack Aircraft/ Ground Attack Aircraft

PLATFORM	Age Score	Capability Score	MODERNIZATION PROGRAM	Size Score	Health Score
EA-6B Inventory: **6** Fleet age: **29** Date: **1971** The Prowler provides the USMC with an electronic warfare capability. The last squadron will be retired in October 2018.	①		**F-35B/C** Timeline: **2008–2033** The Corps is purchasing 353 F-35Bs and 67 F-35Cs. The F-35B is the USMC version of the Joint Strike Fighter program. It is meant to replace the AV-8B Harrier, completing transition by 2030. The Joint Strike Fighter has had many development issues, including a Nunn–McCurdy cost breach and major development issues. The F-35B in particular has had software development problems and engine problems that led to grounding. The Marine Corps announced IOC of its second F-35B squadron in June 2016. The F-35C is not anticipated to achieve IOC until 2019.	③	❶
AV-8B Inventory: **130** Fleet age: **21** Date: **1985** The Harrier is a vertical/short takeoff and landing aircraft designed to fly from LHA/LHDs. It provides strike and reconnaissance capabilities. The aircraft will be retired around 2024.	⑤	❶			
F-35B Inventory: **50** Fleet age: **3** Date: **2015** The F-35B is the Marine Corps's short takeoff and vertical landing variant meant to replace the AV-8B Harrier. Despite some development problems, the F-35B achieved IOC in July 2015.	⑤				
F/A-18 A-D Inventory: **251** Fleet age: **26** Date: **1978** Many aircraft in the F/A-18 fleet have logged about 8,000 hours compared with the originally intended 6,000. The fleet life has been extended until 2030. This is necessary to bridge the gap to when the F-35Bs and F-35Cs are available.	③				

PROCUREMENT

131   289

SPENDING *($ millions)*

$127,534 $278,597

See Methodology for descriptions of scores.   Fleet age—Average age of fleet   Date—Year fleet first entered service

MARINE CORPS SCORES

Weakest ⟵ ⟶ Strongest

Medium Lift

PLATFORM	Age Score	Capability Score	MODERNIZATION PROGRAM	Size Score	Health Score
MV-22 Inventory: **277** Fleet age: **6** Date: **2007** The Osprey is a vertical takeoff and landing tilt-rotor platform designed to support expeditionary assault, cargo lift, and raid operations. The program is still in production. The life expectancy of the MV-22 is 23 years.	④	⑤	**MV-22B** Timeline: **1997–2031** The Osprey is in production, and the platform is meeting performance requirements. The modernization program is not facing any serious issues. Procurement figures include 48 Navy MV-22s and 50 of the carrier variant CV-22s.	④	⑤

PROCUREMENT   403   59

SPENDING ($ millions) $47,898 $8,341

Heavy Lift

PLATFORM	Age Score	Capability Score	MODERNIZATION PROGRAM	Size Score	Health Score
CH-53E Super Stallion Inventory: **139** Fleet age: **29** Date: **1981** The CH-53E is a heavy-lift rotorcraft. The aircraft will be replaced by the CH-53K, which will have a greater lift capacity. The program life of the CH-53E is 41 years.	②	①	**CH-53K** Timeline: **2017–2028** The program is in development. It is meant to replace the CH-53E and provide increased range, survivability, and payload. The program still has not fully developed the critical technology necessary. The program has experienced delays and cost growth.	⑤	③

PROCUREMENT   6   194

SPENDING ($ millions) $6,969 $24,196

Tanker

PLATFORM	Age Score	Capability Score	MODERNIZATION PROGRAM	Size Score	Health Score
KC-130J Inventory: **45** Fleet age: **10** Date: **2004** The KC-130J is both a tanker and transport aircraft. It can transport troops, provide imagery reconnaissance, and perform tactical aerial refueling. This platform is currently in production. The airframe is expected to last 38 years.	④	⑤	**KC-130J** Timeline: **1997–2028** The KC-130J is both a tanker and transport aircraft. The procurement program for the KC-130J is not facing acquisition problems.	④	④

PROCUREMENT   63   41

SPENDING ($ millions) $4,992 $4,904

NOTES: The total program dollar value reflects the full F–35 joint program, including engine procurement. As part of the F–35 program, the Navy is purchasing 67 F-35Cs for the U.S. Marine Corps, which are included here. The MV-22B program also includes some costs from the U.S. Air Force procurement. The AH–1Z costs include costs of UH–1 procurement.
SOURCE: Heritage Foundation research using data from government documents and websites. See also Dakota L. Wood, ed., *2018 Index of U.S. Military Strength* (Washington, DC: The Heritage Foundation, 2018), http://index.heritage.org/militarystrength/.

See Methodology for descriptions of scores.   Fleet age—Average age of fleet   Date—Year fleet first entered service

Endnotes

1. U.S. Department of the Navy, *Department of the Navy FY 2019 President's Budget*, February 12, 2018, p. 4, http://www.secnav.navy.mil/fmc/fmb/Documents/19pres/DON_Press_Brief.pdf (accessed August 9, 2018).

2. Lieutenant General Ronald L. Bailey, Deputy Commandant for Plans, Policies, and Operations; Lieutenant General Jon M. Davis, Deputy Commandant for Aviation; and Lieutenant General Michael G. Dana, Deputy Commandant for Installations and Logistics, statement on "The Current State of the Marine Corps" before the Subcommittee on Readiness, Committee on Armed Services, U.S. House of Representatives, April 5, 2017, p. 5, http://docs.house.gov/meetings/AS/AS03/20170405/105768/HHRG-115-AS03-Wstate-BaileyUSMCR-20170405.pdf (accessed August 9, 2018).

3. Lieutenant General Steven R. Rudder, Deputy Commandant for Aviation, United States Marine Corps, statement on "Aviation Readiness" before the Subcommittee on Readiness, Committee on Armed Services, U.S. House of Representatives, November 9, 2017, p. 1, https://docs.house.gov/meetings/AS/AS03/20171109/106611/HHRG-115-AS03-Bio-RudderS-20171109.pdf (accessed August 9, 2018).

4. General Joseph Dunford, Commandant, United States Marine Corps, statement on Marine Corps readiness before the Subcommittee on Defense, Committee on Appropriations, U.S. House of Representatives, February 26, 2015, p. 10, http://www.hqmc.marines.mil/Portals/142/Docs/CMC%20Testimony%202015/USMC%20FY16%20Written%20Posture%20Statement_FINAL.pdf (accessed August 9, 2018).

5. U.S. Department of Defense, Office of the Under Secretary of Defense (Comptroller)/Chief Financial Officer, *United States Department of Defense Fiscal Year 2019 Budget Request: Defense Budget Overview*, revised February 13, 2018, p. 3-13, https://comptroller.defense.gov/Portals/45/Documents/defbudget/fy2019/FY2019_Budget_Request_Overview_Book.pdf (accessed August 9, 2018).

6. General Glenn Walters, Assistant Commandant of the Marine Corps, statement on "Marine Corps Readiness" before the Subcommittee on Readiness, Committee on Armed Services, U.S. Senate, February 14, 2018, p. 2, https://www.armed-services.senate.gov/imo/media/doc/Walters_02-14-18.pdf (accessed August 12, 2018).

7. U.S. Department of the Navy, *Department of the Navy Fiscal Year (FY) 2011 Budget Estimates, Justification of Estimates: Military Personnel, Marine Corps*, February 2010, p. 4, http://www.secnav.navy.mil/fmc/fmb/Documents/11pres/MPMC_Book.pdf (accessed August 20, 2018).

8. U.S. Department of Defense, Office of the Under Secretary of Defense (Comptroller)/Chief Financial Officer, *United States Department of Defense Fiscal Year 2016 Budget Request: Overview*, February 2015, p. A-1, http://comptroller.defense.gov/Portals/45/Documents/defbudget/fy2016/FY2016_Budget_Request_Overview_Book.pdf (accessed August 20, 2018).

9. U.S. Department of the Navy, Office of Budget, *Highlights of the Department of the Navy FY 2019 Budget*, 2018, p. 1-4, 2-7, and 2-8, http://www.secnav.navy.mil/fmc/fmb/Documents/19pres/Highlights_book.pdf (accessed August 16, 2018), and U.S. Department of Defense, Office of the Under Secretary of Defense (Comptroller)/Chief Financial Officer, *United States Department of Defense Fiscal Year 2018 Budget Request: Defense Budget Overview*, May 2017, pp. 2-6, 2-8, and 7-14, http://comptroller.defense.gov/Portals/45/Documents/defbudget/fy2018/fy2018_Budget_Request_Overview_Book.pdf (accessed August 16, 2018).

10. General Robert B. Neller, Commandant of the Marine Corps, statement on "The Posture of the United States Marine Corps" before the Committee on Appropriations, U.S. House of Representatives, March 7, 2018, p. 15, https://docs.house.gov/meetings/AP/AP02/20180307/106932/HHRG-115-AP02-Wstate-NellerR-20180307.pdf (accessed August 16, 2018).

11. Rudder, statement on "Aviation Readiness," November 9, 2017, p. 2.

12. General John Paxton, Assistant Commandant of the Marine Corps, statement on "U.S. Marine Corps Readiness" before the Subcommittee on Readiness, Committee on Armed Services, U.S. Senate, March 15, 2016, p. 8, https://www.armed-services.senate.gov/imo/media/doc/Paxton_03-15-16.pdf (accessed August 14, 2018).

13. Neller, statement on "The Posture of the United States Marine Corps," March 7, 2018, p. 16.

14. Testimony of General Joseph F. Dunford, Jr., Commandant of the Marine Corps, in stenographic transcript of *Hearing to Receive Testimony on the Impact of the Budget Control Act of 2011 and Sequestration on National Security*, Committee on Armed Services, U.S. Senate, January 28, 2015, p. 74, http://www.armed-services.senate.gov/imo/media/doc/15-04%20-%201-28-15.pdf (accessed August 16, 2018).

15. U.S. Marine Corps, *2018 Marine Aviation Plan*, p. 23, https://www.aviation.marines.mil/Portals/11/2018%20AvPlan%20FINAL.pdf (accessed August 16, 2018).

16. U.S. Marine Corps, *2017 Marine Aviation Plan*, p. 54, www.aviation.marines.mil/Portals/11/2017%20MARINE%20AVIATIOIN%20PLAN.pdf (accessed August 13, 2017).

17. Congressional Quarterly, "House Armed Services Committee Holds Hearing on Aviation Readiness," CQ Congressional Transcripts, July 6, 2016, http://www.cq.com/doc/congressionaltranscripts-4922435?3&search=IXd1KGHk (accessed August 17, 2017).

18. Paxton, statement on "U.S. Marine Corps Readiness," March 15, 2016, p. 9.

19. Rudder, statement on "Aviation Readiness," November 9, 2017, p. 4.

20. Ibid.

21. Ibid., p. 7.

22. U.S. Marine Corps, *2018 Marine Aviation Plan*, p. 10.

23. Rudder, statement on "Aviation Readiness," November 9, 2017, p. 7.

24. U.S. Marine Corps, *2018 Marine Aviation Plan*, p. 78.

25. U.S. Marine Corps, *2017 Marine Aviation Plan*, pp. 70 and 76.

26. Lieutenant General Jon Davis, "Naval Aviation Reflections," Naval Aviation News, Vol. 99, No. 3 (Summer 2017), p. 5, http://navalaviationnews.navylive.dodlive.mil/files/2017/08/NAN-Summer2017_web.pdf (accessed August 20, 2018).

27. Kris Osborn, "Marines: 'We Plan To Have the MV-22B Osprey for at Least the Next 40 Years,'" *National Interest,* May 2, 2018, https://nationalinterest.org/blog/the-buzz/marines-%E2%80%9Cwe-plan-have-the-mv-22b-osprey-least-the-next-40-25654 (accessed August 16, 2018).

28. Vice Admiral Paul Grosklags, Principal Military Deputy, Assistant Secretary of the Navy (Research, Development and Acquisition); Rear Admiral Michael C. Manazir, Director, Air Warfare; and Lieutenant General Jon Davis, Deputy Commandant for Aviation, statement on "Department of the Navy's Aviation Programs" before the Subcommittee on Seapower, Committee on Armed Services, U.S. Senate, March 25, 2015, p. 10, http://www.armed-services.senate.gov/imo/media/doc/Grosklags_Manazir_Davis_03-25-15.pdf (accessed August 13, 2017).

29. Lieutenant General Brian D. Beaudreault, Deputy Commandant, Plans, Policies, and Operations, statement on "Amphibious Warfare Readiness and Training—Interoperability, Shortfalls, and the Way Ahead" before the Subcommittee on Readiness, Committee on Armed Services, U.S. House of Representatives, December 1, 2017, p. 3, https://docs.house.gov/meetings/AS/AS03/20171201/106681/HHRG-115-AS03-Wstate-BeaudreaultB-20171201.pdf (accessed August 16, 2018).

30. Ibid., pp. 4–5.

31. General Glenn Walters, Assistant Commandant of the Marine Corps, statement on "Marine Corps Readiness" before the Subcommittee on Readiness, Committee on Armed Services, U.S. Senate, February 8, 2017, p. 5, https://www.armed-services.senate.gov/imo/media/doc/Walters_02-08-17.pdf (accessed August 19, 2018).

32. General John Paxton, Assistant Commandant, United States Marine Corps, statement on Marine Corps readiness and FY 2016 budget request before the Subcommittee on Readiness and Management Support, Committee on Armed Services, U.S. Senate, March 25, 2015, pp. 10–11, http://www.armed-services.senate.gov/imo/media/doc/Paxton_03-25-15.pdf (accessed August 14, 2018).

33. U.S. Department of the Navy, *Department of the Navy FY 2019 President's Budget*, p. 8.

34. U.S. Department of Defense, Office of the Under Secretary of Defense (Comptroller)/Chief Financial Officer, *United States Department of Defense Fiscal Year 2019 Budget Request: Defense Budget Overview*, pp. 8-1 and 8-12.

35. Lieutenant General Michael Dana, Deputy Commandant, Installations and Logistics, statement on "Marine Corps Readiness" before the Subcommittee on Readiness, Committee on Armed Services, U.S. House of Representatives, March 6, 2018, p. 3, https://docs.house.gov/meetings/AS/AS03/20180306/106942/HHRG-115-AS03-Wstate-DanaM-20180306.pdf (accessed August 14, 2018).

36. U.S. Marine Corps, "Assault Amphibious Vehicle (AAV)," http://www.candp.marines.mil/Programs/Focus-Area-4-Modernization-Technology/Part-3-Ground-Combat-Tactical-Vehicles/Assault-Amphibious-Vehicle/ (accessed August 3, 2018).

37. U.S. Department of the Navy, *Department of Defense Fiscal Year (FY) 2019 Budget Estimates, Navy, Justification Book Volume 1 of 1: Procurement, Marine Corps*, February 2018, p. 2, http://www.secnav.navy.mil/fmc/fmb/Documents/19pres/PMC_Book.pdf (accessed August 16, 2018).

38. U.S. Marine Corps, "Assault Amphibious Vehicle (AAV)."

39. Lieutenant General Robert S. Walsh, Deputy Commandant, Combat Development and Integration, and Commanding General, Marine Corps Combat Development Command; Brigadier General Joseph Shrader, Commander, Marine Corps Systems Command; and John Garner, Program Executive Officer, Land Systems Marine Corps, statement on "Marine Corps Ground Programs" before the Subcommittee on Seapower, Committee on Armed Services, U.S. Senate, June 6, 2017, p. 5, https://www.armed-services.senate.gov/imo/media/doc/Walsh-Shrader-Garner_06-06-17.pdf (accessed August 16, 2018).

40. Walters, statement on "Marine Corps Readiness" February 8, 2017, pp. 7–8.

41. Lieutenant General Robert S. Walsh, Deputy Commandant, Combat Development and Integration, and Brigadier General Joseph Shrader, Commander, Marine Corps Systems Command, statement on "Fiscal Year 2019 Ground Forces Modernization Programs" before the Subcommittee on Tactical Air and Land Forces, Committee on Armed Services, U.S. House of Representatives, April 18, 2018, p. 10, https://docs.house.gov/meetings/AS/AS25/20180418/108159/HHRG-115-AS25-Wstate-ShraderJ-20180418.pdf (accessed August 17 2018).

42. The average age of the M1A1 was 26 in 2016. Paxton, statement on "U.S. Marine Corps Readiness," March 15, 2016, p. 15. No new M1A1 Abrams have been commissioned since that time, so the average age is estimated as 28 in 2018.

43. U.S. Marine Corps, Concepts and Programs, "Ground Equipment Age," last revised April 3, 2014, http://proposed.marinecorpsconceptsandprograms.com/resources/ground-equipment-age (accessed August 17, 2018).

44. U.S. Department of the Navy, *Department of the Navy Fiscal Year (FY) 2019 Budget Estimates, Justification of Estimates: Operations and Maintenance, Marine Corps Reserve OMMCR)*, February 2018, p. 28, http://www.secnav.navy.mil/fmc/fmb/Documents/19pres/OMMCR_Book.pdf (accessed August 17, 2018).

45. Walsh and Shrader, statement on "Fiscal Year 2019 Ground Forces Modernization Programs," April 18, 2018, p. 9.

46. International Institute for Strategic Studies, *The Military Balance 2018: The Annual Assessment of Global Military Capabilities and Defence Economics* (London: Routledge, 2017) pp. 53.

47. U.S. Marine Corps, *2018 Marine Aviation Plan*, p. 45.

48. Shawn Snow, "The Corps Is Down to One Final EA-6B Prowler Squadron," *Marine Corps Times*, May 16, 2018, https://www.marinecorpstimes.com/news/your-marine-corps/2018/05/16/the-corps-is-down-to-one-final-ea-6b-prowler-squadron/ (accessed August 17, 2018).

49. U.S. Marine Corps, *2018 Marine Aviation Plan*, p. 44.

50. GlobalSecurity.org, "F/A-18 Hornet Service Life," last modified May 2, 2018, https://www.globalsecurity.org/military/systems/aircraft/f-18-service-life.htm (accessed August 17, 2018).

51. Paxton, statement on "U.S. Marine Corps Readiness," March 15, 2016, p. 9.

52. Vice Admiral Paul Grosklags, Representing the Assistant Secretary of the Navy (Research, Development and Acquisition); Lieutenant General Steven Rudder, Deputy Commandant for Aviation; and Rear Admiral Scott Conn, Director, Air Warfare, statement on "Department of the Navy's Aviation Programs" before the Subcommittee on Tactical Air and Land Forces, Committee on Armed Services, U.S. House of Representatives, April 12, 2018, p. 3, https://docs.house.gov/meetings/AS/AS25/20180412/108078/HHRG-115-AS25-Wstate-RudderS-20180412.pdf (accessed August 17, 2018).

53. U.S. Marine Corps, *2018 Marine Aviation Plan*, p. 56.

54. Vice Admiral Paul Grosklags, Representing Assistant Secretary of the Navy (Research, Development and Acquisition); Lieutenant General Jon Davis, Deputy Commandant for Aviation; and Rear Admiral Michael C. Manazir, Director Air Warfare, statement on "Department of the Navy's Aviation Programs" before the Subcommittee on Seapower, Committee on Armed Services, U.S. Senate, April 20, 2016, p. 3, http://www.armed-services.senate.gov/imo/media/doc/Grosklags-Davis-Manazir_04-20-16.pdf (accessed August 13, 2017).

55. U.S. Marine Corps, *2018 Marine Aviation Plan*, p. 35.

56. Megan Eckstein, "Marines Declare Initial Operational Capability on F-35B Joint Strike Fighter," U.S. Naval Institute News, July 31, 2015, https://news.usni.org/2015/07/31/marines-declare-initial-operational-capability-on-f-35b-joint-strike-fighter (accessed August 17, 2018).

57. U.S. Marine Corps, *2018 Marine Aviation Plan*, p. 23.

58. U.S. Department of Defense, Office of the Under Secretary of Defense (Comptroller)/Chief Financial Officer, *United States Department of Defense Fiscal Year 2018 Budget Request: Program Acquisition Cost by Weapon System*, May 2017, pp. 3-2 and 3-9, http://comptroller.defense.gov/Portals/45/Documents/defbudget/fy2018/fy2018_Weapons.pdf (accessed August 17, 2018).

59. Andrew Feickert, "Joint Light Tactical Vehicle (JLTV): Background and Issues for Congress," Congressional Research Service *Report for Members and Committees Congress*, February 27, 2018, p. 1, https://fas.org/sgp/crs/weapons/RS22942.pdf (accessed August 17, 2018).

60. Joe Gould, "Oshkosh Awaits Protest After JLTV Win," *Defense News*, August 29, 2015, http://www.defensenews.com/story/defense/land/vehicles/2015/08/29/oshkosh-awaits-protests-jltv-win/71325838 (accessed July 27, 2017).

61. Testimony of John M. Garner, Program Executive Office, Land Systems Marine Corps, in stenographic transcript of *Hearing to Receive Testimony on Marine Corps Ground Modernization in Review of the Defense Authorization Request for Fiscal Year 2018 and the Future Years Defense Program*, Subcommittee on Seapower, Committee on Armed Services, U.S. Senate, June 6, 2017, p. 63, https://www.armed-services.senate.gov/imo/media/doc/17-56_06-06-17.pdf (accessed August 18, 2018).

62. U.S. Department of Defense, Office of the Under Secretary of Defense (Comptroller)/Chief Financial Officer, *United States Department of Defense Fiscal Year 2018 Budget Request: Program Acquisition Cost by Weapon* System, p. 3-1.

63. U.S. Department of Defense, Office of the Under Secretary of Defense (Comptroller)/Chief Financial Officer, *United States Department of Defense Fiscal Year 2019 Budget Request: Program Acquisition Cost by Weapon* System, February 2018, p. 3-2, https://comptroller.defense.gov/Portals/45/documents/defbudget/FY2019/FY2019_Weapons.pdf (accessed August 18, 2018).

64. Feickert, "Joint Light Tactical Vehicle (JLTV): Background and Issues for Congress," p. 1.

65. U.S. Department of Defense, "Department of Defense Comprehensive Selected Acquisition Reports (SARs) for the December 31, 2017 Reporting Requirement as Updated by the President's FY 2019 Budget," March 16, 2018, p. 4, https://www.acq.osd.mil/ara/am/sar/SST-2017-12.pdf (accessed August 18, 2018).

66. Garner testimony in stenographic transcript of *Hearing to Receive Testimony on Marine Corps Ground Modernization in Review of the Defense Authorization Request for Fiscal Year 2018 and the Future Years Defense Program*, p. 63.

67. Congressional Quarterly, "Senate Armed Services Committee Holds Hearing on the Marine Corps," CQ Congressional Transcripts, June 6, 2017, http://www.cq.com/doc/congressionaltranscripts-5117362?2 (accessed August 18, 2018).

68. U.S. Department of the Navy, *Department of Defense Fiscal Year (FY) 2018 Budget Estimates, Navy, Justification Book Volume 1 of 1: Procurement, Marine Corps*, May 2017, p. 211, http://www.secnav.navy.mil/fmc/fmb/Documents/18pres/PMC_Book.pdf (accessed August 17, 2018); U.S. Marine Corps, Concepts and Programs, "Joint Light Tactical Vehicle," http://www.candp.marines.mil/Programs/Focus-Area-4-Modernization-Technology/Part-3-Ground-Combat-Tactical-Vehicles/Joint-Light-Tactical-Vehicle-Family-of-Vehicles/ (accessed August 18, 2018).

69. Feickert, "Joint Light Tactical Vehicle (JLTV)," p. 9.

70. Ibid., pp. 4 and 6.

71. Ibid., p. 6.

72. U.S. Department of Defense, "Department of Defense Comprehensive Selected Acquisition Reports (SARs) for the December 31, 2017 Reporting Requirement as Updated by the President's FY 2019 Budget," p. 4.

73. Andrew Feickert, "Marine Corps Amphibious Combat Vehicle (ACV) and Marine Personnel Carrier (MPC): Background and Issues for Congress," Congressional Research Service *Report for Members and Committees of Congress*, March 7, 2018, p. 5, https://www.fas.org/sgp/crs/weapons/R42723.pdf (accessed August 18, 2018); U.S. Department of Defense, Office of the Under Secretary of Defense (Comptroller)/Chief Financial Officer, *United States Department of Defense Fiscal Year 2018 Budget Request: Program Acquisition Cost by Weapon System*, p. 3-9.

74. U.S. Department of Defense, Office of the Under Secretary of Defense (Comptroller)/Chief Financial Officer, *United States Department of Defense Fiscal Year 2018 Budget Request: Program Acquisition Cost by Weapon System*, p. 3-9.

75. Feickert, "Marine Corps Amphibious Combat Vehicle (ACV) and Marine Personnel Carrier (MPC)," Summary.

76. Lieutenant General Kenneth J. Glueck Jr., Deputy Commandant, Combat Development and Integration, and Commanding General, Marine Corps Combat Development Command, and Thomas P. Dee, Deputy Assistant Secretary of the Navy, Expeditionary Programs and Logistics Management, statement on "Marine Corps Modernization" before the Subcommittee on Seapower, Committee on Armed Services, U.S. Senate, March 11, 2015, pp. 8–9, https://www.armed-services.senate.gov/imo/media/doc/Glueck-Dee_03-11-15.pdf (accessed August 18, 2017).

77. With regard to this overall requirement—armored lift for 10 battalions of infantry—the AAV Survivability Upgrade Program would provide for four battalions, and ACV 1.1 and ACV 1.2 would account for six battalions. Ibid., pp. 7–8.

78. Jen Judson, "BAE Wins Marine Corps Contract to Build New Amphibious Combat Vehicle," *Defense News,* June 19, 2018, https://www.defensenews.com/land/2018/06/19/bae-wins-marine-corps-contract-to-build-new-amphibious-combat-vehicle/ (accessed August 3, 2018).

79. Feickert, "Marine Corps Amphibious Combat Vehicle (ACV): Background and Issues for Congress," p. 7.

80. Dunford, statement on Marine Corps readiness, February 26, 2015, p. 28.

81. Walsh, Shrader, and Garner, statement on "Marine Corps Ground Programs," June 6, 2017, p. 5.

82. Lieutenant General Brian Beaudreault, Deputy Commandant, Plans, Policies, and Operations, statement on "Marine Corps Readiness" before the Subcommittee on Readiness, Committee on Armed Services, U.S. House of Representatives, March 6, 2018, p. 5, https://docs.house.gov/meetings/AS/AS03/20180306/106942/HHRG-115-AS03-Wstate-BeaudreaultB-20180306.pdf (accessed August 18, 2018).

83. Grosklags, Davis, and Manazir, statement on "Department of the Navy's Aviation Programs," April 20, 2016, p. 7.

84. Vice Admiral Paul Grosklags, Representing Assistant Secretary of the Navy (Research, Development and Acquisition); Lieutenant General Jon Davis, Deputy Commandant for Aviation; and Rear Admiral DeWolfe H, Miller III, Director, Air Warfare, statement on "Department of the Navy's Aviation Programs" before the Subcommittee on Seapower, Committee on Armed Services, U.S. Senate, June 13, 2017, pp. 13–14, https://www.armed-services.senate.gov/imo/media/doc/Grosklags-Davis-Miller_06-13-17.pdf (accessed August 13, 2017).

85. U.S. Department of Defense *Selected Acquisition Report (SAR): V-22 Osprey Joint Services Advanced Vertical Lift Aircraft (V22) as of FY 2017 President's Budget*, RCS: DD-A&T(Q&A)823-212, March 21, 2016, p. 61, http://www.dod.mil/pubs/foi/Reading_Room/Selected_Acquisition_Reports/16-F-0402_DOC_64_V-22_DEC_2015_SAR.pdf (accessed August 30, 2016).

86. U.S. Marine Corps, *2018 Marine Aviation Plan*, p. 78.

87. U.S. Marine Corps, *2017 Marine Aviation Plan*, p. 78.

88. U.S. Marine Corps, *2018 Marine Aviation Plan*, pp. 76 and 84.

89. Ibid., p. 84.

90. Grosklags, Davis, and Manazir, statement on "Department of the Navy's Aviation Programs," April 20, 2016, p. 21.

91. U.S. Government Accountability Office, *Defense Acquisitions: Assessments of Selected Weapons Programs*, GAO-16-329SP, March 2016, p. 93, http://www.gao.gov/assets/680/676281.pdf (accessed August 13, 2017).

92. U.S. Department of Defense, Office of the Under Secretary of Defense (Comptroller)/Chief Financial Officer, *United States Department of Defense Fiscal Year 2019 Budget Request: Program Acquisition Cost by Weapon System*, February 2018, p. 1-16.

93. U.S. Government Accountability Office, *Defense Acquisitions: Assessments of Selected Weapons Programs*, p. 93.

94. International Institute for Strategic Studies, *The Military Balance 2017: The Annual Assessment of Global Military Capabilities and Defence Economics* (London: Routledge, 2017) p. 53.

95. Lieutenant General Jon M. Davis, Deputy Commandant for Aviation, statement on "Aviation Readiness and Safety" before the Subcommittee on Readiness, Committee on Armed Services, U.S. House of Representatives, July 6, 2016, pp. [5] and [9], http://docs.house.gov/meetings/AS/AS03/20160706/105159/HHRG-114-AS03-Wstate-DavisJ-20160706.pdf (accessed August 13, 2017).

96. Rudder, statement on "Aviation Readiness," November 9, 2017, p. 7. https://docs.house.gov/meetings/AS/AS03/20171109/106611/HHRG-115-AS03-Bio-RudderS-20171109.pdf (accessed August 3, 2018).

97. Beaudreault, statement on "Marine Corps Readiness," March 6, 2018, p. 5.

98. Another six aircraft will be procured with research and development funding, bringing the program of record to 200 aircraft. U.S. Department of Defense, Office of the Under Secretary of Defense (Comptroller)/Chief Financial Officer, *United States Department of Defense Fiscal Year 2019 Budget Request: Program Acquisition Cost by Weapon System*, p. 1-16.

99. U.S. Marine Corps, "The Commandant's Posture of the United States Marine Corps President's Budget 2018," p. 1, https://www.hqmc.marines.mil/Portals/142/Docs/CMC%20PB18%20Posture%20Written%20Testimony%20Final%20edited%20for%20web.pdf?ver=2017-07-28-161000-643 (accessed August 18, 2018).

100. Walters, statement on "Marine Corps Readiness," February 8, 2017, p. 9.

101. U.S. Marine Corps, *Commander's Readiness Handbook*, May 2014, p. iv, https://www.hqmc.marines.mil/Portals/138/HiRes%20Commanders%20Readiness%20Handbook.pdf (accessed August 18, 2018).

102. Beaudreault, statement on "Amphibious Warfare Readiness and Training (Interoperability, Shortfalls, and the Way Ahead)," December 1, 2017, p. 7.

103. Cary B. Russell, Director, Defense Capabilities and Management, U.S. Government Accountability Office, "Navy and Marine Corps Training: Further Planning Needed for Amphibious Operations Training," GAO-18-212T, testimony before the Subcommittee on Readiness, Committee on Armed Services, U.S. House of Representatives, December 1, 2017, p. 5, https://docs.house.gov/meetings/AS/AS03/20171201/106681/HHRG-115-AS03-Wstate-RussellC-20171201.pdf (accessed August 13, 2018).

104. Beaudreault, statement on "Amphibious Warfare Readiness and Training—Interoperability, Shortfalls, and the Way Ahead," December 1, 2017, p. 4.

105. U.S. Marine Corps, *2018 Marine Aviation Plan*, p. 8.

106. Rudder, statement on "Aviation Readiness" November 9, 2017, p. 3.

107. Ibid., p. 4.

108. Ibid.

109. Ibid.

110. Ibid., p. 6.

111. Ibid., p. 4.

112. Ibid., p. 5.

113. Ibid., p. 7.

114. Ibid., p. 6.

115. Ibid., p. 4.

116. U.S. Department of the Navy, *Highlights of the Department of the Navy FY 2018 Budget*, 2017, p. 1-4, http://www.secnav.navy.mil/fmc/fmb/Documents/18pres/Highlights_book.pdf (accessed August 18, 2018).

117. Neller, statement on "Posture of the Department of the Navy," June 15, 2017, p. 9.

118. Paxton, statement on "U.S. Marine Corps Readiness," March 15, 2016, p. 7.

119. General Robert B. Neller, Commandant of the Marine Corps, statement on "The Posture of the United States Marine Corps" before the Committee on Armed Services, U.S. Senate, April 19, 2018, p. 13, https://www.armed-services.senate.gov/imo/media/doc/Neller_04-19-18.pdf (accessed August 13, 2018). Emphasis in original.

120. Dana, statement on "Marine Corps Readiness," March 6, 2018, p. 3.

121. This count is based on an average number of 1.5 divisions deployed to major wars (see Table 3, pp. 311–312) and an average of 10–11 battalions per division.

U.S. Nuclear Weapons Capability

Assessing the state of U.S. nuclear weapons capabilities presents several challenges.

First, instead of taking advantage of technological developments to field new warheads that could be designed to be safer and more secure and could give the United States improved options for guaranteeing a credible deterrent, the U.S. has elected to maintain (extend the service life of) nuclear warheads—based on designs from the 1960s, 1970s, and 1980s—that were in the stockpile when the Cold War ended.

Second, the lack of detailed publicly available data about the readiness of nuclear forces, their capabilities, and weapon reliability makes analysis difficult.

Third, the U.S. nuclear enterprise has many components, some of which are also involved in supporting conventional missions. For example, dual-capable bombers do not fly airborne alert with nuclear weapons today, although they did so routinely during the 1960s (and are capable of doing so again should the decision ever be made to resume this practice). Additionally, the national security laboratories do not focus solely on the nuclear weapons mission; as they did during the Cold War, they also perform a variety of functions related to nuclear nonproliferation, medical research, threat reduction, and countering nuclear terrorism, including nuclear detection. The National Command and Control System performs nuclear command and control in addition to supporting ongoing conventional operations.

Thus, assessing the extent to which any one piece of the nuclear enterprise is sufficiently funded, focused, and effective with regard to the nuclear mission is problematic.

In today's rapidly changing world, the U.S. nuclear weapons enterprise must be flexible and resilient to underpin the U.S. nuclear deterrent. If the U.S. detects a game-changing nuclear weapons development in another country or experiences a technical problem with a warhead or delivery system, its nuclear weapons complex must be able to provide a timely response.

The U.S. maintains an inactive stockpile that includes near-term hedge warheads that can be put back into operational status within six to 24 months; extended hedge warheads are said to be ready within 24 to 60 months.[1] The U.S. also preserves significant upload capability on its strategic delivery vehicles so that the nation can increase the number of nuclear warheads on each type of its delivery vehicles if contingencies warrant. For example, the U.S. Minuteman III intercontinental ballistic missile (ICBM) can carry up to three nuclear warheads, although it is currently deployed with only one.[2]

Presidential Decision Directive-15 (PDD-15) requires that the U.S. maintain the ability to conduct a nuclear test within 24 to 36 months of a presidential decision to do so.[3] However, successive government reports have noted the continued deterioration of technical and diagnostics equipment and the inability to fill technical positions that support nuclear testing readiness.[4] A lack of congressional support for improving technical readiness further undermines efforts by the National Nuclear Security Administration (NNSA) to comply with the directive.

The weapons labs face demographic challenges of their own. Most scientists and engineers with practical nuclear weapon design and testing experience are retired. This means that for the first time since the dawn of the nuclear age, the U.S. will have to rely on the scientific judgment of people who were not directly involved in underground nuclear explosive tests of weapons that they designed, developed, and are certifying.

The shift of focus away from the nuclear mission after the end of the Cold War caused the NNSA laboratories to lose their sense of purpose and to feel compelled to reorient and broaden their mission focus. According to a number of studies, their relationship with the government also evolved in ways that reduce output and increase costs.

Both the lack of resources and the lack of sound, consistent policy guidance have undermined workforce morale. The Congressional Advisory Panel on the Governance of the Nuclear Security Enterprise recommended fundamental changes in the nuclear weapons enterprise's culture, business practices, project management, and organization. Others proposed moving the NNSA to the Department of Defense.[5]

Another important indication of the health of the overall force is the readiness of forces that operate U.S. nuclear systems. In 2006, the Air Force mistakenly shipped non-nuclear warhead components to Taiwan.[6] A year later, it transported nuclear-armed cruise missiles across the U.S. without authorization (or apparently even awareness that it was doing so, mistaking them for conventional cruise missiles).[7] These serious incidents led to the establishment of a Task Force on DOD Nuclear Weapons Management, which found that "there has been an unambiguous, dramatic, and unacceptable decline in the Air Force's commitment to perform the nuclear mission"; that "until very recently, little has been done to reverse it"; and that "the readiness of forces assigned the nuclear mission has seriously eroded."[8]

Following these incidents, the Air Force instituted broad changes to improve oversight and management of the nuclear mission and the inventory of nuclear weapons, including creating the Air Force Global Strike Command to organize, train, and equip intercontinental-range ballistic missile and nuclear-capable bomber crews as well as other personnel to fulfill the nuclear mission and implement a stringent inspection regime. Then, in January 2014, the Air Force discovered widespread cheating on nuclear proficiency exams and charged over 100 officers with misconduct. The Navy had a similar problem, albeit on a smaller scale.[9]

The Department of Defense conducted two nuclear enterprise reviews, one internal and one external. Both reviews identified a lack of leadership attention, a lack of resources to modernize the atrophied infrastructure, and unduly burdensome implementation of the personnel reliability program as some of the core challenges preventing a sole focus on accomplishing the nuclear mission.[10] The Navy and Air Force took steps to address these concerns, but if changes in the nuclear enterprise are to be effective, leaders across the executive and legislative branches will have to continue to provide sufficient resources to mitigate readiness and morale issues within the force.

Fiscal uncertainty and a steady decline in resources for the nuclear weapons enterprise (trends that have begun to reverse in recent years) have negatively affected the nuclear deterrence mission. Under Secretary of Defense for Policy John Rood testified in March 2018 that:

> The U.S. military remains the strongest in the world. However, our advantages are eroding as potential adversaries modernize and build up their conventional and nuclear forces. They now field a broad arsenal of advanced missiles, including variants that can reach the American homeland....
>
> While this picture is unsettling and clearly not what we desire, as Secretary of Defense [James] Mattis has pointed out, "We must look reality in the eye and see the world as it is, not as we wish it to be."[11]

CHART 15

A Smaller and Less Diverse Nuclear Arsenal

TYPES OF WARHEADS IN THE U.S. NUCLEAR STOCKPILE

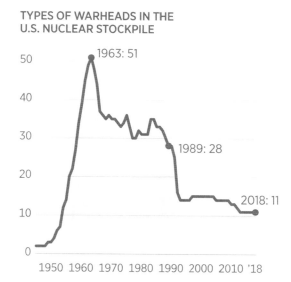

TOTAL WARHEADS IN THE U.S. NUCLEAR STOCKPILE

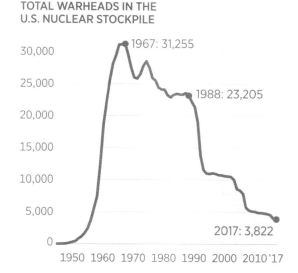

SOURCES: Robert S. Norris and Hans M. Kristensen, "U.S. Nuclear Warheads, 1945–2009," *Bulletin of the Atomic Scientists,* 2009, https://www.tandfonline.com/doi/full/10.2968/065004008 (accessed April 20, 2018); U.S. Department of Energy, "Stockpile Stewardship and Management Plan," *Report to Congress,* November 2017, https://www.energy.gov/sites/prod/files/2017/11/f46/fy18ssmp_final_november_2017%5B1%5D_0.pdf (accessed April 23, 2018; U.S. Department of Energy, "Restricted Data Declassification Decisions, 1946 to the Present," https://fas.org/sgp/library/rdd-5.html (accessed April 23, 2018); and U.S. Department of Defense, "Stockpile Numbers," http://open.defense.gov/Portals/23/Documents/frddwg/2017_Tables_UNCLASS.pdf (accessed April 23, 2018).

☎ heritage.org

The Trump Administration has inherited a comprehensive modernization program for nuclear forces: warheads, delivery systems, and command and control. The Obama Administration included this program in its budget requests, and Congress to a significant extent has funded it. Because such modernization activities require long-term funding commitments, it is important that this commitment continue.

The Trump Administration's reassessment of the U.S. nuclear force posture has included correcting some of the more questionable elements of the 2010 Nuclear Posture Review (NPR). Most specifically, the 2018 NPR recognizes that Russia's aggressive international policies and both Russia's and China's robust nuclear weapon modernization programs should inform the U.S. nuclear posture.[12] The 2018 NPR calls for tailoring U.S. nuclear deterrence strategies and restores deterring a large-scale attack against the U.S. homeland and its allies as the first priority of U.S. nuclear weapons policy. To that end, the 2018 NPR supports modernization of nuclear weapons and the nuclear weapons complex, as well as the sustainment of a nuclear triad, and proposes two low-yield options: a submarine-launched low-yield warhead in the short term and a nuclear-armed sea-launched cruise missile in the long term.

It is not clear how the additional workload created by these capabilities will affect the NNSA complex. Despite these departures from the 2010 NPR, however, the 2018 NPR is "clearly in the mainstream of U.S. nuclear policy as it has evolved through nearly eight decades of the nuclear age."[13]

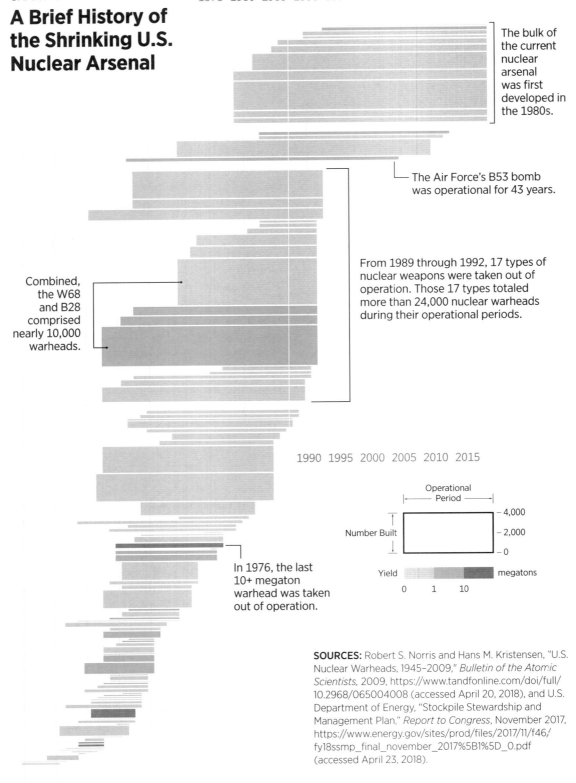

CHART 16

A Brief History of the Shrinking U.S. Nuclear Arsenal

1975 1980 1985 1990 1995 2000 2005 2010 2015

The bulk of the current nuclear arsenal was first developed in the 1980s.

The Air Force's B53 bomb was operational for 43 years.

From 1989 through 1992, 17 types of nuclear weapons were taken out of operation. Those 17 types totaled more than 24,000 nuclear warheads during their operational periods.

Combined, the W68 and B28 comprised nearly 10,000 warheads.

1990 1995 2000 2005 2010 2015

Operational Period

Number Built

— 4,000

— 2,000

— 0

Yield

0   1   10   megatons

In 1976, the last 10+ megaton warhead was taken out of operation.

SOURCES: Robert S. Norris and Hans M. Kristensen, "U.S. Nuclear Warheads, 1945–2009," *Bulletin of the Atomic Scientists,* 2009, https://www.tandfonline.com/doi/full/10.2968/065004008 (accessed April 20, 2018), and U.S. Department of Energy, "Stockpile Stewardship and Management Plan," *Report to Congress,* November 2017, https://www.energy.gov/sites/prod/files/2017/11/f46/fy18ssmp_final_november_2017%5B1%5D_0.pdf (accessed April 23, 2018).

1945 1950 1955 1960 1965 1970 1975 1980 1985

☎ heritage.org

Implications for U.S. National Security

U.S. nuclear forces and U.S. military forces in general are not designed to shield the nation from all types of attacks from all adversaries. They are designed to deter large-scale conventional and nuclear attacks that threaten America's sovereignty, forward-deployed troops, and allies.

U.S. nuclear forces play an important role in the global nonproliferation regime by providing U.S. security guarantees and assurances to NATO, Japan, and South Korea that lead these allies either to keep the number of their nuclear weapons lower than might otherwise be the case (France and the United Kingdom) or to forgo their development and deployment altogether. North Korea has proven that a country with very limited intellectual and financial resources can develop a nuclear weapon if it decides to do so. Iran continues on the path to obtaining a nuclear weapon.

This makes U.S. nuclear guarantees and assurances to allies and partners ever more important. Should the credibility of American nuclear forces continue to degrade, countries like South Korea could pursue an independent nuclear option, which would raise several thorny issues including possible additional instability across the region.

Certain negative trends could undermine U.S. nuclear deterrence if problems are not addressed. There is no shortage of challenges on the horizon, from an aging nuclear weapons infrastructure and unchallenged workforce to the need to recapitalize all three legs (land, air, and sea) of the nuclear triad, and from the need to conduct life-extension programs while maintaining a self-imposed nuclear weapons test moratorium to limiting the spread of nuclear know-how and the means to deliver nuclear weapons. Additionally, the United States must take account of adversaries that are modernizing their nuclear forces, particularly Russia and China.

The 2018 NPR observes that the global strategic security environment has become increasingly dangerous. Russia is now engaged in an aggressive nuclear buildup. Concurrently, Moscow is using its capabilities to threaten the sovereignty of U.S. allies in Eastern Europe and the Baltics. China is engaging in a similar nuclear buildup as it projects power into the South China Sea. North Korea and Iran have taken an aggressive posture toward the West as they attempt to shift from being nuclear proliferators to being nuclear-armed states.

Deterrence is an intricate interaction between U.S. conventional and nuclear forces and the psychology of both allies and adversaries that the U.S. uses these forces to defend the interests of the U.S. and its allies. Nuclear deterrence must reflect the mindset of the adversary the U.S. seeks to deter. If an adversary believes that he can fight and win a limited nuclear war, the task for U.S. leaders is to convince that adversary otherwise even if U.S. leaders think it is not possible to control escalation. The U.S. nuclear portfolio must be structured in terms of capacity, capability, variety, flexibility, and readiness to achieve this objective. In addition, military requirements and specifications for nuclear weapons will be different depending on who is being deterred, what he values, and what the U.S. seeks to deter him from doing.

Due to the complex interplay among strategy, policy, actions that states take in international relations, and other actors' perceptions of the world around them, one might never know precisely if and when a nuclear or conventional deterrent provided by U.S. forces loses credibility. Nuclear weapons capabilities take years or decades to develop, as does the infrastructure supporting them—an infrastructure that the U.S. has neglected for decades. We can be reasonably certain that a robust, well-resourced, focused, and modern nuclear enterprise is more likely to sustain its deterrent value than is an outdated one with questionable capabilities.

The U.S. is capable of incredible mobilization when danger materializes. The nuclear threat environment is dynamic and proliferating, with old and new actors developing advanced capabilities while the U.S. enterprise is relatively static, potentially leaving the United

States at a technological disadvantage. This is worrisome because of its implications both for the security of the United States and for the security of its allies and the free world.

Scoring U.S. Nuclear Weapons Capabilities

The U.S. nuclear weapons enterprise is composed of several key elements that include warheads; delivery systems; nuclear command and control; intelligence, surveillance, and reconnaissance; aerial refueling; and the research and development and manufacturing infrastructure that designs, manufactures, and maintains U.S. nuclear weapons. The complex also includes the experienced people, from physicists to engineers, maintainers, and operators, without whom the continuous maintenance of the nuclear infrastructure would not be possible.

The factors selected below are the most important elements of the nuclear weapons complex. They are judged on a five-grade scale, where "very strong" means that a sustainable, viable, and funded plan is in place and "very weak" means that the U.S. is not meeting its security requirements and has no program in place to redress the shortfall, which is very likely to damage vital national interests if the situation is not corrected.

Current U.S. Nuclear Stockpile Score: Strong

U.S. warheads must be safe, secure, effective, and reliable. The Department of Energy (DOE) defines reliability as "the ability of the weapon to perform its intended function at the intended time under environments considered to be normal" and as "the probability of achieving the specified yield, at the target, across the Stockpile-To-Target Sequence of environments, throughout the weapon's lifetime, assuming proper inputs."[14] Since 1993, reliability has been determined through an intensive warhead surveillance program; non-nuclear experiments (that is, without the use of experiments producing nuclear explosive yield); sophisticated calculations using high-performance computing; and related evaluations.

The reliability of nuclear warheads and delivery systems becomes more important as the number and diversity of nuclear weapons in the stockpile decrease, because fewer types of nuclear weapons means a greater risk of a "common mode failure" that could affect one or more of the remaining warhead types, coupled with the absence of sufficient hedge warheads to replace operational warheads until they can be repaired. Americans, allies, and adversaries must be confident that U.S. nuclear warheads will perform as expected.[15]

As warheads age, aging components must be replaced before they begin to degrade warhead reliability. Otherwise, military planning and employment of these warheads become much more complex. Despite creating impressive amounts of knowledge about nuclear weapons physics and materials chemistry, the long-term effect of aging components that comprise a nuclear weapon, including plutonium pits, is uncertain. As General Kevin Chilton (Ret.), former Commander, U.S. Strategic Command, has stated, "We cannot life extend these [nuclear weapons] forever.... [W]e better know how to do it when we get there...and the only way to be assured of that is to exercise that muscle in the near term."[16]

The United States has the world's safest and most secure stockpile, but security of long-term domestic and overseas storage sites, potential problems introduced by improper handling, or unanticipated effects stemming from long-term handling could compromise the integrity of U.S. warheads. The nuclear warheads themselves contain security measures that are designed to make it difficult, if not impossible, to detonate a weapon absent a proper authorization.

Grade: The Department of Energy and Department of Defense are required to assess the reliability of the nuclear stockpile annually.

This assessment does not include delivery systems, although the U.S. Strategic Command assesses overall weapons system reliability, which includes both the warhead and delivery platforms.

Absent nuclear weapons testing, the assessment of weapons reliability becomes more subjective over time, albeit based on experience, non-nuclear experiments, and simulations. While certainly an educated opinion, some argue that it is not a substitute for the type of objective data that is obtained through nuclear testing. Testing was used to diagnose potential problems and to certify the effectiveness of fixes to those problems. A continuous cycle of replacement of aging components with modern versions will inevitably introduce changes that take weapons away from the designs that were tested in the 1960s through 1980s. This risk must be weighed against the downside risks entailed in a U.S. resumption of nuclear testing.

"[I]n the past," according to the late Major General Robert Smolen, some of the nuclear weapon problems that the U.S. now faces "would have [been] resolved with nuclear tests."[17] By 2005, a consensus emerged in the NNSA, informed by the nuclear weapons labs, that it would "be increasingly difficult and risky to attempt to replicate exactly existing warheads without nuclear testing and that creating a reliable replacement warhead should be explored."[18] When the U.S. did conduct nuclear tests, it frequently found that small changes in a weapon's tested configuration had a dramatic impact on weapons performance. In fact, the 1958–1961 testing moratorium resulted in weapons with serious problems being introduced into the U.S. stockpile.[19]

In fiscal year (FY) 2018, the NNSA nuclear weapons lab directors and the Commander of U.S. Strategic Command, advised by his Strategic Advisory Group, assessed that the stockpile "remains safe, secure, and reliable."[20]

The lack of nuclear weapons testing creates some uncertainty concerning the adequacy of fixes to the stockpile when problems are found. This includes updates that are made in order to correct problems found in the weapons or changes in the weapons resulting from life-extension programs. It is simply impossible to duplicate exactly weapons that were designed and built many decades ago. According to former Defense Threat Reduction Agency Director Dr. Stephen Younger, we have had to fix "a number of problems that were never anticipated" by using "similar but not quite identical parts."[21] Political decisions made by successive Administrations have resulted in fewer types of weapons and, consequently, the potential for a greater impact across the inventory if an error is found during the certification process.

"To be blunt," warned Secretary of Defense Robert Gates in October 2008, "there is absolutely no way we can maintain a credible deterrent and reduce the number of weapons in our stockpile without either resorting to testing our stockpile or pursuing a modernization program."[22] The U.S. is pursuing warhead life-extension programs that replace aging components before they can cause reliability problems, but the national commitment to this modernization program, including the necessary long-term funding, continues to be uncertain.

In light of our overall assessment, we grade the U.S. stockpile as "strong." We are concerned that this rating may be revised downward in future years if the nation lags further in providing challenging nuclear weapons design and development opportunities as means to hone the skills of a next generation of weapons scientists and engineers.

Reliability of U.S. Delivery Platforms Score: Marginal

Reliability encompasses not only the warhead, but strategic delivery vehicles as well. In addition to a successful missile launch, this includes the separation of missile boost stages, performance of the missile guidance system, separation of the multiple re-entry vehicle warheads from the missile post-boost vehicle, and accuracy of the final re-entry vehicle in reaching its target.[23]

The U.S. tries to conduct flight tests of ICBMs and submarine-launched ballistic missiles (SLBMs) every year to ensure the reliability of its systems. Anything from electrical wiring to faulty booster separations could degrade the efficiency and safety of the U.S. strategic deterrent if it were to malfunction. U.S. strategic, long-range bombers regularly conduct intercontinental training and receive upgrades in order to sustain a high level of combat readiness, but potential challenges are on the horizon.

Grade: There was one U.S. ICBM test during the time period covered, and that test was successful. However, another test scheduled for February 2018 was cancelled with no explanation.[24] The ICBM test force has also been struggling with test kit supply. SLBM tests were successful in 2017 and 2018. To the extent that data from these tests are publicly available, they provide objective evidence of the delivery systems' reliability and send a message to U.S. adversaries that the system works. The aged systems, however, occasionally have reliability problems.[25] Overall, this factor earns a grade of "marginal," which is lower than the previous year's score, because of emerging problems with the ICBM test program and a lower number of overall launches. Additional future concerns stem from advanced networked air defense systems and their potential to increase risk to manned bombers.

Nuclear Warhead
Modernization Score: Weak

During the Cold War, the United States maintained a strong focus on designing and developing new nuclear warhead designs in order to counter Soviet advances and modernization efforts and to leverage advances in understanding the physics, chemistry, and design of nuclear weapons. Today, the United States is focused on sustaining the existing stockpile, not on developing new warheads, even though all of its nuclear-armed adversaries are developing new nuclear warheads and capabilities and accruing new knowledge in areas in which the U.S. used to lead.

Since the collapse of the Soviet Union, nuclear warheads and delivery vehicles have not been replaced despite being well beyond their designed service lives. This could increase the risk of failure due to aging components and signal to adversaries that the United States is less committed to nuclear deterrence.

New warhead designs could allow American engineers and scientists to improve previous designs and devise more effective means to address existing military requirements (for example, the need to destroy deeply buried and hardened targets) that have emerged in recent years. New warheads could also enhance the safety and security of American weapons.

An ability to work on new warhead designs would also help American experts to remain engaged and knowledgeable, would help to attract the best talent to the nuclear enterprise and retain that talent, and could help the nation to gain additional insights into foreign nations' nuclear weapon programs. As the Panel to Assess the Reliability, Safety, and Security of the United States Nuclear Stockpile noted, "Only through work on advanced designs will it be possible to train the next generation of weapon designers and producers. Such efforts are also needed to exercise the DoD/NNSA weapon development interface."[26]

Other nations maintain their levels of proficiency by having their scientists work on new nuclear warheads and possibly by conducting very low-yield nuclear weapons tests. At the urging of Congress, the NNSA is increasing its focus on programs to exercise skills that are needed to develop and potentially build new nuclear warheads through the Stockpile Responsiveness Program. These efforts ought to be expanded and sustained in the future.

Grade: The lack of plans to modernize nuclear warheads—life-extension programs are not modernization—and restrictions on thinking about new weapon designs that might accomplish the deterrence mission in the 21st century more effectively earn nuclear warhead modernization a grade of "weak."

Nuclear Delivery Systems
Modernization Score: Strong

Today, the United States fields a triad of nuclear forces with delivery systems that are safe and reliable, but as these systems age, there is increased risk of a significantly negative impact on operational capabilities. The older weapons are, the more at risk they are that faulty components, malfunctioning equipment, or technological developments will limit their reliability in the operating environment. Age can degrade reliability by increasing the potential for systems to break down or fail to respond correctly. Corrupted systems, defective electronics, or performance degradation due to long-term storage defects (including for nuclear warheads) can have serious implications for American deterrence and assurance. If it cannot be assumed that a strategic delivery vehicle will operate reliably at all times, that vehicle's deterrence and assurance value is significantly reduced.

The U.S. Air Force and Navy plan to modernize or replace each leg of the nuclear triad in the next several decades, but fiscal constraints are likely to make such efforts difficult. The Navy is fully funding its programs to replace the *Ohio*-class submarine with the *Columbia*-class submarine and to extend the life of and eventually replace the Trident SLBM. Existing ICBMs and SLBMs are expected to remain in service until 2032 and 2042, respectively, and new bombers are not planned to enter into service until 2023 at the earliest. Budgetary shortfalls are leading to uncertainty as to whether the nation will be able to modernize all three legs of the nuclear triad. The U.S. Strategic Command says that a triad is a "requirement."[27] This requirement, validated by all U.S. NPRs since the end of the Cold War, gives U.S. leadership credibility and flexibility, attributes that are necessary for any future deterrence scenarios.

Maintenance issues caused by the aging of American SSBNs and long-range bombers could make it difficult to deploy units overseas for long periods or remain stealthy in enemy hot spots. At present, the United States can send only a limited number of bombers on missions at any one time. Remanufacturing some weapon parts is difficult and expensive either because some of the manufacturers are no longer in business or because the materials

that constituted the original weapons are no longer available (for example, due to environmental restrictions). The ability of the U.S. to produce solid-fuel rocket engines and continued U.S. dependence on Russia as a source of such engines are other long-range concerns.[28]

Grade: U.S. nuclear platforms are in dire need of recapitalization. Plans for modernization of the U.S. nuclear triad are in place, and funding for these programs has been sustained so far by Congress and by the services, notwithstanding difficulties caused by sequestration. This demonstration of commitment to nuclear weapons modernization earns this indicator a grade of "strong."

Nuclear Weapons Complex Score: Weak

Maintaining a reliable and effective nuclear stockpile depends in large part on the facilities where U.S. devices and components are developed, tested, and produced. These facilities constitute the foundation of our strategic arsenal and include the:

- Los Alamos National Laboratories,

- Lawrence Livermore National Laboratory,

- Sandia National Laboratory,

- Nevada National Security Site,

- Pantex Plant,

- Kansas City Plant,

- Savannah River Site, and

- Y-12 National Security Complex.

In addition to these government sites, the defense industrial base supports the development and maintenance of American delivery platforms.

These complexes design, develop, test, and produce the weapons in the U.S. nuclear arsenal, and their maintenance is of critical importance. As the 2018 NPR states:

An effective, responsive, and resilient nuclear weapons infrastructure is essential to the U.S. capacity to adapt flexibly to shifting requirements. Such an infrastructure offers tangible evidence to both allies and potential adversaries of U.S. nuclear weapons capabilities and thus contributes to deterrence, assurance, and hedging against adverse developments. It also discourages adversary interest in arms competition.[29]

A flexible and resilient infrastructure is an essential hedge in the event that components fail or the U.S. is surprised by the nuclear weapon capabilities of potential adversaries. U.S. research and development efforts and the industrial base that supports modernization of delivery systems and warheads are important parts of this indicator.

Maintaining a safe, secure, effective, and reliable nuclear stockpile requires modern facilities, technical expertise, and tools both to repair any malfunctions quickly, safely, and securely and to produce new nuclear weapons if required. The existing nuclear weapons complex, however, is not fully functional. The U.S. cannot produce more than a few new plutonium pits (one of the core components of nuclear warheads) per year; there are limits on the ability to conduct life-extension programs; and Dr. John S. Foster, Jr., former director of the Lawrence Livermore National Laboratory, has reported that the U.S. no longer can "serially produce many crucial components of our nuclear weapons."[30]

If the facilities are not properly funded, the U.S. will gradually lose the ability to conduct high-quality experiments. In addition to demoralizing the workforce and hampering further recruitment, obsolete facilities and poor working environments make maintaining a safe, secure, reliable, and militarily effective nuclear stockpile exceedingly difficult. NNSA facilities are old: In 2016, the agency reported that "[m]ore than 50 percent of its facilities are over 40 years old, nearly 30 percent date to the Manhattan Project era, and 12 percent are currently excess and no longer needed."[31] Deferred maintenance can indicate "aging infrastructure and associated challenges, such as those relating to reliability, mission readiness, and health and safety."[32] The state of the NNSA's infrastructure did not change during the covered period, although the agency did manage to halt growth in deferred maintenance.[33]

Since 1993, the DOE has not had a facility dedicated to production of plutonium pits. The U.S. currently keeps about 5,000 plutonium pits in strategic reserve. There are significant disagreements as to the effect of aging on pits and whether the U.S. will be able to maintain them indefinitely without nuclear weapons testing. Currently, the U.S. can produce no more than about 10 plutonium pits a year at the Los Alamos PF-4 facility. Infrastructure modernization plans for PF-4, if funded, will boost that number to about 30 by the middle of the next decade and to between 50 and 80 by the end of the following decade. Russia reportedly can produce approximately 1,000 pits a year.[34]

Manufacturing non-nuclear components can be extremely challenging either because some materials may no longer exist or because manufacturing processes have been forgotten and must be retrieved. There is a certain element of art to building a nuclear weapon, and such a skill can be acquired and maintained only through hands-on experience.

Grade: On one hand, the U.S. maintains some of the world's most advanced nuclear facilities. On the other, some parts of the complex—most importantly, parts of the plutonium and highly enriched uranium component manufacturing infrastructure—have not been modernized since the 1950s, and plans for long-term infrastructure recapitalization remain uncertain. The infrastructure therefore receives a grade of "weak."

Personnel Challenges Within the National Nuclear Laboratories
Score: Marginal[35]

Combined with nuclear facilities, U.S. nuclear weapons scientists and engineers are critical to the health of the complex and the stockpile. The 2018 NPR emphasizes that:

The nuclear weapons infrastructure depends on a highly skilled, world-class workforce from a broad array of disciplines, including engineering, physical sciences, mathematics, and computer science. Maintaining the necessary critical skills and retaining personnel with the needed expertise requires sufficient opportunities to exercise those skills.[36]

The ability to maintain and attract a high-quality workforce is critical to assuring the future of the American nuclear deterrent. Today's weapons designers and engineers are first-rate, but they also are aging and retiring, and their knowledge must be passed on to the next generation that will take on this mission. This means that young designers need challenging warhead design and development programs to hone their skills, but only a very limited number of such challenging programs are in place today. The next generation must be given opportunities to develop and maintain the skills that the future nuclear enterprise needs. The NNSA and its weapons labs understand this problem and, with the support of Congress and despite significant challenges, including a fiscally constrained environment, are taking initial steps to mentor and train the next generation.

The U.S. currently relies on non-yield-producing laboratory experiments, flight tests, and the judgment of experienced nuclear scientists and engineers to ensure continued confidence in the safety, security, effectiveness, and reliability of its nuclear deterrent. Without their experience, the nuclear weapons complex could not function.

A basic problem is that few scientists or engineers at the NNSA weapons labs have had the experience of taking a warhead from initial concept to a "clean sheet" design, engineering development, and production. The complex must attract and retain the best and brightest. The average age of the NNSA's workforce remained 48.1 years as of August 2017.[37] Even more worrisome is that over a third of the NNSA workforce will be eligible for retirement in the next four years. Given the distribution of workforce by age, these retirements will create a significant knowledge and experience gap.[38]

Grade: In addition to employing world-class experts, the NNSA labs have had recent success in attracting and retaining talent. However, because many scientists and engineers with practical nuclear weapon design and testing experience are retired or retiring very soon, nuclear warhead certifications will rely largely on the judgments of people who have never tested or designed a nuclear warhead. Management challenges and a lack of focus on the nuclear weapon mission contribute to the lowering of morale in the NNSA complex. In light of these issues, which have to do more with policy than with the quality of people, the complex earns a score of "marginal."

Readiness of Forces Score: Marginal

The readiness of forces is a vital component of America's strategic forces. The military personnel operating the three legs of the nuclear triad must be properly trained and equipped. It is also essential that these systems are maintained in a high state of readiness.

During FY 2017, the services have continued to align resources in order to preserve strategic capabilities in the short term, but long-term impacts remain uncertain. Continued decline in U.S. general-purpose forces eventually could affect nuclear forces, especially the bomber leg of the nuclear triad. Changes prompted by the 2014 Navy and Air Force cheating scandals have begun to address some of the morale issues. A sustained attention to the situation in the nuclear enterprise is critical.

Grade: Uncertainty regarding the further potential impacts of budgetary shortfalls, as part of the overall assessment, earns this indicator a grade of "marginal."

Allied Assurance Score: Strong

The number of weapons held by U.S. allies is an important element when speaking about the credibility of America's extended deterrence. Allies that already have nuclear weapons can coordinate action with other powers or act independently. During the Cold War, the U.S. and the U.K. cooperated to the point where joint targeting was included.[39] France maintains its own independent nuclear arsenal, partly as a hedge against the uncertainty of American credibility. The U.S. also deploys nuclear gravity bombs in Europe as a visible manifestation of its commitment to its NATO allies.

The U.S., however, must also concern itself with its Asian allies. The United States provides nuclear assurances to Japan and South Korea, both of which are technologically advanced industrial economies facing nuclear-armed adversaries and potential adversaries. If they do not perceive U.S. assurances and guarantees as credible, they have the capability and know-how to build their own nuclear weapons and to do so quickly. That would be a major setback for U.S. nonproliferation policies.

The 2018 NPR takes a step in a good direction when it places "[a]ssurance of allies and partners" second on its list of four "critical roles" (immediately following "[d]eterrence of nuclear and non-nuclear attack") that nuclear forces play in America's national security strategy. The 2018 NPR proposes two supplements to existing capabilities—a low-yield SLBM warhead and a new nuclear sea-launched cruise missile—as important initiatives that act to strengthen assurance along with the Obama and Trump Administrations' initiatives to bolster conventional forces in NATO.[40]

Grade: At this time, most U.S. allies are not seriously considering developing their own nuclear weapons. European members of NATO continue to express their commitment to and appreciation of NATO as a nuclear alliance. Doubts about the modernization of dual-capable aircraft and even about the weapons themselves, as well as NATO's lack of attention to the nuclear mission and its intellectual underpinning, preclude assigning a score of "very strong." An unequivocal articulation of U.S. commitment to extended deterrence leads to an improvement in this year's score, raising it to "strong."

Nuclear Test Readiness Score: Weak

In the past, underground nuclear testing was one of the key elements of a safe, secure, effective, and reliable nuclear deterrent. For three decades, however, the U.S. has been under a self-imposed nuclear testing moratorium but with a commitment to return to nuclear testing if required to identify a problem, or confirm the fix to a problem, for a warhead critical to the nation's deterrent. Among other potential reasons to resume nuclear testing, the U.S. might need to test to develop a weapon with new characteristics that can be validated only by testing or to verify render-safe procedures. Nuclear tests and yield-producing experiments can also play an important role if the U.S. needs to react strongly to other nations' nuclear weapons tests and communicate its resolve or to understand other countries' new nuclear weapons.

To ensure a capability to resume testing if required, the U.S. maintains a low level of nuclear test readiness at the Nevada National Security Site (formerly Nevada Test Site). Current law requires that the U.S. be prepared to conduct a nuclear weapons test within a maximum of 36 months after a presidential decision to do so. The current state of test readiness is intended to be between 24 and 36 months, although it is doubtful that NNSA has achieved that goal. In the past, the requirement was 18 months.[41] The U.S. could meet the 18-month requirement only if certain domestic regulations, agreements, and laws were waived.[42] Because the United States is rapidly losing its remaining practical nuclear testing experience, including instrumentation of very sensitive equipment, the process would likely have to be reinvented from scratch.[43]

"Test readiness" seeks to facilitate a single test or a very short series of tests, not a sustained nuclear testing program. Because of a shortage of resources, the NNSA has been unable to achieve the goal of 24 to 36 months. The test readiness program is supported by experimental programs at the Nevada National Security Site, nuclear laboratory experiments, and advanced diagnostics development.[44]

Grade: As noted, the U.S. can meet the readiness requirement mandated by the law only if certain domestic regulations, agreements, and laws are waived. In addition, the U.S. is not prepared to sustain testing activities beyond a few limited experiments, which certain scenarios might require. Thus, testing readiness earns a grade of "weak."

Overall U.S. Nuclear Weapons Capability Score: "Marginal" Trending Toward "Strong"

It should be emphasized that "trending toward strong" assumes that the U.S. maintains its commitment to modernization and allocates needed resources accordingly. Absent this commitment, this overall score will degrade rapidly to "weak." Continued attention to this mission is therefore critical.

Although a bipartisan commitment has led to continued progress on U.S. nuclear forces modernization and warhead sustainment, these programs remain threatened by potential future fiscal uncertainties. The infrastructure that supports nuclear programs is aged, and nuclear test readiness has revealed troubling problems within the forces. Additionally, the United States has conducted fewer test launches than in previous years.

On the plus side, the 2018 NPR articulates nuclear weapons policy grounded in realities of international developments and clearly articulates commitment to extended deterrence. The commitment to warhead life-extension programs, the exercise of skills that are critical for the development of new nuclear warheads, and the modernization of nuclear delivery platforms represent a positive trend that should be maintained. Averaging the subscores across the nuclear enterprise in light of our concerns about the future results in an overall score of "marginal."

U.S. Military Power: Nuclear

	VERY WEAK	WEAK	MARGINAL	STRONG	VERY STRONG
Nuclear Stockpile				✔	
Delivery Platform Reliability			✔		
Warhead Modernization		✔			
Delivery Systems Modernization				✔	
Nuclear Weapons Complex		✔			
National Labs Talent			✔		
Force Readiness			✔		
Allied Assurance				✔	
Nuclear Test Readiness		✔			
OVERALL			✔		

Endnotes

1. "U.S. Nuclear Forces," Chapter 3 in U.S. Department of Defense, Office of the Secretary of Defense, Office of the Assistant Secretary of Defense for Nuclear, Chemical, and Biological Programs, *The Nuclear Matters Handbook, Expanded Edition*, 2011, http://www.acq.osd.mil/ncbdp/nm/nm_book_5_11/chapter_3.htm (accessed September 17, 2014).

2. George C. Marshall Institute, "LGM-30G Minuteman III," Missile Threat website, https://missilethreat.csis.org/missile/minuteman-iii/ (accessed June 13, 2017).

3. "Test Readiness," in Chapter 1, "Safety, Security, and Reliability of the U.S. Nuclear Weapons Stockpile," in National Research Council, Committee on Reviewing and Updating Technical Issues Related to the Comprehensive Nuclear Test Ban Treaty, *The Comprehensive Nuclear Test Ban Treaty: Technical Issues for the United States* (Washington: National Academies Press, 2012), p. 30, http://www.nap.edu/openbook.php?record_id=12849&page=30 (accessed June 22, 2018).

4. Memorandum, "Report on the 'Follow-up Audit of the Test Readiness at the Nevada Test Site,'" U.S. Department of Energy, Office of Inspector General, Audit Report No. OAS-L-10-02, October 21, 2009, http://energy.gov/sites/prod/files/igprod/documents/OAS-L-10-02.pdf (accessed June 13, 2017).

5. The report also recommends that the Department of Energy be renamed the "Department of Energy and Nuclear Security" to "highlight the prominence and importance of the Department's nuclear security mission." Congressional Advisory Panel on the Governance of the Nuclear Security Enterprise, *A New Foundation for the Nuclear Enterprise: Report of the Congressional Advisory Panel on the Governance of the Nuclear Security Enterprise*, November 2014, p. xii, http://cdn.knoxblogs.com/atomiccity/wp-content/uploads/sites/11/2014/12/Governance.pdf?_ga=1.83182294.1320535883.1415285934 (accessed June 13, 2017).

6. Associated Press, "US Mistakenly Ships ICBM Parts to Taiwan," March 25, 2008, http://www.military.com/NewsContent/0,13319,164694,00.html (accessed June 13, 2017).

7. Associated Press, "Air Force Official Fired After 6 Nukes Fly over US," updated September 5, 2007, http://www.nbcnews.com/id/20427730/ns/us_news-military/t/air-force-official-fired-after-nukes-fly-over%20us/#.WT (accessed June 13, 2017).

8. U.S. Department of Defense, Secretary of Defense Task Force on DoD Nuclear Weapons Management, *Report of the Secretary of Defense Task Force on DoD Nuclear Weapons Management, Phase I: The Air Force's Nuclear Mission*, September 2008, p. 2, http://www.defense.gov/Portals/1/Documents/pubs/Phase_I_Report_Sept_10.pdf (accessed June 22, 2018).

9. Kevin Liptak, "U.S. Navy Discloses Nuclear Exam Cheating," CNN, February 4, 2014, http://www.cnn.com/2014/02/04/us/navy-cheating-investigation/index.html (accessed September 11, 2017).

10. U.S. Department of Defense, *Independent Review of the Department of Defense Nuclear Enterprise*, June 2, 2014, https://www.defense.gov/Portals/1/Documents/pubs/Independent-Nuclear-Enterprise-Review-Report-30-June-2014.pdf (accessed June 22, 2018).

11. John Rood, Under Secretary of Defense for Policy, statement on "President's Fiscal Year 2019 Budget Request for Nuclear Forces and Atomic Energy Defense Activities" before the Subcommittee on Strategic Forces, Committee on Armed Services, U.S. House of Representatives, March 22, 2018, p. 1, https://armedservices.house.gov/hearings/fiscal-year-2019-budget-request-nuclear-forces-and-atomic-energy-defense-activities (accessed June 22, 2018).

12. U.S. Department of Defense, *Nuclear Posture Review*, February 2018, https://media.defense.gov/2018/Feb/02/2001872886/-1/-1/1/2018-NUCLEAR-POSTURE-REVIEW-FINAL-REPORT.PDF (accessed June 22, 2018).

13. John R. Harvey, Franklin C. Miller, Keith B. Payne, and Bradley H. Roberts, "Continuity and Change in U.S. Nuclear Policy," *RealClear Defense*, February 7, 2018, https://www.realcleardefense.com/articles/2018/02/07/continuity_and_change_in_us_nuclear_policy_113025.html (accessed June 22, 2018).

14. R. L. Bierbaum, J. J. Cashen, T. J. Kerschen, J. M. Sjulin, and D. L. Wright, "DOE Nuclear Weapon Reliability Definition: History, Description, and Implementation," Sandia National Laboratories, *Sandia Report* No. SAND99-8240, April 1999, pp. 7 and 8, http://www.wslfweb.org/docs/usg/reli99.pdf (accessed June 22, 2018).

15. U.S. Department of Defense, *Nuclear Posture Review Report*, April 2010, https://www.defense.gov/Portals/1/features/defenseReviews/NPR/2010_Nuclear_Posture_Review_Report.pdf (accessed June 13, 2017).

16. Jennifer-Leigh Oprihory, "Chilton on US Nuclear Posture, Deterring Russia, Apollo Astronaut John Young's Legacy," *Defense & Aerospace Report*, January 18, 2018, https://defaeroreport.com/2018/01/23/chilton-us-nuclear-posture-deterring-russia-apollo-astronaut-john-youngs-legacy/ (accessed June 22, 2018).

17. Major General Robert Smolen, USAF (Ret.), Deputy Administrator for Defense Programs, U.S. Department of Energy, National Nuclear Security Administration, remarks at AIAA Strategic and Tactical Missile Systems Conference, January 23, 2008, p. 9, https://www.aiaa.org/uploadedFiles/About-AIAA/Press_Room/Key_Speeches-Reports-and-Presentations/Smolen.pdf (accessed June 22, 2018).

18. Thomas Scheber, *Reliable Replacement Warheads: Perspectives and Issues*, United States Nuclear Strategy Forum Publication No. 0005 (Fairfax, VA: National Institute Press, 2007), p. 2, http://www.nipp.org/National%20Institute%20Press/Current%20Publications/PDF/RRW%20final%20with%20foreword%207.30.07.pdf (accessed September 17, 2014); Thomas D'Agostino, Deputy Administrator for Defense Programs, National Nuclear Security Administration, U.S. Department of Energy, presentation at program on "The Reliable Replacement Warhead and the Future of the U.S. Weapons Program," Woodrow Wilson International Center for Scholars, June 15, 2007, https://www.wilsoncenter.org/event/the-reliable-replacement-warhead-and-the-future-the-us-weapons-program (accessed July 20, 2018).

19. National Institute for Public Policy, *The Comprehensive Test Ban Treaty: An Assessment of the Benefits, Costs, and Risks* (Fairfax, VA: National Institute Press, 2011), pp. 24–25, http://www.nipp.org/wp-content/uploads/2014/12/CTBT-3.11.11-electronic-version.pdf (accessed June 13, 2017).

20. U.S. Department of Energy, National Nuclear Security Administration, *Fiscal Year 2018 Stockpile Stewardship and Management Plan: Report to Congress*, November 2017, p. v, https://www.energy.gov/sites/prod/files/2017/11/f46/fy18ssmp_final_november_2017%5B1%5D_0.pdf (accessed June 22, 2018).

21. Stephen M. Younger, *The Bomb: A New History* (New York: HarperCollins, 2009), p. 192.

22. Robert M. Gates, speech delivered at Carnegie Endowment for International Peace, Washington, D.C., October 28, 2008, http://archive.defense.gov/Speeches/Speech.aspx?SpeechID=1305 (accessed June 13, 2017).

23. Robert W. Nelson, "What Does Reliability Mean?" in "If It Ain't Broke: The Already Reliable U.S. Nuclear Arsenal," Arms Control Association, April 1, 2006, http://www.armscontrol.org/print/2026 (accessed June 13, 2017).

24. Gary Robbins, "Tuesday Night's Minuteman Launch Abruptly Cancelled," *The San Diego Union-Tribune*, February 6, 2018, http://www.sandiegouniontribune.com/news/science/sd-me-vandeberg-test-20180205-story.html (accessed June 22, 2018).

25. For example, the U.S. lost contact with 50 intercontinental-range ballistic missiles in October 2010. For more information, see NTI Global Security Newswire, "Air Force Loses Contact with 50 ICBMs at Wyoming Base," October 27, 2010, http://www.nti.org/gsn/article/air-force-loses-contact-with-50-icbms-at-wyoming-base/ (accessed June 13, 2017).

26. Panel to Assess the Reliability, Safety, and Security of the United States Nuclear Stockpile, *Expectations for the U.S. Nuclear Stockpile Program: FY 2001 Report of the Panel to Assess the Reliability, Safety, and Security of the United States Nuclear Stockpile*, 2002, p. 9, http://fas.org/programs/ssp/nukes/testing/fosterpnlrpt01.pdf (accessed June 22, 2018).

27. Admiral C. D. Haney, Commander, United States Strategic Command, statement before the Committee on Armed Services, U.S. Senate, March 10, 2016, p. 3, http://www.armed-services.senate.gov/imo/media/doc/Haney_03-10-16.pdf (accessed June 13, 2017).

28. Sydney J. Freedberg Jr., "Fading Solid Fuel Engine Biz Threatens Navy's Trident Missile," *Breaking Defense*, June 16, 2014, http://breakingdefense.com/2014/06/fading-solid-fuel-engine-biz-threatens-navys-trident-missile/ (accessed June 13, 2017).

29. U.S. Department of Defense, *Nuclear Posture Review*, February 2018, pp. xiv.

30. John S. Foster, Jr., "Nuclear Weapons and the New Triad," in conference proceedings, *Implementing the New Triad: Nuclear Security in Twenty-First Century Deterrence, Final Report*, Institute for Foreign Policy Analysis and International Security Studies Program of the Fletcher School, Tufts University, December 14–15, 2005, p. 69.

31. U.S. Department of Energy, National Nuclear Security Administration, *Prevent, Counter, and Respond—A Strategic Plan to Reduce Global Nuclear Threats, FY 2017–FY 2021: Report to Congress*, March 2016, p. 2-16, https://www.energy.gov/sites/prod/files/2017/09/f36/NPCR%2520FINAL%25203-29-16%2520%28with%2520signatures%29_Revised%25204%252020_Redacted%5B1%5D.pdf (accessed June 22, 2018). The most recent version of this report notes only "the necessity of repairing and recapitalizing DOE/NNSA's aging infrastructure, some of which dates to the Manhattan Project era." See U.S. Department of Energy, National Nuclear Security Administration, *Prevent, Counter, and Respond—A Strategic Plan to Reduce Global Nuclear Threats, FY 2018–FY 2022: Report to Congress*, November 2017, p. i, https://www.energy.gov/sites/prod/files/2017/11/f46/fy18npcr_final_november_2017%5B1%5D_0.pdf (accessed June 22, 2018).

32. U.S. Department of Energy, *Annual Infrastructure Executive Committee Report to the Laboratory Operations Board*, September 8, 2017, p. 7, https://www.energy.gov/sites/prod/files/2017/09/f36/MAAsset_MA50_IECReport_2017-09-21.pdf (accessed June 22, 2018).

33. U.S. Department of Energy, National Nuclear Security Administration, *Fiscal Year 2018 Stockpile Stewardship and Management Plan: Report to Congress*, November 2017, p. 4-3.

34. Houston Hawkins, "Nuclear Vigor: Russia, China and Iran," American Center for Democracy, December 10, 2014, http://acdemocracy.org/nuclear-vigor-russia-china-and-iran/ (accessed July 20, 2018).

35. The name of this category has been changed to reflect that although the NNSA workforce is of the highest quality, the nuclear complex struggles to retain and train future workforce.

36. U.S. Department of Defense, *Nuclear Posture Review*, February 2018, p. 63.

37. U.S. Department of Energy, National Nuclear Security Administration, workforce data as of August 22, 2017, https://www.energy.gov/sites/prod/files/2017/10/f39/nnsa_fy17%5B1%5D.pdf (accessed April 18, 2018).

38. U.S. Department of Energy, National Nuclear Security Administration, *Fiscal Year 2018 Stockpile Stewardship and Management Plan, Report to Congress*, November 2017, p. 1-17.

39. See, for example, U.K. House of Commons, Foreign Affairs Committee, *Global Security: UK–US Relations, Sixth Report of Session 2009–10* (London: The Stationery Office Limited, March 28, 2010), p. Ev 92, http://www.publications.parliament.uk/pa/cm200910/cmselect/cmfaff/114/114.pdf (accessed June 13, 2017).

40. U.S. Department of Defense, *Nuclear Posture Review*, February 2018, pp. vii and 54.

41. Mary Beth D. Nikitin, "Comprehensive Nuclear-Test-Ban Treaty: Background and Current Developments," Congressional Research Service *Report for Members and Committees of Congress*, September 1, 2016, http://fas.org/sgp/crs/nuke/RL33548.pdf (accessed June 15, 2017).

42. National Research Council, *The Comprehensive Nuclear Test Ban Treaty: Technical Issues for the United States*, p. 30.

43. John C. Hopkins, "Nuclear Test Readiness. What Is Needed? Why?" *National Security Science*, December 2016, http://www.lanl.gov/discover/publications/national-security-science/2016-december/_assets/docs/NSS-dec2016_nuclear-test-readiness.pdf (accessed June 12, 2017).

44. U.S. Department of Energy, National Nuclear Security Administration, Nevada National Security Site, "Stockpile Stewardship Program," https://www.nnss.gov/pages/programs/StockpileStewardship.html (accessed June 22, 2018).

Ballistic Missile Defense

Missile defense is a critical component of the U.S. national security architecture that enables U.S. military efforts and can protect national critical infrastructure, from population and industrial centers to politically and historically important sites. It can strengthen U.S. diplomatic and deterrence efforts and provide both time and options to senior decision-makers.

Ballistic missiles remain a weapon of choice for many U.S. adversaries because they possess important attributes like extraordinarily high speed (against which the U.S. has a very limited ability to defend) and relative cost-effectiveness compared to other types of conventional attacks.[1] The number of states that possess ballistic missiles will continue to increase, and so will the sophistication of these weapons as modern technologies become cheaper and more widely available. An additional concern is ballistic missile cooperation between state and non-state actors, which furthers the spread of sophisticated technologies and compounds challenges to U.S. defense planning.[2]

The ability to deter an enemy from attacking depends on convincing him that his attack will fail, that the cost of carrying out a successful attack is prohibitively high, or that the consequences of an attack will be so painful that they will outweigh the perceived benefit of attacking. A U.S. missile defense system strengthens deterrence by offering a degree of protection to the American people and the economic base on which their well-being depends, as well as forward-deployed troops and allies, making it harder for an adversary to threaten them with ballistic missiles. A missile defense system also provides a decision-maker with a significant political advantage. By protecting key elements of U.S. well-being, it mitigates an adversary's ability to intimidate the United States into conceding important security, diplomatic, or economic interests.

A missile defense system gives decision-makers more time to choose the most de-escalatory course of action from an array of options that can range from preemptively attacking an adversary to attacking his ballistic missiles on launch pads or even conceding to an enemy's demands or actions. Though engaging in a preemptive attack would likely be seen as an act of war by U.S. adversaries and could result in highly escalatory scenarios, the United States would do so if there was a substantiated concern that an adversary was about to attack the United States with a nuclear-armed missile. The United States would have an option to back down, thus handing a "win" to the enemy, but at the cost of losing credibility in its many alliance relationships.

Backing down could also undermine U.S. nonproliferation efforts. More than 30 allies around the world rely on U.S. nuclear security guarantees, and questioning the U.S. commitment to allied safety in the face of a ballistic missile threat would translate into questioning the U.S. commitment to allied nuclear safety in the most fundamental sense. A robust missile defense system would change the dynamics of decision-making, creating additional options and providing more time to sort through them and their implications to arrive at the option that best serves U.S. security interests.

Ballistic missile defense is also an important enabler in nonproliferation efforts and alliance management. Many U.S. allies have the technological capability and expertise to produce their own nuclear weapons. They have not done so because of their belief in U.S. assurances to protect them. U.S. missile defense systems are seen as an integral part of the United States' visible commitment to its allies' security.

The U.S. missile defense system comprises three critical physical parts: sensors, interceptors, and command and control infrastructure that provides data from sensors to interceptors. Of these, interceptors receive much of the public's attention because of their very visible and kinetic nature. Different physical components of a ballistic missile defense system are designed with the phase of flight in which an intercept occurs in mind, although some of them—for example, the command and control infrastructure or radars—can support intercepts in various phases of a ballistic missile flight. Interceptors can shoot down an adversarial missile in the boost, ascent, midcourse, or terminal phase of its flight.

Another way to consider missile defense is by the range of an incoming ballistic missile (short-range, medium-range, intermediate-range, or long-range) that an interceptor is designed to shoot down, since the length of the interceptor's flight time determines how much time is available to conduct an intercept and where the various components of a defense system must be placed to improve the probability of such an intercept. With long-range ballistic missiles, the United States has no more than 33 minutes to detect the missile, track it, provide the information to the missile defense system, come up with the most optimal firing solution, launch an interceptor, and shoot down an incoming missile, ideally with enough time to fire another interceptor if the first attempt fails. The timeframe is shorter when it comes to medium-range and short-range ballistic missiles.

Finally, missile defense can be framed by the origin of interceptor launch. At present, U.S. interceptors are launched from the ground or from the sea. In the past, the United States explored concepts to launch interceptors from the air or from space, but limited efforts have been made on that front since the U.S. withdrawal from the Anti-Ballistic Missile Treaty in 2002.[3] There is renewed interest in airborne missile defense concepts within the Trump Administration, particularly for boost-phase intercepts.

The current U.S. missile defense system is a result of investments made by successive U.S. Administrations. President Ronald Reagan's vision for the program was to have a layered ballistic missile defense system that would render nuclear weapons "impotent and obsolete," including ballistic missile defense interceptors in space.[4] These layers would include boost, ascent, midcourse, and terminal interceptors so that the United States would have more than one opportunity to shoot down an incoming missile.

The United States stopped far short of this goal, despite tremendous technological advances and benefits that came out of the Strategic Defense Initiative (SDI) program.[5] Instead of a comprehensive layered system, the U.S. has no boost phase ballistic missile defense systems and is unable to handle more qualitatively and quantitatively advanced ballistic missile threats like those from China or Russia.

Regrettably, the volatility and inconsistency of priority and funding for ballistic missile defense by successive Administrations and Congresses controlled by both major political parties have led to the current system, which is numerically and technologically limited and cannot address more sophisticated or more numerous long-range ballistic missile attacks. Until the 2017 National Defense Authorization Act (NDAA), U.S. policy was one of protection only from a "limited" ballistic missile attack.[6] The 2017 NDAA dropped the word "limited" that had been a fixture of policy since the National Missile Defense Act of 1999. In the future, as technological trends progress and modern technologies become cheaper and more widely available, North Korean or

Iranian ballistic missiles may rival in sophistication if not numbers those of Russia or China. Consequently, the U.S. must remain aware of how such threats are evolving and alter its missile defense posture accordingly.

In fiscal year (FY) 2018, the Trump Administration requested $7.9 billion for the Missile Defense Agency (MDA), the primary government agency responsible for developing, testing, fielding, and integrating a layered ballistic missile defense system. The request was not that different from the Obama Administration's FY 2017 request for $7.5 billion but below the Bush Administration's budget requests.[7] Additionally, the Administration requested permission to reprogram about $440 million of unspent FY 2017 funds from different accounts toward missile defense technologies, to be divided among different parts of the missile defense system based on policy priorities set by the President and Congress.

Interceptors

A limited U.S. missile defense system has been supported by Administrations and Congresses controlled by both major political parties, Republican and Democrat, as all have found such a system to be of immense importance in dealing with some of the most challenging national security problems of our time, including the North Korean and Iranian ballistic missile threats. That said, different types of interceptors have been emphasized over the years, and these choices are reflected in the composition of today's U.S. missile defense.

Ballistic missile defense interceptors are designed to intercept ballistic missiles in three different phases of their flight.

- The boost phase is from the launch of a missile from its platform until its engines stop thrusting.

- The midcourse phase is the longest and thus offers a unique opportunity to intercept an incoming threat and, depending on other circumstances like the trajectory of the incoming threat and quality of U.S.

tracking data, even a second shot at it should the first intercept attempt fail.

- The terminal phase is less than one minute long and offers a very limited opportunity to intercept a ballistic missile threat.

Boost Phase Interceptors. The United States currently has no capability to shoot down ballistic missiles in their boost phase. Boost phase intercept is the most challenging option technologically because of the very short timeframe in which a missile is boosting, the missile's extraordinary rate of acceleration during this brief window of time, and the need to have the interceptor close to the launch site.[8] It is, however, also the most beneficial time to strike. A boosting ballistic missile is at its slowest speed compared to other phases; it is therefore not yet able to maneuver evasively and has not yet deployed decoys that complicate the targeting and intercept problem.

In the past, the United States pursued several boost phase programs, including the Airborne Laser; the Network Centric Air Defense Element (NCADE); the Kinetic Energy Interceptor (KEI); and the Air Launched Hit-to-Kill (ALHK) missile. Each of these programs was eventually cancelled because of insurmountable technical challenges, unworkable operational concepts, or unaffordable costs.

The MDA is working to leverage unmanned and space-based sensor technologies to utilize existing SM-3 interceptors (typically carried aboard ships for long-range anti-aircraft defense) for a boost phase ballistic missile intercept, but these sensors are years from being deployed. The current budget environment also presents a challenge as it does not adequately fund research into future missile defense technologies and is barely enough to keep the existing missile defense programs going or enable their marginal improvement.

Midcourse Phase Interceptors. The United States deploys two systems that can shoot down incoming ballistic missiles in the midcourse phase of flight. This phase offers more predictability as to where the missile is headed than is possible in the boost phase, but it also allows the missile time to deploy decoys and countermeasures designed to complicate interception by confusing sensors and radars.

The Ground-Based Midcourse Defense (GMD) system is the only system capable of shooting down a long-range ballistic missile headed for the U.S. homeland. In June 2017, Vice Admiral James Syring, then Director of the Missile Defense Agency, testified before the House Armed Services Subcommittee on Strategic Forces that:

> I would not say we are comfortably ahead of the threat. I would say we are addressing the threat that we know today. And the advancements in the last six months have caused great concern to me and others in the advancement of and demonstration of technology, ballistic missiles from North Korea.[9]

The United States currently deploys 40 interceptors in Alaska and four in California and is planning to increase the number of deployed interceptors in the coming years. At about $70 million apiece, the GMD interceptors are rather expensive–but a lot cheaper than a successful ballistic missile attack. The system has struggled with reliability issues during its tests and is unsuited to addressing larger-scale ballistic missile threats.

The Aegis ballistic missile defense system is a sea-based component of the U.S. missile defense system that is designed to address the threat of short-range, medium-range (1,000–3,000 kilometers), and intermediate-range (3,000–5,500 kilometers) ballistic missiles. It utilizes different versions of the Standard Missile-3 (SM-3) depending on the threat and other considerations like the ship location and the quality of tracking data. The U.S. Navy was scheduled to operate 36 Aegis missile defense–capable ships by the end of FY 2018, but temporary loss of two missile defense destroyers, the USS *Fitzgerald* and USS *John S McCain*, involved in separate ship collisions during 2017, will make this goal harder to achieve.[10]

The Aegis-Ashore system being deployed to Poland and Romania will relieve some of the stress on the fleet because missile defense–capable cruisers and destroyers are multi-mission and are used for other purposes, such as anti-piracy operations, when released from ballistic missile missions by the shore-based systems. The Aegis-Ashore site is meant to protect U.S. European allies and U.S. forces in Europe from the Iranian ballistic missile threat.

In order to increase the probability of an intercept, the United States has to shoot multiple interceptors at each incoming ballistic missile. At present, because its inventory of ballistic missile defense interceptors is limited, the United States can shoot down only a handful of ballistic missiles that have relatively unsophisticated countermeasures. Different technological solutions will have to be found to address more comprehensive and advanced ballistic missile threats like those from China or Russia.

Terminal Phase Interceptors. The United States currently deploys three terminal-phase missile defense systems: Terminal High Altitude Area Defense (THAAD); Patriot Advanced Capability-3 (PAC-3); and Aegis BMD. The THAAD system is capable of shooting down short-range and intermediate-range ballistic missiles inside and just outside of the atmosphere.[11] It consists of a launcher, interceptors, AN/TPY-2 radar, and fire control. The system is transportable and rapidly deployable. DOD's FY 2018 program "[c]ontinues fielding and sustainment activities for seven THAAD Batteries."[12] THAAD batteries have been deployed to such countries and regions as Japan, South Korea, and the Middle East.

The PAC-3 is an air-defense and short-range ballistic missile defense system. A battery is comprised of a launcher, interceptors, AN/MPQ-53/65 radar, engagement control station, and diesel-powered generator units. The system is transportable, and the United States currently deploys 15 battalions in several theaters around the world.[13] The system is the most mature of the U.S. missile defense systems.

The predecessor of the PAC-3 system, the Patriot, played a critical role in allied assurance during the First Gulf War when it was deployed to Israel. The purpose was to assure Israeli citizens by protecting them from Iraqi missiles, thereby decreasing the pressure on Israel's government to enter the war against Iraq. In so doing, the U.S. sought to prevent Israel from joining the U.S. coalition against Saddam Hussein's forces in Iraq, which would have fractured the Arab coalition.

The Aegis ballistic missile defense system also provides terminal capability against short-range and medium-range ballistic missiles.[14]

Sensors

The space sensor component of the U.S. ballistic missile defense system is distributed across three major domains—land, sea, and space—that are meant to provide the U.S. and its allies with the earliest possible warning of a launch of enemy ballistic missiles. Sensors can also provide information about activities preceding the launch itself, but from the intercept perspective, those are less relevant for the missile defense system. The sensors do this by detecting the heat generated by a missile's engine, or booster. They can detect a missile launch, acquire and track a missile in flight, and even classify the type of projectile, its speed, and the target against which the missile has been directed. The sensors relay this information to the command and control stations that operate interceptor systems, like Aegis (primarily a sea-based system) or THAAD (a land-based system).

On land, the major sensor installations are the upgraded early warning radars (UEWRs), which are concentrated along the North Atlantic and Pacific corridors that present the most direct flight path for a missile aimed at the U.S. This includes the phased array early warning radars based in California, the United Kingdom, and Greenland that scan objects up to 3,000 miles away.[15] These sensors focus on threats that can be detected starting in the missile's boost or launch phase when the release of exhaust gases creates a heat trail that is "relatively easy for sensors to detect and track."[16]

A shorter-range (2,000-mile) radar is based in Shemya, Alaska. Two additional sites, one in Cape Cod, Massachusetts, and the other in Clear, Alaska, are being modernized for use in the layered ballistic missile defense system.[17]

The other land-based sensors are mobile. These sensors are known as the Army Navy/Transportable Radar Surveillance and Control Model 2 (AN/TPY-2) and can be forward-deployed for early threat detection or retained closer to the homeland to track missiles in their terminal phase. Of the United States' 11 AN/TPY-2 systems, five are forward-deployed with U.S. allies (one to the Central Command area of operations, two in Japan, and one apiece in Turkey and Israel); two are deployed with THAAD in Guam and the Republic of Korea; and four are in the United States.[18]

In March 2017, in cooperation with the Republic of Korea, the United States deployed a THAAD missile system to the Korean peninsula that was accompanied in April by an AN/TPY-2. The THAAD deployment was heavily criticized by China for allegedly destabilizing China's nuclear deterrence credibility because the system would allegedly be able to shoot down any Chinese nuclear-tipped missiles after a U.S. first strike.[19] However, the THAAD system deployed in South Korea for the purposes of intercepting North Korean missiles is not set up in a way that could track or shoot down Chinese ICBMs directed toward the United States, which calls into question why China would be so opposed.[20]

There are two types of sea-based sensors. The first is the Sea-Based X-band (SBX) radar, mounted on an oil-drilling platform, which can be relocated to different parts of the globe as threats evolve.[21] SBX is used primarily in the Pacific. The second radar is the SPY-1 radar system that is mounted on all 85 U.S. Navy vessels equipped with the Aegis Combat system, which means they can provide data that can be utilized for ballistic missile missions. Of these 85 ships, 34 are BMD-capable vessels that carry missile defense interceptors.[22]

The final domain in which U.S. missile defense operates is space. In a July 2017 conference call with reporters, the head of U.S. Strategic Command, General John Hyten, stated that space-based sensors are "the most important thing for [the U.S. government] to invest in right now."[23] Control of the space BMD system is divided between the MDA and the U.S. Air Force.

The oldest system that contributes to the missile defense mission is the Defense Support Program (DSP) constellation of satellites, which use infrared sensors to identify heat from booster and missile plumes. The DSP satellite system is set to be replaced by the Space-Based Infrared Radar System (SBIRS) to improve the delivery of missile defense and battlefield intelligence.[24] One of the advantages of SBIRS is its ability to scan a wide swath of territory while simultaneously tracking a specific target, making it a good scanner for observing tactical, or short-range, ballistic missiles.[25] However, congressional funding delays have left SBIRS underfunded and hampered the system's full development and deployment.[26]

Finally, the MDA operates the Space Tracking and Surveillance System-Demonstrators (STSS-D) satellite system. Two STSS-D satellites were launched into orbit in 2009 to track ballistic missiles that exit and reenter the Earth's atmosphere during the midcourse phase.[27] Although still considered an experimental system, STSS-D satellites provide operational surveillance and tracking capabilities and have the advantage of a variable waveband infrared system to maximize their detection capabilities. Data obtained by STSS-D have been used in ballistic missile defense tests.

Command and Control

The command and control architecture established for the U.S. ballistic missile defense system brings together data from U.S. sensors and relays them to interceptor operators to enable them to destroy incoming missile threats against the U.S. and its allies. The operational hub of missile defense command and control is assigned to the Joint Functional Component Command for Integrated Missile Defense

(JFCC IMD) housed at Schriever Air Force Base, Colorado.

Under the jurisdiction of U.S. Strategic Command, JFCC IMD brings together Army, Navy, Marine Corps, and Air Force personnel. It is co-located with the MDA's Missile Defense Integration and Operation Center (MDIOC). This concentration of leadership from across the various agencies helps to streamline decision-making for those who command and operate the U.S. missile defense system.[28]

Command and control operates through a series of data collection and communication relay nodes between military operators, sensors, radars, and missile interceptors. The first step is the Ground-based Midcourse Defense Fire Control (GFC) process, which involves assimilating data on missile movement from the United States' global network of sensors.

Missile tracking data travel through the Defense Satellite Communications System (DSCS), which is operated from Fort Greeley, Alaska, and Vandenberg Air Force Base, or ground-based redundant communication lines to the Command Launch Equipment (CLE) software that develops fire response options, telling interceptors where and when to fire. Once U.S. Strategic Command, in consultation with the President, has determined the most effective response to a missile threat, the CLE fire response option is relayed to the appropriate Ground-based Interceptors in the field. When the selected missiles have been fired, they maintain contact with an In-Flight Interceptor Communications System (IFICS) Data Terminal (IDT) to receive updated flight correction guidance to ensure that they hit their target.[29]

Overlaying the Command and Control operation is the Command and Control, Battle Management and Communication (C2BMC) program. Through its software and network systems, C2BMC feeds information to and synchronizes coordination between the multiple layers of the ballistic missile defense system.[30] More than 70 C2BMC workstations are distributed throughout the world at U.S. military bases.[31] C2BMC has undergone multiple technical upgrades since 2004, and a major update is scheduled for completion in 2018.

Conclusion

By successive choices of post–Cold War Administrations and Congresses, the United States does not have in place a comprehensive ballistic missile defense system that would be capable of defending the homeland and allies from robust ballistic missile threats. U.S. efforts have focused on a limited architecture protecting the homeland and on deploying and advancing regional missile defense systems.

The pace of the development of ballistic missile threats, both qualitative and quantitative, outpaces the speed of ballistic missile defense research, development, and deployment. To make matters worse, the United States has not invested sufficiently in future ballistic missile defense technologies, has canceled future missile defense programs like the Airborne Laser and the Multiple Kill Vehicle, and has never invested in space-based interceptors that would make U.S. defenses more robust and comprehensive.

Endnotes

1. U.S. Air Force, National Air and Space Intelligence Center (NASIC), and Defense Intelligence Ballistic Missile Analysis Committee, *2017 Ballistic and Cruise Missile Threat*, June 2017, pp. 38–39, http://www.nasic.af.mil/Portals/19/images/Fact%20Sheet%20Images/2017%20Ballistic%20and%20Cruise%20Missile%20Threat_Final_small.pdf?ver=2017-07-21-083234-343 (accessed May 27, 2018).

2. "Moreover, these potentially peer strategic competitors [Russia and China] are 'root sources' for enabling rogue states and non-state armed groups that are developing asymmetrical strategies and capabilities to employ cyber and EMP attacks to disrupt or destroy critically important space systems and essential civil infrastructure, such as electric power grids, communication, financial, transportation, and food distribution systems—as well as key military systems. Such an attack would represent the ultimate asymmetrical act by a smaller state or terrorists against the United States." Henry F. Cooper, Malcolm R. O'Neill, Robert L. Pfaltzgraff, Jr., and Rowland H. Worrell, "Missile Defense: Challenges and Opportunities for the Trump Administration," Institute for Foreign Policy Analysis, Independent Working Group on Missile Defense *White Paper*, 2016, pp. 12–13, http://www.ifpa.org/pdf/IWGWhitePaper16.pdf (accessed May 29, 2018).

3. The platform carrying air-launched ballistic missile interceptors has to be close to the launch area, aloft, oriented in a proper way, and generally within the range of enemies' anti-access/area-denial systems because of payload limits on airborne platforms themselves. These requirements make airborne intercepts particularly challenging.

4. Ronald Reagan, "Address to the Nation on National Security," March 23, 1983, https://reaganlibrary.archives.gov/archives/speeches/1983/32383d.htm (accessed May 27, 2018).

5. For example, SDI Organization investment contributed to making certain electronic and optical components cheaper and more effective. It helped to reduce the cost per pixel on a display screen by a factor of 20. Additional advances were made in areas of sensor technology, communications, and computers. For more information, see James A. Abrahamson and Henry F. Cooper, *What Did We Get for Our $30-Billion Investment in SDI/BMD?*" National Institute for Public Policy, September 1993, pp. 9–11, http://www.nipp.org/wp-content/uploads/2014/11/What-for-30B_.pdf (accessed May 27, 2018).

6. National Defense Authorization Act for Fiscal Year 2017, Public Law 114–328, 114th Cong., December 23, 2016, https://www.congress.gov/114/plaws/publ328/PLAW-114publ328.pdf (accessed May 27, 2018). The understanding of the word "limited" itself changed over time, from scaling a missile defense system to shoot down about 200 reentry vehicles right after the end of the Cold War (because that is how many a rogue Soviet commander was believed to be able to launch from a submarine) to only a handful of relatively less sophisticated North Korean or Iranian ballistic missiles. For more information, see Independent Working Group on Missile Defense, the Space Relationship, and the Twenty-First Century, *2009 Report*, Institute for Foreign Policy Research and Analysis, 2009, p. 17, http://www.ifpa.org/pdf/IWG2009.pdf (accessed May 27, 2018).

7. U.S. Department of Defense, Missile Defense Agency, "Historical Funding for MDA FY85–17," https://www.mda.mil/global/documents/pdf/FY17_histfunds.pdf (accessed May 27, 2018).

8. U.S. Department of Defense, Missile Defense Agency, "Ballistic Missile Defense Challenge," MDA *Facts*, January 30, 2004, http://www.nti.org/media/pdfs/10_5.pdf?_=1316627913 (accessed May 27, 2018).

9. Vice General James Syring, U.S. Navy, Director, Missile Defense Agency, transcript of testimony on Missile Defense Agency budget request before the Subcommittee on Strategic Forces, Committee on Armed Services, U.S. House of Representatives, June 7, 2017, https://www.c-span.org/video/?429388-1/senior-military-officials-testify-missile-defeat-programs (accessed May 27, 2018).

10. Ronald O'Rourke, "Navy Aegis Ballistic Defense (BMD) Program: Background and Issues for Congress," Congressional Research Service *Report for Members and Committees of Congress*, October 13, 2017, p. 12, https://www.hsdl.org/?view&did=805028(accessed on May 27, 2018).

11. Fact Sheet, "Terminal High Altitude Area Defense (THAAD)," U.S. Department of Defense, Missile Defense Agency, approved for release July 28, 2016, https://mda.mil/global/documents/pdf/thaad.pdf (accessed May 27, 2018); Phil Stewart and Idrees Ali, "U.S. THAAD Missile Defenses Hit Test Target as North Korea Tension Rises," Reuters, July 11, 2017, https://www.reuters.com/article/us-northkorea-missiles-usa-defenses/u-s-thaad-missile-defenses-hit-test-target-as-north-korea-tension-rises-idUSKBN19W15R (accessed May 27, 2018).

12. U.S. Department of Defense, Office of the Under Secretary of Defense (Comptroller)/Chief Financial Officer, *United States Department of Defense Fiscal Year 2018 Budget Request: Program Acquisition Cost by Weapon System*, May 2017, p. 4-3, http://comptroller.defense.gov/Portals/45/Documents/defbudget/fy2018/fy2018_Weapons.pdf (accessed May 27, 2018).

13. Fact Sheet, "Patriot Advanced Capability-3," U.S. Department of Defense, Missile Defense Agency, approved for release July 18, 2016, https://www.mda.mil/global/documents/pdf/pac3.pdf (accessed May 27, 2018).

14. Fact Sheet, "Aegis Ballistic Missile Defense," U.S. Department of Defense, Missile Defense Agency, approved for release July 28, 2016, https://www.mda.mil/global/documents/pdf/aegis.pdf (accessed May 27, 2018).

15. Fact Sheet, "Upgraded Early Warning Radars, AN/FPS-132," U.S. Department of Defense, Missile Defense Agency, approved for release July 28, 2016, https://www.mda.mil/global/documents/pdf/uewr1.pdf (accessed May 27, 2018).

16. Cooper, O'Neill, Pfaltzgraff, and Worrell, "Missile Defense: Challenges and Opportunities for the Trump Administration," p. 23, note 47.

17. Fact Sheet, "Cobra Dane," U.S. Department of Defense, Missile Defense Agency, approved for release July 28, 2016, https://www.mda.mil/global/documents/pdf/cobradane.pdf (accessed May 27, 2018).

18. Fact Sheet, "Army Navy/Transportable Radar Surveillance (AN/TYP-2)," approved for release July 28, 2016, https://www.mda.mil/global/documents/pdf/an_tpy2.pdf (accessed May 27, 2018); Zach Berger, "Army/Navy Transportable Radar Surveillance (AN/TPY-2)," Missile Defense Advocacy Alliance, March 2017, http://missiledefenseadvocacy.org/missile-defense-systems-2/missile-defense-systems/u-s-deployed-sensor-systems/armynavy-transportable-radar-surveillance-antpy-2/ (accessed May 27, 2018).

19. Ankit Panda, "THAAD and China's Nuclear Second-Strike Capability," *The Diplomat*, March 8, 2017, https://thediplomat.com/2017/03/thaad-and-chinas-nuclear-second-strike-capability/ (accessed May 27, 2018).

20. Bruce Klingner, "South Korea Needs THAAD Missile Defense," Heritage Foundation *Backgrounder* No. 3024, June 12, 2015, http://www.heritage.org/defense/report/south-korea-needs-thaad-missile-defense.

21. Fact Sheet, "Sea-Based X-Band Radar," approved for release February 1, 2018, https://www.mda.mil/global/documents/pdf/sbx.pdf (accessed May 27, 2018).

22. Thomas Karako, Ian Williams, and Wes Rumbaugh, *Missile Defense 2020: Next Steps for Defending the Homeland*, Center for Strategic and International Studies, Missile Defense Project, April 2017, https://missilethreat.csis.org/wp-content/uploads/2017/04/170406_Karako_MissileDefense2020_Web.pdf (accessed May 27, 2018); Fact Sheet, "Aegis Ballistic Missile Defense,"; Zach Berger, "AN/SPY-1 Radar," Missile Defense Advocacy Alliance, February 2016, http://missiledefenseadvocacy.org/missile-defense-systems-2/missile-defense-systems/u-s-deployed-sensor-systems/anspy-1-radar/ (accessed May 27, 2018).

23. Wilson Brissett, "U.S. Missile Defense Needs Space-Based Sensors, Hyten Says," *Air Force Magazine*, July 27, 2017, http://www.airforcemag.com/Features/Pages/2017/July%202017/US-Missile-Defense-Needs-Space-Based-Sensors-Hyten-Says.aspx (accessed May 27, 2018).

24. U.S. Air Force, Air Force Space Command, "Space Based Infrared System," March 22, 2017, http://www.afspc.af.mil/About-Us/Fact-Sheets/Display/Article/1012596/space-based-infrared-system/ (accessed on May 27, 2018).

25. Center for Strategic and International Studies, Missile Defense Project, "Space-based Infrared System (SBIRS)," last updated August 11, 2016, https://missilethreat.csis.org/defsys/sbirs/ (accessed May 27, 2018).

26. Sandra Erwin, "Production of New Missile Warning Satellites Likely Delayed by Budget Impasse," *SpaceNews*, October 20, 2017, http://spacenews.com/production-of-new-missile-warning-satellites-likely-delayed-by-budget-impasse/ (accessed May 27, 2018).

27. Fact Sheet, "Space Tracking and Surveillance System," U.S. Department of Defense, Missile Defense Agency, approved for release March 27, 2017, https://www.mda.mil/global/documents/pdf/stss.pdf (accessed May 27, 2018).

28. U.S. Strategic Command, "Joint Functional Component Command for Integrated Missile Defense (JFCC IMD)," current as of February 2016, http://www.stratcom.mil/Portals/8/Documents/JFCC%20IMD%20Fact%20Sheet.pdf (accessed May 27, 2018).

29. Karako, Williams, and Rumbaugh, *Missile Defense 2020: Next Steps for Defending the Homeland*, pp. 101–103.

30. Fact Sheet, "Command and Control, Battle Management, and Communications," U.S. Department of Defense, Missile Defense Agency, approved for release July 28, 2016, https://www.mda.mil/global/documents/pdf/c2bmc.pdf (accessed May 27, 2018).

31. Defense Industry Daily Staff, "C2BMC: Putting the 'System' in Ballistic Missile Defense," *Defense Industry Daily*, May 11, 2017, https://www.defenseindustrydaily.com/c2bmc-putting-the-system-in-ballistic-missile-defense-06323/ (accessed May 27, 2018).

Conclusion: U.S. Military Power

The Active Component of the U.S. military is two-thirds the size it should be, operates equipment that is older than should be the case, and is burdened by readiness levels that are problematic. Accordingly, this *Index* assesses the:

- **Army as "Marginal."** The Army's score returned to "marginal" in the 2019 *Index*, primarily due to an increase in readiness. The Army continues to struggle to rebuild end strength and modernization for improved readiness in some units for current operations, accepting risks in these areas to keep roughly half of its force at acceptable levels of readiness.

- **Navy as "Marginal."** The Navy's overall score is the same as in the *2018 Index*. The Navy's emphasis on restoring readiness and increasing its capacity signals that its overall score could improve in the near future if needed levels of funding are sustained. The Navy's decision to defer maintenance has kept ships at sea but also has affected the Navy's ability to deploy, and the service has little ability to surge to meet wartime demands. The Navy remained just able to meet operational requirements in 2018.

- **Air Force as "Marginal."** This score has trended downward over the past few years largely because of a drop in "capacity" that has not effectively changed and a readiness score of "weak." Shortages of pilots and flying time have degraded the ability of the Air Force to generate the air power that would be needed to meet wartime requirements.

- **Marine Corps as "Weak."** The Corps continues to deal with readiness challenges driven by the combination of high operational tempo and the lingering effects of procurement delays. The Marine Corps has cited modernization of its aviation platforms as the single most effective means to increase readiness within the service. Marine operating forces as a whole continue to average a two-to-one deployment-to-dwell ratio, consuming readiness as quickly as it is built and leaving minimal flexibility to respond to contingencies.

- **Nuclear Capabilities as "Marginal."** The U.S. nuclear complex is "trending toward strong," but this assumes that the U.S. maintains its commitment to modernization and allocates needed resources accordingly. Although a bipartisan commitment has led to continued progress on U.S. nuclear forces modernization and warhead sustainment, these programs remain threatened by potential future fiscal uncertainties, as are the infrastructure, testing regime, and manpower pool on which the nuclear enterprise depends.

In the aggregate, the United States' military posture is rated "marginal." The *2019 Index* concludes that the current U.S. military force is likely capable of meeting the

demands of a single major regional conflict while also attending to various presence and engagement activities but that it would be very hard-pressed to do more and certainly would be ill-equipped to handle two nearly simultaneous major regional contingencies.

The military services have continued to prioritize readiness for current operations by shifting funding to deployed or soon-to-deploy units while sacrificing the ability to keep non-deployed units in "ready" condition; delaying, reducing, extending, or canceling modernization programs; and sustaining the reduction in size and number of military units. While Congress and the new Administration took positive steps to stabilize funding for 2018 and 2019 through the Bipartisan Budget Agreement of 2018, they have not overturned the Budget Control Act that otherwise caps defense spending and that, absent additional legislative action, will reassert its damaging effects in 2020. Without a real commitment to increases in modernization, capacity, and readiness accounts over the next few years, a significant positive turn in the threat environment, or a reassessment of core U.S. security interests, America's military branches will continue to be strained to meet the missions they are called upon to fulfill.

U.S. Military Power: Army

	VERY WEAK	WEAK	MARGINAL	STRONG	VERY STRONG
Capacity		✓			
Capability			✓		
Readiness				✓	
OVERALL			✓		

U.S. Military Power: Navy

	VERY WEAK	WEAK	MARGINAL	STRONG	VERY STRONG
Capacity		✓			
Capability			✓		
Readiness			✓		
OVERALL			✓		

U.S. Military Power: Air Force

	VERY WEAK	WEAK	MARGINAL	STRONG	VERY STRONG
Capacity			✓		
Capability			✓		
Readiness		✓			
OVERALL			✓		

U.S. Military Power: Marine Corps

	VERY WEAK	WEAK	MARGINAL	STRONG	VERY STRONG
Capacity		✓			
Capability			✓		
Readiness		✓			
OVERALL		✓			

U.S. Military Power: Nuclear

	VERY WEAK	WEAK	MARGINAL	STRONG	VERY STRONG
Nuclear Stockpile				✓	
Delivery Platform Reliability			✓		
Warhead Modernization		✓			
Delivery Systems Modernization				✓	
Nuclear Weapons Complex		✓			
National Labs Talent			✓		
Force Readiness			✓		
Allied Assurance				✓	
Nuclear Test Readiness		✓			
OVERALL			✓		

U.S. Military Power

	VERY WEAK	WEAK	MARGINAL	STRONG	VERY STRONG
Army			✓		
Navy			✓		
Air Force			✓		
Marine Corps		✓			
Nuclear			✓		
OVERALL			✓		

Glossary of Abbreviations

A

A2/AD	anti-access/area-denial
AAMDS	Aegis Ashore Missile Defense System
AAV	Amphibious Assault Vehicle
ABM	Ansar Bayt al-Maqdis
ACF	Army contingency force
ACV	Amphibious Combat Vehicle
ADIZ	Air Defense Identification Zone
AEHF	Advanced Extremely High Frequency (satellite system)
AEW	airborne early warning
AFAFRICA	U.S. Air Forces Africa
AFP	Armed Forces of the Philippines
AFRICOM	U.S. Africa Command
AFSOC	U.S. Air Force Special Operations Command
AIP	Air Independent Propulsion
AIT	American Institute in Taiwan
AMDR	Air and Missile Defense Radar
AMPV	Armored Multipurpose Vehicle
ANSF	Afghan National Security Forces
AN/TPY-2	Army Navy/Transportable Radar Surveillance
ANZUS	Australia–New Zealand–U.S. Security Treaty
AUSMIN	Australia–United States Ministerial
AOR	area of responsibility
APC	armored personnel carrier
APS	Army Prepositioned Stocks
AQAP	Al-Qaeda in the Arabian Peninsula
AQI	Al-Qaeda in Iraq
AQIM	Al-Qaeda in the Islamic Maghreb
ARG	amphibious ready group
ASBM	Anti-ship ballistic missile
ASEAN	Association of Southeast Asian Nations
ASW	anti-submarine warfare
ASUW	anti-surface warfare
AW	air warfare

B

BBA	Bipartisan Budget Act of 2015
BCA	Budget Control Act of 2011
BCT	brigade combat team
BDCA	border defense cooperation agreement
BJP	Bharatiya Janata Party
BMD	ballistic missile defense
BUR	Bottom-Up Review
BVR	beyond visual recognition

C

C2	command and control
C4ISR	command, control, communications, computers, intelligence, surveillance, and reconnaissance
CA	civil affairs
CAB	combat aviation brigade
CBO	Congressional Budget Office
CCT	Combat Controller
CELAC	Community of Latin American and Caribbean States
CENTCOM	U.S. Central Command
CFC	Combined Forces Command (South Korea–U.S.)
CIA	Central Intelligence Agency
CJTF-HOA	Combined Joint Task Force–Horn of Africa
CLF	Combat Logistics Force
CMRR	Chemistry and Metallurgy Research Replacement
CMT	combat mission team
COCOM	Combatant Command
CONUS	continental United States
CPMIEC	China Precision Machinery Import–Export Corporation
CPT	Cyber Protection Team
CSF	coalition support funds
CSG	carrier strike group
CSO	Critical Skills Operator
CT	counterterrorism
CTC	Combat Training Centers
CTF	Combined Task Force
CTIC	Counter Terrorism Information Center
CVN	Aircraft Carriers

CVW	carrier air wing
CW	chemical warfare
CYBERCOM	U.S. Cyber Command

D

D2D	deployment-to-dwell
DA-KKV	direct-ascent kinetic-kill vehicle
DDPR	Deterrence and Defense Posture Review
DIME	diplomatic, informational, military, and economic
DMZ	demilitarized zone
DNI	Director of National Intelligence
DOD	U.S. Department of Defense
DOE	U.S. Department of Energy
DOS	denial of service
DDOS	distributed denial of service
DPRK	Democratic People's Republic of Korea (North Korea)
DTTI	Defense Trade and Technology Initiative
DSG	Defense Strategic Guidance
DSR	Defense Strategic Review

E

EAS	European Activity Set
EBO	effects-based operations
ECP	engineering change proposal
EDCA	Enhanced Defense Cooperation Agreement
EEZ	exclusive economic zone
EFV	Expeditionary Fighting Vehicle
EOD	explosive ordinance disposal
EMD	engineering and manufacturing development
EMP	electromagnetic pulse
ERI	European Reassurance Initiative
ESG	Expeditionary Strike Group
EUCOM	U.S. European Command
EW	electronic warfare

F

FATA	Federally Administered Tribal Areas
FCS	Future Combat Systems
FOC	full operational capability
FONOPS	freedom of navigation exercises
FTA	free trade agreement

G

GAO	Government Accountability Office (formerly General Accounting Office)
GATOR	Ground/Air Task Oriented Radar
GCC	geographic combatant commander
GCC	Gulf Cooperation Council
GCV	Ground Combat Vehicle
GDP	Gross Domestic Product
GFMAP	Global Force Management Allocation Plan
GEO	geosynchronous orbit
GPF	general purpose forces
GPS	Global Positioning System

H

HA/DR	humanitarian assistance/disaster relief
HEO	highly elliptical orbit
HMMWV	High Mobility Multipurpose Wheeled Vehicle ("HUMVEE")
HVE	homegrown violent extremist

I

ICBM	intercontinental ballistic missile
ICS	industrial control systems
IDF	Israel Defense Forces
IED	Improvised Explosive Device
IFV	infantry fighting vehicle
IMF	International Monetary Fund
INEW	Integrated Network Electronic Warfare
INF	Intermediate-Range Nuclear Forces (treaty)
IOC	initial operating capability

IRGC	Islamic Revolutionary Guard Corps
ISAF	International Security Assistance Force
ISIL	Islamic State of Iraq and the Levant
ISIS	Islamic State of Iraq and Syria
ISR	intelligence, surveillance, and reconnaissance

J

JOAC	Joint Operational Access Concept
JeM	Jaish-e-Mohammed
JP	joint publication
JSF	Joint Strike Fighter (F-35 Lightning II)
JSOC	Joint Special Operations Command
JSTAR	Joint Surveillance and Target Attack Radar System
JLTV	Joint Light Tactical Vehicle
JTF North	Joint Task Force North
JuD	Jamaat-ud-Dawa

K

KATUSA	Korean Augmentees to the United States Army

L

LAC	Line of Actual Control
LAF	Lebanese Armed Forces
LAV	Light Armored Vehicle
LCAC	Landing Craft Air Cushion Vehicle
LCS	Littoral Combat Ship
LeT	Lashkar-e-Taiba
LHA	landing helicopter assault (amphibious ship)
LHD	landing helicopter dock (amphibious ship)
LNG	liquefied natural gas
LoC	Line of Control
LPD	landing platform/dock or amphibious transport dock (amphibious ship)
LRA	Lord's Resistance Army
LRS-B	Long-Range Strike Bomber
LRIP	Low-Rate Initial Production
LSD	landing ship, dock (amphibious ship)

M

MAGTF	Marine Air-Ground Task Force
MANPADS	man-portable air-defense systems
MARCENT	U.S. Marine Corps Forces Central Command
MARFORAF	U.S. Marine Corps Forces Africa
MARFOREUR	U.S. Marine Corps Forces Europe and Africa
MARFORPAC	U.S. Marine Corps Forces, Pacific
MARSOC	U.S. Marine Corps Special Operations Command
MCM	mine countermeasure (ship)
MCO	major combat operation (see MRC, MTW)
MCMV	mine countermeasure vessel (ship)
MDAP	Major Defense Acquisition Program
MEB	Marine Expeditionary Brigade
MEF	Marine Expeditionary Force
MISO	Military Information Special Operations
MNLA	National Movement for the Liberation of Azawad
MNLF	Moro National Liberation Front
MNNA	major non-NATO ally
MOJWA	Movement for Oneness and Jihad in West Africa
MPC	Marine Personnel Carrier
MPS	Maritime Prepositioning Ships
MRC	major regional conflict (see MTW, MCO)
MRAP	Mine-Resistant Ambush-Protected (vehicle)
MRBM	medium-range ballistic missile
MRF	Marine Rotational Force
MTW	major theater war (see MCO, MRC)

N

NAP	National Action Plan
NATO	North Atlantic Treaty Organization
NAVAF	U.S. Naval Forces Africa
NAVEUR	U.S. Naval Forces Europe
NDN	Northern Distribution Network
NDAA	National Defense Authorization Act
NDP	National Defense Panel
New START	New Strategic Arms Reduction Treaty
NNSA	National Nuclear Security Administration

NPR	Nuclear Posture Review
NPRIS	Nuclear Posture Review Implementation Study
NSC	National Security Council
NSR	Northern Sea Route
NSWC	Naval Special Warfare Command

O

OAS	Organization of American States
OCO	overseas contingency operations
OEF	Operation Enduring Freedom
OIF	Operation Iraqi Freedom
O-FRP	Optimized Fleet Response Plan
ONA	Office of Net Assessment
ONE	Operation Noble Eagle
OPCON	operational control
OPLAN	operational plan
OPTEMPO	operational tempo
OSCE	Organization for Security and Co-operation In Europe

P

PACAF	U.S. Pacific Air Forces
PACFLT	U.S. Pacific Fleet
PACOM	U.S. Pacific Command
PAF	Philippine Air Force
PDD-15	Presidential Decision Directive-15
PIM	Paladin Integrated Management
PLFP	Popular Front for the Liberation of Palestine
PLFP-GC	Popular Front for the Liberation of Palestine–General Command
PKO	peacekeeping operation
PLA	People's Liberation Army
PLAAF	People's Liberation Army Air Force
PLAN	People's Liberation Army Navy
PLO	Palestine Liberation Organization
PNI	Presidential Nuclear Initiative
PNT	positioning, navigation, and timing
PRC	People's Republic of China

PRT	Provisional Reconstruction Team
PSA	Port of Singapore Authority
PSF	Peninsula Shield Force

Q

QDR	Quadrennial Defense Review
QNSTR	Quadrennial National Security Threats and Trends

R

RAF	Royal Air Force
RBA	Ready Basic Aircraft
RCOH	refueling and complex overhaul (nuclear-powered ship)
RDJTF	Rapid Deployment Joint Task Force
RFP	Request for Proposals
RMA	revolution In military affairs
ROK	Republic of Korea (South Korea)
RP	Republic of the Philippines

S

SAARC	South Asia Association of Regional Cooperation
SAM	surface-to-air missile
SAR	search and rescue
SBIRS	Space-Based Infrared System (satellite system)
SCN	Shipbuilding and Conversion, Navy (budget category)
SEAL	Sea Air Land operator (Navy)
SEATO	Southeast Asia Treaty Organization
SFA	Strategic Framework Agreement
SIGINT	signals intelligence
SLBM	submarine-launched ballistic missile
SMU	special mission unit
SOCAFRICA	U.S. Special Operations Command Africa
SOCCENT	U.S. Special Operations Command Central
SOCEUR	U.S. Special Operations Command Europe
SOCPAC	U.S. Special Operations Command Pacific
SOF	U.S. Special Operations Forces
SOP	Standard Operating Procedure

SORT	Strategic Offensive Reductions Treaty
SOTFE	Support Operations Task Force Europe
SPE	Sony Pictures Entertainment
SPMAGTF	Special-Purpose Marine Air–Ground Task Force–Crisis Response–Africa
SRBM	short-range ballistic missile
SSBN	ballistic missile submarine, nuclear-powered
SSGN	guided missile submarine, nuclear-powered
SSN	attack submarine, nuclear-powered
SSP	Stockpile Stewardship Program
STRATCOM	U.S. Strategic Command
SUW	surface warfare

T

TACAIR	tactical air
TAI	total active inventory
TANAP	Trans-Anatolian Natural Gas Pipeline
TAP	Trans-Adriatic Pipeline
TCO	transnational criminal organization
TPP	Trans-Pacific Partnership
TTP	Tehrik-e-Taliban Pakistan
TLAM/N	Tomahawk Land Attack Missile/Nuclear
TMP	technical modernization program
TNW	tactical nuclear weapon
TRA	Taiwan Relations Act
TRANSCOM	U.S. Transportation Command
TSOC	Theater Special Operations Command

U

UAV	unmanned aerial vehicle
UAE	United Arab Emirates
UCLASS	Unmanned Carrier-Launched Airborne Surveillance and Strike
UNASUR	Unión de Naciones Suramericanas (Union of South American Nations)
UNC	United Nations Council
USAF	U.S. Air Force
USAFCENT	U.S. Air Forces Central
USAFE	U.S. Air Forces Europe
USARAF	U.S. Army Africa

USARCENT	U.S. Army Central
USARPAC	U.S. Army Pacific
USAREUR	U.S. Army Europe
USASOC	U.S. Army Special Operations Command
USFJ	U.S. Forces Japan
USFK	U.S. Forces Korea
USNAVCENT	U.S. Naval Forces Central
USNORTHCOM	U.S. Northern Command
USSOCOM	U.S. Special Operations Command
USSOUTHCOM	U.S. Southern Command
USW	undersea warfare

V

VEO	violent extremist organizations
VLS	vertical launching system

W

WGS	Wideband Global SATCOM (satellite system)
WMD	weapons of mass destruction
WRM	wartime readiness materials
WWTA	Worldwide Threat Assessment

Methodology

The assessment portion of the *Index of U.S. Military Strength* is composed of three major sections that address America's military power, the operating environments within or through which that power must operate, and threats to U.S. vital national interests.

The authors of this study used a five-category scoring system that ranged from "very poor" to "excellent" or "very weak" to "very strong" as appropriate to each topic. This particular approach was selected to capture meaningful gradations while avoiding the appearance that a high level of precision was possible given the nature of the issues and the information that was publicly available.

Some factors are quantitative and lend themselves to discrete measurement; others are very qualitative in nature and can be assessed only through an informed understanding of the material that leads to a judgment call. In addition, conditions in each of the areas assessed are changing throughout the year, so any measurement is based on the information at hand and must necessarily be viewed as a snapshot in time. While this is not entirely satisfactory when it comes to reaching conclusions on the status of a given matter, especially the adequacy of military power, and will be quite unsatisfactory for some readers, we understand that senior officials in decision-making positions will never have a comprehensive set of inarguable hard data on which to base a decision.

Purely quantitative measures alone tell only part of the story when it comes to the relevance, utility, and effectiveness of hard power. In fact, assessing military power or the nature of an operating environment using only quantitative metrics can lead to misinformed conclusions. Raw numbers are a very important component, but they tell only a part of the story of war. Similarly, experience and demonstrated proficiency are often decisive factors in war, but they are nearly impossible to measure.

This *Index*'s assessment of the **global operating environment** focused on three key regions—Europe, the Middle East, and Asia—because of their importance relative to U.S. vital security interests.

For **threats to U.S. vital interests**, the *Index* identifies the countries that pose the greatest current or potential threats to U.S. vital interests based on two overarching factors: their behavior and their capability. The classic definition of "threat" considers the combination of intent and capability, but intent cannot be clearly measured, so "observed behavior" is used as a reasonable surrogate because it is the clearest manifestation of intent. The selection of threat countries is based on their historical behavior and explicit policies or formal statements vis-à-vis U.S. interests, scoring them in two areas: the degree of provocative behavior that they exhibited during the year and their ability to pose a credible threat to U.S. interests irrespective of intent.

Finally, the **status of U.S. military power** is addressed in three areas: capability (or modernity); capacity; and readiness. All three are fundamental to success even if they are not de facto determinants of success, something we explain further in the section. Also addressed are the condition of the United States' nuclear weapons capability, assessing it in areas that are unique to this military component and critical to understanding its real-world viability and effectiveness as a strategic deterrent, and the country's ballistic missile defense (BMD) capabilities.

With regard to BMD specifically, it is beyond the scope of this *Index* to "score" strategic and operational, or theater, BMD capabilities given the lack of publicly available comprehensive studies. Rather, the *Index* provides an overview of the subject so that the reader can obtain an informed understanding of the scope, scale, and current status of the ballistic missile defense challenge.

Assessing the Global Operating Environment

Not all of the factors that characterize an operating environment are equal, but each contributes to the degree to which a particular operating environment is favorable or unfavorable to future U.S. military operations. Our assessment of the operating environment utilized a five-point scale, ranging from "very poor" to "excellent" conditions and covering four regional characteristics of greatest relevance to the conduct of military operations:

1. **Very Poor.** Significant hurdles exist for military operations. Physical infrastructure is insufficient or nonexistent, and the region is politically unstable. The U.S. military is poorly placed or absent, and alliances are nonexistent or diffuse.

2. **Unfavorable.** A challenging operating environment for military operations is marked by inadequate infrastructure, weak alliances, and recurring political instability. The U.S. military is inadequately placed in the region.

3. **Moderate.** A neutral to moderately favorable operating environment is characterized by adequate infrastructure, a moderate alliance structure, and acceptable levels of regional political stability. The U.S. military is adequately placed.

4. **Favorable.** A favorable operating environment includes good infrastructure, strong alliances, and a stable political environment. The U.S. military is well placed in the region for future operations.

5. **Excellent.** An extremely favorable operating environment includes well-established and well-maintained infrastructure; strong, capable allies; and a stable political environment. The U.S. military is exceptionally well placed to defend U.S. interests.

The key regional characteristics consisted of:

a. **Alliances.** Alliances are important for interoperability and collective defense, as allies would be more likely to lend support to U.S. military operations. Various indicators provide insight into the strength or health of an alliance. These include whether the U.S. trains regularly with countries in the region, has good interoperability with the forces of an ally, and shares intelligence with nations in the region.

b. **Political Stability.** Political stability brings predictability for military planners when considering such things as transit, basing, and overflight rights for U.S. military operations. The overall degree of political stability indicates whether U.S. military actions would be hindered or enabled and considers, for example, whether transfers of power in the region are generally peaceful and whether there been any recent instances of political instability in the region.

c. **U.S. Military Positioning.** Having military forces based or equipment and supplies staged in a region greatly facilitates the ability of the United States to respond to crises and, presumably, achieve successes in critical "first battles" more quickly. Being routinely present in a region also assists in maintaining familiarity with its characteristics and the various actors that might try to assist or thwart U.S. actions. With this in mind, we assessed whether or not the U.S. military was well-positioned in the region. Again, indicators included bases, troop presence, prepositioned equipment, and recent examples of military operations (including training and humanitarian) launched from the region.

d. **Infrastructure.** Modern, reliable, and suitable infrastructure is essential to military operations. Airfields, ports, rail lines, canals, and paved roads enable the U.S. to stage, launch operations, and logistically sustain combat operations. We combined expert knowledge of regions with publicly available information on critical infrastructure to arrive at our overall assessment of this metric.

Assessing Threats to U.S. Vital Interests

To make the threats identified in the *Index* measurable and relatable to the challenges of operating environments and adequacy of American military power, *Index* staff and outside reviewers evaluated separately the threats according to their level of provocation (i.e., their observed behavior) and their actual capability to pose a credible threat to U.S. interests on a scale of 1 to 5, with 1 representing a very high threat capability or level of belligerency. This scale corresponds to the tone of the five-point scales used to score the operating environment and military capabilities in that 1 is bad for U.S. interests and 5 is very favorable.

Based on these evaluations, provocative behavior was characterized according to five descending categories: benign (5); assertive (4); testing (3); aggressive (2); and hostile (1). Staff also characterized the capabilities of a threat actor according to five categories: marginal (5); aspirational (4); capable (3); gathering (2); and formidable (1). Those characterizations—behavior and capability—form two halves of the overall threat level.

Assessing U.S. Military Power

Also assessed is the adequacy of the United States' defense posture as it pertains to a conventional understanding of "hard power," defined as the ability of American military forces to engage and defeat an enemy's forces in battle at a scale commensurate with the vital national interests of the U.S. The assessment draws on both quantitative and qualitative aspects of military forces, informed by an experience-based understanding of military operations and the expertise of the authors and internal and external reviewers.

It is important to note that military effectiveness is as much an art as it is a science. Specific military capabilities represented in weapons, platforms, and military units can be used individually to some effect. Practitioners of war, however, have learned that combining the tools of war in various ways and orchestrating their tactical employment in series or simultaneously can dramatically amplify the effectiveness of the force committed to battle.

The point is that a great number of factors make it possible for a military force to locate, close with, and destroy an enemy, but not many of them are easily measured. The scope of this specific project does not extend to analysis of everything that makes hard power possible; it focuses on the status of the hard power itself.

This *Index* assesses the state of military affairs for U.S. forces in three areas: capability, capacity, and readiness.

Capability. Capability is scored based on the current state of combat equipment. This involves four factors: the age of key platforms relative to their expected life spans; whether the required capability is being met by legacy or modern equipment; the scope of improvement or replacement programs relative to the operational requirement; and the overall health and stability (financial and technological) of modernization programs.

This *Index* focused on primary combat units and combat platforms (e.g., tanks, ships, and airplanes) and elected not to include the array of system and component upgrades that keep an older platform viable over time, such as a new radar, missile, or communications suite. New technologies grafted onto aging platforms ensure that U.S. military forces keep pace with technological innovations relevant to the modern battlefield, but at some point, the platforms themselves are no longer viable and must be replaced. Modernized sub-systems and components do not entirely substitute for aging platforms, and it is the platform itself that is usually the more challenging item to field. In this sense, primary combat platforms serve as representative measures of force modernity just as combat forces are a useful surrogate measure for the overall military that includes a range of support units, systems, and infrastructure.

In addition, it is assumed that modernization programs should replace current capacity at a one-to-one ratio; less than a one-to-one replacement assumes risk, because even if the newer system is presumably better than the older, until it is proven in actual combat, having fewer systems lessens the capacity of the force, which is an important factor if combat against a peer competitor carries with it the likelihood of attrition. For modernization programs, only Major Defense Acquisition Programs (MDAPs) are scored.

The capability score uses a five-grade scale. Each service receives one capability score that is a non-weighted aggregate of scores for four categories: (1) age of equipment; (2) modernity of capability; (3) size of modernization program; and (4) health of modernization program. General criteria for the capability categories are:

Age of Equipment
- **Very Weak:** Equipment age is past 80 percent of expected life span.

- **Weak:** Equipment age is 61 percent–80 percent of expected life span.

- **Marginal:** Equipment age is 41 percent–60 percent of expected life span.

- **Strong:** Equipment age is 21 percent–40 percent of expected life span.

- **Very Strong:** Equipment age is 20 percent or less of expected life span.

Capability of Equipment
- **Very Weak:** Majority (over 80 percent) of capability relies on legacy platforms.

- **Weak:** 60 percent–79 percent of capability relies on legacy platforms.

- **Marginal:** 40 percent–59 percent of capability is legacy platforms.

- **Strong:** 20 percent–39 percent of capability is legacy platforms.

- **Very Strong:** Less than 20 percent of capability is legacy platforms.

Size of Modernization Program
- **Very Weak:** Modernization program is significantly too small or inappropriate to sustain current capability or program in place.

- **Weak:** Modernization programs are smaller than current capability size.

- **Marginal:** Modernization programs are appropriate to sustain current capability size.

- **Strong:** Modernization programs will increase current capability size.

- **Very Strong:** Modernization programs will vastly expand capability size.

Health of Modernization Program
- **Very Weak:** Modernization programs facing significant problems; too far behind schedule (five-plus years); cannot replace current capability before retirement; lacking sufficient investment to advance; cost overruns including Nunn–McCurdy breach. (A Nunn–McCurdy breach occurs when the cost of a new item exceeds the most recently approved amount by 25

percent or more or if it exceeds the originally approved amount by 50 percent or more. See Title 10, U.S.C. § 2433, Unit Cost Reports (UCRs).)

- **Weak:** Facing procurement problems; behind schedule (three–five years); difficult to replace current equipment on time or insufficient funding; cost overruns enough to trigger an Acquisition Program Baseline (APB) breach.

- **Marginal:** Facing few problems; behind schedule by one–two years but can replace equipment with some delay or experience some funding cuts; some cost growth but not within objectives.

- **Strong:** Facing no procurement problems; can replace equipment with no delays; within cost estimates.

- **Very Strong:** Performing better than DOD plans, including lower actual costs.

Capacity. To score capacity, the service's size (be it end strength or number of platforms) is compared to the force size required to meet a simultaneous or nearly simultaneous two-war or two–major regional contingency (MRC) benchmark. This benchmark consists of the force needed to fight and win two MRCs and a 20 percent margin that serves as a strategic reserve. A strategic reserve is necessary because deployment of 100 percent of the force at any one time is highly unlikely. Not only do ongoing requirements like training or sustainment and maintenance of equipment make it infeasible for the entirety of the force to be available for deployment, but committing 100 percent of the force would leave no resources available to handle unexpected situations.

Thus, a "marginal" capacity score would exactly meet a two-MRC force size, a "strong" capacity score would equate to a plus–10 percent margin for strategic reserve, and a "very strong" score would equate to a 20 percent margin.

Capacity Score Definitions

- **Very Weak:** 0 percent–37 percent of the two-MRC benchmark.

- **Weak:** 38 percent–74 percent of the two-MRC benchmark.

- **Marginal:** 75 percent–82 percent of the two-MRC benchmark.

- **Strong:** 83 percent–91 percent of the two-MRC benchmark.

- **Very Strong:** 92 percent–100 percent of the two-MRC benchmark.

Readiness. The readiness scores are from the military services' own assessments of readiness based on their requirements. These are not comprehensive reviews of all readiness input factors, but rather rely on the public statements of the military services regarding the state of their readiness.

It should be noted that even a "strong" or "very strong" score does not indicate that 100 percent of the force is ready; it simply indicates that the service is meeting 100 percent of its own readiness requirements. Often, these requirements assume that a percentage of the military at any one time will not be fit for deployment. Because of this, even if readiness is graded as "strong" or "marginal," there is still a gap in readiness that will have significant implications for immediate combat effectiveness and the ability to deploy quickly. Thus, anything short of meeting 100 percent of readiness requirements assumes risk and is therefore problematic.

Further, a service's assessment of its readiness occurs within its size or capacity at that time and as dictated by the Defense Strategic Guidance, National Military Strategy, and related top-level documents generated by the Administration and senior Defense officials. It does not account for the size-related "readiness" of the force to meet national security requirements assessed as needed by this *Index*. Thus, for a service to be assessed as "very strong" would mean that 80 percent–100 percent of the existing force in a service meets that service's requirements for being "ready" even if the size of the service is less than that required to meet the two-MRC benchmark. Therefore, it is important for the reader to keep this in mind when considering the actual readiness of the force to protect U.S. national security interests against the challenges presented by threats around the world.

Readiness Score Definitions

- **Very Weak:** 0 percent–19 percent of service's requirements.

- **Weak:** 20 percent–39 percent of service's requirements.

- **Marginal:** 40 percent–59 percent of service's requirements.

- **Strong:** 60 percent–79 percent of service's requirements.

- **Very Strong:** 80 percent–100 percent of service's requirements.